MARTIAL ARTS:

TRADITIONS, HISTORY, PEOPLE

MARTIAL ARTS

TRADITIONS, HISTORY, PEOPLE

John Corcoran and Emil Farkas

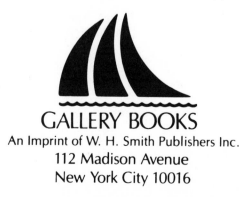

GALLERY BOOKS
An Imprint of W. H. Smith Publishers Inc.
112 Madison Avenue
New York City 10016

To Joe Hyams and Albert and Antonia

Published by Gallery Books, an imprint of W.H. Smith Publishers, Inc.,
112 Madison Avenue, New York, New York 10016

Manufactured in the U.S.A.

4   5   6   7   8   9   10

08317-5805-8
LCC: 82-11940

CONTENTS

ABOUT THE AUTHORS

FARKAS, EMIL (1946-) Hungarian-born American martial arts instructor, writer, and motion picture promoter. Farkas started his martial arts career while still a youngster, and before age 20 he had earned his black belt in both judo and karate. An opportunity to work for a famous record producer (Phil Spector) brought him to Hollywood, where his teaching skills were soon recognized. Musicians and other entertainers sought out Farkas's instruction in the martial arts. He began to teach privately while finishing his college degree in geography and anthropology. In 1970 Farkas opened his own dojo, the Beverly Hills Karate Academy. He is also a U.C.L.A. instructor in women's self-defense.

As martial arts became more popular, Farkas was sought out by TV and film companies to supervise and instruct their stars. Today his knowledge of martial arts choreography demands much of his time and talent, the rest going into teaching or writing.

Farkas has worked on dozens of films, from *Easy Rider* to *The Killer Elite*. Television viewers have seen his work in such series as "Mannix," "Spiderman," "The Hulk," "Mission Impossible," and "The Rockford Files."

Farkas's students include Herb Alpert, Lou Adler, Phil Spector, the Beach Boys, Gary Puckett, Buffalo Springfield, Paul Williams, Dennis Hopper, Mike Connors, Jimmy Caan, Fred Williamson, Raymond St. Jacques, and Lalo Schifrin.

Among the younger set under Farkas's instruction are children of such celebrities as Polly Bergen, Kirk Douglas, Jack Carter, Mike Connors, Buddy Hacket, Barry Gordi, Barbara Mandrell, Michael Landon, and Mel Brooks.

He has written a number of books, including *The Complete Martial Arts Catalogue,* co-authored with John Corcoran; *Fight Back: A Woman's Guide to Self Defense; The Overlook Martial Arts Dictionary; The Illustrated Encyclopedia of Martial Arts;* and *Training and Fighting Skills,* with champion Benny Urquidez. He wrote the original world screenplay for *Force: Five* with George Goldsmith; and *The Magnificent 10,* with Joe Hyams. He is a regular columnist for *Inside Kung-Fu, Kick Illustrated,* and *Official Karate* magazines. Farkas is the founder and president of Creative Action Inc., a multifaceted company dealing with management, promotion, and motion picture production.

CORCORAN, JOHN (1948-) American martial arts writer and pioneer. Following graduation from high school in 1967, Corcoran was visiting a relative in Cleveland when he saw the James Bond movie *You Only Live Twice,* whose realistic depiction of martial arts action ignited his interest in karate. Returning to Pittsburgh, his hometown, he enrolled at the Academy of Oriental Defenses in Oct. 1967; his first instructor was Thomas Voelker, who taught the isshinryu style.

In late 1970, as a brown belt, Corcoran sought out Glenn Premru to learn Premru's flamboyant style of shorin-ryu karate. Under Premru's guidance, he began entering intermediate form competition, winning or placing in more than 30 tournaments. He was also a member of Premru's demonstration team. Then a struggling drafts-man, Corcoran paid for his lessons by writing publicity releases for Premru. In 1971 he wrote his first published magazine article, a personality piece on Premru for *Official Karate.* After moving to Los Angeles in 1972, Corcoran was promoted to black belt; his achievement was further embellished when Premru bestowed his personal black belt upon Corcoran.

In 1973 Corcoran compiled the first set of national Top Ten ratings for American karate form competitors, which appeared that year in the *Official Karate Yearbook.* He was hired as the first book editor for Ohara Publications, the book publishing branch of Rainbow Publications, publishers of *Black Belt* and other martial arts magazines. By the end of 1973, he transferred to the magazines as assistant editor; he was the first karate black belt to become an editor of *Black Belt* and *Karate Illustrated.*

In early 1974 Corcoran helped expose the unethical financial scheme underlying Eugene Forte's $40,000 PAWAK Karate Championships in Long Beach.

Corcoran left *Black Belt's* employ in Aug. 1974 to become managing editor of Mike Anderson's *Professional Karate Magazine.* At the same time, Corcoran worked on the promotion of Anderson's World Professional Karate Championships, the event where full-contact karate was spawned.

In June 1975 Corcoran collaborated with Bob Wall on his self-published book *Who's Who in the Martial Arts.*

SPECIAL CONSULTANTS

JAPANESE ENTRIES
Richard Kim
  author, *The Weaponless Warriors: An Informal History of Okinawan Karate;* technical committee member, American Amateur Karate Federation; representative, Dai Nippon Butokukai; member, Black Belt Hall of Fame (Instructor of the Year 1973)

KOREAN ENTRIES
Ken (Kyung Ho) Min
  physical education director, University of California, Berkeley; founder, American Collegiate Tae Kwon Do Association; former chairman, National AAU Tae Kwon Do Association; former chairman, National AAU Tae Kwon Do Committee; president, National Collegiate Judo Association and National Collegiate Tae Kwon Do Association; editor, *Tae Kwon Do Journal, Judo—USA*

CHINESE ENTRIES
Michael P. Staples
  author, *White Crane Kung-Fu, Wu Shu of China, Hop Gar Kung-Fu, Tibetan Kung-Fu, The Elegant Wu Shu of China;* contributing editor, *Inside Kung Fu, Kick Illustrated*

JUDO ENTRIES
Emilio Bruno
  founder, intercollegiate judo competition (1940), Judo program (Cornell University 1944), AAU judo program (1950), U.S. Air Force Academy judo program (1955); former director, AAU Judo Committee, Strategic Air Command Physical Conditioning, U.S. Judo Black Belt Federation; former coach, U.S. Olympic Judo Team (1964)

TECHNICAL CONSULTANT
Joe Lewis
  retired world heavyweight karate champion; co-founder, full-contact karate; co-author, *Martial Arts for the Masses* (with John Corcoran)

EDITORIAL CONSULTANT
Joe Hyams
  author, journalist, and screenwriter; author, *Zen in the Martial Arts*

EDITORIAL COORDINATOR
Stuart Sobel
  martial arts journalist and photographer; contributing editor, *Kick Illustrated;* vice-president, Creative Action, Inc.; co-author, *Training and Fighting Skills* (with Benny Urquidez and Emil Farkas)

AMERICAN CONTRIBUTORS
Yoshiaki Ajari
  chief instructor, U.S. Wado-kai Karate-do Federation
Sam Allred
  member, Black Belt Hall of Fame
Mike Anderson
  founder, *Professional Karate Magazine;* co-founder, full-contact karate
Steve Armstrong
  president, American-Okinawan Karate Association; author, *Seisan Kata of Isshinryu Karate*
Jim Arvanitis
  founder, Mu tau
Aaron Banks
  founder, World Professional Karate Organization; editor, *World Karate Magazine*
Richard Barathy
  chief instructor, American combat karate
Renardo Barden
  editor, *Karate Illustrated*
Jerry Beasley
  karate coach, Radford University; correspondent, *Kick Illustrated*
Norman Borine
  curator, Bruce Lee Museum
Michael Brodman
  Pennsylvania state director, Okinawan Karate Federation
Jim Butin
  top 10-ranked karate fighter
Sid Campbell
  instructor, shorin-ryu karate
Roger Carpenter
  American karate pioneer
Tom Conners
  founder, Traco International

Joe Corley
  president, South East Karate Association; promoter, Battle of Atlanta; American karate pioneer
William Cox
  former contributing editor, *Kick Illustrated*
Milo Dailey
  national chief of publications, American Tae Kwon Do Association
Fumio Demura
  Author, *Nunchaku, Karate Weapon of Self-Defense, Sai, Karate Weapon of Self-Defense, Shito-ryu Karate;* chief instructor, Japan Karate Federation (U.S. branch)
William Dometrich
  founder, U.S. Chito-kai
Duane Ethington
  correspondent, *Black Belt, Karate Illustrated. Official Karate*
Jack Farr
  founder, All-American Indian Karate Association
George Foon
  former art director, *Inside Kung Fu*
Neva Friedenn
  American film distributor; contributing editor, *Kick Illustrated;* consulting editor, *Martial Arts Movies*
Brian Frost
  instructor, Koei-kan karate
Daniel M. Furuya
  book editor, Unique Publications; specialist in Chinese and Japanese culture
Albert Goldman
  author, *Elvis*
George Goldsmith
  scriptwriter, *Force: Five* (with Emil Farkas)
Jerry Gould
  chief instructor, U.S. Shorin-ryu Karate
Joe Griffith
  staff photographer, *Official Karate Magazine*
Bong Soo Han
  author, *Hapkido, Korean Art of Self-Defense;* co-star, *Force Five;* martial arts choreographer, *Billy Jack, Trial of Billy Jack*
Howard Hanson
  president, World Karate Association
George Harris
  four-time National AAU Judo Champion, Pan-American Judo Champion, U.S. Air Force Judo Champion
Randall Hassell
  author, *The Karate Spirit; The Karate Experience; Zen, Pen and Sword* (with John Corcoran)
Stephen K. Hayes
  Shidoshi, Togakure ryu ninjutsu; author, *Ninja, Spirit of the Shadow Warrior, The Ninja and Their Secret Fighting Art*
Mauricio Hernandez
  public relations director, American Amateur Karate Federation
Dr. William C.C. Hu
  Chinese martial arts scholar and historian
John Huppuch
  manager, World Hwarang-do Association
Ed Ikuta
  staff photographer, Unique Publications
Dan Inosanto
  senior instructor, jeet kune do; guro, Filipino kali; author, *Jeet Kune Do, The Filipino Martial Arts*
Dan Ivan
  former president, Japan Karate Federation (U.S. branch); American karate pioneer; co-author, *Advanced Nunchaku* (with Fumio Demura)
A. Jose Jones
  former contributing editor, *Professional Karate Magazine*
Edward Kaloudis
  American director, International Koei-kan Karate-do Association
Rex Kimball
  instructor, Wu ming ta and kojasho
He-Young Kimm
  hapkido coach, Louisiana State University; president, American Hapkido Association
Dave King
  photo editor, Unique Publications
Ken Knudson
  former president, American Karate Association; founder, Midwest Karate Association

Mark Komura
    art director, Unique Publications
Ted Kresge
    author, *The Encyclopedia of Karate and Related Arts*
Takayuki Kubota
    founder, Gosokuryu karate; author, *Gosokuryu Karate, Kumite 1*
Gene LeBell
    American judo pioneer; author, *Handbook of Judo, Self-Defense for the Young Adult*
Alan Lee
    author, *Kung-Fu Wu Su*
Jeong Sook Lee
    board of directors, U.S. Tang Soo Do Moo Duk Kwan Federation
Joo Bang Lee
    supreme grandmaster, Hwarang-do
Joo Sang Lee
    head grandmaster, Hwarang-do
Linda Lee (Mrs. Bruce Lee)
    author, *Bruce Lee, The Man Only I Knew*
James Lew
    author, *The Art of Stretching and Kicking*
Ernest Lieb
    founder, American Karate Association; member, Black Belt Hall of Fame
Andrew Linick
    author, *Nunchaku, Karate's Deadliest Fighting Sticks*
John Maberry
    correspondent, *Kick Illustrated*
Terry Maccarrone
    instructor, shorin-ryu karate
Ron Marchini
    member, Black Belt Hall of Fame; author, *Renbukan Karate*
Paul Maruyama
    U.S. National Judo Champion, Pan-American Judo Champion, U.S. Olympic Judo coach
Paul Maslak
    former editor, *Inside Kung Fu;* author, *Strategy in Unarmed Combat, What the Masters Know*
George Mattson
    author, *Uechi-ryu Karate, The Way of Karate*
Bill McDonald
    vice-president, South East Karate Association
Chris McLoughlin
    associate director, South East Karate Association; southern correspondent, *Official Karate Magazine;* co-author, *Personal Defense* (with Blackie Collins)
Chuck Merriman
    chairman, Karate International; coach, U.S. World Karate Team
Jenice Miller
    former top 10-ranked karate fighter; member, *Who's Who in the Martial Arts*
Anthony Mirakian
    American karate pioneer; president, (Western branch) Meibukan Goju-ryu Karate-do Association
Hidetaka Nishiyama
    founder, American Amateur Karate Federation; co-founder, Pan-American Karate Union; executive director, International Amateur Karate Federation; author, *Karate, the Art of Empty-Hand Fighting*
Hidy Ochiai
    master instructor, Washin-ryu karate-do; author, *The Essence of Self-Defense*
Hironori Ohtsuka
    founder, Wado-ryu karate-do
Teruyuki Okazaki
    chairman, East Coast Karate Association and International Shotokan Karate Federation
John Pachivas
    Florida karate pioneer
Ed Parker
    American kenpo pioneer; author, *Kenpo Karate, Secrets of Chinese Karate*
Kevin Parsons
    author, *Police Procedures and Defensive Tactics Training Manual*
Cecil Patterson
    author, *An Introduction to Wado-ryu Karate*
Sam Pearson
    instructor, shorin-ryu karate
George Pesare
    American karate pioneer; member, *Who's Who in the Martial Arts*
David Praim
    instructor, Tang soo do
Glenn Premru
    former top 10-ranked karate form champion; instructor, shorin-ryu karate
Jhoon Rhee
    founder, Tae kwon do in America; member, Black Belt Hall of Fame and *Who's Who in the Martial Arts*

Robin Rielly
    author, *The History of American Karate*
W. Scott Russell
    president, Society of Black Belts International; author, *Karate, the Energy Connection*
Tom Schlesinger
    instructor, Renbukan karate
Steve Scott
    National AAU Secretary, Sambo wrestling; author, *Sambo Wrestling, A Coach's Guide*
Sandra Segal
    editor, *Martial Arts Movies*
Harold Sharp
    American judo instructor; author, *Sport of Judo, The Techniques of Judo*
Stirling Silliphant
    author, scriptwriter, and producer; Academy Award winner, *In the Heat of the Night* (screenplay)
Alex Sternberg
    president, Jewish Karate Federation of America; karate chairman, Maccabiah Games; coach, American team for the Maccabiah Games
Dr. John L. Stump
    instructor, shorinji kempo
Kazumi Tabata
    Founder, North American Karate Federation
Lucille Tajiri
    former assistant editor, *Kick Illustrated, Black Belt, Karate Illustrated*
Thomas Tannenbaum
    president, MGM Television; co-founder, full-contact karate
Bruce Terrill
    founder, Wu ying tao
Mary Townsley
    midwest correspondent, *Official Karate Magazine*
Robert Trias
    president/founder, United States Karate Association; author, *The Hand Is My Sword, The Pinnacle of Karate, Methods of Okinawan Shuri-ryu;* founder, karate in the U.S.
Peter Urban
    American karate pioneer; founder, USA Goju; author, *The Karate Dojo, Karate Psychology*
Benny Urquidez
    World Super-Lightweight Karate Champion (full-contact)
Bob Wall
    author, *Who's Who in the Martial Arts;* co-star, *Enter the Dragon, Return of the Dragon, Game of Death*
Bill Wallace
    retired World Middleweight Karate Champion (full-contact)
Al Weiss
    founder/editor, *Official Karate Magazine* and *Warriors;* co-author, *Kung Fu Wu Su* (with Alan Lee) and *Clan of Death: Ninja* (with Tom Philbin)
Jay T. Will
    author, *Kenpo Karate for Self-Defense, Advanced Kenpo Karate*
Curtis Wong
    founder/publisher, *Inside Kung Fu, Kick Illustrated, Martial Arts Movies,* and Unique Publications (martial arts books)
James Wooley
    American judo champion
John Worley
    former editor, *Sport Karate*
Gosei Yamaguchi
    author, *Goju-ryu Karate* (I and II)

FOREIGN CONTRIBUTORS

Jacquest Boudrehault (Canada)
    Canadian martial arts historian
John Conway (Ireland)
    chief instructor, Irish Karate Association
Al Dacascos (Germany)
    founder, won hop kuen do; former top 10-ranked American karate fighter and form champion; European kung-fu pioneer
Bob Dalgleish (Canada)
    former director, Goju-ryu Karate Federation
Ennio Falsoni (Italy)
    editor, *Samurai* (formerly *Banzai*)
Ronald Forrester (Canada)
    president, Canadian Jiu-jitsu Association
Rolland Guillac (France)
    former editor, *Karate*
Alex Kwok (Canada)
    former top 10-ranked American form champion
Zarko Modric (Yugoslavia/Japan)
    European karate and judo pioneer; former European correspondent, *Black Belt*

David Moon (Mexico)
  Mexican tae kwon do pioneer; former top 10-ranked American karate fighter
Bo Munthe (Sweden)
  founder, ninjutsu in Sweden
Mariane Noher (Switzerland)
  secretary, Swiss Judo Association
Terry O'Neill (England)
  editor/publisher, *Fighting Arts Magazine*
Henri Seriesse (Netherlands)
  co-founder, Netherlands Karate Union
Waldemar Sikorsky (Poland)
  coach, National Polish Judo Team
Tom Sulak (Germany)
  former editor, *Karate Illustrated*
John Therien (Canada)
  Canadian kick-boxing coach and pioneer

ABBREVIATIONS

AAF	American Aikido Federation
AAKF	American Amateur Karate Federation
AAU	Amateur Athletic Union
ABA	American Bando Association
ACTA	American Collegiate Tae Kwon Do Association
ACTCA	American Collegiate Tae Kwon Do Coaches Association
AEKF	All European Karate Federation
AFJA	Armed Forces Judo Association
AFKA	Armed Forces Karate Association
AJCKF	All-Japan Collegiate Karate-do Federation
AJJF	All-Japan Juken-do Federation
AJKA	All Japan Karate-do Association
AJKF	All-Japan Karate-do Federation
	All Japan Kendo Federation
	All-Japan Kyudo Federation
AJKO	All Japan Karate-do Organization
AJKR	All Japan Kyudo Renmei
AJNF	All Japan Naginata-do Federation
AKA	American Karate Association
AKBBA	American Karate Black Belt Association
AKF	American Kendo Federation
AOKA	American-Okinawan Karate Association
AOKF	All Okinawa Karate-do Federation
AOKKL	All Okinawa Kenpo Karate-do League
BAA	British Aikido Association
BJA	British Judo Association
BKF	Black Karate Federation
BKR	British Kendo Renmei
CJU	Canadian Jiu-Jitsu Union
CKBBA	Canadian Kodokan Black Belt Association
CPCA	Chinese Physical Culture Association
ECKA	East Coast Karate Alliance
EJU	European Judo Union
EKU	European Karate Union
FAJKO	Federation of All-Japan Karate-do Organizations
FBBA	Florida Black Belt Association
FKU	Feminist Karate Union
FPJ	Federation of Practicing Jujutsuans
GAISF	General Assembly of International Sports Federation
IAKF	International Amateur Karate Federation
IBA	International Bando Association
IIKA	International Isshinryu Karate Association
IJF	International Judo Federation
IKA	International Karate Association
IKF	International Kendo Federation
IKKA	International Kenpo Karate Association
ITF	International Taekwondo Federation
JBBF	Judo Black Belt Federation
JKA	Japan Karate Association
JKF	Japan Karate Federation
KISI	Kebudajaan Ilmu Silat Indonesia
KRANE	Karate Referees Association of New England
KTA	Korea Taekwondo Association
KYA	Korean Yudo Association
MAHF	Martial Arts for the Handicapped Federation
MEKA	Mid-East Karate Association
MKA	Mexican Karate Association
NATU	North American Tae Kwon Do Union
NCJA	National Collegiate Judo Association
NCKRA	Northern California Karate Referees Association
NKL	National Karate League
NKUGB	National Karate Union of Great Britain
ODAA	Oriental Defensive Arts Association
OKF	Okinawan Karate Federation
PAKU	Pan-American Karate Union
PATU	Pan-American Tae Kwon Do Union
PKA	Professional Karate Association
PMAA	Physicians Martial Arts Association
SEKA	South East Karate Association
SEPKC	South East Professional Karate Commission
SKA	Shotokan Karate of America
TJBBA	Texas Judo Black Belt Association
UKF	United Karate Federation
USJA	United States Judo Association
USJF	United States Judo Federation
USKA	United States Karate Association
USMA	United States Maccabiah Association
USOJC	United States Olympic Judo Committee
USTAA	United States Tomiki Aikido Association
WBBL	World Black Belt League .
WKA	World Karate Association
WKU	World Karate Union
WPKO	World Professional Karate Organization
WSMAC	World Series of Martial Arts Championships
WTF	World Taekwondo Federation
WUKO	World Union of Karate-do Organizations
YKA	Yoshinkan Karate Association

PREFACE

It took ten years to compile this work, because of our desire to include in it much information that can be found elsewhere only in a wide variety of sources or that is treated superficially in other works. Hence, this is the most comprehensive one-volume study of world martial arts ever published in the English language.

Over the years, we sought the professional advice and direction of eminent authorities in specific aspects of the martial arts from every corner of the globe. Some 125 distinguished contributors submitted previously unpublished information and photographs to this work. This panel represents, in fact, the greatest international martial arts brain trust assembled for a single book in this field.

We have concentrated on a remarkable scope of material about martial artists and martial arts with, we belive, a good balance of American, European and Asian subjects.

This book's focus encompasses the artistic, technical, historical, spiritual, and esoteric dimensions of the Asian fighting arts since their inception more than 2,000 years ago. Its major features include more than 1,000 biographies of prominent administrators, champions and ranked competitors, instructors, film stars, masters, officials, performers, pioneers, promoters, and writers; historical essays on martial arts development in many major countries of the world, including the most extensive ever compiled for the United States, Okinawa, and Europe; hundreds of major and minor arts, styles, and schools; and the most exhaustive bibliography of Martial Arts books ever compiled.

For every hour of actual writing time that went into the preparation of this book, we must have spent five or more hours of research—checking, cross-checking, and rechecking every fact in and out of our own vast libraries. We have tried, to the best of our abilities, to resolve conflicts between sources of information and to correct factual distortions that have been perpetuated in martial arts literature over the years. But in a work of this size, a degree of oversight and minor errors is inevitable. We beg the indulgence of the reader, if, after all, some inaccuracies have crept in.

As with any work on this magnitude, this book was seen into print with the aid of many people, and we are deeply indebted to all of them. Our grateful thanks, first of all, is extended to our distinguished panel of special consultants whose generous help over the years was instrumental in making this work a reality. Likewise, we are indebted to our eminent contributors from around the world. We owe a very special acknowledgment to Stuart Sobel, whose devoted, meticulous care to the various stages of the manuscript was indispensable, and to best-selling autor Joe Hyams, whose wise direction in critical areas proved invaluable. Finally, an appreciation to the president of W. H. Smith, Richard W. Kislak, and to the staff of W. H. Smith—Malki Stein, Steven Weitzen, Harvey Markowitz, Laura Dempsey, Lori Abrams, Lynn Bond and John Van Nort.

EMIL FARKAS and JOHN CORCORAN
Los Angeles, California

GUIDE TO CONTENTS

Traditions: Each major art is immediately followed by branches, forms, styles and derivations of it.

Biographies Hundreds of biographies of major martial artists—from all arts and styles—are included in this book. Preeminent figures, as a rule, are the subject of extensive entries consonant with the scope and importance of their activities and contributions. To be included herein, a figure was required to have performed some service of national significance in at least one of eight categories: instruction, business, promotion, competition, writing, films, officiating, or creation of a new concept.

In all cases, a painstaking attempt was made to collect accurate facts and present those that are vital. Regrettably, the information available for a number of figures was inconsistent or unreliable.

Bold face Bold-face terms within an entry indicate their appearance elsewhere in the book; an index is provided at the end of the book to help you locate particular subjects.

Further Reading Indicates specific books and magazine editions containing more elaborate information about a particular subject. While these guides are not intended to represent an extensive bibliography on a given subject, an attempt was made to refer the reader to the most reliable sources. Hence, a number of the same sources appear repeatedly, where applicable, throughout this book. Extensive sources are cited for major entries.

Capitalization Names of arts and styles are capitalized only when they derive from a person's name, i.e., Shotokan (Gichin Funakoshi's pen name was Shoto).

Spelling Foreign martial arts nomenclature, as well as the names of some foreign martial artists, have suffered inconsistency due to the varied methods of translation to English. Not even the most scholarly and meticulous panel of authorities could agree on some spellings. The authors went to great pains to spell all foreign words and names consistently throughout this book. In so doing, final decisions were based on how the majority of reliable sources and authorities have presented them most often in the past.

Wherever an important term bears multiple and diverse spellings, usually as a result of translation from more than one dialect, all common versions in widespread use are presented, i.e., tae kwon do, taekwon-do, taekwondo.

Hyphens and Punctuation Like spelling, punctuation defies consistent translation from East to West. Here, too, the authors based their final decision on the majority usage by reliable sources.

TRADITIONS

The Principles of the Martial Arts

Oriental martial arts mirror many of the beliefs and customs of the Orient. More than merely combat techiques, most martial arts offer their practitioners a way life based on Eastern philosophy. Martial arts can be best understood if the following aspects of Oriental thought are understood.

The expression "martial arts" refers to numerous styles of combat originating in the Orient. The most common martial arts are aikido, judo, jujutsu, karate, kung-fu, and tae kwon do. All of these many arts share certain customs and practices with which the student should become familiar.

BELT In most Okinawan, Japanese and Korean martial arts practitioners wear a long colored cloth belt around their waist. They are generally long enough to be wrapped twice around the wearer's waist and then tied in a square knot, with 10 to 15 inches hanging from either side of the knot. Before the 20th century most belts were colorless, but since students were prohibited from washing their belts, belts grew steadily darker through years of accumulated sweat and soil. When the colored belt system of rank was incorporated, it was arranged so that the belt color became darker as the student advanced in rank, ending with the black belt. the highest level of proficiency. Belts vary according to style and type of martial art; in some schools there is only a small colored tip on the end of the belt to show rank. In each case the color represents a different established rank; for example, brown in Japanese and Okinawan karate corresponds to red in Korean tae kwon do. The most common colors used in martial arts are white, yellow, orange, blue, green, purple, brown, and black.

If the belt, called **obi** in Japanese, becomes undone during practice, martial arts etiquette is observed. The wearer turns around, facing away from his partner, and while kneeling on one knee reties his belt before again facing his partner. See also dan; gup; kyu.

BLACK BELT Color of belt worn in the Japanese, Okinawan, and Korean martial arts. Its wearer is generally recognized as an expert. In most styles there are 10 degrees of black belt, called **dan** (rank; degree), in which the latter five are honorary. In some styles, the recognized master, a 10th- degree black belt, will at his option wear a red belt.

Judo black belts are typically awarded by a national governing body whose standards are relatively high and competitive with that of other international bodies. In other martial arts, especially karate, certification of a black belt is not controlled by any single organization. Often, therefore, the standards required to achieve a black belt greatly vary. Since the mid-1960s, large numbers of karate black belts have emerged, many with questionable qualifications. There are major karate organizations whose membership maintains a high standard, but frequently one instructor will promote his students to black belt status based strictly on his own criteria. Similar problems exist in jujutsu, tae kwon do, and other martial arts in which a sole governing association is absent. An especially acute problem is the large number of high-ranking black belts whose only achievement has come through self-promotion of rank. *See also* belt; dan.

BUDO Broad term encompassing the Japanese **do** (way) arts. Unlike fighting systems before the 20th century, the do were designed not necessarily to be used in warfare, but as a means of physical and spiritual perfection.

Budo, from the mid-18th century, grew out of more deadly arts, called **bujutsu** (military arts), as a dispassionate, idealized discipline. Its goal is to free the mind of fear and consciousness of self. Budo requires continuous study of technique. It demands continuous effort in creating the ideal psychological state; constant striving is required to remove any emotion obstructing correct judgment and the reflexes of the body.

The budo arts can be considered the antithesis of those practices included under **bujutsu.** The most popular budo arts are aikido, judo, karate-do, kendo, kyudo, and iaido. *Further reading: Modern Bujutsu and Budo,* Donn F. Draeger, 1974; *Classical Budo,* Donn F. Draeger, 1973; *Secrets of the Samurai,* Oscar Ratti and Adele Westbrook, 1973.

CH'I There are many definitions of the msyterious ch'i, the biophysical energy said to be generated by respiratory rhythm. The concept was probably introduced by Mencius (*Chinese Medicine,* Pierre Huard and Ming Wong). Ch'i manifests itself in the five elements of the universe to give substance to the world, but flows through the elements in the form of a life energy which, if understood, can be controlled. Ch'i is everywhere. It can be seen in one's handwriting or calligraphy. The Chinese calligrapher strove to impart his control over ch'i through his brush to his writing. It might be thought of as a force which gives life, or which holds the moon in place, or which holds an atom to an electron. The concept of ch'i was fundamental to the philosophies of China (Taoism and Buddhism) and, therefore, to its martial arts. Internal systems of kung-fu were very concerned with ch'i-kung (spirit manipulation); the external styles, in contrast, concentrated less on principles of ch'i-kung. (MICHAEL P. STAPLES) *See also* ki. *Further reading: The Secret of the Golden Flower,* C.G. Jung, 1962.

CHING Both ching and **ch'i** (spirit, breath) are terms used by Taoist philosophical alchemists seeking immortality. Ching, in this context, is the product of properly developed ch'i. It can also mean semen or, in another sense, and according to a different Chinese character, "muscular force." Sometimes they are contrasted, as between the ch'i of the internal kung-fu systems and the ching of the external styles, but more often ching is thought to be of a nature directly related to ch'i. *Further reading: Taoist Yoga,* Lu K'uan Yu, 1970; *The Yellow Emperor's Classic of Internal Medicine,* Ilza Veith, 1972.

DAN Category of rank in the Japanese, Okinawan, and Korean martial arts that classifies students, instructors, and masters who wear the black belt. It usually takes three to four years of ascent through the **kyu** or **gup** grades to reach 1st-degree black belt, at which the dan ranks commence in some systems, 6th degree and upward are awarded for merit or accomplishment, instead of physical proficiency.

The dan ranks for Japanese and Okinawan martial arts are:
shodan—1st degree
nidan—2nd degree
sandan—3rd degree
yodan—4th degree
godan—5th degree
rokudan—6th degree
shichidan—7th degree
hachidan—8th degree
kudan—9th degree
judan—10th degree
juichidan—11th degree (judo only)
junidan—12th degree (judo only)
The dan ranks for tae kwon do (Korean) are:
illdan—1st degree
yeedan—2nd degree
samdan—3rd degree
sahdan—4th degree
ohdan—5th degree
yookdan—6th degree
childan—7th degree
paldan—8th degree
koodan—9th degree
shibdan—10th degree
or:
chodan—1st degree
ea dan—2nd degree
samdan—3rd degree
sadan—4th degree
ohdan—5th degree
yukdan—6th degree
childan—7th degree
paldan—8th degree
kudan—9th degree
shipdan—10th degree

DEGREE Black belt rank given in a martial art to one who has completed a prescribed course of study. Though no such ranks were issued originally in the Chinese styles, other than master and student, many American kung-fu instructors have adopted a system similar to that used in karate and other arts. *See also* dan.

DO When it follows any particular style of the Japanese martial arts, this term means the "way," or more clearly, "the way to enlightenment, self-realization, and understanding." Do implies that a martial art has been transformed from a practical means of combat to an educational form with emphasis on perfection of human character. Kendo breastplate; constructed chiefly of heavy strips of bamboo covered by lacquered leather. The leatherwork and lacquer are often beautifully decorated.

DOJO Facility in which karate, judo, aikido, and other Japanese **do** arts are practiced; also called a gakko (school). In early Japan, it was the name of a place, usually part of a Zen temple, devoted to religious exercise. Its original Sanskrit meaning, bodhimandala, is the "place of enlightenment." This name was adopted by the Japanese warrior to identify all the halls where he practiced the martial arts.

The four sides of a dojo have special names and functions. The central locale is called kamiza, implying "upper seat"; it is the place of honor reserved for instructors, honored guests, and judo officials. Opposite the kamiza is the shimoza, or "lower seat," the meeting place for all students. During official ceremonies and instructional periods, students are assembled in ranks along this side.

When facing the kamiza, the side of the dojo to the right is called joseki, or "upper side"; on the left is the shimoseki, or "lower side." When instructed, students line up along the shimoseki, while instructors face them from the joseki.

DOJO ETIQUETTE Some of the rules common to all dojo are:
1. Students must bow when entering or leaving the workout area.
2. Students must wear the traditional uniform to all practice sessions.
3. All uniforms must be clean and in good condition.
4. Students must keep their bodies clean and nails trimmed.
5. Students must not wear jewelry or sharp objects when working out.
6. Students must not chew gum or candy, or eat while in the dojo.
7. Students must not engage in idle talk while in the dojo and should remain attentive at all times.
8. Students must always be courteous and helpful to each other.
9. Students should never use their skills, except in self-defense.

DOJO OATH Code of conduct in the dojo and a guide to everyday life It was written by **isshinryu's** founder **Tatsuo Shimabuku.**

We will train our hearts and bodies for a firm, unshaking spirit.

We will pursue the true meaning of the martial way so that in time our senses may be alert.

With true vigor, we will seek to cultivate a spirit of self-denial.

We will observe the rules of courtesy, respect our superiors, and refrain from violence.

We will pay homage to our creator and never forget the true virtue of humility.

We will look upwards to wisdom and strength, not seeking other desires.

All our lives, through the disciplines of karate, we will seek to fulfill the true meaning of the way.

FIVE ELEMENTS THEORY Water, fire, wood, metal, and earth. Working through these five elements, **ch'i** or **ki** produce the five atmospheric conditions, the five grains, the five planets, the five metals, the five colors, the five tastes, and so on. *See also* hsing-i. *Further reading: Chinese Reader's Manual, Part II,* Mayers; *Tibetan Kung-Fu,* Michael P. Staples, 1976.

HORSE STANCE A basic posture in all of the martial arts. Legs spread approximately twice the width of the shoulders, body weight evenly distributed, and toes pointed straight forward. One's "horse" is thought to be the center of strength (in conjunction with the **tan-tien** and small of the back). Although not all stances fall into the category of the horse stance proper, which refers specifically to such stances as the horse-riding stance, chi-ma-pu, and **kung-**

chien-pu, the strength of one's stances in general is often referred to as horse strength.

In many styles, students are required to stand in a horse position for an hour or more before beginning training. Others systems have a horse "set," as in Choy-Li-Fut and Hop-Gar, in which a succession of horse stances are assumed. (MICHAEL P. STAPLES)

JU Applied to combat, the principle of ju is one of adaptation, taking advantage of an opponent's method and force to defeat or neutralize his purpose. Martial arts chronicles confirm, through ju, a Chinese influence upon that school of thought in Japan which held the principle of nonresistence to be superior, not only in a moral sense, but in the practical reality of combat. *See also* jujutsu; judo.

JUTSU Fighting method with the **bugei,** arts of war, rather than with sporting or aesthetic values, which are generally linked to the **do** (way) methods developed in Japan after the mid-18th century. Some of the more popular were karate-jutsu, kenjutsu, aiki-jutso, and jujutsu; these were the antecedents of karate-do, kendo, aikido, and judo. Also spelled jitsu.

KATA COMPETITION Multi-divisional martial arts competition; participants perform individually chosen kata, which are judged usually by five officials under a point system. Judging of kata is generally based on poise, balance, stance, and precise control of movement. Eye movement must parallel body moves, attention must not stray, and power is a prerequisite. Speed and rhythm must be maintained throughout the performance. Judges deduct points for faults, awarding marks between one and ten. In the U.S. most kata competitions are divided into hard, soft, and weapons.

KI Japanese word meaning "spirit"; energy believed to be the source of life. It was generally held that this powerful source of energy could be tapped only if a man had stabilized that position of inner centralization in the **hara.** In India this vital force has been known for centuries as prajna, in China as ch'i, and in Japan as ki.

The coordinated energy of the hara could infuse a man with tremendous vitality and make him powerful in action, more so that the man who had developed muscular power alone. As might be expected, the range of the methods of using these inner techniques is considerable, but all of them included, in addition to meditation and concentration, the fundamental exercise of abdominal breathing.

In ancient texts, the word itself is translated as air, atmosphere, breath. The doctrine was a main source of metaphysical and intellectual speculation for Indian, Chinese, Tibetan, and Japanese scholars, philosophers, and religious leaders. Finally, it was adopted by almost all the important schools of martial arts.

Ki, or ch'i, is a concept that is both natural and simple. Those who make of it something mysterious and akin to magical power miscomprehend what is essentially a common property of all human beings. Learning to release and utilize ki is where the difficulty lies. Its function in the human body has been described as "electricity that flows back and forth along the wires of our nerves," and as "the psycho-physiological power associated with blood, breath and mind; the biophysical energy generated by respiratory rhythm." *Further reading: Modern Bujutsu and Budo,* Donn F. Draeger, 1974; *Secrets of the Samurai,* Oscar Ratti and Adele Westbrook, 1973; *The Book of Ki,* Koichi Tohei, 1976; *Ki In Daily Life,* Koichi Tohei, 1978; *Kick Illustrated,* July 1980.

RHYTHM An essential element in the performance of martial arts techniques. Rhythm is more complicated than, and cannot be expressed in terms of, musical rhythm. It is especially necessary in the performance of both **kata** and fighting. In the latter, however, it is just as important to learn to break the rhythm and create unpredictability.

The three most important aspects of kata are the application of strength at the correct instances, the control of speed in and between techniques, and the smooth transition of the body from one technique to the next. All of these requirements cannot be fulfilled without rhythm. *See also* broken rhythm; rhythm-changing.

SEISHIN Spiritual energy. Generated through training in classical Japanese disciplines, seishin was expected to heighten courage and patriotic spirit, particularly for the soldier or sailor. Every fighter came to believe that seishin would enable him to perform on the battlefield in a state of mind that would conquer any emergency. The concept of seishin helped to fabricate the myth that the Japanese fighter was invincible in battle.

SENSEI Japanese martial arts teacher. The martial arts have always been indebted to the sensei, who spent the greater part of his life immersed in the forms of **bujutsu.** He tested the techniques and strategies of the various styles in actual combat, experimented with its weapons, and devised new methods of coping with life-threatening situations. Above all, he taught his methods to others.

Little is known about the criteria adopted to evaluate a candidate for assignment as a sensei. It is assumed that the most naturally inclined and talented men from the members of a clan were appointed. In Chinese culture this appointment depended on merit, ascertained through a series of public examinations, and upon constant supervision of a candidate's performance during his official career. In Japan, however, it became largely hereditary and, consequently, was passed from the original teacher to his natural or adopted son. While the records of masters of arms in China abound with names of individual fighters known for their prowess in various systems, in Japan such records point primarily to schools and families of bujutsu experts who took considerable pride in recalling a long line of professional ancestors and whose written or oral instructions they tended to follow quite closely.

In Japan, a sharp distinction can be made between the teachers of the military class and those belonging to other classes. The sensei of the first category comprised the majority, and their specialties included, in order of importance, archery, spearmanship, swordsmanship, general strategy, and several subordinate styles of unarmed combat, such as jujutsu and **aikijutsu,** used in combination with the traditional armed styles. The latter category formed the minority, being men who usually specialized in arts of combat that could be practiced without arousing the attention and concern of the military authorities. Among these teachers were specialists in instruments of various social classes: the staff, fan, iron pipes, and chained blades.

Within his **dojo** a sensei was in a position of supreme authority and unchallenged prestige. A student registered in a particular **ryu** was principally a pupil of the instructor who accepted him as a disciple. Thus personal discipleship, rather than institutional membership, was the working relationship. It has been observed that even today one seldom witnesses a more pronounced form of respect, often virtually indistinguishable from actual subservience, than that accorded to a Japanese master of any martial art by his Japanese students. There have been many attempts to export and transplant this type of relationship to the West in certain judo, karate, aikido, kendo schools, etc. More often than not, the results have been frustrating and disappointing to both the Japanese instructor and his Western students, since the necessary cultural promises simply are not present in the West.

SPINNING KICKS Used in the majority of Asian martial arts, kicks which are delivered with a half or full spin of the body. They are especially prevalent in tae kwon do and numerous forms of kung-fu. Spinning kicks can be performed from several positions including standing, crouching, and while jumping. They can be extremely powerful since the force of the kick is combined with the force of the spin. Many traditional Japanese karate systems use few spinning kicks since the body turn necessary to perform the kicks can leave the user vulnerable to an attack. *Further reading: The Complete Martial Artist*, Hee Il Cho, 1981; *Karate, The Art of Empty-Hand Fighting*, Hidetaka Nishiyama and Richard Brown, 1960; *Taekwon-Do*, Choi Hong Hi, 1972; *Advanced Explosive Kicks*, Chong Lee, 1978; *Super Dynamic Kicks*, Chong Lee, 1980.

STYLE An expression that usually refers to the type of martial arts one practices, e.g. judo, karate, aikido, etc. In karate, the word style refers to the system or school in which one practices. Since there are hundreds of different types of karate, each with different characteristics, the word "style" has become common among practitioners when referring to the specific kind of karate they are engaged in such as **Shotokan, goju-ryu, tae kwon do, shorin-ryu, Chito-ryu, renbukan,** etc.

A growing number of styles are created each year, adding to the confusing array of martial systems. Today, as in the past, as a master perfects a style, he adds techniques of his liking and deletes those that are incompatible. In other cases, two or more styles are combined to give rise to yet another variety. There are also multitudinous styles built around weapons.

The earliest Okinawan karate styles were typically named after the masters who created them. Around 1830, **Sokon Matsumura** became the first Okinawan karate master to call his style by a name other than his own, **Shuri-te**. From that point, Okinawan karate styles were called Shuri-te, **Naha-te**, and **Tomari-te**, forms of **te** (hand), the early name for karate, which were named after the cities where they were created and practiced. Although minor variations exist, the most prominent Okinawan styles are **shorin-ryu** (which entails three primary subdivisions, shobayashi-ryu, kobayashi-ryu, and matsubayashi-ryu, plus one secondary subdivision, matsumura orthodox); **Okinawan goju-ryu; shorei-ryu; Uechi-ryu;** and **isshinryu**.

In Japan, karate is divided into **karate-jutsu** (which focuses strictly on self-defense and combat) and the more popular **karate-do** (which embraces spiritual and philosophical dimensions). According to the late martial scholar, **Donn F. Draeger**, there were more than 70 styles of karate-do extant in Japan by the early 1970s. There are today four major styles of karate-do: **Shotokan; Shito-ryu; wado-ryu**; and **goju-ryu**. Other important styles include **kyokushinkai; renbukai; Chito-ryu; sankukai; koei-kan; shukokai;** and **shudokan**.

In Korea, the umbrella term tae kwon do is primarily representative of Korean karate, followed by **tang soo do** and **hapkido**. The term tae kwon do was coined in 1955 when an undetermined number of the eight existing **kwans** (schools) merged to form this art. Five kwans have remained within tae kwon do: chang moo kwan; chung do kwan; chi do kwan; ji do kwan; and oh do kwan. Tang soo do, like tae kwon do, has spread prolifically throughout the world, while hapkido's internationalization has been much slower. *See also* judo; karate; karate-do; kung-fu; kwans; Olinawa, history of martial arts in; tae kwon do.

TAISO Limbering, stretching, and warm-up exercises performed by martial artists before a class. Taiso is necessary to prepare the body for the spontaneous movements demanded in a training session. Since different martial arts emphasize different movements, taiso varies from school to school. In most karate and tae kwon do schools, considerable time is devoted to vigorous stretching routines, especially for the legs. In judo schools, however, the emphasis is placed on push-ups, sit-ups, etc., to increase strength and stamina. Sometimes, these exercises are performed at the end of a class as well. The main objective of taiso is to eliminate stiffness and promote flexibility so as to prevent muscle injuries during a workout.

UKEMI Breakfalls used in judo and other Japanese martial arts to avoid injury when being thrown. Ukemi has been called the key to judo. Until the fear of falling is eliminated, the judoka has not the confidence to attempt advanced feats. There are two types of ukemi in judo: falls in which the arm strikes the mat; falls in which the body rolls like a ball.

In mastering ukemi, a student first learns to strike the mat with both arms and hands while falling backwards. The arms are held straight about 45 degrees from the body. The head is kept tucked upward to prevent injury. Next, breakfalls to the left and right side are practiced, in which only one hand and arm strike the mat. In a side breakfall, the leg and foot also strike the mat simultaneously with the arms. Finally, the rolling breakfall is perfected, in which the arms and feet strike the mat as the body rolls forward in a somersaulting motion.

YIN-YANG Two opposite forces that exist in harmony, complement each other, and are dependent on each other. Yin is characterized as the negative force of darkness, coldness and emptiness; yang as the positive force of light, warmth and fullness. Yin-yang represents the two primal, opposite forces: hard and soft, masculine and feminine. The binary list is endless.

There are two yin-yang symbols which represent both the philosophy and the marwtial arts aspect of kung-fu: the spiral and the double fish.

Both configurations are enclosed in a circle, which is indicative of the cyclical evolution in nature. The transmutation of two opposites is represented by the dark area blending into the white. Harmony between these opposite attributes is shown by the equality of the two areas. The white dot in the dark area and the dark dot in the white area of the double fish configuration show the interdependency of the two. Obviously these same principles are applicable to the spiral configuration, but its origin is not as clear. However, it is generally believed that it did exist before the double fish diagram and was derived from the **I-Ching**. During kung-fu's evolution, the spiral configuration was adopted by the intellectuals and scholars, and the double fish configuration became synonymous with the commoners.

The pugilist who understands the yin-yang principles, it is said, has unlimited resources in the application of his techniques. *Further reading: The History and Philosophy of Kung-Fu*, Ear C. Medeiros, 1974; *Kung-Fu: History, Philosophy and Technique*, David Chow and Richard Spangler, 1977; *Tibetan Kung-Fu: Way of the Monk*, Michael P. Staples, 1977.

ZANSHIN State of total awareness cultivated in all martial arts. Zanshin is not a state achieved through analysis, but rather through experience and instinct. By an intense and intuitive use of the senses some exponents seem to achieve a state of awareness that almost suggests a sixth sense. It produces an intriguing calmness of mind and an apparent detachment even in threatening situations, when fear or anger might seem a more natural reaction. Through zanshin the Japanese bushi achieved the proper mental and physical attitude with which to dominate his adversary. The Japanese refer to Zanshin as an all-seeing "mind like the moon."

ZEN Discipline that stresses meditation, and direct transmission of teachings from master to student. Zen, as it is known to Japan, was introduced there by Buddhist monks returning from China in the 13th century. Attracted by its austerity, many **samurai** sought to perfect themselves in its study. They hoped in this way to face battle and even death without expressing fear.

The aim of Zen is complete control of the mind—to attain a state of enlightenment and a sense of detachment from the physical world. This is achieved by constant meditation and strict self-discipline.

It is generally claimed that Zen was the foundation of martial arts in feudal Japan, that it provided the doctrine of **bujutsu** with a theory and a philosophy, and that it provided the martial artist with proper disciplines for developing a strong character and personality. A man thoroughly versed in the techniques of concentration and meditation might achieve complete indifference to physical discomfort, pain, and eventually even death. It is no wonder, then, that Japanese warriors, who were professionally fascinated by the various ways of meeting death, came to believe that Zen masters made "sport of death."

The most important contribution of Japanese Zen to the martial arts was its insistence upon intuition, believed by Zen masters to be the most direct way of reaching truth. Intuition was the quality the feudal warrior needed to develop most particularly to respond quickly to the promptings of a dangerous situation.

Finally, Zen seems to have also influenced the style of recording the techniques of the various **ryu** (schools). The task of writing them, of preserving and guarding them, was generally assigned to a Zen priest residing in a nearby monastery, when not performed by the master of the school himself.

In relation to moral conduct, however, Zen had little or nothing to add to the code of loyalty and obedience that ruled the life of a samurai. Instead, it sustained them morally and philosophically. Morally, because Zen teaches one not to look backward once the course is decided upon; and philosophically, because it treats life and death indifferently. *Further reading: Secrets of the Samurai*, Oscar Ratti and Adele Westbrook, 1973; *Zen*, Eugen Herrigel, 1960; *Zen and Zen Classics*, R.H. Blyth, 1962; *The Practice of Zen*, Garma C.C. Chang, 1959.

AIKIDO

A method of unarmed self-defense, Aikido offers four basic advantages to its practitioners: it develops rhythmic movement and physical fitness, both integral parts of self-defense training; it encourages discipline and a nonviolent attitude; it promotes strength and suppleness in the joints and limbs through twisting, bending, and stretching—movements that also free the limbs from harmful adhesions; and it increases the practitioner's awareness of posture and good body alignment, and improves reactions, perception, and coordination. In aikido a student learns to use an opponent's force by bringing it into his own circle, neutralizing aggressive action by gaining control of the attacker.

Grading in aikido is much like grading in most martial arts and is categorized either as **kyu** grades—the student grades which graduate from the lowest, usually 5th or 6th kyu, and **dan** ranks—indicated by a black belt, ascending from the 1st dan to the 8th dan, and in rare cases, above.   In the Ueshiba and Shioda schools, black belts wear a **hakama.** In the Tomiki school, wearing a ha kama is optional.

The beginning levels emphasize fundamental techniques and exercises, and breakfalling skills. Exercises are designed to improve flexibility, breath, and stamina. At the advanced levels, emphasis is placed on a higher and more intense degree of training and greater self-study and introspection. The general direction is always toward polishing the technique and achieving greater awareness into the art as a way of life. Serious study is given to the philosophy of the art as well as its psychological application in training and daily life. Aikido's roots are deep in the tradition of Japanese martial arts and the Japanese view of nature. Water flows and takes any shape or course, yet it is always consistent with its own nature. The aikidoist admires this quality of living. In training, the aikidoist becomes sensitive to the flow and movement of his mind and body and achieves insight into his own fundamental nature. Aikido, as a way of life, is the final transformation of the martial discipline.

That aikido developed from Zen philosophy is evident in the belief that the center of meditation and the source of mental strength or power, **ki,** is centered in the body, about 1½ inches above the navel, the **tanden.**   Several names are given to this power, the most common being **ki.** In both the Ueshiba and the Yoshin schools, students are taught to understand this power, and exercises, such as the unbendable arm, are used to develop it. Special breathing techniques and meditation are intrinsic parts of the training.

Aikido is essentially noncombative, emphasizing throwing and joint techniques over striking and kicking techniques. It emphasizes principles of nonconflict and the cultivation of ki. Aikido's primary aim is a healthy mind and body and a wholesome spirit. In aikido, nonresistance is not only physical; it is also mental and spiritual. To the Western mind, the word *pliable* is perhaps a better way to describe this state; if pushed, move with the push, if pulled, move with that motion, blending with an opponent's movement and direction of power. Because it is instinctive to react against a push by pushing, or against a pull by pulling, the aikido student must learn to overcome this natural tendency.

Aikido has founded in Tokyo in 1942 by **Morihei Ueshiba**

With the death of Ueshiba in 1969 the development of aikido was taken over by his son, **Kisshomaru Ueshiba,** who presides at the general headquarters and the International Aikido Federation, representing all the countries of the free world. Through this organization, the quality of the art and the black belt ranks are strictly regulated. More than 14 different sects of aikido exist today.

The teachings of the **Daito-ryu aiki-jutsu,** the roots of aikido, continue today, and Tokimune Takeda is its current headmaster in Japan. The leading exponents of this traditional sect are Kotaro Horikawa, Yukiyoshi Agawa, Takuma Hisa, Hosaku Matsuda Tomekichi Yamamoto, and **Richard Kim** in the U.S. Matsuda trained two other leading proponents of aiki-jutsu, Yoshiji Okuyama

Aikido techniques

Aikido techniques

and Sachiyuki Oba; Okuyama is the founder of Hakko ryu jujutsu, a modern **bujutsu,** and includes among his many disciples Michiomi Nakano, who, as **Doshin So,** is the founder of the **Nippon Shorinji kempo** system.

Among Ueshiba's senior disciples, in addition to his son, Kisshomaru, are **Koichi Tohei,** Yuso Murasige, **Gozo Shioda,** Minoru Mochizuki, **Kenji Tomiki,** Minoru Hirai, and Yoichiro Inoue. The foremost innovators of Ueshiba's aikido are Shioda, Tomiki, Hirai, and Inoue. Shioda's **yoshin** style is combat-oriented and closely approximates the classical sect of aiki-jutsu, though its spiritual purpose is like Ueshiba's. **Tomiki aikido** is a system of physical education including practical elements of self-defense, and is practiced competitively. Hirai's korindo aikido concentrates on self-defense. The Inoue style is called shinwa taido, a blend of self-defense and sport.

Other students of Ueshiba have developed their own eclectic styles of aikido. Yutaka Otsuki developed Otsuki ryu aikido, and Tetsuomi Hoshi created a system he calls kobu-jutsu; both are occupied with self-defense. Setaro Tanaka is the founder of the shin riaku heiho, also a self-defense system. Students of Tanaka are currently designing other systems of combat based on aikido. The shindo iten ryu is still being formalized, while the yae ryu of Harunosuke Fukui is steadily growing in popularity. Ueshiba's last disciple through direct teaching, Senryuken Noguchi, is the founder of shindo rokugo ryu, another self-defense form of aikido. Contemporary masters of aikido include Ueshiba's son, Kisshomaru; his grandson, Moriteru Ueshiba; Kisaburo Ohsawa; Seigo Yamaguchi; and Mitsunari Kanai. *See also* Tomiki aikido; Ueshiba aikido; Yoshin aikido. *Further reading: Aikido: An Introduction to Tomiki Style,* M.J. Clapton, 1974; *Modern*

Bujutsu and Budo, Donn F. Draeger, 1974; *Martial Arts of the Orient,* James Elkin, 1975; *Aikido, Its Heart and Appearance,* Morihiro Saito, 1973; *Dynamic Aikido,* Gozo Shioda, 1968; *What Is Aikido?* Koichi Tohei, 1962; *Judo with Aikido,* Kenji Tomiki, 1959; *Aikido and The Dynamic Sphere,* Adele Westbrook and Oscar Ratti, 1974.

AIKIKAI Name given to the central dojo of **aikido** in the Shinjuku district of Tokyo. The modern four-story building houses offices, sleeping quarters, and a number of training rooms. Classes are conducted six days a week and on Sunday mornings. The chief instructor is **Kishomaru Ueshiba,** the aikido founder's son, who teaches the first class each day. The Aikikai also houses the headquarters of the International Aikido Federation, which has branches throughout Japan and the world. Qualified instructors from the Aikikai are dispatched internationally to disseminate Ueshiba's aikido. Foreign students constantly travel to the Aikikai for training.

FORMS OF AIKIDO

TOMIKI AIKIDO The Tomiki school of aikido, founded by **Kenji Tomiki.** Its distinctive characteristic is competition. Prof. Tomiki believed that even if a competitive element were introduced into aikido, the basic principles could remain undegraded.

There are four types of competition in Tomiki aikido, designed for participation by all ages. The first is **kata** competition, in which competitors choose kata they wish to demonstrate. Performed in pairs, it involves coordinated movement in kneeling and standing positions. A scoring system similar to that of gymnastics is used, with five judges awarding points. **Ninin-dori** competition is a freestyle event with three players; **tanto randori** is a competition in which participants defend against a knife or short sword; and in **randori kyoghi** two unarmed players attempt to score against each other with skillfully applied techniques. *Further reading: Judo with Aikido, Kenji Tomiki, 1956.*

NININ-DORI Freestyle competition in **Tomiki aikido** with three players, each of whom in turn takes the part of defender against the other

two. Players are judged on variation of technique and attack, speed of performance, and general reaction under stress. Duration of this event is 3 minutes. It is considered poor control if a defender permits both opponents to attack simultaneously, unless he can use such a situation to his own advantage. This is one of four types of competition in Tomiki aikido.

RANDORI KYOGHI Form of **Tomiki aikido** competition; two unarmed players compete, attempting to score through skillful application of aikido techniques. If a player scores twice before time is called, he is declared the winner. Action must be continuous, since non-activity—or playing a waiting game—can lead to disqualification. Only senior grades are permitted to enter this event. Randori kyoghi is one of four types of competition in Tomiki aikido.

Aikido technique

9

Rolling techniques of aikido

TANTO RANDORI Form of competition in **Tomiki aikido** affording participants the opportunity of defending themselves against a knife or short sword, which for the purpose of this event is made of rubber. Two contestants are involved, each in turn acting the part of the defender, who is unarmed, and the attacker, who is armed. The defender scores by demonstrating ability in avoiding the knife attack and applying a skillful aikido technique. The attacker scores by making a positive strike on the target area, which is any part of the trunk between the shoulders and the waistline. The arms, legs, and face are not attacked. Tanto randori is one of four types of competition in Tomiki aikido.

YOSHIN AIKIDO Style of aikido founded by **Gozo Shioda.** It follows a slightly different approach, both ethically and physically, than **Morihei Ueshiba's** aikido, maintaining that through the study of correct technique the gentle can control the strong.

Instruction follows a set pattern, starting with postural exercises that stress positioning and the avoidance of direct lines of attack. There are many exercises for developing strong, supple joints and limbs, followed by study of the basic "controls," all concerned with wrist action and holds. Each control has many variations, and students soon acquire an extensive repertoire.

The Shioda school has some 150 basic techniques, which are practiced repeatedly. These enable the student to master the remaining ones, which total some 3,000 overall. Competition is not advocated in this system; emphasis is instead placed on "mental harmony." The system teaches aikido to many universities and businesses in Japan and has branches overseas, especially in the U.S.

Shioda's dojo, founded after World War II, came to be called the Yoshinkan (house for cultivating the spirit). His aikido is occasionally called the "hard" style because his training methods are a product of the grueling period he spent as Ueshiba's **uke** (receiver of the techniques). At the core of Shioda's training is the concept of agatsu, which, loosely translated, means "control myself." Shite (the performer of the technique) must be in perfect control of himself, blending his mind, strength, energy and ego with that of the uke's. The goal of Shioda's hard training is harmony. The approach is to instill correct technique in the student, so that he may discover on his own the underlying harmony in all aikido movements.

Yoshin aikido places less emphasis on ki than most aikido styles. Like Ueshiba, Shioda embraces aikido as a way of life, rather than a practice confined to the dojo. "Where to go, where to live, where to rest, where to sleep; everywhere is the best dojo," he says.

Yoshin aikido students are not taught to conceptualize sets of movements or analytically study various defensive counters to a specific attack. What is instead emphasized is the development of an intuitive natural understanding of aikido's essence. Students learn several techniques, usually variations of a common form, during each class. Over the course of many years' training, they can grasp the principles underlying the art. To do so, they assume both roles of attacker (uke) and defender (shite) to study a technique.

Yoshin aikido is represented in the U.S. by **Takashi Kushida,** the style's heir apparent who founded the Aikido Yoshinkai Association of North America in the mid-1970s, and in Canada by Takeshi Kimeda. *Further reading: Black Belt Magazine,* Nov. 1982; *Dynamic Aikido,* Gozo Shioda, 1968.

ARNIS

Originally known as kali, arnis is the most popular martial art of the Philippines. It is known as estocada, in the Tagalog provinces, and estogue, or fraile, in other regions. Arnis techniques are executed empty-handed or with such weapons as a stick or a blade. Practiced by Filipinos for centuries, some combat historians think arnis is derived from tjakalele, an Indonesian method of combat.

As a fighting art, arnis has three forms of combat: espada y daga

Two Filipino students practicing arnis, the stick-fighting art of the Philippines

(sword and dagger), using a long wooden sword and a short wooden dagger; solo baston (single stick), employing a long stick made of wood or a rattan cane; and sinawali, a native term relating the intricate movements of two muton (sticks) to the crisscross weave of a sawali, the bamboo-split pattern used in walling and matting.

Arnis is the most effective in close-range combat, and stresses striking and parrying skills. The expert use of the leg and the leg-hip fulcrum maneuver to offset balance and throw an opponent is very important. Unlike other martial arts, which make use of the entire body, early kali and modern arnis emphasize use of the stick and hand-arm movements.

Arnis embraces three principal training methods. Muestrasion, or pandalag, teaches in repetitive drills the artistic execution of swinging movements and stroking for offense and defense; sangga at patama, or sombra tabak, teaches striking, thrusting, and parrying in prearranged series; and larga muton, or labanang totohanan, allows two trainees to engage in free-style practice. The larga muton is the ultimate phase of arnis.

The principles of arnis are divided into two categories: physical and psychological. Physically, the practitioner, known as a bastonero or estocador, must strive for speed when delivering the strokes, speed of the hands and feet, and even speed of the eyes in spotting an opponent's weak points. The practitioner is conditioned to stare for long periods without blinking, for a blink in combat could prove fatal. When swinging the club, the grip must be firm and the stroke delivered with a jerk; the wrist must be relaxed after each stroke. Finally, a player should not allow distance to separate him from his opponent.

Psychologically, the student must learn to be calm and composed, so that he may concentrate completely on his opponent. Above all, he must have the will to fight and win. The presence of an opening will have no meaning if the player does not possess the will to seize and exploit it to his advantage.

Many of the techniques of the "old" arnis have been changed to avoid risk of injury to students; in modern arnis some of the weapons have been altered. Major changes were introduced by **Remy Presas,** the so-called founder of modern arnis. Although the art occasionally uses the itak, or bolo, the cane has become the primary self-defense weapon. A long-bladed weapon, however, is still sometimes employed in arnis competition. The predominant use of the cane in the art of arnis is in keeping with the aims and programs of the New Society of the Philippines, which abhors the use of guns and bladed weapons. *Further reading: The Filipino Martial Arts,* Dan Inosanto, 1978; *Modern Arnis: Philippine Style of Stick Fighting,* Remy Presas, 1974.

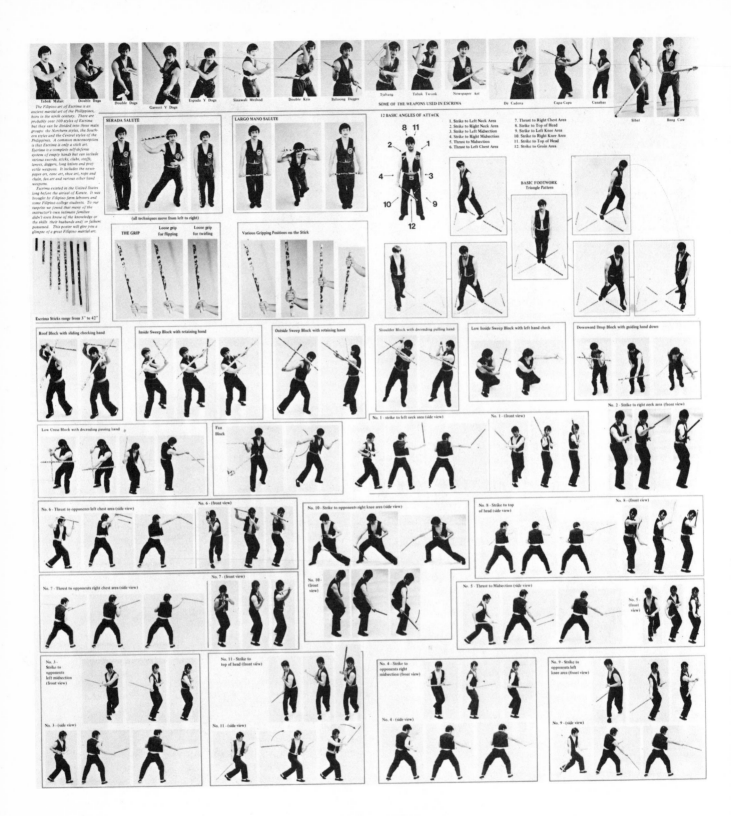

Arnis techniques

FORMS OF ARNIS

KALI is an ancient Philippine martial art, spawned before the arrival of the Chinese of the T'ang dynasty in the 9th century, before the Arab wave of the 15th century, kali was flourishing at the arrival of the Spanish conquistadores in the 16th century.

Kali is a complete self-defense system employing empty-hand techniques and the use of various swords, sticks, clubs, staves, lances, daggers, long knives, and projectile weapons. It embraces the rolled newspaper art, cane art, shoe art, rope art, chain art, fan art, palm stick art, and other weapons.

There are perhaps 100 different styles of kali in the Philippines, but all of them can be classified within four major divisions: northern styles; eastern central styles; western central styles; and southern styles. Kali is sometimes known as **escrima; arnis;** arnis de mano; **silat;** kaliradman, by the Visayans; kalirongan, by the Pangasinese; pagkalikali, by the Ibanags; garote, by the Cebuanos; baston, by the people of Penay and Negroes Occidental; and sinawali, by the Pampangenos.

In kali training practitioners first learn weapons before progressing to the weaponless techniques of hand and foot. The first weapon is usually the stick or dagger. Systems include the sinawali sticks (two sticks usually about 30 inches), single or double dagger methods, and espada y daga, the stick and dagger method. A 27 inch to 30 inch stick is held in the right hand and a 12 inch dagger in the left.

Kicking is taught from inside range to outside range, using the heel in a multitude of ways. Kicking is also done with the shin and knee, as well as in a stomping manner. The use of the palm, finger jab, elbow, and head or shoulder smashes are favored over the fist in many of the empty-hand systems. Experts are able to choke, strangle, throw, sweep, and secure various locks with or without the assistance of a weapon.

Kali declined in popularity as early as 1696; Spanish authorities discouraged and eventually banned its practice in 1764. Kali was practiced secretly during the Spanish reign of 311 years in the northern islands. In southern and central parts of the Philippines, the Moros (Moslem Filipinos) remained unconquered. Their kali arts (silat and kuntaw) were never banned and are still practiced in the south.

Kali (as escrima) was brought to the U.S. and Hawaii in the early 1900s by Filipino college students, farm workers, merchant marines, and stevedores. Jack Santos, an escrima master, formally introduced the art to the U.S. in 1909. He was followed by numerous kali and escrima men, but the art was then highly secretive and was usually taught only to Filipinos. The few non-Filipinos who did learn it did so only through Filipino friends. Just how many learned and how much they were taught is unknown. It is known, however, that during this early period many Filipinos were taught the stick and dagger phases, but were not taught the empty-hand aspects of the art.

Escrima master Angel Caballes opened the first public academy in 1964 in Stockton, Calif. Ben Largusa gave the first public demonstration of kali and escrima at the 1964 **International Karate Championships** in Long Beach, Calif. Probably the best known kali masters today, besides Largusa, are Floro Villabrille and John LaCaste. And perhaps the best known school is the Filipino Kali Academy in Torrance, Calif. under the direction of **Dan Inosanto** and Richard Bustillo. The directors owe the bulk of their knowledge to a long list of instructors: Largusa, Caballes, LaCoste, Villabrille, Pedro Apilado, Leo Giron, Regino Illustrisimo, Pasqual Ovalles, Braulio Pedoy, Max Sarmiento, Telesporo Subing, Subing, Dentoy Revillar, Dioncio Canete, Sam Tendencia, and Leo Gajae.

In an unusual application of the Filipino martial arts, Dr. Bob Ward, conditioning coach for the Dallas Cowboys, invited Inosanto and Bustillo to the Cowboys training camp with the intention of improving players' hand to eye coordination through training in stick fighting.

The foremost exponents of this art in the Philippines are the Canete brothers of Cebu, particularly Cacao and Momoy. (DAN INOSANTO) See also arnis. *Further reading: The Filipino Martial Arts,* Dan Inosanto, 1979; *Black Belt Magazine,* Sept. 1975; *Inside Kung Fu,* Jan. 1981.

SINAWALI Form of **arnis** performed by two players holding a club in each hand; play is characterized by crisscrossing movement of the clubs. The sinawali derives its name from "sawali," a native Filipino woven bamboo thatch. There are two types of sinawali, single and double. The Pampangenos use the term sinawali in place of **kali** or arnis.

YAW YAN Philippine martial art founded in the early 1970s by Napoleon Fernandez. Noted for its variety of spectacular kicks, its hand techniques are patterned after the movements of **arnis.** *Further reading: Inside Kung Fu,* Nov. 1982.

RANKS

DAYANG Black belt ranks given to female students in **arnis de mano.** The belt has a red trim, and is only awarded after one year of continuous training. To attain the rank of dayang-isa (1st-degree black belt), the student must master the 12 basic striking techniques, blocking tactics, the 4 anyos (forms), and all the offensive and defensive technqiues. She also must be able to teach the art, and have taken part in arnis competition. Dayang ranks are as follows:

dayang-isa—1st degree
dayang-dalawa—2nd degree
dayang-tatlo—3rd degree
dayang-apat—4th degree
dayang-lima—5th degree
dayang-anim—6th degree
dayang-pito—7th degree
dayang-walo—8th degree
dayang-siyam—9th degree
dayang-sampa—10th degree

Belts through 5th degree are black with widening red rims to indicate progressively higher rank; 6th and up can wear either a red belt or black trimmed with orange. *See also* arnis.

LAKAN Male black belt ranks in the Filipino art of **arnis** (harness). Rimmed with a red trim, the belt is awarded after one year of continuous training. To attain the rank of lakan (equivalent to 1st-degree black belt) a student must master the 12 basic striking techniques, blocking techniques, the four anyos (forms), and other offensive and defensive techniques. He must be proficient enough to teach the art, and tested in tournament competition.

Lakan ranks are divided into ten progressive categories from 1st-degree black belt through 10th degree. Each is distinguished from its predecessor by a widening of the red rims that border the belt. The ranks are:

lakan-isa—1st	lakan-anim—6th
kalan-dalawa—2nd	lakan-pito—7th
lakan-tatlo—3rd	lakan-walo—8th
lakan-apat—4th	lakan-siyam—9th
lakan-lima—5th	lakan-sampu—10th

Holders of 7th to 10th degree may wear either a red belt or a black belt rimmed with orange.

BANDO

Despite the Chinese influences, bando is credited as a style of armed and unarmed combat native to Burma. It is an assimilation of karatelike striking and kicking techniques, judolike throwing techniques, swordplay and fighting with knives, spears and sticks.

There are numerous interpretations of the term *bando,* and different linguistic and ethnic groups hold to diverse translations. It is generally interpreted in three ways: "way of discpline," "systems of defense," and "art of fighting or combat." Some bando groups have combined all three translations in one, making it similar to the Japanese term *budo* (stop conflict) the Chinese word *wu-shu* (war art), or the English terms *military arts* or *martial arts.* Some etymologists believe the term *bando* derives from Chinese, while others claim Indian or even Tibetan origins. Bando is also called thaing.

There are many styles of bando, but most follow basic instructional patterns. The art emphasizes initial withdrawal followed by an attack

— KALI TERMINOLOGY —

BALANGO – Top student
GURO – Instructor
PANGULO – Head instructor
SARGENTO de ARMAS – Sergeant at Arms
TUHAN – Master
NUMERADO – Close-quarters infighting – METHOD & STYLE
PRAELE – Defensive method
LITERADA – Defensive method
CABISEDARIO – Outside fighting – METHOD & STYLE
SUMBRADA – Counter-for-counter – STYLE
BARTIKAL – One attacks/other defends
KARANSA – Freestyle workout; sparring session
KENOLDAS – Mixed numbers
ESTOKA – Form
PARADA – Stance
DOBLIKARA – Double weapon or 2-fisted method
SINAWALI – Interwoven motion; Doblicara
TAYADA – To encircle opponent
MOHARA – To encircle opponent

— KALI TERMINOLOGY —

PALAD – Palm.
TINDOLO – Finger. (same as Tudlo)
KAMUT – Hand.
BOTES – Leg.
SEMUD – Mouth (same as Ba'ba').
GOSOK – Ribs.
KULIS – Line.
ORASCION – Pray (same as Sumbayan).
MASELA ATAO – Rank.
TAMING – Shield.
BELOK – Lance; spear; staff.
UTBONG – Tip.
APA – Wait; freeze; attention (same as Mangukay).
SENANG – Light; sun.
BEJUCO – Rattan.
BAHI – Palm tree.

— KALI TERMINOLOGY —

ABANTI – To advance
SULOD – To move in
ATARAS – To move back; retreat
DUL – To sparr; a match or contest
DULAK – Exercise
TINDUG – To stand; to get up
LINGKOD – Sit
TAMBAK – Path; forward/backward movement
TABAS – Strike from right side
ORDABIS – Strike from left side
TIGBAS – Strike w/bladed/non-bladed weapon
BUNAL – Strike w/non-bladed weapon
DUNGAB – To stab; thrust
LABTIK – Whip-like strike w/motion follow-through
WITIK – Whip-like strike w/motion pull-back
PITIK – Flick w/finger(s)
SAGGANG – Defensive X-block
PAYONG – Defensive parry

Kali practitioners usually learn the weapons phase of the art
before progressing to the weaponless techniques. Here, Dan
Inosanto shows the use of the stick.
Courtesy of *Inside Kung-Fu*

outside the opponent's reach. All parts of the body are employed in these attacks, and once the initial technique is delivered, grappling and locking techniques are used. Techniques are learned first through formal exercises in some systems and only later through sparring.

When the Japanese invaded Burma in 1942, they encouraged the practice and proliferation of bando and influenced it by exchanging techniques from judo, jujutsu, and aikido. After World War II, bando was furthered through a large number of competitions.

Bando was introduced in the U.S. by Dr. **Maung Gyi,** a college professor who began teaching the art on April 3, 1960, in Washington, D.C. Later, bando classes were formally conducted at American University until the fall of 1966. Dr. Gyi organized the American Bando Association on June 15, 1968, at Ohio University. Members present at this initiation ceremony took a blood oath.

The International Bando Association was officially formed on Mar. 9, 1946, by U Ba Than, then the director of physical education and athletics for the Union of Burma. The IBA was organized in honor of those servicemen who fought and died in the China-Burma-India theater of World War II. (ROBERT MAXWELL) *Further reading: Asian Fighting Arts,* Donn F. Draeger and Robert W. Smith, 1969.

Bojutsu

BERSILAT

Bersilat is a Malaysian form of self-defense dating to the 15th century. It consists of two forms; silat pulot and silat buah. Silat pulot is a dancelike series of movements usually performed at weddings and other ceremonies; graceful in appearance and devoid of combat realism, percussion instruments are used to lend rhythmic background to its movements. Silat buah is the combat form of bersilat. Conducted barefoot, it makes great use of the legs and is quite acrobatic. Training in this phase of the art is given to select students, who are forbidden to divulge its secrets.

Students of bersilat wear a black uniform consisting of a short-sleeved shirt, baggy trousers, and a headband. A belt (bengkong), ranging in color from white (beginners) through green, red, yellow, and finally black, denotes the wearer's rank.

Much of the training and exercises used today have been handed down from generation to generation. According to Malayan folk legend, Huang Tuah of Malaca, a 15th-century traveler, is considered the father of bersilat.

In bersilat, all types of techniques are used to subdue an opponent: karatelike kicks and punches, judolike throws and trips, and jujutsulike holds.

Bersilat embraces numerous styles, teaching the use of weapons such as stick, blade, and staff. It is slowly evolving into a sport form, and is said to promote spiritual development. Today it is regulated by the Silat Seni Gayong Association, founded in 1962. *Further reading: Asian Fighting Arts,* Donn F. Draeger and Robert W. Smith, 1969; *Black Belt Magazine,* Sept. 1967.

FORMS OF BERSILAT

LINTAN Malaysian **bersilat** style; two opponents fight without weapons.

MEDAN Style of **bersilat;** weapons are used in mass fighting.

SILAT BUAH Secondary form of Malaysian **bersilat**, used in actual combat. Generally practiced in semi-seclusion, its moves are passed from master to disciple under a vow of secrecy, reminiscent of Chinese kung-fu. Various forms of silat buah can be found throughout the narrow peninsula of Malaysia, but the most popular forms are fist and finger attacking, grappling and gripping, and a spectacular style with high leaps and flying kicks.

TERELAK Style of **bersilat**; breathing is stressed and great strength is required.

BOJUTSU

BOJUTSU System of armed combat using the **bo**, a staff 5′ long in Japan and 6′ long in Okinawa. Bojutsu was practiced by Japanese feudal warriors, although systematic bojutsu did not develop until the late Kamakura (1192-1333) or early Muromachi (1338-1598) periods. The katori Shinto-ryu style, founded by Izasha Inenao, is the root from which most other systems grew.

Gripping the staff with both hands, bojutsu is executed by striking, poking, blocking, parrying, deflecting, sweeping, and holding. The position of the hands on the staff determines whether the strike is made from long or short distances, making the weapon, or **bo,** and bojutsu, itself, suitable for close-range or long-range combat. **Kata** (formal exercise) is the sole training method. Ranging in size and shape from a simple club to a spearlike shaft, the bo is an ancient weapon. An entire arsenal of armed or spiked staves, shafts, and poles, generally of wood bound with iron, were developed concommitantly with the art of Japanese spearfighting.

Because they were comparatively less dangerous in practice sessions than a blade, the staff and various other wooden weapons were often used in the training halls of **bujutsu** (military arts) schools, where techniques of spearfighting and swordsmanship were taught. This fact helps explain the popularity of the bo among members of those social classes that abhorred bloodshed. Priests, monks, travelers, and even poets used the staff. In time, use of wooden weaponry became so well developed that real combat using the staff or a wooden sword could be engaged in by skilled warriors.

There are as many styles in the use of the staff as there are in the use of arms, since there was a wooden substitute for nearly every weapon. Each, however, also developed independently of the weapon to which it was directly related, even producing its own lore and body of literature. One aspect of the bo is the art of the long staff, whose length was that of either the spear, called hasaku-bo, or the halberd, called the **rokushaku-bo.** A second specialty is the art of the long stick, whose length was that of the long sword (jo or bo) or the regular sword (ham-bo). A particular method of using the long stick, one that is practiced today, is a discipline called **jodo** (way of the stave).

A third development is the art of the wooden sword known as the **bokken,** a staff carved and shaped like a real sword. Its practice is not mentioned very frequently, because it was linked so closely to **kenjutsu** (art of the sword). Yet, most duels among masters of different schools, all tournaments among clansmen, and all rank examinations involved the use of the bokken, so that every Japanese warrior employed it as a part of his training equipment. In certain special cases, the bokken could become a complete symbolic substitute for the katana (sword), as might be necessary for self-defense when skilled swordsmen became itinerant monks or men of peace and developed an aversion to bloodshed under any circumstances.

In Okinawa, use of the bo, heightened during the Satsuma clan's occupation (17th-18th centuries), became popular along with other implements including the **sai** (short sword), **tonfa** (handle), **kama** (sickle), and **nunchaku**. These became the five systematized weapons employed by the early developers of **te** (hand).

In Okinawa today, there are more than 10 varieties of the art of the bo, most of which have been considerably popularized. One form of the bo is preserved in a folk dance presented at local festivals. *Further reading: Asian Fighting Arts,* Donn F. Draeger and Robert W. Smith, 1969; *Secrets of the Samurai,* Oscar Ratti and Adele Westbrook, 1973.

Bojutsu demonstrated by Jerry Gould and one of his students.
Courtesy of Jerry Gould

Bojutsu practitioners often engage in using the bo against other weapons. Here, Jerry Gould uses a sai against a student wielding a bo.

CAPOEIRA

Brazilian martial art founded more than 300 years ago by African slaves and banned by the government for most of its history. Capoeira is beautiful to watch, encompassing such moves as back flips, cartwheels, sweeping movements, and spectacular kicks. Most of its defensive techniques are elusive and devoid of blocking motions. Capoeira practitioners are extremely adept at evading an opponent's attack then countering with any number of hand or foot movements. Many of the foot motions entail leg sweeps, leg blocks, and kicks performed while assuming a handstand position. Although 90 percent of capoeira consists of leg movements the hands must also be trained, especially since they were often used to help the practitioner's balance while upside down.

There is a form of capoeira often seen by tourists in which practitioners perform alternate attacking and defending maneuvers to the sound of the berimbau, a Brazilian bow-shaped instrument. The tempo of the music determines the speed and the type of action to be performed.

According to authoritative sources, capoeira was originated by Negroes in Angola, who performed the movements as a religious dance. During the 16th century, slave traders brought many of these people to Brazil, where they continued to practice their "dance." Because of the brutality of many slave traders, the blacks soon transformed the capoeira moves into a devastating self-defense system. Since their hands were often chained, they placed emphasis on leg and head-butting techniques.

In the 17th century a large number of slaves formed thier own republic but were eventually subdued. Many were killed or escaped to cities and villages around Brazil, disseminating the practice of capoeira wherever they settled. The art reached its height in the 19th century, when many capoeira practitioners roamed the streets in criminal pursuits. At one point during the early 1800s, fines were levied against those who practiced capoeira. Then, in the mid-1800s, the art once again rose to prominence; by 1890, however, the threat of imprisonment was decreed against anyone practicing it, and many capoeirasts were deported.

In 1928, finally, the art was formally recognized by the Brazilian government and in 1972 it became an official Brazilian sport, at which time rules and regulations for its competitive aspect were implemented. Only in the 1970s did capoeira begin to spread outside of Brazil. There are now a small number of schools teaching this art in the United States. *Further reading: Inside Kung Fu,* March 1982; *Black Belt Magazine,* Apr. 1964; June 1969.

Capoeira experts learn how to kick to the head while in a handstand po[...]

Many of the moves of hapkido are similar to aikido techniques and inv[...] wrist and joint twisting as well as throws, sweeps, and karatelike kicks [...] punches.
Courtesy of *Inside Kun[...]*

HAPKIDO

In hapkido, a Korean martial art, one kicks but does not withdraw the leg swiftly as in other styles. Hapkido is distinguished by three essential techniques: passivity when opposing force; countering and attacking with circular movements; and absolute penetration of an opponent's defenses, the water principle. For example, if the attack is strong, one must receive it gently, and likewise, if the attack is gentle, one must counter powerfully. This complementary manner of reacting establishes a perpetual and liquid rhythm as well as constant mobility, the hallmarks of hapkido.

Hapkido is a selective combination of several martial systems: from karate, it derives power; from judo, smooth leverage; from aikido, the "flowing power," or **ki** (spirit).

Hapkido was founded by **Yong Shul Choi**, who, from 1919 to the beginning of World War II, had studied **Daito-ryu aiki-jutsu** (Daito school of harmony art) in Japan, one of the arts **Morihei Ueshiba** synthesized into **aikido.** Around 1939-40, Choi combined his knowledge of aiki-jutsu with the native Korean styles of **hwarang-do** and **taekyon,** the latter chiefly a kicking art. Until the 1960s, hapkido was known by various names: yu kwon sool, **yu-sool,** ho shin sool, and bi sool. In the early 1960s, under Choi's leadership, the Korean Kido Association was formed. Choi was assisted by his students Han-jai Ji, **In Hyuk Su,** and Moo-wung Kim. Later, a number of his students left and formed a rival organization, the Korean Hapkido Association. Today there are reportedly one million members in each association.

There are three major hapkido pioneers in the U.S.: **Sea Oh Choi, Bong Soo Han,** and Louisiana's **He-Young Kimm.** Hapkido was introduced in America by Sea Oh Choi, who immigrated to Los Angeles in 1964, but the style only became popular after the motion picture *Billy Jack* featured hapkido in its fight scenes, realistically choreographed by Bong Soo Han, who came to the U.S. in 1968. *Further reading: Hapkido, Korean Art of Self-Defense,* Bong Soo Han, 1974; *Introduction to Hapkido,* Joon M. Jee, 1974; *Hapkido: The Korean Art of Self-Defense,* Jae M. Lee and David Wayf, 1976; *Korean Hapkido: Ancient Art of the Masters,* Kwang Sik Myung, 1976.

HWARANG-DO

An ancient Korean martial art and healing art, hwarang-do is one of the most complex martial arts systems. The original Korean system of hand-to-hand combat, hwarang-do was conceived 1,800 years ago by the famous Buddhist priest, Won Kwang Bopsa; it is

Grandmaster of hwarang-do, Joo Bang Lee.
Courtesy of *Inside Kung-Fu*

Bong Soo Han, noted hapkido master, demonstrates one of the spectacular kicks for which hapkido is famous.
Courtesy of *Inside Kung-Fu*

based on the twin laws of nature, uum and yang. Korea was then divided into three kingdoms—Paekche, Koguryo, and Silla. King Chinghung of Silla called upon Bopsa to instruct young members of the royal family in the martial arts, religion, and intellectual and artistic pursuits. These young warriors were to become the generals, statesmen, and leaders of the kingdom, and were known collectively as the **hwarang.** The ferocious spirit of the hwarang warrior became legendary; there are thousands of tales concerning their heroic deeds. Memorable figures include Gen. Yoo Shin Kim, Kwan Chang, Sa Da Ham, Moo Kwan Rang, and Won Sool.

Literally, hwarang-do is "flower-man-way" or "the way of the flowering of manhood." Bopsa developed a code of ethics still adhered to by practitioners of the art: loyalty to country, loyalty to parents, trust and brotherhood among friends, courage in the face of an enemy, and justice.

The governing forces of the Yi Dynasty (1392-1910) disbanded the hwarang, so that training continued in the secrecy of Buddhist monasteries in mountainous regions. Here the art was preserved and carried on from master to student until the present day, when two brothers, **Joo Bang Lee** and **Joo Sang Lee,** undertook training from the 57th successor to the title of supreme grandmaster of hwarang-do, a Buddhist monk named Suahm Dosa. After twenty years of instruction, both brothers received permission and the necessary sanctions from the Korean government to teach publicly. In 1960 they opened the first public school in centuries, in Seoul. Since that time, hwarang-do has spread to the rest of the world under the direct control of the World Hwarang-do Association and supreme grandmaster Joo Bang Lee (58th successor).

Though interrelated, applications of hwarang-do can be subdivided into four major paths of study: internal power (nae gong); external power (wae gong); weapon power (moo gi gong); and mental power (shin gong). Nae gong deals with developing and controlling inner energy—ki—through specialized breathing and meditation exercises and physical techniques. At more advanced levels this power can be controlled by the thought processes and transmitted from one individual to another, for combative or healing applications.

Wae gong comprises over 4,000 offensive and defensive combative techniques. Combining elements tense and linear in nature (yang) with those soft and circular (uum), they form a natural, compatible fighting system. This phase includes instruction in all forms of hand strikes and blocks; 365 individual kicks; throws and falls from any position and onto any surface; human anatomy; joint manipulation; joint breaking; finger pressure point applications; prisoner arrest and control forms; offensive choking techniques; defense against multiple opponents; advanced killing techniques; counter-defense and counter-attacks; and advanced, secret techniques.

Moo gi gong is offensive and defensive training in 108 individual weapons in 20 categories. An advanced practitioner can effectively utilize any available object as a weapon.

Shin gong is the study, development, and control of the mind. Techniques seek to increase awareness and concentration levels. This realm includes: ESP; clairvoyance; development of the sixth sense; the natural laws of the universe; the study of human types; the art of concealment (sulsa); and advanced, secret arts.

The in sul aspects of hwarang-do, the study of oriental healing arts, are as complex and demanding as the study of occidental medicine. To most effectively defend himself, the hwarang-do student must have the capacity to heal himself and others. First aid and revival techniques are taught in conjunction with traditional **acupuncture,** royal family finger acupressure, herbal and natural medicines, and bone setting.

Because of its diverse nature, portions of hwarang-do study appeal to nearly everyone. The World Hwarang-do Association offers courses and options tailored to the specific needs of groups, in addition to its all-inclusive courses. The world headquarters for hwarang-do is in Downey, Calif. (JOHN HUPPUCH. JR., GRANDMASTER JOO BANG LEE. MASTER JOO SANG LEE) *Further reading: Special Tactics Series* (3 vols); Michael D. Echanis, 1977-78; *The Ancient Martial Arts of Hwarang-Do* (3 vols), Joo Bang Lee, 1978-80; *Kick Illustrated,* June 1981.

BULKUKSA Buddhist temple built during the Silra Kingdom era; it is closely connected with **hwarang-do,** the forerunner of Korean martial arts.

IAIDO

Iaido. Practice of skillfully drawing the Japanese sword from its scabbard. As used by **samurai,** it was called **iaijutsu** (sword-drawing art), but as a spiritual, almost religious art it was known as iaido (way of the sword), a name still used in schools where the ancient **kata** of iaijutsu, in somewhat modified form, are practiced. The most prominent schools are the Katori-Shinto, Hasegawa, Yagyu, Omori, and Mukai. The art is supervised by the Zen Nihon Iaido Remnei (All Japan Iaido Federation). *Further reading: Martial Arts of the Orient,* Roald Knutsen, 1975; *Modern Bujutsu & Budo,* Donn F. Draeger, 1974; *Secrets of the Samurai,* Oscar Ratti and Adele Westbrook, 1973.

Art McConnel demonstrates a movement from a sword kata from hasegawa ryu style of iaido.

Kiyoshi Yamazaki demonstrates one of the postures used in traditional Iaido.

FORMS OF IAIDO

GUNTO SOHO is a form of combat using the Japanese Army sword. It is popularly called toyama ryu iai. The art grew chiefly from the techniques of **Omori-ryu iai,** or drawing and using the sword from a standing posture. Seven techniques comprise gunto-soho; all are practical methods to be used to kill an enemy instantly.

OMORI-RYU IAI Popular modern style of **iaido.** Comprised of 11 forms, this style was developed in the late 17th century from the Eishin-ryu iai. All but one of these forms commence from seiza, the full kneeling posture, the only exception being a walking posture called koranto, or tiger stalking sword. The 7th form is a direct link to feudal times, the technique used by a swordsman acting as assistant to a man committing **hara-kiri.**

Yoshiteru Otani is one of the leading iaido experts in the United States

IAIJUTSU

In Iaijutsu, Japanese swordsmanship. the opening movement must be   perfect and combined with an instantaneous strike. Particularly suited to an armed encounter in daily life, as opposed to the battlefield, where weapons were already unsheathed, jaijutsu could be used without warning against an unwary foe or opponents preparing to attack. In this context—against an adversary who had not yet drawn his own weapon—a sense of disrepute attached to the art. Many a warrior and commoner were said to take professional advantage of tactical surprise, or merely to test the sharp edge of the **katana** (long sword). The latter indulgence became known as "crossroad cutting," "practice murder," or "swordtesting murder."

On the other hand, many Japanese **bujutsu** (military arts) students contended that iaijutsu was a legitimate part of **kenjutsu** (art of the sword), since a warrior should be prepared to confront danger at any moment, especially in a nation dominated by the professional fighter. Iaijutsu appears to have been perfectly acceptable when used in simultaneous counterattack against an enemy who was about to, or in the act of, unsheathing his sword with deadly intent. An iaijutsu expert had to discern instantly the technique his foe would employ, so that he might direct his counter unimpeded by his opponent's blade.

Four stages of sword mechanics are emphasized in iaijutsu: nukitsuke, or draw; kiritsuke, or cutting action; chiburi, or removal of blood from the blade; and noto, or return of the blade to its scabbard. The techniques and training exercises of this art were presented in a progressively more difficult series of action and reaction against mobile and static targets. Training programs were developed and transmitted in the utmost secrecy to those students who would remain linked to the school, or who would swear never to reveal the method. This discipline was expanded and refined until it entered spiritual and even religious dimensions, and became known as **iaido** (way of the sword). See also battojutsu; iaido; kenjutsu. **Further reading: Classical Budo,** Donn F. Draeger, 1973; **Classical Bujutsu,** Donn F. Draeger, 1973; **Modern Bujutsu & Budo,** Donn F. Draeger, 1974; **Martial Arts of the Orient,** Roald Knutsen, 1975; **Secrets of the Samurai,** Oscar Ratti and Adele Westbrook, 1973.

FORMS OF IAIJUTSU

EISHIN-RYU Parent style of **iaijutsu** (sword-drawing art). Eishin-ryu was originated by a pupil of **Hojo Jinsuke** in the 17th century. In this school, there are four series of **kata** as well as six **kenjutsu** (art of the sword) kata. Until 1868 this style and the related **Omori-ryu** remained a secret of the warlike Tosa clan.

MUSO RYU Iaijutsu style; considered the first school of this art. Founded by **Hojo Jinsuke** in the 16th century.

The starting position for iaijutsu.

21

JEET KUNE DO

Jeet Kune Do was conceived by the late **Bruce Lee** in 1967; literally "way of the intercepting fist." Unlike many other martial arts, there are no series of rules or techniques that constitute a distinct jeet kune do (jkd) method of fighting; jkd utilizes all ways and means to serve its end. It is bound by none and therefore "free." It possesses everything, but in itself is possessed by nothing. Those who understand jkd are primarily interested in its effects of liberation when it is used as a mirror for self-examination.

In the past, many have tried to define jkd in terms of a distinct style, i.e., Bruce Lee's gung-fu, Bruce Lee's karate, Bruce Lee's kick-boxing, or Bruce Lee's street fighting. To label jkd Bruce Lee's martial art is to miss its meaning; its concepts cannot be confined within a system. To understand this, a martial artist must transcend from the duality of the "for" and "against" into one unity which is without distinction. The understanding of jkd is a direct intuition of this unity. Truth cannot be perceived until we have come to full understanding of ourselves and our potential. According to Lee, knowledge in the martial arts ultimately means self knowledge.

Jeet kune do is not a new style of karate or kung-fu. Bruce Lee did not invent a new style or a composite, or modify any style to set it apart from any existing method. His main concept was to free his followers from clinging to a style, pattern, or mold.

It must be emphasized that jeet kune do is merely a name; a mirror in which we see ourselves. There is some sort of progressive approach to its training, but as Lee said, "To create a method of fighting is pretty much like putting a pound of water into wrapping paper and shaping it." Structurally, many people tend to mistake jkd as a composite style because of its efficiency. At any given time, it can resemble Thai boxing, wing chun, wrestling, or karate. Its weaponry resembles Filipino escrima and kali, and, at long range, northern Chinese gung-fu or tae kwon do. According to Lee, the efficiency of style depends upon circumstances and range: a staff, for example, would be the wrong weapon to bring into a telephone booth to fight, whereas a knife would be appropriate.

A good jkd practitioner must develop intuition. According to Lee, a style should never be like a bible in which the principles and laws of which can never be violated. There will always be a difference with regards to quality of training, physical make-up, level of understanding, environmental conditioning, and likes and dislikes. Thus jkd is not an organization or an institution to which one can belong. "Either you understand or you don't, and that is that," in Lee's words.

When Lee was teaching a Chinese system of gung-fu upon his arrival in the U.S., he did have an institute of learning; but after that he didn't believe in a style or system, Chinese or otherwise. According to him, to reach the masses some sort of organization had to be formed, both domestic and foreign branches with affiliations; but he also felt it was not necessary to have these because a martial artist finds himself more often in places that are contrary. To reach the growing numbers of students some sort of pre-conformed sets had to be established as the standard for these branches. As a result, many members will be conditioned according to the prescribed system; many will probably end up as prisoners of systematic drilling.

Jeet Kune Do instructors (*left to right*):
Ted Wong, Dan Inosanto, Dan Lee.
Courtesy of *Inside Kung-Fu*

22

Jeet Kune Do 1

Founder: BRUCE LEE

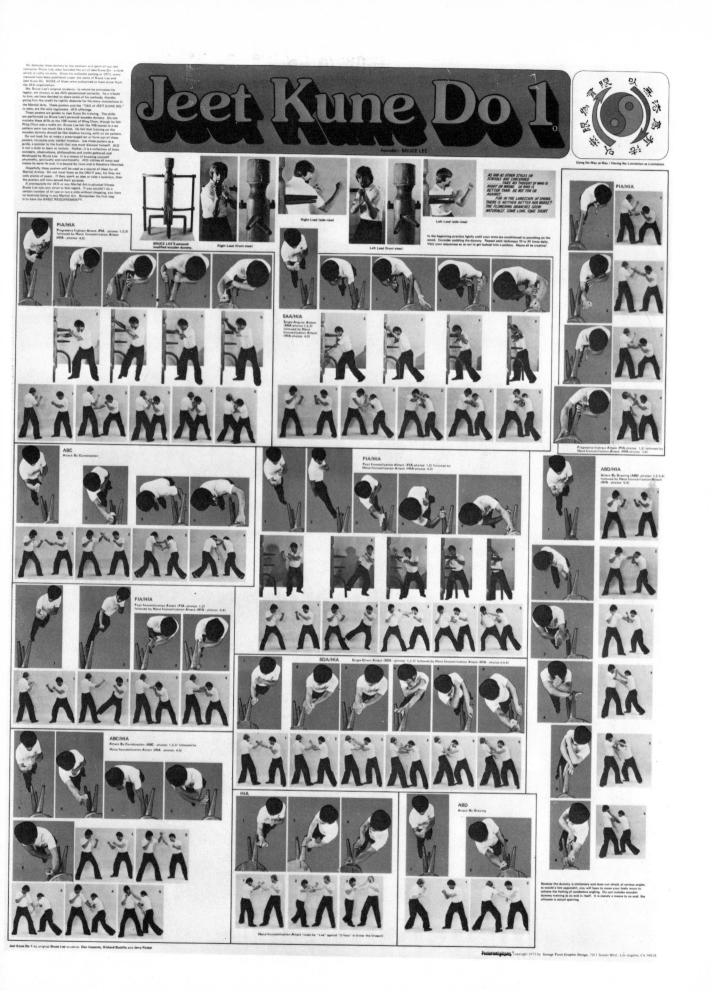

AS FAR AS OTHER STYLES OR
SCHOOLS ARE CONCERNED
TAKE NO THOUGHT OF WHO IS
RIGHT OR WRONG. OR WHO IS
BETTER THAN. BE NOT FOR OR
AGAINST.
FOR IN THE LANDSCAPE OF SPRING
THERE IS NEITHER BETTER NOR WORSE?
THE FLOWERING BRANCHES GROW
NATURALLY SOME LONG. SOME SHORT

BRUCE LEE'S personal
modified wooden dummy.

Right Lead (front view)

Right Lead (side view)

Left Lead (front view)

Left Lead (side view)

In the beginning practice lightly until your arms are conditioned to pounding on the
wood. Consider padding the dummy. Repeat each technique 10 to 24 times daily.
Vary your sequences so as not to get locked into a pattern. Above all be creative!

PIA/HIA
Progressive Indirect Attack (PIA - photos 1,2,3)
followed by Hand Immobilization Attack
(HIA - photos 4,5)

SAA/HIA
Single Angular Attack
(SAA - photos 1,2,3)
followed by Hand
Immobilization Attack
(HIA - photos 4,5)

PIA/HIA

Progressive Indirect Attack (PIA - photos 1,2) followed by
Hand Immobilization Attack (HIA - photos 3,4)

ABC
Attack By Combination

FIA/HIA
Foot Immobilization Attack (FIA - photos 1,3) followed by
Hand Immobilization Attack (HIA - photos 4,5)

ABD/HIA
Attack By Drawing (ABD - photos 1,2,3,4)
followed by Hand Immobilization Attack
(HIA - photos 5,6)

FIA/HIA
Foot Immobilization Attack (FIA - photos 1,2)
followed by Hand Immobilization Attack (HIA - photos 3,4)

SDA/HIA
Single Direct Attack (SDA - photos 1,2,3) followed by Hand Immobilization Attack (HIA - photos 4,5,6)

ABC/HIA
Attack By Combination (ABC - photos 1,2,3) followed by
Hand Immobilization Attack (HIA - photos 4,5)

HIA

ABD
Attack By Drawing

Hand Immobilization Attack (Used by "Lee" against "O'hara" in Enter the Dragon)

Because the dummy is stationary and does not attack at various angles,
as would a live opponent, you will have to move your body more to
achieve the feeling of combative angling. Do not mistake wooden
dummy training as an end in itself. It is merely a means to an end: the
ultimate is actual sparring.

Jeet Kune Do 1 by original Bruce Lee students: Dan Inosanto, Richard Bustillo and Jerry Poteet.

This is why Lee believed in having only a few students at one time, because it requires constant alert observation of each student in order to establish a direct relationship. A good teacher can never be fixed at a routine, and today many instructors are just that. As Lee so often said, "A good instructor functions as a pointer of the truth espousing the student's vulnerability, causing him to explore both internally and externally, and finally, integrating himself with his being.

Martial arts, like life itself, are a constant unrhythmic movement, as well as constant change. Flowing with this change is very important. Finally a jeet kune do man who says jkd is exclusively jkd is simply "not in with it." He is still "hung up" on his own self-closing resistance, anchored to reactionary pattern and naturally bound by another modified pattern and can move only within its limits. He has not digested the simple fact that the truth exists outside of all molds and patterns. An awareness is never exclusive. To quote Lee, "Jeet kune do is just a name, a boat to get one across the river. Once across it is to be discarded and not to be carried on one's back."

In 1981 jkd concepts were taught in only three places: by **Dan Inosanto** and Richard Bustillo at the Filipino Kali Academy in Torrance, Calif.; by Larry Hartsell in Charlotte, N.C.; and by Taki Kimura in Seattle, Wash. As taught in Torrance, the curriculum includes western boxing and Bruce Lee's method of kick-boxing, called Jun Fan boxing. It is felt that students should gather experience rather than technique. In other words, a karate practitioner who has never before boxed needs to experience sparring with a boxer. What he learns from this experience is strictly up to him. According to Lee, a teacher is not a giver of truth; he is merely a guide to the truth and the student must discover for himself.

The total picture Lee wanted to present to his pupil was that above everything else he must find his own way. He always said, "Your truth is not my truth, and my truth is not yours." Lee did not have a blueprint, but rather a series of guidelines to lead to proficiency. Using equipment, there was a systematic approach in which you could develop speed, distance, power, timing, coordination, endurance, and footwork.

Jeet kune do, for Lee, was not an end in itself nor was it merely a by-product; it was a means of self-discovery; a prescription for personal growth, and an investigation of freedom, freedom to act naturally and effectively not only in combat but in life. In life, to absorb what is useful, to reject what is useless, ideally, a student will seek experience in many arts—judo, jujutsu, aikido, western boxing, kicking styles, wing chun, kali, escrima, arnis, pentjak silat, Thai boxing, French savate, etc.—and to understand the strengths and weaknesses of each. It is not necessary to study all of these arts, but to understand the high and low points of each, as well as the range, distance, and effectiveness of each. There is a distance in which western boxing is superior to any kicking style, whether it be from Korean karate or northern Chinese styles of kicking.

No art is inferior or superior to any other. This is the object of jeet kune do: to be bound by no style and in combat to use no style as style. In the Zen maxim: "In the landscape of spring there is neither better nor worse. The flowering branches grow, some short, some long." (DAN INOSANTO) *See also* Bruce Lee. *Further reading: Jeet Kune Do,* Dan Inosanto, 1980; *Tao of Jeet Kune Do,* Bruce Lee, 1975.

In Jeet Kune Do, kicks are delivered low, usually to the opponent's shin or knee, because this is much quicker than the high kicks used in many other martial arts
Courtesy of *inside Kung-Fu*

JOJUTSU

Japanese method of using the jo (long stick), practiced at Waseda University in Tokyo and in lesser known dojo in Japan and abroad. Jojutsu is reputed to have been invented by the great swordsman **Muso Gunnosuke** about 400 years ago, after a bout with wooden swords won by the legendary **Miyamoto Musashi.**

According to this tradition, Gunnosuke withdrew to a Shinto shrine and after a period of purification, meditation, and training with the staff, created the art of the jo, blending techniques of spearfighting and swordsmanship with those of other, minor methods of combat. He named his style Shindo-Muso ryu and challenged Musashi again. This time, Gunnosuke mounted an effective defense and penetrated Musashi's own two-sword strategy.

Gunnosuke is reputed to have trained continually until he had perfected the 12 basic blows and blocks that are the technical patrimony of modern jojutsu, and which he later combined into more than 70 advanced techniques. These basic blows usually are practiced in kata (formal exercises) performed with a wooden sword, bokken, against the jo. These kata include straight (honto-uchi) and reverse (gyaku-uchi) blows to the upper body; response to a block (hiki-otoshi); switch-hand (kaeshi-tsuki) and reverse (gyakute-tsuki) thrusts straight (tsuki-hazushi) and round (maki-otoshi) parries; body pressure (kune-tsuke); body push (kure-hanashi); body whirl (tai-atari); middle body parry and counter (do-harai-uchi); and the spinning evasion and counter (tai-hazushi-uchi).

The modern study of the jo, known as **jodo** (way of the stick), usually leads to other arts and weapons, such as the heavy club (tanjo), the chained sickle (kusari-gama), the fast draw (iai), as well as to blows in karate and kempo or throws in judo and aikido.

Jojutsu, as adapted for modern police purposes, is referred to as **keibo soho,** or police stick art. *Further reading: Asian Fighting Arts,* Donn F. Draeger and Robert W. Smith, 1969.

Jobajutsu

FORMS OF JOJUTSU

JODO Japanese art of stick fighting that grew out of **jojutsu** (art of the long stick). Banned immediately after World War II, it was revived in the 1950s. A staff about 4 feet 2 inches long, usually made of white oak, its methods were created more than 400 years ago by a great swordsman, **Muso Gunnosuke,** and kept secret for centuries by the Kuroda clan of Fukoda. Today the jo is studied as an art rather than self-defense, since carrying the stick is illegal. According to legend the famous swordsman, Muso Gonnosuke was defeated

and went into meditation, during which time the idea of using a short stick came to him. He practiced with the new weapon, then challenged Musashi to another match. Using the jo, Gunnosuke defeated Musashi who, up to that time, had never been beaten. Gunnosuke went on to refine the jo techniques.

The 12 basic blows and blocks of jodo are: normal grip blow (honte uchi); reverse grip blow (gyaku-uchi); back blocking blow (hiki-otoshi); switch hand thrust (kyashi-zuki); reverse grip thrust (gyakute-zuki); wrapping drop block (maki-otoshi); pressing stick to the body (kure-tsuke); pushing stick to the body (kure-hanashi); body check (tai-atari); blocking thrust (tsuke-hazushi); middle body block and counter (doh-harai-uchi); and shifting block and counter (tai-hazushi-uchi).

Jodo techniques include striking, poking, blocking, parrying, deflecting, intercepting, and sweeping. There are 12 basic blows and blocks, and these can be mastered in four to six months. Students learn 70 more advanced techniques, mostly elaborations of the basic moves. Jodo has no free-sparring like judo or karate: students practice against one another in prearranged sets; one student uses the bo while the other wields a sword. Advanced students practice other weapons, such as tenjo jitsu (heavy club) and kuon-gama (chain). Technical supervision is by the All Japan Jodo Federation.

During the Tokugawa period, jojutsu, the forerunner of jodo, was employed by the **bushi** particularly when nonlethal results were wanted. *See also* keibo soho; jojutsu.

JOBAJUTSU

Japanese art of horsemanship, Jobajutsu, also called bajutsu, existed in the early feudal era, as evidenced by bronze and iron cheek-plates and muzzles found in Japanese dolmens. The mounted **bushi** (warriors) usually wore a special type of armor called uma-yoroi, lighter and more functional than later, decorative examples.

Unlike the mounts of the European armored knights of the middle ages, the bushi's horse was not burdened with heavy armor. Its head was generally protected by contoured chamfrons of iron, steel, or lacquered leather; the bard, or body armor, was composed of small scales of padded or lacquered leather sewn onto cloth. The flanchards at the sides (hanging from the saddle) were made of large pieces of the same material molded and gilded. The crupper was usually rectangular in shape and covered the beast's hindquarters.

A warrior held the reins in both hands until he was ready to engage the enemy at close quarters, at which time he hooked them onto rings or hooks on his breastplate and controlled his steed with his knees. He would move toward enemy lines tacking evasively to foil enemy archers, all the while releasing his own arrows. At close quarters, he used his spear or long sword as he wove in and out of enemy groups or engaged in individual combat.

Under perfect conditions the horse is said to have been so united to his master's personality that he would seem to act instinctively. In full synchronization with his rider's movements, he would withdraw, whirling on his hindquarters, before a charge, rear up to offer his rider the advantage of height for delivering a blow, or charge if need be into the thick of battle. At night, the horse might be used to stalk the enemy silently, his bridle bound with cloth and his mouth muffled in a special bag. These animals were specially trained to ford the rivers, streams, and lakes that abound in Japan.

Japanese military horsemanship had a marked effect upon **bujutsu** (military arts). Archery, swordsmanship, spearmanship, and unarmed combat techniques were all directly affected, from the standpoints both of horsemen fighting one another and horsemen battling unmounted warriors.

The use of horses was comparatively restricted, even among high-ranking bushi, because of the prohibitive cost of breeding and keeping horses. After 1600 the relative tranquility of the Tokugawa period reduced horsemanship to a limited role, primarily ceremonial. By the time Japan entered the modern era, the noble steed had disappeared into the history books. *Further reading: Classical Bujutsu,* Donn F. Draeger, 1973; *Secrets of the Samurai,* Oscar Ratti and Adele Westbrook, 1973.

JUDO

An art of self-defense founded in Japan by **Jigoro Kano** and a worldwide sport. Judo received Olympic recognition in 1964 and is governed by the **International Judo Federation,** which regulates judo activities throughout the world. Japan has remained judo's stronghold, with millions of participants, but the U.S., the U.S.S.R., and France, each with more than 200,000 registered judoka, lead the rest of the world. Judo's terminology, however, remains strictly Japanese and its lexicon is standard across the globe.

Like jujutsu, its forerunner, judo is a method of turning an opponent's strength against him, thereby defeating him in an efficient manner. Jujutsu was practiced in Japan for hundreds of years, but with the advent of modern warefare and the diminished need for **hand-to-hand combat,** jujutsu declined.

In 1882, Jigoro Kano, a student of jujutsu, formulated a new system of barehanded fighting called judo (gentle way). Although it comprises many of the eeective throwing, strangling and joint-locking technqiues of jujutsu, the development of guiding principles and strict rules regulating the use of these techniques distinguishes judo the sport from jujutsu the combative art. It is this emphasis on the manner in which techniques are applied that makes judo a popular activity and an international sport.

The two principles upon which Kano based his new art were **seiryoku zenyo** (maximum efficiency with minimum effort) and juta kyoei (mutual welfare and benefit). The former occurs when one can skillfully defeat a stronger opponent by yielding to his attack while maintaining his own balance, thus throwing him off balance so he becomes vulnerable to one's counterattack. In juta kyoei, Kano advocated that judo's purpose was not to win a contest, but to perfect one's mind and body for the mutual benefit and welfare of all mankind.

Judo is practiced in a **dojo** (training hall), the floor of which is covered with **tatami** (straw mat) or with a newer type of plastic foam mat. Practitioners are barefooted and wear a suit (**judogi**) consisting of a loose fitting, strongly woven cotton jacket and a cotton trouser that reaches at least half way down the lower leg. The jacket is secured by an **obi** (belt) wrapped around the waist twice and tied with a square knot in the front.

Etiquette plays an important part in judo. It is customary for all judoka to execute a standing bow (ritsu-rei) upon both entering and leaving the dojo. A standing bow is also exchange dbetween judoka at the beginning and end of a contest, free practice, or formal practice. Furthermore, formal classes always begin and end with a kneeling bow (za-rei) to the sensei (teacher).

The first thing one is taught in judo is **ukemi** (falling), in which the arms are used as a shock absorber by striking the mat when the body impacts with the ground. The head must never touch the ground and the body must be totally relaxed. Falling is learned to the left and right side (yoko-ukemi), backward (ushiro-ukemi), forward (mae-ukemi), as well as in a roling manner (zempo-kaiten-ukemi).

The judoka next learns kumikata (methods of gripping the opponent). The standard grip consists of grasping the opponent's sleeve near the elbow with one hand, while the other hand grips the lapel at chest level. Although this is the most common grip, in contest a number of variations are used. Sometimes both sleeves or both lapels are gripped, and sometimes one hand holds the sleeves while the other grips the collar at the nape of the neck. The only action prohibited is grasping the same side of the opponent's jacket with both hands while moving about the mat.

Shisei (posture) is taught together with kumikata. There are three positions from which most throws are performed: shizentai (natural posture), migi-shizentai (right natural posture), or hidari-shizentai (left natural posture). In shizentai the feet are placed about shoulder width apart, the knees are bent slightly with the body straight and weight evenly distributed. In migi-shizentai the stance is almost the same as in shizentai except the right foot is palced slightly forward, while in hidari-shizentai the left foot is placed slightly forward. Each posture is used in relation to the movement of the opponent's body.

Jigotai (defensive posture) is used when trying to make it difficult for one to be thrown. In this posutre the legs are spread wide and the weight of the body is placed low by bending the knees. This stance is often seen in competition.

Next the judoka must master shintai (walking action), which is divided into two basic types. In the first, ayumi-ashi, each foot moves in turn ahead of the other. In the second, tsugi-ashi, one foot follows but does not pass the other. In both actions, the feet must slide over the mat.

Since throwing techniques are the most extensive and most often used phase of judo, it is the next phase of learning. Judo throws are divided into three parts: **kuzushi,** or breaking the opponent's balance; **tsukuri,** the entry of the body into a position preventing the opponent from regaining his balance; and **kake,** the actual execution of the throw. These three stages are always performed as one continuous movement from beginning to end.

Judo techniques are divided into three categories. The largest is called tachi-waza (standing techniques) or nage-waza (throwing techniques). Within this category are all the methods of throwing an opponent with quick, fluid actions of the body. These throwing techniques are further subdivided into te-waza (hand techniques), koshi-waza (hip techniques), ashi-waza (foot and leg techniques), and sutemi-waza (sacrifice techniques).

In using te-waza, unbalancing techniques are of primary importance. They are particularly effective against larger opponents. Two of these hand techniques, seoi-nage and tai-otoshi, are among the half dozen most frequently used throws in sport judo. Other te-waza are: kata-guruma; uki-otoshi; sumi-otoship; and soto-makikomi.

In koshi-waza, the object is to place the hip underr the opponent's center of gravity and, raising him up off the mat, throw his body in a circular motion. Koshi-waza are extremely effective and compose some of the most popular throws used in judo: harai-goshi and hane-goshi are among the dozen most often used throws in contests. Other hip techniques include: uki-goshi; o-goshi; kuki-nage; tsuri-komi-goshi; ushiro-goshi; koshi-guruma; and sode-tsuri-komi-goshi.

Most ashi-waza are applied by sweeping, or by hooking the opponent's foot or leg with the user's foot or leg. In judo, foot techniques are generally the simplest and easiest to master and beginners are often taught some of these techniques first. Among the most commonly used foot throws in competition are the uchi-mata; o-soto-gari; okuri-ashi-barai; o-uchi-gari; and ko-uchi-gari. Other foot throws include: hiza-guruma; harai-tsurikomi-ashi; kosotogari; kosotogake; de-ashi-barai; and ashi-guruma.

Sutemi-waza are executed with the back or side of the body touching the ground. It is a subdivision of nage-waza and is further subdivided into two branches: masutemi-waza (throwing with one's back on the ground) and yoko-sutemi-waza (throwing with one's side on the ground). Some sutemi-waza are: tomoe-nage; ura-nage; sumi-gaeshi; sore-yokosutemi-waza-ari; tani-otoshi; yoko-otoshi; uki-waza; yokogake; and yoko-guruma. These techniques are sometimes called "suicide throws" by judoka because, should the throw fail, an opponent is ideally positioned to counter with a grappling technique.

The next major judo division is ne-waza (ground techniques), and concerns fighting while on the ground but differs from sacrifice techniques. Ne-waza is subdivided into osaekomi-waza (holding techniques), shime-waza (strangling techniques), and kansetsu-waza (armlock techniques).

Osaekomi-waza (aka osae-waza) is a collective name for all techniques in which an opponent is held or immobilized on his back for 30 seconds. They are usually applied when one or both opponents, having failed to apply a standing technique, successfully carry the match to the mat. Some osaekomi-waza are: kuzure-kesa-gatame; kesa-gatame; ushiro-kesa-gatame; kata-gatame; kami-shiho-gatame; kuzure-kami-shiho-gatame; yoko-shiho-gatame; and tate-shiho-gatame.

Shime-waza techniques include all choking techniques in judo and can be applied while standing, sitting, squatting, lying, and from ahead or behind an opponent. In actual competition, when an opponent is about to pass out he must give a sign of surrender, either clapping his hands or feet against the mat or by shouting "maitta" ("I am beaten"). The most common shime-waza are: nami-juji-jime; kata-juji-jime; gyaku-juji-jime; hadaka-jime; okuri-eri-jime; and kata-ha-jime.

Kansetsu-waza (aka gyaku) includes all the techniques in which pressure or locks are employed against body joints. Because of

Ettiquette plays an important part in judo, and it is customary for all judoka
to bow to each other at the beginning and end of a contest. Gene LeBell (*right*)
at the Kodokan.
Courtesy of Gene LeBell

Immobilization techniques are an important part of judo.
Here, S. Kotai demonstrates shime-waza.
Courtesy of E. Bruno

Ushiro kesa-gatame, judo holddown technique.

Gleeson performing kata.

Dinner in honor of Pop Moore shows gathering of highest-degree black belts alive in the world at that time—1935. *Seated, from left:* Tabata, Izuka, Nagaoka, Jigoro Kano, Yamashita, Samura and Mifune, all 10th dan. *Standing, from left:* Utou Torao, 9th; Ishiguro, 7th; skipping to R. Moore and T. Yamauchi, *(standing behind Kano).*

Kime-no-kata, the third kata in judo.

potential injury in their use, only elbow locks are permitted in judo competition, and even these are restricted to higher-ranked practitioners. Kansetsu-waza are divided into: ude-waza (armlocks); yuki-waza (finger locks); ashikubi-waza (ankle locks); kote-waza (wrist locks); hiza-waza (knee locks); sekizui-waza (spine locks). Some kansetsu-waza are ude-garami (entrapped armlock); ude-gatame; juji-gatame (cross armlock); and hishigi-hiza-gatame (armlock with knee).

The last major division in judo is atemi-waza (vital point techniques), also called ate-waza or just atemi. The object of these techniques is to cause excruciating temporary pain or paralysis to an attacker. Blows are delivered with a sharp recoiling action to different bodily parts using the fingertips, fists, elbows, edge of the hand, knees, ball of the foot, and the heel. Most of these strikes are delivered to the bridge of the nose, temple, ear lobe, upper lip, windpipe, solar plexus, kidney, groin and knees. Founder Jigoro Kano incorporated these techniques into judo after learning them from **Gichin Funakoshi**, the father of modern karate, in 1921. Since atemi-waza can cause severe injury they are usually taught to black belts and are never used in competition. Atemi-waza is one of the three groups of techniques constituting judo; it is subdivided into ude-waza (hand techniques) and ashi-ate (leg or foot strikes).

Ude-waza are used to bring pressure against the elbow. Ude-waza is divided into ude-hishigi (arm crushing) and ude-garami (arm entangling). The former is applied to a straight arm, with the elbow and wrist pressed exactly in opposite directions, the latter is applied to a bent arm, levering the forearm to cause stress at the elbow joint. Both are applicable standing or on the ground. In ashi-ate different parts of the foot are used to kick an attacker so as to subdue or incapacitate him. Ashi-ate is subdivided into hizagashira-ate (attack with the knee cap), sekito-ate (attack with the ball of the foot), and kekito-ate (attack with the heel).

Judo training consists of randori (free exercise), kata (formal exercise(s)), and uchi-komi (inner winding exercise).

Kagamibiraki at the Kodokan.

Judo contests are conducted in an area 9 or 10 meters square with a center referee and four judges.

Randori is a form of training in which two judoka attack and defend against each other at will. All judo techniques are applied including throws, pins, chokes and armlocks. The object of randori is to apply all the basic skills one has learned, such as unbalancing, footwork, timing, as well as the actual techniques themselves. Although randori is competitive, the object is not to win or lose, but to practice judo so as to improve one's ability to attack and defend against an opponent. In proper randori, the emphasis is on correct posture, the use of proper and natural technique, footwork, hip twisting and body twisting. Randori is considered the most valuable method of improving judo skill. It is practiced with many different partners, focing each one to deal with a wide variety of height and weight factors in order to learn effectiveness. Often practiced as a preparation for competition, it can also be practiced less strenuously, with both partners offering less resistance, as a means of physical fitness.

Uchi-komi are non-throwing attack drills of which there are two types: static and dynamic. In the former, one man stands erect while the other assumes the position for the throw without actually throwing him. The partner gives only a semi-resistance to the attacker's entry. In dynamic uchi-komi, both partners move about in order to simulate an actual contest. The attacker continually attacks, taking his partner to the point just prior to throwing him. Both types are beneficial to the student because they refine and train reflexes; strengthen the muscles; increase endurance and speed; and instill confidence. The secret of uchi-komi is repetition; some Japanese judoka can perform 500 without stopping, no simple feat.

Kata embraces all the forms of throwing, grappling, and vital point attacks, together with cutting and thrusting with dagger and sword. Kata is the art and science of judo, and many judoka refer to it as the "grammar of judo." In these prearranged routines, tori (the performer) applies a technique on uke (the receiver). Uke gives tori a perfect opportunity to apply the technique, and tori's application must be absolutely accurate. They work together in harmony to practice timing, form, and body control.

As judo players advance in rank they must master certain kata and at the time they reach black belt status, kata is a required part of grading. The following are kata generally taught at the **Kodokan:**

1. **Nage-no-kata** (throwing)
2. **Katame-no-kata** (grappling and holding)
3. **Go-no-sen-no-kata** (throw and counter throw)
4. **Kime-no-kata** (self-defense)
5. **Ju-no-kata** (gentle forms)
6. **Koshiki-no-kata** (antique forms)
7. **Kodokan-goshin-jutsu** (Kodokan forms of self-defense)
8. **Seiyoku-zenyo kokumin-taiiku-no-kata** (national physical education forms)
9. **Fujoshi-yo goshin-no-kata** (self-defense for women)
10. **Ippan-yo goshin-no-kata** (self-defense for men)

Grading in judo is based on both proficiency in contest and knowledge of the art. Levels of grading are indicated by the different colors of the belt wron around the judogi. The **kyu** (grade) ranks begin with white belt, for a novice, and progress, after examiantion, through yellow, orange, green, blue, and brown belts. Ultimately, the student is graded for black belt. Black belt ranks, technicalled called **dan** (degree), range from 1st degree, the lowest, to 12th degree, the highest level.

Fighting ability and technical knowledge may elevate a judoka to 5th dan, after which advancement depends on service to the sport. In fact, leading international fighters are usually 4th or 5th dans. The highest grade ever awarded by the Kodokan is 10th dan. Special belts are worn by highly advanced practitioners—red and white from 6th through 8th dan, and red for 9th and 10th dans. Twelfth is signified by a white belt, the same as for a beginner.

Shaiai, or judo contests, always begin with the contestants in a standing position. They face each other about 10' apart, perform a standing bow, then meet in the middle of the square contest mat. Here they grasp each other's jackets and strive to throw one another. The contest mat in judo measures 9 or 10 meters square. Surrounding the contest area is a safety zone, also matted, about 2½ meters wide. An opponent can be thrown into this safety zone, but for the throw to be recognized the thrower must remain within the contest area. A 1-meter-wide red margin, running along each side of the mat, warns competitors that they are nearing the boundaries.

Officials for a judo contest include a referee, two judges, and a scorekeeper. The referee, who stays within the contest area, has the sole responsibility for conducting the amtch and making judgements. Either of the two judges, who sit in opposite corners outside the contest area, can disagree with any call made by the referee. If both judges oppose the referee's call, the majority rule prevails. If scores are even at the end of a match the referee calls on the judges to deliver a hantei (decision). The two judges, using flags, indicate the competitor who showe dyuseigachi (superiority). If the judges disagree, the referee renders the final decision.

There are no rounds in judo competition; the duration of a match can vary from 3 to 20 minutes depending on the organizers. National contests are normally 6 to 10 minutes long, while Olympic competition bouts can last 15 or 20 minutes. If within the allotted time any competitor gains an **ippon** (full point), the contest comes to an end regardless of time elapsed. Ippon is awarded to the contestant who throws his opponent on the mat largely on his back with considerable force or impetus. Ippon can also be scored by holding or immobilizing an opponent on the ground for 30 seconds, or by applying a choke or armlock until the opponent surrenders, or the referee sees the effect of the technique and stops the match.

Another way the match ends before the allotted time is if either contestant can gain two waza-ari, or half points, which can be added together to make an ippon. A waza-ari is awarded when a throw does not quite warrant a full score, or when an opponent is held on the ground for at least 25, but under 30 seconds. If two waza-ari are gained by either contestant the referee calls out "waza-ari awasete ippon" (two waza-ari score ippon) and the match ends.

Other scores given in judo competition include yuko (almost waza-ari) and koka (almost yuko). These scores are accumulative and no matter how many are gained the contest does not end until the allotted time, at which point these are tallied to determine the winner. Yuko is given when an opponent is thrown down with a partially successful throw, in which some part of his back lands on the mat. It is also given if an opponent is held on the amt for at least 20, but not less than 25 seconds. Koka is given if an opponent is thrown so that his stomach, side, thighs, or buttocks land on the mat. Koka is also given if an opponent is held on the mat from 10 to 19 seconds before getting free. No number of koka can be added to make a yuko, just as no number of yuko can be added to make a waza-ari.

In the past few years an elaborate penalty system has been introduced, which gives a positive score to the non-penalized contestant, who can win the match through the penalties assessed to his opponent. Penalties that can be imposed are: shido, which, for a minor breach of the rules, gives the opponent the score of koka; chui, which, for further minor breaches or a moderade one, gives the opponent the score of yuko; keikoku, which, for a more serious breach or further moderate ones, gives the opponent the score of waza-ari; and hansoku-make (disqualification), which, for a grave breach, gives the opponent the match by an ippon.

Up until the 1960s there were no weight categories in judo competition, but since then numerous classes have been established. Since 1977, the following weight classes have been used in international competition:

1. Up to 60 kg.
2. Between 61 and 65 kg.
3. Between 66 and 71 kg.
4. Between 72 and 78 kg.
5. Between 79 and 86 kg.
6. Between 87 and 95 kg.
7. Over 95 kg.
8. Open weight

The two major judo championships are the World Championships, held every two years, and the Olympic Games, held every four years. The annual European Championships is another major international tournament. In modern competition, most fighters use a tokui-waza (favorite technique), as well as renraku-waza (combination techniques). Feinting is also frequently used to set up an opponent for a favorite move. Although there are a large number of throws in judo, studies show that only a few throws account for most wins in a contest. These include seoi-nage (shoulder throw), uchi-mata (inner thigh throw), o-soto-gari (major outer reaping

Pariset and Ford at the 1961 World Championships.

throw), harai-goshi (sweeping hip throw), tai-otoshi (body drop), and hane-goshi (springing hip throw).

Up until the early 1970s, women's judo competition was minimal and confined to kata contests in which the women were judged on their technique and fluence of movement. Today there is international competition for women in which they compete under rules similar to those used in male competition, except the duration of the matches are shorter. Children and teenagers compete under rules similar to those for the adults, except that during groundwork chokes and armlocks are prohibited.

HISTORY: Judo was developed by Dr. Jigoro Kano from the ancient schools of jujutsu. Kano, who studied various jujutsu styles including the **kito** and the **tenjin-shinyo** schools, combined what he felt was their best features and named his new style Kodokan judo. In one of his lectures Dr. Kano explained the reason for selecting the name judo:

"The reason why I adopted the name judo instead of jujutsu is that my system is not simply a jutsu, or art, but a **do** (literally, "way," and figuratively, doctrine). Of course, the art is cultivated, but my judo is essentially a do. People today speak of judo rather than jujutsu, but up to that time when I began to expound by judo before the world, the term was but rarely used, except by the jikishin-ryu. In purposefully adopting a rarely used name for my judo, I wanted to distinguish it from the different schools of jujutsu then prevailing in the country. Further, my reason for not coining a purely new name is that my Kodokan judo, when comapred to the old jujutsu schools, has a wider scope for its object and the training is different. From these considerations, I might have been justified if I had christened my system with a quite novel word. I was, however, unwilling to do so since my judo was on the whole based on what I had learned from my jujutsu teacher.

"There were two other considerations that induced me to choose that step. One was that many jujutsu schools indulged in dangerous practices such as throwing by rather unfair means or by wrenching limbs. This led some people to feel that jujutsu was dangerous and harmful to the body. Add to this that there were several ill-disciplined jujutsu schools where the pupils themselves were obnoxious to the public by willingly throwing down innocent people or by seeking quarrels. It thus turned out that the word jujutsu carried with it an unfavorable association in the minds of some classes. Hence my desire was to show that my teaching, in marked contrast to jujutsu such as was interpreted by the men of those classes, was quite free from danger and was not to be used as a means of reckless aggressiveness.

"The other reason was that about the time I began my judo propagation, jujutsu had fallen into such an utter ruin that several former jujutsu masters lost their former dignity, and after a fashion of showmen, gave exhibitions of their art by making their disciples battle wrestlers, charging a fee for admission. These amateur showmen became the object of amusement and quite naturally earned public scorn and disgrace. The situation, then, was really such that I was led to think that my own system, if taught under the name jujutsu, might prove unacceptable to persons of the higher classes. Hence the adoption of the word judo."

Kano opened his first dojo, the Kodokan, in 1882. For some time, judo was regarded as another style of jujutsu, but in 1886 the Kodokan gained independent recognition when the Tokyo Metropolitan Police Board held a tournament between the Kodokan and the Totsuka, the largest of the jujutsu schools. Out of 15 contests, the Kodokan won 13 and tied 2. From that date judo grew in Japan.

The formulation of the Kodokan style was completed by 1887. Kano's new art was soon accepted by the Japanese Ministry of Education, which adopted judo as a sport within the school system. To further popularize judo, Kano traveled to Britain in 1885, and by 1902, one of his students, Yamashita, began teaching in the U.S. By 1905, some of Paris' police were being instructed in the art. Judo took firm hold in the west in 1918 when **Gunji Koizumi** founded a London-based club, the **Budokwai.** The club's first instructor was a jujutsu expert, **Yukio Tani,** who, together with Koizumi, converted to teaching Kano's judo upon the latter's visit to Britain.

The first international judo competition took place in London in 1929 between the Budokwai and the German national team. The Budokwai won, enhancing its status within European judo circles.

Koizumi, the club's chief instructor, toured Europe, instructing and establishing new schools.

By 1949, the European Judo Union was founded, and two years later, in 1951, the **International Judo Federation,** the world governing body for the sport, was created. In 1950, the first European Championships were held; France, Great Britain, and Holland dominated the event for the first five years.

The All Japan Judo Championships were first conducted in 1930, but were interrupted during World War II, resuming in 1948 with a new, multi-divisional, no-age-limit format. Because of the Kodokan's leaderrship in Japan, the Japanese Judo Federation was not founded until 1949. Many universities and smaller dojo affiliated, breaking the dominance of the Kodokan.

Judo reached Australia in 1928, when the Brisbane Judo Club was founded by Dr. Ross. In India, judo began in 1929 and spread to Africa two years later. Thus by 1956, when the 1st World Championships were conducted in Tokyo, judo was truly an international sport.

Prof. Kotani applying an advanced application of okuri-eri-shime-waza on Prof. Otaki. Courtesy of E. Bruno

In the 1st World Championships, no non-Japanese entrant reached the finals. The 1958 World Championships, again held in Tokyo, produced a similar result, although **Anton Geesink** of Holland and Pariset of France showed great potential.

In 1961 the 3rd World Championships were staged in Paris. For many years it had been believed a small skillful man could beat an equally skilled big man. Geesink, 6 feet 6 inches and an excellent judo player, disproved this premise, winning the championships once dominated by the smaller Japanese players. With the issue out in the open, a move to adopt weight categories for the Olympic Games and the World and European Championships was set afoot.

Geesink's victory destroyed the myth of Japanese invincibility. In additon to Geesink, the Japanese had to contend with the Russians, who had displayed remarkable skill at the 1962 European Championships. By 1963, grade classes at the European Championships were replaced by weight categories that included lightweight, middleweight, and heavyweight classes; team events were fought with two entrants in each class. Russia took the team title, as they did every year until 1967.

At the 1964 Olympic Games in Tokyo, judo was included for the first time. The Japanese had no new fighter to oppose Geesink in the open category, but lightweight Nakatani, middleweight **Isao Okano,** and heavyweight **Isai Inokuma** won gold medals. In the open event, Geesink pinned Japan's **A. Kaminaga** for a 30-second hold down, winning the gold medal.

The 1965 Championships were held in Rio de Janeiro—a sign that judo's inclusion in the Olympics had broadened world interest. The Japanese hoped to match Inokuma against Geesink in the openweight category. Geesink chose to compete in the heavyweight class instead and defeated all comers, including the two large Japanese entrants, Sakaguchi and Matsunaga. Inokuma won the gold medal in the open division, while middleweight Okano and lightweight Matsuda took gold medals in their divisions.

In the 1966 European Championships, revised weight categories were introduced: lightweight, welterweight, middleweight, light heavyweight, and heavyweight. Geesink was not present at the tournament, having temporarily retired, but Holland won three of the titles; the others, including the team title, went to Russia.

The 1967 European Championships ushered in a new force, the West Germans. They upset the Russians in the semi-finals and went on to win the team championship, defeating France. The year 1967 also marked Geesink's last European Championships. He retired a winner, defeating **Anzor Kiknadze** of Russia in the open class. One of Geesink's countrymen, **Wilheim Russka,** won the heavyweight title.

Although European judo kept improving, the Japanese were still stronger overall. This was proved at the 1967 World Championships in Salt Lake City, Utah, where the Japanese won five out of six medals. The only non-Japanese who won was Russka; he took the heavyweight title. In the 1969 World Championships in Mexico City, the Japanese ousted even Russka and captured all the first-place medals.

In the next three European tournaments, France won the team title in 1968, West Germany in 1969, and Russia in 1970. In 1971 Britain on the European title and two of its best competitors, **David Starbrook** and **Keith Remfry,** went on to win bronze medals at that year's World Championships in Ludwigshafen. Again, the only Japanese to win a gold medal was Holland's Russka, who regained the heavyweight title.

At the 1972 Olympic Games, staged in Munich, Japan's domination dwindled somewhat. Europeans sent their top players into competition, among them Russia's **Shota Chochoshvili** and Vitali Kuznetsov, both heavyweights, Russka of Holland, and **Klaus Glahn** of West Germany. France sent **Jean-Jacques Mounier** and **Jean Paul Coche.** The British sent Starbrook, **Angelo Parisi,** and **Brian Jacks.** The Japanese captured only half of the gold medals and these in the three lighter weight categories. After the event, all the Japanese coaches were fired and World and Olympic Champion Isao Okano became the team's coach. By 1973 the Japanese again stood supreme, capturing all the gold medals at the World Championships.

By the 1976 Olympic Games in Montreal the rest of the world began to catch up. The lightweight title went to Hector Rodriguez of Cuba, with Eunkyung Chan of Korea second and Italy's Falice Maiani third. The welterweight class was won by Russia's **Vladimir Nevzorov.** Japan's Koji Kuramoto placed second and Frenchman

Hane-goshi is one of judo's most often used throws.
Courtesy of E. Bruno

Patrick Vial third. Japan's **Isamu Sonoda** won the middleweight division, with Russia's Valeriy Dvoinokov second and Yugoslavia's Slavko Obador third. The light heavyweight class was captured by Japan's **Kazuhiro Ninomiya,** with Russia's Ramaz Harshiladze second and Britain's Starbrook third. In the heavyweight class, Russian Sergie Novikov took the gold, followed by East Germany's Gunther Neureuther in second and Sumio Endo in third. The openweight category was dominated by **Haruki Uemura,** with Britain's Remfry second and Russia's Chochoshvili third.

The 1977 World Championships, scheduled for Madrid, were cancelled, so the world's top players met again in 1979 at the 11th World Championships in Paris. Two more weight divisions were added. Out of eight gold medals, the Japanese took only four. The rest went to France, East Germany, and two to Russia.

Because Japan did not compete in the 1980 Olympic Games in Moscow the gold medals were more widely distributed. France, Italy, Belgium, Switzerland, and Germany each took one and Russia took two. *See also* Europe, history of judo; Olympic Games; U.S., history of judo in. *Further reading: Judo, Japanese Physical Culture,* Sumitomo ARima, 1908; *Judo,* Eric Dominy, 1955; *Anatomy of Judo,* G. R. Gleeson, 1969; *Manual of Judo,* E. J. Harrison, 1952; *Judo for Women,* Ruth Horan, 1965; *Judo Training Methods,* Takahiko Ishikawa and Donn F. Draeger, 1961; *Judo,* Jigoro Kano, 1973; *The Sport of Judo,* Kiyoshi Kobayashi and Harold E. Sharp, 1956; *Illustrated Kodokan Judo,* Kodokan, ed., 1967; *My Study of Judo,* Gunji Koizumi, 1960; *Dynamic Judo, Vol. II,* Kazuzo Kudo, 1967; *Championship Judo,* Tamio Kurihara, 1969; *Contest Judo,* Saburo Matsushita and Stepto Warwick, 1961; *Canon of Judo,* Kyuzo Mifune, 1957; *Judo for Young Men,* Tadao Otaki and Donn F. Draeger, 1965; *Judo Coaching Manual,* F. W. Pearson, 1966; *Vital Judo,* T. Sato and I. Okano, 1973; *Judo Dictionary,* Ken Smith, 1968; *A Complete Course to Judo,* Robert W. Smith, 1958; *The Techniques of Judo,* Shinzo Takagaki and Harold E. Sharp, 1958; *Secrets of Judo,* Jiichi Watanabi and Lindy Avakian, 1960; *The Judo Textbook,* Hayward Nishioka and James R. West, 1979.

Japanese champion Ishikawa applying Ude-juju-gatame. Courtesy of E. Bruno

Kata-guruma performed by England's G. Gleeson.

Tao toshi

NAGE-WAZA—JUDO THROWING TECHNIQUES

JAPANESE	ENGLISH	DIRECTION OF UNBALANCE	DIRECTION OF THROW	CLASSIFI-CATION	COMMENTS
Ashi-guruma	Leg Wheel	right front	Forward in a circle	Leg Throw	Throw is over Toris extended leg. Move is similar to Harai-goshi
De-ashi-harai	Advanced Foot Sweep	front or right front	to the side	Leg Throw	ukes leading foot must be swept before his weight is on it. Often called Ashi-harai
Eri-seoi-nage	Collar Shoulder Throw	front	forward over shoulder	Hand Throw	A variation of Morote-seio-nage.
Hane-goshi	Spring Hip Throw	front or right front	forward in a circle over hip	Hip Throw	A spectacular throw, used often in competition
Hane-maki-komi	Outer Winding Spring Hip Throw	right front	forward in a circle over leg and hip	Hip Throw	A combination of Soto-maki-komi and Hane-goshi
Harai-goshi	Sweeping Hip Throw	right front	forward in a circle over hip and leg	Hip Throw	Effective against tall and short opponents. Popular in competition.
Harai-makikomi	Sweeping Winding Throw	right front	forward over the body	Sacrifice Throw	To throw opponent you must throw your own body
Harai-tsurikomi-ashi	Sweeping Drawing Ankle Throw	forward	forward in a circle over foot	Foot Throw	used when uke is stepping backward
Hiza-guruma	Kneel Wheel	right front	forward in a circular motion	Foot Throw	One of the swiftest techniques in judo. Often used to open an opponent's stance in preparation for other attacks.
Ippon-seoi-nage	One Arm Shoulder Throw	front	forward over the shoulder	Hand Throw	A popular throw, en-sures a full point in competition. Especially effective against tall opponents.
Kani-basami	Scissors Throw	right front	to the side	Foot Throw	A good move against a rigid opponent. Tori must keep his feet wide apart when scissoring Uke.
Kata-guruma	Shoulder Wheel	forward	forward over shoulders	Hand Throw	Rarely used in contest
Koshi-guruma	Hip Wheel	forward	forward over hips	Hip Throw	Tori grabs Uke around the neck and throws him.
Ko-soto-gake	Minor Outside Hook	backward	backward	Foot Throw	Similar to osotogari. Good to loosen oppo-nent's balance for other potential throws.
Ko-soto-gari	Minor Outside Reap	backward right-back	backward	Foot Throw	Good to loosen oppo-nent's balance. Also good as a counter.
Ko-uchi-gake	Minor Inner Hook	forward	backward	Foot Throw	Ideal for a small man against a long legged opponent.

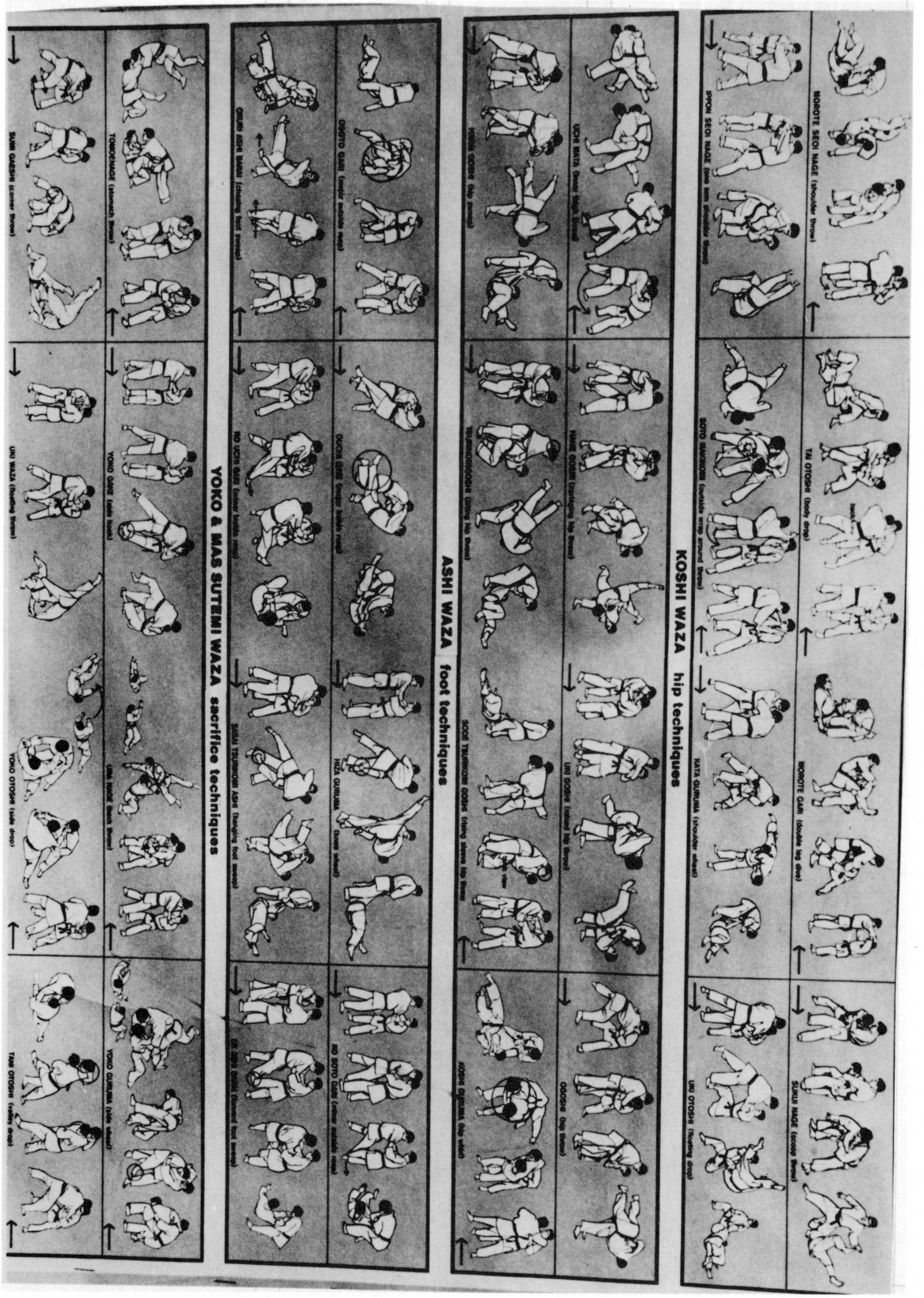

TE WAZA hand techniques (partial, upper section)

MOROTE SEOI NAGE (shoulder throw)

IPPON SEOI NAGE (one arm shoulder throw)

SOTO MAKIKOMI (outside wrap around throw)

TAI OTOSHI (body drop)

MOROTE GARI (double leg dive)

KATA GURUMA (shoulder wheel)

UKI OTOSHI (floating drop)

SUKUI NAGE (scoop throw)

KOSHI WAZA hip techniques

HANE GOSHI (spring hip throw)

UCHI MATA (inner thigh throw)

HARAI GOSHI (sweeping hip throw)

TSURIKOMI GOSHI (lifting pulling hip throw)

SEOI GOSHI (back hip throw)

UKI GOSHI (floating hip throw)

SODE TSURIKOMI GOSHI (sleeve lifting pulling hip throw)

KOSHI GURUMA (hip wheel)

O GOSHI (big hip throw)

O GURUMA (big wheel)

ASHI WAZA foot techniques

OKURI ASHI BARAI (following foot sweep)

DE ASHI BARAI (advanced foot sweep)

OUCHI GARI (large inside reap)

KOUCHI GARI (minor inner reaping throw)

OSOTO GARI (large outer reap)

HIZA GURUMA (knee wheel)

SASAE TSURIKOMI ASHI (propping drawing ankle throw)

ASHI GURUMA (leg wheel)

KOSOTO GARI (minor outer hook)

KO SOTO GAKE (minor outer hook)

YOKO & MA SUTEMI WAZA sacrifice techniques

SUMI GAESHI (corner throw)

TOMOE NAGE (stomach throw)

URA NAGE (floating throw)

YOKO GAKE (side hook)

YOKO OTOSHI (side drop)

YOKO GURUMA (side wheel)

TANI OTOSHI (valley drop)

37

JAPANESE	ENGLISH	DIRECTION OF UNBALANCE	DIRECTION OF THROW	CLASSIFI-CATION	COMMENTS
Ko-uchi-gari	Minor Inner Reaping Throw	left back	backward	Foot Throw	Often referred to as Ko-uchi. Effective technique for small men, it is used often in competition.
Kuchiki-daoshi	Decayed Tree Throw	backward	backward	Hand Throw	Used against a tall opponent often used as an entry to other techniques or to secure a holdown.
Morote-gari	Two Handed Reaping Throw	backward	backward	Hand Throw	Both of opponent's legs are grabbed from the front and he is dumped on his back.
Morote-seoi-nage	Two Handed Shoulder Throw	forward	forward over shoulder	Hand Throw	Effective against taller persons. Clean throw ensures an ippon in competition.
O-goshi	Major Hip Throw	right front	forward over the hip	Hip Throw	Not used in contest, but effective teaching technique to develop full hip movement.
O-Guruma	Major Wheel Throw	right front	forward in a circle over the leg	Foot Throw	Opponent is thrown by pulling twisting motion over Toris extended leg.
Okuri-ashi-harai	Sweeping Ankle Throw	right side	sideways	Foot Throw	Effective when uke is moving sideways.
O-soto-gari	Major Outer Reaping Throw	right back	backward	Foot Throw	Used frequently in contest. Especially popular with big men.
O-Soto-Guruma	Major Outer Wheel	backward	backward	Foot Throw	Similar to O-soto-gari except both of ukes feet are swept away.
O-soto-otoshi	Major Outer Drop	backward	backward	Foot Throw	Similar to O-soto-gari
O-uchi-gari	Major Inner Reaping Throw	left-back	backward	Foot Throw	Called O-uchi, often used by smaller men against bigger opponents. Often used in contest especially to open up a defensive opponent.
Sasae-tsurikomi-ashi	Propping Drawing Ankle Throw	right-front	forward in a big circle	Foot Throw	Best used when uke steps forward. Big pulling twisting motion of hand is required. Anton Geesing was noted for this throw.
Seio-Otoshi	Shoulder Drop	forward	forward over shoulder	Hand Throw	Similar to seoi-nage, except performed on on knee while throwing opponent over the shoulders.

JAPANESE	ENGLISH	DIRECTION OF UNBALANCE	DIRECTION OF THROW	CLASSIFI-CATION	COMMENTS
Sode-Tsurikomi-goshi	Sleeve Lifting Hip Throw	forward	forward over hip	Hip Throw	A variation of tsurikomi-goshi, done while gripping both of ukes sleeves.
Soto-makikomi	Outer Winding Throw	right front	forward over hip	Sacrifice Throw	Similar to a hip throw, except ukes one arm is held tightly under armpit as Tori rolls his body falling and throwing uke over himself.
Sukui-nage	Scooping Throw	backward	backward	Sacrifice Throw	Almost always used as a counter, or when grabbed from behind.
Sumi-gaeshi	Corner Throw	forward	forward while falling on the back	Sacrifice Throw	Applied when uke assumes a defensive posture.
Sumi-otoshi	Corner Drop	right-back	backward	Hand Throw	Similar to uki-otoshi. Not often used in contest. Also known as Kuki-nage.
Tai-otoshi	Body Drop	right-front	forward over extended leg	Hand Throw	A spectacular throw often used in contest, and favored by smaller men.
Tani-otoshi	Valley Drop	right-back	backward	Sacrifice Throw	Applied when uke assumes a defensive position.
Tomoe-nage	Stomach Throw	forward	forward, while falling back	Sacrifice Throw	A very impressive throw, used in competition, but requires superb timing.
Tsuri-goshi	Lifting Hip Throw	right front	forward over hip	Hip Throw	Can be done two ways, by placing hand over opponent's arm to grip his belt (o-tsuri goshi) or by placing hand under opponent's arm to grip his belt (Ko-tsuri-goshi).
Tsuri-komi-goshi	Lifting Pulling Hip Throw	front or right-front	forward over hip	Hip Throw	A popular contest throw referred to as "a small man's giant killer." Often just called Tsuri-Komi.
Uchi-makikomi	Inner Winding Throw	right-front	forward over hip	Sacrifice Throw	Similar to soto-makikomi except Toris arm is under ukes when rolling.
Uchi-mata	Inner Thigh Throw Throw	front or right-front	forward over foot and hips	Leg Throw	One of the most popular throws in judo.

JAPANESE	ENGLISH	DIRECTION OF UNBALANCE	DIRECTION OF THROW	CLASSIFI- CATION	COMMENTS
Uki-goshi	Floating Hip Throw	right-front	forward over hip	Hip Throw	This throw is the basis of all hip techniques. Not used in contest.
Uki-otoshi	Floating Drop	right-front	forward in a big circle	Hand Throw	Used in the Nage no Rata with one knee on the ground.
Ura-nage	Rear Throw	upward	forward	Sacrifice Throw	The fall to Tori could be very heavy.
Ushiro-goshi	Rear Hip Throw		up and straight down	Hip Throw	This is used as a counter throw.
Utsuri-goshi	Changing Hip Throw		forward over hip	Hip Throw	Used as a counter throw against loin or hip techniques.
Yoko-gake	Side Body Drop	right front	to the side	Sacrifice Throw	Tori sweeps ukes ankle while dropping on his side.
Yoko-guruma	Side Wheel		forward	Sacrifice Throw	Used as a counter to the front.
Yoko-otoshi	Side Drop	right	sideways	Sacrifice Throw	Usually done as uke moves to the side.
Yoko-wakare	Side Separation	forward	sideways	Sacrifice Throw	

Ju-no-kata is performed by two female members of the Kodokan.

Anton Geesink was the first non-Japanese to capture the world judo championships. Here he footsweeps American V. Tamura.

Tsumazukasu-waza, or tripping techniques, are an important part of a judo player's repertoire and are often used in competition. Here Gene Le Bell tries to trip his opponent with a harai tsuri komi ashi.

JUJUTSU

Literally, jujutsu is the technique or art (jutsu) of suppleness, flexibility, gentleness; also spelled jiu jitsu or jujitsu. Judo founder **Jigoro Kano** traced the art's emergence to the period between 1600 and 1650. In its golden age—late 17th to mid-19th century—more than 700 jujutsu systems appeared in Japan. Among those mentioned prominently in martial arts chronicles are: **Tenjin-Shinyo-ryu, Takenouchi ryu, Sousuishitsu ryu,** the **Kito ryu,** and the **Sekiguchi ryu.** Many other ancient and reputable schools, such as the Yagyu-Shingan ryu or the Date clan and the Juki ryu or Sawa Dochi, are listed within the doctrine of jujutsu.

The vital issue in jujutsu was effectiveness in combat. Methods were tested in duels and public competitions among members of various schools. These encounters were frequently lethal. Such testing not only improved weapons and ways of employing them, but established the reputations of the survivors.

Jujutsu techniques include kicking, striking, kneeing, throwing, choking, joint locking, holding, and tying, as well as use of certain weapons. Most systems emphasized only one or two major techniques. Jujutsu was always a secondary method of combat to the warrior, since he relied so heavily on his sword.

Although jujutsu techniques are initially learned individually, in a static position, the essence of jujutsu is the ability to move from one technique to another, or a second or even a third as needed—and as quickly and as often as necessary to control an attacker. Since each system emphasizes only a few major techniques (or **waza**), the principle behind each technique can be applied in numerous situations, not just in the manner in which it is learned in a certain technique. Each technique, in fact, is designed to illustrate and teach a specific principle.

In 1905 the majority of the old schools merged with Kano's school, the famed **Kodokan.** The schools of **aiki-jutsu,** however, did not join Kano's movement toward synthesis in jutsu arts. Today, as in the past, they·remain independent in matters of organization and public affiliation, although instructional exchanges are taking place with increasing regularity. *Further reading: Classical Budo,* Donn F. Draeger, 1973; *Modern Bujutsu & Budo,* Donn F. Drager, 1974; *The Complete Kano Jiu Jitsu,* Higashi Katsukuma, 1926; *Secrets of the Samurai,* Oscar Ratti and Adele Westbrook, 1973; *Jujutsu Secrets,* Allan C. Smith, 1920.

FORMS OF JUJUTSU

AIKI-JUTSU Ancient system of combat based on jujutsu; founded by Shinra Saburo Yoshimitsu during the Kamakura period (1185-1336) in Japan. Also known as aiki-jutjutsu, it is the art from which aikido developed.

Sometime during the 13th century, a school existed to the north of Mt. Fuji that specialized in the teaching of aiki-jutsu. It was kept secret except to a few disciples, for the most part Japanese nobles of ancient lineage. This art had originated from **kenjutsu,** and is said to have gradually become a method of combat superior to jujutsu.

The term *aiki,* like *ju,* indicates a principle, a way of using the body as a weapon of combat. The method of aiki is to use the coordinated power of **ki** in harmony with the circumstances of combat; by blending one's strategy with an opponent's, to attain full control over him and over the encounter. *See also* aikido. *Further reading: Secrets of the Samurai,* Adele Westbrook and Oscar Ratti, 1973.

DAITOKAN School of **aiki-jutsu** (harmony art). In late-19th-century Japan, Sokaku Takeda, 32nd in line of the Takeda family, revived the family's system of **Daito-ryu aiki-jutsu.** After traveling throughout Japan to teach his system he opened a school at Hokkaido. Renamed Daitokan by his son, Tokimune Takeda, it continues to operate. Aikido founder Morihei Ueshiba studied here.

DAITO-RYU AIKI-JUTSU One of the earliest known Japanese disciplines to supplement weapons techniques with empty-hand combat methods, the Daito-ryu was a renowned school of ancient **aiki-jutsu.** According to modern sources, the instructional manuscripts of certain secret martial arts, compiled during the feudal era, refer to the aiki-jutsu practiced by this school as dating to the Kamakura

In jujutsu, besides throws (*top photo*) there are numerous joint-locking moves (*above*) that are used to render an opponent totally helpless.

period (1185-1333). Daito-ryu was reportedly founded by Minamoto Yoshimitsu (d. 1120), better known in several Japanese epics as Yoshitsune. The art was practiced by warriors of the Minamoto clan for several centuries before being inherited by the Takeda family, part of the military clan of the Aizu. (However, the specific doctrine of aikido, a modern derivative of aiki-jutsu founded by Morihei Ueshiba, links the origin of Daito-ryu to the sixth son of Emperor Seiwa, Prince Sadasumi, who lived in the 9th century.) Yoshimitsu, a brilliant tactician, was knowledgeable in many martial arts. He is said to have improved and extended aiki-jutsu. He realized that a warrior's hands and wrists, uncovered and unprotected as they were, could be especially vulnerable, and he therefore developed techniques to be applied against these points. It is thought he called his system Daito-ryu aiki-jutsu after his estate, Daito.

Yoshimitsu's son, Yoshikiyo, also an accomplished warrior, enlarged the system's number of techniques. During his lifetime the family's name was said to have been changed to Takeda. The system developed further, but continued to be kept exclusively within the family and among a small number of trusted retainers. After the family moved to Aizu in the late 14th century, the name Aizu-todome was attached to this style.

How the concept of **ai** (harmony) was actually embodied in the ancient techniques of Daito-ryu aiki-jutsu is not known. The fluid beauty and efficiency of this system, however, are still evident in modern interpretations of technique. *See also* Daitokan.

GOSHINJUTSU; GOSHIN-JUTSU Form of jujutsu developed by Tatsu Tanaka, who opened a dojo in Tokyo in 1952. Finding classical jujutsu unsuited to his tastes, he decided to modernize the system by eliminating injurious techniques. Kicking and striking techniques were removed, as was leg tripping, and emphasis placed on **atemi-waza** (vital point technique), **kansetsu-waza** (locking techniques), and **nage-waza** (throwing techniques). Tanaka's main purpose is to promote good health through vigorous exercise and proper knowledge of self-defense. There are some 150 basic techniques in goshinjutsu.

2. Goshin-jutsu is a **kata** in judo, also referred to as the Kodokan goshin-jutsu. These forms, established in 1958, include defense against grabs, chokes, strikes, and kicks, as well as attacks with weapons such as a dagger, stick, or gun. The kata has two divisions: the first comprises 9 techniques against an opponent bearing a weapon; the second comprises 12 techniques against an unarmed assailant.

Against a dagger
1. tsukkake (dagger thrust)
2. choku-zuki (straight thrust)
3. naname-zuki (dagger thrust at the side of the head)
Against a stick
4. furi-gae (upward block)
5. furi-oroshi (downward block)
6. morote-zuki (two-handed thrust)
Against a gun
7. shomen-zuke (pointing gun from front)
8. koshi-gamae (holding pistol at the side)
9. haimen-zuke (pointing gun from behind)
Unarmed at close range
10. ryote-dori (two-hand seizure)
11. hidari-eri-dori (left collar grab)
12. migi-eri-dori (right collar grab)
13. kata-ude-dori (one-hand grab)
14. ushiro-eri-dori (back collar grab)
15. ushiro-jime (choking from behind)
16. kake-dori (rear bear hug)
Unarmed at long range
17. waname-uchi (oblique blow)
18. ago-tsuki (uppercut at the chin)
19. ganmen-tsuki (thrust at the face)
20. mae-geri (front kick)
21. yoko-geri (side kick)

HAKKO-RYU Style of jujutsu founded on June 1, 1941 by **Ryuho Okuyama** in Japan. It is designed to handle attacks by applying pressure on the body's keiraku (meridians) to cause intense but nondamaging pain and thus destroy the attacker's will to continue. The aim of hakko-ryu technique is to neutralize, control and discourage an attacker with techniques that employ minimal strength yet generate maximum efficiency. Okuyama created his system upon the belief that the successful application of technique versus the application of physical strength could overcome attacks in a self-defense context. The ability to neutralize and control both the attacker and the situation is the hallmark of hakko-ryu jujutsu, which translates as ''school of the eighth light.''

Hakko-ryu techniques are taught in two basic ways: suwari-waza (kneeling) and tachi-waza (standing). The former teaches the student to master the hand techniques predominant in this style; in the latter, the student integrates the hand technique with footwork and tai-sabaki (body movement). Here, tensing and the use of power are discouraged in favor of suppleness and flexibility. The principle behind each technique compensates for power. Hakko-ryu does not teach specific techniques and defenses for a myriad of possible attacks, but instead a thorough mastery of the principles upon which the techniques are based.

The most important aspect of the hakko-ryu principles and their application is the emphasis placed on the little finger side of the hand. All gripping techniques stress the pulling motion of the little finger side of the hand, where blocking and pinning, etc. are also performed. Many of hakko-ryu's control techniques do not involve an unnatural twisting of the joints, but rather a bending of the joints in a natural direction—which requires less strength, is much more difficult to resist physically, and results in a sharp piercing pain. **Atemi** techniques in hakko-ryu are based on the principles of **koho shiatsu**, a form of Japanese finger-pressure therapy created by Ryuho Okuyama. Atemi strikes and touches are directed to the tensed areas of an opponent's body.

Kicks, seldom used, are directed to the lower body from the waist down. Open-hand strikes, particularly the knife hand, are typical. The forefist strike, or seiken, is not used.

There are four levels of black belt: shodan, nidan, sandan, and yondan (1st through 4th degree). Advanced training and promotions beyond these ranks can be acquired only at the Hakko Juku Honbu, the style's headquarters in Saitama Prefecture, and only under the direction of founder Ryuho Okuyama or his eldest son and heir apparent, **Toshio Okuyama**. Four levels of advanced instruction take place at the honbu: shihan (master teacher), renshi shihan (senior master teacher), kaiden shihan (master teacher of the deepest mysteries), and sandaikichi (three great foundation pillars). The actual advanced training is called soden kai (transmission ceremonies). Usually, no more than five students ranked yondan or higher participate in the soden kai. They are designated **uchideshi** (special disciples). At the conclusion of this training a formal ceremony is conducted in which Shinto services are performed and advanced teachers throughout Japan are invited to watch the uchideshi demonstrate hakko-ryu techniques.

In Japan, hakko-ryu students include government officials, industrial leaders, executives, attorneys, and police officers who appreciate the range of responses offered to them through hakko-ryu techniques. Okuyama Sr. remains active by teaching and writing, while his son supervises the headquarters and admnistrates the style. Once a year the Okuyamas conduct a public demonstration to crowds are large as 800. Both also treat patients with koho shiatsu therapy. Two well-known Americans in this style of Dennis G. Palumbo, who holds a menkyo-kaiden (teaching certificate), and Brian Workman, a former uchideshi who holds the title of kaiden shihan sandaikichu. *Further reading: Black Belt Magazine*, Nov. 1982; *Hakko-Ryu Jujutsu*, Dennis G. Palumbo, 1983; *Kick Illustrated*, Dec. 1982, Jan. 1983.

KITO RYU Jujutsu style that merits a particular place in the doctrine of unarmed martial arts because of its esoteric elements, elements similar to those of **aikijutsu.** Of particular interest in this regard are the **kata** that have been preserved by the modern inheritors of kito ryu. Some of the available records trace the origin of this school to a Chinese combat based upon the principle of ju (suppleness), as explained and illustrated by **Chin Gempin** to selected warriors of 17th century Japan. Another version associates this method with two other noted jujutsu experts, Yoshimura and Takenaka.

These techniques, generally performed in full armor or in formal robes resembling armor, are centered upon throwing an opponent to the ground. They were considered difficult even by masters such as judo's **Jigoro Kano** and aikido's **Morihei Ueshiba,** both of whom had studied them at great length before incorporating any of their features into their own modern methods.

KOSHI MAWARI Ancient form of combat resembling jujutsu.

KORYU KATA Jujutsu form of the Edo period (1603-1867). It includes unarmed defenses against a knife, sword, spear, and stick, as well as sword against sword.

SAPPO Old system of attacking weak areas of the body so as to disable an attacker. These methods were taught in the old jujutsu systems, handed down by word of mouth from master to pupil in sworn secrecy.

SEKIGUCHI RYU Ju-jutsu style. Sekiguchi ryu originated in 17th century Japan where the stern **Jushin Sekiguchi,** a teacher of warriors, is said to have excelled in the martial virtues of honesty and objectivity—virtues he seems to have successfully transmitted to his sons along with the techniques of his school. The words of his eldest son, Rohaku, to a powerful baron in Edo in 1716 were recorded and indicate the son's contempt for martial arts masters who "threw dust in people's eyes" by performing tricks to advertise their schools, thus debasing **bujutsu** as a whole and bringing dishonor upon the "real" masters.

SHINDO YOSHIN RYU JUJUTSU One of the major jujutsu systems of Japan.

SHIN-NO-SHINDO Early school of jujutsu believed to have been founded by **Yamamoto Tamizaemon,** of the Osaka police, during the Tokugawa era (1600-1867); he added other techniques, especially those of immobilization, to the repertoire of the **yoshin ryu** school. Shin-no-shindo is one of the two arts combined to form the **tenjin-shinyo** school of jujutsu.

SHINTO-YOSHI-RYU Form of jujutsu practiced in Japan at the turn of the 20th century. The school specialized in **atemi** striking and kicking, and is one of the styles from which **Hironori Ohtsuka** created **wado-ryu** karate-do.

TAKENOUCHI RYU Form of jujutsu founded by Toichiro Takeuchi (aka **Hisamori Takenouchi**) in the 16th century. He studied a number of different combat systems, from which he formed his own style, stressing immobilization techniques, as well as those of close combat with daggers. His style soon developed a large following and was taught for many generations.

SOSUISHITSU RYU Variation of Takenouchi ryu jujutsu, this branch of jujutsu was reputedly founded by a **samurai** named Fugatami Hannosuke in 1650. Fugatami, after a period of purification in the Yoshino mountains, named his method after the "pure flowing waters" of the Yoshino River. He taught it to Shitama Mataichi, members of whose family, whether by direct lineage or by adoption, appear to have been masters of this art for centuries. Eventually, their school joined **Jigoro Kano's** successful synthesis of "ju" arts, called judo.

TENJIN-SHINYO-RYU School of jujutsu founded by Iso Mataemon (also known as **Masatari Yanagi**). It is particularly famous for its vital-point attacks (**atemi-waza**), immobilization methods (torae), and strangleholds (shime). It is generally considered to have been the result of a fusion of two ancient schools, the **Yoshin ryu** and the **Shin-no-Shindo. Jigoro Kano**, founder of modern judo, began his martial arts training by studying tenjin shinyo ryu in 1877.

YAWARA Precursor to a form of jujutsu believed by Japanese historians to be the earliest native bare-handed fighting art. In some forms of yawara a short rod is used. Little else is known about this art, and it remains one of the most esoteric of all the existing Japanese **bujutsu.**

YOSHIN-RYU Style of jujutsu known as the willow school. The origins of yoshin-ryu jujutsu are still the object of much debate. Many historians believe the founder of the art to have been a physician of Nagasaki, one Shirobei Yoshitoki Akiyama, who went to China in the 17th century to further his knowledge of medicine. While studying various methods of resuscitation, called hassei-ho (later to become the complex science of katsu), he was exposed to Chinese martial arts and to their principles of strategic application. In particular, he studied the methods of striking externally, which then became the chief technical concern of his school of yoshin-ryu.

It is said that Akiyama then returned to Japan, where he elaborated upon these techniques in complete isolation. His personal training program included both physical exercises and meditation. In time, he developed about 300 combat techniques.

Other sources claim Yoshin Miura founded this system, but there is practically no documentation to substantiate this claim.

The image of the flexible, swaying willow, which snaps back even after the fiercest hurricane, while the sturdy but rigid oak falls before the storm, was recorded in the chronicles of the martial arts.

JUKENDO

JUKEN-DO Systematic use of the bayonet, known as **juken-jutsu** (bayonet art), appeared druing the Meiji era. This method was taught in the Toyama Gakko, a special miltary training school in Tokyo. Prohibited by the Allied occupation in 1945, juken-jutsu was revived among military and ex-military personnel as juken-do (way of the bayonet), a spiritual and physical discipline designed for competition.

The fundamental juken-do technique is the straight thrust. In a shiai (contest) combatants don protective gear to withstand the sock of the mokuju, or wooden rifle and simulated bayonet. The object, under the rules, is to register a lethal attack in any one of the three target areas: the heart, the lower left side, and the throat. **Kata** (formal exercises) exist. *Further reading: Modern Bujutsu and Budo,* Donn F. Draeger, 1974.

FORMS OF JUKENDO

JUKEN-JUTSU Japanese bayonet techniques. Originating in the feudal era, it came to be used on modern rifles, borrowing movements from **sojutsu** (art of the spear). *See also* juken-do.

KALARI PAYAT

Literally, "gymnasium," and payat, "exercises," kalari payat is an ancient form of combat practiced in southern India. Numerous legends exist regarding the origin of this art. Medieval ballads describe a method of fighting believed to have been kalari payat. The art reached its zenith in the late 16th century, in the days of Tacholi Othenan, a celebrated chieftain of North Malabar. Both boys and girls were enrolled in the kalaris from about the age of 10.

Kalari payat's use in warfare faded with the European introduction of firearms. Today, kalari payat is a method of physical fitness and an empty-handed means of self-defense. Yet, it is bound in traditional ceremonies and ritual. Students enter the kalari right foot first and

Juken-do practitioners in action.

bow before certain parts of the gym that serve as seats for ancient deities. Before practice commences, pupils touch the feet of their guru (teacher).

The foundation of the art is meithozhil, a series of conditioning drills for toughness and quick reflexes. The next stage is kolthari, consisting of exercises with wooden staves of various lengths and shapes. Staff drills are performed individually or in pairs. Students also practice with the munchan, a tapered 2 foot staff and learn to employ the otta, an s-shaped staff of the same length.

In the third stage, a group of exercises called angathari, weapons are studied. First is valvari, a solo performance with sword and shield, followed by valpayat, sword-and-shield tactics practiced in pairs. Among the weaponry in the angathari branch is urumi, a deadly instrument best described as a coiled spring. It is worn around the waist. The most dangerous of angathari exercises is kattara payat—attack and defense with daggers.

The final branch of kalari payat is verumkai, bare-handed exercise. Although carrying a dagger or sword is now illegal, verumkai teaches defense against an armed opponent. *Further reading: Black Belt Magazine,* July 1973.

KARATE

An art of self-defense and a sport, which has in recent decades proliferated world wide. It is now the most widely practiced of the Oriental martial arts, with a large following in Japan, the U.S. and Europe.

Unlike other martial arts such as judo, aikido or jujutsu, karate is not a grappling art. Its practitioners learn to deliver blows with their hands and feet as well as using many parts of the body in blocking and defensive movements.

Modern karate originated in Okinawa and was introduced to Japan in the early part of the 20th century by Gichin Funakoshi. From here it was spread world wide after World War II. Unlike judo, there are a large number of styles in karate. Basically divided into Okinawan or Japanese styles, the most widely practiced ones include:

OKINAWAN —	Shotokan
Goju-ryu	Wado-ryu
Isshin-ryu	Other minor styles of Japanese
Shorei-ryu|	karate include:
Shorin-ryu	Chito-ryu
Uechi-ryu	Koei-kan
JAPANESE	Renbukan
Goju-ryu	Sankukai
Kyokushinkai	Shudokan
Shito-ryu	Shukokai

Because rivalry among these groups is intense, karate is the most fragmented of all the martial arts. Even among specific styles disagreements occur, much of it over minor technical points or over the amount of influence the sport should have over the art.

In order to attempt some unification at least in the sport two major world organizations were formed in the early 1970s, the World Union of Karate-Do Organizations (WUKO) and the International Amateur Karate Federation (IAKF). Both organizations have large followings world wide, and between them control Amateur Karate worldwide.

Karate is practiced in bare feet in a dojo. Most dojo have a hardwood floor, although some of the more modern clubs use mats. Equipment found in most karate dojo included the makiwara (straw padded striking post) used to perfect punching and kicking and for toughening parts of the body, punching and kicking bags of various sizes, dumbells, iron clogs for leg strengthening, stretching bars, and mirrors, to aid in movement analysis.

Since karate is an oriental martial art, proper etiquette in a dojo is important. It is customary for all karate-ka to execute a standing bow (ritsu-rei) upon entering and leaving the dojo. A standing bow is also exchanged between practitioners at the beginning and end of a contest, free practice or formal practice. Classes always begin and end with a kneeling bow (za-rei) to the sensei (teacher), and students always line up according to rank—highest belts always sitting on the right side of lower ranks. In traditional schools students wait for the highest ranking belt in line to call out Sensei, ni-rei (bow to sensei) at which point both students and sensei bow to each other.

The karate-gi in which training takes place is usually all white (although in some styles colored gis are used) and made up of a light jacket, pants and a belt. Unlike the judo-gi which is of heavy woven material, the karate-gi is much lighter for easy movement and since little or no grappling takes place it is much less durable, and easier to tear.

The color of the belt or obi indicates the grade of the wearer. In all styles dan grades wear a black belt. These dan grades progress from first to usually 10th dan, the highest level in most styles. The dan ranks are:

Shodan — 1st degree	Rokudan — 6th degree
Nidan — 2nd degree	Shichidan — 7th degree
Sandan — 3rd degree	Hachidan — 8th degree
Yodan — 4th degree	Kudan — 9th degree
Godan — 5th degree	Judan — 10th degree

The color of belt worn by kyu grades (below black belt) vary from style to style, with only the white belt being universally used for beginners. Most styles also use the brown belt for the color just before black. In the kyu grades the progression is from highest to lowest. Most styles start with 10th kyu (white) and work toward 1st kyu (brown). The kyu grades are:

Jukyu — tenth grade	Gokyu — fifth grade
Kyukyu — ninth grade	Yonkyu — fourth grade
Hachikyu — eighth grade	Sankyu — third grade
Shichikyu — seventh grade	Nikyu — second grade
Rokkyu — sixth grade	Ikkyu — first grade

The inbetween colors vary from style to style. The most common colors used are yellow or orange, purple, blue, green and brown. In traditional Japanese styles the black belts have special titles which denote levels of achievement. The chief instructor of a world wide organization of styles is known as Kancho. Instructors above 6th dan are known as shihan; black belts from 2nd to 5th dans are called sempai (senior). It is the sempai who set the example for the junior grade or Kohai to follow.

To move from one rank to another, there are periodic examinations given in which the student must perform basic techniques relevant to their grade. At the earliest stages basic blocks, punches and strikes are required on the test; later kata as well as one point sparring is a requirement and as one advances—good form, power, speed and accuracy all become mandatory for performing all karate techniques.

For black belt, free sparring as well as a thorough knowledge of kata and basics are mandatory. Some styles insist on elements such as breaking for rank advancement especially at the black belt level. Also many styles judge an aspiring black belt on his character, spirit, confidence and ability to fully control all his movements, which include stopping all of his techniques just inches from its intended target.

Karate techniques consist basically of hand techniques and foot techniques. Hand techniques are divided into defensive or offensive moves. Defensive moves, known as Uke-Waza or blocking techniques include a variety of methods by which the hand or forearm is utilized to block, sweep, deflect, or hook an opponent's attacking weapon.

Some styles emphasize circular movements in their blocks, while others place emphasis on linear blocking movements. In general circular blocks are soft, while linear blocks are hard. The softer blocks tend to deflect an attack, while the harder blocks meet the attacking limb, often with enough force to render the limb useless. Most styles of karate include both hard and soft blocks, but tend to emphasize one or the other.

Offensive or attacking hand techniques are divided into purching techniques (Zuki-waza) and striking techniques (Uchi-waza).

Punching techniques are delivered in a straight line, usually from the hip to the target. The fore fist (seiken) is most often employed as the striking point, but punching techniques can also be done with the palm heel (teisho), fingers (nukite) or fore knuckles (hiraken).

Striking techniques usually follow a circular path to the target, and are performed with a snapping motion of the elbow. There are many striking techniques in karate, and they employ all parts of the hand and arm including the back of the fist (riken), bottom of the fist (tettsui), back of the hand (haishu), side edge of hand (shuto), ridge part of hand (haito) and elbow (empi).

Foot techniques are divided into kicking techniques (keri-waza) and leg blocking techniques.

Kicking techniques are usually divided into snap kicks and thrust kicks.

Snap kicks are performed by kicking and then immediately retracting the foot. These kicks make use of the snapping motion of the knee, and enable one to execute a series of kicks in quick succession. Thrust kicks are delivered in a straight line to the target, with the kicking leg locked out for a second, adding more power to the kick.

Kicks can be further subdivided into straight and circular kicks. Straight kicks are delivered in a straight line to the front, side, back or downward. Circular kicks are delivered usually with a snapping motion of the knee and the swinging of the hips. These kicks travel in a circular path before hitting their target. Some styles of karate further divide their kicks into spinning kicks—in which the kick is delivered with a full or half-spin before hitting the target; wheel kicks—in which the kick is executed by swinging the whole leg at the opponent with little knee action.

Stomping kicks—in which the kicks are delivered from close in by lifting the knee high and then driving the heel into an opponent's knee, shin, ankle or instep. These kicks can also be used to kick a downed opponent.

Jumping or Flying kicks—these are kicks which are executed

Kara (*top*) means "empty"; Te (*bottom*) means "hand." Karate therefore means "empty hands."

while in mid air and can be done in any direction in a straight line or circularly. Some styles of karate even have spinning-jumping kicks in which the kicks are delivered while in mid air with a full spin of the body.

Leg Blocking techniques utilize the feet or leg to stop an opponent's kicking or punching attack. These blocks are usually used by jamming or sweeping to the side an opponent's attacking limb. They are valuable especially to low attacks to the legs or groin where the hands have difficulty reaching. Foot techniques utilize all parts of the leg, including the ball of the foot (koshi), side edge of the foot (sokuto), heel (kakato), instep (haisoku), sole (teisoku), toes (tsumasaki) and the knee (hittsui).

Other important elements of karate include stances, posture and body shifting. Since there are a multitude of moves in karate there are different stances for each situation. Stance must be flexible; it must be changed with direction and type of movement.

The stability of a stance depends to a great extent on the area included within its base. And, as the center of gravity is lowered, stability increases. Therefore, stances in which the hips are relatively low tend to be more stable than those in which the hips are high. A particular stance loses stability as the center of gravity is raised, but conversely, aids mobility. No one stance is suitable for all occasions. Generally, when moving from one stance to another, the hips remain at the same level and the feet slide lightly across the floor.

Some styles of karate, like Shotokan, advocate low, deep stances while others, like Shukokai, prefer higher more mobile stances. Some are in between the two. The stances found in a style reflect the emphasis which the style places on such things as speed, power and hip movement.

In competition many of the traditionally deep stances are abandoned in favor of high mobile ones, since in sport karate speed is more important than power.

In most traditional styles the three main types of stances used are:
NATURAL STANCES—in which the muscles of the leg are relaxed (e.g. informal attention stance, open leg stance)
OUTSIDE TENSION STANCES—in which tension is put on the legs by forcing the knees outward (e.g. forward stance, back stance, horse stance)
INSIDE TENSION STANCES—in which tension is placed on the leg by forcing the knees inward (e.g. cat stance, hourglass stance)

Postures used in Karate include front facing—in which an opponent is faced straight on, with hips locked forward; and shoulders parallel to the target., half front facing—in which the opponent is faced forward but the shoulders and hips are turned away at a 45 degree angle. This is the most widely used position when moving and getting ready for attacking, as well as when defending against an attack.

Side facing—in which the opponent is to the side. The shoulders are perpendicular to the target. This position has become widely used lately by karate competitors especially of non-traditional styles.

Body shifting consists of moving from one position to another. In karate this can be done in a number of ways: by stepping, hopping, sliding, shuffling, jumping or turning.

Another important aspect of karate is hip rotation. Destructive force in karate is generated by turning the body and especially by rotating the hips. To deliver a karate punch a smooth, swift, and level turn of the hips is essential to effectiveness. In karate the trunk works as the drive shaft giving the body greater motion which creates a larger and faster movement and more power.

Abdominal muscles play a major role in turning the hips and thigh muscles contribute. Power generated by rotating the hips is conveyed to the backbone then to the muscles of the chest and shoulders and finally arm and fist.

Breathing is also an essential part of karate training. Inhaling is deep and full, through the nose and into the stomach. Exhaling is through the mouth and gradually down toward the stomach. Karate breathing is designed not only to refresh the respiratory system and to conserve bodily energy but most importantly to strengthen the lower abdominal areas so that maximum internal strength can be used when delivering a blow.

When first beginning karate, a new student learns basic stances, punches, kicks and blocks. He works on improving his balance and muscle control and learns how to increase speed and power in his techniques. Breathing—when to inhale and when to exhale as a

technique is delivered—is vital and students must begin to learn its proper application early in training.

Once basics have been mastered, multiple techniques are learned as well as the more difficult blocks, punches, strikes and kicks.

At this stage students begin to work with a partner to perfect not just technique but distancing, timing, speed, power, and eye-body co-ordination. Known as Kumite, or sparring, this type of training puts all the moves of Karate into practical application. There are two types of kumite: pre-arranged (Yakusoku-Kumite) or free (Jiyu-Kumite).

In pre-arranged sparring, often called Kihon Kumite (basic sparring), the mode of attack and defense is always determined in advance. There are a number of pre-arranged sparring methods.

Ippon Kumite or one point sparring consists of participants facing each other from a fixed distance and taking turns in attacking and defending against pre-determined attacks. Usually one participant assumes a fighting position while the defender remains in a natural stance. As the attacker steps forward and delivers his attack the defender steps either backward, forward, or to the side and blocks the move and then immediately counter attacks.

Gohon Kumite or five step sparring consists of one participant attacking five times in a row with the same technique while his partner moving back blocks the attacks and after the last attack he counters with a forceful counter attack.

Sanbon Kumite or three step sparring, consists of one participant attacking, with three pre-arranged techniques of any type and the defender retreats and blocks the attacks—at the end of the three attacks he delivers a forceful counterattack of his own.

Jiyu-ippon-kumite, semi-free one-step sparring, is the midway point between basic and freestyle sparring. Here both partners move around freely and one person attacks with a pre-arranged target. The defender blocks and counters the attack. A more advanced variation occurs in this category, when both the attacker and defender are pre-determined, but the method of attack and choice of weapon remain undisclosed.

Yiyu-Kumite or free style sparring is the most advanced form of karate training. Here both partners move around freely and exchange blows, blocks and counter attacks at random until one of them gets in a focused attack at his opponent's vital point. Here all aspects of karate come into play: punching, kicking, blocking, shifting, distancing, timing, and strategy. Jiyu-Kumite differs from competitive karate in that it is still a method of training whereby students should work with each other in perfecting their skills in a realistic situation. When attacks are thrown they are pulled just short of contact—so injury is avoided.

There are many different methods of free sparring, among them slow sparring in which all attacks are done slowly or done quickly with no power, kick sparring in which only the feet are used, or hand sparring in which only hands are used to attack and counter.

Another way of losing is Shikkaku or disqualification which is given for a number of prohibited acts such as disagreeing with the referee, showing up late, etc., or for not being able to continue his match due to illness or other problems.

Another important training method in karate is KATA, formal exercises. In kata a number of pre-arranged defensive and offensive moves are performed in a fixed order of succession against several imaginary opponents. Kata include all the various hand and foot techniques used in karate, and incorporate rapid changes of technique, speed, balance, posture, position, breathing and muscle tension.

All kata begins with a defensive technique, followed by an attacking movement. Katas are of varying lengths, but all of them terminate in their initial positions.

All styles of karate have kata but some emphasize its practice more than others. Although kata differs from style to style in most of the traditional karate styles, the katas have a lot of similarity because they originate from Okinawan karate masters. Although recently the practice of kata has been on the decline, its practice is still important, especially in the Japanese and Okinawan systems.

Karate today has become an international sport and is practiced in almost every country in the world.

There are two types of karate competition: (Shidi) Kumite (sparring) and Kata (form).

Kumite competition is conducted between two individuals of equal rank and weight on a flat surface usually about 8 meters (26 ft.) square. The actual sparring, which is called non-contact in America, is a free exchange of blows, blocks and counter-attacks until one player directs a blow to within a fraction of an inch of a target area on an opponent's body. If the blow is delivered with the proper posture, balance and distance and is appropriately focused, an ippon (one point) is awarded. A waza-ari (half technique), or half point is given for a well-timed punch or kick that is slightly off center. This half point system is only used by the traditional Japanese styles. Among the non-traditional styles various rules and scoring systems exist. Often especially in the U.S. bouts last 2 or 3 minutes and the winner is the contestant with the most points at the end of the bout. There is usually one referee with from 2 to 4 judges. Majority decision is used to score a point. Bouts are rarely set for more than one round, with the exception of black belt grand championships. Other types of contests include the one point system, in which the person gaining the first full point (ippon) wins.

WUKO (World Union of Karate Do) which is one of the leading non professional karate organizations in the world has established a set of rules which is now used by close to 70 countries. In a WUKO contest there is one referee in the fight area, four judges, one seated at each corner of the match area and one arbitrator, seated to one side of the match area. The referee conducts the match, awards points, announces fouls, and issues warnings and disciplinary actions. The judges act as arbitrators in the awarding of points and the majority can override a referee's decision. They are also the ones to help make a decision (Hantei) in case there is no clear winner.

A winner is declared as soon as a contestant has 3 points (sanbon); or if the match is over and the score is 2 (nihon) to 0. The fighter with 2 points is declared the winner.

Hantei (decision) is used to declare a winner if at the end of the contest the score is 2 to 1; or if the score is tied, or if the score is 1 to 0.

There are a number of penalties a fighter can receive, which can make him lose points and thus the match: Jogai, Huboki, Hansoku, Hansoku-Chui and Shikkaku.

Jogai—occurs when a contestant steps outside the perimeter of the match area. If three jogais are called a point is lost.

Huboki—is given when a contestant does not take up a defensive position for an opponent's attack. If he receives mobobi twice, a loss of point follows.

Hansoku or Foul is given for the following prohibited acts:
heavy contact to opponent's vital area
persistent kicking to shins

attacks to joints
dangerous sweeping attacks
continued clenching
insulting behavior

Once Hansoku is called, the contestant loses the match and his opponent is declared the winner.

Hansoku Chui — is given to a minor infringement of the above rules and two of them bring a loss of a point.

A large group, the Kyokushinkai, have their own knockdown rules which they compete under. Here full contact is allowed to the head and body with kicks and full contact to the body is allowed with punches. In case of a tie the person capable of breaking the most boards is declared the winner.

Another form of competition especially in the U.S. is semi-contact karate. Here protective gear is worn and light contact is allowed. Rules vary according to the area, but usually an accumulated point system is used with a 2 minute match. Excessive contact ends in disqualification.

Professional karate, or full contact karate, is another version of the sport. Here professional contestants wearing boxing gloves and foot gear fight to the knockout. These bouts vary in their number of rounds from 3 to 9 to 12 depending on the organization.

In international amateur competition, teams also compete for the championships. Usually there are 5 men on a team and the team that gains the greatest number of points wins. In case of a draw, one member is chosen from each team to fight in decisive bout.

Another major form of karate competition is Kata competition. Here contestants perform a chosen kata and are graded by 5 or 6 judges on a scale of 0 to 10. Each judge awards a score and usually the top and bottom scores are deleted. The remainder is added together to form an overall score for the contestant. After everyone has competed, the highest scoring kata competitor is declared the winner.

Kata is usually judged on good form, appropriate speed and power, correct breath control and correct direction of movement.

In the U.S., Kata competition is often divided into soft style, hard style and weapons. Recently a new innovation, musical kata, has come into prominence. Here contestants perform kata music and are judged not just on form but on showmanship and how well the music and kata coincide.

Another aspect of karate which is still practiced by certain styles is Tameshiwara or breaking. Today, a difference of opinion exists within karate circles as to its merits. All practitioners agree that karate-ka should be capable of breaking boards or even bricks, but many believe that its public performance, which is merely showmanship, has been responsible for projecting a false image of karate. Advocates of Tameshiwara, such as the Kyokushinkai practitioners, claim that the various parts of the body possess remarkable power, which can be released only when the practitioner has rid himself of the fear of striking something hard.

HISTORY

While sport karate is a product of the 20th century its roots can be traced to ancient India, China, and Okinawa. India, which developed yoga and its diaphragmatic breathing methods, has exerted influence on numerous combative techniques throughout the Orient. Many martial scholars consider India the birthplace of all martial arts. During the 5th and 6th centuries B.C. Indian combat techniques similar to modern karate were transmitted to China by Zen Buddhist monks.

It is thought that at the end of the 5th century A.D. a Buddhist priest named **Bodhidharma** travelled to China from India to instruct at the Shaolin monastery. There he taught the monks a combination of yoga and Indian fist-fighting that became the kung-fu system of **Shao-lin.** As the art proliferated throughout China, variation and local style appeared.

The fighting techniques of China were subsequently carried to the offshore islands, most notably Okinawa, by waves of immigrants, refugees, and priests. Weaponless combat, called te (hand), had already existed on Okinawa; with the ban against carrying arms issued by the Japanese occupation in 1470, these empty-hand techniques thrived.

Left: Karate is an art form as well as a means of combat. Here, A. Mirakian demonstrates one of the beautiful moves of karate. *Above*: J. Jennings performing a jumping side kick. Jumping side kicks are used in most styles of karate. Although very flashy, they are considered impractical in everyday combat and are used mostly for training of coordination and balance. *Below*: Doshin So, leader of Shorinji kempo in Japan until his death in 1980.

Later, with the aid of Chinese kung-fu masters who fled from China, te developed into a crude form of karate. At first the new art was translated to mean T'ang hand, or China hand, to indicate its Chinese origin. It was not until the 20th century, when **Gichin Funakoshi**—an Okinawan karate instructor—introduced Okinawa-te to Japan, that it acquired the name karate. **Yasutsune Itosu** of Okinawa, an exponent of shuri-te (**shorei-ryu**), is generally acknowledged as the first to teach karate as a sport. Itosu made this innovation in 1905 for middle-school students when occupying Japanese authorized karate for inclusion in the physical education curriculum. But it is the Japanese who are cited as the pioneers in the use of **karate-do** as an amateur sport, and the Americans to use of karate as a professional form of competition.

In the years following Funakoshi's arrival in Japan, other styles of karate-do were developed. Many Okinawan masters brought their styles to Japan, among them **Kenwa Mabuni,** who introduced **Shito-ryu** in 1930, and **Chojun Miyagi,** who combined hard Okinawan karate with soft Chinese forms and called it **goju-ryu** (hard-soft way). Other styles arising in Japan include **wado-ryu, shukukai, and kyokushinkai.** Rivalry among these groups was so intense that each style practiced its art in secret.

Following World War II, owing to the presence of many western servicemen in Japan and Okinawa, karate gradually acquired devotees in America and Europe. By the late 1950s and early 1960s, karate was well established, and by the 1970s, the art was practiced extensively throughout the world. *See also:* jiyu kumite; kata; kihon; kyu; dan; dojo; makiwara; Gichin Funakoshi; Japan Karate Association; kiai; te; Bodhidharma; noncontact; semicontact; full-contact; Kenwa Mabuni; Chojun Miyagi; goju ryu; Shito ryu; Shotokan; wado-ryu; U.S., history of karate in. *Further reading: Classical Bujutsu,* Donn F. Draeger, 1973; *Modern Bujutsu and Budo,* Donn F. Draeger, 1974; *Karate-Do Kyohan, The Master Text,* Gichin Funakoshi, 1973; *Karate's History and Traditions,* Bruce A. Haines, 1968; *Dynamic Karate,* Masatoshi Nakayama, 1966; *Karate, The Art of Empty-Hand Fighting,* Hidetaka Nishiyama and Richard C. Brown, 1960; *The History of American Karate,* Robin L. Rielly, 1970; *The Karate Dojo,* Peter Urban, 1967; *Black Belt Magazine,* May-July 1977; *Karate Illustrated Magazine,* April 1977, May 1977.

KARATE-DO Type of karate practiced in Japan that embraces spiritual discipline, self-defense, and a form of competition. From the traditionalist's point of view, **Gichin Funakoshi** must be considered the "father of Japanese karate-do," insofar as he is responsible for making important innovations in Okinawan karate that have brought this art closer to the Japanese taste.

In 1933 Funakoshi changed the concept of kara, which was originally written with an ideogram meaning "T'ang," or China, substituting another ideogram, also pronounced kara, meaning "empty"—thus, "empty-hand art." Two years later, in 1935, he discarded the word jutsu in favor of "do," and karate-do was born in Japan. Funakoshi's changes angered many Okinawan exponents, who considered them insults to tradition.

The linking of Okinawan fighting arts, and of Japanese karate-do and karate-jutsu, to Buddhist religion or philosophy, especially **Zen,** is a modern contrivance. In particular, the quasi-Buddhist teachings sometimes associated with Japanese karate-do are without foundation in the original form established by Funakoshi. Imaginative writers, inexperienced in karatelike disciplines, have enhanced the false belief that karate-do and Buddhism are inseparable.

Funakoshi had very specific points in mind when he renamed the art. The fact that pure Japanese karate-do does not involve the use of weapons other than parts of the body gives literal substance to its newer translation; Okinawan karate systems had always included the use of weapons. Funakoshi clarified his position and gained the support of his countrymen by declaring that the use of the ideogram kara was based on the concept of "hollowness," meaning "unselfishness." Therefore, the "emptyness" suggested by the newly chosen ideogram refers to rendering oneself empty, or egoless, to further development of spiritual insight. But he never intended that theosophical abstractions be made of his kara concept. He leaves a clear definition in his writings: "As a mirror's polished surface reflects whatever stands before it and a quiet valley carries even small sounds, so must the student of karate-do render of his mind empty of selfishness and wickedness in an effort to react appropriately toward anything he might encounter. This is the meaning of kara, or 'empty,' of karate-do."

In America there also has been a great deal of confusion over what constitutes "true" karate-do. Funakoshi wrote: "True karate-do is this: that in daily life, one's mind and body be trained and developed in a spirit of humility; and that in critical times, one be devoted utterly to the cause of justice." *Further reading: Modern Bujutsu and Budo,* Donn F. Draeger, 1974.

SIX RULES OF KARATE-DO Six principles laid down by **Gichin Funakoshi**, the strict observance of which is absolutely essential to achieve an understanding of **karate-do.** While Funakoshi spoke of six rules in his original writings, his book, *Karate-Do: My Way of Life,* lists only five; number three is omitted.

The rules: 1. Be deadly serious in training. Your opponent must always be present in your mind, whether you sit or stand or walk or raise your arms. Should you in combat strike a karate blow, you must have no doubt whatsoever that the one blow decides everything. If you have made an error, you will be the one who falls. You must always be prepared for such an eventuality.

2. Train with heart and soul without worrying about theory. Very often the man who lacks that essential quality of deadly seriousness will take refuge in theory.

The kibadachi (horse-riding stance), for instance, looks extremely easy but the fact is that no one could possibly master it even if he practiced every day for an entire year. What nonsense, then, for a man to complain after a couple of months practice that he is incapable of mastering a **kata.**

Karate-do consists of a great number of kata and basic skills and techniques that no human being is capable of assimilating in a short space of time. Further, unless you understand the meaning of each technique and kata, you will never be able to remember, no matter how much you practice, all the various skills and techniques. All are interrelated and if you fail to understand each completely, you will fail in the long run.

But once you have completely mastered one technique, you will realize its close relation to other techniques. You will, in other words, come to understand that all of the more than 20 kata (in Shotokan) may be distilled into only a few basic ones. If therefore you become a master of one kata, you will soon gain an understanding of all the others merely by watching them being performed or by being taught them in an instruction period.

4. Avoid self-conceit and dogmatism. A man who brags in booming tones or swaggers down the street as though he owned it will never earn true respect even though he may actually be very capable in karate or some other martial art. It is even more absurd to hear the self-aggrandizing of one who is without capability. In karate it is usually the beginner who cannot resist the temptation to brag or show off; by doing so, he dishonors not only himself, but also his chosen art.

5. Try to see yourself as you truly are and try to adopt what is meritorious in the work of others. As a karateka, you will of course often watch others practice. When you do and you see strong points in the performance of others, try to incorporate them into your own technique. At the same time, if the trainee you are watching seems to be doing less than his best, ask yourself whether you too may not be failing to practice with diligence. Each of us has good qualities and bad; the wise man seeks to emulate the good he perceives in others and avoid the bad.

6. Abide by the rules of ethics in your daily life, whether in public or private. This is a principle that demands the strictest observance. With the martial arts, most particularly with karate-do, many neophytes will exhibit great progress, and in the end some may turn out to be better karateka than their instructors. All too frequently one hears teachers speak of trainees as oshiego (pupil), or montei (follower), or deshi (disciple), or kohai (junior). Such terms should be avoided, for the time may well come when the trainee will surpass his instructor. The instructor, meanwhile, in using such expressions runs the risk of complacency, the danger of forgetting that some day the young man he has spoken of rather slightingly will not only catch up with him, but go beyond him—in the art of karate or in other fields of human endeavor. No one can attain perfection in karate-do until he finally comes to realize that it is, above all else, a faith, a way of life.

When a man enters upon an undertaking, he prays fervently that he will achieve success in it. Further, he knows that he requires the help of others and, by accepting it from them, acquires the ability to elevate the art into a faith wherein he perfects both body and soul and so comes finally to recognize the true meaning of karate-do.

Inasmuch as karate-do aims at perfection of mind as well as body, expressions that extol only physical prowess should never be used in connection with it. As one Buddhist saint, Nichiren, has so aptly said, everyone who studies the Sutras should read them not only with the eyes that are in his head, but also with those of his soul. This is the perfect admonition for a trainee of karate-do to always keep in mind.

To attain true proficiency in the art of karate-do, the karateka must control his mind and conquer himself. The Zen doctrine is central to Okinawan goju-ryu karate-do. Intuitive understanding cannot be taught, but is awakened in the karate student's mind after many years of dedicated training, discipline, and meditation.

Traditionally, on Okinawa, goju-ryu karate is taught as **karate-do,** a "way of life."

Do is the Japanese pronunciation of the Chinese ideograph Tao (pronounced *dow*). Tao, or the "way" is the dominant idea in all Chinese philosophy, the foundation of the ancient Chinese world-concept. All things are indissolubly interrelated and mutually influence each other. In karate-do, the training will become, in some measure, the practitioner, and the practitioner will become the training. The balance between karateka and his art is the manner of his training—karate seeks, therefore, to attain that most harmonious joining. (ANTHONY MIRAKIAN) *See also* goju-ryu; Okinawa, history of martial arts in.

KARATE TECHNIQUES

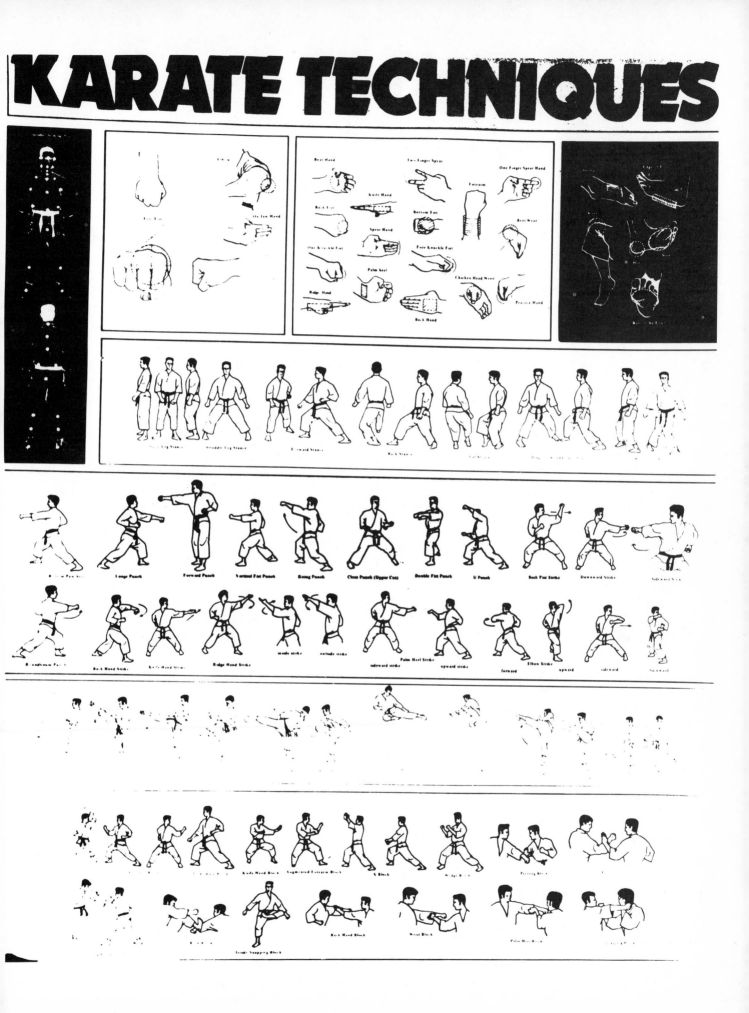

KARATE TECHNIQUES

STANCES—DACHI

JAPANESE	ENGLISH	WEIGHT	KNEES	LEGS	TOES	REMARKS
Fudo-dachi	Rooted stance	Equal	Fully bent and tensed outward	Wide	front—forward rear—45° outward	also known as Sochin-dachi
Hachiji-dachi	Open leg stance	Equal	Relaxed/straight	Medium	45% outward	a basic stance
Hangetsu-dachi	Wide hour glass stance	Equal	Bent and tensed inward	Wide	front—forward rear—45° inward	a defensive stance
Heisoku-dachi	Informal attention stance	Equal	Straight/relaxed	Close together	forward	
Kiba-dachi	Straddle leg or Horse stance	Equal	Bent and tensed outward	Wide	forward	strong stance, used when fighting opponent sideways
Kokutsu-dachi	Back stance	70% on back foot 30% on front	Front bent slightly rear bent over toes	Narrow	Ft. fwd. bck. sideways 90°	Strong defensive stance
Neko-ashi-dachi	Cat stance	90% on back foot	Bent	Narrow	Ft. fwd. Bck. sideways 45°	A very flexible stance. Front heel is off the ground.
Renoji-dachi	L stance	Equal	Straight	Narrow	Ft. fwd. bck. sideways 90°	Rarely used stance
Sanchin-dachi	Hour glass stance	Equal	Bent and tensed inward	Medium	Inward	Strong defensive stance
Shiko-dachi	Square stance	Equal	Deeply bent	Wide	45° outward	Similar to Kiba-dachi
Teji-dachi	T stance	Equal	Straight	Narrow	Frt. fwd. Bck. sideways	feet form a reverse "T"
Uchi-hachiji-dachi	Inverted open leg stance	Equal	Slightly bent	Medium	45° inward	
Zenkutsu-dachi	Forward stance	60% on front foot 40% on back	Front bent Rear straight	Medium	slightly inward	Most often used stance in karate

JAPANESE	ENGLISH	BLOCKING SURFACE	DEFENSE AGAINST	DIRECTION OF BLOCK	COMMENTS
Age-uke	Upward or rising block	outer surface of forearm	attack to the face	upward	a major block used mainly to block attacks from the front
Ashibo-kake-uke	Leg Hooking Block	shin	side kicks	up and inward	not an often used technique
Ashikubi-kake-uke	Ankle Hooking Block	front of ankle	front kick	upward and forward	not used frequently
Gedan-barai	Downward Block	outer surface of forearm	kicks or punches against groin or solar plexus	downward	also known as Gedan-uke one of the major blocks in karate
Gedan-kake-uke	Downward Hooking Block	inner surface of forearm	kicks to the front	circular	hands make a big circle when blocking
Haishu-uke	Back Hand Block	back of the hand	punch to chest	circular/ outward	not used frequently
Haiwan-nagashi-uke	Back Arm Sweeping Block	bottom of fore-arm	punch to face	upward	similar to an upward block
Hiji-suri-uke	Elbow Sliding Block	outer surface of forearm	punch to face	upward/ forward	also known as Tsuki-uke this is a combination block and punch
Juji-uki	X Block	hands crossed at the wrist	punch to face or front kick	upward or downward	very strong block can be used against punching or kicking attacks
Kake-shuto-uke	Hooking knife-hand Block	side edge of hand	punch to the chest	circular/ forward	can be used against front or side attacks
Kakiwake-uke	Reverse Wedge Block	outer surface of both wrists	a grab or choke	down and outward	often used from a back stance to allow an immediate kick
Kakuto-uke	Bent Wrist Block	top of the bent wrist	punch to face or upper chest	upward	not used frequently
Keito-uke	Chicken Head Wrist Block	top of thumb near wrist	punch to face or upper chest	upward	not used frequently
Maeude-deai-osae-uke	Forearm Pressing Block	forearm	punch to body	forward	the block is delivered hard into opponents attacking arm
Maeude-hineri-uke	Forearm Twist Block	forearm	punch to face or chest	upward and circular	not used frequently
Morote-sukui-uke	Two Handed Scooping Block	hands	front kick	inward/ circular	not used frequently
Morote-uke	Augmented Forearm Block	inner surface of forearm	punching attack to the chest area	circular/ outward	second hand helps brace the block against a very strong attack

JAPANESE	ENGLISH	BLOCKING SURFACE	DEFENSE AGAINST	DIRECTION OF BLOCK	COMMENTS
Nagashi-uke	Sweeping Block	palm	punch to chest	straight-sideways	also called Te-nagashi-uke
Osae-uke	Pressing Block	palm	punch to abdomen or groin	downward	also known as Te-osae-uke
Seiryuto-uke	Oxjaw Hand Block	top part of the edge of hand— near wrist	straight punch or kick	downward	not widely used
Shuto-uke	Knife Hand Block	side edge of hand	punch to solar plexus or chest	downward diagonally	a very quick block
Sokumen-awase-uke	Side Combined Block	palm	punch to face	straight sideways	blocking palm is reinforced by the back hand of the other arm
Sokutei-mawashi-uke	Circular Sole Block	sole of feet	punch to chest	circular	performed same as a crescent kick also called Mikazuki-geri-uke
Sokutei-osae-uke	Pressing Sole Block	sole of feet	kick to groin	down and forward	good technique to attack before it begins
Sokuto-osae-uke	Pressing Sword Foot Block	side edge of feet	kick to groin	forward	used mainly while facing sideways
Soto-ude-uke	Outside Forearm Block	outer surface of forearm	punch to chest or face	circular	very powerful block one of the most often used
Sukui-uke	Scooping Block	outer surface of forearm	kick to chest or face	circular	good method of un-balancing opponent
Tate-shuto-uke	Vertical Knife Hand Block	side edge of hand	punch to chest	circular/ forward	almost the same as Keke-shuto-uke
Teisho-awase-uke	Combined Palm Heel Block	palm	front kick	downward & forward	strong block against a low kick
Teisho-uke	Palm Heel Block	palm	punch to face or chest	upward/ downward or sideways	strong quick block not used often
Tekubi-kake-uke	Wrist Hook Block	back of wrist	punch to chest	circular	used while moving away from opponents attack
Tettsui-uke	Bottom-Fist-Block	bottom of fist	punches, or kicking attacks	down or sideways	very powerful block especially aimed at hard parts of opponents anatomy
Tsukami-uke	Grasping Block	palm of both hands	punch to the chest	circular	also called Morote-tsukami-uke (Two handed Grasping Block)
Uchi-ude-uke	Inside Forearm Block	inner surface of forearml	punch to chest or face	circular	an often used block

TSUKI-WAZA — PUNCHING TECHNIQUES

JAPANESE	ENGLISH	STRIKING SURFACE	TARGET AREA	DIRECTION	COMMENTS
Age-zuki	Rising Punch	Fore fist	face or chin	half circle forward	
Awase-zuki	U-Punch	fore fist	face and solar plexus	straight forward	both hands hit target simultaneously
Choku-zuki	Straight Punch	fore fist	anywhere	straight forward	very basic punch
Gyaku-zuki	Reverse Punch	fore fist	anywhere	straight forward	punching hand is on opposite side to forward foot—most widely used technique in karate
Hasami-zuki	Scissors Punch	fore fist	front & back of body	circular	both fists hit target together
Heiko-zuki	Parallel Punch	fore fist	ribs and chest	straight forward	both fists hit target together
Hiraken-zuki	Fore Knuckle-Fist Punch	fore knuckles	below nose—temple—ribs	straight	
Ippon-ken-zuki	One Knuckle Fist Punch	middle joint of index finger	bridge of nose—temple etc.	straight forward	
Kagi-zuki	Hook Punch	fore fist	temple, ribs, solar plexus	angular	punch is delivered sideward at very close range
Kizami-zuki	Jab	fore fist	face	straight forward	mostly a diversionary tactic
Mdwashi-zuki	Roundhouse Punch	fore fist	side of face	circular	
Nagashi-zuki	Flowing Punch	fore fist	usually face	straight forward	power comes from body movement
Nakadate-ippon-ken-zuki	Middle Finger One Knuckle Punch	middle joint of middle finger	below the nose—ribcage	straight forward	
Nukite	Spear Hand	fingertips	throat, solar plexus, ribs, eyes	straight forward	there are a number of variations—one finger 2 fingers, all 5 fingers
Oi-zuki	Lunge Punch	fore fist	face or chest	straight forward	punching hand is on the same side as forward foot and punch comes at the end of a step
Tate-zuki	Vertical Fist Punch	fist held vertically	face, solar plexus	straight forward	useful at close range
Teisho-zuki	Palm Heel Punch	heel of palm	chin, nose	straight forward	very powerful technique
Ura-zuki	Close Punch	reverse fist	ribs, solar plexus	straight and upward	used mostly at close range
Yama-zuki	Wide U Punch	fist	face and solar plexus	circular/ straight forward	both fists hit target together

UCHI-WAZA — STRIKING TECHNIQUES

JAPANESE	ENGLISH	STRIKING SURFACE	TARGET AREA	DIRECTION	COMMENTS
Haishu-uchi	Backhand Strike	back of the open hand	ears, solar plexus, ribs, face	half circle	similar to back fist strike
Haito-uchi	Ridgehand Strike	index finger, side of the open hand	ribs, temple, ear, throat	circular	is performed 2 ways, inside or outside
Hiraken-uchi	Fore Knuckle Fist Strike	all of the fore knuckles of hand	under nose, ribs, temple, solar plexus	straight forward	
Ippon-ken-uchi	One Knuckle Fist Strike	middle joint of index finger	temple, eyes, bridge of nose	straight forward	not used often
Koko-uchi	Tiger Mouth Hand Strike	index finger/ side of hand	adams apple	straight forward	not used often
Kumade-uchi	Bear Hand Strike	palm of hand with fingers bent	face, ears	straight or circular	not used often
Mae-empi-uchi	Forward Elbow Strike	Elbow	ribs, chin, solar plexus	half circle	used in close-in fighting also called Mae-hiji-ate
Mawashi-Empi-uchi	Roundhouse Elbow Strike	Elbow	face, chest	half circle	also called Yoko-mawashi-hiji-ate
Nakadate-ippon-ken-uchi	Middle Finger One Knuckle Fist Strike	middle joint of middle finger	temple, bridge of nose etc.	straight forward	not used often
Otoshi-empi-uchi	Downward Elbow	Elbow	face, back of head, middle of back	straight down	usually used after a block
Seiryuto-uchi	Oxjaw Hand Strike	edge of hand near wrist	collar bone, face	straight	not used often
Shuto-uchi	Knife Hand or Sword Hand Strike	side edge of hand	temple, neck, throat, nose	half circle	often called a "judo" chop
Tate-empi-uchi	Upward-Elbow Strike	Elbow	chin, solar plexus	half-circle up	very powerful technique
Teisho-uchi	Palm Heel Strike	palm of hand	face, chin, ribs, solar plexus	semi-circle	not used often
Tettsui-uchi	Bottom or Hammer Fist Strike	bottom of fist	head, ribs, nose, solar plexus	straight or circular	very powerful technique also known as Kentsui-uchi
Urakan-uchi	Back Fist Strike	back of hand and knuckles	face, ribs, ear	circular	used from close in
Ushiro-empi-uchi	Back Elbow Strike	elbow	chest, solar plexus	straight back	used against rear attacks
Yoko-empi-uchi	Side Elbow Strike	elbow	chest, abdomen	straight	used against opponent at side

KERI-WAZA—KICKING TECHNIQUES

JAPANESE	ENGLISH	STRIKING SURFACE	TARGET AREA	TYPE OF KICK	DIREC- TION	COMMENTS
Fumi Komi	Stamping Kick	heel—edge of feet	leg or instep	thrust	straight & down	knee must be lifted high
Gyaku-mawashi- geri	Reverse Round- house Kick	ball of foot	groin—solar plexus	snap	circular	foot travels opposite to roundhouse kick
Hitsui-geri	Knee Kick	knee cap	groin, abdomen, ribs, face	thrust	straight or circular	effective for close in combat
Kesa-geri	Diagonal Kick	edge of feet	face	thrust	straight while in air	
Mae-geri-keagi	Front Snap Kick	ball of feet	groin-abdomen	snap	straight forward	kicking leg must be pulled back instantly
Mae-geri-kekomi	Front Thrust Kick	heel or ball of feet	groin, chest, abdomen	thrust	straight forward	hip driven into kick knee locked out momentarily
Mae-tobi-geri	Jumping Front Kick	ball of feet	face, abdomen	snap	straight while in the air	kick is done when one reaches the highest point of jump
Mawashi-geri	Roundhouse Kick	ball of feet	ribs, head, solar plexus, chest	snap	circular	can be done with either forward or rear leg
Mikazuki-geri	Crescent Kick	ball or flat of feet	ribs, chest, face	snap	circular	often used for blocking
Nidan-geri	Double Jump Kick	ball of feet	face, abdomen	snap	straight while in the air	two quick kicks are delivered while jumping one to chest one to face
Ushiro-geri- keage	Back Snap Kick	heel	groin, abdomen	snap	straight back	leg is snapped back quickly after the kick
Ushiro-geri- kekomi	Back Thrust Kick	heel	groin, stomach, face	thrust	straight back	hips are thrust into the kick
Ushiro-mawashi- geri	Back Round- house Kick	heel	chest, head	snap	circular	very effective as a surprise kick—often done while spinning
Yoko-geri-keage	Side Snap Kick	edge of feet	armpits, groin, jaw	snap	straight	can be done to the side or with a turn to an opponent in front
Yoko-geri- kekomi	Side Thrust Kick	edge of feet	ribs, chest, face	thrust	straight	hips are thrust into kick for added power a very often used technique
Yoko-tobi-geri	Jumping Side Kick	edge of feet	face, neck	thrust	straight while in the air	usually used as a surprise attack—kick is done while body is at its highest

FULL-CONTACT KARATE Sport karate contest between two combatants in which the outcome is determined by kick-knockout, knockout, judge's decision or draw, or a technical equivalent of the same, much as in professional boxing. Participants are required to wear padded gloves (usually the 8-10 oz. boxing variety) and foot gear, and must execute a specific number of above-the-belt kicks (currently eight) per round. Chokes, head butts, knee and elbow strikes, biting, holding and striking, and striking when an opponent is down are prohibited. Matches are conducted in a 16-20 square foot roped ring, similar to boxing, and range from 3 two-minute rounds (for amateurs) to 12 rounds (for professional world championships) in length, with a one-minute rest period between rounds.

Each bout is controlled by a referee, monitored by an attending physician, and scored by three judges. The judges award round by round point advantages to the contestants for greater overall effectiveness, exceptional above-the-belt kicking skills, and for effecting knockdowns. Then, if the referee does not stop the bout early as the result of a knockout or injury, a decision is rendered based upon the tallied scores of the three judges. Should both contestants receive an equal number of points, a draw is declared.

Most of the techniques in full-contact karate, although taken from traditional karate roots, have been significantly modified. The introduction of padded gloves and foot gear at the sport's inception to minimize unsightly facial cuts, based upon the experinece of 19th-century bareknuckle boxing, also enabled contestants to impart a greater concussive jolt in their punches with significantly less risk of injury to their hands. Thus the emphasis in hand techniques changed from focusing a maiming blow on an opponent's vital point (nerve center, joint, or fragile bone) to reinforce each punch with body leverage, like a boxer, in order to effect a knockout. Kicking techniques on the other hand became more streamlined to eliminate telegraphic motions and, in part due to the minimum kick requirement, more importance was placed on combinations of kicks from the same foot before returning the kicking leg to a stance on the ground.

The safety record of full-contact karate is better than most contact sports, despite its lack of uniform regulation. When compared with the related sport of boxing—ranked seventh by the National Board of Insurance Underwriters on the list of most hazardous sports—full-contact karate has been shown to be significantly safer. For example, most serious injuries and deaths in boxing result from brain damage. Between 1975 and 1982 some 60 boxers (an average of 5-10 per year) lost their lives in the boxing ring worldwide, most from causes related to the competition. During the same period only four karate competitors died in the ring. None of these deaths was from causes directly related to the karate competition.

The following table compares the outcomes of world class boxing bouts in 1982 with the outcomes of world class karate bouts in the same year. Fight result data for boxing were drawn from *The Ring* magazine whereas fight result data for karate were taken from the **STAR System**

The table demonstrates that the outcomes of top full-contact karate bouts tend to be less severe than the outcomes of comparable boxing matches. If knockouts are considered to be generally the result of a competitor being knocked unconscious, and technical knockouts are considered to be the result of referee intervention, then clearly full-contact karate competitors tend to be knocked unconscious 45-50% less frequently than boxing competitors. Further, some 13% of all knockouts in karate are caused by kicks. Most kick-knockouts (KKOs) result from blows to the body which shock a competitor's nervous and respiratory systems, but do not cause unconsciousness. Hence full-contact karate competitors enjoy a smaller risk of brain damage than do boxing competitors.

Full-contact karate first surfaced as American kick-boxing in January 1970 when **Joe Lewis,** influenced by his training sessions in boxing and with **Bruce Lee,** staged the first contact bout, knocking out Greg Baines to become the first heavyweight champion. The sport died out one year later. Lewis and **Tom Tannenbaum,** then of Universal Studios, organized a revival, laying the groundwork for a full-contact event on Sept. 14, 1974, at the Los Angeles Sports Arena. Produced by karate tournament promoter **Mike Anderson,** the event aired as a 90-minute special on ABC's *Wide World of Entertainment,* receiving the highest ratings for a *Wide World Special* in 1974.

Today full-contact karate has grown into a large international sport. The STAR System estimates that between 350-450 full-contact karate events are promoted throughout the world each year, featuring some 3,000 individual karate bouts. The US is the largest center of full-contact activity, accounting for at least 51% of

THE OUTCOMES OF WORLD CLASS BOUTS IN 1982
(Expressed in Percentages)

SPORT	KNOCKOUTS	TECHNICAL KNOCKOUTS	DECISIONS	OTHER (DRAWS, DISQ.)	
Boxing Worldwide	34%	23%	37%	6%	100%
Karate Worldwide	19%	29%	45%	7%	100%
PKA Karate Alone	17%	25%	53%	5%	100%
WKA Karate Alone	19%	33%	38%	10%	100%

THE LEADING SANCTIONING BODIES IN 1982
(According to the STAR System)

ORGANIZATION	% OF EVENTS SANCTIONED WORLDWIDE	% OF WORLD CLASS BOUTS SANCTIONED WORLDWIDE
Professional Karate Association (PKA)	43-45%	40-44%
World Karate Association (WKA)	21-25%	32-36%
World All-Style Karate Organization (WAKO) Nederlandse Kick Boxing Bond (NKBB) Federation Nationale de Boxe Americaine (FNBA) European Professional Karate Association (EPKA)	15-20%	12-16%
Independent Promoters and Organizations	5-10%	2-4%
	100%	100%

Left: A dramatic example of breaking. *Below*: The ability to deliver kicks as well as punches is what makes karate such an ideal form of combat Here, K. Tanaka delivers a classic side kick against a punching attack. *Bottom*: Tanaka (*left*).

59

all promotions, followed by Europe with 28%, Canada with 7%, Japan with 6%, and Australia with 2%.

There are two major sanctioning bodies in the US: the **Professional Karate Association** (PKA) and the **World Karate Association** (WKA). The PKA was formed in August 1974 by **Don** and **Judy Quine** in association with Mike Anderson. Although the PKA operates almost exclusively in the US and Canada, in 1982 it sanctioned approximately 43% of all events worldwide.

The PKA retains rights to television revenues from most of its sanctioned events while the event promoter retains the gate revenues. Since 1980 PKA events have aired weekly on cable television. Also, PKA events have been broadcast periodically by major networks. The organization's principal karate stars have included **Bill "Superfoot" Wallace** and **Jean-Yves Theriault.**

The WKA was conceived in late October 1976 by **Howard Hanson** and **Arnold Urquidez.** The WKA differs from the PKA in that its rules permit footsweeps below the knee and roundhouse kicks to the outside of the thigh above the knee. (The PKA's rules permit no kicks below the belt.) Further, the WKA operates internationally with some 14 member nations, the most active being the US, Canada, Mexico, Australia, Japan, Hong Kong, Holland and the United Kingdom. American and European fighters are frequently matched with Japanese and Thai kick-boxers. Altogether, in 1982 the WKA sanctioned between 20-25% of all events worldwide.

WKA promoters retain all gate revenues from sanctioned events as well as a negotiable percentage of any television revenues. The organization has secured network broadcasts in the US and Japan as well as an assortment of syndication arrangements. The WKA's principal karate stars have included **Benny** "The Jet" **Urquidez** and **Don Wilson.**

A third sanctioning body, called the Karate International Council for Kick-boxing (KICK), has begun to emerge in the US. KICK was formed in late 1982 by Frank Babcock and **Fred Wren.** This organization has secured satellite-linked syndication to independent television stations throughout the US.

Since US sanctioning bodies are organized for the purpose of television production, organizational rivalry frequently prohibits top caliber competition. Champions are signed to exclusivity contracts and major contenders are discouraged from fighting in rival events—an organizational behavior pattern reminiscent of the treatment of movie stars in the early days of the Hollywood film studio. Resultantly, the best fighters in a weight category may never fight. Moreover, the competition between sanctioning bodies tends to depress television revenues in general, especially since the sport has yet to produce a charismatic mainstream personality for whose services the television networks are in turn willing to compete.

Europe has four sanctioning bodies in the forefront: the World All-Style Karate Organization (WAKO), the Nederlandse Kick Boxing Bond (NKBB), the Federation Nationale de Boxe Americaine (FNBA), and the European Professional Karate Association (EPKA). WAKO was formed in 1975 by a group of black belts from 12 European nations. Principal leadership of the organization immediately fell to West Germany's George Bruckner and his tae kwon do instructor, U.S.'s Mike Anderson, a founder of the PKA.

Since in many European countries professional athletics connotes predetermined outcomes, much like professional wrestling in the US, WAKO officially classifies its full-contact karate promotions as amateur. However, competitors are given substantial "training fees," especially competitors from those countries which do not attach a stigma to the idea of professionalism. Still, the organization's amateur status has earned it governmental recognition from several European nations, making WAKO the largest sanctioning body in Europe. Most WAKO activity is centered in West Germany, Yugoslavia, Italy and Austria, although WAKO promotions are frequently found in France, Switzerland, the United Kingdom, Holland, Norway, and even in the Dominican Republic.

WAKO rules differ from those used in the US in that judo throws and footsweeps are permitted, although thigh kicks are not, and further there is no minimum kick requirement. Bouts are sometimes held on an open mat, instead of within a roped ring. World title bouts last six rounds, while contender bouts last five. Once a year, top competitors are required to participate in two-round, tournament

style eliminations to determine the year's top ten in each weight division.

Yugoslavia's Branimir Sikatic, Italy's Franz Haller and Germany's Ferdinan Mack rank among WAKO's most highly regarded karate stars, although many American champions have held the WAKO spotlight as well, including **Gordon Franks,** Ross Scott, Billy Jackson and Dave Johnston.

The NKBB, the Dutch initials for "Netherlands Kick-Boxing Federation," was formed in 1977 by more than a dozen full-contact gymnasiums throughout Holland. The organization was loosely affiliated with both Kenji Kurosaki's kick-boxing league in Japan and George Bruckner's WAKO throughout Europe. Today, Chakuriki gym's Tom Harink and Mejiro Gym's Jan Plas occupy leadership roles in the NKBB.

The NKBB sanctions Japanese-style kick-boxing bouts, which allow round kicks to both the inside and the outside of the thigh, as well as knee strikes to the body. Matches consist of five three-minute rounds. The NKBB also sanctions WAKO-style competition.

NKBB competitors are willing to compete anywhere, for any organization, under any rules, making them among the most respected in Europe. Among the NKBB's leading stars are Lucien Carbin and Rob Kaman.

The FNBA, the French initials for "National Federation of American Boxing (full-contact karate)," grew out of the Comite National du Full Contact which was formed in 1978 under the direction of **Dominique Valera,** just prior to Valera's unsuccessful attempt to dethrone PKA world champion **Jeff Smith.** Subsequently, the FNBA began to sanction full-contact promotions in and around Paris. The rules were patterned after those of the PKA, although the minimum kick requirement was raised to 10 per round.

By 1981 the FNBA, now under the direction of Daniel Rennesson, had gained considerable public attention, and its sanctioned events had spread throughout France. The FNBA gained added momentum from the actions of the Federation de Boxe Francaise et Savate, which promotes amateur savate competition. Since the savate organization refuses to sanction professional events, many savate champions gradually turn to the FNBA for fighting careers. The FNBA's foremost karate stars have included Dominique Valera and Youseff Zenaf.

Another significant sanctioning body in Europe is the European Professional Karate Association (EPKA). The EPKA was formed in Switzerland in November 1978 by Jerome Canabate, a "guest worker" from Portugal. Although the smallest of the major sanctioning bodies, the EPKA sanctions events in Switzerland, Belgium, Spain, Northern Italy and Southern France. At one time or another, the EPKA has attempted to merge with both America's PKA and WKA, but a formal affiliation with either organization has yet to be finalized. Among the EPKA's leading karate stars are Emond Ardissone and John Canabate.

Finally, both the PKA and WKA have attempted to make promotional inroads into Europe, but with limited success. Unlike the US, the development of full-contact karate in Europe has been more influenced by nationalism and governmental interference than by the pursuit of television revenues. Altogther, in 1982 European organizations sanctioned between 15-20% of all full-contact events worldwide.

In Canada, full-contact karate falls under the influence and regulation of the American sanctioning bodies. In eastern Canada, **John Therien** promotes under the PKA banner with Jean-Yves Theriault as his principal star; while in western Canada, Jim Wright and Frank Lee promote with the WKA, featuring Tony Morelli and Billy Chau among the leading karate stars.

In Japan, full-contact competition first arrived in the mid-1960s in the form of Thai kick-boxing (**muay Thai**). The sport gradually grew into one of the nation's top spectator sports, reaching its peak in 1976 with some 6,000 active Japanese kick-boxers. Three major sanctioning bodies quickly emerged: the All-Japan Kick Boxing Association (AJKBA), the World Kick Boxing Association (WKBA), and Kenji Kurosaki's Katogi Kick Boxing League.

In 1977, the WKA and the AJKBA agreed to affiliate for the purpose of international competition, conducted under compromise rules which prohibited elbow and knee strikes, and to recognize each other's champions. Benny Urquidez, Kunimasa Nagae, **Alvin**

Prouder, and **Howard Jackson** became the first internationaly recognized world champions.

In 1981, a scandal swept Japan which linked certain kick-boxing promoters to organized crime. Kick-boxing lost public favor and the WKBA as well as Kurosaki's organization were dissolved. The AJKBA, on the other hand, survived the scandal and subsequently merged with the WKA, fully adopted the American rules. Today, the WKA Japan is the only major sanctioning body in the nation. WKA Japan frequently broadcasts bouts over Japanese television networks, and also promotes events outside of Japan, in Korea, Thailand, Pakistan, and Hong Kong. WKA Japan's leading karate stars have included Kunimatsu Okao, Yoshimitsu Tamashiro, Benny Urquidez, Kunimasa Nagai, Genshu Igari, Yasuo Tabata, and Hiroshi Takahashi.

In Australia, full-contact karate is conducted under the auspices of the WKA. WKA Australia is headed by **Bob Jones** and **Malcolm Lomax.** Australian karate stars have included Tony Quinn and Dave Hedgecock.

Full-contact promotions are also periodically found in Mexico, the Bahamas, Brazil, Venezuela, and Colombia.

Common full-contact karate techniques include:
HAND TECHNIQUES
jab
cross
hook
uppercut
ridge hand
spinning backfist
LEG TECHNIQUES
side kick
round kick
hook kick
front kick
leg kick
spin kick
jump kick
footsweep
(PAUL MASLAK) *See Also,* U.S., history of karate in.

Sake (*left*) versus Jake

Smith (*left*) versus Fujikawa

Gelson (*left*) versus Oishi

Tabaka (*left*) versus Fujikawa

FORMS OF KARATE

CHINESE GOJU Eclectic karate style which incorporates kung-fu, tae kwon do, and **aiki-jutsu** around the central core of the **goju-ryu** system Founded by New York karate instructor **Ron Van Clief** in 1971, Chinese goju combines Chinese, Japanese and American ideologies and teaches fluidity and flexibility of both mind and body. The system is based on blocking of the soft, circular goju type and that of the harder Japanese forms of karate. All blocking and countering is done in one motion. Some 40 percent of this style is based on kicks. There are six levels below black belt (which has eight degrees). There are also two degrees of red belt, the highest rank in the system. *Further reading: Manual of the Martial Arts*, Ron Van Clief, 1981

CHITO-RYU Japanese system of karate founded by **Dr. Tsuyoshi Chitose.** Chito-ryu emphasizes conditioning of mind and body before the actual practice of self-defense. A combination of **goju-ryu** (hard-soft school) and **shorin-ryu** karate, Chito-ryu is structured according to medical principles. Its moral code stresses fairness, tolerance, patience, diligence, courtesy, sincerity, and constant striving to better oneself spiritually, mentally, and physically.

The style's supervising body is the All Japan Karate-Do Federation, Chito-kai, headquartered in Kunamoto City, Japan. Promotion examinations grade technical skill over fighting ability, in the belief that fighting ability decreases with age, while technical skill improves. (WILLIAM DOMETRICH)

CUONG NHU Vietnamese style of karate combining hard, linear karate techniques with the soft techniques of aikido. It was founded by Vietnamese martial artist Ngo Dong in 1965. Dong studied **Shotokan** karate and aikido before formulating his style.

GOJU-RYU Style of Japanese karate-do based on maintaining a balance of resistive and flexible actions. In countering a full force blow, a goju-ryu practitioner never meets the onslaught with an equally hard block; instead he waits until the attack is nearly at full extension and parries with a softer block, conserving his strength and forcing the opponent to commit himself.

Goju-ryu stylists seek to develop timing and reaction speed. Blows are delivered quickly and in rapid succession. There is a great deal of weaving from side to side, in contrast to other hard-style karate schools, in which straightforward movements predominate.

Goju-ryu is noted for its dramatic breathing methods; two types are practied; in-ibuki, soft but firm breathing from deep in the abdomen, and yo-ibuki, the hard form. A student is taught never to exhale all at once. The most advanced breathing form has a spiritual purpose, to focus on a specific feeling or thought.

The word "goju," a common Chinese idiom, has two contrasting meanings: go, "hard" and ju, "soft." Akin to **ying-yang,** this traditional Chinese concept posts a universal balance, as between positive and negative poles, enabling each to exist.

Kanryo Higashionna (d. 1915) may be the earliest to originate a form of the goju school. Having mastered **Naha-te,** Higashionna combined the art with a form of Chinese boxing, which some historians call "chi-chi." **Chojun Miyagi** (d. 1953) reformed the art he learned from Higashionna in the 1920s named it goju-ryu karate, after he had studied Chinese kempo. **Gogen Yamaguchi** (b. 1909) systemized instructional and ranking methods by adopting traditional Japanese administrative procedures. It was Yamaguchi who in 1935 originated **jiyu-kumite** (free sparring), in which students practice techniques against one another. This was the basis for sport karate as it is known today, and was adopted worldwide by every karate style. Yamaguchi later established competitive tournament methods to popularize the art as a contemporary sport form.

Among the various karate styles originally practiced in Okinawa, goju-ryu is the first to adopt a specific name for itself. Until then, Okinawans had referred to karate as **te** (hand) or to-de (Chinese hand) and had recognized style distinctions by their school locations, such as Naha-te, Shuri-te, and Tomari-te.

In 1929 Chojun Miyagi, the founder of goju-ryu, was invited to Japan by Yamaguchi, founder and chief instructor of the Ritsumei-kan University Karate Club in Kyoto. Yamaguchi became the successor of the goju school in mainland Japan, while **Meitoku Yagi** was designated Miyagi's successor in Okinawa.

Yamaguchi established an institute in Kyoto, quartered in an historically famous building called "Shinsen Gumi Tonsho." He had tried to incorporate karate as a section within the **Butokukai,** a goal he achieved in 1930. That same year, Yamaguchi set up the goju headquarters next to the Giho-kai, the famed judo institute. From then until 1938, when he was sent to Manchuria for the government, he established a nation-wide organization and many goju schools throughout Japan.

In May of 1950, he reorganized his organization, calling it the Karate-Do Goju-Kai, and established new headquarters in Tokyo.

By 1970 registered membership in the All Japan Karate-Do Goju-Kai exceeded 450,000. Regional goju-kai institutes in Japan in 1970 numbered 112, with 29 public organizations, 24 college clubs, and 29 high school clubs. The overseas regions are centered in Indonesia, Thailand, Hong Kong, Korea, Formosa, the Philippines, Australia, Great Britain, Sweden, West Germany, France, Spain, South Africa, Chili, Brazil, Mexico, Canada, and the U.S.

Japanese goju-ryu was introduced to the U.S. in 1959 by **Peter Urban,** who later broke away to form his own U.S.A. Goju Association. In 1964, **Gosei Yamaguchi,** first son of Gogen, immigrated to San Francisco, where he established the Goju-Kai Karate-Do U.S.A., the American headquarters of goju-ryu.

Gogen has two other sons, Gosen and Goshi, and two daughters, Wakako and Gogyoku, all of whom assist Yamaguchi in Tokyo. The Goju-Kai, presided over by Gogen Yamaguchi, standardizes instructional programs and preserves traditional kata at the College of Goju within the international headquarters.

Basic to goju are the kata **Sanchin** and tensho. Both forms demonstrate respiratory and isotonic drills; tensho moves are circular; while in Sanchin they are straightforward, striking with the head of the knuckle. The series of **taikyoku,** pronounced t'ai-chi in Chinese, is rooted in one of the Taoist soft styles, **t'ai-chi ch'uan.** Forms in the taikyoku series do not, however, resemble any of the t'ai-chi forms. Sanseiru, seipai, and suparunpei are significant numbers in Zen Buddhism. Kata **Seisan,** on the other hand, also a number, is significant in Taoism. These kata names are legacies, indications that Taoism had permeated the predominantly Zen Buddhist style of **Okinawa-te.**

Goju-ryu kata authorized by Yamaguchi's Karate-Do Goju-Kai are as follows:

Fukyu Gata (fundamentals)	Kihon Gata (basic kata)
taikyoku judan I & II	sanchin
taikyoku chudan I & II	tensho
taikyoku gedan I & II	
taikyoku kake uke I & II	
taikyoku mawashi uke I & II	
Gekisai I & II	

Kaishu Gata (advanced kata)	
saifa	seisan
seinchin	seipai
sanseiru	kururunfa
shisochin	suparunpei

(© GOSEI YAMAGUCHI). *See also* Okinawa, history of martial arts in; Okinawan goju-ryu. *Further reading: Modern Bujutsu & Budo,* Donn F. Draeger, 1974; *Karate: Goju-Ryu By the Cat,* Gogen Yamaguchi, 1966; *Goju-Ryu Karate* (2 vols.), Gosei Yamaguchi, 1974.

GOSOKU RYU Karate style founded by **Tak Kubota.** Best translated as *fast and hard,* the style relies on quick and powerful techniques.

It is a realistic school of fighting, developed to assure survival in the streets. Since a realistic fighting style aims first at being effective, gosoku ryu stresses free-style sparring, or **kumite.** In kumite a student refines and interprets traditional movements according to his own abilities. Gosoku ryu opposes rigid adherence to traditional forms. Kubota developed gosoku ryu kata that are a blend of several other styles, incorporating tight kicks and punches of **Shotokan,** the defense from **goju-ryu** and short stances of **Shito-ryu.** The gosoku ryu kata are: 1. uke no kata; 2. gosoku; 3. gosoku yodan; 4. gosoku ryu; 5. denko getsu; 6. tamashi; 7. sanchin; 8. ri kyu; 9. gosoku godan. *Further reading: Gosoku Ryu Karate,* Takayuki Kubota, 1980.

ISSHINRYU Eclectic form of Okinawan karate combining elements of **shorin-ryu** and **goju-ryu;** founded by the late **Tatsuo Shimabuku,**

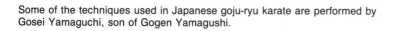

Some of the techniques used in Japanese goju-ryu karate are performed by Gosei Yamaguchi, son of Gogen Yamagushi.

The side thrust kick (*right*) and the roundhouse kick (*left*) are two kicking techniques used by most styles of Karate. Here, leading Shotokan instructor Teruyuki Okazaki demonstrates both kicks. Courtesy of Inside Kung-Fu.

on January 16, 1954. Specifically, isshinryu karate emphasizes: 1. elimination of fancy techniques; 2. low-line kicks, all below the waist; 3. short natural stances without wasted motion and major body shifting (said to be more suited to the American physique); 4. even application of hand and foot techniques, about 50 percent each in the katas; 5. close-range techniques, useful for streetfighting; 6. snap punches and snap kicks, limb extended 90 percent and immediately retracted (preventing excessive strain on the hinge joints); 7. both hard and soft blocking; 8. blocks with the muscular portion of the forearm rather than the bone; 9. fist formed with the thumb on top of the clenched fist rather than wrapped over the first two fingers, (helps prevent the fist from buckling at the wrist on impact); 10. the vertical punch, which increases speed and focus; 11. multiple-purpose technique, allowing a block to become a blow and vice versa.

Proponents of isshinryu karate follow an eight-point code. Within the code are some of the basic principles of the isshinryu system: 1. A person's heart is the same as heaven and earth (*harmony*); 2. The blood circulating is similar to the moon and sun (*movement*); 3. A manner of drinking and spitting is either hard of soft; (*blocking and deflecting*); 4. A person's unbalance is the same as weight; 5. The body should be able to change direction at any time; 6. The time to strike is when opportunity presents itself; 7. The eye must see all sides; 8. The ear must listen in all directions. *Further reading: The Seisan Kata of Isshinryu Karate,* Steve Armstrong, 1974; *The Dynamics of Isshinryu Karate,* Harold Long and Allen Wheeler, 1978.

KEMPO Kempo, read **ch'uan fa** in Mandarin and ken fat in Cantonese, designates a Chinese form of self-defense and self-development similar to karate. Kempo is simply the Japanese way of pronouncing Chinese ideographs for ch'uan fa. Kempo training traditionally consists of instruction in Buddhist philosophy, general education, and the human body and its systems, as well as training in kendo (fencing), kyudo (archery), ikebana (flower arranging), tree-climbing, swimming, horsemanship, use of the blowgun, and weaponless forms of **Shao-lin** kung-fu.

KENPO Kenpo, as spelled is a more modern term describing one of the more innovative systems practiced on Hawaii, Europe, New Zealand and the Americas. It employs linear as well as circular moves, using intermittent power when and where needed, interspersed with major and minor moves that flow with continuity. It is flexible in thought and action so as to blend with encounters as they occur. Kenpo is the first Americanized martial art. Students are encouraged to alter moves, but not the underlying principles, to fit individual body structure, or to compensate for handicaps. Teaching methods also are Americanized, relying on practical demonstration, everyday experience, and familiar nomenclature.

Historically, kenpo, as kenpo jiu-jitsu, was introduced into the Hawaiian Islands by **James M. Mitose** on December 7, 1941, at the beginning of World War II. As taught by Mitose, kenpo emphasized the attacking of vital anatomical areas by punching, striking, chopping, thrusting and poking. Similar to Japanese **atei-waza** in that it also employed throws, locks and takedowns, it differed technically and philosophically. Kenpo teaches how to maneuver so that the opponent unwittingly places himself in a precarious and vulnerable position.

Mitose taught **William K.S. Chow**, who had also studied Chinese concepts from his father. It was Chow who Americanized kenpo by adapting Mitose's aproach to the American environment. **Ed Parker**, a Hawaii native and disciple of Chow, greatly revised the old methods to cope with modern day fighting situations. While Parker's teachings retain a traditional flavor, he has contributed practical, realistic, applicable concepts and principles.

Parker, recognizing the need for an updated approach to the martial arts, experimented with more logical and practical means of combating modern methods of fighting and thus emerged with his own interpretation of the art. To reach his conclusions, he analyzed combative predicaments from the viewpoints of the attacker, the defender, and, uniquely, the bystander or spectator. From these observations, Parker disproved theories and concepts which had earlier been considered combat effective. His greatest insights came by studying himself on film in reverse.

Parker then systematized and categorized all the basic kenpo elements into a logical order of progress for step-by-step instruction. Eventually, he conceived one of the most in-depth and sophisticated training manuals for instructors to date. It gives a clear, precise and thorough understanding of what kenpo entails, with every move within this system methodically and scientifically thought out. Kenpo basics fall into eight categories: stances, blocks, parries, punches, strikes, finger techniques, kicks, and foot maneuvers. The system is divided into three major divisions with relative subdivisions: basics (including forms); self-defense (divided into methods of attack and methods of training for an attack, both of which are further subdivided); and freestyle (tournament and street, with the former subdivided into light contact and full contact).

Kenpo belt ranks are: white; yellow; yellow with orange tip; orange; orange with purple tip; purple; purple with blue tip; blue; blue with green tip; green; green with brown tip; brown with one, two, then three black tops. The kenpo black belt ranks, which progress from 1st degree to 10th degree, are: black with red tips up to 4th degree; a solid 5″ strip for 5th degree; additional tips above the strip for 6th to 9th degrees; and two 5″ strips separated by a 1″ space for 10th degree. In order to become a black belt, all kenpo students affiliated with Parker's **International Kenpo Karate Association**, the governing body of kenpo, must write a thesis on a subject usually selected by each student, and must create a new form.

Unique to this style are Parker's teaching methods wherein he parallels the moves of the martial arts with the study of music or the alphabet. Each move learned, for example, whether offensive or defensive, can be considered an "alphabet of motion." When these are combined they form "words of motion." Combinations of these then form "sentences of motion" and so on, allowing a kenpo practitioner to draw upon a large "vocabulary of motion." (ED PARKER) *See also* International Kenpo Karate Association; U.S., history of karate in. *Further reading: Advanced Kenpo Karate,* Jay T. Will, 1980; *Infinite Insights Into Kenpo,* Ed Parker, 1982; *Kenpo Karate for Self-Defense,* Jay T. Will, 1977.

Chuck Merriman performing a goju kata.
Courtesy of Chuck Merriman

Ishin-ryu karate master Angi-Vezu

Ed Parker ("father of American kenpo") demonstrates some of the style's intricate movements.

The sanchin stance, demonstrated here by Chuck Merriman, is the trademark of goju-ryu karate.

KOEI-KAN Japanese karate style founded by **Eizo Onishi** in 1952. In the koei-kan system the individual is stressed, and each koei-kan student is taught to strive for the highest degree of self-attainment. In Japanese, this philosophy is a blend of bun (obedience), shi (divergence), and shu (separation). Naturally, there is some uniformity during each stage of learning; however, after the fundamentals have been mastered, new methods are encouraged as they pertain to a student's particular needs. Koei-kan teachings embrace the ethics of budo: humility, truth, self-discipline, self-reliance, peace, respect, unselfishness, honor, and courage.

In koei-kan, physical training is composed of: taiso (calesthenics), naza (techniques), and the application of techniques, which are divided into **kata** (form), and **kumite** (free-sparring). Techniques are classified as kihon (basic) and kaishu (advanced).

In kihon renshu (basic training), instruction progresses through three levels. The first is kihon dai ichi (basic one), in which techniques are executed singly, i.e., one reverse punch, one front kick, etc. The second is kihon dai ni (basic two), with techniques delivered in combinations of two, i.e., reverse punch-front kick, roundhouse kick-back fist, etc. In the third stage, kihon dai san (basic three), techniques are executed in groups of three or more.

Kata is stressed in the koei-kan system to develop speed, timing, coordination, balance, focus, precise breathing, eye contact, and quick reflexes. Koei-kan teaches the history and origin of kata, and their practical importance. Five Naha-te kata created by **Kanryo Higashionna** and 16 Shuri-te kata created by **Yasutsune Itosu** are taught.

The next phase of training, kumite, improves the ability to maintain a state of mushin (empty mind), a Zen-like concept dealing with heightened powers of concentration. Neither hand nor leg techniques predominate; instead, the student is taught to adopt the technique most fitted to the moment.

A unique aspect of koei-kan is the use of **bogu** (armor or protective gear) during full-contact fighting. Bogu was invented by Eizo Onishi in 1955 and first tested at the All Japan Karate-Do Shikoku Regional Championships in 1957. The gear resembles somewhat the protection worn by Japanese and European fencers, as well as that used by **kendo** practitioners. It consists of: men (helmet), a steel-mesh face mask and heavy padding on the sides and neck; do (body protector), a large cushioned pad extending from neck to waist; te (gloves), padded; kinteki-ate (groin protector). Koei-kan theory considers full-contact fighting a training necessity. Although the gear is heavy and confining, practice for speed, focus, timing, and power while the bogu is worn can only result in greater mastery when the bogu is discarded.

Tenshin waza (body transfer techniques), applied both defensively and offensively to evade, attack, and counterattack one or more opponents, are to be used on opponents who are larger and stronger, armed, or numerous. There are 15 basic tenshin waza exercises and many variations. They are first practiced singly in all directions, then combined with blocking, striking, kicking, and punching. Koei-kan teaches that proper execution of tenshin waza enables the best use of body weight, distance, and an opponent's power. The techniques are taught, practiced, and researched until quickness and fluidity are achieved. Some of the methods are easily visualized by name and include: tsuri-ashi (dragging the feet), fumi-dashi (lunge step), hineri (hip twist), oshi-fumikkomi (push step), kosa su su mi (intersecting or cross step), and yoko-ido (side step).

The koei-kan system—like all substantial karate systems—is physically demanding; its philosophical and ethical teachings help the student endure the hardships and trials of training. The academic aspects of training include medical, cultural, and historical components. All shodan candidates write a culminative paper that is sent to Japan for sensei Onishi's approval.

History: Eizo Onishi, known as kancho (head of the system) sensei to his followers, established the first koei-kan dojo in Kanagawa-ken, Japan, on April 2, 1954. The founding of the koei-kan system was the crystalization of years of training and study by Onishi under the auspices of two great masters: **Kanken Toyama** (1888-1966) and Juhatsu Kiyoda (1888-1967).

Under their supervision Onishi became an expert in his own right, and was graded hachidan (8th-degree black belt). Prior to his death, Toyama awarded Onishi the **menkyo-kaiden** (hand-written scroll), and appointed him chairman of the All-Japan Karate-Do Association.

Top: Koei-kan practitioners put on a demonstration wearing bogu (protective armor), a unique aspect of the koei-kan system.
Center: Winners of the 1980 All Japan Kyokushinkai Open Karate Tournament: Keiji Sanpei (first); Makoto Nakamura (second); and Takashi Yoshinaga (third).

KYOKUSHINKAI Karate style founded by **Masutatsu Oyama.** Strongly influenced by circular Chinese techniques and the powerful karate of **Gichin Funakoshi,** kyokushinkai advocates body contact to help students overcome fear. Because substantial body contact is allowed, masks and pads are sometimes worn in training to avoid injury. Kyokushinkai puts considerable emphasis on **tameshiwari** (breaking), and before being promoted students must prove their breaking ability. (There is even tameshiwari competition.) Kyokushinkai has a very large following in Japan and in Europe. *See also* Oyama, Masutatsu. *Further reading: Advanced Karate,* Mas Oyama, 1970; *The Kyokushin Way,* Mas Oyama, 1980; *This Is Karate,* Mas Oyama, 1965; *What Is Karate,* Mas Oyama, 1966.

In his continuing search for knowledge and martial wisdom, Onishi traveled to Okinawa to observe the training methods of other karate exponents, including the late master **Choshin Chibana.** Later, Onishi visited Peking, Hong Kong, and Taiwan, where he studied Chinese **chuan fa** with various teachers. Of these, the most notable was Koichi Kyo, an expert in the northern **Shao-lin** style, Yue derivative. Onishi also traveled to Southeast Asia, the U.S., and Europe in his capacity as president of the International Koei-kan Karate-Do Federation, which is headquartered in Tokyo.

Edward Kaloudis is the U.S. director of the koei-kan system. He operates from the national headquarters in Clifton, New Jersey, which is under the auspices of the International Karate-do Gaku Federation and the All Japan Karate-Do Association. Other major U.S. representatives are Brian Frost, the 1972 All Japan Koei-kan Champion, who serves as chief technical instructor, and Richard Woodgeard, a senior instructor and advisor who also studied in Japan under master Onishi.

Koei-kan is currently practiced in Europe and South America also. The style and its representative emblems are trademarked. Only certified instructors are granted permission to use the koei-kan name, emblems, and training materials. The phrase "karate-do gaku" was coined by Onishi to describe koei-kan; it represents the improvement of karate through research, experimentation, and individual adaptation of conclusions. (EDWARD KALOUDIS) *Further reading: Kick Illustrated,* July 1981.

Top: Karate master Kanken Toyama *(seated at right wearing glasses)* and Master E. Onishi *(in center wearing black karate gi).*
Center: Karate master Juhatsu Kiyoda. *Bottom:* Kyokushinkai advocates body contact in sparring.

OKINAWAN GOJU-RYU Founded in the late 1920s by Grandmaster **Chojun Miyagi,** Okinawan goju-ryu karate-do is one of the four major systems of karate on Okinawa belonging to the All Okinawa Karate-do Association, and was the first style of karate on Okinawa to be given a name. The world's foremost living authority on the subject is **Meitoku Yagi,** who resides in Naha City, Okinawa.

Okinawan goju-ryu karate has its own unique kata, techniques, and breathing exercises. Literally, goju means: *go,* sturdiness, firmness, and hardness; and *ju,* gentleness, flexibility, and speed. Goju-ryu is the only Okinawan karate system that consists of hard and soft, slow and fast movements, performed with deep abdominal breathing. Every movement is one of studied symmetry and grace; head, hands, body, and feet move in smooth coordination and harmony.

Characteristic of Okinawan goju-ryu karate is that in most techniques the body is kept upright, and short steps are used when advancing or retreating. It is ideally suited to close-range fighting.

Repertoire of the style comprises roughly 85 percent hand techniques (punching, striking, and elbowing) and 15 percent kicking techniques. The main kicks are the front snap kick and the sideways kick. While limbering up in the **dojo,** kicks are thrown as high and as close to the body as possible. In actual fighting, however, kicks are not aimed any higher than the waist. Stances include: sanchin-dachi (front foot pigeon-toed), hachiji-dachi (natural stance), neko-ashi-dachi (cat-foot stance), kiba-dachi (horse stance), shiko-dachi (square stance), and zenkutsu-dachi (elongated front stance). When practicing stances the body is kept relaxed but ready, coiled to spring; the mind is calm.

The sanchin-dachi position is used for punching, striking, and blocking. The body is erect, the front foot pointed slightly inward and a slight inner bend to the knees.

Versatile and graceful is the neko-ashi-dachi. In this stance most of the weight of the body is on the rear foot, and the ball of the front foot lightly touches the floor, ready instantly to launch a kicking blow. Neko-ashi may be employed to retreat backward or sideways, to close on an opponent, to perform a hooking block, or to push as in the mawashi-uke (round-house block).

The Okinawan goju-ryu system consists of 14 **kata** (formal exercises), in which all karate techniques (waza) are contained. Practice of the kata is of utmost importance for mastery of the art. At least three years of daily practice are needed to perfect a kata; advanced kata require more. The Okinawan goju-ryu kata are: Sanchin, fukyu I, fukyu II, gekisai I, gekisai II, saifa, shisochin, seisan, seipai, sanseru, seiunchin, kururunfa, suparinpe (also known as pechurin), and tensho. (Fukyu I and II were developed recently by Meitoku Yagi.)

Anthony Mirakian practicing goju-ryu kumites with one of his top students, Timothy O'Connor. Courtesy of A. Mirakian

Anthony Mirakian instructs class in goju-ryu gekisai, first kata.

The Sanchin and the tensho kata are breathing exercises undertaken to harden the entire body through deep, slow abdominal breathing while maintaining the correct kind of body tension. Once mastered—they are among the most difficult kata—a karate practitioner can take a punch or kick in almost any part of the body without pain or injury. Originally, the Sanchin, as taught by **Kanryo Higashionna,** was practiced open-handed. Later modified to a closed-fist Sanchin, it has been practiced since with the closed fist.

The tensho (revolving hands) breathing kata was developed by the late grandmaster Miyagi for middle-aged or older people. It is a soft way of breathing and contains many blocking movements performed with open hands.

Fukyu I and fukyu II, developed by Meitoku Yagi around 1974, are designed for beginning students. Fukyu I emphasizes vertical punches, blocking with both hands at once, and striking with fingertips (nukite). Fukyu II concentrates upon the horse stance and slow blocking movements; the body assumes slanted postures.

Gekisai means to destroy, to demolish. The kata was created by Miyagi in 1940, but with notable influence from technical aspects of Shuri-te as taught by **Yasutsune Itosu.** Gekisai I is a beginner's kata containing two upper blocks, executed close to the forehead; two Sanchin-dachi steps, executed with slow chest blocks; and a front snap kick followed by elbowing to the chest and a back-hand strike. This kata ends with three closed-fisted pushing movements in three directions.

The gekisai II kata is essentially the same as gekisai I but the ending is performed in neko-ashi-dachi (cat-foot stance), with round-house blocking.

The saifa (tearing) kata, of typical Chinese origin, calls for two hammer blows (tetsui) performed with circular movements to the top of an opponent's head, two double punches to the chest, and two kicks accomplished while standing on one foot.

The shisochin (four peaceful facing) kata is a typical Chinese kata that commences with three open-handed movements. In this kata are finger strikes (nukite) and four movements performed from zenkutsu-dachi with four palm-heel strikes. The kata terminates in neko-ashi-dachi (cat-foot stance) with an open-hand, down-and-under blocking technique.

The Seisan kata demonstrates 13 techniques: three initial fast chest punches in Sanchin-dachi stance, chest block, two kicks to the knee, and assorted quick punching from the horse stance. It ends with a front kick followed by a punch to the chest and drop into the neko-ashi-dachi with mawashi-uke technique. An advanced kata.

The seipai kata is also an advanced kata, with 18 body-twisting movements. Beginning slowly with open hands, the kata progresses through a shuto (chop) to the neck, a front snap kick with horizontal elbow, and back-hand strike to the face.

The sanseru kata has 36 techniques: three initial slow chest punches, performed with deep abdominal breath control; a leg tackle; a jump kick from zenkutsu-dachi; and a right-arm elbow with simultaneous left-hand punch to the chest. Sanseru is a difficult advanced kata.

Seiunchin means "marching far quietly." This kata is very old; its significance has been lost, though it is elegant and beautiful in performance. Its origins may lie in the **hsing-i** school (one of the three Chinese internal systems). The first three movements are done slowly from the horse stance (kiba-dachi) with rigid open hands and deep breath control. There is in this kata a certain amount of raising and lowering of the body, and an exacting series of movements. All of the movements are hand techniques, an unusual feature.

Kururunfa means "forever stops, peacefulness, and tearing." A very advanced kata, it comprises two open-handed blocks and sideways kicks to the knee, three blocking movements with the hands down and under, and two hooking blocks from the cat-foot stance. Kururunfa includes a curious movement in which the hands are raised back to back above the head.

With 108 techniques, the highest and most difficult kata in Okinawan goju-ryu karate is the suparinpe (or pechurin). Beginning with three slow chest punches, it continues through many open-hand and closed-hand revolving techniques. Suparinpe requires great breath control and skill for the execution of its slow and fast, hard and soft movements.

Kumite (sparring) are composed matches or sets of karate techniques usually performed in the dojo by two students. Patterns are formulated for training purposes by breaking down a kata. In Okinawan goju-ryu karate there is no practice of free fighting (jiyu kumite). Patterned matches (yakusoku kumite) practiced are: ippon kumite (one attack sparring), sanbon kumite (three-step, three-attack sparring), kata bunkai kumite (piecemeal kata sparring), and kake-uke kumite (wrist-strengthening exercise sparring).

To attain true proficiency in the art of karate-do, the karateka must control his mind and conquer himself. The Zen doctrine is central to Okinawan goju-ryu karate-do. Intuitive understanding cannot be taught, but is awakened in the karate student's mind after many years of dedicated training, discipline, and meditation.

Traditionally, on Okinawa, goju-ryu karate is taught as **karate-do,** a "way of life."

Do is the Japanese pronunciation of the Chinese ideograph Tao (pronounced *dow*). Tao, or the "way" is the dominant idea in all Chinese philosophy, the foundation of the ancient Chinese world-concept. All things are indissolubly interrelated and mutually influence each other. In karate-do, the training will become, in some measure, the practitioner, and the practitioner will become the training. The balance between karateka and his art is the manner of his training—karate seeks, therefore, to attain that most harmonious joining. (ANTHONY MIRAKIAN) *See also* goju-ryu; Okinawa, history of martial arts in.

Rare picture of karate instructors Meitatsu Yagi and Yushun Tamaki practicing unique goju-ryu techniques on Okinawa. Courtesy of A. Mirakian

Anthony Mirakian, representing the Meibukan Goju-ryu Karate School, demonstrates the goju-ryu sisochin kata at the Annual Martial Arts event in Ginoza, central Okinawa, in 1958. Courtesy of A. Mirakian

RENBUKAI; RENBUKAN Japanese karate style; literally "training martial arts association." Renbukai has no single founder: it was developed by several masters of various arts. First known as kanbukan, "Korean martial arts place," it was merely a place where martial artists went to practice and exchange thoughts. The "place" was headed by a Korean instructor, Geka Yung. An influential teacher was Hiroyasu Tamae, a student of Shiroma Gusukuma (himself a student of **Yasutsune Itosu**). Tamae was trained in Chinese kempo, Naha-te, and the **bo.**

In 1950, under Norio Nakamura, a 4th dan in **kendo** and judo, the school became known as the renbukan, "training martial arts place." It was not until 1964 that the school took the name of renbukai, becoming a distinct style. At that time, renbukai joined **Shotokan, wado-ryu, Shito-ryu,** and others in becoming the All Japan Karate-Do Federation. Nakamura became at that time the first director of renbukai. There are approximately 300,000 practitioners of renbukai in Japan, though it is not popular in the Western world since no English is spoken in the renbukai schools. Renbukai instructors must have attained 4th dan or higher.

Renbukai is one of the few styles in Japan to practice full-contact; with protective gear. The first full-contact tournament was held in 1954. Renbukai stresses the physical techniques of striking, kicking, and throwing by strong offensive action. Karate champion **Ron Marchini,** a renbukai stylist, attracted attention to this system in the U.S. when he was ranked the number one fighter in America by *Black Belt Magazine.*

Renbukai competition with participants wearing full body armor

SEIKIDOJO Karate style formulated by T. Fujiwara of Japan; its headquarters is in Fukuoka, Japan. Opponents in seikidojo engage in **full-contact,** but to avoid injury wear **kendo** armor and padded gloves. The system combines Japanese and Okinawan karate with foot movements of kendo. There are a few schools in the U.S. James Glassburn of Little Rock, Ark. is the American head of seikidojo. *Further reading: Official Karate,* Oct. 1974.

SHITO-RYU One of the four major styles of Japanese karate founded in 1930 by **Kenwa Mabuni,** an Okinawan karate master. Mabuni studied under two famous Okinawan masters: **Yasutsune Itosu** (Shuri-te) and **Kanryo Higashionna** (Naha-te), blending their teachings into a new system he called Shito-ryu, a name composed of Japanese characters from both instructor's names. Predominately a hard style, Shito-ryu embraces **kata** from the hard **shorin-ryu** as well as the softer **goju-ryu** styles. Training is divided equally between kata, basics, and sparring; hand and foot techniques also find equal emphasis. The style also stresses **kobu-jutsu** (art of weaponry). **Fumio Demura** introduced this system to the U.S. in 1965, and is president of the Japan Karate Federation which supervises Shito-ryu in the West (FUMIO DEMURA)

Fumio Demura *(left),* national karate champion of Japan, who introduced shito-ryu to the United States in 1965.

Ryusho Sakagami

Shito-ryu Grandmaster Kenwa Mabuni, founder of Shito-ryu karate. Courtesy of A. Mirakian

SHOREI-RYU Major Okinawan karate style stemming from Naha-te. Shorei-ryu embraces a meticulous repertoire of techniques. Its basics encompass punching, striking, clawing, ripping, kicking, jumping, blocking, reaping, sweeping, throwing, holding, grappling, falling, choking, joint-locking and twisting, and feinting. It includes 17 major stances for balance, power, and stability. The system is based on five major animal strengths, developed through the practice of kamae with specific fist forms: the dragon (body strength), the tiger (bone strength), the leopard (inner and outer strength), the snake (breath strength), and the crane (spiritual strength).

There are eight performance categories in this system. Ippon kumite kata (standing sparring forms) consist of a series of 26 detailed exercises against a partner designed to develop power. The taezu naru waza (continuous motion techniques) are a set of 10 combinations against a partner to develop speed and fluidity. The kihon kumite kata (basic sparring forms) consist of a series of 30 exercises also performed against a partner. Jiju undo (free exercise), done individually, is a method of form sparring. Kime dachi kumite (focus stance sparring) allows for the development of control and reflex responses while working with a partner. Kata kumite (form sparring) develops sparring ability with precise form and technique. **Kata** (formal exercises), the mainstay of this system, develops the individual mentally and physically. Juji kumite (free-style sparring) is the final category.

Once acquainted with the basic principles of sparring, shorei-ryu students learn eight types of attack, 47 basic and advanced rules, and seven kogeki hoho (attacking methods), to deliver techniques swiftly, accurately, and with maximum power.

Shorei-ryu emphasizes three preparatory exercises (taikyoku I-III) and 15 formal kata. Of the latter, some function to develop physical perfection, balance, speed, power, and form (wan su, ananku, naihanchi I-II, and tsue sho); others develop mental and physical coordination (empi sho, bassai dai, gopei sho, dan en sho, and Sanchin); the remainder develop mental and spiritual awareness (nan dan sho, naihanchi III, tegatana, kanku sho, and tensho).

Shorei-ryu kata are employed on three levels: the mental, which embodies sequence and performance; the spiritual, which embodies the execution of movements against an opponent; and the universal, whereby the practitioner seeks to interpret and understand every movement of each kata against opponents moving at full speed in rapid succession. The shorei-ryu kata include hidden physical and spiritual movements.

Shorei-ryu also emphasizes the study and application of ancient sources like the *I Chin Ching* for the development of **ki** (internal energy), as well as a multitude of breathing methods to cultivate this power. Finally, it emphasizes the mastery of six martial arts weapons: the **bo, sai, nunchaku, tonfa, kama,** and teko (claws). These weapons are perfected to the extent where each can be performed within the unarmed kata of shorei-ryu.

Shorei-ryu's origins can be traced back to **Bodhidharma** and the **Shao-lin Temple.** In 1790 **Sokon Matsumura** divided the various Okinawan styles then taught in Okinawa into two categories, Naha-te and Shuri-te. Karate master **Choki Motubu,** a student of Matsumura and later **Yasutsune Itosu,** is considered the "father of shorei-ryu." Also important in the evolution of shorei-ryu is the Chinese master Shang Tsao Hsiang, who integrated the internal Chinese systems of **hsing-i** and **pa-kua** with the external systems of **Shao-lin** kung-fu and others. The elder Hsiang passed on his knowledge to his nephew, T'ung Gee Hsiang. When T'ung Gee Hsiang was living in the Chinese settlement of Kume Mura in Okinawa, he was sought by Motobu for training.

In 1940 Hsiang traveled to the Soloman Islands as a missionary, seeking to convert the natives. There, in 1942, he met **Robert Trias,** an American serviceman who was a middleweight boxing champion in the U.S. Navy during the war. Following a memorable sparring encounter, Trias began training with Hsiang. Following his discharge, Trias was in 1946 the first to introduce karate of any kind, as well as the shorei-ryu system, in the U.S. Masters Trias and Yasuhiro Konishi, one of Motobu's instructors, are today the two oldest and active links in the shorei-ryu style. (ROBERT A. TRIAS) *Further reading: The Pinnacle of Karate: Okinawan Methods of Shuri-Ryu,* Robert A. Trias, 1980.

SHORIN-RYU One of the two original karate styles formally systematized in Okinawa and considered by some authorities to have had the most influential impact on the development of all modern karate systems. Following its emergence in Okinawa, shorin-ryu eventually splintered into three main branches: shobayashi-ryu (small forest school), kobayashi-ryu (young forest school), and matsubayashi-ryu (pine forest school). All three names refer to the small pine forest where the original **Shao-lin Temple** was located in China, and all three are still interpreted as shorin-ryu, or "Shao-lin way," reflecting their Chinese heritage. There exists also a less popular, fourth branch of shorin-ryu called matsumura orthodox, founded by **Hohan Soken.**

Shobayashi-ryu

Shobayashi-ryu was first taught by **Chotoku Kyan,** a famous student of **Yasutsune Itosu.** Kyan trained several notable students, among them **Shoshin Nagamine,** who in 1947 founded the matsubayashi-ryu branch of shorin-ryu. Another Kyan student, **Eizo Shimabuku (ro)** inherited leadership of shobayashi-ryu. This master has been responsible for turning out many prominent karate figures. His most famous student is full-contact world champion **Joe Lewis. Jerry Gould** of Renton, Wash. is the U.S. chief instructor for Shimabuku's shobayashi-ryu.

Kobayashi-ryu

Another of Itosu's students, **Choshin Chibana,** is credited as the first to teach kobayashi-ryu. According to at least one authority, this system is identical to shobayashi-ryu: it is believed Chibana simply misspelled the kanji characters, which changed the pronunciation from *shobayashi*-ryu to *kobayashi*-ryu. Today, these two systems remain virtually interchangeable, with the same form and patterns visible in their respective **kata.**

Upon Chibana's death **Shugoro Nakazato** assumed leadership of the kobayashi-ryu. From Nakazato's line of descent emerged world light-contact champion **Mike Stone,** who trained with Herbert Peters, a Nakazato disciple.

Matsubayashi-ryu

Shoshin Nagamine, a disciple of Chotoku Kyan, founded matsubayashi-ryu in 1947. Its U.S. headquarters is supervised by Robert Scaglione of New York.

Matsumura Orthodox

A minor form of shorin-ryu, this style was founded by Hohan Soken (b. 1889) one of the oldest living karate masters. Reportedly, some of this style's followers have changed its name to sukunai hayashi. Because of the master's advanced age, he passed on responsibility for supervising this style to his chief disciple, Fusi Kisi.

Technically, the shorin-ryu styles tend to use more upright stances than the Japanese styles, giving the Okinawan stylist more mobility. Unlike the Japanese stylist, the Okinawan shorin-ryu stylist does not emphasize constant forward pressure when engaging in a confrontation, or like the Chinese stylist, indirect countering; rather, he maintains enough flexibility to use both approaches. Shorin-ryu kicking techniques are usually low-line. These stylists typically rely on hand techniques. (JERRY GOULD) *See also* Okinawa, history of martial arts in. *Further reading: Kick Illustrated,* Sept. 1981.

SHORINJI-RYU Japanese style of karate-do founded by Kori Hisataka after World War II. Hisataka named this style after its two main sources of stylistic inspiration: **shorin-ryu** karate and **Shorinji kempo.** Techniques are thrown, for the most part, in rapid, successive combinations. This style is taught in the U.S. by **Richard Kim** of San Francisco.

KOBAYASHI-RYU Okinawan system of unarmed combat derived from shuri-te; now one of the three branches of **shorin-ryu** karate. One source claims kobayashi-ryu was named after its founder, who studied for nine years in northern China before organizing his school in Okinawa. This form of shorin-ryu, translated as "small forest," should not be confused with other branches known as "pine forest" and "young forest." *See also* shorin-ryu.

MATSUBAYASHI-RYU Sokon Matsumura of Tomari, Okinawa, founded this style of karate, later renamed **shorin-ryu;** one of the major systems of Okinawan karate. *See* shorin-ryu.

SHORINJI KEMPO According to present claims, the first established martial art to bear the Japanese name of its origin, the **Shao-lin Temple.** Shorinji kempo is a combination of religion, martial art, and Zen meditation; for many ages it was taught only to those who had entered the Buddhist priesthood. Imbued with the theory of calm in action—seated Zen meditation represents the calm and kempo the action—Shorinji thought maintains that neither of these aspects of the whole can exist independently. In Shorinji kempo both are given equal importance.

At present, there are 2,600 chapters of Shorinji kempo in Japan with a reported membership of 920,000; it is taught in colleges and high schools throughout Japan. There are an additional 300 chapters in 17 countries.

The traditional 28th patriarch of Buddhism, **Bodhidharma,** also known as Daruma and Tamo, traveled from India to the kingdom of Wei and ultimately settled at the Shao-lin ("Shorinji" in Japanese) Temple, a monastery on Hao-shan mountain near Loyang, in what is now Honan province, China. The Buddhism Bodhidharma introduced to China valued equally zazen (seated meditation) and kempo. During the early stages of its development, the kempo practiced at the Shao-lin monastery had several names. It was sometimes referred to as nalo-jan and also as arohan. Later, it was called i-jinsin to distinguish it from zazen.

Government persecutions and repeated burnings destroyed the temple and dispersed the monks. Gradually, kempo, devoid of its **ch'an**, or **Zen,** elements, spread to other parts of China. The techniques were transmitted either in fragments or one by one, but the temple itself seems to have little connection with the later history of kempo.

From the latter part of the Sung Dynasty (947-1279) until the Ch'ing Dynasty (1662-1912) kempo enjoyed what is sometimes called its golden era. So numerous were kempo exponents among the anti-dynastic rebels that in the Yuan dynasty (1279-1368) emperors banned the practice of kempo. Kempo was associated with popular resistance until the Ch'ing, or Manchu Dynasty, which ended in the early 20th century. While the art appeared to vanish during these turbulent times, secret societies continued its practice.

The form of Chinese kempo thought to have been introduced into Japan during the Kamakura period (1192-1333) was in fact not a martial art but a set of calisthenics. Although later, after every Chinese rebellion or dynastic change, monks, patriots, and rebels seeking refuge in Japan brought with them various kinds of kempo, Shorinji kempo, the pure form, is said to have never been among them.

Shorinji was given its present form by the late **Doshin So.** Born in 1911, in Oakayama Prefecture in Japan, the eldest son of a customs officer, So was sent to live in Manchuria with his grandfather. When he was 17, his grandfather's death forced him to return to Japan under the patronage of Mitsura Toyama, founder of the ultrapatriotic Amur River Society (called Black Dragon Society). In 1928 So returned to Manchuria, this time as a member of a secret organization. To facilitate his covert activities, he became a disciple of a Taoist priest who was also a leader in the Zaijari secret society and a master of the byakurenmonken, a branch of kempo originating at the Shorinji temple in Honan province of China.

A trip to Peking brought young So into contact with the 20th master of the North Shorinji Giwamonken temple of kempo, whose disciple he immediately became. Late in 1936, in a ceremony at the Shorinji temple, So was officially designated successor to the master of the North Shorinji temple. After the war, in 1946, he revised, expanded, and systematized the many forms of kempo to which he had been exposed while in China, creating Shorinji kempo as it exists today. So established Shorinji kempo headquarters at Tadotsu, in Kagawa Prefecture, on the Island of Shikoku, in Japan.

So's Shorinji kempo is but one of 12 styles in Japan that claim to have ancestral roots in Chinese Shao-lin. So's claims to teach a traditional form of Shao-lin have been called ludicrous by at least one noted martial scholar. A 1972 decision of the Japanese courts barred So's use of the name "Shorinji kempo"; Chinese groups disproved So's claim to Chinese affiliation. As a result, he now calls his system "Nippon Shorinji kempo," meaning "Japanese Shao-lin fist-way."

Shorinji kempo in the U.S. was founded in 1967 by Hirokazu Yamamori. By 1976 there were about ten centers across the U.S. with growing memberships. The orthodox teachings of Doshin So have been spread by several instructors, among them Dr. Shingo Fukinbara, a chiropractor and acupuncturist from Kobe, Japan. A student of Yamamori, he established doins in several states.

The name Shao-lin and Shorinji kempo, as well as its insignia, the 5,000-year-old Buddhist manji, are copyrighted. Every leading practitioner in this martial art belongs to the general headquarters at the Shikoku Hombu in Japan, and instruction throughout the world is organized under the auspices of the Nippon Shorinji Kempo Federation, which issues instructor certificates. (Dr John L. Stump) *Further reading: What Is Shorinji Kempo,* Doshin So, 1972; *Modern Bujutsu and Budo,* Donn F. Draeger, *Black Belt Magazine,* 1968 Yearbook.

OKINAWAN KEMPO An offspring of Chinese **kempo.** In the early 1900s Shigeru Nakimura and Zenryoku Shimabuku began karate training in the first middle school, called Iichu, in Shuri, Okinawa. **Chojun Miyagi,** the founder of **Okinawan goju-ryu,** was a senior student and president of the school's karate club at the time. He helped both men in their early karate development, although their actual instructors at the club were Chomo Hanashiro and **Kentsu Yabu.** Once a week, one of the foremost Okinawan karate masters, **Kanryo Higashionna,** taught some members privately, including Nakimura and Shimabuku. Thus, the two students were fortunate enough to have begun their training under the greatest of Okinawan masters.

Following his graduation, Nakimura studied with yet another noted karate master, Shinkichi Kuniyoshi, a Peichin (Knight) of the Ryukyu king, Sho. Nakimura returned to his home town, Nago City, to teach his interpretation of karate, called Okinawan kempo karate-do.

After leaving school Shimabuku trained with **Chotoku Kyan** and, in 1916, traveled to Fukien province in China to study with a master of northern sil-lum. In the mid-1920s he returned to Naha City and opened his own dojo where he taught his interpretation of karate, called Okinawan shorinji-ryu karate-do.

In 1962 Shimabuku and Nakimura united to form the Okinawan Kempo Association. Besides freely teaching at each other's schools, they invited other masters to teach there as well. Both, and especially Nakimura, felt that through full-contact sparring, the original quality of combat efficiency would be preserved. At the same time, Shimabuku emphasized Chinese leg techniques, which he believed were are important addition to Okinawan interpretations of the original karate.

With Nakimura's death in 1970, the Okinawan Kempo Association was disbanded. Shimabuku had died one year earlier. Nakimura's followers formed a new association, the All Okinawa Kempo Karate-do League, which continues to operate. Shimabuku's students founded a different school, the Okinawan kempo-ryu karate-do, which is also currently active. (Michael Brodman)

NIOKEN Practice method of defense and counterattack in the **Shorinji kempo** school.

OKINAWA-TE Martial art developed from shorinji-kempo, or **Shao-lin** kung-fu as it is known in Chinese. Okinawa-te is considered the forerunner of modern karate.

SHOTOKAN Japanese style of karate founded by **Gichin Funakoshi.** He brought together two systems of open-hand fighting that flourished in his native Okinawa to form a new system he called **karate-do** (way of the empty hand); his followers refer to it as Shotokan. Shotokan means "hall of Shoto," Shoto being the penname Funakoshi adopted in calligraphic works. In fusing together his new style, Funakoshi continually edited, revised, and updated the various kicks, punches, strikes, blocks, and body dynamics until the day he

Master Gichin Funakoshi, founder of Shotokan karate.
Courtesy of E. Bruno

Shotokan Karate

died in 1957.

As a teacher assigned to instruct in many schools in different parts of Okinawa, Funakoshi was forced to travel extensively, passing through the major centers of martial arts on the island. As a result, he was able to study under excellent masters from different backgrounds over a long period of time. After a period of many years, Funakoshi synthesized the best elements of the techniques and kata that he was taught and created a new system.

Shotokan karate, with 16 kata, teaches relatively fewer techniques than other styles. Instructors adhere to the concept of teaching a thorough knowledge of a few techniques, rather than superficial familiarity with numerous techniques. Students first learn to assume strong stances and to snap punches without lifting the shoulders. After months of practice, a student is ready to integrate various stances with punching and kicking techniques and to begin moving forward and backward while using combination techniques. In each technique he combines breathing, timing, muscle control, and momentum to produce the greatest speed and power of which he is capable.

Shotokan karate emphasizes two ideas in its training: balance and muscle control, and a belief that proper study eliminates ego and promotes hard, honest work, humility, and excellence.

Shotokan is physically distinguished from other karate systems in adapting nearly every one of its techniques to a linear fighting style, its philosophy being that the shortest distance between two points is a straight line. This contrasts with **goju-ryu,** which is based upon a circular pattern of movement, or the kung-fu forms, which are also circular, criss-cross patterns of fighting. Shotokan maintains that a direct line of attack is the quickest, safest, and most effective. While Shotokan fighters may circle an opponent during a match, it is a diversionary tactic.

Shotokan fighters are recognized by their excellent posture, low stances, and hip power—a trademark of Japanese karate in general and Shotokan karate in particular. Foot sweeps and reverse punches are important weapons in a Shotokan fighter's arsenal, as are lunge punches, front kicks, side kicks, and round kicks. A Shotokan student will use the rotating power of the hips in every technique he can, whether spinning the hips around for the round kick or snapping out the hip on impact to generate extra thrust in the side kick. The dramatic, high kicks of tae kwon do are not seen in Shotokan. Many times the highest kick is not the most effective; body kicks do far more damage. Shotokan students are taught "iken hisatsu" (to kill with one blow) and are not unfamiliar with jumping, spinning, and slashing.

Shotokan advocates advancement, but in technique rather than quantitative knowledge. After a student practices reverse punches for six months, for example, he will have four or five of the necessary muscles under control, achieving speed and power in the technique. If he practices another six months, he may control another four or five muscles and also perfect his balance to a greater degree. He will have then advanced this technique to a higher level of excellence—yet he may still be only a green belt.

What is important in Shotokan, then, is to develop each technique to its maximum, not necessarily scoring a point in a match but scoring it well. When a Shotokan stylist has reached the highest possible level of development with a certain technique, he continues training to maintain its quality.

HISTORY The history of Shotokan karate actually began with Gichin Funakoshi's 1917 trip to Kyoto, where karate was demonstrated for the first time in Japan, at the **Butokuden.** While the demonstration was successful and the Japanese interest was high, there was no immediate rush to bring the Okinawan art to Japan on a formal basis. As taken as they were with it, the Japanese still tended to be suspicious of anything purely Okinawan, and they found it expedient to view karate as an interesting sideshow.

This attitude could have been the end of karate in Japan had it not been for a fortuitous event on Mar. 6, 1921. On that date, the Crown Prince (the Emperor Hirohito) of Japan visited Okinawa on his way to Europe. Seeking to impress the Prince with the rich culture of Okinawa, the Department of Education asked Funakoshi to give a karate demonstration for him in the Great Hall of Shuri Castle. So fascinated was the prince by the demonstration, that he spoke of it excitedly throughout the rest of his voyage. Thus the Ministry of Education formally requested a karate demonstration be performed at the first National Athletic Exhibition in Tokyo. Funakoshi was of course chosen to perform.

On the same day he gave the demonstration, he was approached

Shotokan champion Tanaba *(right)* is one of the top karate competitors in the world.

by members of the Sho family, direct descendants of Shotai, the last king of Okinawa, and asked to extend his visit. Humbled and inspired by their supplications, Funakoshi agreed to stay for a few weeks. From **Jigoro Kano,** the founder of judo, came a request to demonstrate karate at the **Kodokan,** the judo headquarters. To assist him with the demonstration, Funakoshi prevailed upon Shinkin Gima, a student at Tokyo Shoka Daigaku, who had attained a high degree of proficiency in karate while still in Okinawa. At a private demonstration for Kano and selected members of the Kodokan, Funakoshi performed the kata, **kanku dai,** and Gima performed **naihanchi** (now known to the Japanese as **tekki**). So impressed was Kano by the demonstration that he enthusiastically asked Funakoshi to prolong his stay in Japan and to teach him the basics of karate. Funakoshi indeed taught Kano some basic blocks, punches, strikes, and kicks, and Kano later incorporated some of these into an advanced judo kata.

The demonstration at the National Athletic Exhibition, and Kano's introductions to influential Japanese, soon led to official requests for karate instruction by the military academy, the Tokyo Bar Association, and the Society for Research in High School Physical Education. While eager to demonstrate before these groups, Funakoshi was struggling with homesickness, worry about his family, and guilt over leaving his responsibilities behind. After correspondence with his wife, in which she gave her blessing, Funakoshi decided to stay in Japan and fulfill what he now perceived to be his destiny: to teach karate to the Japanese people.

While the Japanese in general were reluctant to endorse anything of Okinawan extraction, they were more than eager to pursue almost anything popular with the upper classes. In less than nine months, karate had become a fad with the intelligentsia. In 1922 Funakoshi established the first formal Japanese karate club at the Meisei Juku, a dormitory and school for newly arrived Okinawan students in the Suidobata section of Tokyo. To support himself, he cleaned the dormitory during the day, often tending the garden and lawns, and taught karate in a lecture hall in the evening. Throwing himself completely into his mission, he wrote the first book on karate, *Ryukyu Kempo: Karate,* published by Bukyo-sha in 1922.

An instant best-seller (by textbook standards), it went out of print prematurely, for a time, when the book's plates were destroyed in the great Kanto earthquake of Sept. 1, 1923. The book was not printed again until 1926, when it was re-issued by Kobundo as *Rentan Goshin Karate-jitsu ("Strengthening of Willpower and Self-defense Through Techniques of Karate").*

Many of Funakoshi's finest pupils were lost in the earthquake also, and he was forced to take a job making stencils at the Daiichi Sogo Bank in Kyobashi. Since this was some distance from the Meisei Juku, Funakoshi was invited to move his dojo to the dojo of Hiromichi Nakayama, the great **kendo** teacher. For a great kendo sensei to allow another art to be practiced in his dojo was quite unprecedented.

In 1924, at the age of 56, when most men are contemplating retirement, Funakoshi entered and qualified in the Tokyo Invitational Prize Contest for Athletes. Throughout the 1920s and early 1930s, Funakoshi continued to teach at Nakayama's kendo dojo. The number of active students increased steadily, until his fame brought him an invitation to demonstrate karate before the Imperial Household.

In 1924, Funakoshi was asked by Prof. Shinyo Kasuya of the department of German language and literature at Keio University to teach a group of students at the university. A club was soon organized with the sanction of the university. The Keio club was the first collegiate karate club in Japan, and it is active to this day. By 1926 the Tokyo University Karate Club was officially chartered, followed in the early 1930s by clubs at Takushoku, Chuo, Shodai (now called Hitotsubashi University), Gakushu-in, Hosei, Nihon, Meiji, and others, until today there are over 200 collegiate karate clubs in Japan. Karate made its greatest headway on campuses, but also through instruction to employee groups at companies such as the Tokyo Department Store, Tokyo Railroad Co., the Matsuzakaya Department Stores, and others.

As karate grew in the 1930s, it spawned several **ryu** (schools or styles). **Chojun Miyagi** and **Kenwa Mabuni** brought the **goju-ryu** and **Shito-ryu** styles from Okinawa, and in 1935 one of Funakoshi's most brilliant senior students, **Hironishi Ohtsuka,** broke away, forming his own **wado-ryu** style. Many others formed styles, of course, but these four—Shotokan, goju, wado, and Shito—comprise

the bulk of Japanese karate. Early on, at least, there was very little bickering among the leaders of the varous schools. It was perfectly acceptable, they believed, for different masters to teach in different ways; after all, they were striving toward the same goal: perfection of human character through karate-do.

In 1935 karatemen from all over Japan formed a committee that solicited funds to build a free-standing karate dojo. Construction on the building in Zoshigaya, Toshima Ward, began in mid-1935, and was completed in the spring of 1936. Gichin Funakoshi, at the age of 68, bowed and entered the world's first karate dojo in the spring of 1936. As a tribute to him from karate students all over Japan, a plaque was hung over the door inscribed with the characters for "Shoto-kan," ("the hall of Shoto").

By 1940, with Japan engaged in war on several fronts, Funakoshi's dojo was filled with eager young men. Following the Japanese attack on Pearl Harbor, Funakoshi's dojo was so crowded with students that they frequently spilled over into the street and neighboring yards. Japan's defeat in World War II of course brought to a temporary halt the development of virtualy all the martial arts, but only for a short time.

In 1949 Funakoshi's students—the university clubs, the Old Boys clubs, and the private dojos all over Japan—officially organized themselves into the *Nihon Karate Kyokai* (**Japan Karate Association,** or JKA) and named Funakoshi their chief instructor emeritus. **Isao Obata**, the chairman, was the wealthy president of his own trading company; the first JKA president, Kichinosuke Saigo, was a wealthy politician with major political influence. These men had neither the time nor the inclination to administer the affairs of such a large and burgeoning organization, and the board of directors immediately hired a full-time, paid staff to run the organization. Masatomo Takagi, a business manager and a 5th dan in karate, was hired as general secretary. **Masatoshi Nakayama** was made chief instructor, to conduct day-to-day training at the headquarters; Kimio Ito was appointed director of administration; and **Hidetaka Nishiyama** was named chief of the instruction committee.

To understand what happened next to the JKA and its export of karate to the rest of the world some background will be useful. Both ancestry and wealth contributed to a man's position within the class structure, and Japanese institutions, especially the colleges and universitites, reflect this state of affairs. Even today, a family's wealth and position determine to a large degree which university the children will attend, and a graduate's chances for success are strongly influenced thereby. The "Big Three" colleges, in terms of social and political prestige, are Keio, Waseda, and Hosei. These three, along with Takushoku, also represented the best collegiate karate in Japan. Takushoku, however, was not part of the "establishment" of colleges. Commonly called Takudai, it was created before World War II expressly for the purpose of training administrators for overseas work. Takudai men therefore typically majored in economics, importing and exporting, and international law.

The types of jobs available to Takudai graduates were not considered prestigious by the old-line university graduates, and a good deal of class friction was evident in the JKA between upper echelon Old Boys and highly expert (in karate) but "lower class" Takudai men. Disputes arose over business practices, philosophy, and training methods. The class division among administrators crystallized around the fact that the Takudai staff, Takagi and Nakayama among them, was being paid for teaching karate.

In April 1955 the JKA opened its first commercial dojo in the preview room of the Kataoka Movie Center, and a strong campaign was launched for the recruitment of new students. Many old-line masters, chief among them Isao Obata of Keio, felt it was absolutely immoral for a man to accept money for teaching the art. Even those who would not deny a man the right to be paid voiced opposition to placing karate on the market.

The Hosei Old Boys were the first to leave the JKA, followed by Obata and the Keio group. Unburdened of the conservative Old Boys, the Takudai men pursued the development of karate in their own way; not surprisingly, in view of their training, they chose to internationalize the art.

The Tadukai group thought the best way for an art like karate to gain international acceptance was to give it a sporting aspect. Turning karate into a sport with rules for competition was not new. Since 1936 college clubs had been conducting *kokangeiko* (exchange of courtesies and practice), in which they tested their techniques against each other on a free-style basis. Without formal rules or supervision, however, these exchange and training sessions were, more often than not, bloodbaths. The Old Boys refused to acknowledge the existence of such shenanigans because these bouts were obviously opposed to the principles of karate as Funakoshi taught them.

Nevertheless, the JKA directors and leaders in other styles brought free-sparring into the open, experimenting with it, debating it, and, finally, encouraging it. By 1950, virtually all the major styles of karate in Japan were practicing some form of free-style sparring. The JKA contest rules, comprising three chapters and 16 articles, were completed in Aug. 1956. Collegiate clubs and branch dojo immediately commenced staging tournaments to try contestant skills and to train judges. This flurry of activity culminated in the 1st All Japan Karate-do Championship Tournament in June 1957.

Concurrent with their efforts to devise a workable set of contest rules, the JKA instituted a stringent instructor training program. Only the cream of young karatemen were admitted to the program, and only after graduating honorably from college and attaining 2nd dan rank. In an intensive year of study, candidates were instructed not only in karate but in psychology, physics, anatomy, business management, history and philosophy of physical education and sports, and other subjects. On completing the training program (with 3rd dan and a dissertation) they were assigned to a year's teaching internship. The results of this difficult apprenticeship were a dozen or so highly proficient karatemen, well prepared to plant and nourish their art overseas.

First to arrive in the U.S. were Hidetaka Nishiyama, Los Angeles, and **Teruyuki Okazaki**, Philadelphia, both in 1961. Others followed in rapid succession: **Takayuki Mikami**, twice All Japan Champion, went first to Kansas City and later to New Orleans; Yutaka Yaguchi was assigned to Denver after a brief stay in Los Angeles; and **Hirokazu Kanazawa**, also twice All Japan Champion, brought the JKA to Hawaii. Kanazawa was replaced after two years by Masataka Mori, who ultimately went to New York, relinquishing the Hawaii province to Tetsuhiko Asai. Shojiro Sugiyama, not a graduate of the instructor program, founded a strong organization in Chicago. Later arrivals were Masaaki Ueki and Shigeru Takashina in Florida, Katsuya Kisaka in New Jersey, and Shojiro Koyama in Arizona.

By the mid-1970s, American students were themselves achieving instructor status. The most senior of these, and the most successful, was **Robert Fusaro** of Minneapolis. Other notables include Robert Graves of Oregon, Greer Golden of Ohio, **Ray Dalke, Frank Smith**, and **James Yabe** of California, and **Gerald Evans** of Philadelphia.

The **All America Karate Federation** (now the American Amateur Karate Federation) finally opened its doors to non-JKA karate people in the late 1960s, but too late to salvage an American karate unified under the guidance of the JKA. Indeed, internal strife led in the 1970s to a split in the organization, with master Okazaki spearheading a separate JKA organization, the **International Shotokan Karate Federation.** Both organizations continue to prosper, but there is no indication of reunification.

Outside the U.S. the JKA is stronger as an international organization. **Taiji Kase**, from the European branch in Paris, oversees Hideki Ochi in Germany, Hiroshi Shirai in Italy, **Keinosuke Enoeda** in Great Britain, and Satoshi Miyazaki in Belgium. JKA is represented around the world by Higashino in Brazil, Ishiyama in Venezuela, **Stan Schmidt** (the first non-Japanese 5th dan) in South Africa, Hideki Okamoto in Syria and Lebanon, Tanaka in Denmark, Sasaki in the Philippines, **Hiroshi Matsuura** in Mexico, and others. JKA Shotokan karate-do is now practiced daily by approximately 5,000,000 people in almost every country in the world.

While the JKA has led the way in internationalizing karate, still there is a large, unaffiliated contingent practicing Gichin Funakoshi's karate. Several of Funakoshi's best pupils chose to leave the Shotokan altogether and develop their own, eclectic systems. Notable among these are Ryosuke Konishi, who founded the **shindo-jinen-ryu** (commonly known as the Ryobukan), and Hironishi Ohtsuka, who developed wado-ryu.

But the most significant faction outside the JKA has grown from the unmollified Old Boys in Japan. Prior to leaving the JKA, Isao Obata, head of the Old Boys at Keio University, was instrumental in organizing the Zen Nihon Gakusei Karate-do Renmei (All Japan

Shotokan karate is noted for its wide, strong stances, as demonstrated by Italian karate champion Falsoni.

University Students Karate League). This organization hoped to unite collegiate practitioners from all styles. Ultimately, it evolved into a loose structure sheltering disaffected Shotokan students who wished to pursue their art free from the directives of the JKA. They called themselves the **Shotokai**, and their principal leaders included **Shigeru Egami** and Genshin Hironishi of Chuo University, and Hiroshi Noguchi at Waseda. It was from Waseda University that **Tsutomu Oshima** came to the U.S. in 1956 and founded Shotokan Karate of America. Hirokazu Kanazawa broke with the JKA in the 1970s, establishing Shotokan Karate International. Among the famous practitioners who remained within the JKA are: Minoru Miyata, Osamu Ozawa and Junpei Sugano of Hosei, Kimio Ito, Motokun Sugiura, and Hiroshi Shoji.

Technically, there are some gaps between JKA Shotokan and the Shotokai; practically, the gaps are very narrow. While most of the Shotokai groups still regularly practice the taikyoku and ten-no-kata that were so dear to Funakoshi, the JKA has abandoned them as repetitious and of questionable value. Stances among most of the Shotokai groups are generally higher than those seen in the JKA, and there is relatively little emphasis on free-style sparring in Shotokai dojo. From about 1960 forward, the JKA has pursued the study of karate from a scientific viewpoint—body mechanics, kinesiology, anatomy, physics, and modern psychology. This, contend most of the Shotokai people, is unnecessary and detrimental to the traditional ways taught by Funakoshi. Each group continues to insist that it practices karate exactly as Funakoshi would practice it were he alive today. The present authors, based on the writings of the master, lean toward the JKA claim. Funakoshi frequently said that karate was an unfinished art; it would continue to grow and change, he said, as man's knowledge and circumstances grew and changed. *See also* Funakoshi, Gichin; Japan Karate Association; karate-do. *Further reading: The Way of Karate, Beyond Technique,* Shigeru Egami, 1976; *Shotokan Karate: Free-Fighting Techniques,* K. Enoeda and C.J. Mack, 1974; *Karate-Do Kyohan,* Gichin Funakoshi, 1973; *Karate-Do, My Way of Life,* Gichin Funakoshi, 1977; *Karate: The Art of Empty-Hand Fighting,* Hidetaka Nishiyama and Richard Brown, 1959; *Shotokan Karate,* Peter Ventresca, 1970; *Kick Illustrated,* Oct. 1981-Jan. 1982; *Best Karate,* H. Nakayama, 1978 (8 vols.); *Black Belt Karate,* Jordan Roth, 1974. (technical material by GARY GOLDSTEIN and ALEX STERNBERG; historical material by RANDALL G. HASSELL).

SHOTOKAN KARATE IN THE UNITED STATES
(Regional Instructors)

NISHIYAMA, Hidetaka   OKAZAKI, Teruyuki

MIKAMI, Takayuki (New Orleans)	YAGUCHI, Yutaka (Denver)	MORI, Masataka (New York)	KISAKA, Katsuya (New Jersey)	SUGIYAMA, Shojiro (Chicago)	KOYAMA, Shojiro (Arizona)	TAKASHINA, Shigeru (Florida)
GOLDEN, Greer (Ohio)	DALKE, Ray (Calif.)	SMITH, Frank (Calif.)	FUSARO, Robert (Minneapolis)	RALLO, Vito (Missouri)	HASSELL, Randall (Missouri)	GRAVES, Robert (Oregon)
KANAZAWA, Hirokazu (Hawaii)	ASAI, Tetsuhiko (Hawaii)	NOZAKI, Takehiko (Hasaii)	MORI, Torajiro (Arkansas, Calif.)	HARAMOTO, Kenichi (San Francisco)	TAKAHASHI, George (AFISK)*	IWAKABE, Hideki (AFISK)*

*American Federation of Independent Shotokan Karate-do

SHOTOKAN KARATE IN JAPAN
(Major Students of Gichin Funakoshi)

FUNAKOSHI, Giko	NAKAYAMA Masatoshi (JKA)	TAKAGI, Masatomo (JKA)	NISHIYAMA, Hidetaka (JKA)	OBATA, Isao (Shotokai, Keio)	OKAZAKI, Teruyuki (ISKF, USA)	ITO, Kimio (JKA)
EGAMI, Shigeru	HIRONISHI, Genshin	NOGUCHI, Hiroshi (Shoto-Kai, Waseda)	OHTSUKA, Hironishi (Wado-ryu)	MIYATA, Minoru (JKA)	HIGUCHI, Kunio	GIMA, Shinkin
(Shotokai, Chuo, Senshu)		Ohshima, Tsutomu (SKA,* USA)				

*Shotokan Karate of America

THE 15 BASIC KATA OF SHOTOKAN KARATE

Listed below are the 15 kata which Gichin Funakoshi brought to Japan in 1922, along with the original names, and the main value of the kata as described on Funakoshi.

NAME OF KATA	MEANING OF NAME	ORIGINAL NAME(S)	MAIN POINTS TO BE LEARNED
Heian 1	Peaceful Mind	Pinan 2	Front stance, back stance, stepping patterns, lunge punch.
Heian 2	Peaceful Mind	Pinan 1	Front kick, side kick while changing directions.
Heian 3	Peaceful Mind	Pinan 3	Body connections in forearm blocking, back-fist strike.
Heian 4	Peaceful Mind	Pinan 4	Balance and variation in techniques.
Heian 5	Peaceful Mind	Pinan 5	Balance and jumping.
Tekki 1	Horse Riding	Naihanchi 1	Straddle-leg stance, hip vibration.
Tekki 2	Horse Riding	Naihanchi 2	Grasping and Hooking blocks.
Tekki 3	Horse Riding	Naihanchi 3	Continous middle-level blocking.
Bassai Dai	To Penetrate a a Fortress	Patsai	Changing disadvantage into advantage by use of switching blocks and differing degrees of power.
Kanku Dai	Sky Viewing	Kushanku, Kokuson	Variation in fast and slow techniques; jumping.
Jion	(Name of Originator)	Jion	Turning, shifting, variations in stepping patterns.
Jutte	10 Hands	Jutte	Powerful hip action, use of the staff. (May be performed with a staff in the hands.)
Empi	Flying Swallow	Wanshu	Fast slow movements, high and low body positions, reversal of body positions.
Hangetsu	Crescent or Half Moon	Sanchin	Inside tension stance; coordination of breathing with stepping, blocking and punching; circular arm and leg movements.
Gankaku	Crane on a Rock	Chinto	Balancing on one leg; side kick; back fist strike.

Other, more advanced kata, which are frequently practiced are Sochin (Immovable), Chinte (Small Hands), Niju-shiho (24 Directions), Bassai-Sho (The Lesser Bassai), Kanku-Sho (The Lesser Kanku), Goju-Shiho-Dai (The Greater 54 Directions), Goju-Shiho-Sho (The Lesser 54 Directions), and Unsu (Hands in the Clouds or Cloud-Water).

Other basic kata practiced by many Shotokan practitioners include Taikyoku and Ten-no-kata.

Shotokan karate students must develop strong, powerful stances. Here, a class is seen practicing the kiba dachi, or straddle leg, stance. Courtesy of E. Bruno

Jiyu-ippon kumite, semi-free one point sparring, is a widely practiced exercise in Shotokan karate.

SHUKOKAI Japanese karate style founded by **Chojiro Tani,** who earlier studied **Shito-ryu** with **Kenwa Mabuni.** In 1950 Tani founded shukokai, translated as "way for all." This style focuses on speed and is well suited to competition; full control during sparring is mandatory. Shukokai stances are designed for mobility and are higher and not quite as wide as those in **Shotokan.** Practitioners, when sparring, face each other almost squarely and rely on quick whiplike movements of the hips to generate power in techniques.

TANG SOO DO Tang soo do (art of the knife hand; way of the Chinese hand) is relatively modern. Its basis, however, the Korean art of Soo Bahk Do, dates back many centuries. Tan soo do is a composite style, being 60 percent Soo Bahk Do, 30 percent northern Chinese, and 10 percent southern Chinese. Kicking techniques are based on Soo Bahk. Soo Bahk was first developed during the Silla Dynasty (A.D. 618-935), but enjoyed its flowering during the Koryo Dynasty (A.D. 935-1392).

Tang soo do is both a hard and soft style, deriving its hardness in part from Soo Bahk and its soft flowing movements from the northern Chinese systems.

The man who developed Tang Soo Do Moo Duk Kwan, Grandmaster Hwang Kee, is a martial arts prodigy, having mastered Tae Kyun (another Korean system not related to Tae Kwon Do) and Soo Bahk Do in 1936 at the age of 22. At that time, he traveled to northern China. There he encountered a Chinese variation of martial artistry called the T'ang method. From 1936 to 1945 he combined Soo Bahk Do with the T'ang method and developed what was to be known as Tang Soo Do Moo Duk Kwan.

Tang Soo Do Moo Duk Kwan (a brotherhood and school of stopping inner and outer conflict and developing virtue according to the way of the worthy hand) is not a sport. Though it is not essentially competitive, it has great combat applications. It is a classical martial art, and its purpose is to develop every aspect of the self, in order to create a mature personality who totally integrates his intellect, body, emotions and spirit. This total integration helps to creat a person who is free from inner conflict and who can deal with the outside world in a mature, intelligent, forthright and virtuous manner.

Over the past twenty years thousands of Americans have studied Tang Soo Do in Korea. Korean instructors have been sent around the world, and there are now major Tang Soo Do organizations in many countries of the world. In the U.S. the most famous Tang Soo Do practitioner is **Chuck Norris.** *Further reading: Tong Soo Do,* Hwang Kee, 1978. (JEONG SOOK LEE)

George Mattson introduced uechi-ryu karate to the United States in 1958. Courtesy of *Inside Kung-Fu*

Uechi-ryu, unlike most Japanese styles, uses predominantly circular blocks when defending against an attack. Stances are much higher than usual, with a narrow "sanchin" stance the most often used.

UECHI-RYU Okinawan system of karate founded by and named after **Kanbum Uechi,** an Okinawan who studied in the Fukien province of China from 1897 to 1910 with an instructor named Chou-Tzu-ho. He studied a style called pangai-noon (half hard/half soft) and the Phoenix-eye punch system. Uechi taught in China for two years before returning to Okinawa. In 1924 the Uechi family moved to Wakayam prefecture near Osaka, Japan, where Uechi taught his son, **Kanei Uechi,** and other Okinawans. In April 1942 Kanei returned to Okinawa and began teaching Uechi-ryu there in 1949.

Uechi-ryu is composed of interwoven movements of the tiger, crane, and dragon. It is a specialized method of self-defense that concentrates on the use of the single-knuckle punch, spear-hand strike, the pointed kick, and the circular block. The style emphasizes strong conditioning methods designed to make the body impervious to kicks or punches. The system stresses low front kicks directed to the legs and lower body. The legs as well as the arms are used to block kicks. Uechi-ryu is extremely effective for close-range fighting.

Sanchin, the first and foremost **kata** of Uechi-ryu, develops inner strength, proper stance, posture, blocking and punching ability, and composure. The other two kata that are the heart of this system are **Seisan** and sanseirui.

Uechi-ryu emphasizes sparring in its training in an unusual way. Strong grabbing techniques, coupled with takedowns, are permitted in Uechi-ryu sparring, as well as hard kicks to the legs and midsection.

George Mattson, the first American to receive a black belt from the Uechi-ryu school, in 1958, introduced this style to the U.S. that same year. Since then, hundreds of students, trained in Okinawa or by Mattson, have established Uechi-ryu schools throughout the world.

The All Okinawa Karate Federation is the major association on Okinawa to which all major styles, including Uechi-ryu, belong. The Uechi-ryu Karate-do Association is the parent organization to which all Uechi schools belong; Kanei Uechi is president. The governing U.S. body is the North American Uechi Karate Association (NAUKA), whose chairman is George Mattson. *Further reading: The Way of Karate,* George Mattson, 1962; *Uechi-Ryu Karate,* George Mattson, 1975.

WADO-RYU Japanese karate style founded in 1939 by **Hironori Ohtsuka.** Wado-ryu, meaning "way of harmony," is one of the four major Japanese karate styles and perhaps the purest form of karate-do. Steeped in classical **bujutsu,** founder Ohtsuka applied this outlook and experience to his teachings. Some of the harsher resistive elements of sparring technique, typical of most karate styles, are absent in wado-ryu. Ohtsuka rejects hardening certain parts of the body, such as hand conditioning, believing it a useless preparation. The aim of wado-ryu karate-do is not perfection of physical technique but development of a mind that is tranquil yet alive, able to react intuitively and without hesitation to any situation. In wado-ryu, as skill and knowledge are acquired through training and concentrated effort, the student is said to develop inner strength and calmness of character, as well as the virtues of self-control, respect for others, and true humility.

Karate-do for Ohtsuka is primarily a spiritual discipline: "Violent action may be understood as the way of martial arts, but the true meaning of martial arts is to seek and attain the way of peace and harmony."

Basics—punching, kicking, blocking, guarding, striking, joint twisting, and throwing techniques—**kata,** and prearranged and freestyle sparring comprise the training foundation of this system. Equally emphasized and fundamental to wado-ryu is taisabaki, body shifting to avoid the full brunt of an attack, a technique derived from swordsmanship. Blocking movements are often transformed instantly into attacks, and practitioners of this style tend to employ a large number of feints.

In 1939 Ohtsuka organized the All Japan Karate-do Federation, Wado-Kai, with headquarters in Tokyo. In 1960 **Yoshiaki Ajari,** a student of Ohtsuka, opened a non-profit, cooperative karate-do dojo in conjunction with a judo club in Hayward, Calif., the first school in the U.S. to teach the wado-ryu system. **Cecil Patterson,** who had trained with Kazuo Sakura, a high-ranking wado-ryu black belt, established in 1962 the first of an eventual chain of wado-ryu dojo in Nashville, Tenn. In April 1963 Ajari founded his own exclusively wado-ryu studio in Berkeley, Calif., which he called the University School of Karate-Berkeley Dojo. A year later, in May 1964, he formed the U.S. Wado-Kai Karate-do Federation; it is affiliated with the All Japan Karate-do Federation, Wado-Kai in Japan. In 1968, at the insistence of Ohtsuka, Patterson established the U.S. Eastern Wado-Kai Federation, headquartered in Nashville. Patterson has since served as its president and head instructor.

According to Ajari, most wado-ryu dojo in America operate independently of one another, there being no real central organization. However, instructors do cooperate and occasionally visit one another.

Jiro Ohtsuka, Ohtsuka's second son, took over as chief instructor of the wado-ryu system because of his father's advanced age. (YOSHIAKI AJARI) *Further reading: An Introduction to Wado-Ryu Karate,* Cecil T. Patterson, 1974.

WASHIN-RYU Style of empty hand karate-do based on **kubudo** (weapons way) from a Zen temple whose monks have studied it for health and self-defense for more than 400 years. While the founder of washin-ryu is unknown, Master So-An is its first known proponent; he reputedly studied under C.Y. Yen in 1569. Yen, a visiting Chinese merchant and martial artist, taught the washin-ryu monks many intricate forms, including those which employ washin-ryu's favorite weapon, the **bo** (staff).

The washin-ryu student strives to attain harmony of mind and body as a means to inner peace. Washin-ryu has no specific emphasis. As taught by **Hidy Ochiai,** the style places equal importance on form, sparring, and self-defense training.

Ochiai, the style's leader, began his martial arts training at six in a

Zen temple in Hiroshima. Earlier, Ochiai had studied with his father, said to be one of the foremost **kendo** and jujutsu masters of pre-war Japan. Ochiai learned much of what he now teaches from Kanabe Saito.

Ochiai opened his first karate school in Binghamton, N.Y. After operating three store-front dojos in the Binghamton area, Ochiai secured a permanent, 6,000 square foot, custom-built headquarters in Vestal, N.Y. It is today one of the largest martial arts facilities in the U.S. Ochiai is currently the only master teaching washin-ryu outside of the temple in Japan. He teaches thousands of active students at his headquarters and 13 affiliated branches throughout the eastern U.S. (HIDY OCHIAI)

Washin-ryu master Hidy Ochiai demonstrating a backstance.

Standing on the right is the founder of wado-ryu karate, Hironari Ohtsuka. In the middle is Shotokan master M. Nakayama, and on the left is shito-ryu master K. Mabuni.

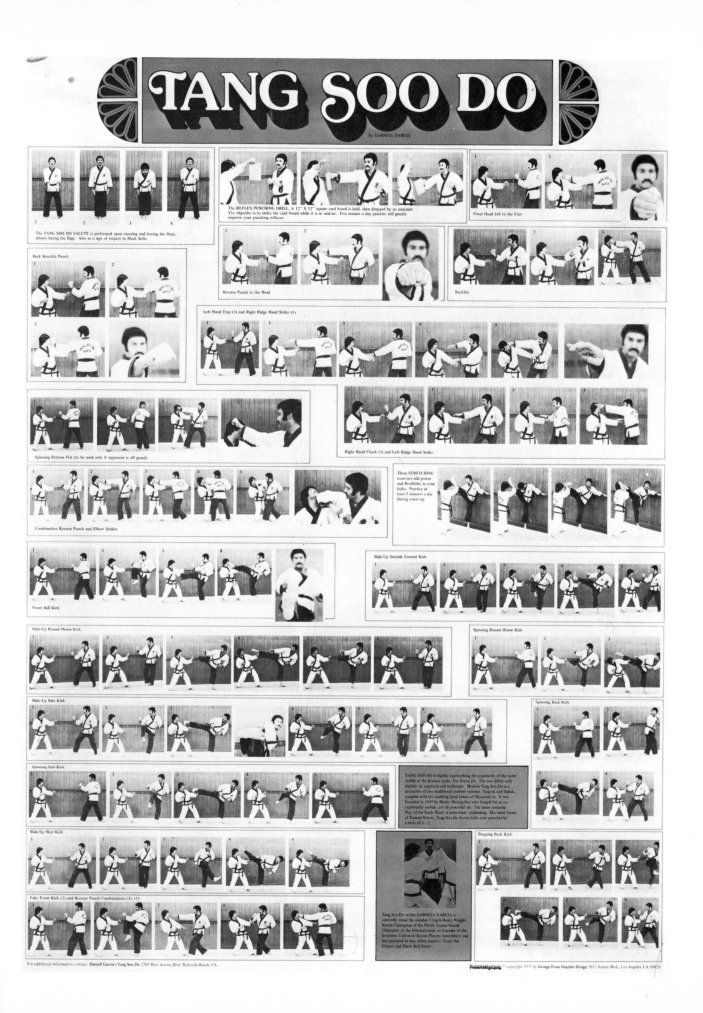

TANG SOO DO

by DARNELL GARCIA

The TANG SOO DO SALUTE is performed upon entering and leaving the Dojo, always facing the flags. Also as a sign of respect to Black Belts.

The REFLEX PUNCHING DRILL, A 12" X 12" square card board is held, then dropped by an assistant. The objective is to strike the card board while it is in mid-air. Five minute a day practice will greatly improve your punching reflexes.

Front Hand Jab to the Face

Back Knuckle Punch

Reverse Punch to the Head

Backfist

Left Hand Trap (3) and Right Ridge Hand Strike (5)

Spinning Bottom Fist (to be used only if opponent is off guard)

Right Hand Check (3) and Left Ridge Hand Strike

These STRETCHING exercises add power and flexibility to your kicks. Practice at least 5 minutes a day during warm up.

Combination Reverse Punch and Elbow Strikes

Slide-Up Outside Cresent Kick

Front Ball Kick

Slide-Up Round House Kick

Spinning Round House Kick

Slide-Up Side Kick

Spinning Back Kick

Spinning Side Kick

TANG SOO DO is rapidly approaching the popularity of the most visible of the Korean styles, Tae Kwon Do. The two differ only slightly in emphasis and technique. Modern Tang Soo Do is a derivative of two traditional combat systems: Tang-su and Subak, coupled with the crushing hand forms of Okinawan te. It was founded in 1949 by Master Hwang Kee who longed for an exceptionally mobile, yet all powerful art. The name meaning Way of the Knife Hand, is somewhat misleading - like most forms of Korean Karate, Tang Soo Do favors kicks over punches by a ratio of 3 : 2.

Slide-Up Heel Kick

Stepping Back Kick

Fake Front Kick (2) and Reverse Punch Combinations (3), (5)

Tang Soo Do stylist DARNELL GARCIA is currently rated the number 3 Light-Heavy Weight Karate Champion of the World, former Grand Champion of the Internationals, co-founder of the Southern California Karate Players Association and has appeared in box office smashes: Enter the Dragon and Black Belt Jones.

For additional information contact, Darnell Garcia's Tang Soo Do 2703 West Artesia Blvd. Redondo Beach, CA.

KENBU

Kenbu. Art of sword dancing. Dancers pantomine legendary heroes or famous **samurai** and the battles they fought. The movements, although graceful, are strong and masculine, unlike most Japanese classical dance forms.

Kenbu was formally begun during the reign of the Shogun Tokugawa Keiki (1866-68), who felt that the unemployed samurai were becoming a menace to society. To ameliorate this he sponsored Shobu, or military arts, contests among the various martial arts training halls. Warriors and the best classical singers and musicians were gathered for the occasions. Surprisingly, many samurai participated in the dances, and their combat technique improved, as well as their conduct. They studied the lives of the warriors, and reflected on how badly they had misbehaved. Samurai discovered that kenbu was excellent training in balance, timing, coordination, and breathing.

Kenbu's popularity declined abruptly in 1867, and not until 1904, when the Russo-Japanese war began, did nationalistic feeling revive it. Kenbu remained a minor art until after World War II; it is today practiced in most cities of Japan.

KENJUTSU

KENJUTSU is the art of samurai swordmasnhip; Kenjutsu schools proliferated from the 9th century onward. Many of these **ryu** appear repeatedly in the chronicles of **bujutsu.** By the end of the Tokugawa period (1600-1867), there were more than 200 active kenjutsu schools.

Notwithstanding the policy of strict secrecy adopted by various masters, the methods and techniques practiced in each school of kenjutsu were usually influenced by those popularized in other fencing schools. There was perpetual effort on the part of hundreds of experts to discover and perfect new methods in swordsmanship. Out of this effort grew a habit that was perpetuated to modern times: When a warrior had mastered one system of sword-play, he set himself to study all others by travelling through the provinces, fencing against other experts and, in the event of defeat, constituting himself the victor's student.

Competition was merciless, since defeat often meant ruin. A kenjutsu master with a well attended school and a substantial income from the lord of a fief stood to lose everything in an encounter with an itinerant expert. Victory, on the other hand, meant opportunity, income, and a prestigious position. Many a kenjutsu student risked his life repeatedly to establish a reputation that would enable him to become the leader of his own school. Naturally, there was a noticeable reluctance on the part of established sensei to partake in direct confrontations with other fencing teachers or with the wandering champions who were always ready, if not eager, to issue a challenge at the mere mention of a reputation.

Gradually, legislation was enacted to curb the bloodshed in these personal contests of fencing skill. Training with live blades in the dojo of pre-Tokugawa Japan had already been restricted to inanimate targets, such as the makiwara, made of rice straw, or to controlled kata performances—still employed in schools where kenjutsu with a live blade is practiced.

The main phase of kenjutsu was training with the katana, the regular sword. Ancient sword techniques appear to have been first systematized in 1350 by Choisai and Join. Techniques were generally divided into two groups, the first comprising cutting (kiri) and thrusting (tsuki) used in attack and counterattack, the second comprising parries used in defense. Targets were clearly identified.

According to orthodox laws of fencing, no warrior was proud of wounding an enemy in any manner other than established by strict samurai code. The long sword was to be directed at only four points: the top of the head, the wrist, the side, and the leg below the knee. Stern warnings issued by many sensei concerning the degrading use of certain practices, would seem to indicate that observance of the code was by no means a general phenomenon. Unpredictable cuts, thrusts, and parries directed against any available target; psychological ploys; and reliance upon tactical surprise were all said to have been so widely employed that they appear to have been the norm rather than the exception. Almost every student of kenjutsu fancied himself the possessor of a secret, unique, and irresistible method of penetrating every other swordsman's defense. Sensei were constantly devising new strategies for the katana, alone or in conjunction with other weapons, which accounts for the many styles associated with this weapon.

A warrior also learned the techniques of other, minor specializations of kenjutsu. He could usually fence equally well with the wakizashi (short sword) or the intermediate sword (chisa-katana), and explored in detail the efficiency of the nodachi, the long sword generally worn on the back with the handle jutting out behind the shoulder. Kenjutsu reached heights of beauty and efficiency with the simultaneous use of two blades—the katana and the wakizashi, or chisa-katana—in the two-sword style made famous by **Miyamoto Musashi** in his school, nito-ryu. Immensely difficult were those techniques which called for the use of one or two swords against several opponents armed with swords or spears. Gliding pivots and spins predominated in such exercises.

Today, of the ancient kenjutsu and all its specializations, there are only a few, strongly modified forms extant in Japan, many of which are embodied in the highly ritualized kata of **kumi-tachi.** Bouts with wooden swords, called **bokken,** are also staged between students of ancient sword disciplines. **Kendo** is the most popular modern derivation of feudal fencing. Kendo has its own weapons, techniques, ranks, and purposes, all of which are heavily impregnated with the traditions of ancient Japanese swordsmanship. *See also* kendo; sword, Japanese. *Further reading: Classical Bujutsu,* Donn F. Draeger, 1973; *Secrets of the Samurai,* Oscar Ratti and Adele Westbrook, 1973.

Kenjutsu

FORMS OF KENJUTSU

JIGEN RYU Aggressive style of **kenjutsu** founded by Togo Bizen no Kami in the 16th century; the foremost martial tradition for the Japanese warriors of Satsuma.

SHINGEN-RYU Traditional **kenjutsu** school dating from the 16th century under the patronage of the Nanbu clan.

KENDO Known as the "way of the sword," it developed from **kenjutsu** (art of the sword). Kendoka wear traditional samurai dress. The feet are bare. A **hakama** (divided skirt) is worn with a tare (apron or groin protector). The **keikogi** (kendo jacket) is similar to the one used in judo, but is worn tucked into the trousers. Hands and forearms are protected by kote (wrist gloves) and the chest is covered by a do (breastplate), held in place by cords fastened around the shoulders. Finally, the men (head-guard), a steel visor and padded cloth, protects the head, throat, and shoulders.

The kendoka uses a **shinai** (practice sword)—four polished staves of bamboo held together by a long sheath that forms the handle. There is a small leather cup at the tip and a cord to the handle holding the sword together. The shinai is sometimes as long as 3 feet 10 inches. When performing **kata,** a practitioner dispenses with body armor and wears only the hakama and keikogi, and uses the **bokken.** For important, formal demonstrations a real sword, mainly the **katana** (long sword), is often used.

The keikogi's color denotes grade. There is less emphasis on rank here than in other martial arts. A white keikogi indicates the lower **kyu** (grades), beginning at 6th and progressing to 1st. A black keikogi denotes the higher **dan** (rank), starting at 1st dan and working up ultimately to 10th. From 4th to 6th dan, a kendoka may be awarded the title of **renshi** (polished expert); and from 8th to 10th,

that of **hanshi** (master). Contest ability, mental discipline, and technical knowledge take a practitioner to 6th dan, after which advancement is obtained through teaching ability and service to the art. For the **hanshi** degree, a kendoka must make original research and take an examination set by the technical board of the **All-Japan Kendo Association.** The hanshi and renshi awards can be authorized only in Japan.

The object of a kendo contest is to land two scoring blows on a target area. There are eight target areas: o-shomen, center of the head; hidari-men, left side of the head; migi-men, right side of the head; hidari-kote, left forearm; migi-kote, right forearm; gyaku-do, left side of the rib cage; migi-do, right side of the rib cage; tsuki, the throat. All are attacked by cuts except the throat, which can be threatened only by a lunge. Competitors often use only one hand on the shinai—to obtain extra distance—but powerful blows are performed with two hands. All blows are called kiri (cuts) in which a kendoka attacks with the cutting edge of the shinai. When striking, the arms should be fully extended, hips remaining square to the target. After striking, the shinai should slide freely up the target without being disengaged.

The **kiai** (yell) is even more important in kendo than in other martial arts. A score cannot be registered without the shout that accompanies the blow. The kiai has three functions: attack, to aid mental and physical coordination, and to unnerve the opponent.

HISTORY

Kendo originated more than 1,500 years ago. The first references to kenjutsu, in fact, are contained in the three volumes of the Kojiki, a medieval history. The earliest reference to any non-lethal practice weapon is about 400 A.D., and the weapon mentioned was the bokken (wooden sword), whose weight, length, and balance were approximately the same as the real one.

Kenjutsu

Like other Japanese martial arts, kendo has innumerable **ryu** (schools). The earliest of these was **Nen-ryu,** founded in 1350. There is some dispute as to who originated the style; some authorities claim **Kamisaka Yasuhisa** and others **Somashior Yoshimoto.** This particular style was taught until the 18th century by the Higuchi family, but has now disappeared. In the 20th century kendo has spread to most parts of the world, including Europe and North and South America. Apart from Japan, the U.S., Canada, and Brazil are the strongest nations.

Kendo, as practiced today, is neither a fighting art nor a pure sport; many consider it primarily a spiritual discipline. Many instructors claim the real purpose of kendo is to learn to settle the problems of life without ever having to draw the sword. *See also* kenjutsu. *Further reading: Fundamental Kendo,* All Japan Kendo Federation, 1973; *Asian Fighting Arts,* Donn F. Draeger and Robert W. Smith, 1969; *Modern Bujutsu and Budo,* Donn F. Draeger, 1974; *Secrets of the Samurai,* Oscar Ratti and Adele Westbrook, 1973; *Martial Arts of the Orient,* Roald Knutsen, 1975; *This is Kendo,* Junzo Sasamori and Gordon Warner, 1964; *Official Karate Magazine,* Nov. 1968.

GEKKEN Common name for **kendo** (way of the sword) during the Meiji era (1868-1912) in Japan. While higher institutions of learning preferred to develop what they called kendo, gekken was used by militarists to bolster a sense of nationalism among the people.

HOKUSHIN ITTO RYU Style of **kendo** (art of the sword).

HOZAN-RYU Style of **kendo** (way of the sword).

KEN-NO-MICHI Variant of the word **kendo** (way of the sword) that arose in the early Tokugawa period, from about 1600-1750.

KENDO, FOUR POISONS OF The four deep-rooted emotional or intellectual problems to be overcome in kendo; fear, doubt, surprise, and confusion. By resolutely confronting many opponents, a student tries to foster objectivity and a calmness of mind in which every situation is perceived with equal clarity.

KUM DO Korean sword art and sport identical to Japanese **kendo.** The **Korean Kum Do Association** was established in June 1948, and the National Kum Do Championships were inaugurated in 1953. The foremost kum do master is Haksuh Jung.

KUMITACHI Sword exercise practiced in Japan as long ago as A.D. 789, when kumitachi entered the curriculum of the sons of kuge, or noblemen, at the capital city of Nara. The introduction of kumitachi is still commemorated each year in the Boy's Festival held on May 5, and marked annually by a large **kendo** meeting in Kyoto.

NIHON KENDO KATA "Japan Kendo Formal Exercise." Known as the Dai Nippon Teikoku Kendo Kata (Great Japan Imperial Kendo Formal Exercise) when it was founded in 1912, it consists of 12 techniques, 9 with the odachi (long sword) and 3 with the kodachi (short sword). This kata, created by a cross-section of high-ranking swordsmen of the **Butokukai,** is the foundation of all modern kendo practice.

SHINAI-GEIKO Swordsmanship training using the **shinai.** It was developed during the latter Edo period (early 1700s) in Japan and is the direct forerunner of modern **kendo.** Opponents attacked each other vigorously but always observing certain rules to ensure safety. Kaho, or prearranged forms, was reduced in importance. *Further reading: Modern Bujutsu and Budo,* Donn F. Draeger, 1974.

KIAIJUSTU

Kiajustu is combat based upon the employment of the voice as a weapon. Even in feudal Japan, where the merely mystical was commonplace, the art of **kiai** was considered esoteric. Kiai, like **aiki,** embraces the familiar concepts of harmony and spirit, or energy. The word itself denotes a condition in which two minds are

A blow directly in the center of the head is one of the eight point areas that score in kendo.

Kendo training in Japan. Courtesy of E. Bruno

united into one in such a way that the stronger controls the weaker.

Unfortunately, very little is known in Japan, and even less elsewhere, about the art of kiai. There are many examples in the annals of the martial arts, especially in connection with **kenjutsu** (art of the sword), of extraordinary powers displayed by self-styled experts— though perhaps only expert in the arts of misrepresentation. Indirect indications suggest that **Zen** masters were particularly accomplished teachers of kiai.

The shout has undoubtedly been one of man's first reactions to danger, whether in an effort to summon assistance or to warn friends. In the east, from India to China, Tibet, Korea, and Japan, the tactical value of the shout in determining or influencing the outcome in battle has never been underestimated. The shout that the Japanese warrior endeavored to develop and control summoned all his powers, fused and channeled through the pitch, tone, and vibration of his voice. Quality, not volume, seems to have been the essential element. Long years of training were required to produce the exact vocal integration that reportedly could kill, defeat, or even cure. *See also* ki. *Further reading: Secrets of the Samurai,* Oscar Ratti and Adele Westbrook, 1973; *Kick Illustrated,* Aug.-Oct. 1981.

Kendo

KOBU-JUTSU

Kobu-Jutsu, also known as Ryukyukobu-jutsu, an outgrowth of Okinawan karate, is a style that employs a variety of weapons, primarily the bo (staff), sai (short sword), nunchaku (flail), tonfa (handle), and kama (sickle).

MAJOR WEAPONS: Bo (staff). Known also as the rokushakubo, the bo can be a formidable weapon. The Okinawan staff is a smooth 6 foot length of hard oak with tapered ends. (Length was limited by the ceiling height in Okinawan rooms, so the weapons could be handled indoors.) There is a distinction between Okinawan staff techniques and Japanese **bojutsu** (art of the staff). The former relies on the body for increased power while the latter concentrates more on the weapon itself.

Kata is the heart of Okinawan bo practice; the best known is Sakugawa-no-kon, created several hundred years ago by "Tode" Sakugawa. More recent kata is Sueyoshi-no-kon, named after Sueyoshi, a contemporary of **Gichin Funakoshi.**

Sai (short sword). A short pointed weapon, made from metal. Usually between 15 and 20 inches in length, it weighs from one to three pounds. The shaft may be pointed or blunted. It has two tapered tines projecting from the main shaft opposite each other, and bent toward the forward end of the weapon. While its exact origin is uncertain, it has been traced to southern China and even to Indonesia, where it is known as **tjabang.** Sailors probably introduced the sai to Okinawa. The weapon was much used in the waterfront areas of Naha and Tomari. Prior to 1870 it was carried by Okinawan police. Only elite units were issued the sai, normal constables being equipped with the bo. Usually three sai were carried, in case one was lost in struggle or thrown.

Of all the kobu-jutsu weapons, the sai most readily lends itself to karate. Almost all the hand techniques can be performed with the sai; blocks particularly can be augmented with the steel shaft of the sai fixed along the forearm. Sai techniques, however, require practice in strikes, wrist snaps, thrusts with both ends, drawing the weapon, flipping the weapon, and so on.

A variation of the weapon is the manji-no-sai in which one tine, or fork, is reversed and the shaft pointed at both ends. The manji-no-sai is sometimes lashed to a bo to produce a composite weapon.

Kama (sickle). A long handle of wood tapering at the butt for a secure grip; to its top is affixed a curved blade at right angles; the blade has a single edge on the inside of the arc. Unlike Japanese sickles, there is no hand guard. Although the weapon can be used singly, it is customarily employed in pairs. Because the weapon is potentially dangerous to the user, in most dojos only advanced students train with the sickle. In the hands of a novice the sharp blades moving around at head level could be fatal.

Blocks and deflections are performed with the shaft or by hooking with the blade. Offensive maneuvers include chopping attacks to the kidney and throat. At close range the weapon is often reversed, the shaft lying along the forearm, blade pointing outward like an extension of the elbow. In this fashion the user simply employs karate type elbow-strikes to his attacker. The kama is practiced in kata (formal exercises).

Tonfa (handle). A weapon of agricultural origin, also known as the tui-fa or ton-kwa, it was used to grind grain. Normally grasped by short handles, it is possible to use a reverse grip, called yaku-te, in which the shaft is held and the projecting handles are used to hook, smash, and deflect.

The basic action is a crisp rotation of the shaft in a full or half strike, vertically or horizontally. Thrusts and blocks can be executed with the shaft along the forearm, or by striking out to block an oncoming attack.

Nunchaku (flail). Composed of two pieces of hard wood, usually connected by rope or chain, this weapon is usually about 14 inches in length. The length of the connecting links is critical because it controls the swing-arc of the weapon. In earlier times, the link was leather, silk, horse hair, rope, chain, or kanda vine. Today, nylon parachute cord is most often used.

The nunchaku can be employed like a baton, chiefly at close range, with both rods held in the same hand. But the singular feature

The bo vs. the sai.

The kama vs. the sword.

The nunchaku.

of the nunchaku are swing techniques, called furi waza. Its arcs, loops, and patterns produce a bewildering barrier to an opponent. Within patterns are blocks, chokes, locks, and strikes. Because of the variety of its techniques, the weapon is ideal for defense. Arms and knees are struck to inflict maximum damage. There are no traditional nunchaku kata; some instructors have introduced their own forms.

MINOR WEAPONS: Timbei (shield). An oval or circular shield used in conjunction with a short spear, rochin, sometimes seen in traditional island dances. One of its more interesting maneuvers is a roll on the ground, over the shield, bringing it up to cover and slicing the leg tendons with the rochin.

Eku (oar). Used by island boatmen, the eku is employed much as the bo (staff), with few modifications owing to its odd shape. One technique involves shoveling a blinding cloud of sand into an opponent's eyes prior to attacking with the narrow end. Also known as the tusuna-gake.

Surushin (weighted chain). A length of forged chain with a weight attached to either end, identical in design to the Japanese **manriki-gusari,** it is used in similar fashion.

Teko (knuckleduster; brass knuckles). Usually employed in pairs, the basic technique is a punch to the face terminating in a rapid ripping vibration.

Pair of kamas.

The tonfa vs. the bo.

KUNG-FU

Kung-fu means simply skill or ability, such as that possessed by a painter, cook, or an adept in the fighting arts; the term refers to no specific style or martial art. Some feel its synonymity with the martial arts is a recent vogue originating in Hong Kong and Kwangtung province. But as early as the 17th century, the Jesuit priest, Pere Amiot, wrote of the "peculiar exercises," which he called "Cong Fou," practiced by the Taoist priests of his area. A more precise term for the martial arts in China is **wu shu,** although there have been other terms used in China through the years whose meanings are equally clear. **Kuo-shu,** according to the martial historian **Robert W. Smith,** was a popular term until 1928; kuo-chi has also been used. (Terms such as chien-shu (way of the sword), tao-fa (way of the knife), or **ch'uan-fa** (way of the fist) do not signify a martial art.) Wu shu is currently the official term for martial arts adopted by the People's Republic of China.

Kung-fu is composed of a number of martially inspired systems for fighting, health development, and dance. There are several hundred styles of kung-fu; most, however, were formed around a more limited number of approaches to a specific subject, be it combat, health, or whatever. Some systems of kung-fu emphasize strenuous, energetic kicking and punching, while others stress more subtle techniques. Indeed, some are nearly static.

At first glance, there are three main types of kung-fu: for fighting, for show, for health. Classification becomes progressively more complex under the surface. Styles can be divided and classified roughly by geographical origin, religious tenets, and technical genre (e.g., linear, circular, etc.). Kung-fu also was influenced to varying degrees by smaller factions of specific periods, non-religious and military organizations, family clans, and theatrical and operatic troupes. Thus kung-fu is just too extensive, too deeply embedded in Chinese culture to be sensibly sketched. It would be highly impractical to include all the medicines, weapons, techniques, historically significant events, personalities, and terminology that have played important parts in the development of kung-fu. The nomenclature alone requires, for its study, a respectable amount of at least one dialect of the Chinese language.

Exactly when kung-fu first surfaced is not known, though the subject continues to be disputed. Some traditional historians date it as far back as the Shang dynasty (16th century B.C.) Others place it in the period of the Contending States (475-221 B.C.) and the Yellow Emperor, Huang Ti. Perhaps its origins are bound up in the unique way China learned to absorb aspects of her conquerors' cultures. Contemporary kung-fu certainly exhibits distinct traces of Mongolian, Tibetan, Indian, and other cultural ideologies.

Geography also played an enormous role in kung-fu's development. Those who lived in the tropical rain forests of the south, for instance, would naturally develop different approaches to living and thinking than those who nomadically wandered the arid northern plains.

With the collapse of the Ch'ing dynasty and the establishment of the People's Republic of China (PRC), many changes have taken place in kung-fu as an institution. All thought of using the art, now called a sport, as an implement of war is considered incorrect. The aims of the PRC are to make kung-fu conducive to competition and available to large numbers of people.

Thus far, kung-fu has been classified by geography (e.g., northern and southern) and philosophical roots (e.g., Buddhist, Taoist, communist). The systems may be further subdivided by the way in which they deal with force (e.g., the internal family in the south, and the external family in the north). All of these general categories are useful for making distinctions among styles presently used for fighting (e.g., the **Hop-Gar** style), for gymnastics or theater (Chang-Ch'uan and other styles from the PRC), or for health (e.g., **t'ai-chi-ch'uan**). Styles may be again divided by techniques employed: those based on linear movement (from which karate sprang), or circular movement, or long-arm and short-arm systems.

The northern, Buddhist systems leaned more toward the linear, with short-hand tactics built upon series of linear attacks and retreats; they rely on strength and speed. Southern, Taoist systems were markedly more circular, with both long- and short-arm styles employing intricately patterned footwork. While not contesting the northern notion that a straight line is the shortest distance between two

Cynthia Rothrock using the double hook swords, one of the many weapons in kung-fu.

To be loose and limber is a requirement of many kung-fu systems. The leg is used to attack targets such as the head.

Many kung-fu styles involve intricate body movements. Most of these movements are attempts to imitate the fighting styles of animals, such as the tiger, snake, praying mantis, crane. Courtesy of *Inside Kung-Fu*

Erick Lee *(right)* showing the fighting aspect of kung-fu with John Corcoran. Courtesy of *Inside Kung-Fu*

Grandmaster Ark Y. Wong

points, southern adherents maintain it is not necessarily the most *practical* technique. The circular, internal, soft systems were based on timing and internal strength, as opposed to speed and muscular strength. (Slight lateral angles or simple, circular hand maneuvers do not make a circular system; styles claiming otherwise have lost track not only of their lineage, but of their very essence.)

The Shao-lin and t'ai-chi-ch'uan styles of kung-fu are often pointed to as exemplary of northern and southern Chinese styles. Shao-lin represents the hard style of the north, while t'ai-chi, the soft southern style. As a geographic shorthand, one may remember, but with reservation, the kung-fu expression, "nan-ch'uan pei-t'ui" (hands in the south, kicks in the north). Between the two extremes lie many degrees of hard, soft, long-arm, and short-arm systems.

It is difficult to say which styles may have originated for combat, which for show, and which for health. Fighting is in vogue now, except in the PRC, and at the moment nearly every style claims to be a combat system. Some noted **sifu** (teacher, instructor) have separated the fighting systems from the more theatrical styles by the terms "wide" and "narrow" kung-fu. In this classification scheme, a style that employs a large number of movements to link a single defensive maneuver to each possible attack is called "narrow," and, as a system, is placed in the non-fighting category. "Wide" kung-fu, on the other hand, employs fewer moves, but relies on "changes," or alternative uses, of a technique. One may note the relative simplicity of **wing-chun, Pat Mei, Tibetan white crane,** or Hop-Gar, all of which, using this scheme, would be considered fighting styles. Hop-Gar, for instance, has only 24 hand techniques instead of the hundreds found in some narrow styles.

Thus, the classification of kung-fu systems into northern, southern, internal, external, long-arm, short-arm, soft, hard, wide, or narrow is generally accepted and understood as it relates to actual performance in a given style. Classifications by philosophical promptings— Confucian, Taoist, Buddhist, or communist—is not thought germane. And classification by originating intent—martial, theatrical, or medicinal—is controversial.

But there are numerous subdivisions relating directly to the specialized techniques for which a particular system or school was known. Although a proficient boxer studied a variety of systems, often traveling from province to province seeking different styles and teachers, nearly every boxer of repute made use of a special technique he favored over all others. It might have been a technique of the sword, or some other weapon; it may have been a hand tactic, a kick, or any number of other techniques. Master Ku-Yu-Cheong, for example, specialized in the iron palm; Cheng-Hua of the Hung-Gar style in the tiger-tail kick; Lau-Fat-Mang in the Chin-na hand of the Eagle Claw Fan-Tzu system; and so on. A specializing student often broke with his original school to found a new style or branch revolving around his specialty. These specialized hand or foot maneuvers then became the trademark of the style. A person who trained certain parts of his arm or hand, for instance, could be identified with a specific style. Like the differences in the salutation or the uniform, a specialty became the index of yet another distinction within kung-fu.

Four great philosophical systems stand out as primary influences in kung-fu's development. First was Confucianism, with its ancient theories of change acting upon the principles of full and empty, or **yin and yang** (often traced to the ruler Fu-Hsi, who lived during the Chou dynasty, ca. 900-800 B.C.). Taoism, the second, promoted philosophical, magical, and religious transformation within a Confucian cosmology. Mahayana Buddhism, the third influence, absorbed some of both, moving into the Taoist sections of northern and eastern China in the form of Chan Buddhism and assimilating itself into the western Tibetan tantric faith.

"Tao," "the way," appears in the poetic Taoist text, **Tao-Te-Ching** (The Way and the Power), which asserts that when life takes its natural course, harmony with nature and the correct flow of existence are assured. Achieving harmony with Tao requires first achieving harmony within one's self.

By the 1st century A.D., Taoism had acquired a strong flavor of magic, and alchemical practices emerged, which were greatly to affect the martial arts. Taoist alchemy sought immortality through the cultivation of the life force known as **ch'i** (air, breath—a concept probably introduced by the Chinese philosopher Mencius, born about 100 years after the death of Confucius). Ch'i was thought to be a spiritual or psychic energy giving substance to all things, acting through the **five elements:** wood, fire, earth, metal, water. The ei-jya (also **nei-chia**), or internal family of kung-fu styles, was constructed around such beliefs. The gold of Chinese alchemists was in the soul. Techniques for manipulating psychic and spiritual qualities comprised an enormous segment of not only Taoist religion but also of Chinese traditional medicine (which overlaps kung-fu).

Special meditative exercises were used in kung-fu for the conversion of elements. They varied in form and usually required an experienced teahcer. Ch'i was drawn up through the base of the spine, called the "first gate," and circulated through the body. Passing through the second gate, between the kidneys, the third gate, in the back of the head, and finally down the front of the body, it returned to its origin. Circulation and breath control were to draw generative forces, related to man's sexual nature, into the lower t'an-t'ien cavity, called the "cavity of the dragon" or the "golden stove." Here, ch'i was converted into an alchemical agent that completed the process, first in the middle t'an-t'ien, called the "yellow hall," then in the brain. In t'ieh-sha-chang, the **Iron palm,** a dramatic example of such kung-fu alchemy, the ch'i force was drawn from the t'an-t'ien, to the palm of the hand. A relaxed slap with the open palm would suffice, as in the case of Ku-Yu-Cheong of the northern **Shao-lin** school, to shatter the spine of a wild horse.

During the magical phase of Taoism, just pre-dating the appearance of Buddhism, a surgeon named **Hua-T'o** (A.D. 190-165) laid the groundwork for the southern, long-hand styles of kung-fu. Making animal attitudes his mental and physical models, and adopting Taoist breathing techniques, Hua-T'o developed a set of gymnastics called the wu-ch'in-hsi (frlic of the five animals). This system was later refined by Tai-Chung, first emperor of the Sung dynasty.

The later Han dynasty, dissolving in the warring upheaval that produced the era of the Three Kingdoms (A.D. 220-280), witnessed a surge of Buddhist missionaries flooding into China with Mahayana doctrine. By the 4th century A.D. the religion had captured the favor of the Chinese, especially in the north, where governmental instability produced special sympathy for the Buddhist's optimistic doctrines. The south, however, maintained a decidedly more Taoist philosophy. As a result, a hybrid form of Buddhism, called Chan in Chinese and **Zen** in Japanese, emerged, exhibiting a Buddhist structure but with Taoist embellishments.

As these religious developments occurred, the effects upon kung-fu were marked. In the 6th century A.D. the monk Ta-Mo (**Bodhidharma** in Indian) of the Chan school came to the Shao-lin monastery in the Shao-Shi mountains of Honan province. Legends of Ta-Mo in Chinese mythology are elaborate. He was, for example, said to have sat staring at a cave wall for nine years in meditation. After accidentally falling asleep, he became so angered with himself that he tore off his eyelids and cast them to the ground. Tea shrubs grew from where his eyelids fell, and thereafter, the monks of the temples used tea to deter sleep.

Ta-Mo may have authored the series of 18 exercises contained in a manuscript, the **I-Chin-Ching,** outlining the Shao-lin method of Chinese boxing. The method that emerged from the Shao-lin Temple, which is representative of the northern Chinese styles in general, was called the "wai-jya" (also **wai-chia**), or external family of Chinese boxing. Noted for its harsh training, and in contrast to southern forms of boxing, Shao-lin strove to increase speed, strength, and elasticity. It was vigorous and calisthenic, and became the basis from which karate, in Okinawa, and the Korean martial arts were derived.

See also Bodhidharma; ch'i, five elements; Hua-T'o; Hop-Gar; I-Chin-Ching; iron palm; karate; kuo-shu; nei-chia; Pak-Mei; sifu; t'ai-chi-ch'uan; Tao-Te-Ching; Tibetan white crane; wai-chia; wing-chun; wu shu; yin and yang. (MICHAEL P. STAPLES) Further reading: Chinese Medicine, Huard and Wong, 1968; Stretching and Kicking Techniques, James Lew, 1977; Basic Broadsword, Mark-Bow-Sim, 1976; Modified Tai-Chi-Ch'uan, Mark-Bow-Sim, 1977; Hop Gar Kung-Fu, Michael P. Staples, 1976; Tibetan Kung-Fu, Michael P. Staples, 1976; White Crane Gung-Fu, Michael P. Staples, 1974; Wu Shu of China, Michael P. Staples and Anthony Chan, 1976.

KUNG-FU, WESTERN MIGRATION OF Many historians trace kung-fu's origin to the **Shao-lin Temples** of China, but actually kung-fu, or **wu shu,** the proper name for the Chinese martial arts, extends much further back in the middle kingdom's history. The temples housed a large number of kung-fu styles, but many others were born in Taoist retreats, Tibetan lamaseries, and non-religious military encampments.

Much of the Shao-lin's colorful reputation as being the birthplace of kung-fu originates in the Ch'ing dynasty, when many of the temples were used as training camps and hideouts for anti-government revolutionaries. Kung-fu flourished as a means of uniting underground organizations like the pa-kua and harmonious fist sects, established to answer Chu-Hung-Tang's call to overthrow the Ching and restore the Ming government to power (see Triads).

The decline of the Ch'ing dynasty brought revolutionary uprisings led by kung-fu societies, culminating in the Boxer Rebellion. Many kung-fu practitioners fled the country, their alternative being a gruesome death by torture.

Dating back to early California, in the days following the gold rush of 1848, kung-fu was an integral part of the lifestyle in Chinese labor camps and mining towns. Activity increased dramatically in 1863 with the importation of Chinese laborers to work on the Central Pacific Railroad. The center of Chinese migration was San Francisco, which now boasts the second-largest Chinese population outside mainlaind China (Hong Kong is first).

Within four years after the first Chinese arrived in California in 1848, the Chinese population had multiplied to 25,000. With them came the benevolent society structure, first appearing in the form of the Chinese Six Companies—comparable to a traveler's aid society—then in the form of Tong brotherhoods, which were overseas extensions of the old country secret societies. With the Tong, kung-fu had unquestionably arrived in America.

Within the Tong factions, bitter conflict over who would control gambling, prostitution, and the like was commonplace. The results were the notorious "tong wars" between rival societies, which did not completely end until 1906.

These internecine wars, much like the struggles between different Mafia families, were fought by "hatchetmen." They were in reality hit men or assassins who used hatchets and meat cleavers to slay their targets. They were also skilled at kung-fu, at the art of "pin-blowing," and at the throwing of lethal razor-sharp coins. Later, these hatchetmen remained in the U.S. and made their livelihood as a secretive group. Since, obviously, they never became legal American citizens, it is impossible to trace them or their transmission of kung-fu.

Any accurate attempt at tracing the early practice of kung-fu in the U.S. would therefore prove fruitless. The American-Chinese societies that sponsored kung-fu practices limited participation to those of immediate ancestry. The slow opening of it to non-Chinese did not take place until two decades after World War II, in the early 1960s.

Early kung-fu schools in America perpetuated the secret society mystique. Few people, even Chinese, were allowed to study the art. As time passed, however, the strict tenets eased and kung-fu slowly came into the public light. Shao-lin was probably the first style to emerge through teachers such as **Alan Lee** of New York, **Ark-Yueh Wong** of Los Angeles, and T.Y. Wong of San Francisco.

T'ai-chi ch'uan instructor Tinn Chan Lee was the first known Chinese sifu to have opened his teachings to the Hawaiian general public when he initiated his classes in Honolulu in 1957. The aforementioned Ark-Yueh Wong is largely credited by the martial arts media for breaking from the traditional "color line" in Los Angeles in 1964 and accepting students of all races.

Choy-Li-Fut and t'ai-chi ch'uan on the mainland U.S. soon followed suit, then the various branches of northern and southern Shao-lin. Sifus Peter Quong and **Brendan Lai** were instrumental in establishing the praying mantis system in northern California, as Y.C. Wong did the Hung Gar and tiger crane systems; Kuo-Lien-Ying did t'ai-chi ch'uan; **George Long** did the white crane style; and Lau Bun and the Luk Mo Studio did the Choy-Li-Fut style.

Throughout the U.S., kung-fu spread gradually, then rapidly during the **Bruce Lee** era of the early and mid-1970s. During this period, due to Lee's films and television's Kung-Fu series, the Chinese martial arts reached an all time apex in popularity. But the vast majority of styles remain secluded even today. (MICHAEL P. STAPLES) See also: U.S., history of karate in; motion pictures and television. Further reading: Karate's History and Traditions, Bruce Haines, 1968.

FORMS OF KUNG FU

BAK-SING CHOY-LI-FUT A combination of two of China's most renowned martial arts styles: Choy-Li-Fut and northern Shao-lin. Bak-sing was founded by Tam-Sam during the Ch'ing dynasty. Tam-Sam had learned the Hung-Sing style of Choy-Li-Fut. Hung-Sing had been a student of the founder of the style, Chan Heung, who had combined the three family systems of Chou, Li, and Fut into the Choy-Li-Fut system.

Master Ku, a kung-fu practitioner famous for his remarkable "iron palm" was challenged by Tam-Sam to fight. Ku accepted, but neither fighter could best the other. They became friends, and Tam-Sam merged his Choy-Li-Fut style with Ku's Shao-lin, christening it the bak-sing Choy-Li-Fut system.

Bak-sing places heavy emphasis on sparring, kicking and long-arm movements. A wide horse stance is most often used and force is believed to come mostly from the waist and shoulders. Many techniques involve simultaneous blocking and punching, or blocking and kicking. Bak-sing techniques are graceful and the fluidity of the supple long-arm movements, combined with the speed and dexterity of the quick, short-hand techniques, give this style a very artistic appearance. (MICHAEL P. STAPLES) *Further reading: Inside Kung Fu,* May 1975.

CH'A CH'UAN is an ancient Chinese martial art, considered a Northern style. Practitioners contend from long range, darting swiftly to the attack. High, long leaps are important in ch'a ch'uan to cover distances quickly. Not widely practiced in China today, it was developed in the 14th to the 17th centuries by Chinese Moslems of Sinkiang, Chinghai, and Kansu, in the west and south of China, and is primarily still practiced by them.

CH'O CHIAO Northern Chinese style of kung-fu originating in the Gao-Yang county of Hopei province, where it is still practiced. Ch'o chiao contains difficult, high-kicking movements, perhaps more than any other system of kung-fu. Because of its flamboyance, the style is suited to the Chinese opera, whose members are often practitioners. Wang-Yu is a famous exponent of the style in China.

CHOW-GAR Style of kung-fu from southern China. It was founded by Chow Lung, who learned **hung-gar,** one of the five basic southern systems originating in the Shao-lin Temple, from his uncle, who added the **pa-kua** (eight trigrams) staff maneuvers to his nephew's training before passing away. The Choy style was taught to him by Choy-Kau. Later, after a three-year residence in one of the Shao-lin temples, he opened his own school in Canton. In 1915 Gen. Lee-Fook-Lam appointed Chow-Lung an instructor in the Chinese Army.

CHOY-LI-FUT Cantonese name for a popular southern Chinese kung-fu system. Choy-Li-Fut derives from the **Shao-lin Temple.**

In Choy-Li-Fut the contenders oppose from some distance, which requires of each the proficient and expert development of long-hand abilities, as well as firm and solid grounding of the body, though the feet must be versatile. The arms are wielded freely and powerfully in a variety of styles: uppercut blows, backfist strikes, roundhouse blows, and overhead foreknuckle thrusts.

The Baat Gaw lance, willow leaf double swords, and "18" staff may be used in this aggressive kung-fu style. *See also* bak-sing Choy-Li-Fut. (MICHAEL P. STAPLES)

CRANE STYLE Also called hok or hork yang; form of kung-fu utilizing one-legged stance. *See also* white crane (Tibetan style).

DRUNKEN STYLE System of Chinese fighting patterned after the conventional movements of a drunkard. The actions appear wild and illogical. The practitioner wobbles unsteadily and occasionally seems to stumble to the ground, where he will lash out with a combination of foot and leg techniques.

Many styles have drunken sets, which are reserved for the highest levels of training. There is a drunken monkey set, a drunken praying mantis set, a drunken white crane set, and so on. The Eight Drunken Fairies set—extremely difficult—was developed by the famous eagle claw master Lau-Fat-Mang, who used it to win the competition at civil examinations in Peking. (MICHAEL P. STAPLES) *See also* t'sui-ch'uan.

EAGLE CLAW SYSTEM Style of kung-fu visible in the highly acrobatic fann tzu system. Teaching the style for the famous Ching Wu (jing Mo, in Cantonese) Athletic Association in Shanghai, China, Grandmaster Liu Fa Mang catapulted the style to its present popularity.

FAN-TZU Northern style of kung-fu; dates at least to the Ming period. It is very simple in its approach. Also called ba-fan.

FIVE ELDERS Style of kung-fu; also, the five priests who escaped the burning of the original **Shao-lin Temple.**

FONG NGAN Style of Chinese kung-fu, known as the Phoenix Eye, originating in China's Hopu province and developed by Kew Soong. In the fong ngan system, the basic blow is delivered with the fore-knuckle fist (from which the style takes its name). Palm fist, finger poke, ridge hand, and knife hand techniques also are taught. The style's only kick is the front snap kick, delivered low to the groin area. There are no formal stances in the style. Instead, practitioners learn to crowd an opponent, enticing him to make a wrong move.

A fong ngan practitioner never retreats from an attack, but moves into it or, if necessary, jumps to the side while counterattacking. Fong ngan employs tripping and leg-hooking throws, techniques that are always followed up by a "killing" blow or strike. The style emphasizes **kuen** (forms), proper breathing, speed, and form. There are four-man and two-man exercises, the latter closely resembling sparring.

FU-CHIAO PAI A tiger claw system of kung-fu; the style emulates the movement of the tiger. There is a fu-chiao federation in New York City headed by Wai Hong.

HOP GAR Also known as Lama kung-fu, Hop-Gar became prominent during the Ch'ing dynasty in China as the official martial system of the Manchu Emperor and his guard. It was, and still is, a style for fighting, not for exercise or dancing. More than three hundred years ago, in the Ming dynasty, a Tibetan priest named Dai-Dot laid the groundwork for the Lama kung-fu style, creating the "lion roar" martial system. According to legend, Dai-Dot was stricken with enlightenment one day and, pointing one finger toward the sky and one toward the earth, he fell to his hands and knees and roared like a lion.

Lion roar, composed of eight fists, eight steps, eight fingers, eight grips, and eight kicks, was taught in the Ting-Juck-Lui-Yam Temple by the Kay-Lam Buddha. Lama passed through many generations of Tibetan priests at the temple before reaching the hands of the Lama Jickbowloklowtow, whose Chinese name was Ng-Mui, a famous personality in Chinese kung-fu novels. He is credited with devising the mui-fa-jeong (plumflower stumps) atop which kung-fu was practiced.

The Lama style is composed of four main subdivisions: **white crane,** ta-mo, wei-t'ol, and law-horn. Ng-Mui taught the complete Lama style to only one student, named Hing-Duk, leaving his four other disciples to make full styles of their respective subdivisions.

Hing-Duk passed the Lama style to Wong-Yan-Lum, who brought it to the emperor's palace in Peking, where he was employed to instruct the Imperial guard. When the Manchu dynasty collapsed, Wong left the Forbidden City and changed the style's name to Hop-Gar. To establish a reputation in southern China, he constructed a stage in Canton, challenging all comers and besting more than 150 kung-fu masters. For this he gained the number-one seat in the

Two of the stances used in Hop-Gar kung-fu.

prestigious group of martial artists known as the Canton-Ten-Tigers.

Wong-Yan-Lum passed the Hop-Gar style to Ng-Yim-Ming, who brought it to the U.S. Ng-Yim-Ming, before his death in the early 1970s, appointed one official representative to carry on the Hop-Gar system, Chin-Dai-Wei (David Chin).

Hop-Gar is composed of 12 short-hand and 12 long-hand maneuvers, and 8 forms employing empty-hand and weaponry techniques. The most important aspect of the style is its footwork, called kay-men-bo, used atop Ng-Mui's mui-fa-jeong, a series of stumps driven into the ground. Technique and form, according to Hop-Gar philosophy, are a means to an end; one learns through formalized training but, finally becomes free, discarding all that is not natural and spontaneous. (MICHAEL P. STAPLES)

HOU CH'UAN Northern Chinese style of kung-fu requiring great agility; the monkey style of kung-fu. *See also* ta-sheng pi-kua.

HSING-I; HSING-YI Literally, the "mind form" style, a kung-fu system found chiefly in the north, originating in San-Shih province. It spread to Hepei, then to Hunan, and eventually reached Peking. Based on the five-element philosophy of Chinese cosmology, it is a simple, practical style. Major weapons in hsing-i are the knife (tao) and sword (chien). It uses single movements in training, repeated on both left and right sides, and contains short basic forms, unlike other northern systems.

Important figures in the Hepei style (which stems from the San-Shih, original style) are Li-Tsun-I, who taught San-Yuen-Shiang, who taught Tsau-Ke-Li, Chiao-Liang-Feng (now in Taiwan), and Adam Hsu (in San Francisco). Contemporaries of Li-Tsun-I were Sun-Lu-

Tang, who taught Shuen-Chian-Yuen, now in the People's Republic of China; and Chiao-Liang-Feng, who taught Li-Ming-Shan, now in Taiwan. (MICHAEL P. STAPLES) *Further reading: Hsing-I, Chinese Mind-Body Boxing,* Robert W. Smith, 1974; *Inside Kung Fu,* Oct. 1982.

HUNG-CHIA Southern style of Chinese kung-fu stressing powerful hand techniques, delivered from strong low stances. As the story goes, five monks, called the **Five Ancestors,** escaped from the **Shao-lin Temple** during its destruction by government troops. One monk, Chi-Sim, made his way to southern China, taking refuge among the boat people, where he was recruited by a floating opera troupe to teach martial arts. Chi-Sim reportedly modified his Shao-lin style accordingly; kicks and the more intricate balancing maneuvers found in northern strains of Shao-lin were excluded.

The origination of the style is credited to Fong-T'sai after his escape from the Shao-lin Temple. Another source holds that the originators of the style were Ng-Mui and Mui-Hin.

The system is based on the movements of the five animals: dragon, snake, tiger, leopard, and crane. A famous exponent of this system is Yuen-Yik-Kai, in Hong Kong. (MICHAEL P. STAPLES)

HUNG CH'UAN Form of northern Chinese kung-fu dating to the 12th or 13th century. *See also* wai chia; triads.

INTERNAL SYSTEM Any of the Chinese kung-fu styles whose emphasis is mostly defensive, with circular soft techniques and regulated breathing patterns. **T'ai-chi ch'uan, pa-kua,** and **hsing-i**

are the best known of the internal systems. *See also* nei-chia.

KE-CHIA Southern form of Chinese kung-fu, composed of three styles: lung-hsing (dragon); bai-mei (white eyebrow; also bak-mei in Cantonese); and tsu-chia (also known as southern praying mantis). Ke-chia literally means "guest family," as the originators of these styles were not from the Kwang-Tung province area.

KUNG-KI-CH'UAN Northern style of Chinese kung-fu originating in the Chang county, Hopei province, where it is still practiced. Practice is quite slow and very difficult, consisting of low horse stances. Famous for its staff and knife routines, it is a rare style in which a practitioner will often strike his own body. Because of this, and its extreme difficulty, the nickname Sa-Dung-Li, or "stupid Kung-Li practitioners," has been applied. The system has three forms, Liu-Twei-Jya, Kung-Li-Jya, and Kung-Li-Ch'uan.

KUO-CH'UAN Dog Boxing; a northern form of Chinese kung-fu originating in Shan-Tung province. The system is not particularly popular and is mostly done for fun. Practitioners stay close to the ground, often barking like a dog. Used in demonstrations.

LEOPARD STYLE Kung-fu style, also called pao; movements are fast and deceptive. The style contains narrow stances and clenched fists.

LI GAR Southern short-hand style of kung-fu; characterized by slapping and poking motions with rapid stance changes. In Mandarin, called li-chia.

LION, CHINESE KUNG-FU (northern and southern) In the south, a large, papier-mache, highly decorated head operated by a kung-fu practitioner from inside. Attached to this head is a long-silken "body" under which a second practitioner crouches, aiding the lion's maneuvers. There are, principally, two kinds of southern lion, the young, or black lion, and the old, or multicolored. The former is considered a mark of hostility by the school that displays it. Horns, birds, tassels, and mirrors (into which any local demons will stare and be frightened away by their own reflections) may adorn lion heads. By contrast, the northern lion is more animal-like; its costume is a form-fitting suit. The head is less stylized than that of its southern relative.

The lion traditionally represents the "soul" of the kung-fu school. A school's prowess is tested by testing the lion when it roams the streets, usually during festivals or opening ceremonies. Lion head colors may follow those attributed to Kwan-Kung and his brothers, Chang and Liu. These are white face, eyebrows, and beard; red face with black beard; or black beard with green nose. Often seen accompanying the lion are the large kung-fu drum (ta-gu), with cymbals and gong, a buddha head or antagonist dressed like a buddha, and the kung-fu school "guards." (Michael P. Staples) *See also* lion dance.

LIU-HE "Six methods." The best forms of liu-he come from Chang County, Hopei province, in China. This is a difficult style of northern Chinese kung-fu; weapon routines include the spear, staff, and knife. It is composed, as the name implies, of three internal and three external principles which, as it turns out, can be applied to many other martial arts. In Shantung, liu-he was combined with tang-lang (praying mantis), forming the liu-he tang-lang style. Important figures in the liu-he style are Teng-Cheng-I and Liu-Te-Kwan, who taught Chiao-Shin-Chou, who taught Wan-Lai-Sin (who wrote a popular book on the liu-he system). (Michael P. Staples)

LIU HO CH'UAN Kung-fu style originating ca. A.D. 1100; also known as six-combination boxing.

LIU-HO-PA-FA "Six Harmonies, Eight Steps," a northern form of Chinese kung-fu comprised of the styles known as liu-ho and pa-fa. The development of this system is rooted in folklore. Essentially, it is similar to yueh-fei-ch'uan. A soft form of kung-fu, this style's origin is somewhat of a mystery. Until 1929, when master Wu-I-Hwei brought the system to Nan-Hing, nobody had seen it. Even when Wu brought

it into the open, the lineage and development were unclear. The style is popular primarily in the Hong Kong area. The system favors fingertip strikes with a minimum use of the legs. Kicks are directed only to leg areas of an opponent. It also favors hand-trapping elbow strikes and wrist-locking tactics. *See also* liu-ho-ch'uan. (Michael P. Staples) *Further reading: Inside Kung Fu,* Feb. 1982.

LO-HAN-CH'UAN Literally the Buddha style, a Chinese kung-fu form with northern and southern variants. The most famous is the northern style, which is itself composed of several systems. Basically, the style is similar to **chang-ch'uan.** Emphasis is placed upon positioning rather than movement (a concept peculiar for kung-fu styles). The southern strain is especially popular in Fukien province; it too stresses positioning, but with more liberal movement. *See also* Lohan, Chinese. (Michael P. Staples)

MIEN-CH'UAN Literally, "cotton fist," a northern style of Chinese kung-fu. Notions of softness, smoothness, slowness, warmth, and even weakness are conveyed in its name. Practitioners train very slowly. Emphasis here is on soft training, training the legs, perfecting a low horse stance. A saying about this style warns "Mein-ch'uan, ten years stay in the home"—ten years of practice before one can use it.

Important figures in the mien-ch'uan style are Luo-Tsen-Li, who taught Wen-Chin-Mong (now in the People's Republic of China) and Fu-Shu-Yuen (in Taiwan). Of the same generation as Fu-Shu-Yuen is Lan-Shu-Chen (also in the People's Republic of China). (Michael P. Staples)

MI-T'SUNG-I Northern style of Chinese kung-fu founded around the end of the Sung dynasty. Its mythical founder, Yen-Ching, was actually a character in a famous Chinese novel entitled *Water Margin.* Emphasis in mi-t'sung is on changing direction, speed, and footwork to confuse the enemy. Aspects of both hard and soft kung-fu are included. Its most noted weapon is the knife (tao). The style was made famous by master Hou-Yuan-Chia, who founded the T'sing Wu Athletic Association in Shanghai during the early part of this century. Although Hou's academy housed several different styles, he never included his prized mi-t'sung in curriculum. To this day, the system is quite rate. The most famous master of this style in the U.S., **Adam Hsu,** teaches in San Francisco; he learned his mi-t'sung from Liu-Yen-Chiao, who in turn studied under Chiang-Yao-Ting. (Michael P. Staples)

MONKEY STYLE Kung-fu style known in Chinese as tai-sing pek kwar; founded by Kou Tze, a Chinese martial artist, in the early 19th century. Kou Tze formulated his art through observation of monkeys' habits during an eight-year imprisonment. He analyzed and classified their movements and combined them with the grand earth style of kung-fu, which he had studied previously. The style consists of five species, each utilizing a different principle of movement. Kou Tze named these forms "the lost monkey," "the drunken monkey," "the tall monkey," "the stone monkey," and "the wood monkey."

Lost monkey deals with surprise attacks and self-defense situations. Drunken monkey, perhaps the most bizarre of all kung-fu sets, simulates imbalance and broken rhythm. In reality, the performer is alert, his stance solid, and his movements evasive and deceptive—thus unpredictable. The drunken monkey cannot be hit; he rolls with each blow and gets up again to do battle. Tall monkey features long distance sweeping, swinging arm movements, and low, deep stances. Stone monkey relies on power and brute strength; it is characterized by somersaults, rolling, and falling—usually taught only to students with strong physiques, who can take the punishing movements. Wood monkey is the primary form of deception. It requires quick wits and cleverness to lure an opponent into the trap. Generally only one set is taught to a student, the one which the instructor feels best suits the student's body and ability. (Michael P. Stapes)

NEI-CHIA 1. Chinese kung-fu styles that approach the development of strength through the cultivation of **ch'i.** Prime examples are **t'ai-chi-ch'uan, pa-kua** and **hsing-i.** These are also referred to as "soft" schools of kung fu. Most systems, using this definition, fall

Master Chan Sau Chung performs the monkey style, one of the most colorful systems of kung-fu.

into a mixed category, in which "hard" and "soft" techniques are combined. Some authorities believe the divisions "inner" and "outer," defined in this way, are erroneous, that most systems, if not all, contain aspects of both the "hard" and the "soft," that no clear division among schools can be drawn. 2. Chinese kung-fu styles that base their philosophical attitudes primarily upon Confucian thought. This definition is vague; though Confucianist, Taoist, Buddhist, and Hindu strains become intertwined, significant influences can sometimes be identified. *See also* wai-chia. (MICHAEL P. STAPLES)

NORTHERN SYSTEMS Name given to kung-fu styles originating in northern China. Northern systems emphasize leg techniques and complex body maneuvers.

PA-KUA One of the three branches of **nei-chia** (internal family or system) of Chinese boxing. The other two branches are **t'ai-chi ch'uan** (grand ultimate fist) and **hsing-i** (form of mind). The name pa-kua, as well as its rationale, derive from the philosophy growing out of the **I Ching** *(Book of Changes)*, but one need not comprehend the *Book of Changes* to practice pa-kua boxing. Pa-kua's philosophy is concerned with continuous change: all is in flux, nothing stands still.

The origin of pa-kua is unknown; it is known only that Tung Hai-ch'uan (A.D. 1798-1879) of Wenan Hsien, in Hopei province, during the Ch'ing Dynasty learned this art from an anonymous Taoist in the mountainous stronghold of Kiangsu province. A young man then barely in his 20s, Tung is reputed to have been nearly dead of starvation when the hermit found him. The Taoist ministered to him, and Tung remained with him several years learning a "divine" boxing.

After becoming famous in Peking, Tung was challenged by **Kuo Yun-shen** ("Divine Crushing Hand") of the hsing-i school. Through two days of the duel, Kuo, who had killed men with his notorious crushing hand, could not gain any advantage. On the third day, Tung finally took the offensive and so completely defeated Kuo that he made him a lifelong friend. At once they signed a brotherhood pact requiring hsing-i students to take pa-kua training and vice versa. For this reason, the two styles are to this day coupled.

Tung's most famous pupils were: **Yin Fu**, Ch'eng T'ing-hua, Ma Wei-chi, Liu Feng-ch'un, and Shih Liu. The best known pa-kua boxers in Taiwan today are Wang Shu-chin, Chang Chuan-feng, Ch'en P'an-ling, Kuo Feng-ch'ih, and Hung I-hsing.

Pa-kua is one of the three internal methods of Chinese boxing emphasizing displacement of horizontal strength and turning of the palms. Pa-kua (eight trigrams) is comprised of various circling postures named after and based on the movements of the snake, stork, dragon, hawk, lion, monkey, and bear. *Further reading: Pa-Kua Chang*, Lee-Ying-Arng, 1972; *Pa-Kua, Chinese Boxing*, Robert W. Smith, 1965.

PI-KUA Northern style of Chinese kung-fu emphasizing use of the palm for striking. Pi-Kua spends a great deal of time teaching one to receive punishment as well as to dish it out. A practitioner may even strike himself, following through with all his force. Noted weapons of pi-kua are the single and double knife.

Important figures in the tung-pei strain of pi-kua are Chiang-Tze, who taught Chiang-Dz; and Chiang-Hsiau-Tang, who taught Meng-Tsau-Shuen (currently in Taiwan). (MICHAEL P. STAPLES)

POC KHEK New style of kung-fu popular in Malaysia. The art has been developed in the past thirty years by a Chinese sifu (teacher), **Nip Chee Fei.** Its resilience is drawn from **t'ai-chi-ch'uan,** its strength from **Shao-lin.** Poc khek has its own kata; leg techniques are employed, but hand techniques predominate. During sparring, punches and kicks are not pulled, and protective gear is worn.

POISON FINGER TECHNIQUES According to kung-fu legends, killing an opponent by the mere touch of a finger on certain parts of the body. Many of these techniques were supposed to cause delayed death, as in the **dim mak.**

PRAYING MANTIS Kung-fu system founded in the 17th century by Wong Long in the southern part of China. Praying mantis relies heavily on fierce grasping movements, clawing attacks, and punches, both for offense and defense. There is, however, a great variety within the style, using as it does the firmness of stance found in **hung gar,** a number of movements from the monkey systems, and something of the litheness and antennae like actions of its namesake.

According to legend, Wang Lang captured a praying mantis and took it home, where he studied its movements. He blended these movements with the monkey style to form his new system.

PRAYING MANTIS (six harmonies style) Northern style of Chinese kung-fu. The original seven stars praying mantis was combined with the **liu-ho** system of Chinese kung-fu, probably by Wei-Shan in Shan-Tung province or his teacher. Wei-Shan taught Ling-Shih-Chen, who taught Tin-Dz-Chen, who taught Chang-Shan-San in Taiwan, and T'sau-Chan-I, T'sau-Chu-Li, and Liu-Yen-Chiao, who taught San Francisco-based Hsu-Chi (**Adam Hsu**).

This system of praying mantis is softer than the original seven stars style, smoother, more circular, and not as clear in usage. In Shantung province it is called "soft t'ang-lang," while the seven stars style is called "hard t'ang-lang." The six harmonies style does not use the "hook" hand as much as the seven stars system; rather, it employs the palm, called the kawan-pai t'ang-lang style at times. Neither does it use as much of the monkey step as the original system, but a step called the "floating river," moving in and out rather than side to side. Basically, it is still praying mantis, not liu-ho.

The six harmonies style of praying mantis has six important forms, different only slightly. The first is tieh-tz, literally "iron teeth," referring to the use of the arm rather than the hooklike hand that is the praying mantis trademark. Second is san-shou-peng; third is ching-li-t'sang-hua (flower hiding in the mirror, i.e., the "image" of the flower, referring to feints and trick moves); fourth is chieh-shou-ch'uan, cutting and circling techniques; fifth is yeh-li-t'sang-hua (flower hiding beneath the leaf, a reference to hiding and techniques behind another); and sixth is shuang-feng (double block, left-right, turning and twisting, changing of direction). (Michael P. STAPLES)

PRAYING MANTIS (eight steps style) Northern Chinese kung-fu style founded near the end of the Ch'ing dynasty by Chiang-Hwa-Lung, perhaps the leading praying mantis master of his time. As Chiang grew older and more knowledgeable, he became dissatisfied with the existing praying mantis system. He had two friends, one a **hsing-i** practitioner and one a t'ung-pei master, whom he trusted enough to ask for advice while formulating a new style.

The "horse-monkey" footwork patterns of the original system Chiang believed inadequate; he therefore introduced the eight steps footwork pattern. It is significant that he, as most other kung-fu grandmasters, always saw the footwork of the style as most important.

Chiang also modified the original seven stars forms known as shau-fan-she (the small rolling wheel) and ta-fan-she (the big rolling wheel). Though still considered seven stars, it was tightened up, fighting was at closer range. Chiang also extended the seven stars form t'sai-yau to over 360 movements presented in six sets, deemphasized the hooklike mantis-shaped hand so often considered a trademark of the t'ang-lang style, and introduced more techniques using the palm.

Famous masters of this style include Chiang-Hwa-Lung, who taught Feng-Wan-I, who taught Wei-Shau-Tang, currently living in Taiwan. (MICHAEL P. STAPLES)

PRAYING MANTIS (seven stars style). Northern style of Chinese kung fu. The "seven stars" style of praying mantis is the original system, so called because of its footwork pattern. The pattern takes its name from the constellation Ursa Major, a conspicious zig-zag star arrangement in the northern firmament suggesting the angular positions adopted during combat. The Chinese name for this style is chi-hsing t'ang-lang. A common misconception holds that the style's founder noticed a starlike pattern of dots on the back of a mantis he had captured to study.

Chi-hsing t'ang-lang is also known as mei-hwa t'ang-lang (plum-flower praying mantis), essentially the same system as the seven-stars style. Its name finds a similarity of form in the branching of plum blossoms and the hand configurations of the style. Mei-hwa t'ang-lang, however, is not a popular style. Yet another name for chi-hsing t'ang-lang is t'ang-lang-gou-dz (t'ang-lang hook), because of the hooklike way in which the hand is used.

Praying mantis was founded by master Wang Lang during the end of the Ming and beginning of the Ch'ing dynasty. Already a master of the Shao-lin style of Chinese kung-fu, he combined "monkey" footwork with praying mantis hand techniques. He called the footwork "horse-monkey" after a species of large monkey whose habits he had observed. The style is quite clear and direct as contrasted with pa-kua or t'ai-chi, which are ambiguous in application. Chi-hsing T'ang-Lang has also been known as Shwei-Shou T'ang-Lang, a branch of the seven stars system.

Seven stars praying mantis has three important forms and numerous minor ones. The Mei-hwa subcategory has three forms: Mei-Hwa-Lu, Mei-Hwa-Ch'uan, and Mei-Hwa-Shou; there is little real difference among them. Chi-Hsing also has three important forms: Peng-Pu (the most important), Lua-Che (literally meaning the free arrangement, so named because in the old days the sifu asked students to arrange the routines themselves—the reason there are so many arranged sets today), and the T'sai-Yau, using elbows and hips. A subcategory of T'sai-Yau is Pa-Sou, or eight elbows, emphasizing a complex use of elbows, hips, and knees.

Important practitioners of the chi-hsing t'ang-lang style are Chiang-Hwa-Lung, who taught Li-Kwun-Shan, and Lo-Kwang-Yu, who taught Wang-Han-Hsun, who taught San Francisco sifu **Brendan Lai.** The same generation as Wang Han-Hsun was Chen-Chiu-I. Li-Kwun-Shan also taught Li-Teng-Wu, now in Taiwan, and Chiang-Te-Hwei, who taught Hsu-Yu-Chiang (now in Caracas). (MICHAEL P. STAPLES)

SAN-HWANG PAO-CH'UI Northern style of Chinese kung-fu originating in the Three Kingdoms period; literally means "cannon fist." The style is also known as hsing-kung-ch'uan, and is still practiced in Peking.

SHAU WAN CH'UAN Kung-fu style originating in a northern **Shao-lin** monastery. It combines quick, accurate foot techniques with fist movements.

SHUAI CHIAO Chinese form of wrestling dating back to about 700 B.C. Unlike Western wrestling or judo, shuai chiao uses throws and takedowns, as well as strikes, kicks, and blocks similar to those in kung-fu. Throwing is often done by a combination of sweeping and throwing actions, thus making the opponent fall hard. Instead of grabbing an opponent's uniform, as in judo, shuai chiao wrestlers grab the arms, legs, shoulders or other bodily parts to execute moves.

Shuai chiao stances are very low and solid. Freestyle fighting is practiced, with kicks, strikes and throws combined. Because of the heavy falling, shuai chao students, of course, learn to fall and tumble. Today, students are graded by colored belts. the art is taught as a means of combat, not as a sport. There are numerous styles practiced in different parts of China.

SIU-LUM Cantonese for **Shao-lin,** a soft style of kung-fu. Performed from a rooted stance, the hands are constantly in motion, used as feints to cover a sudden kick or other attacks.

TA-CHENG CH'UAN Internal boxing system created from **hsing-i** by Wang Hsiang-chai after the death of Chang Chao-tung. Also known as the "great achievement" boxing.

TAI-CH'I (Ch'eng style) Highly philosophical system of Chinese kung-fu founded by Chen-Wong-Ting in the Ming dynasty and closely held for many years within the Ch'en family. A relatively recent creation compared to many other styles, it grew out of five basic forms. The first is soft, designed to change the "way" one moves. The second form begins development of power and circular movement. The third and subsequent forms concentrate heavily on strength and power. (MICHAEL P. STAPLES)

T'AI-CHI-CH'UAN (Ch'en style) Style of "long boxing" in the tradition of t'ai-chi kung-fu. The reader should note that the origin of Ch'en-Chia t'ai-chi is disputed among martial arts historians. The 'Yang' school of t'ai-chi has, according to at least one noted authority, always subscribed to the traditional story of **Chang San Feng's** being the founder of t'ai-chi, in the Sung dynasty. This is probably myth. A second theory suggests that t'ai-chi arose as a natural outgrowth of the four boxing schools of Hsu, Yu, Ch'eng, and Yin. Yet another traces the founding to Wang-Tsung-Yueh. All that is known for sure,

Sifu Brendan Lai doing a sequence from the praying mantis system of kung-fu.
Courtesy of *Inside Kung-Fu*

Part of a tai-chi set

T'ai-chi-ch'uan techniques are based on movements that are applicable to self-defense even though when practicing them they are often performed slowly. At left is kung-fu master Tung Kai Ying

however, is that as far back as historians have been able to trace the style, it has been practiced by the Ch'en family of Ch'en-Chia Kou village, Honan province, in China. (MICHAEL P. STAPLES)

T'AI-CHI-CH'UAN (Fu style) System of Chinese t'ai-chi kung-fu developed by master Fu-Chen-Shung, who passed the art to his son, Fu-Wing-Fay, it is now taught in the People's Republic of China. The style is also taught by Fu-Wing-Fay's former colleague, **Mark-Bow-Sim,** in Boston, who also teaches "combined" and "simplified" t'ai-chi-ch'uan. *See also* t'ai-chi-ch'uan (Simplified and General).

T'AI-CHI CH'UAN (General) Northern style of Chinese kung-fu; it cultivates **chi** as the seat of power and force behind the techniques it employs. There are several theories of its origin: that the Taoist priest **Chang San Feng** of the Yuan dynasty created the style; that it emerged during the T'ang dynasty and developed through the Hsu, Yu, Ch'eng and Yin schools; that the Ch'en family of Ch'en-Chia-Kou in Honan province created it during the Ming dynasty. A fourth theory attributes its development to Wang-Tsung-Yueh, during the Ch'ien-Lung period of the Ch'ing dynasty. Ch'en-Chia-Kou, it is safe to say, was the first t'ai-chi-ch'uan master.

Essentially, Ch'en is the original style. Important figures in this style are Chen-Chiang Shuen, who taught Chen Gen-Yuan, who taught Chen-Yuan-Shih, who taught Chen-Fa-Ke. Chen-Fa-Ke then had three students of note: Chen-Chiao-Shu, who taught Chen-Shiao-Wang (now in the People's Republic of China); Chen-Tsau-Kuei; and Wang-Men-Pi (in Taiwan), who taught Rei-Mu-Ni (now in the Peoples Republic of China), Feng-Tz-Chiao (also in China), and Tien-Shou-Chen was Tu-Yu-Tse in Taiwan, who taught San Francisco-based **Adam Hsu.**

Two major and important schools of t'ai-chi emerged from Ch'en style, namely the Yang and Wu styles. Actually, Wu, Li, Hao, Tsuen, and Sun styles all derive from the Wu system which, in turn, comes from Yang. In one way or another, styles of t'ai-chi originate with Ch'en.

Following the Yang style through Yang-Lu-Ch'an, who learned from Ch'en-Ch'ang-Hsing, we find that Yang had two students of importance: Yang-Chien-Hou and Yang-Pan-Hou. Yang-Chien-Hou taught Yang Ch'eng-Fu, who taught **Cheng-Man-Ch'ing,** Ch'en-Wei-Ming, Li-Ya-Hsuan, Tung-Ying-Chieh, and Wu Hui-Ch'uan. Cheng Man-Ch'ing taught Ben Lo, who taught Tung Ying-Chieh, who taught Tung-Kai-Ying in Los Angeles.

This is but a partial listing of important figures in the lineage of t'ai-chi-ch'uan. There are many schools of t'ai-chi, with members too numerous to mention here. (MICHAEL P. STAPLES)

T'AI-CHI-CH'UAN (Hsu style) Style of "long boxing" originating in the T'ang dynasty with Hsu-Hsuan-P'ing. Hsu was born in Chi-Hsien, An-Hwei, and promulgated a style of t'ai-chi comprised of 37 basic maneuvers. According to one authority, these maneuvers were taught one at a time until a complete understanding of the system as a whole was learned. *See also* t'ai-chi ch'uan (General).

The techniques of Takenouchi ryu were so effective that warriors flocked to Takenouchi's dojo. According to ancient scrolls and manuscripts of this school, Takenuchi's son was requested to perform techniques from his father's program of instruction, which included more than 600 techniques, before Emperor Gomizuno (1611-1629). Following the performance, the emperor bestowed upon the art the title of "supreme and unsurpassed art of combat," granting the disciples of Takenouchi permission to use the imperial color, purple, for the cords employed in the school's immobilization techniques.

T'AN-T'UI Northern form of Chinese kung-fu from the Chang-Ch'uan Islamic style. This is actually not a system in itself, but the first form of Chang-Ch'uan. T'an-tui was adopted by several other northern systems (e.g., erh-lang-men, mei-hwa-ch'uan) in their basics. This Chinese boxing system is characterized by low kicking techniques and an emphasis on strong yet mobile horse stances. Training stresses repeating movements left and right, always ending each move with a kick.

TAO YIN Early Chinese art, purportedly the forerunner of **t'ai-chi-ch'uan.** It was a breathing exercise similar to the Zen Buddhist method. **Chang San-feng,** a Taoist priest (1279-1368), is credited with spreading the art.

T'ai-chi-ch'uan is one of the internal systems of kung-fu. In most styles, the movements are continuous and are performed very slowly with relaxed muscles. Above is Sifu Y. C. Chang.

TA-SHENG-MEN Kung-fu style, known as the **monkey style.** In A.D. 629, Hsuan Tsang, a Buddhist monk, was traveling from China to India. According to legend Sun Wu-k'ung, a monkey, was his body guard. From his methods, so folklore says, the kung-fu system of ta-sheng-men developed. The stances of a monkey are adopted in this style, which also employs rolls, crouching defensive postures, and aggressive leaps.

TA-SHENG-MEN Kung-fu style, known as the **monkey style.** In 629 A.D., Hsuan Tsang, a Buddhist monk, was traveling from China to these styles were supposedly put together in Hong Kong, many feel they are still taught and learned as two separate systems. The pi-kua in this case is not the original sytle but chang-ch'uan pi-kua, which is itself a mixture of pi-kua and the "long fist" of chang-ch'uan. *See also* chang-ch'uan pi-kua.

TI T'ANG Northern Chinese boxing system; techniques of fighting while falling or lying on the ground. Emphasis is on kicking and falling techniques. Balance is considered from three standpoints: keeping comfortable balance; using difficult movements, yet maintaining balance; and breaking balance, falling, and yet maintaining composure. This training is seen as practical in circumstances in which one cannot follow the usual methods of fighting, when injured or taken off guard, for example. Ti-T'ang is also known as Ti-Kung and Bai-Ma-Sya-Shan; its most well-known exponent is Hwa-Che. (MICHAEL P. STAPLES)

WAH KUEN Northern Chinese style of boxing emphasizing high kicks and long-range hand techniques. Students learn to close the gap quickly. Besides kicking and striking, the system also adopts joint locks and throwing techniques. Forms are practiced alone or as two-man sets.

WHITE CRANE Style of Chinese kung-fu based on the movements of the crane and the ape. Tibetan white crane, as opposed to Fukeinese white crane from the **Shao-lin Temple,** is called pak-hoc in Chinese. It stems from the Tibetan Lama, or **Hop Gar** martial system.

Sing-Lung, a Biddhist priest, is credited by many with introducing white crane to China. From him the style was passed to Wong-Lum-Hoi, then Ng-Siu-Chung, the last great patriarch of the system. After Ng's death in 1968, the Pak-Hoc Athletic Federation was formed in Hong Kong, extending authority to all white crane teachers in the absence of Master Ng, who died without appointing a successor. Today white crane is closely overseen by federations in Hong Kong and Singapore, although more and more non-Orientals are being permitted to study the system.

Ng-Siu-Chung taught three prominent students who became key figures in the migration of white crane kung-fu to the U.S.: Cheuk-Tiang-Tse, in Hawaii; Chan-Hoc-Fu, whose student, George Long, was the first person to open his kwoon (Chinese school) to non-Orientals in San Francisco; and Lak-Chi-Fu, whose student, Quentin Fong, is well known in the U.S., and whose son, Lak-Chung-Mau, teaches the art in Canada. Tang-Chak-Ming's students William Siu

Dr. Cheng Man-ching (who died in 1975), famous t'ai-chi-ch'uan master of the Yang style, demonstrates techniques.

Courtesy of A. Mirakian

and Raymond Mar are also well known within the Chinese martial arts.

White crane is a combination of long- and short-hand techniques. It employs both internal and external methods of training and is composed of 24 sets, 10 empty-hand and 14 weaponry, utilizing a wide range of hand and leg maneuvers. As a rule the techniques apply methods of cutting nerves and striking pressure points. White crane footwork, like that of Hop-Gar, is based on moves developed for the mui-fa-jeong (plum-flower stumps), a series of tree-stumps driven into the ground atop which students practiced kung-fu. This philosophy of white crane, identical to that of Hop-Gar, is based on four words: chon (to destroy), sim (to evade), chun (to penetrate), and jeet (to intercept). (MICHAEL P. STAPLES)

WING CHUN Wing Chun is a southern style of Chinese kung-fu, the most influential Chinese martial art in modern times. Wing chun emphasizes self-defense reduced to its most streamlined rudiments: simultaneous attack and defense with multiple straight-line strikes at extremely close range. Every punch, poke, strike, slap, or kick in the system has been designed to serve as a defense; similarly every block, deflection, or evasion has been designed to double as an attack. Rapid hand techniques combined with low kicks tend to be featured in an aggressive array of constant forward pressure.

Wing chun students are taught to insure the most effective deployment of their striking techniques by controlling, or "trapping," one or more of an opponent's limbs whenever possible. Trapping skills are developed through a competitive form of resistance training called chi sao, or "sticking hands," which besides strengthening the upper body tends to make a student combat-effective faster than students in most other fighting arts.

Formal wing chun training also includes instruction in three shadow-boxing sets, a wooden dummy set, and two weapon sets. The first shadow-boxing set called sil lum tao, or "way of the small idea," contains the core of the art's techniques although the routine focuses primarily on breathing, balance, coordination as well as correct hand and arm positions. The second set, called chum kil, or "searching for the bridge," teaches defensive maneuvering skills and closing techniques. The last shadow-boxing set, called bil gee, or "thrusting fingers," develops fingers strikes.

The wooden dummy set (muk yan chong) is performed on a training device unique to wing chun composed of a wooden trunk,

three arms, and one leg. This set teaches the applications of trapping, controlling, and basic combat techniques.

The two weapons sets develop fighting skills with an eight-foot-long pole (luk dim boun kwan), which is especially useful against multiple opponents, and with the twin butterfly knives (pak charn dao).

According to semilegendary accounts, wing chun originated in the early 1700s at the Shaolin Temple in Honan Province. At that time in Chinese history, the Shaolin Temple with its long established tradition of martial arts training had become a sanctuary for dissidents, revolutionaries, and secret societies dedicated to the overthrow of the Manchu dynasty. The Manchu government employed professional soldiers who were highly skilled in the martial arts and well versed in the fighting tactics of the Shaolin Temple. Whenever they were sent into an area of Shaolin activity to enforce the Manchu will, they quickly put a halt to the Robin Hood operations of the rebellious monks.

The Shaolin monks eventually realized that they could not rapidly train a young rebel to match the fighting skills of the Manchu soldiers since full mastery of the Shaolin martial arts required approximately eighteen years. A solution to this problem needed to be found. The elders of the temple convened a meeting and agreed to develop a new fighting art which would overcome all others, and which would take a much shorter period of time to learn.

The elders met regularly and engaged in lengthy discussions during which each elder revealed his or her most secret fighting techniques. Soon the elders became so encouraged by the progress of these discussions that they renamed the martial arts training room in which they met *Wing Chun Hall* , or Forever Springtime Hall. The words "wing chun" expressed their hopes for a renaissance in Shaolin martial arts instruction, as well as for a more effective weapon in their struggle against the Manchus.

However before the new fighting art could be completely developed, a Shaolin traitor tipped off the government and Manchu soldiers were sent to destroy the temple. Most of the temple residents were killed in the attack, and the few who survived quickly fled to clandestine locations throughout China.

Among the survivors was a nun named Ng Mui who had been one of the temple elders. After the raid, she hid herself at a nunery on Tai Leung Mountain between Szechwan and Yunan provinces. She spent her time there finalizing the movements of the new fighting art. Once completed, Ng Mui decided to call the art "wing chun" after the Wing Chun Hall in which she and the other elders had held their discussions.

Ng Mui taught the new art to the teenage daughter of bean-curd vendor Yim Yee Gung who lived in the village at the bottom of Tai Leung Mountain. Shortly before Ng Mui's death, she named her student Yim Wing Chun since the girl had been entrusted with the art's future. For the next two hundred years, wing chun remained a private kung-fu system, taught only to family and friends, until 1952 in Hong Kong when grandmaster Yip Man first offered commercial instruction.

Although over 90 percent of the wing chun schools in the world today can be traced directly to the efforts of Yip Man and his stu-

Wing Chun exercises

White crane techniques are mirrored in others styles but are usually limited to short fists (hon kuen), pecking hands, and kicks. There are also weapons. White crane has ten weapon sets, each with approximately 100 moves.

dents, the art has evolved into two branches of instruction. The first, which may be termed *centerline wing chun* , represents the form of the art taught to Yip Man by Chan Wah Shun. Chan had been an extraordinarily large and powerful man. His teaching stressed direct and overpowering aggression.

Centerline wing chun, therefore, is based on an imaginary straight line, called the "centerline," which is drawn from the wing chun practitioner's solar plexus to the opponent's chin. The centerline forms the axis for all attacks and defenses. As long as the centerline remains in alignment directly in front of an opponent, the wing chun practitioner can attack in a straight charge, with straight punches, straight up the opponent's middle. The clenched fist becomes the primary offensive weapon, reinforced by secondary open hand work and low kicks.

The formal sets in centerline wing chun lack standardization since Yip Man changed them over the years and frequently modified them in accordance with each student's abilities.

Grandmaster Wong Shun Leung of Hong Kong is generally regarded as the foremost exponent of centerline wing chun, although other prominent instructors include Koo Sang (Hong Kong), Leung Ting (Hong Kong), Lo Lan Kam (Taiwan), Lee Sing (Britain), Moy Yat (New York), Jason Lau (New York), Alan Lamb (California), Hawkins Cheung (California), Keith Kernspect (West Germany), and Greco Wong (South Africa).

PAUL MASLAK

KYUJUTSU

Kyujutsu is the name given to classical combat archery of the Japanese feudal era. Kyujutsu training required an archer to shoot 1,000 arrows daily, and to handle all types of bow with full draw. Correct yugamae, or posture, was essential in battle, giving the shooter psychological advantage over his enemy. Archers practiced all the mechanics of kyujutsu: gripping the bowstring (tsurugami), viewing the mark (monomi), raising and drawing (uchiokoshi kikitori), completed drawing (daisan), full draw hold (jiman), and release (hanane). A warrior was trained to "feel" the bow and arrow and his own hands as a unit; even after releasing the arrow, he was taught not to relax his vigil.

Target shooting made use of moving and stationary targets. Live targets were especially popular, as in taka inu, in which mounted archers shoot at a fleeing dog. After the introduction of firearms in the mid-16th century, military kyujutsu declined and was gradually adopted as a sport, **kyudo.** *Further reading: The Martial Arts,* Andre Sollier and Zsolt Gyorbiro, 1978; *Secrets of the Samurai,* Adele Westbrook and Oscar Ratti, 1973.

FORMS OF KYUJUTSU

KYUDO Japanese archery. It combines the physical art with the philosophical principles of Zen Buddhism. Hitting the bull's-eye is not the main object: like all Japanese martial arts, the important point is style and manner. Most important are the benefits to a man's character derived through study of the bow. Japanese archery dates back more than 1,400 years, and its influence has been great in Japanese history. It is one of the 18 martial arts in which a Japanese samurai was expected to be proficient.

The Japanese bow is almost 7½ feet of laminated bamboo and wood. The grip is not centered, but is approximately one-third of the distance from the bottom of the bow. The bowstring is made of hemp. Arrow lengths range from 36 inches to 40 inches, with 5-inch feathers. The shooting glove (yugake) is made of buckskin. Traditional costume consists of a long blouse (monpoku) tucked into a long skirt (hakama). Footwear varies: many men go barefoot. Although the practical purpose o kyudo is to hit the target, one must also stand erect, in the proper posture, and handle the bow with deep concentration.

Shooting is divided into eight stages (hasetsu). Positioning of the

Kyudoka are ranked from 1st to 10th **dan,** as in karate. **Kyu** ranks are 1st and 2nd. Usually no rank is worn by the archers. There are three basic types of target shooting in kyudo: the close target, chikamato, a 14-inch target set up at 85 feet; distant target, enteki, a 32-inch target at 180 feet; and flight shooting, inagashi. *See also* kyujutsu. *Further reading: Asian Fighting Arts,* Donn F. Draeger and Robert W. Smith, 1969; *Zen Combat,* Jay Gluck, 1962; *Zen in the Art of Archery,* Eugen Herrigel, 1973; *The Martial Arts,* Michael Random, 1978; *Japanese Archery, Zen in Action,* Andre Sollier and Zsolt Gyorbiro, 1969; *Martial Arts of the Orient,* Byrn Williams, 1975.

feet (ashibumi): Getting into position for shooting. This is usually performed from a stance in which the target is faced sideways. Both feet point 45 degrees outward, heels aligned, and feet spread about shoulder width. Steadying the bow (dozukuri): The body weight is centered. The archer adjusts his breathing and prepares for the next step. Holding the bow (yugamae): The archer sets the bow in place. He places the arrow in the string and checks his hold on the bow. Raising the bow (uchiokoshi): The bow is raised at arm's length, slowly, high above the head. Drawing the bow (hikiwake): The gripping hand pushes the bow toward the target. The arrow is then pulled back behind the ear. The union (kai): When the bowstring is pulled fully back the archer holds this position. It is the moment when mind and body unite. Release (hanare): The arrow is released. It must be a natural discharge, one not forced by the archer. Follow through (zanshin): The archer watches the arrow while remaining motionless. This is the moment of enlightenment.

The yumi (bow) used in kyudo is the longest bow used anywhere in the world. It often measures eight feet in length and the arrow is what from about one-third from the bottom.

Dressed in samurai armor that dates back to feudal times, this kosiyakumiyumi (infantry archer) demonstrates military archery tactics at Tokyo's Budokan.

LUA

Lua is a Hawaiian martial art which incorporated elements of jujutsu, judo, karate and **aikido**. It strongly relied on knowledge of anatomy and nerve and muscle centers. Lua has come to bear different meanings over the years. To some it refers to the entire range of exotic defensive arts prolific in ancient Hawaii. These included various forms of boxing, wrestling, spear throwing, and staff fighting. To others, the narrow version of lua refers to one specific art, translated as "bonebreaking," a secret form of combat that had many elements in common with the rugged forms of jujutsu flourishing toward the end of the 19th century in Japan. This art was taught only to a select few and, like Chinese kung-fu, what is generally known about it has been transmitted mainly by word of mouth.

During the period called Makahiki, the Hawaiians conducted an annual festival spread roughly over three onths, from October 15 to January 15. As part of this festival, the youth of different villages gathered on the kahua, or playground, to compete in martial sports. A ring area was marked off by spears stuck into the ground. One of the favorite sports was mokomo, a form of boxing that was probably integrated into lua at some point. Lua was never performed publicly.

Lua was taught only to those who were known to be able to control their tempers, and reputedly was never to be used except in defense of life. According to Lorrin Andrews, author of *The Dictionary of Hawaiian Language*, lua employed a technique called "noosing," probably a method of cord strangulation.

King Kamehameha, who united the Hawaiian Islands under one rule in a series of spectacular battles between 1790 and 1910, is known to have established three lua schools, and smaller ones may have also existed. A school was placed under the supervision of a kahuna, or priest, who is usually described as a combination of priest, wizard and medicine man. However, there were various classes of kahuna, and each tended to specialize in a given field such as praying, healing, prophecy or lua.

Lua is today a lost art, with no specific descriptions of actual techniques, although researchers are now exploring data on the subject. Its decline and gradual extinction is chiefly attributed to the influence of Christian missionaries, who arrived in 1820. The introduction of firearms also contributed to its decline. One of the last lua schools, at Waialua, was suppressed by the authorities in the 1840s, according to a March 27, 1904 article in the Hawaiian newspaper, the *Sunday Advertiser*, one of the rare written accounts of this art. The historical description of lua ran as follows:

"To be successful in war, all Hawaiians were taught the lua. First of all, they became adept at the hula, for it was with the soft, cadenced rhythm of the hula, and the sonorous, measured, monotonous tones of the mele, that the victims were often disarmed of suspicion, until suddenly the dancer and singer seized the unsuspecting spectator by the wrist or hand, and with the wonderful knowledge they possessed of the muscles, nerves and bones, the thumb and little finger would be disjointed, the wrist bones displaced or the shoulder thrown into agonizing dislocation. the victim became a physical wreck in a few minutes, or often times in a few seconds.

"On the plains of Mokuleia and Lihue on the way to Waialua, the students hovered in quest of victims upon whom to practice. A lone traveler was often attracted by the lovely music of the hula kui or mele . . . He listened in rapt attention to the singer, all suspicion disarmed.

"Suddenly the traveler's wrist was seized, the thumb and little finger of a hand disjointed and a nerve in the palm was pressed until pain shot through the entire body; a muscle in the biceps was dug into by wiry fingers until faintness came. The process of disjointing and dislocating went on, the wrist, elbow, shoulder and toes being treated likewise. In extreme cases the eyes were gouged, and at last having gone through the entire list of accomplishments in the lua, the victim was helpless, stunned, insensible. The rehabilitation of the body was gone through by the students afterwards, until all the bones were restored to their normal positions, but oftener still the victim was left to die.

"The modern hula kui of the present day contains a few of the steps which belonged to the war dance common to the lua." *Further reading: Black Belt Magazine*, Nov. 1966; *The Book of Mormon*, John Smith.

NAGINATA-JUTSU

Naginata-jutsu is one of the combat systems used by the **bushi,** or Japanese feudal warriors. The **naginata,** a spearlike weapon, was used for cutting, parrying, blocking, thrusting, and evasion. Once the basics were mastered, armored trainees were pitted against partners armed with the wooden sword (**bokken**). Actual combat methods were practiced in **kata** form. Naginata-jutsu became a popular pastime for women; they engaged men in regulated contests wearing protective armor similar to that worn in kendo. Eventually naginata-jutsu was replaced by naginata-do. *See also* yari.

The sport weapon consists of a 6½ foot pole and 1¾ foot bamboo blade. Each end is covered with a leather tip. Protective equipment consists of helmet mask (men), breastplate (do), arm guards (kote), shin guards(sune ate), and a girdle of protective padding around the lower torso.

In the fundamentals, students learn basic postures and stepping techniques, at first in solo practice. In contests a point is scored only when the naginata blade contacts the face, top of the head, forearms, trunk, or shins. An effective thrust at the throat may also score a point. There is a chief referee and two assistants; two out of the three must agree before a point is allowed. Proper form and fighting spirit are important in determining the winner.

NAGINATA-DO Naginata art form. It arose with the decline of the naginata as a combat weapon. A most difficult discipline, it has become a popular form of physical education and sport for women. *See also* yari.

Naginata is controlled by the **Zen Nihon Naginata-do Remnei,** which brought under one leadership all the various styles. Although various styles maintain their own **kata** (forms), a uniform competition system has been worked out to make possible National Championships. In 1967 Naginata became a physical education subject in senior high schools and colleges in Japan. *Further reading: Classical Bujutsu,* Donn F. Draeger, 1973; *Modern Bujutsu and Budo,* Donn F. Draeger, 1974; *Martial Arts of the Orient,* Roald Knutsen, 1975; *Fighting Arts Magazine* Vol. I No. 4.

A demonstration of naginata-do by female practitioners in Japan.

104

NINJUTSU

Ninjutsu is Feudal Japanese discipline embracing **bushido,** espionage, commando warfare, occult powers, and numerous martial arts practices. As a result of extensive religious and territorial wars, Japanese mountain mystics were forced to develop the art to provide security for their families. As Japan entered its war-torn feudal period, from the late 13th to the early 17th centuries, ninjutsu, the "art of stealing in" or "espionage," grew sophisticated in the cloak and dagger arts.

Children born into the Iga and Koga systems, both powerful **ninja** organizations, were trained early as spies and continued in their craft for life. A ninja concealed his name, objectives, and techniques even to the point of death. One never appeared in public without a disguise. For three centuries this clandestine band supplied warlords with information gathering and sabotage networks. (STEPHEN K. HAYES) *Further reading: Ninjutsu: The Art of Invisibility,* Donn F. Draeger, 1971; *Ninja, Spirit of the Shadow Warrior,* Stephen K. Hayes, 1980; *Ninja Realm Magazine,* Shadows of Iga Society of Ninjutsu Enthusiasts, 1980; *Black Belt Magazine,* Aug., Nov. 1967; Jan. 1978; Aug. 1979; Jan., June, July, Aug. 1980 and 1980 Yearbook; and Jan.-Mar. 1981; *Inside Kung Fu,* July-Aug. 1977; Apr. 1980; *Kick Illustrated,* Aug. 1981; *Official Karate,* Winter Annual 1977-78; Apr. 1979.

Ninja in full uniform with short ninja sword.

Ninjutsu back-handed sword grip.

Ninjutsu fighting pose Doko no kamae.

Cultural opposites of the samurai, the ninja in his art, ninjutsu, not only mastered all of the traditional weapons, but also had to be adept at using the special weapons and devices of his trade, among them daggers, dirks, darts, **shuriken,** brass knuckles, caltrops, rope ladders, grappling hooks, smoke bombs, and a variety of poisons. His physical training was intense and varied, enabling him to scale walls, remain underwater for several minutes, or even feign death convincingly.

Because of his constant training, which began in early childhood, the ninja could walk farther, run faster, jump higher, and swim longer and faster than ordinary men. Out of necessity, the ninja was a superb escape artist, who could manipulate his joints to slip out of the most complicated knots. He hid under floors, above ceilings, in trees and wells, underwater, and might even disguise himself as a rock or a tree stump. His ability to disappear into the scenery and his ingenious use of storms, fog, and darkness gave rise to legends claiming the ninja could become "invisible." It was because of this talent that ninjutsu has also been defined as the "art of invisibility."

The ninja was a great actor and master of disguise: a priest one day, a carpenter the next, and an enemy solider the day after. Geogras uniform and equipment were white. On long missions, the ninja carried concentrated food. He was an expert at survival, an excellent cook, a proficient pharmacist, and a chemist as well—not only did he prepare his own food, but poisons, medicines, explosives, and other necessities.

Ninja were often sent out to steal information, track enemy movements, and mislead the enemy. If necessary for the success of their cause, ninja would not hesitate to sneak into an enemy camp and commit arson, sabotage, or assassinate an opposing ,leader. The ninja placed no limits on what he could or would do for the sake of winning.

A man was born a ninja and died one; there were few outsiders among the ninja clans. Since staying alive depended upon secrecy, few ninja masters ever achieved renown. Traitors were hunted down by other agents, perhaps a relative, and killed. A ninja on the verge of capture usually committed suicide rather than face inevitable torture. It was a favorite practice of the warlords to boil a captured ninja alive or slowly skin him to death.

The Tokugawa family's unification of Japan brought an end to ninja activities, and in the 17th century the practice of ninjutsu was banned. Ninjutsu was so feared by the government that even mention of it brought the death penalty. A handful of men continued to practice secretly, however, well away from the Tokugawa capital in Edo (Tokyo today). Recently, with the increasing popularity of the martial arts, there has been great interest in the exploits of the ninja and his art. The relatively few remaining practioners are now in heavy demand. (Stephen K. Hayes) *Further reading: Ninja; The Invisible Assassins,* Andrew Adams, 1970; *Asian Fighting Arts,* Donn F. Draeger and Robert W. Smith, 1969; *Ninjutsu: The Art of Invisibility,* Donn F. Draeger, 1971; *Ninja, Spirit of the Shadow Warrior,* Stephen K. Hayes, 1980; *The Ninja and Their Secret Fighting Art,* Stephen K. Hayes, 1981; *Secrets of the Samurai,* Oscar Ratti and Adele Westbrook, 1973; *Clan of Death: Ninja,* Al Weiss and Tom Philbin, 1981; *Ninjutsu, History and Tradition,* Dr. Masaaki Hatsumi, 1981.

NINJA WEAPONS AND EQUIPMENT
FUKIYA — Blow guns used with deadly accuracy by the ninjas. Used to take out sentries to stop a pursuing attacker. They were often disguised as flutes, canes or umbrellas. Special darts often with poisoned tips were used.

FUKUMI-BARI — Tiny dirks which the ninjas kept in his mouth, and then blew it at an antagonist with great accuracy.

HANKYU — A small bow used by the ninja often to shoot arrows carrying incendiary devices, with which to set fire to enemy encampments.

HITO WASHI — A gliding device used by the ninjas to jump from high points and glide over wall or enemy encampments. Made of bamboo and cloth, it enabled the ninjas to take on the form of human eagles.

HYAKURAI-JU — A weapon in which a number of guns were placed circularly inside a wooden barrel. Ignited by a fuse the loud noise was effective in startling and confusing a ninja's enemy.

IGADAMA — scattered on the ground to stop a pursuing enemy. Also used by the ninja as a throwing weapon usually effective when thrown in the face.

JIRAI — Feudal land mines used by the ninjas to cause confusion and damage to his enemies. These mines were buried underground and used a fused explosive charge to set it off.

KAMA-IKADA — A small one man raft which could be folded and carried by the ninja.

KITO GAN — A pill used by the ninjas which could delay thirst for a number of days.

KUMADE — A ninja climbing device made of collapsible bamboo and rope. About 9 or 10 pieces of bamboo are joined by a rope which runs through the center of the bamboo pieces. When the end of the rope is pulled it causes the collapsible device to stiffen into a single long staff. At the top there is a hook which can be positioned anywhere and facilitate climbing.

KUSARIFUNDO — Weighted short chain, ranging between eighteen and thirty inches in length. It consisted of a chain with two weighted ends. It was used by the ninja to strike an enemy or to entangle his weapon, or to choke him.

KYOBAKO-FUNE — A water crossing device which resembled a wooden chest. Covered by fur it was waterproof and could easily be carried by the ninja.

KYOKETSU-SHOGE — A small hand sickle which has an additional blade projecting from the blade itself. Attached to the butt of the sickle was a braided length of cord made often of animal hair. The end of the cord held a ring like device which could be hurled at an opponent and entangle his arm or neck. Then the ninja pulled his attacker close and used the sickle to finish him off. The KYOKETSU-SHOGE was also used in climbing, binding an enemy, raising equipment or dragging heavy loads.

METSUBUSHI — Blinding powders, used by the ninja to throw into an enemy's face blinding him momentarily and allowing the ninja to escape.

MIZUGUMO — Water crossing device in which a ninja could stand erect and virtually look like he was walking on water.

MIZUKAKI — Flipper like devices tied to a ninja's feet while swimming to hlep them move quicker through the water.

MIZU-TAIMATSU — A torch used by the ninjas, which could continue to burn even in the rain.

MIZUZUTSU — A bamboo snorkle tube, which the ninjas used while submerged. Often it was disguised as a smoking pipe.

MUSUBINAWA — A length of twisted horse's hair, it was used by the ninja to pull himself up into inaccessible places. It was very strong and easily concealed.

NAGE TEPPO — A hand grenade like device thrown into enemy encampments to cause damage and confusion.

NEKODE — A cat claw like device with a spiked surface worn on the hands by the ninja. It allowed him to grip hard surfaces for climbing, even up stone walls. The device was also used to grip or scrape an opponent's face.

NERU-KAWA ITO — A laminated leather shield used by ninjas to hide behind when shot at by an enemy.

NINJA-TO — Sometimes called SHINOBIGATANA. The sword used by the ninja. Its length was shorter than swords used by the samurai, to allow the ninja to fight in close quarters, and to allow him to move easier through small narrow spaces. The scabbard of the sword was longer than the blade, which provided the ninja with a place to conceal items such as chemicals, or powders which he would use to overpower enemies. The scabbard could also be used as a club, a breathing tube used while underwater, a lever, a hearing aid or a blow gun. The headguard (tsuba) of the ninja sword was large, which enabled the ninja to use it as a sort of step ladder by leaning it against a wall then stepping up on to the headguard, he could get over walls. Then using the extra long scabbard cord he'd pull the sword up after him. This scabbard cord was also often used to bind enemies. Because of its short length the ninjas used the sword with

Ninja with swords

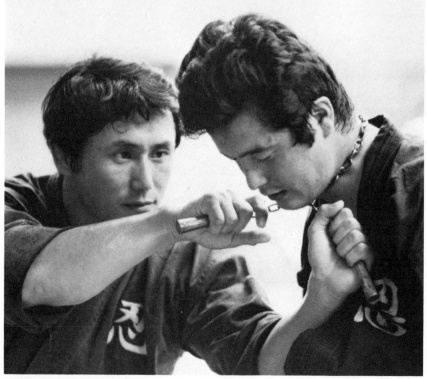

Ninja using kusarifundo

a full extended arm position, a practice not common by the samurai. Also because the blade was not nearly as sharp as samurai swords, ninjas relied on body swing to get power out of their sword movements.

SHIKORO — A saw with a pointed end used to cut through wood or metal.

SHINOBI-KAI — A bamboo weapon used by the ninja consisting of a short piece of bamboo, it held a weighted chain which could easily ensnare an attacker at close range.

SHINOBI-KUMADE — A climbing device used by the ninjas. It consisted or short pieces of bamboo which telescoped and retracted into a length easily concealable. A rope the length of the device and one of its ends contained a grappling hook to make climbing relatively easy.

SHINOBI-ZUE — A weapon made out of a hollow staff. Inside it was a length of weighted chain, and this could be flung at an attacker surprising him. The chain could be used to ensnare an opponent or his weapon, or it could be used to wrap around a protruding object and thus function as a climbing device.

SHUKO — Spiked bands which could slip over the hand or foot used mostly for climbing up walls, trees, etc. It could also be used to grab an attacker's sword, or to just rake an attacker's face or limbs. Also known as ASHIKO.

SHURIKEN — Small multipointed throwing weapons such as dirks, darts, stars, etc. These weapons were an integral part of a ninja's arsenal. The weapons vary in design from three to ten points. The two major types of Shuriken were the HIRA SHURIKEN—which were flat with three to eight points radiating from the center; and the BO SHURIKEN—which were straight blades either with one or two points. Most shuriken were aimed at the eyes, temple, throat, and arms to slow an attacker.

TO KI — Ninja climbing gear, which included numerous devices to get a ninja up or down almost anywhere.

TSUBA-GIRI — A fork shaped instrument used to open doors and cut locks.

TETSU BISHI — see entry.

TORINOKO — An egg shaped firecracker which emitted a loud bang, was used by the ninjas to confuse his enemies.

UKIDARU — Floating pots, which were used by ninjas to travel across the water. The ninjas would step into these pots and literally walk across a body of water while the pots were almost submerged.

YAMI-DOKO — A large kite used by the ninjas to fly over enemy positions or castles. Ninjas would often drop bombs from the kites or fly directly into the enemy territory.

YOKO-ARUKI — A unique method of walking sideways used by the ninja to traverse narrow passages, as well as to confuse an enemy, since his tracks would not reveal his direction of travel.

YUMI — Bow. The ninja bow and arrows (ya) were about half the size of the conventional Japanese longbow. These shorter bows were much easier to carry and conceal. Besides being used for assassination, the weapon was often used for signaling, setting fires, or creating diversions. Special arrows were equipped with bombs, flares, etc. and were very effective in creating havoc among enemy troops.

TRAINING SKILLS

The following were some of the expertise which most ninjas had to master.

BA-JUTSU — Horsemanship was an important part of training. Not only did a ninja master riding, he became proficient at all forms of combat from horseback.

BO-JUTSU — Stick and staff fighting were an important art to the ninja. They learned how to use sticks and canes of all sizes, and often used specially constructed canes which concealed chains, spears or darts that were effective in combat.

BO-RYAKU — Strategy was very important when infiltrating enemy lines. Deception and unconventional warfare gave the ninja the edge over his more conservative enemy.

Ninjas were famous for their climbing ability, much of which was due to their use of the shuko, or hand claws.

Ninja Bo-Shuriken

A ninja's Kuji-in energy channeling hand pose performed by
S. Hayes.

CHI-MON — The study of geography. It gave the ninja the skills to use the land and terrain around him to help accomplish his missions.

CHO HO — Methods of espionage were practiced by the ninja, and all means and ways of spy recruiting were studied.

HENSHO-JUTSU — Disguises and impersonations were an important element in ninjutsu. A ninja had to be able to move undetected through any area. To do this he had to literally take on the characteristics of the person he was to become.

INTON-JUTSU — Escape and concealment techniques were constantly practiced, refined and perfected. Ninjas became the ultimate masters at these techniques, which often mad epeople think of them as invisible.

KAYAKU-JUTSU — Fire and explosives were studied and used constantly. Placement of explosive devices as well as efficient ways of rigging and detonating them were practiced and perfected.

NAGINATA-JUTSU — Halbend fighting was practiced to allow ninjas to defeat an opponent at long to medium range.

SHINOBI-IRI — Stealth and methods of entering an enemy's stronghold was an important part of any ninja's knowledge. Special

ways of walking, running and jumping were learned. Climbing almost impenetrable walls became a ninja specialty.

SHURIKEN-JUTSU — Throwing blades of all shapes and sizes were used by ninjas to stop an enemy. Ninjas became extremely accurate with these throwing weapons which could be easily concealed on their person.

SUI-REN — Water training of all sorts were constantly practiced by the ninja. Swimming, using special flotation devices, underwater combat all were skills ninjas had to perfect.

TAI-JUTSU — Unarmed combat of all sorts were mastered by the ninja. Punching, kicking, striking as well as grappling were constantly practiced.

TEN-MON — Meteorology was a study undertaken by most ninja. Understanding weather patterns and the ability to observe environmental conditions were an important tool when planning any strategy.

YARI-JUTSU — Spear fighting was standard training for the ninja, who used all sorts of lances and spears in combat.

Dr. Masaaki Hatsumi (*center*), 34th Grandmaster of Togakure Ryu ninjutsu.

PENTJAK-SILAT

PENTJAK-SILAT National defense sport of the Indonesian archipelago. Pentjak is practiced as a solo exercise or with a training partner, sometimes with percussion instruments providing background music. It is often performed at festivals or weddings. Training varies with styles, but a typical method might include: **juris** (fundamentals), attacks against the weak points of the body, with fingers, knuckles, elbows, knees, head and feet; **langkah**, posture and footwork, students learn to move in all directions or to stand their ground in different positions; **bunga**, formal etiquette used prior to engagement; **sambut**, sparring exercise against one or more opponents; **rhasia**, advanced training in vital point attack and defense, a student learns the use of weapons (knife, sword, stick, rope, chain, etc.); and **kebatinau,** spiritual training, the final phase of training.

Many Indonesian combat authorities maintain that Indonesian combatives began on Riouw. The old Riouw combatives, in use as early as the 6th century A.D., are today called silat Melayu. Their concepts were carried to the Menangkabau kingdom at Priangan and to the Srividjaya empire centered at Palembang. In the former area silat Melayu underwent progressive change and diversification, eventually becoming pentjak-silat. While perhaps still a crude combat form in the 11th century, pentjak-silat was by the 14th century a polished property of the nobility—the Majapahit sultans and their court officials. Commoners were excluded from learning its tactics.

During the late 1940s anti-Dutch sentiment intensified development of the fighting arts and weapons of Indonesia. By and large, the old weapons of pentjak-silat remained unchanged but took on new applications in modern hand-to-hand combat. These systems were a product, as was "te" in Okinawa, of the drive for independence.

All systems of pentjak-silat are based on the use of weapons and are not considered empty-hand styles in the purest sense. Empty-hand motions may be performed, however, while wielding one or more weapons. Standard weapons in pentjak-silat are a mixture of transplanted and indigenous types and include: **pisau, parang, kris, tjabang,** and **toya.** In addition, geographically localized types exist; they include the **tongkat** (gada or gala), **pedang, arit, golok, kelewang,** and **tombak.** *Further reading: Fighting Arts of the Indonesian Archipelago,* Donn F. Draeger, 1972.

PANDEKAR Master teacher of Indonesian **pentjak-silat.** Besides his great technical skills, the pandekar is a spiritualist around whom legends have been born. His alleged supernatural powers include telepathy, mystic healing, and clairvoyance. He is also throught invulnerable. The world pandekar derives from the Menangkabau expression, pandai akal, meaning "clever mind."

FORMS OF PENTJAK-SILAT

BAGALOMBANG DUA-BLAS SILAT Form of **pentjak silat** practiced in Sumatra; its movements resemble the constant motion of waves.

BARU SILAT Form of Sumatran **pentjak-silat**, an evasive, defensive system, emphasizing hand actions to block, parry, and cover, as well as trapping and seizure tactics. Its name implies "new place."

BHAKTI NEGARA Southern Balinese style of **pentjak-silat** founded in 1955 by Ida Bagus Oka Dinwangkara. A synthesis of older pentjak-silat styles and Japanese methods of karate, aikido, and jujutsu, its name suggests "sacrifice/exclusive dedication/state." Sometimes written bakti negara. *Further reading: Weapons and Fighting Arts of the Indonesian Archipelago,* Donn F. Draeger, 1972.

BUDOJA INDONESIA MATARM Pentjak-silat combative form of central Java characterized by ground-rolling and high leaping. The name suggests "culture place of Indonesia."

CHAMPAKA PUTIH Style of **pentjak-silat** practiced in the Tjikabon area of central Java and extending to Jogjakarta. It is an unusual style in which practitioners assume the low squatting postures called sempok and depok. From these stances the champaka

putih practitioner can spin on one leg while extending the other, knocking an opponent's feet out from under him. This style finds its roots in the Menangkabau of Sumatra.

CHAMPAKA PUTIH White flower form of **pentjak silat,** practiced in the Tijikabon area of Central Java. It is an unusual style in which the practitioners, while crouching low to the ground, spin with an extended leg to knock an opponent's feet from under him.

DELIMA Form of east Javanese **pentjak-silat** practiced by inhabitants of the Ponorogo village. Named after a type of fruit, delima was created by Binpadgar in 1943 to fight the Dutch colonists on Java. *Further reading: Weapons and Fighting Arts of the Indonesian Archipelago,* Donn F. Draeger, 1972.

EKA SENTOSA SETITI Known simply as ESSTI, a **pentjak-silat** style and association founded on Bali by I. Made Regog, alias Pak Gunung. The first organization on Bali for pentjak-silat, it was created in 1937 out of the underground movement against the Dutch. Its methods, finalized by 1950, stem from southern Chinese kuntao, specifically **Shao-lin** (young forest). Eka implies "one," sentosa means "contact" or "secure," and setiti translates as "accurate." *Further reading: Weapons and Fighting Arts of the Indonesian Archipelago,* Donn F. Draeger, 1972.

ENDE The name of a port city of Southern Flores, off Indonesia, as well as that of a form of **pentjak-silat,** suggesting that the style traveled from Flores to Lombok and Bali. Ende practitioners are armed with a shield (tameng) and club (**pet jut**), which can be replaced by a whip. Combatants take three hard blows to the trunk and legs, but always keep the shield protecting the head. The contest, without time limit, is decided by knockout or surrender. *Further reading: Weapons and Fighting Arts of the Indonesian Archipelago* by Donn F. Draeger, 1972.

HARIMAU SILAT Unusual style of Sumatran **pentjak-silat;** practitioners assume positions in imitation of a tiger's stalking its prey. This style of silat, whose name translates as "tiger," is thought to have evolved for combat on wet, slippery surfaces where upright stances are insecure. *Further reading: Weapons and Fighting Arts of the Indonesian Archipelago,* Donn F. Draeger, 1972.

JOKUK Moslem form of **pentjak-silat** practiced in western Bali which uses mystic, trancelike states to make its combatants fanatical fighters. In precombat ceremonies, participants inflict wounds upon themselves, usually with a **kris,** to become insensitive to pain. *Further reading: Weapons and Fighting Arts of the Indonesian Archipelago,* Donn F. Draeger, 1972.

KARENA MATJANG Pentjak-silat style practiced in southwestern Celebes. Its name implies "to perform like a tiger." Karena matjang is related to **kuntao.**

KENDARI SILAT Pentjak-silat style centered in the city of the same name in the Celebes. It is characterized by cross-legged stances for use in cramped quarters, as on small boats.

KEROJOK Test of skill imposed in Javanese **pentjak-silat** against multiple attack. Known as tawur in East Java, this unrehearsed test pits as many as eight attackers against a solitary defender in both armed and unarmed encounters. The name kerojok implies "a fight of one against many."

KUMANGO SILAT Form of Sumatran **pentjak-silat;** a close-range method. *Further reading: Weapons and Fighting Arts of the Indonesian Archipelago,* Donn F. Draeger, 1972.

LANGKA-TIGA-SILAT Its name suggests "three steps"; this form of Sumatran **pentjak-silat** employs three-step fundamental positioning patterns.

LINTOW Pentjak-silat style practiced in Sumatra.

MUSTIKA KWITANG Pentjak-silat style practiced in West Java.

PAMUR Form of **pentjak-silat** practiced by the people of Madura, an island off the northeastern corner of Java. Founded in 1951 by Hasan Hubudin, pamur is headquartered at the founder's residence in Pamekasan.

The pamur system is synthesized from a variety of pentjak-silat forms, especially those of Sumatra. It borrows some of its technical intricacies from Chinese kuntao. Pamur silat categories:

isi (feeling)
    tangkapan—to catch the enemy
    bantingang—to throw the enemy
    sambut pukui—to evade, parry, and strike
    pombas mian—to kill
dasar (fundamentals)
    juris—step by step elements
    alis plarian—to dodge and escape
    kamasukan—successful entry into an enemy's defense
    harimau—tiger movements, such as *harimau kumbang,* or tiger and elephant

PARAIMAN SILAT Style of Sumatran **pentjak-silat** relying chiefly on foot techniques. Kicking has two phases: feinting and contact, both with the same foot.

PATAI SILAT Form of Indonesian **pentjak-silat** created around the turn of the 20th century by an unknown founder. Today, it is headed by Munap Malin Mudo. *Further reading: Weapons and Fighting Arts of the Indonesian Archipelago,* Donn F. Draeger, 1972.

PAUH SILAT Form of Sumatran **pentjak-silat** characterized by a square pattern of stepping movements. During combat one hand usually protects the groin; the locked thumb is the primary striking point to vital areas along an opponent's center line.

PERISAI DIRI Modern refinement of Central Javanese **pentjak-silat** systems; founded by R.M.S. Dirdjoatmodjo in 1955. Its tactics form the basis of self-defense training for Indonesian military personnel. With members throughout Indonesia, and branches in France and Italy, it is headed by eight master teachers. Practitioners are identified by traditional short trousers extending halfway below the knees; the jacket is without lapel, and sleeves end just above the wrist. Uniform colors are white for experts and black for students. *Further reading: Fighting Arts of the Indonesian Archipelago,* Donn F. Draeger, 1972.

PERSATRIAN HATI Central Javanese style of **pentjak-silat.**

PORBIKAWA Eastern Javanese system of combat that has synthesized elements of kuntao, **pentjak-silat,** and jujutsu.

PRISAI SAKTI Founded in 1946 by J. Widjihartani of Jagjakart, prisai sakti, implying "holy shield," is a synthesis of Javanese **pentjak-silat** forms and Japanese martial arts. In its modern interpretation, it is connected both to Christian religion and Indonesian nationalism, and stresses a philosophy called tri-sakti.

Outside of the conventional weapons common to all pentjak-silat systems, prisai sakti practitioners use the **piau,** pendjepit, and rante ber gangedug. *Further reading: Weapons and Fighting Arts of the Indonesian Archipelago,* Donn F. Draeger, 1972.

PUTIMANDI SILAT Literally "princess bathing," this form of Sumatran **pentjak-silat** is particularly noted for its toya (staff fighting) tactics.

RANDAI Indonesian form of combat that borrows movements from, but is not part of, **pentjak-silat.**

SANDANG SILAT Form of Sumatran **pentjak-silat** developed as counter to the powerful **sterlak silat.** It is a mysterious, rarely exhibited style.

SET HATI Pentjak-silat style practiced in central Java.

SETIA HATI TERATE East Javanese Muslim derivative of the **setia hati** form of **pentjak-silat.** It was originally called sedulur tunggal ketjer when founded in 1903 by Ki Ngabehi Soerodiwirjo (Pak Soero) in Surabaja. The style possesses a philosophical and religious as well as mechanical basis. *Further reading: Fighting Arts of the Indonesian Archipelago,* Donn F. Draeger, 1972.

SILAT MAKASSAR General name for **pentjak-silat** in southern Celebes.

SILAT MENANGKABAU Generally known as silat Menangkabau or silat padang, the Menangkabau styles are the technical core for all Sematran **pentjak-silat.**

SILAT ORGANASI National **pentjak-silat** association, under the technical guidance of Ali Al-habsi, which united the many pentjak-silat systems in 1947.

SILAT PUTRA Pentjak-silat style catering to the youth of Central Java.

SISEMBA Known also as sempak or semba, this sportive style of **pentjak-silat** is one of the most unusual in the Celebes. "Sisemba," ranks and lines of opposing factions, square off at one another in the middle of a level field, usually a muddy, slippery rice paddy. Lines and ranks, in various combinations, maneuver and close with opposing lines and ranks. A line once formed must remain a line with combatants clasping hands. Upon approaching one another, the opposing forces kick in any manner, endeavoring to knock down or out their selected targets, thus breaking the line of the opposing force. *Further reading: Weapons and Fighting Arts of the Indonesian Archipelago,* Donn F. Draeger, 1972.

STERLAK SILAT Sumatran **pentjak-silat** style; practitioners train to apply the entire body force behind the fist, foot, or head in executing their attacks.

SULAT Form of **pentjak-silat** native to the island of Sumbawa. Participants, clad in short loincloths, engage in brief freestyle confrontations. Each combatant attempts to wound the other with a flexible pineapple leaf (serrated edges) wrapped in one hand.

SUNDRA SILAT Term for **pentjak-silat** systems in West Java. Sundra silat is also called bundung silat, which in turn is sometimes loosely referred to as main-po, or "to do po." Po implies "self-defense."

TAPAK SUTJI Complicated form of **pentjak-silat,** founded in 1963 by Ifan Badjam; practiced in Central Java. This style is characterized by use of the Japanese **katana** and an indigenous weapon called the **segu.** *Further reading: Weapons and Fighting Arts of the Indonesian Archipelago,* Donn F. Draeger, 1972.

TAPU SILAT Highly secret form of **pentjak-silat** practiced in the Celebes. Revealed only to experts in self-defense, it specializes in countering unanticipated attacks from the rear.

TJAMPUR Synthesis form of Sumatran **pentjak-silat** whose underlying precept is aggressiveness based on premeditated assault. It depends wholly on close-range surprise tactics. Its name implies the world "combined." *Further reading: Weapons and Fighting Arts of the Indonesian Archipelago,* Donn F. Draeger, 1972.

TJATJI Known also as tjatjing, and formally as main tjatji, meaning "to do" and "strike the enemy," this form of **pentjak-silat** appears to be indigenous to the island of Flores, bordering Indonesia. There are several methods of tjatji, one of which uses a hardwood stick and a buffalo hide shield. *Further reading: Weapons and Fighting Arts of the Indonesian Archipelago,* Donn F. Draeger, 1972.

TJI Sundanese variation of the word tjai, meaning "river water." It was used originally to prefix the names of **pentjak-silat** systems of West Java because many of those systems were developed in the lowland basin areas. The prefix tji was always suffixed by a word identifying an animal, the characteristics of which made up the distinctive actions of each system, such as kabon (bat), matjan (tiger), uler

Weaponry of *pentjak-silat*

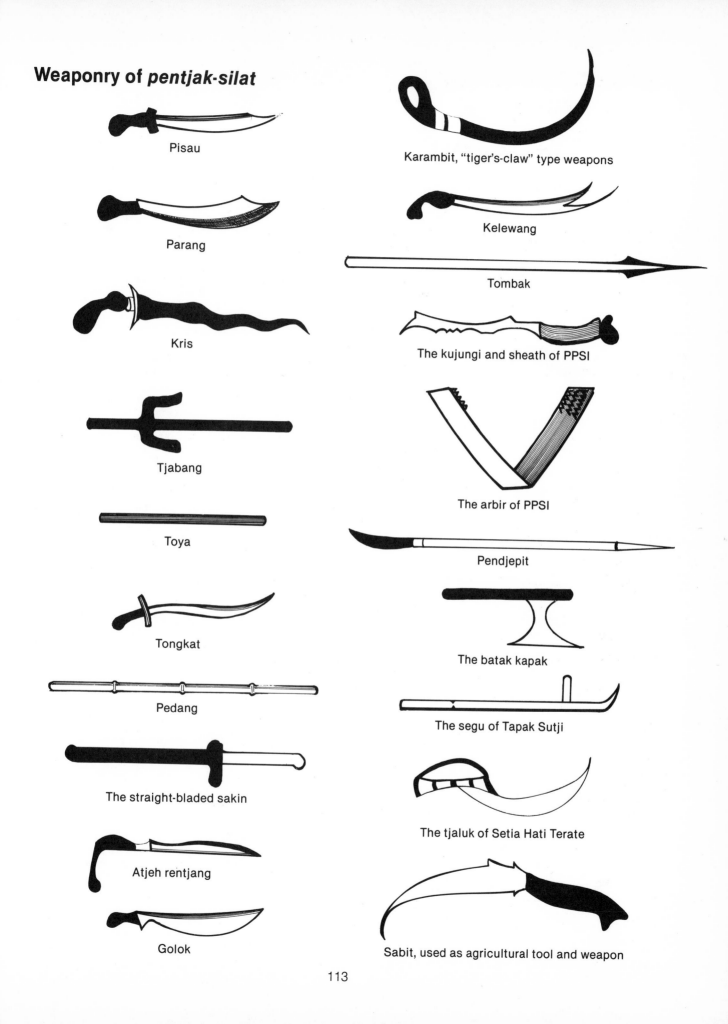

Pisau

Parang

Kris

Tjabang

Toya

Tongkat

Pedang

The straight-bladed sakin

Atjeh rentjang

Golok

Karambit, "tiger's-claw" type weapons

Kelewang

Tombak

The kujungi and sheath of PPSI

The arbir of PPSI

Pendjepit

The batak kapak

The segu of Tapak Sutji

The tjaluk of Setia Hati Terate

Sabit, used as agricultural tool and weapon

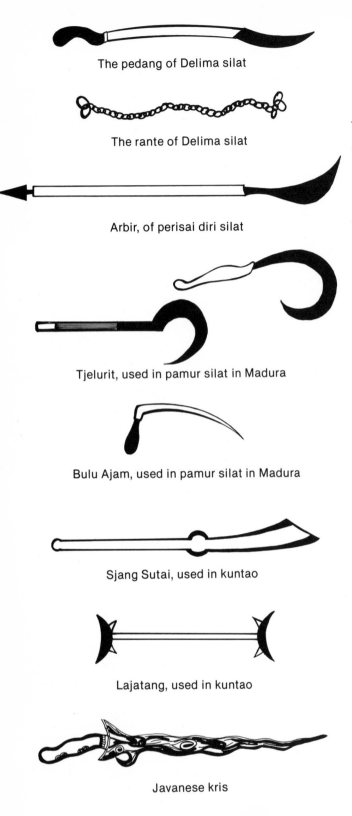

The pedang of Delima silat

The rante of Delima silat

Arbir, of perisai diri silat

Tjelurit, used in pamur silat in Madura

Bulu Ajam, used in pamur silat in Madura

Sjang Sutai, used in kuntao

Lajatang, used in kuntao

Javanese kris

The batak raut

(snake), etc. Some West Javanese forms are tjikampek, **tjikalong, tjimande,** tjimatjan, tjiuler, tjipetir, tjibedujut, tjimalaja, and tjikabon.

Belying their origins, tji systems can be found on the innermost high plateaus and mountain ranges of Central and West Java. All are classified under Sundra silat, a general term for pentjak-silat in West Java. *Further reading: Weapons and the Fighting Arts of the Indonesian Archipelato,* Donn F. Draeger, 1972.

TJIANDUR Style of **pentjak-silat** practiced in West Java.

TJIKALONG Form of West Javanese **pentjak-silat** characterized by open-hand blows and augmented blocks. According to Chinese legend, this system was born when a visiting **kuntao** master exhibited his skill in dodging blowpipe missiles, and students sought him out for instruction. *See also* pukulan.

TJIMANDE Form of West Javanese **pentjak-silat** known also as pentcha, pentcha-silat, or pentjak betwai. Tjimande, which was conceived in the 19th century by a man named Kair, is chiefly an arm-hand system with frontal kicks aimed at low target areas, with secondary emphasis on weapons. *Further reading: Weapons and the Fighting Arts of the Indonesian Archipelago,* Donn F. Draeger, 1972.

TJINGKRIK Form of West Javanese **pentjak-silat** characterized by evasive footwork, open-hand actions, and acrobatic tactics.

TJIWARINGIN Rare form of West Javanese **pentjak-silat** derived from **tjimande.**

TRIDHARMA Northern Balinese system of **pentjak-silat** whose name means "three-honesty/peaceful." It is a balanced system including both the traditional weapons of pentjak-silat and empty-hand techniques. *Further reading: Weapons and Fighting Arts of the Indonesian Archipelago,* Donn F. Draeger, 1972.

TUNGGAL HATI Central Javanese style of **pentjak-silat.**

UNDUKAYAM SILAT Highly unusual form of Sumatran **pentjak-silat** whose mechanical base imitates the actions of a hen. Footwork is used only for displacement and like that of a hen's, is short and choppy. Hand actions are defensive, somewhat like the scratching of a hen searching the ground for food.

PUKULAN

Indonesian martial arts are known as Pukulan. Pukulan is strictly an East Java term; in the west fighting styles are known as **pentjak**, and in the midlands as **silat.** Pukulan is similar to karate, blows are delivered to all parts of the body with either the hands or feet. Like karate this martial art has its **kata** (forms), attacks, and blocks. Styles include serak (decoy), petjut (whipstyle), mina kabauw (dance style), tjemantik (classic style), si matjan (tiger style), suchi hati (big-hearted style), kuntao (Chinese style), tiji monjet (ape style), and klipap (thunder style), against nerve centers.

Use of weapons is also taught, including staff (7 foot), siku-siku (small fork), bedok (curved knife), and **kris** (wavy bladed short sword). These styles have been greatly influenced by Chinese systems that emphasize animal-like movement. It was brought to the U.S. by two Dutch-Indonesians, Paul deThoars and Rudy Ter Linden.

FORMS OF PUKULAN

SERAK Style of **pukulan,** meaning "decoy," very much like Chinese fist and foot fighting. In this particular style the object is not to back off, but to move in on an opponent, then to rely on great speed and reflexes to counter the blow being delivered and retaliate with a strike or trip. Serak was devised by a Sudanese named Mas Ojut, who lived and taught in West Java around the turn of the century. He was originally trained in the kilap "thunder clap" style of nerve center strikes. Legend claims he could kill animals at a distance, or sense the approach of attackers. He was supposed to be a Pendekai "priest master."

SAMBO; SOMBO; CAMBO

A style of jacket wrestling that originated in Russia in the 1930s, Sambo combines techniques from over 20 styles of folk wrestling known in the various republics of the Soviet Union at that time, together with elements from both international wrestling styles and several martial arts. Styles of combat that influenced sambo include Greco-Roman wrestling from the Baltic states; Georgian and Armenian jacket-throwing; Turkish kuresh wrestling from Azerbaijan; and "kokh," the national wrestling of Armenia. Aspects of international freestyle wrestling, judo, and jujutsu are also evident in sambo. The term sambo is an acronym for the Russian phrase "self-defense without weapons" (sam-oborona Bes Orusyia).

Sambo was initially conceived as a means of unarmed crowd control, used by domestic police and soldiers for training in hand-to-hand combat. The initial rules governing sport sambo were drawn up by Anatoly A. Kharlampfief, the father of sambo. He was assisted in this effort by A. Oshichenikov, a 2nd-degree black belt who taught judo to the Red Army in 1917, and V. Speredonov, who began teaching judo in Moscow in 1923. Sambo was officially adopted as a separate All-Union sport in the Soviet Union by the Soviet National Sports Committee on June 9, 1938. The following year, the first sambo championships in the U.S.S.R. were held in Leningrad.

The International Amateur Wrestling Federation (FILA) first recognized sambo as a sport of world stature alongside freestyle and Greco-Roman wrestling in 1968, adopting it as wrestling's third discipline. In 1972 the first European Championships were held in Russia. In 1973 FILA sponsored the first World Championships in Teheran. Four U.S. wrestlers competed in that tournament, with two placing third, one fifth, and one sixth. In 1975 the U.S. took one third place, one fourth, and one fifth at the World Championships in Minsk, Russia. In 1977, the U.S. captured the Pan-American title in Puerto Rico, with seven gold and three silver medals, then repeated as champions in San Diego in 1979 with eight gold and two silver. In 1979 the U.S. placed fifth in the World Championships in Madrid, sending its first full team to a world sambo championships. Eight of the ten U.S. wrestlers in that event placed in the top 6 positions in their weight classes, including two third place finishes, two fourths, one fifth, and three sixths. The U.S. finished third in Madrid at the 1980 Sambo World Cup Championships, with two silver and three bronze medals. Subsequent World Championships were scheduled for Tokyo (1981) and Moscow (1982). In World Cup Competition, as of 1980, the U.S. had earned two silver and three gold medals.

Russians dominated international competition in sambo in the early years, winning all ten weight classes in the 1st World Championships in 1973. In 1975 the Russians won eight gold medals, the Mongolians one, and the British one. In 1979 the Russians had seven world champions to two for Mongolia and one for Spain. In both World Cup Competitions held in 1977 and 1980, the Russians won all ten gold medals. Bulgaria, Mongolia, Japan, the U.S., and Spain consistently had teams ranked in the top 5 or 6 places at world championships between 1973 and 1979.

Like judo, sambo began in the U.S. as a committee of the Wrestling Division of the Amateur Athletic Union. Russ Winer (Ariz.) was appointed the first sambo committee chairman in 1973. He was succeeded by Bobby Douglas (Ariz.) in 1975 and Ivan Olsen (Calif.) in 1977. In 1975 Jamison Devel (Ariz.) and Josiah Henson (Alaska) became the first two internationally qualified American FILA sambo referees.

The First National AAU Senior Men's Sambo Championships were held in Phoenix in 1975. Subsequent national championships were held in Phoenix (1976); San Diego (1977); Chula Vista, Calif. (1978); Walnut, Calif. (1979), and Potomac, Md. (1980). The first National AAU Junior (20 and under) sambo competition was held in Walnut, Calif. in 1979, in preparation for the inaugural FILA World Junior Championships that year in Madrid. The first National AAU Senior Women's and Age Group (under 16) Championships were held in Kansas City, Mo. in 1980.

Sambo wrestlers compete in outfits that combine the wrestling uniform and the judogi: soleless or soft, thin-soled shoes, trunks or wrestling singlet, and a tight fitting jacket, known as kurtka. The official sambo jacket differs from a judogi in the following ways: sleeves extend to the wrist; the body of the jacket is tighter and slightly shorter; the jacket has epaulets or shoulder cuffs sewn into it (for grasping); the belt is worn through loops that keep it in place, since the belt can be grabbed in sambo.

Sambo jackets, like international wrestling singlets, come in red and blue. Each competitor must have one of each for competition. Sambo differs from international freestyle and Greco-Roman wrestling in three principal respects: jackets may be held while executing techniques; sambo allows "submission" holds, or joint locks on both arms and legs, designed to force an opponent to submit or give up; the object of sambo is not to pin—a holddown may earn a maximum of four points, but will not end the match.

Sambo differs from judo in the following ways: sambo wrestlers compete in shoes, with trunks or singlets instead of barefoot and in pants; no choking is permitted; submission holds or joint locks are permitted on the leg; wrestling takedowns and direct leg attacks are permitted.

A sambo bout consists of two periods of three minutes each, with a one minute rest in between. A match ends immediately following a "total victory." A total victory occurs when a perfect throw is executed—the opponent lands on his back and the thrower remains standing; when an opponent surrenders by calling out or tapping the mat twice, when one wrestler gains twelve technical points in excess of his opponent's total, referred to as a technical victory; or when one of the contestants forfeits the match due to injury or disqualification.

There are four types of maneuvers in sambo that will result in total victory or points. These are:

1) *Holddown (Immobilization):* similar to the judo holddown or an extended wrestling near fall. One wrestler must hold the other's back towards the mat in a danger position (less than 90 degrees) with both chests in contact to score. A 10-second holddown is worth two points; a 20-second holddown is worth four points. A maximum of four points can be earned for holding down in a single match and a wrestler who has scored a four-point holddown will not be allowed to attempt further holddowns. Holddowns do not end the match.

A holddown is broken in one of two ways: by turning to the side or chest and off the back, or by breaking chest contact so the chests of both wrestlers no longer touch. Wrapping legs around an opponent will not break a sambo holddown, unlike judo.

In the case of a tie score, various tie-breaking criteria determine the winner of a match. One tie-breaking criteria is which wrestler has scored the highest technical point maneuver. In a tie situation, the wrestler with one four-point holddown will be declared the winner over a wrestler with two two-point holddowns. Accordingly, a wrestler with one or two "two-point" holddowns will be allowed to attempt to substitute a "four-point" holddown even though he has already two "two-point" holddowns and as a result has reached the four point allowable maximum for holding down. If a wrestler successfully completes a "four-point" holddown, that holddown will be scored and any previous holddown points will be erased.

2) *Takedown:* Similar to a freestyle wrestling takedown, except that both wrestlers must start on their feet and the takedown must be completed in a single, continuous motion. The attacking wrestler must 1. unbalance his opponent and 2. take the opponent to the mat, ending up in control. The key element is unbalancing the opponent; gaining control is not enough. Many freestyle takedowns will not score points in sambo. No takedown points can be scored unless the attacker begins the move on his feet. A wrestler may score while on his knees only by lifting the opponent so that the maneuver can qualify as a throw instead of a takedown. Takedowns do not end the match.

3) *Submission Hold* (pressure hold, luxation, arm or leg bag, torture grip, joint-lock, etc.): Applicable to either arms or legs, similar to arm bars in judo. The attacking wrestler applies pressure against the ankle, knee, or elbow joint to force an opponent to surrender. Submission holds may not be applied while standing. A successful submission hold ends the match by total victory.

4) *Throw:* Similar to judo throws, except that the throw is evaluated according to two criteria: the position of the attacking wrestler after the throw is completed (whether he remains on his feet or falls to the mat), and how the thrown wrestler lands on the mat (whether he lands on his back, his side, or his front). This ends the match by total victory. Other throws, in which the attacker falls or the attacked wrestler ends up in a better defensive position than on his back, are awarded one to four points. The impact of a throw is not a factor in

the award of points as it is in judo, nor is arch, amplitude, or style as in freestyle and Greco-Roman wrestling. Only the final positions of the wrestlers are important; a soft throw is scored the same as a hard throw. Unless both wrestlers are on their feet, the attacker must lift the defender for the move to be throw.

In 1979 FILA established a promotion program for sambo wrestling that recognizes proficiency in sambo with the award of colored belts. Unlike belts in many martial arts, sambo belt ranks are determined exclusively by competition. The belt rankings are: 1st degree (white); 2nd degree (yellow); 3rd degree (green); 4th degree (blue); 5th degree (red); 6th degree (black); 7th degree (black with national color); 8th degree (bronze with FILA emblem); 9th degree (silver with FILA emblem); 10th degree (gold with FILA emblem); 11th degree (gold with FILA emblem and honor band). The first three belts are awarded by certified local club instructors with the approval of the regional federation. Fourth and 5th degrees are awarded by regional coaches with approval by the national federation. The 6th-degree black belt is awarded by national coaches to national caliber sambo wrestlers; 7th degree is awarded by the national federation to national sambo champions. The 8th-degree belt is awarded by the World Sambo Committee to wrestlers who have placed third in a continental or world championship. The 9th-degree belt is awarded to those placing second in a continental or world championship, and 10th to continental champions, world cup winners, and world champions. The 11th-degree belt is given exclusively to those with formidable competitive records (several world or continental championships), international masters of sambo, or foremost referees. In sambo, coaches can be awarded belts based on the performance of their wrestlers.

Sambo wrestling

SAVATE

Savate is a French style of foot and fist fighting. Systematized in post-Napoleonic France, savate is the only martial arts native to Europe that still exists in both sport and combative forms. The precise origin of the art is unknown, and puzzled even its earliest practitioners. It is known that 17th-century sailors of Marseilles were required to practice stretch-kicks to keep them in condition for ocean voyages. Some historians speculate that these sailors were influenced by contact with the Asian martial arts during their occasional visits to Burma, Thailand, and China. Certainly, street fighting in the barrooms and alleys of French seaports did begin to feature crescent kicks to the head, body, and legs—though they lacked power and often missed the opponent altogether. Sailors called this form of foot-fighting "chausson," or "slipper," in reference to the felt slippers they wore when practicing stretch-kicks.

Meanwhile, perhaps influenced by chausson, the soldiers in Napoleon's army developed an unofficial punishment for regimental misfits. A group of soldiers would hold the offender in place while another kicked him severely in the buttocks. The punishment was called "la savate," literally "old shoe," but might be best translated as "booting." Perhaps Parisian soldiers introduced savate to the public, booting undesirables in the shins or confronting the disorderly with a leg kick. Whatever the case, by the beginning of the 19th century the ruffian elements of Paris brawled with their feet rather than their fists, and their kick-fighting was popularly called savate.

Eventually, a young man named Michael Casseuse sought out the better street fighters and observed and categorized their techniques. The result was a refined fighting system. His offensive techniques emphasized front, side, and round kicks to the knee, shin, or instep. The hands were held low and open to defend against groin attacks. Palm heel strikes were used to attack the face, nose, and eyes.

In 1824 Casseuse authored a pamphlet on savate that caught the attention of Parisian polite society. Almost overnight he became the country's most sought after master of self-defense. His clientele ranged from the wealthy to the noble and included both Lord Seymour and the Duke of Orleans (heir to the French throne). Street fighters throughout Paris and across France, many of them chausson practitioners, regularly descended upon his school to challenge his mastery. Fortunately, Casseuse, himself an excellent fighter, always rose to the occasion. But as a result of these encounters with chausson, savate came to include both mid-level and high-level kicks, in addition to Casseuse's low kicks.

Later, Charles Lecour, one of Casseuse's best students, journeyed to London to study bare-knuckle boxing from England's most respected teachers, Adams and Smith. Upon his return to Paris in 1832, he synthesized English boxing and Casseuse's savate to create "la boxe Francaise," or "French boxing." Lecour also introduced the use of boxing gloves for training, which minimized accidents and increased the art's popularity. Again, France's elite took notice and Lecour became a sought after fight master.

Lecour and other major teachers regularly opened their schools for public viewing of full-contact competition patterned after the London Prize Ring rules. And in 1850, Louis Vignezon, nicknamed the "Cannonman," emerged as savate's first major ring champion. Vignezon carried a cannon on his shoulders as he made his way into the ring, to dishearten his opponents. His greatest fame came from knocking out the giant wrestler "Arpin the Terrible" with only four kicks.

One of the few men who could stay in the ring with Vignezon, and thus serve as an adequate sparring partner, was his best student, Joseph Charlemont. In 1862 Charlemont toured Europe, challenging fighters of all stylistic persuasions. He was undefeated in the ring. When Charlemont returned to France he introduced fencing theory and footwork, added wrestling techniques, and improved kicking and punching techniques. He was the first to prove the value of high kicks. He is still considered the greatest savateur of all time.

Charlemont's fighting system used the same fighting stance found in modern fencing. His punches were based on a forward lunge and included straights, swings, and uppercuts. His kicks, on the other hand, stressed speed and accuracy above power. The leg was lifted straight from the floor to the target with little preparatory recoil.

Characteristic of these kicks, again influenced by fencing, was a peculiar counterbalancing movement of the arms to improve accuracy.

Charlemont taught his system around the concept of four ranges. The first range, for the cane, is derived from fencing. (The sword itself had been forbidden by law; its role as part of the dress of the fashionable French gentleman was replaced by the cane.) Charlemont could deliver 140 cane blows in 80 seconds. The cane, or "la canne," is still taught to savate students. The second range deals with long-distance techniques, such as kicking. The third range is a medium-distance, with hand techniques. And the last range consists of wrestling techniques.

By the turn of the 19th century, inspired by the example of Joseph Charlemont, savateurs throughout France began to make an effort to promote their art around the world. The great John L. Sullivan was once staggered, and then knocked to the ground by the kicks of a savateur. Charlemont's son, Charles, fought a world-class British prize fighter named Jerry Driscoll and won by knockout in the 6th round. Georges Carpentier, who challenged Jack Dempsey for the world heavyweight boxing championship, was also a savateur.

During the two world wars, thousands of savateurs were killed, and the art was threatened with extinction. In 1945 Count Pierre Baruzy, a student of Charles Charlemont and an eleven-time French national champion, attempted to revive savate. Since the Count was also a black belt in judo, and had had some exposure to karate, he solicited help from the growing numbers of post-war French judo instructors. By the mid-1960s there were enough savate schools to justify the creation of a national organization. The Count became its founder and first president.

A savate club was started in Genoa, Italy, as long ago as 1830. Today, there is a modern French boxing/savate center in Milan. The art was established in Belgium when Joseph Charlemont traveled there in the 1880s and taught the novelist Alexandre Dumas.

To practice savate today, one wears a T-shirt, gym tights or tracksuit trousers, sneakerlike boots, and special boxing gloves (usually 16 oz). The wrist of the savate glove extends half-way up the forearm and is used for blocking. Since World War II, savate has had a grading system: grade is indicated by an inch-wide colored band around the glove's wrist; these grades are called "gloves." The first grade is purple glove, followed by blue, green, red, white, and yellow. The average student reaches yellow glove in about two years. Above this, there is the silver glove of the instructor, and the golden glove of the "professeur."

Today's savate incorporates all of the innovations of the 20th century boxing ring, from Jack Dempsey to Muhammad Ali. Kicking techniques have been designed that are compatible with a boxer's hand techniques. And the unusual counterbalancing actions of the arms have been eliminated from ring use. Competitively, sport savate uses **full-contact** rules and emphasizes fast kicking combinations. As a self-defense system, open-hand and bare-knuckle techniques are still taught, and combined with weapons skills (cane). (Paul Maslak) *See also* Europe, history of karate in. *Further reading: Black Belt Magazine,* March 1967.

BOXE, FRANCAIS Francais Boxe, or French boxing, is a regional style of combat in which both gloved fists and feet are employed. Derived from **savate** and chausson, it is performed, like boxing, in a roped ring. It is now little more than an exhibition sport.

Savate

Savate

118

SUMO

A Japanese combative sport, sumo is practiced by men of gigantic proportions; originally it was known as **sumai** (struggle). According to Nihon Shoki (23 B.C.), combat sumai began on a beach at Iaumo in Shimane prefecture, where Tajima-no-Kehaya met Nomi-no-Sukune in a fierce fight. Sukune defeated Kehaya, fracturing his ribs with a kick, knocking him to the ground, and crushing his hipbone. (Kehaya died from these injuries.)

Sumai evolved into a stylized form of military training, emerging finally as sumo. Sumo is practiced in Japan today, and the various elements of its long tradition are faithfully preserved. Prior to the period between 1570 and 1600, wrestling appears to have been a relatively comprehensive form of combat which, although modified in regard to lethal blows and kicks, did not seem to differ substantially from forms of Mongolian wrestling or even certain European styles. In 1570, however, the ring (dohyo) was introduced and with it fundamental rules establishing ranks, purposes, and basic techniques. The organization of sumo today maintains the ancient division of its professional adherents into three groups: wrestlers, referees, and judges.

Sumo wrestlers (rikishi) are unusually tall, and powerful men selected for their size and then conditioned through training and diet until they reach gargantuan proportions. Since there are no weight limits, it is possible for a wrestler to find himself pitted against an opponent twice his own weight. According to their wrestling performance they are given titles ranging from novice to grand champion.

The ring is an elevated circular area, 2 feet high, once formed by linking 16 rice bales to make a diameter of 15 feet. The floor is constructed of a special clay, and is covered by a thin layer of sand. The tourney begins with an announcement of the program by a professional speaker whose style of delivery resembles narration in religious events or theatrical presentations. There are ceremonies involving the public presentation of the wrestlers and preliminary bouts, which build to a peak of excitement as the grand champions perform the ancient rituals of purification and preparation. For the match the wrestlers are naked except for a silken loincloth (mawashi),

which is wrapped around their waist four to seven times. The mawashi is approximately two feet wide and is made of heavy silk folded in six.

The rules of the contest are simple. Victory is achieved by either forcing the opponent out of the ring, or forcing him to touch the floor within the boundaries of the ring with any part of his body above the knee. This may be accomplished by the use of any one or a combination of approximately 200 movements based upon 32 key techniques. They include pushing the hands only (tsuki), pushing with the entire body (oshi), and clinching (yori).

Starting from a squatting position with their toes on certain marks and bodies resting on their heels, the wrestlers shift to the low position of readiness (shikiri) with feet and fists on the ground. From this position they attempt to launch various attacks, employing weight, strength, suppleness, and strategy in whatever measure they are capable.

Sumo techniques can be divided into two groups: those with limited body contact, such as slapping (tsuppari), side-stepping (hataki-komo), leg sweeps (ketaguri), and leg holds (ashi-tori); and those with extended or full body contact. This last group includes a seemingly infinite number of head throws, arm throws, and hip throws performed by sacrificing one's own position to displace the opponent (utchari). In accordance with the rules, however, if an utchari technique is to be successful, the wrestler attempting it must not touch the floor with his body until after his opponent has already done so. Sumo matches have one referee (gyoji) who is in the ring overseeing the match and five judges who watch from the side. The Gyoji wears a kimono and carries a fan, the various colors of its tassel determining his rank.

The military influence of the past is still vividly present in sumo costumes, particularly in that of the judges and the sword bearer (tachi-mochi) who accompanies the grand champion, in the hair styles worn by the wrestlers, in the water ceremony (mizu-sakazuki), performed before the contest, and finally in the bow ceremony (**yumitori-shiki**), which closes the tournament. *See also* sumai; sumo tori. *Further reading: The Book of Sumo,* Doug Kenrick, 1969; *Takamiyama, The World of Sumo,* Jesse Kuhaulua and John Wheeler, 1973; *Martial Arts of the Orient,* Jeffrey Somers, 1975; *Secrets of the Samurai,* Adele Westbrook and Oscar Ratti, 1973.

Sumo throw

120

Slapping techniques (tsuppari) are often seen in sumo matches. The wrestlers repeatedly slap each other in the face, trying to force one another off balance. Sometimes these exchanges result in blood being drawn.

Sumo ring

SUMO TOURNAMENTS

There are six Grand Tournaments each year in Tokyo, one in Osaka, Nagoya, and Kyushu. Each tournament lasts fifteen days, and every wrestler fights once every day with a different opponent. All matches start in the morning, with the lowest ranking wrestlers followed by those of progressively higher and higher rank, until toward the end of the day the bouts featuring the Yokozuna (grand champions) occur.

The winner of the tournament is awarded the Emperor cup on the final day. He also receives the championship flag. The Emperor cup is made of pure silver and was first as awarded in 1926.

Since 1947, three additional prizes are awarded to wrestlers who have won at least eight of their fifteen matches. The shukunsho is awarded to the wrestler who defeats the most Yokozuna or Ozeki (champions).

The Kantosho is given to the wrestler with the best record or to the wrestler who displayed the best fighting spirit.

The ginosho is given to the wrestler who displayed the best sumo technique in the tournament.

Sumo Rankings All sumo wrestlers are graded into five classifications or rankings. At the top are the Makuuchi, or champion, classes, headed by the Yokozuna, Ozeki, Sekiwake, and Komusubi. Those The wrestlers with these titles receive many special privileges. The wrestlers below the titled ranks are called the Maegashira.

The group below the Makuuchi is headed by the Juryo ranks. All sumo wrestlers aspiring to the Makuuchi group must pass through the Juryo ranks.

The lower ranks include the Sandamme, Jonidan, and Jonokuchi.

BANZUKE After each tournament, the Banzuke (rankings) are revised and wrestlers are either promoted or demoted, depending on their performance during the fifteen-day competition. The Yokozuna, alone of all the ranks, can never be demoted.

For a wrestler to be considered for promotion to Yokozuna he must have won two or more tournaments while holding the rank of Ozeki (champion).

The rank of a wrestler determines the style in which his long hair is dressed. The higher the rank, the more elaborate the hairstyle.

DOHYO-IRI Every day of a sumo tournament before the matches begin, the dohyo-iri (entering the ring) ceremony takes place. Down the aisle in reverse order of their rank comes one team of wrestlers.

The wrestlers wear their kesho-mawashi (ceremonial aprons). These aprons are beautifully made of silk and are richly embroidered with different designs and hemmed with gold fringe. The wrestlers climb into the ring and go through a short ritual. After they depart, another team of wrestlers enters from the opposite aisle and repeats the ritual.

The major ceremony takes place when the Yokozuna enter the ring. A Yokozuna comes down the aisle attended by a senior gyoji (referee) and two lower-class wrestlers, one of whom bears a sword. Over his kesho-mawashi the Yokozuna wears a massive braided-hemp rope weighing from 25 to 35 pounds tied in a bow at the back and ornamented in the front with strips of paper hanging in zigzag patterns.

While the gyoji and the attendants crouch in the ring, the Yokozuna performs the dohyo-iri ceremony. He first claps his hands together to attract the attention of the gods. He then extends his arms to the sides and turns his palms upward to show he has no weapons. He lifts one leg high in the air, sideways, then the other, bringing each leg down with a resounding stamp. After he finishes his ceremony, he and his attendant leave the ring, and the other Yokozuna enter and repeat the ceremony.

YUMITORI-SHIKI After the final match of the day in a sumo tournament, a wrestler climbs into the ring and is handed a bow with which he performs the yumitori-shiki (bow dance). The ceremony was introduced during the Edo period when winning wrestlers were awarded a prize of a bow and to express their happiness they performed a bow dance.

SHIKIRI The preliminary posturing ritual in sumo: the wrestlers stoop almost with their noses in the earth—pound the floor with their fists, and fix each other with piercing looks. They do not begin the match at once but work themselves and the spectators up into the proper pitch of excitement. The rules specify that this may last at the most only four minutes.

TEGATANA Tegatana is a ritual performed by the winning wrestler when receiving his prize. The wrestler squats in the sonkyo (basic) position at the place where the ring is broken (nijiguchi) and, using one hand like a sword, he cuts to the left, right, and middle, a gesture thanking god for the match.

CHIRI A dusting-off ritual performed by each wrestler before his match in which the hands are slapped hard, rubbed together, then spread wide apart to the sides at shoulder height. This is an old custom from days when sumo matches were held in open fields and wrestlers snatched up blades of grass to clean their hands.

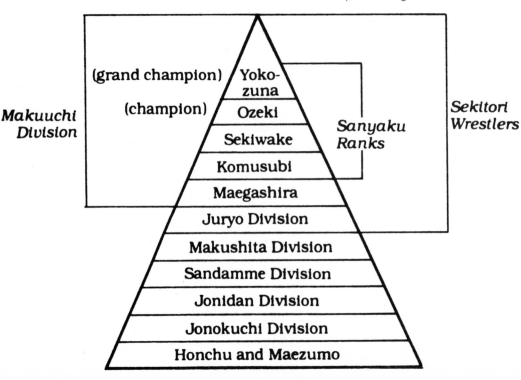

TECHNIQUES

In sumo there is a set of traditional forms called shujihatte (48 maneuvers). These techniques form the foundation of sumo, but there are countless other moves or variations that sumo wrestlers employ.

Most sumo techniques can be divided into throws, trips, twists, or backward maneuvers.

Some common sumo techniques include:

Tsukidashi

Oshidashi

Shitatenage

Uwatenage

Sukuinage

Kotenage

Hatakikomi

Tsuradashi

Tsukiotoshi

Tottari

Sotogake

Uchigake

Nodowa

Utchari

Yorikiri

Okuridashi

TAE KWON DO; TAEKWON-DO; TAEKWON DO

Literally, "Art of kicking and punching," tae kwon do is a native Korean form of fighting that embraces kicking, punching, jumping, blocking, dodging, and parrying. It is a system for training both the mind and body, with an emphasis on the development of moral character. Modern tae kwon do is a combination of the **hyung** (patterns) of its ancestral combative arts, **taekyon** and **subak**, and the **kata** (formal exercises) of the Okinawan Shuri and the Naha schools of karate. Tae kwon do incorporates the abrupt linear movements of karate and the flowing, circular patterns of kung-fu with native kicking techniques.

In modern times, hand techniques have become increasingly more important in this art. The use of the feet, however, remains the trademark and beauty of tae kwon do. When a new student enters a **dojang** (practice gym), he becomes part of a family in which he is the youngest member. This concept applies to everyone, regardless of sex. The instructor is the head of the family and all who study with him or her are children at different levels of development designated by means of colored belts: white (novice); 1st gold; 2nd gold; 1st green; 2nd green; 1st blue; 2nd blue; 1st red or brown; 2nd red or brown; and 1st black through 9th black. All grade levels below black belt are called **gup** or kub; black belt ranks are called **dan.**

Since tae kwon do is basically a kicking art, every practitioner must devote substantial time developing the legs, hips and back. The first step in training is a lengthy period of stretching exercises designed to make the practitioner limber and able to kick head high. The stretching varies in position and direction.

The tae kwon do student also uses wide stances to develop strength in the thighs, a common practice in most martial arts. The length of time the student maintains these stanes while practicing techniques increases as the individual's strength becomes greater.

Tae kwon do kicking techniques are divided into direct and circular. The direct kick travels in a straight line from the kicker to the target area (front kick, side kick, back kick, etc.). The most common of these is the front kick. The circular kick travels in any direction other than a straight line (wheel kick, crescent kick, roundhouse kick, etc.). The most common of these is the roundhouse kick.

Both direct and circular kicks can be delivered in any nubmer of ways, from one foot planted firmly on the ground to jumping with the entire body in the air, to spinning 180 degrees. Most commonly, tae kown do kicks are delivered from the back stance with the body's weight distributed anywhere from 60-80 percent on the back leg. The front foot points toward the target; the toes of the rear foot angle outward from 45-90 degrees. Unlike Okinawan and Japanese karate systems, tae kwon do advocates a broader array of kicks with an emphasis on spinning kicks. Many tae kwon do kicks are aimed at head level, which is relatively rare in other martial arts.

Tae kwon do is famous for its flying kicks, a spectacular assortment of techniques which, when executed by an expert, are devastating. All of the basic tae kwon do kicks can be delivered in a jumping or flying motion. Flying kicks are considered the ultimate in the tae kwon do practitioner's arsenal of weapons. Although noted for its kicks, tae kwon do practitioners also use a large array of hand techniques to punch, strike or block. As in karate, all parts of the hand and arm are used in attacking as well defending.

The Yi dynasty rulers held scholarship and learning in high esteem and military related pursuits fell into disrepute. Examples of martial arts training are therefore rare during this period. The martial arts for the most part were practiced secretly and passed on by forms from father to son. The final blow came in 1909 with teh Japanese annexation of Korea. During the Japanese occupation, which spanned 36 years until 1945, the Resident General banned the practice of martial arts and imprisoned many patriots. Patriotic young men secretly visited Buddhist temples in remote mountain and rural areas to learn the martial arts and organize underground revolutionary groups. Other Koreans went to China and Japan to work and study, where no restrictions on martial arts training existed. There they were exposed first to kung-fu and in the 1920s to karate in Japan. They became the first to blend Korea's

style with others in over one thousand years. Back in Korea, **Duk Ki Song** and Il Dong Han managed to keep taekyon alive.

In 1943, rapidly following judo, Japanese karate and Chinese kung-fu were introduced to Korea and enjoyed temporary popularity until Korea's liberation in 1945. That Sept., the **Korean Judo Association** (also called the Korean Yudo Association) was formed. The end of World War II saw thousands of post-occupation Korean emigrants, fired by intense patriotism and nationalistic pride, return home from other parts of the Orient. As part of the national movement to restore Korean traditions, the martial arts were revived and many experts established schools. According to one scholar, the martial arts at this time were often used as an excuse to cover up unrelated business enterprises.

Various names which emphasized one part or another of taekyon became common: kwon bop, **bang soo do,** kong soo do, soo bahk gi, and tae soo do. **Dojang** (gymnasiums), or schools, also adopted different names. The teachings differed in each of them; some founders who had trained in China or Japan taught a synthesis of karate, kung-fu, and earlier Korean self-defense methodology. Thus were born the **kwans** (schools) of Korean martial arts.

The kwans were the most important institution in the post-World War II status and evolution of Korea's fighting arts between 1945-55. Much confusion reigns over the names, the number, and the subsequent roles of these kwans in the formation of tae kwon do. The two most reliable information sources appeared in magazine articles: the first was written by **Jhoon Rhee,** the father of American tae kwon do, for *Action Karate* in 1969; the second by editor D.W. Kang for the *Traditional Taekwon-Do* 1977 yearbook.

Master Won Kook Lee opened the first post-war dojang in 1945 in Yong Chun, Seoul; he called it the chung do kwan. Soon after, Hwang Kee established the moo duk kwan in Seoul, teaching tang soo do. Later that year, Sup Chun Sang (aka Sup Jun Sang) established the yun moo kwan in Seoul. In 1946, In Yun Pyung (aka In Yoon Byung) founded the chang moo kwan at a YMCA. And, finally, Yon Kue Pyang founded the chi do kwan in 1946. These were the five original kwans. Three more, all major, followed after 1953, and in the early 1960s, at least another four were established. Fragmented by the pre-war secrecy of their teachings and the post-war confusion of reconstruction, it took some ten years before these stylistic spinoffs and adaptations were able to consolidate into a single martial art, tae kwon do. Actually, they never did completely consolidate.

The Korean Armed Forces were formed in 1945, and in January 1946, **Choi Hong Hi,** a second lieutenant in the Korean Army, began teaching taekyon to the Korean military in Kwang Ju. Americans were first introduced to taekyon when Choi later instructed Korean Army troops and some American soldiers stationed with the 2nd Infantry Regiment. In 1949, Choi, now a lieutenant colonel, attended Ground General School at Ft. Riley, near Topeka, Ks., in the U.S. There he gave a public taekyon demonstration for the troops, the first display of this art in America.

The Communist forces in North Korea and non-Communists in the south erupted into civil conflict, bringing about the Korean War from June 25, 1950 to June 27, 1953. In the south, martial arts-trained commandos were dispatched across the lines to spy and occasionally to execute. The cost to the arts was high. By war's end Sup Chun Sang and In Yun Pyung, respective founders of yun moo kwan and chang moo kwan, were missing. Nam Suk Lee took over Pyung's school in Seoul and for some time chang moo kwan was the leading self-defense method. Woo Lee Chong succeeded Sang in the yun moo kwan.

In 1953-54, three more kwans emerged. Gae Byang Yun founded the ji do kwan (aka jee do kwan), Byung Chik Ro the song moo kwan (sometimes translated as sang moo kwan) at Kae Sung, and Choi Hong Hi, with the help of **Tae Hi Nam,** the oh do kwan. Counting the original five schools, there were now eight kwans, all apparently espousing a different style.

A classical roundhouse kick performed by Ernie Reyes.
Courtesy of *Inside Kung-Fu*

The origins of tae kwon do can be traced to the Koguryo dynasty, founded in 37 B.C. The ceiling of the Muyong-chong (a royal tomb) bore a painting depicting two men facing each other in tae kwon do practice, while the mural paintings of Kakchu-chong (another royal tomb) depict two men wrestling. In reference to this particular painting, Tatashi Saito, a Japanese historian, in the *Study of Culture in Ancient Korea,* wrote: "The painting either shows us that the person buried in the tomb practiced tae kwon do while he was alive or it tells us that people practiced it, along with dancing and singing, for the purpose of consoling the soul of the dead."

The construction of these tombs dates to the period between A.D. 3 and 427, during which historians maintain that Hwando province was the capital of Koguryo. It can be inferred that the Koguryo people began practicing tae kwon do during that period.

Tae kwon do was also practiced during the Silla dynasty (668-935). Silla was a kingdom founded in the southeastern part of the land some twenty years before Koguryo in the north. At Kyongju, the ancient capital of Silla, two Buddhist images are inscribed on the Keumkang Ginat Tower at Sokkuram in Pulkuk-Sa Temple, portraying two giants facing each other in a tae kwon do stance.

Silla was famous for its **hwarang** warriors. These knights trained their bodies and minds by devoting themselves to hunting, studying, and the martial arts. **Hwarang-do** (way of the flower of manhood) was an essential part of Silla's struggle to unify the country. Scattered references in the *Samguk Yusa,* the two oldest documents of Korea's history, show that the hwarang practiced tae kwon do in their basic training.

Tae kwon do maintained its popularity after the Koguryo and Silla dynasties through the Koryo dynasty (935-1392). During this dynasty, tae kwon do, as subak, was practiced not only as a skill to improve health and as a sports activity, but encouraged as a martial art.

Subak is believed to have peaked in popularity during the reign of King Uijong, between 1147 and 1170. This period includes part of

Song Duk Ki (*left*) is the sole surviving authority of taekyon. Courtesy of D. W. Kang and *Traditional Taekwon-Do*

Breaking is widely practiced in tae kwon do.

126

Jhoon Rhee was the first Korean tae kwon do master to teach this style in the United States.

the Chinese Sung and Ming dynasties, during which Chinese kung-fu became widely popular after developing into two advanced systems, namely **nei-chia** (internal school) and **wai-chia** (external school). (These two systems differ chiefly in that the one employs more defensive skills than the other.) The above fact is worthy of attention since it further shows that tae kwon do is not only of pure Korean origin, but has achieved independent development throughout Korea's long history.

During the Yi dynasty (1392-1907), there is some speculation that envoys from Okinawa learned subak and introduced it to their people. *The Historical Record of Chosun* (Chosun is another name for the Yi dynasty) mentions these envoys and their frequent visits to bring tribute to the kings of Chosun. The speculation that subak, then, could be the forerunner of **Okinawa-te** is not altogether unlikely, especially since "Nul," the Korean see-saw game, was also adopted from Korea by Okinawans.

A book about subak, written in the Yi dynasty, was published to teach the sport as a martial art. The art became more popular among the general public, whereas it had been to a certain degree monopolized by the military during the preceding Koryo era. An historical record indicates that people from both Chung-chong and Cholla provinces once gathered at the village of Chakji, located along the provincial boundary, to compete in subak.

People who aspired to be employed by the military department of the royal government were eager to learn subak because it was one of the major subjects of the test taken by applicants. Meanwhile, King Chongjo published *Muye Dobo Tongji*, an illustrated textbook on martial arts, which included tae kwon do as one of the major chapters. During the latter half of this era, subak, as a martial art, began to decline due to the negligence of the royal court, which was constantly torn by strife between feuding political factions. Subak survived merely as a recreational activity for the masses.

In 1943, rapidly following judo, Japanese karate and Chinese kung-fu were introduced to Korea and enjoyed temporary popularity until Korea's liberation in 1945. That year, a move was made to unify the fighting arts of Korea under one name in an effort to revitalize the traditional Korean art of subak. Ten years later, in 1955, a conference of chung do kwan masters decided to standardly adopt the term "tae kwon do," which had been created and submitted for acceptance by **Gen. Choi Hong Hi.** The name was chosen for its resemblance to taekyon.

In 1952, during the Korean War, a demonstration before President Syngman Rhee evolved into the most significant turning point for Korean martial arts. Rhee watched a 30-minute performance by Korean martial arts masters, and was especially impressed when Tae Hi Nam broke 13 roof tiles with a single punch. When the demonstration ended, Rhee asked Choi Hong Hi some questions about the martial arts. So impressed was Rhee he immediately turned to his military chiefs of staff and ordered that all Korean soldiers receive training in these arts. This dictate ultimately accounted for a tremendous surge in schools and students. Later that year, Nam, who had impressed the president with his tile breaking, was assigned to Ft. Benning, Georgia for radio communications training. There he demonstrated before military troops and the public, receiving considerable media publicity.

In 1954, Gen. Choi Hong Hi organized the 29th Infantry on Che Ju Island, off the Korean coast, as a spearhead and center for taekyon training in the military.

On April 11, 1955, at a pivotal conference of kwan masters, historians, and taekyon promoters, it was decided to standardly adopt the term "tae kwon do," which had been created and submitted by Gen. Hi. The name was approved because of its resemblance to taekyon, and so provides continuity and maintains tradition. Further, it describes both hand and foot techniques. The number of kwans which then consolidated into tae kwon do is the subject of much debate and historical confusion. Not all of the eight major kwans extant at that time merged, and to this day they still have not.

According to Jhoon Rhee, dissension among the various kwans carried on for six years, and it wasnt until Sept. 14, 1961 that the groups once again organized into a single association, as ordered by an official decree of the new military government. It was called the **Korea Taekwondo Association** (KTA), with Gen. Hi elected its first president. The new association soon gained official recognition

Gen. Choi Hong Hi, the father of tae kwon do.

by the major kwans, but not for long. Hwang Kee, the founder of tang soo do, maintained the Korean Soo Bahk Do Association and became a competing body to the KTA. The Chi Do Kwan Association also seceded. By 1962, however, many of the individual instructors rejoined the KTA, possibly because that year the KTA re-examined all the black belt ranks to determine national standards, and they did not wish to be omitted.

As KTA president, Hi dispatched many demonstration teams and instructors throughout the world. Jhoon Rhee introduced tae kwon do in America when, in 1956, he attended San Marcos Southwest Texas State College. He was called back to Korea for one year of remaining active duty with the army, after which he returned again to San Marcos in 1957, where he taught a non-accredited tae kwon do course at the college. Rhee founded his first public tae kwon do club in San Marcos in 1958.

Meanwhile, in Korea, tae kwon do spread from military posts to universities and high schools. Public dojangs proliferated, all with abundant student enrollment. In their war against Communism, South Vietnamese requested tae kwon do instructors to teach their troops. On March 22, 1966, Hi founded the **International Taekwon-do Federation** (ITF), for which he also served as president. He later resigned as KTA president and moved his ITF headquarters to Montreal, Canada, from where he has concentrated on organizing tae kwon do internationally. His emphasis is on self-defense methodology, not particularly on the sport.

Tae kwon do's international expansion started with the Republic of Vietnam in 1962 when four instructors, headed by **Tae Hi Nam,** began teaching 50 hand-picked soldiers from various Vietnamese Armed Forces branches. After six months, two of these instructors returned to Korea; Nam and Seung Kyu Kim remained for six more months, returning on Dec. 24, 1963. Tae kwon do next migrated to Thailand, Malaysia, and Hong Kong in 1962-63. It was pioneered in Canada by Chong Lee in 1964, the same year it hit Singapore. The art was introduced to Europe by Park Jong Soo in 1965, first in West Germany, then in the Netherlands in 1966. Tae kwon do entered the Middle East in 1966, and Taiwan in 1967.

Mass expansion to the U.S. started in the early 1960s. In 1963, a tae kwon do demonstration was performed at the United Nations headquarters in New York City, and on Nov. 26, 1967 the U.S. Taekwon-do Association was formed (superseded in 1974 by the **U.S. Taekwon-do Federation**).

Although tae kwon do practitioners are noted for their foot techniques, hand techniques are also widely practiced. Here, Master Bong Yu delivers a bottom fist to one of his students.

One of the most difficult and spectacular kicks in tae kwon do is the scissor kick, performed here by Jim Chong.

Thousands of tae kwon do demonstrations were performed internationally in the late 1960s, and more ITF and KTA instructors were exported to foreign countries than at any other period. These demonstrations were normally the first step in spreading tae kwon do to a new country. Following such exhibitions were invitations from governments to send qualified instructors. The plan worked brilliantly. In 1968, the United Kingdom Taekwon-do Association was formed, followed by organizations in Spain, Canada, Belgium, India, Yugoslavia, and Hungary. By 1974, Gen. Hi reported that some 600 qualified international instructors, all afffiliated with the ITF, were distributed throughout the world.

Young-wun Kim was elected the new KTA president. Feeling that Korea was the mother country of tae kwon do and that the world headquarters should be located there, he dissolved the ITF's connection with the KTA and on May 28, 1973 created a new international governing body called the **World Taekwon-do Federation** (WTF).

Since the official birth of tae kwon do in 1955, and especially in the 1960s under Gen. Hi's expansionistic vision, the art has spread to almost every country in the world and in 1980 claimed a reported 15 million practitioners, more than any other martial art, in 62 countries. By 1975, more than 700,000 were reportedly practicing tae kwon do in the U.S. alone. Furthermore, under the supervision of the WTF, its evolution and development as a sport has been rapid. In 1962, tae kwon do became one of the official events in the annual National Athletic Meet in Korea. This development, as far as can be determined, was the first truly national tae kwon do championship in Korea. The first World Tae Kwon Do Championships were conducted in Seoul in May 1973, which led to the formation of the WTF. The WTF is the body officially recognized by the Korean government. Today, tae kwon do, tang soo do and **hapkido** are the three major kicking and punching arts in Korea.

Tae kwon do develops in a practitioner the power to disable an antagonist with the bare hands and feet. But it is also a study in discipline. A tae kwon do master can make a punch, forcible enough to smash boards, touch a sheet of fragile rice paper without breaking it.

The Korean word do (also **do** in Japanese, tao in Chinese), translated "art," means more literally "way." Thus, tae kwon do can be interpreted as "way of being in the world," as opposed to simply a method one practices or a proficiency in self-defense.

The mind must be relaxed and open to perceive an opponent's intentions clearly, and one must practice the techniques relentlessly to develop a responsiveness that is instantaneous and correct, an intuitive reflex, requiring no thought or preparation. Response should be synchronized with perception: defense should begin as the opponent's attack begins. A practitioner must realize and accept the fact that to stand and defend his life means to risk losing it. Accepting the likelihood of death, fear cannot distract him, an opponent cannot intimidate him, and he is free to perceive and concentrate on the opponent's weaknesses, rather than his own.

Tae kwon do is a method of self-defense without weapons. Flesh and bone, the natural, vulnerable equipment of the body, are the only resources of the tae kwon do practitioner. What is "soft" is pliable and is therefore not used to resist an attack so much as to give way before the onslaught, allowing the opponent's own momentum to carry him off balance. What is "soft" is also movable and is therefore trained to react with speed and agility. What is "hard" is naturally resistant and is therefore used to fend off blows to which the soft parts of the body should be vulnerable. What is "hard" is also forcible and is thus a logical striking point.

The center of force is in the abdomen, and it is at this point that the flow of energy begins, and it is from here that it goes outward, through the body, to the extremities. Thus, concentration—the integration of strength, speed, and muscular coordination—begins at the center.

History: Korean ancestors who settled in several tribal states in the kingdom of Koguryo, after the neolithic age, enjoyed various games, especially in the form of religious rites. Yongko in Puyo state, Tongmaeng in Koguryo, Muchon in Ye and Mahan, and Kabi in the Silla dynasty are examples of "sports activities" that ancient Koreans practiced as part of their religious rites. These eventually were developed into exercises to improve health or martial abilities.

The long, intense experience of ancient people in defending themselves against animal attacks, as well as their imitation of the offensive and defensive positions assumed by animals, slowly led them to develop more effective skills of their own, creating a primitive form of combat called taekyon, an early name for tae kwon do.

Since its official birth on Apr. 11, 1955, tae kwon do has spread to almost every country in the world and in 1980 claimed a reported 15 million students. Furthermore, its evolution and development as a sport has been rapid. In 1962 tae kwon do became one of the official events in the annual National Athletic Meet in Korea. The first World Tae Kwon Do Championships were conducted in Seoul in May 1973, leading to the formation of the **World Taekwon-do Federation** (WTF), which has worked to make tae kwon do a modern world sport. A second faction exists, Gen. Hi's **International Taekwon-do Federation** (ITF), overseen by Hi from his headquarters in Toronto. The WTF is the body officially recognized by the Korean government.

In the short space of a few years, tae kwon do has made major progress toward official status as an international amateur sport, both in the U.S. and other countries. Since the formulation of the WTF, a major effort has been made to standardize tournament rules and organize world class competitions. The inaugural meeting elected Un Yong Kim as president and drafted a charter for the federation.

Two years later, in 1975, after conducting the 2nd World Championships in Seoul, the WTF became an affiliate of the General Assembly of the International Sports Federation (GAIF). The International Military Sports Council (CISM) recognized tae kwon do as an official sport in 1977. In 1980, the International Olympic Committee (IOC) recognized tae kwon do as a sport worthy of Olympic competition, which made it eligible for selection into the Olympic Games. This development makes it possible for tae kwon do to become a part of the 1988 Olympics. (KEN [KYUNG HO] MIN; additional historical material by JHOON RHEE, D.W. KANG, and HE-YOUNG KIMM) *See also* amateur tae kwon do; kwans; ITF; style; U.S., history of karate in; WTF. *Further reading: Action Karate,* Jan. 1969; *The Complete Book of Tae Kwon Do Forms,* Keith Yates, 1982; *The Complete Martial Artist,* Hee Il Cho, 1981; *The Making of a Martial Artist,* San Kyu Shim, 1981; *Man of Contrasts,* Hee Il Cho, 1977; *Promise and Fulfillment in the Art of Tae Kwon Do,* San Kyu Shim, 1974; *Official Karate Annual,* Spring 1982; *Taekwon-Do,* Gen. Choi Hong Hi, 1972; *Taekwon-Do, The Art of Self-Defense,* Gen. Choi Hong Hi, 1965; *Tae Kwon Do: The Korean Martial Art and National Sport,* Richard Chun with Paul Wilson, 1976; *Taekwondo (Poomse),* World Taekwon-do Federation, 1975; *Traditional Taekwon-Do,* 1977 Yearbook.

AMATEUR TAE KWON DO When karate was accepted as an official Amateur Athletic Union (AAU) sport in 1972, the karate leaders required tae kwon do participants, instructors, and students to follow karate tournament rules and administrative guidelines. **Ken Min,** of the University of California at Berkeley, and a few other tae kwon do leaders approached the AAU to request independent recognition of tae kwon do for four reasons: 1) tae kwon do was popular and distinct, utilizing more leg techniques than hand techniques; 2) competition rules were entirely different, since tae kwon do is bound by regulations of the **World Taekwondo Federation** (WTF), which uses three-round contact matches with body protection, as opposed to karate, which follows the rules of the **World Union of Karate-Do Organizations** (WUKO) and the **International Amateur Karate Federation** (IAKF), with one-round noncontact matches; 3) administratively, tae kwon do is regulated internationally by the WTF (which was later recognized by the GAIF and the International Olympic Committee before the WUKO); and 4) athletes have one more avenue for recognition in fistic competition.

The 86th annual AAU convention in 1973, in West Yellowstone, Mont., was the site of the official introduction of tae kwon do to AAU Executive Committee members. Following this initial display, and through the ensuing year, Ken Min, David Rivenes, at the time National AAU president, and other AAU leaders throughout the country, combined their efforts to gain official recognition of tae kwon do as an independent sport. These efforts were rewarded in 1974, when the AAU membership at the general meeting of the AAU convention approved by an overwhelming majority the establishment of tae kwon do as a separate AAU sport. They created an AAU National Tae Kwon Do Committee, electing Ken Min, chairman (four years), and **Jay Hyun** as vice-chairman

The 1st AAU Invitational Championships was held in Berkeley, Calif., in May, 1974, and in 1975 the 1st National AAU Championship was held at Yale University, New Haven, Conn.

The AAU Tae Kwon Do Committee conducted more than fifty referee clinics nationwide for the unification of tournament rules. AAU tae kwon do has been represented in all international events since 1974 and hosted the North American Championships (Berkeley, 1977), the 1st International Invitational Championships (Berkeley, 1980), the 2nd Pan-American Championships (Houston, 1981), and the 3rd World Tae Kwon Do Championships (Chicago, 1977). AAU tae kwon do is the governing body recognized by the Kukkiwon in Korea and affiliated with the WTF in rank promotion, as well as technical and instructional matters within the U.S. (KEN MIN)

The flying side kick (which is practiced in many styles of karate) is a trademark of tae kwon do and is widely practiced in it. Jim Chong is shown here performing a flying side kick.

FORMS OF TAE KWAN DO

TAEKYON A forerunner of tae kwon do; it can be traced to the Koguryo dynasty, which began in 37 B.C. It matured during the Koryo dynasty, encompassing some 25 fundamental movements with emphasis on hand, leg, jumping, rolling, and punching techniques. Taekyon, along with **cireum,** a form of wrestling, are the two most popular combat sports practiced in Korea today. While cireum has remained in its original form, taekyon has undergone a great transformation.

Taekyon was banned in Korea during its occupation by Japan but re-emerged, after Korea's independence, in a modernized version called tae kwon do. Hong Shik Kim (b. 1902) and Kuk Ki Song (b. 1903) are two of the oldest surviving masters of taekyon.

There were no **hyung** (patterns) in taekyon, and no standard uniforms were worn. Students simply wore the traditional Korean garb, including gibshin (slippers woven from rice straw). It was practiced strictly as a self-defense form, its techiques controlled without making hard contact. There were also no breaking techniques using the hands and head, so often seen in modern tae kwon do. Also unlike tae kwon do, taekyon did not involve the sophisticated combinations of techniques.

Basic taekyon embraced 18 movements. Students specialized in a few of these moves and mastered them with full confidence. Some of the taekyon techniques which have been transmitted to tae kwon do are the roundhouse kick, stomach punch, and the jumping front snap kick with both feet.

WU SHU

Wu shu is the proper name for that which is usually called kung-fu in the Western Hemisphere. The latter term denotes little more than ability or skill. The People's Republic of China has formally adopted the term wu shu as the official name for martial arts on the Chinese mainland.

The early 1950s sparked renewed interest in kung-fu on the mainland. But the ideals of the old society art form were not conducive to the promotion of the "modern ethics." A special wu shu committee was established to review all of the Chinese kung-fu styles and synthesize the essence of each into a new, nationally acceptable form.

A National Traditional Sports Meet was conducted in 1953, which laid the foundation for the further study and improvement of wu shu. In 1955, the Physical Culture and Sports Commission of China started a systematic research to discover more forms of the art and improve on them in accordance with the Party's policies on cultural heritage.

Wu shu today is composed of basic offensive and defensive movements executed either bare-handed or with weapons according to set patterns. It may be classified as follows:

1. Bare-handed Exercises. Each has a style of its own and consists of dozens of regulated basic movements. Exercises of this category include **ch'ang ch'uan, t'ai-chi-ch'uan,** nan ch'uan, **hsing-i** ch'uan, fantzu ch'uan, tungpi ch'uan, pakua ch'uan, pikua ch'uan, pachi ch'uan, and ti-t'ang ch'uan. Exercises emulating the characteristic movement of animals (e.g., monkey, praying mantis) also belong to this group.

2. Exercises with Weapons.

a) Long weapons: spears, cudgels, scimitars (one with a short blade and long hilt, the other with long blade and short hilt);

b) Short weapons (with long or short tassels): broadswords and daggers;

c) Double weapons: double swords (with long or short tassels), double broadsword, double hooks, double halberds, double whips, double-headed spears, and single broadsword plus whip; and

d) Flexible weapons: nine-section whips, three-sectional staffs or cudgels, meteor hammers, and rope darts.

3. Exercises with Partners. These are performed by two or more persons according to set patterns designed for both offensive and defensive purposes. They include:

a) Bare-handed fights, such as in kung-fu and "gripping" (grappling) with a partner;

b) Combat with weapons: broadsword vs. broadsword, spear vs. spear, sword vs. sword, cudgel vs. cudgel, single broadsword vs. spear, double broadsword vs. spear, three-sectional staff vs. spear, bare-handed trio vs. cudgel, and single broadsword vs. spear and cudgel; and

c) Bare hands against weapons—spear, dagger, and double spears.

4. Group Exercises. Performed bare-handed or with one or more types of weapons by three or more persons, sometimes set to musical acocmpaniment.

Wu shu is taught at all physical culture institutes and a number of middle and primary schools in China. Physiological studies have been carried out in connection with the sport. Numerous publications on wu shu since the liberation have helped popularize it. In Peking, Shanghai, Canton, Harbin, and other cities, it is common to see people of all ages performing wu shu exercises morning or evening. Many wu shu centers have been established in the towns and smaller cities, with workers or pensioners offering free coaching.

In 1974, the west's first glimpse of wu shu came when the 32-member Mainland Chinese Troupe, sponsored by the National Committee for U.S./China Relations and the New York Center for Music and Drama, toured the U.S. giving performances on both coasts. A second, six-city U.S. tour was set up in mid-1980. This troupe was composed of 15 male and 13 female members, none more than 18 years of age, the youngest 8.

Wu shu sets or forms have become popular in the U.S.; they were first introduced to west coast tournament competition in 1975 by **Anthony Chan** of San Francisco. He performed the ch'ang-ch'uan set and a variety of weapon, compulsory, and optional routines in events throughout northern and southern California. (MICHAEL P. STAPLES) *Further reading: Wu Shu of China,* Michael P. Staples, 1976; *Black Belt Magazine,* Nov. 1974; *Kick Illustrated,* Dec. 1980; *The Elegant Wu Shu of China,* Michael P. Staples and Anthony Chan, 1981.

FORMS OF WU SHU

BA JI Form of **wu shu** that makes use of uppercuts, elbows, holds, circular parries, and bent-elbow locks.

DI TANG Form of **wu shu** employing tumbling skills for both attack and defense.

FAN ZI Form of **wu shu,** characterized by short routines.

NAN CH'UAN Form of **wu shu** popular in China's southern provinces. It uses vigorous, rhythmic movements, mostly for the upper limbs.

TUNG BI Form of **wu shu** (national arts) popular in the northern provinces of China. It consists of 5 basic movements: backhand blow, slap, thrust, palm cut, and corkscrew blow. Executed with the shoulders relaxed, the movements are quick and powerful.

XING YI Form of **wu shu** (national arts) evolved through integrating the characteristic movements of the tiger, monkey, eagle, horse, and bear into boxing exercises. Its basic movements include the palm-cut, the straight blow, the corkscrew blow, the oblique thrust, and the swing.

Anthony Chan, the first to use wu-shu forms in western tournament competition.

A spectacular jump by a Wu Shu practitioner. Courtesy of *Inside Kung-Fu*

MISCELLANEOUS ARTS

BOXING, GREEK Ancient sport and form of combat in which the fists were employed as the primary weapon. Since the use of some type of covering or protection for the hand necessarily determines the style of fighting, it is possible to distinguish three periods in the history of ancient boxing. The first is the period of soft thongs made of ox-hide, and extends from Homer to the close of the 5th century B.C. During this period, in 688 B.C., the sport entered the Olympic Games. The second period is that of the sphairai, or "sharp thongs," lasting from the 4th century B.C. into late Roman times. The third is that of the Roman cestus, the brutal spiked and weighted glove. The classic era of Greek boxing is undoubtedly that of the first period, 6th and 5th centuries B.C.

In Greek boxing there was no ring, so there was no opportunity for cornering an opponent or fighting on the ropes. This discouraged close-range fighting and encouraged defensive tactics. Competitors fought without rest periods, and sometimes, exhausted, would pause to take a breath, but usually the fight continued until one acknowledged defeat by raising his hand.

As there was no rule against hitting a falling opponent, caution was the rule of Greek boxing, and the fighting thus tended to become slow paced. Also, classification by weight was unknown to the Greeks, and competitions were open to all comers, so boxing became the monopoly of the heavyweight fighter.

The boxer took a position with his body upright, head erect, and left foot advanced. The left leg was usually slightly bent, the foot pointing forward, while the right foot was approximately at right angles to the left—the position of a lunge as in fencing. The left arm, used for guarding, was extended almost straight, the hand sometimes clenched, more often open. The right arm was drawn back for striking, as in delivering the chopping blow performed in karate. The elbow sometimes dropped, but usually was raised level with the shoulder.

The Greek boxer confined his attention to his opponent's head and made no use of body blows. Even where in-fighting is depicted on period vases, the boxers are always shown pummeling each other's heads, never the body. The position of the right arm on these vases indicates that it was employed chiefly for hooks, uppercuts, and chopping blows.

With the introduction in Hellenistic and Roman times of the murderous cestus, boxing became more brutal and declined as a scientific sport. Greek boxing is the forerunner of the pre-Christian martial art of **pankration** (all powers). It may be the first art of combat known to have utilized open-hand methods. At the very least, Greek boxing is the only pre-Christian form of hand-to-hand fighting to have been documented through vases and paintings and through records from the early Olympic Games. *Further reading: Athletics of the Ancient World,* Norman E. Gardiner, 1930; *Greek Athletic Sports and Festivals,* Norman E. Gardiner, 1910.

PANKRATION Pre-Christian form of Greek fighting. Pankration, sometimes spelled pancration, or pancratium or even pankratium, was a combination of earlier forms of boxing and wrestling practiced by the Greeks. Some historians trace its origin to the Indian **vajramushti** system. It should be noted, however, that pankration and the **Pyrrhic dance,** a Greek armed and unarmed war-dance similar to modern karate **kata** (formal exercises), both antedate Indian statues depicting temple guardians in poses similar to those used in latter-day fighting arts.

In 648 B.C. pankration was introduced to the Greek Olympic Games. A subdivision, boy's pankration, was added in the 2nd century B.C., which attests to the popularity of the sport.

The object was, as in boxing, to force an opponent to acknowledge defeat, and to this end almost any means might be applied. Though rules were enforced by officials with a switch or stout rod, a whipping must have been more desirable than being killed, for the rules were

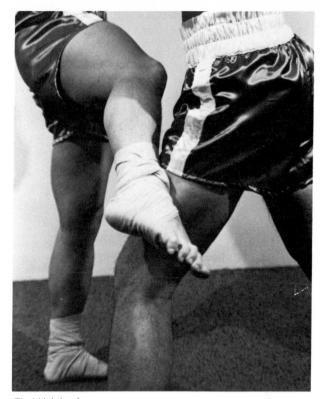

Thai kick boxing

often broken. Serious injuries and fatal accidents did occur, but they were rare, rarer probably than in ancient **Greek boxing.**

Facing one another, much as in the position taken by wrestlers, pankratiasts, as they were called, tried to bring one another violently to the ground by grappling, hitting, kicking, leg-sweeping, choking, or joint-locking. There was much preliminary sparring. Hands were bare and generally held open, although the clenched fist was used for hitting; feet were also bare. As in Greek boxing, there were no rules against hitting a man when down. More often than not, the contest was decided on the ground, even though, when both fighters were down, hitting was usually ineffective. Biting and gouging were prohibited. Kicking was an essential part of pankration and the stomach area was a common target. Because of this comparatively rare tactic, historians speculate that pankration may have been one of the first, if not the first, total martial art known to mankind.

Such throws as the flying mare and various foot-and-leg holds, although too risky for Greek wrestling proper, were freely employed in the pankration. A pankratiast sometimes threw himself on his back to accomplish a throw. Much later, these techniques became common in judo, called **sacrifice throws.** Another type of sacrifice throw was the stomach throw. Seizing his opponent by the shoulders or arms, the pankratiast threw himself backwards, simultaneously planting his foot in his opponent's stomach, pulling him over his head. This technique, later a favorite among the Japanese, is depicted in the tombs of Beni-Hassan, giving rise to the belief that it may have been used by the ancient Egyptians.

Locks applied to an opponent's limbs or neck were as common in pankration as in jujutsu. Opportunities for applying them were more frequent when one or both combatants were on the ground, where the struggle was usually decided. The Eleans especially commended strangling as a means of defeating the adversary. The favorite stranglehold of pankratiasts was the "ladder-trick": the attacker jumped on his opponent's back, entwined his legs around the body, and his arms around the neck. A trained pankratiast realized when his opponent had secured an injurious grip and acknowledged defeat at once.

The decisive struggle on the ground was said to be as long and as complicated as it is in modern wrestling. It was to this aspect of pankration that Plato objected, saying it "did not teach men to keep their feet."

In the palaestra, the Greek wrestling school, pankration was given a separate training room, known as the Korykeion, equipped with punching and kicking balls, called korykos, suspended from the ceiling beams. The Greek boxer and the pankratiast used the punch-ball much as the modern boxer does. Another larger ball, used for kicking practice, hung about 2 feet from the floor. Pankration was taught progressively: when a student had thoroughly learned the movements and their combinations, he would be permitted to engage in "loose play," as it is called in fencing.

As would be expected in such a brutal sport, pankration did not escape criticism—principally due to the advent of professionalism. An excess of purses and honors in all Greek sports had precipitated social complications. The "evil" effects of professionalism were considered worst in boxing, wrestling, and pankration. In Greece itself, the problem was increased by the absence of weight classifications, making these events the monopoly of heavyweights.

In 1973 **Jim Arvanitis** and martial arts journalist Massad Ayoob wrote an account of this little-known, but historically important, discipline. They pointed out that Alexander the Great made friends with Dioxippus, the champion pankratiast who won the Olympic crown by default in 336 B.C. because no one dared compete against him. Later, as Alexander marched in conquest across the world, his armies carried with them elaborate tents, more like collapsible amphitheaters, in which they could practice and play athletic games, foremost among them pankration. Some martial scholars and authorities—the number is growing—believe Alexander's armies, in carrying pankration across the Himalayas in 326 B.C., laid the groundwork for kung-fu in China. Still, due to inadequate evidence, the links in martial arts evolution remain unsubstantiated. *See also* boxing, Greek; India, martial arts in; mu tau; Pyrrhic dance; vajramushti. (JIM ARVANITIS)*Further reading: Mu Tau: The Modern Greek Karate,* Jim Arvanitis, 1980; *Athletics of the Ancient World,* Norman E. Gardiner, 1930; *Greek Athletic Sports and Festivals,* Norman E. Gardiner, 1910; *The History of American Karate,* Robin L. Rielly, 1970; *Black Belt Magazine,* Nov. 1973; *Inside Kung-Fu Magazine,* Feb. 1980; *Official Karate Magazine,* June 1977.

CORNISH WRESTLING Known also as Corno-Breton wrestling, it has been practiced in Cornwall, England, for over 15 centuries. Contestants try to throw each other from a standing position. If a hand or knee should touch the ground, the hold is broken, and players must start again. All holds must be above the waist; chokeholds are not allowed. Each bout lasts ten minutes, with a ten-minute extension if no winner is declared. Should there still be no clear victor at the end of the second ten-minute period, the three referees decide a winner. Cornish wrestling tournaments are conducted annually

DUMOG is a form of wrestling practiced by natives of the Philippine Islands. Opponents grapple and attempt to throw or unbalance one another until one is sent to the ground squarely on his back.

GLIMAE Icelandic wrestling; established in 1888 as an organized sport. Matches are held on a wooden floor 20′ to 26′ square. The "climubelti" is a leather belt with straps fastened to the thighs; wrestlers grasp each other by the belt and do not let go until a throw is completed. A wrestler loses if any portion of his body above the knee or above the elbow touches the ground or if both hands touch the ground. The match is declared a draw if both men continue to hold onto the belts as one falls. Movements in glimae are called "tricks" and include body trick, heel trick, leg trick, beginning of the knee trick, side throw down trick, hip trick, and split trick. Glimae championships are held annually in Iceland and the sport appears to be gaining popularity.

GO-TI Form of wrestling practiced in China as early as 260 B.C. and considered by some scholars the forerunner of Chinese boxing. Practitioners of this art wore horned head-gear as they sparred.

GULAT Indonesian wrestling form with sportive aspects; it combines elements of Iranian free-style wrestling, Korean **cireum,** and Japanese **sumo.**

MAIN TINDJU is a peculiar boxing style native to the island of Flores, off Indonesia, whose name translates "to do boxing." Sometimes referred to as Bajawah box, after a local area, two participants attempt to defeat each other using hands, arms, and shoulders while being steered from behind, each by a partner who clutches the combatant's waistband. *Further reading: Weapons and Fighting Arts of the Indonesian Archipelago,* Donn, F. Draeger, 1972.

TEGUMI is a style of wrestling native to Okinawa. As with karate, its origins are unknown, and many Okinawans suppose that there must have been a relationship between the two. In writing the word tegumi, one would use the same two characters used to write karate's "kumite" (sparring), except that they are reversed.

Tegumi is a far simpler and more primitive sport than karate. There are few rules except for certain prohibitions: the use of the fists, feet, or legs to strike an opponent. Nor are opponents permitted to grab each other's hair or pinch one another. Prohibited also are the knife hand blow, and the elbow blow.

Unlike most forms of wrestling, in which participants are lightly clad, contestants in tegumi bouts remain fully clothed. There is no special ring; a contest may be held anywhere. The match begins as sumo does, with the two opponents pushing against each other. As it proceeds, grappling and throwing techniques are employed. Referees are usually those who also act as seconds, their principal role being to insure that neither participant is seriously injured or knocked unconscious.

THAI KICK-BOXING, or Muay Thai, as it is called in Thailand, is the most popular spectator sport in Thailand. Its real origins probably never will be known, since Thailand's early historical records were lost forever in 1769 when Burmese armies laid siege to Siam's ancient capital, Ayutthaya. According to stories from the reign of King Naresuen the Great (1590-1605), Muay Thai was a part of military training. The king was an expert in individual combat techniques; he won several contests and became a national hero at 22.

Warriors learned Muay Thai to supplement the sword and pike in close-range fighting. Muay Thai reached its height in popularity during the reign of Pra Chau Sua (1703-09). Siam was at peace and Muay Thai became the favorite pasttime of the population. Prizefights were staged in every village. In those days it was customary to bind hands and forearms with strips of horse hide, to protect one's own skin and to inflict the maximum damage to an opponent's face. In the 1970s modern boxing gloves were introduced and metal groin protectors added for safety.

The contest always begins with a rite or invocation that is typically Indian in nature. A bout consists of five 3-minute rounds with 2-minute rest periods. The fight is controlled by a referee and two judges, who keep score cards. Decisions are arrived at by a knockout (count of 10), a technical knockout—the result of serious injury, or of throwing in the towel—or on points tallied by the official. Points are awarded for any legitimate attack that weakens the opponent. If the contestants have an equal number of points a draw is declared. The referee's decision is final, and judges have no right to dispute the result. "No contest" is declared when a boxer shows poor technique or lacks fighting spirit. Hip and shoulder throws are not allowed, neither are head butts, choking, or biting, or attacking when an opponent is down.

Modern Thai boxing has about 30 major basic techniques. There are 6 "ways of the fist," 5 elbow techniques, 7 different kicks, and 5 ways of using the foot for pushing or thrusting. Training sessions are strict; boxers work out every day after their regular jobs. Except for a few camps, all training is conducted outside.

Thai kick boxers use every part of their bodies, including the
shin, when fighting in the ring.

Unlike karate and kung-fu, Thai boxing has no set forms or **kata** and training is done by constant sparring and bag hitting.

Kick-boxing is considered big business and a major tourist attraction in Thailand. It is not only popular in Thailand, but is becoming extremely popular in Japan as well. *Further reading: Karate Illustrated,* Nov. 1971; *Muay Thai Kick-Boxing: The Art of Siamese Unarmed Combat,* Hardy Stockmann, 1976; *Thai Boxing, The Devastating Fighting Art of Thailand,* Samyon Tanjaworn, 1975. *Muay Thai,* Harris Malben, 1976.

Thai kick boxers are among the best-conditioned martial artists in the world. Since every part of their body can be a target, they must train themselves to absorb a terrific amount of punishment, especially to their legs.
Courtesy of *Inside Kung-Fu*

ECLECTIC ARTS

AIKIKENDO Style of martial art, founded by **Momoji Sudoh,** that combines aikido, karate, and jujutsu techniques. Sudoh developed aikikendo because he felt that aikido took too long to master and lacked the element of contest; aikikendo has a wider range of defensive techniques and a more aggressive training method. Competition is held in a manner similar to karate, but students wear chest protectors. The style is taught in numerous Japanese universities as well as private dojos.

CHA-YON RYU is an eclectic style of martial arts founded and taught by **Kim Pyung Soo** of Houston, Tex. Its range of kicking techniques is evolved from tae kwon do and **hapkido;** hand tactics from Chinese **Shao-lin** kung-fu and Japanese **Shito-ryu** karate. The basic principles of judo and aikido are present in the techniques of the cha-yon style. Its forms include **hyung** (patterns) from tae kwon do, **kata** (formal exercises) from Japanese and Okinawan karate, and **kuen** (forms) from Shao-lin kung-fu.

KAJUKENBO is an eclectic form of unarmed combat formulated in 1947 by five Hawaiian martial artists: Walter Choo of karate, Joseph Holke of judo, Frank Ordonez of jujutsu, **Adriano Emperado** of kenpo, and Clarence Chang of Chinese boxing. The name was derived from the martial disciplines of its founders: *ka* from karate, *ju* from judo and jujutsu, *ken* from kenpo, and *bo* from Chinese boxing.

KEIBO-SOHO Japanese police method of using the **keibo,** the patrolman's short wooden club, in hand-to-hand combat. It became a part of the policeman's arsenal in 1946, during the Allied occupation of Japan. At first many types of wooden club were employed, but in 1956 the short stick used by the U.S. Navy shore patrol was adopted. Shimizu Takaji, an authority on stick and club techniques, headed a commission to devise a style for the new weapon.

Although keibo soho incorporates many of the defensive techniques of **jojutsu** (art of the long stick), actual keibo soho techniques are closely allied to **jutte-jutsu** (art of the iron truncheon). The techniques taught to policemen include striking, thrusting, parrying, and blocking actions. *Further reading: Modern Bujutsu and Budo,* Donn F. Draeger, 1974.

KYUK-KI-DO, or Trithlon is a martial art combining judo, karate, wrestling, and other bare-handed fighting systems. Founded and developed by **Ken Min,** physical education instructor of the University of California at Berkeley, the trithlon is a well-rounded, balanced physical pursuit. Kyuk-ki-do, in addition to being a comprehensive self-defense system simulating actual fighting conditions, shares aesthetic features of such martial arts as karate, tae kwon do, and kung-fu.

Every trithlon contest consists of three rounds of 3 minutes each with a 1-minute rest period between rounds. A maximum of ten points may be scored by a contestant in one period; if one contestant has accumulated ten points within one period, that period ends, regardless of elapsed time. At the end of the third period, points are tallied and the high scorer is declared the winner. In the event of tied scores a "sudden death" overtime breaks the tie—a rotation of 1-minute rounds until a point is scored.

Official personnel for a trithlon match are a referee, two timekeepers, and one scorekeeper. Responsibility for awarding points, imposing penalties, declaring time-outs (not to exceed 3 minutes per contestant during the 9 minutes of regulation time) to allow recovery from injuries, rests entirely with the referee. Required uniform is the judogi. The prime directive for trithlon competition is the safety of the competitors. (KEN [KYUNG HO] MIN)

LIMA LAMA American martial art of Polynesian descent; founded by **Tino Tuilosega.** Known as the "Hand of Wisdom," lima lama employs certain modifications from other arts of which Tuilosega is a master. Lima lama resembles arts such as aikido, boxing, and certain forms of kung-fu, with quick, smooth, powerful techniques.

MU-TAU is an eclectic martial arts system derived from the ancient Greek fighting system **pankration.** Developed by **Jim Arvanitis,** an expert in pankration, it is a modification of the ancient art to meet the unrestrained and unpredictable nature of modern combat. (Its name arises from a Green acronym for "martial truth.")

Mu tau techniques are based on a simplicity and economy of motion, blending a subtle defense with a penetrating attack. In mu tau the legs are a major offensive weapon. High kicks, however, are sparingly used; most kicks are to the shin, knee, groin, or ribs. Hand techniques are based on the same principles as western boxing, with deceptive combinations. Grappling is appropriate at close range. Throws are seldom used—takedowns, immobilizing holds, and joint breaks are preferred.

There are no **kata** in mu tau training, and very little reduced contact beyond the earliest levels. Almost all sparring is full-contact, with protective gear to avoid serious injury. Physical conditioning is mandatory and much time is spent improving flexibility, strength, and endurance. Heavy bags are a staple in mu tau training, as are more sophisticated devices seldom seen in traditional karate **dojo.**

Mu tau philosophy advocates self-expression and adaptability. Each student is free tó select those aspects of the system most suited to his own physical and psychological nature.

Besides being one of the most practical of the combative disciplines, mu tau is also one of the more selective. Only two of Arvanitis' best pupils have been authorized to teach the art. It is hoped in this way to preserve high standards within the academies, which are located in New Hampshire. Also referred to as the "modern Greek karate," mu tau is the sole descendant of pankration. *See also* pankration. (JIM ARVANITIS)

NIPPON KENPO Amalgamation of several arts including judo, karate, and aikido. Kicking, striking, throwing, and reverse holds are chief techniques. Full protective gear (gloves, chest protector, face mask, groin protector) is worn in full-contact practice. Nippon kenpo was founded in Japan in 1928 by Mumeomi Sawayama; it was brought to the U.S. in 1961 by Goki Kinuya, a student of Sawayama.

SHINTAIDO Relatively new martial art founded in 1966 by Hiroyuki Aoki. It combines techniques from karate, judo, jujutsu, **kendo, bojutsu,** and shiatsu. Shintaido movements tend to be soft and circular.

TAIDO New, eclectic Japanese system of fighting planned to develop attacks and defenses against an opponent by means of changing the body axis. It is based on three principles of movement: on the ground, on the feet, and in the air. A basic premise is that anything that can be done on the ground also can be done in the air. There is no economy of motion in taido; the object is to perform a difficult and beautiful technique. Ordinary straight karate punches and kicks are not allowed in taido competition, although basic karate techniques are required learning for beginning students.

Taido was originated in the late 1960s by Seiken Shukumine, a student of Okinawan gensei-ryu karate. Its name consisted of "tai," meaning "one's external element," and "do," meaning "the way of ethically attaining an objective."

Taido, mastered properly, is too difficult to be used as self-defense; it is an art form. Movement, patterned after natural forces—waves, tornadoes, clouds, whirlpools, and lightning—is divided into five classes:

untai—movement of ascent and descent; including all flying techniques.
sentai—spinning actions
hentai—falling or topping techniques
nentai—spiral movements
tentai—the movement of a sphere

Like other martial arts, taido has ten **kyu** ranks leading to black belt. There is a taido association in Japan with thousands of members. An annual national tournament stages competition in **kata,** mass kata, and free fighting. Only black belts compete in the freestyle part of the tournament. In a unique event, called tenkai-kyosi, is a six-person kata in which a single man fends off five attackers, who use the most spectacular techniques they can muster. *Further reading: Karate Illustrated,* May 1975.

TAIHO-JUTSU Self-defense system used by the Japanese police. It consists of techniques from judo, jujutsu, kendo, aikido, karate and **bojutsu.** After World War II, a technical committee comprised of five experts in various martial arts was appointed by the Tokyo Police to unite the best methods from various arts into a workable self-defense for police. Born thus in 1947, taiho-jutsu is constantly being revised and changed. *Further reading: Modern Bujutsu and Budo,* Donn F. Draeger, 1974.

TOKUSHU KEIBO SOHO Japanese police combat art using a weapon called the tokushu keibo (special police club), a collapsible tubular truncheon made of metal alloy. Because of its telescoping property it is sometimes referred to as tobi-dashi jutte (jump out truncheon). First appearing in 1961, by 1966 a standard series of techniques were presented. The truncheon was given to police officers who were assigned special missions.

The basic techniques of tokushu keibo are borrowed from Ikaku-ryu, a **jutte** specialty. Emphasis is placed on defensive action against unprovoked attacks. Policemen are trained in body movements, posture, and stance, and instructed in methods of avoiding an aggressor's attack or countering with the truncheon. *Further reading: Modern Bujutsu and Budo,* Donn F. Draeger, 1974.

KUK SOOL WON "Korean Traditional Martial Arts Association" founded in 1966. Kuk Sool Won combines karate kicking and hand techniques with judolike throws, and locks and bars similar to those in jujutsu. Practitioners of Kuk Sool Won endorse the superiority of this style because of its many tactical options; none require more strength than a woman or an elderly man can be expected to possess. Additionally, serious students learn the healing arts.

In Hyuk Su, the grandmaster of Kuk Sool Won, established the world headquarters in San Francisco. After verifying the moral character of each beginning student, Su teaches them a small number of simple, yet effective techniques. Advanced students learn as many as 3,608 techniques, which are divided into 270 sections, which in turn are derived by In Hyuk Su from three traditions: Sado Mu Soo (tribal martial arts), Buldo Mu Sool (Buddhist temple martial arts), and Koong Joong Mu Sool (royal court martial arts).

Sado Mu Sool reputedly originated during the close of the stone age in Korea, about 2000 B.C. Understandably, its most important weapons were the stone knife, the stone spear, and the stone axe. During this period, Korean tribes living in northern Korea and southern Manchuria united into the Puyo confederation, an organization very similar to the Iroquois confederation in North America. During spring and autumn ceremonies, martial arts tournaments between tribes took place. As stone weapons were gradually replaced by those of bronze, then iron, then steel; as agriculture replaced hunting as the chief food source; and as the larger villages became towns, then cities, Sado Mu Sool was preserved by a small number of initiates. In A.D. 987 King Sung Jong outlawed the use of weapons by the citizenry. As is frequently the case under such prohibition, there was renewed interest in unarmed fighting, and Sado Mu Sool enjoyed a revival in popularity. When the Japanese invaded Korea in 1592, they met strong resistance from tribal troups skilled in this art.

Buldo Mu Sool has a history similar to those styles of kung-fu that grew out of the Shao-lin temples in China. Buddhist monks had to maintain good health to practice their long, intense meditation sessions, and they had to be able to defend themselves when traveling. Some of the monks were already skilled in the martial arts when they joined the monasteries, but most were taught after they entered.

Koong Joong Mu Sool has its roots in the military training given officers and soldiers in the armies of the three war-torn Korean kingdoms founded in the first century: Silla (57 B.C.), Koguryo (37 B.C.), Paikje (17 B.C.). Warfare encouraged the study and development of Koong Joong Mu Sool, which included education in armed and unarmed tactics and a thorough grounding in the classics, creating men who were both scholars and soldiers. When the Silla kingdom conquered the other two in 688 A.D., this martial tradition declined, but with the Japanese invasion in 1592 interest was renewed.

In 1790 King Jung Jo instructed martial arts teacher Lee Duk Moo to compile an introduction to Korean martial arts techniques. His first three books concern weapons fighting. A fourth dealt with unarmed combat: he described vital pressure points and warned that no one should be taught these techniques unless he could be trusted.

In 1910 the Japanese conquered Korea. When they abolished the Korean Royal Court Army, the master instructor, Myung Deuk Suh, returned to his hometown in Kyung Sang province in order to

preserve what he had learned of Koong Joong Mu Sool. His grandson, In Hyuk Su, began the study of Korean martial arts when he was 6. Kuk Sool Won has spread throughout Korea in an estimated 153 schools, each presided over by an authorized master trained by Su.

Kuk Sool Won uniforms are patterned after the traditional dress of Korean military generals. The twin dragon emblem worn by the grandmaster is a well-known symbol of the heavenly mandate, or legitimacy of the king's power. Its colors—gold, green, and lavender—are symbolic of the royal household. *Further reading: Inside Kung-Fu,* July 1980.

Taido technique: flying hentai.
Photo by Christian Peacock

Taido

Members of the U.S. Air Force watch as Emilio Bruno (*left*) and Professor Hosokawa demonstrate taiho-jutsu (police self-defence) techniques. Courtesy of E. Bruno

WEAPONS, EQUIPMENT AND TRAINING DEVICES

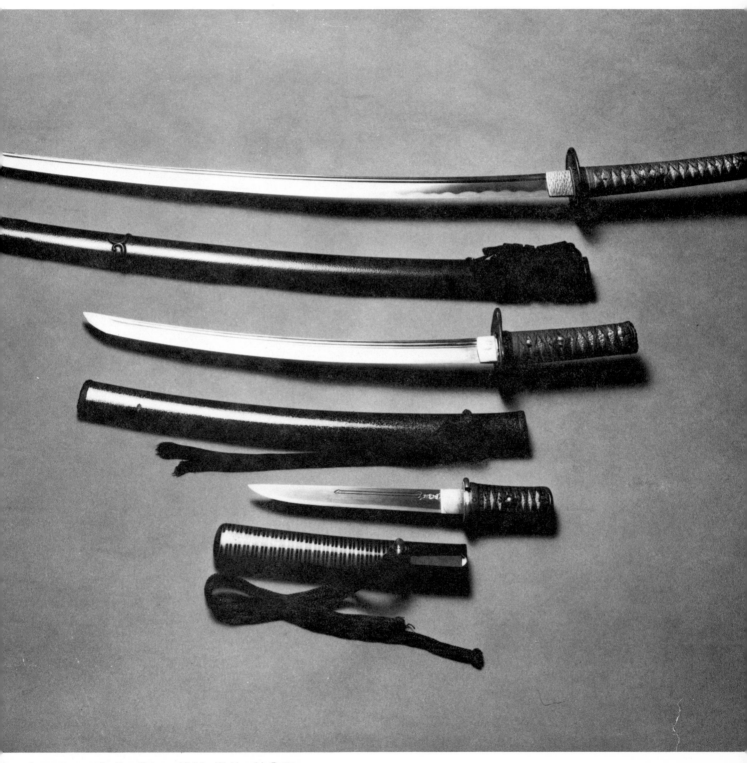

Japanese swords. *Top:* Katana. *Middle:* Wakizashi. *Bottom:*
Tanto. weapons, first pages;

CHINESE WEAPONRY

The use and development of weapons in kung-fu (skill, ability) varied with the time and place in which each weapon originated and flourished. Different weapons were used in northern China, for instance, than were used in the south, and at different periods, for different reasons. Weapons were developed, of course, for use in combat; over the centuries, however, they have found new employment. The massive **Kwan-tao,** for example, helps the kung-fu student develop strength in the arms and wrists, while the **three-sectional staff** promotes timing and control.

The current trend in the People's Republic of China (PRC) eliminates altogether any combative qualities in weaponry, and they are thought of as tools or props, to be employed in the strictly gymnastic **wu shu** (national art) routines.

Originally, kung-fu weaponry was composed of 18 classical weapons introduced by the 18 Lo-han or Buddhas, popular deities of the Chan Buddhist religion. Literally hundreds of different kinds of weapons were accumulated over the centuries, however, which fall into five categories: long, short, soft, double, and throwing. Additionally, there are miscellaneous weapons that defy orderly classification; examples are the wooden benches and smoking pipes employed in **Choy-Li-Fut.**

The staff, known as the father of long weapons, is probably the precedessor to all others. There are several famous routines in China employing this weapon. The Ng-Long-Kwan set, for instance, was developed by the fifth son of the Yang family, who converted the well-known family spear sets into staff sets when he became a priest. (Religious orders considered spears to be implements of war and forbade their use, forcing the majority of monks to develop other means of defense.) The Ng-Long-Kwan sets became fundamental to the Fut-Gar style of kung-fu. Also well known in the south of China are the look-dim-buen (six-pointed staff) and the bing-kuai-kwan staff set of Choy-Li-Fut kung-fu.

Staff maneuvers are called "single headed" when only one end of the stick is used, and it is single-headed maneuvers that are usually related to combat as opposed to dancing. When both ends of the staff are used, and the weapon grasped at its center and twirled, as in the routines of the **monkey** style of kung-fu, the maneuvers are called "double headed" and are considered more suitable for theatrical purposes.

The first military weapon was probably the spear, or jyang, which was known as the king of long weapons. Spears fall into several categories, pertaining to their use defensively and offensively, or the era of origin. The early spear is one of the wu-ping, or five weapons

The Kwan-tao, or Kwan-do in Cantonese, is a large halberd named after the famous general, Kwan-Yu. This weapon is used primarily by males, and, usually, by those of large build, for it requires a good deal of strength in the arms, shoulders, and wrists.

The tiger-fork is another relatively heavy weapon primarily used by men. Originally, this three-pronged fork was used in southern China to hunt tigers, but there is also a northern version called the "horn-big-fork," distinguished by the smaller radius formed by its two outer prongs.

Northern fork maneuvers contain more ostentatious movements than do those of the south, and are less commonly seen in the U.S. The fork is generally pitted against the traditional knife and rattan shield in demonstrations. (The knife and shield were developed by Lau-Fat-Mang of the Eagle Claw Fan-Tzu style of kung-fu during World War II, who led the notorious Big Sword Unit against the Japanese invaders.)

The jyan, or gim in Cantonese, is a sword known as the king of the short weapons. It is a straight, double-bladed implement with three cutting edges, one on each side and at the tip. Said to have been invented by Ch'ih Yu, who forged it from the gold that he found in a certain mountain in China, it is essentially a badge of scholars and the upper class, more decorative than combative. It also is used in the PRC for wu shu competition.

Traditionally, the dancing sword, unlike the combat sword, has a tassel attached to it, which may be either long or short. There are numbers of tales and legends concerning sword-wielding heroes in China's history. Lu-Tung-Bin of the **Eight Immortals,** for instance, possessed a magic sword that would leave its scabbard, do its work, and return to the scabbard by itself.

The single-edged knife, or tao, looks something like a stylized machete, with a single cutting edge used for slicing rather than thrusting. One source considers the knife a descendant of the ta-tao (darn-do in Cantonese), or long-handled halberd, such as that carried by **Kwan-Kung,** while another source ascribes the invention to Sui-Jean-Shih, who made the weapon by melting gold. Still another authority places its origin with the famous Emperor Chou-Muk-Wong during the Chow dynasty.

Many single weapons can be placed in a double-weapon category. The knife, sword, and spear all have single and double counterparts. Some weapons are rarely used singly, such as the butterfly knives, double axes, or twin daggers.

Soft weapons are those which are joined together, such as the steel whip and three-sectional staff, which became the trademarks of guards in old China.

The last category of Chinese weapons are those which are thrown. The practice of throwing weapons was closely related to the study of poisons, another category within the kung-fu spectrum. But the dart or coin thrower was not held in esteem by the Chinese martial arts community. To throw a dart meant that one's kung-fu abilities were not up to par.

For reference purposes a number of the better-known Chinese weapons are listed below in alphabetical order:

butterfly double knives
Chinese waterpipe
cold night knife (single and double)
cold night sword (single and double)
double-headed spear
dragon sword
fingernail razors
flying crane sword (single and double)
golden coin knife
gold coin spade
gong tin spear
green dragon knife
hero big fork
hidden shoe razor
horn big fork
horn twin daggers
Liu-Po spear
Marshal's spear
meteor hammer
mixed gold twin daggers
monk's rake
nine ring knife
pa-kua circular knives
phoenix sword
pirate's twin daggers
razor coins
red tasseled spear
seven stars knife
seven stars sword
Shao-lin monk's spade
shooting star rope dart
short axe (single and double)
sin bin crutch
steel flute
stiff-jointed iron whip
3, 5, 7, 9, and 11 section steel whip
tiger head double hook
twin dragons double knives
vagabond fork
Wah-Shan axe
waist sword
Wai-Tieh spear
white tiger knife
willow leaf knife (single and double)
wooden bench

It should be noted that even though many different weapons relating to Chinese kung-fu have been presented in this Encyclopedia, many prominent kung-fu masters consider only the spear, staff, knife, and sword to be of any importance. The progressive wu shu in vogue on the mainland has built its basic routines around these four implements. (MICHAEL P. STAPLES) *Further reading: Basic Broadsword,* Mark-Bow-Sim, 1977; *Tibetan Kung-Fu,* Michael P. Staples, 1977; *Wu Shu of China,* Michael P. Staples, 1977; *Inside Kung-Fu Magazine,* July 1977.

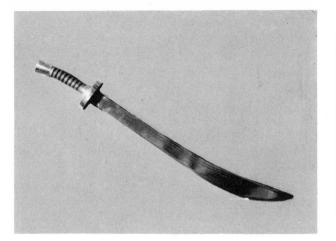

Ox tail knife
Photo by M. Staples

The shinai, or bamboo sword, used in kendo varies in length from 25 inches to 46 inches.

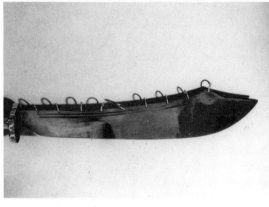

Nine ring big sword
Photo by M. Staples

Master Jew Leong explaining the finer points of the tiger fork as it is used against a shield and butterfly knife.
Courtesy of *Inside Kung-Fu*

The three sectional staff versus the long staff.
Courtesy of *Inside Kung-Fu*

Courtesy of *Inside Kung-Fu*

Sifu Dock Fai Wong with a nine dragon trident

AIKUCHI Short dagger with a cutting edge of about nine inches carried by the samurai, or warrior class; popular especially during the 15th century. During infighting and close-range grappling, the aikuchi was used to dispatch an opponent after throwing him to the ground. It is recognized by its length and the absence of a hilt guard. A much thicker version, called a yori toshi (armor piercer), was strong enough to cut through armor in close-range combat. Another type, the moroha zukuri (double-edged style), was usually six to seven inches long and sharpened on both sides. The best of these knives were made by famous swordsmiths in the Osafune school of Bizen province. Today they are rare and valuable.

ARBIR Halberd approximately five feet long. The plane of the blade has a shallow groove running along it that allows the user to determine exactly where the cutting edge is at all times. The arbir is one of three special weapons used by members of the **Persatuan Pentjak Silat Selurah Indonesia** (PPSI).

ARIT Sickle with a short handle and crescent-shaped blade. Wielded with one or both hands, the arit is used regionally in some systems of Indonesian **pentjak-silat.**

ARMOR The armor worn by the warriors of ancient Japan, as well as various other types of protective equipment used during the latter part of the feudal era, both reflected and influenced the evolution and use of those weapons employed against him in combat. At its most advanced levels, judo contains stylized **kata,** such as the **koshiki-no-kata** (forms of antique), clearly derived from combat strategies for forcing a heavily armored foe to the ground. *Further reading: Secrets of the Samurai,* Adele Westbrook and Oscar Ratti, 1973.

ARROW, SLEEVE Small arrows concealed in the sleeve and used as throwing weapons in some forms of Chinese kung-fu. Called sui-jian.

AXE, SHORT Primarily used by southern kung-fu stylists; the short axes are usually employed in pairs. Also known as hurricane double axes, a name coined by the Sung dynasty figure Li-Kwai. Also called t'uan-ful.

BADIK Also called the butterfly knife, this Malaysian dagger has a flat blade with one cutting edge, but it comes in many sizes and shapes. It is used by various tribes in the Celebes and is ideal for close combat. Known also as bade, badi, badek, and badit. *Further reading: Weapons and Fighting Arts of the Indonesian Archipelago,* Donn F. Draeger, 1972.

BALISONG Philippine fan knife considered a martial arts weapon with both offensive and defensive capabilities. The knife has a locking system that allows quick one-hand opening. It can be used as a primary weapon or a secondary weapon when the forward hand is wielding a stick or a sword. The balisong first gained recognition

following World War II when American servicemen purchased them. Today, the Philippine government has banned the weapon because of its lethal nature. Although it is against the law, many towns in the Batangas continue to produce this weapon.

BARONG A sword used in the Philippines and in Indonesia by the Moslem Moros. It is about 18 inches long with a single edge. Carried in a sheath, the hilt is often fancy and made of precious metal.

BENCH Wooden bench used as a weapon, primarily in the **Choy-Li-Fut** style of Chinese kung-fu.

BERLADAU A knife used in Sumatra for close combat. Usually manipulated in a ripping fashion to attack the midsection.

BISENTO Ninja weapon; a long stick with a blade at one end.

BO Japanese name for the wooden long staff, about 5' in length (6' in Okinawa). The bo was used by bushi (military warriors) of feudal Japan. In Okinawa the bo was commonly practiced by early karate adherents. *See also* bojutsu; kobudo; kobujutsu.

BOGU Protective equipment used, for both practice and competition, in several styles of Japanese karate. Bogu consists of the do, the upper protection that covers chest and stomach; and the kin-ate, which covers the lower abdomen and groin. Bogu is similar to equipment used in kendo and is used in karate during bogu kumite (armor sparring).

BOKKEN Wooden sword carved and shaped in accordance with the contours of a steel sword. It is used as a practice tool today, but during the era of the Japanese feudal warrior, the bokken was employed very effectively in combat, and was in some respects superior to metal swords.

The use of an exercise sword made of wood, called bokuto, which later became generally known as the bokken, greatly increased the range of **kenjutsu** (art of the sword) practice in feudal Japan. In time, the bokken itself grew to be a weapon with lethal possibilities in the hands of an expert who knew how to concentrate the full force of his blows on the vital points of his opponent's anatomy.

Contests of skill with wooden swords, which often resembled bloody duels with live blades, became increasingly frequent. And, since a student's natural tendency was to exercise less restraint when employing the bokken, certain sensei adopted protective

BROADSWORD Chinese weapon used in many styles of kung-fu. Large, with a curved single edge, its techniques include a variety of cuts, swings, blows, thrusts, and parries worked through an intricate set of footwork patterns. *See also* weapons, Chinese.

BRUSH, JUSTICE Set of painting brushes used as weapons in some forms of Chinese kung-fu. Also called pan-gwan-bi.

BUTTERFLY KNIFE Weapon used in kung-fu; short and used in pairs. They are also known as butterfly double knives. *See also* weapons, Chinese.

CALTHROP Small weapon made of four spikes set in a sphere; favorite of the Japanese **ninja,** who could throw it with deadly accuracy.

CERN-DO Paired broad swords used in Chinese kung-fu. Also known as swang-tao, the modern cern-do has a slight curve and ranges from 25 to 29 inches and weighs about four pounds. One sword is used for defense while the other attacks. Techniques includ parrying, slashing, blocking, cutting, stabbing and chopping. The use of the waist is important in using the cern-do because of the power in helps generate.

CHAIN, ART OF THE Group of weapons noted for their efficiency in neutralizing the sword at close range, or reducing the advantage of the spear at long range. The chain, known in Japan as kusari, was forged of iron or steel. Its application to combat, singly or in combination with other weapons, seems to have been ancient, perhaps originating in the far northern regions of China.

Attached to approximately 12 feet of chain was a metal weight, about one pound, the size of a large acorn, with metal rings crowning its base. Used offensively, it could crack bones. Ordinarily, this Chinese chain was swung around in unpredictable patterns at great speed; it could be withdrawn at will. As a defensive weapon, it was used to keep enemies at bay.

Exactly when the chain reached Japan is not known. It appears to have evolved into a number of other weapons, such as the **nage-gama,** though it was frequently employed alone as a primary weapon. The chain is a difficult weapon to master because even the slightest error in judgement can mean harm to its user—modern versions use a rope in place of the traditional chain. *See also* manriki-gusari.

CHASHI A training device originating in China which is used to strengthen the wrist and forearm. Usually made of a circular cement block, it weighs anywhere from 5 to 15 pounds. The cement block has a protruding handle which the practitioner grasps and performs different swinging movements. Kata movements can be practiced with the chashi. Today, this device, which is similar to the Okinawan **chikaraishi**, is used rarely in karate.

CHEMETI Whiplike weapon used in **tjambuk,** constructed of buffalo leather, metal chain, or sometimes human hair. Its overall length, including the handle, varies from three to five feet.

CHER-KHI Worn in the turbans of Sikh warriors of India and Pakistan, these flat metal rings have razor-sharp outer edges and can be thrown with deadly accuracy.

CHI Specialized long weapon with a hooklike spearhead used in Chinese kung-fu.

CH'IAN One of the major Chinese weapons used by practitioners of **wu shu.**

CHIEN Chinese double-edged sword.

CHIGIRIKI A deadly feudal Japanese weapon consisting of a chain 3 to 10 feet long with a lead or cast-iron weight attached to one end. The other end was fixed to a staff which varied in length. It could be used to ensnare a sword, snatching it from the opponent's hands, or to propel the metal weight against an opponent's body, causing severe damage or even death. If necessary the opponent could be immobilized without great damage by entangling his arms and legs with the chigiriki. This weapon was often employed by the **samurai** to keep a number of attackers at bay. It is rarely practiced today.

The **kusarigama,** a similar weapon, consisted of the weighted chain attached to the shaft of a razor-sharp sickle. One hand held the sickle while the other swung the chain. Used much in the same fashion as the chigiriki, it was a favorite weapon of the **ninja,** as well as Japanese farmers and police. Today the kusarigama has been modified to make it less lethal. A rope has replaced the chain and a wooden sickle replaced the steel one. There are still practitioners, mainly in Japan. *See also* chain, art of the.

CHIKARAISHI Training device used in Okinawa by karateka to strengthen wrists, forearms, elbows, and shoulders. Similar to the **chashi,** it consists of a 10-pound stone with a protruding handle. The chikaraishi is employed to perform basic karate techniques, as well as body-strengthening exercises such as arm lifts, arm circles, etc. **Kata** can be performed while holding this device.

CHI SHING CHUNG A kung fu training device used for hardening the legs. Consisting of seven logs two and a half inches in diameter and three feet long, they are inserted into the ground so that one and a half feet stick out. The practitioner wraps his legs with some cloth to insulate his legs and then commences in kicking the logs with various kicking techniques. After a few months the cloth is removed and the logs are wrapped with rope to cushion the impact. Later the ropes are removed and the practitioner should be able to break the logs with any kick. Few if any kung fu practitioners are still known to practice on the Chi shing.

CLAW, FLYING Specialized weapon used in some styles of Chinese kung-fu.

CRIPPLED-MAN'S CRUTCH Short weapon resembling a crutch; used in some styles of kung-fu.

CUDGEL, TWO SECTION Two-section staff, linked at the ends; the Chinese precursor of the Okinawan **nunchaku.**

CUDGEL, WOLF TEETH Cudgel tipped with metal thorns; used in some styles of kung-fu.

DAAB Thai foil used in the art of krabi-krabong.

DAGGER Short knife used in Chinese kung-fu.

DAI KISSAKI The long point of the samurai sword; the part of the sword most often used to cut. *See also* sword, Japanese.

DAITO Japanese samurai sword roughly 4' in length. There are two types, the **tachi,** worn slung over the shoulder, and the **katana,** with less curvature. *See also* sword, Japanese.

DAGGER Short knife used in Chinese kung-fu.

DART, ROPE Weapon, in some styles of kung-fu, consisting of a long rope with a metal dart at one end. The practitioner winds the rope around his body during the various specialized maneuvers used with this weapon, then unwinding it at high velocity, shoots the dart out at his enemy.

DART, SLEEVE Small, razor-sharp dart hidden in the sleeve; used in some styles of Chinese kung-fu.

DOBOK White uniform worn when practicing tae kwon do. It consists of loose-fitting jacket and pants with a belt to hold the jacket in place. Often there is a thick stripe down the collar and around the cuffs of the jacket. *See also* gi.

DOGI Uniform worn by aikidoka who have not yet achieved black belt.

DUNG Leather shield used in krabi krabong.

ENHERO Name for a spear used throughout Burn Island, near Celebes.

ESPADA Y DAGA Filipino words for sword and dagger; one of three forms of sparring in arnis, utilizing a long wooden sword and a short wooden dagger.

FAN Popular weapon in kung-fu. A man's fan contained 9, 16, 20, or 24 ribs, and was carried in the sleeve or waistband. It is the emblem of Chang-li-Chuan of the **Eight Immortals.**

FAY TIAN-CHI Specialized weapon combining sword, spear, and axe; used against the spear with a hooking action. There are both long and short styles.

FINGERNAIL RAZORS Weapon used in some styles of kung-fu; razors inserted under the fingernails. *See also* weapons, Chinese.

FLUTE Popular weapon in Chinese kung-fu. The practitioner of this art could, it is said, transmit the power of ch'i through the music of his flute and drive an opponent mad. The flute also is the emblem of Han-Hsiang-Tsu of the **Eight Immortals.**

FONG-BIN-CHARN Spade-like weapon once used by Chinese monks for both burying the dead and fighting. *See also* weapons, Chinese.

FORK, TIGER (hu-cha) Large trident originally used to kill tigers in southern China. Planted in the ground as a tiger charged, the animal impaled itself on the three sharpened prongs. Eventually, the fork entered the arsenal of long kung-fu weapons. It is often wielded by performing lion dance groups. Southern forks are larger than those used in the north, their techniques demonstrating power rather than style. Northern forks were designed for mounted soldiers; the southern were used primarily on foot. (MICHAEL P. STAPLES) *See also* weapons, Chinese.

FOU-TOU-OU Hook and crescent sword; a weapon used in Chinese kung-fu.

FUCHI Metal sleeve on a Japanese sword.

FUKIYA Poisoned pins and darts shot through blowguns; used by the **ninja** of feudal Japan.

FUKUMI-BARI Small dirks concealed in the mouth and blown at an enemy's eyes or face; used by the **ninja** of feudal Japan.

FUKUSHIKI Known as a double **makiwara** (striking post), a solid piece of wood imbedded in the ground or fastened to a solid base. Unlike the **tanshiki** the top of the fukushiki has a 2' vertical slot. The pad is mounted on the first half of the wood, which provides a second resistence during the strike and gives the feeling of penetration.

FUNDOSHI Tight-fitting loincloth worn by judo practitioners to avoid injury.

FUTAMATA-YARI Japanese spear with a forked head classified broadly in the category of **yari** (spear).

GADUBONG One-handed Sumatran sword ranging in length from 30" to 51".

GANJA Raised collar guard of the Indonesian **kris;** it generally forms the base of the blade.

GARROTE Weapon of Spanish origin, causing silent strangulation or breaking of the neck. Materials for the garrote may include thong, cord, string, wire, or silk. Use of the garrote was taught in the armed forces as a method of disposing of sentries. *See also* kali.

GETA Clogs worn while walking on ice to practice balance and silent treading. Geta were used by **ninja** in training. Today iron geta are worn by some martial artists to strengthen the feet and legs.

GOLDEN COIN Small mock sword comprised of many Chinese coins linked together. A talisman and good luck charm. *See also* sword, Chinese.

GOLDEN HELON HAMMER Specialized kung-fu weapon, a cudgel with a large metal ball at one end.

GOLOK Heavy, cleaver-like knife with a curved blade ranging in length from 10" to 20". It is used in some systems of Indonesian **pentjak-silat.**

GONTAR Short wooden instrument used to sound the village drum, and secondarily employed as a club by **pentjak-silat** experts.

GU-TANG Ancient weapon used in some styles of Chinese kung-fu.

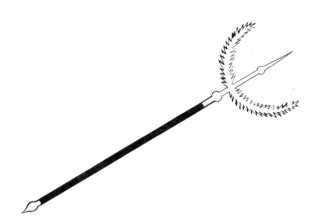

HAMMER, COPPER Set of short cudgels with large copper balls attached to one end; a weapon in some kung-fu styles.

HANDACHI NO KOSHIRAE A mounting for the Japanese sword that marks an evolution in sword wearing. Once slung from the waist in the Chinese manner, later the sword was thrust into the belt edge upward. This enabled a warrior to draw and cut in a single motion and eventually led to the development of **iaido,** the Japanese art of the fast draw.

HASSAKU-BO Wooden spear, one of the subdivisions of the Japanese art of the long staff. *See also* bojutsu.

HIDARI-YOKO-ERI Left side collar of the judo gi (uniform).

HO-GOO Protective sparring garments developed by the Korean Taekwon-do Association. Use is mandatory in all KTA-sanctioned contests and exhibitions.

HOJUTSU Firearms used by Japanese feudal warriors.

HOKO Special, spearlike weapon or halberd thought to be Japan's oldest bladed weapon. The hoko's head is fitted perfectly into the shaft. It was used either from a standing or mounted position. Although not a formidable weapon in individual confrontations, it was effective in mass deployment. *See also* yari.

HACHIKYU In most traditional karate and martial arts systems, a white belt; in hybrid systems, a yellow belt. *See also* kyu.

HACHIMAKI Light cotton towel, also called tenugui, worn in **kendo.** It is both additional protection, beneath the inner men (mask) padding, and a sop for perspiration.

HAKAMA Pleated skirt worn as formal attire; shirtlike trousers inherited from the **samurai,** who wore them while practicing the martial arts. They are worn in modern kendo, aikido, iaido, and in some styles of jujutsu. In most of these arts, all students wear the hakama; in aikido, however, only those holding black belt rank wear them.

HALASAN Long Sumatran knife.

HALBERD, COIN-SHAPED Large halberd with a sharpened coin-shaped head. This rare weapon, used in some styles of Chinese kung-fu, was designed to catch an enemy's spear. Also known as golden coin halberd.

HON-BO Traditional wooden staff, similar to the **rokushaku-bo** (6-foot staff), but only about 3 feet long. Hon means half. It is used to strike, entangle, or even throw an opponent. Made of any hardwood, it measures about 1 inch in diameter. The hon-bo is usually gripped in both hands; strikes and blocks can be delivered in rapid succession.

HOOK, CENTIPEDE Sword with a hook at its tip, used in some forms of Chinese kung-fu. Also known as wu-gung-go.

HOOK-SWORD Much like a conventional sword, this Chinese weapon has a double edged cutting blade and a hook extending from one side at the point.

HAM-BO Wooden sword of regulation length and a subdivision of **bojutsu** (art of the staff).

HUI-THO Whiplike weapon consisting of a sharpened metal piece attached to a 1-yard length of cord; used in the Celebes.

JITTE Also known as jittei, jutte, or jutta, this 15-inch Japanese weapon usually consists of an iron or steel rod, a long hilt, and a characteristically square hook jutting from the rod at the hilt. It is often fitted with a guard (tsuba) and a scabbard; in certain rare cases it is even mounted as a sword, complete with blade. Some sources report that it is carried hanging from the belt or in a scabbard inserted in the waistband or sash; others claim it is generally hung from the wrist by a cord tied to a ring on the hilt.

The jitte's origins are unclear: Okinawan and Japanese provenance are both claimed. Whatever its origins, this weapon gave rise to a sophisticated method of combat known in Japan as jittejutsu. Its techniques included parries, blows, and thrusts, and on occasion the weapon was hurled. The hilt of the jitte could also be used with devastating effect in delivering reverse blows to maim or even kill an unwary opponent.

Mastery of jittejutsu depended upon skill in the art of displacement, called **tai-sabaki** (body movement), which made it possible for an expert to change positions quickly, sliding or whirling away from an opponent, whose reach normally extended to the tip of his long sword. Since the techniques of **kenjutsu** (art of the sword) are numerous, the techniques of jittejutsu of necessity had to be sufficiently inclusive to cover all threatening contingencies.

Official use of the jitte was restricted to police officers of the feudal era, for whom it was a symbol of position. Warriors were said to have dutifully acknowledged the efficiency of this instrument, which, in the hands of experts, could snap a steel blade or send it whirling away. *Further reading: Classical Budo,* Donn F. Draeger, 1973; *Secrets of the Samurai,* Oscar Ratti and Adele Westbrook, 1973.

JIU SHING DORSIEN CHUNG A kung fu training device used to train in the techniques of shunning. The device consists of about 9 logs about one inch in diameter, which are stuck in the ground so about six feet protrude. They are placed in different patterns fairly close to each other, and the practitioner must slip through the spaces among the logs swiftly, but without touching any of them.

JO Staff used in the Japanese art of **jojutsu.**

JUDOGI Uniform worn by judo players. The standard judo costume consists of a white jacket and trousers secured by a colored **obi** (belt), signifying the wearer's rank. The entire jacket is made of two layers of cotton material. For strength, double stitches of cotton string are woven through the jacket material, covering the entire upper half of the garment and the sleeves. From the waistline to the bottom of the jacket, front and back, a small diamond-shaped design is woven into the fabric.

From the bottom of the right side, around the neck and down the left side, runs a continuous lapel approximately 2 inches wide, stitched to the body of the jacket. Extra heavy stitching in each armpit prevents the seams from opening or deteriorating from perspiration. A slit of about 7 inches up each side frees the hips. The sleeves must be loose, at least 1½ inches between cuff and forearm.

The trousers usually are made of cotton fabric, with a string drawn through the top to hold them in place. They too must fit loosely, with at least 2 inches between the bottom edge and the leg. The belt, also made of cotton fabric, is about 1½ inches wide and 8 or 9 feet long, wound twice around the waist and tied in a square knot in front.

JU-I Short sword, also known as a scepter, symbolic of the lotus in Buddhist religion. The ju-i pattern often decorates kung-fu uniforms.

KAGI-YARI Japanese hooked spear classified under the broad category of the **yari** (spear). The kagi-yari is used mostly in parrying, hooking, and deflecting.

KALUS Whip of about 3 feet used in the **tjatji** (strike the enemy) system of **pentjak-silat.**

KAMA Okinawan rice harvesting implement; one of the five systematized weapons used by the early developers of **te** (hand). The kama was used either singly or in pairs, one in each hand, for close-range combat, where it could be employed to slash, hook, rake, chop, deflect, or block. The kama has a short blade set perpendicular to a hardwood handle. Its use is related to **kusarigama.** Its practice now consists primarily of **kata** (formal exercise). *See also* bo; kobu-jutsu; nunchaku; sai; tonfa.

KAMA-YARI Japanese spear with a sickle-shaped blade.

KAME Weighted jars, used by Okinawan karateka to increase the strength of fingers and grip. These jars are lifted empty or weighted, the wrists turning side to side.

KAMEIKADA One-man rafts, made with crossed bamboo or timber sections, kept afloat by four large, sealed ceramic jars. Used by the **ninja** of feudal Japan.

KAMPILAN Swordlike weapon used in the Filipino art of **silat.**

KAN-SHU Karate training device, used chiefly by **Uechi-ryu** practitioners, a pail into which the karateka thrusts his fist or fingers to toughen them. The progression is usually from damp sand, through dried peas or beans, to gravel.

KANZASHI Sharp-pointed ornamental hairpin employed by women in feudal Japan for self-protection. The sides were spoon-shaped and usually contained some form of lethal poison.

KAPA; KAPAK Small throwing hachet used by the Batak tribe of Sumatra. The metal weapon is carried inconspicuously at the back of the neck, or on the forearm inside the sleeves. A Batak can pin an enemy's foot to the ground with the kapa at a distance of 15 feet.

KARAMBIT Curved knife used in Sumatra. The forefinger is inserted in a hole at the head of the hilt.

KARIS Short knife of Moorish design used in Sumatra.

KATANA Long, curved, single-edged Japanes sword with a blade a little over two feet long, it was usually carried by the **samurai** in a scabbard on his left side. The katana's hilt, made typically of wood and covered with skin and silk cords, was removable. Between the skin and cords were placed decorative figures. the katana's guard (tsuba) was often beautifully decorated and made from expensive metals. Many katanas were forged by master swordsmen, many of whom kept their art a secret. **Kenjutsu** (art of the sword) was practiced mainly with the katana. *See also* kenjutsu; sword, Japanese. *Further reading: The Samurai Sword, A Handbook*, John Yumoto, 1958.

KEIKOGI Jacket worn in kendo. The novice wears a lightweight cotton jacket, white with criss-cross black stitching; the instructor wears a heavier or hand-made quilted keikogi, usually black or navy blue. Karate practitioners may refer to their practice uniforms as keikogi, but most often they are called gi.

KEIKO-NAGINATA Comparatively light **naginata** with a curved bamboo blade similar to the kendo shinai (bamboo sword). This practice spear is generally about 6 feet 8 inches in length, though longer staffs are recommended for taller practitioners.

KELEWANG Long sword with a single cutting edge and a protruding notch near its tip; blade lengths vary from 15 inches to 30 inches. Used locally in some systems of Indonesian **pentjak-silat.**

KESHO MAWASHI Ceremonial apron worn by high-ranking **sumo** wrestlers just prior to their bouts. the aprons are worn during the **dohyo-iri** ceremony and are made of silk, richly embroidered with different designs and hemmed with gold fringe.

KNIFE, BUTTERFLY Also known as southern style short sabres, it originated from the butcher's chopping cleaver. These variably shaped weapons are usually seen in pairs and often attached to the large kung-fu drum played at lion dance ceremonies. They are primarily used in southern kung-fu styles. The top of the knife hilt is turned forward so that the practitioner can flip the knife around his thumb, much like the Okinawan **sai.**

KNIFE, CHINESE Unlike the sword, whose tip thrusts and jabs, the knife, or sabre, cuts and slashes at its target. It is often ascribed to the Emperor Chou-Muk-Wong, of the Chow dynasty, who was presented with a large sabre while traveling through Shi-Kiang province. The knife, in various lengths and sizes, has much the same mystique about it as does the sword, on a less grand scale. If the sword was the emblem of the upper classes, the knife was the mark of the warrior.

The most popular knife is the willow leaf; also popular is the white ghost and, in northern China, the grain leaf sabre, all of which can be used with other weapons, most often with the shield.

KNIFE, NINE RING Broad knife (tao) used in Chinese kung-fu, especially the southern styles, with a series of metal rings attached to its dorsal edge. The rings are used to catch an opponent's weapons (e.g. spear) and to create a din.

KNIFE, SPREAD THE WATER Circular knife used in some forms of kung-fu.

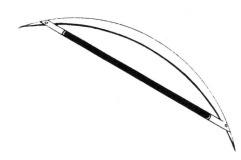

KNIFE, SPRING AND AUTUMN Specialized weapon in some styles of kung-fu; resembles the **Kwan tao.**

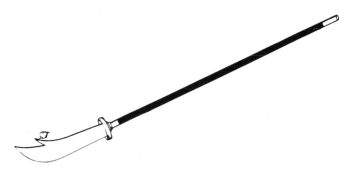

KNIFE, WILLOW LEAF Thin, curved knife (tao) in some forms of kung-fu.

KODACHI One of the swords worn by the Japanese **bushi** or feudal warrior. A forerunner of the **wakizashi** (short sword), the kodachi has a blade ranging between 30 inches and 60 inches.

KO-GATANA Knife fitted into one side of the scabbard of the Japanese **wakizashi** (short sword). Samurai swordsmen were proficient at hurling the ko-gatana and employing it at close range.

KON Chinese term for the staff. *See also* bo.

KONGOKEN Karate training device used mostly in **Okinawan goju-ryu.** An oblong iron ring of 100 lbs., it accustoms practitioners to handling the weight of a man.

KONSAIBO Hardwood staff reinforced with metal strips and often studded with heavy iron nubs along its upper portion. The konsaibo was a lighter version of the Japanese **tetsubo** (iron staff).

KORUNG Another name for the Indonesian tombak.

KOWLIUM Weapon indigenous to Indonesian kwitang silat. Similar to a boat hook, it is a short shaft tipped by an iron spearhead from which a small hook projects a few inches below the tip.

KRABI Thai version of the western sabre, used in the art of **krabi-krabong.**

KRIS Double-edged Malaysian dagger with blades ranging from 5 inches to 30 inches. It is a standard weapon of all classical Indonesian **pentjak-silat** styles and can be said to be the national weapon of Java. Primarily designed for thrusting, this weapon is known also as creese, creis, cris, crise, crisi, dawang, keris, and querix. All kris possess hantu (spirit), and many are said to be capable of tuju, "sorcery by pointing." These qualities are imparted by the secret and mystical forging process of the pande (expert), as the smith is called, but can only be activated by the owner. Purportedly lethal even when stabbed into the victim's shadow or footprints, legends tell of the kris rattling in the owner's sheath to warn him of approaching danger or leaping from its sheath to fight for its owner.

Size, shape, and workmanship of the weapon vary. The kris is unique among weapons in two ways: its blade widens suddenly, just below the base, which is set almost perpendicular to it; and, in all but the earliest, one-piece (blade-handle) models, the blade is not set firmly to the handle. All early kris were straight-bladed; undulating blades are said to be adopted from Indian weapons. The deadliness of a kris in combat increases with the number of waves it possesses. A wavy blade causes a larger wound and penetrates more readily between bones. *Further reading: Weapons and Fighting Arts of the Indonesian Archipelago*, Donn F. Draeger, 1972.

KRIS BAHARI One of two types of **kris** popular in Sumatra. It is a relatively large kris.

KRIS BALENGKO Kris with a long, undulating blade used by the Atjeh tribe.

KRIS MAJAPAHIT Possible prototype of the Indonesian **kris.**

KRIS PANGANG One of two types of **kris** popular in Sumatra. It features a decorative handle and a long, flat, narrow blade, often with a raised rib running the length of the blade.

KRIS PICHIT Possible prototype of the Indonesian **kris.**

KUJUNGI Short-handled Indonesian knife with a blade of irregular design. It is one of the three special weapons used by members of the **Persatuan Pentjak Silat Selurah Indonesia** (PPSI).

KUJUR Sumatran spear; also known as kunjur.

KUKRI Knife invented in India but a favorite weapon in Burmese bando. It has a recurved blade with a somewhat rounded point; weighted toward the tip, it is an excellent throwing weapon. Used by the famous Gurkas of Nepal.

KUSARIGAMA Japanese weapon consisting of a chain with a metal weight at one end with the other end attached to the shaft of a razor-sharp sickle. When facing a sword-bearing opponent, the kusarigama user held the sickle with one hand, while the other swung the chain in such a way as to ensnare the opponent's weapon and snatch it from his grasp. The metal weight was simply used to strike any part of the opponent's body and cause serious damage. An expert with the kusarigama could entangle his foe's arms or legs to immobilize him without causing excessive injury, if so desired.

This weapon was employed by the **samurai**, by peasants, and often by police forces. The **ninja** were extremely adept at handling it. A variation of the kusarigama was the **chigiriki**, a weighted chain attached to the end of a staff. It was used in a manner similar to the kusarigama and could be whirled to keep a number of attackers at bay simultaneously. *See also* chain, art of the.

KWAN-TAO Literally "Kwan's knife"; a large halberd used in kung-fu, named after the famous general **Kwan-Kung.** The weapon is thought to build strength in the forearms and wrists.

LADING Double-edged Sumatran knife; length varies from 8 inches to 16 inches.

LAMBING Spear used by the Menangkabau warriors of Sumatra.

LOH Leather shield used in **krabi krabong.**

LOPU Type of **parang** used on the island of Cream. *Further reading: Weapons and Fighting Arts of the Indonesian Archipelago*, Donn F Draeger, 1972.

LURIS PEDANG One-handed Sumatran sword ranging in length from 15 inches to 30 inches.

MAE-TATEMITSU That part of the **sumo** wrestler's attire that sweeps down at right angles to the abdomen and covers the vital organs.

MAGARI-YARI Japanese spear, similar in appearance to a trident; the side blades are set at right angles to the central blade, points turning slightly inward. This weapon is classified broadly among the **yari.** It was invented by Matsumoto Bizen-no-kami Naokatsu.

MAISUM Pair of 18 inch wooden clubs similar to the **tonfa;** used in **krabi krabong.**

MAKIGAE-GU Training instrument used in Okinawan karate to strengthen the wrist; a rack with a revolving horizontal wooden bar. A weight suspended on a rope is hung from the bar; a student; with double-handed grip, winds the weight up or down by rotating the bar.

MANDAU Twenty inch single-edged knife of the Dyak warriors of Borneo. The handle is hewn from deer antlers and carved with scenes of snakes devouring fish; human hair hangs from the handle. Mandau sheaths are made of bamboo with circular imprints representing the number of heads taken. The weapon resembles a machete. *See also* kenjah.

MANRIKI-GUSARI Japanese weapon; a chain 2 feet in length with weights at either end. Masaki Toshimitsu Donnoshin, a famous swordsman of Japan's feudal era, devised a method of disarming and subduing an opponent with this weapon. He named his weapon manriki-gusari (10,000 power chain) because he felt it possessed

certain systems of Chinese kung-fu (e.g. white crane, hop-gar, etc.) for both training and actual fighting atop these stumps. Lion dancing can also be performed upon them, as can lion fighting. According to some references, sharpened spikes have at times been planted around them, making any fall a fatal one. The placement pattern of the stumps signifies the particular type of chuang. Chi-hsing-chuang employs seven stumps placed in the so-called "seven star" pattern. The traditional mei-hwa pattern consists of five stumps, arranged like the five dots on a dice cube. (MICHAEL P. STAPLES)

MEN Face mask used in **kendo.**

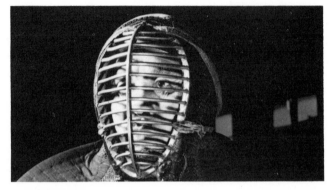

MITSU-DOGU Three classical Japanese weapons used in unison for restraining swordsmen; they are **sasumata,** a forked device; **sodegarami,** a barbed instrument; and **tsukubo,** a T-shaped device. All three had long shafts to protect their operators from the blade of a skillful swordsman. In the Tokugawa period (1600-1867), these weapons became merely ornamental and were replaced by three different weapons, used chiefly against bushi by Tokugawa policemen: **jutte, manriki-gusari,** and **rokushakubo.**

MIZUGUMO Wooden floats attached to each leg used by **ninja** to "walk" across water.

MON-FAT-JONG Kung-fu training device resembling a human figure, complete with a spring-mounted head. A single knee extends outward and down from the base. The body is designed to recoil upon impact and return to its normal, upright position. All striking areas are padded with form rubber. With the mon-fat-jong, a student can practice virtually any type of punching, blocking, or kicking technique. Also called mook jong.

MOOK JONG Wooden dummy used by Chinese kung-fu practitioners to practice blocks and counters. It has protruding extensions resembling arms and legs. *See* mon-fat-jong.

the power and ingenuity of 10,000 persons. In his school, the Masaki-ryu, students learned to fight many armed and unarmed opponents simultaneously, the weights of their chains whirling ominously as they wove in and out among their attackers.

The weapon could be used to hobble, choke, and immobilize an opponent, or to hook his clothing or weapon. Like the **jitte,** it served well to parry and deflect a sword by stretching the chain taut before an oncoming blade and striking the wielder with the weights connected to the chain. Other schools evolved from the Masaki-ryu, whose techniques, as well as the weapon employed, underwent several modifications, affecting mainly the length of the chain, its thickness, the shape and size of its weights, and finally, the methods of actually using the weapon. Some of these are: Hoen-ryu, Toda-ryu, Shuchin-ryu, Kyoshin-Meichi-ryu, Shindo-ryu, and Hikida-ryu. The manriki-gusari also is referred to as kusari-bundo, ryo-bundo, kusari-sode-kusari, tama-kusari, and kusari-jutte; in Okinawa, it is called the surushin (weighted chain).

Especially popular with samurai of the palace guard, it was sacrilege to spill blood on palace grounds, but the chain could strike, strangle, or entrap without wounding. *Further reading: Spike and Chain,* C.V. Gruzanski, 1968. *See also* chain, art of the.

MATA KRIS Blade of the Indonesian **kris;** straight (dapur bener) or wavy (dapur lug; dapur parung).

MAWASHI Loin cloth worn by **sumo** wrestlers; it has a long stripped fringe, called sagari, at the front.

MEI-HWA-CHUANG Literally the "plum flower stumps," a series of wooden posts driven into the ground. Special techniques exist in

MU-CHUANG Large wooden dummy used for striking practice in some forms of Chinese kung-fu, especially the **wing-chun** style.

MUNE-ATE Chest protectors used in **kendo** were once called mune-ate; today known as **do.**

MUTON Short staff used in Philippine **arnis de mano.** *See also* baston.

NAGE-GAMA Javelin with a short, sicklelike blade set at right angles to one end and a long chain attached to the other. Some sources believe this weapon was used chiefly in defending Japanese castles and bastions, being thrown, for example, at besiegers and then retrieved by a quick pull on its chain. Others hold that it was employed as a walking stick that could be instantly transformed into a lethal weapon. Militant monks and the formidable **ninja** favored the nage-gama, disguised in various ways, one of which consisted of a bamboo pole from whose hollow tip the chain would snap out to engangle an opponent.

NAGEMAKI Type of **naginata** (long sword) with heavy, very long blade mounted on a shorter, sturdy staff. The earliest known Japanese halberd.

NAGINATA Scimitarlike blade, 3 feet in length, fixed to a slightly longer shaft. From the 11th century, when the Monamoto and the Taira clans started their long struggle, the naginata became popular among military men because of its combined powers of cutting and thrusting. Early naginata consisted of simply a blade and shaft, a handguard was added later. Double-edged blades and blades set at right angles (jumon-ji naginata) became the most popular type.

There were three major forms; the first appears to have been the ancient tsukushi-naginata, whose shaft was inserted into a metal loop on the back of the blade; the second, and most common, was secured to the shaft; and the third, and rarest, had a socket at the base into which the shaft was inserted (ta-no-saki). Their shafts were heavily lacquered and decorated with metal fittings. The naginata is usually employed with propellerlike slashes directed to all parts of the enemy's anatomy. From a safe distance the naginata could keep a sword-bearing enemy at bay. It is believed that the introduction of protective armor for the legs and the lower part of the body was owed to the effectiveness of the naginata.

During the Muromachi Period (1392-1573) hundreds of styles of naginata developed, but with the arrival of firearms in 1542 began a decline. By 1600 it was relegated to a symbolic position.

The naginata, interestingly enough, was also referred to as the "woman's spear," because women of the Japanese military class were expected to have perfected its use by age 18. Even in modern Japan, it is said there are few more graceful or interesting spectacles than the manipulation of this weapon by an expert female fencer. Today it is practiced as a sport and a form of physical education by women.

NAKAE Shaft of the Japanese spear. *See also* yari.

NGOW Ax or halberd with a 7 foot handle; used in the art of **krabi-krabong.**

NINE-SECTION WHIP Wu shu weapon chiefly employed in coiling, stretching, and sweeping movements. Double whips require great dexterity, as does wielding a whip and a broadsword simultaneously. *See also* weapons, Chinese.

NINSHOKUDAI Candles on iron-spiked holders shaped like the letter "L" so they could be wedged into a wall projection or tree. Used by the **ninja.**

NIO BODHISATTVAS Statues of the so-called Nio deities, they are found in Buddhist temples of Japan and posed in unmistakable similarity to karate stances. These replicas of early Indian prototypes are protectors of the Buddhist faith. A large number guard the entrances to Buddhist temples.

NODACHI An extra sword, quite heavy and generally longer than the normal **katana,** carried by the feudal Japanese warrior. The nodachi was usually strapped to the back and accompanied the customary **wakizashi** (short sword) and the **tachi** (long sword). Its use, once almost universal, became increasingly rare during the Tokugawa era (1600-1876). *See also* sword, Japanese.

NINE DRAGON TRIDENT Chinese weapon known as gao loon cha; used by practitioners of **Choy-Li-Fut** kung-fu. the weapon weighs about 20 pounds and is approximately six feet long. It can be used for striking, poking or cutting, or in a spiraling motion to entangle an opponent's weapon. the hooks of the trident are sharp-edged and can be used for cutting. *Further reading: Inside Kung Fu,* Oct. 1982.

NUNCHAKU Okinawan weapon composed of two pieces of hardwood connected by rope or chain. The length of the weapon varies, but is usually around 12″ to 14″. Although the connecting link is never very long, its length does vary from one inch to as much as 4 or 5″. Earlier, the link was made of horsehair, leather, silk, or rope; today, nylon cord or chain is most often used. Although the most common nunchaku is octagonal (hjakakuei), with eight sides, there are variations: round (maru-gat) in which both pieces are round and of even length; long-short (so-setsu-kon) in which one piece is about half the length of th eother; half-size (han-kei) in which the two sides, when placed together, form one circular piece of wood; three piece (san-setsu-kon) in which all three pieces are about 14″ long, or a variation in which one side is long, but the other is composed of two smaller pieces; four piece (yon-setsu-kon) in which there are two longer and two shorter pieces all hinged together. Modern nunchaku, especially those made in the U.S., often have fancy handgrips and employ such innovations as ball-bearing swivels.

NUNTE Okinawan weapon with a central shaft and two prongs, one pointing away and the other toward its wielder. Though often attached to a long staff, the nunte is roughly 15 inches in length and was developed by Okinawans. It was employed either to hook the samurai sword and snap its blade, or to twist the sword from an attacker's hand. Also called manji-no-sai.

O-DACHI Long sword used by the Japanese samurai.

OMI-GARI Japanese spear within the category of the **yari.**

PAKSI Pin projecting through the collar guard of the Indonesian **kris.**

PAKU Indonesian weapon, originally 2 inches or 3 inches in length with sharp points at both ends, of Chinese derivation. Similar to the Japanese **shuriken,** the paku is concealed in the hands or garments and thrown at an enemy. Today it ranges from 4 inches to 6 inches with one sharply pointed end. The paku is one of three special weapons used by members of the **Persatuan Pentjak Silat Selurah Indonesia.**

PA-KUA CIRCULAR KNIVES Literally "eight trigrams knife," a moon-shaped set of knives used in the pa-kua style of Chinese kung-fu.

PAMOR Special design obtained by welding metals of various compositions in an ingenious manner to the core of the **kris** blade.

PARANG Cleaverlike weapon used in Indonesia and Malaya; blades range from 10 inches-36 inches in length. It is a standard weapon of all classical Indonesian **pentjak-silat** styles. The parang is known as the belo in times of peace; belo-leong, meaning "ear parang," during wartime. Sometimes the name "nume" is attached to the parang employed combatively.

PENTJONG Short hardwood stick or club used in the bhakti negara style of **pentjak-silat.**

PETJAT Whip of 4 feet to 6 feet in length used in **udung.** It is made of sturdy fibers, such as twisted coconut palm.

PETJUT Weapon consisting of a hardwood handle fastened to a short leather thong tipped by a ball of knotted leather; used in **ende.**

PEUDEUENG One-handed Sumatran sword ranging in length from 15 inches to 30 inches.

PIAU Unusually-shaped piece of metal for throwing; one of three special weapons of the **sakti** style of **pentjak-silat.**

PLONG Six foot quarterstaff used in **krabi-krabong.**

PRINGAPUS Bamboo knife used in the Singaraja area of northern Bali; possibly derived from the metal-bladed knife called tadji. Both are short in overall length and used in stiletto fashion. Poison is occasionally applied to the tip of the blade.

PROSECUTOR Police weapon, a combination of the standard billy club and the Okinawan **tonfa.** It is approximately 24 inches in length with a 5¾ inch handle. Police departments throughout America are adopting the new weapon.

PUTTHA Gauntlet sword developed by the people of Decca, India. Today it is no longer used combatively but practiced in formal exercises.

RANTE Chain weapon used in the **tridharma** style of **pentjak-silat.** Affixed to one end is a sawtoothed gearlike metal weight. The rante is whirled at different lengths while held in one hand. By changing hands, the swing may be lengthened to its full extension, approximately one yard. This weapon is said to be inherited from the Chinese by practitioners of **delima,** another form of pentjak-silat.

RANTE BER GANGEDUG Metal chain, one of three special weapons in the **prisai sakti** style of **pentjak-silat.**

RAUT Short-bladed knife with a pistol grip used by the Batak tribe of Sumatra.

RAZOR COINS Weapon thrown by practitioners of some schools of Chinese kung-fu. These coins varied in size and weight; their edges were filed sharp. Also known as "hidden coin" technique. *See also* weapons, Chinese.

RED TASSELED SPEAR Spear with a red tassel at one end, often seen in Chinese kung-fu. *See also* spear.

RENTJONG Unusually shaped Sumatran weapon, whose blade carries distinct markings, generally Arabic characters suggesting mystic powers. The rentjong is used according to its length, which varies from about 5 inches to 20 inches. The shorter lengths, because of easy concealment, are favored.
   In some styles of **pentjak silat** the rentjong is gripped with the toes and, after much practice, kicks can be delivered with the knife remaining in place. *Further reading: Weapons and Fighting Arts of the Indonesian Archipelago,* Donn F. Draeger, 1972.

RINGS Set of rings used as weapons in some forms of kung-fu.

RING, FLYING Specialized weapon in some styles of Chinese kung-fu.

ROKUSHAKU-BO Hardwood, polelike weapon about 6 feet in length; also the name of an Okinawan fighting system employing the rokushakubo. Developed from Chinese preecursors, it utilizes basic karate movements. The staff is employed mostly in striking and thrusting, though because of its length its effectiveness is inhibited in crowded areas. Good staff skill requires at least five years' training. After the fundamentals are learned, students embark on prearranged combat practice against other weapons. *See also* bo.

ROPE-DART Weapon in Chinese **wu shu** (national arts); a dart attached to one end of a long rope. The weapon is swung in circular patterns to gather speed before being flung at its target.

ROTI KALONG Brass knuckle-type weapon, not unlike the hilt of the World War I trench knife, used in the **perisai diri** style of Indonesian **pentjak-silat.**

RUDUS Sword used by the Menangkabau warriors of Sumatra.

RULER, IRON Weapon resembling a large ruler used in some forms of kung-fu.

SAFE-T-CHOP; SAFE-T-FACE; SAFE-T-KICK Foam rubber safety pads worn on the hands a feet to protect martial artists from injury, especially during sparring. Invented by Korean instructor **Jhoon Rhee** in 1972, the equipment revolutionized sport karate, allowing fighters to make moderate contact without injury and making possible **semi-contact** tournaments.

SAGARI Short string skirt of starch-stiffened lengths of silk hanging from the **sumotori's mawashi**.

SAI Short, forklike metal weapon approximately 15″ to 20″ in length and weighing about 3 lbs. The weapon consists of a shaft, pointed in front and tapered to a blunt lipped end, and two tines projecting forward from about a quarter of the distance from the end of the shaft. The sai is primarily a defensive weapon, used rather like a truncheon, to strike, poke, jab, or hook (with the tines). The tines may catch the blade of a sword. Often two or three sai were carried, one in each hand and a third thrust into the waistband in reserve.

The sai has a long history found in India, China, Malaysia, and Indonesia; the weapon migrated to Okinawa, where it became one of the five systemetized weapons of the early "te" developers of Okinawa—the other weapons being the **bo, nunchaku, kama,** and **tonfa**. *See also* kobujutsu. *Further reading: Sai, Karate Weapon of Self-Defense*, Fumio Demura, 1974.

SAKIN Slender, straight-bladed weapon used in Sumatra.

SAM Traditional uniform worn in Chinese kung-fu.

SAN-CHIAN LIANG-REN-TAO Three-pointed double-bladed sword, a specialized long weapon used in some forms of Chinese kung-fu.

SAN-CHIEH-PANG Three short cudgels linked at the ends. Also called **three-section staff,** sam jeet gwun, and dragon sticks.

SANOKAT Spear of the warriors of Ceram.

SASH Silk waistband worn by kung-fu practitioners to show skill levels.

SASHI Okinawan karate training implements, usually in pairs, for a powerful punch. Often referred to as a "thrusting stone."

SASUMATA Japanese spear with a forked head and hooks or spikes at its base. This weapon is classified broadly with the **yari** (spear).

SAYA Scabbard of the Japanese sword.

SEGU Metal truncheon with a short flexible shaft somewhat more than a foot in length. It is a special weapon of **tapak sutji,** an Indonesian combative. Also known as serba or guna.

SCARF In judo, the part of the jacket around the neck; often used to choke out an opponent. Choke holds are sometimes called scarf holds.

SEWAR Slender, arch-bladed weapon used in Sumatra.

SHAKEN Star-shaped **shuriken** with three points, six points, and sometimes eight points. They are thrown or held in the fist so that the points protrude beyond the fingers to attack certain vital points. In feudal Japan, when employed by the **samurai**, poison or horse dung was applied to the points. Occasionally, a fuse and explosive compound was attached to the weapon and ignited before throwing. The shaken were also referred to as "five-vehicle knives"—used for igniting fires from a distance.

SHIELD, RATTAN Large rattan shield used in conjunction with the knife (tao) in some styles of kung-fu. A specialized set of rolling techniques were designed for the shield against the fork (cha).

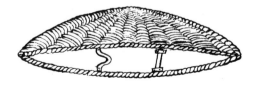

SHIKOMI-ZUE Special sword can used by **ninja** while pretending to be blind.

SHINAI Sword made of four sections of bamboo tightly fastened together in the shape of a straight sword, with a guard (tsuba) and a long handle for double-handed grasping. It is the weapon commonly employed in **kendo.** Known in ancient Japan as the chikuto, the shinai is said to have been invented by Nakanishi Chuzo of Edo in 1750, to minimize the dangers of sword practice.

SHINOBI-ZUE Ninja staff weapon with a chain hidden in one end and a lead weight in the other.

SHINOBU SHOZOKU Ninja uniform; usually black and often reversible in another color. The ninja wore a hood that covered most of his face and dark shoes split at the toe. Often the uniform had hidden pockets for weapons.

SHORT SWORD Common name for the Okinawan weapon known as the **sai,** as well as the Japanese swords **kodachi** and **wakizashi.**

SHOVEL, CONVENIENT Fang Bian Tsang; a weapon used in some forms of kung-fu—originally a peasant weapon.

SHU-KE Javelinlike spear in some forms of Chinese kung-fu. *See also* spear, Chinese.

SHUKO The ninja of Japan wore these brass knuckles, which were made of a metal plate adorned with four spikes extending from the palm. Not always a weapon, sometimes used to grasp when climbing.

SHURIKEN Small, multipointed throwing weapons, such as dirks, darts, stars, etc. They vary in design from three to ten points. These weapons were an integral part of a **ninja's** arsenal. Most shurikens were aimed at the eyes, temple, throat, and arms to slow an attacker.

SICKLE Farming tool also used by the Okinawans as a weapon. Sickle fighting became a standardized art still practiced in Japan and Okinawa. *See also* kama; kobu-jutsu.

SIKIM GALA Long, single-edged Sumatran blade.

SODEGARAMI Japanese spear with barbed hooks attached to one end for entangling the sleeves of a swordsman or spearman. Sodegarami is also the name of an intertwining sleeve choke used by some jujutsu schools.

SPEAR Traditionally referred to in China as the "king of weapons," it is as old as China herself. Spear techniques consist of a series of outward and inward parries and thrusts. *See also* weapons, Chinese.

SPEAR, DOUBLE HEADED *See* weapons, Chinese.

SPEAR, EYEBROW Specialized spear, used in some styles of Chinese kung-fu, with a sickle-shaped head.

SPEAR, SNAKE Specialized spear, tipped with a curved blade, used in some styles of Chinese kung-fu.

SPEAR, WITH HOOK Specialized weapon used in some forms of Chinese kung-fu.

STAFF Wooden rod almost 6 feet in length; used by the Okinawans as a weapon and later turned into a systematized fighting art. It is practiced in Japan today as **bojutsu.**

STAFF, CHINESE Developed by a priest who thought other weapons too warlike, the staff can be used as a single weapon (i.e., one end of a spear) or a double-headed weapon (both ends). Double-headed technique is principally for show.

STAFF, THORN Swordlike weapon covered with metal thorns, used in some forms of kung-fu.

STAFF WITH CHAIN Specialized weapon, used in some styles of Chinese kung-fu, consisting of a staff with chains at either end.

STEEL WHIP Used in some styles of Chinese kung-fu, it is composed of 3, 5, 7, or 9 linked steel sections with a dart at one end. The whip is easily concealed.

SUMPING; SUMPIT; SUMPITAN Blowpipe used by the Batak tribe of Sumatra. Constructed of special lengths of bamboo with joints five feet apart, it is used more for hunting than warfare. In Toradja, it is called sumpi; in the Buru Islands, sumping.

SU-YARI Japanese spear classified under the straight-spearhead category of the **yari**; frequently used from horseback.

SWORD, CHINESE The double-edged sword is known as the mother of weapons. Said to have been invented by Ch'ih-Yu, who forged his sword from gold found in nearby mountains, the weapon often has supernatural qualities attributed to it—to chase away evil demons, etc. Use of the sword was traditionally reserved to the upper classes. It was the emblem of the sage, varying from 1½ feet to 3 feet in length.

The best swordsmiths in China were Che-Yen, 2600 B.C., and Kan-Chiang, who lived in the state of Wu in the 3rd century B.C. They are said to have forged magic swords of steel, regarded as supernatural because they were so much sharper than earlier bronze weapons. A rock still exists in Kashing that was, as the story goes, split in two by Kan-Chian, who was testing the blade of a sword. Also famous for his sword is Lu-Tung-Pin, one of the **Eight Immortals,** who was given a magic sword by his teacher, Chung-Li-Chuan. Lu could hold the scabbard of his weapon while the blade jumped from its sheath to obey his commands.

Many swords have poetic names pertaining to a specific hilt design or method of use. The god of the sword, Fei-Yang, ruled both male and female swords. According to legend, the sword retained the ability to change into a dragon. The sword's handle was called T'an, its end called Feng, the scabbard called Fu-Yao or Ru-Yao-Mu. Materials from which swords were made were gold, jade, silver, iron, oyster shells, brass or, in the case of the chien talisman, coins.

The sword traditionally includes some 16 methods of use. **Wu shu** styles adapt the sword to their own principles of boxing, making the weapon an extension of their particular techniques.

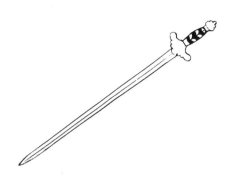

Sword techniques fall into four general categories: single-sword, double-sword, long-tasseled sword, and short-tasseled sword. *See also* weapons, Chinese. (Michael P. Staples)

SWORD, DOUBLE-HOOKING Also known as tiger's head hooks; the written characters for the double-hooking sword actually refer to the large crescent-shaped handguard, but because the sound of the word for this handguard is similar to the sound of the Chinese word for double-hooking sword (hu-tou-gou)—also a synonym for tiger's head—the weapon is loosely referred to as the tiger's head hook. A weapon primarily found in the northern styles of Chinese kung-fu.

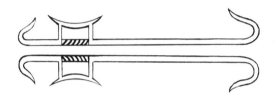

SWORD, ELEPHANT TRUNK Sword used in some forms of Chinese kung-fu, which is curled over at its tip.

SWORD, GHOST HAT Knife (tao) similar to the nine-ring sword, but with a thick dorsal edge. Used in some styles of Chinese kung-fu.

SWORD, HORSE LEG CHOPPING Also known as double-hand big sword, a large sabrelike weapon used to chop off the legs of a horse—a method of bringing down a mounted opponent.

SWORD, JAPANESE There is perhaps no country in the world where the sword has, in its time, received so much attention as it has in Japan. All warriors, regardless of rank, were trained in swordsmanship.

It was well established in ancient times that gifts to the Gods must possess three very important elements: purity, rarity and value. The Japanese sword was believed to have all three of these characteristics, and it was not uncommon to dedicate one as a votive offering in religious ceremonies. Ancient records reveal that the first such offering was made to the deities around 3 B.C. Later, when the sword symbolized the samurai code, it acquired even richer spiritual qualities.

The legendary swordsmith Amakuni is supposed to have forged the first curved sword blade about A.D. 700. The straight-edged blades had been chiefly used for stabbing, but calvary was becoming increasingly more important in battle at this time, and the horsemen wanted a weapon designed for slashing. Yatsutsuna is the first authentic swordsmith whose name has been documented. He worked around A.D. 900 and the blades he created were so superb that the Japanese sword has changed little since his time.

Other forms of straight double-edged swords, heavily ornamented, appeared almost simultaneously with the spread of **Buddhism** to Japan during the Nara period. They also closely resemble the pre-Buddhist symbolic swords used in religious ceremonies in central Asia, particularly in the northern Indian territories of Nepal and Tibet, as well as in China.

As in almost every aspect of Japanese culture, China also influenced the Japanese sword. The shape, as well as the names of Japanese swords, are related, directly or indirectly, to Chinese sources. The ancient Chinese ideograms for **chien** (double-edged sword) and **tao** (single-edged sword or knife) are considered semantic and phonic roots of both the Japanese renditions "ken" and "to," which were to evolve into "**katana**"—the Japanese reading of tao that supplanted the more ancient rendition "to." Placed together, in reverse order, the Japanese "to-ken" was also a general term for all types of swords.

An exclusive privilege granted the **bushi** the right to carry two swords: the long sword, or katana, and the short sword, or **wakizashi.** The katana measured 2 feet or more in length, the short sword 16 to 20 inches. The katana was used for fighting, the wakizashi, an auxiliary weapon, for beheading a defeated enemy or committing ritual suicide. Both were worn on the left side and secured at the waist to facilitate quick and easy draw. Later, both blades were thrust through the waist sash, edge upward, the katana on the left side and the wakizashi across the stomach.

The **bushi** usually carried two swords: the long sword, or katana, and the short sword, called **wakizashi.** These were the two blades **(daisho)** that he alone was privileged by law to wear and employ, and they symbolized his position in Japanese society. The long sword, ranging from the long **nodachi** or dai-katana to the standard-sized katana, measured 2 feet or more in length. This was the weapon used for close-quarter combat. The short sword or wakizashi measured from 16 inches to 20 inches and could be used in combat as an auxiliary weapon or for other purposes, such as beheading an enemy or performing ritual suicide. Both were worn on the left side and secured at the waist to facilitate quick and easy draw. In later periods, both blades were thrust through the waist sash, edge upward, the katana on the left side and the wakizashi.

The wakizashi seldom left the bushi's belt for any reason; the katana could be removed when custom required: when at home, while visiting another bushi's home, or within the confines of the ruling lord's palace.

Considering the exaggerated veneration in which the native katana has been held from the earliest times, it is not surprising that the occupation of swordsmith should have been regarded in feudal days as an honorable profession. Casting of the sword blade was even considered a religious cremony, complete with traditional costume. The forging of blades was surrounded with ritual secrecy, and technical details were passed down from father to son. In fact, the personality of the individual smith was thought to be reflected or animistically embodied in the blades he forged.

It is not surprising, then, considering the importance of this weapon in the eyes of the samurai, that the capacity to read a blade, seeing and knowing the marks that indicate its maker and age, became a highly sophisticated art, requiring special facilities and knowledge, and long experience.

It was believed a great swordsmith imbued his swords with qualities beyond the physical. A fine sword was thought to have a character of its own, and a samurai who owned such a sword had to live up to it. More than an instrument of killing, it was an instrument to elad the samurai who owned it to spiritual enlightenment. A Japanese proverb states, "katana wa no tamashii": The sword is the soul of the samurai.

Regarded as a treasured family heirloom, the sword was carefully preserved and passed on to each succeeding generation. Even in modern times, these swords have been carried into battle by officers and men of the Japanese armed services. Outlooks differ regarding the swords that were confiscated during the tenure of the Allied Occupation in Japan after World War II. Many American soldiers thought they were collecting mere war souvenirs and seldom understood or suspected the value and deep meaning of the swords. Eventually, most of the confiscated swords that had been collected en masse and which were known to have special artistic or historical value were returned to their original owners to be preserved as objects d'art.

The Japanese sword lost much of its prestige as a sidearm after World War II, but it still remains the most finely wrought steel weapon in the world. The legendary Damascus and Toledo blades or the Excalibur of English literature diminish when compared with the craftsmanship and quality invested in the ritual manufacture of the Japanese sword. In 1965 a museum of Japanese swords was founded in Tokyo. There is also a Japanese society for preserving swords of beauty. *Further reading: Art of the Japanese Sword,* Robinson, 1961; *Black Belt Magazine,* July 1975, 1982 Yearbook; *Classical Bujutsu,* Donn F. Draeger, 1973; *Japanese Sword Blades,* A Dobree, 1967; *Japanese Swordsmiths,* W.M. Hawley; *A Primer of Japanese Sword Blades,* B.W. Robinson, 1955; *The Samurai Sword, A Handbook,* John Yumoto, 1958; *Secrets of the Samurai,* Oscar Ratti and Adele Westbrook, 1973.

SWORD, SEAGULL (yan-ling-tao) Specialized sword used in some forms of kung-fu.

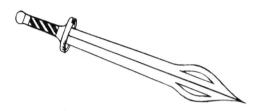

TACHI 1. A long sword worn by **samurai.** 2. Second series of judo defense techniques in **kime-no-kata.**

TADJI Balinese short metal knife and the forerunner of the bamboo knife called the pringapus. It is used in stiletto fashion.

TA-GU Large, black, leather-toppeed drum played in conjunction with the **lion dance** and kung-fu forms. The drum holds a position of prestige within the kung-fu musical group, which consists of the drum, cymbals, and the brass gong.

TALWAR Short sword, similar to the Arab scimitar. It has a double knife sheath and was used for close-range combat in India and Pakistan. Today it is no longer used combatively, but is practiced in formal exercises.

TANBONG Korean name for the short staff.

TANTO Fighting knife used by the Japanese warrior. About 9" long, the tanto had no hand guard (tsuba). It was employed in close combat and to commit **hara-kiri** (belly-cutting). It is the weapon around which **tantojutsu** was created.

TAPAK KUDAK Long, single-edged Sumatran blade.

TARE Apron worn by keno and naginata-do practitioners, which helps to protect the hips and abdomen.

TA-SHAO-DZ Weapon similar to the Okinawan **nunchaku** but longer; precursor to the san-chieh-pang, or **three-section staff.**

TEKAGI Hook worn on the hands like a metal band; useful for gripping when climbing walls, trees, and so on. Also used as a weapon to rake an enemy's face. The tekagi was employed by the **ninja** of feudal Japan.

TEKKEN Walking cane used as a weapon by exponents of **perisai diri,** a style of Indonesian **pentjak-silat.**

TEKO 1. Japanese knuckleduster (like brass knuckles) used in **kobu-jutsu.** 2. Form of aikido founded by Tetsumi Hoshi.

TETSU BISHI Four-pointed caltrop, used by the **ninja** of feudal Japan. These vicious weapons were especially effective to slow a pursuing enemy. Since no matter which way they landed, one spine always pointed upward, the pursuers, who generally wore straw sandals, were constantly harried. These caltrops also were sprinkled around an encampment or castle wall to prevent an enemy's stealthy approach.

TETSUBO One of the early weapons transferred from the Asian continent to Japan. The tetsubo, or iron staff, came in various shapes and lengths, with circular, hexagonal, or octagonal cross-sections. Its systematic use was known as tetsubo-jutsu. The tetsubo could be employed mounted or afoot, but only the strongest warriors were able to become proficient in its use. *Further reading: Classical Bujutsu,* Donn F. Draeger, 1973.

THININ Long, single-edged Sumatran blade.

THREE-SECTIONAL STAFF Chinese weapon constructed from three pieces of wood connected by metal rings at their ends. Lengths of sections are roughly equal, each about the length of an arm, and the diameter is a little over an inch. It can be used as a long-range weapon when held at one end and swung freely, or a short-range weapon when two of the sections are held and used to strike or parry. *Further reading: Technique and Form of the Three-Sectional Staff,* Kam Yuen, 1979.

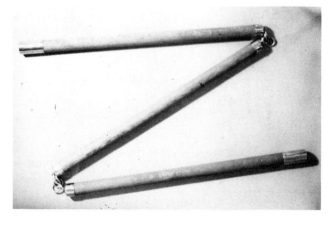

TI In the Korean martial arts, the belt signifying rank. *See also* obi.

TJABANG Iron truncheon with two tines, similar to the Okinawan **sai** and possibly its precursor. The weapon, used in Indonesia and Malaysia, originated within the Hindu culture, which entered Indonesia around A.D. 300 to 400. The weapon is used with **pentjak-silat** techniques, sometimes against the sword, staff, or stick or to attack by striking, thrusting, or hooking. Usually tjabang is used in pairs, one in each hand. *Further reading: Weapons and Fighting Arts of the Indonesian Archipelago,* Donn F. Draeger, 1972.

TJALUK Semi-sickle shaped knife with a reverse cutting edge. Of Muslim origin, it is found in **setia hati terate,** a form of East Javanese **pentjak-silat.**

TO Karate training device used in Okinawa prior to the introduction of the punching bag; a sturdy circular post sunk in the ground, covered thickly in bamboo with a leather sheet.

TOBOK Practice uniform worn in tae kwon do; the counterpart of the **gi.**

TODO Chief bladed weapon of the natives of Buru Island.

TONFA Old Okinawan farming implement, the tonfa was used as a handle to turn the manually operated millstone when grinding rice. It is a tapered hardwood billet between 15 inches and 20 inches in length, with a short projecting side-handle set about 6 inches down from the thicker end.

When employed as a weapon, with the short or long end lying along the underside of the forearm, the tonfa permits effective punching or striking; the opposite end is employed to jab. The tonfa, commonly in pairs, is also used to block and parry.

The tonfa, also called tuifa or ton-kwa, is one of the five systematized weapons of the early **te** developers in Okinawa, along with the **bo, kama, nunchaku,** and **sai.** Today tonfa experts are rare in Okinawa, and there is a chance of this art becoming extinct. *Further reading: Black Belt Magazine,* July 1969; *The Technique of the Tonfa,* I.S. MacLaren and G. D. Thompson, 1977. *See also* kobu-jutsu.

TONGKAT Name commonly applied to sticks and clubs of various lengths used locally in some systems of Indonesian **pentjak-silat.** Also known as gada or gala.

TONGKAT PEMUKUL Hardwood stick employed in the tjatji style of **pentjak-silat.** It is used against a shield called agang or nggiling if made of buffalo hide, prisai kayu if made of wood. Two participants alternately attack and defend, one using the stick, the other the shield. The tongkat pemukul operator attempts to beat the shield bearer into submission; the shield bearer attempts to disarm the stick wielder.

TONKI Small metal throwing weapons such as dirks, daggers, and darts, often used by the **ninja** of feudal Japan to delay and harry pursuers.

TORINOKO Firecrackers shaped like eggs; used by the **ninja** to surprise the enemy with a loud noise.

TOYA Wooden staff, usually of rattan, some 5 feet to 6 feet in length and from 1½ inches to 2 inches in diameter; a standard weapon of all classical Indonesian **pentjak-silat** styles.

TOYAK Halberdlike weapon whose special usage involves slashing attacks. It is found in bhakti negara, a form of **pentjak-silat.**

TSUKA Handle of a samurai sword. *See also* sword, Japanese.

TSUKA ITO Decorative binding around the handle of a samurai sword; it serves as a grip. *See also* sword, Japanese.

TSUKUBO Japanese spear with a crossed-shaped head containing sharp teeth; classified within the broad category of **yari** (spear).

TSUKUSHI-BOKO Large type of bronze spearhead used by Japanese feudal warriors. This weapon is classified under the straight spearhead category of the Japanese **yari.**

T'UAN-TANG Specialized kung-fu weapon consisting of two moon-shaped cudgels.

TUI-FA Another name for the **tonfa.**

UKIDARU Water crossing devices of waterproof reed pots for the feet, used with fanlike bamboo oars; used by the **ninja.**

ULU Handle of the Indonesian **kris.** Today, it is a status symbol for, as the social status of a Javanese alters, so does his ulu design. Older kris handles featured human figures and animals; later designs were geometrical shapes.

WAIST SWORD Sword (actually a knife, tao) made of spring steel, flexible enough to be worn around the waist like a belt. *See also* weapons, Chinese.

WAKIZASHI Short sword worn by the Japanese warrior. It was about 16" to 20" long and was worn together with the longer **katana.** As well as its use in combat, the wakizashi was also used to commit **hara-kiri.** Worn on the left side of the body along with the katana, it was seldom taken off by the warrior. Together, these two swords were known as the daisho. *See also* sword, Japanese.

WATERPIPE Long smoking pipe used as a weapon in the **Choy-Li-Fut** style of kung-fu.

YARI The Japanese spear, known generally as the yari, was a weapon second in traditional significance only to the bow and arrow. The very first samples of this weapon were apparently drawn from Chinese models with large blades and long thick poles. At least one source mentions the hoko (halberd) as being the oldest recorded form of spear to evolve from continental models. **Bujutsu** schools specializing in the use of this weapon abounded in Japan. Certain manuscripts, in fact, explicitly refer to ancient masters who traveled to China and studied the various methods of handling the hoko.

The Japanese spear, in both design and structure, was similar to all Japanese blades in the high quality of its tempering, its lightness, and ease of handling. The spear blades were carefully protected by sheaths. The shafts (nakae) of these spears came in many weights and lengths. Made of excellent wood, they were carefully seasoned and treated, usually reinforced by and decorated with strips or rings of metal.

Spearheads were cast of the same high quality steel used for making swords and came in a variety of lengths and sizes. They can be divided into three main groups: straight, curved, and a miscellaneous category of shapes. The straight spearhead was the most common; it was double-edged and its decoration and length, design of point, type of casting, and quality of steel gave rise to several specific types.

At a point of transition between the straight spearhead and the curved spearhead is the blade of the nakamaki, which closely resembles the popular **naginata.** (The naginata is often erroneously referred to in English as a halberd.) The third group of spearheads includes a confusing variety of shapes, generally extremely specialized.

The Japanese **bushi** of the higher rank carried his spear when on horseback, fastened to his leg or stirrup in an iron or copper spear nest called yari-ate. Foot soldiers carried their spears, and often those of their officers, on their shoulders.

There were two major arts of using the spear: **yari-jutsu,** the art of the straight spear, and **naginata-jutsu,** the art of the curved spear. Each art was subdivided into numerous styles concerned with the use of various long and short spears and javelins. All of these styles shared a substantial number of basic techniques, such as strikes, thrusts, and parries—found also in swordsmanship. Many ready positions and angular attack methods, however, varied not only from school to school, but from teacher to teacher.

What has been passed down from feudal yari-jutsu is found in the exceptionally modified techniques of **jojutsu,** the art of the staff, practiced in several modern schools of **jodo,** the way of the staff, and also as a supplementary exercise in certain aikido schools. Naginata-jutsu added to the techniques of the yari those circular cuts particularly applicable and practical to the curved shape of the naginata.

Spearmanship continued to be taught professionally and practiced in the bujutsu schools for some time; very few remain active today.

Students now wear protective equipment, as in kendo, with safety elements based on the ancient suit of Japanese armor. This equipment includes a head protector (men), a breastplate (do), arm guards (kote), a padded apron (aidate), and shin guards (sune-ate). While formerly razor sharp, the contemporary naginata is made of oak 6½ feet long with a bamboo blade 21 inches long, encased at the tip by a leather cap. This, and longer naginatas, are used against a partner/opponent in training and competition or alone in a **kata.** It can even be employed against life-sized dummies. Today these same schools, frequented for the most part by women, use the naginata not so much as a method of combat, but rather as a discipline of mental and spiritual integration (naginata-do), linking these schools to the mysticism and esotericism that are intrinsic to the traditional culture of Japan. *Further reading: Secrets of the Samurai,* Oscar Ratti and Adele Westbrook, 1973.

YUEH-YA-T'SAN Half-moon shaped long weapon used in some forms of Chinese kung-fu.

YUGAKE Shooting glove worn by practitioners of **kyudo,** usually made of buckskin and worn on the right hand. The thumb is made of deerhorn with soft leather on the inside. An attached strap wrapped around the wrist holds the glove in place.

YUMI The Japanese bow. It varies in length from five feet to eight feet and, unlike western bows, as the grip (nigiri) about two thirds of the way down. This bow is used today in Kyudo and was used by the Japanese feudal warriors either from horse back or while in a kneeling position. The yumi is the longest bow in the world.

ZORI Known as judo slippers, they are made of rubber or straw and held to the feet by a cord between the first and second toes.

ZUBON Judo trousers made of cotton, usually extending only to the mid-calf.

Jigoro Kano (*seated left*) with a number of his early students at the time he founded the Kodokan, ca. 1885.

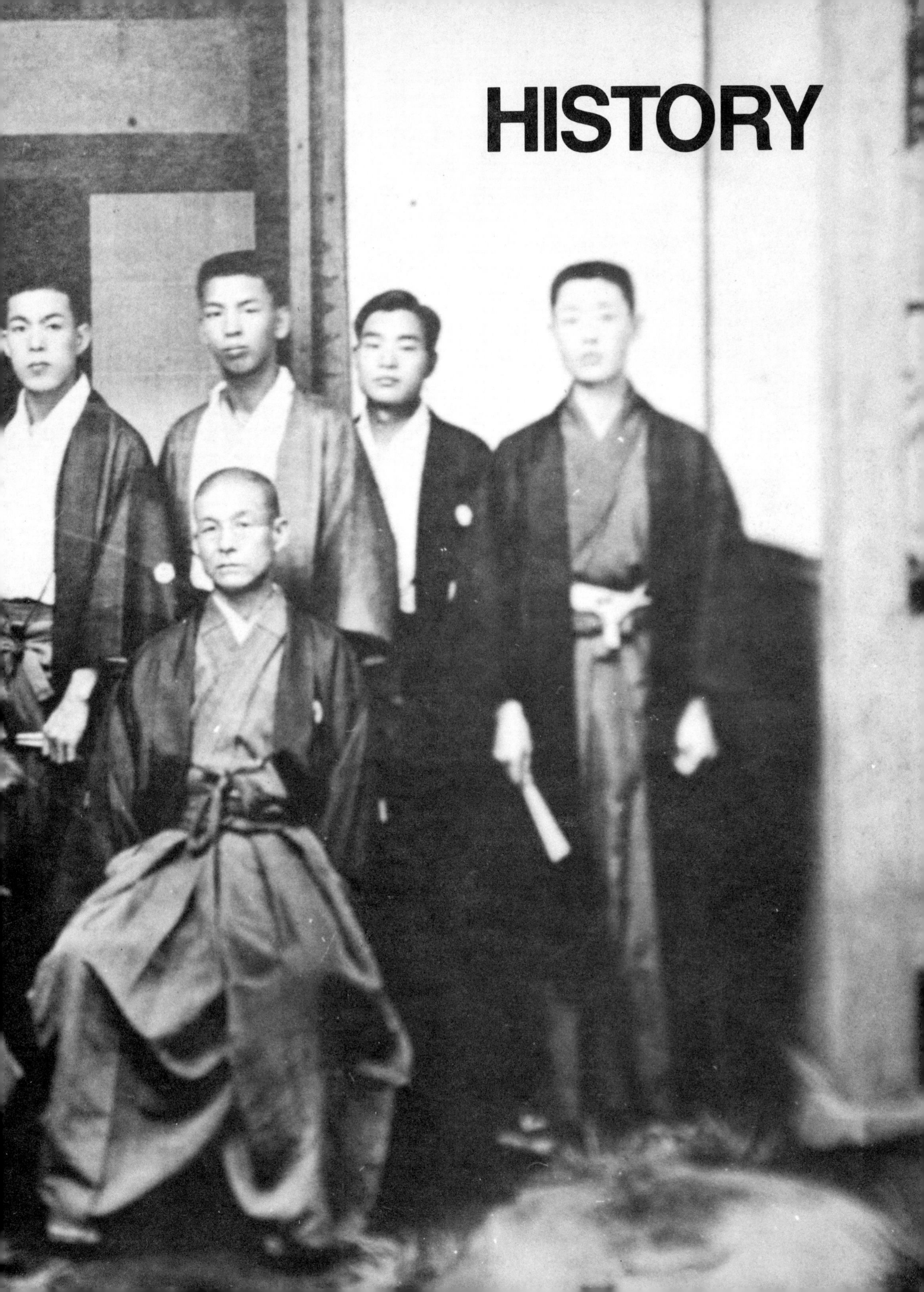

HISTORY

THE ROOTS OF MARTIAL ARTS

The histories of the various martial arts are inextricably entwined with the histories of the countries in which they originated and practiced today. For example, the Shao-lin Temple, built by emperor Hsiao-when, was a focal point in the evolution of martial arts in China.

SHAO-LIN TEMPLE Chinese Buddhist monastery of the "Chan" school located in the Sung-Shan mountains of Tung-Feng county, Honan province. The temple is named after its surrounding "small forest" of trees. Built by Emperor Hsiao-Wen in the late 5th century A.D., its construction honored the Indian monk Bodhiruchi. **Robert W. Smith**, in his book *Asian Fighting Arts*, quotes a source describing the temple: "(It) had twelve upper and lower courts and was ringed almost completely by mountains, festooned with bamboo, casia, and cedar trees, and laced with waterfalls."

In the Sui dynasty, early Ch'ing, and once again in the early 20th century, the temple was seriously damaged. Surviving structures renovated by the People's Republic of China include the front gate, guest hall, Bodhidharma pavillion, and the white-robe hall, with two frescoes depicting monks exercising and sparring—the northern wall depicts sparring exercises of the liu-he ch'uan (six-methods boxing) and on the southern wall are a number of monks engaged in weapons training. Also surviving are the thousand-Buddha hall and the forest of stone tablets.

This temple became a focal point for martial arts training at one period in China, but not on the grand scale Western journalists and filmmakers depicted. More often than not, kung-fu styles have little if any religious background. Religion's role in the martial arts was quite small in the overall scheme of things. The Shao-lin order was the exception, not the rule.

Evidence identifying the creators of the Shao-lin style itself is inconclusive. Three theories have emerged. The first attributes the creation to the Indian priest Ta-mo **(Bodhidharma)**, who followed his predecessor, Bodhiruchi, to the middle-kingdom several decades after the construction of the temple. This story, though unsubstantiated, is the most popular. It paints a colorful picture of Ta-mo as a staunch ascetic, confining himself to a cave for nine years, where he sat facing the wall in meditation (the cave can still be viewed). The second theory attributes its creation to Hwei-Kuang and Sung-Chou, monks preceding Ta-mo's arrival in China by several years. Yet another theory, the most probable, attributes the style's origin not to any single individual, but to the collective efforts of the priests over the years.

The People's Republic of China has been investigating the temple's origins and development. One source, the *History of the Shao-lin Monastery*, appeared as a four-volume work. Yang-Ya-Shan referred to this work in a translated article, stating that the Shao-lin school was actually the oldest school of ch'uan-shu (kung-fu), and that it originated in the Southern and Northern dynasties (420-589), flourished in the Sui (581-618) and T'ang (618-907) dynasties, after which it branched into a number of subsystems.

"Shao-lin," he explains, "first served military purposes in the early T'ang dynasty when the first emperor, T'ai-chung, appealed to the Shao-lin monastery for reinforcements against Wang'She-Ch'ung, who sought to establish a separate regime in Lo-Yang. Joining the punitive expedition, the Shao-lin monk-soldiers captured Wang alive. Thirteen of them were cited for meritorious service, including monk T'an-chung, on whom was conferred the title of Major General. In addition, the monastery was granted 400 mu of land and allowed to set up barracks to give the monks military training. At its peak, Shao-lin boasted a force of 5,000 monk-soldiers. It was known far and wide as the 'number-one monastery under heaven.'

"Apart from the barehand Shao-lin ch'uan exercises, monks also learned **chi-kung** (breathing exercises), horsemanship, and combat with weapons. They became, in effect, a special detachment of the Imperial army.

"In the middle of the Ming dynasty, China's coastal areas were subjected to frequent Japanese harassment. In 522, monk Yueh-kung led a crack force of 40 Shao-lin monks to the Sun-Chiang river area to resist the invaders. Using iron rods as weapons, they won many battles before patriotically laying down their lives. As willing tools of the court, the Shao-lin monk-soldiers were not exempt from being used as elements of repression: in 1341, they attacked the Red Turbans—an army of peasant insurgents (and a secret society which opposed the Ch'ing government). The battle is portrayed in a mural in the white-robe hall.

"Though monks are supposed to lead a secluded life, those in Shao-lin, being versed in the martial arts, were often involved in political strife. Using them for its own end, the ruling class kept a wary eye on them. During the Ch'ing dynasty, the monks were once forbidden to practice martial arts. In 1723, when the monastery was to be rebuilt, the blueprint had to be submitted to examination by the Emperor. He decreed the monks be placed under strict supervision by a court-appointed abbot."

Yang-Ya-Shan is here referring to the monastery located in Honan province. Several authorities have claimed the existence of a second Shao-lin Temple located in Fukien, south of the original. Indeed, there is a Buddhist temple at this location, though not of the grand scale of its alleged sister temple in the north. Several other authorities dispute the existence of an authentic Shao-lin order in Fukien. Be that as it may, many stories concerning this Fukien-based temple are told.

One tradition concerns a Shao-lin monk's aid to the emperor of the K'ang-hsi reign, i.e., the Emperor Sheng-Tsu, who turned back one of the western border raids, and the subsequent praise lavished upon the temple. Another is the story of the later destruction of this temple. Supposedly, five monks, who later became known as the **"Five Ancestors,"** escaped this destruction.

Concerning the temple's destruction, however, there are two accounts. The first is an oral tradition passed down through the **"Triad"** society, a secret society reputedly formed by the members of the temple who escaped its destruction, the second is handed down through the martial arts community in general. According to Leung-Ting in his book *Wing Tsun*, the story perpetuated by the Triads lists the "Five Ancestors" as Choy-Tak-Chung, Fong-Tai-Hung, Wu-Tak-Tei, Ma-Chiu-Hing, and Li-Sik-Hoi (note: their Mandarin romanizations would be T'sai-Teh-Chung, Mang-Ta-Hung, Ma-Ch'ao-Hsing, Hu-Teh-Ti, and Li-Shih-Kai). "But according to the story retold by people of the martial arts circle," he explains, "they were Ng-Mui, the Buddhist nun; Chi-Shin, the Zen master; Pat-Mei, the Taoist master; Fung-To-Tak, the Taoist master; and Miu-Hin, an unshaved Siu-Lam follower. These two sources greatly differ in details regarding names, identities, and sex."

In addition, the first story is supported by authors such as Shuai-Hsueh-Fu in his *Chung-kuo pang-hui shih (History of Chinese Secret Society)*, and Hsu-K'o in his *Ch'ing-pei lei-ch'go (Incidents of the Ch'ing period)*. Both of these works, however, seem primarily interested in recounting the history of secret societies. Still other sources support the probably less accurate second story. One noted authority believes this second story to have stemmed directly from the fictional novel *Ch'ien-lung huang yu Chiang-nan (The Ch'ien-lung Emperor Visits the South)*, in which the monk Chih-Shan (or Chi-Shen) is portrayed as the abbot of the Shao-lin Monastery who is killed by the monk Pak-Mei—before the destruction of the temple ever took place.

The facts in kung-fu, for several reasons, have often been systematically distorted. In the much quoted *Chung-kuo pang-hui shih*, Shuai-Hsueh-Fu states that in the eleventh year of the K'ang-hsi emperor (1662-1723), Tibetans invaded China's borders and were successful enough to prompt the government to place posters before the public requesting volunteers to bolster its army. At the lesser Shao-lin Temple in Fukien, one of the priests, Cheng Chun-Ta, rallied behind him some 128 other monks to aid the effort. His plan, however, was not to help strengthen the current Ch'ing government. He and his fellow monks were "Ming' loyalists who, in fact, opposed the government. Cheng had in mind a plan to infiltrate the government by gaining political favor through this particular war effort to attack the government from within. The 128 Shao-lin priests managed to push back the Tibetan invasion without help from the Ch'ing troops. For this, official titles were conferred upon them. Only Cheng, however, accepted a title, in accordance with his plan. The other monks allowed the emperor to help renovate the Fukien temple.

An antagonist appears in this story, a monk named Ma Fu-I, who seduced Cheng's wife and sister. He was, consequently, ostracized from the temple. Ma later came to be known as A-tsat (literally, seven) in the secret society vernacular, because he had ranked seventh in the temple in physical prowess. The Triads considered the number seven taboo due to its relationship to Ma. In its place, the word "kat" (good luck) was substituted while the name A-tsat was given to a white rooster, sacrificed during an inductee's blood oath to the secret organization (signifying "should I prove a traitor, may I perish as did A-tsat"). Ma sought revenge after being ousted from the temple. He went to the governor of the province, who was himself jealous of the attention Shao-lin was getting. He convinced the governor and his two officers, Ch'en-Wen-Yao and Chang-Chin-Ch'in, to appeal directly to the emperor for support in destroying the temple.

Stories differ here once again. Shuai-Hsueh-Fu states that K'ang-hsi was the emperor who received the appeal from the governor and his officers, and who eventually was responsible for destroying the Shao-lin Temple. Other sources place K'ang-hsi's successor, Yung-Cheng, in this position, while still another source insists the whole event was drummed up as a ploy to foment anti-government feeling. Accounts seem to agree that the official formation of the Hung-Men-Hui or Triad society (which could only have been formed after the fall of the temple, if we are to believe the story), was in 1674. If this is the case, it is reasonable to assume the burning of Shao-lin could not have occurred in the reign of Yung-Cheng, who did not come to the throne until after K'ang-hsi died in 1723.

Some 3,000 Ch'ing troops were sent to destroy the Shao-lin Temple. Led by Ma, they successfully entered the temple grounds and killed all but eighteen of the monks. Thirteen more died soon after escaping. The remaining five became known as the "Five Ancestors" and formed the Triad secret society.

The distinctive features of the Shao-lin style of kung-fu, according to Yang-Ya-Shan, include a blending of both the hard and soft elements of movement, following six core principles including skill, tact, boldness, quickness, ferocity, and practicality. "In a word," Yang explained, "emphasis is on striking effectively. Naturally, this involves long years of painstaking practice, as is evidenced by the three rows of 20 hollows—each about 50 centimeters in diameter—on the brick floor of the thousand-Buddha hall of the Shao-lin Monastery. It is said that these were shaped through generations by the monk's stamping their feet during training." (MICHAEL P. STAPLES)

In Japan, many martial arts developed as outgrowths of the samurai tradition.

Samurai were feudal Japanese warriors who adhered to a code of ethics called **bushido.** The symbol of the samurai was the sword, but his skills included the use of the spear, the bow, horsemanship, hand-to-hand combat, and other military arts. During the dictatorship of the Tokugawa clan (1600-1867), the samurai were placed in the service of the shogun (military dictators), or stationed in the provinces under the command of various daimyo (territorial lords). From the humblest foot soldier to the mounted warriors of the upper ranks, they all belonged to the same warrior class (buke), and were known as bushi. After 1869, they were qualified as former military subjects, but the world at large continued to refer to them by that Chinese name usually translated as "vassal" (samurahi; samurai). In earlier times, the title of samurai had been assigned to leaders of armed clans in the north, and in a somewhat modified form, to warriors of aristrocratic clans attached to the imperial court during the Muromachi period. The term was later expanded to include all warriors permitted to wear the long and short swords (daisho) in the service of a lord, and was more specifically translated as "one who serves."

Their principal function was that of carrying out any and all orders issued by those superiors to whom they had pledged loyalty. This obligatory tie between master and samurai constituted a serious threat to national unity after the restoration in 1868, when it was necessary to transfer the bond of loyalty from the clan leader to the head of the Japanese national family, the emperor.

So strong was this bond that when a master died many of his retainers took their own lives, to follow him in death as they had in life. The practice became so widespread that it had to be forbidden by law and enforced by inflicting severe penalties upon the samurai's surviving family. In battle, the retainer fought under his direct superior's command. If his superior chose to elude capture by committing **hara-kiri,** the samurai acted as his second, shortening the agony of a self-inflicted mortal wound by severing his master's head with a single sword stroke. Usually, the samurai would flee with the severed head to prevent enemies from making a war trophy of it. Often, however, a retainer would facilitate his superior's escape by donning his lord's armor and fleeing, drawing off the enemy.

Japanese warriors have always displayed a preference for death over capture. His contempt for death was fostered from infancy. A military household's child was exposed to cold in winter and expected to endure without complaint the heat of summer. He was often sent on purposely difficult errands. His fear of death and of the supernatural was substantially reduced, it is told, by sending him to such locations as cemeteries and places of execution at night, even while quite young. Physical pain was endured without betraying the slightest emotion.

The eagerness with which the thoroughly conditioned warrior of the early feudal period engaged in combat is proverbial. In times of peace, particularly during the Tokugawa period, that eagerness turned to murderous disdain for all other social classes, as well as an hysterical tendency to overreact to even imagined indications of lack of respect. A retainer's servility toward his masters within the clan was in startling contrast to his arrogance outside this hierarchy.

The status of a warrior within the clan of his birth or the clan to which he had been assigned was generally immutable. Only exceptional circumstances might release him from the bond of loyalty and turn him into a masterless warrior (**ronin**). But according to ancient ordinances, any warrior who severed ties with his clan without permission could not be accepted into the ranks of any other clan. Thus, no matter where he turned, the samurai met obstacles, insuring that he would cling to the position assinged him within the social order.

While the upper ranks of the military class were exposed to education, their retainers seem to have concentrated almost exclusively upon perfecting military skills. The lower samurai was trained at home or in clan centers for military instruction. His education in the literary sense was neglected; there was a continuing condition of illiteracy among the lower samurai. The Tokugawa encouraged the establishment of schools of lower samurai, but with a limited curriculum. During this period, the noticeably inferior quality of the education of low ranking retainers only widened with respect to the attainments of ranking leaders. *Further reading: Samurai, The Invincible Warriors,* Cap. F. Brinkley, 1975; *Bushido, The Soul of Japan,* Inazo Nitobe, 1969; *The Martial Arts,* Michael Random, 1978; *Secrets of the Samurai,* Oscar Ratti and Adele Westbrook, 1973; *The Samurai—A Military History,* Stephen Turnbull, 1977; *Samurai,* H. Paul Varley and Nobuku Morris, 1970.

A MARTIAL ARTS CHRONOLOGY

Date	Asia	U.S.	Europe	Other
720	Japan: the *Nihon Shoki*, first chronicle concerning Japanese wrestling, compiled.			
800–	Japan: Kenjutsu schools proliferate.			
900–1200				Indonesia: silat transmitted from China.
c. 900				Philippines: Kali founded.
900	Japan: ch'in-na transmitted from China; becomes the basis for aiki-jutsu.			
1147–1170	Korea: subak reaches its peak in popularity.			
1185–1336	Japan: aiki-jutsu founded by Shinra Saburo Yoshimitsu.			
1192	Japan: Bushido emerges.			
1271–1368	China: kung-fu used by anti-government resistance groups.			
13th century	Japan: Zen transmitted by Chinese Buddhist monks.			
c. 1300	China: Chang San-Feng introduces soft elements to Shao-lin kung-fu and reputedly founds t'ai-chi-ch'uan.			
1350	Japan: Nen-ryu, earliest recorded school of swordsmanship, founded. Japan: sword techniques systematized for the first time by Choisai and Jion.			
1368–1644	China: ch'in-na recorded as a self-defense system.			
1372	Okinawa: Ryukyu Islands become a Chinese satellite and from this year foward kung-fu mingles with Okinawan tode.			
1392	Kume-mura, Okinawa: 36 Chinese families immigrate and teach Chinese boxing to Okinawans.			
c. 1400	Japan: Ninjutsu emerges, flourishing for four centruies.			
15th century	Japan: atemi becomes popular.			Malaya: Huan Tuah purportedly founds bersilat.
1477	Okinawa: Sho Shin bans all weapons, which stimulates underground training in unarmed combat.			
16th century	China: win chun founded by Yim Wing Chun, a Buddhist nun.			Brazil: African slaves develop capoeira.
c.1550	Japan: jojutsu founded by Muso Gunnosuke.			
1570	Japan: sumo emerges.			

Date	Asia	U.S.	Europe	Other
1600–1650	Japan: jujutsu emerges.			
17th century	China: Wong Long founds praying mantis kung-fu.			
1609	Okinawa: Japan's Satsuma clan bans the use of weapons. Okinawan improve weaponless fighting methods and create kobu-jutsu from farm tools.			
1629	Okinawa: tode and ch'uan fa synthesized into a new art called te.			
1644–48	Japan: China's Ch'en Yuan-pin reputedly introduces a form of jujutsu and the sai.			
1645	Japan: Miyamoto Musashi, one of Japan's greatest samurai, dies.			
1662–1723	China: the Triads, a secret society which perpetuates kung-fu, emerges.			
1692	Okinawa: Ko Sokun, a ship-wrecked Chinese boxer, introduces kumiai-jutsu.			
c.1700	Okinawa: modern characteristics of Okinawan karate begin to emerge.			
1703–09	Thailand: muay Thai, in its early form, reaches its peak in popularity.			
1710	Japan: *Hagakure Bushido*, classic work on samurai ethics and conduct, written by Tsunetomo Yamamoto.			
1730	China: Ching Edict drives kung-fu underground where it propagates secretly from generation to generation.			
1750	Japan: budo disciplines emerge from bujutsu. Edo, Japan: shinai invented by Chuzo Nakanishi.			
1761	Okinawa: China's Kusanku begins traching a form of kung-fu.			
1764			Phillipines: Spanish authories ban kali.	
c.1800			Paris, France: savate emerges.	
1815	Okinawa: "Tode" Sakugawa dies; he is believed to have been the first to combine ch'uan fa and tode to form Okinawa-te.			
c.1830	Okinawa: Sokon Matsumura is first master to systemize karate and to call his style by a name (Shuri-te) other than his own.			

Date	Asia	U.S.	Europe	Other
1830			Genoa, Italy: first savate club founded.	
c.1831	China: Chan Heung founds Choy-Li-Fut.			
1832			Paris: Charles Lecour synthesizes English boxing and savate to create French boxing.	
1848		California: kung-fu secretly transmitted to the U.S. by Chinese laborers imported for the Gold Rush.		
1868	Japan: samurai prohibited from wearing swords; end of samurai era.			
1882	Tokyo: Jigoro Kano founds judo and establishes his first school, the Kodokan, at the Eisho-Ji Temple.			
1884	Japan: judo contest conducted for the first time, within jujutsu dojo.			
c. 1887–89	Okinawa: the word "karate" (T'ang hand) replaces te.			
1887	Tokyo: technical formulation of Kodokan judo completed.			
1889	Tokyo: Prof. Ladd of Yale University becomes first American to study judo at the Kodokan.			
c. 1890	Okinawa: Kanryo Higashionna introduces Naha-te and a breathing exercise called Sanchin.			
1890	Japan: sumo, judo and kendo introduced into Japanese scholastic system for boys; naginata-do for girls.			
1895	Kyoto, Japan: Dai Nippon Butokukai founded.			
1896	Tokyo: Jigoro Kano devises the go-kyo-no-waza, a systemized approach for teaching judo.			
1899	Kyoto: Butokuden established.			
1900	China: during the Boxer Rebellion, the martial arts are virtually eliminated from the mainland.			
1901–02	Okinawa: karate becomes part of the physical education curriculum at two schools. Okinawa: Yasutsune Itosu becomes the first karate master to instruct publicly.			
1902		Yoshiaki Yamashita introduces judo in the U.S.		

Date	Asia	U.S.	Europe	Other
c.1903		Washington, D.C.: Yoshiaki Yamashita demonstrates judo at the White House.		
1903		Shumeshiro Tomita, an influential judo pioneer, arrives in the U.S.		
1904				
1905	Okinawa: Chomo Hanashiro breaks tradition and writes book using new characters for karate which translate "empty hand(s)." Tokyo: majority of jujutsu schools merge with the Kodokan. Okinawa: karate taught as a sport for the first time by Yasutsune Itosu in middle schools.		France: jujutsu introduced by writer Re-Nie Guy de Montgaillard. Paris: judo taught to police.	
1906	Okinawa: first public karate exhibition conducted by Gichin Funakoshi.		England: Gunji Koizumi, father of European judo, arrives.	
1906			Berlin, Germany: Erich Rahn becomes European to teach judo extensively, at his jujutsu school. Berlin; Lichterfelde: Agitaro Ono begins teaching jujutsu at military academies.	
1907	Japan: University Kendo Fed. founded.	Seattle, Washington: America's first judo dojo founded by Takugoro Ito.		
1909		Kali introduced in the U.S. by Jack Santos.		Honolulu: Hawaii's first judo called the Shunyokan, founded by Shigen Teshima and Naomatsu Kaneshiga.
1911	Tokyo: Judo Teacher's Training Department established at the Kodokan. Jigoro Kano founds Japan Athletic Assn. Kendo and judo named compulsory subjects in Japanese middle schools.			
1912	China: kung-fu restored and instituted in all areas of Chinese learning. Japan: Nihon Kendo Kata, foundation of all modern kendo practice, created.		England: E. J. Harrison, first Westerner to write prolifically about the martial arts, authors his classic book *The Fighting Spirit of Japan*.	
1914			Brussels, Belgium: judo introduced by Ito and Maurice Minne.	
1915	Okinawa: Yasutsune Itosu and Kanryo Higashionna, the two most important 19th century Okinawan karate masters, die.			
1917	Kyoto: Gichin Funakoshi performs the first karate demonstration in Japan, at the Butokuden.			

Date	Asia	U.S.	Europe	Other
1918			London, England: Europe's first judo club, the Budokwai, founded by Gunji Koizumi.	
1920			Rome. Italy: judo introduced by Carolo Oletti.	Hawaii: Okinawan Kentsu Yabu performs karate demonstrations here and in Los Angeles, marking the first international exposure of this art.
1921	Okinawa: Okinawan Assn. for the Spirit of the Martial Arts founded by Gichin Funakoshi and others.	Oriental martial arts exposed to Western audiences for the first time in the film *Outside Woman*.		
1922	Tokyo: Gichin Funakoshi demonstrates karate at the 1st National Athletic Exhibition; he then remains in Japan to teach his art. Tokyo: Funakoshi establishes the first karate club in Japan at the Meisei Juku; he also writes the first book on karate, *Ryukyu Kempo: Karate*. Japan: Kodokan Dan Grade Holder's Assn. founded. Seoul: Korea Archery Assn. founded.		Germany: Erich Rahn defeats Hans Reuter of Munich to become first professional German Jujutsu champion.	Honolulu: Chinese Physical Culture Assn. becomes the first club in the West to teach a form of Kung-fu.
1924	Japan: first Japanese collegiate karate club founded at Keio University by Gichin Funakoshi.		Germany: Reichsverbandes for Jiu-Jitsu founded.	
1925			Germany: first illustrated martial arts magazine, *Jiu Jitsu*, published.	
1926	Tokyo: women's judo section established at the Kodokan.			
c. 1927–28	Okinawa: Chojun Miyagi founds goju-ryu karate; he's the first to give his style a name apart from the city in which it is practiced.			
1927				Honolulu: Kentsu Yabu gives the first public karate demonstration in Hawaii, and introduces Shuri-te.
1928	Japan: All Japan Kendo Fed. founded. Japan: Chojun Miyagi teaches karate at universities. Japan: Nippon kempo founded by Muneomi Sawayama. Okinawa: Choshin Chibana becomes the first to name his karate style shorin-ryu. China: kung-fu is renamed wu shu and becomes formalized.			Australia: judo introduced by Dr. A. J. Ross; Australian Council of Judo founded.
1929			London: Europe's first international judo meet conducted between the Budokwai and the Jiu-Jitsu Club of Frankfurt on Main.	India: judo is introduced.

Date	Asia	U.S.	Europe	Other
1930	Tokyo: Gogen Yamaguchi establishes Japanese goju-ryu headquarters. Osaka, Japan: Kenwas Mabuni founds Shito-ryu karate. 1st All Japan Judo Championships conducted. Okinawan Prefecture Athletic Assn. founded; Chojun Miyagi named karate division chairman.	Los Angeles: Wong Wen Sun Chinese Benevolent Assn., the earliest known group of kung-fu students in the U.S., founded by Ark-Yuey Wong.	Hungary: judo introduced by Tibor Vincze. Europe's first intercollegiate judo match conducted between Oxford and Cambridge universities.	
1931	Tokyo: police adopt modern hojo-jutsu. Tokyo: Kanken Toyama founds shudokan karate.		Hungary: First judo club founded.	Africa: judo introduced.
1932	Japan: Judo Medical Research Society founded.		Europe's first judo organization, the European Judo Fed., founded. Frankfurt, Germany: first international judo summer school founded by Alfred Rhode.	Hawaii: first known kendo school outside of Japan founded by Shuji Mikami.
1933	Japan: karate recognized as one of the official martial arts of Japan with the founding of the Dai Nippon Butokukai, Okinawa Branch.		Judo founder Jigoro Kano tours Europe; the term "judo" begins to replace "jiu-jitsu."	Hawaii: Choki Motobu promotes Okinawan karate. Zuiho Mutsu and Kamesuke Higaonna cofound Hawaii Karate Seinin Kai, first known Caucasian group to openly study and promote karate.
1934			Holland: judo introduced by Maurice Van Nieuwenhuizen.	Hawaii: Cojun Miyagi lectures and teaches goju-ryu karate. Brazil: judo master Ryuzo Ogawa immigrates and becomes chief instructor of the Jukendore-nei Assn.
1935	All Japan Goju-kai karate-do Assn. founded by Gogen Yamaguchi. All Japan Kempo Fed. founded by Muneomi Sawayama. Japan: Jigoro Kano receives Asashi Prize for outstanding contributions to art, science and sport.		Paris: France's first judo club, the Club Franco-Japonais, founded by Mikonosuke Kawaishi.	
1936	Naha, Okinawa: at a conference of distinguished karate masters it is decided to officially adopt the term "karate" for the national martial art of Okinawa. Zoshigaya, Japan: first free-standing karate dojo, "The Shotokan," established by Gichin Funakoshi's students. Japan: Funakoshi adopts Chomo Hanashiro's translation of karate, "empty hand," and popularizes it. Japan: Chojun Miyagi receives a medal for "Excellence in the Martial Arts" from the Ministry of Education.	Los Angeles: Toaro Mori immigrates and teaches kendo.	France: Jiu-Jitsu Club de France, still operating today, founded by M. Feldenkrais, with Mikonosuke Kawaishi its chief instructor.	
1937	Korea: han pol, a branch of hapkido, founded by Chung Yun Kim.			

Date	Asia	U.S.	Europe	Other
1938	Japan: judo founder Jigoro Kano dies; Nango Jiro named his successor.			Soviet Union: sambo recognized as an official sport.
1939	Japan: Hironori Ohtsuka founds wado-ryu karate and the All Japan Karate-do Fed., Wado-kai.			Leningrad: first sambo championships conducted.
1940	Okinawa: karate becomes the official martial art of the Okinawan Police Academy.	San Jose, California: Emilio Bruno and Henry Stone conduct the first intercollegiate judo competition.	France: Jiu-Jitsu Fed. of France founded by scientist Paul Maury-Bonet.	
1941	Japan: kendo named a compulsory subject in Japanese primary schools.			
1942	Tokyo: Morihei Ueshiba founds aikido.			Honolulu: James Mitose founds the Official Self-Defense Club.
1943	Korea: Japanese karate and Chinese kung fu introduced.		Paris: 1st French Judo Championships conducted at Walgram Hall.	
1944				Hawaii: Prof. William K. S. Chow teaches kenpo for the first time.
1945–50	Japan: The Allied occupation bans the practice and teaching of all martial arts and ways.		Germany: judo practice prohibited by the Allied occupation.	
c. 1945	Korea: Hwang Kee founds tang soo do.		European Judo Union founded.	
1945	Okinawa: Eizo Shimabuku(ro) designated the grandmaster of shobayashi shorin-ryu. Korea: Won Kook Lee founds chung do kwan. Seoul: Korean Judo Assn. founded. China Communism overtakes the mainland; kung-fu masters retreat to Hong and Taiwan and disseminate their arts.			
1946	Korea: Byung In Yoon founds chang moo kwan. Shikoku, Japan: Doshin So systematizes Shorin-ji-kempo. All Japan Karate-do Assn. founded by Kanken Toyama. Tokyo: the Kuramae Kokugi-kan constructed for sumo competition.	Phoenix, Arizona: Robert Trias introduces karate in America, and becomes the first Caucasian to teach it.		Rangoon, Burma: U Ba Than founds International Bando Assn.
1947	Okinawa: Shoshin Nagamine founds matsubayashi shorin-ryu.		French Fed. of Judo and Associated Sports founded by Paul Maury-Bonet.	Djakarta: Ikatan Pentjak Silat Indonesia founded.

Date	Asia	U.S.	Europe	Other
1947				Indo nesia: Silat Organasi, which united pentjak-silat systems, founded. Hawaii: kajukenbo co-founded by five instructors.
1948	Seoul: Korean Kum Do Assn. founded 1st All Japan Judo Chamionships conducted. All Japan Kyudo Fed. founded.	Phoenix: Robert Trias founds America's first karate organization, the United States Karate Assn. Berkeley, California: Henry Stone devises weight divisions for judo competition.		New Zealand: judo introduced by George and Keith Grundy.
1949	Japan: the Shotokai founded. Tokyo: Japan Karate Assn. founded. All Japan Judo Fed. founded.	Judo recognized as an official sport by the Amateur Athletic Union.	European Judo Union and British Judo Assn. founded.	
1950	Japan: Chojiro Tani Founds shukokai karate. Japan: Butokukai reestablished with the official removal of the SCAP ban. Tokyo: Gogen Yamaguchi founds the Karate-Do Goju-Kai.		Venice, Italy: International Judo Fed. founded.	Hawaii: Adriano Emperado founds the first and subsequently largest chain of karate schools.
1951–52	Tokyo: American Air Force personnel receive martial arts training at the Kodokan.			
1951	Tokyo: Japan Karate Assn. adopts kumite (free-sparring) practice. Japan: Mas Oyama founds kyokushinkai karate.		Stockholm, Sweden: judo introduced by Bruno Adler. Paris: 1st European Judo Championships conducted.	Pamekasan: Hasan Hubudin founds pamur, a form of pentjak-silat.
1951			Yugoslavia: first judo dojo founded in Angreb.	
1952	Tokyo: Tatsu Tanaka founds goshin-jutsu, a form of ju-jutsu. Japan: Eizo Onishi founds koei-kan karate. Japan: Chibana Sanshu founds toshu kakuto. Seoul: Dr. Je-Hwang Lee founds the Korean Yudo College.	Mas Oyama tours 32 states and introduces karate on a widespread basis to the American public for the first time Amateur Judo Assn., the first national governing body for Judo, founded.	International Judo Fed. founded; Risei Kano named president. Hungary: National Judo Fed. founded. Ireland: judo introduced at a small club in Phoenix Park.	
1953	All Japan Naginata-do Fed. founded. Korea: 1st National Kum Do Championships conducted. Naha: Shoshin Nagamine founds first matsubayashi-ryu karate dojo.	Berkeley: first collegiate judo tournament (Pacific Coast Intercollegiate Judo Championships, conducted San Jose: 1st National AAU Judo Championships conducted. Emilio Bruno organizes a tour of SAC bases by ten Japanese martial arts instructors; this marked the second broad-based introduction of the martial arts in the U.S.	European Judo Union reformed; Dr. Aldo Torti of Italy elected president. Hamburg: German Judo Bundes founded.	Hawaii: aikido introduced by Koichi Tohei.

Date	Asia	U.S.	Europe	Other
c. 1954			Paris: Europe's first karate club, the Academie Francaise d' Arts Martiaux, founded by Henry D. Plee. Plee also founds the French Fed. for Free Boxing and Karate.	
1954	Hong Kong: Bruce Lee begins studying wing chun. Kanagawa-ken: Eizo Onishi founds first koei-kan karate dojo.	New York: Edward Kaloudis introduces karate on the East Coast. Covington, Kentucky: Chito-ryu karate introduced in the U.S. by William Dometrich.		Hawaii: Mas Oyama visits and with Bobby Lowe founds the first overseas branch of kyokushinkai karate
1954	Okinawa: Tatsuo Shimabuku founds isshinryu karate.	Provo, Utah: kenpo karate introduced in the U.S. by Ed Parker		
1955	Tokyo: Japan Karate Assn. founds its first dojo, and begins sending Shotokan instructors abroad to establish schools. Korea: seven styles merge to form tae kwon do, a name coined by Choi Hong Hi. Tokyo: Masatoshi Nakayama appointed chief instructor of the JKA. Japan: Mas Oyama founds his first dojo, the Kyokushin-kaikan.	Phoenix: Robert Trias conducts the first karate tournament in America (Arizona Karate Championships). Judo Black Belt Fed. founded, replacing the Amateur Judo Assn. Los Angeles: Tsutomu Ohshima introduces Shotokan karate in the U.S.		
1956	All Japan Collegiate Karate Fed. founded by Yoshiaki Ajari. Tokyo: 1st World Judo Championships conducted. All Okinawa Karate-do Assn. founded. All Japan Juken-do Fed. founded.	Los Angeles: Ohishima founds Shotokan Karate of America. San Marcos, Texas: Jhoon Rhee introduces tae kwon do in America. Pasadena, California: Ed Parker establishes his first West Coast kenpo school.		New Zealand Judo Fed. Founded.
1957	Tokyo: Gichin Funakoshi dies. Tokyo: 1st All Japan Karate Championships conducted.	Tennessee: wado-ryu instructor Cecil Patterson becomes one of the South's first karate teachers. Los Angeles: Gordon Doversola introduces Okinawa-te in America St. Louis, Missouri: Louis Kowlowski founds the first karate dojo in the Midwest. Jacksonville, N.C.: Don Nagle introduces issihinryu karate in America.	Paris: Tetsuji Murakami founds a Shotokan dojo Germany: Juergen Seydel introduces karate. Sweden: Gerhard Gosen introduces aikido, karate and t'ai-chi-ch'uan.	Honolulu: t'ai-chi-ch'uan instructor Tinn Chan Lee becomes first to teach Kung-fu to the general public.
1958	Tokyo: Kodokan moves to a new seven-story building.	Los Angeles: Nisei Week Karate Championships, today the longest running annual karate event in the U.S., conducted by Tsutomu Ohshima. Boston, Massachusetts: George Mattson introduces Uechi-rye karate in America, and becomes the first karate teacher in the New England states.		Canada: Mas Tsuroka, father of Canadian karate, begins teaching in Toronto, Ontario.

Date	Asia	U.S.	Europe	Other
1959	Korea: Gen. Choi Hong Hi writes and publishes his first Korean-language textbook. Okinawa: Eizo Shimabuku(ro) named chairman of the All Japan Karate-do League, Okinawa branch. Japan: Isao Inokuma, 21, becomes youngest ever to win All Japan Judo Championship title	Hawaii becomes the 50th state of the U.S. Jersey City, N.J.: Don Nagle establishes isshinryu's U.S. headquarters. New York: Hiroshi Orito introduces renbukai karate in America. Union City, N.J.: Peter Urban introduces Japanese goju-ryu karate in America. Seattle, Washington: Bruce Lee immigrates to America to attend school. New York: Alan Lee introduces Shaolin kung-fu on the East Coast.		
1960	Seoul: Joo Bang Lee and Joo Sang Lee found first public hwarang-do school	U.S. Judo Fed. replaces the Judo Black Belt Fed. Seattle: Bruce Lee establishes his first gym, in Chinatown. Hayward, California: wado-ryu karate-do taught publicly for the first time by Yoshiaki Ajari.	Yugoslavia: Trin Tam Tam introduces karate in Zagreb.	
1960		Washington, D.C.: Dr. Maung Gyi introduces bando in America. Watertown, Massachusetts: Anthony Mirakian introduces Okinawan gojuryu in America New York: S. Henry Cho founds first tae kwon do dojang on the East Coast Pacific Northwest: Steve Armstrong of Tacoma, Washington and Bruce Terrill of Portland, Oregon, two influential karate poineers, begin teaching. *American Judoman Magazine* founded by Philip Porter. Elvis Presley becomes the first known celebrity to earn legitimate karate black belt; he's promoted to 1st dan in Chito-ryu by Hank Slemansky.		Austrualia: William Cheung indruduces wing chun kung-fu, in Canberra.
1961	Korea Taekwondo Assn. founded.	Los Angeles Mito and Jim Uyehara found *Black Belt Magazine*. San Francisco: Shorinji-ryu karate introduced in America by Richard Kim. Philadelphia, Pennsylvania: Teruyuki Okazaki becomes the first official JKA Shotokan instructor in America. Los Angeles: Hidetaka Nishiyama founds the All America Karate Fed. Florida: John Pachivas becomes first known karate teacher on the Southeast Coast.	German Karate Fed. founded by Juergen Seydel. Paris: Holland's Anton Geesink becomes first non-japanese world judo champion. 1st French Karate Championships conducted.	

Date	Asia	U.S.	Europe	Other
1962	Korea: tae kwon do becomes official event at the 43rd National Games.	New York: North American Karate Championships, America's first open tournament, conducted. Philadelphia: Teruyuki Okazaki founds the East Coast Karate Assn. New York: Al Weiss and John Kuhl produce the first exclusive karate magazine, *Combat Karate*. Washington, D.C.: tae kwon do pioneer Jhoon Rhee moves from Texas and begins building a martial arts empire. Texas: Allen Steen establishes his first karate school and begins building an empire in the Southwest. National Collegiate Judo Assn. founded; 1st National Collegiate Judo Championships conducted at U.S. Air Force Academy.	Turku, Finland: first judo school, Turan Judoseura, founded. Mas Oyama tours Europe, establishing kyokushinkai karate schools.	Malaya: Silat Seni Gayong Assn., the regulating body for bersilat, founded Toronto: 1st Canadian Karate Championships conducted by Mas Tsuroka
1963		Chicago: first national karate tournament in the U.S. (1st World Karate Championships) conducted. Torrance, California: Chuck Norris opens the first of an eventual chain of tang soo do schools.	Irish Judo Assn. founded. Sweden: kendo introduced by Robert von Sandor and Ronald Knutsen. Weight categories instituted for the first time at the European Judo Championships. First international karate meet conducted between European countries; national teams of France, Belgium and England participate.	Canadian Jiujitsu Assn. founded.
1964	Japan: renbukai karate founded. Tokyo: judo enters the Olympic Games for the first time; Jim Bregman becomes first American to win bronze medal. Tokyo: the Budokai erected for the Olympics. Tokyo: Fed. of All Japan Karate-do Organizations founded. All Japan Karate-do Organization founded.	Los Angeles: Sea Oh Choi introduces hapkido in America. San Francisco: Gosei Yamaguchi begins teaching gojo-ryu karate. Pasadena: America's first accredited collegiate karate course founded by Tsutomu Ohshima at the Institute of Technology. Washington, D.C.: 1st U.S. National Karate Championships conducted by Jhoon Rhee. Long Beach, California: 1st International Karate Championships conducted by Ed Parker; Bruce Lee is the featured kung-fu performer. Texas: J. Pat Burleson creates ''belt goal'' karate courses, which becomes a standard in American karate schools.	Sweden: first karate dojo founded by Attila Mezsaros. Yugoslavia: Tetsuji Murakami pioneers karate on a widespread basis.	Montreal: tae kwon do introduced to Canada by Chong Lee.

Date	Asia	U.S.	Europe	Other
1965	Japanese government awards "Order of the Purple Ribbon" to judo's Kazuzo Kudo for service to the martial arts.	Santa Ana, California: Fumio Demura introduces Shito-ryu karate in America. Portland, Oregon: Pauline Short founds the first karate school exclusively for women. Washington, D.C.: karate matches televised nationally for the first time at Jhoon Rhee's 2nd U.S. Nationals.	Charles Palmer becomes first non-Japanese president of the International Judo Fed. France: Count Pierre Baruzy founds first national savate organization.	
1966–67		Hollywood: Bruce Lee plays Kato in TV's "The Green Hornet"; the show results in the first boom in martial arts interest by the American public.		
1966	Seoul: International Taekwon-do Fed. founded. Korea: In Hyuk Su founds the Kuk Sool Won.	New York: Peter Urban founds USA goju.	European Karate Union founded; Paris lawyer Jacques Delcourt elected president. Paris: 1st European Karate Championships conducted. Germany: kendo introduced by Gerd Wischnewski. Karate Union of Great Britain founded. German Karate Union founded by Mike Anderson and Juergen Seydel. Netherlands Tae Kwon Do Assn. founded by Park Jong Soo. Dominique Valera, Europe's greatest karate champion, wins his first major title at the European Championships.	Karate Assn. of Malaya founded by Chew Choo Soot.
1967	Japan: naginata-do becomes a physical education course in senior high schools and colleges. Okinawa: Shuguro Nakazato inherits from Choshin Chibana leadership of the Okinawan Shorin-ryu Shunakai Assn. Japan: Hironori Ohtsuka awarded the Fifth Order of Merit of the Sacred Treasure from the emperor.	Los Angeles: Bruce Lee founds jeet kune do, and establishes the Jun Fan Gung-Fu School in Chinatown. Ninja presented to mainstream movie audiences for the first time in *You Only Live Twice*. Los Angeles: Joe Lewis conceives the first set of Top 10 ratings for American karate fighters in *Black Belt Magazine*. New York: Aaron Banks promotes first open karate team competition. Hirokazu Yamamori introduces Shorin-ji kempo in America. Kentucky: U.S. Chito-kai founded by William Dometrich.	Rome: Anton Geesink retires after winning the openweight title of the European Judo Championships. Finland: first karate dojo, the Wadokan ryu, founded. England: 1st Karate Union of Great Britain Championships conducted.	

Date	Asia	U.S.	Europe	Other
1968		New York: Joe Lewis, Chuck Norris, Mike Stone and Skipper Mullins win professional world karate titles. New York: Al Weiss founds *Official Karate Magazine.* Los Angeles: Mito Uyehara founds the Black Belt Hall of Fame. Kansas City, Kansas: Jim Harrison conducts the first professional karate tournament in America. Ohio: Dr. Maung Gyi founds American Bando Assn. at Ohio University. Oakland, California: Al Dacascos founds won hop kuen do.	All European Karate Fed. founded. Germany: aikido introduced.	Sambo recognized as a third form of wrestling by the International Amateur Wrestling Fed.
1969	Tokyo: aikido founder Morihei Ueshiba dies; Kishomaru Ueshiba inherits aikido leadership Japan: Seiken Shukumine founds taido.	Los Angeles: Mito Uyehara founds *Karate Illustrated.* San Jose: Tracy's Karate Studios launches the world's largest franchised school operation, eventually expanding to 70 commercial studios. American Tae Kwon Do Assn. founded by Haeng Ung Lee. U.S. Judo Assn. founded.	Yugoslav Karate Fed. founded. Hamburg: kyudo introduced in Germany. Sweden: European Kendo Fed. founded; Swedish Budo Fed. founded.	Modern Arnis Fed. of the Phillippines founded by Remy Presas in Manila.
1970	Tokyo: World Union of Karate-do Organizations (WUKO) founded; 1st WUKO World Championships conducted. Tokyo: International Kendo Fed. founded.	Long Beach: Professional full-contact karate founded by Joe Lewis; Chuck Norris engages in his final noncontact match at the same event.		
1970		Albuquerque, N.M.: Pat Johnson creates the penalty point system for excessive contact, ending the "Blood-n-Guts" era of American karate tournaments. Atlanta, Georgia: Battle of Atlanta founded by Joe Corley and Chris McLoughlin.		
1971	Japan: International Kendo Fed. founded. Japan: aikido master Koichi Tohei founds the Ki Society. Hong Kong: Bruce Lee in two films, *Fists* of Fury and *The Chinese Connection.*	Dallas: Bill Wallace rises to prominence by winning grand title of Allen Steen's U.S. Karate Championships.		
1972	Hong Kong: Bruce Lee stars in his third film, *Return of the Dragon,* in which Chuck Norris makes his film debut; Lee then shoots incomplete footage for *Game of Death.* Seoul: the Kukkiwon, tae kwon do's mecca, founded Korea: Choi Hong Hi writes *Taekwon-Do,* the most extensive work on a single martial art.	Hollywood: Bong Soo Han's potent hapkido scenes in *Billy Jack* result in the beginning of the second and by far the biggest martial arts boom in America: Hollywood: the first pure martial arts television series,"Kung Fu'," airs; the arts reach an all-time apex in popularity.	All Europe Karate Fed. reorganized as the European Amateur Karate Fed. Munich, Germany: judo reinstated in the Olympic Games. Paris: 2nd WUKO World Karate Championships conducted.	Brazil: capoeira recognized as an official sport. Soviet Union: 1st European Sambo Championships conducted.

Date	Asia	U.S.	Europe	Other
	Japan: first American sumo champion, Jesse Kuhaulua, wins the Emperor's Cup, sumo's highest honor. Japan: Hironori Ohtsuka receives the Hanshi Award from Japan's emperor.	Washington, D.C.: Jhoon Rhee invents Safe-T-Equipment, which revolutionizes sport karate. Karate recognized as an official sport by the Amateur Athletic Union. *Karate-Do Dyohan: The Master Text,* Gichin Funakoshi's posthumous book translated by Tsutomu Ohshima, Published in English.		
1972		American Tae Kwon Do Coaches Assn. and American Collegiate Tae Kwon Do Assn. founded.		
1973	Korea: National High School and Middle School Taekwondo Fed. and National Collegiate Taekwondo Fed. founded. Seoul: 1st World Tae Kwon Do Championships conducted; World Tae Kwon Do Fed. founded Hong Kong: Bruce Lee dies on July 20. Korea: tae kwon do included in the physical education curriculum of primary and middle schools.	"Bruce Lee Era" begins with the release and widespread success of his Hong Kong films. *Enter the Dragon*, released in August, becomes the classic martial arts film, eventually grossing over $100 million worldwide and making Bruce Lee a superstar. Hollywood: Curtis Wong founds *Inside Kung Fu* magazine. Los Angeles: Mito Uyehara founds *Fighting Stars Magazine.* Oklahoma City: Mike Anderson founds *Professional Karate Magazine,* which revives the sport. St. Louis: Mike Anderson founds semi-contact competition at the Top Ten Nationals. Long Beach: biggest grand championships purse in karate tournament history, $2,500, won by John Natividad at the International Karate Championships. Los Angeles: Howard Jackson becomes first semi-contact karate fighter to be ranked number-one in the U.S.	British Kendo Renmei founded. Liverpool, England: Terry O'Neill founds *Fighting Arts Magazine.*	Judo Karate Fed. of Pakistan founded. Tehran, Iran: 1st World Sambo Championships conducted.
1974	Seoul: 1st Asian Tae Kwon Do Championships conducted.	Chinese wu shu troupe tours the U.S. for the first time, performing extraordinary demonstations. New York: International Amateur Karate Fed. founded; Hidetaka Nishiyama named executive directive. Tae kwon do recognized as an official sport by the Amateur Athletic Union; Ken Min named chairman of the AAU Tae Kwon Do Committee.	Sweden: tae kwon do introduced by Lee Joo Suh. Germany: George Bruckner selects and coaches the first full-contact European team to meet Americans in Los Angeles.	Toronto: Gen. Choi Hong Hi moves International Taekwon-Do Fed. headquarters from Korea.

Date	Asia	U.S.	Europe	Other
		New York: Aaron Banks' Oriental World of Self-Defense generates a $100,000 live gate, largest in American martial arts history.		
		Los Angeles: Professional Karate Assn. founded by Don and Judo Quine and Mike Anderson.		
		Los Angeles: Mike Anderson promotes the World Professional Karate Championships at which full-contact karate is revived.		
		Long Beach: International Karate Championships draws a reported 6,000 competitors, biggest draw in karate history.		
		Honolulu: Tommy Lee creates the World Series of Martial Arts Championships; Benny Urquidez makes his professional full-contact debut.		
		Knoxville, Tennessee: International Isshinryu Karate Assn. founded by Harold Long.		
1975		New Haven, Connecticut: 1st National AAU Tae Kwon Do Championships conducted at Yale University.	Yugoslavia full-contact karate established by Zarko Modric and others.	
		Washington, D.C.: Jeff Smith and Karriem Allah fight 11-round full-contact bout as preliminary to the Muhammad Ali/Joe Frazier boxing match in Manila: audience was estimated at 50 million.	West Berlin: American Gordon Franks wins inaugural PKA world super lightweight (full-contact) title, beating Mexican Ramiro Guzman.	
		Phoenix: 1st National AAU Senior Men's Sambo Championships conducted.		
		Los Angeles: 1st IAKE World Karate Championships conducted by Hidetake Nishiyama.		
		The end of the martial arts movie boom creates a serious slump in the martial arts industry.		
c. 1976–77			West Berlin: World All-Style Karate Organization founded by George Bruckner and Mike Anderson.	
1976	Seoul: *World Taekwondo*, official organ of the World Taekwon-do Fed., published.	Los Angeles: World Karate Assn. founded by Howard Hanson and Arnold Urquidez.	Paris: World Champion All Star Team Tournament conducted.	Bolivariana Karate Fed. founded.
		Bill Wallace becomes first karate athlete to represent his sport in the nationally televised ''Superstars'' competition.	Barcelona, Spain: European Taekwon-do Union founded.	
		Los Angeles: John Corcoran creates *Karate Illustrated's* Regional Ratings, which become a standard in the sport.		

Date	Asia	U.S.	Europe	Other
1976		California: Calif. State Athletic Commission begins regulating full-contact karate, the first time a government body oversees any form of American martial arts. Thibodaux, Louisiana: 1st National Collegiate Tae Kwon Do Championships conducted.		
1977	Tokyo: Benny Uriquidez title defense yields $500,000, largest live gate in professional karate history; he becomes first American to beat Japanese kick-boxers at their own sport. Tokyo: Dutchman Otti Roetoff becomes first non-Oriental to win the WUKO World Karate Championships. Asia/Oceania Amateur Karate Fed. founded.	Los Angeles: John Corcoran becomes world's foremost martial arts magazine writer, syndicating articles to seven countries in six languages. Las Vegas, Nevada: first live television broadcast of martial arts in any form for Bill Wallace's full-contact title fight against Blinky Rodriquez. Philadelphia: International Shotokan Karate Fed. founded; Teruyuki Okazaki elected chairman and chief instructor. Berkeley: North American Tae Kwon Do Union founded. Chicago: Pan-American Tae Kwon Do Union founded.		Central America/Caribbean Karate Conducted fed. founded.
1978	Hong Kong: Jackie Chan becomes Asia's biggest martial arts film star.	Hollywood: Chuck Norris becomes a box-office star with the release of *Good Guys Wear Black*; Norris restores the martial arts film genre in Hollywoood. Los Angeles: All America Karate Fed. reorganized as the American Amateur Karate Fed.	European Jujutsu Fed. founded. Swedish Wu Shu Fed. founded.	Mexico City: 1st Pan-American Tae Kwon Do Championships conducted.
1979		*The Silent Flute,* a film originally written by and for Bruce Lee, released as *Circle of Iron,* starring David Carradine. Los Angeles: editor Renardo Barden improves *Karate Illustrated's* Regional and National Ratings; they become the most widely accepted ratings for point tournaments. New York:*Official Karate's* Legion of Honor founded by Al Weiss. Hollywood: joe Lewis makes his starring debut in *Jaguar Lives.* Las Vegas: Graciela Casillas becomes first female full-contact world champion. Semi-contact competition in the U.S. rejuvenated through the rivalry of two great point fighters, Atlanta's Keith Vitali and Dallas' Ray McCallum.	West Berlin: 1st WAKO Full-Contact World Championships conducted by George Bruckner.	Soviet Union joins the European Karate Union.

Date	Asia	U.S.	Europe	Other
		Bruce Lee's final film, *Game of Death*, featuri four Lee doubles, released in U.S. theaters.		
		A martial arts resurgence begins.		
		Los Angeles: ESPN, a 24-hour all-sports cable network, signs pact with the PKA to broadcast full-contact karate matches. By March 1980, the bouts air weekly.		
1980	Tokyo: a conference between the rival WUKO and IAKF results in their unification of amateur karate in Japan.	Hollywood: Jackie Chan, Asia's martial arts box-office star, makes his American film debut in *The Big Brawl*.	Paris: European Kung-Fu Union founded.	
	International Olympic Committee recognizes tae kwon do, making the sport eligible for entry into the Olympic Games.	Los Angeles: *Kick Illustrated* and *Martial Arts Movies* founded by Curtis Wong; John Corcoran is founding editor.	Madrid, Spain: Tokey Hill becomes first American to win the WUKO World Karate Championships.	
		Los Angeles: Paul Maslak and John Corcoran create the STAR System independent full-contact ratings.		
		Shogun, a five-part TV mini-series focusing on the Japanese samurai, earns the second highest ratings in television history.		
		Mainland Chinese wu shu troupe tours six cities, presenting spectacular exhibitions of rare martial arts.		
1981		Hollywood: Benny Urquidez makes his film debut in *Force: Five*.		South American Karate Confed. founded.

Two early students of judo practicing sasae-tsurikome-ashi.

ASIA

JAPAN

Japan, though not the birthplace of karate, had since ancient times a tradition of exotic military arts. In Japan's mythological era, before A.D. 500, legend relates that the demi-gods Takeminakatano Kami and Takemikazuchino Kami engaged in some sort of hand-to-hand combat that the stories refer to as a "strength contest." During the dawning of the historical age, another famous duel occurred between Nomi-No-Sukune and Taemonokehaya, again without weapons. References to such contests abound in Japan's early literature; although these tales are steeped in the symbolism of Japanese mythology, there is every likelihood that many were based on actual struggles.

Buddhism was first brought to Japan by bands of Chinese and Korean travelers in the 6th century. Japan became enamored with China and Chinese culture as early as A.D. 607, when the first official embassy was sent to China. With the founding of China's T'ang dynasty in 608, there began a period of close contact. As in the history of the martial arts in Okinawa, there exists a theory that shipwrecked Buddhist monks brought a weaponless self-defense system to the Ryukyu Islands. Another theory holds that during the 7th and 14th centuries, when it was common for Japanese youths to study Buddhism in China, they learned kung-fu and brought knowledge of this art back to their homeland—in view of the close ties between kung-fu and Buddhist philosophy, this hypothesis is not improbable.

In the Heian period (A.D. 794-1184), Buddhist monasteries employed armed bands to settle local disputes, and there are sketchy reports of priests of rival temples clashing with such violence in the streets of Heian-kyo (Kyoto) that government intervention was needed to preserve order. During the classical age of Japanese martial arts (1500-1868), the leading **bujutsu** (military arts) men were often Buddhist monks. In fact, **ch'uan fa** (**kempo,** in Japanese) was not known by many people outside of the Buddhist priesthood until the latter part of the 16th century.

In 1952 Hideyoshi Toyotomi, the great warlord general of Japan, implemented his plan for the complete conquest of China. For the next six years Japan waged an overseas war against a combined Korean-Chinese resistance. In 1598, when Hideyoshi died, the remnants of his army returned home without ever setting foot on Chinese soil. In Japanese oral tradition it is recorded that many of Hideyoshi's returning samurai brought with them a working knowledge of ch'uan fa, and from the 16th century onward part of the **samurai's** armament included a punching and nerve-striking technique based on Chinese kung-fu.

The relationship of Chinese military arts to the rise of a Japanese system of weaponless self-defense is vague and not fully documented. One date, however, has been authenticated. During the Tokugawa period, in 1698, a Chinese pottery master, **Ch'en Yuan-pin,** came from China to serve as ceramics instructor for the daimyo of Owari. Ch'en's duties included teaching several ronin (masterless samurai) an art of seizing without weapons. Ch'en's work is often cited as the beginning of a karatelike art in Japan. Some historians, however, feel that an esoteric weaponless technique called **yawara** was the first martial discipline to take root in Japan.

In the early decades of the 20th century, Japanese martial arts groups invited the Okinawans to send a representative who could teach their highly developed technique of empty-hand fighting. **Gichin Funakoshi,** of Naha, was chosen in 1917, and again in 1922, to demonstrate Okinawan karate at the annual Japanese exposition of martial arts. Pressed to stay, Funakoshi taught at judo founder Jigoro Kano's **Kodokan** and at the Butokukai Military Arts College in Kyoto. Keis University in Tokyo became interested in this new art, and soon Funakoshi was teaching on campus. In time, more than 200 campus karate groups came under Funakoshi's direct supervision, or that of his senior disciples. His students included virtually all of the subsequently important karate masters of Japan, and his **Shotokan** style, similar to its antecedent, Shuri-te, is the most widespread style of karate in Japan and throughout the world.

Karate styles formulated in Japan are all derivatives of the earlier Okinawan systems, though influenced by jujutsu, samurai bujutsu, and Chinese and Korean fighting arts. There are presently four or five major styles, numerous minor ones, and countless spin-off styles. In 1949 the **Japan Karate Association** (JKA) was founded;

Master Gichin Funakoshi *(third from left)* seen here in the late 1920s with Gemuja Nakazumi *(left),* Tsoyoshi Chiose *(second from left),* and Kunish Kou *(right).*

A samurai's most important weapon was his sword, or katana, with which he became extremely efficient.

A samurai warrior in full battle dress.

Funakoshi was chief instructor. This organization established strict standards for instructors and members. Moreover, in 1955 it began sending these superbly trained instructors abroad to establish clubs in other countries. The JKA is today headed by chief instructor **Masatoshi Nakayama.**

Some of Funakoshi's senior students declined to join the association and continued teaching as they felt they should, without unifying. Among them were **Isao Obata, Shigeru Egami,** Genshin Hironishi, Kichinosuge Saigo, and Toshio Kamata.

Second in popularity in Japan is Japanese **goju-ryu,** headed by **Gogen "The Cat" Yamaguchi.** Yamaguchi blended the Okinawan goju-ryu of **Chojun Miyagi,** with Chinese techniques, yoga, and Shinto elements. His innovations created a typically Japanese style of karate-do. While Yamaguchi's claims to seniority in the goju system are disputed by Okinawans, he has built a strong, unified, worldwide organization. Among Yamaguchi's senior students are Shojo Ujita, Tomoharu Kizaka, Kenjo Uchiage, and Yamaguchi's three sons, **Gosei, Gosen,** and **Goshi.**

In 1930 **Kenwa Mabuni** came from Okinawa to Osaka and established a style he called **Shito-ryu,** a name derived from the names of two masters with whom he studied. This style, now headed by the master's son, Kenei Mabuni, also enjoys popularity in Japan.

Shito-ryu employs **kobu-jutsu** (art of weapons) and a balance between hard and soft techniques.

In 1935 one of Funakoshi's disciples, **Hironori Ohtsuka,** broke away and founded the **wado-ryu** style, another major form of Japanese karate-do. Ohtsuka had been in line of succession for the shinto-yoshin-ryu jujutsu system, and by blending this with Funakoshi's teachings he created his system. Ohtuka's senior students include Tatsuo Suzuki, the chief instructor in Japan, **Yoshiaki Ajari** in the U.S., and Hidetaka Abe.

Kyokushinkai, the style founded by **Masutatsu Oyama,** has enjoyed growing popularity. Oyama, a student of Korean goju-ryu master So Neichu, of Gogen Yamaguchi, and of Funakoshi, combined what he learned from these masters with his knowledge of Korean fighting arts (he is a Korean by birth), and with certain Chinese techniques and strategies. Oyama, one of the most famous karate masters in the world, popularized karate through spectacular tests of strength such as killing bulls barehanded and winning public challenge matches against pro wrestlers.

Some of the minor styles of Japan include the **shudokan** of Toshio Hanaue and the **koei-kan** of **Eizo Onishi.** Both masters had been students of **Kanken Toyama,** who in turn was a student of **Kentsu Yabu** and **Choshin Chibana.** Another minor style is the **Chito-ryu** of **Tsuyoshi Chitose,** a disciple of four great masters:

I. Obata, one of Gichen Funakoshi's instructors hired by S.A.C. to teach American airmen karate during the 1950s. He was among the first high ranking Japanese karate instructors to travel outside Japan to demonstrate karate.
Courtesy of E. Bruno

M. Nakayama, seen here with Mel Bruno, was a student of Gichin Funakoshi's. He is today the head of the JKA and is one of the most respected karate masters of the world.
Courtesy of E. Bruno

184

In December of 1980, some of Japan's top karate leaders met in a
historic conference to discuss the unification of karate in Japan.
Some of the participants included (*top photo, left to right*):
Zentaro Kosaka, IAKF and JKA President; Matsuhei Mohri, Kyokushin-Kai
President; Ryoichi Sasakawa, WUKO and FAJKO President; and Nihon Budokan
Director Yamanaka. *Bottom photo, left to right*: Mas Oyama, founder of Kyokushinkai
karate; Kimio Itho, IAKF director and General Secretary of the JKA:
Fajiro Takagi, FAJKO Executive Director; and Eichi Eriguchi, WUKO General

Choki Motobu, Chotoku Kyan, Chojun Miyagi, and Funakoshi.
Numerous other styles exist, but most of them can be traced either
directly or indirectly to the Okinawan **shorin-ryu** systems, or
Okinawan goju-ryu.

By 1940 about 30 percent of Japanese colleges and universities
had campus karate clubs allied with one of the principal ryus
(schools) of karate. After World War II, Gen. MacArthur outlawed all
martial arts, and though karate was practiced in secret its
development was retarded until 1947 or 1948, when the ban was
lifted.

In 1951 the JKA adopted **kumite** (free sparring), developed in
1936 by Gogen Yamaguchi. With free sparring, karate became a
recognized sport and, as with judo, competition began to spread
throughout Japan. In 1958 the first All Japan Karate Championships
were conducted; by the 1970s the **World Union of Karate-Do
Association** (WUKO) was holding world championships.

According to martial scholar, **Donn F. Draeger,** there are more
than 70 different Japanese systems of **karate-do** today; some 30
more systems prefer to designate their teachings karate-jutsu.
Originally a plebian Okinawan form of combat, distinctive Japanese
taste has altered the original teachings to produce a kind of karate-do
that is primarily concerned with unarmed methods of close-quarter
fighting and grappling. Japanese karate-do, properly taught, is a
balanced mix of spiritual discipline, physical education, self-defense,
and competitive sport.

The amazing proliferation of karatelike systems in Japan today
has led to the involvement of more than 2 million Japanese enthusiasts.
Karate-do is largely a sport, according to Draeger, and has the
largest following; karate-jutsu is fundamentally the study of self-
defense. Adaptation of karatelike techniques to fit the requirements
of sport began with the teachings of **Yoshitaka Funakoshi,** Gichin's
son. The elder Funakoshi's techniques were oriented toward self-
defense, while the younger Funakoshi taught a style based more on
upright stances and fluid postures, eventually only a quasi-combat
form, as both weapons and throwing techniques were discarded.

The JKA style, the most prevalent in Japanese karate-do, has
influenced almost all karate-do sects in the nation, forcing them to
adopt similar patterns of technique to attract new members and
keep pace. *See also* karate; karate-do; SCAP Ban. *Further reading:
The Illustrated Guide to Karate,* PMV Morris, 1979; *Modern Bujutsu
& Budo,* Donn F. Draeger, 1974.

OKINAWA

By the 7th century, China had officially recognized Japan as an independent political entity. At various times diplomatic and cultural missions made up of Japanese priests, soldiers, and statesmen passed between the Chinese mainland and Japan. It is plausible that these and other travelers introduced a martial art to Okinawa. Japanese Buddhism students in Chinese monasteries were undoubtedly exposed to the **Shao-lin** kung-fu techniques of **Bodhidharma**; it is reputed that the more adventurous of them, following their training, set sail eastward to spread the teachings to the known world. But such possibilities remain in the realm of conjecture.

There is a widely held view that kung-fu entered the Ryukyus by way of China's Foochow district during the 6th- and 7th-century reign of China's Sui dynasty. Such Chinese-Ryukyuan contacts are first mentioned in the section on Eastern Barbarians of the *Sui Shu,* the dynastic history of the Sui rulers. The definitive Japanese encyclopedia, *Dekai Dai-Hyakkajiten,* states that karate or a type of kung-fu was probably brought to Okinawa from China during the T'ang dynasty (A.D. 618-906). From the end of the T'ang dynasty to the beginning of the Ming period in 1368, a span of 450 years, development of karate in the Ryukyus is unrecorded. Perhaps the strongest support for the claim that karate is innately Okinawan is based on some of the Ryukyu islander's classical dances.

In 1372, official Chinese-Okinawan channels were opened when Okinawa's King Sho-en established a tributary relationship between his domain and China. With Okinawa now a Chinese satellite, cultural proselytization began in earnest. Kung-fu mingled with an indigenous Okinawan form of fist fighting called **tode.** Oral traditions cite the beginning of the 14th century as the period when a karatelike art began to be generally practiced. This budding art was greatly stimulated by the large mission of Chinese officials and their entourage, sent to Okinawa by Emperor Hung Wu-ti in 1372.

During the Ming period (1368-1644) a permanent Okinawan settlement grew up at the Chinese capital of Ch'uan-Chou. Commuting Okinawan citizens brought artifacts and customs back to their islands, and a general belief that all things Chinese were superior. A major contribution to the founding of Okinawan karate was the migration in 1392 of 36 Chinese families from Fukien province, China, to Kume-mura, a suburb of Naha, Okinawa. They established the community called the **Thirty-Six Families.** Here, Chinese masters taught their own systems of Chinese boxing (**kempo**) to Okinawans. (One of **Meitoku Yagi's** ancestors, a Chinese kempo master, arrived with this group.)

Before 1429 Okinawa was divided into three kingdoms: Hokuzan, Chuzan, and Nanzan. King Hashi from Chuzan conquered the kingdoms of Nanzan and Hokuzan and unified Okinawa; he banned all weapons on the island. With the subsequent opening of trade, Arabs, Malays, Indonesians, and Thais brought to Okinawa glimpses of Southeast Asian forms of unarmed self-defense.

In 1477 Sho Shin, the grandson of Sho Hashi, reimposed the weapons ban, placing all weapons in a storehouse under his supervision. The ban stimulated training in weaponless fighting.

Records in Okinawa's national archives, which were unfortunately destroyed during World War II, indicated that between 1432 and 1570 Okinawa established forty-four official embassies in Annam (Vietnam), Thailand, Malaya, and many of the lesser kingdoms of Java. This intercourse supports the conviction that modern karate kicking techniques were imported from Indochina (i.e., Vietnam, Cambodia, and Laos), whereas the open-handed and finger-stabbing techniques in offensive karate movements originated in other locations.

In 1592, Toyotomi Hideyoshi, a Japanese general, raised an army to invade the Asian mainland. In 1599 Sho Nei, king of Okinawa, asked the Chinese court to send an embassy to his royal investiture. Because of the Japanese military threat to China, the Chinese Imperial court sent military men in this and subsequent embassies to Okinawa. Army generals who were prominent in martial arts taught Chinese kempo to the Okinawans.

A Japanese military expedition in 1609 ended Okinawan automony. The subjugated Okinawans were again denied weapons. In clashes with the victors, the Okinawans used the only weapons they possessed, their bare hands and feet. Okinawans, especially the owners of property, trained diligently to make thier hands and feet into weapons in order to protect their lives and property. Martial arts experts never exchanged their techniques with other experts; therefore the development of fighting techniques proceeded in secret. At night, Okinawans went to caves or mountain hideouts and trained, using the trees as their enemies. On the trunk and shoots of the tree called "gajimaru" (banyan tree) they practiced jump kicks, kicks, punching and chopping, and hardened their fists. The "kakidameshi" was a fight to the death between two experts. Relatives of the slain expert would never seek revenge because they were ashamed to be seen. Many techniques were developed at the expense of human life.

Gaining little from such disunited resistance, the various Okinawan **ch'uan fa** groups and tode societies banded together in 1629; the result was a new fighting style, a combination of Okinawa-te and ch'uan fa, called simply **te.** During this period, and after, many Okinawans were secretly sent to China to learn fighting systems; such famous Chinese as Saifa, Seiunchin, Ason, Waishinzan, Ananku, **Chinto,** and **Kusanku** either taught the Okinawans or provided inspiration by their deeds.

The third book of the *Oshima Hikki,* a reliable chronicle, mentions that a shipwrecked Chinese boxer named Ko Sokun (Kung Hsiang-Chun) with a group of followers introduced in 1692 a special kind of martial art to Okinawa. It uses not the term karate, but the word kumiai-jutsu, meaning "fighting technique."' At any rate, a monument to karate exists at the foot of Chuzan Castle (Shuri Castle), containing written evidence that the Chinese lion and tiger schools of boxing were brought to Okinawa. (Written accounts of the development of karate are rare; one of the few is an 1830 book entitled *Gokansen Tode Ko,* or *Okansen Karate Ko,* by Sennan Choho.)

In the early days in Okinawa, there were three styles of unarmed fighting: **Naha-te, Shuri-te,** and **Tomari-te,** named after the three principal cities in which they flourished. Even today, little is known about Tomari-te, a style somewhat similar to Naha-te.

By the 18th century, the modern characteristics of Okinawan karate began to emerge. Because of the secrecy under which te was practiced, it is not clearly known how the different styles emerged. Okinawan karate today, however, is traced back to two major original groups. One is **shorin-ryu** (or Shuri-te) and the other is **shorei-ryu** (or Naha-te).

Naha-te is itself divided into two styles: **goju-ryu** and **Uechi-ryu.** Shuri-te is divided into three styles: shobayashi-ryu shorin-ryu, kobayashi-ryu shorin-ryu, and matsubayashi-ryu shorin-ryu. The general distinction between the two major branches in Naha-te's emphasis on flexibility in movement, while Shuri-te emphasizes speed.

By the late 1880s, the term **karate** (T'ang hand) came into use in Okinawa, replacing the word te (hand). In 1905, Chomo Hanashiro broke with tradition and wrote a book using the new character for karate. The characters were pronounced alike, but Hanashiro's translation was "empty hand(s)." This angered some of the purists, who felt they should acknowledge their debt to the Chinese who had taught them. **Gichin Funakoshi**, who popularized the use of Hanashiro's character, is usually given credit for first using it. A conference sponsored by the *Ryukyu Shimpo* newspaper in Oct. 1936 brought together karate leaders including: **Kentsu Yabu, Chotoku Kyan,** Hanashiro, **Choki Motobu, Chojun Miyagi, Juhatsu Kiyoda, Choshin Chibana,** Mashige Shiroma, Asatada Koyoshi, Eijo Shin, Miyashiro, Nakutsune, and Nakamora. At this important conference it was officially decided to adopt the term "karate" for the national martial art of Okinawa.

Several modern karate authorities claim that the intense seclusion of karate was maintained until about 1903. Others feel that in 1875, when the occupation of Okinawa ended, and the Ryukyu Islands became a part of the Japanese Empire, secrecy was relaxed. In any event, karate was opened up to the public. The period just prior to World War II saw a great popularization of karate on Okinawa. Between 1915 and 1940, in fact, almost all the major karate styles in existence today were founded.

In 1901-02, when the First Middle School and Men's Normal School opened on Okinawa, karate was officially installed as a part of the physical education curriculum. Karate grandmaster of Shuri-te, **Yasutsune "Ankoh" Itosu,** was the first karate master to instruct

Historical photograph of Okinawan karate masters taken in 1936. *Seated left to right:* Shorin-ryu karate masters Chotoku Kyan, Kentsu Yabu, Chomo Hanashiro, and founder of goju-ryu karate, Master Chojun Miyagi. *Standing, left to right:* Shimpan Shiroma and *(second from right)* Chosin Chibana.

Photograph taken in 1946 at Master Chojun Miyagi's residence. Master Miyagi is standing at far left instructing kumite practice. Students *(left to right)* are: Meitoku Yagi, Eiichi Miyasato, Seikichi Toguchi, and Eiko Miyasato.

187

Bust of Chojun Miyagi, Grand Master of Okinawan Goju-ryu, which was installed permanently in the Police Department Gymnasium (Old Budokan Martial Arts Exercise Hall) on Okinawa.

publicly on Okinawa. It is known also that in April 1901 the Shurijijo Elementary School on Okinawa had introduced karate training into its gym glasses. This was the first time karate was taught in a group.

In 1905, karate clubs were founded in the following schools on Okinawa: Okinawa-ken Junior High, Naha City School of Commerce, Okinawa-ken Trainers School, Prefectural Agricultural School, Prefectural Engineering School, and the Prefectural Fisheries College. Karate on Okinawa was quickly accepted on the strength of its introduction into, and evaluation by, the Okinawan scholastic system.

From 1900 to 1912, Okinawan karate had a great impact on the Budokai (Martial Arts Association), and on the navy of Okinawa. In the spring of 1912, when the First Fleet, under Admiral Izuha, anchored in Nakagusuku Bay, about ten petty officers were sent for a week of karate training at the First Middle School.

In Feb. 1920 Kentsu Yabu, a karate instructor for many years in the Normal School and earlier an army lieutenant, was invited to the U.S., where he successfully exhibited karate in Hawaii and Los Angeles. This marks the first international exposure of Okinawan karate.

Emperor Seijo visited Okinawa on March 10, 1922, while on his way to Europe. A group of Okinawan karate masters, among them Chojun Miyagi, had the honor of demonstrating karate in front of him at the Teachers School. In May 1926 the royal family visited and observed karate training at the same school.

In 1923 karate training was given in the Okinawan Police Academy, and in 1940 karate became the official martial art at the academy. On Nov. 21, 1930 the Okinawa Taiiku Kyokai (Okinawan Athletic Association) was founded; its karate division combined with the Okinawan Karate Club, founded in March 1927.

On Okinawa today there are estimated to be more than 200 dojos. New schools crop up regularly. The main styles on the island are: kobayashi shorin-ryu, matsubayashi shorin-ryu, shobayashi shorin-ryu, Uechi-ryu, goju-ryu, matsumura orthodox, Okinawan kempo, and isshinryu. Less prominent offshoots of these styles can be found, as well as hybrid systems of recent invention.

STYLES: As previously indicated above, Naha-te is divided into two main styles: Uechi-ryu and goju-ryu. Uechi-ryu was founded by **Kanbun Uechi,** who had gone to China as a result of an unhappy love affair. He returned ten years later and opened a school. His style was based on the pangai-noon system of China and today is headed by his son, **Kanei Uechi,** who assumed leadership upon his father's death in 1947, and by one of the original students, Ryuko Tomoyose.

Okinawan **kempo,** the least organized of the fighting systems, enjoys some following in the islands, but is little known outside the Ryukyus.

Another relatively small system is **isshinryu. Tatsuo Shimabuku,** after studying under such famed masters as Chotoku Kyan of Shuri-te and Choki Motobu of shorei-ryu, modified and combined the two styles to form the isshinryu (one-heart style). Though its following is small here, in the U.S. it is quite large because of the large number of American servicemen who studied this style while stationed in Okinawa.

The **goju-ryu** (hard-soft school) traces its origin to the external (hung style) and internal (**pa-kua** chang, **hsing-i** ch'uan, and **mi tsung-i**) systems of China. The great Okinawan karate master, **Kanryo Higashionna** (also known as Higaonna and West Higashionna) trained in Chinese kempo, or ch'uan fa. (The Chinese ideograph for ch'uan fa is read by the Japanese and Okinawans as kempo, meaning "fist way.") Higashionna sailed from Okinawa in 1866 at the age of 15 to Fukien province, China, to learn Chinese kempo. With over twenty years of training under the famous Chinese kempo master Liu Liu Ko, Higashionna mastered the art. He returned to Okinawa during the middle of the Meiji Era (1868-1911) and introduced a new school of karate there. The new style, called Naha-te, integrated go-no kempo and ju-no kempo (hard and soft); incorporated hard and soft, slow and fast movements. Higashionna also introduced a special breathing exercise called **Sanchin.** In 1915, Master Higashionna died, leaving many devoted students. **Chojun Miyagi,** Higashionna's top student, became his successor as head of the Naha-te school of karate; Seiko Higa assisted.

Miyagi traveled several times to China after Higashionna died and remained a few years each time to train in the Chinese martial arts. Miyagi's unusual dedication to the martial arts earned deep respect

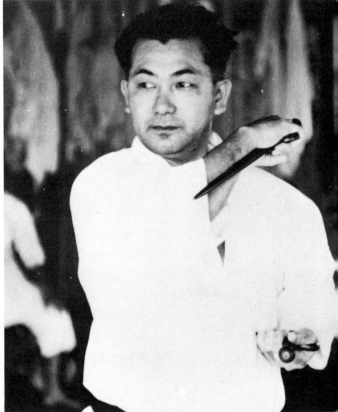

Shugoro Nakazato, Okinawan karate master, president of the Okinawan Shorin-ryu Shumakai Association. Courtesy of Sid Campbell

from the Chinese kempo masters. He was considered an outstanding karate master of great skill, strength, and spirit. Miyagi further improved and developed the theory and techniques of Naha-te and scrutinized it scientifically for martial arts training on Okinawa.

In the late 1920s, Miyagi founded goju-ryu karate on Okinawa. He named the system "goju-ryu" (hard-soft style) from the old Chinese book *Wu pei chih (Army Account of Military Arts and Science)* by Yuan-i Mao, published in 1636. The term "goju" appears in the sentence: "The successful method required both give and take (go-ju)." Miyagi was teaching and promoting goju-ryu karate-do up to the time of his death on Oct. 8, 1953, at the age of 66. He was called the last great samurai warrior of Okinawa because of his legendary strength and skill as well as his intense dedication to the martial arts. **Meitoku Yagi** received the style's **menkyo-kaiden** from Chojun Miyagi and succeeded to the leadership of goju-ryu.

Meitoku Yagi is the foremost living Okinawan goju-ryu karate master. President of the Meibukan School of goju-ryu karate-do at Naha City, Okinawa, he and his two sons, Meitatsu and Meitetsu, continue in the strict tradition of goju-ryu. His school has branches on Okinawa and in other parts of the world. Its North American headquarters is in Watertown, Mass., under the direction of **Anthony Mirakian,** who first introduced Meibukan goju-ryu karate to the U.S. in 1960.

Shorin-ryu, a popular style of karate on Okinawa, traces its descent through distinguished Chinese fighting systems.

Legend traces the history of shorin-ryu to two ancient Chinese masters, Iwah and Wai Shin-zan. Iwah's students were chiefly citizens of Kume (Maesato and Kogusuku), but included **Sokon Matsumura** of Shuri, whose descendants were to be influential in the formation of Okinawan karate. With the exception of Shimabuku of Uemdon, all of Master Waishinzan's students were from Kunenhoya (Senaha, Gushi, Nagahama, Arakaki, Hijaunna, and Kuwae). **Kusanku,** an 18th-century Chinese military official, is said to have learned from a Shao-lin monk the Chinese art of ch'uan fa. In 1761, he was sent to Okinawa, and it is through his subsequent teaching efforts that the art became more widespread.

"Tode" **Sakugawa** (1733-1815), born in Shuri Toribori, was first a student of Peichin Takahara (1683-1760), but on his teacher's death continued his training with Kusanku, traveling many times to China. During this period he is said to have combined ch'uan fa and tode to form Okinawa-te. Sakugawa left the oldest surviving kata still in use today, the Sakugawa no kun, or staff form. He also passed down the Kusanku kata and is credited with founding the dojo kun (dojo etiquette).

After Sakugawa the record of transmission becomes vague. Known are the names of three masters who came between Sakugawa and the acknowledged founder of Shuri-te, Sokon Matsumura. Sometime between the death of Sakugawa and the rise of Shuri-te, Urazoe Mayamoto, Chogun Suekata, and Makabe Chyan lived and taught. Surfacing for the first time are the names Gusukuma, the teacher of Azato, Kanagusuku, Oyatomari, Yamada, and especially Matsumura, Nakazato, and Toguchi.

Sakugawa had befriended a political leader on Okinawa by the name of Matsumura. At the time of his death in 1799, he asked Sakugawa to raise his 3-year-old son, Sokon Matsumura (1796-1884), who became the most important karate master of the mid-Meiji era (1867-1912). Sakugawa, training the child, affectionately dubbed him the Bushi, a term meaning Warrior. Matsumura is credited with creating all of the kata of the system that came to be called Shuri-te. Still taught in the shobayashi shorin-ryu system of karate, these include: **Seisan, naihanchin** (I through III), **ananku, wanshu, gojushiho, Chinto, passai,** and Kusanku. Living into his 90s, he left many disciples, among the most famous: **Yasutsune Itosu** and **Yasutsune Azato.** Of still other pupils little is known but their descendants, Choshin Chibana and **Ankichi Arakaki,** were prominent.

According to family tradition, Nabe Matsumura, the grandson of Sokon Matsumura, received all the so-called secret techniques and knowledge of his grandfather. The chief instructor of this style, now called the matsumura orthodox system (of shorin-ryu), is Hohan Soken (b. 1889), Nabe's nephew. While this system teaches the traditional basic and advanced kata, it also makes use of the hukutsuri, or "white crane" forms. Miraculous skill is reputed to derive from proper practice of this technique, such as the ability to stand or even

Anthony Mirakian while on Okinawa. *Front row, left to right:* Shosei Shiroma, Meitatsu Yagi. *Standing, left to right:* Anthony Mirakian, Yushun Tamaki, Master Shinken Taira, famous Kobujutsu Master (black gi), Karate Master Meitoku Yagi, and Mr. Tamaki. Courtesy of A. Mirakian

189

fight on a small board afloat in rough water. Great emphasis is placed on **kobu-jutsu** (art of weapons).

Another famous student of Sokon Matsumura is **Yasutsune "Anko" Itosu** (1830-1915). Itosu, a student also of master Gusukuma, created the **pinan** kata and developed the naihanchi kata to such an extent that he became known as the "Anko" or "Iron Horse," rooting himself uncannily in immobility. His senior student, **Kentsu Yabu** (b. ca. 1870), taught only a few years before retiring and leaving the style to Itosu's second-ranking student. Perhaps because so many students had attained high levels of proficiency during Itosu's long life, or perhaps due to the unsettled times (late Meiji and early Taisho eras), each master felt he should assume leadership. Consequently, several distinct styles of shorin-ryu emerged. Splinter groups, of whom very little is known outside Okinawa, are Chomo Hanashiro, Choran Yamakawa, Shinei Shiroma (the short-term instructor of Shugoro Nakazato), Ambun Tokuda, Chotei Soryoku, and Yabiku.

Conflicting stories exist about Yabu: that he was gentle and a good teacher; that he enjoyed shinken shobu or shobishi kumite (fight to the death or knockout). Legend says Yabu killed more than sixty men in unarmed combat, and even defeated the famous eccentric and enormous Okinawan shorei-ryu master, **Choki Motobu.** Yabu left two well-remembered students, Shinken Taira and **Kanken Toyama** (1888-1966), the founder of shudokan karate.

Choshin Chibana (1887-1969), Yabu's successor, first named his style shorin-ryu in 1928. Master Chibana was universally respected on Okinawa, and was even decorated by the Emperor of Japan as a great karate master. Chibana left behind three kudan (9th-degree) students, several splinter students, and two kata: Kusanku-dai and gojushiho. At Chibana's death two followers disputed over seniority. Presently Katsuya Miyahira heads the **kobayashi** shorin-ryu (small forest shorin style) and **Shugoro Nakazato** heads the kobayashi shorin kan shuwakai (small forest shorin school of all Shugoro's students).

Shoshin Nagamine is the present head of **matsubayashi** shorin-ryu (pine forest shorin style). Nagamine had studied with Ankichi Arakaki, **Chotoku Kyan,** and Choki Motobu. His system is chiefly distinguished from the others by a typically faster, lighter movement; the kobayashi styles emphasize more power and less mobility.

Chotoku Kyan, another student of master Itosu, is remembered primarily as an outstanding instructor. Kyan's students included Tatsuo Shimabuku, founder of isshinryu, and Choshin Chibana himself.

Gichin Funakoshi (1868-1957) is perhaps the best known of the Shuri-te masters. Having trained under Itosu and Azato, he became widely known throughout Japanese society not only for his considerable skill in the fighting arts but for his dignity, academic acumen, and nobility of character. Funakoshi was chosen in 1917, and again in 1922, to demonstrate Okinawan karate at the annual Japanese exposition of martial arts conducted at the great **Butokuden** in Kyoto. He counted among his personal friends **Jigoro Kano,** the founder of judo; his students included virtually all of the subsequently important karate masters in Japan. Funakoshi's teachings formed the nucleus of the style, similar to Shuri-te, called **Shotokan** after his death. It is now the most prolific karate system in Japan and has since 1955 spread throughout the world. Funakoshi emphasized three things above all else: basic technique, kata, and improvement of character.

A contemporary and friendly rival of Funakoshi was **Kenwa Mabuni** (b. 1889). In addition to his Shuri-te studies with Itosu, he trained in Naha-te under Kanryo Higashionna, and in goju-ryu under Chojun Miyagi. He later migrated to Japan and formed the **Shito-ryu** system in Osaka.

The Zen Okinawa Karate-do Remmei (All Okinawa Karate-do Association) was founded on Okinawa in 1956; it is the official body for Okinawan karate. The charter members were goju-ryu, Uechi-ryu, and two styles of shorin-ryu, matsubayashi and kobayashi. The members meet regularly in Naha City to establish karate policies governing the qualifications for grades, ranks, and titles for students, instructors, and masters.

In World War II, more than 90 percent of Okinawa's structures were destroyed by bombardment; 42,000 civilians were killed, among them several leading karate exponents. Following the Japanese surrender on Sept. 2, 1945, Okinawa was recognized as a U.S. territory under residual Japanese sovereignty. Several American military bases, including the huge Kadena Airbase, were established. The Taiwan tensions following 1949 and the Korean War of 1950-53 underlined the continuing strategic importance of the island and U.S. military units were constantly stationed there.

It was U.S. servicemen seeking involvement in Okinawan culture who found karate a viable practice and pastime, particularly those serving in the U.S. Marine Corps. So taken were many servicemen with Okinawan karate that they requested and frequently received extensions of duty in Okinawa to further pursue karate training. With these extensions came an increase in the number of marriages between American marines and Okinawan women, who would then immigrate to the U.S. in droves with their new husbands. The situation reached a saturation point and the reigning marine commander prohibited extensions of duty in Okinawa after 13 months of service.

According to **Joe Lewis,** a U.S. Marine who trained in Okinawa with Eizo Shimabuku(ro) in 1964-66, at every karate school but one the servicemen paid their own tuition. The exception was Tatsuo Shimabuku's isshinryu school. **Steve Armstrong,** one of Tatsuo's senior students, established a contract for his instructor wherein the U.S. government paid the $5 per month training fee for each marine enrolled at Shimabuku's dojo. Hence, more isshinryu black belts were produced than in any other Okinawan style at that time, which subsequently accounted for the widespread proliferation of isshinryu in the U.S. by returning servicemen.

Also according to Lewis, the advent of the Vietnam War in March 1965 greatly reduced the number of servicemen stationed in Okinawa, for the ground and air forces were committed to Vietnam in strength. Lewis, in fact, was a member of the first marine division that left Okinawa for Vietnam. In April 1972, Okinawa returned to Japanese rule. (RICHARD KIM, ANTHONY MIRAKIAN, GLENN PREMRU) *See also* te. *Further reading: Fighting Arts,* Vol. 1, No. 6 to Vol. 2, No. 6; *Karate's History and Traditions,* Bruce A. Haines, 1968; *Okinawa: The History of an Island People,* George H. Kerr, 1958; *The Weaponless Warriors, An Informal History of Okinawan Karate,* Richard Kim, 1975.

Master Eizo Shimabukaro who teaches the Shobayashi shorin-ryu style.

190

Two great Okinawan masters, Fusei Kisei *(left)* and Hohen Soken.

PAKISTAN

The Pakistani government until 1971 prohibited all martial arts. In 1971, however, a native Pakistani, **Saleem Jehangir,** with the help of Khwaja Saleem Almed, then director of the National Sports Training and Coaching Center, convinced the government to lift its ban. In Oct. 1971 Jehangir taught the first karate class in Pakistan. The school enjoyed moderate success, and in 1972 local police began to study the martial arts. In 1973, the Pakistan Sports Board, similar to the AAU in America, formed the Judo-Karate Federation of Pakistan to propagate the martial arts and prepare teams for international competition. With the arts in favor, instructors from Burma and Taiwan opened schools in Karachi. In 1974, the first All Pakistan Karate Championships were held, receiving coverage on national television.

INDIA

The origin of organized systems of weaponless self-defense in India is undetermined, though historians speculate that the martial arts reached a high degree of sophistication in India thousands of years ago. Some modern authorities feel that Greek **pankration** and the **Pyrrhic** war-dance may have antedated any Indian form of combat. Indian folklore, history, dance, and drama are replete with tales of warriors, princes, and gods who accomplished incredible battlefield feats with their bare hands. In works of art, particularly ancient Buddhist temple sculpture, warriors are depicted in positions strongly evocative of modern karate **kata** (formal exercises).

The Kshatriya (warrior caste), comparable to the Japanese **samurai** and the European knight, were the dominant class in Indian society. As a class they antedate the rise of Buddhism and played the leading cultural role in India until the rise of the Brahmana (circa 300 B.C.), or priestly caste. Authorities agree that at least one early fighting method, **vajramushti,** is attributable to the Kshatriya. Its physical techniques are said to have been similar to the punches used in karate as we know it today.

Buddhist literature also confirms the existence of Indian bare-handed fighting. The first mention appears in thue Buddhist chronicle, **Lotus Sutra,** which refers both to a pugilistic art and to a form of fighting called nata, meaning "a manly character; a dancer or performer." Another early Buddhist sutra, the *Hongyo-kyo,* indicates that more than one type of weaponless fighting was extant and popularly practiced in India before being noted in either Chinese or Japanese literature. *See also Lotus Sutra;* pankration; Pyrrhic; vajramushti. *Further reading: Karate's History and Traditions,* Bruce A. Haines, 1968.

OTHER SOUTHEAST ASIAN COUNTRIES

Only recently have students of Asian history discovered that empty-hand fighting techniques existed in Southeast Asia for hundreds of years. Archaeological expeditions, sifting through large caches of temple friezes, wall carvings, and religious and secular statuary of recently uncovered remains, brought to light the first real evidence of early martial arts development.

Cambodia Present-day Cambodia was once at the center of the Khmer Empire. For more than 600 years (A.D. 802-1432) the Khmers dominated much of Southeast Asia. Probably the most magnificent structures erected during this period were Suryavarman II's awe inspiring temple at Angkor Wat, Jayavarman VII's walled city at Angkor Thom, and the strikingly detailed Bayon Temple. Throughout these ruins statues and animated reliefs were found depicting various stages of weaponless fighting. Figures portrayed in some form of close combat number in the thousands, among which are many posed in fighting stances that are unmistakably of Chinese kung-fu.

The early Indian martial arts of hsiang ch'a hsiang p'u, nata, and **vajramushti** seem to have no visual representation in Southeast Asia. Although it is known that there was a certain amount of intercourse between early India and Southeast Asia, there is no tangible evidence that early Khmer styles of fighting were descendents of any Indian combative forms. It is probable, therefore, that Khmer bare-hand fighting may have borrowed from India and China, and perhaps gave to each in turn, but nevertheless remained a unique style unto itself.

Vietnam A form of kung-fu is practiced in modern Vietnam, but the exact period of its origin is not known. There is little doubt that this Vietnamese form was strongly influenced by the Chinese, who have subjugated this small, narrow country for the past 2,000 years.

A certain amount of Japanese influence in unarmed fighting undoubtedly took place during the Japanese occupation of Indochina during World War II. Judo is also popularly pursued in present day South Vietnam, and is known by the indigenous term, nhu dao.

Little else can be said about the martial arts in Vietnam; there is a general dearth of written material on the subject in Southeast Asia, but sources dealing with Vietnam in particular are virtually non-existent.

Thailand Numerous forms of unarmed combat are found in modern Thailand, most notably **Thai boxing,** or kick-boxing. Thailand has been the sole Southeast Asian country to escape colonialism, either eastern or western. Even without such direct rule, however, the country adopted customs and traditions that bear unmistakable signs of Indian and Chinese influence. Thai weaponless fighting arts are in many instances indistinguishable from the Chinese and Indian.

Indonesia There is insufficient historical evidence from which to infer with certainty whether India or China, the two great sources for Indonesia's unarmed fighting arts, gave Indonesia its first exposure to a martial art. The situation is further complicated by the fact that Chinese, Malay, Arab, and Filipino pirates continually disrupted the rather sublime life of the Indonesians both at sea and among the coastal inhabitants.

In present-day Indonesia four terms—**pukulan, pentjak, silat,** and Chinese kun-tao—indicate unarmed combat in general, much as in the western world we may refer to essentially the same sport in terms such as boxing, fisticuffs, pugilism, etc. There are a multitude of variations on the general themes of pukulan, silat, and pentjak, in contrast to the relatively few forms of Chinese kuntao. A style is usually representative of a practitioner's home city or village, and since village rivalry is often intense, a master of one of these four martial systems allegedly never teaches his village's style to an outsider.

Malaya It is very likely that India influenced the development of a weaponless fighting art called **bersilat;** however, there is presently more direct evidence for the hypothesis that China was the real spiritual force behind the emergence of bersilat in Malaya. Bersilat varies from state to state in Malaysia, and indeed from teacher to teacher, but the east coast is generally considered to produce the finest men in the art. Kuntao is also practiced in the larger cities, where there are numerous Chinese clubs, and where a reputed rivalry between kuntao associations and bersilat groups exists.

Bersilat is today one of the rarest martial arts because of the secrecy with which it evolved. *Further reading: Weapons and Fighting Arts of the Indonesian Archipelago,* Donn F. Draeger, 1972.

191

EUROPE

Gunji Koizumi, father of judo in Europe

JUDO

First contacts between Asian and European wrestling arts are lost in the early history of travels and wars, but Japanese wrestling as a system appears at the beginning of the 20th century, with the early development of **Jigoro Kano's** judo.

As early as 1901 Japanese wrestlers performed in circuses in England, France, and Germany, "fighting against any man" and amazing audiences with their skill. German Kaizer Wilhelm II was so impressed he invited two Japanese instructors to teach in the military school at Kiel, and later Agitaro Ono taught jujutsu at the Berlin Military Academy.

Katsukuma Higashi, another Japanese judo expert, taught in Britain, Germany, and other European countries. His biggest contribution to the development of judo in Europe was *The Complete Kano's Jiu Jitsu,* which he published with Irving Hancock in 1905. A reprint edition, more than 60 years after the first publication, is still selling in many European countries.

Yukio Tani, a small jujutsuka from Japan, was the first to bring judo to Britain. Barton Wright, famous British sportsman, persuaded Tani to begin teaching jujutsu. In 1904 he was fighting wrestlers for money, but failed to start a regular gym. Though he was active until his death in 1950, other interests limited his participation.

Gunji Koizumi arrived in England in 1906. Koizumi became the father of British and also European judo. He stayed a year in England, visited the U.S., but returned to London by 1910, and with Tani started to teach jujutsu. In 1918 Koizumi founded the **Budokwai**, the oldest judo dojo in Europe, still the center of British judo.

An important British member of the Budokwai, journalist, writer, and diplomat E.J. Harrison lived in Japan and has written judo and karate textbooks. Harrison joined the Budokwai in 1919 and remained active in the dojo until he died in 1961, at the age of 88. Miss White Cooper, probably the first woman in Europe, and perhaps the world, to practice judo, joined in 1919. Trevor P. Leggett, another famous Budokwai member, was the highest graded Caucasian in Kodokan judo for many years. He was a 5th dan before World War II, an extremely high grade for that time. The first female black belt in the Budokwai was Dame Enid Russel-Smith.

Other Japanese teachers toured Europe, introducing jujutsu or judo. Lasting impressions were made by Raku Uyenichi and Taro Mayaki in Germany, and Kichisaburo Sasaki in Austria and Hungary.

The first European to teach judo extensively was a German, Erich Rahn, who opened a jujutsu school in Berlin in 1906. The school is still open, in newer quarters at Berlin Hohenzollerndam, 111. At the invitation of Berlin police president Von Jagow, Rahn started teaching jujutsu to policemen in 1910, and in 1913 taught unarmed combat to the Army. Rahn's pupil, Alfred Rhode, opened the Jiu Jitsu Club of Frankfurt on Main in 1922.

Judo pioneers throughout Europe were often not aware of each other, and only in the 1920s did they begin to organize and communicate. Powerful German judo was soon the axis of international cooperation. The first judo matches were named "professional championships." Two were organized in the Sports Palace of Berlin. In 1922 Erich Rahn defeated Hans Reuter of Munich in 4 minutes to become the first professional German Jiu Jitsu Champion. In 1923 Rahn again defeated his challenger, Australian-German Charles Buse, to keep his title. In 1926, in Cologne, the first national tournament, with 7 weight classes, was held under the title "All German Jujutsu Championships." The first international tournament was a friendly match held between London's Budokwai and the Jiu Jitsu Club of Frankfurt on Main on November 15, 1929.

Judo was developing in almost all central European countries. Dr. Hanho Rhi, a Korean instructor, taught in Switzerland. Hungarian judo was developed by Tibor Vincze, a fighter who returned home from Japan with a 4th dan, a high grade in 1930. Maurice Minne and his brother Ito founded the Judo Club de Belge in Brussels in 1914, and again in 1918. Carolo Oletti started teaching Japanese wrestling in 1920 in Rome. A group of Czechoslovakians learned jujutsu in Germany, and in 1925 they began teaching physical education instructors in Prague and the military. In 1936 they founded a Jiu Jitsu Union; its first president was Dr. Franktisek Smotlachy. In Holland, Maurice Van Nieuwenhuizen, a pupil of Gunji Koizumi, opened the first dojo, the Judokwai, in 1934.

Germany had three federations and more than 110 clubs in 1930. Alfred Rhode organized an international summer camp in Frankfurt on Main in 1932, and nearly every judo instructor in Europe attended. Koizumi and Tani arrived from London, Ishiguro from Paris, and Dr. Kitabatake from Berlin. Judomen from Germany, Britain, Hungary, and Switzerland formed the first European Judo Federation. (By 1933, when Jigoro Kano visited Europe, the term judo was beginning to replace jujutsu.)

Germans pushed hard for more international meetings, and in 1934 they organized the 1st European Judo Championships, in Dresden. Czechoslovakians, Hungarians, Swiss, and German judomen participated, but all five titles in five weight classes were easily won by Germans—the runner-ups were Germans as well. Among the

Terry O'Neil *(left)* one of Britain's top karate competitors and instructors, with Emil Farkas.

Gus Glahn, the most successful German judoka.

French judo champion Jean-Jacques Mouiner.

first German champions were Stenzel, Lehman, Gasch, Wittwer, and Woble. Referees were Max Hoppe and Alfred Rhode of Germany, Hanho Rhi of Switzerland, and Von Loross of Hungary.

France was comparatively late in taking up judo. In 1905 jujutsu was introduced by writer Re-Nie (Guy de Montgaillard,)and later by a Navy officer, Le Prieur, who had been awarded a black belt in Japan. Neither had any success, and several Japanese instructors, including the Kodokan's Ishiguro in 1924 and Hikoichi Aida in 1925, fared only slightly better. Jigoro Kano demonstrated judo at the Joinville Military School in 1932, again with disappointing results.

Mikonosuke Kawaishi, a judoka from the famous Kyoto Butokukai, who was briefly in the U.S. in 1926 and 1927, arrived in Paris in 1935. He founded the first regular dojo in France, the Club Franco-Japonais, and one of his first pupils, M. Feldenkrais, founded the Jiu Jitsu Club de France in 1936. Kawaishi joined this club, which is still open today.

Kawaishi taught classical judo at first, but soon developed his own teaching method. He believed Europeans could not remember complicated Japanese names, therefore he numbered throws: 5th leg throw, 1st hip throw, 2nd armlock, etc. Kawaishi also developed his own way of grading, which included colored belts, and even formulated his own kata. One of Kawaishi's star pupils, scientist Paul Bonet-Maury, formed the Jiu Jitsu Federation of France in 1940, and in 1943, at Wagram Hall in Paris, the first French Judo Championships was organized. Jean DeHerdt, another Kawaishi pupil, defeated Jean Beaujean to take the first title; the Paris Police Club won the team title. When World War II started, Kawaishi left France, returning to Japan in 1943.

Soon after the war ended, at the famous London Budokwai, judomen from Britain, Italy, Holland, and Switzerland gathered to form the European Judo Union (EJU). French representatives were there as observers only, though French judo was at the time far more developed than that of any other European country. Paul Bonet-Maury founded the French Federation of Judo and Jiu Jitsu in 1947; the federation was recognized and aided by the government. Kawaishi, who returned to France in 1948, published several books on his method of judo and self-defense, and all became best sellers.

In 1949 leaders of European judo gathered in the Dutch city of Bloemendael, where Italian judoka Dr. Aldo Torti was elected president of the European Judo Union. In 1950, at the European Judo Union's 3rd Congress, in Venice, representatives of Italy, Britain, Switzerland, Belgium, France, and Germany formed the International Judo Federation (IJF). The federation at the time had no contact with countries outside of Europe.

In 1951, when EJU leaders met in London, two more countries joined the organization: Austria and Holland. Here, inclusion of judo in the Olympic Games was first mentioned, and Germany proposed that weight classes be used in competition. Young French publisher **Henry D. Plee** suggested that he print a translation of the Kodokan's monthly magazine in English and French; the EJU agreed to make it an official organ of the EJU. The French also proposed to hold the first European Judo Championships and invite Japanese judo leaders to the event. On December 5 and 6, 1951, at the Palais des Sports in Paris, the first in this series took place. Kodokan President Risei Kano led a large Japanese delegation that included All Japan Judo Champion Toshiro Daigo. Judomen from France, Holland, Belgium, Switzerland, Britain, Italy, Germany, and Austria fought in front of 13,000 spectators for team and individual titles. The French dominated, defeating the heavily favored British team 4-0. Individual titles all went to France as well. Dupre of France defeated a young giant from Holland to take the 1st-kyu title. (The young man was **Anton Geesink,** later a dominant figure in the sport.) The 1st-dan title went to Pariset, 2nd-dan to Cauquil, and both 3rd-dan and All-Grade Championships to French champion Jean Deherdt, who defeated perhaps the finest European judoman of that time, **Geoffrey Gleeson** of London's Budokwai.

The Japanese delegation claimed that the IJF could not properly represent world judo without the Japanese, and they hinted that the Europeans should ask Risei Kano, son of Jigoro Kano and president of the Kodokan, to assume the presidency. When Aldo Torti resigned in 1952, the IJF Congress bestowed the presidency upon Risei Kano. The U.S., Cuba, and Canada, along with Japan, became members of the IJF. The European Judo Union was formed again, and Dr. Aldo Torti was elected president.

Europe's most famous judo champion, Anton Geesink *(right)*, faces Henry Courtine

Perhaps the best European judoka of all time: Soviet lightweight Vladimir Nevzorov, winner of World Championships and Olympic Games. Courtesy of Z. Modric

Wilhelm Ruska, successor to Anton Geesink. Courtesy of Z. Modric

Vladlen Andreev, longtime coach of the Soviet Union's judo team, is one of the best European judo experts. Courtesy of Z. Modric

Two powerful Soviet judomen: Vladimir Novikov *(left)* and Shota Chochoshvili. Courtesy of Z. Modric

The most influential man in European and world judo: Charles Palmer, famous Budokwai judoka who succeeded Risei Kano as International Judo Federation president. Courtesy of Z. Modric

In 1952, at the 2nd European Judo Championships, Anton Geesink won the 1st-dan title and Jacquemond, an Austrian, won another title, but the rest of the medals went to the French, including the team title. When the Pan-American Judo Federation sent a team to Europe in 1953, the EJU had 13 members. The French team easily won over the Pan-American team, 3-0 with 3 ties. (The Pan-American team, composed of judomen from the U.S., Cuba, and Argentina, beat only the Belgian team, 2-1 with 3 ties.)

More Japanese judo instructors visited Europe. Teizo Kawamura came to London, and Noritomo Ken Otani came to stay in Italy. Ichiro Abe and Shozo Awazu taught in France. Already strong, French judo was further assisted by a state law in 1954 permitting only teachers with a degree in both judo and physical education to teach judo professionally.

Aging Mikonosuke Kawaishi was one of the first victims of the growing popularity of Kodokan judo in France. Although responsible for the high development of French judo, he was suddenly considered old-fashioned. As more instructors switched to true Kodokan judo, Kawaishi finally broke away from the French federation in 1957, and died almost forgotten in 1969, a bitter man of 71. His club, Jiu Jitsu Club de France, is still open, and his son Norikazu Kawaishi, born in France in 1948, teaches the Kawaishi method, but he too holds the state license, as does every other French judo coach.

The 1st World Judo Championships, in Tokyo in 1956, proved the superiority of Japanese judo. This was repeated at the 2nd World Judo Championships, but at the 3rd World Judo Championships, Paris, 1961, Anton Geesink won landmark victories over Japanese opponents. In the intercontinental matches organized in Paris after the World Championships, European teams defeated American and Asian teams, proving European judo was mature, if still not technically up to Japanese standards.

Another important development for European judo was the presence of Soviet representatives at Paris in 1961. They sensed judo was soon to be an Olympic sport, and hungry for medals, decided to participate. Judo was not new to the Soviet Union. Russian wrestlers were often in Japan, and some gained a marked proficiency in judo. Kodokan files record gifted Russian pupils, but Soviet isolation following the revolution had separated them from developments in Europe. A prominent judoka, V.S. Oshchepkoff, and famous wrestler H. Haralampieff, had prepared a course of self-defense and unarmed combat for the Red Army in 1920. They developed it as a sport in 1923, calling it **sambo.** It looked identical to early judo but with some wrestling added along with influences of Asiatic and Siberian wrestling arts. In 1930 sambo was accepted as an official sport, and by 1935 tournaments were organized in all Soviet republics.

Sambo contest rules closely resemble judo, but of the 1920 variety. Samboists wear a judogi top but prefer shorts to long trousers and fight in wrestling shoes, not barefoot. Strangulations are barred, but throws, leglocks, armlocks, and holds are allowed. Throwing techniques differ slightly, since belt-holding, barred in judo, is legal. Points in sambo are awarded only for throws achieved while standing.

It was easy for Soviet samboists to learn judo rules, and they invited the best Europeans, the French national team, to three friendly matches in the Soviet Union. The French were so easily defeated that "sambo" became a frightening word for European judomen. Superior physical training and unorthodox techniques surprised even the best European team. But the French and other Europeans learned quickly from the Soviets.

The success of Geesink, and of his countryman Jon Bluming—banned from international competition because of factional quarrels within the Dutch judo community—and later the emergence of Geesink's successor, **Wilhelm Ruska,** proved the Japanese were not invincible. Still the Europeans trained only three or four times a week to participate in tournaments. When the Soviet Union sent fighters with more intensive training and unorthodox techniques, the Europeans started to change their approach to high-level competition judo. Now it was necessary to train twice a day, seven days a week, to compete.

Soviet fighters, especially the gifted Georgians, were a bigger threat to Japanese dominance than the one-man Dutch army. The Tokyo Olympic Games in 1960 affirmed Geesink still the best judoka outside of Japan, but as a team the Russians were superior. The Soviet Union entered four fighters, the maximum allowed, and all four won bronze medals, impressive for virtual beginners. At

The most crucial moment of Munich Olympics in 1976. Young Soviet judoka Shota Chochoshvili throws Japanese and World Champion Fumio Sasahara to win a gold medal.

French champion Henry Courtine attempts an ippon-seoi-nage at the 1961 World Judo Championships in Paris

European tournaments, Russians adopted even better techniques. At the 1976 Munich Olympic Games, a young reserve on the Soviet team, **Shota Chochoshvili,** did the impossible: he threw Japanese and World Champion Fumio Sasahara, winning a gold medal.

In France, as in several other European countries, judo is the most popular individual sport. In 1951 there were 16,281 boxers, 7,542 judomen, and 1,994 wrestlers registered in the official federation. In 1958 the number of judomen jumped to 30,000; in 1960 41,000, and in 1970 over 340,000 judomen held licenses. By 1981 the number of paid licenses in France was close to 400,000. Britain follows with some 200,000 members in 1981, but the number was close to 100,000 in 1960. Germany now boasts 200,000 registered judomen. Most impressive, however, is tiny Holland where judo is surpassed only by soccer in popularity. (There is an Anton Geesink Street in Utrecht.)

Europeans lead the world in development of judo. New rules, for better or worse, were invented and introduced by Europeans, and they actively rule the International Judo Federation. **Charles Palmer,** a famous Budokwai judoman, was IJF president after Risei Kano, who left his mark on the development of judo. Europeans do most of the research, and they have the best experts. Japan is still the number one power, but in big tournaments they have to work very hard to stop not only the Soviets, but other European judomen: East Germans, French, Italians, or British.

Women in judo, long a European phenomenon, are now accepted all over the world. Japanese women competed at the Women's World Judo Championships in New York. Women will probably soon compete at the Olympics, thanks to the efforts of Europeans.

Proposals to change judo even more are still far from being accepted. Anton Geesink wants to discard the traditional white judogi and introduce red and blue judogis for fighters, to make television coverage of judo tournaments more interesting to the general public. Weight classes were unacceptable to the Japanese only 20 years ago, but now there are seven. Change and development for this sport reflect the increased strength of judo in Europe. (ZARKO MODRIC)

K. Kobayashi, head technical adviser for judo in Europe and chief of Portuguese judo

Three of Europe's top judomen at the Kodokan in the mid-1950s *(left to right):* G. Gleeson and C. Palmer of England and Gouell of France

KARATE

French documents indicate early contacts of Europeans with what is known today as karate. Napoleon once made a remark about the fighting abilities of the people of Okinawa; he did not, however, mention the word karate. Sailors or travelers, Europeans living in Asia, and Asians coming to Europe brought some elements of Chinese boxing. Before the end of the 19th century the Asian martial arts were rarely taught, although they were seen in circuses.

In the first decades of the 20th century, rudimentary judo, most often called jujutsu or Japanese wrestling, was introduced to many European countries. Even people who learned some kind of Chinese boxing, or similar fighting art based on kicks and punches, simply called the art jujutsu, or later, judo.

After World War II, as Europe was engulfed in rebuilding shattered economies, sports were not very popular, but in the early 1950s magazine articles from the Far East and the U.S. introduced a new term—karate. France was the first European nation to adopt this new fighting art, and two judomen were responsible for its introduction.

One of them was Jim Alscheik, a Frenchman of Turkish descent who studied judo, karate, kendo, and aikido in Japan with Minoru Mochizuki, head of the Yoseikan school of martial arts. Alscheik briefly taught karate in France and several North African countries, but died in Algiers during the 1961 uprising.

Henry D. Plee, owner of a publicity agency in Paris, started karate in France and many other European countries. Nearly all of today's European karate leaders are his pupils, or pupils of his pupils. When he learned the rudiments of karate from Japanese karateka Rikutaro Fukuda in 1950, he began inviting Japanese teachers to Europe. In the early 1950s, karate was an unknown term; fellow judomen called the art "karaplee," but Plee was not easily discouraged. His guest teachers were first-rate: **Tsutomu Ohshima,** a karate pioneer in the U.S.; Harada; Minoru Mochizuki's son Hiroo; Tetsugi Murakami; Ogashara; Yoshinaro Nanbu; Chojiro Tani; **Taiji Kase;** and others. The first French karate club, also the first in Europe, was the Academie Francaise d'Arts Martiaux (AFAM), which Plee opened in his house in the 5th arrondisement of Paris.

In September 1954, Plee formed the Federation Francaise de Boxe Libre et Karate (French Federation for Free Boxing and Karate), linking the almost forgotten art of French boxing, sometimes called **savate,** and the new Asian fighting art of karate. The combination was not particularly happy for either, but both probably profited from it. Even today the tradition of French boxing can be found in any French karate development.

The first official French karate championships took place in 1961. Plee's AFAM easily took first place in the team event among five competing contingents, and the individual winner was Ohshima's star French pupil. Thirty-two fighters from seven clubs participated in the tournament. The Japanese rules, used here for the first time, remained the basis for European karate matches and have been only slightly modified over the years.

French karatemen soon broke their links with French boxing and joined the highly developed French Judo Federation, a government-financed body. It was renamed the French Federation for Judo and Similar Sports, and later included aikido, kendo, tae kwon do, and other Asian martial arts. French judo was at that time the most developed in Europe; judomen coming to France from other countries were introduced to karate.

The 3rd World Judo Championships, in 1961, was the first big international tournament outside Japan, and nearly every European judo instructor felt obligated to come to Paris and see how champion **Anton Geesink** would deal with Japanese judomen. Some of them established contact with French karatemen, and later helped karatemen within their own countries contact the well developed karate organization in France. The result was the first international karate tournament, in 1963. National teams of France, Belgium, and Great Britain participated. France won both contests: 3-1 against Britain and 4-0 against Belgium. The Belgians defeated the British 2-1.

Between 1963 and 1965, representatives of France, Belgium, Germany, and Spain met twice for European Karate Union (EKU) congresses, and at the 3rd Congress, in Paris in 1966, the EKU was formally inaugurated by representatives of eight European countries. Its first president was Paris lawyer and amateur karateka, Jacques Delcourt. Holland, Yugoslavia, and Portugal submitted official letters of support. The EKU also elected two technical advisors: Tatsuo Suzuki, a Japanese wado-ryu instructor living in Britain, and Hiroo Mochizuki of France. Henry Plee, the French karate pioneer, was later elected a technical advisor. Some other Japanese instructors, most of them wado-ryu stylists, were present: Kono from Holland, Yamashita from Italy, and Yutaka Toyama from Germany. Most French and European karatemen, however, were then practicing the **Shotokan** style.

National delegates at the 1966 EKU congress submitted short reports of the state of karate development in their countries:

Spain: Mr. Pallacio reports that karate is banned in his country because authorities think it is brutal and savage. He requests the EKU's help to explain to the authorities that karate is a safe sport.

Switzerland: Mr. Cherix, president of the karate section of the Swiss Judo Federation, reports there are 300 karatemen in 12 clubs. Five are black belts.

Italy: Mr. Basile, president of the Accademia di Karate Internazionale, reports there are 300 karatemen, and this number grows quickly, so it will soon reach 1,000. His organization has no connection with a judo organization.

Great Britain: Mr. Sommers reports his organization has between 3 and 4,000 members in 34 clubs, and about 10 black belts. There is another organization supervised by a Mr. Bell, but it is a "private and commercial affair."

Germany: Two representatives from two organizations, Mr. Kiltz and Mr. Brandt, explain that there are several organizations; some are recognized by the judo federation, others are not. Mr. Tatsuo Suzuki, who was invited to teach by an unauthorized group, adds to the confusion. The EKU decides to grant a six-month grace period to all German organizations to form a union.

Austria: Mr. Neveceral reports that he formed a federation in 1965, and his group is recognized by the judo federation. There are 300 karatemen in three clubs.

France: Jacques Delcourt reports there are more than 7,000 members in more than 200 clubs. Nearly 200 karatemen are 1st-degree black belts, and more than 20 are 2nd-degree.

The European Karate Union was modeled after the older European Judo Union (EJO). The bylaws were borrowed from the EJU with only slight modifications, and most member organizations were linked to a judo federation in their country. Realizing the danger of feuds between Japanese karate styles and organizations, the EKU congress decided to ban individuals and clubs from contacting Japanese organizations without first checking with their respective karate federations. This policy helped, but within several years Japanese instructors were so numerous and so powerful that the EKU could not prevent rank-hungry Europeans from accepting more Japanese meddling with European karate organizations.

Conflict began when instructors belonging to the **Japan Karate Association** (JKA) formed their own European branch organization in 1968, called the All Europe Karate Federation (AEKF); it was controlled by Japanese instructors. Later, all other Japanese karate styles formed their own separate bodies for wado-ryu, goju-ryu, kyokushinkai, and other styles. The Vietnamese organized the Vietvodao Union, and even rare Chinese boxing instructors began forming their own organizations. (The first notable Chinese boxing organization was formed in France, where veteran Vietnamese instructor Hoang Nam had been teaching Chinese boxing since the early 1960s.)

The first European Karate Championships in 1966, in Paris, demonstrated French superiority over the other European entrants. Only four countries sent full teams of five fighters each. France easily disposed of Britain, 5-0, while Switzerland defeated Italy, 3-1. In the finals, France again won, 4-0, with only one draw. In the individual tournament, each country could field four fighters but some of them sent less. Altogether there were 22 fighters from France, Britain, Austria, Germany, Switzerland, and Italy. After the first two rounds three Frenchmen remained, but one semifinalist was Britain's big Peter Spanton, who defeated the French hope, **Dominique Valera.** Small, fiery **Guy Sauvin** of France defeated Spanton, while in the other semifinals match, Patrick Baroux, who had never won a French championship, defeated French champion Guy Sauvin to take the first title of European champion. Baroux, a clever, modern fighter repeated this victory in 1967.

In 1968 the EKU organized a refereeing clinic in Rome. Referees

198

Dominic Valera, Europe's most famous traditional karate competitor.

from all over Europe gathered to discuss rules and to practice. The clinic was repeated the next year in Split, Yugoslavia, and from 1970 it has been an annual event. Every international referee is expected to participate in at least one annual clinic every two years to have his referee's license validated.

A poll taken at the 1968 European Karate Championships ascertained the Japanese Shotokan style was by far the leading one. Of eight French team members five were Shotokan; the other three belonged to the wado-ryu, kyokushinkai, and shukokai styles—all of them Japanese. Only one member of the German team was a kyokushinkai stylist, all others were Shotokan. The Belgian and Swiss teams were all Shotokan. Britain, however, had one Shotokan, three wado-ryu, and four kyokushinkai stylists (all pupils of the celebrated Steve Arneil). The Italian team had only one Shotokan member, while four were wado-ryu, and the Yugoslav team was all Shotokan except for one shukokai member. Few of the Shotokan stylists belonged to the Japan Karate Association, the organization claiming to represent true Shotokan. All karatemen who belonged to the JKA were grouped in the small AEKF, and they remained outside true international karate in Europe.

In the late 1960s, tae kwon do was introduced to several European countries. American GIs were the first teachers of tae kwon do, which they taught as a form of karate. It was widely accepted, and in Germany Americans like **Arthur Hisatake** (kyokushinkai) and **Mike Anderson** (tae kwon do) could work with other karatemen without problems. But when Koreans began to arrive in Europe, conflicts arose. Korean tae kwon do instructors refused to have anything to do with karate, shunning karate tournaments and organizations. Two groups—the JKA Shotokan stylists and the tae kwon do stylists—refused to participate in any activity with the main karate groups and continued separate development. All other styles, wado-ryu, kyokushinkai, shukokai, and others, produced their own tournaments, but never refused to participate in open EKU events. Tae kwon do was relatively successful in its isolated development, and in many European countries is accepted as a sport separate from karate.

Ticky Donovan, seen here delivering a flying side kick, is one of England's top karate competitors and instructors.

EKU efforts to organize a world karate body finally resulted in the 1st World Karate Championships, conducted in Tokyo in 1970. France next hosted karatemen from all over the world, in 1972, at the 2nd World Karate Championships, organized by the **World Union of Karate-do Organizations** (WUKO). The Japanese team was soundly defeated by the British, though the French beat the British to win the team championships. Japanese team members belonging to the JKA left the tournament in protest, followed by some Americans. The result was a split in the **Federation of All Japan Karate-do Organizations** (FAJKO), and the rise of more factions in Europe. All followers of the JKA, ex-members of the already defunct AEKF, convened again and formed the European Amateur Karate Federation (EAKF).

The EKU continued to grow and is today a powerful body open to all styles. It is still shunned by the JKA-controlled Shotokan stylists and most of the tae kwon do stylists, but nearly all traditional karate followers in Europe accept it as a controlling body.

A boost to the EKU format and worldwide influence is the latest development in Eastern Europe. Karate was long banned in the U.S.S.R., but when the government legalized karate—secret clubs had long existed—the EKU and EAKF competed to enlist the Soviet Union. The Soviet Union was quick to recognize the EKU's democratic framework and joined in 1979. Soon Poland, Hungary, and Czechoslovakia will follow. Soviet karate is still young, but with government support and scientific research facilities for sports, karate will soon parallel the development of other sports in the U.S.S.R.

American influence, particularly via the popular *Black Belt Magazine,* opened the door for modern full-contact karate in Europe. Berlin tae kwon do and karate instructor Georg Bruckner, in 1974, was the first to select and coach a team of Europeans to meet Americans in full-contact. His inexperienced team lost at the 1974 World Professional Karate Championships at Los Angeles. In 1976, he invited an American team to Paris, where Europeans got their first look at the new sport.

One of the best martial artists in Europe is Italy's Pio Gaddi, high official in the Vatican City and international referee in both judo and karate. Courtesy Z. Modric

Two French pioneers: *(left)* Jacques Jouys *(right)* referee Max Vichet. Courtesy of Z. Modric

French karate team during the late 1960s in Henry D. Plee's famous A.F.A.M. dojo in Paris. *Standing left to right:* Patrick Baroux, Guy Desnoes, Albert Boutboul, Alfred Doudou, Alain Setrouk, coach Taiji Kase, Henry D. Plee, Jean Pierre Lavorato. *Kneeling left to right:* Guy Sauvin, Abdelhafid Saidane. Courtesy of Z. Modric

Tom Harinck, controversial Dutch karate and kick-boxing coach whose "Chakuriki" fighters are perhaps the most ferocious contact fighters in Europe. Courtesy of Z. Modric

Some of Europe's finest fighters left the ranks of traditional karate competition to take up full-contact. The most celebrated was Dominique Valera, a Frenchman, with 658 victories, 11 defeats, and 10 ties in his long career. Valera denounced the quality of traditional karate refereeing and made a loud, controversial exit from traditional karate at the 3rd WUKO World Championships in 1975 at Long Beach, Calif. When Valera took up full-contact karate, many younger karatemen showed interest.

Germany's Georg Bruckner organized the World All-Style Karate Organization (WAKO), the first international body for the development of amateur full-contact and semicontact karate. France and Britain did not join, but following the German lead were: Holland, where Jan Stoker and Tom Harinck headed the two most prominent groups; Switzerland, where Jean-Pierre Schuepp popularized full-contact; Yugoslavia, where full-contact was introduced by Emin Topic and **Zarko Modric;** Norway, where Bruckner's pupil, Wolfgang Wedde, brought full-contact; Italy, where ex-Shotokan karateka **Ennio Falsoni** converted to full-contact; and Austria, with pioneers Berndt Zimmerman and Peter Land.

Belgium, France, and Britain joined later, but while the WAKO is strong in amateur full- and semicontact karate, professional fights are organized by many small promoters. The Chakuriki group in Holland, led by Tom Harinck, left WAKO early and now organizes professional tournaments featuring kick-boxing, full-contact, and so on. WAKO amateurs are generally of high technical level, and some of them can stand against better Americans, as the 1979 1st Full-Contact World Championships in Berlin indicated.

It is broadly correct to say that all the best in European karate is under the roof of two organizations: the EKU, in traditional karate, and the WAKO, in contact karate. There are fine fighters outside these two organizations, but the future will see many small federations and styles growing smaller and smaller, until they disappear, just as they did in judo.

Tae kwon do keeps its own name and identity. The split between the two major world organizations of tae kwon do—the **World Taekwon-do Federation** and the **International Taekwon-do Federation**—has been felt in Europe, too, and has hurt both tae kwon do groups in their struggle for recognition. Chinese boxing is by and large considered self-defense, not a sport, and it develops accordingly; although there are some organizations, especially in Britain, which have tried to initiate kung-fu competition. (ZARKO MODRIC)

The founders of the World Union of Karate-do Organizations—the W.U.K.O.—in Paris in 1972. *Right to left:* Jacques Delcourt, France, Chairman; Eiichi Eriguchi, Japan, Secretary General; Ryoichi Sasagawa, Japan, President. Courtesy of Z. Modric

Emin Topic of Yugoslavia developed his own karate style mixing karate with judo and other Asian martial arts. His students are successful in full-contact matches all over Europe. Courtesy of Z. Modric

Georg Bruckner, Berlin tae-kwon-do and karate instructor, was the pioneer of full-contact karate in Europe. He brought Americans to Europe and organized W.A.K.O.—the leading amateur full-contact organization in the world. Courtesy of Z. Modric

The final match of the European Karate Championships 1968: Dominic Valera *(right)* is attacking Guy Sauvin. Italian referee Augusto Basile *(far left)* awarded the victory to Sauvin.

Chojiro Tani, head of Shukokai karate organizations from Japan, has a big following in Europe. Courtesy of Z. Modric

Big Dutchman Jon Bluming was considered one of the world's strongest judomen, but feuding among several factions in Dutch judo prevented him from participating in judo tournaments. Bluming turned to karate and is one of the strongest kyokushunkai karatemen (Oyama-ryu) in Europe. Courtesy of Z. Modric

Yugoslav karate pioneer Zarco Modric is also one of the leading martial arts journalists in the world. Courtesy of Z. Modric

Hiroo Mochizuki, wado-ryu instructor, is the most influential Japanese teacher in France. Courtesy of Z. Modric

Ennio Falsoni, one of the best Italian Shotokan stylists, turned to full-contact in the late 1970s. Courtesy of Z. Modric

Tetsugi Murakami of Japan

Steve Arneil of Britian *(left)* with Holland's Jan Kallenbach—two prominent kyokushinkai (Oyama-ryu) karatemen in Europe. Courtesy of Z. Modric.

Ex-G.I. Mike Anderson *(right)* was instrumental in the early development of tae-kwon-do in Germany and later helped Georg Bruckner introduce full-contact karate to Europe. Courtesy of *Official Karate Magazine*

FINLAND

Judo is the most popular martial art in Finland. In 1954 Shigemi Tagami, secretary to the Japanese embassy in Helsinki, began teaching a few students. In 1958 Torsten Muren, a cabinet member, founded the Suomen Judoliitto, offering judo courses.

The first full-time judo club, called Turun Judoseura, was opened in 1962 in Turku, southwest Finland. By 1963, a number of clubs existed in Helsinki. In Feb. 1963, the first Finnish Championships were held in Turku; winners were Timo Korpiola (68 kg.), Max Jensen (80 kg. and open div.), and Pauli Hissa (over 80 kg.).

Finland has participated in Olympic judo since 1972, but so far no medals have been won. Finnish players have been more successful in the European Championships and Nordic Championships, in which Finnish judomen monopolized the gold medals in 1978 and 1980. In 1975, Finland hosted the Junior European Championships, and in 1978 the senior event was held there.

Max Jensen, a black belt in judo, was the first to practice karate in Finland; he began teaching in 1967. Later in 1967, the first karate dojo in Finland, called Wadokan ry, was opened by Taisto Raumala, Ilkka Rautavirta, and Pekka Jokinen. Siurala, Kari Kuula, and Taisto Raumala founded the Finnish Karate Federation in 1969. By 1971, the first tournament between Finland and Sweden took place and in the following year the first Finnish Championships was organized.

GERMANY

From 1894-1905, through various military incidents in Asia (the Boxer Rebellion in China, the Russian-Japanese War, etc.), came reports to Europe about esoteric empty-hand fighting techniques called jiu-jitsu (jujutsu). In 1906 two Japanese warships arrived in Kiel, Germany, for a goodwill visit; a judo demonstration so impressed Emperor Wilhelm II that he issued an order to hire an instructor. Agitaro Ono came to Germany from Japan in the same year and started teaching jujutsu at the military academies in Berlin and Lichterfelde. Four other Japanese arrived to teach privately.

The most notable early student was Erich Rahn, who in 1906 established the first German jujutsu school, in Berlin. (It still exists at Hohenzollerndamm III, Berlin.) In 1910, Rahn taught detectives of the Berlin Police.

October 10, 1922, marked the founding of the first jujutsu club in Frankfurt, through Alfred Rhode. Clubs were formed soon thereafter in Wiesbaden, Berlin, and at the Frankfurt Police Athletes Club. In that year, at the Berliner Sportspalast, Rahn won the first German Professional Jujutsu Championship, using a leg scissors against Reuter of Munich.

In 1924, the Reichsverbandes for Jiu Jitsu (RFJ) was founded. The first illustrated martial arts magazine, *Jiu Jitsu*, was published in 1925. That same year, through Rhode, the first contact was made with judo clubs in England and Italy. A Berlin high school adopted jujutsu for its exercise program—the instructor was Rudolf Krotki—and, on October 26, 1925, the RFJ excluded all professionals and independent teachers unless they belonged to an amateur club. On November 17, 1929, the first tournament between English and German teams resulted in a loss for Germany and the first realization of jujutsu's unsuitability as a sport relative to judo.

In 1932, the first international judo summer school was established in Frankfurt, under Alfred Rhode's direction. The instructors were Professors **Gunji Koizumi** of Japan, **Yukio Tani** of London, Ishiguro of Paris, and Dr. Kitabatake of Berlin. The school remained in operation until August 1939, three weeks before the outbreak of World War II. Also in 1932, Rhode originated the German Judo Ring (DJR).

An international judo championship between England, Switzerland, and Germany, at which Frankfurt was the victor, was conducted in 1935. By 1939, there were forty-four instructional books published on the subject of jujutsu.

From 1945-48, judo practice was prohibited by the Allied occupation. Following the ban, from 1948-56, small martial arts groups formed in Germany. In 1953, Ilse Brief became the first woman in Germany to earn shodan (1st-degree black belt) rank. The year also marked the founding of the German Judo Bundes (DJB), in Hamburg. By 1957, the organization had 10,500 members. In 1964 Germany participated in the first Olympic judo. One year later, the DJB had more than 30,000 members; its chief instructors, in succession, have been: Han So Han (1964-66), Yutaka Toyama (1966-73), and Yasuwasa Kaneda (1973-   ).

Kendo was transmitted to Germany in 1966 by Gerd Wischnewski, holder of black belts in judo, karate, aikido, and kendo. Also that year, the German national team won the European Judo Championships in Rome, and Peter Hermann won the middleweight title. Aikido arrived in Germany in 1968.

In 1970, at its annual convention, the DJB lifted its ban on women's free-sparring in judo. In May of that year, Klaus Glahn won a gold medal and Engelbert Doerbandt a bronze at the European Judo Championships. The inaugural European Karate Championships were conducted in Hamburg.

In 1971, the World Judo Championships were held in Ludwigshafen. Later, the Sportordnung Tae Kwon Do (SOT) was founded, an organization that regulates and administers tae kwon do, along with the European Tae Kwon Do Union (ETU), in West Berlin.

In 1969, a kendo section had been added to the DJB: Eberhard Riemann, a study of Wischnewski, was named president. the first kendo competition was conducted on October 9, 1971, in Wiesbaden, between Berlin/Hamburg and Wiesbaden/Mannheim. The latter won by a narrow margin.

Aikido was introduced in Germany in 1951 by Eugen Holzel, a German judo pioneer and the country's first judo champion. Holzel was asked by Christian Koch, head of the prison administration for the city of Hamburg, to establish self-defense methods for the protection of his staff. Holzel then attended the first officially organized teaching session for aikido in Europe, at the International Judo Summer Session in Neuchatel, Switzerland, given by **Minoru Mochizuki.** Holzel eventually became Mochizuki's best student.

In 1956, Holzel traveled to southern France for further instruction from M. Nakazone, who, like Mohizuki, had studied under **Morihei Uyeshiba.** Upon Holzel's return to nothern Germany, he began teaching aikido to prison employees, and later, at the University of Hamburg, and a number of other cities including Kiel, Einbeck, Elmshorn, Bremen, and Hanover. Holzel's wife, also an aikido black belt, taught the art to women.

By 1966, aikido had come under the auspices of the DJB and had about 750 active students throughout Germany. Several Japanese instructors had also been dispatched from the **Aikikai** in Tokyo to teach the art in Germany.

Kyudo was introduced in 1969 at the Heki School in Hamburg, and has been a DJB member since 1974. Prof. Genshiro Inagaki is responsible for its growth. In 1976 Karl Bockstahler co-founded *Karate Revue,* Germany's leading martial arts magazine.

HUNGARY

In the early 1900s a Japanese judo instructor, Kisisaburo, came to Hungary at the invitation of Miklos Seemere and instructed about sixty students at the BEAC Sports Club. The students tired of instruction quickly, and at the end of three months only four remained.

The first sustained judo instruction was given by Tibor Vince beginning in 1928. In 1931 the first judo club was formed; among the first competitors were Vorosmartly, Vince, Tallian, Ravdics, and Dr. Saary. They achieved a draw in 1933 against an Austrian team. In 1938, at a national black belt ranking held in Frankfurt, Germany, two Hungarians were present, Vince, who received his 2nd dan, and John Purman who received his 1st dan.

After World War II Vince and Purman continued to teach judo at a gym on Domonkos Street in Budapest. These and other groups eventually united to form the Electricians Sports Federation Judo Club; in 1950 Purman became its coach. After 1946 a number of sports organizations began to teach judo. By 1950 the first national grading was held, and at the end of the year the first invitational tournament was conducted in Budapest.

The National Judo Federation was established in 1952. On November 16, 1952, the Bastya Sportsclub of Budapest sponsored at the police academy the first national competition for individuals as well as teams. In 1956 the Judo Federation formed the first national team, unsuccessfully competing against Czechoslovakia. Hungarian teams had little success until 1958, when a few Hungarians managed victories at the first European University Championships.

In 1958 the Hungarian Judo Federation became a member of the European Judo Union, and the Hungarian team competed at the 1959 European Championships. As judo in Hungary continued to grow, the caliber of competitors improved; in 1961 a Hungarian judoka, John Kovacs, won the silver medal at the Milano Junior

Championships. At the 1962 European Championships, Thomas David finished third in the 1st dan division.

At the Berlin Junior Championships in 1964, Laslo Nadas took the bronze medal. In 1966 the **Kodokan** sent one of its top judo men, Toshio Daigo, to instruct and lecture. A little more than two months after Daigo's departure, the Hungarian national coach, Akos Kovacs, and four team members, Antol Bodor, Benjamin Farago, John Kovacs, and Miklos Nagy, were killed in a plane crash while en route to a competition in Prague.

In the summer of 1968 the Japanese national team paid a visit to Hungary and put on demonstrations. Since then, a number of top ranking Japanese instructors have visited the country, helping Hungarian judo competitors to reach international level.

At the 1971 European Championships, Ferenc Szabo won a bronze medal in the 63-kg. division; he won the silver in 1977. In the 1972 European Championships, Laszlo Ipacs placed third in the 80 kg division, and at the 1972 Munich Olympics, Antal Heteny placed fifth in the 70-kg division. At the 1976 Montreal Olympics, Jossef Tuncsik won the bronze medal in the 63-kg. division.

The 1978 European Championships at Helsinki were something of a triumph for Hungarian judo; Tuncsik took the bronze in the 65-kg. division, Karoly Molnar the bronze in the 71-kg. division, and Imre Varga the bronze in the 95-kg. division. Varga repeated as a silver medalist at the 1980 European Championships. At the 1980 Olympics in Moscow, Tibor Kincses placed third in the 60-kg. division and Anras Ozsvar third in the open category. *See also* Europe, history of judo in.

IRELAND

Judo was first practiced in Ireland in 1952, when a Dublin man, who had reached the rank of yellow belt in England, established a club near Phoenix Park. Because it was situated in the attic of a small garage it came to be called the Loft. A class of about a dozen people practiced there, and soon a black belt was brought over from England to grade the members. During this embryonic stage the British Judo Association (BJA) regularly sent instructors and examiners to Dublin.

In 1956 a second club was formed, on the other side of Dublin, and friendly competition commenced between the two. In 1957 the Loft moved to much larger premises, renamed Dublin Judo Club, and began in earnest to promote judo in Ireland. Over the next five years, clubs opened in Cork, Limerick, Galway, Belfast, and Londonderry, and in 1962 the first Dublin practitioner, S. Kavanagh, earned his black belt.

The Irish Judo Association (IJA) was formed in 1963 as the national governing body; it joined the **EJU** and **IJF.** The IJA is exclusively an amateur organization; there are no paid administrators.

In 1964, when judo was admitted to the Olympics, Ireland was represented in Tokyo by one man, John Ryan, a Sligo-born black belt living in London. Ryan fought to the quarter-finals in the middleweight division, losing to Ted Boronoskis of Australia. Since then, Ireland has competed nearly every year, either in the European Championships, the World Championships, or in various international opens. In the 1972 Olympic Games, Ireland was represented by a full five-man team.

There are approximately 65 judo clubs in Ireland today, affiliated with the IJA, and 35 more in Northern Ireland affiliated with the BJA. Approximately 10,000 people practice judo in Ireland—female players number about 35 percent—and there are an estimated 120 black belts in the country. (John Conway)

POLAND

Judo in Poland really began when Adam Nidzgorski, a judo student, returned to Poland after the war and began to teach judo at the Academy of Physical Education in Warsaw. Judo clubs opened thereafter in various parts of the country, including Krakow, Wroclaw, and Gdansk.

The Polish Judo Association was founded in 1957; the first Polish Individual Judo Championships were held in the same year. In 1958, there were only eight clubs, with approximately 100 judoka, but by 1964 there were 32 clubs, with almost 1,700 members. In 1959 two Polish judoka, Kazimierz Jaremczak and Ryszard Zieniawa, took part in the European Judo Championships. Not until 1963, when Jan Okroj won a silver medal, did Polish competitors register a major success.

Since 1977, judo has developed in Poland due partially to top notch Japanese judoka such as Hiromi Tomita, Masao Watanabe, Mahito Ogho, and Saburo Matsushita, who have visited and contributed a great deal of their technical experience. The Polish judoka picked up quickly the best example of Japanese skill and flexibility, and also adopted the power techniques of Russian judoka. With these two systems they trained in a style that fitted their constitution and mentality. Waldeman Sikorsky was made national team coach in 1967.

Since 1968 Polish competitors have brought home medals from each of the European Championships, as well as from the World Championships and the Olympic Games. The bronze medal at the 1971 World Championships went to **Antoni Zajkowski,** who a year later placed second in the lightweight division at the Olympics. **Antoni Reiter** was third at the 1973 World Championships as a middleweight; **Adam Adamczyk** placed third at the 1975 World Championships in Vienna. A year later Marian Talaj won a bronze medal in the Montreal Olympics. **Janus Pawloski** took bronze medals at the 1979 World Championships and 1980 Olympics. (Waldemar Sikorski) See also Europe, history of judo in.

SWEDEN

Judo and budo: Martial arts in Sweden have certainly existed, in a small way, since the 1920s, but not until the late 1940s was judo at all known, chiefly through the efforts of the late Viking Cronholm and Maj. Einar Thunander.

In a way, one can say that judo really came to sweden in a basement; the man who brought it was Bruno Adler. Born in Vienna, Adler learned his jujutsu in the front lines, in Beirut during the so-called religious wars between Christians and Moslems. He arrived in Stockholm in 1951 and practiced with Prof. C. Marten at a school called the Swedish Jujutsu Institute.

In 1956, 14 people who had read a newspaper article about judo

Sweden's top judo competitor, Ann Lof.

that Adler had written showed up for Sweden's first organized judo—in a basement belonging to a well-known tradesman of oriental carpets. Adler soon rented a studio and founded the first dojo in Sweden, the Hie Gou.

In 1957, a Dutchman, the late Gerhard Gosen, founded a school, the Stockholm Judo and Jujutsu club, in which he introduced to Sweden other budo arts, including aikido, karate, and **t'ai-chi-ch'uan.** His students, Attila Meszaros, popularized **kyokushinkai** karate around the country. Another, Zsolt Gyorobiro, who lived in Japan for two years and received a 5th dan in **shorinji kempo,** introduced that art to the Swedes. Johnny Grimstal, who currently has the largest karate studio in Stockholm also emerged from Gosen's school.

The first federation, the Swedish Judo Federation, came into being in 1964. During the following years many new budo forms entered the federation, and the name was changed in 1969 to the Swedish Budo Federation; the arts of judo, karate-do, aikido, kendo and jujutsu are represented. There are about 23,000 students practicing the arts, divided as follows: judo, 52 percent; karate, 32 percent; jujutsu, 10 percent; aikido, 5 percent; kendo, 0.5 percent. Non-Japanese sports in the federation include kung-fu and tae

kwon do; some others have been refused membership, such as **full-contact** karate and **Thai boxing.** Some arts have chosen not to enter the federation—**ninjutsu,** jushin-jutsu, and jujutsu-Durewall system, to name a few.

Among noted Swedish competitors are S.A. "Sassa" Alsen, Lars Holm, Rolf Johansson, Bo Holm, Ton Geels, Larry Edgren, and Istvan Hambalek. But the most memorable is Ann Lof. Born in 1959, she began practice at the age of 10. In international competition she has won 11 gold, 5 silver, and 6 bronze medals; she dominated national competition, winning 80 gold and 5 silver medals. She took one memorable Swedish championship—three matches—in 56 effective seconds.

Lennart and Solveig Malmqvist, black belts in judo and leaders in one of the biggest judo schools in Sweden, Sodra Judoklubben, teach a special judo for blind children called Tomteboda.

Karate: Gosen's club, of course, was the starting place for karate in Sweden. Of his students, previously mentioned, Zsolt Gyorbiro and especially Attila Mezsaros were most active in broadening Swedish karate. Mezsaros, born in 1940, had found judo not entirely satisfying. In Stockholm, around 1962, he first encountered karate. Enthusiastically he pursued the subject across Europe, receiving

his 1st kyu from **Jon Bluming** in Amsterdam, his 1st and 2nd dan from Steve Arneil in London, and 3rd dan, signed by **Mas Oyama,** again from Bluming. Between excursions he opened Sweden's first karate dojo, the Gothenburgs Karate Kai, in 1964.

Two years after Mezsaros started the club in Gothenburg another kyokushinkai club, the Oyama Karate Kai, was opened in Stockholm by an immigrant from New Zealand, Marshall Macdonagh. In 1970, the Stockholm Karate Kai was founded by Johnny Grimstol, another Gosen student and a convert from the **Shito-ryu** style. The Stockholm Karate Kai has more than 4,000 members. Chief instructor is the well-known Englishman, **Brian Fitkin.** Kyokushinkai remains the most popular of styles practiced in Sweden, with **Shotokan** a close second.

Ninjutsu: Togakure ryu ninjutsu first became known to the Swedish in 1975. Bo Munthe, who had studied the martial arts since 1960, read a book by **Andrew Adams,** *Ninja, the Invisible Assassins,* and one called *Stick Fighting,* by **Masaaki Hatsumi** and Quinton Chambers. He wrote to the publishers of *Stick Fighting* and through them contacted Hatsumi. In 1976 Munthe went to Japan to practice at Hatsumi's dojo in Noda; he graduated 1st dan in Togakure ryu ninjutsu.

Although ninjutsu in Sweden is growing, it has left the Swedish Budo Federation, preferring to follow the rules of bujinkan, made up by Hatsumi. The practical problem in Sweden with arts outside of the federation is that they tend to be small. Perhaps the problem is more inside the federation, since it cannot control those who enjoy practicing the **nunchaku,** which is prohibited by law, as well as other popular martial arts weapons.

Jujutsu: Modern jujutsu dates from 1970, when the present chief instructor, Hans Greger, was commissioned to organize and coordinate a jujutsu system for Sweden. At the same time, jujutsu joined the Swedish Budo Federation. From 1970 to 1981, Swedish jujutsu enrollment has increased to about 3,000 practitioners divided into 40 clubs. In 1978 Sweden took part in founding the European Jujutsu Federation (EJP) in which Greger, now 4th dan, presides over the technical committee. Several European championships have already taken place and participation in competitions is steadily increasing.

Hans Greger was born in 1945 and began judo instruction in 1964. He continued with jujutsu from 1967 both in Sweden and Europe. He has been Chairman in the jujutsu section of the Swedish Budo Federation since 1973, Chairman in the budo club Budokwai's jujutsu section since 1970. National instructor on jujutsu in Sweden since 1970. He also holds the rank of 4th dan in jujutsu since 1978.

Jujutsu, Durewall system: Kurt Durewall, trained in jujutsu since 1940, began in the late 1950s to devise a less brutal, "softer" form of the art. The resulting style was brought in 1966 into the Swedish Budo Federation, where he worked as chief instructor in self-defense. He left this organization in 1970, however, to devote more time to his own system. His softer jujutsu was the platform for the founding of a new group, the Swedish Jujutsu Federation, in 1971.

Judo entered the SJF as an exercise sport, now called SJF-judo, with the guidance of Mahito Ogho, 5th dan. Activity in the SJF is based on the theory that violence must be dealt with by non-violence. Special programs are offered for the needs of various professions—lifting techniques, self-defense, dealing with conflict situations. Prison guards, policemen, hospital workers, and others learn useful skills.

Aikido: In 1963 Gerhard Gosen invited the Japanese aikido instructor M. Noro to Stockholm for a week-long seminar. One of those in attendance was Jan Beime, who became interested enough to journey to France and study with masters M. Nakazono and N. Tamura. Upon his return to Sweden he started his own dojo, the Stockholm Aiki Kai. In 1966 Beime invited instructor T. Ichimura from Japan; Ichimura is still teaching in Sweden as well as in Finland, Denmark, and Poland. T. Tomita, another Japanese aikido instructor, arrived in 1969; he now has his dojos in Stockholm and Denmark. In 1981, about 1,200 students practiced aikido in Sweden.

Shorinji kempo karate-do: Zsolt Gyorbiro, a Hungarian refugee living in Sweden, traveled to Japan, where he had the good fortune to study **shorinji kempo** for two years under Isamu Tamutsu, 10th dan, and **hanshi** Kasuo Akai, 8th dan. He and fellow student Andre Sollier wrote the book, *Japanese Archery—Zen in Action.* In 1965, having earned his 5th dan, he returned to Sweden. With Lars Ryhammar in 1969 he founded a karate section in Ryhammar's jujutso club in

Katrineholm. There are now about six or seven clubs in Sweden. Gyorbiro is the head of the art in Europe, organized as the International Shorinji-ryu Karate-do Federation.

Thai boxing: Christer Bergenhall, an attorney working in the suburbs of Stockholm, began western-style boxing in 1967. By 1975 he was studying shorinji kempo under Zsolt Gyorbiro. During a visit to Thailand in 1977 he first observed Thai boxing. He began to practice and at the end of 1980 returned to Thailand to enter competition, in the course of which he became the first European to knock out a native Thai boxer.

Tae kwon do: Tae kwon do was introduced to Sweden in 1974 by instructor Lee Joo Suh, a 5th dan from Korea. The style's high flying, spectacular kicking techniques quickly aroused interest. Though tae kwon do entered a slump with the eventual departure of Suh, the arrival of Korean instructor Lim Won Sup, 6th dan, revived the sport. The Swedish team and individual practitioners compete internationally under his guidance. Currently there are a couple of Swedish clubs, which meet every year in competition.

Ju shin jutsu ryu: This style of self-defense, developed in Sweden beginning in 1972, was evolved to accord with the culture and laws of Sweden. A soft technique, practitioners are taught to meet attacks with a minimum use of force. Students must become knowledgeable in physiology, to appreciate the bodily effects of various techniques; in psychology, to read through body language and other clues of aggressive levels and intent; and in Swedish law, to know the limits of response permissible. Ju shin jutsu attempts to retain the oriental philosophy and original thoughts of budo within its higher ranks. The name means "school of physical and psychological defense." Georg Irenius is credited as the principal designer of the art.

Wu shu: **Wu shu** was unknown in Sweden until 1975, although a few Chinese did instruct, often in the cellars of Chinese restaurants. In Stockholm, Taiwanese **sifu** Louis Lin opened the first club in 1975. In six years the number of students grew from 30 to over 2,000 in Stockholm alone. Additional clubs were formed in Upsala, Skovde, Karlsborg, Jonkoping, and Norrkoping. The style taught in these clubs is Shao-lin wu shin ch'uan (Shao-lin five animal). The Swedish Wu shu Federation was established in 1978; besides Lin, also hand-to-hand combat instructor for the Swedish marines, participating in the federation's founding were Dr. William Dockens III, proficient in western boxing, hsun na, and t'ai-chi-ch'uan; Lim Yoo-Jik; and Dr. Tien Lung. Sweden has two delegates in the European Kung-Fu Unions, founded in Paris in 1980.

Kendo: As far as is known, kendo was practiced in Sweden for the first time in 1963 in the new Stockholm Kendoclub; the instructors were Robert von Sandor and his guest **Roald M. Knudsen,** England's leading kendoka. In 1969 the European Kendo Federation was founded by Sandor and Knudsen. Sweden joined the International Kendo Federation (IKF) at its inception in 1970 during the World Championships in Tokyo; Sandor was elected vice-president.

Kendo is practiced in 11 clubs in which the membership, as of 1981, has never exceeded 200 people. Lack of instructors has been a problem, but lengthy visits by such well-known teachers as Akio Watanabe and Zen-Ken-Runs have kept the sport alive. The policy for the kendo section in the Swedish Budo Federation has been to concentrate on quality for its smaller membership. Allied with kendo in the federation have been related arts, such as **iaido, naginata,** and **kyudo.** (Bo MUNTHE)

YUGOSLAVIA

The Japanese martial arts were introduced to Yugoslavia in the beginning of the 20th century by seamen who had visited the Far East and by several police officers trained in jujutsu. Though chiefly self-defense based on judo and jujutsu, some elements of Chinese boxing were also taught. Until 1950, however, martial arts were not popular.

No schools emerged until 1951, when the first judo dojo was established in Zagreb, then in 1952 in Belgrade and Ljubljana. Judo flourished on a relatively small scale until some judoka came into contact with karate, witnessing demonstrations in several European countries during the late 1950s, as well as through the release of several popular books, especially **Mas Oyama's** *What is Karate?*

When Vietnamese karateka Trin Tam Tam came to Zagreb from Paris in 1960, he visited the Mladost Judo Club and found several members practicing the rudiments of karate. He remained for several months, teaching a handful of judoka, but only **Zarko Modric** continued to teach the new art when Tam left Yugoslavia.

At the same time, when a Belgrade student, Dorde Duricic, was sent to Switzerland to mend an injured arm, his doctors recommended karate as a suitable exercise. Duricic learned the art, and upon his return to Belgrade in 1961, he began to teach it.

Two distinct groups formed in Zagreb and Belgrade, both of which united in 1964 to invite Japanese **Shotokan** instructor **Tetsuji Murakami** to teach in Yugoslavia. Murakami laid the foundation for karate in this country, and his pupils subsequently spread the art throughout Yugoslavia. His foremost disciples were Modric, Dr. Emin Topic, Zeljko Iljadica, and Nikola Pecko—all from Zagreb—and Duricic, Vojislav Bilbija, and brothers Ilija and Vladimir Jorga of Belgrade.

The Jorga brothers maintained traditional Shotokan policies and linked themselves with the **JKA.** Topic established budokai, an independent Yugoslav style of martial arts based on karate and Chinese boxing and which incorporated some of the country's ancient weapons. Iljadica, with another ex-judoka, Slavko Truntic, started teaching pure Chinese boxing. Pecko turned to Korean tae kwon do with Mikola Podhraski. And Modric integrated several Japanese systems including Shotokan, **Shito-ryu, kyokushinkai,** and **sankukai,** before he introduced **full-contact karate** in the mid-1970s.

Almost every major Japanese, Korean, or Chinese style today has at least a token number of practitioners, but the majority of the country's 20,000 karateka belong to two groups. In the eastern part of Yugoslavia (Serbia, Montenegro, Bosnia, Herzegovina, and Macedonia), traditional JKA Shotokan combined with some **wado-ryu** is the dominant karate style. While in the western part (Croatia and Slovenia), Topic's budokai system, with some Shotokan and **shukokai** influence, is the most popular. More than 70 percent of all Yugoslav karateka belong to these styles. Tae kwon do is popular only in Croatia, while Chinese boxing is limited to several small groups.

Yugoslavia was one of the nine countries represented in the inaugural **PKA** World Professional Karate Championships of 1974 in Los Angeles, the event at which **full-contact** karate was conceived. By virtue of winning a European elimination, two Yugoslavians were among the 14 fighters who vied for the four original world titles. Both, however, were defeated in the first elimination round.

Full-contact karate is organized in Croatia and Slovenia, but in other parts of Yugoslavia only a handful of fighters emerged by the late 1970s.

The first official body was formed in 1967 within the framework of the Yugoslav Judo Federation. But in 1969 karatemen split from this judo-controlled organization and formed the Yugoslav Karate Federation (YKF). Receiving the support of the Union of Sports Organizations of Yugoslavia, this body joined the powerful **European Karate Union** (EKU) and began participating in international contests. During the late 1960s, the nation was ranked third in European karate.

A series of conflicts forced the EKU to oust the Yugoslav Karate Federation; it promptly joined the Shotokan group connected with the JKA and, later, the newly formed **International Amateur Karate Federation** (IAKF). The official YKF is today an affiliated member of the IAKF, while the budokai group, which is developing full-contact karate, joined the World All-Styles Karate Organization (WAKO), headquartered in West Berlin.

Karate in Yugoslavia enjoys popularity as a sport, but most of the 1,000 dojo are very small. All are non-profit organizations subsidized by local youth or sports organizations. Only a few dojo have permanent facilities, while the majority rent school physical education halls on a several-hours-per-week basis. Only a handful of instructors are paid, and then only a small fee.

While traditional karate is supported by state and local sports organizations, full-contact is frowned upon. Occasionally the authorities have banned full-contact contests. All full-contact fighters are amateurs, except for a few who went abroad to seek professional careers—with little or no success. Most Yugoslav fighters, traditional and full-contact, are of large build and have therefore developed a powerful, aggressive fighting style. (Zarko Modric) *See also* Europe, history of karate in.

SOUTH AFRICA

The first known karate instructor was **Stan Schmidt**, who had learned **Shotokan** karate in Tokyo and returned to South Africa to begin teaching in 1963. At that time, fewer than 100 South Africans were studying karate. By the beginning of 1976 there were five or six major styles practiced, led by Schmidt's Shotokan headquartered in Johannesburg, **shukokai** and **wado-ryu** in Durban, and **kyokushinkai** in Cape Town. Each style is affiliated with the National Amateur Karate Association (NAKA) of South Africa the country's only officially recognized body. The NAKA is composed of an administrative and executive committee with eight members, all of whom are 4th dan and above and have trained in Japan. Each is in charge of a province.

Each style conducts its own provincial and national tournaments each year, and the NAKA promotes an annual national tournament to choose the South African champion. The NAKA also encourages teams to travel to and from South Africa. Various resolutions boycotting South Africa on racial grounds have over the years hindered karate's full development. However, black instructors do teach if they are qualified, and black students practice karate in their own areas for geographical, not political reasons. In 1973, an Italian team came to South Africa to enter a multiracial tournament which was part of the South African Games.

South Africa has hosted many karate dignitaries over the years, especially Shotokan masters. The first to arrive was **Taiji Kase** in 1964, who returned in 1965 accompanied by **Keinosuke Enoeda**, **Hirokazu Kanazawa**, and Hiroshi Shirai. In 1974, **Masatoshi Nakayama** conducted a special instructor's seminar. By 1976, there were approximately 8,000 Shotokan practitioners, 350 of whom were black belts.

NEW ZEALAND

George Grundy and his son Keith, members of the London **Budokwai,** emigrated to New Zealand in 1948 and formed the Judokai NZ Judo Club in Auckland. They were joined soon after by Alf Morton, also of the Budokwai. Immigrant judoka of the early 1950s include Feiko Sjoerds, Simon Tump, Peter Roovers, and Hans Bontje from Holland; and Des Tarring, Pat Toner, Len Wood, and Rita Johnson from England. Servicemen returning from occupation duty in Japan, such as Eric Cresswell and Lawrie Hargrave, had studied judo in its homeland; Hargrave had been a student of **Kodokan** sensei Ogata, 9th dan. In 1956, with nine clubs throughout New Zealand, the New Zealand Judo Federation was founded in Lower Hutt, Wellington.

The first international representative was Feiko Sjoerds, who competed in the Goodwill Tournament in Japan in 1958. Since that time the NZJF has been represented at most World Championships and major international events. New Zealand's first National Championships were held in 1957, and the first Oceania Union Championships in 1965. Leading national and international champions have included: Feiko Sjoerds, John Oosterman, David Delay, John Burke, Mick Yarrow, Bruce McCoombe, Gerry van Cuylenborg, Joe Fisher, Garrick Littlewood, Hands van Duyan, Barry Madden, David Clark, Elaine Bryson, Dianne Frame, and Sandra Manderson.

In 1980 the NZJF National Instructors Register listed 200 club instructors. The National Referee's Association includes two IJF referees, ten Continental Union Referees, including Clare Hargrave who became the first Union Woman Referee in 1975, and eighteen National Referees within New Zealand.

From its start in 1956, the NZJF has developed steadily to a membership of 100 judo clubs with 10,000 members. Judo has been introduced into the educational curriculum in many schools, largely through the efforts of former English judoka, Ivan Willis. The annual National Championships attract over 500 competitors. In addition, there are regular tournaments at Island level and within each of the eight affiliated member associations that make up the NZJF. International contact may be made through the president: Lawrie Hargrave, 145 Calliope Road, Stanley Bay, Auckland 9, New Zealand.

Stan Schmidt (*center*) is one of the highest ranking non-Japanese Shotokan practitioners in the world. He heads Shotokan karate in South Africa. On his left and right are two leading Japanese karate champions, Oishi (*left*) and Iida (*right*).

Twice Olympic medalist David Starbrook (*left*) and Tony MacConnel.

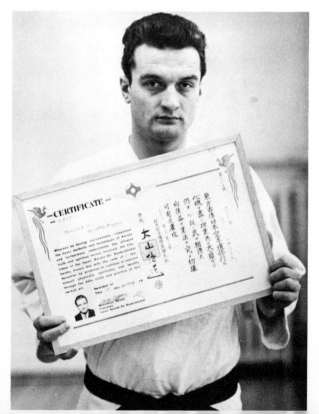

Hungarian-born Attila Meszaros brought Kyukoshinkai to Sweden. He's seen here with his 3rd dan certificate from Mas Oyama.

U.S.

JUDO

The first known meeting of **Kodokan** judo and any American occurred in 1879, when President U.S. Grant was in Japan on a state visit and observed a demonstration of judo techniques by 19-year-old **Jigoro Kano.** The official date given for the start of kodokan judo is 1882, and most likely Kano did not explain his Kodokan Judo then but may have lectured on his study of jujutsu. In any case, President Grant was exposed to the judo master at a very fertile and productive period in pre-Kodokan judo's history.

The next contact came in 1889, when Kano lectured on the educational values of judo before a group of foreign dignitaries. There were several Americans present but this contact had no discernible result.

The first American to study seriously at the Kodokan was Prof. Ladd from Yale University. Ladd came to the Kodokan sometime during 1889, ten years after Kano's demonstration for President Grant. Ladd studied **nage** (throwing), **katame** (mat work), **atemi-waza** (striking techniques), and **koshiki-no-kata** (self-defense forms).

The number of Americans at the Kodokan did not rise immediately after Ladd's visit. By 1908, the Kodokan had a total of 13 American members studying in Japan. During 1919 Prof. John Dewey of Columbia University went to the Kodokan to observe a demonstration. Dewey discussed Kodokan judo with Kano and may have been instrumental in the beginning of a pioneering judo program at Columbia University.

Yoshiaki Yamashita, then 6th dan, was the first person to teach judo in the U.S. He arrived in 1902 at the invitation of Mr. Graham Hill, director of the Great Northern Railroad. Hill contacted a Mr. Fujiya, who contacted Mr. Shibata, who was a student of Prof. Yamashita, concerning Yamashita's coming to the U.S. to teach his children judo. After Yamashita arrived, the Hill family decided that judo was much too dangerous for their children. Mr. Hill arranged for judo demonstrations in New York and Chicago. He also tried to arrange for Harvard University to hire Yamashita as a judo teacher.

At the same time, Sen. Lee's wife and Mrs. Wadsworth started taking judo lessons from Yamashita. They had the sixth floor of a building covered with tatami mats. The women mostly practiced **nage-no-kata.** These few women started the first judo class in the country. A men's judo group made up from various embassies in the area appeared. Thus judo traveled in prominent circles in its embryonic stage in America. For lack of wider participation this judo mission died out with Yamashita's return to Japan in 1907.

Mrs. Wadsworth was a fine horsewoman and went to the same country club as did President Theodore Roosevelt. She mentioned to the president that Yamashita was teaching judo and that Roosevelt might be interested in the art. Yamashita was subsequently invited to Washington to give a demonstration at the White House. There was a contest with a wrestler by the name of John Graft, who was the coach at the U.S. Naval Academy and who was teaching President

George Harris, one of America's top judo competitors, practices with M. Tajika at the Kodokan.

The first ever U.S. judo team immediately following the 1964 Olympics trials at the New York World's Fair. *Left to right:* Paul Maruyama, Jim Bregman, George Harris, Ben Campbell. Courtesy of Paul Marayuma

Roosevelt wrestling. Although Yamashita threw him time after time, Graft continued to get up. Finally, Yamashita decided that he would do mat work with Graft, since there seemed to be no end to the match. In the mat work, Yamashita got an arm lock on Graft, but the wrestler would not give up. Yamashita kept up the pressure until Graft groaned as his arm came close to breaking. President Roosevelt was impressed and took judo lessons. After leaving office, he kept mats in his home. Roosevelt studied judo for about a year, earning a brown belt in the process. Through the help of the president, Yamashita taught judo at the Naval Academy. In 1935, Yamashita was promoted to 10th dan, the first person to hold that rank. He died later that year.

Pacific Northwest In 1903, one year after Yamashita's arrival in America, Shumeshiro Tomita journeyed to the U.S. He was the first person to sign the rolls of the Kodokan; he was instrumental in establishing judo in the U.S. as well as in Japan. Tomita stayed in the U.S. for seven years and taught judo at Princeton and Columbia Universities. After the arrival of Tomita and Yamashita, many judo instructors came to America. Among the very first were Miada Kousen, Sataki Nobushitam, and Ito Takugoro. Judo in the U.S. first flourished on the West Coast because of its large Japanese population.

Judo in the Pacific Northwest dates back to the beginning of the century, when judo was practiced in small, scattered clubs. The first dojo was opened in the Seattle area by a judoka named Kano in 1903, but this club closed after only a few months. Prof. Takugoro Ito, then 4th dan, arrived in America in 1907 and opened the Seattle Dojo.

Ito, like many other early judoka, was a wrestler. He held challenge matches, in which he was unbeatable. After several years he left the Seattle area, traveling to South America. Eisei Media, Akitoro Ono, Satake, and Matsuura traveled with him, touring South America as professional wrestlers, and returned to San Francisco in 1914. (Eisei Media stayed in Brazil and the Brazillian government gave him a quarter-million acres near the Amazon for his wrestling feats.)

In the 1920s, there were two dojos in the state of Washington, the Seattle Dojo and the Tacoma Dojo, operated mainly by yudansha of the respective communities, businessmen, farmers, and laborers. Yoshida sensei of Tacoma, then 3rd dan, was the best judo player. He was employed as a laborer in a sawmill. The other black belts were 1st and 2nd dans. Factions within the Seattle Dojo had difficulty working together. It is not known what the exact problem was but, around 1930, some members of the Seattle Dojo withdrew and formed their own Tentokukan Dojo. Each club hired teachers from Japan. Among the Seattle Dojo's teachers in the 1920s and early 1930s were senseis: Miyazawa, Shibata, Kaimon Kudo, and Suzuki.

Before Wrold War II, three main styles of judo were prominent in North America. The Budokan style and the Kodokan style predominated in the U.S. In Canada the Kito-ryu was strong, especially in Vancouver, B.C. The Seattle Judo Black Belt Association was organized around 1935 by Kumagai and Sakata senseis, tending to unite the two rival American factions. The two instructors were also responsible for organizing the bi-annual 24-man team contests with the Nanka (southern California) team. Southern California and the Northwest had the strongest judo groups at that time.

After World War II, the Tentokukan Dojo was not re-activated because the former membership was spread around the country. This closed out a pioneering judo effort on the West Coast. The Seattle Dojo owned their building and were able to continue with practice after the war.

The Washington team competed against the Vancouver B.C. team annually, against sailors from the visiting Japanese training ships, and occasionally with college teams from Japan. Eventually, nisei yudansha were hired when dojos were opened in Spokane, Yakima Valley, Eatonville, and cities in Oregon and Idaho. In the late 1930s, some dojos existed in the state of Washington, and each sponsored an annual tournament.

Judo in the Tacoma, Washington, area was started by Prof. Iwakiri, who was born in Japan, and who came here in 1912. Iwakiri exhibited such skill that he received his 1st dan from Prof. Kano at the age of 13. The Fife-Tacoma Dojo was originally formed as the St. Regis Dojo and was located in the St. Regis lumberyard sawdust pit. (The dojo was later moved from the lumberyard to the corner of 17th and Market Streets). Prof. Kano made two trips to the Fife-Tacoma dojo, in 1932 and 1938, in recognition of its outstanding achievements. In 1932 he presented the dojo a scroll and in 1938 another was given

to the yudanshakai. In the 1938 scroll Kano wrote "return to the source," and the ambiguity of his phrase still causes debate. Most opinion holds that the statement refers to Zen training.

Rev. Yukawa was the first yudanshakai president and served the Fife-Tacoma, Washington area from 1924 to 1925. After Rev. Yukawa, Prof. Iwakiri served as president from 1940 to 1958.

Before World War II, there were six dojos in the state of Oregon: Shudo-Kan Dojo, Obukan Dojo, Salem Judo Club, Milwaukee Dojo, G. T. Dojo, and the Shobukan Dojo. The Shobukan Dojo was the first, and was organized under Mits Nikata, then a 2nd dan. Prof. Kano visited the Portland area in 1932; during this visit he took the occasion to rename the Portland Dojo the Obukan Dojo. Some of the pioneering judo specialists in the Portland area were Mr. Nishizim of the Kito-ryu; Mr. Kobayashi of the Kito-ryu; Mr. Sakano Ichiro, 3rd dan from the Kodokan; Mr. Sazaki Ojiro, 2nd dan from the Kodokan; and Mr. Tomori, 2nd dan from the Kokodan.

After World War II, Buddy Ikata gathered together some of the people who knew judo and got the Portland-Obukan Dojo going again. The Obukan was re-established in 1952. Rev. Homma, a Buddhist priest, started judo at the YMCA and the YWCA. The Guiki Dojo started practice again in the spring of 1953 under Mr. Kato and Mr. Hamado, both 2nd dans, and Rev. Homma and Nakata, 3rd dans. March 3, 1960, was the 42nd anniversary of the Obukan Dojo.

Hawaii During the era of Japanese immigration to Hawaii, in the late 1800s and the early 1900s, many Japanese immigrants trained in the art of Kodokan judo arrived. The first judo club in Hawaii, the Shunyo-Kan, was formed on March 17, 1909, by Shigemi Teshima and Naomatsu Kaneshige. Consul-General Isami Shishido, 7th dan, joined the club in 1919 and served as chairman of the club's board of directors for many years.

The Shobu Kan judo club was founded by Yajiro Kitayama, Nakajiro Mino, and others. Its first dojo site was the basement of the Ono Bakery on Beretania Street, followed by several locations in Honolulu, until it was moved to its present location on Kunawai Lane in the Liliha area.

Other clubs were subsequently established, and in 1929, three of the major judo clubs, Shunyo Kan, Shobu Kan, and Hawaii Chuugakko (junior high school) initiated an effort to organize judo in the territory of Hawaii. The organization hoped to demonstrate a united effort to the community and to be recognized as an instrument through which the social and cultural significance of this martial art would be transmitted and perpetuated. Organized judo grew rapidly under the supervision of this body, the Hawaii Judo Kyokai. In 1925, the Kodokan issued the first certificates for black belts to judoka in Hawaii. In 1927, a judo seminar was conducted by a visiting Waseda University judo group, headed by Mr. Makino, 6th dan. By 1932, the Hawaii Judo Association had several active clubs, and received official recognition from Prof. Kano during one of his stopovers in Honolulu. The certificate of recognition, #76, issued by the Kodokan Judo Institute on November 15, 1932, was the first such authorization granted to a yudanshakai outside of Japan.

The Los Angeles Area The story of judo in southern California begins with Prof. Ito. Prof. Yamashita and Tomita were his contemporaries in American judo, but of the three only Ito made a lasting contribution to the development of American judo. Wherever Ito stayed, judo took hold and flourished. In 1915 he moved to Los Angeles and established the Rafu Dojo on the first floor of the Yamato Hall, near Jackson and San Pedro Streets. When Prof. Ito returned to Japan after seven years in Los Angeles, the Rafu Dojo continued under the management of Prof. Seigoro Murakami, Dr. Matsutaro Nitta, and Ryuii Tatsuno. In July 1917, there were still only two dojos in southern California.

The Nanka Judo Yudanshakai was organized in 1928. In 1930, the Kodokan Nanka Judo Yudanshakai was formed and Yasutaro Matsuura, then 4th dan, was elected president. Still only eight dojos and fewer than twenty black belts existed in southern California.

The Kodokan Nanka Judo Yudanshakai was reorganized at the direction of Prof. Jigoro Kano in 1932 while he was visiting the Los Angeles Olympic Games. The yudanshakai was renamed once more, this time the Hokubei Judo Yudanshakai or Southern California Judo Black Belt Association of North America; its presidency to devolve permanently upon the Los Angeles Consul General of Japan. A formal organization of judo occurred as a result of Prof. Kano's visit, and four yudanshakais, or judo black belt associations, were formed: Southern California, Northern California, Seattle, and Hawaii.

When World War II started in Dec. 1941, there were twenty-six dojo in southern California, with 422 black belts and about 2,000 students. The black belts were distributed in the following manner: 6th dan—2; 5th dan—5; 4th dan—6; 3rd dan—42; 2nd dan—101; 1st dan—264; and 2 honorary black belts.

During World War II, judo continued to flourish in relocation camps such as Manzanar, Heart Mountain, Post Gila River, and Rule Lake. Although all other judo clubs ceased operations during the war years, Seinan Dojo kept its doors open. Jack Sirgel, then a 2nd dan, the head instructor, visited the Manzanar Relocation Camp with his students to improve their judo techniques, even though the war was at its peak.

San Diego As the last major port of entry for the Japanese on the west coast of the U.S., the pacific southwest failed to develop the large judo communities characteristic of northern cities. According to oral reports, the only judo club or judo activity in the San Diego area before World War II was begun in 1925, and continued for several years, upstairs in the Taiikuki Hall on 6th and Market Streets. The first instructor, Mikinishake Kawaushi, taught for several years; Mizuzaki Showa, 5th dan, taught for about one year before the organization ceased activities. The only other organized martial arts activity in the San Diego area before World War II was a kendo society located in the buddhist temple at 29th and Market Streets. This organization ceased activities affter outbreak of the war.

Judo activity after World War II comenced in the San Diego area in April 1946 with the opening of classes in the city YMCA by Al C. Holtmann. From 1946-54 much prejudice against the Japanese existed. The promotion of judo in the San Diego area proved difficult during the early post-war years. In 1952, with hostility abating, the general public expressed an interest in Japanese goods, culture, arts, and sports. The San Diego Judo Club joined the Nanka Judo Yudanshakai (Los Angeles) in 1954, at the invitation of Mr. Kenneth Kuniyuki. Under Nanka's jurisdiction much assistance was given the San Diego area in the way of advice, promotions, and technical help. An open invitation to all of Nanka's tournaments was extended also to the San Diego judoka. The Sanshi Judo Club, located in Oceanside, in 1955, taught by Sachio Matsuhara, joined Nanka in 1955. In that year Benso Tsuji, now a 7th dan, became technical director for the San Diego Judo Club. As the highest graded black belt in the area, he brought his technical knowledge to bear on the teaching and promoting of Judo in the community.

Western United States The earliest record of judo being taught in the Denver area is that of Dr. T. Ito. Ito had learned his judo in Hawaii and was teaching in the early 1930s. James Fukumitsu, who had studied judo in Japan, was in the area and teaching judo to put himself through college from 1937-40. Some of the other early area judoka were Bill Ohikuma, Don Tanabe, and Nob Ito.

During World War II, judo activity ceased in the area. In 1944, George Kuramoto left the Amachi Relocation Center and with Fred Okimoto started judo classes in the local gymnasium, in the 20th Street Recreation Building, during 1950. During this time Toro Takematsu, 4th dan, had moved to the Denver area and notice an announcement in the Japanese community paper. Takematsu introduced himself to Geroge Kuramoto and Fred Okimoto. Together, they purchased straw mats and started the original Denver Dojo, located between 19th and 20th Streets and Lawrence, the heart of the Japanese community. As the dojo developed, a larger building was rented and renovated.

During 1954, the Judo Black Belt Federation started to establish local chapters, or yudanshakais. The Rocky Mountain Regional Black Belt Association was recognized as the local governing body.

Intermountain Area The first, post-war judo club in the Salt Lake area was formed in 1950 by Frank Nishimura and George Akimoto. Hot Springs, Utah, had a judo club that was started in 1954 by Mr. Mimya and Mr. Okawa, both 1st dans. Their club was active for about three years. In 1955, Mr. Ichi Isogi started judo in Corinne, Utah. It was later started up again under Mr. Yamasaki. In Ogden, Utah, judo was started in 1956 through the efforts of Mr. Masaichiro Manomoto, 4th, Ted Sakawa, 1st, Tom Kimomoto, 1st dan, and Mr. Yonetani, 1st dan.

Frank Oryu, an old pioneer in the area, started the first Oregon dojo. An older 4th dan by the name of Muramoto, who also worked

for Oryu, helped Oryu organize judo in 1949 and the Ontario Dojo was founded in 1950. The Ontario Dojo had a membership of about twenty black belts.

According to a report from Mas Yamashita, judo in the Caldwell-Boise Valley area started about two years after judo in Ontario, Oregon. Judo experienced a strong growth and was doing well when the first tournament was held in 1952.

Judo in Omaha began during the mid-1950s. Mike Meriweather taught at the YMCA and Dr. Ashida (at 22 one of the youngest 5th-degree black belts) taught at the University in Lincoln. Also, a number of black belts practiced judo at Offutt Air Force Base. Among the better known military judoka were Sgt. Mann, Augie Hauso, Phil Porter, Carl Flood, and La Verne Raab. The military people did not get involved in civilian judo until about 1958. Around 1960, Darrell Darling, Phil Porter, Paul Own, Wally Barber, who was director of the local YMCA, and Mike Manly met at Dr. Ashida's house and decided to form a yudanshakai. They framed a constitution and made contacts with the yudanshakai officers in Chicago and Denver to implement the project. In 1961 the yudanshakai, which covered the greater part of six states, was formed. The first president of the Midwest Judo Association was Dr. Ashida. The second was La Verne Raab. The third, Ike Wakadayashi, had a strong judo program established at Kansas University. The fourth president was Dr. Loren Braught. The fifth and sixth presidents were Bill Stites and Darrell Darling respectively.

The first commercial judo school, the Omaha Judo Academy, was opened by La Verne Raab and Carl Flood after they left the military. Mel Bruno, who later became head of judo for SAC, taught judo at the Omaha YWCA and at the Omaha Athletic Club.

Chicago Judo first arrived in the Chicago area in Sept. 1903, when Mr. Graham Hill arranged for a judo demonstration by Prof. Yamashita in the cities of New York and Chicao. According to Prof. Kotani, in 1916, Heita Okabe, 4th dan; Toshitaka Yamauchi, 4th dan; and Ken Kawabara, 4th dan were teaching judo while studying at the University of Chicago; this would be the earliest organized judo activity in the midwest.

Mr. Harry Auspitz incorporated the first judo club in the Chicago area in 1938, the Jiu Jitsu Institute. Prior to 1939, judo was practiced sporadically by members of the Japanese Counsulate and other interested individuals. The Ju JitŠu Institute became the first Kodokan Judo Club in Chicago, Whie Auspitz opened the dojo, the first instructor was Ralph Mori, who eventually opened his own judo club in 1941. Mori named his dojo the International Judo Club. Mr. Shozo Kuwashima came from New York in 1939 to teach at the institute; he later opened his own dojo. Also in 1941, Mr. Yasushi Tomonari came from New York to teach at the institute. During May of that year, Mr. Masato Tamura, then a 4th dan, came to Chicago from Fife, Washington, and also taught at the institute. With the illness of Mr. Auspitz in 1944, Mr. Tamura became the owner of the Jiu Jitsu Institute.

The Chicago Judo Club was founded by Shozo Kuwashima in 1941. When Kuwashima moved to the West Coast, the Chicago Judo Club was taken over by John Osako and Ruth Gardner.

After World War II, judo in Chicago received numbers of Japanese who were relocating in the midwest section of the country. Vince Tamura came to Chicago and helped out at the Jiu Jitsu Institute. In 1944, Mr. Yoshitaro Sakai moved to the area, and Hiro Iwamoto arrived in 1945 as the relocation camps closed. Hank Okamura relocated close to the Lawson YMCA in 1946 and joined the "Y." Okamura, wrestling at the YMCA, met Kenji Okimoto; and the two men, who discovered they were both judoka, began to practice together. From this start, judo remained at Lawson YMCA for the next twenty years.

The Chicago Judo Black Belt Association was formed during 1947 and a charter was received directly from the Kodokan. (As a recognized judo organization the yudanshakai could promote up to 3rd-degree black belt.) At that time the Chicago Judo Black Belt Association covered the states of Wisconsin, Missouri, Minnesota, Ohio, Indiana, Arkansas, Louisiana, and Michigan. The first constitution for Chicago, a rather informal document, stated that **John Osako** would be president of the association, and the vice-president would be Mas Tamura. There was not much more to the constitution than that. The charter members of the Chicago Judo Black Belt Association were Masato Tamura, Hank Okamura, Hik Nagao, Yosh Sakai, Carl

Group of judo players from Nanka (southern California) and a group of wrestlers on their way to Japan to compete, in 1937

Top Air Force judo champions of the late 1950s. *Left:* Boone. *Center standing:* Williams. *Center kneeling:* T. Seino. *Right:* R. Reeves.

Judo training at the Norfolk Naval Training Station in 1942. The instructor is E. Bruno.

Yoshiaki Yamashita was among the first instructors of judo in the U.S. Among his students was President Theodore Roosevelt.

This 1937 edition of *Collegiate Digest* was one of the first U.S. magazines to feature judo on its cover. The picture is of Emilio Bruno throwing Walt Kuehenis.

The 1937 San Jose State College team, one of the first judo teams organized in the U.S. Emilio Bruno *(far right)* was the first instructor and coach of judo at San Jose and was the man most responsible for promoting intercollegiate judo on the Pacific Coast.

Shojii, Carl Kalaskai, Jack Ohashi, and Tom Watanabe.

In 1949, Masato Tamura became the president of the yudanshakai and remained in that office for the next fourteen years. During the late 1940s the Oak Park YMCA started under Bob Matsuoka. Some noted members of the Chicago Judo Club were Hik Nagao, Tom Watenabe, Jim Beres, John Osako, and Art Broadbent. At the Lawson YMCA were the Benson brothers, the Fletcher brothers, Hank Okamura, and Kenji Okamoto. The Jiu Jitsu Institute had Masato Tamura, Vince Tamura, Bob Belhatchet, Frnak Leszczynski, Bill Burk, Bill Berndt, and Bill Kaufman. During these years, any team that represented the U.S. was mostly made up of people from the Chicago Judo Black Belt Association. Chicago sent teams to the first two Pan-American Judo Tournaments and one of the two American representatives to the 1st World Tournament in Japan.

Judo was intensively promoted in Chicago during the 1950s. There were a number of self-defense demonstrations conducted for television shows. Tournaments became regular events with the Lawson YMCA providing a central location.

Konan, or Detroit, was encouraged to break away, about 1952. This change relieved Chicago of the responsibility for all of Michigan and some midwestern areas. Milwaukee, Wis., and St. Louis, Mo., were starting to develop judo groups during this time, but, unlike Chicago, these two areas did not have strong Japanese judo players to get the sport going and give guidance to its development.

With the start of the 1950s, judo in Chicago began to develop into a citywide sport as new dojos were opened. Bill Kaufman was discharged from the service in 1952 and came back from Japan as a 2nd-degree black belt. Kaufman worked out at the Jiu Jitsu Institute and started his own club at the Hyde Park YMCA. Later he taught at the University of Chicago. Mr. Hikaru Nagao was teaching judo at the Illinois Institute of Technology. In time, these two clubs combined to form the Uptown Dojo.

In the early 1950s, some students from the original dojos began teaching at various locations around the city, and the Oak Park YMCA was developing a good judo group also. Indiana at this time had a judo community developing under the guidance of Mr. Bill Craig. In local tournaments there would be as many as 80 brown belts competing at one time. National registration was adopted during this period and was run by the Chicago Yudanshakai for a few years. In the late 1950s, Chicago had 2,800 registered members.

In 1954, Vince Tamura represented the Chicago Yudanshakai and the U.S. in the 1st World Tournament. There were no weight divisions in early world competitions, so the matches were rough. Tamura lasted until the semi-finals, defeating heavier and higher ranking people. His only loss was to a future world champion.

Texas In 1957 the Second Air Force held its championship tournament in Austin, Tex., and invited Roy H. "Pop" Moore to officiate the tournament. Pop decided to stay, and, with the help of Col. Walthrop, Beverly Sheffield, from the Austin Recreation Department, and a young competitor, Jerry Reid, from Bergstrom Air Force Base, the Austin Judo Club opened its doors.

With the addition of members such as Bill Nagase and Sam Numahiri in Fort Worth, Karl Geis and Rick Landers in Houston, and Rick Mertens in Shreveport, the Southwestern U.S. Judo Association came into being. The association annexed small areas out of several yudanshakais and covered the states of Texas, Louisiana, Arakansas, Oklahoma, and New Mexico. In 1959 the Southwestern U.S. Championships were held in Austin, Tex., with over 300 competitors attending. In the late 1950s Bill Nagase and Gail Stolzenburg competed in the National AAU Senior Judo Championships.

The sport continued to grow and attracted several talented instructors to Texas—Ace Sukigara, 3rd dan, to Longview, and Vince Tamura, 5th dan, to Dallas. In 1961 the Southwestern U.S. Judo Yudanshakai became the Texas Judo Black Belt Association, and in 1962 the Texas Yudanshakai was approved by the Judo Black Belt Federation as a regional association. The first officers included John Ebell, Rick Landers, Gail Stolzenburg, Karl Geis, and Vince Tamura.

In 1964 the National Collegiate Championships were held in El Paso with Texans Ace Sukigara, John Rowlett, Wes Maxwell, and Joe Rude among the winners. In 1971 Odessa Boys Club hosted the USJF Junior National Championships with many trophies staying in Texas. In 1975 the High School National Championships were held in Houston.

To keep all the clubs informed of the Judo activities in Texas and surrounding areas, the Texas Yudanshakai has produced since 1963 a bi-monthly magazine entitled *Texas Judo News*. (GAIL STOLZENBURG)

Shufu Shufu Yudanshakai at one time had the largest judo area in the U.S. Over the years, new, localized judo organizations grew out of the initial central organization.

James Takemori, 5th dan, has served as rank registration chairman, secretary, and president of Shufu. He related the following information concerning shufu's history:

"I was in Washington before Shufu was organized. There were only a handful of men in the area, approximately ten yudansha. Among the black belts present wer Kenzo Uyeno, Eichi Koiwai, M.D., Nonkey Ishiyama, Donn Draeger, Bill Berndt, Lanny Miyamoto, and Masauki Hashimoto. Mr. Hashimoto became Shufu's first president.

There were five yudanshakais prior to the formation of Shufu. The earlier five were in Chicago, Seattle, Hawaii, Hokka, and Nanka. **Donn Draeger** was an early advocate of a yudanshakai on the East Coast. His efforts resulted in the first meeting of the forming yudanshakai, in the spring of 1953. There were some differences of opinion regarding a name for the new organization. Some felt it should be called, using Japanese terminology, East Coast, while others felt the Japanese for Capitol was more appropriate. The name Capitol finally won, thus Shufu Yudanshakai. The early officers of Shufu were: Mr. Hashimoto, president; Kenzo Uyeno, vice-president; Lanny Miyamoto, secretary-treasurer; and Donn Draeger, chairman of the board of examiners.

Shufu eventually stretched from Maine to Florida, including the Panama Canal Zone. Those seeking examination or further study might have had to travel two days for such an activity. Takemori and Uyeno traveled a great deal during that early period: to North Carolina twice a year for promotional tournaments; to New England twice yearly; and to Dixie states twice yearly. Early applicants for examinations were not very knowledgeable about judo. Many of those tested had learned judo from a book, owing to the small number of instructors on the East Coast. The candidates usually failed to pass the examinations on their first attempt. The exams were designed to develop instructors, which the large area desperately needed. Terminology was very highly stressed.

Shufu, unlike many of the other yudanshakais, did not have a large indigenous Japanese population from which to form the basis of the organization. Many of the judo people came from the military. Often, men recently home from military service overseas, would return to the U.S. from Japan as 1st- or 2nd-degree black belts.

Among the instructors in the area were Dr. Koiwai, teaching in Philadelphia at a YMCA; Lanny Miyamoto in Baltimore; Ken Freeman and George Uchida in New York; and James Takemore, Bill Berndt, Kenzo Uyeno, and Donn Draeger in Washington. There was considerable practice of Judo at military bases as well, especially at Ft. Benning and at Ft. Bragg. In 1957, the Washington Judo club, earlier named the Pentagon Judo Club, established a dojo outside of the Pentagon.

The level of judo awareness and numbers of practicing judokas in the various areas of Shufu increased. It soon became practical for more localized judo organizations to exist. The first to develop a base sufficient to run its own affairs was the Florida area. Next, New England formed its own yudanshakai, followed by the Dixie States, and Allegheny Mountain. As long as the local judo population has sufficient numbers and knowledge to administer judo in its area, the more efficient service of a local yudanshakai is preferred. This concept has motivated the splitting of areas from Shufu's original territory.

Intercollegiate Judo The first record of any U.S. collegiate judo participation was in the early 1930s when **Henry Stone**, a young coach at the University of California, Berkeley, sent a few students to participate in some tournaments held in San Francisco.

In 1937 **Emilio Bruno**, a student, introduced judo as a sport to the physical education department at San Jose State College; later the judo program was taken over by another student, Yosh Uchida. Mr. Uchida took the first group of college judo competitors from San Jose to Southern California to participate in a yudanshakai tournament, the beginning of sectional tournaments.

World War II interrupted all collegiate judo. In 1946, Yosh Uchida

217

Group of Air Force personnel being given a demonstration of judo by some of Japan's top judoka at the Kodokan during the early 1950s

SAC class at the Kodokan in 1954 being demonstrated by S. Kotani

Henry Stone (*left*) and Emilio Bruno.
Courtesy of E. Bruno

Professors for SAC personnel during the mid-1950s. *Left to right:*
Onnegawa, Sato, Tomiki, Kotani, Daigo, and E. Bruno (SAC class
director).

Courtesy of E. Bruno

Courtesy of E. Bruno

Courtesy of E. Bruno

Kata-guruma demonstrated by Prof. S. Kotani at the Kodokan to a
group of U.S. military officers, ca. 1953.

Gen. Thomas S. Power, commander in cheif of the Strategic Air
Command, receiving his 4th dan judo certificate from judo pioneer
Emilio Bruno. Power personally supervised the development of
judo in SAC and the armed forces.

The 1955 AAU American judo team arrives in Japan for a goodwill tour. *Center, with flowers:* Team captain gene LeBell. To the right of LeBell is Emilio Bruno, the team's coach.

The first International Japan-United States judo meet, 1955. Accepting the flowers is Emilio Bruno; looking on (wearing glasses) is Risei Kano, son of Jigoro Kano.

America's Vince Tamura *(left)* competes against Holland's Anton Geesink at the first World Judo Championships, in Tokyo, 1956.

Twice All Japan champion, Ishikawa, who came to the U.S. and became one of the top judo sensei.

The first SAC judo tournament held at OFFUT Air Force base, Omaha, Neb., in 1954. This was the first judo tournament in the history of the U.S. armed forces.

Left to right: G. Harris, Pop Moore, Roy Moore, Jr., Cross, and Evans.

One of SAC's finest competitive judo teams, in 1957. *Standing, left to right:* Maj. Bleakman, Prof. Hosokawa, Hodge, E. Bruno (coach), O'Connor, Seino, unknown, Henderson, unknown, unknown, Reed, Prof. Kotani, Reding, Boone. *Kneeling, left to right:* Raab, Williams, Harris, Meed, and Reed.

Courtesy of E. Bruno

Carl Flood throwing his opponent at a SAC judo tournament

Courtesy of E. Bruno

Jigoro Kano, awards grand championship silver cup to Hayward Nishioka, who went on to become one of the leaders of judo in the U.S.

1955 goodwill tour of Japan. *Seated, facing camera, right to left:* E. Bruno, H. Sharp, J. Lang, G. LeBell, G. Harris, and J.F. Geisenhoff.

1955 reception given by Japanese officials in honor of visiting American judo players. *Seated in center, wearing dark suit:* Risei Kano. *Seated, fifth from left:* E. Bruno. *Standing in the center, rear:* George Harris. *Standing, fourth from right:* Gene LeBell.

Gene LeBell *(right)* competes with Lyle Hunt in the early 1950s

Courtesy of G. LeBell

Chuck Merriman *(right)* with Bernie Lepkofker at Judo Twins in New York City, in 1961.

Front row, left to right: unknown, P. Porter, K. Kuniyuki, Shinahara.
Back row, left to right: G. Harris, H. Nishioka, T. Seino.

Members of the 1975 U.S. team to the world championships in Vienna, Austria. *Left to right, kneeling:* Jimmy Martin, Pat Burris, Steve Cohen, Irwin Cohen, Jim Wooley, Alan Coage.

Left to right, standing: Ken Okada, Paul Marayuma, Clyde Worthen, Shag Okada (coach), Brewster Thompson, Dean Sedgwick, Johnny Watts. Courtesy of Paul Marayuma

講道館派遣柔道普及團歡迎柔道大會記念撮影

Some of Japan's best martial artists, including leading judo instructors (in the front row, wearing gis), on a visit to Los Angeles in 1953 at the invitation of SAC. Many leading American judo sensei are seen in the back.

Prof. S. Kotani *(back row, center)* was the leader as well as the organizer of the group of martial artists invited to the U.S. in 1953 by SAC and the USAF. The purpose of the trip was to train Air Force personnel and to exhibit martial arts at various cities throughout the U.S. This was the beginning of the great expansion of judo together with the lesser-known martial arts, such as karate and aikido, in the U.S. *Standing, left to right:* Prof. Kobayashi (judo), Ishikawa (judo), Kotani (judo), Prof. Tomiki (aikido), and E. Bruno (chief of SAC project). *Kneeling, left to right:* Nishiyama (karate), Kamata (karate).

Gen. Curtis E. LeMay, SAC commander, awards a trophy to Sgt. Dameron, winner of his division at the 1954 SAC judo tournament.

Courtesy of E. Bruno

Top SAC judo leaders. *Left to right:* Pop Moore, W. Arnold, Harold Jones, and Bob Matheny.

Courtesy of E. Bruno

returned to college and helped revive the judo program at San Jose State. Many of the students, who were World War II veterans, had been taught strictly self-defense in the service. Because fine technique was lacking among the judo participants, great force was used on opponents and small competitors were easily injured.

In 1948 Henry Stone devised a weight system that he hoped would aid the growth and development of judo. For several years, the weight system was experimented with at San Jose State in the physical education classes and proved worthwhile. The original weight divisions were: 130, 150, 180 lbs, and unlimited. These weight divisions were adopted by the AAU, but have since been revised several times in an effort to keep up with changes in body size. The weight divisions adopted by the Olympic Judo Committee, and used in the Olympic Games in Tokyo in 1964, were 156, 176, heavyweight, and open.

Most of the early college judo participation and development was carried out on the west coast at San Jose and U.C. Berkeley. Dual meets between the two schools were initiated in the early 1950s. In 1953, the first collegiate judo championships were held at U.C. Berkeley, called the Pacific Coast Intercollegiate Judo Championships. Also in 1953, the first National AAU Judo Championships were held at San Jose State. Lyle Hunt, a San Jose State senior, was the first grand champion of the National AAU Championships. Later in 1953, as a college student, Lyle represented the U.S. in several tournaments in Europe, along with John Osoko from Chicago. Yosh Uchida, from San Jose State, was coach. This was the first U.S. representation abroad in the sport. Judo was recognized as in intercollegiate sport at San Jose in 1954, but the growth of judo was definitely hampered over the years by a general lack of understanding and knowledge of the sport by athletic directors and physical education department chairmen, who have been traditionally reluctant to accept new minor sports.

In 1955 San Jose State hosted the first International All-Star Collegiate competitors. Haruo Imamura, who won the U.S. National AAU Grand Championship in 1960, was a member of that team. The tournament was the first all-college judo participation on an international scale between two countries, although sometime during the mid-1930s, a team from Keio University had participated in a yudanshakai tournament in southern California.

Henry Stone, the great leader of judo, passed away suddenly in 1955 and judo floundered on the university level. A long-smouldering feud between the NCAA and the AAU flared up in 1960, and it became impossible for college teams to compete in AAU-sanctioned tournaments. On May 12, 1962 college leaders met and organized the National Collegiate Judo Association. In 1962 the first National Collegiate Judo Championships were held at the U.S. Air Force Academy, San Jose State, U.C. Berkeley, University of Minnesota, Mankato State College, and the Eastern Collegiate Judo Association. Since then many National Collegiate Judo Championships have been held at various colleges and universities across the country.

In 1967, the National Collegiate Judo Association selected Howard Fish to represent the U.S. in the University Games held in Tokyo. George Uchida, of U.C. Berkeley, was coach and manager. The only U.S. representative, Fish won a bronze medal in both the heavyweight and open divisions. Because of Fish's outstanding performance, the NCJA was invited to send a team to Lisbon, Portugal, in 1968. The U.S. sent Mike Ogata, Doug Graham, Roy Sukimoto, Gary Martin, and Yosh Uchida as coach. Doug Graham won a silver medal in the 205 lb division, and Gary Martin was a silver medalist in the 154 lb division. These two U.S. collegiate judoists lost only to collegiate competitors from Japan.

In 1972 the University Games were held in London. Team members included David Long, John Reed, Tom Cullen, Louis Gonzalez, Tom Masterson, and Tom Tigg. In Soo Hwang, from Yale University, served as coach-manager. Tigg won the silver medal in the 139 lb division.

For all the University Game competition, financial help was received from the USJF. Without this national governing body, U.S. judo would have had a far greater struggle; and certainly, without its financial aid, competitors would never have been able to compete internationally. (YOSH UCHIDA)

The Armed Forces The organized judo program in the U.S. Armed Forces began in the Air Force in 1950 when Gen. **Curtis E. LeMay**, then commander-in-chief of the Strategic Air Command, USAF, directed the setting up of a model physical conditioning unit at Offutt AFB, Neb. In 1951 similar conditioning units were set up at other SAC bases. Gen. LeMay appointed Emilio ("Mel") Bruno, a former National AAU Wrestling Champion and 5th-degree in judo, to direct the program. At this time, civilian judo instructors staffed six SAC bases; the rest had physical conditioning units, but no judo instructors. In direct charge of the judo and conditioning program for SAC was Gen. Thomas Power, later honorary chairman of the National AAU Judo Committee.

Because of an obvious deficiency of instructors, Power sent two classes of airmen (24 men) to the Kodokan Institute in Tokyo in 1952 for several weeks training. This was the first such training for any Armed Forces group.

Air Force judo received added impetus in 1953 when ten experts from Japan, six in judo, three in karate, and one in aikido, gave demonstrations at over 70 U.S. Air Force Bases over a three-month period. The purpose of this tour was to train judo instructors and combat crews and to give exhibitions on and off base. Many civilian judo clubs had their first visit from high-ranking judo teachers as a result of this tour. One of the highlights of the tour was a demonstration at the White House on July 22. The year 1953 was also marked by the first National AAU Judo tournament held at San Jose State College. A SAC team participated in these first Nationals.

In 1954, the first SAC Judo Tournament was held at Offutt AFB; the Grand Champion was Airman Morris Curtis. Also in 1954, 26 SAC Air Police went to the Kodokan to study judo for ten weeks. The curriculum consisted of police tactics, aikido, karate and, of course, judo.

Two SAC judoists advanced to the last few rounds in the 1954 AAU National Championships at Kezar Stadium, San Francisco. The 12-man SAC team won 29 rounds and lost 19 but was unable to place a man. Staff Sgt. Ed Maley, SAC, a member of the 1955 SAC Judo Team, placed in the 1955 AAU National Championships—third in the 150-lb division. The Air Research and Development Command, USAD (ARDC), also entered a team in 1955, after only a year of competition, and A/1C Vern Raab won an unofficial fourth place in the heavyweight division.

The year 1954 also brought a 10-man AAU-Air Force team visit to six Japanese cities to compete in 16 contests. Five members of the team were Air Force, and the most successful member of the team was to be heard from many times in the future. This man, Staff Sgt. George Harris, won all of his 16 contests.

Seventy men from SAC and ARDC journeyed to the Kodokan in 1955 for instruction. Under the guidance of Gen. Power, who had taken over as ARDC Commander, the SAC-ARDC Judo Association was formed and received recognition from the Kodokan in 1956. Emilio Bruno was elected president, and the association was permitted to grant judo rank. This was the first and only Armed Forces judo association to be so recognized by the Kodokan. SAC and ARDC sent 280 Air Policemen for four-week classes at the Kodokan during 1956.

Again in 1956, the Air Force placed one man in the national AAU Judo Tournament at Seattle. Returning from his successful Japanese tour, George Harris, then a 2nd dan, placed third in the heavyweight division.

In 1957, after only five years in judo, Staff Sgt. George Harris won the Grand Championship in the National AAU Judo Championships in Hawaii. Harris was first in the heavyweight division; sweeping the division with him were A/1C Lenwood Williams in second place and A/2C Ed Mede, third. The Air Force also took the National 5-Man Team Championship for the first time.

Winners of the SAC and ARDC tournaments represented the Air Force in the AAU tournaments on April 13 and 14 in Chicago. Twelve Air Force judoists participated, with George Harris successfully defending his Grand Championship, and the Air Force team captured the National 5-Man Team Championship for the second year in a row. Due to the great power of southern California in the lower weight divisions, the Air Force was unable to win the overall team championship.

The SAC Judo Team, consisting of L. Williams, E. Mede, G. Harris, J. Reid, R. Moxley, and M. O'Connor (trainer) was designated as the U.S. Pan-American Judo Team in 1958. Team members won first and fourth in the 3rd dan category (Harris and Williams), third in the 2nd dan (Reid), and second in the 1st dan (Mede). In the fall of 1958, George Harris and Ed Mede represented the U.S. in the 2nd World Tournament, held in Tokyo. Harris's three wins before losing to

Sone, a Japanese 5th degree, placed him in a tie for fifth place along with the four other defeated quarter finalists. As a result of this fine record, George Harris was promoted to 4th degree in judo, the first Armed Forces man to be so honored. (Lt. Agulla Gibbs Dibrell)

The Governance of U.S. Judo The development of a national governing body for U.S. judo started in 1952, through the efforts of Dr. Henry A. Stone, Maj. Draeger, and others. At that time there was no national authority to give guidance to local judo communities and insure the logical and orderly development of judo as a sport. The Amateur Judo Association was a first attempt at establishing a national governing structure. Dr. Stone served as the first president. Authority to grant the most coveted Kodokan judo rank was assumed by the national organization. High ranking individuals were no longer permitted to grant promotions independently. The growth of local judo organizations was encouraged, promotion privileges were granted to yudanshakais, and a national communications avenue was opened.

Until the early 1960s, judo in the U.S. had grown in a haphazard, somewhat informal fashion. Most leaders tended to be purists, preferring the security and recognition offered by their local influence. Judo was structured strictly on rank, and those without the proper credentials were considered outsiders. It was judo rank, that coveted mantle of recognition, which for so many years retarded the formation of a strong, responsive national organization. As judo spread across the nation, false claims to rank and promotions were commonplace, and the existing organization was powerless to take action. Those leaders who had feared a national organization and popularization of judo in time became the strongest voices for change.

The national organization was renamed the Judo Black Belt Federation. President Yosh Uchida (1960-61) delegated the task of laying the groundwork for reorganization to Donald Pohl, a relatively unknown 1st dan from Detroit. Pohl, the executive secretary of the Detroit Judo Club (then the nation's largest non-profit club), had effected a pilot program for a national rank system.

During the brief tenure of President Renyo Uyeno (before his untimely death at the age of 39 on June 1, 1963), the Judo Black Belt Federation launched a national rank registration procedure, which was coupled with a detailed rank identification system. This was the basis for future financial stability of the organization. The Judo Black Belt Federation also adopted a comprehensive constitution and by-laws, established a national communications system and published the *Judo Bulletin.*

Although the early leaders of the Judo Black Belt Federation (then known as the Amateur Judo Association), had actively sought out the Amateur Athletic Union and had been granted the right to represent U.S. judo on the international level, little attention or significance was attached to this accommodation until early in the 1960s when amateurism and sanctions began to become important. As the Judo Black Belt Federation expanded (18 yudanshakais in 1963) and tournaments were more widely attended, the importance and presence of the AAU began to be noticed. The Judo Black Belt Federation and the Amateur Athletic Union succeeded in maintaining an atmosphere of cooperation and mutual assistance during the remainder of the decade.

In 1963 the Judo Black Belt Federation joined the Amateur Athletic Union in producing the first of what were to be five joint handbooks (two published by Phil Porter and three by Don Pohl). Sales of the books, mostly through the Federation, exceeded 100,000 copies. All proceeds were given to the Amateur Athletic Union Judo Committee to help finance its operation. When proceeds from the sale of handbooks failed to provide the necessary funding for the expanding program, the Judo Black Belt Federation authorized grants in excess of $75,000 to the Amateur Athletic Union to help finance international competition and related programs.

In 1964 and 1966, Hiro Fujimoto of Detroit was elected president of the Federation and Dr. Eichi Koiwai of Philadelphia, vice-president. Dr. Koiwai assumed the presidency at the 1968 election, holding office for several terms. During the uncertain years of the 1960s the Federation changed its name to the U.S. Judo Federation, published a book of procedures, rewrote the judo contest rules, adopted a comprehensive promotion procedure, drafted a new referees' certification procedure, and expanded to 25 yudanshakais.

Judo soon grew to the third largest sport in the array of Amateur Athletic Union activities. What were first considered minor contentions between the Union and the Federation soon grew to open disagreement over philosophy, priorities, and control. Amateurism became a bone of contention, considered by many a stumbling block in the way of development. Amateur Athletic Union advocates, on the other hand, questioned the unchallenged control of rank exercised by the U.S. Judo Federation.

In 1969 the differences and positions that had been fought out at the meetings finally culminated in one of the yudanshakais (the Armed Forces Judo Association) withdrawing from the U.S. Judo Federation to start a rival national organization. The Armed Forces Judo Association adopted a name similar to that of the parent organization, the U.S. Judo Association. The association closely aligned itself with the philosophy and position of the Amateur Athletic Union. (Dennis Helm)

KARATE

Kung-fu arrived in the U.S. with the first Chinese immigrants in the mid-19th century, but the growth of karate is largely owed to contact between American servicemen and Japanese experts during the post-World War II occupation of Japan and Okinawa.

Kung-fu: the Forerunner of Karate Kung-fu was a part of the Chinese lifestyle in the labor camps and mining towns that grew up following the gold rush of 1848. With the importation of large numbers of Chinese laborers to work on the Central Pacific Railroad, beginning in 1863, the swelling Chinese communities isolated themselves within their own, transplanted culture. Conflicts over control of gambling, prostitution, and the like, arose; rival secret societies fought each other in the notorious "Tong Wars," which lasted until the 1930s. The troops in these internecine wars were "hatchetmen," so-called because they used meat cleavers and hatchets as weapons. They were skilled also in kung-fu, in the art of "pin-blowing," and in hurling lethal, razor-edged coins. Hatchetmen in the U.S. handed down, from one generation to the next, the secret and sinister practice of kung-fu, the forebearer of modern karate.

Until roughly two decades after World War II, kung-fu was not available to non-Chinese on the U.S. mainland. The early Japanese and Okinawan communities in the U.S. were isolated, introverted, and intensely secretive about their ethnic arts and crafts. Judo was the only exception: **Jigoro Kano,** the founder of judo, encouraged its spread. According to martial arts scholar **Donn F. Draeger,** Kano asked that "judo training be undertaken not only in the dojo but also outside it, and so make of its physical aspects the focus of human endeavor for the progress and development of man." The other martial arts had no such original intention.

The first club to practice kung-fu in organized classes with instructors from Chinese provinces was a branch of the Chinese Physical Culture Association, founded in Honolulu in 1922. This association promoted physical culture among the Islands' Chinese communities, but kung-fu remained unavailable to non-orientals until 1957, when **Tinn Chan Lee,** a t'ai-chi-ch'uan specialist, became the first Chinese sifu to open his teaching to the general public.

In 1964 the closely-guarded doors of kung-fu finally opened in the U.S. mainland. **Ark Y. Wong** of Los Angeles, born in China, broke the traditional kung-fu "color line" by accepting students of all races at jos Wah Que Studio in Los Angeles's old Chinatown. Also in 1964 the movie idol **Bruce Lee** and his one-time partner, **James Yimm Lee,** began accepting non-Orientals at Lee's kwoon in Oakland, Calif. In fact, the notorious **John Keehan,** a.k.a. "Count Dante," claimed to have trained there as early as 1962.

Teachers like New York's **Alan Lee,** Ark Y. Wong, and T.Y. Wong popularized **Shao-lin. Choy-Li-Fut** and t'ai-chi-ch'uan quickly became public and, soon after, the various branches of northern and southern **Shao-lin** kung-fu.

In northern California, sifus Kwong and **Brendan Lai** helped establish the **praying mantis** system. Y.C. Wong promoted the **hung gar** and tiger crane systems; Kuo-Lien-Ying promoted t'ai-chi; George Long, the **white crane**; and Lau Bun and the Luk Mo Studio, the Choy-Li-Fut. Noted scholar Wen-Shan Huang, with his protege Marshall Ho, started the National T'ai-Chi-Ch'uan Association in the early 1960s, opening up instruction in this "soft style" of kung-fu to Caucasians.

Throughout the U.S. kung-fu spread, especially during the Bruce Lee era, when so-called Eastern Westerns dominated American and international movie screens. Even so, the majority of kung-fu styles and teachers still remain hidden.

Many of the first karate students were street fighters. Few of these rough types possessed, however, the discipline necessary to remain with the art and learn it thoroughly. The small number who did found their original attitudes startlingly transformed. Today, karate classes are predominantly composed of businesspersons, professionals, skilled workers, and students—a cross section of American society.

Karate Comes to Hawaii In Hawaii, a great cultural crossroads, karate secured a foothold long before its emergence on the mainland. Although practiced within the Okinawan community, no wider audience had seen karate in Hawaii until 1927, when **Kentsu Yabu,** a famous Okinawan master, introduced **Shuri-te** in a public demonstration at the Nuuana YMCA in Honolulu.

A few "naichi" Japanese (i.e., Japanese from one of the four main islands of Hawaii) who observed the YMCA demonstration adjudged karate a srong fighting art, possibly even stronger than their judo. Interest in karate by non-Okinawans flourished thereafter. Yabu's open teachings also brought together interested groups of Okinawans for practice and recreation, something the rivalries of Naha, Shuri, and Tomari had prevented on Okinawa.

In 1932 **Choki Motobu,** a legendary, eccentric Okinawan karate fighter, was denied entry to Hawaii when a group of Okinawan promoters living in Hawaii tried to import him for a public match against well-known Island fighters. In 1933 Zuiho Mutsu and Kamesuke Higaonna were allowed into Hawaii with the understanding that they would teach and lecture but not compete in the boxing ring. Both refused to engage in public matches and prepared to depart immediately. Thomas Miyashiro, who had studied with Yabu in 1927, convinced other karate enthusiasts to approach the pair collectively and urge that they remain in Hawaii to teach their art. They agreed and, after great initial success at the Asahi Photo Studio, the site of their original school, the two karate masters chose a new facility for their classes, the Izumo Taishi Shinto Mission.

The club formed from these classes, the Hawaii Karate Seinin Kai (Hawaii Young People's Karate Club), subsequently staged a public karate demonstration at the Honolulu Civic Auditorium. A number of Caucasian spectators in attendance, mostly members of the First Methodist Church, became interested in learning karate. Through their efforts, the first known Caucasian group in the Western world to study openly and to sponsor karate activities was formed in 1933. Shortly thereafter, both Mutsu and Higaonna departed for Japan, where they had been teaching previously.

In May 1934 Chinei Kinjo, editor of the Okinawan newspaper *Yoen Fiho Sha,* invited grandmaster **Chojun Miyagi,** the founder of **goju-ryu** karate, to Hawaii. Miyagi lectured and taught to popularize Okinawan goju-ryu karate-do, staying almost a year and returning to Okinawa in Feb. 1935.

The spread of **kempo** to the Islands is largely owed to Dr. **James Mitose,** a Japanese-American born in Hawaii in 1916. At age five he was sent to Kyushu, Japan, for schooling in his ancestral art of self-defense, called "kosho-ryu kempo," said to be based directly on Shao-lin kung-fu. Mitose returned to Hawaii in 1936. In 1942 he organized the Official Self-Defense Club at the Beretania Mission in Honolulu. This club continued under his personal leadership until 1953, when it was assigned to **Thomas Young,** one of his chief students. Only five of his students—Young, **William K.S. Chow,** Paul Yamaguchi, Arthur Keawe, and Edward Lowe—attained the· rank of black belt. But the kempo arts flourished in Hawaii and later on the west coast of the mainland, where three of Mitose's proteges formed clubs of their own. In 1953, before going to the mainland, Mitose wrote *What Is Self-Defense,* reprinted by his students in 1980.

Of Mitose's students, perhaps Chow played the most significant role in the evolution of the American martial arts. Although he had learned kosho-ryu kempo under Mitose, Chow was the first to teach what he called **kenpo** (first law) karate. From 1949 Chow trained a great number of students to the rank of black belt, including **Adriano Emperado,** Ralph Castro, **Bobby Lowe,** John Leone, and Paul Pung. By far the most famous of Chow's students is **Ed Parker,** a leading pioneer in the American karate movement.

Adriano "Sonny" Emperado was a co-founder in 1947 of the **kajukenbo** system, formed by five experts: Walter Choo (karate), Joseph Holke (judo), Frank Ordonez (jujutsu), Emperado (kenpo), and Clarence Chang (Chinese boxing). The name is an acronym derived from the five disciplines of its founders: *ka* from karate, *ju* from judo and jujutsu, *ken* from kenpo, and *bo* from Chinese boxing. Today, this style is one of the most prominent in Hawaii. In 1950 Emperado founded Hawaii's first and largest chain of karate schools, the Kajukenbo Self-Defense Institute, Inc., in which he still holds the

office of vice-president. Probably Emperado's most famous student is **Al Dacascos,** founder of the **won hop kuen do** system.

In 1954 Japan's colorful **Mas Oyama** visited Hawaii for a month to assist Bobby Lowe, a Chinese-American, in setting up the first overseas branch of Oyama's **kyokushinkai** style.

Karate Emerges on the Mainland The first karate school on the U.S. mainland was established by a former sailor, **Robert Trias,** who began teaching karate in Phoenix in 1946. In 1942, while stationed in the Pacific, Trias trained with Tong Gee Hsing, a teacher of **hsing-i** and Shuri tode ryu, and a nephew, according to Trias, of Okinawa's Choki Motobu. The word "karate" was not then in universal use; Shuri tode ryu was a style of Okinawan **shorei-ryu** karate.

Upon his discharge in 1946, Trias returned to the U.S. and established his private, 14-foot-square dojo. He charged a low annual fee for instruction in judo or karate for two to three hours daily, seven days a week. Until the late 1970s, when **John Corcoran** investigated the subject, little acknowledgement was given Trias as the actual founder of karate in America. Later, in 1948, Trias formed the **United States Karate Association** (USKA), the first karate organization on the mainland.

From Mar. to Nov. 1952, Mas Oyama of Japan toured 32 states by invitation of the U.S. Professional Wrestling Association—officials had heard of his exploits in Japan. While in the country he began his famous challenge matches with professional wrestlers and boxers, all of whom he is said to have defeated. Oyama's exhibition bouts and demonstrations, including the breaking of boards, bricks, and stones, received great public attention, including articles in the *New York Times,* which covered his bout with a pro boxer at Madison Square Garden.

In 1951 **Emilio Bruno,** judo teacher, pioneer, and administrator, had been named supervisor of judo and combative measures for the Strategic Air Command (SAC). Bruno formulated a new approach to military combat training, integrating parts of aikido, judo, and karate into a systematic unarmed combat technique. To implement his idea, he suggested a pilot program to Gen. **Curtis LeMay,** then commander of the U.S. Air Force and one of Bruno's judo students. The program had a significant effect on the subsequent propagation of karate in the U.S.

With Gen. LeMay's endorsement and SAC's sponsorship, Bruno initiated eight-week training programs for Air Force instructors at the **Kodokan,** judo's mecca, in Japan. Kodokan officials contacted the **Japan Karate Association** (JKA) to manage the karate instruction, and that organization selected **Hidetaka Nishiyama** as one of the coaches. Financially backed and supported by SAC, Bruno invited ten martial arts instructors of judo and karate to participate in a now famous four-month 1953 tour of every SAC base in the U.S. and Cuba. The touring group included seven judoka and three karate dignitaries: Nishiyama, Toshio Kamata, and the late **Isao Obata,** a JKA co-founder and senior disciple of **Gichin Funakoshi.**

The 1953 SAC tour was responsible for opening up communication between Japan and the U.S., accounting for the migration of dozens of Japanese karate instructors to America. It also influenced other U.S. military branches and departments to adopt similar martial arts programs.

In 1954 the JKA established its first, small headquarters inTokyo, and, with the establishment of a central dojo, Nishiyama was elected chief of the JKA instruction department. He conceived a plan to train large numbers of karate instructors and send them across the world to establish karate. His plan, once put into operation, accounted for the migration, beginning in 1955, of many instructors who pioneered **Shotokan** karate wherever they settled. Nishiyama himself assumed responsibility for furthering karate in the U.S.

In 1954 **Ed Parker,** black belt kenpo student of William Chow, began teaching a karate course at Brigham Young University. Hawaiian-born Parker, who had arrived on the mainland in 1951, limited instruction to Americans attending the university. His evening classes enrolled as many as 72 students: city police, state highway patrolmen, fish and game wardens, and sheriffs' deputies. With some of his students, Parker formed an exhibition team, and through various chambers of commerce, he and his group performed in several Utah cities.

William Dometrich, who began his karate training in Japan in 1951, returned in Dec. 1954, settling in Kentucky. A student of Dr. **Tsuyoshi Chitose,** the founder of **Chito-ryu** karate, Dometrich

Rare photo (ca. 1935) showing master Chojun Miyagi *(standing, fourth from left, in kimono),* who had just come back from Hawaii, where he taught karate for almost a year. To Miyagi's left is master Nakamoto; in front of Miyagi *(seated)* is master Shiroma, and to his right is Mr. Anzama.

Courtesy of Anthony Mirakian

Courtesy of Nick Cerio

William Chow, Hawaiian karate pioneer, taught kenpo karate to a large number of students, who went on to spread the art on the mainland. Ed Parker was one of Chow's students.

Hawaiian karate pioneer Sid Asuncion *(center)* with one of his better-known students, Al Dacascos *(right),* who went on to spread his own won hop kuen do system on the mainland and later in Europe.

Robert Trias *(center)*, "The father of American karate " with a number of his early students, including his daughter Roberta, who was one of the first female karate black belts in the U.S. Trias founded the first karate school in the U.S. in Phoenix, Ariz., in 1946.

In 1953 the Strategic Air Command (SAC) sent a number of personnel to Japan to train under some of the top instructors there. Here a group of airmen receive instruction from Prof. Obata while M. Nakayama *(left)* and H. Nishiyama *(right)* look on. This took place inside the old Kodokan.

Emilio Bruno *(right)* was the man most responsible for getting SAC to send personnel to Japan for training in the martial arts. Many of the instructors who taught the American airmen were students of Gichin Funakoshi *(third from left)* and included such famous masters as M. Nakayama *(left)* and I. Obata *(second from left).* This photo was taken ca. 1953.

In 1953, at the invitation of the U.S. Air Force, some of Japan's top martial artists visited the U.S., giving demonstrations and holding seminars. Here the group is seen while on a stopover at Yosemite Park.

Left to right: Bob Bowles, Jim McLain, Robert Trias, Bill Dometrich, Phil Koeppel, John Townsley, Bob Yarnall, and Glenn Keeney. *Kneeling:* Ross Scott *(left)*; Ron Shaw *(right).*

Photo by Mary Townsley

Stirling Silliphant, one of Hollywood's top screenwriters, is also a martial arts enthusiast. He has written numerous TV and movie scripts in which martial arts are featured and was instrumental in the career of Bruce Lee, with whom he studied for three years.

Don Nagle was among the most important pioneers of karate on the East Coast.

Ed Kaloudis was one of the first instructors to teach karate on the East Coast. A koei-kan stylist, Kaloudis oversees a number of schools in the New York-New Jersey area.

was the first to teach this system in America. He formed the U.S. Chito-Kai in 1967.

Denver's Frank Goody, Jr., who had as early as 1924 started judo lessons with his father, is the first instructor to have taught karate in the Rocky Mountain region. **Jack Farr**, in compiling the history of martial arts in Colorado, reported that between 1945 and 1951, Goody promoted yawara tournaments within his judo school in Denver. While Goody's background is the subject of much confusion, his contribution to karate's growth is not. In 1957, he opened a karate school in Boulder, Colo., and is credited with teaching nearly all the other karate pioneers in the Colorado area.

Dewey Deavers, a jujutsu and karate instructor who reportedly traveled in China and Japan in the 1920s, surfaced around 1954 in Pittsburgh. By then he had already trained two students to the rank of black belt: Warren Siciliano and Larry Williams. Williams in that year introduced karate to a promising student, **Glenn Premru,** who in the late 1960s and early 1970s, became a noted performer and national kata champion.

Another pioneer was Atlee Chittim of Texas. After studying tae kwon do in Korea, Chittim returned as a brown belt in 1955 and taught his art at San Antonio College. (Interestingly, the name "tae kwon do" had only been created in April of that year.) As far as can be determined, Chittim was the first to teach any form of karate in the southwestern U.S. outside of Arizona. And he sponsored the entry of **Jhoon Rhee** to America from Korea in 1956. Rhee, a tae kwon do black belt, came to the U.S. to study engineering at San Marco's Texas State College and began to teach his art on campus, opening a commercial club in 1958. Rhee, known as the "Father of American Tae Kwon Do," went on to become one of the most important leaders in American karate.

In 1955 **Tsutomu Ohshima**, a graduate of Waseda University in Japan, organized a small karate class at the Konko Shinto Church in Los Angeles. A disciple of Gichin Funakoshi's Shotokan style, Ohshima was the first instructor in the U.S. to teach a typically Japanese karate system, and was the first resident karate teacher on the West Coast. In 1956 he opened the first public dojo in Los Angeles. He also founded the Shotokan Karate of America.

The First Karate Tournament Robert Trias in 1955 conducted the first known karate tournament in America, the 1st Arizona Karate Championships. Held at the Butler Boys Club in Phoenix, participants were chiefly members of the Arizona Highway Patrol, Trias' own students.

Karate Comes to Hollywood By 1956 Ed Parker had moved to California, where his growing student list began to include such Hollywood names as Darren McGavin, author **Joe Hyams,** television executive **Tom Tannenbaum,** producer Blake Edwards, and the late film stars Nick Adams, Frank Lovejoy, and Audie Murphy. Both Hyams and Tannenbaum later achieved black belts under different instructors. Each made substantial contributions to karate, Tannenbaum in television and Hyams in print. Through Parker's influence, Blake Edwards directed his writers to add karate scenes to the screenplays for such 1960s hits as *A Shot in the Dark* and *The Pink Panther.* In those days, filmmakers were intrigued primarily by the more spectacular aspects of the martial arts, such as board and brick breaking.

Eventually Parker taught many more celebrities, including **Elvis Presley,** and appeared in motion pictures and television shows. It is difficult to determine whether **Bruce Tegner** or Parker was the first karate expert to work in films. It is a matter of record, however, that Tegner attracted attention to the martial arts early by setting up fight scenes for the 1950s TV series "The Adventures of Ozzie and Harriet," and "The Detectives," starring Robert Taylor. He also wrote a large number of books which had a great influence on the number of Americans that got involved in karate. As early as 1956 **Stirling Silliphant** had begun writing martial arts into many of his films requiring combat action. He first did this in *Five Against the House* in which Brian Keith portrayed a Korean war veteran and karate expert. Later he wrote martial arts roles in TV series like "Naked City" and "Route 66." Silliphant later became largely instrumental in the rise of Bruce Lee, with whom he studied for 3 years.

Karate Pioneers In the years 1956 through 1960 the core of an American establishment came into being. A nucleus of first-rate instructors—immigrants from the Far East and returning U.S.

servicemen—opened the first schools in assorted styles, in their respective regions. In 1957 **Don Nagle** returned from Okinawa, where he studied **isshin-ryu** under **Tatsuo Shimabuku.** He opened a dojo in Jacksonville and trained such well-known black belts as Ed McGrath, **Harold Long, Gary Alexander,** Ron Duncan, Donald Bohan, James Chapman, Lou Lizzotte, Ralph Chirico, and Joe Bucholtz. Nagle became one of the instructors chiefly responsible for the profiferation of karate throughout the Eastern Seaboard.

Louis Kowlowski, an early USKA member, opened the first karate school in the midwest in 1957, in St. Louis, Mo. He was also one of the first to introduce Okinawan **shorin-ryu** (Matsubayashi) into the U.S.

In 1957 **Cecil Patterson,** a **wado-ryu** black belt, opened a private club in Sevierville, Tenn. In 1962 he opened his first commercial school in Nashville, which, by the mid-1970s, expanded to as many as 17 dojo across Tennessee. Patterson also began the Eastern U.S. Wado-Kai Federation.

Okinawa kempo master Zempo (atsu) Shimabuku founded the first known karate dojo in Philadelphia in 1957.

In 1958, Roger Warren, who studied in the Orient, started teaching karate in Chicago and Peoria. **Charles Gruzanski** (d. 1973) also opened a martial arts school in Chicago in the same year. Gruzanski, who spent many years in Japan, was a black belt in a number of different arts and was one of the few Caucasian experts in masaki-ryu-manriki-gusari, a viscous chain and sickle weapon.

In the mid-1950s **Ed Kaloudis** traveled to Japan to improve his judo knowledge. While there he studied **koei-kan** karate from **Eizo Onishi.** In 1958 Kaloudis moved to New York where he began to teach at NYU and also to members of the New York City Police Department. He later moved to New Jersey and opened up schools in Clifton and Caldwell. Today he oversees a large number of affiliated schools.

Robert Fusaro, who trained under Nishiyama in Japan, was the first man to teach karate in Minnesota. He began teaching his shotokan style in 1958 in Minneapolis and founded the Midwest Karate Association. Today he runs a number of schools in Minnesota.

In 1958 **George Mattson** was discharged from the U.S. Army. He returned home to Boston where he became the first **Uechi-ryu** instructor in America, as well as the first karate pioneer in the New England region. Mattson became a leader of karate on the Eastern Seaboard sponsoring the first karate tournament in New England in 1961. Mattson also wrote one of the first books on karate, *The Way of Karate,* published in 1963.

In 1958 in Portland, Oreg., Moon Yo Woo began teaching kong su an obscure Korean style of karate.

In 1958-59 Harry Smith, a student of Don Nagle, opened the first-known karate school in western Pennsylvania. He trained several students including Joe Penneywell, Harry Ackland and James Morabeto.

Around this time Walter Mazak and Joe Hedderman opened a dojo in Pittsburgh, Hedderman was a student of Chito-stylist William Dometrich.

In 1959 **Philip Koeppel** was discharged from the Navy. He had studied karate in Japan with **Richard Kim** and Kajukenbo with Adriano Emperado in Hawaii. In 1960 he joined the USKA and studied under Robert Trias. In 1963 he helped promote the 1st World Karate Championships in Chicago and has since built a strong chain of karate studios throughout the midwest.

In 1959 Natamoro Naikima opened a school in Philadelphia teaching shorin-ryu.

Peter Urban, one of the founders of karate on the East Coast, opened his first goju-ryu karate school in Union City, New Jersey, in Sept. 1959. Urban had studied in Japan with Richard Kim and later became a top student of **Gogen** "The Cat" **Yamaguchi.**

In 1960, Urban moved to New York City and taught karate at the Judo Twins (Bernie and Bob Lepkofker) and later established his own dojo, the famous "Chinatown Dojo." He also broke away from the goju-kai organization and formed his own, which he called USA Goju. Urban probably trained more top black belts than anyone on the East Coast; among them were: **Chuck Merriman,** Al Gotay, **William Louie, Frank Ruiz, John Kuhl,** Lou Angel, Thomas Boddie, Joe Lopez, Joe Hess, **Bill Liquori, Aaron Banks, Ron Van Clief,** Susan Murdock, **Owen Watson,** and **Rick Pascetta.**

Dr. Maung Gyi, a master of Burmese **bando,** founded the American

Bando Association in Washington, D.C., in 1960 This was the first Asian boxing association in the U.S.

Ron Duncan, a karate student of Don Nagle, began teaching in Brooklyn in 1959. Besides karate, he taught jujutsu as well as weaponry.

Another dojo, the Tong Dojo, also opened in Brooklyn in 1959. Founded by **George Cofield,** who got his black belt from Maynard Minor (one of the first shotokan instructors in the U.S. affiliated with the JKA), Cofield taught such well-known students as **Thomas LaPuppet, Alex Sternberg,** and **Hawk Frazier.** LaPuppet went on to become one of America's premier tournament fighters of the 1960s, and is considered one of the greatest champions ever to emerge from New York City.

During this same period, Chris DeBais was teaching karate at the Judo Twins. He later went on to train with Peter Urban.

The New York Karate Club was founded in 1959 by Hiroshi Orita. Orita, a renukan stylist, later switched to shotokan in 1961 and affiliated himself with Philadelphian Teruyuki Okazaki.

Also in 1959, Wallace Reumann began teaching karate at his judo club in Newark, N.J. When he departed a few years later, his senior student, James Cheatham, took over the instruction. Cheatham trained the controversial Karriem Allah who fought **Jeff Smith** in a full-contact bout, which was seen worldwide as part of the Ali/Frazier "Thrilla in Manilla" in 1975.

Don Nagle moved to New Jersey in 1959 and with his partner Joe Bucholtz opened a school in Jersey City.

Upon his discharge from the U.S. Marines, **Harold Long** began teaching isshinryu in eastern Tennessee. In 1962 he opened his first dojo in Knoxville, one of the earliest karate schools in the South.

Finally in 1959, Mas Oyama visited the U.S. for the second time, opening schools across the country. His California affiliate was Don Buck, a rugged individual who generated much attention to Oyama's style over the years.

Dan Ivan, who was one of the first postwar Americans to study at the **Kodokan,** settled in southern California in 1956 and opened a karate school in Orange County. A former C.I.D. agent in Japan, Ivan made periodic trips back to the Orient. In 1963 he saw a karate and weapons demonstration by **Fumio Demura**; impressed, he brought Demura to the U.S. in 1965 to help him teach in his growing chain of schools. In the ensuing years the two would become inseparable partners and would establish more than 20 schools teaching **Shito-ryu** karate. In addition, Demura became one of the most sought after performers—demonstrating his karate and weaponry at Japanese Village, Sea World, and Las Vegas' Hilton Hotel.

The first person to introduce Okinawan goju-ryu karate to the U.S. was **Anthony Mirakian,** who founded the Okinawan Karate-do Academy in Watertown, Mass., in 1960. A quiet individual who learned his karate in Okinawa, Mirakian is one of the most knowledgeable instructors to teach in the U.S. He has, over the years, kept a low profile in the American karate community but was persuaded to make major contributions to this encyclopedia.

Goju-ryu instructor Charles Iverson visited Robert Trias in 1960 and exchanged numerous katas with Trias. This led to the latter's formation of his shorei-goju-ryu style, which became a common style in the USKA.

New York saw the arrival of **Henry Cho** in 1960. Cho was the first to introduce tae kwon do in the eastern U.S. Cho's ability, as well as his keen business sense, made him an instant success, and even today he runs one of the largest schools in Manhattan.

After becoming isshin-ryu founder Tatsuo Shimabuku's number 1 student, **Steve Armstrong**—a former Marine—settled in Seattle, Wash. in 1960. Armstrong taught karate out of his garage for a while and later opened a full-time dojo, which by the 1970s expanded into a chain of nine schools throughout the Pacific Northwest.

Other early pioneers of that region included Bill Ruder, Ernest Brinekee, Morris Menk, Bob Hill, Don Williams, and Bill Weaver.

Another principal force in the area at the time was **Bruce Terrill** of Portland, Oreg. Beginning in 1960, Terrill expanded his one school into a chain of twenty affiliated studios.

Terrill, a founder of his own style of **wu ying tao**, trained nationally ranked **Dan Anderson** and **Pauline Short,** one of the first female black belts in the U.S. Short opened a school exclusively for the instruction of women, one of the first in the U.S.

Virgil Adams was the first to teach karate in the state of Kansas, in

Karate pioneer Peter Urban was one of the most famous instructors on the East Coast. Founder of American goju, he is seen here in 1967 when he ran his famous Chinatown Dojo on Canal Street in Manhattan.

Two of George Cofield's top students, Thomas LaPuppet *(left)* and Alex Sternberg, went on to make names for themselves. LaPuppet became one of America's top competitors in sparring, and Sternberg became a leading kata competitor. Today both men teach karate in the New York area.

Photo by Mary Townsley

Dan Ivan *(left)* and Fumio Demura opened a chain of karate schools in southern California and made it one of the most successful in the nation. A former All Japan Champion, Demura was brought to the U.S. in 1965 by Ivan, who has been teaching here since the early 1960s.

Tsutomu Oshima, seen doing a flying side kick, was the first to teach Shotokan karate in the U.S. He founded the Southern California Karate Association in 1955—it later expanded into a larger organization, the Shotokan Karate of America.

Bill Wallace *(left)* and Joe Lewis at the 1972 USKA Grand Nationals.

Courtesy of *Inside Kung-Fu Magazine*

Photo by Mary Townsley

Joe Corley, an influential karate leader in the south, has his headquarters in Atlanta, Ga.

George Mattson was the first Uechi-ryu karate instructor in the U.S.

Courtesy of Anthony Mirakian

Anthony Mirakian *(left)* introduced Okinaway goju-ryu to the U.S. in 1960. Mirakian, who spent considerable time in Okinawa practicing karate, is one of the most knowledgeable Americans teaching the art in the U.S.

Robert Fusaro, seen judging kata, is a leading Shotokan instructor in the Midwest. He began teaching in Minneapolis in 1958.

Four early karate pioneers seen at the 1965 Nationals. *Left to right:* John Pachivas, one of the first teachers of karate in Florida and one of the leading members of the USKA for a long time; Henry Cho, a leading taekwondo instructor in New York City and a Black Belt Hall of Fame winner; Harold Long, first president of the International Ishinryu Karate Association and one of the first instructors to open a school in the southeast; Sam Pearson, a top Shorin-ryu instructor and one of the most successful competitors in the early days of American karate tournaments.

Left to right: Richard Kim and Hidy Ochiai. Kim and Ochiai, pioneers of Japanese karate, both came to the U.S. in the early 1960s. Kim settled on the West Coast, teaching in San Francisco; Ochiai began teaching his unique style of Washin-ryu on the East Coast.

Mike Stone *(right)* practices with a teammate at Fort Chaffee, Ark., in 1964. Stone went on to become the first superstar of American karate.

New York's Aaron Banks *(right),* one of America's greatest martial arts promoters, and Johnny Kuhl, one of New York's earliest instructors.

Allen Steen delivering a flying side thrust kick, ca. 1965.

Some of the top karateka in North America line up at the 1st World Karate Tournament, July 28, 1963, in Chicago. *Left tor ight:* Roy Oshiro, John Keehan, Phil Koeppel, George Mattson, Mas Tsuroka, Robert Trias, Ed Parker, Anthony Mirakian, Harold Long, Jhoon Rhee, Kim and Wendell Reeves.

Courtesy of Robert Trias

Ron Marchini *(right)* versus Chuck Norris in a tournament in the mid-1960s.

Three U.S. masters of the martial arts: Peter Urban, Ri. Signorelli and D. Nagle.

Dr. Maung Gyi *(center)* brought bando to the United States in 1960. He is seen here with Kim Soo Jin *(left)* and Robert Trias.

Early karate pioneers on the East Coast. *Standing, left to right:* John Kuhl, Gary Alexander, Hawk Frazier, Ed McGrath, Don Bohan, Lou Lizotte. *Kneeling, left to right:* Klein, Andrew Linick, Ralph Lindquist, Glenn Premru, Mr. Joseph.

Some of the top East Coast black belts line up for a group shot at the 1966 East Coast Open Karate Tournament. *Left to right:* Danny Pai, Harold Long, Ralph Lindquist, Steve Armstrong, Ed McGrath, George Cofield, Don Nagel, Rus Kozuki, Thomas LaPuppet, Joel Bucholz, Jerry Thomson, Pete Sirangano, Andrew Linick, Ed Kaloudis.

242

Three top American karate leaders of the 1960s. *Left to right:*
George Minshew, Pat Burleson, and Allen Steen.

Courtesy of Tom Decker

Steve Armstrong, one of the pioneers of Ishin-ryu karate, seen
here in the early 1970s.

Courtesy of *Official Karate Magazine*

Gary Alexander *(left)* was one of karate's early pioneers. A fighting
instructor, he won a number of major tournaments before
becoming one of the country's leading promoters in the 1960s.

Shotokan instructor Hidetaka Nishiyama came to the U.S. in 1961 and soon became one of the early leaders of karate in America.

Teruyuki Okazaki, a high-ranking JKA instructor, came to the U.S. in 1961 and began teaching in Philadelphia. A pioneer of Shotokan karate on the East Coast, Okazaki later founded the I.S.K.F., a leading Shotokan organization affiliated with the JKA.

1960. He operated out of Wichita.

Ralph Lindquist, an isshin-ryu stylist, opened a school in 1960 in New Cumberland, Pa.

In Michigan, Al Horton began teaching his uechi-ryu in Kalamazoo in 1960. Other early pioneers included J. Kim in Lansing; **Ernest Lieb** in Muskegon; **David Praim** in Mt. Clemens (1962), who taught fighters Everett Eddy and Johnny Lee; and Paul and Larry Malo from Detroit who taught Shito-ryu and operated a number of multi-million-dollar karate centers.

As the decade closed, karate was gaining appeal. While no single member of the 1950-60 group of pioneers appears to have been greatly successful, the fact that so many individuals were operating schools, whose enrollments were increasing steadily, proved this new form of self-defense was attractive to the general public. In this decade the foundation was laid for the circulation of styles, instructors, and masters that would in the 1960s see the art of karate surpass judo in numbers of active practitioners.

The 1960s also marked the beginning of an extensive immigration of Korean tae kwon do instructors. After Jhoon Rhee, who introduced tae kwon do in the U.S. in 1956, the first wave included: S. Henry Cho, **Richard Chun**, and Duk Sung Son in New York; D.S. Kim in Georgia; J. Kim and **Sang Kyu Shim** in Michigan; Mahn Suh Park in Pennsylvania; **Haeng Ung Lee** in Omaha; **Ki Whang Kim** in Maryland; and **Jack Hwang** in Oklahoma. In all, it is estimated that more than 25 masters during the early and mid-1960s settled in the U.S. The Vietnam War gave this native Korean art visibility. Pictures of Korean instructors training American GIs in hand-to-hand combat appeared in *Time* and *Newsweek*. While these legitimate instructors were encouraged to emigrate to the U.S., the teaching credential itself was to create an intense controversy in American karate. As more and more Korean tae kwon do instructors and masters arrived in the U.S., it was clearly unlikely that all of them could have taught American military personnel. Yet this claim, coupled with insupportable claims to unreasonably advanced degrees of black belt rank—usually no less than 7th dan—first caused suspicion, then rebellion by American karatemen. More often than not a third claim, that of being an "All Korean Champion," was another of the tae kwon do credentials. It is improbable that there were more than a few dozen All Korean Champions, since tae kwon do embraced no organized competitions until the 1960s—when more than 800 master instructors were teaching tae kwon do in the U.S. The degree and intensity of business competition was undoubtedly the motive for these exorbitant claims. At any rate, potential martial arts students now had a choice of where and with whom to study. By the early 1970s more than 1,200 tae kwon do instructors were reportedly teaching in the U.S.

Such phenomenal growth placed increasing demands on the tae kwon do community as a whole, and the need for a central organization quickly became apparent. In the U.S., as in Korea, the cause of organization was initially obstructed by affiliations of master instructors to parent schools and associations in Korea.

Meanwhile, within the Japanese karate community, Tsutomu Ohshima, who was still traveling, arranged in 1961 for Hidetaka Nishiyama to come to California to preside over his Los Angeles headquarters. Nishiyama arrived in July and within four months struck out on his own to form the **All America Karate Federation** (AAKF), a branch of the powerful Japan Karate Association (JKA). Today, the AAKF is one of the largest karate organizations in the U.S. This development spawned a bitter political rivalry between Ohshima and Nishiyama, which continues under the surface of the international amateur karate movement. Both pioneers, however, are consummate karate masters. Each is responsible for having firmly planted Shotokan karate in the U.S., and for having trained numerous disciples of high technical skill.

Richard Kim, sensei to such American karate pioneers as Peter Urban, Phil Koeppel, and Canada's Benny Allen, came to America from Japan in 1961 and began teaching at the Chinese YMCA in San Francisco, Calif. Later Kim became the foremost karate historian residing in the U.S.

Top JKA instructor **Teruyuki Okazaki** arrived in the U.S. in May 1961 and began teaching Shotokan karate in west Philadelphia. In Sept. 1962 he formed the East Coast Karate Association, a branch of the AAKF. Today he oversees the 50,000-member **International Shotokan Karate Federation.**

Also in Philadelphia that year, Mahn Suh Park established his first tae kwon do dojang, which, like Okazaki's dojo, is still in operation today.

It was around 1961 that **John Keehan**, alias "Count Dante," began teaching karate in the midwest from his base dojo in Chicago, Ill. Keehan joined the USKA in 1961, at age 22, and was instrumental in helping Trias firmly entrench the USKA in the midwest, the association's strongest territory. He taught numerous students all the way to black belt, who opened their own schools and turned out respected students.

On the night of April 23, 1970, he took part in the infamous "dojo war" that ended in the brutal stabbing death of his friend and student, Jim Koncevic, at the Green Dragon's Black Cobra training hall in Chicago. The tragedy left a profound mark on Keehan until his death from bleeding ulcers in 1975.

An early pioneer of karate in the South was John Pachivas, who became the first karate instructor in the Miami Beach area in 1961. Pachivas reportedly has been active in the martial arts since the mid-1940s, and holds degrees in judo, jujutsu, and goju-ryu karate.

In Jan. 1961 **George Pesare** introduced kenpo karate to Rhode Island in Providence. Preceded only by Ted Olsen, Pesare would in time become the foremost instructor in his state and an influential leader in the northeastern U.S.

One of the first New York instructors to be affiliated with Mas Oyama was Augustin DeMello, who opened the New York Kyokushinkai karate club in Greenwich Village in 1961. He later broke away from Oyama and quit teaching.

Daeshik Kim, a judo and tae kwon do instructor, came to Atlanta, Ga., in 1961 where he began teaching tae kwon do in the physical education department of Georgia State College.

Among Kim's students were **Joe Corley, Chris McLoughlin,** "Atlas" Jesse King, Larry McClure, and Dick Lane. In 1966, Kim sold his Institute of Self-Defense, a non-campus club, to McLoughlin and Corley.

Corley and McLoughlin established several branch schools over the years, all in and around Atlanta, and they jointly produced the first **Battle of Atlanta** in 1970. Later, the tournament would become one of the most prestigious in American sport karate.

Individually, Corley would become one of the most influential voices in Southern karate by spearheading the formation of the **Southeast Karate Association** (SEKA). In the 1970s, he would invest most of his time and money in the full-contact karate movement.

McLoughlin would make his mark as one of the first professional martial arts journalists who also was a black belt.

In Los Angeles, Mito Uyehara, an aikido practitioner, and his brother, Jim, published the inaugural issue of *Black Belt Magazine* in 1961. The first issue was in digest form, with articles on judo, karate, aikido, and **kendo.** Though it suffered lean years, the publication became one of the most successful in its field. In the late 1960s, the brothers dissolved their partnership, Jim taking with him the merchandise trade—which later developed into Martial Arts Supplies—and Mito retaining ownership of the magazine. The publication struggled until Mito launched a line of paperback textbooks, which eventually brought large profits. This, coupled with shrewd capitalization on the martial arts movie trend of the early 1970s, made Mito Uyehara one of the few millionaires in the martial arts business.

Out of the Uyehara publishing empire have come some 60 textbooks, the monthly, *Karate Illustrated* (since 1969), and the monthly *Fighting Stars* (since 1973). In 1975 Mito reduced his active involvement and moved to Hawaii.

In 1961 New York's **John Kuhl** wrote, edited, posed for, and published a karate manual/magazine called *Combat Karate*. Kuhl started his karate training in Montreal in 1957 under Ari Anastasiatis. After moving to New York City in 1970, he continued his training with Peter Urban and **Gosei Yamaguchi**, son of Gogen, the goju-ryu teacher. Two of Kuhl's early students were **Aaron Banks** and **Al Weiss.** Kuhl and Weiss co-produced in 1962 a manual entitled *Karate,* the most popular instruction book at its price. Its success prompted the 1968 publishing of *Official Karate Magazine,* a bi-monthly. It soon became a monthly, with international distribution. The magazine's outlook is radical compared to the conservative *Black Belt.* It was an animated voice in the movement toward an Americanized form of karate. And Weiss, its editor, has been recognized for writing the most potent monthly editorials in his field.

Courtesy of Official Karate Magazine

Count Dante, whose real name was John Keehan, was one of the most controversial karate instructors in the U.S.

Grand Champion Joe Hayes

245

Bob Yarnall, a **shorin-ryu** instructor, opened his first dojo in 1962 in St. Louis, Mo., where he has remained to this day. A student of James Wax, Yarnall has instructed such pioneers as **Jim Harrison, Parker Shelton**, and Bill Marsh, who was a successful competitor in the European karate circuit. Yarnall is probably the best-known exponent of Matsubayashi-ryu in the U.S. and has been a long time member of Trias' USKA. His wife, Joyce, assists her husband in the operation of his schools, and is a photographer whose collection includes many historic pictures of the sport and its early champions.

Jhoon Rhee opened his first school in Washington, D.C., in 1962, and within three months had amassed more than 100 students. This, then, became the basis of the Jhoon Rhee empire, which later blossomed into one of the largest privately-owned martial arts enterprises in the world today.

The Jhoon Rhee Institutes have developed many of the most accomplished karate competitors in American karate. Some notable students are: **Larry Carnahan,** Michael Coles, **Gordon Franks, Jeff Smith, Jose Jones,** Wayne Van Buren, **John and Pat Worley,** Otis Hooper, **John Chung** and **Rodney Batiste.**

Rhee would also begin teaching tae kwon do to distinguished members of the U.S. government hierarchy, senators and congressmen among them. Through his endeavors, Rhee would become a genuine celebrity to the D.C. general public.

Allen Steen, Rhee's student, established the first school of his eventual empire in 1962 in Dallas, Tex. Only Johnny Nash preceded him by a few months. No one, however, would dominate the Southwest territory as would Steen. Like Rhee, Steen trained many of America's top karatemen, among them **Mike Anderson, Skipper Mullins, Pat Burleson, Fred Wren, Roy Kurban,** and **Jim** and **Jenice Miller.**

In 1962 after a visit to Pittsburgh by Master Tatsuo Shimabuku, at the invitation of James Morabeto and Harry Smith, disharmony once again set in among the city's isshinryu principals. Morabeto opened several dojo of his own, while Harry Ackland and Joe Penneywell established the Academy of Isshinryu Karate in downtown Pittsburgh. William Duessel and William Wallace, students of Shimabuko, assumed ownership in the late 1960s.

At this time, Nick Long began teaching Okinawan kempo in Greensburg, Pa., where he built a large following of college students.

In Denver, Robert Thompson and Fran Heitmann jointly opened a tang soo do school in 1962. That same year, **Chuck Sereff,** a black belt student of Heitmann's, established his first school and brought in Korean instructor Moon Ku Baek to teach there. Sereff and one of his black belts, **Ralph Krause,** opened another Denver karate school, but later the two went separate ways. Today, Sereff has one of the largest operations in Colorado.

Frank Ruiz earned a chestful of medals including the Purple Heart, Silver Star, and Bronze Star during the Korean War. Upon his release, he became one of Peter Urban's first students in 1960. In 1962, he launched his own teaching career in New York City, and produced two nationally recognized fighters, **Louis Delgado** and Herbie Thompson (of Florida), and East Coast karate champions Ron Van Clief, Owen Watson, and the late Malachi Lee. Ruiz later broke away from Urban to form his own Nisei Goju organization. In 1970 Ruiz cheated death after being struck by a car traveling 80 m.p.h., managing four years later to walk normally and even practice karate.

The Birth of Franchised Karate In 1963 two brothers, Jim and Al Tracy, founded their first kenpo karate school in San Francisco; both had been students of Ed Parker. After spending large sums in development costs, the brothers launched what became the largest chain of karate schools in the world, under the trade name "Tracy's Karate." The Tracy brothers brought big business practices to karate. Their strategy included a proven sales system, adapted from commercial dance studios. At its peak, 1969-73, the Tracy organization was estimated to have 70 studios under its franchise banner. After hiring **Joe Lewis,** one of the sport's brightest stars, as a figurehead for its franchise recruitment program, the organization attracted instructors who, using the knowledge gained in business indoctrination courses, were able to make careers in the martial arts. Among the early corps of Tracy's novitiates were **Jay T. Will, Al Dacascos, Jerry Smith, Jerry Piddington,** Dick Willett, Roger Greene, **Steve LaBounty,** and Ray Klingenberg.

At the same time, throughout the mid- and late 1960s, other instructors and organizations were developing sales systems and

Allen Steen *(left)*, known as "Father of Texas Karate," seen here with Hidetaka Nishiyama in the early 1960s

Jhoon Rhee, "Father of American Tae Kwon Do," receives Martial Arts Man of the Century award from the Washington, D.C., Touchdown Club. Rhee runs one of the most successful chains of karate clubs in the U.S.

246

East Coast's Harry Rosenstein was among the founders of the Nisei goju system, an offshoot of Peter Urban's USA goju.

Courtesy of Ron Taganashi

New York's Frank Ruiz, one of the founders of the Nisei goju system

Courtesy of *Official Karate Magazine*

business practices particularly suited to the martial arts. Jhoon Rhee, Allen Steen, **Chuck Norris,** and Ed Parker soon expanded into franchising. **Bob Wall** of Los Angeles is credited with having helped many martial artists adopt sound business practices in their schools, among them Norris, Rhee, and Colorado's **Jim Harkins.** An astute businessman, Wall developed and manualized a sales system still in use in many professional karate studios across the nation.

In 1963 Chuck Norris, who would become one of the most respected karate fighters in the world, established his first school in Torrance, south of Los Angeles. In 1968 he and Bob Wall bought out Joe Lewis' interest in the Sherman Oaks Karate Studio. From there he launched a chain of seven studios until 1975, when he gave up the operation to concentrate fully on a motion picture career.

Norris was responsible for guiding more than 100 students to black-belt rank and dozens to competitive prominence. Among them are: Jerry Taylor, **Pat Johnson, John Natividad, Howard Jackson, Ralph Alegria, Darnell Garcia,** and Bob Burbidge, among many, many others.

In April 1963 Master Duk Sung Son, president of the World Tae Kwon Do Association, immigrated to the U.S. and began teaching in and around New York City. Within a few years, Son was teaching his art at Princeton, N.Y., Brown and Fordham Universities, and later at the U.S. Military Academy at West Point.

Francisco Conde in 1963 initiated classes exclusively for females at the Women's Karate Club of Fort Meade, Maryland. There his wife, Kathleen, received some of her early training before going on to become one of the premier black belt competitors in her region. Known for his tournament promotions, as early as 1963 Conde became a driving force behind many of the regional activities of the Mid-Atlantic states.

Roger Carpenter, a black belt student of George Pesare, came to Wichita, Kans., in Sept. 1963. Carpenter taught karate for two years at churches, YMCAs, and a National Guard Armory. In the spring of 1965, he opened the first commercial karate school in Wichita. By 1964, Jim Harrison had also established a school in Kansas City.

In Denver, Shotokan stylist Joe Costello (d. 1973), from Hawaii, opened a dojo downtown. That same year, Ralph Krause opened the first of an eventual chain of karate schools in Colorado.

Ki Whang Kim, a highly respected tae kwon do master, organized a YMCA class in Washington, D.C., in 1963. This class produced some outstanding D.C. martial artists including John Camance, **Albert Cheeks, Phil Cunningham, Mike Warren, Furman Marshall,** and John Mickens. During the 1970s Mike Warren was widely considered to be America's best tournament fighter and, indisputably, one of the best technicians in the sport.

Lou Angel, Jack Hwang, and Bill Brisco, all of Oklahoma City, are the recognized pioneers of karate in Oklahoma. Angel, a former U.S. Marine and student of Peter Urban, arrived in Oklahoma at an unspecified date in the early 1960s. He is best known for having produced the Tulsa Southwest Karate Championships in 1963, where **Mike Stone** would launch his impressive fighting career. Stone, then still a brown belt, became an overnight sensation by winning first place in the sparring division and soon rose to prominence as the sport's first superstar.

Jack Hwang, a pioneer of tae kwon do, immigrated to the U.S. in 1960. He taught quietly until opening his first school in Oklahoma City in 1964. In 1965, Hwang produced his inaugural All American Open Karate Championships, which is a highlight of the southwestern karate circuit.

Marine sergeant **Sam Pearson**, a disciple of Master **Eizo Shimabuku,** founded a shorin-ryu karate club in 1963 at Camp LeJeune, N.C. His most famous student is the aforementioned Glenn Premru of Pittsburgh, who would become one of the sport's first corps of great kata champions and flamboyant performers.

Tournaments The early 1960s brought the first American karate tournaments. Until 1963 several local and, at best, regional competitions were organized in different parts of the U.S. Principal among these early events were the All America Karate Championships and the North American Karate Championships. The former was held in Los Angeles in Dec. 1961 by Hidetaka Nishiyama, concurrent with his formulation of the All America Karate Federation. Nishiyama chose as the tournament site the Olympic Auditorium, the West

Courtesy of Tom Decker

Donny Williams delivers a dropping side kick on Howard Jackson, top American karate competitor.

Glen Oyama *(left)* with Ron Marchini at the 2nd Hawaii vs. Mainland karate championships.

Ray Dalke doing a flying side kick soon after receiving his black belt in 1963 from H. Nishiyama. Dalke was among the leading Shotokan competitors in the mid and late 1960s and is today a member of the I.S.K.F. and teaches karate in southern California.

At one of the East Coast karate tournaments, Louis Delgado *(left)* receives a reverse punch from Numano. World champions Joe Lewis (in gi, standing at left) and Chuck Norris (in gi, sitting behind referee) watch.

Photo taken at 1st International Karate Championship, held in Long Beach, Calif., in 1964. *Front row, left to right:* Pat Burleson, Bruce Lee, Anthony Mirakia, Jhoon Rhee. *Back row, left to right:* Allen Steen, George Mattson, Ed Parker, Tatsuo Oshima, Robert Trias.

Chuck Loven *(left),* trainer of many Texas karate champions, with Duane Ethington, one of the top martial arts writers in the U.S.

Coast boxing center. The tournament was produced as a fund-raiser for the March for Muscular Dystrophy. Participants were chiefly members of the Shotokan style of karate, but some came from as far as Canada and Hawaii.

The North American Karate Championships, conducted on Nov. 24, 1962, was the first karate tournament held at Madison Square Garden, and the first open karate competition in America. Here, Mas Oyama appeared for the second time in his illustrious career, and this time the appearance was not for the purpose of demonstrating karate's superiority to professional boxing and wrestling. Preceding the finals, Oyama presented one of his impressive breaking routines, crushing rocks, bricks, and boards with his bare hands, feats even at that time considered phenomenal by the American public. **Gary Alexander,** one of the early wave of "fighting" instructors, won the black belt sparring championship. In 1963 he established his first school in New Jersey and began promoting notable karate tournaments himself.

On July 28, 1963, Robert Trias and John Keehan jointly hosted the 1st World Karate Tournament at the University of Chicago Fieldhouse, gathering contestants and officials from around the country. (The 1963 event was won by **AlGene Caravlia.**) This was the first truly national American karate tournament and the forerunner of the many subsequent tournaments using and abusing the title of "World Championship." To date, this misnomer has been attached by various promoters to more than 20 North American karate tournaments. Clearly, it is an inexact title, since the participants do not come from all over the world.

Tournament titles were not an issue, however, during the embryonic stage. What is important is that Trias' event attracted most of the prominent American karateka. What took place in Chicago set a precedent for the emergence of large-scale, national-caliber competitions. This particular event was retitled the USKA Nationals in 1966, and in 1968 adopted its present title, the **USKA Grand Nationals.** It is one of the longest-running annual karate tournaments in America.

Also in 1963, Texan Allen Steen inaugurated his Dallas Southwest Karate Championships, in which Mike Stone, still a brown belt, won the black belt fighting division. Steen's tournament was retitled in 1965 the U.S. Karate Championships. **David Moon,** one of the few Asian instructors competing in open sparring divisions, won the first of three consecutive grand championships there. The tournament maintained its national prestige until the mid-1970s.

During this period many judo and jujutsu black belts had begun studying karate; their styles were often unrefined. Some were the recipients of "cross-over" ranks, i.e., because of their proficiency in one art they might receive **dan** rank in karate. As each generation of American karate black belts became progressively more polished, fluid, and performance-conscious, the old ex-judo/jujutsu converts appeared out of touch with new developments in the art. Despite criticism, many of these same figures were responsible for introducing the martial arts to individuals who would later make contributions to the growth of American karate. One of these, Jerry Durant, trained top fighter Artis Simmons as well as Art Sykes, William Cavalier and Vince Christeano.

In 1964 Trias again staged his World Championships in Chicago, but this year two new tournaments shared the spotlight. The first was Ed Parker's **International Karate Championships** in Long Beach, Calif. Parker's tournament, like Trias' the year before, attracted the biggest names in American karate. Mike Stone became the event's first grand champion, an accomplishment overshadowed historically by the results of a demonstration presented there by an unknown Chinese stylist named Bruce Lee.

Lee was a sensation. Demonstrating his skills, he sent partners reeling backward with his 1-inch punch, a technique that became a personal trademark. Lee's performance left a lasting impression on many practitioners and non-martial-artist spectators.

Parker's Internationals grew in size and prestige until about 1976, reaching its zenith in 1974, when Parker drew a record-setting 6,000 contestants. In 1975 Parker awarded prize money totaling $16,250, the largest yet at an American Pro/Am tournament.

The second prominent event of 1964 was Jhoon Rhee's U.S. National Karate Championships, held in Washington, D.C. **Pat Burleson** of Texas, winner of the black belt grand championship, joined AlGene Caraulia in becoming the first recognized national

champion of the new sport. Today Burleson is looked upon as the "granddaddy" of tournament fighters and the first genuine star in the sport.

In late 1964 Mahn Suh Park produced the first open tournament in Philadelphia, the Globe Tae Gyun Championships; it became an annual promotion enjoying steady growth.

Jhoon Rhee pulled off a coup in 1965: he persuaded *Wide World of Sports* to film and subsequently broadcast segments of his U.S. National Karate Championships. His was the first American karate tournament to receive television coverage from a network sports program. However, a heated match for the grand championship between Stone and Walt Worthy, in which there was bloodshed and heavy contact, earned the displeasure of the show's producers. Select excerpts only were broadcast. And the program ignored the sport for the next nine years.

It is important to recall here the nature of competition in this period. It was a time of bloodshed and brutality. Historians have called it—suitably—the "blood and guts era" of American sport karate, a period spanning from 1963, when the major open tournaments began, to roughly 1970, when the sport temporarily graduated to its first kick-boxing phase. During this time tournaments were an arena for only the most courageous karate fighters, with a high tolerance for absorbing punishment. The type of sparring then popular is called "non contact" or "light contact." Rules stipulated closely pulled blows to the face and only light body contact. Excessive contact was grounds for disqualification. Despite this general rule, heavy contact to both the face and body was so common that competitors and officials alike appeared to accept it. The techniques, crude and calamitous by today's standards, were as unrefined as the rules governing the infant sport. A fighter might break an opponent's bones or knock him into the grandstand and not be disqualified. If he was a true fighter, the opponent was expected to come back and dish out the same punishment he had received.

The Second Generation In karate instruction a virtual explosion took place from 1964 onward, not only in the U.S., but in Canada, South America, Europe, and Asia. Ex-military personnel, having studied the martial arts in the Orient, returned home en masse to open karate schools. Augmenting this rapid growth were the second generation, students of the original pioneers, who concurrently established studios of their own.

In Sept. 1964 the Institute of Technology in Pasadena adopted a regular course of karate instruction supervised by Tsutomu Ohshima. This is the first known karate program to have been accepted as an accredited course by an American college.

The move to establish karate as part of the educational curriculum had enjoyed widespread success in Japan. Thus, the early Japanese stylists in the U.S. concentrated on this aim. Later, the Korean tae kwon do instructors, perhaps even more meticulously organized, likewise made significant progress toward gaining acceptance for the martial arts in American institutions of higher learning.

In Beaver Falls, Pa., Willie Wetzel, a master of **pukulan**, was one of the first instructors of an Indonesian discipline to surface in the U.S. One of his students, **Barbara Niggel,** in the mid-1970s distinguished herself as a national kata champion.

Pauline Short should probably be called the "mother of American karate." Short opened in 1965 the first karate school exclusively catering to a female clientele, in Portland, Oreg. In 1975 she became one of the nation's top 10 female fighters.

Also in 1964, Bill Readers emerged in Erie, Pa. He trained Art Sykes.

In 1965 Glenn Premru returned to Pittsburgh, having trained with Shorin-ryu instructor Sam Pearson. He opened a dojo in the North Hills section of town.

Mike Stone became the first superstar of the sport. He had dominated competition since 1963, and by the time of his retirement had been active for only eighteen months. Although he competed in a total of nine tournaments, all of them were large-scale events featuring highly rated fighters. Stone won in 1965 what could be considered Karate's Triple Crown: the Internationals in Long Beach, U.S. Nationals in Washington, D.C., and World Championships in Chicago. Although Stone claims to have won 89 consecutive black belt matches, the record shows that he lost a grand championship match in the middle of his run, at the 1964 Western U.S. Karate Championships in Salt Lake City. (Stone won the heavyweight title, but was defeated

Skipper Mullins, seen here breaking five one-inch boards, had the fastest kicks in sport karate during his competitive career.

Tak Kubota *(right)*, leading West Coast sensei, with Chuck Norris at one of Kubota's earliest tournaments.

Left to right: Roger Carpenter, Fred Wren, and Bob Wall.

Joe Lewis *(center)* and Robert Culp *(right)* at the 1967 U.S. Nathals in Washington, D.C.

Left to right: Mike Stone, John Townsley, and Chuck Norris at a clinic in 1969.

by Dave Johnson in the grand championship play-off.)

The first genuine martial arts craze in America began in 1966, when Bruce Lee made his acting debut as Kato in the *Green Hornet* TV series. From Sept. 9, the weekly series remained on the air until Mar. 17, 1967. There were 26 half-hour episodes, and reruns began in 1968. Although this series was short-lived, Lee's provocative kung-fu action in the show's numerous fight scenes stirred the public's imagination. Thousands of new students became involved in the martial arts. This development seemed to prove that the popularity and acceptance of the Asian martial arts was directly related to the degree of its exposure in the visual media.

During the mid- and late 1960s "American karate" emerged. The name describes an openminded practice method and philosophy that challenged time-honored Asian patterns, traditional karate. American karate gained support from both anti-traditionalists, opposed to the strict oriental ideology, and non-traditionalists, a less radical sect, opposed to the study of one system exclusively. Basically, it was traditional karate put to typically American uses.

Until the late 1960s Asian instructors in the U.S. wielded considerable political power, chiefly because they controlled large numbers of students. This status slowly began to change as Trias, Parker, Steen, Urban, Nagle, and other American karate advocates built personal followings, and American names started to become synonymous with karate. After 1969 American athletes dominated the fighting divisions of major tournaments with very few exceptions. This development, in conjunction with the proliferation of American karate instructors, worked to precipitate an important shift in the martial arts hierarchy.

With the rapid growth and diversification of karate during this era, there came about, perhaps inevitably, political fragmentation and an unprecedented degree of stylistic prejudice. There was, and still is, a tendency among various styles and stylists to ignore the merits, however consequential, of other styles. Among karate styles and karate organizations there are factions that multiply alarmingly each year. Out of this dissonance and confusion have emerged three loosely identifiable legions in the U.S.: the traditionalists or purists, the non-traditionalists and anti-traditionalists—both of which have been called the commercialists—and a mixed group that can be called the commercial-traditionalists.

The year 1966 marked the competitive debut of Joe Lewis, who had distinguished himself quickly, earning his black belt in Okinawa in a mere seven months. With just twenty-two months of training, Lewis entered his first tournament in 1966, Rhee's U.S. Nationals. He won the black belt championship, using one technique exclusively, the side kick. Astonishingly, no opponent scored a single point against him. Demonstrating his versatility, Lewis also won the black belt kata championship.

During the late 1960s the number of karate tournaments swelled substantially on a state, regional, and especially, on the national level. Yet, as the sport grew, so did its problems. Promoters disagreed on rules and procedures; the sport suffered from a lack of unification and standardization, a problem that continues to plague it today. These difficulties did not impede two rising tournament stars, both of whom became recognized world champions: **Chuck Norris** and **Skipper Mullins.**

After losing the 1966 Internationals grand championship to Allen Steen, Norris came back to win the grand title two years running, 1967 and 1968. He also won the grand title of the 1967 and 1968 All American Karate Championships, produced by S. Henry Cho in New York. Norris was an innovator in combination techniques; until his arrival fighters usually delivered only one technique to score a point. After his victories combinations became standard in the sport.

Skipper Mullins, 6 feet, 150 lbs., was heralded as the fastest kicker in karate. Many of his victories were the result of whiplike kicks, at a time when punchers dominated the tournament circuit. Mullins rose to prominence on lightweight and middleweight victories in the All American Karate Championships, produced by Jack Hwang in Oklahoma City, and the Top 10 Championships. In one weekend in Feb. 1967 Mullins fought in New York City on Friday, Dallas on Saturday, and Los Angeles on Sunday. Norris and Mullins, with Mike Stone and Joe Lewis, are the great karate champions of the 1960s—only Lewis continued competing into the 1970s.

Team Competition In 1967, in New York City, team competition was introduced. The concept was originated by Aaron Banks, who became karate's most prolific promoter. Banks continued the team competition format, producing the first team event of national caliber in 1968, the East Coast vs. West Coast Team Championships. The victorious West Coast contingent was represented by Joe Lewis, **Steve Sanders,** Chuck Norris, and Jerry Taylor. Representatives for the East Coast were Thomas LaPuppet, **Joe Hayes,** Kazuyoshi Tanaka, and Louis Delgado.

Team competition was soon adopted by karate promoters throughout the country. Banks also deserves credit for keeping sport karate flourishing in New York when others could not: from 1967 to 1975 his over 100 flamboyant productions gave regional exposure to aspiring East Coast competitors.

The Sport Turns Professional For five years, from 1963-68, sport karate had grown strictly on an amateur basis. In 1968 several promoters endeavored independently to add a professional dimension, offering prize money to victorious fighters and meeting the expenses of star names participating in the events.

In Feb. 1968 **Jim Harrison** staged the 1st World Professional Karate Championships (WPKC), the first of a string of tournaments to use this popular title. In principle, at least, this was the first professional tournament in the history of American karate. Harrison conducted the event in his Kansas City dojo, two days after Allen Steen's U.S. Championships in Dallas. Many top fighters were invited, but in view of Harrison's permissive rules, which endorsed heavy contact, only six fighters participated. They were: Joe Lewis, Bob Wall, Skipper Mullins, J. Pat Burleson, David Moon, and Fred Wren. Several fighters suffered broken ribs and noses and were forced to forfeit. Lewis won the title, becoming karate's first paid professional fighter when Harrison awarded him the token sum of one dollar.

In Aug. 1968 Robert Trias and Atlee Chittim produced the World's Hemisphere Karate Championships in San Antonio, Tex. The second professional karate promotion held in the U.S., this was the first to be conducted as a genuine tournament. Victor Moore of Ohio won the grand championship in a spirited battle with Joe Lewis and took a purse of $500. (Lewis also took away $500, a contract guarantee.)

The most important professional karate event of the decade was Aaron Banks' World Professional Karate Championship, produced on Nov. 24, 1968, at the Waldorf Astoria Hotel in New York City. This invitational established four fighters as recognized world champions. In contrast to Harrison's event, each champion was paid $600. And Banks paid all of his ringside personnel, from officials to the announcer. The champions were heavyweight Joe Lewis (over Victor Moore); light-heavyweight Mike Stone (over Bob Taiani); middleweight Chuck Norris (over Louis Delgado); and lightweight Skipper Mullins (over Kazuyoshi Tanaka). There were subsequent protests disputing the event's status as a legitimate world championship, in the sense that the contestants were predominantly American, but no one disputed the world-class skill of the four winners. (Only Norris returned in 1969 to defend—successfully—his title.)

Another karate competitor who made his bid for national prominence at this time was **Ron Marchini** of Stockton, Calif. He won Henry Cho's Tournament of Champions in 1968 in New York City, and then went on to distinguish himself as one of the top competitors of the late 1960s and early 1970s.

Challenges to authority and inconsistent tournament regulations became the rule rather than the exception, though tournament planning was steadily improving. The amount of promiscuous contact in tournaments became a destructive issue, and injuries increased dramatically, often because of inexperienced and intimidated officials. Some believed the sport should encourage contact; others wanted contact barred.

Commercial karate came of age in 1969. Women and children flocked to the schools, as more and more instructors expanded classes to accommodate them.

In 1968, two influential martial artists, **Jay T. Will,** and AlGene Caraulia established schools in Ohio. Will, a student of Ed Parker and Scott Loring, had relocated from San Jose, Calif., to Columbus, opening the very first Tracy's karate franchise in the U.S. Caraulia, the winner of Robert Trias' 1963 World Championships, had relocated to Cleveland from Chicago.

Until 1965 the Japanese styles had the largest following in the U.S., but by 1967 Okinawan karate was attracting more students. In 1969, with the great influx of Korean immigrants, tae kwon do suddenly outdrew the others. More than ever before, practitioners

were changing from one style to another. Consequently, interest in organizations and unification dwindled.

The Birth of Full-Contact Karate Joe Lewis objected to the unrealistic structure of noncontact karate, in which blows were to be pulled short of actual contact. Its nature was to score points without producing results—what Bruce Lee called "swimming on dry land." At the peak of Lewis' disenchantment, which had begun as early as 1969, he started training with, and was influenced by, Bruce Lee and ranked heavyweight boxer Joey Orbill. He began training in various Los Angeles boxing gyms, with the intention of becoming a professional boxer.

In late 1969 Lewis was contacted by Los Angeles promoter Lee Faulkner, who was organizing a major noncontact team contest in which he wanted Lewis to participate. Lewis agreed on the condition that Faulkner permit him to fight also in a **full-contact** match. Faulkner agreed to promote the bout, but only if Lewis fought in the team event as well. Lewis searched frantically for a suitable opponent. After repeated rejections from top karate fighters, he found Greg Baines, a San Jose kenpo stylist, who agreed to meet Lewis under full-contact conditions.

The bout, preceded by the U.S. Team Championship, took place on Jan. 17, 1970, at the Long Beach Sports Arena. Results of the contests were victories for Lewis, by a 2nd-round knockout, and for a West Coast team composed of Lewis, Mike Stone, Bob Wall, Chuck Norris, and Skipper Mullins. And, while the Lewis/Baines bout had been promoted as the "first full-contact" championship, during the fight itself the uninformed announcer inadvertently but repeatedly called it "American kick-boxing." The announcer's blunder caught on, and Lewis became known for having pioneered American kick-boxing. The term "full-contact karate" would not be used until several years later. In this its original form, full-contact karate survived for only a year; Lewis successfully defended his title during that year ten times, with no opponent lasting past the 2nd round. The Jan. 17 team bout also marked the last fight in Chuck Norris' brilliant competitive career.

Karate in the 1970s **Pat Johnson** of Sherman Oaks, Calif., a nationally respected tournament referee, originated the "penalty point" system for excessive contact in 1970. The "Johnson Ruling," as it was called by *Karate Illustrated,* essentially ended the uncontrolled "blood and guts era" of noncontact sport karate. Johnson's innovation, introduced at the National Black Belt Championships in Albuquerque, is used as a standard today in every U.S. karate tournament. Under this rule, competitors who make excessive contact forfeit one point; any degree of dangerous contact results in disqualification.

The year 1970 also marked the emergence of amateur sport karate on a truly international scale: 32 nations took part in the 1st WUKO World Karate Championships at Tokyo's **Budokan.** A conference held prior to the event had resulted in the name of **World Union of Karate-do Organizations** (WUKO). Qualification and participation rules, however, were ill-defined and the competition rules were those used by the Japanese. WUKO had no constitution or organizational rules covering the tournament. As such, Japan was permitted to have four teams competing and the U.S. three. All other nations had one. The U.S. members had been selected by extensive negotiations among the principal U.S. Japanese karate stylists. The only nationally known U.S. member was **Tonny Tulleners** of Los Angeles; he won third place in individual fighting at the WUKO event.

The disorganization of the 1st WUKO World Championships was the chief reason for the eventual existence of two organizations governing international amateur karate: WUKO and the International Amateur Karate Federation (IAKF) with Los Angeles' Hidetaka Nishiyama the elected executive director as of 1974, when the association was formed. The struggle to organize international karate has engaged these two bodies since then. The goal is a worthy one: Olympic recognition and acceptance for the sport.

The AAKF resisted a move in 1973 by the AAU to relinquish its rights as the international karate representative of the U.S. in WUKO, and subsequently resigned its membership in the AAU. Afterwards, the AAU formed its own karate committee with **Caylor Adkins,** a student of Tsutomu Ohshima, named its first chairman. So bitter were the political conflicts that in 1976 Adkins dropped out of karate altogether and moved from Los Angeles to a farm in middle America.

In Thailand, its homeland, kick-boxing, or more properly, Muay

Jim Harrison, one of the Midwest's all-time great instructors and one of the pioneers of karate in Kansas.

Right to left: Green belt Pat Worley and brown belt Jeff Smith at the 1968 U.S. Championships in Dallas, Texas.

Louis Delgado competing in kata

Left to right: Bob Yarnall, John Townsley, Jim Chapman, Robert Trias, Ed Parker, John Kuhl, and Parker Shelton at the Midcontinental Karate Championships in 1969. Photo by Mary Townsley

Thai **(Thai kick-boxing)** was—and is—the national pastime. In America, however, it failed dismally. In 1971 American kick-boxing died almost as suddenly as it had begun. There was virtually no spectator support, and promoters were losing more money than ever before. Along with kick-boxing, professional karate, in its noncontact form, also died. Chuck Norris held perhaps the last important pro tournament of the initial era. His 2nd World Pro/Am Championships of 1971 attracted a large representation of top-rated fighters, but barely 1,000 spectators showed up at the spacious Los Angeles Sports Arena where it was staged.

In the 1970s, the ties between parent schools in Korea and tae kwon do instructors in the U.S. had been weakened by a decade of separation and "Americanization." Consequently, a number of regional tae kwon do associations were born. On the nation's college and university campuses the American Tae Kwon Do Coaches Association and the American Collegiate Tae Kwon Do Association were created in 1972. These organizations worked jointly to send a U.S. team to the inaugural World Tae Kwon Do Championships in 1973, at which the U.S. team placed second, and the 2nd World Championships in 1974, both held in Seoul, Korea.

The most significant development of 1971 was the advent of the "Longstreet" television series, co-starring Bruce Lee. Unlike productions that had preceded it, the one-hour season opener actually identified the art being shown and was the first to explain on screen the philosophy behind the Asian fighting arts. The program was a showcase for Lee's innovative teaching methods. Cast as a martial arts master, Lee taught the blind detective, Longstreet (James Franciscus), how to protect himself, through both the physical maneuvers of **jeet kune do** and Lee's personal philosophy. That particular show is now considered by many martial arts aficianados Bruce Lee's best work on film, and it has become a classic. The season opener was written by **Stirling Silliphant,** one of Lee's students.

This year marked the rise to stardom of **Bill Wallace**, who rocketed from virtual obscurity to America's number-1-ranked karate fighter, a position he also held in 1972 and again in 1974. Wallace won Allen Steen's highly competitive U.S. Championships and the USKA Grand Nationals.

In 1972 an astonishing growth occurred in the martial arts. Much of it was directly attributable to the martial arts' sudden emergence as a bona fide entertainment vehicle. It began when filmmaker Tom Laughlin released *Billy Jack* in which he starred. Although the karate sequences in *Billy Jack* took but a few minutes of screen time, they were climactic. Filmed in slow motion, with hapkido master **Bong Soo Han** doubling for Laughlin, they demonstrated more than any previous motion picture the electrifying visual aspects of the martial arts.

Bruce Lee's *Fists of Fury,* released on the heels of *Billy Jack,* became one of the first Chinese films to be distributed to general movie theaters. In the Orient, it unexpectedly broke all box-office records, eventually surpassing the longstanding hit, *The Sound of Music.* Shortly afterward, Lee's second film venture with Raymond Chow, *Fist of Fury (The Chinese Connection* in the U.S.), eclipsed the success of its predecessor and catapulted Lee to stardom as the biggest box-office draw in the history of Asian cinema.

Back in the U.S., the mounting martial arts mania was accommodated by an influx of Hong Kong kung-fu films that virtually flooded the American market. Critics labeled them "Eastern Westerns" or "chop-sockeys." But the trend found its way into big-budget projects such as *Red Sun,* starring Charles Bronson and Toshiro Mifune, and *The Mechanic,* again starring Bronson and featuring Hollywood karate master **Tak Kubota.**

Kung Fu, starring David Carradine, aired as an ABC-TV *Movie of the Week* on Aug. 8, 1972. This weekly series, which showcased martial arts philosophy as well as physicality, had a positive effect on the trend, introducing martial arts on a regular basis directly to American living rooms.

The need for stuntmen familiar with the martial arts grew. Conventional Hollywood stuntmen were at the time inexperienced in the arts, and martial artists poured into Hollywood casting offices. Some of the more flamboyant and fortunate were catapulted to stardom. With the release of *Melinda,* Los Angeles' **Jim Kelly,** hired as a fight-scene choreographer, was made a co-star. Kelly went on to star in *Enter the Dragon, Black Belt Jones, The Golden Needles,*

Bill Wallace *(right)* during his competitive career in noncontact karate. Wallace was ranked the number one fighter in the U.S. during the early 1970s and went on to become full-contact karate's superstar.

256

Fred Wren wins the 1970 U.S. title in Dallas, Tx.

Truck Turner, Three the Hard Way, Hot Potato, Black Samurai, and *Take a Hard Ride.*

Also in 1972 **Emil Farkas** founded Creative Action Associates, the first martial arts company to cater to the motion picture and television industries. His company set up action sequences for shows such as "The F.B.I.," "Mannix," "Mod Squad," "Mission Impossible," "Spiderman," and many others.

Hungarian-born Farkas came to the U.S. in 1965 with black belts in judo and karate. He began giving private lessons to some of Hollywood's top celebrities, among them Phil Spector, the Beach Boys, Herb Alpert, Jimmy Caan, Dennis Hopper, Fred Williamson, etc. Through his students Farkas gained entrance to Hollywood's inner circle and soon was working regularly on T.V. shows and features as a fight choreographer and stuntman.

Joe Lewis unexpectedly announced his retirement in 1972. During his tenure as champion, Lewis amassed more than 30 major titles. He was the only four-time grand champion of the U.S. National Karate Championships (1966-69) and the only three-time grand champion of the International Karate Championships (1969-71).

Coincidental with the entertainment craze, tournament karate was thriving as never before. In 1972 Mike Stone, now a promoter, conceived the first tournament franchise. Earlier, Stone, together with Chuck Norris and Bob Wall, had created the Four Seasons Karate Championships, a quarterly series of contests held in southern California. When the others lost interest, Stone maintained the tournaments. In 1972 he sold its name and concept to promoters in other parts of the country and created the Four Seasons Nationals in Las Vegas as the culminating event of the network.

Public interest in martial arts reached its zenith in 1973. Thousands of spectators who formerly had no interest in karate supported tournaments as never before. And theaters showcasing martial arts films were doing great box-office business.

Meanwhile, in Hong Kong, Bruce Lee was working constantly. Following *Way of the Dragon,* his third hit, he immediately started production on *Game of Death.* But the film was interrupted when Lee received a co-production offer from Warner Bros. to star in *Enter the Dragon. Enter the Dragon* was the first co-production between Chinese and Hollywood filmmakers. On July 20, 1973, shortly before the U.S. release of *Enter the Dragon,* the world was staggered by the unexpected death of Bruce Lee in Hong Kong. Only 32, he allegedly died from acute brain swelling, the cause of which remains enigmatic. Lee's chief jeet kune do protege is **Dan Inosanto**.

Enter the Dragon became the king of martial arts movies, the unsurpassed classic of the genre. Today, this picture stands out as one of the most profitable in international cinema history. Though numerous imitators attempted to replace Lee, no one could duplicate his spectacular success. By 1974 the martial arts craze, commonly called the "Bruce Lee Era" began tapering off.

Professional Karate Revival The comeback began in the summer of 1973, when Oklahoman **Mike Anderson** published his inaugural edition of Professional Karate Magazine. Anderson openly campaigned for the restoration of professional karate, backed by his quarterly publication and his compilation of national and regional ratings of karate players. Widespread acceptance of these ratings revolutionized the ratings polls, making *Black Belt's* annual Top 10 rating antiquated by comparison.

Shortly after the release of his inaugural issue, Anderson staged his **Top 10 Nationals** in St. Louis. Anderson offered a $1,000 grand championship purse, a precedent immediately adopted by other major promoters. The event was the first to make mandatory the use of Jhoon Rhee's newly created **Safe-T Equipment** in the black belt fighting divisions. This innovation launched a new form of karate fighting, which in 1974 was dubbed **"semicontact"** by martial arts journalist **John Corcoran.** The use of Safe-T Equipment, basically foam rubber hand and foot pads, added excitement to competition, safely permitting moderate contact to both the face and body.

At this event Los Angeles' **Howard Jackson** won the grand championship and prize money. At 5 feet 5 inches, 152 lbs, Jackson became the first lightweight to dominate his sport and professional karate's biggest money winner of 1973.

Jackson had usurped Bill Wallace, at the time America's top tournament fighter. Wallace was a sport karate phenomenon in that he gained most of his victories by relying on one technique exclusively,

Bong Soo Han made hapkido famous by his spectacular demonstration of the art in the film *Billy Jack* in 1972.

Bill Wallace *(left)* jams a kick thrown by Texas champion Roy Kurban.

Jeff Smith *(left)*, America's number-one-ranked karate champion in 1974, competes against top 10 ranked John Natividad. The referee is Steve Armstrong.

Courtesy of Larry Ritchie

Ed Daniels *(left)* vs. Joe Lewis

Ron Marchini *(right)* vs. Joe Hayes at the 1971 Top Ten Nationals

Photo by Phil Pacheco

Mike Warren was one of the top Tae kwon do champions in the U.S.

Courtesy of *Official Karate Magazine*

259

Mike Foster *(left)* and his instructor, Mamarou Yamamoto.
Courtesy of *Official Karate Magazine.*

Mike Anderson, founder of semicontact karate and co-founder of
full-contact karate, delivers a classic flying side kick during the 1960s.

Bruce Lee *(right)* as Kato in the 1966 "Green Hornet" series with
Van Williams, who played the title role.

a left-footed whip-like roundhouse kick. His kicks were clocked at an incredible delivery speed of 60 m.p.h., and when he later became the premier star of full-contact karate, he was aptly nicknamed "Superfoot."

On June 4, 1973, John Corcoran was hired as book editor for Ohara Publications, the sister company of Rainbow Publications, publishers of *Black Belt* and *Karate Illustrated*. By the end of the year, he had begun to work on both magazines as assistant editor. Corcoran was the first karate black belt to become an editor of these publications, and he rose to prominence as one of the first genuine martial arts journalists in America. He was preceded as a black belt editor only by *Official Karate's* Al Weiss. Corcoran was a student of Glenn Premru.

Corcoran was hired the same week as **Jerry Smith**, a commercial artist, who was also a black belt and a disciple of Joe Lewis. The pair formed an intimate friendship and Corcoran continued his martial arts studies with Smith, who was to become recognized as one of the first full-contact karate coaches in the U.S.

In Aug. 1974 Ed Parker offered a winner-take-all purse of $2,500 for the grand champion of his International Karate Championships in Long Beach. In a spectacular 25-point overtime match, **John Natividad,** a student of Chuck Norris and Jerry Taylor, defeated **Benny Urquidez,** 13-12. Even today, spectators debate the outcome of this classic contest; some believe Urquidez, a regional favorite, scored an overtime point against the favored Natividad before the latter landed his conclusive point. Historians call it one of the greatest bouts of the light-contact era.

The continuing martial arts mania kept business flourishing through 1974. Aaron Banks' Oriental World of Self-Defense, an annual production of martial arts demonstrations, set a gate record in its field. The promotion, held at Madison Square Garden, attracted 19,564 spectators, according to Banks. The paid live gate reportedly reached $100,000. The event was aired on ABC's "Wide World of Sports."

Ken Min, of the University of California at Berkeley, conducted the first collegiate survey in 1974 to determine how many schools offered karate, tae kwon do, and kung-fu classes on campus. Judo, which preceded other arts in its American migration, outranked all of them. Of 596 colleges responding to the survey, 278 offered some type of judo program. At the same time, there was equal interest in karate, tae kwon do, and kung-fu. Of 448 colleges reporting, 228 offered some type of program in one of these three disciplines.

Joe Lewis and **Tom Tannenbaum** decided to resurrect full-contact karate. They planned to promote the World Professional Karate Championships. Lewis brought Mike Anderson into the deal and Anderson spent most of 1974 preparing for what was to become the most extraordinary promotion in American karate history. He spent months finding and establishing European and Asian representatives. German karate entrepreneur Georg Bruckner, Anderson's friend and business associate, conducted an elimination contest to determine European full-contact representatives. Three of the four American representatives were selected on the basis of their divisional supremacy in *Professional Karate's* ratings: they were lightweight Howard Jackson of Los Angeles, middleweight Bill Wallace of Memphis, and light heavyweight **Jeff Smith** of Washington, D.C. Joe Lewis, originally scheduled to co-host the event, chose to come out of retirement and fight as the heavyweight representative. Lewis was the only karate fighter with full-contact experience.

Jeff Smith, during this year, had surpassed Jackson to become America's foremost tournament fighter. He was, in fact, named the 1974 "Fighter of the Year" by *Professional Karate Magazine*. A product of the rugged Texas school of karate, Smith had moved to the nation's capital in the early 1970s to teach for Jhoon Rhee.

Two months before the event, in July 1974, Anderson relocated his operation to Los Angeles. In August he formed a promotion company with Beverly Hills business couple, **Don** and **Judy Quine**, who helped finalize negotiations with Universal Television. In late August, the Quines and Anderson formed the **Professional Karate Association** (PKA), the sport's first sanctioning body, to establish full-contact karate as a major professional sport with recognized champions, standardized rules, and network television coverage of its bouts. Anderson also persuaded Bob McLaughlin and John Corcoran, editors of *Black Belt* and *Karate Illustrated,* to work jointly as editors of *Professional Karate*. Instead of editing, however, the two worked feverishly on the fast approaching World Championships.

On the night of Sept. 14, 1974, at the Los Angeles Sports Arena, 14 fighters from eight countries vied in a double elimination for the inaugural titles. Four emerged as world professional full-contact champions: heavyweight Joe Lewis, light heavyweight Jeff Smith, middleweight Bill Wallace, and lightweight **Isaias Duenas** of Mexico City. Among the American entrants, only Howard Jackson, suffering from a severe knee injury, lost his bid for the title. This extravaganza drew one of the largest live gates for competition karate, $50,000, and attracted more than 10,000 spectators. Anderson awarded an unprecedented $20,000 in total prize money. Each champion earned $3,000, while runners-up received a smaller purse. All fourteen participants were given a guaranteed minimum. Much of this impressive news soured, however, when Anderson later reported a personal loss exceeding $60,000. Tom Tannenbaum sold the broadcast rights to ABC's "Wide World of Entertainment." The event aired twice as a 90-minute special, the first time acquiring the highest rating of a "Wide World" special for 1974.

Great controversy ensued. The traditional karate community contended that full-contact degraded the art form and would have a negative influence on school enrollments. This faction felt the television coverage for the sport gave the impression that full-contact was taught in schools everywhere as a required course of learning and would therefore discourage parents from enrolling their children. Moreover, detractors protested the association of the word "karate" with full-contact and vocally sought a name change to "kick-boxing."

It wasn't to be. For one, the sport could only be sold to television because of the popularity of karate. It was a word and an activity with which television executives were familiar. Kick-boxing, on the other hand, was associated with the far more brutal sport popular in Thailand and Japan. When its promoters attempted to get it on American television, they failed. TV executives felt it was too violent. Consequently, the name "full-contact karate" was retained.

In Oct. 1974 tae kwon do was recognized as an amateur sport separate from karate by the AAU. This development was chiefly due to the efforts of Ken Min, tae kwon do coach of Berkeley University, with the support and aid of members of the AAU Judo Committee and a dozen tae kwon do masters. A number of important tournaments—starting with the 1st AAU Invitational Tae Kwon Do Championships in June 1974, held at Berkeley under Min's able direction, through the 1st National AAU Tae Kwon Do Championships, conducted at Yale university in Mar. 1975, and the Mar. 1976 version held in Kansas City—promoted and publicized the sport aspect of this Korean art.

It was in Kansas City that a U.S. tae kwon do federation was conceived with the purpose of supporting the National AAU Tae Kwon Do Committee. Tae Kwon Do programs in American universities reached a new level of progress with the advent of the 1st National Collegiate Tae Kwon Do Championships, held at Nicholls State University in Thibodaux, La., that same year.

From 1975 onward, two activities dominated the martial arts: films and the sport. These continue to be the most active and visible aspects of the industry, based simply on mass exposure through the various media.

The year 1975 was one of economic disaster, signaling the beginning of the end of the martial arts movie boom. The industry suffered a double blow when it was victimized jointly by the depressed national economy and the pronounced tapering off of martial arts in the cinema. Some instructors blamed the new full-contact movement for deteriorating enrollments at the school level. Others felt it was not the sport itself, but poorly conditioned fighters and unprofessional promotions.

Following the inaugural world championships, a rash of full-contact promotions broke out in 1975, spreading to epidemic proportions. At one point in Los Angeles alone, hardly a week passed without a full-contact event. Within a year of its birth, no less than seven full-contact karate organizations sprang up. Their organizers were convinced that the infant sport and its potential sales appeal to television might be the financial salvation of the declining martial arts industry. It wasn't.

In all fairness, the army of inept promoters who tried to capitalize on the young sport were not totally at fault. Some blame has to be shared by the fighters themselves. Many entered the ring preposterously underconditioned, and none of them had any ring

Benny Urquidez *(left)* and John Natividad *(right)* fight it out in a classic match at the 1973 Long Beach Internationals. Natividad went on to win the grand title in a historic 23-point overtime match. The referee is Tadashi Yamashita.

Gathering of black belts at the 1968 Gateway Open in St. Louis. *Kneeling, left to right:* Bill Wallace, Glenn Keeney, unknown. *Standing, left to right:* Unknown, Jim Harrison, Jimmy Jones, Bob Yarnall, unknown, Jim McClain, Parker Shelton, unknown, unknown, unknown, Phil Koeppel, John Pachivas.

Courtesy of Mike Anderson

Kneeling, left to right: Joe Hess, J. Santiago, Owen Watson, Ron Van Clief, and Preston Baker. *Standing, left to right:* Little John Davis, Bill Downs, Jimmy Jones, Joel B. Ward, and Shorty Mills.

Photo by Mary Townsley

The early period of semicontact karate. Jeff Smith *(left)* vs. Howard Jackson. Jackson was America's number-one fighter in 1973, while Jeff Smith became number one the following year.

Jay T. Will opened a school in Ohio in 1968 and became one of the most successful instructors in the U.S. Today he is one of the leading full-contact referees.

experience.

Those organizations that moved into the promotional end of the sport in 1975 were: Tommy Lee's World Series of Martial Arts; Jhoon Rhee's World Black Belt League (WBBL), a team concept; Joe Corley's South East Professional Karate Commission (SEPKC); Aaron Banks' World Professional Karate Organization (WPKO); and Larry Scott's and Valerie Williams' National Karate League (NKL), another team concept. Each association created its own rules, sanctioned its own promotions, and established its own champions. Each independently sought television exposure for its promotions. Of these early organizations only two remain: Banks' WPKO and Rhee's WBBL.

The Scott/Williams NKL featured Benny Urquidez as its premier star. Urquidez quickly accumulated the most impressive record in his sport by virtue of his consistent victories in 3- and 5-round NKL team bouts across the country. However, the NKL was under-financed and suffered major losses. It disbanded in 1976. Its principals left substantial debts in their wake, as well as a negative business reputation for karate in general.

In 1975, 50 million viewers saw full-contact karate when Jeff Smith defeated Karriem Allah. The closed-circuit broadcast was a preliminary card to the Muhammad Ali/Joe Frazier "Thrilla in Manila" fight.

On May 3, 1975, the PKA, in conjunction with Joe Corley's **Battle of Atlanta** in Georgia, produced a full-contact card whose main event was the much-acclaimed bout between Corley himself and Bill Wallace. It marked the first title defense of the new sport and, as in Los Angeles, it attracted more than 10,000 spectators to the Omni Arena. Wallace retained his crown with a 9th-round TKO.

Notable at this event were two new concepts: the addition of professional kata competition to the regular competition, an innovation of Mike Anderson's at his Top 10 Nationals in St. Louis; and the introduction of martial ballet, created by Jhoon Rhee, in which a team of black belts perform a synchronized kata routine to classical music. This latter concept served as the prototype of the musical kata divisions gaining popularity in American karate tournaments today.

One week later, on May 10, Aaron Banks conducted a title defense held under the auspices of his WPKO. Presented at the Nassau Coliseum in New York, Banks' event later aired on ABC's "Wide World of Sports," a development creating a fierce dispute between Banks and the Quines, whose original PKA event had aired as an ABC network special. The PKA felt it was a conflict of interest on the part of ABC to air two different events that declared two different sets of "world champions." Banks' card crowned four divisional champions: heavyweight Joe Hess of New York (now of Florida), light heavyweight **Fred Miller** of New York, middleweight Kasim Dubar of New York, and lightweight Benny Urquidez of Los Angeles. By year's end, Urquidez was the leading money winner of his sport, having earned more than $30,000.

In June 1975, Mike Anderson resigned as an executive officer of the PKA to pursue the promotion of the sport on his own. The Quines assumed complete control of the PKA, while Anderson eventually formed the World All-Style Karate Organization (WAKO) with Georg Bruckner in West Berlin, Germany. At the same time, Anderson's *Professional Karate* magazine was suffering from poor sales. He decided to move his operation back to Oklahoma City. Bob McLaughlin entered the public relations business; John Corcoran joined author Bob Wall as editor of Wall's self-published book, *Who's Who in the Martial Arts.* By autumn, Corcoran launched a full-time career as a free-lance writer specializing in the martial arts.

Professional Karate, it must be emphasized, left a lasting mark in its field. No magazine before or after it had such a profound impact on all aspects of the sport, its participants, and its formation of a professional foundation. Through *Professional Karate,* careers were launched and professional karate athletes began to receive a degree of respect and admiration they had never before known. Most of these benefits can be directly attributed to the magazine's founder and publisher, Mike Anderson, who often put his money where his heart was to promote the sport.

The movies of 1975 included the Stirling Silliphant-scripted *The Killer Elite,* directed by Sam Peckinpah. The film featured a bevy of West Coast martial artists clad in **ninja** disguises engaging in poorly staged fight scenes having nothing to do with **ninjutsu.** *The*

Full-contact champion Bill Wallace *(left)* in action

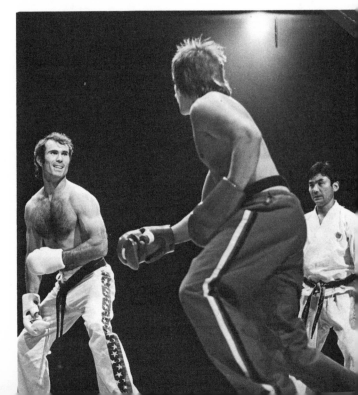

The inaugural PKA World Championships in Los Angeles in 1974.
Here Bill Wallace *(left)* faces Bernd Grothe of Germany while
referee Mikami watches. Wallace won the match.

Darnell Garcia *(right)* vs. Fred Wren. Garcia was a top noncontact fighter during the 1960s.

Left to right: Jim Butin, Jhoon Rhee, Mike Anderson, and Jeff Smith.

Photo by Mary Townsley

Left to right: Fred Wren, Bill Wallace, Glenn Keeney, Owen Watson, Ron Van Clief, and Little John Davis at the Tournament of the Century, in Chicago, 1973.

Courtesy of Ed Kaloudis

Head break by Ed Kaloudis at Madison Square Garden's Oriental World of Self-Defense. This event, promoted by Aaron Banks, gave many East Coast sensei national exposure.

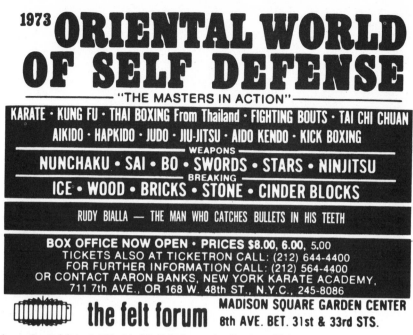

1973 ORIENTAL WORLD OF SELF DEFENSE

"THE MASTERS IN ACTION"

KARATE · KUNG FU · THAI BOXING From Thailand · FIGHTING BOUTS · TAI CHI CHUAN
AIKIDO · HAPKIDO · JUDO · JIU-JITSU · AIDO KENDO · KICK BOXING

WEAPONS
NUNCHAKU · SAI · BO · SWORDS · STARS · NINJITSU
BREAKING
ICE · WOOD · BRICKS · STONE · CINDER BLOCKS

RUDY BIALLA — THE MAN WHO CATCHES BULLETS IN HIS TEETH

BOX OFFICE NOW OPEN · PRICES $8.00, 6.00, 5.00
TICKETS ALSO AT TICKETRON CALL: (212) 644-4400
FOR FURTHER INFORMATION CALL: (212) 564-4400
OR CONTACT AARON BANKS, NEW YORK KARATE ACADEMY,
711 7th AVE., OR 168 W. 48th ST., N.Y.C., 245-8086

the felt forum   MADISON SQUARE GARDEN CENTER
8th AVE. BET. 31st & 33rd STS.

Aaron Banks' Oriental World of Self-Defense, despite the criticism
it received, managed to draw the largest gate in the history of the
martial arts.

Nick Cerio *(right)* with Tadashi Yamashita.
Cerio is a leading instructor in Rhode
Island and studied personally under
William Chow in Hawaii. Today he runs
one of the largest schools in Rhode Island
and teaches the state sheriffs.

Moses Powell, prominent New York martial
artist, performing his famous one-finger roll.

Courtesy of *Official Karate Magazine*

Black Belt Hall of Famer Ernest Lieb *(right)* faces Jim Grady at the
Long Beach Internationals.

Two world champions, Bill Wallace *(right)* and Ernest Hart, put on
a demonstration at the 1980 Battle of Atlanta.

Courtesy of *Official Karate Magazine*

Byong Yu, a top 10 ranked karate champion in both sparring and kata, was noted for his quick kicking ability and for his spectacular breaking demos.

Left to right: Ron Van Clief, Jim Jones, and Jim Kelly. Van Clief and Kelly went from competitive careers to film work, and both have starred in a number of full-length motion pictures.

Steve Fisher *(right)*, one of the West Coast's leading competitors and instructors, with Duane Ethington, martial arts author.

New York's Fred Miller competing in a noncontact tournament while Aaron Banks referees. Miller became light-heavyweight champion of Aaron Banks' WPKO (World Professional Karate Organization) in 1975.

Killer Elite suffered from production disputes and inferior editing. It did average box-office business.

Bruce Lee: His Life and Legend, to which Warner Bros. devoted $200,000 in development costs, never advanced from preproduction. Warners launched a worldwide search for a candidate to play the lead role in this Bruce Lee bio, co-scripted by Linda Lee, Bruce's widow, and director Robert Clouse. Advertisements seeking the candidate were run in major newspapers across the U.S. and thousands of aspiring martial artists swarmed the Burbank studio appying for the role. Denver's Al Dacascos (now of Hamburg, Germany) was given serious consideration. The producers eventually settled on Chinese-Canadian **Alex Kwok** of Vancouver. After changing his name to Alex Kwon, capping his teeth, and paying him a holding fee, the producers dropped the project and the film was never made.

Released films of 1975 included *Paper Tiger,* starring Toshiro Mifune, David Niven and Irene Tsu, and *Hot Potato* and *Take A Hard Ride,* starring Jim Kelly. None left an impression.

The big disappointment of 1975 was the final retirement of superstar Joe Lewis following two back-to-back nontitle defeats. Remarkably, in the last of these bouts, Lewis dislocated his right shoulder after the 1st round and, despite excruciating pain, continued fighting for the duration of the contest. He lost a seven-round decision to Ross Scott because of penalties for insufficient kicks.

Ed Parker's Internationals in Aug. 1975 awarded the largest sum of prize money ever for a Pro/Am karate tournament, a total of $16,250. Kata winners were awarded an overall $1,000 of that sum. The two figures stand as records to this day.

Along with Washington vs. Dominican Republic team matches on Sept. 14, 1975, Jhoon Rhee presented a special politician's semi-contact division pitting a trio of Democrats against a Republican threesome in what was called the Capitol Hill Grudge Bout. Presented under the auspices of Rhee's World Black Belt League, the novel division featured Democrats Rep. Walter Fauntroy (D.C.), Rep. Tom Bevill (Ala.), and Sen. Quentin Burdick (N.D.) against Republicans Rep. Willis Grandison, Jr. (Ohio), Rep. Floyd Spence (S.C.), and Sen. Ted Stevens (Alaska). The Congressmen appeared on behalf of the Freedom of the Press Foundation; they were members of Rhee's twice-weekly classes and have come to be known as the "Capitol Hill karate corps." (The match was drawn.)

On Sept. 21, in conjunction with Georg Bruckner's All European Karate Championships, America's **Gordon Franks** met Mexico's **Ramiro Guzman** to decide who would emerge as the first world super lightweight champion of full-contact karate. Franks, then a 20-year-old college student from Minneapolis, won the title in a unanimous 9-round decision. Promoted at the Deutschlandhalle Arena in West Berlin, it was the first full-contact world title fight to be staged in a foreign country. The promotional budget was reportedly $130,000, the single most expensive karate promotion up to that time. Franks, besides being the original champion in this 139-lb division, was also the first black fighter to become a full-contact world champion.

Also in 1975, the 3rd WUKO World Karate-do Championships were held, for the first time in the U.S., at the Long Beach Arena. It was an uneventful tournament for the U.S. amateur karate athletes. The British team emerged as the new world champions, and the Japanese fighters, as usual, dominated the individual competition.

In *Black Belt's* 1976 survey respondents in karate registered an 11 percent increase in students from 1975-76. Judo and tae kwon do registered no increase or decrease. Yet, many leaders in karate stated that a decline took place. One answer may be that the decline was registered in 1974-75 and that interest had picked up in this year. A statistic of interest was that 18 percent of all students in both 1975 and 1976 were female. Approximately 31 percent of all students were children, 14 or younger. However, it was not clear from the survey that girls age 14 or younger were not also included in the female as well as the children's statistics.

In 1976 the full-contact karate movement continued to be the pacesetter for the industry. By now, most of the smaller promoters found the expense prohibitive, and the more distinguished entrepreneurs took command of the sport. Most of the lavish events were filmed for television and appeared on sports shows such as "The Champions," "CBS Sports Spectacular," and the PKA's 90-minute "Sports Special of the Month."

The year kicked off with champion Bill Wallace becoming the first

Ramiro Guzman

Benny Urquidez became the lightweight full-contact karate champion of the world. After the retirement of Bill Wallace in the late 1970s, Urquidez remained the only superstar of sport karate.

During the 1975 WUKO World Championships held in Long Beach, Calif., an unprecedented event occurred when French champion Dominic Valera made contact with his opponent while sparring. When the judges disqualified Valera, he hit one judge with a chair and kicked another as the crowd went wild. Finally, Long Beach police took Valera away, and he was later dropped from the WUKO.

Ross Scott, PKA world heavyweight champion who succeeded Joe Lewis.

karate athlete ever to participate in ABC's "Superstars" competition. Wallace appeared in the third set of eliminations on Jan. 31, which was broadcast nationwide on Feb. 7. Wallace placed in two events, but finished only tenth out of 11 entrants in his elimination series, besting Lynn Swann of the Pittsburgh Steelers. Despite a disappointing finish, it was an extraordinary endorsement for the sport of karate.

Prior to Wallace's appearance, Don Quine, who now managed the champion, originated the nickname "Superfoot," a nickname attributed to Wallace's uncanny kicking ability.

A PKA event held at the Los Angeles Sports Arena on Oct. 1, 1976, marked the beginning of the association's contractual arrangement with CBS Sports, as well as a merger attempt with promoter **Howard Hanson** of Westminster, Calif. The CBS deal eventually accounted for four network broadcasts per year of PKA-sanctioned world title fights. Critics accused the PKA of conflict of interest. The organization was operating both as a sanctioning body and, through Sport Karate, Inc., a sister corporation, as a promotional body. The PKA principals, Don and Judy Quine, countered by claiming the sport's survival depended on their synthesis of its various activities. The PKA sanctioned a total of 19 events in 1976.

After his merger attempt with the PKA soured, Howard Hanson formed the **World Karate Association** (WKA), a full-contact sanctioning body that became the PKA's strongest competitor. As its president, Hanson survived by arranging promotions in Japan, pitting Japanese kick-boxers against American full-contact karate fighters, using a combination of the two sports' rules. After the PKA stripped Benny Urquidez of his lightweight title in 1977, the champion fought predominantly in the WKA and quickly established himself as a superstar in Asia, where he defeated every kick-boxing challenger and champion he fought.

The most bitter conflict between the PKA and the WKA is a dispute over rules. The WKA advocates the use of leg kicks, while the PKA rigidly opposes them. The issue is one of potential injury to the athletes. The PKA maintains that these techniques are dangerous to the fighter's physical safety and his career longevity. Hanson parries this charge by pointing to the Orient, where some kick-boxing champions remain active after more than 50 fights where leg kicks, at their most vicious, are employed.

In Sept. 1976 California passed a law placing full-contact karate under the jurisdiction of the State Athletic Commission (SAC), which regulates professional and amateur boxing and wrestling. It marked the first time that any form of American karate was regulated by a government body, even though many martial artists had been attempting for years to bring traditional karate under government supervision for licensing of instructors. The California commission sanctioned the organization of the volunteer group called the Full-Contact Karate Advisory Board to assist in the formation of standard rules and practices for the sport.

The state athletic commissions, which regulate professional and amateur boxing and wrestling in 13 of the United States, have gradually begun regulating full-contact karate since 1976.

In California, the SAC generally recognized the PKA's rules and policies as standards for the sport, with the exception of the controversial leg kicks. In July 1978 the North American Boxing Federation, to which all SACs belong, approved a motion to officially recognize the PKA as the international governing body of professional full-contact karate.

Finally in 1976, amateur karate, under the WUKO, was accepted for membership in the General Assembly of International Sports Federations (GAIF), bringing it one step closer to the Olympics. In the following year, however, the General Assembly of the International Olympic Committee (IOC) issued a directive specifying that the two world karate bodies, the WUKO and the IAKF, had to unify before Olympic recognition of karate would be granted. As a result, that recognition was postponed indefinitely.

1976 WORLD TITLE FIGHTS

Date: 2/8; Site: Atlanta, Ga.; Sanction: SEPKA; Division: Lt. Hvywt.; Winner: Jeff Smith; Loser: Wally Slocki; Promoter: Joe Corley; Television: "The Champions" (Syndication).

Date: 3/13; Site: Las Vegas, Nev.; Sanction: PKA; Division: Midwt.; Winner: Bill Wallace; Loser: Jem Echollas; Promoter: SKI; Television: "Sports Special of the Month" (90-minute syndication).

Date: 5/29; Site: Toronto, Can.; Sanction: PKA; Division: Midwt.; Winner: Bill Wallace; Loser: Daniel Richer; Promoter: Jong Soo Park;

Television: Filmed by ABC "Wide World of Sports" but not aired.

Date: 8/28; Site: Honolulu, Hawaii; Sanction: PKA; Division: Hvywt.; Winner: Teddy Limoz; Loser: Mike Arroyo; Division: Ltwt.; Winner: Benny Urquidez; Loser: Earnest Hart, Jr.; Promoter: SKI/Hanson.

Date: 10/1; Site: Los Angeles, Calif.; Sanction: PKA; Division: Mdwt.; Winner: Bill Wallace; Loser: Gary Edens; Division: Ltwt.; Winner: Benny Urquidez; Loser: Eddie Andujar; Promoter: SKI/Hanson; Television: "CBS Sports Spectacular."

Activities in the sport and movies continued to remain at the forefront of the martial arts for 1977. The big news was the starring debut of Chuck Norris, the first karate champion turned actor. Norris was best known to filmgoers for his performance against Bruce Lee in the climactic fight scene of *Return of the Dragon.* His first starring role came in *Breaker, Breaker,* a low-budget exploitation film that attempted to capitalize on Norris' karate name and expertise and the CB radio trend. Filmed for under $250,000, *Breaker, Breaker,* according to director Don Hulette, grossed $10 million.

Before the release of *Breaker, Breaker,* Norris signed a three-picture deal with a new production company called American Cinema and began filming *Good Guys Wear Black.* By the time it had run its course, *Good Guys* had grossed $20 million.

The ramifications of this film are extraordinary. Norris had singlehandedly restored interest in the martial arts genre at a time when Hollywood refused to make such films.

Other filmmaking efforts featuring the martial arts this year included *Revenge of the Pink Panther,* starring Peter Sellers, with Ed Parker as a hired karate assassin. *A Fistful of Yen,* starring Bong Soo Han of *Billy Jack* fame, was one of three vignettes composing the satirical *Kentucky Fried Movie. Yen* is actually a parody of *Enter the Dragon* and is perhaps the first American made comedy related to the martial arts genre. It has become a cult classic.

With two national television broadcasts and a total of ten sanctioned events in 1977, the PKA remained at the forefront of contact karate. The April 23 "Triple Crown" championship from the Las Vegas Hilton was broadcast live by "CBS Sports Spectacular," marking the first live broadcast of karate in any form in U.S. history. But the PKA principals, Don and Judy Quine, were also pressing its world champions to sign exclusive contracts with them. Refusal on the part of several led to the Quines stripping them of their titles. One of these stripped champions was Benny "The Jet" Urquidez.

Howard Hanson, who had just formed his World Karate Association, quickly recruited Urquidez to fight in the Orient under the WKA banner. Urquidez went to Japan and became the first American fighter ever to beat the Japanese kick-boxers at their own game. Urquidez scored a knockout over champion Katsuyuki Suzuki on Aug. 2 before a national television audience in Japan. His victory amounted to a national insult to the Japanese, who take their sport very seriously. Following his win, retired and undefeated champion Kunimatsu Okao publicly challenged Urquidez to a bout for which he would come out of retirement. Urquidez accepted. On Nov. 14, at the prestigious Budokan in Tokyo, the two met in a vicious showdown resulting in an Urquidez victory. Bloody and battered, Okao was knocked out cold in the 4th round and had to be helped from the ring. The bout was carried over Japanese national television and drew an unprecedented $500,000 live gate, the largest on record for professional karate.

The victory brought Urquidez' record to 40-0 with 38 knockouts, the best in his sport, and made him an international celebrity. In Japan, he became a cult hero and the central figure of a series of comic books entitled *Benny the Jet.* He also represented his sport in a Japanese documentary, *Kings of the Square Ring,* which also features boxing's Muhammad Ali and wrestling's Antonio Inoki.

Howard Jackson became the first karate champion to enter professional boxing and win. Within one year, Jackson amassed a pro boxing record of 14-1-2 with 11 knockouts. Jackson's precedent has since 1977 led the way for other karate athletes to pursue dual careers in the boxing and karate rings.

The 4th WUKO World Karate-do Championships in 1977 marked the return of this international event to Tokyo. The tournament, held at the Budokan, featured kata competition for the first time. American players fared better at kata than fighting, but tied for fifth place in team fighting. Japan dominated the kata competition, winning the two top positions, and the strong Dutch contingent surprisingly dominated both the team and individual fighting titles. **Otti Roetof** of

Gary Sproul wins WAKO full-contact light heavyweight title in Tampa, Fla., 1978.

275

Holland defeated Great Britain's **Eugene Codrington** to become the WUKO amateur world champion.

On March 5, 1977, the 3rd National AAU Tae Kwon Do Championships were held at the University of California at Berkeley, in conjunction with the 1st North American Tae Kwon Do Championships. The latter event was highligthed by the first organizational meeting of the North American Tae Kwon Do Union. Later, on Sept. 15-17, at the Amphitheater in Chicago, the World Tae Kwon Do Championships made its debut in America.

1977 WORLD TITLE FIGHTS

Date: 3/12; Site: Los Angeles, Calif.; Sanction: WKA; Division: Spr. Ltwt.; Benny Urquidez/Narong Noi (Declared a no contest); Promoter: Howard Hanson.

Date: 4/23; Site: Las Vegas, Nev.; Division: Hvywt.; Winner: Ross Scott; Loser: Everett Eddy; Division: Midwt.; Winner: Bill Wallace; Loser: Pilinky Rodriguez; Division: Ltwt.; Winner: Benny Urquidez; Loser: Howard Jackson; Promoter: SKI; Television: "CBS Sports Spectacular" (Wallace/Rodriguez aired live).

Date: 5/21; Site: Providence, R.I.; Sanction: PKA; Division: Midwt.; Winner: Bill Wallace; Loser: Ron Thiveridge; Promoter: Hee Il Cho.

Date: 5/21; Site: Charlotte, N.C.; Sanction: PKA; Division: Lt. Hvywt.; Winner: Jeff Smith; Loser: Jim Horsley; Promoter: Jerry Piddington.

Date: 8/2; Site: Tokyo, Japan; Sanction: WKA; Division: Spr. Ltwt.; Winner: Benny Urquidez; Loser: Katsuyuki Suzuki; Promoter: Howard Hanson/Ron Holmes/Hisashi Shima/Antonio Inoki; Television: Japanese national TV.

Date: 10/8; Site: Indianapolis, Ind.; Sanction: PKA; Division: Midwt.; Winner: Bill Wallace; Loser: M. Pat Worley; Division: Welwt.; Winner: Earnest Hart, Jr.; Loser: Eddie Andujar; Promoter: SKI; Television: "CBS Sports Spectacular."

Date: 11/14; Site: Tokyo, Japan; Sanction: WKA; Division: Spr. Ltwt.; Winner: Benny Urquidez; Loser: Kunimatsu Okao; Division: Ltwt.; Winner: Kunimasa Nagae; Loser: Tony Lopez; Promoter: Hanson/Holmes/Shima; Television: Japanese national TV.

Date: 11/28; Site: Honolulu, Hawaii; Sanction: PKA; Division: Mdwt.; Winner: Bill Wallace; Loser: Burnis White; Promoter: Kip Russo.

Participation in the Korean martial arts reached an all-time high from 1977-78, according to *Black Belt's* 1978 survey. Almost 65 percent of the respondents were either students or instructors in hapkido, tae kwon do, or tang soo do. Also at an all-time high was the percentage of practitioners in the category of "others," those from obscure or combination arts. In comparison to previous surveys, response from practitioners of the Japanese arts was at a low, virtually equal to the number of respondents for the Chinese disciplines.

In 1978, while the WKA was idle, the PKA coordinated a sanction for a light-heavyweight title fight between champion Jeff Smith and challenger **Dominic Valera,** for a decade Europe's greatest noncontact karate champion. Valera had made the transition to full-contact fighting in mid-1975 following a fierce dispute with the WUKO's amateur karate politicians. Valera met Smith for the PKA title on May 22 in Paris before a sold-out crowd. Smith won a dull 9-round decision.

Also on the international front, John Corcoran began to syndicate his articles to martial arts magazines across the world. This marked the first time a domestic writer secured mass exposure abroad for American martial artists and events on a regular basis. He became the world's foremost martial arts magazine writer and joined an elite group of syndicated peers: **Zarko Modric** in Yugoslavia and **John Robertson** and **Arthur Tansley** in Japan.

Semicontact (often called "point karate" or "tournament karate") in 1976-77 had sunk to an all-time low in popularity and interest. Chiefly responsible for the decline was the absence of recognizable stars: all of the great fighters had turned to full-contact. In 1978, however, a star emerged. **Keith Vitali** won the grand championships of two of America's most prestigious tournaments: the Battle of Atlanta and the Mid-America Diamond Nationals. The victories catapulted him to the pinnacle of every 1978 Top 10 rating poll in the U.S. Vitali duplicated his number-1 rating for the next two years before retiring in Feb. 1981 at 28. He and Bill Wallace are the only point fighters in U.S. history to have been ranked number 1 for three years; Vitali, however, is the only fighter to occupy the position in consecutive years. Vitali's intense rivalry with Texan **Ray McCallum,** beginning in 1979, infused new life into a sport sorely needing it. Although the pair met only three times in competition, with Vitali

Linda Denley, the leading woman fighter during the last few years.

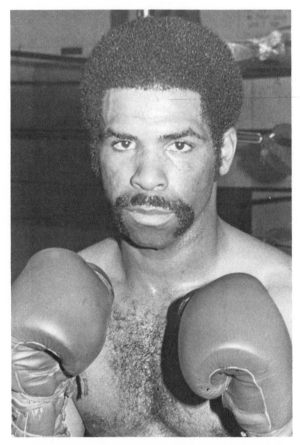

Number one in noncontact karate, Howard Jackson became a formidable opponent when he turned his talent to professional full-contact karate.

276

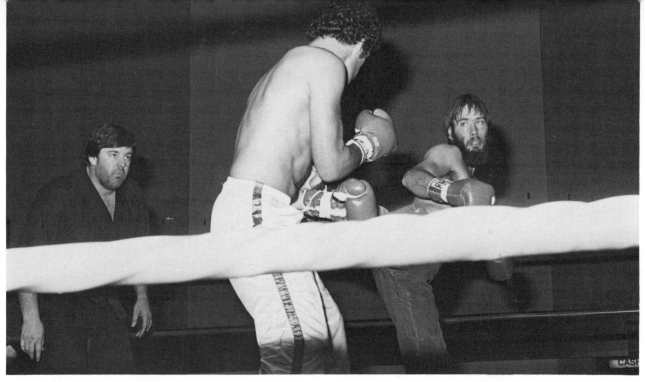

Ray McCallum *(right)*, one of the leading fighters in the late 1970s, helped sport karate rejuvenate itself.

Courtesy of *Kick Illustrated Magazine*

Keith Vitali *(right)* emerged as the semicontact superstar of the late 1970s and helped revitalize sport karate in the U.S.

Tracy's black belt team at the 1970 Long Beach Internationals.
Left to right: Jay T. Will, Dennis Nackord, Joe Lewis, Ray
Klingenberg, Larry Demerrit.

Richard Jackson *(left)* vs. Jerry Blank at the 1980 Battle of Atlanta.

winning twice, the contests were classic encounters. Through their presence and performance, point fighting was rejuvenated and more martial artists took an interest in the sport. Vitali won the rubber match at the 1981 Superstar Nationals in Oakland, Calif., where he was grand champion runner-up and announced his retirement from competition.

1978 WORLD TITLE FIGHTS

Date: 3/11; Site: Providence, R.I.; Sanction: PKA; Division: Midwt.; Winner: Bill Wallace; Loser: Emilio Narvaez; Division: Welwt.; Winner: Bob Ryan; Loser: Earnest Hart, Jr.; Promoter: SKI/George Pesare; Television: "CBS Sports Spectacular."

Date: 5/22; Site: Paris, France; Sanction: PKA; Division: Lt. Hvywt.; Winner: Jeff Smith; Loser: Dominic Valera; Promoter: Guy Jugla/Marc Counil.

Date: 7/22; Site: W. Palm Beach, Fla.; Sanction: PKA; Division: Welwt.; Winner: Steve Shepherd; Loser: Bob Ryan; Promoter: Steve Shepherd/Don Haines.

Date: 11/30; Site: Atlanta, Ga.; Sanction: PKA; Division: Welwt.; Winner: Earnest Hart, Jr.; Loser: Steve Shepherd; Promoter: SKI/Joe Corley; "CBS Sports Spectacular."

The Second Boom By 1979, a martial arts movie renaissance was underway. At the forefront of these films was Chuck Norris, in *A Force of One,* produced by American Cinema. Due to Norris' personal philosophy, *A Force of One* earned a PG (Parental Guidance) rating and consequently reached a huge market of youthful moviegoers. Also starring Jennifer O'Neill and Bill Wallace, who made his film debut, *Force* was a box-office hit from its outset and even received favorable critical reviews.

Joe Lewis, who once competed against Norris in the karate ring, became the second American karate champion to star in a motion picture. Lewis' transition had been expected by martial artists, since it was common knowledge that he had been seriously pursuing an entertainment career since 1970, when he took up acting. Filmed on locations in Europe and Asia, *Jaguar Lives*—Lewis' first film—is a poorly written "travelogue" intended as a spy action adventure in the James Bond tradition.

In 1979, two projects that originally involved Bruce Lee finally appeared in American theaters. *Game of Death,* partially filmed by Lee before *Enter the Dragon* but unfinished at his death, and *Circle of Iron* (a.k.a. *The Silent Flute*), originally written by Lee, Stirling Silliphant, and actor James Coburn, were replete with production complications and controversy.

Back in 1977 producer Raymond Chow decided to string together select footage of Lee from *Game of Death* and integrate it with a film and story line engineered for and around it. The resulting film was an ill-assorted mixture of action by no less than four doubles who played the role of Lee. Nevertheless, the approximately 10 minutes of Bruce Lee footage tacked onto the new footage, however absurd, gave audiences their coveted idol.

The Silent Flute, despite a reported $4 million budget, a host of name actors, countless collaborators, an Oscar-winning screenwriter, and two cult heroes, turned out a weak fantasy/odyssey, and was probably a decade too late to appeal to the martial arts consciousness of the U.S. in the late 1960s and early 1970s. It starred David Carradine.

The martial arts resurgence was not limited to film. Joe Hyams took three years to complete *Zen in the Martial Arts,* a collection of compelling personal anecdotes touching upon the wisdom transmitted by his martial arts master instructors, including the late Bruce Lee. Predicted to become a classic whose lessons will be as relevant in the future as they are now, the book was a sensation in its field.

In October, the PKA signed a pact with the Entertainment and Sports Programming Network (ESPN), a new 24-hour cable company that broadcasts sports exclusively. In Nov. 1979 ESPN broadcast five PKA-sanctioned events from across the country. By Mar. 1980 the PKA was selling weekly bouts for ESPN broadcast. At the time the agreement was signed, ESPN had four million viewers nationwide and anticipated growth based on the pay-TV revolution and the phenomenal American sports appetite.

Finally, in 1979, the International Olympic Committee (IOC) approved tae kwon do as a sport worthy of Olympic recognition. According to Dr. Dong Ja Yang, president and chairman of the National AAU Tae Kwon Do Committee, this development meant that tae kwon do would now "be eligible for selection into the games." The approval

Scene from the film *Force of One* in which Chuck Norris competes with full-contact champion Bill Wallace. The film moved Norris from champion to star and was the film debut for Wallace.

Chief instructor for the JKA, Masatoshi Nakayama *(left)*, on a visit to the U.S. in 1982. He is seen here with Emil Farkas.

Demetrius Havanas in Dallas in 1968. Havanas was one of the leading karate champions from Texas. He was the number one world welterweight contender in 1980-81 when a tragic airplane accident on June 23, 1981, took his life.

came too late for the sport to be included in the 1984 Olympics in Los Angeles, but there was indication that it would enter the 1988 games, which will be hosted by Korea. Another encouraging growth factor was the inclusion of amateur tae kwon do, as well as amateur karate competition, in World Games I, held in July 1981 in San Jose, Calif.

1979 WORLD TITLE FIGHTS

Date: 3/?; Site: Tokyo, Japan; Sanction: WKA; Division: Spr. Welwt.; Winner: Alvin Prouder; Loser: Toshihiro Nishiki; Promoter: Howard Hanson/Hisashi Shima; Television: "NBC Sports World"/Japanese national network.

Date: 5/2; Site: So. Lake Tahoe, Nev.; Sanction: WKA; Divison: Spr. Ltwt.; Winner: Benny Urquidez; Loser: Rick Simerly; Promoter: Howard Hanson; Television: "NBC Sports World."

Date: 5/26; Site: W. Palm Beach, Fla.; Sanction: WKA; Division: Midwt.; Winner: Steve Shepherd; Loser: Chris Gallegos; Promoter: Steve Shepherd.

Date: 10/?; Site: Tokyo, Japan; Sanction: WKA; Division: Spr. Ltwt.; Winner: Benny Urquidez; Loser: Yoshimitsu Tomashiro; Promoter: Howard Hanson/Hisashi Shima; Television: Japanese national network.

Date: 8/25; Site: Hampton, Va.; Sanction: PKA; Division: Banwt.; Winner: Vernon Mason; Loser: ?; Promoter: Frank Hargrove.

Date: 11/7; Site: W. Palm Beach, Fla.; Sanction: PKA; Division Welwt.; Winner: Steve Shepherd; Loser: Earnest Hart, Jr.; Promoter: Steve Shepherd/Don Haines.

Date: 12/?; Site: St. Paul, Minn.; Sanction: PKA; Division: Spt. Ltwt.; Winner: Gordon Franks; Loser: Tony Lopez; Promoter: Superfights Co.

Date: 12/23; Site: Las Vegas, Nev.; Sanction: WKA; Division: Banwt.; Winner: Graciela Casillas; Loser: Irene Garcia; Promoter: Hap Holloway/Ron Holmes.

After a career spanning 12 years, Bill Wallace retired on June 15. He won a 12-round decision over Robert Biggs in a bout broadcast live on "CBS Sports Spectacular."

July marked the release of the inaugural issue of *Kick Illustrated*, the second martial arts magazine published by **Curtis Wong** (his first, in 1973, was *Inside Kung-Fu*). *Kick*, edited by John Corcoran, was an immediate success; it helped restore traditional values to the martial arts media. Late in 1980 Wong and Corcoran produced a one-shot special entitled *Martial Arts Movies*. So impressive were its sales that Wong launched it in July 1981 as a monthly magazine with editor Sandra Segal at the helm.

In Sept. 1979 a group of enterprising karate instructors from St. Paul, Minn., published the first edition of *Sport Karate Magazine*. Its reception by the sports community led to expansion to a monthly magazine format in July 1980. Edited by **Gary Hestilow** and **John Worley**, *Sport Karate* had come closest to duplicating the defunct *Professional Karate* in serving the interests of the sport and its athletes. Limited by regional distribution and direct mail subscriptions, *Sport Karate* ceased publication in June 1981.

Overall, more than 40 PKA-sanctioned events were telecast over the ESPN in 1980, and CBS aired three more. The rival WKA broke into the American network with one broadcast over "NBC Sports World" and signed a television syndication pact with Hollywood Programmed Entertainment for the broadcast of 26 full-contact cards domestically and abroad.

In August, Chuck Norris, with a media blitz and personal appearances, publicized the release of *The Octagon*. Having fulfilled his contract with American Cinema, Norris became a free agent. In 1981-82 he starred in three films—*An Eye For An Eye, Silent Rage,* and *Forced Vengeance*—and formed his own production company.

August also marked the second American tour of a Chinese **wu shu** troupe, through the coordination of San Francisco's **Anthony Chan,** a wu shu stylist and one of America's great form champions. The first visit had been in 1974; the 1980 tour took the Peking troupe to San Francisco, Oakland, Los Angeles, St. Louis, Boston, New York, and Houston. The troupe's San Francisco performance was filmed by ABC's "Wide World of Sports" for later broadcast.

Full-contact karate was televised in two national broadcasts of PKA bouts, one on "NBC Sports World," the other on "CBS Sports Spectacular." NBC aired the unexpected defeat of PKA heavyweight champion Ross Scott by Demetrius Edwards, via a 7th round knockout. This marked the first of three matches within a one-week period in

Supreme Court
STATE OF ARIZONA
Phoenix
85007

CHIEF JUSTICE
JAMES DUKE CAMERON

VICE CHIEF JUSTICE
FRED C. STRUCKMEYER, JR.

JUSTICES
JACK D. H. HAYS
WILLIAM A. HOLOHAN
FRANK X. GORDON, JR.

CLIFFORD H. WARD
CLERK

MARY ANN HOPKINS
CHIEF DEPUTY CLERK

November 8, 1976

Mr. John Corcoran
6530 DeLongtre Avenue, Apt. 1
Hollywood, California   90028

Dear Mr. Corcoran:

I have been contacted by Mr. Robert A. Trias of Phoenix, Arizona, who advises me that you need some information concerning him.

I have been acquainted with Mr. Trias since 1946. In April of that year he opened a commercial school of karate and judo in Phoenix. To my knowledge that school has been continuous since that time, although not at the same address. I was either the first or one of the earliest of Bob Trias' students.

Trusting that this is the information which you need,

Very truly yours,

Fred C. Struckmeyer, Jr.

FCS:fs

Letter *proving* that Robert Trias had in dojo in Arizona as early as 1946, thus making his the oldest karate school in the continental U.S.

Al Gene Carulia, the first world champion in the U.S.

In 1964 Sea Oh Choi (seen demonstrating) brought Hapkido to the U.S.

Left to right: Jhoon Rhee, Pat Burlson, fourth from left, Ed Parker, Maung Yi, Anthony Miriakim. Courtesy of Anthony Miriakim.

Group of karate leaders assembled before the Don Wilson-Andy White title fight in Florida. *Sitting, left to right:* Jim Wilson; Howard Hanson, president of the WKA; Harris Allen, John Barnett, Al Weiss. *Standing, left to right:* Red Carver, Tom Watson, Andy White, Bob Padgett, Jerry Moore, Don Wilson, Steve Shepherd, Paul Maslak, John Ormsey, Dale Merrit, and Clay Teppenpaw.

Jumping side kick performed by Dan Anderson, a leading semicontact fighter of the mid-1970s and early 1980s.

Courtesy of *Inside Kung-Fu Magazine*

In 1980 Tokey Hill became the first American gold medalist at the WUKO World Karate Championships.

US team in Madrid, Spain, in Nov. 1980. *Standing, left to right:* Chuck Merriman, Tokey Hill, Phil McRae, Billy Banks, and J. Thomson. *Kneeling, left to right:* Jose Jordon, Ted Pritchard, Domingo Llanos, Jueng Kim.

which established world champions were defeated by challengers. On August 9, the invincible Benny Urquidez lost his first match. His opponent was Billy Jackson of Dallas, who won the 7-round non-title fight in West Palm Beach, Fla. Also on August 9, challenger Cliff Thomas of El Paso assumed the PKA world super-lightweight title, upsetting Gordon Franks by a 3rd-round TKO.

Perhaps the greatest event of the 1980 martial arts renaissance was the staggering success of the television miniseries *Shogun.* Based on James Clavell's best-selling novel, the $22 million project aired on NBC the week of Sept. 15-19 in five parts, and presented American audiences with the first insight into the world of the feudal Japanese samurai. *Shogun* captured 125 million viewers, or more than half of the total television viewing audience in the U.S. *Shogun's* phenomenal success created a new wave of interest by the American public in learning the "samurai arts." Supply companies reported a sudden boost in orders for samurai swords and other Japanese-related weapons. Karate schools were inundated with phone calls from potential students, and business increased dramatically.

With the 1980 Warner Bros. release of *The Big Brawl,* general American audiences were introduced to the irrepressible new king of kung-fu, **Jackie Chan.** Chan's fame spread from Hong Kong when, beginning in 1978, three of his pictures surpassed the grosses of Bruce Lee's films in Asia: *Drunken Monkey in a Tiger's Eye, Fearless Hyena,* and *The Young Master,* the last having sold more tickets, according to its producers, Golden Harvest, than any picture of any genre ever to play Hong Kong. Chan was quickly discovered by Hollywood and cast in his first American-made film, *The Big Brawl;* his American debut, however, failed to duplicate his international appeal.

When Mexico suffered last-minute sponsorship problems, the 5th WUKO World Championships was picked up by Spain as the host country. The event, originally scheduled for 1979, was delayed one year by this development. The tournament took place in Madrid on Nov. 28-29, with 55 countries represented. The AAU had conducted its team selection tournament in New Jersey, from which America fielded its strongest, most experienced contingent ever. Head coach **Chuck Merriman** anticipated the possibility of returning home with a world championship.

Tokey Hill of Ohio became the first amateur world champion to emerge from the ranks of America's fighters. Not since 1970, at the inaugural WUKO tournament, had an American placed in individual fighting, when Tonny Tulleners won third place. Hill won a gold medal and Pennsylvania's Billy Blanks defeated the Spanish national champion to advance to the finals, where he took a silver medal in the openweight class. Blanks then took a bronze medal in the 80 kg division, making him the only American double medal winner in world class amateur karate competition.

Another new division, in addition to the openweight class, was women's kata competition. Kathy Baxter of New York and Pam Glaser of Massachusetts placed within the top 8 finalists, with Baxter taking a respectable fifth place.

Significantly, the 1980 AAU karate team was composed of players representing a multitude of karate styles, whereas, earlier, most of the U.S. representatives had been predominantly Japanese stylists.

The international rivalry between the WUKO and the IAKF took a bright turn on Dec. 25, 1980, when a unification meeting between the two organizations took place in Tokyo. Zentaro Kosaka, president of the IAKF, and **Ryoichi Sasakawa,** president of the WUKO, initiated talks for the consolidation of international amateur karate-do competition.

Since 1977 the International Olympic Committee had directed that prior to consideration of karate as a recognized non-participatory Olympic sport, application for this status must emanate from only one federation truly representing the great majority of karate federations worldwide. The Dec. 25 conference resulted in unification of the WUKO and the IAKF in Japan only—the intention was to unify amateur karate in those parts of the world still divided between the two organizations. With world unity essential to IOC acceptance, it is believed the organizations can overcome the remaining obstacles to that recognition.

1980 WORLD TITLE FIGHTS
Date: 1/10; Site: Providence, R.I.; Sanction: PKA; Division: Lt. Hvywt.; Winner: Dan Macaruso; Loser: Jeff Smith; Promoter: George Pesare.

Date: 1/26; Site: Las Vegas, Nev.; Sanction: WKA; Division: Welwt.; Winner: Howard Jackson; Loser: Yoshimitsu Tomashiro; Division: Spr. Ltwt.; Winner: Benny Urquidez; Loser: Shinobu Onuki; Promoter: Howard Hanson; Television: "NBC Sports World."

Date: 3/8; Site: Brussels, Belgium; Sanction: PKA; Division: Lt. Hvywt.; Winner: Dan Macaruso; Loser: Dominic Valera.

Date: 3/29; Site: Las Vegas, Nev.; Sanction: WKA; Division: Spr. Midwt.; Winner: Bob Ryan; Loser: Pilinky Rodriguez; Division: Spr. Welwt.; Winner: Alvin Prouder; Loser: Marc Costello; Divison: Banwt.; Winner: Graciela Casillas; Rochelle Raggsdale; Promoter: Howard Hanson; Television: USA Cable.

Date: 4/19; Site: Vancouver, Can.; Sanction: WKA; Division: Spr. Lt. Hvywt.; Winner: Tony Morelli; Loser: Travis Everett; Division: Fthrwt.; Winner: Lily Rodriguez; Loser: Maureen Tatum; Promoter: Jim Wright; Television: USA Cable.

Date: 5/17; Site: W. Palm Beach, Fla.; Sanction: PKA; Divison: Welwt.; Winner: Steve Shepherd; Loser: Mike Brennan; Division: Banwt.; Winner: Larry Sanders; Loser: Vernon Mason; Promoter: Steve Shepherd/Don Haines.

Date: 6/15; Site: Anderson, Ind.; Sanction: PKA; Division: Hvywt.; Winner: Ross Scott; Loser: Jacquet Bazemore; Division: Midwt.; Winner: Bill Wallace; Loser: Robert Biggs; Promoter: SKI/Glenn Keeney; Television: "CBS Sports Spectacular."

Date: 8/9; Site: El Paso, Tex.; Sanction: PKA; Division: Spr. Ltwt.; Winner: Cliff Thomas; Loser: Gordon Franks; Promoter: Tony & Hilary Sandoval; Television: ESPN.

Date: 8/12; Site: Ottawa, Can.; Sanction: PKA; Division: Hvywt.; Winer: Demetrius Edwards; Loser: Ross Scott; Promoter: SKI/John Therien; Television: "NBC Sports World."

Date: 10/13; Site: Cocoa Beach, Fla.; Sanction: WKA; Division: Lt. Hvywt.; Winner: Don Wilson; Loser: Andy White; Promoter: Jim Wilson.

Date: 10/30; Site: Providence, R.I.; Sanction: PKA; Divsion: Lt. Hvywt.; Winner: Dan Macaruso; Loser: Carl Beamon; Promoter: George Pesare; Television: ESPN.

Date: 11/8; Site: W. Palm Beach, Fla.; Sanction: PKA/WKA; Division: Welwt.; Winner: Steve Shepherd; Loser: Earnest Hart, Jr.; Promoter: Steve Shepherd/Don Haines; Television: ESPN.

Date: 11/15; Site: Ottawa, Can.; Sanction: PKA; Division: Midwt.; Winner: Jean Yves Theriault; Loser: Robert Biggs; Promoter: SKI/John Therien; Televison: ESPN.

Date: 11/15; Site: Denver, Colo.; Sanction: PKA; Division: Banwt.; Winner: Felipe Garcia; Loser: Larry Sanders; Promoter: Karyn Turner/Jim Hawkins; Television: ESPN.

Jerry Beasley, a karate historian and writer who teaches a karate program at Radford University in Virginia, has organized American karate's evolution into three distinct phases. They are:

The Traditional Era (Mid-1950s—Mid-1960s) American karate emphasizes conformity, with few practitioners or competitors breaking with tradition.

The Progressive Era (Mid-1960s—1972) Competitors introduce progressive concepts and develop new fighting methods; Americans become recognized as competent fighters and instructors.

The Contemporary Era (from 1972) Evolution can be traced to prominent fighters of the Progressive Era. The reality of combat originally advocated by Joe Lewis and Bruce Lee is synthesized through the introduction of contact competition and the innovative safety equipment designed and marketed by Jhoon Rhee.

(JOHN CORCORAN)See also amateur tae kwon do; motion pictures and television; tournaments, American karate. *Further reading: The Complete Martial Arts Catalogue*, John Corcoran and Emil Farkas, 1977; *the Hatchet Men: The Story of the Tong Wars in San Francisco's Chinatown*, Richard H. Dillon, 1962; *Karate's History & Traditions*, Bruce Haines, 1967; *The Encyclopedia of Karate & Related Arts*, Ted Kresge, 1971; *The History of American Karate*, Robin L. Rielly, 1970; *Karate: The Energy Connection*, W. Scott Russell, 1976; *This Is Karate*, Masutatsu Oyama, 1965; *Who's Who in the Martial Arts*, Bob Wall (John Corcoran ed.), 1975; *Zen Combat*, Jay Cluck, 1962; *Black Belt Magazine*, May-July 1977; *Karate Illustrated*, Jan.-Feb. 1977 and Sept. 1977; *Kick Illustrated*, April 1981.

One of the most exciting finals ever at the 1973 Long Beach
Internationals: Benny Urquidez and John Natividad battle to a
13–12 score. The winner was Natividad.

Steve Sheperd *(left)* and Ernie Hart during PKA World Welterweight title fight.

MOTION PICTURES AND TELEVISION

The first U.S. fight film was made by Thomas Edison in 1894, capturing Gentleman Jim Corbett in the boxing ring with Peter Courtney. Since that primitive era, western martial arts have cut and punched a path from the decks of 1920s Douglas Fairbanks' swashbucklers, through the Sherwood Forest of Errol Flynn's *Robin Hood,* onto the battlefields of medieval England and France, which appeared in epic color in the 1950s and 60s, into gladiatorial arenas for Italian-made muscle extravaganzas starring Steve Reeves and others, and back into the boxing ring with

hit movies such as the Oscar-winning *Rocky* (1976), *Rocky II* (1979), and *Raging Bull* (1980).

Martial arts of the Far East were first exposed on western screens in *Outside Woman* (1921), featuring a Japanese manservant's jujutsu skill. In the mid-1930s, the series of *Charlie Chan* movies frequently showed oriental-style fighting, and almost every one of the *Mr. Moto* films, with Peter Lorre in the title role, displayed some judo.

Actually, the "modern era" of eastern martial arts began in 1945, after World War II had introduced elements of Japanese culture to Americans at large. In *Blood on the Sun,* for the first time a Hollywood

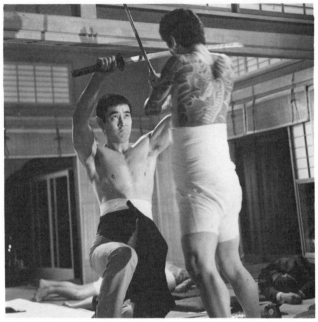

Takura Ken (*left*) battles a yakuza member in the exciting action movie *The Yakuza* (1974). The picture also starred Robert Mitchum and showed some of the most exciting Japanese sword fighting ever filmed for an American movie. It was shot on location in Japan with some of Japan's top sword masters participating in the action.

James Cagney in 1942 practicing judo for his movie role in *Blood on the Sun.* The film featured Cagney in one of the greatest judo fights ever put on the screen.

star, James Cagney, used Asian combative techniques, those of judo, to defeat an antagonist. His attempt to inform the west of imminent war pits him against the Tokyo chief of police for the climactic one-on-one battle.

Bad Day at Black Rock (1954) cast Spencer Tracy as a one-armed war veteran who discovers the corruption of a Western town and uncovers the secret behind it. Suspense builds to a climactic fight sequence in which Tracy uses karate to accomplish justice. Here the art was portrayed clearly and cleverly as part of the story line. The year 1954 also saw the release of Japanese director Akira Kurosawa's classic, *The Seven Samurai,* with Toshiro Mifune. This film was critically acclaimed, and its subsequent attraction for American audiences was the first hint of much broader popularity awaiting martial arts films within the next two decades. *The Seven Samurai* was transformed into a Western, emerging as *The Magnificent Seven.* The concepts of Kurosawa's *Yojimbo* and *Sanjuro* found tremendous profit in the international market remade as the trend-setting "spaghetti Westerns," *A Fistful of Dollars* and *For a Few Dollars More.* When by the end of the 1960s these latter two pictures brought Clint Eastwood home from Italy as a bona fide movie star, it was clear that an oriental perspective on heroism—its ironies no less than its challenges and glories—would eventually win acceptance with the American public.

Yet throughout the 1960s, American-produced films limited the depiction of the eastern martial arts to "novelty" bits, as in a karate attack upon a character played by Frank Sinatra in *The Manchurian Candidate* (1962). Martial arts-styled fights added to the pseudo-macho character of Peter Sellers' Inspector Clouseau (beginning with *The Pink Panther,* 1964) and spiced each of the exhilarating James Bond adventures. In *Goldfinger* (1964), real-life judo black belt Honor Blackman, as Pussy Galore, expertly threw Sean Connery; in *You Only Live Twice* (1967), **ninja** and their exotic skills were presented for the first time to mainstream movie audiences.

Elvis Presley insisted on using the then unknown oriental art of karate in almost every picture he made. At least half a dozen contained martial arts scenes: *G.I. Blues, Wild in the Country, Blue Hawaii, Harum-Scarum, Kid Gallahad,* and *Follow That Dream.* Through these films, Elvis, a real-life black belt, did much to expose karate to the world at large.

James Coburn, before becoming a student of **Bruce Lee,** demonstrated karate while spoofing a hero in *Our Man Flint* (1966). Coburn emphasized the martial arts to an even greater degree in the sequel, *In Like Flint* (1967).

The Green Berets (1968) featured John Wayne in a Vietnam story with martial arts elements distributed around the commando action scenes. *The Wrecking Crew* (1968), starring Dean Martin as Matt Helm, had a surfeit of fight scenes choreographed by Bruce Lee, who was first introduced to viewers via television in *The Green Hornet* series of 1966-67. Karate champions **Chuck Norris, Joe Lewis,** and **Mike Stone** played bit parts as heavies. And *Marlowe* (1969), with James Garner in the title role, is a private detective whose office and equanimity are destroyed by the high-kicking Bruce Lee, here in a cameo role as a Chinese assassin.

The martial arts byplay in American movies of the 1960s served to bring an exotic image of eastern fighting skills to the public eye. However, while heroes were permitted to show their mastery of karate with a few kicks, no film company wanted to risk basing an entire project on martial arts action. Since the stakes were much lower in the production of single television episodes, eastern martial arts had more consistent and extensive exposure on action-adventure television series until the early 70s. Producers and writers rising to the week-to-week challenge of devising new kinds of conflict for the television screen, turned to the martial arts.

One of the first times karate was seen on American television occurred in an early episode of *The Detectives* (1959-61), in which karate instructor **Bruce Tegner** taught Robert Taylor how to proceed against an "empty hand" killer. From the same era, although with less serious intent, an episode of *The Adventures of Ozzie and Harriet* had Rick Nelson performing karate. In the 1960-61 series *The Case of the Dangerous Robin,* **Ed Parker**'s student, Rick Jason, played an insurance investigator and karate expert.

A British syndicated import *The Avengers* (1964-69), introduced U.S. audiences to female secret agent/martial arts expert Emma Peal, played by Diana Rigg. By 1965, three series were regularly

using the martial arts. In *I Spy* (1965-68) Robert Culp and Bill Cosby took karate along with them to exotic locales. *The Wild, Wild West* (1965-69) introduced Robert Conrad as a secret service agent in the Old West mixing karate and judo for fight scenes in virtually every episode. *Honey West* (1965-66) was promoted as a martial arts program and starred Anne Francis as a private investigator and judo expert.

With *The Green Hornet* series (1966-67), a genuine fighting wizard entered television in the person of Bruce Lee, playing Kato and displaying his flamboyant kung-fu. Lee embellished his style with visually stunning kicks, many of them so fast that retakes were necessary. Lee again attracted attention in the one-hour season opener for *Longstreet* (1971-72) written by **Stirling Silliphant.** James Franciscus played the title role, a blind investigator to whom Lee teaches his innovative art of **jeet kune do.** Three additional episodes of the series also featured Bruce Lee.

When "Kung Fu" (1972-75) aired, with David Carradine as a Shao-lin disciple wandering in the Old West, martial arts reached an apex in popularity. The success of this series paved the way in 1973 for the successful reception of four martial arts pictures filmed in Hong Kong, three of which starred Bruce Lee.

Red Sun (1971) exploited the odd, foreign look of martial arts, casting Toshiro Mifune as a full-dress samurai accompanying outlaw Charles Bronson through the West of the 1860s. In *The Mechanic* (1972) hitman Charles Bronson merely observes a karate fight featuring **Tak Kubota.** Mainstream motion pictures rarely employed martial arts as more than good action footage.

That changed in 1972 with the release of *Billy Jack.* The Warner Bros. feature generated domestic net film rentals (U.S.-Canadian box-office gross, less exhibitors' percentage and second feature deductions) of $32 million. Playing a half-breed war veteran, producer-star Tom Laughlin integrated the **hapkido** kicks of master **Bong Soo Han** (who doubled for Laughlin) into the plot. Over the next few months, it became possible to identify pure martial arts movies as a new and potent film genre.

Although the themes of American martial arts movie productions were rarely more sophisticated than the triumph of good over evil, by the early 70s the idea that the martial arts were mental and spiritual disciplines began to influence the new genre. For these new pictures, the goals of the central character are often tempered with Taoist mysticism or Zen irony, always punched across with instantaneous action that conveys the immediacy and intuitive quality of enlightenment.

Pure martial arts movies flowered in the U.S. in 1973 when Warner Bros. imported *The Five Fingers of Death,* which starred Lo Lieh as a tiger-claw stylist who indulges in swordplay on the way to becoming the kung-fu boxing champion of China. With the arrival of *Fists of Fury* and *The Chinese Connection* by mid-1973, the first wave evolved into a "Bruce Lee Boom." In *Fists of Fury,* he wins freedom for himself and his fellow workers from the illegal operations of their factory boss. And in *The Chinese Connection,* Lee fights to defend a kung-fu school against anti-Chinese prejudice and attack in Japanese-occupied Shanghai of 1938.

With *Enter the Dragon,* Bruce Lee mania became a worldwide phenomenon. First released in the U.S. in Aug. 1973, a few short weeks after Lee's death, the Golden Harvest-Warner Bros. production became an instant classic and unqualified hit. Its worldwide box-office gross today totals more than $100 million. Lee's role is that of a Shao-lin disciple with multiple motives for entering the mysterious Mr. Han's karate tournament and for destroying the villain's worldwide drug operation. John Saxon, **Jim Kelly, Bob Wall,** and Angela Mao co-starred. Robert Clouse directed; Raymond Chow and Fred Weintraub were co-producers.

Return of the Dragon (1974), which Lee wrote, directed, and choreographed, and in which he starred, was filmed in Hong Kong and Rome in 1972. As the unsophisticated hero, smashing a Roman syndicate, Lee played the role light, adding another dimension to his hard-edged, cult hero image. Chuck Norris co-starred.

The talents associated with *Enter the Dragon* kept the martial arts movie genre alive throughout the mid-1970s. Fred Weintraub produced *Black Belt Jones* (1974) and *Golden Needles* (1974), starring Los Angeles karate expert and actor Jim Kelly, who also starred in *Melinda* (1972) and *Hot Potato* (1976). Additionally, Tamara Dobson used hapkido as *Cleopatra Jones* (1974), and Jimmy Wang Yu—the

Franco Nero in *Enter the Ninja* (1982), the first American-made film in which ninjas are the central theme of the movie.

biggest name in Hong Kong kung-fu movies prior to Bruce Lee—captured some American attention as the one-armed fighter in *The Master of the Flying Guillotine* (1975).

Leading action director Sam Peckinpaw's *The Killer Elite* (1975) starred James Caan as a CIA agent attempting to prevent the assassination of a government official by ninja killers. The climactic scene, which takes place aboard ships docked in San Francisco Bay, prolifically but ineffectively displayed ninjutsu, karate, and judo by a gathering of some of the best martial artists ever to work in film.

Chuck Norris went from *Return of the Dragon* into the leading role as the karateka trucker in *Breaker, Breaker* (1977). Otherwise, mainstream audiences got their martial arts from a cute action sequence in *The Bad News Bears Go to Japan* (1978) and the satirical vignette "A Fistful of Yen" with Evan Kim and Bong Soo Han, from *Kentucky Fried Movie* (1978). During the same period, martial arts film buffs watched for pictures that independent film distributors had in limited release, such as *The Streetfighter* starring Sonny Chiba—the first picture to be MPAA-rated X for violence—and *Bloody Fists* with the Shaw Brothers' discovery, Alexander Fu Sheng. Hard-core kung-fu movie fans with access to Chinese-language theaters also discovered the high-spirited "Comedy Kung-Fu" genre, featuring the antics of Hong Kong's **Jackie Chan.** Chan's inventive blend of multiple northern Shao-lin styles with Chinese opera acrobatics resulted in two Far East hits in 1978: *Snake in the Eagle's Shadow* and *Drunken Monkey in a Tiger's Eye.*

In 1978 American Cinema's *Good Guys Wear Black* accumulated domestic net rentals in the millions. Chuck Norris starred as a karate expert exposing corruption in high places. American Cinema followed up with *A Force of One* (1979), with again gigantic domestic net rentals. Norris, again, as a karate instructor tracks down a karate killer, played by **full-contact** karate champion **Bill Wallace,** and extracts his own vengeance from the culprit. This movie enjoys a reputation of being one of the most realistic, entertaining films of the genre made in Hollywood.

In 1979 a martial arts movie renaissance began. *Jaguar Lives* (1979) pitted full-contact karate champion Joe Lewis against a sinister mastermind whose ambition is to assassinate the world's leading political figures. Also released in 1979 was Columbia's *Game of Death,* a posthumous pastiche that crossed Bruce Lee fighting footage, from an unfinished film, with a more recently conceived story line. The ill-assorted mixture made necessary the extensive use of doubles in the Lee role. Film Ventures International entered the martial arts movie marketplace in 1980 with the PG-rated *Kill or be Killed,* which exploited the karate tournament formula.

American Cinema's *The Octagon* (1980), the third film in the Chuck Norris trilogy, which began with *Good Guys Wear Black,* has Norris searching out and destroying the secret ninja training camp of **Tadashi Yamashita** (a.k.a. Bronson Lee).

With the spectacular Far East grosses of Jackie Chan's *Fearless Hyena* (1970) and *The Young Master* (1980) in mind, and with confidence in the ability of the Robert Clouse-Fred Weintraub team to recreate their *Enter the Dragon* success, Warner Bros. released their first collective effort in *The Big Brawl.* Ever supple and whimsical as the engaging young hero, Chan goes the distance in a 1930s Texas prizefight to prove his skill and endurance.

In Sept. 1980 NBC aired its five-part television miniseries of James Clavell's novel, *Shogun,* starring Richard Chamberlain and Toshiro Mifune. The television blockbuster won ratings second only to those of *Roots.* New World Pictures joined the trend with the theatrical release of *Shogun Assassin.* Re-edited and specially dubbed for U.S. general release, the film used footage from parts I and II of the six-part Japanese *Sword of Vengeance* or "Baby Cart" series of feature films. Inspired by a samurai comic strip and produced by Shintaro "Zatoichi" Katsu, this unusual plot offers Tomisaburo Wakayama as a superbly skilled swordsman who rebels and takes to the road. He pushes his young son ahead of him in an ingeniously equipped baby carriage while the shogun's ninjas creep closer on all sides.

In addition to re-releases of the Lee classics and the Norris hits, summer 1981 introduced New World's *Firecracker,* with Jullian Kesner; Film Ventures' *Kill and Kill Again,* James Ryan starring in this sequel to *Kill or Be Killed;* American Cinema's *Force: Five,* produced by Fred Weintraub, directed by Robert Clouse, based on a story by martial artist **Emil Farkas** and George Goldsmith, and

starring Joe Lewis, **Benny Urquidez,** and Bong Soo Han; Avco Embassy's first Chuck Norris karate-thriller, *An Eye for an Eye;* and the Cannon Group's *Enter the Ninja,* starring Franco Nero and Sho Kosugi, with Mike Stone providing choreography and doubling for Nero. This film was the first to focus exclusively on ninjutsu and ninja, the mysterious spies and assassins of Japan, who seem likely to become the new heroes in American martial arts movies.

In 1982 Columbia Pictures released *Silent Rage,* with Chuck Norris, then MGM followed with another Norris picture, *Forced Vengeance.* Another relatively high-budget feature is *The Challenge,* from CBS Theatrical Films, starring Toshiro Mifune and directed by John Frankenheimer. In 1982 Johnny June starred in the first full-length martial arts comedy, *Fistfull of Chopsticks.* (Neva Friedenn) *See also* U.S., history of karate in. *Further reading: Kung-Fu: Cinema of Vengeance,* Verina Glaessner, 1974; *The Martial Arts Films,* Marilyn D. Mintz, 1978.

Jackie Chan, the most popular martial arts star in the Orient, starred in *The Big Brawl* (1981), the first role he has had in an American feature.

Spencer Tracy displays his martial arts skills in the 1954 film *Bad Day at Black Rock.*

Bong Soo Han in his role in the comedy spoof *Kentucky Fried Movie* (1978).

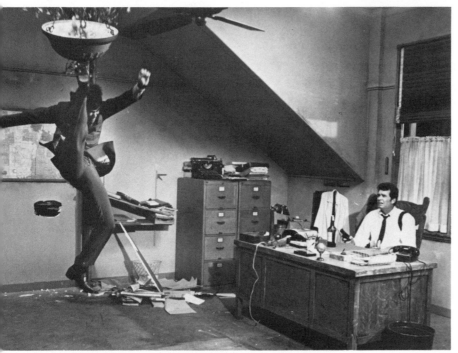

Bruce Lee destroying James Garner's office in the film *Marlowe.* This was Lee's first major American motion picture, filmed in 1969.

Fred Williamson practices his karate behind bars in *That Man Bolt,* a feature for Universal Pictures.

In the 90-minute TV pilot, Emil Farkas matches skills with *The Amazing Spider-Man* (1978). The show has been converted for release to European theaters.

John Saxon and Bruce Lee in *Enter the Dragon* (1973), the biggest grossing martial arts movie ever made. Standing at extreme left is Bob Wall.

Kareem Abdul-Jabbar and Bruce Lee in *Game of Death* (1979),
which was released many years after Lee's death.

Joe Lewis, former heavyweight karate champion of the world,
portrays a secret agent in American International's exciting
action drama, *Jaguar Lives* (1979).

Chuck Norris (*right*) delivers a karate kick in the movie *Breaker,
Breaker* (1977), which was Norris' first starring role in a feature.

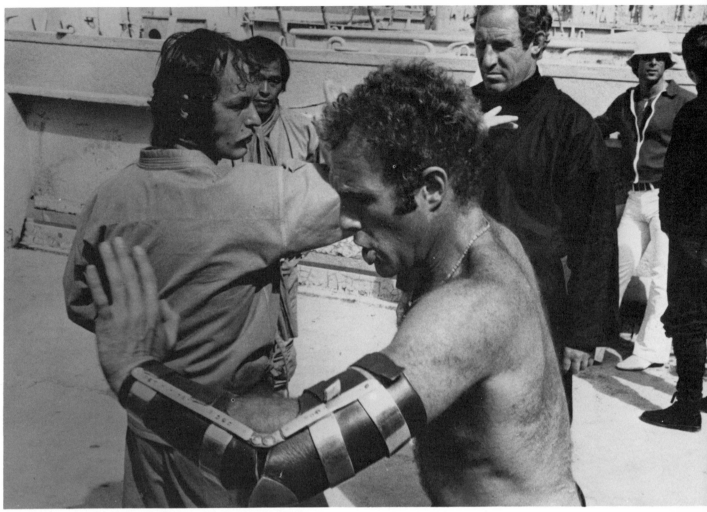

On the set of *The Killer Elite,* the 1975 Sam Peckinpah epic, Emil Farkas shows James Caan the intricacy of an empty-hand blow. Gene LeBell and Tak Kubota look on.

Tomisaburo Wakayama plays Ito Ogami in one of Japan's leading series of samurai films—the baby carriage series. It was released in the U.S. as *Sword of Vengeance* (1981).

Martial arts publisher Curtis Wong (*left*) doubles for David Carradine on the TV show ''Kung-Fu.''

James Coburn demonstrates his martial arts expertise in the movie *Our Man Flint* (1966). Coburn was one of Bruce Lee's students and is an ardent martial arts fan.

Charles Bronson (*right*) with Tak Kubota as they appeared in the film *The Mechanic* (1972).

Roger Moore displays his martial arts skill in the James Bond movie *The Spy Who Loved Me* (1977). Here he delivers a side kick to antagonist Milton Reid during a fight on a Cairo rooftop.

Tamara Dobson uses karate as one of her weapons in her attack on dope traffic in the Warner Bros. action thriller *Cleopatra Jones* (1974).

Five Fingers of Death (1973), starring Lo Lieh (*left*), was the first Chinese-produced kung-fu film distributed widely in the U.S. The film's great success assured the growth of future martial arts movies and showed Hollywood producers the commerciality of this type of film.

Billy Jack (1972), starring Tom Laughlin (*right*), was one of the first American films in which martial arts were prominently featured. The film introduced audiences to the little-known Korean art of hapkido and catapulted Bong Soo Han, the film's fight choreographer, to national fame.

Peter Sellers spoofed the martial arts in his movie *A Shot in the Dark* (1964). The movie was written and directed by Blake Edwards, a karate student for many years under Ed Parker.

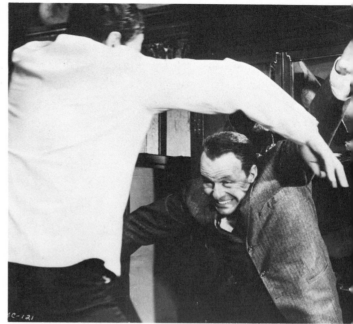

The Manchurian Candidate (1962), with Frank Sinatra (*right*), was one of the first films featuring karate. Here Lawrence Harvey attempts to kill Sinatra using his deadly karate skills.

Donn F. Draeger (*left*), a former American Marine Corps major who is a master of many Japanese martial arts, instructs Sean Connery (*center*) in bojutsu for a scene in *You Only Live Twice* (1967).

Anne Francis, star of the TV show "Honey West," played a female detective who was a judo expert. Here she is about to throw veteran judoman Gene LeBell with a shoulder throw. Courtesy of Gene LeBell.

Sean Connery visits a ninja training center in the James Bond adventure film *You Only Live Twice.*

Force: Five (1981) starred some of the most impressive martial artists ever assembled for a major motion picture. *Left to right:* Benny Urquidez, Sonny Barnes, Richard Norton, actress Pam Huntington, and Joe Lewis. The film also starred Bong Soo Han and arm wrestling champion Bob Schott, both playing villains.

David Carradine stars in the martial arts feature *Circle of Iron*. This film was conceived by Bruce Lee and was originally entitled *The Silent Flute*.

Chuck Norris stars as J. J. McQuade, a maverick Texas Ranger in *Lone Wolf McQuade*.

Chuck Norris and Bruce Lee in *Return of the Dragon*.

The Super Six, Steve Chase (James Ryan), Kandy Kane (Anneline K Gorilla (Ken Gampu), Gypsy Billy (Norman Robinson), The Fly (Stan Schmidt), and Hotdog (Bill Flynn) in *Kill and Kill Again*.

PEOPLE

Bruce Lee

Gogen Yamaguchi

Ed Parker

Bill Wallace

Yip Man

Hidy Ochiai

Chuck Norris

ABDERRAHMAN, JACQUES (1952-) French karate champion. One of the top-ranked competitors in Europe, Abderrahman spent 1974 in Japan and won the Northern Japan Karate Championships. In 1975, after changing his name to Patrice Belhriti, he returned to France and was selected as a member of the French national team. He placed second in the 1975 French Openweight Championships and won the openweight title of the 1975 European Karate Championships.

ABE, KENSHIRO (1916-) Japanese judo champion and pioneer. A 5th dan in judo by 18, Abe also studied aikido, kendo and jukendo. He taught at the Judo College within the **Butokukai** in Kyoto in the late 1930s and by 1945 was a 7th dan. He became chief instructor at Doshisa University as well as instructor to the Kyoto Police Department.

Abe went to England in 1955 at the invitation of the London Judo Society and opened his own club one year later. A leader of the British Judo Council he became a highly sought after instructor; however, because he believed that competition victory was not the ultimate goal of judo, he encountered opposition at a time when judo was gaining popularity as a sport. In 1970, he suffered serious injuries in an automobile accident from which he had not fully recovered four years later when he returned to Japan.

ABE, TADASHI Japanese pioneer of **Morihei Ueshiba's** branch of **aikido.** Abe traveled in Europe, training students in the intricacies of aikido. Like **Koichi Tohei,** Abe encouraged many of his disciples to study in Japan so they could better assist him in spreading aikido. In his first French demonstration he challenged a rapier champion and won the encounter by disarming him, but not before losing the tip of an ear.

ABSHER, FRED (1944-) American karate instructor and leader of the **kojasho** system of Chinese boxing. Absher began his martial arts training in the kojasho system in 1960, under the guidance of Jack B. Goric. After studying Japanese karate-do for three years in the U.S. Army, he was promoted to the rank of 1st degree black belt. In 1965 he began the study of **t'ai-chi-ch'uan, hsing-i, pa-kua,** and cha yon tae kwon do, eventually receiving his 4th degree black belt in tae kwon do from **Soo Kim** of Houston, Tex. Absher established a studio in Albuquerque, N.M., as a member of the World Taekwondo Association and the USKA. He won the New Mexico State Karate Grand Championship three times and served as the U.S. team captain in the 1st World Taekwondo Championships in Seoul, South Korea. In 1972, shortly before his death, Goric named Absher the new leader of the kojasho system. Absher currently teaches kojasho within the framework of a formalized sash system.

ADAMS, ANDY Martial arts author and journalist. Adams has been writing about the martial arts in Japan since 1961 when he began reporting **sumo** for the *Japan Times.* He has been a contributor to *Black Belt Magazine* for many years. Since 1973, he has served as editor and publisher of *Sumo World* and in 1978 he co-edited (with John Robertson and photographer **Arthur Tansley**) the *Japan Sports Guide,* which covered every martial art and sport practiced in Japan. In 1970, Adams authored the first authoritative English-language book on ninjutsu, *Ninja, The Invisible Assassins.* In 1979, with Ryo Hatano, he wrote *Sumo History and Yokuzuna Profiles.* For many years, Adams compiled the top ten fighters in Japan for the ratings appearing in the annual *Black Belt Yearbook.*

ADAMS, HAMISH Scottish karate instructor and competitor; member of the Scottish karate contingent that won the 1973 European Team Championships.

ADAMS, NEIL British judo competitor; won the silver medal at the 1980 Moscow Olympics, the European Senior Judo Championships in 1979 and 1980, and the British Open Championships in 1980.

ADAMS, WILLIE American karate instructor. Owner of one of the largest karate studios in Detroit, Mich., Adams has guided several students to national prominence in sport karate. An **isshin-ryu** stylist, he serves as the vice-president and midwestern representative

Neil Adams

of the American Okinawan Karate Organization. Adams received his black belt in 1964; in 1965 he won both the Pennsylvania State and the Illinois State Karate Championships. In 1966 he won the Michigan State Championships, the American International Karate Championships, and placed second in the Canadian Grand Nationals. He won the Ohio State Championships in 1967.

ADKINS, CAYLOR (1934-) American karate instructor. Chairman of the Amateur Athletic Union (AAU) Karate Committee from 1974-77, Adkins has served as president of **Shotokan Karate of America** since 1969. A student of American Shotokan pioneer **Tsutomu Ohshima,** Adkins founded karate clubs at Long Beach City College in 1965 and at California State University, Long Beach, in 1967. Together with Ohshima, he helped translate and edit **Gichin Funakoshi's** textbook on Shotokan karate.

Instrumental in expanding AAU karate rules to develop programs for women, children, and both light- and full-contact competition, Adkins organized AAU karate tournaments and served as the American representative to **WUKO.** A member of *Who's Who in the Martial Arts,* Adkins directed the WUKO World Karate Championships in Long Beach, Calif., in 1975, and that year organized the first European tour by an AAU karate team.

AHN, KYUNG WON (1937-) Korean-born tae kwon do instructor; head of the U.S. team for the 3rd World Tae Kwon Do Championships in Chicago. In 1978 he served as technical and promotional committee member for AAU tae kwon do.

AISU, ISO (1452-1538) Japanese **kenjutsu** master; founder of the Aisu-kuge-ryu.

AJARI, YOSHIAKI (1933-) Japanese-American karate pioneer. Born in Wakayama City, Japan, Ajari began karate training in the

Yoshiaki Ajari

goju-ryu style at 14, under the guidance of **Gogen Yamaguchi** and Shozi Ujita. At Meiji University in Tokyo, he began his study of **wado-ryu** karate-do under Hironori Ohtsuka, the style's founder. In 1956 Ajari organized the All Japan Collegiate Karate Federation and, as its chairman, formulated rules and regulations for its competitions.

In 1957, equipped with black belts in both goju-ryu and wado-ryu, he immigrated to the U.S., where in 1960, together with a cooperative judo club, he founded a nonprofit wado-ryu dojo in Hayward, Calif. It was the first time this major Japanese style was taught publicly in America. Three years later he established his first dojo. In 1964 he formed the U.S. Wado-Kai Karate-do Federation, an affiliate of the All Japan Karate-do Federation, Wado-kai, in Tokyo.

Ajari has practiced and taught his art for almost 30 years; he is the highest-ranking wado-ryu instructor in America today. In 1968 Ajari served as chairman of the All America Karate Championships, which were sponsored by his Wado-kai. *See also* U.S., history of karate in.

AKIYAMA, SHIROBEI Japanese jujutsu instructor. In the opinion of some authorities, Akiyama was the founder of the **yoshin-ryu** style of jujutsu. According to legend, while Akiyama was meditating, a heavy snow fell, and the limbs of many trees were broken by the weight. Only a solitary willow withstood the storm, its pliant branches rejecting any accumulation of snow. Akiyama was allegedly inspired by the willow's resistance and based his yoshin-ryu school on this principle. *See also* yoshin-ryu.

AKO NO KAMI Lord of Ako, Asano Naganori. Asano, an 18th-century feudal lord in what is now Hiroshima Prefecture, was forced to commit **hara-kiri.** The actions of his retainers, who took revenge for his death, are recounted in the legend of Chushingura, the tale of the 47 loyal retainers.

ALBERTINI, PIERRE French judo champion who first won the French championship in 1966 and has a number of times since. In 1970, at the European Championships, he won the bronze medal both in individual competition and as part of the French team. In 1971 he again won the European title.

ALEXANDER, GARY (1938-) American karate pioneer and competitor, president of the Association of Martial Arts Institutes, and one of the first martial arts instructors to establish himself on the East Coast. Winner of the first karate tournaments conducted in Canada and on the East Coast in 1962, Alexander organized the Karate Olympics and the U.S. Karate Championships in 1963 and the East Coast Open Karate Tournament in 1964. He was selected as "Instructor of the Year" in 1974 and voted into the Black Belt Hall of Fame. A member of *Who's Who in the Martial Arts,* he has designed fighting and training equipment. Alexander currently hosts several tournaments, including the Gary Alexander Invitational Karate Championships, held on a quarterly basis in New Jersey. *See also* U.S., history of karate in.

ALIFAX, CHRISTIAN French karate champion, a wado-ryu stylist; he won the French Championships in 1974, 1975, and 1976, and took first place at the 1973 European Championships.

ALLRED, SAM (1935-) American judo and karate instructor and author. Allred was initially a judo student but later ranked in **kajukenbo** karate; his instructors included **Don Nahoolewa** and **Al Dacascos.**

A former high school science teacher, Allred promoted martial arts among high school students through his Duke City Judo Club, founded in 1958 in Albuquerque, N.M. A member of the editorial staff of *Black Belt* and *Karate Illustrated* magazines in 1973, Allred also served as a contributing editor to *Professional Karate.* He has written two textbooks: *Dynamic Self-Defense* and *Karate for Teenagers, with Techniques of Kung-Fu.* Allred was owner and director of the Karate College of the Southwest and has sponsored and promoted tournaments in his region. He is included in *Who's Who in the Martial Arts* and appeared as a stuntman in the feature film *Black Belt Jones.* In 1969 he was the Black Belt Hall of Fame "Man of the Year."

ALMEIDA, UBIRAJARA Brazilian **capoeira** master. Better known in the capoeira world as Master Acordeon, he is one of the few recognized maestroes of capoeira, having won the Bahia Capoeira Championships twice and the Brazilian National Championships three times. He has visited the U.S. to teach his art, and is currently president of the World Capoeira Association.

ALVARADO, JOE (1944-) American karate instructor and competitor. Winner of the Outstanding Texan Award in 1972, Alvarado is noted as a teacher and motivator of physically handicapped students. He trained in Japan between 1962 and 1965 before opening his first school in Austin, Tex., in 1967. A leading regional fighter before his retirement from competition, he was a member of the team that won titles at the Alamo Open Karate Championships, the Central Texas Karate Championships, and the Texas Karate Championships, all in 1971.

AMAKUNI The father of Japanese swordmaking, he lived in Yamato province during the 8th century. One of his swords, the Kogarasu Maru (Little Black Crow Sword) was a treasure of the Taira family before their defeat in the Gempei Wars of the 12th century. The sword has been handed down through many illustrious families, including the Imperial Court, and is today considered a national treasure in Japan.

AMAKURA Top student of **Amakuni,** he lived in Yamato province during the 8th century.

ANDERSON, DAN (1953-) American karate champion. Anderson began karate training in Oregon in 1967 and received his black belt in 1970 from **Bruce Terrill.** He placed second in the lightweight division at the 1972 Long Beach Internationals, and won the U.S.

Gary Alexander, one of the pioneers of karate on the East Coast

Dan Anderson delivering a jumping side kick. Courtesy of *Inside Kung-Fu Magazine*

Karate Championships in 1973. He has also won such tournaments as the MARS Nationals in Cleveland, the Pacific Northwest Championships, the Central Washington State Championships, and the Vancouver Invitational. He appeared regularly in top-10 polls throughout the mid-1970s and into the early 1980s as a nationally ranked semicontact fighter.

ANDERSON, MIKE (1942-) American karate pioneer and promoter. Anderson trained in the Jhoon Rhee system of tae kwon do under **Allen Steen** in Dallas, then taught karate in Europe from 1963 to 1968. He won the All European Open Karate Championships four times and the U.S. Armed Forces Karate Championships twice. While teaching in Germany, Anderson was awarded a gold medal by President Park Chung Hee of South Korea for his efforts in spreading tae kwon do in Europe.

In 1969 Anderson returned to the U.S., where he continued to teach and compete. He placed high in a number of major American tournaments and trained teams that won several national titles between 1970 and 1973. A member of *Who's Who in the Martial Arts,* Anderson launched **Professional Karate Magazine** in 1972 and was instrumental in the rebirth of professional karate competition in the U.S. His **Top 10 Nationals,** promoted since 1971, was one of the three major elimination tournaments produced in America from 1973 to 1976. In 1973 this event was the first to make use of the foam hand-and-foot pads created by Jhoon Rhee which are standard today in semicontact competition.

On Sept. 14, 1974, in conjunction with Don and Judy Quine of the

Mike Anderson

PKA, Anderson co-produced the World Professional Karate Championships in Los Angeles. The event was televised over ABC's "Wide World of Entertainment" and was responsible for originating full-contact karate competition. Anderson originated several other major tournaments in the U.S. and abroad, including the first title fight to produce a world superlightweight champion, in Berlin in 1975; and the World Champion All Star Team Tournament in Paris in 1976.

In 1973 Anderson founded the Professional Karate Referee's Association; he has been active throughout his career as an official at major events in America and Europe. *See also* U.S., history of karate in; Europe, history of karate in.

ANDRAS, OSVAR (1957-) Hungarian judo champion; won the European Junior Championships in 1977 in the 95-kg. division, and took the bronze medal at the Moscow Olympics in 1980. He currently works as a sports instructor in Budapest.

ANNESI, TONY (1947-) American judo, karate, and aiki-jujutsu instructor and martial arts writer. In 1964 Annesi studied sport judo under Ron K. Siegal, and trained at the Tohoku Judo Club under Charles Chaves and Harry Yanagi, and later under Benny Babineaux and Ray Deon. He instructed in judo at Exeter and Vermont Academy.

Annesi earned his black belts in judo and **aiki-jujutsu** under Dr. Albert C. Church in Charleston, S.C., and was cross-graded in kamishin karate. Church appointed Annesi the Massachusetts representative of the Kamishin-kai International, and his personal ichibon-deshi (number-one student) in aiki-jujutsu.

Annesi wrote the official handbooks for the kamishin aiki-jujutsu style, and two karate manuals; since 1980 he has written technical articles for *Kick Illustrated.* He teaches at his Bushido-Kai Martial Arts Center in Natick, Mass.

ANZAWA Japanese **kyudo** master instrumental in introducing his art to Great Britain, Anzawa was ranked a 10th-degree black belt (judan), the highest rank attainable in kyudo.

ARAKAKI, ANKICHI (1899-1927) Okinawan karate master. Born in Shuri, Okinawa, to a wealthy family, Arakaki began studying karate early under the guidance of Chomo Hanashiro and Shinpan Gusukuma. After dropping out of school, he studied with the legendary **Choshin Chibana.** At 19, Arakaki took part in a sumo tournament in Shuri, and defeated a notorious giant wrestler from Yomitan village. Upon his discharge from military service in 1921, he moved to Kadena and trained with **Chotoku Kyan.** With the death of his father, during a time of declining fortunes in the economic crisis after World War I, Arakaki was faced with the financial difficulties of his family. The hardships were so burdensome that the young Arakaki fell ill and died of ulcers in 1927, at the age of 28. Before his death, he taught **Soshin Nagamine,** who became a leading figure in Matsubayashi-ryu karate. *See also* Okinawa, history of martial arts in.

ARMSTRONG, STEVE (1931-) American karate pioneer and author. Born in Guymon, Okla., Armstrong grew up in Texas, where, as an amateur boxer, he won 68 of 72 bouts. He began studying karate at 16 while stationed in Japan with the Marine Corps. He went to China in 1949 and within 18 months achieved a black belt. Restationed in Japan he continued studying karate, but was required to start over as a white belt in a different style; again, he earned the black belt. Following service in Korea and Washington, D.C., he was sent to Okinawa, where he studied **isshin-ryu** karate under its late founder, Tatsuo Shimabuku, becoming Shimabuku's third-in-command, second only to Harold Mitchum.

In 1964 he opened his first public karate school in Tacoma, Wash., which eventually expanded to several locations including colleges and state universities. He was named Most Outstanding Tournament Referee of the U.S. Championships between 1961 and 1970. Beginning in 1963, Armstrong became a prolific producer of karate events; his annual Seattle Open is the largest tournament in the northwest. Named to *Who's Who in the Martial Arts,* he is the author of *Seisan Kata of Isshin-Ryu Karate* (1973), and has written and self-published *An Introduction to Karate* and *Seiuchin Kata of Isshin-Ryu Karate. See also* U.S., history of karate in.

ARVANITIS, JIM (1948-) Greek-American pankratiast and founder of **mu tau.** Arvanitis began studying the little-known fighting art of his ancestors, **pankration,** as a child. In 1971, after study of various martial art styles and theories, he modified that ancient Greek combat system into a modern concept that he calls mu tau. Arvanitis's mu tau academies in New Hampshire are exclusive establishments; to date he has authorized only two men to teach mu tau: Doug Terry and Nick Hines. In 1979 he established a world record on the nationally televised "Guiness Game," performing 61 pushups on his thumbs in 47 seconds. In 1980 he wrote *Mu Tau: The Modern Greek Karate.*

ASHIDA, DR. SACHIO (1924-) Japanese-American judo coach and administrator. Born in Kyoto, Japan, Dr. Ashida began his training in judo and Zen at 12. In 1938 he won the All Japan Kotoshogakko Championships. Ashida was promoted to black belt in 1940 and won numerous championship titles while studying at Kwansai University in Osaka. Ashida served as assistant judo instructor at Nishinomiya Police Station and the Osaka West Police Station from 1948 to 1953, when he immigrated to the U.S. In 1956 Dr. Ashida helped found the Midwest Judo Association, and in 1960 he founded the Midwest Judo Yudanshakai. Since 1962 he has served on the board of governors of the USJF, on the U.S. Olympic Judo Committee, the Midwestern Judo Conference, and on the AAU National and International Judo Committees. Ashida coached the All American High School Judo Champions during their 1971 tour of Japan, and the All American Junior Judo Champions at the 1972 World Championships in Germany. He was voted into the Black Belt Hall of Fame in 1973 as "Judo Sensei of the Year." *See also* U.S., history of judo in.

AUFRAY, GUY French judo champion. Aufray won the French middleweight title in 1971 and was runner-up in the open weight division. That same year, he captured first place at the prestigious European Judo Championships and won a bronze medal in the World Championships.

AUGUSTINE, MEL (1931-) American judo instructor, official, and administrator. Augustine started training in judo with Henry Okazaki in his native Hawaii. When his family moved to San Francisco, he continued his studies with Mits Kimura and received his black belt at 17. Augustine was one of the original judo teachers for the Strategic Air Command. In 1953, having joined the Army, he became heavyweight boxing champion of the 25th Division.

After visiting the **Kodokan,** Augustine returned to the U.S., where he was appointed San Francisco Judo Institute representative to the AAU. He competed in the National Judo Championships between 1955 and 1965. After retiring from competition, he became president of the Northern California Judo Association and a member of the U.S. Olympic Judo Committee. He also served as vice-president of the USJF, for which he undertook additional responsibilities on its board of governors and board of examiners. An outspoken advocate of the therapeutic value of athletics, he was appointed chairman of the AAU's Correctional Institutional Sports Committee.

AZATO, YASUTSUNE Okinawan karate master, known by the name Tonochi. Governor of the village of Azato, he served as a chief of the military for the king of the Ryukyus and trained under **Sokon "Bushi" Matsumura.** Azato excelled in horsemanship and archery. He belonged by birth to the Tonochi class, one of the two upper classes of the Shizoku families on Okinawa. (The Udon were the highest class, equivalent to the daimyo among clans outside of Okinawa, and the Tonochi were hereditary chiefs of towns and villages.) Azato was unsurpassed in the Ryukyu Islands in the art of karate; he was also a brilliant scholar. In Azato's time karate was strictly forbidden by the government, and karate training was done in secret.

Azato was a highly skilled swordsman of the jigen school of kendo. Though not a braggart, he maintained he could not be bested by any opponent in the Ryukyus. When Azato met Yorin Kanna, the most famous swordsman on Okinawa, a huge, muscular man with great powerful arms and shoulders, he issued a challenge. In the famous duel, Kanna attacked Azato with the **katana** and was surprised to find his attack thwarted by the unarmed Azato who, applying a lightning-fast karate technique with the turning of his hand, managed not only to evade the thrust but to bring Kanna to his knees, defeating him without killing him. When asked to comment on the duel, Azato described Kanna as a swordsman who first terrified his opponent and then went for the kill. Azato explained that if an opponent refuses to be terrified and can remain cool-headed, victory could be achieved.

Azato is noted for saying, "When you practice karate, consider your arms and legs as swords." He kept detailed information about all the karate masters living on Okinawa, including not only names and addresses, but data concerning intelligence, abilities, special skills, and weaknesses. Azato told his karate students that knowledge of an opponent's ability and technical skills was half of the battle. Azato is credited with having contributed to the education of Gichin Funakoshi. (ANTHONY MIRAKIAN)

BANKS, AARON (1928-) American karate pioneer, promoter, and instructor. Banks began his karate studies in 1960 at the Sigward Health Studios under the direction of Shotokan instructor John Slocum. He received his black belt in 1964 from **Peter Urban** and Ramon Duran in the **goju-ryu** style.

Banks has produced nearly 500 events. He began his national career in 1967, when he produced the first important team contest in karate, the East Coast vs. West Coast. Later in 1967 he presented the 1st Oriental World of Self-Defense, a series of martial arts demonstrations, at the Town Hall in New York City. In 1968 Banks brought **Gogen Yamaguchi** from Japan as a featured performer for his Goju-kai National Karate Championships at the Manhattan Center. The legendary Yamaguchi attracted a reported standing-room-only crowd of 10,000 spectators. Also that year, he produced the America

vs. Orient Team Championships, the first of its type, which reached a controversial climax when strong racial prejudice was expressed by the partisan audience.

Banks's World Professional Karate Championships, held Nov. 16, 1968, at the Waldorf Astoria ballroom, presented one of the first professional series of karate fights in the U.S. In this event Joe Lewis, Chuck Norris, Mike Stone, and Skipper Mullins captured their world professional championship titles. It was the first contest to use a three-minute, three-round format for each elimination and each championship match. Banks's Oriental World of Self-Defense moved to the Felt Forum in 1973. In 1974 this event was televised five times over ABC's "Wide World of Sports." This time, Banks moved his show to Madison Square Garden and attracted 19, 564 spectators, recording the highest paying live gate in the history of American martial arts promotions, $100,000. Although criticized for sensationalism, Banks has made this show an annual event and taken some of his performers on tour to England, South America, and major cities throughout the U.S.

In 1975 Banks returned to the promotion of full-contact events. His first, at the Nassau Coliseum, drew 5,000 spectators, and the matches, highlighted by the participation of Benny Urquidez, were broadcast on "Wide World of Sports." Banks was the subject of considerable controversy at this event for matching a woman against a man in a fight to the knockout.

BARATHY, RICHARD (1947-) American karate instructor. Barathy began his martial arts training at age 15 in tae kwon do with Han Ok Shin. At 20 he switched to Nisei goju under Frank Ruiz, from whom he received his black belt in 1969. He later studied with Warren Montenino, who was teaching a version of karate called the American combat system, which stresses street combat as opposed to sport karate. Barathy also trained under Howard Tegg, from whom he learned Tai Zen jujutsu. During the late 1970s Barathy gained national fame by breaking 15 1¼" concrete slabs on the television program "That's Incredible," a feat that has not been equalled. He has performed on television talk shows, such as those of Johnny Carson and Merv Griffin, and in 1979 was the star of a syndicated documentary called "Masters of the Martial Arts."

Richard Barathy

BARON, BRETT American judo competitor. He won the 179-lb. division of the AAU Nationals in 1979, a bronze medal that same year at the Pan-American Games, and finished first at the World Trials.

BARROW, BOB (1943-) American karate instructor and competitor. A consistent tournament winner since 1970, Barrow achieved regional prominence when he was rated in *Professional Karate Magazine* in 1975. After obtaining his black belt from **Chuck Norris,** Barrow began teaching karate in Medford, Ore., in 1971. He has since expanded his classes to the campuses of several local universities and colleges. Barrow has written a college textbook on tang soo do, and a curriculum on intermediate and advanced karate for the Oregon State Board of Higher Education. A member of *Who's Who in the Martial Arts,* Barrow hosts the Oregon Training Tournament every three months and produces the Tang Soo Do Invitational, begun in 1973.

BATEMAN, PY (1947-) American karate instructor. Founder of the Feminist Karate Union, Bateman is a noted social activist and leader in women's karate. Originator of karate schools exclusively for females in Seattle, Wash., she has written a monthly self-defense column for *Pandora,* a news magazine for Washington women. Bateman produced a 13-week instructional series for local cable television and was a member of the faculty in the University of Washington's Women's Studies Department from 1972 to 1974. In 1975 she prepared a program on rape and self-defense for distribution to women's studies departments throughout the U.S. and was named to *Who's Who in the Martial Arts.*

BATES, GILBERT G. American kung-fu practitioner. Bates began his martial arts training in 1960 with judo and **goju-ryu** karate, in Tulsa, Okla. At one time a student of Dr. Fenia Woo, who taught him northern sil-lum kung-fu, he went on to study with Ark-Yuey Wong, from whom he learned a number of styles, including Choy-Li-Fut and southern sil-lum kung-fu. He has also studied t'ai-chi-ch'uan, tae kwon do, and Indian yoga. Bates is a noted lecturer and writer on kung-fu and is the author of *How to Tap the Invisible Force.*

BATES, LAVERNE BARNARD (1934-) American kung-fu instructor and author. She began kung-fu in 1960, receiving her black belt from **Gilbert G. Bates** and her black sash from Fenia Woo. Among the kung-fu systems she has studied are sil-lum-p'ai, white crane, pa-kua, and t'ai-chi-ch'uan. She is the author of a number of books, including *On Being Quiet* (meditation for children), *Why Herbology,* and *Common Sense Self-Defense for Women.*

BATISTE, RODNEY (1953-) American karate competitor and instructor. Batiste began his martial arts studies in 1967 under

Rodney Batiste

Joseph Lopez and continued his instruction while in the U.S. Army. After leaving the service he moved to Washington, D.C., where he competed in point tournaments. He won against top East Coast competitors, such as Mike Gradel, Arnold Mitchell, and Johnny Miller. His most notable full-contact bout occurred in 1977 when he beat previously undefeated Jimmy Horsley at Charlotte, N.C. He has been rated number-three contender by the PKA.

BERMUDEZ, MARION American karate champion. Under the guidance of Fred Stille, of Tempe, Ariz., Bermudez has become the undefeated U.S. Women's Professional Champion. She has won titles in both noncontact and full-contact contests, some against male opponents. In noncontact, Bermudez won the prestigious **International Karate Championships** twice, in 1973 and 1975. She was named to the Black Belt Hall of Fame in 1976 as "Female Fighter of the Year."

BIZEN, MATSUMOTO (d. 1525) Japanese swordsman; one of the greatest masters of *sojutsu.* He founded the kashima shin-ryu, a school of swordsmanship.

BOMBA, RALPH (1948-75) American karate instructor and competitor. A promising young fighter from Rhode Island, Bomba won numerous tournament titles and was rated among the top 10 East Coast karate fighters until 1973, when it was discovered he had a malignant tumor in his right leg. Despite an amputation, Bomba remained active as an instructor and tournament official until his death. In 1973 Bomba was voted "Best Referee of the Year" by the **NEKRA,** an organization in whose development he was instrumental. Named to *Who's Who in the Martial Arts* shortly before his death, Bomba had officiated at such major karate tournaments as the U.S. Championships, the Battle of Atlanta, and the All American Championships.

BRAZIEL, MAUREEN (1946-) American judo champion. Braziel won the gold medal at the 1974 Women's European Championships and in 1976 took a gold medal in the open class and a silver medal in the heavyweight class of the British Open. She has won the AAU Senior Women's Championships a number of times. Braziel has been training in judo since age 20, when she began her studies under Kiyoshi Shina of New York City.

BREGMAN, JIM (1942-) American judo champion and administrator. Bregman undertook the study of judo in 1952 at age 10 in Washington, D.C., and earned a black belt at age 15. Bregman is one of only two Americans to have won a bronze medal for the U.S. in the Olympic Games. His feat, which took place in 1964 in Tokyo, was unequalled until 1976, when Allen Coage of New Jersey won a bronze in Montreal. In 1965 he won a bronze medal in Rio de Janeiro at the World Judo Championships and gold medals at the Pan-American Games and the Maccabiah Games in Israel.

Bregman is founder and director of **Camp Olympus,** a two-week summer practice and seminar in judo, which he has operated since 1970. On ABC's "Wide World of Sports" in 1966 he appeared as play-by-play commentator for the All Japan Judo Championships. He has written several articles for *Black Belt Magazine* and *American Judoman* and formerly served as president of the USJA. In 1973 he was elected to the Black Belt Hall of Fame, and in 1975 he was named to *Who's Who in the Martial Arts.*

BRUNO, EMILIO (1914-) American judo pioneer and instructor. A former AAU wrestling champion, Bruno took up judo in 1932. He competed in the National AAU Judo Championships of 1939, finishing second at 158 pounds, and was scheduled to compete in the 1940 Olympics in Japan, canceled because of the war. Bruno became the fifth American to earn a black belt in **Kodokan** judo when he received the honor personally from the sport's founder, **Jigoro Kano** in 1935. He subsequently became the first American to receive 5th and 6th degrees.

From 1937 to 1941 Bruno served as a part-time judo instructor at the San Jose State College Police School. He formed the nation's first college judo team, and in 1940 he and the late Henry Stone of the University of California at Berkeley brought their teams together for the first intercollegiate judo competition in U.S. history. In 1944 Bruno introduced judo at Cornell University.

In 1946 he was appointed to direct physical training and judo for the California Department of Corrections. As supervisor of judo and combative measures for the Strategic Air Command (SAC) in 1951, he organized Air Force classes for judo training at the Kodokan in Japan and arranged for the Kodokan team's tour of air bases in the U.S. and Puerto Rico in 1953. Bruno received a special commendation for his work in SAC from Gen. Curtis LeMay and Gen. Thomas Power, also a judo student of Bruno's.

Bruno served as coach of the U.S. wrestling team in 1950 for a tour of Japan and at the same time was instrumental in forging ties between the Kodokan and the U.S. Judo Black Belt Federation and AAU. Acting on Bruno's request, in 1949 the AAU Wrestling Committee had already recognized judo, appointing him to develop its judo program. In 1955 Bruno initiated the first judo tournament between the U.S. and Japan; he was selected as coach of the AAU and Air Force teams. He coached the U.S. judo teams competing at both the 1958 World Judo Championships in Tokyo and the 1961 World Championships in Paris. Named to *Who's Who in the Martial Arts* in 1975, Bruno has written numerous manuals on judo training and sports administration. *See also* U.S., history of judo in.

BUCK, DONALD American karate instructor. Already a black belt in judo, Buck entered the U.S. Navy in 1943 and was exposed to kung-fu while stationed in the Admiralty Islands. There he met and befriended **Mas Oyama,** who returned with Buck to the U.S. and lived with him for a year. Promoted to black belt, Buck became one of the first non-Oriental instructors of the **kyokushinkai** style.

He also studied **hung gar** kung-fu under **Y.C. Wong** in San Francisco, who studied along with Buck under Lam Cho in Hong Kong. Buck also studied the Yang family style of **t'ai-chi-ch'uan** with Siufan Chan in Shanghai. He presently resides in Benecia, Calif. where he operates a studio teaching full-contact karate. His most famous student is **Mike Dayton.**

Don Buck, who instructs kyokushinkai karate

BUELL, MARTIN THOMAS (1942-) Hawaiian-born instructor and competitor. Buell began his study of martial arts with judo in 1953 and switched to Chinese kempo in 1957. Studying under Thomas Young, Sonny Emperado, and Walter Godin, he received his black belt from Godin in 1966. He has also studied kajukenbo, but instructs in Godin's Chinese kempo.

Buell formed and organized the Hawaiian Martial Arts Association. From 1970 to 1980 he promoted the Godin's Schools of Self Defense Kempo Championships, as well as the Pacific Black Belt Team Championships and the All Pacific Black Belt Team Championships, between Hawaiian teams.

While active in competition, Buell placed first in the 1968 All American Championships, in which he was named "Outstanding Competitor," the Kajukenbo Championships, and the 1969 Leeward Championships.

In 1978 he coached the Hawaiian Team at the PKA Nationals in Baltimore. He has been a PKA commissioner and a professional chief referee in both professional events and point tournaments. Notable students include Victor Rapoza, Bill Takeuchi, Jonathan Vance, Gilbert Ragudo, Lance Cabanilla, and Garland Johnson. In 1975 he was named to *Who's Who in the Martial Arts.*

BUNDA, CARLOS American karate competitor. Born in Hawaii, Bunda began training in karate in 1958. In 1964 he won the black belt lightweight title of the 1st **International Karate Championships** in Long Beach, Calif., but had to retire from competition due to failing eyesight.

BURLESON, J. PAT (1936-) American karate champion, instructor, and promoter. Burleson is acknowledged as the "grandfather" of open tournament fighting in America, having won numerous national titles before retiring from competition in 1966. He was the 1962 East Coast Championships runner-up, the 1963 Southwest Championships runner-up, and a participant in the 1st World Karate Championships in Chicago in 1963.

In 1964 Burleson won the inaugural U.S. National Karate Championships in Washington, D.C., and in 1965 became the Texas State Grand Champion and Southwest Karate Grand Champion. Following several other victories in 1965 and 1966, at the All American Open Championships in Oklahoma City and the U.S. Championships in Dallas, he retired.

Burleson's students have included **Jim Butin, Chuck Loven, Steve Stavroff, Phylis Evetts, Pam Watson, Bill Watson,** and **Ron Moffett.** He has also taught special classes for airline stewardesses, federal riot control squads, and women's task forces in rape prevention. Burleson has been a leader in the business of karate; he originated "belt-goal" courses in 1964 to increase enrollment and lower dropout rates, an innovation now used throughout the U.S.

Highly regarded as a referee, Burleson received 12 Outstanding Officiating awards from other tournament promoters and was a member of the original rules committee for the state of Texas. As a promoter, he has launched since 1965 the Texas State Karate Championships and the Tournament of Champions, the first in karate to invite only champions of other tournaments to compete. Named to *Who's Who in the Martial Arts* in 1975, Burleson also appeared in the 1974 Warner Bros. film *Black Belt Jones. See also* U.S., history of karate in.

BURRIS, PATRICK (1951-) American judo champion. Burris began his judo career in Hawaii at age 9, and won the National High School Judo Championships in 1966 and 1968. In 1970 Burris won his weight division title at the Pan-American Games in Brazil, and in 1971 competed in the World Judo Championships in Munich. He took first place at the 1972 AAU Nationals and represented the U.S. in the 1972 Olympics. He was a member of the U.S. judo team at the 1973 World Championships in Switzerland, the same year he won the AAU Senior Judo Championships. The following year, 1974, Burris competed again in the Pan-American Games, bringing home the gold medal in the 154 lb. class. In 1975, once again a member of the U.S. Pan-American team, he helped win a bronze medal. That same year he became a gold medalist in the Pre-Olympics at Montreal, defeating world champion Vladimir Nevzorov of the Soviet Union.

In 1976 Burris repeated his victory at the National Judo Championships and was chosen a member of the U.S. Olympic team to compete in Montreal. Burris is a two-time member of the Black Belt Hall of Fame, where he was cited as "Judo Instructor of the Year" in 1976. *See also* U.S., history of judo in.

BUTIN, JIM (1949-) American karate competitor, instructor, and promoter. Butin began his martial arts training under **Pat Burleson** in Ft. Worth, Tex., and received his black belt in American karate from Burleson in 1968. He is affiliated with American Karate Black Belt Association.

In 1973 he fought on the U.S. team at the World Tae Kwon Do Championships; the team placed second out of 26 competing countries. In 1974 he competed alongside Bill Wallace, Jeff Smith, Howard Jackson, and Joe Lewis in Europe and was undefeated in six contests. He has won 36 major karate championships to date, which include Roy Kurban's 1980 National Pro/Am in Ft. Worth; 1976 light heavyweight champion in the Battle of Atlanta; 1974 and 1975 Top 10 Nationals in St. Louis, where he won the grand champion title.

Currently he promotes the Oklahoma State Championships, which began in 1973. In 1975 Butin was named to *Who's Who in the Martial Arts.*

CAHILL, WILLIE American judo instructor. He first studied jujutsu with his father in Hawaii. In 1947, the family moved to the U.S. mainland, where Willie continued under his father's instruction, taking over the school at his death. Over the years, Cahill has greatly contributed to the development of judo for youths. By 1975, when he was named "Judo Instructor of the Year" and entered in the **Black Belt Hall of Fame**, his judo team had amassed more than 500 trophies and medals and took home more awards in the USJA Junior Nationals than any other team.

CAMPBELL, BEN (1933-) American judo instructor and champion. Campbell started judo practice in 1952 in South Korea, where he earned his black belt. He was three times a National Judo Champion: 1961, in the 180-pound class; 1962 in the heavyweight division; and 1963, in the openweight division. He also won at the Pan-American Games in 1963. A pioneer in introducing judo in California high schools, Campbell produced nationally rated students. An author and promoter, he has written several articles for *Black Belt Magazine* and *American Judoman.* Named to *Who's Who in the Martial Arts* in 1975, he also wrote *Championship Judo Drills* in 1974, and with **Phil Porter** co-authored *Championship Judo Drill Training.* Campbell is secretary of the U.S. Olympic Judo Committee and a member of both the U.S. Judo Association and the U.S. Judo Federation. He is also on the staff of the **Camp Olympus** summer judo retreat. *See also* U.S., history of judo in.

CAMPBELL, SID (1944-) American karate pioneer and promoter; named California's most outstanding Okinawan-style instructor in 1974 at the Golden Fist Awards. He established his first school in Oakland, Calif., in 1967. Campbell created the first karate program for deaf students in the Oakland area. One of the organizers and original members of the Northern Californian Karate Referee's Association, he has produced several tournaments including the United Karate Championships in 1974. In 1975 he was named to *Who's Who in the Martial Arts.*

Sid Campbell

CARAULIA, ALGENE (1940-) Hawaiian-born American karate champion, instructor, and promoter. Winner of numerous early major tournaments including the 1st World Karate Championships, held in Chicago in 1963, Caraulia began studying martial arts at 14. A student of **Adriano Emperado** of the **kajukenbo** system, he also won the Midwest Championships in 1965, and the Illinois State Judo Championships. He swept the lightweight title at the **International Karate Championships** in 1965, 1966, and 1968. Active in the first rules committee for professional karate, he is founder of the Cleveland Karate Championships and director of the Midwest Four Seasons Karate Championships. He was elected to *Professional Karate's* Hall of Fame in 1974, and named to *Who's Who in the Martial Arts* in 1975. *See also* U.S., history of karate in.

CARNAHAN, LARRY R. (1949-) American karate fighter, writer, photographer, and instructor. Born in Paris, Tex., he began his martial arts training under **Chuck Loven** of Ft. Worth, Tex., in 1967. In 1970 he received his black belt from **Pat Burleson** of Ft. Worth. Carnahan began full-contact competition in 1975, achieving Professional Karate Association world ratings as high as number three in the lightweight category. Carnahan has won such semicontact tournaments as the U.S. Championships in Dallas (1973), and the Battle of Atlanta (1973).

CARPENTER, ROGER (1940-) American karate competitor and instructor. A student of **George Pesare,** Carpenter became the first New England Karate Champion in 1970 and later captained the

Roger Carpenter *(right)* vs. Demetrius Havanis. Photo by Tom Decker

winning team from that region at the U.S. Championships in Dallas in 1973. A winner in 1968, 1970, and 1972 of the heavyweight title at the All American Open in Oklahoma City, he twice won Pat Burleson's Tournament of Champions, in 1969 and 1970. He gained notoriety in a full-contact 1973 grudge match fought without protective equipment, after which his opponent, John Bal'ee, required hospitalization.

A member of *Who's Who in the Martial Arts,* Carpenter teaches self-defense to the Wichita Police Department. *See also* U.S., history of karate in.

CARTER, PRESTON, SR. (-1977) American karate instructor. Carter began his long martial arts career at 11 in Trenton, N.J., studied overseas at **Mas Oyama**'s dojo, and then with Ray Nishida for six years. He returned to the U.S. in 1960, and began teaching karate regularly in 1967. On the karate tournament circuit he became known for breaking boards, bricks, and concrete slabs. In 1972, while working as a bouncer at a lounge in N.J., he was shot, paralyzing him from the waist down. In spite of his confinement to a wheelchair and his frequent operations, Carter continued to practice karate and to operate his karate schools with the help of friends. Because of his condition, Carter decided to create the **Martial Arts for the Handicapped Federation** with members throughout the U.S.

CASEL, TAYARI American kung-fu instructor, competitor, and performer. Casel has won national form and fighting titles since the mid-1970s. His style is derived from two major systems: kupigana-ngumi, a rhythmical and acrobatic martial art developed by African slaves and their descendants; and **ch'ang ch'uan.**

In 1976 and again in 1979 he won the kung-fu form championship as well as the 1976 form grand championship at the Battle of Atlanta. In 1980 he won the nonmusical form division of the Mid-America Diamond Nationals, and was runner-up to grand champion John Chung. As a performer, he appeared on "Wide World of Sports" in 1975 as part of the Oriental World of Self-Defense show, and was a featured performer from 1973 to 1978. At present he lives and teaches in Las Vegas, Nev.

Casel wrote *A Snake's Eye View: Sweeping and Groundfighting Techniques,* which is still in compilation.

Tayari Casel

CASILLAS, GRACIELA (1956-) Mexican-American karate champion; first female world champion of professional **full-contact karate**. Born in Bellflower, Calif., Casillas began her martial arts training at 17 with a tae kwon do class sponsored by her church. A year later, in 1974, when Casillas began attending Ventura College, she continued her martial arts training in **hwarang-do** with **Joo Bang Lee**.

In 1976, Casillas began to compete in full-contact karate against other women. Over a period of years, she won a string of six karate bouts, all by knockout within two rounds.

In May 1979, since there were no professional titles yet established in women's karate, she turned to boxing and signed to fight Karen Bennet, the Women's International Boxing Association (WIBA) Bantamweight World Champion. Bennet, unaware of Casillas's full-contact karate record, was preparing to defend her title against the number-two contender, Ginger Kaufman. She intended to use the Casillas bout as a tune-up for Kaufman. On July 13, 1979, Casillas stunned the world of women's boxing by defeating Bennet in a unanimous six-round decision. Two weeks later, the new champion substituted for the old champion, defending her world title with a unanimous decision over Kaufman.

On December 23, 1979, with two world championship divisions established for women's karate, Casillas defeated Irene Garcia by a six-round unanimous decision, becoming the first **WKA** Women's Bantamweight World Champion. As champion, Casillas

made ring appearances across the U.S. and abroad, in Mexico, Thailand, Japan, and Hong Kong. Her most significant karate title defenses were seven-round victories over Cookie Melendez in 1980 and Cheryl Wheeler in 1981.

In 1982, Casillas became a **kali** instructor and personal disciple of **Dan Inosanto**, and developed an elite clientele of private students which included pop vocalist Helen Reddy. As of December 1982, her karate record stood at 15-0-1 with nine knockouts; her boxing record was 8-0 with five knockouts. (PAUL MASLAK)

Graciela Casillas

CASS, MIKE American karate competitor; winner of the USKA Grand Nationals in 1976 and first place in the 1975 and 1976 AKA Nationals. He won his division at the 1974 Battle of Atlanta and took second place in 1976. In 1975 he appeared in *Professional Karate Magazine*'s full-contact ratings.

CASTALDO, JOHN American karate competitor. Castaldo won the the 1971 **USKA Grand Nationals,** placed second at the 1972 U.S. Karate Championships in Dallas, and won the grand championship of the AKA Nationals the same year.

CASTELLANOS, RALPH (1935-) American karate competitor. Castellanos was born in San Jose, Calif., and started his karate training under Al Tracy in 1958. He won the California State Championships in 1967 and 1969, and the 1969 Central California Championships, as well as the U.S. Open in Salt Lake City. In 1970 he placed first in the U.S. All American Championships and was a member of the West Coast All Stars in a Madison Square Garden event of 1969. In 1971 Castellanos won the National Black Belt Championships in Albuquerque; N.M.

CATTLE, STEVE English karate competitor. Cattle first trained in judo, winning the European Students Judo Championships. He earned his karate black belt in 1966 from **Hirokazu Kanazawa** and later continued his training with **Keinosuke Enoeda.** Since 1969 he has been a member of the English karate team. Among his important victories are the 1971 BKCC Senior individual crown and the 1974 KUGB (Karate Union of Great Britain) Championships. He also won the SKU Kata Championships in 1971 and 1972.

CEMOVIC, RADOSLAV (1946-) Yugoslavian karate competitor.

Cemovic, once rated among the best European karate fighters, defeated notables Jean Dehaes of Belgium, Gerald Gross-Etete of Switzerland, Geert Lemmens, and Gilbert Gruss. At the height of his career, in 1969 and 1970, he was often disqualified for lack of control in noncontact contests.

CERIO, NICK American karate instructor, one of the leaders of karate in Rhode Island. Cerio began his martial arts training over twenty years ago and has studied Judo, Jujutsu, Sil-Lum Kung-fu and Chinese Kempo. He has studied with such renowned masters as William Chow of Hawaii, and Master Gan Fong Chin. A highly respected instructor, he runs his own school in Rhode Island as well as being the self-defense instructor to the Rhode Island state police.

CHA, PETER (1934-   ) Korean-born tae kwon do instructor and administrator. Cha is president of the Mu Duk Kwan Brothers Society of the United States and technical advisor of AAU Tae Kwon Do.

CHAANINE, DAVID (1945-   ) Lebanese tae kwon do instructor and pioneer. He learned tae kwon do from Kwon Jae Hwa and in 1965 became head instructor at the YMCA in Beirut, and in 1971 at the American University of Beirut. He also taught at the Lebanese University of Fine Arts in Beirut, and served as president, tae kwon do branch, Lebanese Federation of Judo and Karate. During this time, he was instructor to some 75 black belts. His work was praised in an official proclamation by the director-general of youth and sports for the Lebanese Ministry of Education and Fine Arts, in which Chaanine was cited as a pioneer.

He moved to San Diego, Cal., in the mid-1970s, where he taught at the YMCA, Coronado Recreation Dept., and the Chula Vista Police Dept.

CHAMBERS, QUINTIN British martial arts authority. Chambers studied judo in his early twenties and captained the Cambridge University team in 1958-59. In 1961 he went to Japan and has since then been a lecturer at Satima University. He has made a special study of the classical martial arts and holds teacher licenses in shindo muso ryu, jodo, tenshin shoden katori shinto ryu, and kukishin ryu. Also an authority on the fighting arts of Indonesia, Chambers is co-author of *Stick-Fighting.*

CHAN, ANTHONY K. (1954-   ) Chinese-American kung-fu champion. Chan began his martial arts training in Hong Kong, eventually

Anthony Chan performing a Chinese kung-fu routine. Courtesy of *Kick Illustrated Magazine*

studying **wu shu,** tae kwon do, and **pa-kua.** While a member of the Chung-Ngai Lion Dance Troupe of San Francisco's Chinatown, Chan studied the Hung-ga style. The first to use the new wu shu forms from the People's Republic of China in American martial arts competition, he rose to be the U.S. soft-style form champion.

In 1976 Chan co-authored with martial arts journalist **Michael Staples** *Wu Shu of China.* In 1981 they collaborated on a special magazine edition entitled **The Elegant Wu Shu of China.** In 1980 he was voted into the Black Belt Hall of Fame as "Kung-Fu Artist of the Year." Among Chan's important competition victories are the grand kata championship in the 1978-80 International Karate Championships, the 1980 American Karate Association Grand Nationals, and the 1980 West Coast Nationals. (MICHAEL P. STAPLES)

CHAN, HAK-FU Chinese kung-fu master and pioneer. Chan was born in Canton, China. He learned white crane kung-fu from Ng Shou-Jone and served as a chief instructor of kung-fu to the Chinese Air Force during World War II. In 1954, at the request of a Hong Kong athletic organization in Macao to raise funds for charity, he staged a "life or death" bout with the late **t'ai-chi** master Ng Kung-Yee. Although it resulted in a draw, the bout thrilled thousands of spectators, for such a contest had not been seen during the previous 50 years.

In 1972 Chan settled in Australia and established his Pak-Hok Kung-Fu International Association, expanding it in 1976 to include schools in New York, and later in San Francisco. He is the first Sifu to have established studios on three continents.

CHAN, JACKIE (1954-   ) Chinese martial artist and motion picture star. Chan was born in Hong Kong and entered the China Drama Academy at 7. His first screen appearance, at 8, was in a Cantonese movie, *The Big and Little Wong Tin-Bar.* While still a child, Chan appeared in *The Love Eternal* (1963) and *The Story of Qui Xianglin* (1964). After leaving the drama academy he worked as a character actor and martial artist in films such as *Not Scared To Die* (1973), *Heroine* (1973), *All in the Family* (1973), *Count Down in Kung-fu* (1976).

In 1976 Chan signed with Lo Wei Film Company, where he starred in *New Fists of Fury* (1976), *Shaolin Wooden Man* (1976), *To Kill With Intrigue* (1977), *Snake and Crane Arts of Shaolin* (1978), *Spiritual Kung-fu,* and *The Magnificent Bodyguard* (1977/78). In 1978, working for Seasonal Film Corporation, he starred in *Snake in the Eagle's Shadow* and *The Drunken Master.* He wrote, directed, and starred in *Fearless Hyena* in 1979, and signed with Raymond Chow's Golden Harvest, for whom he has directed and starred in *Young Master.*

When three of his pictures broke all box-office records in the Orient, surpassing the grosses previously set by the late Bruce Lee, Chan was brought to Hollywood by Chow to star in his first English-language picture, *The Big Brawl.* (NEVA FRIEDENN) *See also* U.S., history of karate in.

Jackie Chan as he appears in one of his numerous films

CHAN, SOU CHUNG Chinese kung-fu master. Known in the Orient as the "Monkey King," Chan is a grand master of tai-sing pek kwar, the monkey style of Chinese boxing. He has appeared in Chinese films, including *Monkey Fist* and *The Story of Monkey Boxing*. A former board member of Hong Kong's Martial Arts Association, Chan at present heads two schools, one in Hong Kong and the other in Kowloon.

CHAN-CHIK SHEUNG Chinese kung-fu master in Hong Kong known for his mastery of the pat mei (white eyebrows) style of Chinese martial arts.

CHANG, SOON-HO (1937-) Korean-born American tae kwon do and judo instructor. Chang served as Regional Chairman of the National AAU Tae Kwon Do Committee and has produced outstanding competitors, including Tom Seabourn, for the U.S. amateur tae kwon do team.

CHANG-I-TE A well-known master of the white crane (fukien style) system of Chinese kung-fu in the Republic of China.

CHANG SAN-FENG (1279-1368) Taoist priest said to be the founder of **t'ai-chi-ch'uan.** According to Chinese legend, Chang San-Feng possessed a face like a turtle, a beard like steel wool, and the bones of a crane. He was given to his mother by a giant crane one night while she slept. He learned t'ai-chi from the Fire-Dragon men atop a mountain. Also known as Chang Chun Chih. *See also* t'ai-chi-ch'uan (general). *Further reading: Hop-Gar Kung-Fu,* David Chin and Michael P. Staples, 1976.

CHANG-SHIH-JUNG A well-known master of the **t'ai-chi, pa-kua,** and **hsing** styles of Chinese kung-fu in the Republic of China.

CHAN-KWUN-TAI Chinese practitioner of kung-fu in Hong Kong; known for his skill in the monkey style of martial arts. A student of Chan-Shau-Chung, he is also noted for competition in Eastern tournaments and roles in Chinese movies.

CHAN-SHAU-CHUNG Famous practitioner of the monkey style of Chinese kung-fu in Hong Kong. Chan studied under Gan-Duc-Hoi, who in turn learned his art from Kau-Sei.

CHAN-TAT-FU Chinese kung-fu master in Hong Kong; known for his mastery of the t'sai-li-fu style of Chinese kung-fu.

CHAN-YICK-YAN Chinese kung-fu master in Hong Kong; known for his mastery of the liu-ho pa-fa style of Chinese martial arts.

CHAPMAN, BECKY (1955-) American karate competitor and instructor from Greenville, S.C. Chapman began instruction in 1975 under **Sam Chapman** (her husband). She is affiliated with the **South East Karate Association** and is an associate director for that organization. Chapman has been SEKA's top fighter for five years (1975-80). Her tournament wins include the 1978 PKA Nationals in Baltimore; Battle of Atlanta—twice; Atlanta Pro/Am—three times; Greenville Pro/Am—twice. In more than 100 tournaments, she failed to win or place in only two. She has been rated as one of America's Top Ten fighters since 1979.

CHAPMAN, SAM (1942-) American karate competitor, promoter, and instructor. Chapman began martial arts training in 1962 under Ron Waters in Camp LeJune, N.C., and in 1969 received his black belt from Ron Morris. Chapman instructs in American Karate, but has also studied tae kwon do and kempo.

From 1973 through 1976, he won or placed in virtually every tournament in the south; in 1974, and again in 1975, he was voted the **South East Karate Association's** number-one-ranked middleweight black belt. He is a director of SEKA and a commissioner of the PKA. In 1980 he was inducted into *Official Karate Magazine*'s Legion of Honor.

CHARTIER, GEORGE American karate instructor and promoter. After 18 months of study in Okinawa, he received a black belt in **shorin-ryu** and returned to the U.S. In 1956 he began studying Chinese Shao-lin under James Cheatham of Newark, N.J., and in 1961 took up the sikaran style under Louis Lagadrejos. Promoting annual tournaments for charity, he earned a citation from the Governor of New Hampshire. Cartier formed the first dojo in New Hampshire,

Sam Chapman

and is president and director of the New Hampshire Black Belt Federation, founded and chartered in 1974.

CHEEKS, ALBERT American karate competitor. Cheeks began karate at 14 under tae kwon do instructor Ki Whang Kim of Silver Springs, Md. He won the grand championship of Henry Cho's All American Championships in New York in 1973. Later that year, he represented the U.S. at the World Tae Kwon Do Championships in Seoul, Korea, placing third in the heavyweight division. Cheeks was rated among the top 10 competitors of sport karate in the U.S. in 1973 by *Black Belt Magazine*.

CHEN, WILLIAM Chinese t'ai-chi-ch'uan instructor. Chen studied under t'ai-chi-ch'uan master Man-Ch'ing Cheng in Taiwan from 1955 to 1958. He immigrated to the U.S. in 1962. After teaching his art in Hawaii and San Francisco, he moved to New York.

CH'EN, YUAN-PIN (1587-1671) Chinese martial artist and pottery master. According to legend, in 1638, during the Tokugawa period, a Chinese pottery master named Yuan-pin Ch'en arrived from China to serve as a ceramics instructor for the **daimyo** of Owari, Japan. Among his other duties, Ch'en instructed **ronin** in the art of seizing a man without the use of weapons. Some sources credit Ch'en with the introduction of **ch'uan-fa** and jujutsu to Japan, a theory that is disputed on the grounds that a weaponless technique called **yawara** was in existence long before Ch'en came to Japan. Ch'en probably introduced the Okinawan sai, later adopted and modified by the Japanese police into the jitte. Ch'en is also referred to as Chin Gempin, Chen Yuan Ping, Ch'en Yuan-Pin, and Ching-Ping.

CHENG, MAN-CH'ING (1902-75) Chinese **t'ai-chi-ch'uan** master. Cheng was a painter, calligrapher, poet, and grandmaster of t'ai-chi-ch'uan. An attack of tuberculosis turned Cheng's attention to t'ai-chi-ch'uan, and he credited it with restoring his health. He continued his study of the discipline, becoming head of the Yang school of t'ai-chi-ch'uan. Consonant with the aims of his art, Cheng was skilled in traditional Chinese medicine, and at one time was director of the Chinese Medical Association.

311

On several occasions while visiting the U.S., he lectured and demonstrated t'ai-chi-ch'uan, including a 1968 demonstration at the United Nations. He wrote *Cheng-Tzu T'ai-Chi Ch'uan Shih-San P'ien. See also* t'ai-chi-ch'uan. (ANTHONY MIRAKIAN)

CHENG-CHUN-KI Chinese kung-fu master in Hong Kong; known for his mastery of the pai-mei (white eyebrows) style of Chinese martial arts.

CHEUK-TONG TSE Prominent Cantonese master of the white crane style of Chinese kung-fu. A student first of Ng Siu Chung, he also studied the hop-gar style under Ng-Yim-Ming, who appointed him the style's representative in Hawaii.

CHEUNG-WING-FAI Chinese kung-fu master in Hong Kong; known for his mastery of the mo-chia style of Chinese martial arts.

CHI, HSU Chinese kung-fu master. Now teaching in San Francisco, Calif., Chi has served as an editor of two kung-fu magazines, a columnist for the "National Sporting" newspaper column, and a senior editor of the *Kung-Fu Library.* Chi was chosen a member of the R.O.C. National Kung-Fu Delegation that staged demonstrations in many Asian countries, and directed kung-fu for action movies in Taiwan.

Chi, a disciple of Liu Yun-Chiao, studied pa-chi (eight ultimate), pi-qua (palm striking), mi-chung (lost track), and **pa-kua** (eight trigrams) systems; he is expert in Chen's tai-chi and liu-h'or tarn larn (six harmony praying mantis) systems. (MICHAEL P. STAPLES)

CHIANG, YUN CHUNG Chinese kung-fu master. When he was 28, Chiang became a student of Kuo Lien-Yin, with whom he spent 15 years learning t'ai-chi-ch'uan, Shao-lin, hsing-i ch'uan, pa-kua ch'uan, and weapons. Chiang also studied with Chih-Chien Wang, who perfected his t'ai-chi, hsing-i, pa-kua, and praying mantis. From Wang he learned slow, medium, and fast t'ai-chi, the five kinds of t'ui shou (pushing hands), and san shou. At 42 he began to learn the white crane style from Ch'en K'ai Shan, the eighth in a direct line of white crane masters descending from the **Shao-lin Temple.** In his two years with Ch'en, Chiang learned both internal and external aspects of white crane boxing, including secrets rarely taught even to advanced students.

In addition to the martial arts, Chiang exhibits internationally painting, calligraphy, and seal-stone carving. He is currently living in Berkeley, Calif. (MICHAEL P. STAPLES)

CHIBA, KAZUO (1940-   ) Japanese **aikido** master. As a youth, he began training in **Omori-ryu** iaido. In 1958 he witnessed a demonstration by **Morihei Ueshiba** and took up aikido under the founder's direct instruction. Later he served as Ueshiba's kaban-mochi (baggage carrier), accompanying the master on instructional tours as his **uke** (receiver) in demonstrations and to carry his luggage and sword while traveling.

In 1966, Chiba was sent to England to teach and develop aikido. He remained there for ten years, establishing the Aikikai of Great Britain with more than 2,000 students. He returned to Japan in 1976 and resumed teaching at the aikido hombu. Then, after spending two years in the country farming and practicing meditation, he came to the U.S. and settled in San Diego, Calif. in 1981, where he established a dojo. He is one of only four direct disciples of Ueshiba to teach aikido in the U.S. (DANIEL M. FURUYA)

CHIBA, SHUSAKO (1794-1855) Japanese master swordsman; founded the Hokushin Itto ryu of **kenjutsu** (art of the sword). Chiba made shinai-shiai (bamboo-sword contests) a sport, pitting men and women armed with the wooden **naginata** against swordsmen armed with the **shinai.**

CHIBANA, CHOSHIN (1887-1969) Okinawan karate master. Born in Shuri, Okinawa, Chibana left high school at 15 to study karate under **Yasutsune Itosu,** remaining with Itosu 15 years, until his master's death.

In 1956 Chibana formed the Karate-Do Renmei and was appointed its first president. By 1957 he had received the title of **hanshi** (master), the highest accolade granted to a martial artist in Japan, from the **Butokukai.** Chibana withdrew from the Okinawan Karate-Do

Choshin Chibana

Renmei, in 1961, to form the Okinawan Shorin-Ryu Karate Kyokai, for which he served as president until he died.

According to Okinawan karate authorities, it was Chibana who first named his style "shorin-ryu," in 1928. And it is from Chibana that most of the **shorin-ryu** styles derive. He also left behind three 9th dan students, several disciples who broke away from his teachings, and two kata: Kusanku-dai and gojushiho (54 steps). *See also* Okinawa, history of martial arts in; shorin-ryu.

CHING, KUANG NAM (James Ching) (1953-   ) Chinese-American amateur Muay Thai champion. Currently living in the U.S., Ching, a true Shao-lin monk, has spent over half of his life in a monastery 60 miles south of Bangkok, Thailand, where he mastered the art of kung-fu. Under Chao Kunaz Chiz, Ching mastered the crane, dragon, snake, and tiger styles of kung-fu. He is also noted for his skill in Shao-lin kung-fu and t'ai-chi-ch'uan. Ching is an expert in **Thai kick-boxing** and reigned as amateur lightweight champion for six years. In 1979 he immigrated to the U.S. and settled in Costa Mesa, Calif., where he teaches kung-fu and Muay Thai.

CHINTO A Chinese military attache who influenced the early development of **te** (hand) in Okinawa; an Okinawan **kata,** "fighting toward the east." Originating in the Okinawan **shorin-ryu** style, chinto is recognized by numerous kicks and one-legged stances. The name of the kata was changed to **gankaku** by karate master Gichin Funakoshi after he moved to Japan. *Further reading: The Essence of Okinawan Karate-Do,* Shoshin Nagamine, 1976.

CHITOSE, TSUYOSHI, DR. (1898-   ) Japanese karate master. Dr. Chitose is at present Supreme Instructor and President of the All Japan Karate-Do Federation, Chito-kai. His initial learning experience was with the kata **Seisan,** which he is said to have practiced for seven years before being taught another at age 14. Prior to World War II, Chitose was regarded as one of the most outstanding kata masters in the Japanese empire. He studied **kobu-jutsu** (art of weapons) with **Gichin Funakoshi** and another unnamed instructor at the Okinawan Engineering School. He studied **goju-ryu** (hard-soft school) with **Chojun Miyagi** and **shorin-ryu** karate with **Choki Motobu.**

312

Dr. Tsuyoshi Chitose

Chitose began teaching karate in Japan while still a student at the Tokyo Medical Center. He integrated shorin-ryu and goju-ryu to formulate his own system, **Chito-ryu.** Although the style is not one of Japan's most popular, it has spread throughout the world. **Mas Tsuroka** and Shane Higashi, both of Canada, and **Wiliam Dometrich** of Kentucky are leading Western exponents of the style. Its greatest Japanese following is in the southernmost part of Kyushu, where the membership is reported to be 42,000.

CHO, HEE IL (1940-   ) Korean-American tae kwon do master, competitor, and author. One of the world's most celebrated tae kwon do masters, Cho was raised in Korea during the depressed times that followed the Korean War. His initiation into the martial arts came when he was severely beaten by five other youths at a local fair. When he recovered, he began studying **tang soo do,** a form of Korean karate, training incessantly for five to six hours daily.

Three years after he'd joined the school, Cho earned his black belt. Shortly thereafter, his family moved to Ichon, near the South Korean capital of Seoul, and it was there that he began studying tae kwon do. At 21, by then a 4th degree black belt, Cho joined the Korean military, where he taught tae kwon do to servicemen. In 1962 Cho won the Northern Korean Championships, and in 1964, the National Korean Championships. Upon his release from the military, Cho continued his studies with Gen. **Choi Hong Hi,** president of the International Taekwon-do Federation. In 1969 Cho traveled extensively throughout Europe, teaching tae kwon do. Then the

Hee Il Cho

federation asked him to go to the U.S. as part of a demonstration team. Cho secured his first job in Chicago, working as an assistant instructor. He moved to South Bend, Ind., in 1970 and worked evenings. The pay was poor, and he was forced to work in a factory. He competed in his first tournament that year and won first place sparring at the Illinois State Championships.

Cho then moved to Milwaukee, Wis., where he opened his first school. That summer he won first place in both the sparring and breaking divisions in the USKA Grand Nationals.

In 1971 Cho relocated to Providence, R.I., where he opened a permanent tae kwon do school. He also won first place titles in sparring and form at the 1972 Northern American Tae Kwon Do Championships in Canada, and the form championship of the 1974 All American Open in New York City.

Cho moved to California in 1975 and bought a studio formerly owned by Chuck Norris in West Los Angeles. In 1979 he expanded to another location, opening a combination tae kwon do studio and health spa in Houston, Tex., which is operated by his brother.

Cho's books include *Man of Contrasts* (1977); *The Complete Martial Artist* (1981); and *The Complete Tae Kwon Do Forms* (1981).

Cho formed his Action International Martial Arts Association in 1981. Open to all styles and systems, the organization offers membership to students and offers instructors guidance and assistance in establishing and maintaining a successful school.

CHO, S. HENRY (1934-   ) Korean-American tae kwon do instructor and promoter. After coming to the U.S. in 1958, Cho attended the University of Illinois before moving to New York City, where he began teaching tae kwon do in 1960. In 1965 he inaugurated the All American Championships. Cho was decorated in 1970 by President Park Chung Hee for his promotion of tae kwon do in the U.S. In 1971 he was elected to the Black Belt Hall of Fame as "Man of the Year." Cho has conducted tae kwon do classes at several New York colleges.

A member of *Who's Who in the Martial Arts,* Cho has written three books: *Korean Karate, Free Fighting Techniques; Better Karate For Boys;* and *Self-Defense Karate.*

S. Henry Cho

CHO, SANG MIN Korean-born tae kwon do instructor and pioneer. He began studying tae kwon do in his native Korea in the mid-1950s, and in 1968 was named an instructor for the tae kwon do instructor's school in Seoul. In 1970, Cho was sent to Sao Paulo, Brazil, where he introduced tae kwon do in that country. By 1977, he supervised some 80 schools with more than 50,000 students.

CHOCHOSHVILI, SHOTA (1950-) Russian judo champion. Chochoshvili upset world champion Fumio Sasahara in the Munich Olympics of 1972, and won the gold medal in the light-heavyweight class. Chochoshvili, who stands 6'3", often scores with powerful counterthrows and is noted for his solid defense. He won the bronze medal in the openweight division of the 1976 Montreal Olympic Games. *See also* Europe, history of judo in.

CHOI, CHANG KEUN Korean tae kwon do instructor and champion; first All Korean National Heavyweight Champion in 1963. He began his study of tae kwon do in the early 1950s. He was an instructor of the Korean Army Training Camp for two years. From 1964 -69, Choi was the national tae kwon do instructor of Malaysia; two of his students were champions of the first and second Asian Tae Kwon Do Championships in 1969 and 1970. In 1970, he moved to Vancouver, Canada where, by 1974, he had established four schools, as well as tae kwon do programs at Simon Frazier University and the University of British Columbia. He is chairman of the umpire committee for the **International Taekwon-do Federation**, and was a member of the ITF exhibition team that conducted a world tour in 1973.

CHOI, DAN (1943-) Korean-born American tae kwon do instructor. Choi was the U.S. team coach for the 3rd World Tae Kwon Do Championships.

CHOI, JOON PYO Korean-born American tae kwon do instructor. Choi served as the U.S. team coach for the 3rd World Tae Kwon Do Championships in 1977, and for the 1978 Pre-World Games Invitational Tae Kwon Do Championships in Seoul, South Korea.

CHOI, SEA OH Korean **hapkido** pioneer and administrator. He studied hapkido under the style's founder, **Yong Shul Choi**. While a student at Han Yang University in Korea, he taught hapkido at the Korean Military Academy and to the U.S. Army 7th Division.

Choi moved to Los Angeles in 1964 and introduced hapkido in the U.S. Later he formed the All American Hapkido Federation and the Hapkido Karate Federation. President of the Korean Amateur Sports Association, Choi was selected three times by that organization to participate in their national games in Korea, in 1971-73.

CHOI, TAE HONG (1935-) Korean-born American tae kwon do instructor. Currently living in Portland, Ore., he has served as northwest regional chairman of the National AAU Tae Kwon Do Committee and produced national-caliber tae kwon do competitors, including Scott Roh.

CHOI, YONG SHUL (1890-) Korean founder of **hapkido.** Choi studied an art called **Daito-ryu aiki-jutsu** from **Shokaku Takeda** in Japan. After 40 years of study and practice, he developed a new form of combat he called hapkido (way of coordinated power).

CHOISAI and JION (ca A.D. 1350) Acknowledged originators of the major system of fencing with the sword used in individual confrontations in feudal Japan. Choisai and Jion codified these sword techniques as early as A.D. 1350. Their system was one of the most rigorous and precise, based upon the warrior's code of ethics and employing its norms to regulate all phases of swordplay: initial preparation for combat; posture and unsheathing of the weapon; basic displacements and strategies of attack, defense, and counterattack; and choice of targets.

Warriors who respected themselves, their opponents, and the rules of orthodox fencing were required to introduce themselves and state their reasons for engaging in combat. When possible, this ethical practice was honored even in the heat of battlefield combat.

After composing themselves, the duelists would unsheath their weapons and advance slowly to the proper distance from each other. Each then would assume the posture appropriate to the strategy he intended to apply. The resolution would usually follow with blinding speed and total commitment.

Certain techniques were identified by number, name, or function. There were 16 varieties of cutting, each with a specific though fanciful name, such as the ''four-sides cut,'' ''the wheel stroke,'' and

so on. While these names appear exotic, they convey an exact meaning to Japanese ears. *Further reading: Secrets of the Samurai,* Oscar Ratti and Adele Westbrook, 1973.

CHOISAI IENAO (d. 1488) Japanese **yarijutsu** pioneer. Choisai is regarded as one of Japan's greatest spearmen, both with the yari (spear) and the **naginata.** He founded the tenshin shoden katori shinto-ryu.

CHONG, HWA (1939-) Korean-born American tae kwon do instructor. Chong is the national vice-chairman of the AAU Tae Kwon Do Committee. He is a certified international referee for amateur tae kwon do competition.

Jun Chong

CHONG, JUN (1948-) Korean-born American karate instructor. Chong began martial arts study at 7, and moved to the U.S. with his family in 1967. During the early 1970s, Chong opened his first tae kwon do and hapkido studio in Rosemead, Calif., moving in 1975 to larger quarters in Los Angeles. He has made three films in the Orient, one of them, *Visitor of America,* released in the U.S. as *Bruce Lee Fights Back from the Grave.* In 1974 Chong was nominated ''Best Instructor of the Year'' by the U.S.A. Tae Kwon Do Federation, and has been awarded certificates of appreciation from the WTF of Korea for his work to promote this art in the U.S.

CHOW, DAVID Chinese-American martial artist. Born in Shanghai, China, Chow began learning the rudiments of judo at 12. In 1949 he became a Hong Kong regional judo champion. Chow immigrated to Los Angeles in 1950. While obtaining a master's degree, he was instrumental in initiating judo classes on campus at both UCLA and the University of Southern California. He served as the first technical advisor to the ''Kung-Fu'' television series, from 1972 to 1974, and works as a fight choreographer in both television and feature films. With Richard Spangler, he wrote *Kung-Fu: History, Philosophy and Technique.*

CHOW, WILLIAM K.S. (1914-) Hawaiian kenpo pioneer and instructor. Chow began the study of martial arts at 7 under the guidance of his father. During his youth, Chow studied boxing, wrestling, jujutsu, sumo, kempo (fist way; fist law), and karate. He learned **kosho-ryu** kempo under **James Mitose,** one of only five students to attain a black belt under Mitose. Chow started teaching what he called **kenpo** (fist law) karate in 1944. His first school was at the Nuuano YMCA.

This school is unusual in uniting itself with karate; Mitose had never associated his kosho-ryu kempo with any form of karate. Chow went on to train and award black belt ranks to a great number

Hawaiian kenpo pioneer William Chow

of students since 1949, including **Ed Parker, Joseph (Adriano) Emperado,** Paul Yamaguchi, Bobby Lowe, Ralph Castro, John Leone, and Paul Pung. *See also* kenpo; U.S., history of karate in.

CHOW, YUT-LUNG Chinese kung-fu master. The top student of Hak-Fu Chan, Chow studied the white crane kung-fu system for over ten years. He served as a coach in the Chan Hok-Fu Athletic Club and participated in local Hong Kong kung-fu exhibitions. Chow came to the U.S. in 1967, and is now teaching at the Pak-Hok Kung-Fu International Association in New York.

CH'UEH, YUAN SHANG-JEN Kung-fu master responsible for verifying the existence of **Bodhidharma**'s "eighteen hands of the lo-han" exercise and combining these movements with numerous forms of his own style. Ch'ueh is credited with increasing the original movements from 18 to 72. After Ch'ueh had spent time popularizing his expanded version of **Shao-lin** kung-fu, he traveled to Shensi province where he met another martial arts master named Li-Shao. The two allegedly enlarged the 72 strokes to 170, and gave the best of these movements such names as dragon, tiger, snake, and crane. *See also* Yuan, Kiao.

CHUN, RICHARD (1935-) Korean-American tae kwon do instructor and author. Arriving in the U.S. in 1962, Chun has trained hundreds

Richard Chun

of black belts, including **Joe Hayes.** Chun served as head coach for the U.S. team at the 1st World Tae Kwon Do Championships (Seoul, 1973) and as regional chairman of the AAU Tae Kwon Do Committee. In 1954 Chun was grand champion of the Moo Duk Kwan National Tournament in Seoul. In the mid-1960s, he organized his annual Universal Open Karate Championships, held in New York. He has written *Moo Duk Kwan, the Korean Art of Self Defense,* and *Tae Kwon Do, Korean Martial Art.* In 1975 he was named to *Who's Who in the Martial Arts. See also* U.S., history of karate in.

CHUNG, GEORGE H. (1961-) Korean-American karate champion. Chung began his study of the martial arts in 1974 under **Ernie Reyes** in San Jose, Calif. Chung now instructs in moo duk kwan and tae kwon do. His list of first place and grand championship victories is extensive, including every major tournament throughout the U.S. in 1980 and 1981. He received the AKA award for Top Kata and the California Karate League "Competitor of the Year" in 1980. Also in 1980 Chung was named the STAR System's National Grand Champion of kata and was rated number one in American form competition by *Karate Illustrated Magazine.*

CHUNG, JOHN Korean-American tae kwon do champion; America's number-one form champion in 1981 and 1982. A fabulous technician trained by **Jhoon Rhee** in Washington, D.C., Chung was ranked second in the nation to **George Chung,** his perennial rival, in 1980. He was rated number-one in the U.S. by *Karate Illustrated* in 1981, surpassing George Chung. That year he was grand champion in seven of the magazine's A-rated (national caliber) tournaments: the Southern California Championships, Top Ten Nationals, AKA Grand Nationals, Ft. Worth Nationals, National Karate Circuit Finals, U.S. Open, and **Battle of Atlanta**. He was runner-up at every other A-rated event he attended.

In 1981, he moved to North Carolina to attend Wake Forest University. In 1982 he captured a remarkable seven grand championships in A-rated tournaments and was runner-up in two more. He reprised his position as *Karate Illustrated*'s number-one form champion in America, and was named to the **Black Belt Hall of Fame** for 1982 as "Forms Competitor of the Year."

CHUNG, SUK (1939-) Korean-born tae kwon do instructor and champion. He started training in 1950 at the kyung ki school under Hyun Jong Myong. In 1963, he won the ko ki gup division (reportedly, 3rd dan and up) of the National College Team Tournament and Memorial Day Championships. In 1964, he won first place in the Superior Players Selective Series.

Chung captained a tae kwon do team which in 1965 toured Asia, Africa and Europe. Afterward, he came to the U.S. to study journalism in Illinois. In 1969, he established his first school in Cambridge, Mass.

CHURCH, ALBERT (1930-80) American karate instructor. Church studied an obscure system called shorinji tetsuken do kanda ha kamishin for 20 years under the direction of C.C. Wang of Korea. Upon Wang's death in Japan in 1967, Church inherited the sokeship (leadership) of the system and had the art formally recognized by the Japanese government. In 1969 he returned to the U.S. and founded his system's U.S. branch in Charleston, S.C. He also established the Kamishin-Kai International (KKI), an organization that by 1980 reported 7,000 members, primarily on the eastern seaboard. With Church's death the presidency of the KKI and sokeship of the art were passed on to his wife, Catherine Church, who continues teaching.

The kamishin style is primarily a self-defense system, with elements from hard fist, **aiki-jutsu, iaido, kempo,** and **kobudo.**

CLEMENT, PATRICK French judo champion; winner of the prestigious French Championships a number of times, and a silver medalist at the 1968 European Championships.

COAGE, ALLEN (1942-) American judo champion; the second American to win an Olympic medal, the bronze at the 1976 games. Coage was National AAU Champion four times, won gold medals twice at the Pan-American Games (1968-69), and represented the U.S. in the World Championships. *Black Belt Magazine*'s annual Top Ten poll rated Coage 8th in 1968, 1st in 1969 and

1970, and 7th in 1971. He injured his knee in the 1972 Olympic Trials and underwent corrective surgery, returning to prominence in 1977 as America's number-one-rated judo champion. With karate's **Bill Wallace**, Coage holds the distinction of being one of the first martial artists voted into the **Black Belt Hall of Fame** twice in the same category: "Judo Player of the Year" in 1970 and 1077.

COBB, RANDALL (1955-   ) American karate competitor; first black belt to fight for the world heavyweight boxing championship. Cobb began training in tae kwon do at the age of seventeen in Abilene, Texas, with Ken McDowell. He received additional training in kojasho kung-fu and cha yon tae kwon do from first Rex Kimball, and later from **Fred Absher** in Albuquerque, New Mexico, earning his black belt in 1975. He subsequently turned to **full-contact karate** competition, establishing a reputation as a kick-knockout artist by winning a string of five bouts, all by kick-knockout within two rounds. Following one of these karate bouts, he was approached by a professional boxing scout who sent him to Philadelphia to train in boxing under George Benton out of Joe Frazier's Boxing Gym.

In 1979, while beginning to climb up the ranks in boxing, Cobb was cast in the role of the heavyweight boxing champion of the world, opposite Academy Award-winner Jon Voight, in the climactic fight scene to MGM's *The Champ.*

In July 1980, Cobb broke into boxing's top ten world ranks with a TKO victory over Earnie Shavers in the eighth round, then on November 26, 1982, in a prime-time ABC-TV network broadcast, he became the first black belt to contend for the world heavyweight boxing championship when he lost a fifteen-round decision to Larry Holmes.

Cobb currently remains an active top ten contender in both boxing and full-contact karate. As of December 1982, his boxing record stood at 20-3 with eighteen knockouts. His karate record was 6-0 with six knockouts, five by kick-knockout. (PAUL MASLAK)

COCHE, JEAN PAUL French middleweight judo champion. Coche won the European Judo Championships in 1972 and 1974, and a bronze medal at the 1972 Munich Olympic Games.

CODRINGTON, EUGENE British karate competitor. Known for his use of the roundhouse kick, Codrington won in 1975 the European Wado-Ryu Championships and the European Karate Championships, upsetting champion **Dominic Valera.** In 1977 he was runner-up at the 4th World Karate Championships, losing to Otti Roetoff of Holland.

COFIELD, GEORGE (1935-   ) American karate pioneer and instructor. Cofield is noted for his work organizing and teaching black ghetto youth. Having trained outstanding students such as **Thomas LaPuppet,** Hawk Frazier, and **Alex Sternberg,** Cofield formed a popular demonstration team, performing at regional tournaments. Founder of the celebrated Tong Dojo in Brooklyn, he has promoted nearly 80 students to the rank of black belt. He briefly appeared with his students in the movie, *The Landlord,* and is a member of *Who's Who in the Martial Arts.*

George Cofield *(right)* and Peter Urban during the 1960s. Cofield's Tong Dojo was among the leading schools on the East Coast and was noted for the number of its outstanding students. Courtesy of Gary Alexander

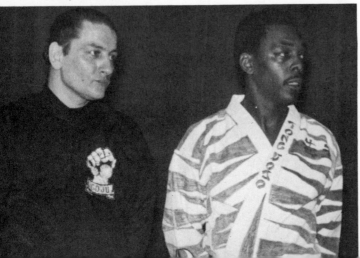

COHEN, IRWIN (1952-   ) American middleweight judo champion. Cohen captured first place at the Junior Nationals in 1965 and 1968. In 1969 and 1970 he was grand champion of the High School Nationals. In 1971 he won the grand championship in the Collegiate Nationals. He won first place at the Senior Nationals in 1971, 1972, and 1974, and was a member of the 1972 U.S. Olympic judo team. Five times national judo champion and voted into Black Belt Hall of Fame in 1978 as "Judo Competitor of the Year," he won the gold medal at the 1973 and 1977 Maccabiah Games in Israel and a silver medal in the 1975 Pan/Am Judo Championships.

COLES, MICHAEL PEYTON (1953-   ) American karate competitor. Coles began his martial arts training in 1968 under **Jhoon Rhee.** In 1975 he entered professional full-contact karate, compiling (to 1980) a 20-2 record. He holds the **PKA** U.S. welterweight title.

CONDE, FRANCISCO (1931-   ) American karate instructor, pioneer, and promoter. Conde began teaching karate in 1963 to women at the Women's Karate Club of Forte Meade, Md. He began producing karate tournaments in 1965 with the Baltimore Invitational and now averages four tournaments each year. He and his wife performed demonstrations at the Tri-State Invitational; the **Internationals;** and, for the Heart Fund, the Boy Scouts and the Association for Retarded Children. Conde, named to *Who's Who in the Martial Arts* in 1975, is director of the Oriental Defensive Arts Association. In 1978 he co-produced the inaugural PKA Nationals with **John Corcoran.** See also U.S., history of karate in.

CONFUCIUS (c. 551-479) Chinese ethical teacher; founder of Confucianism. Confucianism, along with Taoism and Buddhism, were the instrumental philosophies in the evolution of kung-fu. Confucianism was a doctrine of humanism, based on the efficacy of ritual and conformity as the means to salvation. Its contributions to kung-fu are proper breathing, hygiene, **ch'i,** inner strength, proper respect for man and his emotions, and a better understanding of life and its relationship to everything else.

Confucius authored five classics: *I-Ching* (Book of Changes); *Shu Ching (Book of Poetry); Shih Ching (Book of History); Li Chi (Book of Ceremonies and Rites);* and *Ch'un Ch'iu (Spring and Autumn Annals).* Only the last book was written entirely by Confucius and is basically an historical text. The others are believed to have been edited by him or compiled by later followers.

There are an additional four books which comprise the Confucian school of thought: *Lun Yu (Analects); Ta Hsueh (Great Learning); Chung Yung (Doctrine of the Mean);* and *Meng-tse Shu (Book of Mencius). See also* I Ching; kung-fu. *Further reading: The History and Philosophy of Kung-Fu,* Earl C. Medeiros, 1974; *A Path to Oriental Wisdom,* George R. Parulski, 1976.

CONNER, TOMAS American karate pioneer. Born in New York City, Conner studied jujutsu from age 7 at a local Boys Club. At 13 he entered amateur boxing, winning the Golden Gloves in his division. Conner opened his first karate school in 1964 in Phoenix, Ariz., under the name Traco International, becoming one of the first American karate instructors to launch a chain-school operation. In 1968 he was promoted to an advanced black belt rank by American, kenpo pioneer **Ed Parker.** In late 1974 he helped found the Arizona Authentic Karate and Martial Arts Council (AAKMAC), and he has periodically produced the Arizona State Karate Championships since 1969.

CONWAY, JOHN Irish karate instructor and administrator. Conway began in 1961 an accelerated training program under John McSweeney, an American **kenpo** instructor enrolled at the University of Dublin. After earning his black belt, Conway commuted to the U.S. for annual seminars with American kenpo founder **Ed Parker.** In 1966 Conway captained an Irish team which won its division at the All America Karate Championships. He is currently chief instructor of the Irish Karate Association.

COOK, DALE (1956-   ) American karate competitor in full-contact and point competition. Cook began his study of the martial arts in 1974 under D.W. Kang of Tulsa, receiving his black belt in 1975. He has written articles for *World Tae Kwon Do Journal* and *Traditional*

Tae Kwon Do magazine. In 1980-81 he was the number-one ranked middleweight in the STAR System's full-contact ratings.

COOK, JAMES, JR. (1947-   ) American karate competitor from Cleveland. Cook began his training in judo and **Isshin-ryu** karate. In Vietnam he trained in tae kwon do with Korean soldiers; later transferred to Korea, he earned a 3rd dan. Cook took first place at the 1977 USKA Grand Nationals in weapons and sparring, and was ranked nationally by that organization.

CORCORAN, MARYANNE (1952-   ) American karate competitor. Born in Pittsburgh, Pa., Corcoran began her karate training in 1970 with **Glenn Premru.** She received her black belt from Premru in 1973, in the shorin-ryu style. She trained in innovative forms with **Steve Fisher** and worked out with Eric Lee and Malia Dacascos.

In 1975 Corcoran was the only woman kata competitor to place in three of the largest elimination tournaments in the U.S.: the Battle of Atlanta, the Internationals, and the Top 10 Nationals. She was cited as one of America's top ten form competitors in both 1975 and 1976.

She and **John Corcoran,** married since 1973, met at Premru's dojo in 1971, were divorced in 1977. She retired from karate after moving to Fulton, N.Y., in 1980.

CORLEY, JOE (1947-   ) American karate competitor, instructor, pioneer, and promoter. Corley was the first challenger to participate in a full-contact world-title fight. On May 3, 1975, Corley met world middleweight champion Bill Wallace in nine rounds of furious exchanges and lost by a ninth-round TKO.

Among other titles, he won the National Karate Grand Championships (1969, 1971, 1972), the 1967 Southeast Grand Championship, and the 1969 Southern U.S. Open. In 1971-2 he was twice rated among the top 10 fighters in the nation by *Black Belt Magazine*. He created in 1970 the **Battle of Atlanta,** with the help of co-promoter **Chris McLoughlin.** Corley was voted "Man of the Year" for 1974 by **SEKA,** an organization he helped found in 1972. Corley was named to *Who's Who in the Martial Arts* in 1975. In 1979 he became a partner in the **Professional Karate Association.** He has trained champions Keith Vitali, Richard Jackson, and Jeff Grippen. *See also* U.S., history of karate in.

COSTELLO, MARC (1956-   ) American karate champion. Costello entered martial arts in 1968 in Spokane, Wash., under Frank Giles. In 1974 he received his black belt from Jonathon David. He later studied with **Arnold Urquidez.** He fought throughout the U.S. and Japan, winning the WKA U.S. middleweight title from Demetrius Havanas in 1978, and the WKA U.S. super welterweight title from Chris Gallegos in 1979.

COURTINE, HENRY (1930-   ) French judo champion. Courtine was a member of the French team that won the European Judo Championships in 1952, 1954, 1955 and 1962. In individual competition, Courtine was a World Championship semifinalist in 1958, the European Champion of 1959, and a middleweight gold medalist in 1962. He is said to have possessed remarkable timing in executing ankle sweeps. *See also* Europe, history of judo in.

CROMPTON, PAUL H. (1936-   ) British writer, author, publisher, and martial arts practitioner. Born in Leeds, England, Crompton studied boxing as a young man, then judo and jujutsu. He continued his judo studies in London at the **Budokwai.** In the 1960s **Tatsuo Suzuki** and Masafumi Shiomitsu instructed Crompton in **wado-ryu** karate. Later studies included kung-fu and the Yang and Wu styles of t'ai-chi-ch'uan. Most recently, he trained with Dr. Lee Ah Loi of the famous Yawara Tomiki Aikido dojo in London.

In April 1966 Crompton founded a bi-monthly magazine, *Karate and the Oriental Arts,* today the oldest regularly published martial arts periodical in Great Britain. In 1968 Crompton founded his own martial arts book publishing firm, Paul H. Crompton Ltd., which regularly produces titles on a wide variety of styles, arts, sets, and weapons. Crompton has written two books: *Karate Training Methods* and *Kung-Fu Theory and Practice.* In 1975 he was a contributor to the book *Martial Arts of the Orient.*

DACASCOS, AL (1942-   ) American kung-fu instructor and competitor, the first to enter American karate tournaments. Dacascos began competing in the late 1960s and retired in 1973 as a top 10 fighter and a kata competitor. He was. Central North American Grand Champion three times (1969-70) and Rocky Mountain Grand Champion twice (1971 and 1972). At the 1972 **Internationals** in Long Beach, Calif., he won five trophies: kata grand champion, Chinese kata champion, lightweight freestyle runner-up, best sportsmanship award, and the decathlon title for most points accumulated. He had previously won the Chinese kata championship in 1966, 1970, and 1971.

Dacascos' style is now **won hop kuen do,** which means "way of the combined fists." He overhauled **kajukenbo** karate as a result of his discussions with Ron Lew, who instructs in fu-jow pai (tiger claw), Paul Eng (t'ai mantis), Kam Yuen (Praying Mantis), and Won Jack Man (the internal systems). By 1969 this exchange between instructors led to his informing Prof. Emperado, founder of the kajukenbo style, that he no longer wished to call his art kajukenbo. Expanding kajukenbo beyond its ch'uan-fa component, he developed a new style, won hop kuen do.

In 1977 he was inducted into the Black Belt Hall of Fame as Kung Fu Artist of the Year. Dacascos and his family moved to Germany in 1975 and opened a school in Hamburg. He was named to *Who's Who in the Martial Arts* in 1975. He has trained a host of outstanding champions, including **Malia Dacascos,** his wife, **Eric Lee, Karyn Turner, Karen Sheperd,** Peter Morales, and Christian Wulf.

Al Dacascos

Courtesy of *Inside Kung-Fu Magazine*

DACASCOS, MALIA (1943-) American kung-fu champion and instructor. Dacascos was rated the top U.S. female competitor by *Professional Karate Magazine* in 1974, and ranked among the top 10 women in the 1975 *Black Belt Yearbook*. She won first place in kata five times at the **International Karate Championships** and, in 1969 and 1970, won the women's sparring title in addition to kata. She won first in kata at the 1974 U.S. Championships in Dallas.

Dacascos retired from competition in 1975 to concentrate on teaching kung-fu; her students include Cindi Peterson, Karyn Turner, and Karen Sheperd. Since 1975 she has taught kung-fu with her husband in Hamburg, Germany.

Malia Dacascos

DAIGO, TOSHIRO (1926-) Japanese judo champion. In 1950 Daigo was promoted to 6th dan, the youngest judoka to be awarded this grade at the time. His powerful build and fine technique, particularly a precise **kouchigari** (minor inner reaping throw), brought him success in the early 1950s. He won the All Japan Judo Championships twice, in 1951 and 1954, and the Tokyo Championships in 1950 and 1951. Later, Daigo was head of the **Kodokan** kenshuei (special students).

DALGLEISH, BOB (-1978) Canadian karate instructor. A representative of the goju-ryu system and a member of the U.S. Karate Association (USKA), Dalgleish studied under such famous teachers as Canadian karate pioneer **Masami Tsuroka, Hidetake Nishiyama, Gosei Yamaguchi,** and **Peter Urban.** He was chief instructor for the Sudbury Goju-kai.

DALKE, RAY (1939-) American karate champion and instructor. Dalke began karate training with **Dan Ivan** in 1960 and **Hidetaka Nishiyama** in 1961 and received 1st dan by 1963. He was for ten years a member of the U.S. karate team and competed widely here and abroad. In 1965 and 1969 he was the National Karate Champion in the **Shotokan** style; in 1969 he also won the national kata championship. In 1967 Dalke became a full-time student of the **Japan Karate Association**'s Instructor's Institute and after 30 months received his instructor's certificate. In 1970 he withdrew

Ray Dalke *(left)* with Emil Farkas

from competition to coach and promote karate.

Dalke became an associate professor at the University of Riverside (Calif.) in 1972, where he currently teaches karate and other related martial arts. In 1967 he formed the West Coast Karate Association with branch schools throughout southern California. Today he is one of the most highly ranked non-Japanese Shotokan karate instructors in the U.S. and is the southwest representative of the **International Shotokan Karate Federation**, under **Teruyuki Okazaki**. *See also* Shotokan.

DALTON, THOMAS F. American judo champion and official. One of the few authorized IJF referees in the U.S., Dalton worked with the Pan-American judo team in 1967 and 1968, and the U.S. team in the 1967 World Championships. Dalton studied with **Donn F. Draeger,** and later with Takaniko Ishikawa. As a competitor, he won the gold medal at the 1955 Pan-American Games, and in 1956, the silver medal at the same event.

DANIEL, HERVE French karate champion; **shotokan** stylist. A lightweight competitor in the 1976 French Championships, he took first place; in the same year he won the silver medal at the European Championships.

DANIELS, ED (1933-) American karate competitor and instructor. Daniels is perhaps best known for his battles in so-called noncontact competition with Jim Harrison during the 1960s. As a tournament competitor he won the 1964 Southwestern Karate Championships in Dallas. In 1968 he became the Texas State heavyweight champion, Olympic Karate Champion (not to be confused with the Olympic Games), and the Texas State Professional Champion. He received "Outstanding Official" awards at the U.S. Karate Championships in Dallas in 1968, 1969, and 1971, and helped create the professional full-contact rules used in Texas since 1975.

DAYTON, MIKE American martial artist, bodybuilder, and performer. Dayton won the Mr. America bodybuilding title in 1976. Earlier, he had begun martial arts training with **Don Buck,** working chiefly on concentration and the manifestation of **ki** (also called **ch'i**), or internal energy, in which state a person can be void of pain and promote unlimited strength. Once able to refine this power, Dayton began performing public feats of internal and external strength; breaking regulation police handcuffs attached to both wrists, surviving a six-foot drop from the gallows, allowing audience members to perform a tug of war with his neck encircled by a rope held between then, and restraining by a chain a 2,400-horsepower dragster.

He has performed these and other feats on the *Merv Griffin Show* and *That's Incredible*. He also competed in the World's Strongest Men contest, nationally televised, winning first place in the hand strength event. In late 1978, he set a Guinness World Record for "object smashing" by breaking, bending, smashing and destroying eight objects in two minutes. In so doing, he broke two baseball bats, tore a Los Angeles telephone book lengthwise, snapped a file in three places, bent a large screwdriver, broke a pair of bolt cutters, and ripped a license plate in two. His feat aired on "The Guinness Game" in the fall of 1970.

In 1976, afer considerable consultation with his superiors, Buck was vested with the authority to award Dayton the title of "Master of Ch'i."

DEE, (DiCalogero) JOHN (1944-) American karate instructor and promoter. Dee began martial arts in 1963 under Ed Mede. He has studied both **Shotokan** and **kenpo,** but instructs in kenpo. Dee has been a **KRANE** board member and promoted the 1973-76 Massachusetts State Regional Karate Championships and 1974 NEKRA New England Grand Karate Championships.

DELGADO, LOUIS (1948-) American karate competitor. Delgado was a top fighter in the U.S. during the late 1960s and early 1970s. He studied with a number of leading instructors, including **Peter Urban, Hidetaka Nishiyama,** Chris DeBaise, **Moses Powell,** and **Frank Ruiz.** Noted for his aggressive-offensive fighting style, Delgado was also one of the best kata competitors in the nation. He now teaches karate in the New York area.

DE MELLO, AUGUSTIN American karate pioneer and instructor. De Mello opened his first dojo in New York in 1962. He studied karate in Okinawa, later personally under **Mas Oyama.** He sponsored the North American Karate Tournament in 1962, with Oyama as chief referee. After receiving a 4th dan in **kyokushinkai,** he dedicated himself to teaching karate, but was forced to quit due to ill health.

DEMILE, JAMES (1938-) American kung-fu instructor and promoter. An original student of the late **Bruce Lee,** DeMile taught his own system of wing chun kung-fu at the Hawaii Martial Arts Academy, which he founded in Honolulu in 1974. DeMile wrote a series of books entitled *Tao of Wing Chun Do* and *Bruce Lee's 1 and 3 Inch Power Punch.*

DeMile produced several full-contact tournaments in Hawaii in 1975, and performed for the Muscular Dystrophy Telethon. He assisted with and appeared in Lee's early book, *Chinese Gung-Fu, The Philosophical Art of Self-Defense,* published in 1963. DeMile was named to *Who's Who in the Martial Arts* in 1975.

DEMURA, FUMIO (1940-) Japanese-American karate instructor, weapons expert, and performer. A former All Japan Karate Champion, Demura immigrated to the U.S. in 1965. He was named to the **Black Belt Hall of Fame** in 1969 as "Karate Instructor of the Year" and was also named by that publication as the 1975 "Martial Artist of the Year." Chief instructor of the American branch of the Japanese Karate Federation, Demura and his partner, **Dan Ivan,** own and operate a chain of karate studios in Orange County, Calif. Demura is recognized as American karate's first professional performer.

Demura produced the University of California at Irvine Karate Championships in 1967, the Japanese Village Championships in 1969, and the Orange Coast College Championships in 1971. In 1973 he was the recipient of a Golden Fist Award as California's outstanding tournament official. In addition to *Nunchaku: Karate Weapon of Self-Defense,* Demura has written texts on the basics of **Shito-ryu** karate, the **sai** (short sword), and the **bo** (staff). In 1975 Demura was named to the *Who's Who in the Martial Arts. See also* U.S., history of karate in.

Fumio Demura demonstrates his famous front kick. Courtesy of *Official Karate Magazine*

DENLEY, LINDA American karate champion. Denley began her martial arts training in 1973 under Robert Torres of Houston, receiving a black belt in tang soo do in 1975. From 1977-81, she was rated America's number-one female fighter by *Karate Illustrated.* In 1980 she was named to the **Black Belt Hall of Fame** as "Fighter of the Year," and named the **STAR System's** "National Grand Champion" by *Kick Illustrated.*

Denley's grand championship victories in major tournaments include: the Battle of Atlanta (1977, 1979, 1980, and 1981—making her the only four-time champion of this event), the Fort Worth National Pro/Am (1977, 1979, and 1980), the PKA Nationals (Los Angeles, 1979), the U.S. Open (St. Petersburg, Fla., 1979), the AKA Nationals

(Chicago, 1980), the National Karate Finals (Oklahoma City, 1980 and 1981), and the West Coast Nationals (San Jose, Calif., 1981).

DEPASQUALE, ARNOLD (1949-) American jujutsu and judo competitor and instructor. DePasquale began martial arts in 1957 under his father, **Michael DePasquale,** and subsequently studied in New York dojos until 1964, when he founded Dojo Yoshitsune. In 1968 and 1969, he won the heavyweight division of the Rockland County College Invitational Karate Tournament. In 1980 DePasquale was awarded a 5th degree ranking from Jun Saito, international representative of hakkoryu jujutsu. He demonstrated in over 300 expositions and tournaments, including the 1964 New York World's Fair at the Japanese Pavilion, and appeared in a Paramount sports special entitled *Chop-Chop.*

DEPASQUALE, MIKE (1925-) American jujutsu instructor. At the New York World's Fair in 1964, DePasquale performed daily for six weeks in the Japanese Pavilion, sponsored by the Japanese Exhibitors Association. A hakkoryu jujutsu instructor, he has appeared as a demonstrator at regional karate tournaments and lectured at northeastern colleges. DePasquale appeared in a 1967 Paramount sports special entitled *Sports in Action.* He sponsored the annual U.S. Invitational Karate Championships in 1971 at Asbury Park, N.J. In 1975, he was named to *Who's Who in the Martial Arts.*

DEWALLE, ROBERT VAN Belgian judo champion. DeWalle was a gold medal winner at the 1980 Olympic Games in Moscow, defeating Russia's Tengiz Khubulouri. He has won gold, silver, and bronze medals in the Senior European Judo Championships, and a silver medal at the World Championships.

DIDIER, FRANCIS (1949-) French karate champion. Rated among Europe's top 10 karate competitors by *Black Belt Magazine* during the early 1970s, Didier was a member and coach of the French contingent that took the team title of the 1974 European Championships. He placed second at the 1972 French Championships and European Championships. In 1973, he was grand champion of Europe.

DILLARD, L. MICHAEL (1950-) American karate promoter and businessman. Dillard earned his black belt while studying in Korea in 1969 under Yong Ho Kim. In 1977 Dillard founded Century Martial Arts Supply, Inc., and has guided the company to a strong position in the industry, manufacturing traditional and professional-style karate uniforms and sparring equipment.

Dillard created and developed the National Karate Circuit (NKC), in 1979, a series of twelve regional tournaments culminating in the

Michael Dillard

National Finals Karate Tournament at Oklahoma City each November. The NKC is the first successful open karate circuit in the sport's history.

DILLMAN, GEORGE American karate instructor. Dillman began Okinawan kempo in 1960 with Robert Tieu at Ft. Knox, Ky., and received his black belt in this style from Charles Cant. Dillman has also studied **isshinryu** with Harry Smith, **shorin-ryu** with James Coffman, and Chinese systems with Daniel Pai. In 1973 Dillman was named one of the country's top 10 kata competitors by *Official Karate Magazine*.

Dillman was featured in "Ripley's Believe It Or Not" in 1975 for a feat that made worldwide wire service coverage: He broke more than 1,000 pounds of ice for a charity function. The Ripley's cartoon featuring Dillman's feat appears at many Ripley's Museums in England, Canada and the U.S.

DJUT, MAS A Sudanese, he was the developer of **serak**, a style of pukulan.

DOIGUCHI, SUKETARO (1886-1960) American judo pioneer. Doiguchi was one of the founders of the Hokka Judo Yudanshakai (Northern California Judo Association); in 1948 he became its president, later serving as chairman of the board until his death. Doiguchi received the honorary rank of yudansha taigu, only twice conferred in the U.S. (The other was to Gen. Curtis E. Lemay.) *See also* U.S., history of judo in.

DOMETRICH, WILLIAM (1935-) American karate instructor and pioneer. Dometrich started his karate training in Japan in 1951; he was a student of **Dr. Tsuyoshi Chitose,** the founder of **Chito-ryu** and his early promotions were under Chitose and **Gichin Funakoshi.** Dometrich earned his kyoshi (teacher grade) degree before returning to Covington, Ky., in 1954, the first to introduce Chito-ryu karate in America. At present, he is the highest-ranking non-Japanese in his style. *See also* U.S., history of karate in.

DONG, NGO Vietnamese **cuong nhu** instructor. After studying a number of martial arts including **Shotokan** karate, he founded cuong nhu in 1965. As a professor of biology at the University of Hue in Vietnam he traveled to the U.S. to attend the University of Florida, earning a Ph.D. in entomology in 1971. Upon his return to Vietnam, he was appointed president of Quang Da College, and in 1975 was arrested by the Communist government. After a daring escape, Dong arrived in the U.S. in Nov. 1977, where he subsequently founded the Cuong Nhu Karate Association in Gainesville, Florida. By 1980, Dong directed 15 schools in Florida, California and South Carolina.

DONOVAN, TICKY (1946-) English karate champion. A three-time winner of the prestigious British Karate Championships (1973, 1974, and 1975), Donovan began his training in **Shotokan** karate in 1965, later swtiching to the **isshinryu** system. He received his black belt in 1967 and became British Junior Champion in 1966. Donovan has frequently been a member of British teams; representing England in the South African Games, he took a silver medal in individual competition. At the 1973 Eastern Regional Open Championships he won first place in team events, kata, and individual competition.

In 1974 he won a British Karate Association Black Belt Open competition, and in 1973 and 1974 he captained teams at the B.K.C.C. British Open Championships, capturing first place in 1974. In 1975 he won the Midland Open Championships. He co-authored *Special Competition Karate* with **Dominic Valera.**

DOUGLAS, DICK (1935-) American karate competitor and promoter. A student of **Chuck Norris,** Douglas is a karate pioneer in Nevada, having founded his first school in 1967. He is a three-time grand champion of the Las Vegas Invitational Karate Championships. Douglas re-established Norris' Las Vegas National Karate Championships in 1971 after a four-year hiatus. In 1975 he was named to *Who's Who in the Martial Arts.*

DOVERSOLA, GORDON American karate instructor and pioneer. Born in Honolulu, Doversola began jujutsu at 11, and at 19 changed to **kempo** under **James Mitose.** After teaching kempo for several years, Doversola met Teiken Nagusuko of Okinawa, with whom he studied Okinawa-te for three years.

Doversola moved to Los Angeles in 1957 and opened an Okinawa-te school. **Joe Lewis**, the retired world heavyweight champion; karate pioneer **Bob Wall**; and actor **Jim Kelly** trained with him. Doversola was technical advisor for karate scenes in *The Manchurian Candidate,* one of the first films to make use of martial arts.

Gordon Doversola was one of the earliest karate instructors on the West Coast.

DRAEGER, DONN F. Martial arts author, historian, and pioneer. Draeger is regarded as the foremost Western scholar of the Japanese classical disciplines, in which he holds numerous black belt ranks and teaching licenses. Draeger has lived in Japan, China, Mongolia, Korea, Malaysia, and Indonesia. His works include: *Judo Training Methods, Practical Karate* (six volumes), *Judo for Young Men, Pentjak-Silat, Weapons & Fighting Arts of the Indonesian Archipelago, Classical Bujutsu, Classical Budo, Modern Budo & Bujutsu,* and with Robert W. Smith, *Asian Fighting Arts.*

In 1967 Draeger doubled for actor Sean Connery and was a stunt choreographer for the James Bond film *You Only Live Twice.* He has for some time been engaged in research for his doctoral dissertation in hoplology, the science of weapons. *See also* U.S., history of judo in.

Don F. Draeger

DUENAS R., ISAIAS (1950-) Mexican karate champion. Duenas began martial arts under Dai Won Moon (**David Moon**) in Mexico City in 1969. Mr. Moon awarded Duenas with his black belt in 1972. He was in 1974 the PKA's first world champion in the lightweight division. His wins include the 1973 1st World Taekwondo Championships in Seoul; 1973 and 1974 Mexico National Team Championships in Mexico City; 1974 Central America Taekwondo Championships in Guatemala; 1976 Dual Meet American Team vs. European Team in Paris.

Isaias R. Duenas

DUNCAN, RONALD American weapons expert. One of the pioneers of the martial arts on the East Coast, Duncan began teaching in New York City in 1956. He is noted in the U.S. for his exciting weapons demonstrations and holds black belt ranks in karate, jujutsu, and judo. *See also* U.S., history of karate in.

DUTCHER, JOHN (1939-) American karate and judo instructor. Dutcher began his study of judo in 1957 at the University of Hiroshima while serving in the U.S. Armed Forces. He received his black belt in 1958. He studied tae kwon do in the U.S. with **Jhoon Rhee.** At the Tae Gyun Global Karate Championships in Philadelphia in 1968, Dutcher defeated Joe Hayes, Ulysses Edwards, and Mitchell Bobrow for the grand championship. Dutcher's most noted pupil is Lawrence Kuss, who, in 1975, was rated among America's top 10 kata competitors.

John Dutcher

EADS, VALERIE (1943-) American martial arts journalist. Eads has studied kendo, but is most noted for her numerous articles in martial arts publications in the U.S. The publisher and editor of *Fighting Woman News* since 1975, she has always championed the woman's cause in the martial arts.

EAGLING, DALE Tasmanian tae kwon do instructor and pioneer. Chairman of the Tasmania Taekwondo Association and vice-president of the Australian Taekwondo Association, he was appointed in Sept. 1975 the Australian team supervisor for the 2nd World Tae Kwon Do Championships in Seoul, Korea. By 1977, Eagling had taught more than 15,000 students in Hobart, New Norfolk, Launceston, Devonport, and Burnie.

ECHANIS, MICHAEL (1950-1978) American martial arts instructor and author. Echanis was considered a leading authority in **hand-to-hand combat** and was a former senior instructor for the Special Forces and the U.S. Navy Seals. Specializing in unconventional warfare, Echanis taught throughout the world. It was while he was training in Nicaragua that he was killed. A former member of the 75th Ranger Special Forces, Echanis served in Vietnam and was wounded in 1970. He studied un shin bup, a Korean version of **ninjutsu**, under **hwarang-do** grandmaster **Joo Bang Lee** and developed this discipline for use by the U.S. Special Forces, Seals, VDTs, and so on. Echanis wrote three books: *Knife Self-Defense for Combat; Knife Fighting, Knife Throwing for Combat;* and *Basic Stick Fighting for Combat.*

EGAMI, SHIGERU (1912-) Japanese karate master. Egami started his karate training while a student at Waseda University, whose karate club he helped to establish. In 1937 he was appointed by **Gichin Funakoshi,** the "father of modern Japanese karate," to the Shotokan's committee for evaluation.

After World War II he studied under Funakoshi and assisted him in teaching. Egami lectured in physical education at Waseda University, taught karate at Gakushuin, Toho, and Chuo Universities, and was active in establishing numerous karate organizations in Japan and overseas.

Among Egami's books are *Karate-do: For the Specialist* and *The Way of Karate, Beyond Technique.* Egami was named Funakoshi's successor as chief instructor of the **Shotokan.** *See also* Shotokan.

ELDER, RAY American kick-boxing champion. A former U.S. Marine before disembarking in Japan, he undertook kick-boxing in Jan. 1969 and turned professional nine months later. He fought his way up the ranks to become the first non-Asian ever to win a Japanese kick-boxing title, capturing the middleweight crown on Nov. 5, 1971 by knocking out T. Furuya in the 4th round. He successfully defended his title on Feb. 26, 1972, this time with a 1st-round knockout. After an unsuccessful bid for the overall middleweight title of the Orient, he retired as Japanese middleweight champion on Nov. 4, 1972.

ELKIN, JAMES British aikidoist. The general secretary and national coach to the British Aikido Association, Elkin has studied aikido for some 18 years. In 1975 he was a contributor on aikido to the book *Martial Arts of the Orient.*

EMPERADO, ADRIANO D. "Sonny" (1926-) American karate master and pioneer. A kenpo master trained by **William K.S. Chow,** Emperado is one of five founding members of the kajukenbo system. His more famous students include **Al Dacascos, AlGene Caraulia, Sam Allred, Jim Roberts, Sr.,** and **Phil Koeppel.** Emperado started Hawaii's first and largest chain of karate schools. A member of the *Who's Who in the Martial Arts,* he served as chief referee of the Hawaii State Championships from 1971 through 1973. *See also* U.S., history of karate in.

Adriano D. Emperado

Courtesy of *Inside Kung-Fu Magazine*

ENDO, SUMIO Japanese heavyweight judo champion, winner of the 1975 World Championships. Winner of the 1974 and 1976 All Japan Judo Championships, he was also a bronze medalist at the 1976 Montreal Olympics. A former All Japan College Champion as well, Endo is famous for his **seoinage,** but is also respected for such moves as **kosotogari, osotogari,** and **uchimata.**

Sumio Endo

ENOEDA, KEINOSUKE (1935-) Japanese karate instructor and champion. Born in Kyushu, Japan, he began judo at 7, eventually earning a black belt and placing in the finals of the All Japan High School Judo Championships. At 17, Enoeda saw a karate demonstration by **Teruyuki Okazaki** and a partner from Takushoku University, where Enoeda soon enrolled because of its outstanding karate section. He earned his black belt in **Shotokan** karate in two years; two years later, at 21, he was named captain of the university's karate team.

Graduating from Takushoku with a degree in economics, he soon joined the **Japan Karate Association**'s three-year instructor's program, training under **Masatoshi Nakayama** and **Hidetaka Nishiyama.** In 1961, he entered the JKA's All Japan Championships, sharing third place in sparring with **Takayuki Mikami**; in 1962 he placed second to champion Hiroshi Shirai, whom Enoeda defeated in 1963 to finally become All Japan Champion.

Among the spectators who witnessed Enoeda win his title in Tokyo was President Sukarno of Indonesia, who immediately negotiated for Enoeda's services in troubled Indonesia. Nakayama, the JKA's chief instructor, and Enoeda spent four months in Indonesia teaching Sukarno's personal bodyguards and at police and military establishments. Another overseas spectator at the 1963 tournament was South African **Stan Schmidt,** who brought Enoeda to his country to teach for three months.

After a brief stint in Hawaii, Enoeda was invited to Great Britain to assist **Hirokazu Kanazawa** in propagating Shotokan. He taught chiefly in Liverpool. Gradually, the Shotokan organization grew into the country's strongest. In 1966-67, Enoeda traveled to the U.S. to assist Hidetaka Nishiyama, one of his teachers. He returned to Great Britain and, when Kanazawa returned to Japan in 1971, Enoeda inherited leadership of Shotokan in Great Britain. Soon, he was appointed chief instructor to all Europe, throughout which he made frequent teaching trips. He has coached many celebrities behind the cameras for fight scenes in films such as *Day of the Jackal* and *Countess Dracula,* and he appeared briefly in the opening sequence of the James Bond thriller, *Diamonds Are Forever. See also* Shotokan. (TERRY O'NEILL)

ENSLOW, DAVE American cartoonist and a black belt in judo, he is noted for the martial arts cartoons he drew for *Black Belt Magazine* in the 1960s.

ERIGUCHI, EIICHI (—) Japanese martial arts administrator, one of the founders of WUKO. A high ranking member of F.A.J.K.O. Eriguchi is a high ranking karate black belt. He has been active in karate since his student days at Tokyo Imperial University as a member of its Karate Club. He continued his interest in karate becoming chairman of the Wado-Kai Karate Association, as well as being vice president for the All Self Defense Force Karate Federation. He is a former Lt. General of the Japanese Self Defense Forces.

ETHINGTON, DUANE R. (1937-) American martial arts journalist and karate instructor. Ethington began his study of the arts in 1966 in Dallas, earning his black belt in 1973, and originated a radio show in Las Vegas during the late 1970s called "Duane's Tips on Self-Defense." One of the early martial arts journalists in the U.S., Ethington has been a correspondent for major American martial arts magazines including *Black Belt, Karate Illustrated,* and *Official Karate.*

EVANS, FLEM (1945-) American semicontact karate competitor. Evans began his study of karate under **Ken Knudson** in the mid-1960s. Winner of the 1974 USKA Grand Nationals, he was rated in the top 10 by *Black Belt Magazine* and *Professional Karate Magazine* during the mid-1970s.

EVANS, GERALD American karate competitor. A member of the AAKF and a **Shotokan** stylist, Evans began training with **Teryuyuki Okazaki** in 1967 in Philadelphia. He won the All American Karate Championships in 1972 and 1973 and has competed at JKA contests in Japan, reaching the finals in every tournament he entered. Evans has also been the captain of the American team representing the U.S. in Tokyo. *See also* Shotokan.

FALSONI, ENNIO (1946-) Italian karate champion. A pupil of Hiroshi Shirai of the JKA, Falsoni won numerous championships throughout Europe. He operates his own dojo in Milan and is editor of *Bansai,* an Italian-language martial arts magazine. *See also* Europe, history of karate in.

FARNSWORTH, TERRY (1943-) Canadian judo instructor and champion. He has devoted most of his life to judo, including a six-year tenure in Japan where he studied judo at Chuo University under **Hiroshi Nakamura.** In 1969, Farnsworth won the gold medal at the Maccabiah Games in Israel in the lightweight division. He represented Canada in the 1971 World Championships and at the 1972 Summer Olympics in Munich.

FARR, JACK (1945-) American martial arts instructor and administrator. Farr studied kung-fu, tae kwon do, **Shotokan, pentjak silat,** and **kenpo.** At various times he was president of the Martial Arts Society, the Chinese Karate Federation, and the IKKA, founded by **Ed Parker.** He produced the Dallas Kenpo Karate Invitational in 1974, the U.S. Golden Karate Championships in 1976 and 1977, and the Lookout Mountain Invitational in 1976 and 1977.

FEI, NIP CHEE (1930-) Chinese kung-fu master and founder of **poc khek.** A native of Hong-Kong, Nip Chee Fei began studying kung-fu at an early age, but later drifted into **t'ai-chi-ch'uan.** While teaching t'ai-chi in Malaysia, Fei created the more combat-oriented poc khek.

FERGUSON, LINNY (1957-) American semicontact karate competitor. Ferguson won the grand championship of the 1975 International Karate Championships, the last year that this tournament enjoyed truly national prestige. As a full-contact fighter, Ferguson was considered the leading contender to world super lightweight champion Gordon Franks in the years 1975-76.

FIELD, JAMES American karate instructor, one of the first four Americans to become a certified instructor of the **Japan Karate Association.** Field was captain of the U.S. international karate team for several

James Field (*right*) and Emil Farkas

years and has won such titles as National Collegiate Champion (1968), National Grand Champion (1971-73), and Pan-America Champion (1973-74). He placed 3rd at the 1976 World Championships. He teaches at his own dojo and is a karate coach at U.C.L.A.

FISHER, MICKEY (1946-) American karate instructor, promoter, and competitor. He received his black belt from **Jhoon Rhee** in 1964. Besides tae kwon do, Fisher studied a number of styles, among them **kenpo, goju-ryu, Okinawa-te,** and **hapkido.** He recently formed his own system, which he calls shin-toshi. Among other tournament engagements, Fisher has been director and announcer of Jack Hwang's All American Karate Championships since 1969. He promoted the Southern United States Martial Arts Championships and is also a full-contact trainer and manager.

FISHER, STEVE (1953-) American karate competitor, instructor, and promoter. In 1971 and 1972, Fisher received black belt rankings from **Steve Sanders, Mike Stone,** and Phil Skornia. Fisher also trained under **Hidetaka Nishiyama** and **Tadashi Yamashita.**

Since 1977 he has been ranked in various top 10 polls for both kata and semicontact. In 1977 he won the kata grand championship of the International Karate Championships, in 1978 the grand championship in fighting. He won both the light heavyweight division and the grand championship in fighting at the 1979 Fort Worth National Pro/Am, in Texas.

In 1978, *Black Belt Magazine* rated Fisher among their top 10 fighters, and in both 1979 and 1980 he held fifth place among America's top 10, according to *Black Belt.* In 1980 the STAR System rated him third for the year in the light heavyweight division, according to *Kick Illustrated.* In 1981, in a poll taken by *Sport Karate Magazine,* he was rated seventh in the nation. He was a co-trainer of nationally ranked kata competitor **Maryanne Corcoran.** He promotes the annual Steve Fisher Karate Championships, one of the ten top tournaments in the U.S.

California's Steve Fisher *(left)* is one of the state's top karate competitors. Courtesy of *Official Karate Magazine*

FITKIN, BRIAN (1947-) British karate champion. Fitkin caused a stir, when as a 22-year-old green belt, he defeated several well-known European black-belt fighters, and led his team to a 1969 European Karate Championship title over the previously undefeated French contingent. He later studied in Japan with kyokushinkai founder **Mas Oyama.** Though only sporadically active, he was a member of the victorious British team at the 1975 WUKO World Championships in Long Beach, Calif.

FONG, LEO T. (1928-) American kung-fu promoter, author, film producer, and actor. A former Methodist minister, Leo Fong taught martial arts to delinquent youths as part of rehabilitational training. He wrote *Sil lum Kung-Fu, Choy Lay Fut Kung-Fu* and, with **Ron Marchini,** *Power Training in Kung-Fu and Karate.* Currently Fong owns a film production company, producing action-adventure martial arts films. He has starred in or produced: *Murder in the Orient, Bamboo Trap, Blind Rage, Tiger's Revenge,* and *Revenge of the Bushido Blade.* In 1975 Fong was named to *Who's Who in the Martial Arts.*

Leo T. Fong

FONG-T'SAI-YUK The son of Miu-T'sui-Fa who, in a popular Chinese story, beat Lui-Lo-Fu in combat. Fong-T'sai-Yuk supposedly escaped from the burning **Shao-lin Temple** with the **Five Ancestors** to found the five patterns style of **hung-chia** kung-fu.

FONTAINE, KYUNG-AE Korean-born female tae kwon do instructor. Fontaine, of Burlington, Vt., is active as the Women's Subcommittee Chairman of the AAU Tae Kwon Do Committee. She created the first women's international tae kwon do team.

FOSTER, MIKE American karate pioneer and instructor. Foster trained in Japan and returned, after ten years, to the U.S. in the mid-1960s, where he established one of the first karate schools in Florida. Beginning in 1967, Foster set up accredited karate programs at St. Leo's University, Florida State, the University of Southern Florida, Tampa University, and Florida Atlantic University. Foster heads the U.S. branch of the Yoshukai Karate Association. *See also* U.S., history of karate in.

FRANKS, GORDON (1955-) American karate champion, businessman, and instructor. Franks began karate in 1969 in Washington, D.C., under **Pat Worley.** After winning the 1975 PKA super-lightweight world title, he was undefeated for five years. His record from 1974 through 1980 was 18-1.

He is a co-owner of the Mid-America Karate Schools in Minneapolis-St. Paul, and a founder of *Sport Karate Magazine.* Franks and his partners produce the Mid-America Diamond Nationals. In 1980 Franks was selected by the members of the PKA Players Committee as its chairman. *See also* U.S., history of karate in.

FRAZIER, DWIGHT (1949-) American karate competitor. At 14 Frazier began karate with **George Cofield.** Nicknamed the "Hawk" because of his sensational airborne kicks, he was ranked ninth in the U.S. in 1969-70 by *Black Belt Magazine.*

FREEMAN, KEN American judo instructor. Freeman began training at the **Budokwai** with **Gunji Koizumi** and **Yukio Tani.** Arriving in the U.S. in 1946, he trained under **George Yoshida** for three years. Freeman was instrumental in forming the New York Judo Yudanshakai. With Yoshida, he was its coach for three years and president for four. He was a founder and president of the Eastern College Judo Association, and served as coach of the judo team at Princeton University. *See also* U.S., history of judo in.

FUJIWARA, T. Japanese karate instructor, founder of the **seikidojo** system of karate. Fujiwara received advanced rankings in Okinawan shorin-ryu and Japanese goju-ryu karate, and is well versed in **kendo.** He combined these three arts to form seikidojo.

FUKII, SHOZO (1951-) Japanese judo champion; winner of the middleweight division of the 1971 and 1973 World Judo Championships.

FUKUDA, KEIKO (1913-) Japanese judo instructor. One of the highest-ranked female judoka in the world, Fukuda at 22, persuaded by Jigoro Kano, undertook judo at the **Kodokan.** Since 1965, Fukuda has traveled throughout the world teaching judo and giving demonstrations. She has been the senior instructor at the Kodokan women's section, and was the first woman to achieve 6th-degree black belt—an honor prompted by petitions sent to the Kodokan from instructors across the world. Fukuda wrote *Born for the Mat,* a history of judo and women's position in the Kodokan.

FUKUI, HARUNOSUKE Aikido disciple of **Morihei Ueshiba** and the founder of shindo iten ryu aikido.

FULLERTON, FRANK American judo administrator. Named "Man of the Year" in 1968 in the Black Belt Hall of Fame, Fullerton is an attorney by profession who received his black belt in judo from the **Kodokan.** He has served as president of the Texas Judo Black Belt Association, sponsor of the 1964 National Collegiate Judo Championships, and member of the AAU judo executive committee. He also holds a black belt in karate from the JKA.

FUNAKOSHI, GICHIN (1868-1957) Okinawan-born karate master and pioneer, regarded universally as the father of modern karate. Born to a privileged class (shizoku) in Shuri, Funakoshi began his karate training while attending primary school with Yasutsune Azato, a great scholar and karate master. Under Azato's tutelage, Funakoshi studied not only karate but Chinese classics and Confucian dialectics. Because of his association with Azato, Funakoshi was able to meet and train under many of the best Okinawan karate masters, among them master **Yasutsune Itosu,** Kiyuna, Niigaki, and Toonno.

In 1902 Funakoshi held the first recorded karate demonstration on Okinawa, for Shintaro Ozawa, commissioner of schools for Kagoshima Prefecture. So successful was the demonstration that by 1903 karate became part of the physical education program at the Men's Normal School in Shuri and at the prefectural Daiichi Middle School. Because of Funakoshi's philosophical approach to karate, the art quickly attracted the interest of intellectuals and educators.

In 1906 Funakoshi conducted the first public exhibition of karate, and by 1913 the interest in karate had grown to such proportions that Funakoshi organized a demonstration team comprised of the most active karate masters of the day. This group included such masters as Gusuku, Mabuni, Motobu, Kyan, Ogusuku, Ishikawa, Tokumura, and Yahiku. They toured Okinawa constantly between 1914 and 1915.

In 1917, at the request of the ministry of education, Funakoshi traveled to Kyoto, Japan, where he performed at the **Butokuden.** While the demonstration was a success, there was no immediate

Keiko Fukuda

Gichin Funakoshi (*right*) with Isao Obata during S.A.C. training class

FUKUHARA, LARRY American judo champion. Larry Fukuhara was chosen number-one judo player in the U.S. for 1967-68 by *Black Belt Magazine.* A lightweight known for his versatile array of throws, Fukuhara won the bronze medal at the 1967 Pan-American Games in Winnipeg, Canada.

rush to bring the Okinawan art to Japan on a formal basis. In 1921, after an exhibition before the visiting Crown Prince of Japan at Shuri Castle, Funakoshi was invited to appear at the First National Athletic Exhibition in Tokyo in 1922. He was asked to stay on in Japan by several prominent people, among them Jigoro Kano, the founder of judo, who asked Funakoshi to demonstrate karate at the **Kodokan.** Kano later incorporated some karate movements into an advanced judo kata.

Deciding to remain in Japan, he taught, at first for an artist's guild, and established the first Japanese karate club at the Meisei Juku, a dormitory and school for newly arrived Okinawan students in the Suidobata section of Tokyo. In 1922 he wrote his *Ryukyu Kempo: Karate,* later re-issued as *Rentan Goshin Karate-jitsu* ("Strengthening of Willpower and Self-defense through Techniques of Karate").

In 1924, Funakoshi established the first collegiate karate club, at Keio University, and soon was teaching at a number of schools and commercial dojos. In 1936, Funakoshi's students solicited funds and constructed for him the world's first free-standing karate dojo. The dojo was named "Shotokan" (the hall of Shoto)—Shoto was the pen name used by Funakoshi when signing his poetry.

Funakoshi's second book, *Karate-Do-Kyohan,* in which he changed the ideographs for kara from "Chinese" to "empty," appeared in 1936. Although controversial among Okinawan karate masters, from that time forward karate became "empty hand" instead of the previous "China hand."

After the war Funakoshi rebuilt karate in Japan. In 1953, asked to the U.S., he instead sent a number of his top students including Isao Obata, Masatoshi Nakayama, Kamata, and Hidetaka Nishiyama. In 1955, two years before his death, Funakoshi presided over the opening of the first dojo of the **Japan Karate Association.** On April 26, 1957, Funakoshi died in Tokyo. *See also* Japan, karate in; karate-do; Shotokan. *Further reading: Karate-Do: My Way of Life,* Gichin Funakoshi, 1975; *Kick Illustrated,* Oct. 1981-Jan. 1982.

FUNAKOSHI, GIGO (-1945) Japanese karate instructor. The third eldest son of **Gichin Funakoshi,** Gigo replaced Takeshi Shimoda as his father's assistant after the latter's sudden death in 1934. Winning the admiration and respect of his students, they affectionately referred to him as waka sensei, or "young teacher." Gigo died while yet in his thirties.

Gigo adapted karate techniques to fit the requirements of sport. His style was based on upright, fluid postures and made abundant use of full-leg-extension kicking at high target areas, such as the roundhouse kick, side thrust kick, and back kick. This is said to be the basis of the current style of JKA exponents.

FUNAKOSHI, KEN (1938-   ) Japanese-American karate instructor, competitor, and referee. Funakoshi is a distant descendant of **Gichin**

Ken Funakoshi (*left*) fights Frank Smith at the 1967 All America Karate Championships.

Funakoshi, founder of modern Japanese karate-do. Funakoshi became proficient in judo, kenpo, and Shotokan karate under well-known instructors, including **Sonny Emperado** and **Hirokazu Kanazawa.** Funakoshi was the first American citizen to be elected chief instructor of the Karate Association of Hawaii, a branch of the JKA. He was three times a first-place winner of kumite and kata at the All Hawaii Championships in 1964 through 1966. A member of *Who's Who in the Martial Arts,* in 1978, he was named to the Black Belt Hall of Fame as "Instructor of the Year."

FUNG, GARY Chinese-American kung-fu actor. Fung learned several styles of Chinese kung-fu while growing up in San Francisco. His father, a theatrical consultant in Hollywood during the Charlie Chan era and himself versed in the hung gar style of boxing, supported Gary in his kung-fu studies and eventual turn to acting. Experimenting with techniques, he worked with stunt fighter Rocky Capella and kicking expert Winsley "Kato" Yee.

In 1975, he won the first West Coast Full-Contact Gung-Fu championship, and formed the first kung-fu program for the Police Activities League in San Francisco. Fung has since appeared on numerous television programs including *Streets of San Francisco, Stuntmen,* and *Charlie Chan and the Curse of the Dragon Lady.* He starred and worked as martial arts coordinator in *Kill Squad* with Cameron Mitchell. He also worked with Eric Lee in *Falcon's Claw* and with Chuck Norris in *An Eye For An Eye.*

FURUYA, DANIEL M. (1948-   ) Japanese-American aikidoist and martial arts scholar. Daniel Furuya began training at 10 in kendo and aikido, in Los Angeles. He was selected under the federally sponsored Carnegie Project to study Chinese at the University of California at San Francisco. In 1966 he entered the University of Southern California under scholarship to study Asian history and philosophy. In 1968, under the National Defense Act, Furuya was sent to Harvard University in Cambridge to further study Eastern philosophy and literature. He graduated in 1970 from the University of Southern California with a degree in Asian Studies.

In 1969 Furuya was granted permission by **Morihei Ueshiba,** the founder of aikido, to study at the Aikido World Headquarters in Tokyo. Two months later, Ueshiba died, and Furuya continued his studies under the founder's son, **Kisshomaru Ueshiba.**

In addition to aikido, Furuya has a deep interest in Eastern philosophy, history, and art. He is considered an authority on the Japanese sword, as well as Chinese and Japanese art through the 1800s. On the staff of Unique Publications as book editor since 1980, he serves as consultant for *Kick Illustrated* and *Inside Kung Fu* and contributing editor to *Martial Arts Movies,* three national magazines published by the company. In 1981 he was a technical advisor for *The Overlook Martial Arts Dictionary* and *The World Encyclopedia of Martial Arts.*

FUSARO, ROBERT American karate instructor, administrator, and pioneer. Fusaro began his training in 1955 at the **Japan Karate Association** while serving in the U.S. Army in Japan. Returning to Minneapolis in 1958, he was the first to teach karate in Minnesota, and one of the first in the midwest. He founded the Midwest Karate Association in 1961. Accredited karate instructor at the University of Minnesota since 1965, Fusaro received a 5th-degree black belt in 1972. Fusaro is chairman and chief instructor of the North Central Region of the American Amateur Karate Federation. *See also* U.S., history of karate in; Shotokan.

FUZY, ERNEST ALLEN American karate instructor and promoter. Fuzy began martial arts with Robert Moore and Curtis Herrington in Lakewood, Ohio, in 1968, and earned his black belt in 1972 from Herrington. He currently teaches ji do kwan and t'ai-chi ch'uan. Fuzy promoted the Northern States Karate Championships in 1974, 1975, 1980, and 1981; the USKA Regional in 1976; and the AKBBA Regionals in 1980. Fuzy and Herrington annually co-produce the "Karate Pioneer Awards," which honors men and women who have contributed to the advancement of the martial arts. He also directs a martial arts entertainment team called Kicks.

GAILLAC, ROLLAND (1945-   ) French martial arts writer. Gaillac undertook judo and karate in 1960 with Romeu-Toulouse; he later studied Shotokan, tai-jutsu, and full-contact. Gaillac served as editor of *Karate,* a French martial arts magazine with a peak circulation of a quarter million during his tenure.

GALINDO, JOSE LUIS TORRES (1951-   ) Mexican karate competitor. Galindo began martial arts in 1968, earning a black belt under his original tae kwon do instructor, **David Moon,** in 1973. Affiliated with the **WTF** and **Jhoon Rhee's** World Black Belt League, Galindo was a member of Mexico City's professional team, the Aztecs. He is also Mexico's pioneer instructor in Europe, having taught in Germany, Austria and Spain. He was the 3rd-ranked world middleweight in *Professional Karate Magazine's* full-contact ratings in 1975.

GARCIA, DARNELL (1946-   ) American semicontact karate competitor. Garcia began martial arts study in 1966, receiving his black belt in 1971 from **Chuck Norris.** In 1972, Garcia won the grand championship of the **International Karate Championships.** During the years 1973 and 1974 he was rated among the top ten semicontact competitors by *Professional Karate Magazine.*

GEESINK, ANTON (1934-   ) Dutch world judo champion. The first man to best the Japanese at their own sport, Geesink dominated the sport from 1961, when he secured his first world title, until his retirement six years later. Between 1952 and 1967 he won 18 European individual titles. In addition, he was an openweight gold medalist in the 1964 Olympic Games.

In 1961, after strong showings in earlier matches, Geesink took the world title in Paris, defeating in successive rounds the three Japanese entrants, Kaminaga, Koga, and Sone. In 1964, when the sport first appeared in the Olympics, Geesink twice defeated Kaminaga, pinning him with a kesa gatame (scarf hold) in the finals.

In the 1965 World Judo Championships, held in Rio de Janeiro, Geesink defeated Matsunaga for the heavyweight title. He won his last major title in Rome, against Kiknadze of the USSR at the 1967 European Championships. Geesink retired from competition to become a professional judo instructor in Holland. He is the author of *Go-Kyo: Principles of Judo, Judo Principles: Newaza,* and *My Championship Judo. See also* Europe, history of judo in.

Anton Geesink of Holland, a living legend in European judo
Courtesy of Z. Modric

GEHLSON, JOHN (1937-73) American karate competitor; vice-president of the IKA. Gehlson began karate under **Tak Kubota.** A Shotokan stylist, he competed at the 1st WUKO World Karate Championships in Tokyo in 1970 as a member of the American team, and in 1972, at the 2nd World Championships in Paris.

GLAHN, KLAUS (1942-   ) West German judo heavyweight champion. Glahn won a bronze medal in the openweight category at the 1964 Olympic Games in Tokyo. At the 1972 Olympics he captured a silver medal, losing to world champion **Wilhelm Ruska.** Glahn has been European Judo Champion in 1963, 1968, and 1970, and has won silver medals at the 1967 and 1969 World Championships. Glahn is noted for his devastating **tai-otoshi** and superior matwork. *See also* Germany, history of martial arts in.

GLEESON, GEOFFREY ROBERT (1927-   ) British judo instructor and coach of the British National Judo Team. He was the first non-Oriental to become a special research student at the **Kodokan,** studying there from 1952 to 1955. In 1955, he was appointed chief instructor of the **Budokwai,** and two years later, captained a British team that won the European Judo Championships. He is the author of *Judo for the West, The Anatomy of Judo,* and *Better Judo. See also* Europe, history of judo in.

GONZALES, LATINO (1910-   ) Filipino karate master and pioneer; one of the world's most senior **shorin-ryu** masters. Gonzales was the first Filipino to learn shorin-ryu and subsequently introduced this style in the Philippines. He is the holder of the highest black belt rank issued by the Okinawan Shorin-ryu Karate-do Organization. He wrote a book, *Techniques of Okinawa Shorin-ryu Karate.*

GOTAY, ALBERT American karate instructor; student of **Peter Urban.** Gotay is an instructor of martial arts at the New York Police Academy, where he teaches judo, karate, jujutsu, and other self-defense sciences. He also teaches karate at several New York colleges.

GOULD, JERRY (1943-   ) American karate instructor and administrator. Gould began martial arts in 1966 with Norm Hamilton in Seattle, Wash. Presently he is chief instructor of the shobayashi shorin-ryu system in the U.S., as authorized by **Eizo Shimabuku,** and president of the Northwest Shorin-ryu Karate Association.

Besides winning numerous kata and weapons kata titles regionally Gould has been producer of the West Coast Regional Karate Championships since 1978 and the Shorin-ryu Open Karate Championships since 1974.

Jerry Gould, U.S. chief instructor of shorinryu karate, with kama. Gould is regarded as the Northwest's number-one competitor in weapons competition.

GRAHAM, DOUG (1944-   ) American judo champion. Winner of the 1972 AAU National Judo Championships, Doug·Graham began studying judo in 1960 while in high school. Graham received his black belt from George Wilson in 1961, and that same year, won his first of six Pacific Northwest Championships. Later he trained under **George Uchida** at San Jose State College in northern California. Graham won first place at the 1967 Pan-American Games; in 1970 he won the National Collegiate AAU Championships. He was named "Judo Player of the Year" in 1972 and inducted into the **Black Belt Hall of Fame.**

GRUSS, GILBERT (1943-   ) French heavyweight karate champion. A past amateur champion of France, of Europe, and the world. He was considered one of the best European fighters until his retirement in 1973. Second only to **Dominique Valera** in the 1970-71 European Championships, Gruss defeated Valera for the 1973 European title. A **wado-ryu** stylist, Gruss became coach of the French karate team after he retired from competition.

Gilbert Gruss

GRUZANSKI, CHARLES (-1976) American author and **manriki-gusari** expert. While stationed in Japan he began study of the traditional Japanese martial arts, a pursuit he continued for over 26 years. He is believed to have been the only non-Japanese to hold instructor's credentials in the esoteric art of masaki-ryu manriki-gusari. Gruzanski was a police officer and a self-defense instructor for the Chicago Police Academy, where he taught for more than ten years. During off-duty hours, he operated two large martial arts schools. He authored numerous magazine articles on police self-defense and in 1965 wrote *Knife Throwing as a Modern Sport.*

GUZMAN, RAMIRO (1954-   ) Mexican karate champion. Guzman began martial arts in 1967 and received his black belt in 1972 from **David Moon** in Houston, Tex. He now teaches tae kwon do and moo duk kwan in Mexico City and is technical director for the Association Moo Duk Kwan De Mexico.

Guzman's team placed first at the 1973 and 1974 Mexico Team Championships in Mexico City, where he also finished first in individual forms. His team also won the 1975 dual full-contact meet, Mexico vs. Dominican Republic.

In 1975, ranked number 1 contender, Guzman lost his bid for the inaugural world super-lightweight title in a 9-round decision won by **Gordon Franks** in West Berlin.

GWON, PU GILL (1936-   ) Korean-American tae kwon do instructor and author. With the outbreak of the Korean War in 1950, the Gwon family moved to Pusan, Korea, where the young Pu Gill took up Western boxing. In 1953, he won the Junior Boxing Championship at his school and began studying tae kwon do with Ha Dae Yong. In 1954, he also studied judo with Ko Tae Baek. Following graduation from high school, he trained in ji do kwan.

In 1964, Gwon began teaching judo under the auspices of the Kyung Ki Do Judo Association, and in 1966 was named director of the organization. In 1971, he visited the U.S., performing demonstrations, particularly breaking, at numerous martial arts expositions. He remained here and opened his first dojang in Baltimore, Md. By 1977, Gwon had moved to Los Angeles with eight schools throughout the U.S. under his supervision. He has written three books, *The Dynamic Art of Breaking, Skill in Counterattacks,* and *Basic Training for Kicking.*

GYI, DR. MAUNG (1933-   ) Burmese-American bando and karate instructor and author; founder of the **American Bando Association,** Maung Gyi came to the U.S. in 1960 after training in Burma and Japan, and competing in the 1956 World Olympics in Melbourne. He is a contributor to *Black Belt Magazine* and has written: *The Manual of Bando Discipline; Training for Kick Boxing;* and *The Art and Science of Burmese Bando Boxing.* A highly regarded tournament official, he was referee for the historic full-contact match between Bill Wallace and Joe Corley in 1975. *See also* U.S., history of karate in.

HALL, MARCIA (1956-   ) American tae kwon do world champion and instructor; first American to win a gold medal in international AAU tae kwon do competition. Hall began training in **Shotokan** karate in 1975 under John Stevenson of Mt. View, California, and in 1977 concurrently studied moo duk kwan tae kwon do with Marty Mackowski of San Mateo. In 1978 she received a black belt in both fighting arts and subsequently became active in AAU competition. She won the AAU Women's Middleweight US National Tae Kwon Do Championship in 1978, 1979, and 1980. She became the first American to win a gold medal in AAU tae kwon do competition when, in 1978, she defeated the Korean champion in Seoul, Korea, on Korean national television, for the AAU Women's Middleweight World Tae Kwon Do Championship. She successfully defended her world title in Taiwan one year later, winning a second gold medal.

In 1980, the women's division was cancelled at the AAU World Games, and Hall retired undefeated in AAU competition.

In 1981 Hall received an advanced black belt degree in moo duk kwan, a B.S. degree in human performance (kinesiology and physiology) from San Jose State, and a California coaching certificate. She currently teaches tae kwon do classes, specializing in industrial fitness and women's self-defense, throughout the Mt. View area of California. (Paul Maslak)

HALLIBURTON, ROBERT (1944-   ) American karate instructor and competitor. Halliburton is noted for his design of a comprehensive program to teach karate to the blind and for his work with the National Association for Mental Retardation. His handicapped students have demonstrated their self-defense expertise before social and civic groups. In competition, Halliburton's victories include the heavyweight title of the 1971 International Karate Championships. In 1975 he was named to *Who's Who in the Martial Arts.*

HAMA, HIDEO (1900-   ) Japanese-born American judo pioneer. In the early 1930s he was assistant to Kurozawa at the Tentokukan Dojo; after Kurozawa's death he took over the dojo, instructing there and in a number of other schools in the Seattle area. While interned in a wartime relocation center he taught American army officers. *See also* U.S., history of judo in.

HAMILTON, FRED (1925-   ) American karate instructor and promoter. Hamilton began karate in 1961 with John Slocum, receiving his black belt in **Shotokan** in 1965. In 1975 he hosted the first bare-knuckle full-contact professional tournament in the country. He was the first to allow women full participation in all categories of karate competition. From 1968 to 1973 Hamilton used karate in conjunction with Operation Helping Hand, a program for ghetto youth, and demonstrated the art at prisons and colleges. Currently, he operates a dojo in New York's Harlem area. Member of *Who's Who in the Martial Arts.*

HAMISH, ADAM Scottish karate champion and instructor. He was European Wado-ryu Champion in 1970, 1972, and 1974, and Scottish individual champion twice.

HAN, BONG SOO (1931-   ) Korean-born American **hapkido** instructor. Han studied hapkido in his native country under **Yong Shul Choi.** He immigrated to the U.S. in 1968. In 1971, while giving a demonstration in Los Angeles, Han met filmmaker Tom Laughlin. As a result of the meeting hapkido was incorporated into the film *Billy Jack,* in which Han directed fight scenes and doubled for Laughlin. It was the first motion picture to employ martial arts as a significant part of the story line, and it paved the way for what has been called the first martial arts movie boom, which lasted until mid-1974 and accounted for a tremendous surge in popularity for the arts worldwide.

Han served as technical advisor for *Cleopatra Jones* and *Shanks.* In *The Trial of Billy Jack,* the 1975 sequel, he appeared in a supporting role in addition to creating and directing fight scenes. In 1976 Han starred in the satire *A Fistful of Yen* (a take-off on Bruce Lee's *Enter the Dragon),* part of the trilogy for *The Kentucky Fried Movie,* a cult classic. Han starred opposite world karate champion **Joe Lewis** in *Force: Five,* a martial arts adventure filmed in 1981.

In 1974 he wrote *Hapkido: The Korean Art of Self-Defense.* Named to *Who's Who in the Martial Arts* in 1975. *See also* motion pictures and television.

HAN HSING-TZU One of the **Eight Immortals;** said to have the power to make flowers grow and blossom instantly.

HANSON, HOWARD (1933-   ) American karate pioneer, instructor, and promoter. Hanson's formal training did not begin until 1970, at 37, in the Okinawan art of **shorin-ryu** karate. In 1973 he was promoted to black belt by **Mike Stone.** In 1974 he began co-promoting independent **semicontact** events in Hawaii with Mike Stone, Henry Awau, and Arnold Urquidez. Later he attempted to promote **full-contact** karate on a national basis through the **PKA.** But in late October 1976, after co-promoting Bill Wallace's title defense against Gary Edens and Benny Urquidez' title defense against Eddie Andujar, Hanson broke away to form the **World Karate Association** (WKA) with his original co-promoters, Arnold Urquidez and Henry Awau.

He was responsible for bringing countries from the Orient into professional karate by requiring the use of the outer thigh kick and sweeps in world title bouts. He treated professional fighters as free-agents, barred management contracts as a condition for title challengership, required that titles be won only in the ring, and lost only through a ring defeat or voluntary retirement. He required that champions defend their titles against the highest ranked contender available.

Hanson established the first world championship divisions for women. He replaced the WKA world rating list with the independently controlled **STAR System.** And he incorporated the WKA as the first non-profit governing body for professional karate. In October 1979 Hanson was awarded an advanced dan ranking by Masafumi Suzuki for his contributions to the martial arts.

As a promoter, Hanson, by 1981, had produced three professional karate events for national broadcast on NBC-TV, three events for live telecast on Japanese national television, five events which established a WKA world champion in various divisions, a large number of events that featured a WKA world title defense, and over 52 taped events that were in national and international syndication. On November 14, 1977, Hanson co-promoted the Benny Urquidez title defense against Kunimatsu Okao, which yielded the largest live gate on record for professional karate, $500,000. Hanson was promotionally responsible for the international stardom of Benny Urquidez. (PAUL MASLAK) *See also* full-contact; U.S., history of karate in; World Karate Association.

HARKINS, JIM (1947-) American karate competitor and instructor. Harkins trained, beginning in 1964, under **Pat Burleson** and **Fred Wren.** As a brown belt, Harkins won first place in the 1969 U.S. Championships in Dallas. Harkins promoted the Colorado State Championships, Rocky Mountain Pro/Am, Four Seasons Championships, and the Colorado Open Championships. In 1975 he was named to *Who's Who in the Martial Arts.*

He is a member of Karyn Turner's Hard Knocks, a martial arts performing troupe, which has performed on television and at major karate tournaments in the U.S.

HARRIS, GEORGE American judo champion. Member of the 1964 U.S. Olympic team, Harris is a three-time gold medal winner in the Pan-American Games and placed fifth twice in the World Championships in Paris and Japan. He reigned as heavyweight champion of the U.S. in 1957, 1958, 1960, and 1961, and overall champion in 1957, 1958, and 1961. Harris began his training while at Travis Air Force base, where he was stationed with the Strategic Air Command. He has traveled to Japan to study and has been one of the leaders in the Armed Forces judo program. *See also* U.S., history of judo in.

HARRISON, ERNEST JOHN (1883-1971) British journalist, author, diplomat, linguist, and martial artist. In 1919, Harrison joined London's **Budokwai,** England's judo mecca, and remained an active member until his death at age 88. He was the first Caucasian to become a 3rd-degree black belt in judo, during the mid-1900s. The first Westerner to write prolifically about the martial arts, Harrison wrote his classic, *The Fighting Spirit of Japan,* in 1912. The book examines the esoteric principles of the Japanese martial arts.

Harrison's other books include: *The Art of Ju-Jitsu* (1932); *Judo* (1930); *Judo-At-A-Glance* (1954); *Judo for Beginners* (1954); *Judo for Girls* (1954); *Judo for Women* (1957); *Judo on the Ground* (1954); *Junior Judo* (1958); *Kodokan Judo* (1956); *The Manual of Judo* (1952); *The Manual of Karate* (1959); *My Method of Judo* (1955); *My Method of Self-Defense* (1957); and *Theory and Practice of Judo* (1928). He also translated a number of judo books into English, including two by Mikonosuke Kawaishi.

HARRISON, JANET WALGREN (1947-) American karate champion and instructor. Winning or placing in every tournament she entered, Harrison has won numerous national championships and in 1969 was named "Women's National Tournament Champion" by the **USKA.** Her wins include: 1968 Central State Championships; 1968 and 1969 USKA National Championships; and the 1969 National Open Championships. A member of the *Who's Who in the Martial Arts,* she served as coordinator for the USKA Nationals in 1967, 1968, and 1969. She also created the Miss Karate Beauty Pageant presented in conjunction with the 1969 Nationals.

HARRISON, JIM (1936-) American karate and judo champion, instructor, and referee. A former AAU judo champion, Harrison has won numerous national karate titles and was the 1970 U.S. light-heavyweight kick-boxing champion. He has officiated at every major tournament in America and served as co-chief referee of the 1974 World Professional Karate Championship, where **full-contact** karate

was spawned. He trained several national champions including his former wife, **Janet Walgren Harrison,** and judo champion Harry Parker. Sponsor of a number of major tournaments, including the very first professional karate tournament in the U.S. in 1968 in Kansas City, Kans., Harrison is a member of *Who's Who in the Martial Arts* and author of *Professional Karate Magazine's* "Self-Defense Textbook" series. *See also* U.S., history of karate in.

HASSELL, RANDALL G. (1948-) American karate instructor, author, and writer, a student of **Hidetaka Nishiyama** since 1961, under whose tutelage he has studied **Shotokan** karate. In addition to his karate training, he has over twelve years of experience in jujutsu, judo, and aikido.

While majoring in English Literature at Washington University in St. Louis, he began an intense, formal study of the history and philosophy of the martial arts in general, and karate-do in particular. This study led to the publication of numerous articles on the history and philosophy of karate-do and more than a dozen technical manuals, many of which are in use today by thousands of karate students. In 1979 he devised the "Self Protection for Women" program for the Greater St. Louis YWCA's, and wrote *Rape Prevention: A Study Guide.* This program has trained thousands of women in the mechanics and psychology of rape prevention.

He organized the first Shotokan karate club in the St. Louis area in 1962, and served as chairman of the Missouri Karate Association from 1966-72. In 1973 he was appointed chief instructor and regional director of the Central Region (Missouri, Kansas, Iowa, Nebraska, Oklahoma) of the **American Amateur Karate Federation** and the Japan Karate Association International of America. Hassell has served as tournament director at over 100 tournaments, and holds a judge's license from the International Amateur Karate Federation. In addition to technical manuals, he has written extensively for martial arts publications and is the author of *The Karate Experience, A Way of Life* and *The Karate Spirit: Tradition and Science.*

HATASHITA, FRANK Japanese-Canadian judo champion and instructor. Hatashita began judo at six under 7th dan S. Sasaki in Vancouver. He has won the All Canada Judo Championships three times. President of the Canadian Kodokan Black Belt Association (CKBBA), Hatashita was a Kodokan kenshusei (research student). He coached Canadian teams for the Olympics and the World Championships.

HATSUMI, MASAAKI DR. (1931-) Japanese **ninjutsu** master and author. Thirty-fourth grandmaster of Togakure ryu ninjutsu. Hatsumi

Dr. Masaaki Hatsumi

earned black belt teacher rank in judo, kendo, karate, and aikido. Dissatisfied with these styles he tried western boxing, classical **kobudo,** and finally ninjutsu, under Toshitsugu Takamatsu, 33rd grandmaster of Tokagure ryu.

Hatsumi journeyed weekly across the countryside from his home in Noda City to the training hall of Takamatsu in Kashiwara City. Before his death in 1972, Takamatsu awarded his title of soke, or head of the family, to Hatsumi. Having since trained a new generation of master teachers, Dr. Hatsumi has retired from active teaching. He devoted his first twenty years in the martial arts to what he calls the "front," or omote—rigorous training, unquestioning respect for seniors, and traditional concepts of the Japanese warrior morality. His next twenty years were devoted to the "back," or ura—the warrior's capabilities. In 1971 he co-authored *Stick Fighting,* and in 1981 he wrote *Ninjutsu: History and Tradition.* (STEPHEN K. HAYES) *See also* ninja; ninjutsu.

HAVANAS, DEMETRIUS (1950-81) American karate champion and instructor. In 1967 Havanas, also known as the "Greek" or the "Golden Greek of Texas," began martial arts training at one of **Allen Steen's** karate schools in Dallas. Over the years he trained with Jerry Wiseman, Tim Tiah, Larry Caster, **Skipper Mullins,** and **Fred Wren.** As a brown belt he won 90 straight tournaments in both form and fighting competition. He received his black belt in 1971, and won thirteen grand championships in the same year. From 1971-75 Havanas was consistently rated among America's top 10 karate fighters.

In 1975, entering **full-contact** competition, he won the PKA U.S. Welterweight Championship. He amassed a record of 39-4 with 24 knockouts, and the **STAR System** ranked him number-one world welterweight contender in 1980-81.

Scheduled for a world title fight against champion Howard Jackson, he was killed on June 23, 1981, in an airplane accident. (DUANE ETHINGTON)

HAYAKAWA, NORIMASA (1947-   ) Japanese karate competitor. A **Shotokan** stylist, he was second in the All Japan Championships in 1975 and won the Asian Pacific Ocean Championships.

HAYASHI, TERUO Okinawan karate instructor, a foremost exponent of the Okinawan system of **kubudo.** Hayashi trained in judo and karate under such masters as Kosei Kokuba (Shito-ryu), **Shoshin Nagamine** (shorin-ryu), and Seiko Higa (goju-ryu). With difficulty, he persuaded Kenko Nakaima, a great weapons expert, to instruct him in kobudo. He demonstrated at the 1st World Karate Championships in Japan, and again at the 2nd World Championships in Paris. He now travels, teaching in his many dojos in the U.S. and Europe.

HAYASHIZAKI, JINSUKE SHIGENOBU (1543-1616) Japanese **iaijutsu** pioneer. Considered by historians the father of modern schools of iaijutsu (sword drawing art), Hayashizaki was a **samurai** whose deeds have been lost to time.

HAYES, BILL American karate instructor. Hayes began karate in 1962 with Ron Taganashi and studied **bando** until 1967 when he was sent to Vietnam, where he taught his art. In Okinawa he undertook **shorin-ryu** karate with **Eizo Shimabuku.** Hayes became the Dai Sempai, or "right-hand man" of the master. He was named military affairs director of the USKA.

HAYES, JOSEPH (1946-   ) American karate competitor. A one-time boxer and cross-country runner, Hayes began martial arts at 17, receiving his black belt in 1966 from **Richard Chun.** A three-time member of *Black Belt Magazine's* U.S. top 10 (second in 1970 and 1971 and fourth in 1969), he won the Universal Open Championships, from 1967-72; the All American Karate Championships in 1969, 1971; American Tang Soo Do Championships in 1970; and placed second at the 1973 World Tae Kwon Do Championships in Seoul, Korea. Hayes also has won awards for kata and sportsmanship. He was named to the **Black Belt Hall of Fame** in 1972 as "Karate Player of the Year."

HAYES, STEPHEN KURTZ (1949-   ) American **ninjutsu** instructor and author, sole American disciple of Togakure ryu ninjutsu

grandmaster **Masaaki Hatsumi.** Hayes began his formal martial arts training at Oxford, Ohio's Miami University karate club. Hayes earned his black belt and taught beginner karate classes for the Miami University Physical Education Department. He traveled in the U.S., Europe, Arctic, and Mediterranean regions, studying with martial arts teachers as he found them. Hayes journeyed to Japan in 1975 to seek instruction in the art of ninjutsu and was accepted as a student of Tsunehisa Tanemura, a master teacher of the Togakure ryu ninja tradition and began his training in Noda City, Japan. He later returned to Atlanta, Ga., and brought Tanemura to his U.S. dojo to teach a select group of his students. In 1977 Hayes was invited to become a personal student of Tsunehisa Tanemura's teacher, Dr. Masaaki Hatsumi; he put his dojo in Atlanta under the direction of Joseph Beaver and moved to Japan for intensive training.

While living in Japan, Hayes worked as an actor and stuntman in Japanese television and movie productions and appeared in NBC's miniseries *Shogun.* He became the only American to attain the rank of shidoshi, or "teacher of the warrior ways of enlightenment," in a Japanese ninja ryu. In 1980 Hayes wrote *Ninja, Spirit of the Shadow Warrior,* and in 1981 *The Ninja and Their Secret Fighting Art.* Hayes travels between homes in Kumamoto, Japan, and Ohio, and supervises ninja training in his Shadows of Iga dojos.

HEBLER, DAVE American karate instructor and one-time personal bodyguard to the late **Elvis Presley.** Hebler began karate in 1958 under **Ed Parker** and later opened his own dojo in Glendora, Calif., where he taught for eleven years. He met Presley in 1972 while practicing at Parker's studio in West Los Angeles. Hired as a full-time bodyguard, a position he maintained until 1976, Hebler was one of four karate instructors who actually taught Presley.

Shortly after being fired by Presley, Hebler collaborated with Red and Sonny West and writer Steve Dunleavy in 1976 to produce the controversial book, *Elvis, What Happened?* Today he teaches karate in San Clemente, Calif.

HEINTZ, PIERRE French karate competitor, a **wado-ryu** stylist. He was French university champion in 1971, 1972, and 1974, and a member of the winning French team at the 1975 European Championships.

HERRINGTON, CURTIS RAY (1936-   ) American karate instructor and promoter. Herrington began martial arts in 1956 while stationed in Korea, receiving his black belt from Robert Moore in 1964. He instructs in ji do kwan, but also studied judo, jujutsu, isshinryu, Shotokan, shorin-ryu, and hapkido. He promoted the 1968 Texas State Karate Championships, the 1967 USKA Invitational, the 1974, 1975, 1980, and 1981 Northern States Karate Championships, and the 1976 USKA Regionals as well as the 1980 AKBBA Regionals.

HERRMAN, PETER West German judo champion; a light-heavyweight who won bronze medals in the light-heavyweight and openweight divisions at the 5th World Championships in 1967. He won the West German Championships a number of times and gold medals at the European Judo Championships. Herrman has also won the European Police Championships several times. Noted for his **taiotoshi, ouchigari,** and **newaza.** *See also* Germany, history of martial arts in.

HEUNG, CHAN (1806-75) Chinese kung-fu master, founder of the **Choy-Li-Fut** system. Heung was born in the village of King Mui and began training at an early age with his uncle, a famous boxer. By 15 he was a skilled fighter enrolled for study with Lee Yau-shan. In a few years he surpassed his teacher and sought instruction from a monk, Choy Fok. After eight years spent learning martial arts, he returned to his village, where he created the Choy-Li-Fut style.

In 1864 Heung traveled to San Francisco, where he taught martial arts to the Chinese. He remained in the U.S. for four years, returning at age 63 to his homeland.

HI, GEN. CHOI HONG (1918-   ) Korean founder of tae kwon do. As a frail and sickly youth, he studied calligraphy and **taekyon** under the tutelage of Han II Dong. His turbulent political and military career began with an expulsion at 12 for organizing a student walkout, and includes a Japanese imprisonment for complicity in plans to overthrow the wartime military government of Korea.

In 1937 Hi was sent to Japan to further his education and subsequently met a countryman by the name of Kim who taught Japanese karate. There followed a period of both mental and physical training, preparatory school, and finally the university in Tokyo.

With the outbreak of World War II, Hi was forced to join the Japanese Army as a student volunteer. Toward the latter part of the war, he received a seven-year prison sentence when his plans to overthrow the Japanese military through the Pyongyang student soldier's movement were discovered. Korea's liberation from Japanese rule in August 1945 spared Hi from serving a full sentence. That same year, he enrolled in an English military school, which was later to become the Korean Military Academy. On January 15, 1946, he was commissioned a second lieutenant in the new Korean Army.

Hi was promoted to captain and then major in 1947. The next year he was stationed in Seoul as head of logistics and became tae kwon do instructor for the American Military Police School there. In late 1948 he became a lieutenant colonel. In 1949, Hi was promoted to full colonel, and in 1951, brigadier general. He was named Chief of Staff in 1952, and was responsible for briefing General MacArthur during the latter's visit to Kang Nung.

While engaged in military duties, Gen. Hi conducted research on ancient Korean taekyon, Japanese karate, and Chinese kung-fu. In 1955 he christened tae kwon do, both in name and organized practice, spreading it to universities and military posts throughout Korea. In March 1959 Gen. Hi led the ROK (Republic of Korea) Army Tae Kwon Do Team, consisting of nineteen members, on a demonstration tour to the Republic of China and to Vietnam. Also in 1959, he published his first Korean-language text on the subject, which became the model for his 1965 edition.

In 1965 Ambassador Hi, a retired two-star general, was appointed by the ROK to lead a tae kwon do goodwill mission to Europe, the Middle East, Africa, and Asia. This led to the formation of the **International Taekwon-Do Federation** (ITF) in March 1966.

In August 1967 he visited the All American Tae Kwon Do Championships, a visit which led to the establishment of the U.S. Tae Kwon Do Association in Washington, D.C., with **Jhoon Rhee** appointed as its first Secretary General. Following numerous trips around the world to establish, promote, and solidify his art, Gen. Hi was also instrumental in introducing it to many universities in Europe, the Americas, the Middle East, and the Far East.

In 1974 Gen. Hi moved the headquarters of his ITF from Korea to Toronto and reported that his organization no longer had any affiliation with Korea. Since his departure a new organization, the **World Taekwon-do Federation,** has been formed and is now considered the administrative body for worldwide tae kwon do. His publications include *Taekwon-Do Guidelines, A Taekwon-Do Manual* (1965) and *Taekwon-Do* (1972)—518 pages with nearly 3,300 photographs, the most ambitious work yet written on a single martial art. *See also* tae kwon do.

HIGA, TERUYUKI Okinawan-born karate and weapons instructor. He holds a black belt in **Okinawan kempo**. Higa immigrated to the U.S. in 1967, eventually settling in New York. He is director of the All Okinawa Kempo Karate-do League and the All Okinawa Classical Weapons Association.

HIGA (SHI) ONNA, KANRYO (1851-1915) Okinawan karate pioneer; a Naha-te master, regarded as one of the most influential karate instructors in Okinawan history. He sailed from Okinawa in 1866, at 15, to Fukien province, China. There he is said to have spent more than twenty years training under a famous Chinese kempo master, Liu Liu Ko. He returned to Okinawa during the middle of the Meiji era (1868-1911) and introduced a new school of karate there, distinguished from other styles by its integration of go-no (soft) kempo and ju-no (hard) kempo into one system.

Higashionna's reputation rivalled that of Shuri-te's **Yastusune Itosu** (they were good friends throughout their lives). A Confucian scholar as well, he counseled future generations: "Those who learn karate should help others. Karate contains 'jutsu' (art) and 'do' (spirit). Never seek trouble and refrain from quarrels." Most prominent among his disciples was **Chojun Miyagi,** his top student and the founder of **goju-ryu;** others include **Juhatsu Kyoda** (a Naha-te exponent), Seiko Higa (Miyagi's assistant), **Kenwa Mabuni** (founder of **Shito-ryu** karate), **Kanken Toyama** (founder of **shudokan** karate),and **Tatsuo Shimabuku** (founder of **isshinryu**).

Grandmaster Kanryo Higashionna, the highest authority of Naha-te.

Higashionna was noted for his powerful **Sanchin** kata. Sometimes he would permit four men to attempt to push him out of his stance, but they were always unable to move him. It is said that after finishing his Sanchin form, the wooden floor would be hot from the mere gripping of his toes. (ANTHONY MIRAKIAN) *See also* Okinawa, history of martial arts in.

HIGAONNA, MORIO Okinawan karate master, a high ranking **goju-ryu** stylist. Higaonna began karate at 14 with his father, at first in **shorin-ryu,** but later, in high school, in goju-ryu. After the death of **Chojun Miyagi,** the founder of goju, his heir, **Meitoku Yagi,** invited Higaonna, then 17, to study with him. During his high school years, he also began the study of Okinawan **kobujutsu** (weaponry) with Kasahara. While at Takushoku University in Japan he taught Okinawan goju at a Japanese dojo, attracting a large following. He has visited the U.S., South Africa, England, and Portugal.

HIGGINS, WILLIAM (1946-) British karate champion; ranked among the top karate fighters of Europe. A European middleweight champion in 1974 and 1975, he was a runner-up at the 1972 World Championships in Paris. A karate instructor in England, Higgins has been ranked in the European Top Ten since 1970. He captained the British team which won the title at the 1975 World Championships in Long Beach, Calif. Standing 5'7", 155 pounds, he is especially effective and accurate with the reverse punch and is known for his aggressive style.

HIKIDA, BUNGORO (ca. 1537-1606) Japanese master swordsman and founder of the Hikida ryu (known also as the Hikida-kage ryu). Hikida was the first swordsman known to have used the **shinai.** He is immortalized as one of the **shi tenno** or "four kings" of the sword.

HILL, TARRENCE "TOKEY" (1957-) American karate champion. Winner of the 1980 WUKO World Championships in Madrid. Tokey began martial arts training in 1972 under Don Madden, and received his black belt from that same sensei in 1976. He earned his 3rd dan from Katsmi Niikura in Japan. Hill is currently affiliated with the USKA and the Seui-kan.

Traveling the world competing in noncontact competition, Tokey won the All Japan Karate Championships in 1978 as well as the Caracaz Kata International title. He was AAU National Champion for 1978, 1979, and 1980. In 1980, he also won the USKA light-heavyweight title, the Trias International Award, and "Competitor of the Year" award.

The most notable award that he won in 1980 was the 5th WUKO World Championships, the first American competitor ever to do so. *See also* U.S., history of karate in.

HIRAI, MINORU Japanese aikido instructor. One of the senior disciples of **Morihei Ueshiba**, founder of the korindo style of aikido.

HIRANO, KIYOHISA Japanese-American karate instructor. Kiyohisa Hirano studied **wado-ryu** in Japan, earning his black belt at 15. In 1960 he won the All Japan Karate Championships and captained a winning Nihon University team in 1961. Hirano came to Hawaii in 1962, on a demonstration tour with his instructor, and decided to stay. He now runs the Japanese International Karate Center there.

HIRANO, TAKEMICHI (1947-) Japanese karate champion; **wado-ryu** stylist. Hirano is winner of the 1973 and 1974 All Japan Wado-Kai tournaments, and three-time winner of the East Japan Tournament, held by the All Japan Karate-do Federation, in 1970, 1971, and 1972. In 1972 and 1973 he also won the All Japan Non-Student Karate Tournament.

HISAMORI, TAKENOUCHI Japanese jujutsu master; founder of **Takenouchi-ryu**, which some historians regard as the seminal system for all jujutsu. He established his style in 1532, borrowing heavily from **sumo** techniques.

HISATAKA, KORI (1907-) Okinawan born karate master, founder of **Kentokan** karate-do. He began his martial arts training while very young and studied under such reknowned masters as Choyun Kyamu. In 1929 he toured Taiwan where he competed against top kempo practitioners, then returned to Japan where he entered the Kodokan and reached a 4th dan black belt. He also studied kendo and Shorinryu kempo. After the war he formulated his system of kenko-kan and opened his first dojo, the Kenkokan School of Karate-do in Kyushu.

HISATAKA, MASAYUKI (1940-) Japanese karate-do instructor, author, and champion. Hisataka, a descendent of Kyowa, the 56th Emperor of Japan, his training in judo and karate-do at the age of 3. He obtained his black belt in both disciplines at 13. Although successful in full-contact matches—he won all of his fights by knockout—he left this sport to dedicate his time to karate-do.

Hisataka never lost in noncontact competition, winning the All Japan Open Karate-Do Championships in 1961 and 1962, and the Shorinji-ryu Kenkokan Karate-Do Championships five consecutive years, from 1958-62. The Japanese government selected Hisataka to represent Japanese martial arts at the World's Fairs of 1964 and 1967. In 1976 he wrote *Scientific Karate-do*, a description of the style he helped found, Shorinji-ryu kenkokan.

HISATAKE, ARTHUR KOJI (-1972) Hawaiian-born karate instructor. A former U.S. Army sergeant serving in Korea and Europe, Hisatake taught **kyokushinkai** karate all over Europe. He was also a top referee, often giving refereeing clinics.

HITOTSUYANAGI, ORIBE Japanese jujutsu instructor of the 19th century, a master of the **yoshin-ryu** style.

HOFFMAN, WOLFGANG West German middleweight judo champion. Many times a winner of the German Judo Championships, he became an international star when he won a silver medal at the 1964 Olympic Games, losing only to All Japan Champion Isao Okano. At the 1965 European Championships he won the gold medal. In the 1969 European Games, he was a member of the winning West German team, defeating Anatoly Bondarenbo, a strong Soviet competitor. Hoffman favors **uchimata** and **seoinage**, and is especially strong on the mat. *See also* Europe, history of judo in.

HOLTMANN, AL American judo pioneer. He began studying judo in Hawaii in 1940. Having served as a sergeant major in the U.S. Marines during World War II, he enrolled at San Diego State University after the war and began giving instruction in judo. He opened the first judo school in San Diego in 1949, still in operation today at the same location. Two of his students, Tokuji Hirata and Ben Tsuji, were technical advisors for the maiden issues of *Black Belt Magazine* in 1961. Holtmann estimates he has taught some 60,000 students over the years, and he has former students in every state in the country.

HO-NGAU Chinese kung-fu master in Hong Kong known for his mastery of the T'sai-Li-Fu style of Chinese martial arts.

HON-SAN Chinese kung-fu master in Hong Kong known for his mastery of several styles of Chinese martial arts.

HOMMA, JOYEMON Nineteenth century Japanese jujutsu master of the **shin-no-shindo** style.

HONG, WAI Chinese-born kung-fu instructor, founder of the Fu Jow Pai Federation. Hong began kung-fu at 5 with his grandfather and father. He studied other styles, including the fu jow (tiger claw) system under grandmaster Wong Moon Toy. In 1960, when Toy died, Hong became his successor; he teaches in the U.S.

HONG, WAI A kung-fu master, he is the third generation successor to the Fu-Jow Pai system. Born in Canton, China, he began his training as a child, learning hung gar, mi-chung-i, choy li fut, and t'ai-chi-ch'uan. He is the founder of the Eastern U.S. Kung-fu Federation as well as the author of *The Secret of Fu-Jow Pai.* He teaches today out of New York City, and has trained a number of high quality students as well as instructors many of whom now teach all over the world.

HOO, MARSHAL An American t'ai-chi-ch'uan instructor, he has studied with such masters as Huang Wen-shan and Tun Fu-lin. He was chosen to the Black Belt Hall of Fame in 1973 and has taught at the California Institute for the Arts. He teaches at the Aspen Academy of the Martial Arts and is also an acupuncturist.

HOTGER, DIETMAR East German judo champion. A welterweight, Hotger has won the European Championships a number of times and a bronze medal at the 1972 Olympic Games. At the 1973 World Championships he was a silver medalist.

HSU-CHI (HSU, ADAM) Chinese kung-fu master, martial arts columnist, and editor. Hsu grew up in Taiwan, although he was born in Shanghai. He was chosen a member of the R.O.C. National Kung-fu Delegation

Hsu-Chi

that performed in Asian countries. Hsu studied several northern styles of kung-fu, which he teaches in San Francisco.

He learned pa-chi and pi-kua from master Liu-Yun-Chiao, who in turn studied under Li-Su-Wen. He also learned **Mi-T'sung-I** from Liu, who acquired the art from Chiang-Yao-Ting, and **pa-kua,** whose lineage descends through Liu from Kang-Pao-Tien, who learned from Yin-Fu, a student of Tung-Hai-Chuan. He learned Ch'en t'ai-chi from Tu-Yu-Tze, the line reaching back to Chen-Yen-Hsi and Chen-Gen-Yuan; he learned **hsing-i** from Chao-lian-feng, and chang-ch'uan from Han-Ching-Tang. Finally, Hsu learned three systems of **praying mantis:** the seven stars style from Li-Kwun-San, the eight steps style from Wei-Shau-Tang, and the six harmonies style from Chang-Hsian-San.

Hsu is noted for his ability with the single broadsword, single sword, long staff, and large spear. (MICHAEL P. STAPLES)

HU, WILLIAM C.C. Chinese-American kung-fu historian, scholar, and writer. Hu was born in Honolulu, Hawaii, and was educated in China, Japan, and the U.S. He earned several degrees and is currently a consultant in authenticating Oriental art, in Saline, Mich.

Hu began his study of the martial arts in the 1930s with Fang Yu-Shu in China. He trained in **t'ai-chi ch'uan** (Chen school) and tao-chia ch'uan, and pa-chi ch'uan. He is affiliated with the Chinese Physical Culture Association, in which he has held various offices including director of martial arts, senior instructor, and Chinese secretary. He was also trained in the Peking Opera, where he specialized in military roles; his stage name is Shao-wen Hu.

A noted scholar and one of the first martial arts writers in America, he has written historical articles for *Black Belt Magazine* beginning in 1960 and contributed to *Karate Illustrated, Fighting Stars,* and *Inside Kung Fu.*

HUANG-TI The Yellow Emperor, who wrote *Huang-Ti Nei-Ching Su-Wen (Yellow Emperor's Classic of Internal Medicine).* According to legend, he had a transparent navel to better observe the effects of different herbs on his metabolism.

HUA T'O (190-265) Famous Chinese surgeon believed to have devised breathing and physical exercises to tone the body and relieve emotional stress. His method was based on the movements of five animals: tiger, bird, deer, bear, and monkey.

HUNG, LEE KOON Chinese kung-fu instructor. He began Choy-Li-Fut at 12 under the late master Dic Pon. After eight years of study he became an instructor, and six years later was given permission to open his own school.

In 1975 Hung participated in the 4th Asian Full-Contact Kung-Fu Competition in Singapore. His students took first, second, and third places in different weight categories. In 1978 he represented Hong Kong at the 2nd International Mardi Gras Festival in Paris, winning second place among the thirteen nations present.

HUO YUAN-CHIA (1862-1909) Famous Chinese boxer who established the Ching Wu Athletic Association in Shanghai, the most influential **wu shu** institution in China other than the **Shao-lin Temple.**

HURLEY, CARSON (1939-) American karate instructor, competitor, and organizer; founder of the Mid-East Karate Association (MEKA) in 1973. Hurley won the 1972 Tae Kwon Do Grand Championships and the North Carolina Grand Championships in 1968. In 1974 he was rated among the top 10 competitors in his region by *Professional Karate Magazine.* A member of the *Who's Who in the Martial Arts,* Hurley established karate courses at two Virginia colleges.

HWANG, IN-SOO (1933-) Korean-American tae kwon do and judo instructor. Hwang was tournament director of the 1st National AAU Tae Kwon Do Championships, and is the vice-president of the **USJF.**

HWANG, JACK (1931-) Korean-American tae kwon do instructor, pioneer, and promoter. Hwang is president of the American Tae Kwon Do Federation and founder of the All-American Open Karate Championships in Oklahoma City. A recipient of *Official Karate Magazine's* "Instructor of the Year" award, he was coach of the American team that competed in Seoul, Korea, in 1973. Hwang

staged a number of benefit demonstrations to help charities raise money. Member of *Who's Who in the Martial Arts. See also* U.S., history of karate in.

HYAMS, JOE (1923-) American author and karate pioneer. A World War II combat correspondent and a syndicated columnist, Hyams began martial arts in 1952 as a **kenpo** student of **Ed Parker.** He was influential in introducing the martial arts to Hollywood, occasionally including them in his own screenplays. He co-wrote a 1978 "Quincy" episode, *Touch of Death,* which focused on the delayed death touch as a mysterious means of murder. In 1980 he wrote *Zen in the Martial Arts,* composed of anecdotes of his personal learning experiences with prominent masters including Parker, **Bruce Lee,** and **Bong Soo Han.** A best-seller in its field, the book was immediately recognized as a modern classic. In 1981 he wrote *Playboy's Book of Practical Self-defense.*

In October 1972, vacationing in Europe with his wife, actress Elke Sommer, Hyams suffered a severe attack of Weill's disease, a rare and usually fatal virus. In the intensive-care unit of a German hospital, lapsing in and out of consciousness, Hyams exercised a Zen breathing technique he had learned in aikido training. "The more I concentrated on my breathing, the more immune I became to the fear that I was dying," he says. Three weeks later he was discharged. Zen breathing had, perhaps miraculously, saved his life.

Hyams was an editorial consultant for this encyclopedia. *See also* U.S., history of karate in.

Left to right: Bill Wallace, Emil Farkas, Joe Hyams, and John Corcoran

HYON, JAY (1936-) Korean-born American tae kwon do instructor. Hyon emigrated from Seoul in 1966, settling in Minneapolis and opening a dojo. In 1974 and 1975 he served as the national vice chairman of the AAU Tae Kwon Do Committee, and was team coach for the 2nd World Tae Kwon Do Championships.

IMRE, VARGA (1945-) Hungarian judo competitor. Varga fights in the 95-kg. category and in the open division. He placed third at the 1979 World Championships, second at the 1978 European Championships, and second at the 1980 European Championships.

INOKUMA, ISAO (1938-) Japanese judo champion. Inokuma was the youngest person ever to win the **All Japan Judo Championships,** in 1959 at 21. His use of the shoulder throw and the body drop upset **A. Kaminaga** in 1959, but in 1960 and 1961, Kaminaga defeated him in the finals. Inokuma regained the title in 1963, and at the 1964 Olympic Games in Tokyo, he won the heavyweight gold medal. In the 1965 World Judo Championships, he defeated the Russian Kibrotsashvili to win the openweight gold medal and his last major title. Inokuma is currently a professor of physical education at Tokai University and an international referee. In 1979 he co-authored *Best Judo.*

INOSANTO, DAN (1936-) American **jeet kune do** and **arnis** instructor and author. One of two surviving original instructors of jeet kune do (way of the intercepting fist), **Bruce Lee's** personal combat method, Inosanto worked closely with Lee in developing the art and its training methods. Under the guidance of **Ed Parker** he studied conventional forms of karate, including **kenpo.** Inosanto is also an instructor in the Philippine arts of escrima, **arnis de mano, kali, silat, kuntao,** dumog, and sikaran, and he founded the only Philippine martial arts academy in southern California. Located in Carson, a suburb of Los Angeles, the academy serves as the world headquarters of jeet kune do.

He has written *Escrima,* co-authored with Ciraco Cadiente, *Filipino Escrima, The Art of Combat,* and *Jeet Kune Do;* he co-authored *The Flying Phalanges, Boxing and Kick-Boxing,* and collaborated with editor Gilbert Johnson on Bruce Lee's posthumous *The Tao of Jeet Kune Do.* In the years 1966 through 1970, Inosanto was instrumental in developing jun fan kick-boxing, the method of contact sparring in jeet kune do. Film appearances include roles in the "Green Hornet"; the final Bruce Lee film, *Game of Death;* Sam Peckinpah's *The Killer Elite;* and *Sharky's Machine* with Burt Reynolds. Inosanto was named to *Who's Who in the Martial Arts* in 1975. *See also* U.S., history of karate in; jeet kune do; kali.

INOUE, MOTOKATSU Japanese **kobu-jutsu** master. Inoue began jujutsu at 10, with Seiko Fujita. He later joined his university **sumo** club and studied karate with Tasuhiro Konishi. He next took up aikido, with **Gozo Shioda,** and studied Okinawan weapons with one of the greatest experts of the time, **Shinken Taira.** When Taira died in 1970, Inoue became the president of the Society for Promotion and Preservation of Ryukyu Martial Arts. Inoue has written three books on Ryukyu kobu-jutsu.

INOUE, YOICHIRO Japanese aikido instructor. One of the senior disciples of **Morihei Ueshiba,** he founded the shinwa taido style of aikido.

ISA, KAISHU Okinawan **kobudo** master. When his father died soon after Isa's birth, in the first year of World War II, Isa's grandfather began raising him and started teaching the boy karate at 3. Isa grew up with a reputation as a neighborhood bully. As punishment, he was once hung by his hands from a tree and was rescued by Shosei Kina, a martial arts instructor with whom Isa eventually began studying kobudo. At Kina's death in 1981, Isa inherited the **menkyo-kaiden** of this style, which was founded by **Kanakushiku Ufuchiku.**

ISHIKAWA, TAKANIKO Japanese-American judo champion and instructor; All-Japan Judo Champion in 1949 and 1950, and co-author of Judo Training methods. One of the highest-ranking judoka in the U.S., Ishikawa undertook judo at 12, later enrolled at the Judo College and stayed on as an assistant professor. He came to the U.S. in 1957 at the invitation of the U.S. Air Force to train servicemen as judo instructors.

ITO, KAZUO (1898-) Japanese judo master. Ito began jujutsu as a child with his father. He entered the **Kodokan** in 1920 and received his 9th dan in 1958. One of the Kodokan's senior instructors, he wrote the authoritative *This Is Judo.*

ITOSU, YASUTSUNE "ANKO" (1830-1915) Okinawan karate pioneer. Itosu was born in 1830 in Shuri; he trained under karate masters Sokon Matsumura and Kosaku Matsumora. His good friend, **Yasutsune Azato,** recommended him to become secretary to the king of the Ryukyus. Around 1901-02, when karate was introduced in the Okinawan Daiichi Junior High and the Teachers Boy's School, he became the first instructor.

This barrel-chested master was famous for the strength of his arms, hands, and chops; it is said he appeared not to feel the blows of other karate masters, and even walked as if in the **horse stance** (from which his nickname, Anko, derives). Shuri-te karate master Itosu and Naha-te karate master **Kanryo Higashionna** are considered the most important figures in Okinawan karate of the 19th century. Certainly Itosu restored karate to a high technical level and devised **kata** still in use.

Among Itosu's eminent students were **Gichin Funakoshi, Chotoku Kyan,** Chomo Hanashiro, **Choshin Chibana,** Anbun Tokuda (who became assistant to Itosu), Shinpan Gusukuma, **Kentsu Yabu,** Moden Yabiku, **Kenwa Mabuni,** and **Kanken Toyama.**

Describing the art in his own words: "Karate means not only to develop one's physical strength but to learn how to defend oneself. Be helpful to all people and never fight against one person. Never try to strike, if possible, even when taken unawares, as perhaps meeting a robber or a deranged person. Never face others with fists and feet. As you practice karate, try to open your eyes brightly and keep your shoulders down, stiffen your body as if you are on the battleground. Imagine that you are facing the enemy when you practice the punching or blocking techniques. Soon you will find your own striking performance. Always concentrate attention around you. A man of character will avoid any quarrels and loves peace. Thus the more a karateka practices the more modest he should be with others. This is the true karateka. (ANTHONY MIRAKIAN) *See also* Okinawa, history of martial arts in. *Further reading: The Weaponless Warriors,* Richard Kim, 1975.

ITTOSAI, ITO (1560-1653) Japanese swordsman; founder of the Itto ryu method of swordsmanship. Ittosai believed that those without wholesome moral character could not achieve great skill in swordsmanship.

IVAN, DAN (1929-) American karate pioneer. Elected to the **Black Belt Hall of Fame** in 1973 as "Man of the Year," Ivan holds black belts in karate, judo, aikido, and kendo. A former member of the CID of the American occupational forces, Ivan was first exposed to the martial arts in Japan, where he was stationed from 1948 to 1956. He was one of the first postwar Americans to study judo at the **Kodokan** and he holds the distinction of being the first American issued black-belt rank in aikido.

Upon his return to California in 1956, Ivan established one of the first karate clubs in the U.S., located in Orange County. In 1965, he brought **Fumio Demura** from Japan to act as chief instructor. As partners, the pair established some twenty additional dojo. He produced karate and samurai shows at Japanese Village and Sea World, California tourist attractions, and in Las Vegas. Ivan wrote a novel, *Tokyo Undercover,* based on his own experiences as an undercover investigator with the CID in Tokyo, and the martial arts figure prominently in the story line. With Demura, he co-authored *Advanced Nunchaku.* In 1975, he was named to *Who's Who in the Martial Arts. See also* U.S., history of karate in.

IWATA, MANZO Japanese karate instructor and administrator. A member of the technical examination committee of F.A.J.K.O. He has studied Shito ryu karate under Kenwa Mabuni, and became chief instructor of the Shito Kai Karate Association.

IZUMIGAWA, KANKI Okinawan karate master. Izumigawa was taught at an early age by Seiko Higa and **Kanken Toyama.** After World War II, Izumigawa was active in teaching **goju-ryu** karate at the Okinawa Hall in Kawasaki, Japan, directing Okinawan youth. *See also* Okinawa, history of martial arts in.

JACKS, BRIAN (1946-) British judo champion. The Londoner took up judo at 11 and went to Japan four years later. He won the European junior titles in 1964-65 and competed in the Tokyo Olympic Games. A disputed decision at the 1967 World Championships resulted in his winning the bronze medal. In 1970 he won the European middleweight title, the first Englishman to win a weight category in that event. He placed third in the Munich Olympics in 1972 and regained his European crown in 1973.

Brian Jacks

JACKSON, HOWARD (1951-　) American karate champion. Jackson began martial arts in 1968 under Harold Williams of Detroit, Mich. In 1970 he received a black belt from Hwang Kee in the Korean style of tang soo do.

After moving to southern California and gaining some notoriety as a fast-rising regional point fighter, Jackson trained with senior members of the Chuck Norris Studios and also with world heavyweight champion **Joe Lewis,** who had a profound influence on Jackson.

In 1973, when **Mike Anderson** introduced **semicontact** fighting at his **Top 10 Nationals** in St. Louis, Jackson won the grand championship and the first $1,000 purse in semicontact competition. *Black Belt* and *Professional Karate* magazines rated him the number-1 U.S. karate fighter of 1973; he was inducted into the **Black Belt Hall of Fame** as "Fighter of the Year," the first black fighter to be ranked number-one in the history of the sport. He is also the only two-time grand champion of the prestigious **Battle of Atlanta** (1973 and 1974).

Howard Jackson

A severe knee injury destroyed Jackson's chances of winning an inaugural world championship title at the World Professional Karate Championships of 1974, the event at which **full-contact** karate was spawned. He limped through a one-legged performance and retired bitter and frustrated shortly afterward. After two years of surgery and therapy, Jackson launched a comeback in 1976, competing in professional boxing, karate, and kick-boxing.

On January 26, 1980, Jackson, now with a record of 15-1 in full-contact karate and 21 wins in pro boxing, won a unanimous nine-round decision over Japan's Yoshimitsu Tamashiro to capture the WKA full-contact welterweight title. And in January 1981 he won against Miyaso Chiba in Tokyo to become the world junior welterweight champion of the World Kick-Boxing Association. *See also* U.S., history of karate in.

JACKSON, LYNN (1937-　) American karate instructor and referee. Jackson began training in Korea in 1960 as a member of the armed forces. He has since founded several karate clubs in his native Ohio, and won regional titles in kata and sparring. Jackson is a noted karate referee. In 1975 he was named to *Who's Who in the Martial Arts.*

JAY, WALLY (1917-　) American judo and jujutsu instructor and administrator. Jay began training in 1935 with Paul Kaelemakule in Honolulu and received his black belt in 1944. He is a past president of Jujitsu America and technical director and international head of jujutsu for the **Butokukai,** Kyoto, Japan. He is also technical advisor and black belt grading consultant of the Norwegian Jiu Jitsu Federation, technical advisor of jujutsu for the Independent Karate Association of London, and technical director of the Canadian Jiu Jitsu Association. An exponent of a "small circle theory," he was inducted into the **Black Belt Hall of Fame** in 1969 and entered *Who's Who in the Martial Arts* in 1975.

JEHANGIR, SALEEM Pakistani karate pioneer and instructor; founder and president of the Tae Kwon Do Karate Association of Pakistan. While studying in the U.S. he began tae kwon do with Hwa Chong in Ann Arbor. He received his black belt in 1970, and in 1971 he returned to Karachi, Pakistan, to work for an American oil company. Jehangir overcame Pakistani government objections to establish martial arts in his homeland. In 1971 he taught the first karate class held in Pakistan. Although he now lives in the U.S., he still returns to Pakistan to help promote the martial arts.

JINSUKE, HOJO Father of modern **iaijutsu.** Jinsuke founded the shin muso hayashizake ryu (also known as muso ryu), where he taught defensive swordsmanship. Some historians dispute that Jinsuke founded iaijutsu, but clear evidence has not come to light.

JIROKICHI, YAMADA (1863-1931) Japanese kendo master; 15th headmaster of the jikishin-kage ryu. All of his efforts in teaching went toward maintaining kendo's intrinsic spiritual essence. He devoted his life to kendo and influenced many people who were instrumental in the art's later development.

JIRO, NANGO (　-1951) Japanese judo administrator; past president of the **Kodokan.** He began studying judo with founder **Jigoro Kano** in judo's embryonic era and received his black belt in 1884 while continuing a career in the navy, from which he retired as a rear admiral.

In 1938, when Prof. Kano died, the Kodokan board of trustees unanimously chose Jiro his successor, a post he held until September, 1946, when he retired due to bad health. While president he established a system of judo for juveniles, fixed the kata of self-defense for women, and founded the institute for the training of teachers of judo. He was one of the few judans, 10th-degree black belts.

JOHNSON, PAT (1939-　) American karate instructor, competitor, and referee; originator of the Johnson Rule, a penalty point system

Pat Johnson, kneeling, center

to discourage excessive contact in light-contact matches. Johnson received a Golden Fist Award in 1973 and 1974 as an outstanding official. Middleweight champion of the 1969 California State Karate Championships, Johnson was selected captain of the undefeated **Chuck Norris** team from 1969-73.

He has written articles for *Black Belt* and *Professional Karate* magazines, and is a member of *Who's Who in the Martial Arts.* Johnson is a part-time actor, stuntman, and technical advisor for fight scenes; he has appeared in *Enter the Dragon, Golden Needles, Black Belt Jones, A Force of One, The Big Brawl,* and *Force: Five.*

Johnson keeps active with films, writing, and private instruction. His most famous pupil was Steve McQueen. *See also* U.S., history of karate in.

JONES, A. JOSE (1932-) American karate instructor, official, and writer. Founder of the Wheelkickers Tae Kwon Do Club and the Woodrow Wilson High School Karate Club, Jones formerly taught at the **Jhoon Rhee** Institute. He contributed to the training of prominent fighters such as **Wayne Van Buren, Mike Warren,** Otis Hooper, and **Albert Cheeks.** Jones, a university professor, established martial arts programs for ghetto youths and families of workers affiliated with the Department of Housing and Urban Development. A member of *Who's Who in the Martial Arts,* he was a noted regional fighter for ten years, undefeated in team competition.

JONES, BOB Australian karate instructor and businessman. Jones began tae kwon do in 1965 with Jack Rozinsky. In 1969 he received his black belt from Tino Ceberana, and has since studied various styles with instructors such as **Pat Johnson, Chuck Norris, Mike Stone, Steve Armstrong,** and **Aaron Banks.** Jones, occasionally a bodyguard for rock and roll artists, is one of Australia's leading karate promoters and school owners, and runs a martial arts supply company with manufacturing facilities in Melbourne. Currently he is the Australian director of the **WKA.**

JONES, JIMMIE (1940-) American karate instructor and promoter. Appointed chief instructor in Chicago for the **USKA** in 1966, his students include top 10 kata competitor and fighter **Tayari Casel,** regional fighter Preston Baker, regional kata standout Ben Peacock, 1967 Grand Nationals runner-up John Norman, and 1967 Grand Nationals winner James Pitchford.

Jones's competitive career began in 1963 and ended in 1972. A runner-up as a brown belt in Robert Trias's 1963 World Championships, he won frequently as a black belt in midwest tournaments, competing in both kata and sparring. In 1963 he won first place at the Midwest Championships and the Tri-State Championships; he finished second in kata at Jhoon Rhee's 1968 U.S. Nationals in Washington, D.C. In 1972 he won the top coach award at the Midwest Challenges the East & West Coast Tournament.

Jones has hosted the Midwest Nationals Karate Championships and the Midwest Pre-Nationals since 1973, and has promoted two events a year since 1964. In 1975, he was named to *Who's Who in the Martial Arts.*

JORGA, ILIJA (1942-) Yugoslavian karate champion. Jorga was a top European competitor in the early 1970s. He placed third at the European Championships in 1969 and has been coach of the Yugoslavian national karate team. *See also* Yugoslavia, history of karate in.

JUBEI, YAGYU (ca. 1607-50) Japanese swordsman. Jubei, an aggressive combatant during a time when the trend was toward a tamer approach, obtained permission to challenge a group of seven swordsmen. After insulting and provoking them into a fight, Jubei dismembered two and killed another outright; the remaining four fled. As a result of the confrontation, many aspiring swordsmen sought him out for instruction.

KAICHIRO, SAMURA (1880-1964) Japanese judo master, one of the few judo 10th dans. He began judo at the **Kodokan** in 1898. After receiving his black belt he traveled in Japan, introducing judo to places where only jujutsu was practiced. In 1907 he became famous by defeating Kozoburo Tokata, a great champion of that time. He returned to the Kodokan in 1932, where he continued his career as a teacher.

KAIHEWALU, SOLOMAN (1935-) American karate instructor and promoter. Known in California for his work in developing children into champion competitors, Kaihewalu received two Golden Fist Awards, one for best instructor of children. In 1968, Kaihewalu founded the Polynesian-Chinese Karate Association, headquartered in Orange, Calif. An innovative promoter, he originated the All Pee-Wee/Junior Championships in 1970 and conceived the Women's Pro/Am Championships in 1973, one of the first events in America to award cash prizes to black belt women in both sparring and kata. He was named to *Who's Who in the Martial Arts* in 1975.

KAJIYAMA, RICHARD T. (1929-) American karate instructor. A native of Hawaii, he and one of his instructors, Mikio Maruyama, introduced **Shito-ryu** karate-do to the Hawaiian islands in 1957. He began the martial arts in 1945, receiving black belts in judo and jujutsu in 1949. The Shito-ryu organization in Kobe, Japan, awarded him his present grade, 7th dan.

Kajiyama is the overseas representative of the Shito Ryu Karate-do, Abe School and the World Karate-do Union in Japan.

KALLENBACH, JAN (1943-) Dutch karate champion. Kallenbach has several times been rated among Europe's top 10 karate fighters by *Black Belt Magazine.* He is a student of **Mas Oyama** and teaches

Jimmy Jones

karate in Holland. In 1974 he won the openweight division of the European Karate Championships.

KALOUDIS, EDWARD (1936-) Greek-born American karate instructor and pioneer. Kaloudis studied karate from age 10 and came to the U.S. in 1954, becoming the first-known instructor in New York. He was the first non-Oriental to study the **koeikan** system in Japan and the first to introduce this style outside of its native country. While in Japan Kaloudis trained under **Eizo Onishi.** He has been the representative of the International Koeikan Karate-do Federation in the Western Hemisphere since 1954 and since 1968 has been a representative of the All Japan Karate-do Association.

Kaloudis is a director of physical education in the North Caldwell School System and is also a member of the faculty at Fairleigh Dickinson University and at Montclair college. He has promoted a large number of students to black belt rank, many of whom now teach in Europe as well as South America. He is a contributing author to the *Handbook of Martial Arts and Self-defense* as well as the *Essential Elements of Koeikan Karate. See also* U.S., history of karate in; koeikan.

Edward Kaloudis, pioneer of karate on the East Coast

KAMI TOGO BIZEN NO (1563-1643) Japanese sword master. Founder of the jigen ryu style of **kenjutsu** (art of the sword).

KAMIIZUMI, ISE NO KAMI (1508-78) Founder of the shinkage ryu style of **kenjutsu.**

KAMIKADO, OSAMU (1950-) Japanese karate champion. A rengo-kai stylist and physical education instructor, Osamu Kamikado won the All Japan Rengo-Kai Championships in 1975; the Osaka All Styles Tournament in 1974, and was a member of the Osaka team that was runner-up at the 1973 All Japan All-Styles Championships. He also won the All Japan Student Karate Championships in 1972. Kamikado holds black belts in judo, kendo, and karate.

KAMINAGA, A. (1937-) Japanese judo champion. Kaminaga won the **All Japan Judo Championships** three times, in 1960, 1961, and 1964, but lost the Olympic openweight finals in Tokyo to **Anton Geesink.** Although extremely shortsighted, he was particularly proficient at the tai otoshi (body drop) and uchimata (inner-thigh throw). Kaminaga was an Olympic silver medalist in the open class at Tokyo in 1964.

A. Kaminaga

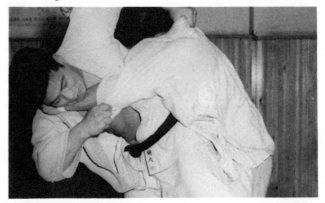

KAM-TUNG Chinese kung-fu master in Hong Kong known for his mastery of the liu-ho pa-fa and ho-chia (hop-ga) styles and for his roles in Chinese movies. Kam-Tung learned ho-chia from Ng-Yim-Ming.

KANASHIRO, KENSEI Okinawan karate master; founder of the tozan-ryu style of karate. Kanashiro studied with **Choshin Chibana,** the founder of **shorin-ryu.**

KANAZAWA, HIROKAZU Japanese karate champion, one of the top **Shotokan** instructors. Kanazawa won the All Japan Championships in 1957 and 1958. He reached 2nd-degree judo black belt while still in high school and studied karate at Takushoku University in 1951. In 1955 he began training at the **JKA** headquarters, becoming one of their instructors in 1957. That same year he won the All Japan Championships, despite a broken right hand. The next year he faced fellow instructor **Takayuki Mikami** in the finals, but the two were so evenly matched that both were declared winners. Kanazawa also won the kata event, becoming grand champion.

He taught in Hawaii for two years, and then in South Africa. For five years he promoted the growth of karate in England and in Europe generally. In 1971 he returned to Japan where he became chief technical advisor and team coach to the JKA. Many claim he has come closest to having "perfect technique." *See also* Shotokan.

Hirokazu Kanazawa, twice All Japan Champion, is today a leading Shotokan instructor.

KANG, DONG WON (1942–   ) Korean-American tae kwon do instructor, publisher, and writer. Born in Seoul, Korea, he began studying at 7 and achieved a junior black belt in 1950. He was graduated from the University of Han Yang with a degree in movie directing and scriptwriting. He immigrated to the U.S. in 1970, first settling in Los Angeles where he taught tae kwon do. In 1971, while on holiday to the southwest, he was invited to teach at a school in Tulsa, Okla. He opened his own school in Tulsa in 1972. In the mid-1970s, Kang founded *Traditional Taekwon-do* magazine, serving as both publisher and editor; it is the leading publication devoted to the Korean martial arts. In August 1978, Kang opened his fitness complex in Tulsa, a posh training center costing $850,000. More than 500 tae kwon do students train there. Perhaps Kang's most prominent student is **Dale Cook.** Kang promotes the annual Mid-America Taekwon-Do Championships in Tulsa.

KANG, MYUNG KYU (1934-) Korean-American tae kwon do instructor. Since 1964, Kang has taught tae kwon do at Sacramento State University. He has served as technical advisor and teachers training committee chairman, National AAU Tae Kwon Do Committee. Among his students are **Byong Yu** and **Dan Choi.**

Jigaro Kano

KANO, JIGORO (1860-1938) Japanese educator and founder of judo. Born October 28, 1860, in Kobe, Japan, to a wealthy family, Kano was physically weak during his childhood. His training in the martial arts began under the direction of Teinosuke Yagi, and later Hachinosuke Fukuda, a master of the Tenjin-Shinyo school of jujutsu. Fukuda stressed technique over **kata,** which influenced Kano, who in his own system emphasized **randori** (free practice). In 1879, after Fukuda's death, Kano joined a dojo operated by Masatomo Iso, a school known for its excellence in the performance of kata. By 21 he had mastered the style. Kano later trained with Tsunetoshi Iikubo, master of the kito school of jujutsu, who was especially skillful at teaching nage-waza (throwing techniques).

In 1881 Kano graduated from the Imperial University and assumed a position as a teacher of literature at Gakushuin (Peer's School), an exclusive establishment for the children of royal Japanese. One year later, Kano established his own dojo in Eisho-ji Temple. The next year, he set up a 20-mat dojo in his home.

In 1884 Kano formulated by-laws and called his new martial system "Kodokan judo," which he envisioned as a complete way of life. Kano also saw judo's potential as a sport, whereas jujutsu was strictly a form of self-defense. The dangerous techniques of jujutsu were eliminated in judo contests, but Kano retained some of them for instructional and self-defense purposes.

By 1884 judo contests were conducted within some jujutsu dojo. In 1886 Kano moved the site of his Kodokan—40 mats by this time, to the Fujimi-cho residence of Meji-era magnate, Baron Yajiro Shinagawa. It was supervised by Kano until 1894, when the Kodokan council was inaugurated.

In August of 1891 Kano married Sumako Takezoe, daughter of a

former ambassador to Korea. They sired nine children; six daughters and three sons.

In May 1909 the Kodokan became a foundation, and by April 1911, the Judo Teacher's Training Department was established. In 1922 the Kodokan Dan Grade Holder's Association was organized, followed by the Judo Medical Research Society in 1932.

By 1912 Kano had made more than nine trips abroad. A fan of many sports, he became the father of modern sports in Japan. In 1911 he founded the Japan Athletic Association and became its first president. He was also named Japan's first member of the International Olympic Committee and attended the 5th Olympiad in Stockholm in 1912, the first Olympics in which Japan participated. In 1935 Kano received the Asashi Prize for "outstanding contribution in the fields of art, science, and sport." In 1938, at Cairo, he was responsible for having Tokyo nominated as the site of the 1940 Olympics. Returning aboard the SS *Hikawa Maru,* Kano died on May 4, 1938. *See also* judo.

KAO-FANG-HSIEN Well-known exponent of the **Shao-lin** style of Chinese kung-fu in the Republic of China.

KAO-SEN-HUANG Well-known master of the **Shao-lin** (southern) style of Chinese kung-fu in the Republic of China.

KASE, TAIJI Japanese karate pioneer and instructor. Kase was one of the first high-ranking Japanese karate teachers to instruct in Europe; he opened a dojo in Paris as a branch of the **JKA.** He studied with **Gichin Funakoshi,** the father of Japanese **karate-do,** and his son, **Yoshitka Funakoshi.** *See also* Europe, history of karate in; Shotokan.

KAWADA, MINORU (1952-) Japanese karate competitor. A **Shotokan** stylist, Minoru Kawada placed third in the All Japan Championships in 1975, and won the Ibaragi Prefectures Championships Tournament in 1974.

KAWAGUCHI, TAKAO (1950-) Japanese judo champion whose crisp throwing techniques won him the world lightweight title in 1971. He was an Olympic gold medalist in 1972 and a silver medalist in the 1973 World Championships.

KAWAISHI, MIKONOSUKE (1899-1969) Japanese-born French judo pioneer. Having achieved a 3rd **dan** from the **Kodokan,** he embarked on a world tour, willingly competing against top boxers and wrestlers. He traveled and taught judo in the U.S., especially in New York and San Diego. In 1931 he travelled to London, where he became judo instructor at Oxford University. While in England he founded the Anglo-Japanese Judo Club. In 1935 Kawaishi, now a 5th dan, taught at the Jujutsu Club of France. He formulated a system of teaching based on numbers rather than the traditional, cumbersome Japanese names.

After the war, and an imprisonment in Manchuria, he returned to Paris and continued to teach. His students put together a special fund to assure his livelihood in his declining years. *See also* Europe, history of judo in.

KEEHAN, JOHN (-1976) American karate pioneer. Alias Count Dante, Keehan was one of the most controversial figures in American karate, billing himself as the "deadliest man alive." He ran a chain of studios in the Chicago area, where he often became involved in disputes with other karate studios, one of which resulted in the stabbing death of Jim Koncevic in 1970.

A former student of **Robert Trias,** Keehan was co-promoter of the 1st World Karate Championships, held at the Chicago Fieldhouse on July 28, 1963. In 1967, in Chicago, he promoted what was supposed to be the first bare-knuckle full-contact event ever conducted in the U.S. It was reportedly supported by only eight black belt contestants. *See also* U.S., history of karate in.

KEENEY, GLENN (1941-) American karate instructor, competitor and promoter. A former lightweight champion of the **United States Karate Association,** Keeney has trained numerous regional and national champions from his school in Anderson, Indiana. In 1972, Keeney was rated fourth among **Black Belt's** Top Ten and in 1972 and 1973 he was the USKA's number-one fighter. His most famous student is Ross Scott, who became the **PKA** world heavyweight champion (**full-contact**).

A member of *Who's Who in the Martial Arts,* Keeney is best known as one of American karate's premier promoters. He has produced on several occasions the **USKA Grand Nationals,** as well as the **Top 10 Nationals.** In June 1980, he produced the live event for **Bill Wallace's** retirement fight.

KELLEY, HUGH K. (1940-   ) American karate instructor. Kelley received his black belt in **Shito-ryu** in 1957 from Shiyogo Kuniba. He later studied **Shotokan** and **kyokushinkai,** but instructs in Shito-ryu.

Kelley wrote *I Bring Death,* and hosted a local television show, *Kelley on Karate.*

Kelley was the recipient of several awards after rescuing a girl from five would-be rapists. During the rescue, he sustained a knife wound and gun-powder burns to his left eye.

KELLY, JIM (1946-   ) American karate instructor, competitor, and actor. Kelly launched a film career in 1972, one year after winning his most important karate title, the middleweight division of the 1971 **International Karate Championships.** As an instructor, he trained Dana Goodson, a world-ranked heavyweight karate fighter. Kelly's movie credits include *Enter the Dragon, Melinda, Three the Hard Way, Hot Potatoe,* and *Black Samurai.* Member of *Who's Who in the Martial Arts. See also* U.S., history of karate in; motion pictures and television.

KERR, GEORGE (1937-   ) Scottish judo champion. Kerr won three European silver and two bronze medals during the 1960s. A member of the British team, in the middleweight category and open events. His excellent range of groundwork techniques, superb **uchi-mata** (inner thigh throw) and knowledge of amateur wrestling (he represented Britain in the 1965 World Championships) contributed to his success. Kerr won the 1966 and 1968 British Open middleweight titles before retiring.

KHARLAMPIEV, ANATOLY ARKADEVICH Russian **sambo** founder. A scholar-sportsman, Anatoly Kharlampiev studied wrestling in his homeland and abroad before devising sambo, which in 1938 became a recognized national sport in Russia.

KIKNADZE, ANZOR (1934-   ) Russian judo champion. Kiknadze won eight European gold medals, four individually and four as a member of the Soviet contingent that won consecutive team titles from 1963-67. He won a bronze medal at both the 1964 Olympic Games and the 1965 World Championships, and a silver medal in the 1968 European Championships before retiring.

KIKUGHI, DAN (1953-   ) American judo champion. Winner of the AAU Junior Nationals in 1969. He became National Intercollegiate Champion for 1973, and the same year won the Pacific AAU Championships and the AAU Western Regionals.

KIM, C.S. Korean **tang soo do** instructor. He studied both boxing and judo in Korea before he was 10, then took up tang soo do under Song Ki Kim. By 1969, he had established two schools in downtown Osan and taught full-time at Osan Air Force Base. He was the subject of a half-hour tang soo do documentary produced by the U.S. Air Force in 1969; 100 copies of the film were distributed to air bases across the world. He captained a team of competitors that scored victories in tournaments in Malaysia and the Philippines.

At the request of tang soo do grandmaster Hwang Kee, Kim moved to the U.S. and founded three schools by 1979. His main school is located in East McKeesport, Pa. He holds the distinction of having promoted almost 1,000 practitioners throughout the world to the rank of blue belt, tang soo do's equivalent to black belt.

KIM, CHAN-YONG (1935-   ) Korean-born tae kwon do and judo instructor, international tae kwon do referee. Currently teaching in the U.S., Kim is a graduate of the Korean Yudo College (1961). He toured much of the Orient, demonstrating and teaching tae kwon do and self-defense; officially representing the Korean Yudo Association, he established the first tae kwon do school in Melbourne.

KIM, DAESHIK (1934-   ) Korean-American tae kwon do and judo instructor. Kim is largely responsible for the early judo and tae kwon do development in the southeastern U.S. He has contributed to leading professional magazines and trained outstanding students, including **Joe Corley** and **Chris McLoughlin.** *See also* U.S., history of karate in.

KIM, IN MOOK (1934-   ) Korean-American tae kwon do instructor. He started taekyon training in grade school in 1946. He also took up judo in 1948 in Bae Jae while attending junior high school. Later, in high school, he continued judo under Pae Kyung Yul. Kim immigrated to the U.S. in August 1968 and began teaching tae kwon do in San Antonio, Tx. Within ten years, he built a chain of 12 schools extending to four states: Missouri, Kansas, Kentucky, and Iowa, in which he established eight of his schools. He also developed tae kwon do programs at Iowa State University and Northern Iowa University. His headquarters is in Des Moines. He has taught more than 7,000 students.

KIM, J.C. (1935-   ) Korean tae kwon do instructor. He first taught tae kwon do in 1957 in a military school. In 1966, when the **ITF** was founded, Kim was named committee coordinator and one of the first ITF instructors. Kim taught the Korean national police and combined military services. He was asked, in 1968, to provide instruction to the Malaysian Tae Kwon-Do Association. After 1970 Kim opened a school in Montreal, where, in 1974, he held the 1st World Tae Kwon Do Championships.

KIM, JAE JOON (1931-   ) Korean-born tae kwon do master; a senior instructor of the moo duk kwan style. Residing in Detroit, he serves as promotional committeeman, National AAU Tae Kwon Do Committee.

KIM, JAY (1935-   ) Korean-American judo and tae kwon do instructor and promoter. Kim is a professor of physical education at Michigan State University, beginning in 1961, and hosted numerous collegiate tournaments, including the 3rd National Collegiate Tae Kwon Do Championships. He is a certified international judo referee.

KIM, KI WHANG (1920-   ) Korean-American tae kwon do instructor and pioneer. Elected to the **Black Belt Hall of Fame** in 1970 as "Instructor of the Year," Kim trained nationally ranked fighters **Mike Warren,** Marshall Collins, **Albert Cheeks,** Mitchell Bobrow, and **George Thanos.** He began judo at 15 in Seoul, and was promoted to black belt five years later by the **Kodokan.** While in college he studied karate and, for two years in China, **kempo.** He came to the U.S. in 1963 and was appointed chairman of the American Moo Duk Kwan Association. Kim also hosts a tournament, the All-American Invitational Karate Championships, in his home state of Maryland. *See also* U.S., history of karate in.

Ki Whang Kim

KIM, KYU-HA (1935-) Korean-American judo and tae kwon do instructor. Kim coached the U.S. judo team at the 1979 Kano Cup International Judo Championships in Japan. He has also served as president of the Korean-American Judo Instructor's Society.

KIM, PYUNG SOO Korean-American tae kwon do instructor. He undertook tae kwon do at an early age under Nam Sok Lee, president of the Chang Mu Kwan Association in Seoul. Kim instructed many students and groups, including the Secret Service of the late Korean president Syngman Rhee, municipal police departments, youth organizations, and students at universities in Korea and Texas. From 1965-67, he served as the first Korean news correspondent to *Black Belt Magazine.*

Kim arrived in the U.S. in 1968, and established a school in Houston. In September 1970 he inaugurated an eclectic tae kwon do style called cha-yon ryu (natural system). Kim wrote two textbooks on the **hyung** (patterns) of tae kwon do: *Palgue 1,2,3 of Tae Kwon Do Hyung* (1973) and *Palgue 4,5,6* (1975).

KIM, RICHARD (1917-) Korean-American martial arts historian, lecturer, and instructor. Kim began the martial arts as a child in Hawaii. In China, he learned **t'ai-chi-ch'uan** and **pa-kua.** He also studied from **Ankichi Arakaki,** a disciple of **Kentsu Yabu,** and a Taoist priest named Chao Hsu Lai. Kim began teaching formally in 1951 in Yokohama; his students include pioneer **Peter Urban,** Canadian karate pioneer Benny Allen, Hawaii's James Miyaji, competitors Richard Lee, Leroy Rodriguez, and John Pereira, and Canadians Don Warrener and Eileen Dennis. A member of the **Dai Nippon Butokukai** (Great Japan Martial Virtues Association) since before World War II, he founded branches of the association in the U.S., Canada, France, and Germany.

After more than 50 years of training, research, and giving instruction, Master Kim is heralded as the foremost karate historian residing in the U.S. and one of the world's premier authorities and respected scholars in the martial arts. In 1976 he wrote his first book, *The Weaponless Warriors: An Informal History of Okinawan Karate.* From 1975-81 he oversaw and edited Japanese/Okinawan entries for *The Illustrated Encyclopedia of the Martial Arts.* Kim is perhaps best known for his long-running monthly column in *Karate Illustrated Magazine.* Master Kim came to the continental U.S. in 1961 and settled in San Francisco, Calif., where he conducted a karate program at the Chinese YMCA until his semiretirement in 1978. He continues to oversee classes in **shorinji-ryu** karate at a dojo near San Francisco.

In 1973 he was inducted into the **Black Belt Hall of Fame** as "Sensei of the Year." He is an executive officer of the **AAKF,** and has served as an arbitrator at international amateur karate tournaments. In 1975 he was named to *Who's Who in the Martial Arts. See also:* U.S., history of karate in.

KIM, UN YONG President of the **WTF** since 1973, member of the Korea Amateur Sports Association, and first vice-president and honorary secretary general of the Korea Olympic Committee. Kim is responsible for the WTF becoming a member of the GAISF and the International Olympic Committee. *See also* World Tae Kwon Do Federation.

KIM, WEY-SENG Korean-American judo instructor and administrator. Kim came to the U.S. in 1960. He served as chairman of the board of examiners for the **USJF** and technical director for the AAU Judo Committee.

KIM, YONG KEIL (1938-) Korean-born American tae kwon do instructor. Kim served as regional chairman of the National AAU Tae Kwon Do Committee and hosted the annual tae kwon do championships in Los Angeles.

KIM, YOO JIN (1944-) Korean tae kwon do instructor. Born in Seoul, Kim began to study jee do kwan in his teens; he moved to Atlanta in 1966. Kim sponsors the annual National Karate Championships.

KIMM, HE-YOUNG (1940-) Korean-born American **hapkido** instructor. President of the American Hapkido Association, and hapkido coach at Louisiana State University, Kimm conducts frequent clinics and demonstrations throughout the U.S. He also owns a martial arts supply company. Kimm wrote a teaching guide for hapkido instructors and translated Korean works into English.

KIMURA, MASHIKO (1918-) Japanese judo champion; he dominated the sport between 1938 and 1949. Kimura was only 5'7", but his use of the osoto-gari (major outer reap) brought him a run of success against larger opponents. He won the young men's division of the All Japan Championships on four occasions, more than any other competitor. The All Japan Championships was a closed competition until 1948; the following year, Kimura, then a 7th **dan,** was joint champion with **Takaniko Ishikawa.**

KIMURA SHIGERU Japanese karate instructor, he is the world's chief instructor of the Shukokai Karate Federation. He began judo when he was twelve, and also studied kendo. At age sixteen he began **Shukokai** karate under the style's founder **Yukio Tani.** In 1962 he won the All Japan Shukokai Karate Championships and in the same year he became world Shukokai champion. In 1964 he again won the All Japan title and then retired unbeaten from competition. At 24 he left Japan and travelled to South Africa and much of Europe spreading Shukokai. In 1971 he became chief instructor of the Shokokai Karate Federation. When not traveling around the world Kimura makes his home in the U.S. where he moved to in 1973.

KIN, SHEK Chinese kung-fu practitioner and motion picture star. Best known for his role as the villain Mr. Han, in the **Bruce Lee** movie *Enter the Dragon,* Kin has appeared in kung-fu films since 1940. He began kung-fu training at 13; his studies included northern **Shao-lin,** eagle claw, northern praying mantis, chien yuen, and lor horn mon. Always cast as a villain, his first prominent role was in *Wong Fai-Hung.* In 1975 Kin, and other kung-fu dignitaries, visited the U.S. giving demonstrations of the Chinese arts. In 1980, he again visited the U.S. as a special guest at the Coliseum World Expo in Oakland, Calif. (MICHAEL P. STAPLES)

Shek Kin

KINA, SHOSEI (1882-) Okinawan karate and **kobudo** instructor. At 18, he became a teacher with a temporary certificate and enrolled in the Okinawan Teacher College in 1904, studying karate at the college first with **Yasutsune Itosu.** Itosu was aged at that time and held classes only once a week, between which the students practiced on their own. Shortly after Kina began his training, Itosu retured and his senior student, **Kentsu Yabu,** took over. Kina studied with Yabu for five years. At the same time, he started training in **kobu-jutsu** (art of weapons) with the famous police commissioner of Shuri, **Kanakushiku Ufuchiku** (aka Kinjo Sanda). Kina became one of Ufuchiku's two chief disciples and qualified to wear the special gold belt indicating expert status in kobudo.

During his teaching career, he taught karate to students in each school's karate club. From 1909-16, he taught at the Kishaba Elementary School; from 1917-23, at the Goeku School; and from 1924 to the early 1930s, he resumed teaching at the Kishaba School. In 1938, at 60, he retired.

Because he had trained in Okinawan karate before the emergence of the grading system, Kina had never received an official rank. In 1974, a special ceremony was held in his honor by the All Okinawan Karate and Kobudo Rengokai, and the highest rank was issued to him by Sotoku Uehara. One year earlier, he was awarded the Sixth Order of Merit by the Japanese emperor, Hirohito, for saving the village of Shimabuku from demolition in World War II. He was the first Okinawan to receive this great honor from the emperor.

KIRBY, GEORGE American jujutsu instructor, promoter, and author. Kirby took charge of the Burbank YMCA jujutsu program in 1968, and started his own jujutsu ad self-defense program in 1974. A promoter of jujutsu tournaments since 1969, Kirby is vice-president of the Samurai Ju-Jitsu Association and a director of the International Judo/Ju-Jitsu League. He wrote *Budoshin Ju-Jitsu Instructor's Manual* (1973); *Applied Self Defense* (1976); and *Budoshin Ju-Jitsu,* revised edition (1977).

KNIGHTON, STANLEY (1950-) British karate competitor who captained the British team in the 1970 European Karate Championships; a **shukokai** stylist.

KNUDSON, KEN (1944-) American karate instructor; founder of the Midwest Karate Association and former president of the AKA. After winning grand championship titles at midwest tournaments during the mid-1960s, Knudson was a member of the three-man team that defeated teams representing the West Coast and the East Coast in 1969 in Chicago. He is still the only fighter to win the **Top 10 Nationals** two years in a row, 1971 and 1972. Knudson's students include Flem Evans, Ken Kolodziej, **Mike Cass,** and Don Hawk. He is an AAU certification deputy, charged with certifying judges for AAU karate competition.

Promoter of a long-standing annual tournament called the Ken Knudson Pro/Am, he has also produced the AKA Grand Nationals (1973-1975), the largest tournament in the midwest. Karate's first audio/visual training kit was produced by Knudson in 1970, and he also wrote and designed a log book for karate training. Other business ventures include 11 karate schools and a martial arts supply house. Named to *Who's Who in the Martial Arts* in 1975.

KNUTSEN, ROALD British kendo founder. Strongly opposed to the sportive element in the martial arts, Knutsen is chairman of the British Kendo Renmei, formed in 1973 to establish a true kendo tradition in Great Britain. At the Meiji in 1968, he was one of eight non-Japanese honored for their contribution to kendo.

KOBAYASHI, MITSUGI Japanese-American karate instructor. With George Miyasaki and Kenneth Murakami, Kobayashi revived **Chojun Miyagi's goju-ryu** karate in the Hawaiian Islands; they established the Senbukan, Hawaiian branch, goju-ryu karate school. Kobayashi trained with Seiko Higa of Okinawa.

KO-DANG Pseudonym of the Korean patriot Cho Man-Sik. The 39 movements of the **hyung** (pattern) named after him symbolize the number of times he was imprisoned and the location of his birthplace on the 39th parallel. Ko-Dang is an official pattern of the **ITF.** *Further reading: Taekwon-Do,* Gen. Choi Hong Hi, 1972.

KOEPPEL, PHIL American karate instructor. A regional director for the **United States Karate Association,** Koeppel began karate with **Richard Kim** and Yahito Kauaguchi in 1956 while serving with the Navy in Japan. He continued his training under **Andriano Emperado** in Hawaii. Koeppel was one of the co-promoters of the 1st World Karate Tournament, held in Chicago in 1963. His foremost student is Randy Holman, a kata competitor. *See also* U.S., history of karate in.

KOGA, BOB American martial arts author and instructor. An investigator and self-defense instructor with the Los Angeles Police Department, Koga holds black belts in judo, aikido, and jujutsu. Considered an expert in self-defense for law enforcement, he wrote *Police Weaponless Control and Defense Techniques* and *Police Baton Techniques.*

Koga was an instructor for the Los Angeles Police Academy for ten years, and for more than 20 years he has taught other law enforcement agencies throughout the U.S. A specialist in one-on-one situations, developing through the observation of the needs of the law enforcement agencies throughout the country the Koga method, a combination of martial arts adapted to the specific needs of law enforcement. His method is based on the principles of control and the concept that the role of the police is essentially defensive.

In 1972, Koga formed the Police Self-Defense Instructors' Association. Because so many individual police officers joined the group, the association was divided into two separate bodies, the Police Self-Defense Training Association and the nonprofit Koga Institute. Instructors make up the training association while the Koga Institute offers a 600-hour course in the Koga method, leading to accreditation as an instructor. The first sessions of the Koga Institute were held June 27, 1975 at San Jose City College. The sessions are an extension of Koga's teachings in the California State College system.

In addition to his duties with the L.A. Police Dept., Koga has taught his method to the Rio Hondo Police Dept., the National Park Rangers, the California Dept. of Alcoholic Beverage Control, the California Marshall's Association, the sheriff departments of Orange, San Bernadino, Monterey, and Los Angeles counties.

KOIWAI, DR. EICHI K. American judo instructor. He began judo at ten, receiving his black belt at 16. Dr. Koiwai has served as chairman of the Middle Atlantic AAU Judo Committee, chairman of the U.S. Judo Federation Medical Committee, and consultant to the Journal of the American Medical Association and American College of Sports Medicine. In addition, he is president of the **USJF.** His many published articles concern prevention of accidents and injuries in judo. Named "Man of the Year" for 1970 in the **Black Belt Hall of Fame.**

Left to right: Paul Maruyama; Matsu Maye, president of the International Judo Federation; T. Kitaura; and Dr. Eichi Koiwai

KOIZUMI, GUNJI (1885-1965) Japanese judo instructor and pioneer; founder of British judo. He arrived in Britain in 1906, and in 1918, founded the **Budokwai** in London. Koizumi was first proficient in jujutsu, but later switched to judo. A dedicated instructor, he founded clubs all over Europe, leading to the establishment of both the British Judo Association and the European Judo Union. Besides judo, Koizumi was an expert in lacquerware and catalogued the Victoria and Albert Museums collection. He also was a calligrapher and a practicing Buddhist. He died in 1965, an 8th dan, by committing hara-kiri, following the tradition of the old samurai. He wrote *My Study of Judo. See also* U.S., history of judo in; Europe, history of judo in.

KONCHIN Karate **kata** practiced in the Okinawan **Uechi-ryu** style; created by **Kanei Uechi** during the 1960s. *Further reading: Uechi-ryu Karate-Do,* George E. Mattson, 1974.

KONG, BUCKSAM (1940-) American kung-fu instructor and pioneer. For his efforts in furthering kung-fu in Hawaii Kong was named to the **Black Belt Hall of Fame** in 1974. Chief instructor of Hawaii's Siu Lum Gung-fu Association, he founded his own school in 1963, the first in Hawaii to accept non-Chinese students. A member of the *Who's Who in the Martial Arts,* Kong made a series of instructional films and wrote *Hung-Gar Gung-Fu* and *Siu-Lum Gung-Fu.*

KONG, YOUNG IL Korean-born tae kwon do instructor. Kong began tae kwon do at 13 and later captained his university team. Immigrating first to Pennsylvania, he moved to Baltimore, where he opened a dojo. In 1972 he staged the Pan-American Tae Kwon do Championships.

KONISHI, YASUHIRO Japanese karate master. A disciple both of **Gichin Funakoshi** and **Choki Motobu,** Konishi founded the Shindo Jinen Ryu in 1934. Konishi, also holder of a **kendo** kyoshi (teacher grade), integrated ideas drawn from swordsmanship into his techniques, which he preferred to call karate-jutsu.

KORTE, BONNIE (1949-) American judo champion. Korte began her studies in 1963, achieving black belt in 1969. She was a silver medalist at the British Women's Open Judo Championships of 1974 and 1976; in 1975 she won the gold medal. Her record includes consistent kata placings in the USJA Nationals.

Bonnie Korte

KOSUGI, SHO (1948-) Japanese-American karate instructor and weapons expert. Kosugi, who operates a school in San Gabriel, Calif., rose to fame in 1981 as the co-star of the first American-made film to focus exclusively on **ninjutsu,** *Enter the Ninja.* So effective was his performance that he was contracted to star in a sequel, *Revenge of the Ninja,* filmed in Los Angeles in late 1982. A flamboyant weapons performer, Kosugi is particularly skillful with the **sai** and the sword.

KOTAKA, CHUZO (1941-) Japanese-born American karate instructor. A former champion in his native Japan and head of the International Karate Federation, he developed new kata, established schools on the mainland, and promoted the popular All Hawaii State Karate Championships since 1973. A member of the *Who's Who in the Martial Arts,* Kotaka has officiated at almost every major amateur and professional karate event in Hawaii.

KOTANI, SUMIYUKI (1903-) Japanese judo master; one of the few 9th-degree black belts. He began judo training at 14, under **Jigoro Kano** and **Shuichi Nagaoka** (10th dan). By 1927 he was a 5th dan; in 1962 he was promoted to 9th dan. In 1932 he participated in the tenth Olympics, not as a judoka, but as a member of the wrestling team. In 1933, together with Prof. Kano, he toured Europe

Sumiyuki Kotani

to promote judo in Austria, Germany, France, Belgium, England, and Russia. In 1939 he visited South America, where for over a year he continued to promote judo. He visited the U.S. on a number of occasions, touring military bases to demonstrate judo. At present, he is a professor at Tokai University, and teaches regularly at the Kodokan. *See also* U.S., history of judo in.

KRAUSE, RALPH American karate instructor and promoter. A black belt in moo duk kwan, he promoted the Rocky Mountain Team Championships, the NGS Pro/Ams, the Pikes Peak Open and the March of Dimes Classic. *See* also U.S., history of karate in.

KRESGE, TED American karate instructor and author. He has studied several styles of karate and Chinese boxing. Kresge was first introduced to the martial arts in 1957, and began teaching karate in Orleans, France, in 1962. In 1963 he was instructing in Germany. One year later he had one of the largest Armed Forces judo clubs in all of Europe and the U.S.

In 1965 Kresge established the Fort Bragg Karate Club. In 1966 he established the NATO Karate Club outside of Paris. Kresge returned to the U.S. in the late 1960s and founded a studio in St. Petersburg, Fla. In the 1970s he published a martial arts encyclopedia. Throughout the 1970s he promoted the annual U.S. Open, a major karate tournament.

KRIEGER, DAVID (1942-) American karate instructor and author. Krieger began his studies in Kobe, Japan, with Kenjiro Moriguchi in 1963. In 1965 he received his black belt from Chojiro Tani, in the style of **Shito-ryu.** Krieger also studied **goju-ryu, Shotokan,** judo, and aikido. He is a director of the Pacific Karate-do Institute. Krieger wrote *Karate-Do, A Student Manual* and *The Empty Hand.* His *Spirit and Basic Techniques of Karate-Do* is in compilation.

KUBOTA, TAKAYUKI (1934-) Japanese-American karate instructor. Born in Kumamoto, Japan, in 1934. It was here at the age of 4 that he began his study of karate and jujutsu on the island of Kyushu, in Kumamoto.

Kubota began his teaching at age 14 and has continued for over four decades.

In addition to holding an 8th dan in karate, Kubota holds a 5th degree in aikido, a 3rd degree in judo, and a 1st degree in kendo. From 1949-59, he was an instructor for the Kamata Police Department in karate, baton techniques, self-defense, and **taiho-jutsu.**

From 1958-64, Kubota instructed the U.S. Military police and other personnel in self-defense techniques at military bases in Japan. Over the years he has trained personnel in the F.B.I. Since his arrival in the U.S. in 1965, he has trained police and F.B.I. personnel in California. Kubota's students, among them the late **John Gehison, Jr.** and **Tonny Tulleners,** were champions in Japanese-style karate tournaments.

Takayuki Kubota is head of the International Karate Association and teaches his own system of gosoku-ryu karate.

A member of *Who's Who in the Martial Arts,* he also promotes the Hollywood Karate Championships. His list of acting credits include *The Mechanic* and *The Killer Elite.* In 1981 he wrote *Fighting Karate.*

KUDO, KAZUZO (1898-) Japanese judo instructor and author of the classic judo book *Judo in Action.* While still in college he became one of **Jigoro Kano**'s outstanding students.

From 1938-39 Kudo, then a 5th dan, won every major tournament in Japan, establishing a yet unequalled record of three successive championships in the annual Great Kodokan Red and White meets. In 1958 he advanced to 9th dan and in 1963 made a tour of Europe and America. He was a judge in the 1964 Tokyo Olympics, and the following year received the "Order of the Purple Ribbon" from the Japanese Government for his long service to the martial arts.

KUDO, NORIE Japanese-born, American judo instructor. He won the Northern Japan High School Judo Championships at 17; in 1959 and 1960, Kudo won the Tokyo Judo Championships. Besides judo, he studied boxing, karate, and kendo. After completing college, Kudo taught judo at Tokyo Keiza University and the Marunochi Police Club. Today he teaches his art in Springfield, Mass.

KUHAULUA, JESSE Born in Hawaii, Kuhaulua entered the clique of Japan's sumo wrestlers and won its highest honor, the Emperor's Cup, in July 1972. He competed at first under his own name, but in March 1964 was honored with a prestigious wrestling name, that of Daigoro Takamiyama, a reformer of the Meiji period. The name means "mountain of the lofty view."

John Kuhl

KUHL, JOHN (1935-) American karate instructor and official. Kuhl began karate in Montreal in 1957, under Ari Anastasiatis and continued, after moving to New York, under **Peter Urban** and **Gosei Yamaguchi**. His own style, which he calls combat karate, draws upon karate, judo, and jujutsu. Kuhl has refereed in nearly all of the important East Coast karate events. In 1962 he packaged what may have been the first exclusive karate magazine, *Combat Karate.* He has also contributed articles to *Official Karate Magazine,* whose editor, **Al Weiss,** was trained by Kuhl. In 1975, he was named to *Who's Who in the Martial Arts. See also* U.S., history of karate in.

KUSANKU Chinese martial artist and teacher of "Tode" **Sakugawa**. Also known as Kushanku, Kouh-Shang-Kouh, and Ko Sokun.

KUSHIDA, TAKASHI (1935-) Japanese **aikido** master; holder of the **menkyo-kaiden** of **Yoshin aikido**. A judo novice, at 18, in 1953 he accompanied another judoka to the Tokyo dojo of **Gozo Shioda**, founder of Yoshin aikido, and joined the Yoshinkai that same day. Encouraged by his father, a calligrapher who had studied **kendo**, Kushida, within six months, was invited by Shioda to live in the dojo and become his personal **uchideshi**. For the next ten years he served as Shioda's assistant and trained as much as 12 hours per day. By the 1960s, Kushida became one of Shioda's principal students and one of the Yoshinkai's chief instructors, teaching full time and accompanying Shioda for demonstrations in New Zealand and Hawaii.

In 1972, Edward Moore and several other Detroit aikidoka who had practiced at the Yoshinkai requested an instructor to teach in the U.S. Shioda sent Kushida, who was to set up a program and return to Japan within three months. He has remained and taught in the U.S. ever since. As founder and chief instructor of the Aikido Yoshinkai Association of North America, Kushida oversees a network of schools with more than 500 students. From the Genyokan, his North American headquarters dojo in Ann Arbor, Michigan, he has introduced thousands of westerners to Yoshin aikido.

In 1982, Kushida was awarded an 8th dan and the menkyo-kaiden from Shioda, establishing him as the heir apparent of this style and the highest-ranking Yoshin aikido instructor in the West. Kushida's student, Masatoshi Morita, a 4th dan, has established a school in San Francisco. Others were established in Chicago by Robert Hackett and Gilbert James, in Philadelphia by Yukio Utada, in Michigan by Jerome Helton, in Toronto, Canada by Takeshi Kimeda. In addition, Kushida's wife, daughter, and son (a 2nd dan) study aikido at the Genyokan, where Kushida frequently teachers more than 26 classes a week. *See also* Yoshin aikido.

KUZNETSOW, VITALLY (ca. 1941-) Russian judo competitor. He has defeated almost every ranking judo champion in the world including world champions **Masatoshi Shinomaki** and **Wilhelm Ruska**. Besides judo, he is also an expert at **sambo**.

KWAN-KUNG General of the later Han dynasty. Kwan-Kung rose from poverty to become one of the most hallowed military figures in Chinese history. Immortalized in the novel "Romance of the Three Kingdoms," Kwan was forced to live as a wandering criminal after slaying an official who was tormenting one of his friends. Kwan and two comrades, Liu-Pei and Chang-Fei—known as the Three Brothers of the Peach Orchard—began a crusade to unite China that elevated them to the ranks of China's great men. Kwan-Kung became the patron saint of the martial arts; his picture is usually found in kung-fu training halls. (MICHAEL P. STAPLES)

KWANG-WING-LAM Chinese kung-fu master in California noted for mastery of the Hung-Chia style.

KWOK, ALEX Chinese-born Canadian kung-fu champion and instructor. He studied the my jong law horn style under Lau Tung Yim of Hong Kong. Although not a full-time instructor or competitor, Kwok won many championship titles and was rated number 1 in North American kata top 10 by *Professional Karate Magazine.* He was chosen at one time by Warner Brothers to play the lead in the life story of Bruce Lee.

KWON, JAE-HWA (1938-   ) Korean-born tae kwon do instructor and author. After earning a black belt in tae kwon do, he was named head of the 1965 Korean Good Will Team which toured Asia, Africa, and Europe. In May 1966, Kwon moved to Germany as chief instructor of the German Tae Kwon Do Association. He built strong followings in Germany, Turkey, Greece, Lebanon, Quwait, Austria, France, Belgium, Holland, and Denmark. In 1972 he was named national coach o fthe tae kwon do branch of the German Judo Federation. He wrote a German-language book, *Zen Buddhims and Self-Defense.*

Kwon moved to the U.S. in 1974, teaching first in New York City. He then established his own school in Ft. Lauderdale, Fla. He has promoted the International Tae Kwon Do Tournament and Demonstration in Ft. Lauderdale.

KYAN, CHOTOKU (1870-1945) Okinawan karate master. Kyan became his father's student in the arts of **sumo** and karate as a teenager. When Kyan was about 20, his father felt it necessary for him to practice karate regularly. At the time, there were three noted Okinawan karate teachers: Sokon Matsumura in Shuri, **Yasutsune "Ankoh" Itosu,** also in Shuri, and Pechin Oyadomari in Naha. Kyan's father asked all three to train his son, although his chief **sensei** is reputed to have been Itosu. Kyan learned rapidly, absorbing both Shuri-te and Tomari-te; his Chinto kata was said to be flawless. He was challenged frequently, but was never defeated.

With the reform of the social system under the Meiji government, Kyan's family sank into poverty. Kyan struggled to make a living by pulling carts and raising silkworms. Later he taught karate at the Kadena Police Station, where he met and trained **Shoshin Nagamine,** who became the most important figure in the matsubayashi-ryu form of **shorin-ryu** karate. Among other prominent students he instructed were **Choshin Chibana, Gichin Funakoshi, Eizo Shimabukuro,** and **Tsuyoshi Chitose.** Kyan founded the shobayashi-ryu branch of shorin-ryu karate. *See also* Okinawa, history of martial arts in; shorin-ryu.

LABOUNTY, STEVE (1942-   ) American karate instructor and official. LaBounty was vice-chairman of the Northern California Karate Referees Association in 1973. A member of *Who's Who in the Martial Arts,* LaBounty was a contributing editor to *Professional Karate Magazine* and wrote a book on kenpo instruction. He is co-promoter of several large western tournaments, including the Superstar Nationals, held annually in Oakland.

LAI, BRENDAN Chinese kung-fu instructor, promoter, and businessman. Lai studied kung-fu in childhood under the late master Hon-Fan Wong, head of the northern praying-mantis system. Immigrating to the U.S. in 1961, he started Brendan Lai's Supplies Co. in 1972. During that time, Lai took part frequently in kung-fu exhibitions and judged **kata** in major karate tournaments. For two terms he was an executive advisory council member of the AAU National Kung-Fu Committee. Lai has served as master of ceremonies at such prestigious events as the Northwest Kung-Fu Exhibition in Seattle in 1974; the U.S. and Hong Kong United Kung-Fu Exhibition in San Francisco in 1975; and the International Martial Arts Exhibition in Oakland, Calif. in 1979. *See also* kung-fu, Western migration of.

LAMB, ALAN (1946-   ) British-born kung-fu master and pioneer; first Western recognized in China as an expert in wing chun. Lamb began martial arts training in 1966 with Danny Chaganis of South Shields, England, in **wado-ryu.** He moved to London in 1968 where he studied **wing chun** for four years with Paul Lam and for one year with Joseph Cheng. Late in 1973, he journeyed to Hong Kong where he underwent an additional year of intensive wing chun training with Koo Sang, a disciple of the fighting art's patriarch, the late **Yip Man.**

In January 1975. Lamb became the first Westerner to be recognized in China as a wing chun master when Koo Sang awarded him an instructor's certification in accordance with the professional standards set by the **Hong Kong Chinese Martial Arts Association,** one of the most prestigious organizations of its kind in China.

Over subsequent years, Lamb became wing chun's most travelled instructor, establishing followings in Britain, Colombia, West Germany, Canada, and the United States. His most notable wing chun students include Alec Au (Hong Kong), Rag Parsonlai (Trinidad), Keith Kernspect (West Germany), and Bob Stevenson (Canada). Further, respected martial artists from other styles who have studied with Lamb include Terry O'Neill (Britian), Danny Connors (Britain), Gary Hemmingway (Britain), Ernest Hyman (New York), Bill Morris (New York), Yuki Wada (Japan), Gario Acosta (Colombia), Rex Kimball (California), and **Paul Maslak** (California). (Paul Maslak)

LAMBOUR, CHARLES American judo administrator and business executive; chairman of the New York Athletic Club and a member of the U.S. Olympic Committee. Lambour began judo training in 1956 with Dennis Kane. In 1964 he received his black belt at the **Kodokan.** He organized a judo program at the New York Athletic Club and was instrumental in establishing judo at West Point. Lambour is also responsible for introducing judo to the Maccabiah Games (the Jewish Olympics conducted in Israel), and is now on the board of directors of the US. Maccabiah Committee.

LAPUPPET, THOMAS (1938-   ) American karate champion, instructor, and referee. Now a practitioner of nisei goju, LaPuppet started in Shotokan under **George Cofield** and later founded the United Shotokan Association. He began his karate training in 1959, and by the time he retired from competition in 1970 had distinguished himself as one of the all-time great competitors in American history. LaPuppet was one of the first to compete on a national and international basis, bringing home trophies from around the country and from Canada. Among his championship wins are the 6th Grand Nationals, the heavyweight title of the All-American Open, and kata titles, including the All-American Open and the Universal Open. He received awards as an outstanding official at the 11th U.S. Championships in 1973, the U.S. Nationwide Open, and the World Karate Open.

LaPuppet co-produced with **Alex Sternberg** the Playboy Open at the Playboy Resort in Great Gorge, N.Y. In 1969 LaPuppet was the second fighter ever to be named to the **Black Belt Hall of Fame;** member of *Who's Who in the Martial Arts. See also* U.S., history of karate in.

Brendan Lai

Thomas LaPuppet, one of the top karate competitors in the U.S., with some of his many awards

LARGUSA, BEN Filipino-American **kali** master. Born and raised in Kauai, Hawaii, he began to study kali during his high school years. In 1951 he became deeply involved in this art while learning it from **Floro Villabrille**. Largusa, who founded a school in San Francisco, is one of the men responsible for opening up the teaching of kali to the public. He gave the first public kali demonstration in the U.S. at the 1964 **International Karate Championships**. See also kali.

LAU, JEANNIE (1951-   ) Chinese kung-fu champion. Lau began her study of the martial arts in Hong Kong from her father, Lau Fat Ming, in 1956. Her style is **eagle claw.** Her tournament wins include grand championships at the 1975 C.K.C. Tournament in San Francisco and 1976 Internationals in Long Beach; and first place in kata and weapons at the 1975 **Internationals,** 1975 Las Vegas Karate Tournament, and 1976 Sacramento Karate Tournament.

LAVORATO, JEAN-PIERRE French karate competitor, French karate champion in 1968. He is a **Shotokan** stylist.

LAW-KAY Chinese kung-fu master in Hong Kong; president of **Choy-Li-Fut,** founder of the Chan Hung Memorial, and vice-chairman of the Chung Wah Chinese Martial Art and Athletic Association.

LEBELL, GENE (1932-   ) American judo champion and instructor. LeBell studied judo, karate, jujutsu, boxing, and wrestling. He won the AAU Nationals twice as a judo heavyweight in 1954 and 1955. He became a professional wrestler, winning pro titles in Hawaii, California, and Texas, and held the North American Heavyweight Champion title. He was World Champion title holder for a record 12 seconds—it would have been longer, but during a ring riot following the bout, he accidentally kicked the Texas wrestling commissioner in the head.

LeBell was a close friend of **Bruce Lee's.** They traded many fighting techniques and training tips. He acts as a stunt coordinator and commentator for films and television. In 1963 LeBell accepted a public challenge to compete as a judo/karate fighter against world-ranked light-heavyweight boxer Milo Savage in Salt Lake City. LeBell scored a 4th round knockout. In June 1976 LeBell refereed at the controversial Muhammad Ali/Antonio Inoki, boxing-versus-wrestling match in Japan. LeBell wrote *The Handbook of Judo* in 1962; *Your Personal Handbook of Self-defense,* 1964; *Judo and Self-defense for the Young Adult,* 1971.

Judo champion Gene LeBell (*left*) working out with Hayward Nishioka

LEE, ALAN Chinese-American kung-fu master. Lee began training at 7 under his father, a specialist in the southern **Shao-lin** style of kung-fu. Later he studied a northern style of kung-fu in Peking. An American resident since 1959, he was chairman of the Second International Convention of the Martial Arts, conducted in 1969 in New York. Lee has since operated kung-fu studios in the New York area and in New Jersey. In 1978 he was chosen "Kung-Fu Artist of the Year" and inducted into the **Black Belt Hall of Fame.** *See also* Kung-fu, Western migration of.

LEE, BRUCE (1940-73) Chinese-American martial arts pioneer and film star. Lee was born in a San Francisco Chinatown hospital on November 27, 1940. His father, Lee Hoi Chuen, a famous actor in the Cantonese opera, and his mother, Grace, were touring with the opera company. The fourth of five children, he was named Lee Jun Fan. The name Bruce was bestowed upon him by a nurse at the hospital, though he did not use it until he began the study of English at age 12. Because he was born in the Chinese year of the dragon, at the hour of the dragon, he later adopted the name Lee Siu Lung (Lee Little Dragon) in acting.

He returned with his parents to Hong Kong at the age of 3 months, having already made his stage debut in the arms of his father. In grammar school, he learned to read and write the Chinese language. He attended St. Francis Xavier and LaSalle College and appeared in several films as a child, the most notable of which was *The Orphan,* in which Lee played a rough-edged, street-wise juvenile delinquent. His charismatic, intense screen presence was already evident, but as a young man Lee did not plan on an acting career.

At 13 he began the **wing chun** style of gung-fu under Yip Man. The five years that followed were his only period of formal instruction in the martial arts. In later years, when his art took on innovative and expanded dimensions, Bruce acknowledged his debt and gratitude to Yip Man for having initiated a process of discovery that was to continue the rest of his life.

When he was 18, Lee went to the U.S. to further his academic career. He left Hong Kong in April 1959, disembarking in San Francisco with but a hundred dollars. Having been the Hong Kong cha-cha champion in 1958, he at first gave dance lessons. After a few months, now in Seattle, he lived and worked in a Chinese restaurant and enrolled in Edison Technical School to complete his high school requirements. He continued to practice gung-fu and soon acquired a small group of students with whom he trained in various garages, parking lots, and other open spaces. A basement in Seattle Chinatown provided the site of his first official gym.

Bruce was soon accepted at the University of Washington, where he majored in philosophy. In his three years of study, he began to integrate philosophical tenets with the martial arts, examining such concepts as the Chinese **yin/yang** principle and its application to physical combat. In an essay entitled *The Tao of Gung-Fu,* he wrote: "Chinese gung-fu is a subtle art of matching the essence of the mind to that of the techniques in which it has to work." In these years he began an intense examination of his art and its impact on his developing "self."

While at college, Lee met Linda Emery, a student in his gung-fu class; they were married in 1964 and would later have two children, Brandon and Shannon. In 1964 they moved to Oakland, Calif., where Bruce opened a gym with his friend and long-time practitioner, **James Lee.** Difference of opinion on how the Chinese martial arts should be taught soon arose among gung-fu sifu in San Francisco, and a challenge was issued by them. Although Lee was victorious in this encounter, he began to feel trapped by the limitations of the wing chun style and its emphasis on hand techniques. He commenced a more complete exploration of combat—Eastern, Western, ancient, and modern—to find what was personally appropriate.

Lee ruffled a good many traditional feathers with his eclectic methods and insistence that any particular style binds and confines the adherent. He disdained the use of rank or belt, feeling that the process of understanding oneself cannot be measured in numbers of techniques one has learned. Lee's personal development resulted in the "way," which is identified with his name, **jeet kune do.** Since jeet kune do is not a formalized body of knowledge or technique, it cannot be classified as a style. Rather, he taught it as a vehicle of self-discovery and personal liberation through rejection of mechanical routine and conditioned limitations. Lee was an exceptional teacher

The certificate of achievement given to Steve McQueen by his instructor, Bruce Lee

Bruce Lee

Bruce Lee as he appeared in his most successful movie, *Enter the Dragon*

Linda Lee

because he could adapt his discussion of martial arts and life situations to the listener's ability to understand. Through his writings and teachings, he was largely responsible for the dispelling of myths that have shrouded the oriental fighting arts and their greater acceptance by the American public.

In August 1964 Lee was invited by **Ed Parker** to give a demonstration at the **International Karate Championships** in Long Beach. A spectator at this tournament was Jay Sebring, hair stylist to many Hollywood personalities. A client of Jay's, William Dozier, was a producer looking for an oriental actor to play the part of Charlie Chan's Number One Son for a planned TV series. The result of these coincidences was that in 1966 20th Century Fox signed Lee to play Kato in the *Green Hornet* television series. The public was intrigued by the practical nonmystical presentation of the oriental martial arts and the wide range of flexibility and tools that they provided over the traditional boxing and wrestling techniques more frequently depicted in movies and TV. The high visibility of his Kato role, combined with Lee's unique physical abilities and spontaneous nature, engendered interest in the martial arts.

From 1967-71 Bruce was featured in several TV shows and movies. He established a Los Angeles branch of the Jun Fan Gung Fu School, where **Dan Inosanto,** his senior student, assisted. Lee also gave private lessons to well-known personalities ranging from Kareem Abdul Jabbar to Steve McQueen. During these years Bruce studied constantly to refine his art; he wrote articles for martial arts publications that trace the evolution of his thinking. He collected an extensive library of books relating to all types of combat, physical fitness, philosophy, and self-improvement. His writings fill several volumes, which were edited and published as *The Tao of Jeet Kune Do* after his death. At some point he decided his art—without curricular maxims and formalized approaches—could not be reproduced in a chain of schools and instead focused on success in the film industry.

In 1971 Bruce returned to Hong Kong to make two films, *The Big Boss* (a.k.a. *Fists of Fury*) and *Fist of Fury (The Chinese Connection).* These films were so successful, breaking all previous box office records in Hong Kong, that in 1972 he formed Concord Productions with Raymond Chow and wrote, directed, produced, and starred in his third film, *The Way of the Dragon* (a.k.a. *Return of the Dragon*). He immediately went into production on the *Game of Death* with Kareem Abdul Jabbar, but this film was incomplete at the time of Lee's death. His last film, *Enter the Dragon,* was a co-production with Concord and Warner Bros. Bruce would not live to see the finished product, which premiered at Mann's Chinese Theater in Hollywood, in August 1973. This film is revered as a classic martial arts picture, as is evidenced not only by its financial success, but by the fact that in the eight years since its release it has not been shown on television and continues to draw crowds when it is reissued in theaters around the world.

Lee died suddenly on July 20, 1973. The official verdict was death by misadventure caused by hypersensitive reaction to a headache-tablet ingredient. More than 20,000 aggrieved fans gathered at his funeral in Hong Kong. He was buried in Seattle, Wash., in a peaceful and natural setting overlooking the University of Washington where he spent many a carefree and simpler day.

In the years since his death, Lee's picture has appeared on the covers of hundreds of martial arts magazines. Worldwide merchandizing, numerous fan clubs, museums, honorary exhibitions, and many attempts to duplicate his success story and to replicate his image all attest to his legendary status. But his achievements have been most appreciated by the martial arts community. Through his physical prowess, his intense study and application, his desire for excellence, and his emphasis on quality, he elevated the ideals of those whose lives he touched. *See also* U.S., history of karate in; jeet kune do; motion pictures and television. (LINDA LEE) *Further reading: The Legend of Bruce Lee,* Alex Ben Block, 1974; *Bruce Lee, The Man Only I Knew,* Linda Lee, 1976.

LEE, CHONG (1938-) Korean-born tae kwon do instructor and pioneer; the "father of Canadian tae kwon do." Lee left Korea in 1962, eventually settling in Montreal, where he began to teach tae kwon do in 1964. Now a Canadian citizen, he operates a chain of schools affiliated with the **World Taekwon-Do Federation.** Lee

won the All Canadian Tae Kwon Do Championships in 1972, and the Battle of Champions in 1973.

Over the years, he has trained dozens of black belts, among them Daniel Richer, a former full-contact world middleweight contender.

LEE, ERIC (1948-) Chinese-American kata and weapons champion. Born in Chung Shan village, Canton province, China, in early 1962, Lee was sent to school in Nicaragua; later he moved to Oakland, Calif. He began tournament competition in 1968 and retired in 1974 as an undefeated kata champion. Lee is proficient in more than 20 different martial arts weapons, including the Chinese double swords, triple irons, spear, steel whip, daggers, and nunchaku.

At one time a Chinese opera performer, he has acted in films such as *The Killer Elite, Death Machines, Good Guys Wear Black, Shame Shame on the Dixie Boys, A Force of One,* and *Americathon;* he had starring roles in *Weapons of Death, Shinubi,* and *The Falcon's Claw.*

He has made training films and has authored a self-defense book, *Eric Lee's Practical Self-Defense.* Before the advent of form ratings, Lee was unofficially considered the number-one form champion in the U.S.

LEE, FRANK PANG (1940-) Chinese-Canadian instructor, promoter, and referee. Lee began his martial arts training under Fan Hung in Hong Kong in 1950. He studied various styles of kung-fu and later created his own system based on the white crane style. Lee promoted full-contact bouts in Edmonton and Calgary from 1970 through 1976.

LEE, HAENG UNG (1935-) Korean-American tae kwon do pioneer and instructor. Born in Manchuria to Korean parents, Lee returned to Seoul after World War II. He began training in tae kwon do as a teenager—he and friends trained in the street until they found expert supervision.

Lee received his 1st-degree black belt in chung do kwan at his third six-month testing. Later, as the martial art burst into widespread popularity in the new Republic of Korea, Lee was drafted into the Korean Army, where he taught tae kwon do as his military duty.

Haeng Ung Lee

After four years in the military, Lee opened a commercial chung do kwan school in Osan. In 1962 he immigrated to the U.S., brought to Omaha, Neb., by an American black belt student, Richard Reed. In 1966 Lee and Reed founded a regional organization that grew into the American Tae Kwon Do Association (ATA) in 1969. The ATA, with headquarters in Little Rock, Ark., has become one of the largest in American martial arts, with an estimated 80,000 members and 250 schools, according to an organization spokesman. In 1980 the national headquarters began using its own IBM computer for rank records and research, perhaps the first American martial arts organization to do so. *See also* U.S., history of karate in. (MILO DAILEY)

LEE, JAE MAN Korean-American hapkido, judo, and tae kwon do instructor. A professor of physical education at Nicholls State University in Thibadaux, La., Lee is president of the American Collegiate Tae Kwon Do Association. He hosted the 2nd National Collegiate Tae Kwon Do Championships.

LEE, JAMES YIMM (1920-72) Chinese-American kung-fu pioneer and author. Lee was active in physical activities as a child and participated in gymnastics and wrestling in high school. While working as a welder in Hawaii during World War II, he undertook judo. He also practiced sil-lum kung-fu in San Francisco for four years before studying **wing chun** kung-fu and **jeet kune do** under **Bruce Lee** in 1962; he was one of the few instructors taught personally by the late martial arts idol.

During the early 1960s, he and Bruce Lee operated a kung-fu studio in Oakland, Calif. In 1964 the pair became one of the first to teach kung-fu to non-orientals in northern California. As early as 1959, Lee founded a martial arts publishing firm, perhaps the first in America, which printed Bruce Lee's first book, *Chinese Gung-Fu: The Philosophical Art of Self-Defense.*

Prior to his death from cancer, James Yimm Lee occasionally taught wing chun and jeet kune do to a small private class. Shortly before his death, he authored *Wing Chun Kung-Fu: Chinese Art of Self-Defense,* published in 1972.

LEE, JOHNNY KWONG MING (1946-) Chinese-born kung-fu instructor. Lee, born in Shanghai, began martial arts in 1956 under Sun Paul Kong. In 1962 he became assistant instructor to Yip Yui Ting. He currently teaches my jong law-horn and is chief instructor of the White Lepord Kung-Fu School in Shreveport, La.

Johnny Kwong Ming Lee

LEE, TINN CHAN Chinese-born kung-fu master. An expert in **t'ai-chi-ch'uan,** Lee is credited as the first Chinese martial arts instructor in Hawaii to open his teachings to non-Asians at the Mun Lum Chinese Language School in Honolulu in 1957. *See also* kung-fu, Western migration of.

LEE, TOMMY (1941-) American martial arts promoter. Proficient in t'ai-chi, kung-fu, and pro boxing, he created the World Series of Martial Arts Championships. Sumo wrestlers, boxers, street-fighters, and karateka, are matched in ring competition. The first event, staged in Hawaii in 1974, marked the first professional appearance of **Benny Urquidez,** a winner in the tournament. Lee served as chairman of the AAU Division 5, South Seas.

LEE-YING-ARNG Chinese kung-fu master in Hong Kong; noted both for his mastery of several Chinese styles and his kung-fu books, several of which have been translated into English (*Iron Palm in 100 Days*).

LEGGETT, TREVOR PRYCE (1914-) British judoka and instructor. Leggett was for many years the highest ranked non-Japanese judoka and was the first Englishman to go to Japan specifically to learn the sport. He was a 3rd dan and captain of the national team when he went to Japan, in 1938; after six months, he was made 4th dan. In 1946 he was appointed head of the Japanese section of the BBS, and during the following fifteen years, trained almost every leading judo fighter in Britain at the **Budokwai.** In 1970 he was promoted to 7th dan. *See also* Europe, history of judo in.

LEMAY, GENERAL CURTIS E. Former Chief of Staff of the U.S. Air Force, Lemay was instrumental in starting judo instruction for Strategic Air Command (SAC) combat crew members in the early 1950s. A practicing judoka himself, he holds the rank of yudansha taigu (an honorary rank presented by the Kodokan to leaders who have contributed to the sport). *See also* U.S., history of judo in.

General Curtis E. Lemay

LEMMENS, GERT (1945-) Belgian karate competitor. One of Europe's top karate fighters since 1970, Lemmens placed several times in the European Championships (third in 1970 and 1972), and captained a Belgian team that placed highly in the same event (second in 1968, third in 1969, second in 1971). He instructs in the **Shotokan** style.

LEONG, ALBERT American kung-fu competitor; noted for performance with kung-fu weaponry. Leong moved to California at 12 and began kung-fu under **Ark-Yuey Wong;** he later joined **Doug Wong's** kwoon. He became the star of a weapons demonstration duo (the other half was **James Lew**). Quan-do, a 2,000-year-old weapon named after the Chinese god Quan, is Leong's specialty.

LEUNG, SHUM Chinese-born kung-fu instructor. He studied the **eagle claw system** in Hong Kong. Leung came to the U.S. and opened a school in New York City in 1972.

LEUNG, TING (ca. 1947-) Chinese kung-fu master, author and pioneer. Born in Hong Kong, Leung Ting began **wing chun** training at 13 with Leung Buk, a student of grandmaster **Yip Man**'s most senior disciple, the late Leung Sheung. In November 1966, he first started teaching kung-fu privately at his uncle's gymnasium in Hunghom, Kowloon, and in 1968 established public classes at Hong Kong Baptist College.

Between 1970 and 1972, Leung served as secretary of the Hong Kong Ving Tsun Athletics Association, the student-run organization which operated Yip Man's kung-fu school during the grandmaster's final years of failing health. In this position, Leung succeeded in preserving many photographs and memorabilia from Yip's lifetime of dedication to the martial arts.

On July 24, 1973, Leung founded the International Wing Tsun Leung Ting Martial Arts Association, a legally registered fraternity of kung-fu schools which today has branches throughout the world (New Zealand, Austria, West Germany, Greece, Yugoslavia, Denmark, Italy, Britain, and the United States). His method of kung-fu instruction became designated by spelling the name of his art as "wing tsun."

Between 1975 and 1976, Leung was an editor for Hong Kong's now defunct English-language martial arts magazine, *Real Kung-Fu*. Having graduated with a B.A. degree in English and Chinese literature in 1973, he quickly used the print media and his facility with the English language to become an outspoken authority on wing chun kung-fu. He authored *Wing Tsun Kuen* in 1968 and *Seven Stars Praying Mantis Kung-Fu* in 1980.

Leung also has worked as a technical director in the Hong Kong film industry, amassing more than two dozen television and film credits. Among his most notable students are Tam Kung Fun (New Zealand), **Keith Kernspect** (West Germany), A.S. Sharif (Denmark), and **Ron Van Clief** (New York). (Paul Maslak)

LEW, JAMES (1952-) American martial arts competitor and performer. He began Korean-style martial arts in 1967, at 14; after a few years he switched to kung-fu and specialized in the five-animal system of Shao-lin and the white lotus system. Lew became a regional kata star, winning numerous grand championships. Drawing upon his training techniques, he authored *The Art of Stretching and Kicking*. He has appeared in television roles, such as *Kung-Fu, The Fall Guy, In Search Of . . ., When Hell Was In Session,* and *Stunt Seven.* His early film credits include John Cassavete's *Killing of a Chinese Bookie* and Hong Kong Production's *Tiger Man.* He recently starred in *The Young Dragon.*

LEWIS, JOE (1944-) American karate pioneer, champion, and instructor. Born March 7, 1944, Lewis grew up on a farm in Knightdale, N.C. As a teenager, he took up body building and wrestling.

Lewis joined the U.S. Marine Corps in 1962 and first saw karate while stationed at Cherry Point. He started karate in 1964, stationed with the Marines in Okinawa, and achieved the extraordinary by earning his black belt in seven months. His instructors on Okinawa were **Eizo Shimabuko (ro),** John Korab, and Kinjo Kinsoku, from whom he learned the side kick that became his competitive trademark.

In 1966, with only twenty-two months of training, Lewis won the grand championship of the first tournament he entered, **Jhoon**

Joe Lewis, one of the all-time greats of American karate

Rhee's U.S. Nationals in Washington, D.C. His feat was remarkable in that he was unfamiliar with the rules and had never before seen a karate tournament. Yet he won every match, including those against nationally reputed fighters, by scoring all of his points with but one technique, the side kick. He also won the black belt kata championship.

Lewis reigned as this tournament's grand champion for four years, through 1969.

In Los Angeles, in 1966, he trained with **Gordon Doversola,** an Okinawa-te stylist. Lewis conceived the first set of top-10 ratings for American karate fighters, which appeared in the April 1967 issue of *Black Belt.* In 1968 Lewis began training with **Bruce Lee** in **jeet kune do** and, intending to become a professional boxer, studied with Joe Orbillo, a world-ranked heavyweight contender. He won the 1968 World Professional Heavyweight Championship (of karate) in New York City. In 1969 Lewis won the first of three consecutive grand championships of the **International Karate Championships** in Long Beach, Calif. To date, he is the only three-time champion of this tournament.

During his tournament fighting career, Lewis amassed more than 30 major titles. With **Mike Stone** and **Chuck Norris,** he is one of the three great American champions of light-contact karate in the 1960s.

He introduced **full-contact** karate in 1970, revolutionizing the sport. In the sport's first bout, conducted at the Long Beach Arena on Jan. 17, Lewis scored a 2nd-round knockout over Greg Baines to become the original heavyweight champion. As U.S. Heavyweight Kick-Boxing Champion, Lewis defended his title ten times, knocking out all of his opponents in the 1st or 2nd round. His ring savvy caught the attention of *Sports Illustrated* and *The Ring,* and in 1970 Lewis became the first karate champion featured in these publications.

Lewis began taking acting lessons in 1971 and in 1973 he co-hosted a *Merv Griffin Show* exclusively devoted to the martial arts.

By 1972 the sport of American kick-boxing had died, and in 1973 Lewis began an effort to resurrect it. He and one of his few black belt students, **Tom Tannenbaum,** a vice-president at Universal Television, created the World Professional Championships as a 90-minute special for ABC's *Wide World of Entertainment.* The event took place Sept. 14, 1974, at the Los Angeles Sports Arena; Lewis won the heavyweight division with a 2nd-round knockout over Yugoslavia's Frank Brodar.

As early as 1968, Lewis had begun presenting sophisticated

348

technical fighting seminars across the U.S. and abroad. In 1973 he created a revolutionary scientific approach to tournament and full-contact fighting. He subsequently taught his unique theories to almost every important American karate champion throughout the 1970s. Today these theories are still used by fighters who consider them the work of genius.

In 1974, shortly before he appeared on the cover of *Playgirl,* Lewis retired from competition, his fighting career spanning almost a decade. Coming out of retirement, he suffered two consecutive full-contact non-title defeats: a 3-round decision to Teddy Limoz in July 1975 in Hawaii, and a 7-round decision to **Ross Scott** in Sept. in New Jersey. In this last match, impaired by a dislocated shoulder, he lost only through penalties assessed against him for failing to make the mandatory six kicks per round.

Following this, Lewis pursued a full-time acting career. Through Bruce Lee, Lewis had gotten a bit part in 1968 in *The Wrecking Crew,* starring Dean Martin.

In 1978 he starred in *Jaguar Lives,* and in 1981 he starred in *Force: Five,* a successful martial arts film that cast leading martial artists in key roles.

Lewis began writing articles concerning his technical theories in 1973 for *Professional Karate Magazine.* His definitions appear throughout this encyclopedia. He is currently writing his first instructional textbook, with **John Corcoran,** entitled *Martial Arts for the Masses.* In 1975 Lewis was named to *Who's Who in the Martial Arts* and inducted into the **Black Belt Hall of Fame** as "Karate Player of the Year." *See also* U.S., history of karate in; motion pictures and television.

LEWIS, LYNNE (1957-   ) American judo champion. Lewis began martial arts in 1972 under Jim Pedro at the Massasoit dojo. She received her black belt in 1975 from Pedro at the High School Nationals in Dallas, Tex. She is affiliated with the AAU, USIF, and the USJA. She was New England grand champion from 1975-77, and Junior National champion in 1972. Other victories include the High School Nationals in 1975, and the Senior Nationals in 1975 and 1976. In addition, Lewis won in successive years an honor never before awarded, for Best Technique. In 1975 she won a gold medal in the British Open Championships and a silver medal in 1976.

Lynne Lewis

LIAO-WAN-PAO Well-known exponent of the white crane (Fukien style) system of Chinese kung-fu in the Republic of China.

LIAO-WU-CH'ANG Well-known master of the Monkey style of Chinese kung-fu in the Republic of China.

LIAO-WU-FANG Well-known master of the Shao-lin (Fukien style) system of Chinese kung-fu in the Republic of China.

LI-CH'ANG-YU (1851-1929) Famous **hsing-i** boxer and disciple of Ch'e I-chai.

LIEB, ERNEST American karate instructor. In 1957 he studied judo but soon switched to jujutsu and karate. In 1962, while stationed with the U.S. Air Force in Korea, he practiced karate under a Mr. Chun. In 1963, he took first place in the Chidokwan Championships in Korea, the first of 12 titles in various tournaments. After his discharge, Lieb opened a dojo in Muskegon, Mich., in 1964 and continued his studies with **Tadashi Yamashita.** Director of the AKA, Lieb was named in 1973 to the **Black Belt Hall of Fame** as "Man of the Year." *See also* U.S., history of karate in.

LI-KIM-SUI Well-known master of the **Shao-lin** (Fukien style) system of Chinese kung-fu in the Republic of China.

LIMAS, ARLENE (1966-   ) American karate competitor. She began studying martial arts at 5 with her brother, Arnold, eventually earning black belt equivalency in **Shao-lin** kung-fu. At just 15, she rose to national prominence by virtue of major victories in national-scale karate tournaments. In 1981, she won the sparring grand championship of the Diamond Nationals, AKA Grand Nationals, the Portland Pro-Am, and Steve Fisher's Karate Championships. She also placed high in form competition. *Karate Illustrated* ranked her the number-two female fighter in the U.S. for 1981, as well as 5th in women's forms and 5th in co-ed weapons.

LIN, WILLY (1938-   ) Chinese-American kung-fu instructor. Lin began martial arts in 1957 under Wang Jue-Jin in Taichung, Taiwan. In 1962 he became Wang's chief disciple and head instructor in kung-fu. He teaches t'ien shan p'ai (northern style) kung-fu. Lin wrote *T'ien Shan P'ai Kung-Fu,* published in 1976. He organized a performing group that stages kung-fu exhibitions.

Willy Lin

LINICK, ANDREW S. (1945-) American karate instructor, author, and administrator. In 1958 he began his study of the martial arts, and in 1965 he received his black belt in both karate and judo. He won numerous regional tournaments, specializing in weapons (**kobu-jutsu**). Linick wrote *Nunchaku, Karate's Deadliest Fighting Sticks* and *Zen, the Realm of Nothingness.* In addition, he is executive director of the U.S. East Coast Karate Alliance; chairman of the Jewish Karate Federation of America, Inc.; co-chairman of the Karate U.S. Committee Sports for Israel, Inc. (sponsors of the U.S. Maccabiah Team); and president of the Okinawan Kobu-jutsu Kyokai.

LIN-KUO-CHUNG Well-known master of the white crane (Fukien style) of Chinese kung-fu in the Republic of China.

LIQUORI, WILLIAM A. (1933-) American karate competitor, instructor, and promoter. Liquori began training in 1958 under **Peter Urban,** earning his black belt in 1969 in the U.S.A. Goju system. He is senior advisor for the FBBA and chairman of its Sanctioning Committee. Among his promotions are the Greater Orlando Karate Classic and the Annual Region 9 Karate Championships. Liquori is chief instructor for the Orlando Police Academy Self-Defense and Physical Conditioning Unit. His noted students include Herb Thompson, Mike Bell, Gene Fry, and Alan Watson.

LIU, YUN CHIAO (1908-)Chinese kung-fu master; the foremost authority of **pa chi** and **pa-kua** kung-fu. A descendant of the Liu clan, a wealthy and influential Chinese family, Yun Chiao Liu began martial arts training in his family's castle in 1913 with his grandfather's bodyguard, Yau Ting Chang, who taught the youth **mi tsung-i** and **tai-tsu-chang-ch'uan.** From 1915-24, Liu learned pa chi from Shu Wen Li, one of northern China's most notorious martial artists.

Following this, Liu and Li went to Shangtung Province, traveling together for another five or six years, during which time Liu met Pao Tien Kung, with whom he was to train for some time in pa-kua. Liu also studied **praying mantis** (six harmonies style) with grandmaster Tsu Teng Ching. And finally, he also studied **t'ai-chi-ch'uan** from Hsiang Wu Chang.

In the 1930s, Liu became a captain of Chinese commando forces at the beginning of the Sino-Japanese war. After World War II, he had advanced to the rank of general. In 1949, when the Communists came into control of China, he, as well as thousands of other once-privileged people, fled, losing property and wealth. He continued service in the armed forces until 1955, after which he founded the Wu Tang Martial Arts Development Center in Taiwan and began teaching martial arts. Today this association includes most of the instructors of northern Chinese martial arts in Taiwan. Besides being recognized as the foremost living authority of two styles, he has also mastered three others. (JAMES NAIL)

LIU-YEN-CHIAO Taiwanese kung-fu teacher, noted for his ability as a swordsman. *See also* praying mantis (six harmonies style).

LOMAX, MALCOLM (1947-) Australian karate instructor. In 1967 he trained in **goju-ryu** under Tino Ceverano. The following year, in Vietnam with the Australian forces, he studied tae kwon do. Also trained in Okinawan karate and **hung gar** kung-fu, he acted as a guard for celebrities, hotels, and night clubs. In 1976 Lomax went to Hong Kong to train in ma'chung lama pei. Within a ten-year span (1971-81), he opened 52 karate clubs throughout Australia. He appeared in 1982 with **Chuck Norris** in *Silent Rage.*

LONG, HAROLD American karate pioneer and instructor. Sent to Okinawa by the Marine Corps in 1956, he sought out **Tatsuo Shimabuku** to study **isshinryu** karate, earning his black belt seventeen months later. Long opened one of the first dojos in the southeast after his discharge in 1959 and return to Tennessee. In August 1974 Long discussed with Shimabuku the inauguration of an association. Long was elected first president of the new organization, the International Isshinryu Karate Association. Although he claims to have taught more than 30,000 students, he also claims to have awarded fewer than 200 black belts. He is the author of a series of books entitled *Dynamics of Isshinryu Karate. See also* U.S., history of karate in.

LONGSTREET, JOHN (1959-) American karate instructor and competitor. He began martial arts in 1973 under **John Worley.** Currently Longstreet is head instructor of the West St. Paul branch of the Mid-America karate chain, instructing in American karate and tae kwon do. His tournament wins include the 1978 Diamond Nationals, the 1979 and 1980 Forth Worth Pro/Am. In professional competition he was rated 6th in the U.S. by *Karate Illustrated* in 1979, and 2nd in 1981.

John Longstreet

LORENZ, DIETMAR German judo champion. Lorenz was European champion in 1977 and 1978 and won the 1980 Moscow Olympics in the open division. He is an expert at **uchimata,** as well as mat work.

LOUIE, WILLIAM (1951-) Chinese-American karate competitor and performer. Famous for his spectacular demonstrations of karate and related martial arts, Louie studied under such instructors as **Peter Urban** (goju); Chan Tai Hing (hung gar); Gin Foo Mark (praying mantis); and Stan Israel (judo). He is also considered a top kata competitor. In the recent past, Louie has been involved in motion pictures, co-starring in films such as *The Intrigue, Death Force, Death Promise,* and *Fist of Fear, Touch of Death.* He starred in the 1980 feature *Bruce vs. Bill,* released by Golden Light Film Co.

LOVEN, CHUCK (1939-) American karate competitor, instructor, and referee. He studied with **Pat Burleson** of Ft. Worth, Tex. Before his retirement in 1972, Loven was nationally rated by *Black Belt Magazine* in 1970 and 1971. He trained world and nationally rated fighters including **Pat Worley, Larry Carnahan,** and also Gary Hestilow, Billy Simmons, Danny Edison, Shelbron Barnes, and Charlotte Hoffman. Member of the *Who's Who in the Martial Arts.*

Bill Watson sidesteps a backfist by Chuck Loven as Ed Daniels officiates.

LOW, KON LIN Malaysian tae kwon do instructor and administrator. He received his original instruction in 1962 from **Gen. Choi Hong Hi**, who was then Korea's ambassador to Malaysia. When Choi returned to Korea in 1965, Low continued his training with the newly arrived ambassador, **Tae Hi Nam**. When Nam left Malaysia In 1970, Low was named chief instructor for that country, overseeing ten tae kwon do institutions. Because Malaysia ranks third in the line of genetic tae kwon do migration, following Korea and Vietnam, respectively, Low holds a prestigious position in the **International Taekwon-do Federation**.

LOWE, EDWARD "BOBBY" American karate pioneer. One of the five original black-belt-ranked students of **James Mitose**, Lowe deviated somewhat from Mitose's **kosho-ryu kempo**. In 1958 Lowe affiliated his school with **Mas Oyama's kyokushinkai** of Tokyo, Japan. *See also* U.S., history of karate in.

MABERRY, JOHN EARL (1958-) American martial artist and journalist. Maberry began martial arts training in 1967 under Joshua J. Johnson, a hapkidoist. He also trained in Shinowara-kan jujutsu, judo, and aikido, also taught at Maberry's parent school, the Ju-Ka-Do Dojo of Philadelphia. He added Sil-Lum pai kung-fu to his repertoire in the early 1970s, training with Kam L. Fong.

He is a contributing editor to both *Inside Kung-Fu* and *Kick Illustrated* magazines, and a frequent contributor to *Black Belt* and *Karate Illustrated*.

MABUNI, KENWA (1889-1957) Okinawan karate master and pioneer. Founder of the **Shito-ryu** style of karate, Mabuni studied **Shuri-te** with **Yasutsune Itosu**, **Naha-te** with **Kanryo Higashionna**, and **goju-ryu** with **Chojun Miyagi**. Descended from a famous **samurai** and wanting to overcome poor health, he began intensive karate training at 13. He also studied techniques of the **bo, sai, tonfa, kama,** and **nunchaku** under Arakaki. By combining the teachings of Itosu and Higashionna, he developed a hybrid system he called Shito-ryu, today one of Japan's four major karate systems

Mabuni taught his art to Okinawan police and self-defense forces. In 1929 he moved permanently to Osaka, teaching regularly at Japanese universities and police departments. His son, Kanei, became Mabuni's best pupil and assumed the responsibility as chief instructor upon his father's death. *See also* Okinawa, history of martial arts in.

MACARUSO, DAN (1957-) American **full-contact** karate champion. Macaruso began martial arts in 1976 under **George Pesare.** In 1979 he received his black belt from Pesare. In noncontact tournament competition, Macaruso won the Annual Kempo Karate Instructor Tournament 1977-80 and the New England Black Belt Tournament in 1979. Turning to full-contact, he defeated fighters such as Ron Thiveridge, from whom he won the New England middleweight championship in 1978, and Rory Bussey, for the 1979 PKA U.S. Light Heavyweight title. On Jan. 10, 1980, he decisioned World Champion **Jeff Smith**; he defended his world title twice in 1980, defeating **Dominic Valera** in Paris and Carl Beamon.

MAGDALENO, RICHARD (1944-) American karate instructor. He began the arts in 1959, receiving his black sash in 1963 from J.Y. Sa in the Sam Sow Che style. In 1966 he won a black belt from **Hwang Kee** in tang soo do and moo duk kwan.

Magdaleno is president of the International Lei Lum Tong, Thunder Dragon Kung-Fu Association; assistant and acting regional examiner for the U.S. Tang Soo Do Federation, and president of the Western Karate Federation. He is also owner of a custom weapons manufacturing company in San Diego and co-authored a book with Chung Wha Yong entitled *Tang Soo Do.*

MALEY, ED American judo instructor. Among his students are Tommy Rigg, silver medalist at the world University Games; Ron Sliner, 1971 Southeast Heavyweight AAU Champion; Tommy Masterson, National Collegiate Champion; Kerry Kins, 10-year-old 1971 Junior Champion; and Gene Garren, Pan-American gold medalist. A certified graduate of the **Kodokan,** Maley was five-time champion of the Eighth Air Force Tournament and undefeated Florida State Champion from 1959-65. *See also* U.S., history of judo in.

MAMI, JEAN LUC (1952-) French karate champion. A member of the winning French National Team at the 1974 and 1975 European Championships, Mami also won the French Championships in 1974, and placed second at the European Championships in the same year. A pupil of European ex-champion **Gilbert Gruss,** he studied karate from the age of 17. Roundhouse kicks and reverse roundhouse kicks are his specialty.

Yip Man

MAN, YIP (- 1972) Grand master of the Wing-Chun style of kung-fu. He was born in Fatshan, in Kwantung province where he began his kung-fu training with Chan Wah Shun at age 13. At 16 he moved to Hong Kong where he studied Wing-Chun under Leung Bik. At age 24 he returned to Fatshan where he lived in relative ease practicing his kung-fu, but not teaching it. After WWII, Yip Man and his family moved to Hong Kong where in 1949 he became kung-fu instructor to the Association of Restaurant Workers. Two years later, he opened his own school, and as his students increased in numbers he was forced to move to bigger facilities. Wing-Chun began to become highly visible and many people began to study the art, especially members of the police force.

In 1967 he founded the Hong Kong Wing-Chun Athletic Association to continue to promote the style. In 1970 he retired from active teaching, and in 1972 he died of throat cancer. Superstar Bruce Lee was a student of Yip Man.

MARCHINI, RON (1945-) American karate instructor, champion, and promoter; member of the **Black Belt Hall of Fame.** A tournament fighter of the late 1960s and early 1970s, among his many victories were grand championships at the 1968 North American Tournament of Champions and at the 1971 National Black Belt Championships, and the middleweight title of the 1971 World Pro/Am Championships. He also won the 1965 Western Karate Championships, 1966-68 California Karate Championships, and 1967 Pacific Coast Invitational; he was a U.S. team member at the 1st and 2nd World Championships and was subsequently the coach for the U.S. team. His ability as an instructor and referee earned him seven Golden Fist awards. Marchini is a member of the *Who's Who in the Martial Arts* and has co-promoted several West Coast tournaments. He was rated America's number-one karate fighter in 1969 and 1970 by *Black Belt Magazine.*

He is the co-author of *Power Training for Kung-Fu and Karate,* and wrote and published *Rembukai* in 1981. He is the only licensed rembukai instructor in the U.S. Retired from active competition, Marchini starred in several films, including *Murder in the Orient, Yellow Faced Tiger, Death Machines* (a film he also produced), and a tournament karate documentary titled *The New Gladiators,* financed by Elvis Presley. *See also* U.S., history of karate in.

American karate champion Ron Marchini

MARK, BOW-SIM Chinese-American **wu-shu** master. Trained from childhood in wu-shu, and completing the standard college course in Chinese wu-shu, Mark composed two sword forms included by several schools in their training. From 1968-73, she assisted Fu Wing-Fay in perfecting Pa-Kua Leung Yee Boxing. In 1973 she became chief instructor of the Women's Wu-Shu Association in Hong Kong. In 1975, while touring in the U.S., she settled in Boston, where she now instructs. Mark lectured in 1976 on wu-shu and **t'ai-chi-ch'uan** at M.I.T. In 1977, she wrote *Simplified Tai Chi Chuan* and *Basic Broad Sword.*

MARSHALL, FURMAN L. (1936-) American karate instructor. Marshall began the martial arts in 1964 and received a black belt in 1967 from **Ki Whang Kim** in tae kwon do.

He and other black belts organized the Brotherhood of Martial Arts, an association for sharing techniques among different styles and systems. He participated in the World Blackbelt League Competition and staged numerous demonstrations in Washington, D.C., Virginia, and Maryland.

MARTIN, JIMMY American judo champion. Fighting in the 143-lb. division, he won the 1977, 1978, and 1979 AAU Nationals. In 1979 he won the Pan-American Trials and the World Trials.

MARTIN, TOMMY (1956-) American judo champion. Martin received his black belt at 15, one of the youngest persons elevated to that status in the U.S. In 1972 Martin placed second in the U.S. Judo Nationals, won the National Championships in his age group, and was an alternate for the U.S. Olympic team. He won a gold medal at the 1974 Pan-American Games and was U.S. National Champion in the following year. In 1976 he represented the U.S. at the Montreal Olympics, finishing in fourth place.

MARUYAMA, PAUL American judo champion and instructor. Born in Japan, where he began judo, he came to the U.S. in 1961, and in 1962 won the national college championships. He won the light-middleweight championships at the 1966 U.S. Nationals and a silver medal at the Pan-American Games in Brazil. Maruyama represented the U.S. at the World Championships in Rio de Janeiro and Salt Lake City, and at the 1968 Olympics. After retiring he became coach at the U.S. Air Force Academy.

Left to right: Paul Maruyama, Tommy Martin, and Jimmy Martin at the 1979 World Judo Championships in Paris

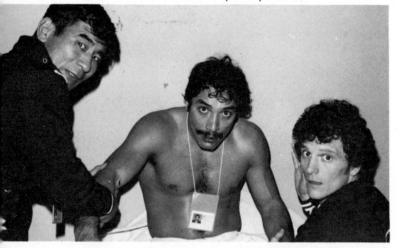

MARX, KARL W. American martial arts instructor. Marx is a graduate of Louisiana College with a degree in psychology. His major contribution to the martial arts has been in the field of education, with special interest in martial arts as a therapeutic recreational and rehabilitative process. He is an author of several books on martial arts, sociology, recreation, and other related fields of martial arts. He is director of the Keichu American Karate Institute, and president of the W.K.C.D. Self Defense Federation of Human Development where research is being conducted in relation to martial arts and crime prevention.

MASLAK, PAUL (1951-) American martial arts writer, author, and statistician. Maslak began martial arts training at 14, with high school wrestling and amateur boxing. While in college, he studied tae kwon do, **shorin-ryu, isshinryu, bando,** judo, and **Shao-lin** kung-fu. Trained in both quantification and systems analysis, Maslak undertook a statistical study of professional boxing, **full-contact** karate, and Japanese kick-boxing. The results of his research, which he calls **positional theory,** comprised the basis for two books: *Strategy in Unarmed Combat* and *What The Masters Know,* published in 1979.

As an editor of *Inside Kung-Fu,* he introduced the use of statistical analysis to sport karate, and with **John Corcoran,** created the **STAR** (Standardized Tournaments And Ratings) **System,** a ratings system for full-contact and tournament karate. Maslak encouraged national adoption of **semicontact** rules for open competitions, mandatory seeding of top competitors, and establishment of separate women's divisions in **kata** and full-contact. With karate official **Tom Schlesinger,** Maslak co-authored the Schlesinger Rules System for point tournaments, and in 1980 wrote the official rules of the **WKA** for full-contact competition.

MASON, TED (1938-) American karate instructor. Mason began **tang soo do** in 1964 under Donald Garrett and attained 1st dan in 1967. Currently a 3rd dan in tang soo do moo duk kwan, he has a kyo-sa (instructor) rating from **Hwang Kee,** the president and founder. Among his black belt students was **Howard Jackson,** rated the number 1 fighter of 1974. Mason was influential, with the help of Roberto Villalba, in the introduction of tang soo do to Argentina, and is known there as ''El Padrino,'' or the ''Godfather.''

MATSUDA, DON American judo competitor; winner of the Northern California Championships and the U.S. Collegiate Grand Championships (1968). He was named among the top 10 U.S. judo players for 1968 by *Black Belt Magazine.*

MATSUMURA, SOKON ''BUSHI'' (1796-1893) Okinawan karate pioneer; founder of **Shuri-te.** He trained in karate under ''Tode'' **Sakugawa** and learned Chinese kempo from a master of the Iwah school. Matsumura served as a chief of the military and a court retainer for the king of the Ryukyus.

Sakugawa gave Matsumura the nickname of ''Bushi'' early in the youngster's training.

Sokon Matsumura was the first karate master to systemize karate and to call his style by a name other than his own. Among his many noteworthy disciples are **Yasutsune Itosu, Chotoku Kyan, Choki Motobu,** and **Choshin Chibana.** He also passed down the **Chinto** kata, the oldest empty-hand form practiced in **shorin-ryu** karate, the descendent of Shuri-te. *See also* Okinawa, history of martial arts in; shorin-ryu.

MATSUNAGA, MITSUO (1939-) Japanese judo champion, 1967 World Openweight Champion at 6 feet, 245 lbs. Matsunaga qualified for the All Japan Open over eight times, winning the tournament in 1966. He competed regularly at the All Japan Police Tournament. Noted for standing armlocks.

MATSUURA, HIROSHI Japanese karate instructor and pioneer. Matsuura's training in karate began at the **Shito-ryu** dojo of Sadachika Tsugikawa, under whose instruction Matsuura remained for 15 years. In February 1966 the Nagasaki native embarked upon a fourteen-year stay in Mexico at the request of some former students. This period was to profoundly influence the tenor and tempo of karate development in Mexico. The national amateur karate teams he coached brought recognition to amateur karate in Mexico; Matsuura is regarded by many as the ''father of modern Mexican karate.'' In 1977 his team captured the gold medal at the Pan-American Championships in Montreal.

MATSUZAKA, TAKESHI (1940-) Japanese judo champion. Matsuzaka, at 5 feet 8 inches, 172 lbs., won the 1968 All Japan Open Championships and the middleweight title of the All Japan University Championships.

MATTSON, GEORGE E. (1937-) American karate instructor, author, and pioneer. He began karate in 1956 in Fatenma, Okinawa, while serving in the U.S. Army, attaining in 1958 a black belt in the **Uechi-ryu** style. Eventually, he opened a chain of schools throughout the New England states. Mattson was chairman of the North American Uechi Karate Association. From 1953-75 he promoted the North East Open Karate Championships, in Boston. In 1975 he began an annual tournament exclusively for Uechi-ryu stylists. Mattson wrote *The Way of Karate* and *Uechi-ryu Karate Do. See also* U.S., history of karate in.

MAURY-BONET, PAUL (-1972) European judo administrator. Maury-Bonet began judo under Mikonosuke Kawaishi. A well-known competitor, instructor, referee, and administrator, he founded the French Federation of Judo and Associated Sports in 1947. During his last fifteen years, he served as secretary-general of both the European Judo Union and the International Judo Federation. *See also* Europe, history of judo in.

McCALLUM, RAY (1958-   ) American karate champion. McCallum began studying karate in Texas in 1972 with several instructors: Ron Cox, Jack White, James Toney, and Max Alsup. He received additional training under Walt Bone, **Roy Kurban, Demetrius Havanas,** and Larry Caster, earning his black belt in chung do kwan in 1974. After winning his last ten tournaments as a junior without being scored on, McCallum graduated to the black belt fighting divisions in 1974.

From 1975-77 he won the middleweight division of the Houston Olympics; from 1976-81, the middleweight division of the All American Championships in Oklahoma City; and from 1975-80, the middleweight division of the Fort Worth Pro/Am.

McCallum's victories in the Fort Worth event brought him national attention, and in 1979 he made his bid for prominence by winning the grand championship runner-up position to **Keith Vitali** at the PKA Nationals in Los Angeles, where he also placed second in the Korean kata division. He was named to the **Black Belt Hall of Fame** as "Fighter of the Year" in 1979. In 1980 McCallum won the grand championship over Vitali at the Mid-America Diamond Nationals; he was named the **STAR System's** "National Light Heavyweight Champion" for **semicontact** karate.

McCallum is one of only a handful of Americans who is a champion in both the semicontact and full-contact aspects of sport karate. His first full-contact match was in March 1975, a National Karate League team event, in which he won a 3-round unanimous decision over Manny Charusan in Fort Worth.

McCallum went to Japan with little more than ten fights to his credit and fought middleweight kick-boxing champion Genshu Igari, who beat McCallum by a 5th-round TKO. On March 1, 1980, McCallum reached a turning point in his fighting career when he faced the legendary **Bill "Superfoot" Wallace** in a non-title fight in Oklahoma City. He lost to the champion in a 5-round decision. Shortly afterward, in July 1980, McCallum won the **PKA's** U.S. Middleweight Championship by virtue of a 2nd-round knockout over Glen McMorris, a title he lost in the spring of 1981 in a 4th-round knockout to **Rodney Batiste.** In Dec. 1980, McCallum won the **WKA's** U.S. Light Heavyweight Championship by a unanimous decision over Ted Pryor in Cocoa Beach, Fla.

Ray McCallum is heralded as one of the greatest fighters of his era. Martial arts journalist **John Corcoran** designated him as "the only fighter to carry on the rough-and-tumble spirit of **Joe Lewis,"** perhaps the greatest champion in the history of American Karate. *See also* U.S., history of karate in.

McDONALD, BILL (1939-   ) American karate pioneer and instructor. Winner of civic citations for a blend of karate and community work, he is also a highly regarded southern referee. A member of the *Who's Who in the Martial Arts,* McDonald sponsored several regional tournaments. He is the coach of PKA World Heavyweight Champion Demetrius Edwards. He opened the first commercial karate school in North Carolina, in Greenville, in 1961.

McFARLANE, ROBIN (1951-   ) Scottish karate competitor, McFarlane is a Shukokai stylist from Glasgow. Runner-up in the heavyweight division of the European Karate Championships, he has been among Europe's top karateka since 1973. His specialty is the sweep-punch combination.

McLOUGHLIN, CHRISTOPHER J. (1944-   ) American karate author and administrator. In 1966 he began the martial arts under **Daeshik Kim** and **Joe Corley** in Atlanta. In 1971 he received his black belt from the Korean Tae Kwon Do Association. His tournament wins include: 1972 Atlanta Open Championships; 1972 Alabama State Karate Championships; 1972 Georgia State Championships; 1973 Florida Open Championships; and the 1975 South Carolina State Championships. Author of *Personal Defense,* he is secretary and treasurer of the South East Karate Association (SEKA).

McLoughlin also writes a monthly column in *Official Karate Magazine* called *Southern Exposure.* He is a co-promoter in various pro karate events including the prestigious **Battle of Atlanta.** He is a contributing writer for the *Atlanta Sportsman Magazine;* SEKA Black Belt Examination Board and official in many of the top fights on the East Coast. McLoughlin has also been instrumental in pioneering a standard scoring system for full-contact karate. *See also* U.S., history of karate in.

MERRIMAN, CHUCK (1933-   ) American karate competitor, referee, and coach. Merriman began judo under In Soo Hwang in 1960. In 1962 he began his karate training under Chris Debaise. He participated as a member of the demo team for the Japanese Pavilion at the 1964 New York World's Fair. In 1973 he was rated nationally in the top 10 in kata by *Official Karate Magazine.*

From 1974-80 he acted as the chief referee or arbitrator for all the National AAU Karate Championships. He went to Japan in 1977, for the 4th WUKO World Championships, as chief referee. Head Coach for the 1978 USA/AAU Karate Team, he also coached the touring U.S. team in 1977 and 1978. In 1980 he was head coach of the U.S. team at the 5th WUKO World Championships in Madrid—where **Tokey Hill** won a gold medal, while two more Americans won silver and bronze. Merriman was inducted in 1980 into the **Black Belt Hall of Fame** as "Instructor of the Year," and is a member of *Who's Who in the Martial Arts. See also* U.S., history of karate in.

MEYER, LOUIS HUBERT (1949-   ) Dutch karate competitor; among the top European karatemen of the early 1970s. A wado stylist, he was noted for a variety of techniques.

MIFUNE, KYUZO (1883-1965) Japanese judo pioneer. In July 1903 he entered the **Kodokan.** Though his father cut off all financial support, Mifune supported himself publishing a popular neighborhood paper. By age 30 he was a rokudan (6th dan) and an instructor at the Kodokan. Three months before he turned 48 he was promoted to hachidan (8th dan) and at 54, reached kudan (9th dan). Mifune's major contributions were new techniques; he invented the **o-guruma.**

After war broke out he instructed at the army and navy military academies, while still teaching at the police dojo and college clubs. On May 25, 1945, at age 62, he became one of only seven men ever

Kyuzo Mifune *(right)* with Emilio Bruno; note tie.

353

Jim and Jenice Miller

to hold the distinction of judan, or 10th-degree black belt. In the late 1950s he was decorated by the government of Japan with the Order of the Rising Sun. At this time he was the head of the Kodokan's instructors and was a permanent member of the Kodokan Dojo Consultive Group. In 1910 he became judo instructor at Tokyo University, as well as a number of other universities. He married Hiratari Ikuko in 1912.

In 1956 he wrote *The Canon of Judo,* in which he set down his martial philosophy and technical theories. During his later years he continued to referee; he served as an official at the 1964 Tokyo Olympics.

In 1959 he received the Academy Prize from the Japan Scholar's Association for his work in the field of physical education.

MIFUNE, TOSHIRO (1920-) Japanese film star; epitome of the Japanese screen warrior. Best known for his dramatic and ironic-comic roles as a samurai, he is by far the best known Japanese screen personality in the world. Although it is unclear whether or not he trained in Japanese sword techniques, his masterful skill with this weapon in films has been instrumental in his samurai characterizations.

Born in Tsing-tao, China to Japanese parents, he entered films after World War II by winning a studio talent contest. His early career was shaped by director Akira Kurosawa. Films in which he depicts a samurai or a martial artist include: *Rashomon* (1950); *Seven Samurai* (1954); *Throne of Blood* (1957); *The Lower Depths* (1957); *Samurai Saga* (1959); *Yojimbo* (1961); *Sanjuro* (1962); *Samurai Pirate* (1964); *Samurai Assassin* (1965); *Red Beard* (1965); *Judo Saga* (1965); *Samurai Banners* (1969); *Red Sun* (1971); *Zato Ichi Meets Yojimbo* (1971); *Paper Tiger* (1975); and *The Bushido Blade* (1978). He also played the title characer in the American television miniseries "Shogun." *See also* chambara; motion pictures and television.

MIKAMI, SHUJI (1892-) American kendo pioneer and instructor. In 1932 he opened in Hawaii the first kendo school outside of Japan. When he retired, his two sons carried on the instruction. In 1968 the Nippon Kendo Remnei in Japan awarded him the honorary title of "Kendo Hanshi." In addition, he was awarded the Japanese Order of Merit for his service to culture. In 1968 he was named to the **Black Belt Hall of Fame.**

MIKAMI, TAKAYUKI (1933-) Japanese-American karate instructor and champion. Mikami was born in Japan and began karate when he entered Hosei University. He captained his university karate club. Prior to graduation, he applied for instructors' training at the **JKA** and was accepted. Between 1958 and 1962 he won five sparring and kata titles at the All Japan Karate Tournament. In 1963 he traveled to Kansas City, Mo., and later moved to New Orleans, where he teaches the **Shotokan** style at his own dojo. He was named in 1975 to *Who's Who in the Martial Arts.* Mikami is affiliated with the **International Shotokan Karate Federation** as well as the JKA, and also holds office for the All South Karate Federation. *See also* Shotokan.

MIKI, MINOBU (1945-) Japanese-born American karate competitor. Miki was born in Nagoya, Japan, and began his study of the martial arts in 1957. In 1961 he received his black belt from Koshi Yamada. He instructs in Hayashi-ha and **Shito-ryu.** He is affiliated with the **Federation of All Japan Karate-do Organizations,** the **World Union of Karate-do Organizations,** and is the vice chairman of the committee of the Japan Karate-do Organization.

His titles include: 1967 Atlantic Coast Grand Champion; 1968 Tennessee Grand Champion; 1969 and 1971 Hawaii Champion; 1969-71 Northwest Grand Champion; 1974 All Japan National Shito-Ryu Champion (held in Japan). In 1974 he was awarded the "President Sasagawa Trophy" by the governor of Osaka.

MILLER, FREDERICK (1950-) American karate competitor. Miller is affiliated with the World Professional Karate Organization and was its original light-heavyweight full-contact champion. A **goju-ryu** stylist, he won numerous regional titles in and around New York.

MILLER, JENICE (1944-) American karate instructor and competitor. Miller was rated among the nation's top 10 women in 1975 by *Black Belt Magazine.* A winner of numerous state and national titles, including the U.S. Championships in Dallas, she is presently an instructor and an outspoken advocate for improvement in women's karate competition. At one time the only female promoter in American karate, she produced the annual Mardi Gras Nationals in New Orleans. Member of *Who's Who in the Martial Arts.*

MILLER, JIM (1944-) American karate instructor and competitor. Miller, a noted heavyweight, was rated among the top 10 competitors in his class by *Professional Karate Magazine* in 1975. Miller and his wife Jenice have greatly assisted the growth of karate in Louisiana. Member of *Who's Who in the Martial Arts.*

MILLERSON, WILLIAM (1953-) Dutch karate competitor. He was among the top 10 karatemen in Europe in 1973 and 1975. A **wado-ryu** stylist, Millerson has consistently placed second in the European Championships.

MIN, KEN (KYUNG HO) (1935-) Korean-American judo and tae kwon do instructor, administrator, and pioneer. Professor Ken Min is most widely recognized as the spearhead for the amateur tae kwon do movement and collegiate judo program in the U.S.

Min served in many capacities including: first national chairman of the AAU Tae Kwon Do Committee; faculty member of the U.S. Sports Academy; president of the National Collegiate Judo Association; first president of the National Collegiate Tae Kwon Do Association.

He is responsible for tae kwon do becoming an AAU sport in 1974, and was honored by the creation of the Annual Ken Min Award. Min is the founder of the **American Collegiate Tae Kwon Do Coaches Association** and the **American Collegiate Tae Kwon Do Association.** He served as team manager for the 1st (1973) and the 2nd (1975) World Tae Kwon Do Championships in Seoul, Korea, and was co-director of the 3rd World Championships in Chicago, Ill., in 1977. He was also the team head, Pre-World Games Invitational Tae Kwon Do Championships in Seoul, in 1978.

Ken Min

Takayuki Mikami, one of the leading Shotokan instructors in the U.S.

A member of *Who's Who in the Martial Arts,* Min has received numerous awards for coaching in both judo and tae kwon do. He is a member of the International Judo Coaching Staff and a certified international referee in tae kwon do. He holds black belts in judo, tae kwon do, **hapkido,** and **kendo.** As martial arts supervisor for the University of California at Berkeley, Prof. Min hosted major tae kwon do and judo championships in Harmon Gym: National AAU Judo Championships (1977, 1980); National Tae Kwon Do Championships (1974, 1979); National Collegiate Judo Championships (1976); 1st North American Tae Kwon Do Championships (1977); 1st U.S. Invitational International Championships (1980).

He contributed articles to professional journals and served as editor of the *Tae Kwon Do Journal* (1978-) and editor of *Judo-USA* (1977-80).

In 1973 Min developed the sport of **kyuk-ki-do** and oversaw its national development. He currently holds a number of administrative offices: president, North American Tae Kwon Do Union (1977-); secretary-general, **Pan-American Tae Kwon Do Union** (1977-); president, National Collegiate Judo Association (1980-); chairman, Collegiate Sub-Committee of the **WTF** (1980-).

In 1976, Prof. Min agreed to become a consultant for this book and for five years supervised Korean-language entries. *See also* U.S., history of karate in.

Anthony Miriakin in his dojo.

MINATOYA, HIROSHI (1943-) Japanese judo champion. A leading welterweight, he won silver medals at the 1965 and 1971 World Championships and gold medals at the 1967 and 1969 World Championships.

MINSHEW, CAROLYN (1946-) American karate instructor. Best known for her work with her husband in developing business procedures for karate schools, Minshew is co-owner of the Houston Black Belt Academies. She won regional titles in competition and has trained champion students. A member of the *Who's Who in the Martial Arts,* she has co-produced the Karate Olympics since 1965.

MINSHEW, GEORGE (1943-) American karate instructor and promoter. A former competitor, he is now an instructor and successful karate businessman. One of his students, **Pat Worley,** became a world-ranked middleweight contender. Minshew, a member of the *Who's Who in the Martial Arts,* developed programs of karate instruction for rape prevention and handicapped children. He has co-promoted the Karate Olympics annually since 1965 with his wife, Carolyn.

MIRAKIAN, ANTHONY (1933-) American karate instructor and pioneer. Mirakian is the representative of Okinawan Meibukan goju-ryu karate in the U.S. and was the first instructor to bring **Okinawan goju-ryu** to America, in 1960. His karate school, in Watertown, Mass., is the U.S. headquarters of Meibukan goju-ryu karate-do.

Mirakian started training in the martial arts in the early 1950s. His first Okinawan goju-ryu karate master was **Seikichi Toguchi,** president of the Shoreikan School of goju-ryu in Nakanomachi, Koza City, Okinawa. Mirakian was also taught in the same school by another master, Ryuritsu Arakaki. He was advised by Arakaki to train under the foremost goju-ryu master, **Meitoku Yagi,** in Naha City. After being interviewed and demonstrating karate for Yagi, Mirakian was accepted to train in his dojo. Mirakian was the first and only westerner ever taught by Yagi, and the only karate student from the U.S. to receive a black belt from him. Workouts in Yagi's dojo were over four hours each night, five times a week.

While on Okinawa, Mirakian demonstrated goju-ryu karate forms many times during the Ryukyu-American Friendship Week. His keen interest in karate led him to travel through many countries while in the Orient, including Japan, Korea, Taiwan, and Hong Kong, where he gathered information, took movies and photographs, all with the desire of broadening his knowledge of the martial arts.

Much of the material Mirakian collected while traveling and studying in the Orient is rare and of historical value today. He contributed more than 150 photographs, as well as previously unpublished information on Okinawan karate, to this book.

Before departing from Okinawa, while preparing for a trip to Taiwan and Hong Kong, Mirakian procured a letter of recommendation from a 70-year-old Chinese master, Mr. Lao, who had many karate friends in Hong Kong. With this letter of reference, Mirakian was able to meet a great Chinese kempo master, Dr. Kwan Tak Hing, with whom he still corresponds.

While in Taiwan, Mirakian had the opportunity to meet many Chinese kempo masters and to discuss the aspects of their systems. He demonstrated goju-ryu forms for some of the Chinese masters, and observed the training for the **pa-kua, t'ai-chi-ch'uan** and other Chinese arts then unknown in the western world, and took movies for his own research.

Mirakian was taught **kobu-jutsu,** specifically **bojutsu** and the **sai,** by the late president of the Ryukyu Kobujutsu Kenkyu Dojo, **Shinken Taira,** one of the foremost masters of Okinawan weaponry. During his travels to the Japanese islands, Mirakian had the honor of meeting and conversing with the late karate master **Juhatsu Kyoda,** one of the top students of grandmaster **Kanryo Higashionna.**

In 1960 Mirakian returned to the U.S. and opened his karate school in Watertown, Mass., where he teaches today. Since then he has continued teaching and is preserving traditional Okinawan Meibukan goju-ryu karate-do as taught in its purest form in Okinawa. *See also* U.S., history of karate in; Okinawan goju-ryu.

MITOSE, DR. JAMES M. (1916-1981) Japanese-American karate pioneer. At the age of 5, Mitose was sent from Hawaii to Kyushu, Japan, for schooling in his ancestral art of self-defense, **kosho-ryu kempo.** From 1921-36 he studied and mastered this art, based directly on **Bodhidharma's Shao-lin** kung-fu. According to Mitose family tradition, clan members in Kumamoto and Nagasaki brought the knowledge of Shao-lin kung-fu from China shortly before the Tokugawa era, which began in 1600. This art is said to have been modified by successive Mitose kempo masters until kosho-ryu, or "old pine tree style," kempo was born.

Mitose claims that his kempo is not Okinawan karate, even though some of the kata of kosho-ryu resemble, and in a few instances are duplicated in, certain karate styles.

After completing his training in Japan, Mitose returned to Hawaii in 1936. In 1942 he organized the Official Self-Defense Club at the Beretania Mission in Honolulu. He presided over the club until 1953, when it was taken over by **Thomas Young,** one of his students. Only five of his students—Young, **William K.S. Chow,** Paul

Yamaguchi, Arthur Keawe, and **Edward Lowe**—had attained 1st-degree black belt.

Mitose authored four books, two of which were published: *What Is Self-Defense? (Kenpo Jiu Jitsu)* and *What Is True Self-Defense? (Kenpo Jiu Jitsu)*. The former, a war-time publication, focused on the fighting aspects of the arts, whereas the latter, written during peacetime, covered philosophy and conflict resolution to prevent physical engagement.

MIURA, MIYUKI (1949-   ) Japanese karate champion, **Kyokushinkai** stylist. At 5 feet 8 inches, 163 lbs., he won the 4th All Japan Karate-do Open Tournament, and endured an extraordinary sparring session against 100 kyokushinkai karateka. He currently teaches his art in Chicago.

MIURA, YOSHIN Japanese jujutsu instructor and physician. Some historians designate him the founder of the yoshin-ryu style of jujutsu.

MIYAGI, CHOJUN (1888-1953) Okinawan karate master and pioneer; founder of **goju-ryu.** When Miyagi was 14 he started training in karate on Okinawa, from Sept. 1902 to Oct. 1915, under the foremost **Naha-te** grandmaster, **Kanryo Higashionna.** After training in karate for 13 years, Miyagi sailed to China and studied chugoku kempo in Foochow, Fukien, from Nov. 1915-17. When he returned to Okinawa he was instructor at the Okinawa-ken Police Training Center, Naha City Commercial School, Okinawa Normal School, Okinawa Recreational and Health Center, and others.

In 1928 Miyagi traveled to Japan and instructed karate at Kyoto Imperial University, Kansai University, and Ritsumeikan University, Kyoto. He was made chairman of the Okinawan-ken Taiiku Kyokai Karate-do (Okinawa Prefecture Athletic Association Karate Division) in 1930. In 1934 he became permanent officer of the Okinawan branch of the **Dai Nippon Butokukai** (Great Japan Martial Virtues Association).

As a result of his efforts, karate was first recognized officially as one of the martial arts of Japan with the formal establishment of the Dai Nippon Butokukai, Okinawa Branch, in Nov. 1933. Chinei Kinjo, editor of the Okinawan newspaper *Yoen Fiho Sha,* invited Miyagi to Hawaii in May 1934. There he gave lectures and taught. He returned to Okinawa in Feb. 1935.

On Jan. 28, 1936, Miyagi gave a lecture in the Sakaisuji Meiji Syoten hall in Japan entitled "Things About Karate-do," in which he said: "Karate is not to be stiff as a steel bar, but to be relaxed, always training your body and mind, prepared for a sudden attack. There is a legend that the principle of karate was based in the saying 'There is no first move in karate.' But in real life this discipline is not enforced much. As time went by, the principle of instruction was altered. Now we abandon the principle called 'Tai Shu Shin Ju' (body first, spirit second; technique first, personality second) and emphasize 'Kenzen Itchi' (hand and Zen are altogether), which suggests Shin Shu Tai Ju (spirit, character, personality first, body second)." In this lecture, Miyagi also said: "The year of secrecy of teaching karate has gone and the year of open-door policy is here. The future for karate looks very promising. I strongly feel that we should abandon the policy to keep karate on Okinawa a secret, and open it to the world."

Miyagi received a medal for "Excellence in the Martial Arts" in 1936 from the Ministry of Education in Japan. Also that year, he studied Chinese martial arts at the Seibu Dai Iku Kai (Great Gymnastic Association, Pure Martial Arts Spirit) in Shanghai.

In May 1937 Prince Moriwasa Nashimoto, Commissioner of the Dai Nippon Butokukai, authorized Miyagi, with the headmaster of Shinto shizen-ryu (jujutsu), and the headmaster of kushin-ryu (also jujutsu), to form the Dai Nippon Butokukai Karate Jukkyoshi (Great Japan Martial Arts Karate Teachers' Association). They inspected and regulated karate throughout Japan until the dissolution of the association. In 1937 Miyagi received the **kyoshi** (assistant professor) degree from the Dai Nippon Butokukai. He was made in 1946 an official of the Okinawa Minsei Taiiku Kan (Okinawa Democratic Athletic Association). In 1953, Miyagi was instructing at the Ryukyu Police Academy in Naha City, Okinawa. He died Oct. 8, 1953, of a heart attack.

Miyagi subjected the art of **Naha-te**, as received from Kanryo Higashionna, to scientific examination. Originally, a martial arts expert was trained for killing with one blow. Karate as such was unsuitable for the contemporary world. Miyagi studied the basic "go" (**Sanchin**) and the six rules and created the "ju" (**tensho**) form, combining soft and hard movements. He also organized auxiliary movements to strengthen the body through calisthenics. He organized these exercises in preparation for practicing the **kaishu** kata. Thus, he formulated the theory for the practice of karate and organized it as an educational subject, an art of self-defense, and as a spiritual exercise.

From the old Chinese book *Wu pei chih,* an *Army Account of Military Arts and Science* published in 1636, Miyagi took the expression "Goju" as it appears in the sentence: "The successful methods required both give and take (Go-ju)," for the name of his school. He was the first karate master to organize a school of karate on Okinawa and give it a name apart from the city in which it was practiced, as in Naha-te, Shuri-te, and Tomari-te.

Miyagi often used the slogan *Nanji Kyokuden,* meaning to apply all one's strength, to be determined in everything that one does; defeat is not the end; losing is not the end of everything. **Meitoku Yagi** was named Miyagi's successor in Okinawan goju-ryu and accordingly inherited the grandmaster's karate gi and belt in 1963. (ANTHONY MIRAKIAN) *See also* Okinawa, history of martial arts in; Okinawan goju-ryu; U.S., history of karate in.

Grandmaster Chojun Miyagi, founder of goju-ryu karate
Courtesy of Anthony Mirakian

MIYAZAKI, TOYOTARO (1944-   ) American karate competitor and instructor. President of the U.S. Kenkyoku Karate Federation, Miyazaki was a leading fighter until a knee injury forced his retirement in 1971. In 1970, he was ranked 7th among the nation's Top-10 fighters by *Black Belt Magazine.* In 1973 he was named among America's top 10 kata competitors in the *Official Karate Yearbook.* Member of the *Who's Who in the Martial Arts.*

MOCHIZUKI, MINORU Japanese martial arts master; founder of yoseikan karate. He studied judo under **Kyuzo Mifune**, and **Daito-ryu aiki-jutsu** under Sokaku Takeda, its headmaster. At Takeda's **dojo**, Mochizuki met **aikido** founder **Morihei Ueshiba**, with whom he later studied aikido, becoming one of Ueshiba's senior disciples. At 26, because of a lung ailment, he retired to the countryside and established a dojo in the town of Shizuoka. Here he founded the yoseikan style of karate. In 1954 he went to Europe, where, in Paris, he taught his art to European karate pioneer **Henry Plee**. Mochizuki also continued teaching Daito-ryu aiki-jutsu. *See also* Europe, history of karate in.

MODRIC, ZARKO (1939-   ) Yugoslavian karate and judo pioneer, instructor, and writer. Modric began judo in 1955 while still in high school and was, in fact, one of the first judoka in all of Yugoslavia. He was both a competitor and an instructor and later an international referee. He began studying karate in the late 1960s—first the **Shotokan** style, then shukokai—and was one of the three pioneers of karate in Yugoslavia. In 1975 Modric and members of his club started **full-contact** karate, one of the first clubs in Europe to do so. He has served as an international karate referee.

Modric has been writing about the martial arts since the mid-1960s and was one of the first martial arts journalists to syndicate his articles internationally. He authored ten books on martial arts including judo, karate, **t'ai-chi ch'uan,** judo refereeing, and **budo** in general; and translated fifteen books from English to Croatian by such esteemed martial arts authors as karate's **Mas Oyama** and judo's **Kazuzo Kudo.**

Modric served as *Black Belt Magazine's* European correspondent for some twelve years and contributed regularly to *Karate Illustrated,* and other American, French, and British publications. He wrote articles for *Physical Culture Encyclopedia* in Yugoslavia, the *Sports Lexicon,* published in Zagreb, and *The Illustrated Encyclopedia of Martial Arts,* for which he provided entries on the development of European judo and karate. Modric was also a founding member of the World All-Style Karate Organization (WAKO), Europe's leading amateur full-contact body. *See also* Europe, history of karate in; Yugoslavia, history of karate in.

MOMOCHI, SANDAYU Famous **ninja** leader of the 16th century. To confuse his enemies and conceal his identity, Momochi maintained three separate homes with a different wife and family in each.

MOON, DAVID (Dai Won) (1943-   ) Korean-born American karate instructor, competitor, and promoter. Moon began studying the martial arts in 1957 under Prof. Young Ha Chon in Korea, receiving his black belt in 1959 from Prof. **Hwang Kee;** his styles are moo duk kwan and tae kwon do. He is secretary-general of the Federation Mexicana de Tae Kwon Do and president of the Association Moo Duk Kwan de Mexico. He trained world champion **Isaias Duenas.**

Moon is a three-time U.S. Karate Grand Champion (1965-67). In 1969 he went to Mexico City, after living in the U.S. for six years. He became a major force in the martial arts of that country and a member of the *Who's Who in the Martial Arts.* At present he directs twenty-six schools throughout Mexico. Moon promoted the Campeonato Nacional de Karate in Mexico City 1969-74, and the Campeonato Nacional de Tae Kwon Do 1975 and 1976. *See also* U.S., history of karate in.

David Moon

MOORE, ROY (1893-1980) American judo pioneer. Moore was taught wrestling by Frank Gotch, world heavyweight champion (1908). At 17, he won the World Wrestling Championships. He began judo instruction under Mattie Matsuda. **Jigoro Kano,** the father of judo, asked Moore to instruct the Japanese wrestling team, which he did. In 1935 he took the first U.S. wrestling team to Japan and helped draft the rules for international judo competition. Moore was one of the pioneers of judo in Texas. He later moved to San Diego, Calif., where he taught in his own dojo. *See also* U.S., history of judo in.

MOORE, VICTOR American karate competitor and instructor. He started judo and jujutsu at 14, then switched to karate. After attending Central State University in Wilburforce, Ohio, he established two schools in Cincinnati, teaching the eclectic shorei-kempo style. Moore was one of the premier tournament fighters of the late 1960s who was unduly overlooked in the nation's Top Ten ratings. His ring battles with **Joe Lewis** are legend. His biggest victory perhaps was the Aug. 1968 World's Fair Karate Championships in San Antonio, Tex. where he defeated Lewis for the title and $500. Lewis in turn defeated him on Nov. 24 that year to win the World Professional Heavyweight Championship in New York City. Moore was also co-captain of the **USKA** competition team. Moore also fought in the early American kickboxing bouts conducted in 1970-71. He won his first bout and lost a second to **Jim Harrison.** *See also* U.S., history of karate in.

MORI, TOARO (1914-69) Japanese-American **kendo** instructor. He began kendo at 6. In 1936 Mori came to the U.S., settling in Los Angeles. He was instrumental in reviving western fencing in Japan after the war years. Returning to the U.S. he helped organize the American Kendo Federation and taught western fencing at U.S.C. and the Los Angeles Health Club. He was asked to head the first Japanese Olympic fencing team. Founder of the Beverly Hills Fencing Academy, he was its chief instructor until his death.

MORI-TOSHIRO (1951-   ) Japanese karate champion; a **Shotokan** stylist (5 feet, 9 inches, 200 lbs.) and **JKA** instructor. He won the 1975 All Japan All Styles Championships, and in 1974, the Tohoku Area Championship tournament.

MORRIS, THOMAS H. European **shukokai** karate instructor; a pioneer of karate in Scotland. A high-ranking black belt, he has studied a number of martial arts. He wrote *Shukokai Karate Kata* in 1979.

MORROW, VIKKI (1951-   ) American karate competitor and instructor. A former student and assistant to **Bill McDonald,** she now operates her own school and directs the U.S. Goju-Shorin Classics. Her tournament wins include first place in the 1974 Battle of Atlanta, the U.S. Goju-Shorin Classics, the North Carolina Goju-Shorin Classics, the North Carolina State Championships, the Atlanta Pro/Am, Atlanta Spring Open, and Southern Coast Championships. She has also officiated at a number of major tournaments. Member of the *Who's Who in the Martial Arts.*

MOSIG, DIRK American karate instructor. Mosig was born in Berlin, Germany, and began his study of karate by age 12. His wins include the Trias' Internationals in Jacksonville, 1968; Southeastern Karate Championships in Chattanooga, 1970; North Carolina Open, 1968—kata; Southeastern Championships, 1968—kata. Mosig was voted "Best National Tournament Coach" of the year 1969 by the **USKA.** in 1968 and 1969 his students captured more than 120 trophies.

MOTOBU, CHOKI (1871-1944) Okinawan karate master. Born in Shuri, Okinawa, third son of a ranking lord, Motobu trained in karate by himself, engaging in **makiwara** exercises and heavy rock lifting. For his exceptional leaping ability he was nicknamed "Saru" (monkey). Motobu habitually started fights to test his expertise; because of this, most Okinawan masters refused to teach him. Kosaku Matsumora of Tomari, however, taught him some **kata,** only because he was impressed with Motobu's ability. In order to learn fighting techniques, Motobu was forced to secretly watch Matsumora nightly through a fence surrounding the **dojo.**

Motobu moved to Osaka, Japan, in 1921. On a trip to Kyoto, he entered a contest in which amateur challengers were invited to pit themselves against professional boxers. He defeated one foreign boxer with such speed as to astound the audience. The match caused a public sensation and the story appeared in a popular magazine, making him known throughout Japan.

Later in life, Motobu underwent a change in attitude and studied karate to seriously seek its true spirit. In 1936, he returned to Okinawa to examine the original Okinawan empty-hand and weapons kata of karate. In this regard, he sought out his senior, **Kentsu Yabu,** to learn the correct original forms. Yabu was one of two men ever to defeat Motobu in a match.

One of Motobu's few authentic students was **Shoshin Nagamine,** leader of the matsubayashi-ryu school of **shorin-ryu** karate. Motobu is also associated with the rise of **kempo** in Hawaii, perhaps through his visit there in 1933 and an unclear link with **James Mitose.** Motobu also trained with Tung Gee Hsing, a Chinese martial artist who later taught U.S. karate pioneer **Robert Trias.** *See also* Okinawa, history of martial arts in.

MOUNIER, JEAN-JACQUES (1946-) French judo champion. He won the European lightweight title in 1971 and 1972, and won a bronze medal at the 1972 Munich Olympics. Mounier also won a gold medal at the 1971 World Military Championships. Skillful evasion and sudden throwing techniques made him one of the few Europeans to match the Japanese in the lighter weight divisions.

MULLEN, EDWARD Scottish judo competitor, member of the British Olympic team in Munich in 1972. Mullen started judo training in 1962 and in 1967 won the Scottish Junior Open and was twice a bronze medalist at the European Junior Championships (1968-69); he won a bronze in the European Senior lightweight category in 1970. In 1971 Mullen was a member of the winning British team at the European Championships and the British Olympic team of 1972.

MULLINS, SKIPPER (1946-) American karate champion and instructor. Rated among karate's top 10 fighters for six of the seven years he competed, Mullins was one of the world's premier competitors until his retirement in 1972. He was also a member of the undefeated 1968 national champion team that featured **Chuck Norris, Mike Stone, Joe Lewis** and **Bob Wall.**

As a noted instructor, Mullins has turned out many world rated and nationally ranked tournament fighters.

His tournament wins include: 1967, 1971, and 1972 All-American Champion, 1967 Top 10 Champion, 1968 International Champion, 1969-71 World Professional Lightweight Champion. Member of *Who's Who in the Martial Arts. See also* U.S., history of karate in.

MURAI, MASAYOSHI (1942-) Japanese judo competitor and coach. A regular qualifier at the All Japan Championships, at 5 feet, 10½ inches, 231 lbs. he was a formidable competitor. Murai was a coach in Eastern Europe in 1966, and also coached in West Germany in 1965.

MURAKAMI, TETSUJI (1927-) Japanese karate pioneer. He began karate studies at 19 under Masaji Yamanuchi, a **Shotokan** stylist. After three years he earned his black belt, and by 1956 he was a leading karateman in Japan. In 1957 he went to Paris, opened a dojo, and soon was teaching all over Europe. Murakami is considered one of the pioneer instructors of Japanese karate in Europe. *See also* Europe, history of karate in.

MURATA, SUMIYA Japanese karate master, developed a form of karate called **tai-jitsu.** The art combines karate, judo and kendo.

MURRAY, JR., JOHN WILLIAM (1934-) American judo writer. Murray began judo in 1957, under John Warhay at the Philadelphia Naval Base; he received his black belt in 1972 from Karl Geis in **Kodokan** judo. He contributed articles on aikido, judo, and karate to *Black Belt Magazine, Official Karate,* and *Karate Illustrated.* Columnist for *The Fighters* and publisher of the *AAU News, Judo U.S.A.,* he was the only American accredited to cover judo at the 1975 Pan-American Games and 1976 Montreal Olympics.

MURUKAMI, KUNIO (1947-) Japanese karate champion. Murukami was the winner of the individual title in the 3rd World Karate Championships, the 1972 and 1973 All Japan All Style Championships, and the 1972 and 1973 All Japan Rengo-Kai Tournament. At 5 feet 9 inches, 150 lbs. Murukami is extremely fast. In 1972, at the All Japan Rengo-Kai Championships, he suffered a badly broken nose but won despite his injury. A rengo-kai stylist, he is currently the owner of the Western Japan Gymnastic Company.

MUSASHI, MIYAMOTO (1584-1645) Japanese swordsman and folk hero of the 17th century. He based his school of instruction on the art of nitoryu—fencing with two swords, one sword in each hand. His greatest exploit was a duel with Sasaki Kojiro, the "Duel on Ganryuto Island," much written about in Japanese literature.

Musashi felt the sword was a part of the person, and the man who mastered the sword after long years of training came to master himself. He recognized, of course, that the sword might equally well become the master of the man. Also a painter, some of his works are treasures of the Japanese government. He wrote *A Book of Five Rings,* a classic psychological guide to strategy.

MUTSU, ZUIHO Okinawan karate pioneer. He and **Kamesuke Higaonna** came to Hawaii in 1933 with the understanding that they were to teach and lecture on the art of karate. Upon their arrival they discovered the Okinawan promoters really wanted them to perform in public matches against well-known island fighters. Both flatly refused. Thomas Miyashiro, an Okinawan who had studied karate with **Kentsu Yabu** in 1927, convinced most of the Okinawan karate enthusiasts to approach Mutsu and Higaonna with a request to stay in Hawaii and teach. They agreed and soon opened a school near Honolulu's Aula Park. The school later moved to larger quarters at the Izumo Taishi Shinto Mission. Mutsu returned to Japan to resume his duties as vice-president of Imperial University's (presently known as Tokyo University) Karate Study Club; Higaonna left soon afterwards. *See also* U.S., history of karate in.

NAGAMINE, SHOSHIN (1907-) Okinawan karate master. Nagamine was a sickly youth until 17, when he undertook the practice of karate; his karate instructors at the time were Taro Shimabura and **Ankichi Arakaki.** After serving with a Japanese artillery unit sent to China in 1928, Nagamine returned to Okinawa to become a policeman in 1931. This appointment permitted him to further his karate studies with the legendary **Chotoku Kyan.** While studying at the Tokyo Metropolitan Police Academy in 1936, he trained with **Choki Motobu,** another famous Okinawan karate figure.

In May 1940 Nagamine passed his qualifying examinations for karate instructor of the **shorin-ryu** (matsubayashi-ryu) style and was awarded a 3rd-degree black belt in **kendo.** He resigned a police superintendency in Jan. 1953 to build a dojo in Naha. He named it the Kodokan Karate-do and Kobu-jutsu Dojo. In honor of his two **sensei,** Nagamine decided in 1947 to adopt the name matsubayashi-ryu for his style.

At 68, Nagamine wrote *The Essence of Okinawan Karate-do* (1976). He operates a worldwide matsubayashi-ryu organization from his headquarters in Okinawa. *See also* Okinawa, history of martial arts in; shorin-ryu.

NAGANO, KIRO Japanese-American judo pioneer. He began judo in his native Japan at 8. By his second high school year he was school judo champion; at 15 he won the Gold Medal at the Hokkaido Judo Tournament; and at 17 he went to Tokyo and joined the **Kodokan** under the sponsorship of Prof. **Kyuzo Mifune.** Nagano came to the U.S. in 1916 as a visiting student but remained in southern California, and became a leader of the Southern California Judo Team for thirty-eight years. He is on the board of examiners for the USJF and served as president of Nanka Yudanshakai (Southern California Judo Association). *See also* U.S., history of judo in.

NAGATOSHI, YASUHIKO Japanese judo competitor, he was born in Fukuoka, Japan. He began to practice judo in high school and in 1961 won the All Japan High School Championships. He graduated from Kansai University where he majored in economics, then came to the U.S. where he won the U.S. Grand Championship in 1967.

NAGLE, DON (1938-) American karate instructor and pioneer; father of **isshinryu** karate in the U.S. Nagle began karate training in 1955 under **Tatsuo Shimabuku** while stationed in Okinawa with the U.S. Marines. He won the Okinawan Karate Championships, besting black belt competitors, as a mere white belt.

In 1957 Nagle opened his first karate school, in Jacksonville, N.C., one of the first karate dojos in the southern U.S. Upon his discharge from the Marines in 1959, he moved to New Jersey, where he established permanent headquarters in Jersey City. Besides introducing the isshinryu style to the U.S., his Jacksonville and Jersey City schools were two of the earliest karate dojo in America. His students include **Gary Alexander,** James Chapman, Louis Lizotte, Ed McGrath, **Don Bohan,** Malachi Lee, Ralph Chirico, and Joseph Bucholtz, who operates Nagle's Jersey City dojo. *See also* U.S., history of karate in.

NAKABARA, TORATARO Japanese-American **kendo** and **iaido** master; the highest-ranked iaido master in the U.S. Born in Kyushu Village, Japan, he began studying sword techniques at 13, and by graduation from high school had attained the rank of nidan (2nd-degree black belt) in kendo at a time when the ultimate rank in all of Japan was 6th dan. In the early 1930s, Nakabara joined the Japanese police force in Korea. As a kendo instructor, he continued teaching through the Second World War until the Allied Occupation prohibited the practice of kendo after the war; when the ban was lifted in 1948 he resumed teaching. He began studying iaido in 1955 and came to the U.S., where he has continued teaching both kendo and iaido from his headquarters at the Japanese Cultural Center in Van Nuys, Calif.

NAKAE, KIYOSE (-1974) Japanese-American jujutsu pioneer. One of the foremost authorities on jujutsu in America, Nakae taught thousands in his studio in New York City for more than 50 years. He wrote *Jiu Jitsu Complete.*

NAKAMURA, HIROSHI (1943-) Japanese judo competitor and instructor, now teaching in Montreal, Quebec. Already a 4th-degree black belt at age 19, he captained the Chuo University Judo Team and in 1965, captured the All Japan Middleweight Championship. In 1967 he was coach of the Japanese University Judo Team.

Nakamura was recognized as one of the finest technicians of judo in Japan, but in 1968 he decided to move to Canada, where his talents were quickly recognized. He became coach of the Canadian World Judo Team and presently coaches judo in Quebec, and runs his own dojo in Montreal.

NAKAMURA, TADASHI Japanese-born karate instructor; founder and chairman of the World Seido Karate Organization. A high-ranking black belt in karate, Nakamura is also a holder of a dan ranking in **kendo** and an expert in oriental weaponry. Nakamura won numerous championships in Japan, both in contact and noncontact events. In recent years he has conducted seminars in the U.S., Latin America, and the South Pacific.

Tadashi Nakamura

NAKANISHI, CHUZO Believed to have been the inventor of the **shinai,** or bamboo staff, used in **kendo.** Nakanishi reputedly created the shinai in Edo, Japan, in 1750.

NAKAYAMA, MASATOSHI (1913-) Japanese karate master; chief instructor of the **Japan Karate Association**. Born to a family of fencing instructors in Yamaguchi City, Japan, he received most of his elementary education in Taipei, Taiwan. His father, Naotoshi, was an army surgeon and **kendo** master who introduced Masatoshi to kendo while he was still a child. After returning to Japan from Taiwan, he was fairly proficient in kendo.

Upon entering Takushoku University, he misinterpreted the schedule for kendo classes and accidentally viewed the campus karate class. Inspired by what he saw, he began studying karate in

Masatoshi Nakayama in the early 1950s. Today he is the chief instructor of the Japan Karate Association.

1932 under **Gichin Funakoshi**, the "father of modern karate." In 1937 he went to Peking to study Chinese language (Mandarin), society and history. He spent nine years there, at which time he also studied various systems of Chinese boxing. Nakayama returned to Japan in 1946.

In 1949, with the founding of the JKA, Nakayama was named its chief technical advisor; in 1955 he was appointed the JKA's chief instructor. Since then he has taught the **Shotokan** style in several southeast Asian countries and throughout the world. He is also professor and director of physical education at Takushoku University, from which he was graduated in 1937. Nakayama has trained many internationally acclaimed karate fighters, including **Teruyuki Okazaki** (U.S.), **Hidetaka Nishiyama** (U.S.), **Takayuki Mikami** (U.S.), **Taiji Kase** (France), Hideki Ochi (Germany), **Hirokazu Kanazawa** (Japan), **Keinosuke Enoeda** (G.B.), Toru Miyazaki (Belgium), Hiroshi Shirai (Italy), and Masahiko Tanaka (Denmark). As chief instructor, he oversees more than six million Shotokan karate practitioners throughout the world.

Nakayama is cited for two great contributions. The first was his creation of a theoretical basis for instruction. He summarized this in his 1965 textbook, *Karatedo Shinkyotei (A New Method for Teaching Karate-do)*, which is now in use in JKA schools throughout the world, and it has been copied by instructors in other organizations virtually everywhere. A condensed English-language version of this book was published as *Dynamic Karate* in 1966. Nakayama's other outstanding contribution was his development of the original rules for karate competition, and it was he who staged the 1st All Japan Karate Championships in Tokyo in 1957.

In addition to the above mentioned book, he has also authored the *Karate Kata Series* of six JKA manuals, a series of eight books entitled *Best Karate*, and with Donn F. Draeger, a series of self-defense books entitled *Practical Karate* (REandall G. Hassell). *See also* Japan, history of karate in; Shotokan. *Further reading: Black Belt Magazine*, Nov. 1982.

NAKAZATO, SHUGORO (1921-) Okinawan karate master. He was sent at 13 to the Japanese mainland to study and while there began martial arts training in judo.

Instead of continuing his studies, Nakazato devoted full time to the study of karate. In 1949, upon the death of his first teacher, Seiiko, Nakazato continued his training under **Choshin Chibana,** who promoted him to 9th dan in 1967. After Chibana's death, Nakazato became head of the Okinawan Shorin-ryu Shunakai Association. Nakazato is expert in the **sai** and **bo.** Two of his better known students are **Tadashi Yamashita** and **Sid Campbell.** *See also* Okinawa, history of martial arts in; shorin-ryu.

NAM, TAE HI Korean tae kwon do pioneer and administrator, president of the Asian Tae Kwon Do Federation from 1968-72. He began teaching Korean self-defense in the 1940s. He served as an army officer during the Korean War, after which he was sent to the U.S. to study military courses. Nam returned to Korea and resumed teaching Korean soldiers. He was instrumental in helping **Gen. Choi Hong Hi** for the **oh do kwan** in 1953, a dojang (gymnasium) for Korea's 29th Infantry Division.

Nam gave superb self-defense demonstrations throughout Korea. One demonstration, viewed by Korean President Syng man Rhee, so interested him that he ordered all his military personnel to learn tae kwon do. In the 1950s, Nam traveled across the world giving demonstrations while serving as chief instructor for the military police forces of Korea. A performance in 1959 in Vietnam by Nam and 16 others was seen by 360,000 people. In 1964 he returned to Korea to serve in the National Sport Division and was selected as a delegate to the Counseil International Du Sport Militarie. In the late 1960s he was chief instructor in Malaysia, and in 1968 became president of the Asia Tae Kwon Do Federation, overseeing nine countries. He also served as chairman of the Provincial Committee of the **International Taekwon-do Federation (ITF).** In the early 1970s, Nam moved to the U.S. and in 1973 established a school in Chicago, Ill., which is also the headquarters of the American Taekwon-do Federation. He has since been named vice-president of the ITF.

NANBU, YOSHINAO (1943-) Japanese karate master, pioneer, and champion; founder of **sankukai** karate. Born in Kobe, Japan, he began karate and **aikidi** training with sensei Someka in the early 1950s. At 18 he entered the Faculty of Economic Sciences in Osaka and began studying **Shito-ryu** karate under sensei Tani. Nanbu became captain of the university karate team and in 1963 was Japanese University Champion.

In 1964, French karate pioneer **Henry Plee** invited nanbu to Paris to teach karate. Nanbu had the ability to break a *makiwara* (striking post), which spread his reputation throughout Europe. At Plee's school, Nanbu taught many of Europe's foremost karate fighters, and he was eventually named coach of the award-winning French team. Nanbu was responsible for teaching fighters the footsweep at a time when the technique was unknown in Europe. Among those who learned this technique from Nanbu were **Dominique Valera,** Europe's greatest karate fighter, **Patrick Baroux, Guy Sauvin,** and **Alain Setrou.** In 1965 he made his first visit to Scotland.

In 1966, Nanbu broke tradition and entered the prestigious French karate tournament, the Cannes Cup, becoming the first Japanese to compete against Europeans on their home ground. He won first place, defeating Baroux. Later that year he returned to Japan and began studying **shukokai** karate with its founder, **Chojiro Tani.** He then began traveling across the world, introducing shukokai to Scotland in 1967 and with sensei Kimura to Britain in 1969. He was named president of the Scottish Karate Federation, and became a member of the Yugoslav karate team. In 1972, following the 2nd World Karate Championships in Paris, he returned to Japan, where he formulated his own style, calling it sankukai. In 1974 he wrote *Sankukau Karate. See also* Europe, history of karate in.

NATIVIDAD, JOHN (1946-) American karate competitor and instructor. A nationally rated fighter until his retirement in 1975, Natividad appeared in the top 10 polls of both *Black Belt Magazine* and *Professional Karate Magazine;* he was especially noted for his array of kicking techniques. He reached national stature in a 1970 defeat of **Joe Lewis** at the All-Star Team Championships in Long Beach, Calif. In 1973 he won grand titles at the **International Championships,** Colorado State Championships, Yamashita Open, and Northern California Karate Championships; and first place at

One of America's top karate competitors, John Natividad (*left*), delivers a high kick to Roy Kurban of Texas.

the Las Vegas Nationals and Black Belt Team Championships. A member of the *Who's Who in the Martial Arts,* he wrote *John Natividad's International Self-Defense Book* (1974). *See also* U.S., history of karate in.

NATSUI, SHOKICHI (1926-) Japanese judo champion; he won the 1st World Championships in 1965 and the All Japan title from **Sone** in 1966.

NEGLIA, LOUIS (1950-) American karate competitor and instructor. Neglia began martial arts in 1964, receiving his black belt from Warren Siciliano; he also holds rank from Ray Skarila in kick-boxing and in Japanese **goju** and jujutsu.

In 1979 he won the world's full-contact championship in the welterweight division sanctioned by the World Professional Karate Organization. He was elected 1980 "Fighter of the Year" by the WPKO.

NELSON, DEVIE (1951-) American judo competitor, Nelson began in judo in 1972, earning her black belt in 1975 under Willy Cahill and a jujutsu black belt in 1974 from the American Jujutsu Institute. She is the author of a research paper on judo injuries and mat surfaces.

Her tournament credits include: Pacific Coast Championships, first place 1974 and 1975; Western States Championships, first place 1974 and 1975; U.S. Judo Federation AAU Nationals, first place 1975. Nelson was chosen among the top 10 female judo players by *Black Belt Magazine* in 1975 and 1976, and was an All American Team member in 1975.

Devie Nelson

NELSON, DOUG (1948-) American judo champion. A three-time national champion (1967, 1971, 1972), he represented the U.S. in the 1970 Pan-American Games, the 1971 World Games, and the 1972 Olympic Games.

NEVZOROV, JLADIMIE Russian judo champion; winner of the welterweight division at the 1975 World Championships. Standing only 5 feet 7 inches, Nevzorov is a calm and intelligent fighter who usually wins his matches with full points.

NEWMAN, EDDIE (1955-) American karate competitor. Newman began martial arts in 1973 under **Steve Sanders** and **Jerry Smith.** His style is **kenpo,** but he studied tae kwon do and boxing as well. His victories include the 1979 and 1980 Long Beach **Internationals,** 1980 National Championships, World Expo of Martial Arts, South Western Championships, Fiesta Bowl Classic (3 times), Top 10 Nationals, and Steve Fisher's 2nd Annual Open.

NEWMAN, JOHN EDWARD BRIAN (1935-) British judo champion. Winner of both the 1st and 2nd Dan Championships of Europe in 1956 and 1958, Newman was a member of the British team that won the European Championships in 1957 and 1958. His career ended during a stay in Japan; Newman was thrown into a post at Tenri University and injured his back. In 1964 he managed the British Olympic judo team.

NG-SIU-CHUNG Grandmaster of the white crane (bai-ho) style of Chinese kung-fu. Ng acquired his kung-fu from Wong-Lum-Hoi, who learned from Sing-Lung, who in turn studied under Jicboloclowto (Ng-Mui). He passed his art on to Chan-Hoc-Fu, Lak-Chi-Fu, and Chuk-Tse. Lak-Chi-Fu taught Quentin Fong, William Su, and Raymond Mar (all prominent **sifu** in the San Francisco area).

NG-YIM-MING Grandmaster of the Ho-Chia (hop-gar, in Cantonese) style of Chinese kung-fu. Ng acquired his kung-fu from master Wong-Yan-Lum, who in turn learned from Hing-Duk, who studied under the lama master Jicboloclowto (Ng-Mui). Occupying the number one seat among the prestigious "Canton Ten Tigers," Ng passed his style on to Chin-Dai-Wei, who had several students including kung-fu movie choreographer Fung Ging Men (Gary Fung).

Hidetaka Nishiyama

NICHOLS, SAM American karate competitor. He began karate at 13 and has since won such tournaments as the Top 10 Nationals, USKA Grand Nationals, and Midwest Open. In 1976-77 he was National Champion of the **USKA,** having the highest number of USKA tournament wins.

NICOL, C.W. Canadian wildlife authority and karate instructor. Nicol has traveled throughout the world pursuing both interests. Born in Wales, he began to study judo at 14, later wrestled professionally, and eventually earned his black belt in Japan. In 1975 he wrote *Moving Zen,* in which he describes the difficulties of a Caucasian karate student in Japan's dojos. Nicol's wife, Sonako, is a black belt in jujutsu.

NIGGEL, BARBARA American karate competitor and instructor. She began karate at 12, receiving her black belt from Willie Wetsel while still a teenager. She is one of the few professional women instructors. A noted kata competitor, Niggel won form competition in men's as well as women's divisions. She was a four-time winner of the women's black belt kata division at the **USKA Grand Nationals,** and trained a number of regional champions. Member of *Who's Who in the Martial Arts.*

NINOMIYA, KAZUHIRO Japanese judo champion, winner of the 1976 Olympic Games in the light-heavyweight division. In 1973 he won the openweight class at the World Championships and the All Japan Police Championships. Ninomiya, standing 6 feet 2 inches, favors techniques such as **osotogari, kosotogari,** and **haraigoshi.**

NISHIOKA, HAYWARD (1942-) Japanese-American judo champion. During the 1960s, Nishioka was a U.S. division champion three times, in 1965, 1966, and 1970. In 1965 he retired as the National AAU Grand Champion. A member of four U.S. international teams, he won a Pan-American Games gold medal in 1967, was the British-Columbian Champion in 1966, and competed in the World Judo Championships in 1965 and 1967, finishing fifth and fourth. Also a black belt in **Shotokan** karate under pioneer **Tsutomu Ohshima,** Nishioka competed briefly in the karate circuit. After retiring from competition, he became a physical education instructor at Los Angeles City College in California, heading its martial arts program as well as coaching wrestling. He continues to officiate at judo events.

Nishioka is the founder and first president of the Southern California Collegiate Judo Conference, and is a board of directors member of the Southern California Judo Association. Author of the isntructional books *Foot Throws* (1973) and *The Judo Textbook* (1979), he has contributed articles to *Black Belt Magazine* and *Karate Illustrated.* He has also produced and directed three martial arts training films.

NISHIYAMA, HIDETAKA (1928-) Japanese-American karate master, author, administrator and pioneer. Born in Tokyo, Nishiyama began his karate training in 1943 under **Gichin Funakoshi** at the **Shotokan.** Two years later, while enrolled at Takushoku University, he became a member of the university's karate team, for which in 1949 he was named captain. He was a co-founder of the **All Japan Collegiate Karate Federation** and was elected its first chairman.

Nishiyama received a Master of Arts degree in economics from Takushoku in 1951. That same year, he was a co-founder of the **Japan Karate Association** (JKA) and was elected to the JKA Board of Directors.

In 1952 he was selected as a member of the martial arts combat instruction staff for the Strategic Air Command (SAC) Combat Training Program. SAC personnel received training in judo, aikido and karate at the Shotokan. The other karate instructors for this program included **Masatoshi Nakayama** and **Isao Obata.**

Karate; The Art of Empty-Hand Fighting, co-written with Nishiyama and published in 1960, is even today considered the definitive textbook on the subject. In its 70th printing, it is believed to be the best selling karate textbook in history.

In 1961, SAC karate students and JKA members residing in the United States joined with **Tsutomu Ohshima** of Los Angeles to invite Nishiyama to visit America. Later that year, he organized the **All America Karate Federation** (AAKF) as a nationally based amateur karate organization. The first AAKF Championships were conducted in Los Angeles that same year. Also establishing his dojo in Los Angeles, Nishiyama has since 1961 been a major force in propagating the Shotokan style of karate in the U.S. and abroad.

1965 marked his organization of the first United States (vs) Japan Goodwill Karate Tournament. Because of the participation of the All

Japan Collegiate Karate Team, this event became the first truly international karate competition.

In 1968, Nishiyama organized the first World Invitational Karate Tournament, held at the Los Angeles Sports Arena in conjunction with the Olympic Commemorative Tournament hosted by the Mexico Karate Federation in Mexico City. A conference held during the tournament culminated in an agreement to form an international karate organization and to hold its first world championship in Tokyo.

In 1973, Nishiyama co-founded the Pan American Karate Union and was elected its first executive director. The first PAKU Championships were staged in Rio de Janeiro.

The next year, based on the 1968 agreement at the Mexico City conference, an international formation meeting was held in New York City. There the **International Amateur Karate Federation** was founded with Nishiyama elected executive director. The first IAKF World Championships were held in Los Angeles in 1975.

He oversaw the formation of the Mediterranean Karate Championship Committee and the Bolivariana Karate Federation in 1976. Also that year, acting on behalf of the IAKF, he submitted an application to the International Olympic Committee seeking Olympic recognition for karate.

Nishiyama then supported the formation in 1977 of the Central America/Caribbean Karate Confederation and the Asia/Oceania Amateur Karate Federation. In 1978, in accordance with U.S. Public Law regulating national amateur sports governing bodies, the All America Karate Federation was succeeded by the **American Amateur Karate Federation.** Nishiyama was elected its first president.

In 1981, he also lent support to the formation of the South American Karate Confederation and the North American Karate Confederation.

Nishiyama's reputation has spread foremost because of his superior technical expertise and his disciplined instruction. Among his former students are past All Japan Champions **Keinosuke Enoeda, Takeshi Onishi** and Hiroshi Shirai. He has also trained a host of national amateur champions in the U.S. including **James Yabe, Frank Smith, James Fields** and **Ray Dalke**. Also among his endless roster of noted black belts is author **Randall Hassell**, and he was the original instructor of **Arnold Urquidez** and actor John Saxon. See also: U.S., history of karate in; Shotokan. (MAURICIO HERNANDEZ)

NOGUCHI, YUKIO Japanese-American aikido instructor; chief of Yoshinkai aikido for all territories outside Japan. Noguchi began martial arts training with **kendo** and took up judo at 15. He won the All Tokyo Judo Championships twice and at 17 began to study karate and **sumo** wrestling. It was not until 1951 that he took up aikido.

NOMURA, TOYOKAZU (1949-) Japanese judo champion; welterweight winner at the 1972 Olympic Games. In 1969 and 1971, Nomura won silver medals at the World Championships and in 1973 became world champion of the welterweight class. Nomura is a specialist in **seoi-nage.**

NORRIS, CHUCK (1940-) American karate champion, pioneer, instructor, and actor. Born in Ryan, Okla. Chuck Norris is one of the greatest champions in the history of American karate. Winner of

By 1981, Chuck Norris was a Hollywood star. This is a scene from his third movie for American Cinema, *The Octagon.* In the background is his brother Aaron, who choreographs all of Norris' movies.

virtually every major title in karate between 1965 and 1970, his grand championship victories include the 1967 and 1968 **International Karate Championships,** the 1967 and 1968 All American Championships, the 1968 National Tournament of Champions, and the 1968 World Professional Middleweight Title. He retired as the undefeated middleweight champion after his last title defense, Jan. 17, 1970.

As an instructor, Norris has been responsible for guiding more than 325 students to black belt and dozens to competitive success. He also coached the only black belt team to go undefeated in 29 tournaments. Among his prominent students are **Bob Wall, Pat Johnson, John Natividad, Howard Jackson,** Ralph and Bob Alegria, **Darnell Garcia,** Bob Burbidge, Jerry Taylor, Vic Martinov, and Aaron Norris, his brother. He also taught celebrities including the late Steve McQueen, Bob Barker, Priscilla Presley, and the Osmond Brothers. It was McQueen who encouraged Norris to try an acting career.

In 1974 he wrote *Chuck Norris' Basic Karate Fundamentals* and, in 1975, *Winning Tournament Karate,* the first manual written on American-style karate. Along with Bob Wall and **Mike Stone,** Norris co-founded in 1967 the Four Seasons Karate Championships, one of the most successful tournament formats in the sport's history. In 1975 he co-founded the National Karate League, with full-contact teams in 12 cities. The league's premier star was **Benny Urquidez,** who later became an individual superstar in his sport.

A graduate of the Lee Strasburg school of acting, Norris made his film debut in 1968 in *The Wrecking Crew.* In 1972 he co-starred with **Bruce Lee** in *Return of the Dragon* (released in 1974). This film's climactic fight scene, filmed in the Roman Coliseum, remains a classic among martial arts film buffs. In 1976 he landed his first starring role, in *Breaker, Breaker.* At this time the genre, following Bruce Lee's death, was suffering a decline. Norris singlehandedly reinstated the interest in martial arts films by convincing Hollywood filmmakers of their marketing potential.

In 1977 he signed a three-picture deal with American Cinema, all of which became big box-office hits: *Good Guys Wear Black* (1978); *A Force of One* (1979), which featured the film debut of another karate champion, **Bill Wallace;** and *The Octagon* (1980). In 1981 he starred in *An Eye for An Eye* for Avco Embassy. In 1982 he starred in and co-produced *Silent Rage* for Columbia Pictures. That same year he also starred in *Forced Vengeance* for MGM Studios.

Norris is the only martial artist to have been named three times to the **Black Belt Hall of Fame:** "Player of the Year" (1968), "Instructor of the Year" (1975), and "Man of the Year" (1977). A member of *Who's Who in the Martial Arts,* he received a Golden Fist Award as an "Outstanding Fighter" for the decade 1960-70. He is the founder of the United Fighting Arts Federation, which by 1982 included 42 affiliated schools. *See also* motion pictures and television; U.S., history of karate in.

NOZAKI, SUMIKICHI Japanese-American judo competitor and five-time U.S. lightweight judo champion.

OAKLEY, MERVYN Australian karate pioneer and instructor. He began studying jujutsu in Sydney, Australia for four years. In early 1963, Oakley traveled to Tokyo with the intention of furthering his jujutsu training when he met some karate students working out in a public park who invited him to their dojo, the **goju-ryu** headquarters of **Gogen Yamaguchi**. He studied goju-ryu intensely for 36 hours per week, occasionally under the personal instruction of Yamaguchi, and earned his black belt within six months.

He returned to Sydney and opened his first dojo in late 1963, in the process introducing goju-ryu karate in Australia. Within one year, Oakley founded three additional goju clubs and seven more by 1969. He also assisted Tino Generano in establishing four goju clubs in Melbourne.

OBATA, ISAO (1904-) Japanese karate pioneer and disciple of **Gichin Funakoshi.** He is co-founder and past chairman of the **JKA.** He joined Keio University's karate club, supervised by Funakoshi. After 1926 Obata assisted Funakoshi in establishing clubs at other Japanese universities. He also practiced **kyudo** and in 1940

Karate pioneer Isao Obata (*right*) and Hidetaka Nishiyama demonstrate in front of Air Force personnel on a visit to the U.S. in 1953.

represented the Manchuria territory in the Japan National Kyudo tournament held in Tokyo; he won the event.

After World War II, he and Funakoshi formed the **JKA,** though Obata dropped out a few years later, feeling that it had become too commercial. In 1953 Obata came to the U.S. at the invitation of the Strategic Air Command (SAC), demonstrating karate techniques to Air Force and Army personnel. In 1968, he returned to the U.S. to be honored by the Southern California Karate Association as one of those most instrumental in furthering American karate. One of Obata's students, **Tsutomu Ohshima,** became a karate pioneer in America. *See also* Shotokan; Japan, history of karate in.

OCHIAI, HIDY (1939-   ) Japanese-born American karate master, champion, and author. He came to the U.S. in 1962 and entered Albright College, from which he received a B.A. in philosophy. In 1966 he opened his first school, in Binghamton, N.Y., and today he owns one of the largest karate schools in the nation, in Vestal, N.Y. He also has dozens of branch schools in the New England states. An instructor in the washin-ryu style, Ochiai began studying martial arts at age 6 in his native Japan.

Best known for his spectacular demonstrations, he is considered one of America's premier martial arts performers and has demonstrated all over the world.

Ochiai has been rated five consecutive times as the number-one kata competitor in the U.S. by *Professional Karate Magazine* and has won this event at tournaments such as the U.S.K.A. Grand Nationals, Southern Grand Nationals, Ohio State Karate Championships, U.S. Championships, Top Ten Nationals, Long Beach Internationals, and the P.K.A. Nationals.

Besides being a consumate karate master, Ochiai is also well versed in different weapons such as the bo, sai, sword, and nunchaku. In 1978 Ochiai began teaching a four credit course, "Zen and the Martial Arts of Japan" at the State University of N.Y. at Binghamton. The course is based on historical, psychological, and philosophical perspectives of Zen and the martial arts.

In 1979 he was named to the Black Belt Hall of Fame as "Instructor of the Year," and the following year he was named "Man of the Year." He authored *The Essence of Self-Defense* in 1979 and is a member of *Who's Who in the Martial Arts. See also* U.S., history of karate in; washin-ryu.

OGAWA, TYUZO (1882-   ) Japanese-born, Brazilian judo instructor and pioneer. In 1929 he gave a demonstration of judo for the emperor of Japan and was awarded the coveted Shield of Excellence. In 1934, he immigrated to Brazil, where he became director of the Jukendore-nei Association and chief judo instructor. He later founded the Brazilian Budokan Association, which produced several champions. The Brazilian Federal Judo Association presented him in 1970 with a 7th-degree black belt. One year later the Budo-kai Association of Japan awarded him 9th dan.

OHGAMI, SHINGO (1942-   ) Japanese karate instructor. He began studying karate in 1960 in Japan, earning his black belt in **Shotokan**. He also trained in **kobu-jutsu** (art of weapons). He immigrated to Sweden in 1969 and established his main school in Goteborg. By 1978, Ohgami had formed several branch schools with an overall membership of some 2,000 students.

OHSHIMA, TSUTOMU (1930-   ) Japanese-American karate pioneer and instructor. A student of **Isao Obata,** Ohshima came to America in 1955. One year later, he founded Shotokan Karate of America, an organization that by 1975 had more than 70 schools internationally. In 1958 Ohshima originated the Neisei Week Karate Championships, one of the first American tournaments and the longest-running annual event in the U.S.

Ohshima spent ten years translating and preparing **Funakoshi's** text, *Karate Do Kyohan: The Master Text,* for publication. It was released in 1972. Ohshima's better known students include **Caylor Adkins,** John Evans, and Jordon Roth. He was named to *Who's Who in the Martial Arts* in 1975. *See also* Shotokan; U.S., history of karate in.

OHTSUKA, HIRONORI (1892-1982) Japanese karate master, founder of the **wado-ryu** system. Ohtsuka began martial arts training at six in Shindo Yoshin-ryu jujutsu. By 1921, at the relatively young age of 29, he was awarded the coveted **menkyo-kaiden,** designating him the successor as master of this style. A year later, he commenced karate under the legendary **Gichin Funakoshi.**

Ohtsuka founded wado-ryu karate-do in 1939, which became one of the four major styles of Japanese karate. As early as 1934, he had developed rules and regulations for competitive free-sparring, which he incorporated into his sytem. In 1939 he organized the All Japan Karate-do Federation, Wado-Kai, which serves as the worldwide sanctioning body for the wado-ryu system and its affiliates.

For his outstanding contributions to karate, the Emperor of Japan awarded Ohtsuka-sensei the Fifth Order of Merit of the Sacred Treasure in 1967; he was the first karate master to receive this distinguished award. In 1972, he was the recipient of the Hanshi Award, an even greater honor. Along with this award came the honor of being ranked at the head of all martial arts systems within the All Japan Karate-do Federation.

Ohtsuka is considered by his disciples to be one of the three men responsible for originating the modern Japanese martial arts.

Ohtsuka's second son, Jiro, assumed duties as chief instructor for the wado system shortly before his father's death. *See also* Japan, history of karate in; wado-ryu.

Hironori Ohtsuka

OISHI, TAKESHI (1941-) Japanese karate champion. Oishi, in addition to having been rated one of Japan's top competitors, is a **JKA** instructor and coach of the Komazawa University Karate Club. He won the 1973 JKA International Championships and the 1970 and 1973 Mas Oyama's World Kyokushinkai Karate Championships. He is a three-time champion of the All Japan Shotokan Championships, 1969-71 and winner of the 1968 Mexico City International Karate Tournament.

OKADA, KENNETH (1950-) American judo champion, member of the 1972 U.S. Olympic Judo Team. Okada began judo at 6 and had already won top honors while attending high school in Garden Grove, Calif. In 1965 he finished fifth in the High School Nationals, but captured first place in 1967 and 1968. Under the instruction of **Shag Okada,** his uncle, he spent some time training in Japan.

OKADA, SHAG (1923-) Japanese-American judo instructor. Okada is perhaps best known for his superior coaching abilities. In 1972 his students, **Pat Burris** and **Kenny Okada** (his nephew), served on the U.S. Olympic judo team. Okada was named coach of the U.S. teams competing at the 1975 Pan-American Championships. His contingent brought back nine medals. Okada's own team has twice swept the Southern California Team Championships, in 1973 and 1974. In 1976 he was elected to the **Black Belt Hall of Fame** as "Judo Instructor of the Year." *See also* U.S., history of judo in.

OKANO, ISAO (1944-) Japanese judo champion. The lightest fighter to win the All Japan Championships, Okano scored victories in 1967 and 1969 over larger opponents. He won the Olympic middleweight gold medal in 1964 and the World Title in 1965.

Okano was especially noted for **seio-nage** and **kouichigari.** He retired in 1969 to concentrate on instructing. In 1972 he was appointed Japan's national team trainer.

OKANO, TOMOSABURU Japanese karate instructor; founded his own style, kenkojuku, in 1942. Okano studied with **Gichin Funakoshi.**

OKAZAKI, TERUYUKI (1931-) Japanese-born American karate pioneer and instructor. Okazaki began his training in the **JKA** in 1947 under **Gichin Funakoshi** and **Masatoshi Nakayama.** His experience as an instructor began in 1955, and while in Japan he taught karate at Takushoku University, Tokyo Toritsu University, Japan Karate Association Instructor's Program, and Boei University, equivalent to West Point.

In 1961 he came to the U.S. as chief instructor of the Philadelphia Karate Club. Shortly after his arrival he founded the East Coast

Karate Association. Okazaki taught the **Shotokan** style at universities and private clubs throughout Pennsylvania.

In 1977, Okazaki was successful in forming a nationwide organization, the **International Shotokan Karate Federation.** The ISKF was officially recognized as a representative member of the JKA in 1979. The ISKF, composed of 150 clubs in the U.S. and member organizations in 12 countries in the Western Hemisphere, has approximately 50,000 members, and about 80 percent, or more than 10,000, of the JKA practitioners in America. In 1982, Okazaki was named "Man of the Year" and inducted into the **Black Belt Hall of Fame.**

In the early 1960s he also organized the East Coast Collegiate Karate Union and served as chief instructor for a number of the clubs. As chief instructor of the ECKU and the ISKF he holds monthly seminars, classes, and ranking exams for clubs from Maine to Virginia. Quarterly seminars are given by him to karate organizations in the West Indies, Canada, and Latin America. He co-authored *The Textbook of Modern Karate.* (ROBIN RIELLY) *See also* U.S., history of karate in; Shotokan.

OKUYAMA, RYUHO Japanese jujutsu master; founder of **hakko-ryu** jujutsu. Also known as Yoshiji Okuyama, he was a leading exponent of **Daito-ryu aiki-jutsu** before founding his system. *See* hakko-ryu.

OKUYAMA, TOSHIO (1944-) Japanese jujutsu master; heir apparent of **hakko-ryu** jujugus. Eldest son of **Ryuho Okuyama,** the founder of hakko-ryu jujutsu, Toshio began training in hakko-ryu and **koho shiatsu** with his father in 1949 at five. Known by the titles nidai imei (second great generation) and waka sensi (young teacher), Toshio supervises the operation of the Hakko Juku Honbu (private headquarters of the hakko-ryu) and helps administrate the branch dojo in and outside of Japan. *See also* hakko-ryu.

ONASHVILI, GIVI Russian judo champion. At 6 feet, 4 inches, 275 lbs., three-time European champion, bronze medal winner at the 1969 World Championships and at the 1972 Olympic Games in Munich. Onashvili favors the **maki-komi** and uses his great bulk to pin his opponents.

O'NEILL, TERRY British karate champion, instructor, and publisher. He began judo at 13 and karate at 15 under Andy Sherry in Liverpool. When Japanese Shotokan karate instructor **Keinosuke Enoeda** visited England, he lived with O'Neill for six months. O'Neill began his competitive career in 1967, at the first Karate Union of Great Britain (KUGB) Championships, an event he has won five times. When the British team competed in South Africa, in 1969, he won a division gold medal. O'Neill was a member of the British Karate team for eight years and its captain for the 1972 World Championships in Paris. In the early 1970s he created and published the magazine *Fighting Arts.*

Teruyuki Okazaki (*right*)

Terry O'Neill (*right*) vs. Norman Robinson of South Africa at the 1973 JKA World Championships

ONISHI, EIZO Japanese karate master; founder of **koei-kan** karate. He began judo, kendo, jujutsu, and jodo as a child, and during his early teens became a pupil of **Kanken Toyama.** At 19 he captained the Matsuyama Dai (Matsuyama Language Institute) Karate Club and trained while attending Keio University in Tokyo. Onishi became Toyama's star pupil, eventually becoming assistant instructor.

Toyama gave him a letter of introduction to **Juhatsu Kiyoda.** Onishi traveled by boat from his home to Beppu City on Kyushu once a month for a year before Kiyoda finally accepted him as a student. Traditional martial arts teachers often tested the sincerity and patience of prospective students in this way.

Onishi continued to study under both Toyama and Kiyoda, and in 1952 founded the koei-kan system. On April 2, 1954 he established the first regular koei-kan dojo, in Kanagawa prefecture. Prior to his death in 1966, Toyama awarded Onishi the **menkyo-kaiden** in the traditional makimono (hand-written scroll) form and appointed him chairman of the All Japan Karate-do Association. As chairman of the International Koei-Kan KArate-do Federation (known also as the International Ken-do Gaku Federation), Onishi visited the U.S., South America, Europe, and Southeast Asia. (EDWARD KALOUDIS)

Eizo Onishi, founder of the koei-kan style of karate

Courtesy of Brian Frost

ONOWO, KAZUO SONNY (1954-   ) Japanese-born American karate competitor. Onowo has been studying martial arts since 1963. It began with saibukan in Tokyo. He received his black belt in 1970 in **goju-ryu,** but also studied tae kwon do, Mid-America Karate, and **washin ryu** under **Hidy Ochiai**. Among his wins are: Mid-America 1976, 1978, 1979—first place black belt forms; Battle of Atlanta

ORITO, HIROSHI Japanese-born karate instructor; founded the New York Karate Club in 1959. He studied the **renbukan** style, but in 1961 joined the East Coast Karate Association and changed to the **Shotokan** style.

OSAKO, JOHN (1921-   ) Japanese-born American judo instructor, champion, and referee. In 1939 Osako was Kagoshima State Champion. After moving to the U.S. he won the heavyweight and grand championships at the 1956 AAU Nationals; in 1955 and 1958 he was the 180-lb. champion. He was also grand champion at the first two Pan-American championships, held in Havana, Cuba, in 1952 and 1954. The first certified referee of the **IJF,** he has since chaired several officiating committees. Osako wrote several handbooks on officiating. Member of Who's Who in the Martial Arts. See also U.S., history of judo in.

OTANI, NAGASAKI (1898-1977) Japanese-born judo pioneer. He came to England in 1919 and practiced at the **Budokwai**. In 1927 he began teaching judo at Oxford and Cambridge Universities, and in 1932 he became instructor at the Anglo-Japanese Club. After the war he taught the military and police forces. In 1958, Otani joined the British Judo Council under **Kenshiro Abe**, becoming its leader in the mid-1960s when Abe returned to Japan. He continued teaching in England until his death.

OTANI, SHIMOSA NO KAMI SEIICHIRO (1789-1844) Japanese master swordsman. Otani was a technician of **menkyo-kaiden** rank whose great skill earned him the honor of cho-ichi-ryu, or supreme swordsman. He became the 13th headmaster of the jikishin-kage-ryu and was head of the Kobusho, a government training school.

OYAMA, MASUTATSU (1923-   ) Korean-born karate master, pioneer, author, and administrator. Known worldwide as Mas Oyama, he was born Yee Hyung in Kimje, Korea. At age 9, while attending Yongee Primary School, he studied chabi (aka **taiken**), a combination of **kempo** and jujutsu. At this time, he also began training in **Shao-lin** kung-fu and chabi with a North Korean farmhand employed by his father, continuing until he was 13.

In 1937, he was sent to Japan to attend a boy's military academy in Yamanashi Prefecture. He changed his name and began studying **Shotokan** karate. Unsatisfied with his training after two years, he moved to Tokyo and enrolled in Takushoku University. He was accepted for further karate training at the Shotokan, the private dojo where **Gichin Funakoshi** and his son taught. There he studied directly under the elder Funakoshi for two years, two hours a day. Oyama was drafted into the Imperial Army at 18. Stationed in Tokyo, he joined the **Butokukai**, the government-sponsored organization comprising all the primary martial arts, where he resumed his karate training. Oyama was a member of the Kihokai, a section of the Butokukai specializing in teaching espionage and guerrilla tactics for wartime use.

After the Kihokai was disbanded, Oyama met **Neichu So** (in Korean, Hyung Ju Cho), a student of **Chojun Miyagi**, who taught Oyama **goju-ryu** karate for two years. During the hectic period following World War II, Oyama resumed his studies with So for one year at a dojo in the Koenji section of Tokyo. After 1948, at the urging of So and statesman Tenshichiro Ozawa, Oyama journeyed to Mt. Kiyosumi in Chiba Prefecture and for 18 months remained in seclusion, devoting himself completely to a spartan existence. Ozawa sent him $50 every month for expenses. Here Oyama followed a strict daily regimen of practicing karate seven hours each day, sleeping for eight hours, and meditating. Through such rigorous training as seated meditation under a waterfall, struggles with wild animals, and smashing trees and stones with his bare hands, Oyama refined his doctrine of karate, as well as his own mind and body.

He returned to civilization in 1951, residing in a beach resort town of Tateyama, where, determined to teach the true meaning of karate to the world, he faced his first monumental challenge. At a local slaughter house, Oyama tested his strength against a bull by attempting to kill it with a single punch. After the first attempt failed, Oyama returned a few days later and this time staggered the bull to its knees with one mighty punch, then knocked off one of its horns with a knife-hand slash. In the ensuing years, he battled a total of 52 bulls in this barehanded manner, slicing the horns from 36 of them, and killing only three; all the bulls were marked for slaughter. A 20-minute film of Oyama's barehanded bull fighting was produced by Shochiku.

As a result of these battles, his fame spread far and wide. He opened a small dojo in Tateyama, but closed it after one year and returned to Tokyo in late 1950. After working as a bodyguard at the South Korean mission in Tokyo, he made the first of many trips to the U.S. From March to Nov. 1952, he toured the country with judoka Kokichi Endo and pro wrestler "The Great Togo" of California, under the auspices of the U.S. Professional Wrestling Association. Beginning in Chicago, the three men challenged pro wrestlers and boxers in public exhibition bouts. Oyama reportedly won every one of his matches by knockout, in the process generating unprecedented media exposure for karate in America. He returned to Chicago in the summer of 1953, where, in front of television cameras, he stunned a bull with his first punch and sliced off a horn. He then went to New York to teach karate for a week, then back to Japan.

By this time, Oyama was an international sensation, the publicity surrounding his feats having made him the most famous karate figure in the world. In 1954, he conducted a three-month tour of Southeast Asia, where he defeated the "Black Cobra," the reigning welterweight Thai kick-boxer, by knocking him out and breaking his jaw in two minutes of the first round. Also that year, he went to hawaii for one month to help his student, **Bobby Lowe**, set up Oyama's first overseas school. Oyama founded his own first school in Japan in 1956, but it wasn't until 1961 that he changed the name of his schools to reflect his newly-created style, kyokushinkai, which emphasizes **Zen, tameshiwari** (breaking), and a rough style of **kumite** (free sparring).

Masutatsu Oyama

He returned to the U.S. in 1959 and 1962 to give demonstrations and establish branches of his school in Chicago, New York, and California, during which he gave karate exhibitions for the FBI at its Washington, D.C., headquarters. Among the techniques he refined for these performances was the breaking of rocks, bricks, boards, bottles, and roofing tiles. He still holds the record for smashing a stack of 30 roofing tiles with a single downward punch. He also toured Europe in 1962.

In 1963, he established his present headquarters, a four-story building in Idebukuro (Prime Minister Eisaku Sato was honorary chairman). By 1980, Oyama claimed some 300,000 students in Japan alone, and more than 1.5 million worldwide. From his headquarters, he oversees a reported network of some 520 kyokushinkai schools around the world, including branches in Iron Curtain countries such as the U.S.S.R., Poland, Yugoslavia, and Czechoslovakia.

Overall, Oyama has written 22 books, all highly successful, which have been translated into 19 languages, most of them noted for lavish, spectacular photography. He wrote his first book, *What Is Karate*, in 1958. Among his works is an autobiographical series which became very popular in Japan. At least one film has been made about his life. *See also* Japan, history of karate in; U.S., history of karate in.

OZAWA, OSAMU (1925-) Japanese karate instructor. Ozawa began the Kobe branch of the **JKA.** Later he was commissioner of the Kansai branch, with over 10,000 students. In 1965 he went to the U.S. and founded the International Karate Organization in San Gabriel, Calif. *See also* Shotokan.

PACHIVAS, JOHN American karate instructor and pioneer. One of the first men to teach karate in the state of Florida, he began his martial arts training in the late 1950s. He received a black belt in judo in 1961, and a black belt in karate from Bob Sasaki in 1963. Pachivas served as chief instructor of the Dade County Police Academy in Miami. In 1966 and 1974 he promoted the **USKA Grand Nationals** and was the seventh inductee to the Trias International Society. *See also* U.S., history of karate in.

John Pachivas

PAINTER, DR. BIFF (1946-) American kung-fu instructor and author. During a brief period after college, Painter traveled throughout the U.S. demonstrating kung-fu, meditation, and his ability to escape from any bonds. In one demonstration, to show the power of meditation, Dr. Painter was buried alive for five hours. He survived by slowing his bodily functions to barely perceptible levels through what he calls ''Tao Chi Meditation.'' The author of three books on Chinese health principles, kung-fu, and Chinese meditation, Painter opened the Tao Chi Ch'uan International Health Club in Arlington, Tex.

Dr. John Biff Painter

PALMER, CHARLES STUART (1930-) British judo competitor and administrator. Palmer was the first non-Japanese to serve as president of the **IJF,** in 1965. From 1951, he studied judo for four years in Japan. In 1957, he was a member of the victorious British team at the European Championships, and in the following two years captained the British team. As president of the IJF, Palmer was chiefly responsible for the reintroduction of judo to the Olympic Games and for standardization of international contest rules (with the collaboration of the **Kodokan**). *See also* Europe, history of judo in.

PARISET, BERNARD (1929-) French judo competitor. The only European to defeat the legendary **Anton Geesink** in a major event, Pariset won a split decision in the 1955 open class final, which was hotly disputed although he had pinned Geesink for 20 seconds. Pariset's **ippon-seoinage** bought him three European titles. He was a member of the European Championships winning team in 1951, 1952, 1954, 1955, and 1962.

PARISI, ANGELO (1953-) British judo champion. He won three European junior titles, a European senior gold medal in the team event, the bronze medal at the 1972 Munich Olympics and the gold medal in the super-heavyweight division at the 1980 Moscow Olympics. He also won the silver medal in the open division. Currently he lives in France and competes internationally for France.

PARISI, LUCIANO (1943-) Italian karate competitor. A Shotokan stylist and student of Hiroshi Shirai, Parisi spent ten years training before entering itnernational competition. Before his retirement in 1973 he was a leading Italian competitor. He operates a dojo in Genoa.

PARK, DONG KEUN Korean-born tae kwon do instructor. After earning a black belt in ji do kwan, he was named to the 1966 Korean Hall of Fame for his athletic prowess. He spent five years in Thailand teaching Thai and American troops, and in 1971 came to the U.S., where he established schools in Kentucky, New York, and New Jersey and taught at the New York University. Two of his students, Gerald Robbins and Dennis Robinson, placed first in their respective divisions of the AAU Tae Kwon Do Championships, earning a place on the American team for the 2nd World Tae Kwon Do Championships in August 1975, in which Robbins won a bronze medal in individual competition.

PARK, KEIL SOON (1937-) Korean-born American judo and tae kwon do instructor. Park won the silver medal in competition at the 1968 World Judo Championships and instructed notable U.S. judo competitors.

PARK, SUNG KEUN (1931-   ) Korean tae kwon do instructor and administrator. He began studying tae kwon do in Sept. 1954 under Byung Sik, Young Mook, and two others. He was personal secretary for **Gen. Choi Hong Hi** from 1969-72, after which he was named under-secretary to the **International Taekwon-do Federation**. He established his first U.S. school in Illinois in July 1973.

PARKER, ED (1931-   ) American karate pioneer, promoter, actor, instructor, and author. Parker founded the first commercial karate school on the West Coast, in Provo, Utah, in 1954. A student of **William K.S. Chow,** he left Hawaii in 1951. After presenting a karate demonstration during a basketball game, he began teaching local law enforcement officers. After graduating from BYU, Parker moved to Pasadena and opened a karate school in 1956, where he taught **kenpo** karate. In Aug. 1964 Parker originated the annual **International Karate Championships** in which the late Bruce Lee first attracted notice. Named "Outstanding Contributor" to karate for the years 1961-70 by the U.S. Championships in Dallas, Parker also received a Golden Fist award as a karate pioneer in southern California. He was named to *Who's Who in the Martial Arts* in 1975.

Parker, who was the first showman to combine a Hollywood flair with his exhibitions, has staged demonstrations for such dignitaries and celebrities as President Ronald Reagan, Gary Cooper, and Mae West, just to name a few.

Some of the celebrities Parker instructed in the art of karate and self-defense include the late **Elvis Presley,** Blake Edwards, Nick Adams, Robert Culp, Robert Wagner, Audie Murphy, Joey Bishop, Warren Beatty, Frank Lovejoy, and author **Joe Hyams.** In 1974, Parker took an American team, sponsored by Elvis Presley, to compete against contingents in England and Belgium. Fighters accompanying him were **Benny Urquidez, John Natividad, Darnell Garcia, Ron Marchini,** and **Tom Kelly.**

As an actor or stunt choreographer, he has worked in: *The Wrecking Crew, Money Jungle, The Devil's Choice, The Revenge of the Pink Panther, Seven,* and *Kill the Golden Goose.* He has appeared in numerous television shows, including *The Rebel, I Spy, I Love Lucy,* and *The Courtship of Eddie's Father.*

He wrote *Kenpo Karate; Secrets of Chinese Karate; The Woman's Guide to Self-Defense: The Basic Booklet; Ed Parker's Guide to the Nunchaku;* and *Manual for Training of Law Enforcement Personnel. See also* U.S., history of karate in; kenpo.

PARSONS, KEVIN American police self-defense authority and author. Parsons serves as Law Enforcement Liaison Director for the **U.S. Karate Association.** Each summer he conducts the National Police Self-Defense Instructors Training Seminar in conjunction with the **USKA Grand Nationals.** In addition to

Ed Parker *(left)* with Sidney Poitier.

sanctioning regional training programs throughout the U.S., he supervises the national certification and licensing program for physical training and defensive tactics instructors.

Author of *Techniques of Vigilance: A Textbook for Police Self-Defense,* Parsons is a frequent contributor to several law enforcement periodicals including *Law and Order Magazine.* He has conducted a year-long evaluation of police weaponry for the federal government and has been employed as an expert witness regarding police weapons usage. He has also conducted training research studies for the U.S. Department of Justice.

PARULSKI, GEORGE R. American author and authority on Oriental culture. A novelist, poet and philosopher, he has spent three years at the Eisho-ji Monastery in the U.S., training under Kuzure Kudo Roshi, and holds degrees in judo and **kito ryu** jujutsu. His books include *Wisdom of the East; A Dictionary of Eastern Experience ; Zen in the Art of Swordsmanship;* and *A Path to Oriental Wisdom.*

PASCETTA, RIC (1950-   ) American karate competitor, instructor, and promoter. Pascetta began the martial arts in 1963 in Melbourne, Fla. under Skip McKuen, receiving his black belt in 1969 from Edward Verycken in U.S.A. goju. He later became a student of **Peter Urban.** He is president of the American Goju Karate Association, international and executive director of the United Martial Arts Referee Association.

From 1977-81 he traveled throughout northern Italy giving demonstrations and seminars sponsored by various Italian karate organizations. He coached and managed a team of fighters called the *Philadelphia Kicks,* from which emerged several prominent full-contact fighters: Eddy Andujar, Emilio Narvaez, Gerry Galarza, Marty Manuel, and Bill Van Cleef.

PASCHY, ROGER (1946-   ) French karate champion and three-time European lightweight champion (1973-75). Paschy is a **Shotokan** stylist and a member of the French karate team. A protege of **Taiji Kase,** Paschy is noted for his kata performances. In 1975 he traveled with the French team to Long Beach, Calif., for the 3rd WUKO World Championships, where he won a bronze medal. Entering **full-contact** karate, he won the European professional lightweight title in May 1976.

PATTERSON, CECIL (1930-   ) American karate pioneer and instructor. While serving in the U.S. Navy at Iwakuni, Japan, Patterson enrolled in a **wado-ryu** karate school under Kazuo Sakura, achieving an advanced black belt rank in 1959. He opened the first known karate school in the state of Tennessee in 1962. In 1968, **Hironori Ohtsuka,** founder and leader of the wado-ryu style, urged Patterson to establish the U.S. Eastern Wado-Kai Federation; he was the organization's president and chief instructor. Patterson also served as state representative and regional director for the **USKA.**

Today Patterson, a criminal investigator, lectures and teaches self-defense at the Tennessee Law Enforcement Training Academy. He is the author of *An Introduction to Wado-Ryu Karate* (1974). *See also* U.S., history of karate in.

Cecil T. Patterson

Sam Pearson

PAUL, BILL American judo competitor and author. Paul represented the U.S. in the 1965 and 1967 World Championships and won a bronze medal at the 1967 Pan-American Games. He promoted judo through various civic organizations and co-authored *The Women's Guide to the Martial Arts.* Member of the *Who's Who in the Martial Arts.*

PEARSON, SAM DURELL (1936-) American karate pioneer and instructor. In 1954, Pearson began his study of the martial arts from a Mr. Watai in Japan. In 1956 he was awarded his black belt by **Eizo Shimabukuro.** A **shorin-ryu** stylist, Pearson is affiliated with the Okinawan Karate Federation. He also holds black belt rank in **kobu-jutsu** (weapons). Pearson's most notable student is **Glenn Premru.** *See also* U.S., history of karate in.

PEDRO, JIMMY American judo competitor and instructor. Winner of bronze medals in the 1973 Pan-American Games, 1974 North American Championships, and national AAU contests, he was inducted in 1978 into the **Black Belt Hall of Fame** as "Judo Instructor of the Year." In 1977 his club swept the U.S. Judo Association Junior Nationals with 7 first- and 6 second-place winners. Among his top students are Amy Kublin, **Lynne Lewis,** and Pamela Adams.

PENA, ALBERTO (1955-) American karate champion. Alberto Pena was born in Maizal, Dominican Republic. In 1970, his family moved to the U.S. where he began his martial arts studies in 1972 with **Chuck Merriman.** Pena has competed internationally since 1975. A member of the AAU's Karate Team, he competed in El Salvador, Dominican Republic, South Africa, France, Spain, and Japan. In 1977 he was undefeated in the 4th World Karate Championship in Japan, helping the U.S. Team to place fifth overall. Pena has won the U.S. AAU National Karate Championships, New York State AAU Karate Championships (three times), and the 1979 AAU Northeastern Regional Championships. He was named the 1980 U.S. Men's Individual Karate Athlete of the Year by the *New York Times.*

PEREIRA, ANTONIO American jujutsu instructor. He learned various martial arts during World War II and from these he formed an eclectic system of combat called miyamaryu jujutsu. He has taught jujutsu in New York for more than 20 years at the Tremont School in the Bronx. Pereira emphasizes practical street defense in an urban context.

PERSON, LEE American judo competitor. Winner of the openweight division at the 1973 AAU Nationals, and nominated to the top 10 list of *Black Belt Magazine.*

PESARE, GEORGE (1939-) American karate instructor and pioneer. Since introducing kempo karate to Rhode Island in 1961, Pesare has turned out champions including **Roger Carpenter,** Dan Macaruso, and Bob Ryan, **Dennis Passaretti,** and the late **Ralph Bomba.** Teams coached by Pesare won the 1967 and 1969 East Coast Intercollegiate Karate Championships, 1973 U.S. Team Championships, and 1975 U.S. Women's Team Championships. Pesare competed actively himself until 1973, and was a member of teams that defeated Canada, Massachusetts, and Connecticut.

His first production was an interschool competition in 1963, the first tournament of any type in Rhode Island. On Oct. 1, 1966, he produced the first major public tournament, the Rhode Island State Karate Championships. Later productions include the first **semicontact** karate tournament in 1973; the New England All-Star Professional Championships in 1974; and the U.S. Women's Karate Team Championships in 1975 and 1976.

In 1969 Pesare formed the **New England Karate Referee Association** (NEKRA), along with Robert Cheezic and **George Mattson.** Member of *Who's Who in the Martial Arts. See also* U.S., history of karate in.

PETHERBRIDGE, DAVID ALLAN (1921-) Welsh judo competitor; the first Welshman to achieve black belt status. He was a European 3rd dan champion in 1962, and a member of the British team that won the European title for three consecutive years in the late 1950s. He competed in the 1964 Olympic Games and retired in 1967.

PETITDEMANGE, FRANCOIS French karate champion. He was a member of seven winning French teams at the European Championships and winner of the 1973 and 1974 European Karate Championships in the heavyweight division.

PIDDINGTON, JERRY (1944-) American karate competitor. Nationally rated as a **noncontact** karate fighter by the *Black Belt Yearbook* and by *Professional Karate Magazine* in 1974, Piddington began his competitive career in 1970, winning the Four Seasons Karate Championships as a brown belt. He was Northeast Grand Champion in 1971 and Mid-American Grand Champion in 1972 and 1973. Piddington captained the five-man winning team at the 1974 **International Karate Championships** in Long Beach. Member of *Who's Who in the Martial Arts.*

PIERCE, DIANE (1945-) American judo champion. Pierce began the martial arts in 1968 under John Holm in Minneapolis. A four-time National AAU judo champion, she has won a gold medal at the Pan-American Championship, a silver medal at the British Open, and first place at the YMCA National Championship and East Coast Championships. During the past five years of competition, she has over 100 first place wins.

PLEE, HENRY D. French karate pioneer, considered the father of European karate. Originally a judoka, Plee learned karate in the early 1950s and invited top Japanese karateka to France at a time when the art was nearly unknown. Plee opened the first karate club in France and in 1954 formed the French Federation for Free Boxing and Karate. Over the years Plee's club has produced many of France's top karate men, and many of today's European karate leaders are his original pupils, or pupils of his pupils. In 1967 Plee wrote *Karate, Beginner to Black Belt.* In addition, Plee is the owner of one of the largest martial art supply stores in Paris called Judo International. *See also* Europe, history of karate in; Europe, history of judo in.

POGLAJEN, MARTIN (1942-) Dutch judo competitor. Poglajen won a silver medal in the 1967 World Championships and a bronze in 1969. He was the European Middleweight Champion of 1965, a bronze medalist in 1969, and silver medalist in 1970.

POHL, DON American judo administrator. Pohl was one of the men responsible for organizing the Detroit Judo Club, one of the largest judo schools in the U.S. and served as its secretary for more than twenty years. In addition, he also helped form the Great Lakes Black Belt Association. Pohl served as national secretary to the **USJF** for more than ten years and was responsible for the establishment of the organization's uniform rank registration and identification system. Pohl conceived and edited the *AAU-USJF Judo Handbook,* and acted as liaison between the AAU and the USJF. He is a member of the U.S. Olympic Committee. *See also* U.S., history of judo in.

POI, CHAN (1939-) Chinese-American kung-fu instructor. He studied the wa lum mantis style with Lee Kwan Shan in China. Later, he moved to Hong Kong and then the U.S., settling in Boston. He built a wa lum temple in Orlando, Florida, where he teaches students as well as instructors from all over the country. Known for his weapons expertise, he has written a book on the **broadsword**. In 1982, he was named to the **Kung-Fu Hall of Fame** as "Kung-fu Instructor of the Year."

POKATAYEV, VLADIMIR Russian judo champion; winner of a gold medal at the 1967 European Championships and a silver medalist at the same event in 1966. Pokatayev is also a **sambo** champion.

PORTER, PHILIP (1924-) American judo author, administrator, and referee. Porter did not begin studying the sport until he was 27, yet he competed regularly until age 41. In 1975 he won the 50-55 class competition at the National Masters Tournament. A graduate of West Point, Porter began his judo career while in the military and wrote the constitution of the United States Air Force Judo Association in 1959. He has founded clubs on Air Force bases all over the world. In 1973, he organized the All American Judo Club in Sacramento. He presently serves as chairman of the U.S. Judo Association National Coaching Staff.

Porter refereed the historic world heavyweight match between **Anton Geesink** and **Mitsuo Matsunaga** in 1956. As technical director of the Pan-American Judo Union, Porter rewrote the first international rules. In 1967 he trained referees for the Pan-American Games in Canada.

Founder and editor of the *American Judoman Magazine* (1960), he is author of the first two judo handbooks ever published in the U.S. He also published two instructional books: *Judo from the Beginning,* which he wrote, and *Championships Judo Drill Training,* which he edited for author **Ben Campbell.** A member of the *Who's Who in the Martial Arts,* he chaired the National AAU Judo Committee and the U.S. Olympic Judo Committee. *See also* U.S., history of judo in.

Maj. Phil Porter, president and founder of the USJA

POWELL, MOSES (1941-) American jujutsu instructor and performer. A veteran showman, he started making appearances at the 1965 World's Fair in the Japanese Pavilion. He was a featured performer

Moses Powell (*right*)

with **Aaron Banks'** Oriental World of Self-Defense from 1973. In 1971, Powell became the first black martial artist to perform at the United Nations.

An instructor in both jujutsu and karate, Powell trained successful students including regionally rated John Davis, **Ron Van Clief,** a former New York champion who now acts in foreign-made karate films, and four-time nationally rated fighter **Louis Delgado.** Member of the *Who's Who in the Martial Arts.*

POWER, GEN. THOMAS S. (1905-) The commander in chief of the Strategic Air Command and a black belt in judo. He was responsible for starting the judo program for SAC. Power sent trainees to the **Kodokan** to become instructors and took a personal interest in the program's growth. *See also* U.S., history of judo in.

PRAIM, DAVID (1939-) American karate instructor. An instructor of **tang soo do** since 1963, Praim had a part in training world-rated fighters such as Everett Eddy and Johnny Lee. Praim, the 1970 American Moo Duk Championships winner, officiated at a number of major U.S. tournaments. Praim promotes three midwest tournaments, including the area Four Seasons Championships. Member *Who's Who in the Martial Arts. See also* U.S., history of karate in.

PREMRU, GLENN (1942-) American karate competitor, performer, and instructor. Premru began formal karate training at a YMCA in Pittsburgh in 1956 with Larry Williams, a **goju-ryu** stylist. During his high school years, he also studied **isshin-ryu** and **Shotokan** karate. He was promoted by Williams to black belt in 1959.

While in the Marine Corps he trained in the **shorin-ryu** style under **Sam Pearson.** He was director of the U.S. Marine Corps Karate Team, and in 1965 he directed a national goodwill tour and recruitment drive for the Navy and Marines. Also during this time, he promoted two karate tournaments at Camp Lejeune, N.C. He also won first place in kata, sparring, and weapons at the 1964 U.S. Marine Corps Championships, at Camp Lejeune.

Premru competed for eleven years, from 1964-75, one of only a handful of Americans to participate in his sport for more than a

Glenn Premru   Photo by Mike Brodman

decade. A consistent kata and weapons **kata** winner, Premru won in 1971 the weapons titles of both the **USKA Grand Nationals** and the **Internationals.** Premru specialized in empty-hand forms, however, and on seven occasions received perfect scores—straight tens—from the five officials. He was named one of America's top 10 form competitors in the 1973 *Official Karate Yearbook,* the first set of national kata ratings for the sport.

Premru was one of the first great karate showmen, putting together touring demonstration teams and memorable dramatic and comedic routines. Even after his retirement from competition, he presented an unusual solo comedy routine at the 1976 **Battle of Atlanta,** which brought down the house.

As a performer, Premru is perhaps best known for his ''Meeting of the Samurai,'' a masterful skit depicting humor, drama, and conflict between two opposing samurai groups. The routine has fostered countless imitations.

In 1972 Premru organized and hosted an historic U.S. visit by grandmaster **Hohan Soken** of the Matsumura orthodox style and his chief disciple Fusi Kisi. In one promotional event, Soken exchanged a pair of his **kama** (sickles) for a baseball with the late Roberto Clemente, before a capacity crowd at Three-Rivers Stadium.

On June 11, 1972 Soken appointed Premru the president of the newly formed Okinawan Karate Federation.

As an instructor, Premru owned and operated various karate schools in and around Pittsburgh from 1966-73. His most noted students were martial arts writer **John Corcoran,** former nationally rated form champion **Maryanne Audley Corcoran,** and John Hamilton. In 1973 Premru moved to Tampa, Fla. and after teaching karate briefly, embarked on a new career as an independent film producer. *See also* U.S., history of karate in.

PRESAS, REMY (1936-   ) Filipino **arnis** master and founder of modern arnis. At 6 he was already learning the fundamentals of **kali,** the forerunner of modern arnis de mano. In Cebu, he studied arnis under Rodolfo Moncal, Timoteo Marranga, and Venancio Bacon, experts in arnis and the ''Balintawak'' style of stick fencing. In addition to arnis, he became proficient in judo, jujutsu, and karate.

In 1968, at one of his summer sessions at the Rizal Memorial Sports Arena in Manila, Presas attracted the attention of Col. Arsenio de Borja, director of the National College of Physical Education, Philip Moncerrat, former president of the Philippine Amateur Athletic Association, and Prof. Jose Gregorio. They asked him to relocate to Manila, where in 1969 Presas established a gymnasium in the heart of its commercial district and founded the National Amateur Karate Organization (NAKO). In the light of other martial arts he had studied, Presas revised the antiquated techniques of arnis, gaining acceptance for the modernized system at the National College of Physical Education in 1969. Presas also founded the Modern Arnis Federation of the Philippines (MAFP), and was elected vice-president of the Philippine Arnis Association.

In 1970 Presas was asked to go to Japan, where he introduced arnis at the Itago Police Academy. Through his efforts, the Bureau of Public and Private Schools has included arnis in the physical education curriculum. Presas wrote and published *Modern Arnis: Philippine Style of Stick Fighting* in 1974.

PRESLEY, ELVIS (1935-77) American karate pioneer. Elvis Presley had two major obsessions in life secondary only to his music: karate and gospel music. In fact, he was by far the most famous celebrity ever to legitimately achieve the rank of black belt. Presley's interest in the martial arts commenced in 1958 when he saw a demonstration of either judo or jujutsu at Fort Hood. His first karate instructor was a German named Seidel, who began teaching Elvis while he was stationed in Germany with the U.S. Army. He also studied briefly with orientals, probably Vietnamese, during his leaves in Paris. He qualified for 1st degree black belt in 1960 in Memphis with the late Hank Slemansky, a **Chito-ryu** stylist. Slemansky was killed on active duty in Vietnam sometime in the mid 1960s. Very little else is known of Presley's early involvement in karate, other than his dedicated practice of his hobby with Rex Mansfield, another U.S. serviceman stationed in Germany.

Whatever endeared Presley to karate also inexplicably endeared him to others physically involved in its practice. Ever since his introduction to it he selected his most intimate companions based

Elvis Presley was one of the few celebrities to attain a black belt in karate. In this photo he is wearing a black karate gi with the kenpo patch on it.

on their own enthusiasm for the martial arts. Upon his release from active duty in 1960, Presley surrounded himself with an entourage, popularly called the ''Memphis Mafia,'' which included his close friend Red West and Red's cousin Sonny West. In their capacity as bodyguards, both Wests took up karate, and Red reached black belt level.

Between 1958 and 1972, Presley starred in thirty-three films. He insisted upon using the then obscure Asian fighting art in many of the pictures he made, realizing early that the use of karate in his fight scenes added a unique element to his films. He was one of the first to pioneer the use of karate in American films.

Ed Parker, one of the five men who actually taught karate to Presley during his lifetime, met the rock 'n' roll idol in 1960 while performing a karate demonstration at the Beverly Wilshire Hotel in Beverly Hills. Although Parker and Elvis met infrequently over the next few years, Presley referred students to him. In 1961, on the set of *Blue Hawaii,* the two met again. Parker demonstrated some revolutionary concepts to Presley, which marked Presley's first karate ''lesson'' with the man who would eventually advise and influence him on all matters pertinent to the martial arts and Presley's part in them. Presley actually affixed Parker's **kenpo** emblem to his guitars.

Throughout the 1960s, Presley and his karate-trained bodyguards never missed an opportunity to exhibit karate skills in front of others, usually as a means of having fun and suppressing boredom. In 1969, following a nine-year absence from live audiences, Elvis returned to public concerts, starting at the Las Vegas Hilton Hotel (then the International Hotel). He introduced karate techniques into all of his routines on stage, uniquely combining them with the suggestive rhythms that had made him a legendary showman. Through this innovation, Presley gave another tremendous endorsement of karate to the general public.

Parker's visits with Presley became more frequent after a trip to one of his Las Vegas shows in late 1969. Elvis began formally training with Parker and continued to do so until his death. During the period from 1970-77, Presley expanded his interest in the nonphysical aspects of the martial arts. He actually quit working out altogether at one point in 1973, only to return to the physical side of it once again. During this period he increased his karate fraternity to include **Dave Hebler, Bill Wallace,** and **George Waite.** Hebler, a student of Ed Parker, was one of Presley's bona fide karate instructors; Wallace, the retired world middleweight full-contact champion, taught Elvis for a few weeks in 1974. Another short-time instructor was **Kang Rhee** of Memphis, Tenn. All members of Presley's karate

370

fraternity were recipients of lavish gifts.

Elvis was a credible black belt, but he was not a karate master, and the 8th-degree black belt rank he was awarded prior to his death was obviously honorary.

In 1973, a year before winning his world middleweight full-contact title, Bill Wallace, karate's fastest kicker, suffered a severe injury to his left knee. Wallace could barely lift his leg, and when conventional medical treatment failed, Presley flew in a Los Angeles acupuncturist to treat the champion at Graceland Manor. Minutes after the acupuncturist stuck needles in Wallace's leg, he kicked normally again.

In Jan. 1972 Presley suggested that his wife Priscilla take up karate. After briefly studying at Ed Parker's school in West Los Angeles, she began taking private lessons from **Chuck Norris** at his West Los Angeles school. Shortly afterward, **Mike Stone** began teaching her. From this relationship blossomed the most talked about break-up in the history of entertainment when Priscilla left Presley for Stone. The romance dissolved in 1975.

Presley had a long-standing desire to make a documentary film about the martial arts, and after meeting George Waite, a black belt student of Parker's, Presley offered full financial backing in 1974 for a project entitled *The New Gladiators*. A great deal of footage was shot by Waite. Only twice did Presley allow photographers to capture him on film during a karate workout. Not only was this the only footage ever taken of Presley demonstrating karate, but according to Waite it is the only footage of the superstar still unreleased. For unexplained reasons, *The New Gladiators* has not been released.

Until his death the facts surrounding Presley's nineteen-year involvement with karate had never been publicly revealed. The first published record of his activities was *Elvis: What Happened,* compiled by Red and Sonny West and Dave Hebler. The trio, all black belts, had been fired by Presley in 1976, and their unauthorized expose of Presley's private life was published in 1977, a week before Elvis's death.

On his own admission, Elvis Presley's love for karate was second only to his music. As a patron and practitioner of the martial arts for almost two decades his involvement was hardly superficial. He was a black belt who unselfishly used his money and influence to enhance the growth of the martial arts. *See also* motion pictures and television. *Further reading: Elvis,* Albert Goldman, 1981; *Inside Kung Fu,* Nov. 77-Jan. 78; *Inside Elvis,* Ed Parker, 1979; *Elvis: What Happened?* Red West, Sonny West, Dave Hebler, as told to Steve Dunleavy, 1977.

PRIOUR, ANNICK French karate champion. A **wado-ryu** stylist, she is one of the top female competitors in France—winner of the French Championships in 1972. She has had some success in **full-contact** karate.

PROUDER, ALVIN (1960-) American **full-contact karate** champion; **WKA** super welterweight and **PKA** welterweight world champion. He began fighting full contact at 17. On September 1, 1978, Prouder won a 9-round unanimous decision over Brendan Leddy in Long Beach, Calif., to become the WKA world super welterweight champion. On July 24, 1982, he became one of the few full-contact champions to hold a double title; he TKOed Jeff Gripper in Atlanta, Ga., winning the PKA world welterweight title. By the end of 1982, Prouder's record was 21-1 with 15 KOs. Six knockouts he scored with kicks to the head. Possessing the talent and potential for superstardom, he has attracted the attention of major boxing promoters, including Don King and the promotinal organizations owned by Muhammad Ali and Sylvester Stallone. He is managed by Bernie Krasnoo, who operates a karate school in Sherman Oaks, Calif. formerly owned by **Chuck Norris**.

PRUZANSKY, DAVID American judo competitor and champion wrestler. In 1973 he took first place in the National AAU Judo Championships (lightweight), Eastern Championships, and Mid-Atlantic AAU Championships. He has two gold medals from the Macabbiah Games in Israel. In addition, the former Temple University wrestling champion won the national AAU Freestyle Wrestling Championships and the Pan-American Wrestling Championships.

QUINE, DON (1938-) American full-contact karate promoter and

pioneer. Don Quine is president and co-founder of the **PKA**, the original sanctioning body of full-contact karate. *See also* U.S., history of karate in; Professional Karate Association.

Don and Judy Quine, founders of the PKA

QUINE, JUDY American full-contact karate promoter and pioneer. Judy Quine is chairperson and co-founder of the **PKA**, the original sanctioning body of full-contact karate. *See also,* U.S., history of karate in; Professional Karate Association.

RAPUE, ROBERT R. American karate pioneer. One of the earliest pioneers of karate and kung-fu training in Colorado, Texas, and New Mexico, Rapue established some of the first commercial training schools in these areas. He holds a high degree from the Kajukenbo Institute in Hawaii in kenpo and Chinese styles; his sifu was **Adriano D. Emperado.** Rapue also holds a black belt in judo from Toro Takamatsu, and a jujutsu black belt in the Hokkoryu style (Ryuho Okuyama, founder). *See also* U.S., history of karate in.

Robert R. Rapue

RASCH, DR. PHILIP J. American sports medicine expert. For many years martial arts book reviewer for *Black Belt Magazine,* he trained in judo under Yaju Yamada. Rasch, with a PhD in physical education, was a director for Biokinetics Research Lab at the California College of Medicine and has published numerous articles and books on the physiological and psychological aspect of exercise. He is a member of the board of Trustees of the American College of Sports Medicine and the research council of the American Association for Health and Physical Education Recreation.

RATTI, OSCAR American martial arts author and commercial illustrator. A university Greek-Roman wrestling champion and member of a championship judo team, he came to the U.S. from Italy and began to study **aikido,** along with his co-author, **Adele Westbrook,** under Yasuo Ohara, one of the first aikido instructors in New York. They collaborated on *Aikido and the Dynamic Sphere* in 1970, and *Secrets of the Samurai* in 1973.

REITER, ANTONI (1950-) Polish middleweight judo champion. Reiter was a bronze medalist at the 1973 World Championships, and a gold medalist at the 1975 European Championships. He won a silver medal at the Students World Championships and represented Poland at the 1976 Olympics in Montreal.

Polish judo champion Antoni Reiter

REMFRY, KEITH (1947-) British judo competitor. Remfry was a heavyweight bronze medalist in the 1971 and 1973 World Championships and placed second in the European Judo Championships. In 1976 he won the silver medal at the Montreal Olympics. On his way to the bronze medal at the 1971 World Championships, Remfry accomplished one of the biggest upsets in judo history by throwing and pinning Kaneo Iwatsuri, the reigning All-Japan Judo Champion.

RENAUD, JEAN SYLVAIN (1956-) French karate champion. In 1978 he won the European Championships, beating world karate champion Otti Roetof of Holland. A former French Junior Champion, Renaud had victories in the 1977 European Team Championships and the 1978 French Senior Championships. Renaud is a **wado-ryu** stylist who trains with Claude Saillou.

REYES, ERNIE (1952-) American karate instructor, performer, and competitor. Reyes began karate in 1971 under Dan Choi of San Jose, Calif. He received his black belt from the **WTF** and has since been a consistent tournament winner. Among his wins are 1974 AAU Tae Kwon Do Championships; 1975 California State Karate Championships; 1977 bronze medalist World Tae Kwon Do Championships; 1978 California State Championships (forms/hard-style); 1978 and 1979 **Internationals** (forms/hardstyle); 1978 **Battle of Atlanta** (forms); and 1979 California State Karate Championships (Grand Champion).

Reyes is head of the popular West Coast Demo Team, a group of young karateka including **George Chung,** a Reyes student, 6-year-old Ernie Reyes, Jr, Belinda Davis, and Margie Betke.

Since 1979, Reyes and his troupe have been recognized as the foremost demonstration team in American martial arts.

RHEE, JHOON (1932-) Korean-American tae kwon do pioneer and master instructor; father of American tae kwon do. In 1956 he came to the U.S. to attend San Marcos Southwest Texas State College. A member of the Korean Army Officer Training Program at the time, Rhee was called back to Korea almost immediately to complete one year of remaining active duty. He returned to San Marcos again in late 1957 and started his freshman year, studying engineering, on Feb. 1, 1958.

Originally teaching a non-accredited tae kwon do course at San Marcos State College, Rhee established his first club in San Marcos, Tex. in 1958 as a sideline to help finance his education. In Sept. 1960 Rhee founded a second tae kwon do club at the University of Texas at Austin. It was here that a young student enrolled who would have a major impact on American karate: **Allen Steen** became one of only six of Rhee's students to earn his black belt by 1962, this out of a class of 184. Rhee left Texas for Washington, D.C., in June 1962, for a summer job at a karate school. Upon his arrival the studio

had only six paying students and the struggling owners were unable even to reimburse him for traveling expenses. He decided to open his own school in Washington, and within three months, had more than 100 students. Today, Rhee oversees eight studios in Washington with an estimated enrollment of more than 2,000, and 30 more schools across the U.S.

Rhee has taught a 13-week course at the Secret Service School in the U.S. Treasury Dept., and from 1965-66 instructed some 50 members of the Officers Athletic Club at the Pentagon. He also established the U.S. Congressional Tae Kwon Do Club on Capitol Hill, where he trains many congressmen. From 1966-70 he promoted the National Karate Championships, one of the most prestigious karate tournaments in America (**Joe Lewis** was its four-time grand champion).

Emphasizing sport competition in all its various aspects, the Jhoon Rhee Institutes have developed some of the most accomplished champions in the world. While the list is far too extensive to print here, some of the more notable Rhee students are: Allen Steen, **Jeff Smith, Gordon Franks, Pat Burleson, Dr. Jose Jones, John** and **Pat Worley, John Chung, Larry Carnahan,** and **Rodney Batiste.**

Rhee's activities have included the production of instructional books and video cassettes, development of foam rubber protective gear, celebrity promotions, and tournament and martial ballet staging. His first full-length feature film appeared in movie houses in Asia and the U.S. in 1973 under the titles *When Tae Kwon Do Strikes* and *The Sting of the Dragon Master.*

In 1976 the Washington, D.C. Touchdown Club awarded Rhee its Sportsman Award—the first time the award was presented to a martial artist. Rhee was also given the flag that flew over the Capitol on the day he earned his U.S. citizenship, Feb. 23, 1973. Member of *Who's Who in the Martial Arts.* *See also* U.S., history of karate in.

RHEE, KI HA Korean tae kwon do instructor and pioneer; father of tae kwon do in the United Kingdom. He began his study of tae kwon do at 15. After graduating from the Nam Institute at the College of Natural Service, University of South Korea, Rhee was one of the first tae kwon do instructors to be sent overseas by the Korean government to teach and promote this art. From 1964-67 he taught in Singapore, Malaysia as instructor for the Royal Air Force.

In 1967, Rhee moved to Coventry, England, the first to introduce tae kwon do in that country. He was named by **Gen. Choi Hong Hi** the director of the European Taekwon-do Federation, and chief instructor for the United Kingdom and the Republic of Ireland. By 1977, he was supervising more than 50 schools and clubs from his headquarters in Glasgow, Scotland, and was teaching at Oxford, Glasgow, and Canton Universities. By early 1980, Rhee was teaching more than 4,000 members through the United Kingdom.

RIELLY, ROBIN L. (1942-) American karate instructor and author. Rielly began his training in the martial arts in 1960 while a student at Fairleigh Dickinson University in Madison, N.J. He studied judo and karate with Sofjan Rophy, an Indonesian exchange student who had formed a club with Jim Gibson at the Perth Amboy YMCA. Between 1961 and 1963, while in the Marine Corps, he trained under Fumio Nagaoka, 8th dan head of the Kobukan School in Yokohama, briefly with **Eizo Onishi** of the All Japan Karate-do Federation, and with Yoshio Kawaguchi, a **wado-ryu** instructor. Upon his return to the U.S. in 1963, he founded a club at Camp Lejeune, N.C. After his discharge in 1964, he became a member of the **JKA** and began training under his present teacher, **Teruyuki Okazaki.**

At present, Rielly is chief instructor of his school, the Kobukan Karate Club in Toms River, N.J. He was 1971-72 chairman of the technical committee for N.J. AAU Karate, and member of the technical committee of the East Coast Karate Association. He is author of *The History of American Karate, The Kobukan Manual,* and *Traditions and Training: A Guide to Understanding Japanese Martial Arts.*

RIGG, TOMMY American judo champion. Rigg is a leading competitor in the 156-lb. division. A former intercollegiate, high school, and junior champion, and a student of Karl Geiss, he won the 1979 World Trials.

ROBERTS, SR., JAMES (1933-) American karate instructor. Roberts received his black belt in 1957 from **Adriano Emperado** in the **kenpo** style. Roberts is the man most responsible for bringing the martial arts to the state of Virginia, in 1964. He has promoted many tournaments, including the annual American Korean Karate Championships, which he has produced since 1969, and the Roberts Pro/Am Championships. Member of *Who's Who in the Martial Arts.*

ROBERTSON, JOHN (1947-) New Zealand born martial artist and correspondent. Working with photographer Arthur Tansley from their base in Japan, Robertson has become one of the few martial arts journalists to syndicate his articles throughout the world.

Numerous European American martial arts magazines including Karate review (Germany), Fighting Arts (England), and Kick Illustrated among others have published articles with Robertson's byline.

Robertson has been involved in judo since he was 15. He was captain of the Wanganui Judo Club in New Zealand, and has practiced Judo in Japan's famed Kodokan. He has travelled extensively and has practiced Thai kick boxing, tai chi chuan and kung-fu. Together with Andy Adams and Arthur Tansley he published the 1978-79 Japan Guide and Directory to the Martial Arts and Modern Sports.

ROGERS, DOUG Canadian judo champion; winner of a silver medal at the 1964 Tokyo Olympics. He studied under a European instructor at the YMCA in Montreal and continued his training at the Japanese Community Center. In 1960 he went to Japan and studied for nearly four years at the **Kodokan.** After the 1964 games he stayed in Japan for another year and studied economics at Takushoku University, becoming a member of the University team that won the All Japan University Championships. He placed third at the 1965 World Championships in Brazil and won first place at the Pan-American Games the same year.

Doug Rogers, Canadian judo champion

ROTHROCK, CYNTHIA ANN (1954-) American karate champion. Rothrock began martial arts in 1973, under Frank Rrojanowicz in Scranton, Pa. In 1975 she received her black belt from Jay Shul Shin, and today instructs in the northern eagle claw style.

In 1980, she became a top 10-ranked form competitor. Among

Cynthia A. Rothrock

her major tournament victories are: Henry Cho's All American Karate, Kung-Fu Championships; Playboy Invitational; **Battle of Atlanta;** Ted Kresge's U.S. Open; M.A.R.S. National Grand Championships; PKA Nationals; Empire State Championships. In 1981 she was ranked America's number-one female kata champion by *Karate Illustrated.* She is now a member of **Ernie Reye's** West Coast Demo Team in San Jose, Calif.

ROUFUS, PATRICK J. (1946-) American karate instructor. Roufus began his formal training under Dukan Yun in Milwaukee, receiving his black belt in 1973 in American karate; he also studied tae kwon do. He is head of fight sanctioning for the **PKA.**

ROUGE, JEAN LUC French judo champion; he won the World Championships in 1969 and was the French and European champion a number of times.

ROWE, MIKIE (1942-) American karate instructor, competitor, and referee. Rowe was rated among the nation's top 10 in 1973 by *Professional Karate Magazine* and again in 1975 by the *Black Belt Yearbook.* The only female member of the Northern California Karate Referees' Association, she officiated in men's and women's competition. In 1977 Rowe came out of retirement to place second in black belt fighting at the **International Karate Championships.** Member of the *Who's Who in the Martial Arts.*

ROYAMA, HATSUO (1948-) Japanese karate competitor. A **kyokushinkai** stylist (5'8"-172 lbs) he was the runner-up in kyokushinkai's 1975 First World Open Tournament in Tokyo, and winner of the 1973 All Japan Kyokushinkai Open Tournament. He shows a preference to attack with an ankle sweep and kicks to the back of the knee.

RUIZ, FRANK (1934-) American karate instructor, competitor, and pioneer. A student of **Peter Urban,** Ruiz is one of the founders of karate on the East Coast and has trained some of the best fighters in the nation, including **Louis Delgado.** A rated regional fighter until his retirement in 1965, Ruiz came out of retirement in 1969 to win the kata competition at the Pan-American Championships in Puerto Rico. He is founder of the Nisei Goju Organization (1969).

Ruiz was struck by a car in 1970 but made a determined recovery over a period of four years. Member of *Who's Who in the Martial Arts.*

Frank Ruiz

Courtesy of Ron Taganashi

RUSKA, WILHELM (1940-) Dutch judo champion. With fellow competitor **Anton Geesink,** Ruska helped to upset the Japanese domination of sport judo. The 6 foot 3 inch fighter from Amsterdam began judo at age 21. In 1967 he took the heavyweight gold medal at the European Championships in Rome. In the same year, at the World Championships in Salt Lake City, he won the heavyweight event by defeating Maejima in the finals. Ruska regained his world title in 1971 and took two Olympic gold medals the following year, one in the heavyweight, the other in the open category. After winning the Olympic medals he announced his retirement from the sport. *See also* Europe, history of judo in.

Courtesy of Z. Modric

Wilhelm Ruska, Dutch judo champion

RUSSELL, W. SCOTT American karate instructor, author and administrator. He began with **aikido** training in 1964, then took up **isshinryu** karate, in which he earned his black belt. Later, he studied kung-fu with William Chung and **kempo** and jujutsu with **Albert Church.** In 1971, he founded the Isshin Kempo Association, a chain of karate schools with headquarters in Summit, N.J. He is also president of the **Society of Black Belts International,** founded in 1966. In 1976, he wrote *Karate: The Energy Connection.*

RYUSAKI, BILL (1937-) American karate instructor. A noted California instructor, Ryusaki has trained several prominent karateka, including the **Urquidez** family and Cecil Peoples. A black belt in both judo and karate, he first began his training in Hawaii with his father. Also a highly regarded referee, he was voted Most Competent Official at the Pacific Coast Karate/Kung-fu Championships by the competitors. Member of the *Who's Who in the Martial Arts.*

SACHARNOSKI, RODNEY (1943-) American martial arts instructor. He attended the judo class of Professor Momoru Noguchi at the **Kodokan** and received a black belt in 1959 from the Okinawa Jujutsu/Kempo Association at Camp Courtney in Okinawa. Sacharnoski instructs in juko ryu, **aiki-jujitsu,** and related arts. He is founder of the Juko Ryu International, an organization dedicated to the **ki** arts of internal energy.

SAIDANE, ALURENT French karate champion. Saidane was a member of the French team that won the European Championships in 1968, 1969, and 1975.

SAIGO, SJORP (1862-) Japanese judo practitioner, one of the early heroes of judo, immortalized in books and films, including *Sugata Sanshiro* by Kurosawa. Saigo joined the **Kodokan** in 1883, when it was just one year old, at age 21. He was a small man, 5'1¾", 136 lbs. Saigo was so supple that he could never be completely thrown; he would turn in the air like a cat and usually land on his feet. His short stature allowed him to throw people over his shoulders easily, without having to lower his hips. His favorite technique was the **yama arashi** combined with **seoi-nage** and **harai-goshi.**

His most memorable bout occurred in 1885, when the jujutsu section of the Tokyo Metropolitan Police Department challenged the Kodokan, with the intention of showing the public that **Jigoro Kano's** judo was inferior to established jujutsu systems. Saigo, using his effective yama arashi, threw his opponent, Terushima, so hard he knocked him unconscious.

Saigo unexpectedly quit judo in 1889 after only eight years as a practitioner. He became an alcoholic and by age 34 was hopelessly lost. The town of Aiyu, where he was born, erected a statue in his honor.

SAKAGAMI, KUNIAKE (1944-) Japanese karate instructor. He began karate at 14, training under a local teacher, achieving brown belt. He then switched to **wado-ryu** karate-do under **Tatsuo Suzuki** at Aichi University, where Sakagami was graduated four years later with a degree in economics. During his tenure there, he reached the quarter finals of the All Japan Collegiate Championships. In 1967, Sakagami taught wado-ryu in West Germany, then, at the request of Suzuki, in Great Britain.

SAKAGAMI, RYUSHO (1915-) Okinawan karate master and administrator. Beginning in 1934, he studied Okinawan karate and **kobudo** under the late Moden Yabiku, Shinken Taira, and later under **Kenwa Mabuni,** founder of **Shito-ryu** karate. In 1941,

Sakagami returned to Japan and established the Gembukan karate dojo.

In 1952, Mabuni instructed him to accept the position of third head of Shito-ryu karate. One year later, Sakagami moved to Yokohama and established the Japan Karate Itosu-kai where, in addition to karate, **kendo, iaido, jodo,** and Okinawan kobudo were taught. In addition to his duties as head of this association, Sakagami was named senior supervisor for the **Federation of All Japan Karate-do Organizations**; the chief supervisor for the Japan Karate-do Rengokai (an affiliate of the FAJKO); chairman of the Association for the Preservation and Promotion of Ancient Okinawan Martial Arts; and a counselor to these and other groups.

In 1974, Sakagami wrote *Nunchaku and Sai: Ancient Okinawan Martial Arts*. Perhaps his most famous student is *Fumio Demura* of Santa Ana, Calif.

SAKUGAWA, "TODE" (1733-1815) Okinawan karate master. He started his training in karate under the Okinawan monk Peichin Takahara in Akata. At 17 Sakugawa trained under the famous Chinese kempo master **Kusanku** (known also as Ko Sokun; Chinese name: Kung Hsiang-chun) who, with a group of followers, is credited with bringing Chinese kempo from China to the Kume-Mura section of Naha in the mid-1700s. Sakugawa also sailed to China, trained in Chinese kempo there, and returned to Okinawa after many years. The Sakugawa no kun kata, a **bojutsu** kata, was named after him. He is also credited with establishing the dojo kun (dojo etiquette) on Okinawa. (ANTHONY MIRAKIAN) *See also* Okinawa, history of martial arts in.

SANDERS, STEVE (1943-) American karate instructor and competitor. Co-founder of the Black Karate Federation (BKF) in 1970, Sanders won numerous national titles, including the 1971 heavyweight title of the **Internationals.** His students include Gary Goodman, Sammy Pace, and Ernest Russell. A member of the *Who's Who in the Martial Arts,* Sanders also appeared in the Bruce Lee film *Enter The Dragon.*

Steve Sanders;

SANSHU, CHIBANA Japanese martial artist; founder of **toshu kakuto.** An expert at classical jujutsu, he is also trained in Japanese kempo, judo, karate, and **aiki-jutsu,** and has studied western boxing and wrestling. In 1952 he combined tactics from these various systems to create toshu kakuto.

SASAHARA, FUMIO Japanese judo champion / winner of the light-heavyweight gold medal at the 1969 and 1971 World Championships. His famous left-side **harai-goshi** made him a favorite at the 1972 Munich Olympics, but he was unexpectedly defeated by the Russian **Chochoshvili.** He retired after the games.

SASAKAWA, RYOICHI Japanese millionaire industrialist and former Diet member. Although not a martial artist himself, Sasakawa has long been involved in such groups. He has held presidential positions in the **Federation of All Japan Karate-do Organizations**, the World Shorinji Kempo Organization, and the **World Union of Karate-do Organizations**, an international governing body for amateur karate. He is most recognized for his support of the WUKO, for which he has provided financial assistance and leadership.

SATO, KATSUAKI (1947-) Japanese karate champion; **kyo-kushinkai** stylist (5 feet 10½ inches, 183 lbs). He was the winner of the 1975 1st World Open Tournament in Tokyo, and the 1971 and 1974 All Japan Kyokushinkai Open Tournaments.

SATO, NOBUYUKI (1944-) Japanese judo champion. The world light-heavyweight champion in 1967 and 1973 and a silver medalist in 1971.

SAUVIN, GUY French karate champion; winner of the French Championships in 1964, 1965, and 1972. In 1968 and 1972 he won the European Championships. Sauvin was a member of the French World Championship team in 1972. *See also* Europe, history of karate in.

SAWAI, KENICHI (1903-) Japanese martial arts instructor. He studied various martial arts from childhood, and by 22 had attained advanced rank in judo, **kendo** and **iaido.** In 1931, in China, he became a student of Wang Hsiang-ch'i. In 1947, with Wang's permission, Sawai founded a taiki-ken school in Japan which still operates today. Sawai wrote *Taiki-Ken: The Essence of Kung-Fu* in 1976.

SAWAYAMA, MUNEOMI Japanese martial arts instructor and founder of nippon kempo, in 1928. Not finding any one art to his total liking, he founded his own school, a mixture of karate, judo, and boxing. Sawayama was one of **Kenwa Mabuni's** top students. In 1935 he founded the All Japan Kempo Federation.

SCHLESINGER, TOM (1946-) American karate referee and promoter. President and co-founder of the Northern California Karate Referees Association (1972), Schlesinger holds black belts in **goju-ryu** and **renbukai.** He is co-promoter (with Steve LaBounty) of the Superstar National Karate Championships. He devised the Schlesinger Rules System for point tournaments. Member of *Who's Who in the Martial Arts.*

SCHMIDT, STAN (1936-) South African karate instructor and pioneer. Schmidt began teaching in 1963, at a time when fewer than 100 South Africans were studying karate. Today Schmidt oversees more

Stan Schmidt is one of the highest ranking Caucasians in Shotokan karate and heads that style in South Africa. In this photo he is flying in at Del Rogers.

than 800 dojo with thousands of members. A **Shotokan** stylist, Schmidt was the first Westerner to receive a 5th dan from the JKA in 1972. In 1979 Stan was awarded his 6th dan. Schmidt authored *Soul of Karate* (1978) and in 1981 completed a masters thesis: *Karate and Communications—A Study in Human Awareness.* He has appeared in the martial arts feature film, *Kill or Be Killed* and *Kill and Kill Again,* both starring James Ryan.

SCHUTTE, DR. G.F.M. (1901-) Dutch judo instructor. Schutte, who began the sport at 46, was the founder of the Netherlands Amateur Judo Association.

SECK, STEVEN (1956-) American judo champion. Seck, who began training at 9 in Minneapolis, traveled to Japan in 1975 where he trained with the Nagasaki riot police for six months, returning as a 3rd-degree black belt. He won the 1977 Naitonal Collegiate Championships, and in 1978, 1979, and 1980, won the U.S. Nationals. He was undefeated at the 1980 U.S. Olympic trials and the only American winner at the U.S. Open Internationals. Named to the **Black Belt Hall of Fame** in 1980.

SEDWICK, DEAN (ca. 1949-) American judo competitor. He won the heavyweight division of the 1973 AAU Nationals. He participated in the 1973 World Championships in Switzerland and has competed with the Tenri University Team while in Japan, where he also practiced with the All Japan Judo Team. He was ranked among the Top Ten judo competitors in the U.S. in 1973 by *Black Belt Magazine.*

SEE, KEITH A. (1941-) American karate competitor. See began his martial arts studies in 1956 in Hawaii. In 1962 he received his black belt from J.T. Nash II and today teaches Chinese kenpo in Waterloo, Iowa. He won the 1964 U.S. Grand Championships in Dallas, 1965 All American Championships, and 1966 Texas State Championships.

SEKIGUCHI, JUSHIN Japanese jujutsu instructor. Related to the Imagawa family, once a powerful military house, Sekiguchi, in his youth, took up fencing and jujutsu, becoming a master of both. In Yedo he founded the **Sekiguchi ryu**.

SEKINE, SHINOBU Japanese judo champion; winner of the All Japan Championships and a gold medalist at the Munich Olympics in the middleweight division.

SEREFF, C.E. (CHUCK) (1933-) American tae kwon do instructor. Sereff began his training under Robert Thomson of Denver; in 1963 he received a black belt in moo duk kwan. Sereff, a member of the **ITF**, was one of the first to open a Korean-style school in the Denver area, and has since promoted hundreds of students to black belt rank, among them **Ralph Krause** and Russel Perone. In 1974, he coached the American team that competed in the Montreal World Championships. *See also* U.S., history of karate in.

SERIESE, HENRI (1937-) Dutch karate pioneer. Born in Indonesia, but now living in Den Haag, Holland, Seriese began judo in 1954 and karate, under **Jon Bluming,** in 1959, receiving black belts in both.

Henri Seriese, coach of the Dutch National Karate Team from 1968 through 1971

Presently he instructs in **kyokushinkai** karate, but he also studied the **goju** style. General secretary of the Netherlands Karate Union, he promoted from 1963-76 all the Dutch karate championships and international tournaments. He placed or won in the 1963 Dutch Open Karate Championships, 1966 International Holland/England teams, 1968 European Karate Championships, and 1970 Dutch Championships—teams. *See also* Holland, history of karate in.

SETROU, ALAIN French karate champion. A frequent winner at the French and European championships, he was a member of the winning French team at the 1972 World Championships. *See also* Europe, history of karate in.

SEYDEL, JUERGEN Known as the "father of German karate." As early as 1939, he took up judo at the university in Bonn. In 1957, Seydel introduced karate in Germany, establishing the Bad Homburg Dojo, which soon became the karate center of Germany. In October 1959, he was awarded 1st dan in karate by the **Yoseikan** Karate Federation of Japan. In 1961, Seydel founded the German Karate Federation and affiliated it with the **Japan Karate Association**. Also that year he wrote the first karate manual in the German language. In 1966 he and **Mike Anderson** founded the German Karate Union.

In 1964, Seydel organized the 1st German Karate Championships, held at the University of Goettingen. The 2nd German Karate Championships, conducted at Bad Godesberg in April 1965 by Seydel, was a landmark in that it generated the participation of prominent **Shotokan** karate teachers **Taiji Kase, Keinosuke Enoeda, Hirokazu Kanazawa**, and Hiroshi Shjirai. *See also* Europe, history of karate in.

SFETAS, GEORGE Greek karate instructor and **full-contact** karate administrator; European coordinator for the **Professional Karate Association**. He earned black belts in Shotokan and wado-ryu under instructor Meji Suzuki, and within four months was teaching at Suzuki's dojo. Later he opened his own club in Brighton and taught at the University of Sussex. In 1980, Sfetas was named European coordinator for the PKA, making him the association's authoritative voice in Europe. In 1980-81, he promoted three PKA-sanctioned events, the last of which featured 60 fighters from all over England.

SHANG-TUNG-SHENG Well-known master of the Shuai-Chiao style of Chinese kung-fu, now living in the Republic of China.

SHANG YUN-HSIANG (1863-1938) Chinese kung-fu master, Li Ts'un-i's greatest student. An extremely powerful man but a poor teacher, he is believed to have killed several students while demonstrating techniques.

SHARP, HAROLD American judo practitioner and author. In 1952 he enrolled at the **Kodokan** and received his 1st-degree black belt in Jan. 1953. Sharp, trained by many of Japan's top instructors, among them Sensei **Oda** (9th dan), won the title Foreign Judo Champion of Japan in 1954. In 1953 he began work on his *Sport of Judo,* subsequently highly successful.

SHELTON, PARKER (1940-) American karate competitor. The number 1 world-rated heavyweight contender in 1975, Shelton was

Parker Shelton, top American karate fighter

USKA number one fighter for 1974 and 1975. He began martial arts in 1959 as a judo student under **John Osako;** Shelton won the World's Fair AAU National Judo Championships in 1964. He earned a black belt in karate from **Robert Yarnall** in 1965. He earned the Trias International Award in 1969 and has been president of the **Trias International Society.** Shelton organized the first rules committee for the USKA. A member of the *Who's Who in the Martial Arts,* he appeared in the 1973 motion picture *Flower Drum Man. See also* U.S., history of karate in.

SHEPERD, KAREN LEE American karate champion. Ranked America's number-one female form champion in 1979 and 1980, Sheperd began her karate training at the University of Oregon. In 1974 she moved to Denver to study **wun hop kuen do** kung-fu with **Al** and **Malia Dacascos.** In 1980 she became the first woman to win the U.S. Open grand championship, beating 17 of the top black belt male and female kata competitors. Among her victories are the 1979 U.S. Open (women's black belt), 1980 AKA Grand Nationals, 1980-81 Diamond Nationals, 1980-81 West Coast Nationals, and 1980 **Battle of Atlanta.** In 1980, she went to Japan to star in a Japanese martial arts film, *The Shinobi.*

SHEPHERD, STEVE (1950-) American karate champion and promoter. He received his black belt in 1974 from Mark Herrman and Carl Stone after two years of study. Shepherd began promoting **full-contact** events in 1977 in West Palm Beach, Fla., where he also owns and operates a karate school. He won the **PKA** World Middleweight title in 1977 and successfully defended it twice against Ernest Hart, Jr. In 1979 he also won the **WKA** World Middleweight title, becoming the first full-contact champion to hold two world titles simultaneously.

SHIM, SANG KYU Korean-American tae kwon do instructor and author. A native of Seoul, Korea, Sang Kyu Shim began teaching tae kwon do to U.S. servicemen stationed in Korea in 1957. In 1961 and 1962 he traveled throughout the U.S. to introduce his art. Since then he has taught both in the U.S. and Canada and today conducts classes in his school in Detroit, Mich., where he has been teaching since 1964.

Best known as a scholarly author, in 1974 he wrote his first book *Promise and Fulfillment in the Art of Tae Kwon Do.* This was followed in 1980 by *The Making of a Martial Artist.* Both are academic works that delve into the intellectual, psychological, and spiritual dimensions of the martial arts.

SHIMABUKU(RO), EIZO (1925-) Okinawan karate master and pioneer; leader of the shobayashi-ryu branch of **shorin-ryu** karate. Shimabuku (later Shimabukuro) studied karate from several renowned Okinawan masters: **Chojun Miyagi, Choki Motobu,** his elder brother **Tatsuo Shimabuku,** and chiefly, **Chotoku Kyan.** He learned **kobu-jutsu** (art of weapons) from **Shinken Taira.**

Eizo Shimabukuro (10th dan) of Okinawa, a grandmaster of shobayashi shorinryu karate

Before Kyan's death in 1945 he named Eizo Shimabuku his successor to and grandmaster of the shobayashi-ryu branch of shorin-ryu karate. In 1959, at age 34, Shimabuku became the youngest man ever to receive the rank of 10th-degree black belt. He was promoted to this rank by **Kangen Toyama,** who also named him chairman of the All Japan Karate-do League, Okinawa branch.

Shimabuku's most famous student was retired world heavyweight champion **Joe Lewis.** His other notable students include **Sam Pearson, Jerry Gould, Phil Skornia, Jerry Smith,** and Mickey Gneck (who first taught **Bill Wallace**). In the early 1960s Shimabuku wrote an account of the great Okinawan karate masters of the past, which is heavily relied upon by karate historians. *See also* Okinawa, history of martial arts in; shorin-ryu. (JERRY GOULD)

SHIMABUKU, KICHERO Okinawan karate instructor, son of **Tatsuo Shimabuku** (founder of **isshinryu**). Kichero took over the leadership of the isshinryu style after his father's death in 1975.

SHIMABUKU, TATSUO (1908-75) Okinawan karate master; founder of **isshinryu** karate. After four years of training with his uncle in **Shuri-te,** he entered formal training in other forms of karate with such masters as **goju-ryu's Chojun Miyagi** and **shorin-ryu's Chotoku Kyan** and **Choki Motobu.** Shimabuku also perfected the use of weapons such as the **bo** and the **sai.** His reputation was such that Japanese officers stationed on Okinawa during World War II prevented his military conscription in exchange for karate lessons.

After the war, U.S. Marines stationed on Okinawa sought him out for lessons. Throughout the succeeding years, he turned out hundreds of black belts, many of whom returned to the U.S. in the 1950s and 1960s to pioneer karate. His prominent students include **Don Nagle, Steve Armstrong, Harold Long,** and **Kichero Shimabuku.**

On Jan. 16, 1954, after consultation with leading karate masters on Okinawa, Shimabuku formed his own system of karate, calling it **isshinryu.** This development was opposed by some of his contemporaries; his brother Eizo left the new style in 1959. *See also* Okinawa, history of martial arts in.

Master Tatsuo Shimabuku (10th dan), founder of the isshin-ryu system of karate

SHIMIZU, TAKAJI (1897-1978) Japanese jujutsu master; the 25th headmaster of the shindo muso ryu of jujutsu. He began jujutsu at 15, and in 1927, with Kenichi Takayama, gave a demonstration of his art before the technical commission of the national police force, leading to his appointment as resident instructor in 1931. In 1947, together with other experts in martial arts, he created a system of self-defense specifically designed for the police force called **taiho-jutsu.** Shimizu was decorated by the emperor of Japan for his contributions to classical and modern martial arts.

SHIMODA, TAKESHI (-1934) Japanese karate instructor. One of **Gichin Funakoshi's** chief assistants, Shimoda was expert in the nen-ryu style of **kendo** and in **ninjutsu.** He became ill following a karate demonstration tour in 1934 and died soon afterwards. His place as Funakoshi's assistant was inhereited by the master's third son, **Gigo Funakoshi.**

SHIMOMI, CARLTON American karate instructor. By organizing the **shorin-ryu** karate club on Kapahulu (Honolulu) in Aug. 1956, Shimomi became the first to reintroduce "pure" karate into the Hawaiian Islands following World War II.

SHIN, BONG YUL (1936-) Korean-born American tae kwon do and judo instructor. He has hosted numerous judo and tae kwon do championships in St. Louis, Mo., including the National AAU Judo Championships.

SHIN, KYUNG SUN (1932-) Korean-born American tae kwon do and judo instructor. Shin of Chicago, a prominent martial arts businessman, hosted the 3rd World Tae Kwon Do Championships in 1977.

SHIN, SOUNG EUI (1942-) Korean-born tae kwon do instructor. He began his martial arts training in 1955, in Korea. Shin also holds an advanced degree in judo. He has an international tae kwon do instructor's rating from the **WTF** and currently teaches at Fort Campbell, Ky. and Nashville, Tenn.

SHINOHARA, KAZUO American judo champion; winner of the National Grand Championships in 1962 and 1963.

SHINOMAKI, MASATOSHI Japanese judo champion, winner of the 1969 and 1971 World Championships in the openweight division. In 1970 Shinomaki won the All Japan Championships.

SHIODA, GOZO (1915-) Japanese aikido master; founder of the **Yoshin aikido** system. A famous student of **Morihei Ueshiba,** Shioda impressed a number of businessmen with his aikido demonstrations who subsequently invited him to become the chief instructor at the Yoshinkan school of aikido. Shioda organized an instructor training program that facilitated the spread of the style to other countries and brought an influx of foreign students to the Yoshinkan Institute. Shioda is also head instructor to the Tokyo Metropolitan Police Department and at various universities, including Takushoku University, from which he graduated. His chief disciple is **Takashi Kushida,** the style's heir apparent who presides over the Aikido Yoshinkai Association of North America. Shioda is the author of *Dynamic Aikido.*

SHIONJA An Okinawan who returned to his homeland from China in 1784 bringing with him **Kushanku,** a famous Chinese martial artist.

SHIPLEY, BOB (1941-) American karate instructor, competitor, and referee. A leading Hawaiian karate and **full-contact** fighter, Shipley was Hawaii State Champion in 1972. Chairman of the Hawaii Tang Soo Do Federation, he assisted in editing and translating the first complete **tang soo do** manual. He is a columnist for *Sportscene Hawaii Magazine* and freelance contributor to other martial arts publications.

Shipley won the Outstanding Officiating Award at the 50th State Open Championships in 1973 and the Hawaiian Martial Arts Championships in 1973 and 1975. A member of *Who's Who in the Martial Arts,* he is also active in various other martial arts organizations including the Hawaii Kendo Federation and Hawaii Amateur Sumo Association.

SHOJI, HIROSHI (1931-) Japanese karate champion, instructor, and author. He took up karate while attending Takushoku University, from which he was graduated in 1954. He is a two time kata champion of the All Japan Championships, in 1957 and 1960. He is a director of the instructors' group at the **Japan Karate Association** headquarters in Tokyo, the mecca of **Shotokan** karate. He has written a series of six volumes on Shotokan kata. *See also* Shotokan.

SHORT, PAULINE (1942-) American karate pioneer, instructor, and competitor. Short is owner and head instructor of Karate For Women, an exclusively female dojo founded in 1965. Named among *Black Belt Yearbook's* top 10 women fighters in 1975, she won numerous tournament titles in both **kata** and sparring. She is author of *Fight Back,* a self-defense program for women published in 1974, and co-produces the annual Northwest Women's Championships. Member of *Who's Who in the Martial Arts. See also* U.S., history of karate in.

SHUKUMINE, SEIKEN Japanese karate instructor, founder of **taido.** He studied gensei-ryu karate in Okinawa under Sokou Kishimoto. After researching a great many of the Japanese martial arts he created his own system.

SIKORSKI, WALDEMAR (1937-) Polish judo instructor. Sikorski received his black belt in 1962 and has been coach of the Polish National Judo Team since 1967. He has written a number of judo books, including *Theoretical Aspects of Judo, Training for Beginners,* and *Remarks About Junior Training.*

SILLIPHANT, STIRLING (1918-) American screenwriter, producer, and martial arts film pioneer. More than a quarter-century ago, when he oversaw a karate scene in television's "Naked City," Silliphant began to employ the martial arts in his projects whenever possible. Of his 20 television productions and 26 motion pictures (by 1981) he introduced the martial arts into some 15 of them.

In the martial arts field, Silliphant is perhaps best known for his close relationship with **Bruce Lee.** Beginning with *Marlowe* in 1970, Silliphant wrote Lee into numerous stories, including "Longstreet," whose first one-hour TV special many aficianados consider Lee's unsurpassed work on film.

Besides having been a three-year private student of Lee's, from 1968-71, Silliphant was one of his closest friends before and during the period when Lee became a star.

Also in 1970, Silliphant collaborated with Lee and actor James Coburn on *The Silent Flute,* eventually released in 1979 as *Circle of Iron,* starring David Carradine. The outcome was a deep disappointment for Silliphant, as was his 1975 effort, *The Killer Elite,* which suffered from production disputes and poor editing.

Author John Corcoran (*left*) with award-winning screenwriter Stirling Silliphant

Photo by Ed Ikuta

Silliphant won an Academy Award in 1968 for his powerful screenplay, *In the Heat of the Night,* two Best Screenplay Awards from the Foreign Press Association, the Edgar Allen Poe Award for mystery/suspense script of the year in 1968, an Image Award from the NAACP, and the Writer of the Year Award from the National Theater Owners of America in 1974.

In 1970 **Jhoon Rhee** and Bruce Lee introduced Silliphant to his wife, actress-writer Tiana Alexandra-Silliphant, today a karate brown belt. He has also studied karate with **Tak Kubota** and tae kwon do with **Byong Yu.**

Projects in which he has cast the martial arts are: Television—"Naked City" (principal writer), "Route 66" (principal writer, co-creator), "Longstreet" (creator, exec. producer, writer). Motion pictures—*The Joe Louis Story* (producer), *Five Against the House* (producer and screenplay), *Marlowe* (screenplay), *Shaft* (exec. producer), *Shaft's Big Score* (exec. prod.), *Shaft in Africa* (exec. prod. and screenplay), *The Killer Elite* (screenplay), *Circle of Iron* (screenplay), and *The Masters* (exec. prod. and screenplay). *Further reading: Kick Illustrated* July-Nov. 1980. *See also* U.S., history of karate in; motion pictures and television.

SIRINGANO, PETE American jujutsu and karate instructor. He began his training in 1943, taking a course in combat judo. In 1956 he opened his first commercial studio, one of the first in New York, and has been teaching ever since.

SITIWATJANA (TODDY), THOHSAPHON Thai kick-boxing instructor and performer; chief instructor of the British Association of Thai Martial Arts (BATMA). At 6, he was permitted to train for a trial period in a Thai boxing camp in Prakanong. At 13, he also began training in tae kwon do at Prakanong under Suk Young Ahn, and two years later was promoted to black belt. He was teaching tae kwon do by the age of 19.

Toddy arrived in England in 1974, settling in Oldham. He enrolled at the Abraham Moss center in Manchester for a compulsory English course, where he opened one of his first tae kwon do clubs. He taught Thai boxing techniques only to his most dedicated students. In 1978, with the sanction of Thiemboon Intrabut, president of the Thailand Professional Boxing Council, Toddy founded the BATMA and began teaching Muay Thai (Thai kick-boxing) exclusively. He and his students are renowned throughout England for spectacular demonstrations, one of which includes performing techniques while standing in burning glass.

SIU, WILLIAM Chinese-born kung-fu instructor. Siu began the **white crane** system at 13 under the famous master Tang Cha-Ming, the last disciple accepted by the late grandmaster Ng Shou-Jone. After settling in San Francisco, in the 1960s he began instructing in white crane kung-fu and participated in almost every major San Francisco kung-fu exhibition, either as performer or manager. He was also frequently asked to judge kata competition. Siu produced the 1979 International Martial Arts Exhibition, held in Oakland, Cal. (MICHAEL P. STAPLES)

SKORNIA, PHILLIP (1941-) American karate instructor and administrator. While stationed in Okinawa in 1959 with the U.S. Army, Skornia started his formal karate training in **shorin-ryu** with **Eizo Shimabuku (ro).** He took up jujutsu at the same time and by 1960 earned black belts in both arts. Returning to the U.S. in 1962, he began teaching in Los Angeles. In 1963 he became one of the first members of **Hidetaka Nishiyama's AAKF.**

In 1968 Skornia founded the Shorinji Zendo-ryu Karate International organization, reportedly the first to open its membership to all karate styles. He was also appointed the international representative for Eizo Shimabuku(ro)'s All Japan Karate Association. Having begun a serious study of **Zen** in 1959, he was ordained a Zen priest under the Rinzai Daihonza Myoshiji division of Honozono University, Japan, in 1972. In 1971 Skornia was selected to represent American karate by the Encyclopedia Brittanica for its Japanese edition. That same year he developed the first accredited black belt course for home study, a four year course; in 1980 he introduced the first black belt course (again, four years) on video tape.

Skornia taught accredited martial arts classes at La Verne College in 1975. The next year he taught one of the first martial arts philosophy courses in the U.S. for graduate-level credit, at the University of Oriental Studies, Los Angeles, under Dr. Thich Thien-an, a Zen master. In 1978 he was appointed chairman of the Public Relations and Membership Committee for the AAKF headquarters. Skornia's most famous black belt student is **Steve Fisher.**

SLOCKI, WALLY Canadian karate champion. Slocki has won every major title in Canada as well as numerous events in the U.S. He received his black belt from **Richard Kim.** Twice, in 1974 and 1976, he challenged and lost to Jeff Smith for the world light heavyweight **full-contact** title. In 1978 he was the first karate athlete to compete in the Canadian *Superstars* competition.

SMALL, ANNE (1950-) American karate instructor. Small was the first female to be named the AAU National Women's Karate Chairperson. She was appointed director of the karate program at the University of Toledo and won outstanding instructor awards from the AKA. Small began her training at Indiana State under Dennis Calahan. She also is the first female black belt accepted by the AKA, in 1969.

SMITH, JEFF (1947-) American karate champion and instructor. A student of **Jhoon Rhee**, he won numerous grand championships on a national and international level. Among his titles and victories are the **PKA** World Light-Heavyweight Championship (1974-80), 1974 Long Beach **Internationals,** 1974 Houston Karate Olympics, 1973 and 1974 U.S. Pro/Am Championships, and 1973 and 1974 **Top 10 Nationals** in St. Louis. Smith was ranked number-1 semi-contact U.S. champion in 1974, and was awarded the Bruce Lee Cup by **Professional Karate Magazine.**

He was coach of the full-contact pro karate team the *Washington Superstars,* and also coached the winning contingent of the 1974 U.S. Team Championships in Dallas.

He officiated at a number of major tournaments including the **Battle of Atlanta,** the U.S. Championships and Top 10 Nationals. A member of the *Who's Who in the Martial Arts. See also* U.S., history of karate in.

SMITH, JERRY (1947-) American karate competitor and instructor. A student of **Joe Lewis** and **Eizo Shimabuku,** Smith is co-founder and one of the first vice-presidents of the Black Karate Federation (BKF). He captained the BKF team that won the **Internationals** three times in a row (1971-73), and is also a well-known referee. An early advocate of **full-contact** karate, Smith wrote a regular column for *The Fighers Magazine.* Smith appeared in the Bruce Lee classic *Enter The Dragon.* Member of *Who's Who in the Martial Arts. See also* U.S., history of karate in.

SMITH, ROBERT W. (1926-) American martial arts instructor, writer, and author. He received his first judo instruction while in the Marine Corps (1944-46), then joined the Chicago Judo Club under **John Osako** in 1946. By 1960 Smith held a third-degree black belt from the **Kodokan.** As a result of his studies in Taiwan (1959-62), he became a leading authority on Chinese fighting forms and techniques. Among his books are *A Complete Guide to Judo* (1958); *Asian Fighting Arts* (with Donn Draeger, 1969); *Pa-kua: Chinese Boxing* (1967); *Chinese Boxing, Masters and Methods* (1974); *Hsing-I; Chinese Mind-Body Boxing; Secrets of Shao-lin Temple Boxing* (1964); and, under the pseudonym John F. Gilbey, *Secret Fighting Arts of the World* (1964). He is one of the foremost Western authorities of the Eastern fighting arts.

SO, DOSHIN (1911-80) Adopted name of Nakano Michiomi, founder and religious leader of the most widely known sect of **Shorinji kempo** in Japan. So was born in Okayama prefecture, became a member of the Black Dragon Society, and was sent to Manchuria to conduct intelligence operations. Here he allegedly practiced Chinese **ch'uan-fa.** He presumably studied under Wen Tai-tsung in Peking and claimed without substantiation that he was named the 21st leader of the **Shao-lin** tradition, a fact disputed by researchers. He combined jujutsu with Chinese ch'uan-fa in 1947 to create a new system called Shorinji kempo. *See also* Shorinji kempo.

SO, NEICHU (1907-) Korean karate master. A student of Okinawa's **Chojun Miyagi** in high school, in 1939 he became a karate instructor in schools and colleges in Kyoto, Japan. He is remembered for having taught **Masutatsu Oyama.**

Stuart Sobel

SOBEL, STUART (1943-) American martial arts promoter, author, and businessman. Sobel began martial arts in 1970 under **Emil Farkas** in Hollywood. In 1975 he became executive vice-president of Creative Action, Inc., which produced and packaged a series of four successful tournaments during the years 1974 and 1975.

The first of these, the Beverly Hills Pro/Am Karate Championships, had many screen and record celebrities in attendance for their first exposure to traditional competition, as well as over 700 competitors. The next event was packaged for *Official Karate Magazine* and was *Western Regional Championships,* which was covered locally by NBC-TV. Famous **hapkido** practitioner and actor **Bong Soo Han** produced his first tournament under the guidance of Sobel and Farkas. Their final event was a joint production and perhaps their most unusual. They teamed with the famous **Urquidez** brothers and presented their Black Belt Invitational in which the point matches were predetermined, as in professional **full-contact** karate.

In addition to all of his other martial arts ventures, Sobel has become a top free-lance writer and photographer, and has been published in every major martial arts publication in the U.S. and throughout the world. Sobel was a contributor to the Emil Farkas-**John Corcoran** bestseller, *The Complete Martial Arts Catalogue,* to Farkas' *Fight Back, A Women's Guide to Self-Defense,* and co-authored with **Benny Urquidez** and Farkas *Training and Fighting Skills.*

Sobel is frequently consulted on matters of business, promotion, and marketing by many of the top people in the industry. In addition he also manages the career of world karate champion Benny Urquidez.

SOKEN, HOHAN (1889-) Okinawan karate master. Soken began training in karate and kobu-jutsu (art of weapons) at 13. By 23 he was experienced enough to be taught the secret art of hakutsura, the white swan, a very deadly style. In the 1920s Soken left Okinawa and travelled extensively through the Far East and South America, settling in Argentina till the end of World War II. He now teaches **shorin-ryu** karate and weaponry and holds demonstrations in the martial arts. *Further reading: Black Belt Magazine,* 1971. *See also* Okinawa, history of martial arts in; shorin-ryu.

SOMERS, JEFFREY British kendoka and karateka. A chairman of the British Karate Association, Somers studied kendo for four years before taking up karate. He is a member of the Japan Society and a fellow of the Royal Asiatic Society. In 1975 Somers was a contributor to *Martial Arts of the Orient.*

SON, DUK SUNG Korean karate instructor and author. Son arrived in the U.S. in 1963 at the invitation of **Jhoon Rhee,** one of his former students. With Robert J. Clark, he wrote a comprehensive book on tae kwon do, *Korean Karate: The Art of Tae Kwon Do* (1968). *See also* U.S., history of karate in.

SONE, KOJI (1928-) Japanese judo champion. Winner of the World Championships in 1958, he was also All Japan Judo Champion the same year.

SONE, TAIZO (-1972) American judo instructor. Sone began judo in 1914 at the **Kodokan.** Sone's work for a trading company brought him to the U.S. in the 1930s; wherever he went he instructed in judo. In 1958 Sone founded the Florida Yudanshakai. At the time of his death he was Florida AAU Judo Chairman, as well as chairman of the board of examiners of the Florida Black Belt Judo Association. Sone was named Sensei of the Year and inducted into the **Black Belt Hall of Fame** in 1972.

SONG, DUK KI (1893-) Korean **taekyon** master; the last surviving practitioner of this art. Born in Sa Chick Don, Seoul, Korea, Song began studying taekyon at 13 under Hue Lim. Taekyon declined during the Japanese occupation of Korea from 1909-45 and was completely prohibited in 1920. During this period, Song practiced the art in secret, teaching it briefly after the Korean independence, to youths who engaged in occasional disputes causing injuries. Hence, taekyon failed to re-emerge as a popular Korean practice.

SONG, JOON HI (1936-) Korean-American judo and tae kwon do instructor. Song hosted the National AAU Judo Championships and served as a member of the **USJF** examination board and vice-chairman of the National AAU Tae Kwon Do Committee.

SONODA, ISAMU Japanese judo champion, gold medalist in the middleweight class at the 1976 Montreal Olympic Games. He was middleweight winner at the 1969 World Championships and a semifinalist at the 1969 and 1970 All Japan Championships.

SOO, PARK JONG (1941-) Korean-born tae kwon do instructor; father of Canadian tae kwon do, Soo is secretary general of the **ITF.** He began his training in tae kwon do at age 14.

He was instructor of the Police Training Center of Chun Bok in Korea, the famed Tiger Division. After 1964 he met **Gen. Choi Hong Hi** and began to study under him. Soo accompanied Gen. Choi on a 1965 goodwill mission, touring Europe, Africa, and Asia and became coach of the German Taekwon-do Association. He founded the Netherland's Tae Kwon do Association in 1966. In 1968 he left for Canada, settling in Toronto, and opened the first tae kwon do school in the country.

Park Jong Soo, a pioneer of tae kwon do in Canada

SOOT, CHEW CHOO Known as the father of Malaysian karate, Soot founded the Karate Association of Malaysia in 1966.

SPREMICH, SHARON (1955-) American karate competitor. Spremich began the martial arts in 1969 with Jeff Wong, eventually receiving black belts in **kajukenbo** and sil lum kung-fu. She won or placed in the California State Karate Championships 1970-75; **International Karate Championships** 1973-75; and the Four Seasons National Karate Championships (Las Vegas) 1974. Spremich was rated in *Karate Illustrated Magazine* as a top 10 female fighter (summer 1975) and also by *Official Karate Magazine* (summer 1976).

STAPLES, MICHAEL P. (1949-   ) American martial arts journalist and kung-fu practitioner. Born in Redlands, California, Staples first became acquainted with the martial arts during the mid-1950s when he learned karate from an instructor at a local YMCA. In 1966, he enlisted in the Marine Corps where he served on the Bomb Disposal Team stateside and overseas. While stationed in the Carribean Islands, Staples's interest in the martial arts was reinforced by a Force Recon sergeant who gave him private karate lessons. But not until returning from Vietnam, where he was awarded a Bronze Star and was promoted to sergeant, did he begin formal training once again. His final months in active duty were spent in San Clemente, California, working with the Secret Service as an EOD representative to assure the security of President Nixon's Western White House. In both San Clemente and Santa Ana, California, he studied **Shito-ryu** karate under the supervision of **Fumio Demura** and his instructors.

Upon his honorable discharge form the Marines, Staples relocated to San Francisco to study the **white crane** style of kung-fu and acupuncture from George Long, chairman of the White Crane Federation. He soon became a chief instructor and began entering sparring divisions of karate tournaments using the unique white crane techniques for the first time in such competition.

In 1972, Staples wrote the first magazine article on white crane kung-fu to appear in a Western periodical, November 1972 *Karate Illustrated*. He followed this by writing a book on the subject, *White Crane Kung-Fu: Chinese Art of Self-Defense*. It was published in 1974 by Ohara Publications, selling over 100,000 copies.

In 1974, Staples was the only martial arts magazine representative on the West Coast to gain a personal interview with the leaders of the Wu Shu Troupe from the People's Republic of China (PRC) during their United States tour. His subsequent article appeared as a cover story in *Black Belt* magazine.

Staples became a contributing editor of *Inside Kung Fu* magazine in 1975, soon after opening his own kung-fu kwoon (school) in San Francisco. He studied the **Hop-Gar** style of kung-fu from the renowned sifu (instructor), **Chin-Dai-Wei** (David Chin), and wrote the first articles on this system to appear in a Western periodical. Soon afterward, Staples authored two books, *Hop-Gar Kung Fu* and *Tibetan Lama: The Way of the Monk*, which were the first works ever to expose the Tibetan kung-fu styles of the Ching Dynasty Imperial family.

In 1976, the prolific writer established his own book publishing firm, Willow Publications, in San Francisco. The company's first title was *Wu Shu of China*. Staples has earned the status as one of the most prominent and accomplished martial arts journalists in the world, and is one of only a handful of writers in the field who is also an actual black belt level practitioner of the arts.

Because of his distinguished background, he was asked to serve as the Chinese entries editor for this encyclopedia. To assure accuracy, Staples edited every Chinese entry contained in the encyclopedia, in addition to the ones he personally wrote.

STARBROOK, DAVID COLIN (1945-   ) British judo champion. In 1971, he was a member of the British team that captured the European title, and he won the bronze medal at the 1971 World Judo Championships. In 1972 he captured the silver medal in the light-heavyweight division of the Munich Olympics and also the European title. The following year, he won a silver medal at the European

Championships and a bronze in the World Championships. In 1976 he won a bronze in the Montreal Olympics. Now retired, he is the joint British national team manager with Tony MacConnel.

STAVROFF, STEVE (1946-   ) American karate competitor and instructor. A competitor for over 12 years, Stavroff took second place at the Battle of Atlanta twice and in 1973 won the lightweight title at the Houston Karate Olympics. He opened his first school in 1965 at the University of Mississippi. Originating there one of the nation's first college tournaments, he moved to Atlanta and finally Texas, where he opened a school in 1971. Member of *Who's Who in the Martial Arts*.

STEELE, DAVID (1944-   ) American martial artist and weapons expert. As a freelance writer Steele traveled widely in the Middle East, Far East, and South Pacific, studying and observing the martial arts. He worked as supervisor of the Police Weapons Center project at the International Association of Chiefs of Police in Washington, D.C. He studied **escrima** with **Dan Inosanto, arnis** with Leo Gaje, and **tanto-jutsu** with Don Angier. He has written extensively about weapons and the martial arts, including *Submachine Guns in Police Work* (1971) and *Secrets of Modern Knife Fighting* (1975) and articles for *Soldier of Fortune, GUNS, Kick Illustrated, Inside Kung-Fu, Warriors, Black Belt, Karate Illustrated,* and *Fighting Stars*.

David E. Steele

STEEN, ALLEN (1940-) American karate instructor, pioneer, competitor, and promoter. Beginning his karate training in 1959 under **Jhoon Rhee,** Steen received his black belt in 1962—one of only six of 184 original students to reach that level of proficiency. He has trained more nationally rated fighters than any other instructor except **Chuck Norris.** His students include **Pat Burleson, Skipper Mullins, Fred Wren,** and **Mike Anderson.**

Entering his first tournament in 1963, Steen became one of the premier fighters in early American karate history. Winner of over 30 titles, he defeated both **Joe Lewis** and Chuck Norris on the way to a grand championship victory at the 1966 Long Beach **Internationals.** A member of the *Who's Who in the Martial Arts,* he is founder of the U.S. Karate Championships, held annually in Dallas since 1964. *See also* U.S., history of karate in.

STERNBERG, ALEX (1950-) Hungarian-born American karate instructor, competitor, author and promoter. He began karate in 1963 under **Richard Chun,** but later switched to Japanese karate

Alex Sternberg

Courtesy of *Official Karate Magazine*

(**Shotokan**) under **George Cofield.** A past vice-president of the United Shotokan Association, Sternberg began teaching in the New York City area in 1966 and was chief instructor to the Jewish Defense League from 1968 through 1972. He was rated among *Professional Karate Magazine's* Kata Top 10 in 1974 and was in 1973 selected by *Official Karate Magazine* as one of America's Top 10 kata competitors. He won titles at over 75 tournaments, including the U.S. Nationals, Canadian Nationals, South American Nationals, New England Championships, and All America Open.

Current karate chairman of the U.S. Maccabiah Association, Sternberg is credited with introducing karate into the World Maccabiah Games in 1977. He is founder of the Jewish Karate Federation and a member of the board of directors of the East Coast Karate Alliance. Sternberg is a class "A" referee with the World Union of Karate-do Organizations (WUKO). In 1980 and 1981 he co-promoted with **Tom LaPuppet** and Charles Reichman, The Playboy Invitational Karate, Kung-Fu, Tae Kwon Do Classic. He wrote *The Complete Karate Textbook,* and is a member of *Who's Who in the Martial Arts.*

STONE, HENRY (1901-55) American judo pioneer. Called by many the "father of American judo," Stone envisioned judo as an Olympic sport as early as 1946. Between 1948 and 1952 he, together with a number of judo leaders, organized the Beikoku Judo Yudanshakai, the first national judo organization. In 1953 this group became the Amateur Judo Association, and in 1955 the name again was changed to the Judo Black Belt Federation of the U.S. This group was later re-named the **U.S. Judo Federation.**

Stone was instrumental in having the AAU recognize **Kodokan** judo as the only official form in the U.S. He devised a weight system in 1948, since revised, but used all over the world. Stone also instituted the grand champion match at all national events, in which judoka of all sizes may compete. *See also* U.S., history of judo in (Intercollegiate Judo).

STONE, MIKE (1943-) American karate champion, instructor, and promoter. Stone began **aikido** in 1961 while in high school in his native Hawaii, and in 1962 started karate training under Herbert Peters in the **shorin-ryu** (kobayashi) style while stationed at Fort Chaffee, Ark. As a brown belt, Stone made his competitive debut at the 1963 Tulsa Southwest Karate Championships and won first places in black belt fighting and forms. Along with **Chuck Norris** and **Joe Lewis,** Stone is considered one of the three great light-contact karate champions of the 1960s. Before retiring for the first time in 1965, Stone dominated his sport for 18 months, competing in a total of nine tournaments. Stone lost only three times in his career.

His fighting history is as follows:

1963 (including the above event)—Dallas Southwest Karate Championships, first place sparring and kata.

1964—U.S. National Karate Championships (Washington, D.C.), first place sparring and kata; Gulf Coast Invitational Championships (Houston), grand champion, sparring; Western U.S. Championships (Salt Lake City), first place heavyweight sparring; lost in grand championship match.

1964-65—International Championships (Long Beach), sparring and kata grand champion both years.

1965—World Karate Championships (Chicago), grand champion, sparring.

1968—World Professional Karate Championships (New York): Came out of retirement and won the World Professional Light Heavyweight Championship.

1970—National Team Championship (Long Beach): Lost team match to Victor Moore when he dislocated his shoulder in the 2nd of a scheduled 3-round fight.

In 1967 Stone began promoting karate tournaments; with Chuck Norris and **Bob Wall,** he originated the Four Seasons Karate Championships, a series of quarterly events whose name and concept Stone franchised nationally in 1972. In 1974 he created the Golden Fist Awards to honor western U.S. martial arts pioneers and champions.

Stone was named in 1971 to the **Black Belt Hall of Fame** as "Karate Player of the Year", in 1975 he was named to *Who's Who in the Martial Arts.* Stone's more notable students are **Steve Fisher, Jerry Piddington** and **Howard Hanson.** In 1981 Stone was martial arts choreographer for the film *Enter the Ninja. See also* U.S., history of karate in.

SU, IN HYUK (1939-) Korean-born founder of **Kuk Sool Won.** Su began his study of Korean martial arts at six under his grandfather, Myung Deuk Suh. Visiting many private studios and monasteries, his primary instruction came from Young Sool Choi, a master in sado mu sool (tribal martial arts); Hai Dong Seu Nim, a master of Buldo mu sool (Buddhist temple martial arts); and Tai Eui Wang, who supplemented what Su had already learned from his grandfather about koong joong mu sool (royal court martial arts). In 1961 Su founded the Kuk Sool Won (Korean Martial Arts Association). Immigrating to the U.S. in 1974, he and his American sponsor, Ken Duncan moved to New Orleans, La., where the first Kuk Sool Won studio had already been established prior to his arrival. In 1975 they opened the World Kuk Sool Won Association Headquarters in San Francisco. Since Su founded the Kuk Sool Won in 1961, it has established studios in Korea, Europe, and North and South America.

SUA, RAY (1954-) American-Samoan karate instructor and competitor. Sua began tae kwon do in 1970 under Yong Suh, receiving a black belt in 1973. A consistent regional fighter in the mid-1970s, his biggest victory was the grand championship of the 1976 Long Beach **Internationals.**

SUDOH, MOMOJI Japanese martial arts instructor; founder of **aikikendo.** He attained black belts in both karate and judo, then studied aikido (yobukai style). Sudoh felt aikido suffered in popularity through lack of a sportive aspect; he created aikikendo to fill such a need.

SUH, BYUNG DAE (1936-) Korean-American tae kwon do and judo instructor. Currently living in Chicago, he is president of the Korean Judo Instructor's Society in the U.S.

SUNG SHIH-JUNG Famous **hsing-i** boxer who passed on his mastery of the art to his son Sung T'ieh-lin.

SULLIVAN, ROBERT Welsh judo champion. He was captain of the Welsh judo team in 1965, and in 1968 he won a silver medal in the Senior European Championships. He was 1968 British open champion. Sullivan represented Great Britain at the 1969 World Championships in Mexico; in 1972 he was a member of the British Olympic team.

SUSLINE, SERGEI Russian lightweight judo champion. Susline won the European Championships in 1966 and 1967, coming in second in 1965 and 1968. He has also won bronze medals at the 1967, 1969, and 1971 World Championships, losing only to top Japanese competitors. Susline, who has long legs and very long arms, specializes in the **tomoenage** (stomach throw).

SUZUKI, MASAFUMI (1929-) Japanese karate master; president of the All Japan Budo Federation. Suzuki, a high-ranking black belt in **goju-ryu** karate, owns and operates one of the largest martial arts academies in Japan, Kyoto's Seibukan, which houses regular classes in karate, judo, **aikido, kendo,** and **iaido.** Between 1978 and 1982, he was the chief official of **World Karate Association** Asian Operations. In this capacity, he served as the referee in most world title bouts held in Tokyo, especially those featuring **Benny Urquidez, Don Wilson,** and Kunimasa Nagae. (PAUL MASLAK)

SUZUKI, SHINICHI American **aikido** leader. Suzuki began studies in 1953 under **Koichi Tohei.** A leader in Hawaiian aikido, he received the Gov. William Quinn Award in 1962 and the Maui Junior Chamber of Commerce Good Citizenship Award in 1963. In 1970 he was named to the **Black Belt Hall of Fame.**

SUZUKI, TATSUO (1928-) Japanese karate master, one of the world's foremost **wado-ryu** stylists. He began training under **Hironori Ohtsuka,** founder of wado-ryu, while still in his teens. By 1951 he achieved the highest grade given to anyone, the 5th dan. In 1965 he became 7th dan, and has traveled since 1952, spreading wado-ryu around the world but especially in England. He is the author of *Karate-do. See also* Europe, history of karate in.

SWAIN, MIKE (1961-) American judo champion; first American to win a gold medal in international judo competition. Swain took up judo for recreation at 8 and continued through high school in New Jersey. In 1977, Swain, only 16, qualified for the World Championships in Barcelona, Spain, and made the 1980 U.S. Olympic team which eventually boycotted the Moscow Games. In March 1982, Swain won his division at the National Collegiate Judo Association Championships and later won the U.S. National title in Indianapolis. In the spring of 1982 he defeated Magomet Parchieu of the USSR for the gold medal in the 71-kilo division of the Dutch Open, a victory which gave the U.S. team credibility in international competition. A student of San Jose State University, he is coached by **Yoshisada Yonezuka** and has twice traveled to Japan to train with champions. He was named "Judo Competitor of the Year" and entered the 1982 **Black Belt Hall of Fame.**

TABARES, JIMMY American karate competitor. Nicknamed Gato ("Cat"), Tabares began his study at 13 under **George Minshew.** He won the U.S. Karate Championships in Dallas in 1979 and 1980, and the lightweight division of **Roy Kurban's** Ft. Worth National Pro-Am in 1979. Other victories include the Karate Olympics (twice), the National Finals Karate Tournament in 1979, and Ted Kresge's U.S. Open.

TABATA, KAZUMI Japanese-American karate instructor. Kazumi received his black belt in **shorinji-ryu** as a freshman in high school; at Wadeda University he took up the study of **Shotokan,** earning a black belt in that style as well. His instructor, **Isao Obata,** chose Tabata as head instructor of the newly formed All American Karate-do Federation. Tabata moved to the Boston area in the 1960s where he founded the **North American Karate Federation** and the New England Collegiate Karate Conference.

TABATA, TETSUO (1948-) Japanese karate competitor and **goju-ryu** stylist. He placed at the 1975 All Japan Championships and the All Kansai Area Championships in 1972.

TACKET, TIMOTHY American kung-fu instructor and author; the first American to bring kuoshu, a Taiwanese art, to the U.S. Tacket studied in Taiwan with C.M.S. Chen for two years. In 1977 he authored a book on this Taiwanese art.

TAGANASHI, RONALD M. American karate instructor. Taganashi began studying martial arts at the age of 8 with Kim Son Rhee, a tang soo do stylist, eventually receiving black belt from Rhee and also in the **goju-ryu** system. Together with **Frank Ruiz** and Harry Rosenstein he founded the Nisei Goju system, which incorporated the best of the "old" along with new techniques, but still maintaining a system based on circle techniques. Besides karate, Taganashi is highly versed in kobudo (weapons).

New York's Ronn Taganashi *(left)* practicing karate on the streets of New York.

TAIRA, SHINKEN (1902-1970) Okinawan martial arts master; one of the greatest weapons experts in Okinawa. He was born Shinken Maezato and later changed his family name to Taira. He studied karate under **Yasutsune Azato, Yasutsune Itosu,** and **Kentsu Yabu,** and was trained in **kobu-jutsu** (art of weapons) by Moden Yabiku. Taira traveled often to Japan, many times remaining there for as long as six months. On one of these trips in 1931, he resided at the Haruna Shrine in Gunma Prefecture. From the Shrine's crest, which resembled a swastika, he developed the manji-no-sai (a variation of the Okinawan **sai**).

In 1935, Taira founded the Kobu-Jutsu Research Society, changing its name in 1940 to the Society for the Promotion and Preservation of Ryukyu Martial Arts. Before his death, he was recognized as the greatest kobu weapons genius of his time. Among his many outstanding kobu-jutsu students are **Eizo Shimabuku(ro), Teruo Hayashi, Ryusho Sakagami, Tatsuo Shimabuku, Fumio Demura,** and **Motokatsu Inoue,** who, at Taira's death, succeeded him as president of the Society.

TAKADA, SHIGERU (1949-   ) Japanese karate champion; a **Shito-ryu** stylist (5 feet 8 inches, 135 lbs.). Takada won the Japan Martial Arts Championships in 1972, the 1971 and 1972 All Japan Shito-ryu Championships, and the 1971 East Japan Student Karate Federation Tournament. Takada was chosen karateka of the year in 1972 by the All Japan Student Karate Federation.

TAKAGAKI, PROF. See U.S., history of judo in.

TAKAGI, CHONOSURE Japanese judo champion, gold medalist in the heavyweight division at the 1973 World Championships, and bronze medalist at the same event in 1975. Takagi was runner-up twice in the All Japan Championships (1973, 1975) but won the openweight in that event in 1971. In 1976 he won the All Japan Police Championships for his division.

TAMURA, MASATO American judo instructor and organizer, he was president of the J.B.B.F. in 1958-59. Masato Tamura began his study of the martial arts at age 11, and in 1936 **Jigoro Kano** personally awarded Tamura his 3rd-degree black belt after he won the Outstanding judo trophy in the 1st Northwest California vs. Southern California Judo Tournament. He first began teaching in the state of Washington and in 1941 moved to Chicago and began helping to get judo established there. He was president of the Chicago Judanshakai for twelve years. In 1969 he entered the **Black Belt Hall of Fame** as "Judo Sensei of the Year."

TANAKA, KATSUTAKA (1946-   ) Japanese karate instructor and promoter. Tanaka began training in 1960, receiving his black belt in **Shito-ryu** karate in 1966; he also studied judo, aikido, kendo, and **kobudo** (weaponry). He captained his university team for two years and was 1968 Central Japanese karate champion. In 1973 he founded the Alaskan Karate Championships, the largest in Alaska. Currently he teaches at his own academy in Anchorage.

Katsutaka Tanaka

TANAKA, MASAHIKO (1940-   ) Japanese karate champion (5 feet 10 inches, 160 lbs); **Shotokan** stylist now employed as an instructor for the **JKA** in Denmark. Among his victories are the 1973 Tokyo All-Style Tournament, 1973 JKA Kyushi Tournament, 1975 World Karate Championships, and 1975 All Japan Shotokan Tournament.

TANI, CHOJIRO (1915-   ) Japanese karate master. He studied under **Kenwa Mabuni,** founder of the **Shito-ryu** style. In 1950 Tani broke away to found the **shukokai** style. He is president of the governing shukokai organization, known as the World Karate Union. See also Europe, history of karate in.

TANI, YUKIO (1881-1950) Japanese judo pioneer. With **Gunji Koizumi,** Tani introduced judo to England and Europe. He studied the **shin-no-shindo** style of jujutsu and went to England in 1899, where he gained fame by defeating all comers in wrestling matches. When in 1918 Koizumi founded the **Budokwai** he appointed Tani chief instructor. Tani remained at the Budokwai until his retirement in 1937 following a stroke. Tani and Taro Miyake wrote one of the first English-language books on jujutsu, *The Game of Jujutsu,* published in 1906. See also Europe, history of judo in.

TANNENBAUM, TOM (1932-   ) American television executive and karate pioneer. In the early 1960s, Tannenbaum began studying karate under **kenpo** pioneer **Ed Parker.** He continued his training with Parker until 1966, when he witnessed a demonstration by **Bruce Lee** at the **International Karate Championships** in Long Beach, California. Soon afterward, he started training with Lee. In 1970 he worked jointly with **Stirling Silliphant** to introduce the "Longstreet" television series, co-starring Lee.

After 1971, when Lee left the U.S., Tannenbaum continued his training under **Joe Lewis.** In 1973 Tannenbaum and Lewis began laying the groundwork for the sport of **full-contact** karate, creating and developing for television the inaugural World Professional Karate Championships. On Sept. 14, 1974 the event was conducted at the Los Angeles Sports Arena, featuring fourteen fighters from nine countries, competing for four world titles. It aired on "ABC's Wide World of Entertainment" as a 90-minute special.

In 1976, again at the Internationals, Tannenbaum engaged in a public full-contact sparring exhibition with Lewis. The exhibition was actually part of Tannenbaum's black belt test, which he passed. See also U.S., history of karate in.

TANSLEY, ARTHUR English photo-journalist and martial artist. In 1951 Arthur Tansley founded the Leicester Judo Club. A member of the London **Budokwai,** in 1968 he traveled to Tokyo, where he continued his judo training at the **Kodokan.** Currently he lives and trains in the Orient; his judo photos have been published in almost every European and American martial arts magazine.

Martial arts journalist Arthur Tansley

TERRILL, BRUCE (1942-) American karate instructor, Terrill opened his first school in 1960 and by 1975 had twenty branches in two states and Canada. His students include **Dan Anderson** and **Pauline Short.** In 1969 he founded the annual Western States Karate and Kung-fu Championships. Member of the *Who's Who in the Martial Arts.* Terrill is founder of **wu ying tao.** *See also* U.S., history of karate in.

TESSHU, YAMAOKA (1837-88) Japanese **kendo** master, founder of the Itto Shoden Mutto Ryu style of kendo. He greatly influenced the concept of "rakazu ni sumu"—settling issues "without drawing a sword." He believed the sword was to be borne for the purpose of maintaining peace and saving life, not for war and taking life. He was, for a while, secretary to Emperor Meiji, in which capacity he was a moderating voice.

THANOS, GEORGE (1952-) American karate competitor. Thanos received his black belt in 1966 from **Ki Whang Kim.** He instructs in tae kwon do, but also studied aikido (yoshinkai) style. Once the 4th-rated light-heavyweight contender by *Professional Karate Magazine,* his tournament wins include: 1968 U.S. National Karate Championship, 1975 All American Open, 1975 Battle of Atlanta, and 1975 Top-10 National Karate Championship.

George Thanos

THERIAULT, JEAN-YVES (1955-) Canadian **full-contact karate** champion; **PKA** world middleweight champion. He began studying karate and jujutsu with **John Therien.** Although he started his competitive career in point-fighting, he was repeatedly disqualified for excessive contact. After witnessing the 1976 full-contact karate fight between **Jeff Smith** and Karriem Allah, a preliminary to the Muhammad Ali/Joe Frazier "Thrilla in Manilla," Theriault immediately took up the sport, fighting and winning his first pro bout in June 1976. He won his world title by virtue of a TKO over Robert Biggs on Nov. 15, 1980, the first Canadian fighter in decades to hold a world title in a combat sport. This status, coupled with his exceptional fighting ability, brought Theriault major recognition as a sports star in Canada, as well as big financial rewards. He has been nominated three times as "French Canadian Athlete of the Year." He has been contracted to endorse products. Unofficial reports placed his 1982 annual earnings at $100,000, the first full-contact karate athlete to reach the six-figure stage.

At the end of 1982, his record stood at 32-2 with 29 KOs.

Date	Opponent	Location	Outcome
6/76	Serge Simard	Ottawa, Canada	TKO
4/77	Murray Sutherland	Ottawa	Lost/TKO
8/77	James Louth	Rochester, N.Y.	TKO
9/77	Roger Hurd	Toronto, Canada	TKO
10/77	Mark Kosycki	Ottawa	KO
10/77	Carl Beamon	Buffalo, N.Y.	Decision
11/77	Victor Hale	Rochester	TKO
3/78	Mike Chapman	Ottawa	KO
3/78	Fritz Matthews	Kitchener, Canada	TKO
5/78	Rob Warcloud	Sorel, Canada	TKO
10/78	Kerry Roop	Windsor, Canada	Decision
11/78	Ralph Hollett	Ottawa	KO
4/79	Kerry Roop	Ottawa	KO
5/79	Blinky Rodriguez	Lake Tahoe, Nev.	Lost/KO
6/79	Emilio Narvaez	Kitchener	KO
7/79	Ace Lewis	Boston, Mass.	KO
10/79	Doug Ware	Ottawa	KO
11/79	Doug Ware	Boston	KO
11/79	Ralph Hollett	Halifax, N.S.	Lost/Split Decision
3/80	Jeff White	Detroit, Mich.	KO
4/80	Ron Thiveridge	Ottawa	KO
7/80	Emilio Narvaez	Boston	KO
8/80	Larry Poore	Ottawa	KO
11/80	Robert Biggs	Ottawa	TKO
2/81	Glenn McMorris	Ottawa	KO
4/81	Rodney Batiste	Ottawa	Decision
11/81	Eddy Durant	Ottawa	TKO
1/82	Jarvis Gardner	Montreal, Canada	KO
2/82	Mark Zacharatos	Windsor	KO
3/82	Ross Scott	Ottawa	TKO
4/82	Andy Brewer	Montreal	KO
6/82	Maurice Moore	Montreal	KO
9/82	Tom Richardson	Ottawa	TKO
10/82	Bernard Clarke	London, Canada	KO
11/82	Kerry Roop	Montreal	TKO

THERIEN, JOHN (1949-) Canadian martial arts instructor, promoter, and writer. Therien began studying in Ottawa under Georges Sylvain; in 1969 he received his black belt from the **Canadian Jiu-Jitsu Association.** An instructor in Can-Ryu, kick-boxing, and jujutsu, he is vice-president of the Canadian Jiu-Jitsu Union and promoter of the John Therien Invitational and Ottawa Inter-Club Championships. He is president and founder of the T.S.S. Promotions, Ltd., the most active full-contact promoters in Canada. He is the Canadian **PKA** representative and manager of Jean-Yves-Theriault, who assumed the vacated title after **Bill Wallace** retired. Therien is a columnist for *Official Karate Magazine.*

Therien is also founder and president of the Canadian-European Jiu-Jitsu Exchange (CEJJEX), a reciprocating learning experience for instructors and students from around the world.

John Therien

THOMSON, JERRY (1941-) American karate instructor and administrator. Thomson began karate in 1960 under Alfred Gossett and **Frank Van Lenten,** and in 1964 received his black belt in goshin kagen goju. In 1972 he became executive director of the Society of Black Belts International. In 1973 he was appointed the East Coast Regional Chairman for the AAU.

Thomson was rated in 1974 one of the 16 international karate referees. The following year he was appointed AAU officials certification chairman for the entire U.S. He was elected in 1977 national AAU karate sports chairman for all U.S. karate programs. Appointed senior referee for Pan-American countries, and chief referee at the 4th **WUKO** World Championships in Tokyo, he was one of five members of an International Referees Board responsible for training, evaluating, and selecting all international referees.

Jerry Thomson

THURMAN, BOB (1960-) American **full-contact karate** champion; **PKA** world super middleweight champion. As an amateur boxer, he amassed a record of 36-1 and made it to the 1980 Golden Gloves national middleweight quarterfinals. He began studying karate with Bob Mackey in Kansas City. He turned to professional full-contact karate in 1979, by late 1982 amassing a 22-1 record, with 15 knockouts. He won his world title in April 1981.

TILLET, GEORGE American judo competitor and instructor. Member of a Marine Corps judo team, he traveled in Japan for two years. In 1964 he won the Far East Championships in the 150-lb division. Tillet returned to the U.S. in 1965, where he won the All Marine Corps Judo Championships in the 139-lb division. He opened the University of Illinois Judo Club a few years later.

TOGUCHI, SEIKICHI (1917-) Okinawan karate instructor. He studied **goju-ryu** karate under **Chojun Miyagi** and Seiko Higa. With Sieihin Yamaguchi, a musician and composer, he developed a series of kata performed to music. He is president of Shoreikan Goju-ryu Karate.

TOHEI, KOICHI (1920-) Japanese **aikido** master and author. He is responsible for spreading aikido throughout the world. In 1953 Tohei visited Hawaii, where he introduced aikido for the first time outside of Japan. He remained for over a year establishing aikido schools all over. In 1961 he visited major cities on the mainland to promote aikido. In 1974 he quit Ueshiba's dojo and founded his own Shishin Toitsu Aikido. Tohei also founded the Ki Society in 1971. His books include: *What is Aikido, Aikido in Daily Life, Aikido, the Art of Self-Defense. Further reading:* "20th Century Warriors," *Black Belt Magazine,* 1971.

TOMIKI, KENJI (1900-) Japanese aikido pioneer and judo instructor. Tomiki studied judo under its founder, **Jigoro Kano,** and after achieving a high level of competence, was asked in 1930 by Kano to learn aikido under founder **Morihei Ueshiba.** After extensive study

he formulated a self-defense system called goshin-jutsu-kata.

Tomiki had delved into the possibilities of aikido as a form of physical exercise, while still respecting Ueshiba's spiritual principles. Already a recognized authority on Japanese **bujutsu,** he devised a system of instruction based on the principles of physical education. Until this time no real system of aikido instruction existed.

Tomiki formulated a series of exercises and a basic kata with many variations. Later, he extended his system (originally of 15 basic techniques), adding 2 more techniques to the **kata** and slightly altering some of the others; he called in the randori-no-kata, or techniques suitable for freestyle fighting. He later devised a series of competitive forms that tested a student's ability to defend himself in freestyle situations, thereby introducing a sport element into aikido. Tomiki further extended the formal side of aikido, modifying several koryus, or ancient forms, techniques against various weapons used in other martial arts.

Tomiki is currently teaching at Waseda University, where he is professor of Physical Education. He authored *Judo with Aikido* in 1956, which was the first English text explaining the principles of aikido. *See also* Tomiki aikido.

TOWNSLEY, JOHN (1936-) American karate instructor and promoter. Townsley began his martial arts training in judo in 1956 at the YMCA and in 1968, he received his black belt in **shorei-ryu** karate. He studied **kenpo** and **Shotokan** karate as well. Townsley is AAU Wisconsin state chairman. Among his tournament promotions were the 1969 Mid-Continental and Illinois State, and 1975 U.S. Team Competitions.

TOWNSLEY, MARY American karate photo-journalist. Wife of **John Townsley,** her photography has appeared in every major martial arts magazine in the U.S. She also has a regular column in *Official Karate Magazine* called "Midwest Scene."

TOYAMA, KANKEN (1888-1966) Okinawan karate master. Toyama (also Kanken Oyadomari in the Okinawan dialect) studied under **Yasutsune Itosu** and, to a lesser degree, **Kanryo Higashionna,** the leading exponents of **Shuri-te** and **Naha-te** respectively. Additionally, he trained with Itarashiki and, in **kobudo** (Okinawan weaponry), with Oshiro, Tana, and **Choshin Chibana,** all of Okinawa.

In 1931, in the Meguro section of Tokyo, he opened a dojo, which he named the Shudokan. Subsequently, he began teaching at Nihon University, and in 1946 formed the All Japan Karate-do Association. This association attempted to unify Okinawan and Japanese karate factions.

Toyama trained Toshio Hanaue, who now is the chief instructor of **shudokan** karate, and **Eizo Onishi,** who founded the **koei-kan** style of karate. *See also* Japan, history of karate in; Okinawa, history of martial arts in.

TOYOKURA, HIROMASA (1940-) Japanese karate champion; a **renbukan** stylist (6 feet, 172 lbs). Toyokura won the 1958 and 1960 All Japan Tournament and the First Asia Championships in Tokyo in 1964. He coached winning teams at the 1967 and 1968 Asian Championships.

Robert Trias

TRIAS, ROBERT (1922-) American karate pioneer, instructor, author, and administrator. Known as the father of American karate, he opened the first karate school in the U.S. in 1946 in Phoenix, Ariz., and founded the **U.S. Karate Association** two years later.

While stationed in the British Solomon Islands during World War II he met T'ung Gee Hsing with whom he trained and received his first instructor's degree. Later, during the war, he trained with Hoy Yuan Ping, a master in **kempo** and jujutsu in Singapore.

Master Trias's first style was shuri karate kempo, which was later called shorei-ryu. In 1964 he incorporated some of the goju-ryu katas into the shorei-ryu style and founded the shorei-goju ryu system, which he still teaches today.

In 1948 he founded the USKA, first karate organization in the U.S., and it became one of the largest in the nation, with almost every early top karate instructor in its membership.

Trias was instrumental in promoting the World Karate Tournament in 1963. Held in Chicago, it was the largest U.S. tournament up to that time. Currently he heads the Okinawan shuri-ryu system and holds a 9th dan. Trias is the author of three books, *Karate Is My Life, The Hand Is My Sword,* and *The Pinnacle of Karate,* and travels world-wide conducting seminars on the shuri system as well as acting as goodwill ambassador for karate. *See also* Trias International Society; U.S., history of karate in; USKA.

TSUKAHARA, BOKUDEN (1491-1571) Japanese swordsman. He was a minor baron from eastern Japan who studied swordsmanship at the famed Kashima Shinto shrine, where his adoptive father was a ritualist. He is recorded as having fought 19 times with the live blade, man-to-man, taken part in 37 battles, and fought several hundred **bokken** (wooden sword) matches. Tsukahara was wounded but 6 times, all by arrows in the heat of battle. During his life he is said to have killed more than 200 enemies.

TSUROKA, MAS (1929-) Japanese-Canadian karate pioneer, known as the "father of Canadian karate." Born in Canada, Tsuroka moved with his parents to Japan in his early teens. There he studied karate under **Dr. Tsuyoshi Chitose** at age 17 and received his black belt in Chito-ryu at age 20. After World War II he returned to Toronto and opened the first dojo in Canada in 1958. He sponsored the Canadian Karate Championship in 1962, one of the earliest in North America. He has promoted many black belts who now run dojo all across Canada. *Further reading:* "20th-Century Warriors," *Black Belt Magazine,* 1971.

TUDELA, MIGUEL A. (1955-) American judo champion. Tudela began judo in 1969, at John Holms Olympian Judo School in Hopkins, Minn. Currently he studies with **Diane Pierce,** his wife, in Los Angeles. Tudela is a two-time national AAU champion, bronze medal winner at the Pan-American Games, Armed Forces Judo Champion, and an Army wrestling champion.

TUILOSEGA, TINO Samoan-American martial arts instructor. In Hawaii, Tuilosega learned Polynesian arts of self-defense from his grandfather and father. He founded the **lima lama** system of martial arts, which he calls an "American martial art of Polynesian descent."

TULLENERS, TONNY (1944-) American karate competitor and instructor. Tulleners was a student of **Tak Kubota.** Rated eighth

Tonny Tulleners

among the 1968 *Black Belt Yearbook's* Top Ten, Tulleners was a noted amateur fighter in the 1960s, achieving a third-place win in individual competition at the 1st **WUKO** World Championships in Tokyo in 1970. A member of *Who's Who in the Martial Arts,* Tulleners authored a book in 1974 entitled *Beginner's Karate.*

TUNCSIK, JOZESF (1949-) Hungarian judo champion. He won a bronze medal at the 1976 Montreal Olympics and in 1976 was European champion. Since 1979 he has retired from competition and is a sports instructor in Budapest.

TUNG, ROGER (1950-) Chinese-American wu shu instructor, pioneer, and competitor. Tung began wu shu training in Shanghai, China, in 1958, majoring in long fists form. After leaving China in 1964, Tung trained in tae kwon do in the U.S. He competed sporadically in major tournaments and singlehandedly introduced wu shu in the U.S. By 1977, he was training future U.S. form champions including **Anthony Chan.** Every legitimate wu shu artist in the nation is either directly or indirectly his student. He is president of the National Chinese Wushu Association of America. In Oct. 1981, and also in June and Sept. 1982, Tung took groups of American martial artists to China to study wu shu. He was named international coordinator of the 1st World Wu Shu Championships in fall 1982 at Nanjing, China. He was named "Kung-Fu Artist of the Year" and inducted into the **Black Belt Hall of Fame** in 1982.

TUNG-YIN-CHIEH Well-known master of **t'ai-chi-ch'uan** and a student of Yang-Ch'ung-Fu. *See also* t'ai-chi-ch'uan (general).

TURNER, KARYN (1947-) American karate champion, performer, and promoter. Turner began martial arts studies in 1972 under **Al Dacascos** in Denver, attaining her black belt in 1974. She organized the traveling martial arts performing troupe, *Hard Knocks,* and is president of Superfights, Inc., based in Denver, which promotes **full-contact** karate events. In form competition 1977-78, she won the Rocky Mountain Championships, Denver Pro/Am, Top 10 Nationals, **Battle of Atlanta,** and Long Beach **Internationals.** Before retiring in 1978, she was the number-1 female form champion in America.

Karyn Turner (*center*)

TZE, KOU Chinese kung-fu master; founder of the **monkey** style. He was originally a practitioner of a northern boxing system called grand earth style. During the Boxer Rebellion of 1911 he was arrested for killing a political assassin. During his eight-year imprisonment he observed a group of monkeys cavorting outside his cell window. For years he watched, analyzed, and studied their movements and behavior. He mixed them with his own grand earth style and called his new system tai-sing. Upon his release he founded the Monkey Boxing Society, later changing the style's name to tai-sing pek kwar. (MICHAEL P. STAPLES)

TZU, LAO (ca. 600 B.C.) Chinese scholar and founder of the school of thought known as Taoism. The philosophy he taught over 2,500 years ago is an influence today upon practitioners of karate, judo, aikido, and other martial arts. A prominent scholar of his day, he held a post as an official of the archives of the empire. Most of his philosophy is contained in a work entitled *Tao te Ch'ing (The Way and the Power)*. He teaches the importance of humility and non-aggressiveness—all part of the martial arts today. Many of his ideas were assimilated into **Buddhism.**

UCHIDA, GEORGE (1923-) American judo coach. While in college he competed for the University of Meiji judo team. His coaching record includes: 1967 World Collegiate Games in Tokyo; 1968 Pan-American Judo Championships in San Juan; U.S. coach for high school teams in international competition from 1967-72. Uchida is a recognized referee of the IJF.

UCHIDA, YOSHIHIRO (Yosh) Japanese-American judo coach and administrator. A high-ranking black belt, Uchida was chairman of the U.S. Olympic Judo Committee and coach of the 1964 U.S. Olympic Judo Team. He is a former president of the Judo Black Belt Federation of America. *See also* U.S., history of judo in.

UECHI, KANBUM (1877-1948) Okinawan karate master; founder of **Uechi-ryu** karate. In 1897 Uechi went to China where he studied a system called pangai-noon, under Chou-tzu-ho, a famous Chinese instructor of the time. After ten years of study, he opened a school in the Chinese province of Nonsoue. He was quite successful until one of his students killed an attacker in a fight. Uechi was blamed for the mishap. Resettling in Okinawa in 1910, he thereafter refused to teach. In 1924 he left for Japan, where he met a fellow Okinawan, Ryuko Tomoyose, who became his student and who finally convinced Uechi to teach his art to the public. *See also* Okinawa, history of martial arts in; Uechi-ryu.

UECHI, KANEI (1911-) Okinawan karate instructor. His father, **Kanbum Uechi,** is the founder of **Uechi-ryu** karate. Uechi took over the leadership of Uechi-ryu karate after the death of his father in 1948. He now oversees the organization from Fatenma, Okinawa.

UEMURA, HARUKI Japanese judo champion. Uemura won openweight gold medals in the 1976 Montreal Olympics and 1975 World Championships. In 1973 and 1975 he won the All Japan Championships. His favorite technique in competition is **seionage.**

UESHIBA, KISHOMARU (1921-) Japanese **aikido** instructor. The son of **Morihei Ueshiba,** aikido's founder, Kishomaru began studying aikido at 14. While attending Waseda University he was already a full-time instructor at his father's dojo. After college he devoted himself strictly to aikido. In 1942 Kishomaru's father moved to a new location leaving him the Tokyo school, which at the time was the largest in the country.

In the early 1960s he spent three months in Hawaii promoting aikido. He visited the mainland U.S. in 1966, traveling to New York and Boston. After his father's death in 1969, Kishomaru inherited an aikido empire comprising close to 1 million students all over the world.

UESHIBA, MORIHEI (1883-1969) Japanese **aikido** founder. Born in a rural area near Osaka, he left home in his late teens for Tokyo to seek martial arts instruction. He investigated many, but concentrated his efforts in three: the sword style of the Yagyu Shinkage ryu **(kenjutsu),** the Hozoin spear style (**sojutsu),** and **tenjin-shinyo ryu**

Morihei Ueshiba

jujutsu. Shortly after the Russo-Japanese war of 1904, upon his discharge from the army, Ueshiba was contracted to lead a group of immigrants to Hokkaido. At this time, Sokaku Takeda, headmaster of **Daito-ryu aiki-jutsu,** had begun to teach his art outside the clan, traveling throughout Japan and finally settling in Hokkaido in 1905. Impressed with the power of Takeda's technique, Ueshiba studied Daito-ryu until he had mastered it and obtained a license to practice its teachings. In addition, he continued his practice of kenjutsu and sojutsu.

After more than a decade in Hokkaido, Ueshiba was called home to his sick father. On the way, he met Oni Subaro Deguchi (also Wani-Saburo Deguchi), leader of the Omotokyo religion, a form of Shintoism. Having grown up in an environment of strict religious discipline and tradition, Ueshiba was very impressed by Deguchi and subsequently became one of his followers.

Throughout his life, Ueshiba sought to unite his spiritual beliefs with his technical skill: to seek and discover the underlying unity. The combination of his budo prowess, his insight, and his deep spirituality led him to the revelation that "the source of budo is God's lover, the spirit of loving protection for all beings. True budo is to accept the spirit of the universe, to keep the peace of the world, and to correctly produce, protect, and cultivate all beings in nature." Ueshiba realized that the truly critical struggle in man was not physical combat, but rather one's internal confrontation with the forces that lead a person out of harmony with the spirit of the universe.

Aiki-jutsu, as it was then taught and practiced, did not comform to Ueshiba's vision of a physical and spiritual unit, balanced and unaggressive. He thus organized his own system and called it aikido (way of the spirit meeting). For his art, Ueshiba laid down the principle of nonresistance, the non-violent way of self-defense.

Once he had fully developed his system, he began teaching selected pupils—some from noble families, others from the armed forces—continuing his instruction until World War II, when he returned to the countryside.

Witnessing his countrymen turn their interests from spiritual to material matters, Ueshiba eventually decided that perhaps through the medium of aikido he could encourage a rebirth of the spirit. His intention was to spread aikido throughout the world; to this end he selected his finest students and sent them abroad to teach.

Shortly before his death Ueshiba appointed his son, **Kishomaru** (also Kisshomaru), director of the world headquarters of aikido, the hombu in Tokyo.

Ueshiba trained a large group of distinguished disciples, many of whom created their own systems. For the most part, the differences between these styles are purely technical. Among Ueshiba's senior disciples are: **Koichi Tohei** (founder of the **Ki Society); Gozo Shioda (Yoshin aikido); Kenji Tomiki (Tomiki aikido); Minoru Hirai** (korindo aikido); **Yoichiro Inoue** (shinwa taido); Yutaka Otsuki (Otsuki ryu aikidi); Tetsuomi Hoshi (kobu-jutsu); **Setaro Tanaka** (shin riaku heiho); **Harunosuke Fukui** (yae ryu); **Senryuken Noguchi** (shindo rokugo ryu); Yuso Murasige; and **Minoru Mochizuki.** As of 1981, four direct students of Ueshiba were teaching in the U.S.: **Yoshimitsu Yamada** of the New York Aikikai; Akira Tohei of the Midwest Aikido Center in Chicago; Mitsunari Hambei Kanai of the New England Aikikai in Cambridge, Mass.; and **Kazuo Chiba** of San Diego. Ueshiba's grandson, Moriteru, is also considered a contemporary aikido master. *See also* aikido. *Further reading: Black Belt Magazine*, Nov. 1982; *Kick Illustrated*, July 1982; *Modern Bujutsu and Budo*, Donn F. Draeger, 1974; *20th Century Warriors*, compiled from *Black Belt Magazine*, 1971.

UESHIRO, ANSEI (1933-) Okinawan-American karate pioneer and instructor. During the World War II invasion of Okinawa, Ueshiro's parents were killed and he himself suffered severe burns throughout his body and lost most of the fingers from both hands. At 13, he was taken in by relatives who enrolled him in a karate school run by **Shoshin Nagamine**, head of matsubayashi **shoriryu**. Ueshiro practiced karate religiously, becoming a flawless kata technician and a passionate devotee of rugged kumite. From other Okinawan masters he learned weapons and despite his handicap, developed extraordinary expertise with the **bo** (staff).

During the late 1950s, Ueshiro, at Nagamine's **dojo** (training hall), became the direct instructor of **James Wax**, a U.S. Marine stationed in Okinawa. Wax became a central pioneer of shorin-ryu karate in the U.S. in the early 1960s and made arrangements to bring Ueshiro to America. Ueshiro arrived in New York in 1962, authorized by Nagamine as the direct link between matsubayashi shorin-ryu in Okinawa and America. Ueshiro first taught at a school located in Queens, then in Hempstead, Long Island, where, by 1964, a group of ten qualified students emerged to begin forging a shoriryu network independent of that created by Wax. These ten opened schools in lower Manhattan's Chinatown, and several other Long Island locations. By late 1964 there were five to six dojo which promulgated shorin-ryu in the eastern U.S. Although Ueshiro's relationship with Nagamine was severed in 1969, his influence has remained an important factor among segments of the U.S. shorin-ryu community. (STEVE SHEAR)

UFUCHIKU, KANAKUSHIKU (1841-1920) Okinawan **kobu-jutsu** master; founder of Ufuchiku kobu-jutsu. As police commissioner of Shuri, Okinawa, and personal bodyguard of Shota-O, the last reigning king of the Ryukyu Islands, Ufuchiku (aka Kinjo Sanda) made an intensive study of weapons. In his official capacities, he was informed about the state of arsenals of Okinawa's neighboring countries, and he carried on military liaisons with both Japan and China. Responsible for the king's safety and the security of the castle grounds, he supervised the police that patrolled the town, men who were usually equipped with spears, sticks, ropes, and stones. Ufuchiku had trained these men himself, passing on a system of kobu-jutsu which was actually an advanced police science. Many of its weapons are believed to have been confiscated and adapted from criminal elements.

Ufuchiku's kobu-jutsu naturally included the five systematized weapons of Okinawa: the **bo** (staff); **sai** (short sword); **nunchaku** (flail); **tonfa** (handle); and **kama** (sickle). However, he also taught the surushin (weighted chain); tetsu (a form of spiked brass knuckles); tetkoo (tiger-claw-shaped iron spikes); rokushaku-kama (a sickle connected to a six-foot handle); the eku (ship oar); the **nunte** (also called the manji-no-sai); and the zinkasa (which evolved into the use of the knife and shield).

In 1912, at 71, Ufuchiku planned to commit **seppuku** out of respect for his king, who had died and left Okinawa under Japanese control. Several Okinawan martial artists approached Ufuchiku and requested that he pass on his knowledge of kobu-jutsu before committing ritual suicide.

Ufuchiku trained two chief disciples: Saburo Takashiki and **Shosei Kina**. When Ufuchiku finally committed seppuku on October 13, 1920, Kina inherited the style's **menkyo-kaiden**. Upon Kina's death in June 1981, the style's leadership was passed on to **Kaishu Isa**, who studied with both of Ufuchiku's senior disciples. *Further reading: Black Belt Magazine*, Nov. 1982.

URBAN, PETER (1935-) American karate instructor and pioneer; he introduced **goju-ryu** karate to the U.S. in 1959, and was one of the first to teach karate in the eastern U.S. He began training at 18 in Japan with **Richard Kim**, later with **Gogen Yamaguchi** and **Mas Oyama**. Urban resigned in 1966 as East Coast goju representative to found his own American Goju Association. His notable students

Peter Urban, American karate pioneer, introduced Japanese goju-ryu to the U.S. in 1959. He later broke away and formed his own American goju system.

include **Chuck Merriman, Aaron Banks, Al Gotay, William Louie, Frank Ruiz**, Ron Van Clief, **Owen Watson, Ric Pascetta**, Joe Hess, Lou Angel, and **John Kuhl**. Urban was one of the few Americans to compete in the All Japan Collegiate Championships, in 1957. In 1965, he wrote *The Karate Dojo* and in 1979, *Karate Psychology*. *See also* U.S., history of karate in.

URQUIDEZ, ARNOLD (1941-) American karate instructor, competitor, and full-contact trainer. Arnold Urquidez is the trainer and driving force behind the Urquidez clan (Benny, Rubin, Smiley, Blinky, Lilly), as well as to a stable of fighters. In 1970 he won the **International** heavyweight division in Long Beach after six years as a top regional fighter in southern California. The Urquidez brothers placed second in the 1971 International Team Championship and second in the 1972 California State Team Championship. Arnold coached the Los Angeles Stars, a now disbanded full-contact team for the National Karate League, also no longer in existence. In 1975, he was named to *Who's Who in the Martial Arts*.

URQUIDEZ, BENNY (1952-) American-born world karate champion, Benny Urquidez began the martial arts at the age of 8. **Bill Ryusaki** was the first formal instructor. At 14 he received his black belt—highly

World champion Benny Urquidez

unusual at that time, but his talents and competitive spirit and a two-day test with his brother **Arnold Urquidez, Ed Parker,** Clarence Akuda, **Tino Tuilosega,** and **Tak Kubota** passed him to a **shodan** level.

An extremely colorful fighter, he captivated audiences in England and Belgium as a member of Ed Parker's 1974 U.S. team. He and **John Natividad** engaged in one of the greatest **non-contact** bouts in history at the 1973 **Internationals.** In an unprecedented 25-point overtime match, Natividad won the grand title, 13-12, and a $2,500 purse.

At the very inception of **full-contact** karate, in 1974, he made the transition and began fighting anybody and everybody he could find. Benny Urquidez was proclaimed world champion within every sanctioning body for which he fought; they include the National Karate League (NLK), **PKA, WKA, Tommy Lee,** and **Aaron Banks.** In Japan he attracted hordes of fans, beating Japanese kick-boxers at their own sport. (He stars in hero comic books under his fighting name, Benny "The Jet," a name given to him during a bout in Madison Square Garden early in his career.) In 1978 *Black Belt* Magazine voted Urquidez "Fighter of the Year" and inducted him into the **Black Belt Hall of Fame.**

Urquidez has been featured in two documentaries on the martial arts, *The New Gladiators,* produced by the late **Elvis Presley,** and *Kings of the Square Ring,* produced and released in Japan. In 1981 he starred in the American Cinema release *Force: Five* with two other martial artists turned actors, **Joe Lewis** and **Bong Soo Han.** His first book, *Training and Fighting Skills,* also appeared in 1981. *See also* U.S., history of karate in.

UYEHARA, MITO(SHI) Japanese-American martial arts publisher, author, and aikido practitioner. He learned **aikido** in his native Hawaii and claims to be a black belt in the Koichi Tohei method. He went to Los Angeles in 1960 intending to teach his art. In 1961, Mito, his brother Jim Uyehara, and two other investors put up $500 apiece to publish *Black Belt Magazine,* the first English-language martial arts publication on the market. Two years later,

Above: Mito Uyehara (*left*) honoring Hayward Nishioka with a Black Belt Hall of Fame plaque. *Right:* Dominic Valera (*right*) and Emil Farkas.

the Uyehara brothers bought out the other investors and by 1964 began showing a profit, only because they had created their own equipmnent company in 1962, called Martial Arts Supplies Co.

In 1969, the Uyehara brothers founded *Karate Illustrated,* which focuses on karate, kung-fu and martial arts competition. By 1970, *Black Belt* had already reached its status as the best-selling

magazine in the martial arts field. The brothers dissolved their partnership, Jim taking the lucrative supply company and Mito the magazines. Mito then launched a line a softbound textbooks which became a huge success. These books, coupled with his astute exploitation of the martial arts fad of the 1970s, made him one of the few millionaires in the martial arts business. Today, Mito's imprint, Ohara Publications, has more than 60 titles.

In 1973 Mito founded *Fighting Stars Magazine,* devoted to martial arts films and film personalities. He has authored a series of books entitled *Bruce Lee's Fighting Method.* In 1966 he began studying **jeet kune do** privately with **Bruce Lee.** In 1975 he moved to Honolulu, from where he oversees his businesses. *See also* U.S., history of karate in.

UYENO, KENZO (1923-63) American judo instructor and administrator; president (1962-63) of the Judo Black Belt Federation of America. He was awarded his 1st-degree black belt at 15, his second dan at 18. During World War II he taught judo at Poston Relocation Center. Uyeno moved to Washington, D.C., where he won the East Coast Black Belt Championship for five consecutive years from 1953 and helped organize, in 1954, the Capital Judo Black Belt Federation (Shufu Yudanshakai). In 1958 he received his godan (5th degree), and in 1963 he represented the JBBF in the Pan-American Games. *See also* U.S., history of judo in.

VACHUN, MICHAL (1944-   ) Czechoslovakian judo instructor and champion. Vachun began his study of the martial art in 1959 and received his black belt in 1964. His **sensei** was Dr. R. Kotva, in Pardubice, but Vachun received his black belt from the Czechoslovak Judo Federation. Vachun is affiliated with the Czechoslovak Judo and Karate Federation, acting as chief technical advisor and national coach.

He took first place in the National Judo Championships of Czechoslovakia in the years 1966, 1970, and 1972. Vachun took part in the 1965 World Judo Championships and in nine European Judo Championships in succession from 1964-72. After retiring from competition he was coach of the Czechoslovakian teams at the 1972 World University Championships and in several international judo tournaments. From 1973-75 he was national coach of Iceland, helping to organize the first national judo team of Iceland.

VALERA, DOMINIC French karate champion; Europe's best known karate competitor. Between 1966 and 1972 he won nine European Championships (four as an individual and five as a member of the French team). Valera also won the individual title at the American Open Championships in 1969 in New York and a bronze medal at the 1970 **WUKO** World Championships in Japan. He was also a member of the victorious French team at the 1972 WUKO World Karate Championships. Valera has been French champion 16 times. In 1978, in Paris, he challenged American **Jeff Smith** for the PKA World Light-Heavyweight Championship of full-contact. Smith won

a 9-round unanimous decision. In 1980, he was scheduled for a rematch when Smith unexpectedly lost his title to **Dan Macaruso**. Valera instead fought the new champion and was knocked out in the 6th round. See also Europe, history of karate in.

VAN CLIEF, RON American karate competitor, actor, and author. From 1953 to 1959, he studied **Shotokan** karate, **hakko-ryu** jujutsu, and **kendo**. After entering the U.S. Marine Corps in 1959, he studied **shorin-ryu** karate with grandmaster **Eizo Shimabuku(ro)** in Okinawa. That same year, he took up **goju-ryu** karate with **Peter Urban**. Much, later he began training in **wing chun** kung-fu with **Ting Leung**.

A successful regional competitor, Van Clief restricted his participation to East Coast tournaments and became one of New York's finest point fighters. In 1971, he founded **Chinese goju**, an eclectic karate style.

Van Clief became a member of the East Coast Stuntman's Association in 1966. He subsequently worked on 20 films as a stuntman, including *Shaft* and *The Anderson Tapes*. He got his first break in 1973 when he signed a five-picture contract with the Hong Kong film company, Yangtze Films, a branch of the Shaw Brothers Studios, starring in a series of Hong Kong movies as the "Black Dragon." He did three additional films by 1981, one of which also starred two Bruce Lee imitators who have become popular in Asia.

In 1981, he wrote *The Manual of the Martial Arts.*

VAN LENTEN, FRANK American karate pioneer; founder of the goshin-do karate system in the U.S. Van Lenten studied **kempo** karate in 1954 while stationed with the Marines in Hawaii. He also studied **isshinryu** in Okinawa under its founder **Tatsuo Shimabuku.** In the early 1960s, on the mainland, he began teaching his new style, selectively derived from other systems.

VILLABRILLE, FLORO Filipino-American **kali** grandmaster; one of the few American kali masters to bring his art from the Philippines. Born and raised in Cebu in the Visayas, he studied kali with his uncle and grandfather as a child. By the time he was 18, he was fighting in mortal contests. Having heard of a tribe that was reputedly the ultimate in kali, he and a friend ventured into the mountains of Samar to find the village of Gandari, where, they were warned, all strangers were killed. Undeterred, they found the village, impressed the officers of the tribe, and were accepted as pupils of the tribe chieftain for two years. Villabrille's greatest kali training was under the direction of the chieftain's daughter, who was blind. So acute was her sensory perception that she could sense when an opponent silently changed his stick from one hand to the other.

Villabrille eventually created his own system by combining all his various types of kali training. He oversees schools in San Francisco, Los Angeles, Hawaii and Washington. His foremost student is **Ben Largusa**. See also kali.

VITALI, KEITH American karate champion and instructor. From 1978 to 1981 Vitali has won or placed in every important karate tournament in the U.S. and in those years was continually ranked as the No. 1 point fighter in the country.

Vitali began karate in 1971 at the University of South Carolina under John Roper. He earned his black belt in Tae kwon do after two years and then taught at the University. In 1977 he moved to Atlanta, where he soon began to teach for Joe Corley. Today he is part owner of a Joe Corley Karate Studio in Forest Park.

After retiring from competition he worked in the Film *Force Five* and was later hired to co-star in Cannon Films *Revenge of the Ninja*. He has authored a number of books on karate for Contempory books. Among Vitalis major wins are: National Tae Kwon Do Championships (1973 and 1976), Mid America Nationals (1978), Battle of Atlanta (1978-79), AKA Grand Nationals (1980), PKA Grand Nationals (1979), Forth Worth Pro-Am (1980), U.S. open (1980)

VIZZIO, PAUL American **full-contact karate** champion; **PKA** world super lightweight champion. He first studied amateur boxing at age 9. Later, he was drawn to kung-fu under the direction of Wai Hong in New York, where he participated in the Chinese version of full-contact fighting. While studying karate with **Toyotaro Miyazake**, a popular tournament fighter and form champion, Vizzio was persuaded by Miyazaki to take up full-contact karate. In just his second fight, Vizzio barely lost (by one point) a non-title fight with the then current world super lightweight champion, **Gordon Franks**, a performance which brought him to the attention of the sport's promotors. On Nov. 13, 1981, he won the PKA world super lightweight title via a 12-round unanimous decision over Cliff Thomas in New York City; this after their first meeting on July 24, 1981, when Thomas had TKOed him in the 5th round. At the end of 1982, Vizzio's record was 188-2 with 9 KOs.

VOSS, WILLY (1953-) German karate competitor. Voss placed third in the 1973 European Championships (openweight) and second in 1975 (lightweight).

WADA, KOJI (1949-) Japanese karate champion. Wada, a **Shotokan** stylist (5 feet 8 inches-154 lbs), was twice champion of the All Japan Student Karate Federation Tournaments, in 1970 and 1971, and winner of the **JKA's** 1971 International Friendship Tournament.

WAITE, GEORGE (1942-) American karate instructor, businessman, and promoter. Waite studied **kenpo** in 1962 under Stephen Fox in Sacramento, Calif. In 1967 he received his black belt from **Ed Parker**. From 1968-71 he studied **Shotokan** karate under Kinji Mimora and fought as a member of his "A" team in northern California. In Aug. 1974, he and Parker produced what is purported to be the largest tournament in the history of American karate, the 11th Annual **International Karate Championships** in Long Beach. The two-day event drew more than 5,000 competitors and 11,000 spectators.

In Sept. 1974 Waite was made producer for **Elvis Presley's** film company, TCB Productions. He and Ed Parker organized and produced a martial arts documentary film entitled *The New Gladiators,* as of 1982 still unreleased. From 1979-81, Waite assisted author **Joe Hyams** in the writing of *Zen in the Martial Arts* and *Practical Self-Defense.*

WAKAYAMA, TOMISABURO Japanese motion picture star. Tomisaburo Wakayama has recently emerged as one of Japan's top film stars, having won that country's Academy Award just last year.

Brought up in a prominent Japanese show business family, Wakayama lived for years in the shadow of his father, the renowned Grand Master of the traditional song genre "Naga-utu," and his brother Shintaro Katsu, an actor-producer-director.

Wakayama persuaded his borther (who is considered the "Clint Eastwood" of Japan, msot famous as Zato-Ichi ("The Blind Swordsman") hero of a perennial series of popular samurai spectaculars) to produce a film he had long dreamed of making: a samurai epic based on the adventures of a legendary assassin, a Superman of medieval Japan called "Lone Wolf With Son," already long-popularized by a best-selling comic book, "Kozure Okami."

The smash hit film has catapulted Wakayama himself into superstardom in Japan. A skilled practitioner of "Kendo" (Japanese fending) in real life, on the screen, his swordplay often defies the imagination.

WALL, ROBERT "BOB" (1939-) American karate instructor, competitor, actor, and promoter. Wall began martial arts in 1958 under James Shimaga, in San Jose, Calif. He studied also under such notables as Al Thomas, **Gordon Doversola, Joe Lewis, Chuck Norris,** and **Bruce Lee,** with whom he worked on a number of films, including *Enter The Dragon* and *Return of the Dragon.* He also co-starred in *Game of Death,* making him the only martial artist to appear in three of Lee's films.

In 1966 Wall and Joe Lewis opened a karate studio in Sherman

Bob Wall *(right)* with one of his best friends and former partners Chuck Norris.

Oaks, Calif.; when Chuck Norris bought out Lewis's share in 1968, the two partners expanded into a successful chain of karate schools. Shortly afterwards, Wall, with Norris and **Mike Stone,** organized the Four Seasons Karate Championships, a series of quarterly events that were eventually nationally franchised.

From 1965 he won trophies in every major karate tournament in the country including the U.S. Nationals in Washington, D.C., the U.S. Championships in Dallas, the **Internationals** in Long Beach, the World Championships in Seattle, and the Tournament of Champions in Fort Worth. In 1970 he joined Chuck Norris, Joe Lewis, **Skipper Mullins,** and Mike Stone in forming a memorable team, which won the National Team Championships. A well-known instructor, he has taught personalities such as Steve McQueen, Jack Palance, Brian Keith, Freddie Prinze, and The Osmond Brothers.

In 1975 Wall compiled and published the *Who's Who in the Martial Arts* (edited by **John Corcoran**), giving recognition to top American martial artists. *See also* motion pictures and television; U.S., history of karate in.

WALLACE, BILL "Superfoot" (1945-) American karate champion, instructor, author, actor, and referee. World professional middleweight champion since 1974 for the **PKA,** Wallace won many point tournament competitions prior to entering the professional ring, including the U.S. Championships and USKA Grand Nationals three times each, and the **Top 10 Nationals** twice. He was rated top fighter in the country three times by *Black Belt Magazine*. A superstar of **full-contact** fighting, he is also a noted official and served as chief referee at the 1975 U.S. Championships.

Bill Wallace   Courtesy of Jay T. Will

Wallace started in judo. He took up karate in 1966 while serving in the U.S. Air Force. His first instructor was Michael Gneck, a **shorin-ryu** stylist who taught Wallace in San Bernadino, Calif. Wallace trained religiously seven days a week on a four-to-midnight schedule and won his black belt in one year. He returned to his home state of Indiana in 1968 where he began working out with **Glenn Keeney** in Anderson. While he never adopted any of Keeney's shorei-goju style, Wallace credits much of his sparring ability to those early workouts. While studying physical education at Ball State University, he entered and won his first tournament as a black belt, the Mid-East Nationals in Lexington, Ky. in Jan. 1968. After losing his next three consecutive tournaments, he launched a spectacular winning streak that continued to Sept. 1974 when he turned to full-contact karate. Wallace received his bachelor's degree in 1972 and completed his master's at Memphis State University, where he then taught a physical education program which included karate and judo.

Wallace conducted seminars in Europe, South America, England, and throughout the U.S. He once taught at the **Elvis Presley**-owned studio, the Tennessee Karate Institute where Presley trained with Wallace briefly. He co-authored a college text, *Karate's Basic Skills and Concepts*. Voted into the **Black Belt Hall of Fame** as "Man of the Year" for 1978, he was twice elected "Karate Player of the Year." Wallace co-starred in the Chuck Norris film, *A Force of One*. Member of *Who's Who in the Martial Arts*.

A combination tae kwon do and **shorin-ryu** stylist, he is noted for his fast left roundhouse kick and left hook kick. In the pro ring he is remembered for his quick left leg, which gave him the name "Superfoot." Wallace's ring history is 21-0, 11 KOs; he is the only full-contact world champion to retire undefeated.

Date	Opponent	Location	Outcome
9/14/74	Bernd Grothe	Los Angeles, Calif.	KO, 2nd round
9/14/74	Daniel Richer	Los Angeles, Calif.	TKO, 3rd
5/3/75	Joe Corley	Atlanta, Ga.	TKO, 9th
3/13/76	Jem Echollas	Las Vegas, Nev.	TKO, 2nd
4/26/76	Greg Hertel	Paris, France	KO, 1st
5/29/76	Daniel Richer	Toronto, Canada	KO, 3rd
10/1/76	Gary Edens	Los Angeles, Calif.	Decision, 9th
4/23/77	Pilinky Rodriguez	Las Vegas, Nev.	Decision, 9th
5/21/77	Ron Thiveridge	Providence, R.I.	TKO, 6th
9/10/77	Herb Thompson	Miami, Fla.	TKO, 2nd
10/8/77	Pat Worley	Indianapolis, Ind.	KO, 2nd
11/28/77	Burnis White	Honolulu, Hawaii	Decision, 9th
3/11/78	Emilio Narvaez	Providence, R.I.	Decision, 9th
4/8/78	Glen Mehlmen	Miami, Fla.	Decision, 7th
6/5/78	Ralph Hollett	Nova Scotia	Decision, 7th
7/18/78	Daryl Tyler	Monte Carlo	TKO, 6th
2/8/80	Steve Mackey	W. Palm Beach, Fla.	Decision, 5th
3/1/80	Ray McCallum	Oklahoma City, Okla.	Decision, 5th
5/24/80	Tom Georgiades	Denver, Colo.	KO, 2nd
6/15/80	Bob Biggs	Anderson, Ind.	Decision, 12th
10/3/81	John Shields	Atlanta, Ga.	Decision, 3rd

See also U.S., history of karate in; Professional Karate Association.

WALTERS, RICHARD American judo champion. Winner of the 1965 AAU Judo Championships, Walters tied Russia's **Anzor Kiknadze** at the World Championships at Rio de Janeiro. Walters was named among the top 10 judo players in the U.S. in 1968 by *Black Belt Magazine*.

WARREN, MIKE American karate champion. Runner-up in the 1973 World Tae Kwon Do Championships and a member of the second-place U.S. team, he won numerous tournaments. Warren was named among the top 10 karate players of 1973 by *Black Belt Magazine,* and was ranked repeatedly in *Professional Karate Magazine's* top ten from 1973-75.

WATANABE, LUIS TASUKE (1948-) Brazilian karate champion. Born in Japan, he emigrated with his family to Brazil when he was 8. Watanabe began karate at 21 with Yasutaka Tanaka in Rio de Janeiro. In Sao Paulo he continued his studies with Sensei Saraga, one of the foremost teachers in Latin America. In 1972 he was a surprise victor at the World Karate Championships (Paris) defeating competitors such as Luciano Parisi, **Ticky Donovan,** Ken Wittstock, **Guy Sauvin,** and William Higgins.

WATSON, BILLY American karate competitor. Watson began training in 1967, earning his black belt under **Pat Burleson.** He was rated among the top ten karatemen of 1971 by *Black Belt Magazine.*

WATSON, OWEN American karate instructor. Watson joined **Frank Ruiz's** dojo in 1966 and studied **Nisei goju.** He studied later with **Peter Urban,** from whom he received a senior expert certificate as chief instructor. He was a frequent winner at numerous East Coast tournaments during the early 1970s.

WATSON, PAM (1952-) American karate competitor and instructor. A student of **Pat Burleson,** she was rated among the top 10 females in the U.S. by *Professional Karate Magazine* in 1974. Watson won first place trophies at the 1972 American Karate Black Belt Association Championships, the 1972 and 1973 Texas State Championships, the 1973 U.S. Championships, and the 1973 Capital City Championships. A former self-defense instructor at the American Airlines Stewardess School in Dallas, she was cited for community work in teaching underprivileged children. Member of *Who's Who in the Martial Arts.*

WATTS, JOHN (1944-) American judo competitor. Watts, 6 feet 4 inches and over 300 lbs, began judo in 1966 while in the Air Force. He reached the finals of the 1968 National A.A.U. Judo Championships. He won the 1971 CISM Judo Championships (a military judo tournament) in Vienna and represented the U.S. in the 1972 Olympics in Munich.

WAX, JAMES American karate pioneer and instructor. While stationed in Okinawa with the U.S. Marines, he began studying matsubayashi **shorin-ryu** with the style's founder, **Shoshin Nagamine**, and with **Ansei Ueshiro**, receiving his black belt in 1958. He also married Nagamine's niece. He returned to the U.S. in 1961, the first to teach shorin-ryu in the eastern U.S. He established his first school in lower Manhattan. He then traveled and taught throughout parts of the U.S., selecting his best student at each school to operate it after he moved on. His most prominent student is **Bob Yarnall.** Wax was instrumental in bringing Ueshiro from Okinawa to the U.S. in 1962. (Steve Shear) *See also* U.S., history of karate in.

WEISS, AL (1926-) American martial arts publisher and editor. Founder and editor of numerous books and magazines pertaining to the martial arts, Weiss is best known for *Official Karate Magazine,* which he started in 1968; his other current magazine is *Warriors.* Among his publications no longer in print are *Fighting Champions* (1973), *Defense Combat* (1975), and the short-lived (two issues) *Martial Arts Illustrated* (1971). Weiss produced two books for author **Alan Lee,** *Tai-Chi* and *Kung-Fu,* and in 1981 co-authored with Tom Philbin *Clan of Death-Ninja.*

In addition, Al Weiss produced regional tournaments throughout the U.S. under the banner of *Official Karate Magazine.*

A black belt under New York sensei **John Kuhl,** Weiss has officiated at a number of tournaments and helped organize the East Coast Karate Alliance. In 1975 Weiss was named to *Who's Who in the Martial Arts. See also* U.S., history of karate in; Official Karate Magazine; Official Karate's Legion of Honor.

WESTBROOK, ADELE Martial arts author. Westbrook studied philosophy at Columbia University at the same time as her co-author, **Oscar Ratti,** was completing graduate work in classical languages. They began to practice **aikido** together and, while training under a variety of instructors in the U.S. and Europe, started a collection of notes and sketches that developed into *Aikido and the Dynamic Sphere,* published in 1973. Westbrook and Ratti then collaborated on the authoritative *Secrets of the Samurai.*

WESTBROOK, HAMES American judo competitor. A wrestler prior to his involvement in judo, Westbrook took a silver medal at the Pan-American Union Games and represented the U.S. at international meets. He was among the top ten judo men in the U.S. in 1968 according to *Black Belt Magazine.*

WHITE, LEO American judo champion. White was 209-lb U.S. Collegiate Champion in 1976, 1977, and 1979. Among his other wins are a bronze medal at the Pan-American Games and a second place at the World Trials in 1979.

WILL, JAY T. (1942-) American karate competitor, instructor, referee, photographer, and author. He obtained his black belt from **Ed Parker.** Elected to *Who's Who in the Martial Arts.* He was also elected into the **Black Belt Hall of Fame** by *Black Belt Magazine* and credited as the principal force in bringing karate to the midwest by *Inside Kung-Fu Magazine.*

Before retiring from competition in 1974, he won a number of midwestern tournaments including the grand championship at the Ohio State Championships, the Kenpo Karate Champoinships, and the Ohio-Pennsylvania Championships. In 1975 he promoted the 5th Mid-American Karate Championships in Columbus and the Ohio State Professional and Regional Championships. Will is also the annual promoter of the Midwest Karate Championships. He wrote two books, *Kenpo Karate,* (1976), and *Advanced Kenpo* (1980). Will has also appeared in numerous television shows and films including *Jaguar Lives* and *Force Five.* He is the foremost **full-contact** referee in the U.S.

WILLIAMS, BYRN British karate administrator. Williams first studied karate in Hong Kong. Subsequently, as a National Sports Council staff member, he performed liaison duties with all the oriental martial arts organizations based in Britain. In 1974 he became treasurer of the **European Karate Union,** the largest karate organization in Europe, and full-time general secretary to the British Karate Control Commission. Williams served as general editor of *Martial Arts of the Orient* (1975).

WILSON, DON (1954-) American karate champion, instructor, and promoter; the first kung-fu stylist to hold a **full-contact** karate world title. Wilson started in **goju-ryu** karate in 1972 with **Chuck Merriman** in New London, Conn. He transferred to Brevard Community College in Cocoa, Fla., where he studied pai-lum kung-fu with his brother, Jim, reaching instructor level in 1975.

Wilson made his professional fighting debut in 1974. In Sept. 1979 in Orlando, Fla., he won by 7th round TKO the PKA U.S. Middleweight Championship, defeating Jimmy Horseley in ESPN's first cable broadcast of the sport. In 1980, Wilson won the WKA World Light Heavyweight Title by virtue of a 2nd round TKO over Andy White in Cocoa Beach. By the end of 1982 he had defended his title five times throughout the world, in New York, Las Vegas, Tokyo, and Hong Kong.

WILSON, GEORGE American judo instructor. He first studied judo in Hawaii with Prof. Higami. In 1955 Wilson introduced the first official American high school judo program at Kent-Meridian Senior High School. He won the Pacific Northwest Black Belt Championships in 1957, and the Western Canadian Black Belt Championships in 1958. He was a member of the board of examiners of the **USJF** and a member of the U.S. Olympic Judo Committee. In 1970 he was selected to the **Black Belt Hall of Fame.** *See also* U.S., history of judo in.

Al Weiss

WOMBLE, JOHN J. (1934-) American karate pioneer and instructor. Womble began martial arts in 1953 while in the Army. He received his black belt in 1955 in Japan under Dr. **Chitose** in **Chito-ryu.** Womble also studied kung-fu, moo duk kwan, judo, and **kenjutsu.** His competition wins include the 1967 Jhoon Rhee Nationals; Francis Conde's Tri State Tournament, 1971-73; Aaron Banks New York Championships, 1965 and 1966; and Ki Whang Kim's All-American Invitational, 1966 and 1967. *See also* U.S., history of karate in.

WONG, ARK-YUEY (1899-) Chinese-American kung-fu instructor and pioneer. Wong began kung-fu in 1907, under Lam Ark Fun and Ho Yeng. He came to the U.S. in 1921 and began teaching his art exclusively to Chinese. In 1929 he moved to Los Angeles, where he was the first kung-fu instructor to allow non-Chinese into his studio, in 1964. He was inducted into the **Black Belt Hall of Fame** in 1970.

Wong's first kwoon (training hall) was established in 1922 in San Francisco's Chinatown. Other schools followed: Oakland, 1926; Stockton, 1928; Los Angeles, 1929. After returning to China for a brief visit, he returned to Los Angeles and opened his Wah Que Studio in 1962 in Chinatown. Since opening his teachings to non-Chinese, his studio has become a famous training establishment. Wong estimates he has taught some 20,000 students in his lifetime. He still teaches private and group lessons, a practice most kung-fu teachers assign to their senior students. He is a master of the **Shao-lin** style, the eighteen classical weapons, herbal medicine, and the lion and dragon dances. *See also* U.S., history of karate in.

WONG, CURTIS F. (19490) Chinese-American kung-fu practitioner and publisher. Wong is the publisher of *Inside Kung-Fu, Kick Illustrated, Martial Arts Movies,* and *Racquetball Illustrated.* He is the owner of Unique Publications, one of America's leading martial arts publishing houses, and Mantis Supply, a martial arts supply company. He is an accomplished kung-fu practitioner and actor, appearing in a number of television shows, feature films, and television commercials, as well as frequent public demonstrations, including one at the Chinese New Year celebration in Los Angeles' Chinatown. Member of *Who's Who in the Martial Arts. See also* U.S., history of karate in.

Curtis Wong, publisher of *Inside Kung-Fu* and *Kick Illustrated*

WONG, DOC-FAI Chinese kung-fu instructor. A sifu of **Choy-Li-Fut** and **t'ai-chi-ch'uan,** Wong trained in America under Lau Bun and in Hong Kong under Woo Van-Cheuk. Based in nothern California, he has taught at Oakland Laney College, San Francisco City College, and the San Francisco Community College Center.

The Hong Kong headquarters appointed Wong as president of the association in memory of Chan Heung, founder of the Choy-Li-Fut Martial Arts, Northern California Chapter. He is also an honorary president and lifetime member of the United Chung Wah Martial Arts Association of Hong Kong, and a lifetime member of the Hong Kong Chinese Martial Arts Association (Michael P. Staples)

WONG, DOUGLAS LIM (1948-) Chinese-American kung-fu author, and instructor. He began kung-fu under Wing-Wong in 1960 and received the black sash from **Ark Wong** in 1972, Hamuea Lifiti in 1973, Wai Doo in 1975, and Hsu Hong Chi in 1975. Wong instructs in the Five Animal Style, Five Family Style, **wing chun,** and white lotus. He is affiliated with Tang Shou Tao Committee of Taipei Athletics Association, as an overseas advisor, and served on the Martial Art Advisory Board for the city of Los Angeles. He sponsored the 1975 and 1976 Los Angeles Martial Arts Tournament, 1974 Lima Lama East West Karate-Kung-Fu Tournament, Western Karate Championships, and 1973 Chapman College Kung-fu Tournament. His noted students include **James Lew,** Carrie Ogawa-Wong, and Al Leong.

Wong has authored *Kung-Fu The Way of Life, Shao-Lin Fighting: Theories and Concepts,* and *Wing Chun: The Deceptive Hand.*

Doug Wong

WONG-FEI-HUNG Noted practitioner of the hung-chia style of Chinese kung-fu; member of the Canton-Ten Tigers of Kwang Tung province. Wong's adventures were immortalized on the movie screen by actor **Kwang-Tak Hing** in one of the longest movie series in Hong Kong cinema history.

WONG, Y.C. Chinese kung-fu master. He began training at 6 in Kwangtung province, China. At 18, he studied in the **hung gar** style (also known as tiger-crane) under Lum Jo in Hong Kong. This is the style for which Wong is most known; however, is is proficient in the northern pek qua style, **t'ai-chi-ch'uan, pa-kua,** and sum-yee. Wong has taught kung-fu in the San Francisco area since the late 1960s.

WOOLEY, JIMMY (1949-) American judo champion. Member of the 1972 U.S. Olympic Team, he is 6 feet, 205 lbs. Wooley began judo at age 10 and has done extensive training in Japan. Wooley won a bronze medal at the 1973 World Championships and was ranked among America's top 10 judo players of 1973 by *Black Belt Magazine.*

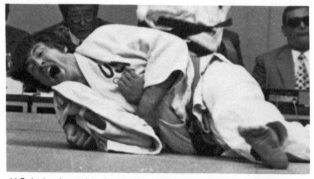

U.S. judo champion James Wooley throws W. Kim at the 1972 Olympics.

WORLEY, JOHN (1944-) American karate instructor, competitor, administrator, promoter, and publisher. A student of **Jhoon Rhee,** Worley began teaching at the Washington, D.C., Jhoon Rhee Institute in 1970, the year he entered competition. Winner of the lightweight division at the Pan-American Championships in Maryland in 1971, Worley also won numerous other regional titles including the 1971 Tae Kyun Championships and the 1972 Virginia State Open. Knee surgery in 1974 prevented him from competing until a year later, when he won first place in sparring and second place in kata at the National Championships in Minnesota.

A member of the *Who's Who in the Martial Arts,* Worley performed demonstrations at the White House (1972). With his brother, **Pat Worley,** he promotes the Diamond Nationals, in which the grand champion wins a diamond ring with the tournament logo designed around it.

Worley, along with his brother Pat, **Larry Carnahan,** and **Gordon Franks** operate a chain of schools in Minnesota called Mid-America Karate. A former editor of *Sport Karate,* Worley promotes the Super Fights, full-contact events. *See also* U.S., history of karate in.

Left to right: John Worley, Gordon Franks, Gary Hestilow, and Floyd Jackson.

WORLEY, PAT (1948-) American karate competitor, instructor, promoter, and publisher. Like his elder brother **John Worley,** Pat Worley was a student of **Jhoon Rhee.** Entering competition in 1970, he won the 1970 National Karate Championships (kata and sparring), 1971 Top 10 Nationals, 1973 North America Open, and 1975 U.S. Championships (light-heavyweight). He was twice named to *Black Belt's* Top 10 (1971, 1975).

Worley and his brother were instrumental in pioneering musical kata performance. They performed at the White House in 1972. Pat and John promote the Diamond Nationals along with the partners **Larry Carnahan** and **Gordon Franks;** they are owners, with the above mentioned partners, of the Mid-America Karate Studios. Member of *Who's Who in the Martial Arts.*

WREN, FRED (1947-) American karate champion, instructor, and promoter. Wren was named to every major Top 10 poll between 1970 and 1975 and ranked number-1 fighter in America by *Professional Karate Magazine* in 1973. His first major victories came at the 1969 and 1970 U.S. Championships in Dallas, where he won the light-weight title. In 1973 he was grand champion at the USKA Grand Nationals and the Mardi Gras Nationals in New Orleans. He repeated the latter victory in 1974 and 1975. Trainer of such regional champions as **Jim Miller,** Harold Gross, Walt Bone, and D.P. Hill, Wren co-founded and promted until 1974 the **Top 10 Nationals** in St. Louis with **Mike Anderson.** Member of the *Who's Who in the Martial Arts.*

WYATT, PAT (1940-74) American karate instructor. In 1971 he was chosen as "Coach of the Year" by the **U.S. Karate Association.** He died of an apparent heart attack while working out in his dojo on April 1, 1974.

Pat Wyatt

YABE, JAMES (1944-) Japanese-American karate champion and instructor. One of the most senior U.S. students of **Hidetaka Nishiyama,** Yabe was the combined champion of the 1st All America Karate Tournament in 1961 while still a brown belt. In 1962, 1963, 1966, and 1967, Yabe added more victories in the All America Karate Tournament competition. He was a member of the U.S. National Team at both the 1st **WUKO** World Championships in 1970 in Tokyo and at the 2nd WUKO World Championships in 1972 in Paris.

A high ranking black belt, he also holds credentials as a duly qualified instructor of the **JKA,** and in 1980 assisted **Richard Kim** on the 1980 U.S. National Karate Team Coaching Staff. (MAURICIO HERNANDEZ) *See also* Shotokan.

YABU, KENTSU (1870-) Okinawan karate master. A student of the legendary **Yasutsune Itosu** and **Sokon Matsumura,** Yabu was one of the first men to teach karate in Okinawan public schools. Yabu introduced Shuri-te (**shorin-ryu**) to Hawaii in 1927, presenting the first public karate demonstration at the Nuuanu YMCA in Honolulu. Although the demonstration was open to the public, nearly all of the spectators were Okinawans. After about seven months of teaching in the islands, Yabu returned to Okinawa.

Interest in karate by non-Okinawans thereafter ebbed and flowed until the post-World War II period. Yabu's open teachings brought together interested groups of Okinawans for practice and recreation. This was something the rivalry of Naha, Shuri, and Tomari had prevented on Okinawa. Yabu's students include **Choshin Chibana, Kanken Toyama,** and **Shinken Taira.** *See also* Okinawa, history of martial arts in.

Shorin master Kentsu Yabu, who introduced karate to Hawaii in 1927

YAGI, MEITOKU (1912-) Okinawan karate master. He started his karate training under **Chojun Miyagi** at 14 after undergoing an eight-month trial period, during which time he performed daily chores for Miyagi, the founder of **goju-ryu** karate. Miyagi never had his own dojo, but taught in his house and in his backyard. During his first year of daily training, Yagi was taught **Sanchin,** the basic breathing form. When Yagi went to the public bathhouse, older strangers, noticing the bruises on his shoulder from training in Sanchin, remarked, "Aha! You have been at Chojun's school," so well known was Miyagi's Sanchin training on Okinawa. Yagi practiced with him until Miyagi's death in 1953.

Yagi is Miyagi's successor and the foremost living goju-ryu karate master; he is president of the Meibukan School of goju-ryu karate-do at Naha City, Okinawa. Because of his dedication and loyalty, the Miyagi family gave Grandmaster Miyagi's karate gi and belt to Yagi in 1963. (ANTHONY MIRAKIAN) *See also* Okinawan goju-ryu; Okinawa, history of martial arts in.

YAGI, TEINOSUKE Japanese jujutsu master; first instructor to **Jigoro Kano,** founder of judo.

Okinawan Goju-ryu karate master Meitoku Yagi, president of the Meibukan Goju-ryu Karate Association

YAGUCHI, YUTAKA Shotokan karate instructor; a member of the **JKA.** Yaguchi came to the U.S. to assist **Hidetaka Nishiyama.** He presently teaches **Shotokan** karate in Denver.

YAMADA, HEIZAEMON (d. 1578) Founder of the Jikishin-kage ryu style of **kenjutsu.**

YAMADA, YOSHIMITSU Japanese **aikido** instructor, one of the early pioneers of **Morihei Ueshiba's** aikido in the U.S. Yamada devised his own system, which slightly differs from that taught at the **hombu** in Tokyo.

Chief instructor of the New York Aiki Kai and president of the American Aikido Federation, Yamada began his studies as an apprentice at the aikido headquarters in Japan. After three years under Morihei Ueshiba he became a full-time instructor, teaching at various universities and army bases. Author of *Aikido Complete,* he was named in 1972 to the **Black Belt Hall of Fame.**

YAMAGUCHI, GOGEN (1909-) Japanese karate master and head of the Japanese **goju-ryu** system of karate; nicknamed "The Cat." He began karate in 1929 under Okinwan karate master **Chojun Miyagi.**

In 1935, he organized the All-Japan Goju-Kai Karate-do Association and became its chief instructor. In 1939, he was sent to Manchuria as an intelligence officer and was captured by the Russians and held prisoner until 1947. Upon his return to Japan, he continued his organization, which is today among the largest in the world.

In 1936, Yamaguchi devised a form of free style fighting that had not existed in the traditional Okinawan goju system. Today this form of free sparring (**jiyu-kumite**) forms the basis of sport karate.

Due principally to Yamaguchi's efforts, the All Japan Karate-do Federation was established in 1964, which has succeeded in unifying some of Japan's karate schools. For his contribution to the martial arts he was decorated by the Emperor with the Ranju-hosho, or Blue Ribbon Medal, and the fifth order of merit. In 1966 he wrote and published *Karate Goju-ryu by the Cat. See also* Japan, history of karate in.

YAMAGUCHI, GOSEI (1935-) Japanese-American karate instructor and author. Founder of Goju-Kai Karate-do U.S.A., Norimi Gosei Yamaguchi is the eldest son of **Gogen Yamaguchi.** Under his father's tutelage he studied Japanese **goju-ryu,** and he earned a judo black belt from the **Kodokan.** Yamaguchi came to the U.S. in 1964 to replace his brother, Gosen, as director of the goju karate club at San Francisco State College. In 1967 he became one of the first martial arts instructors to serve on the faculty at an American college.

Yamaguchi is noted for his teaching of the physically and mentally handicapped. In 1972 he was chosen to the **Black Belt Hall of Fame;** in 1975 he became a member of *Who's Who in the Martial Arts.* He is the author of two books: *Goju-ryu Karate* and *Goju-ryu Karate II.*

Yamaguchi promoted a number of tournaments in the San Francisco area, among them 1966 California Goju-Kai Karate-Do Championships, 1967 North-South California Karate Tournament, 1967 All Goju-Kai Karate-Do Championship, 1968 and 1970 National Goju-Kai Karate-Do Championships, and 1972 AAU National Invitational Karate-Do Championships.

Gosei Yamaguchi, who came to the U.S. in 1964, is the leader of Japanese goju-ryu karate in America.

YAMAGUCHI, GOSEN Second son of **Gogen Yamaguchi.** Gosen came to the U.S. in 1963 and enrolled at San Francisco State College, where he began to instruct in **goju-ryu** karate. His brother **Gosei** replaced him in 1964.

Gogen Yamaguchi

YAMAGUCHI, GOSHI (1943-) Third son of the famous **Gogen Yamaguchi.** Goshi, 5'5" and 143 lbs., won the All Tokyo Goju-Kai Tournament in 1968. He has won the All Japan Karate-do Goju-Kai Tournament ten times. He taught karate at San Francisco State College, then returned to Japan to teach at the Tokyo Goju-Kai.

YAMAMOTO, KANSUKE YORINORI (-1561) Japanese **yari-jutsu** master also known as "one-eyed Yamamoto." He was famous for his ability in to-so-jutsu (sword and spear). It is related that he practiced cutting water in flowing streams, thus contributing to the name of his personal style, doki-ryu.

YAMAMOTO, TAMIZAEMON Police officer in Osaka, Japan, during the Tokugawa period (1600-1867), Yamamoto is reputedly the founder of the **Shin-no-Shindo** school of jujutsu.

YAMASHITA, TADASHI (1942-) Japanese-American karate performer, official, and author. He received two Golden Fist Awards, one for outstanding demonstrator of 1971-73, the second as California's most outstanding official. Yamashita wrote two books, one on **shorin-ryu** karate and the other on the **nunchaku.** Member of *Who's Who in the Martial Arts.*

Byung Yu *(right)* with some of his colleagues Tadashi Yamashita *(center)* and Tino Tuilosega *(left).*

Yamashita began his study of karate at 11. Among his instructors are some of the finest names in Okinawan karate. He trained for two years with **Chosin Chibana,** founder of a branch of **shorin-ryu** karate, and also with Chibana's chief disciple, **Shugoro Nakazato.** Yamashita immigrated to the U.S. in 1964 as a high-ranking shorin-ryu black belt and skilled, flamboyant performer with the **kobujutso** (art of weapons) arsenal of Okinawa. With a combination of showmanship and innovative performances, he rose to prominence as one of America's foremost weapons experts. After two featured appearances on the nationally syndicated *Thrillseekers,* he was given parts in the television movie *Judge Dee,* the *Kung Fu* series and *Mannix.* Since 1974 he has periodically returned to Japan to star in Japanese karate films. He has founded schools in Indiana, Wisconsin, Florida, Virginia, and Orange County, California. His foremost student is Chuck Cavinaugh of Wisconsin.

YAMASHITA, YASUHIRO (1957-) Japanese heavyweight judo champion; winner of the All Japan Judo Championships six times (1977-81 and 1982). He was a gold medalist at the 1976 World Junior Judo Championships, and winner of the World Championships in 1979 and '81. Yamashita is excellent at kosotogari and has an extremely effective ko-uchi-gari. He has the distinction of being the youngest winner in the history of the All Japan Championships.

YAMAUCHI, TOSHITAKA (1894-1971) Japanese judo master. Born into a **samurai** family in Kagoshima, Japan, he began judo at 13, becoming a black belt while still in high school. In college Yamauchi was trained by the great names of the early **Kodokan.**

In 1917 he came to the U.S., sent by **Jigoro Kano,** a judo missionary to the new world. A 1930 reunion with Kano in Los Angeles resulted in the formation of the first U.S. Judo Black Belt Association. After 1932 Yamauchi and Roy Moore, Olympic wrestling coach, took a 14-man wrestling team to Japan—the first time western wrestling was seen in Japan. In 1963 he was promoted to 8th dan, and continued to teach in Fresno till his death. *See also* U.S., history of judo in.

YAMAZAKI, KIYOSHI (1940-) Japanese-American karate instructor and performer. He began his karate studies at 16 under **Yosuhiro Konishi** and within three years had earned a black belt. In 1961 he traveled to Okinawa and trained with **Shugoro Nakazato,** earning a black belt in **kobudo.** He also trained in **aikido,** judo, and **kendo.** He was graduated in 1963 from Senshu University, where he competed on the university black belt team. He crowned his college career as one of two men to represent Tokyo in the All Japan Karate Championships. In 1964 he was chosen one of the top eight karate competitors in Japan and was seeded into the finals of the All Japan Karate Championships. In 1967 he was awarded a teaching certificate from the All Karate Organization, accrediting him as a karate teacher outside of Japan.

Yamazaki immigrated to the U.S. in 1968, and since then has traveled across the world giving instruction and demonstrations of karate and weaponry. He performed with **Fumio Demura** at Japanese Village and Deer Park, an amusement and cultural center in Orange County, California, and has appeared in television commercials and shows. He is the chief instructor of the Japan Karate Federation Ryobu-kay, an organization with schools in the western U.S. and Canada. He is also an instructor at the University of California Irvine and the Los Angeles County Sheriff's Department. He was a technical advisor for the film, *Conan, the Barbarian* in 1982 and taught sword techniques to the film's star, Arnold Schwarzenegger.

YANAGI, SEKIZAI MINAMOTO MASATARI (-1862) Japanese jujutsu master. Through his efforts the jujutsu schools of **yoshin- ryu** and **Shin-no-Shindo** were unified, becoming the tenjin-shinyo-ryu.

Yanagi, also known as Iso Mataemon in his later years, was credited with some rather astonishing feats of prowess in unarmed combat. His deeds fill many vivid pages in the Japanese literature of the martial arts.

After having studied the techniques of the yoshin ryu and the Shin-no-Shindo under the guidance of Masters Hitotsuyanagi and Homma he traveled from school to school to challenge local champions. In the course of his travels he is said to have confronted a group of hired mercenaries who had come to extort a sum of money from peasants who were sheltering him. Perhaps, as was customary under similar circumstances, they had actually hired him. Records describe the encounter as a savage battle in which Yanagi and one of his best students demonstrated the devastating effects of well applied **atemi-waza.**

Yanagi was also a conscientious theorist, who apparently leaned toward an ascetic view of the martial arts. Of particular importance to the development of jujutsu were his ideas concerning the principle of **ju,** or suppleness. According to Yanagi, overdevelopment of the muscles and excessive reliance upon muscular force entailed those qualities of rigidity and slowness usually associated with a suit of armor or with encroaching old age. He preferred to emphasize suppleness, which he felt was the most visible characteristic of life and of action. Accordingly, in combat he recommended that his students apply the techniques of his school quickly, but without undue tension and only when an opponent, by attacking, had weakened his own line of defense. This provided the major part of that force necessary to subdue him.

YANG, DONG JA (1938-) Korean-born American tae kwon do instructor and administrator. A physical education professor at Howard University, Washington, D.C., Yang is responsible for the promotion and unification of tae kwon do competition rules throughout the nation. He is also a certified international referee in tae kwon do.

YANG LU-CH'UAN (1800-73) Well-known master of **t'ai-chi-ch'uan;** often called the "father" of modern t'ai-chi. He was a noted student of Ch'en Ch'ang-shing who breached the barrier of the Ch'en family to become the first outsider to learn t'ai-chi boxing.

YARA, CHATAN Famous **hsing-i** and chi-kung master who, following twenty years of martial arts study in China, returned to Okinawa and introduced the concept of inner strength to Okinawan karate.

YARNALL, BOB (1942-) American karate pioneer, instructor, and competitor. Yarnall was inducted into the **Black Belt Hall of Fame** as 1971 "Instructor of the Year." A **shorin-ryu** teacher in St. Louis since 1962, he trained such noted fighters as **Parker Shelton** and Bill Marsh. Yarnall also holds community classes for handicapped and underprivileged children.

During his competitive career (1960-68) he was grand champion of the 1963 U.S. Open Championships, 1966 and 1967 Central State grand champion, and American Tae Kwon Do grand champion in 1967. An official at almost every tournament in the midwest, including the USKA Grand Nationals and the **Top 10 Nationals,** Yarnall has also refereed at numerous other events around the country. Member of the *Who's Who in the Martial Arts. See also* U.S., history of karate in.

YEE, KWOK (A.D. 25-) Chinese martial artist, he is thought to be one of the earliest Chinese boxers. He practiced chi chi san, or the art of the long hand.

YIN-FU (1840-1909) Nicknamed "thin Yin," a native of I-shien in Hopei province skilled in **pa-kua** boxing. He taught few students. Some sources claim he was a pupil of Ch'eng T'ing-hua; others believe him to be one of the original proteges of Tung Hai-ch'uan, the first known master of pa-kua.

YONEZUKA, YOSHISADA (1937-) Japanese-American judo instructor. He earned his black belt in Japan and, after attending Nihon University in Tokyo, moved to the U.S. in 1960. He taught judo in New York for two years, then for one year at the U.S. Military Academy at West Point, New York, finally settling in New Jersey. A trainer of champions, whose coaching methods have been compared to those of the late football coach, Vince Lombardi, Yonezuka is estimated to have trained 32 national champions by 1982 including **Mike Swain**, the first American to win a gold medal in international competition. He was named to the **Black Belt Hall of Fame** in 1982 as "Judo Instructor of the Year."

YOSHIDA, GEORGE Japanese-American judo pioneer. Yoshida came to the U.S. in 1917 from Japan, settled in New York City, and joined the Nippon Athletic Club, where he began his judo training. In 1923 he achieved a black belt. Yoshida ran the most famous judo clubs in New York—visited by **Jigoro Kano** on his trips to the U.S. Yoshida was instrumental in forming the New York Yudanshakai, of which he became honorary president. *See also* U.S., history of judo in.

George Yoshida

YOSHIDA, KOTARU Japanese jujutsu master. He became the head of the **Daito-ryu** system. An expert with the **yari** and the **halberd**, he was one of the instructors of **Richard Kim**.

YOSHIMATSU, YOSHIHIKO (1921-) Japanese judo champion; the first fighter to win the All Japan Judo Championships on three occasions: 1952, 1953, 1955. In 1965 he placed second in the 1st World Championships.

Japanese judo champion Y. Yoshimatsu

YOUNG, DOUGLAS (1926-) British judo competitor. He was a British team member when Britain won the European title three times in a row and runner-up in the 2nd dan class in 1954 and 1955, and 3rd dan in 1958.

YOUNG, THOMAS American **kempo** instructor. Young was one of the original five black belts of **James Mitose.** He assumed control of the Official Self-Defense Club in Honolulu when Mitose departed for the U.S. mainland in 1953. By 1966 Young had promoted a number of students to black belt, including some who formed kempo clubs in Hawaii and on the mainland U.S. *See also* U.S., history of karate in.

YUAN-PIN, CHEN Chinese martial artist who, according to some legends, was responsible for the introduction of jujutsu into Japan about 1644-48; some authorities believe even earlier. In light of conflicting evidence, many historians do admit that Yuan-pin could have introduced Chinese boxing (kempo) to Japan, which had some influence on jujutsu. *See also* Gempin, Chin.

YUAN-TAO Well-known master of **hsing-i, t'ai-chi** and two element boxing in the Republic of China.

YU, BYONG YONG (1935-   ) Korean-born American karate instructor, competitor, and referee. Winner of the 1970, 1971, and 1973 **International Karate Championships** (lightweight division) and 1971 World Pro/Am Championships in Los Angeles, Yu was also grand champion at both the 1971 Henry Cho's Tournament of Champions and 1972 **Jhoon Rhee** World Tae Kwon Do Championships. His credits as an official include head referee at the 1972 National Black Belt Championships, Kim Loo's 1972 National Tae Kwon Do Championships, 1973 All-American Open, and the 1973 Yamashita Open. Member of the *Who's Who in the Martial Arts*, Yu was named among America's Top 10 Kata competitors in 1973 by *Official Karate*.

YUEN, KAM American kung-fu instructor and technical advisor in films and television. Yuen operates a kung-fu school in Torrance, Calif.; his most noted student is the actor David Carradine. Yuen choreographed fight scenes for television's *Kung-Fu* and the film *Circle of Iron*.

Yuen began his kung-fu training in New York while attending Manhattan College. In 1965 he moved to California and opened his first school in San Jose. In 1969 he returned to his native Hong Kong to further his studies in the tai mantis style of kung-fu. Upon his return he settled in Los Angeles and established a school in Culver City. He has written two books: *Beginning Kung-Fu* and *Technique and Form of the Three Sectional Staff in Kung-Fu.*

YUKIO, MAEDA (1942-   ) Japanese judo champion (5 feet 11 inches, 231 lbs) Yukio was All Japan Police Champion (heavyweight), and in 1963 Openweight Champion at the Japan National Sport Games.

ZAJKOVSKI, ANTONI (1949-   ) Polish judo champion. Zajkovski was a bronze medalist at the 1971 World Championships, and a silver medalist at the 1972 Olympic Games. He also won the European Championships in the lightweight division.

Antoni Zajkowski

ZEELENBERG, RENE American judo competitor. A silver medalist at the 1974 U.S. Nationals, he was born in Belgium and came to the U.S. as a child.

ZIMMERMAN, BERND (1943-   ) German martial arts instructor. Beginning in 1955 he studied under Jurgen Seydel, **Mike Anderson,** Toyama Sumi, **Tadashi Yamashita,** and **Chuck Norris;** Zimmerman received a black belt from each. He studied **Shotokan,** tae kwon do, **wado ryu,** and **kobudo,** and combines all of these styles. President of the Austrian Karate Association, he won several championships in Austria and at the European Championships. He wrote a nunchaku booklet with Tadashi Yamashita. *See also* Europe, history of karate in.

Bernd Zimmerman

ZULU, CHAKA American karate instructor. Zulu began training in the middle 1960s, studying **Nisei-goju** with **Frank Ruiz,** as well as tae-kwon-do and judo. He is noted for his ability in kata performance. Among his many competition wins are the 1969 Annual Professional Karate Tournament, 1970 Montreal Canadian Championships, 1971 Brotherhood of Martial Arts Tournament (New York), and 1971 U.S. Southern Karate Championships (Miami).

Two of New York's old-time karate-ka: sensei Chaka Zulu *(left)* and Ron Taganashi.

ORGANIZATIONS AND ASSOCIATIONS

ALL AMERICA KARATE FEDERATION *See* American Amateur Karate Federation.

ALL CHINA SPORTS FEDERATION Governing body for sports, including **wu-shu,** in the People's Republic of China.

ALL EUROPE KARATE FEDERATION *See* Europe, history of karate in.

ALL JAPAN COLLEGIATE KARATE FEDERATION *See* Ajari, Yoshiaki.

ALL JAPAN GOJU-KAI KARATE-DO ASSOCIATION Japanese karate-do organization founded in 1935 by **Gogen Yamaguchi,** with branches throughout the world that teach the goju-ryu system of karate-do.

ALL JAPAN KARATE-DO ASSOCIATION Chaired by **Eizo Onishi,** this association fosters the **koeikan** style of karate.

ALL JAPAN KARATE-DO ORGANIZATION Formed on November 22, 1964, a federation of the four leading schools of Japanese karate: Shotokan, wado-ryu, goju-ryu, and Shito-ryu. Known in Japan as the Zen Nihon Karate-do Rengo.

ALL JAPAN KEMPO FEDERATION Supervisory organization of the kempo style, founded by **Munemi Sawayama** in 1935. Its U.S. branch is called the **American Nippon Kempo Federation.**

ALL JAPAN KENDO FEDERATION Founded in 1928, the AJKF, known in Japan as the Zen Nippon Kendo Remmei, conducts periodic examinations for the right to hold ranks and teaching licenses and sets standards for kendo techniques and training methods.

ALL JAPAN KYUDO FEDERATION *See* Zen Nihon Kyudo Remmei.

ALL JAPAN NAGINATA-DO FEDERATION *See* Zen Nihon Naginata-do Remmei.

ALL JAPAN SHORINJI KEMPO FEDERATION Founded by **Doshin So,** this federation is headquartered in Kagawa Prefecture in Shikoku, where **Shorinji kempo** is practiced by members of the Zen Kongo sect, a Mahayana Buddhist group.

ALL JAPAN SHORINJI-RYU KENKOKAN KARATE FEDERATION Japan's supervisory organization for the **shorinji-ryu** kenkokan system. **Masayuki Hisataka,** one of the system's founders and president of the federation's U.S. branch, introduced the style to the U.S. in 1963.

AMERICAN AMATEUR KARATE FEDERATION (AAKF) **Hidetaka Nishiyama,** a student of **Gichin Funakoshi,** came to the U.S. in July, 1961. In December of that year he called together the representatives of all Shotokan clubs, and the All America Karate Federation was founded. Concurrent with this conference, the AAKF conducted the inaugural All America Karate Championships at the Olympic Auditorium in Los Angeles, Calif. The title of this organization was later changed to the American Amateur Karate Federation. The Federation is divided into 12 regional districts within the U.S. The AAKF was not conceived as a branch of the influential **Japan Karate Association.** Instead, from its inception, it has retained its own administration, character, and national identity.

Hidetaka Nishiyama, head of the American Amateur Karate Federation

1971, the AAKF expanded its representation to include all karate styles as well as becoming an Allied Member of the A.A.U. In 1973, the AAKF resigned from the A.A.U. and in 1979 was reorganized as the non-profit, public benefit American Amateur Karate Federation in compliance with the U.S. Public Law pertaining to national sports governing bodies.

Since 1961 the AAKF has conducted an annual summer training camp making it one of the ongest running national karate summer camps in the United States. Among its past faculty are included **Masatoshi Nakayama, Richard Kim, Hidetaka Nihsiyama, Keinosuke Enoeda,** Hiroshi Shirai, **Takeshi Ohishi,** Toru Yamaguchi, Masataka Mori. (MAURICO HERNANDEZ)

Members of the All Japan Karate-do Organization at a referee's council of WUKO. *Bottom row, left to right:* Mr. Nowak (Australia), Mr. Hayashi (Japan), and Mr. Thomson (U.S.A.).

AMERICAN BANDO ASSOCIATION Organization founded by **Dr. Maung Gyi,** who introduced **bando** in the U.S. on April 3, 1960, in Washington, D.C. The ABA was officially organized at the 1st Blood Oath Initiation Ceremony at Ohio University on June 15, 1968. It currently has members in nine states and is chaired by **Robert Maxwell** of Baltimore, Md.

AMERICAN COLLEGIATE TAE KWON DO ASSOCIATION; AMERICAN COLLEGIATE TAE KWON DO COACHES ASSOCIATION The two organizations that govern collegiate tae kwon do competition in the U.S. The association handbook was published by **Ken Min.**

AMERICAN NIPPON KEMPO FEDERATION U.S. branch of the **All Japan Kempo Federation,** organized by Goki Kinnya, who introduced his style of kempo to the U.S. in 1961.

AMERICAN-OKINAWAN KARATE ASSOCIATION Organization propogating the **isshin-ryu** system of karate in the U.S. Its eastern director is **Don Nagle** of Jersey City, N.J.; western director is **Steve Armstrong** of Tacoma, Wash.

AMERICAN TAE KWON DO ASSOCIATION Founded in 1969 by **Haeng Ung Lee,** the ATA is one of the largest martial arts organizations in the U.S. In 1980 the association reported a membership of 80,000 practitioners, 1,000 of them black belts, and a chain of 250 schools. The ATA is headquartered in Little Rock, where a computer is used for record keeping. The *ATA News,* a tabloid newspaper, is published regularly and sent to members. Instructors receive business and advertising advice, financial backing, a 100-page instructor manual, and an organizational structure which offers training resources in each individual school from higher-ranking ATA masters. (MILO DAILEY)

BRITISH AIKIDO ASSOCIATION (BAA) founded in 1968 to promote and maintain the ethical and technical standards of aikido and to disseminate knowledge and information relating to it. The BAA, which propagates **Tomiki aikido,** has established a coaching and promotion structure and by 1974 had some 1,200 members. As a governing body it is recognized by the Sports Council, its coaching system is recognized by educational authorities, and its recommendations for rank promotion are accepted by the All Japan Aikido Association. The BAA is supervised by an executive committee composed of the association officers and two members from each of four regions: north, south, midland, and western. Each region has a committee and each member club has a representative serving on that committee.

BRITISH AMATEUR FULL-CONTACT ASSOCIATION Formed in 1979, with Steve Babbs as chief instructor, it is the regulating body for full-contact in England. The body licenses and grades individuals and has a rating system for those who compete in contests. In 1981, it scheduled four regional events, culminating in a national championship.

BRITISH KARATE CONTROL COMMISSION The BKCC founded in 1967 is the governing body for karate in Great Britain.

BRITISH KENDO ASSOCIATION The BKA was founded in 1962 and is one of the two leading Kendo associations in Britain. It was founded by **Roald Knutsen** and R. Lidstone.

BRITISH KENDO RENMEI The BKR founded in 1973 is one of the two leading Kendo associations in Britain. Founded by **Roald Knutsen** who also founded the first Kendo association in Britain, the British Kendo Association, Mr. Knutsen left the BKA to form the new association in order to maintain the traditional art of Kendo.

BUDOKAN Large arena, specially constructed in Tokyo for the 1964 Olympics, used for all forms of martial arts competition.

BUDOKWAI Judo club founded in London in 1918, at 15 Lower Grosvenor Place. The Budokwai was the first judo club established in Europe, and remains the most distinguished. Founded by **Gunji Koizumi,** the "father of European judo," the

club's first chief instructor was judo pioneer **Yukio Tani,** who remained there until 1937. In 1920 the Budokwai was visited by **Jigoro Kano** and strong ties with the **Kodokan,** judo's world headquarters in Tokyo, were instituted. The Budokwai served as the center of European judo until World War II. The first international judo match was conducted in 1926 between a Budokwai team and a German national contingent. The London club won.

In 1949 the Budokwai helped form the British Judo Association and the European Judo Union. It moved from its original site to its present location at 4 Gilston Road, South Kensington, in 1954. The club celebrated its Silver Jubilee in 1968 with its 15th annual display at the Royal Albert Hall in London. Over the years the Budokwai has produced some of Britain's greatest competitors and continually has had some of the most highly-ranked instructors outside of Japan. **Trevor Leggett,** the highest-ranked non-Japanese judoka at the time, taught at the Budokwai from 1947 judoka at the time, taught at the Budokwai from 1947 to 19057, and was instrumental in sending a number of British black belts to the Kodokan for additional study.

When the Budokwai was founded it included instruction not only in judo but in **kendo** as well. Today, again, the club offers classes in various martial arts besides judo. *See also:* Europe, history of judo in.

The interior of the Budokan

CANADIAN JIUJITSU ASSOCIATION (CJJA) Organized in 1963 and incorporated as a nonprofit corporation in 1968, the CJJA is a member of the Sports Federation of Canada and the **Dai Nippon Butokukai.** The association sets standards for black belt promotions, issues rank, sanctions provincial and national tournaments, establishes rules for jujutsu competition, trains qualified referees and judges, and offers training seminars by high-ranking Canadian and international instructors.

CANADIAN KODOKAN BLACK BELT FEDERATION The CKBBF is the governing body for judo in Canada.

CHINESE PHYSICAL CULTURE ASSOCIATION Located in Honolulu, the CPCA was probably the first club in the U.S. to teach a form of kung-fu. It was founded in 1922 as a branch of the parent organization in China and for many years restricted its membership to Chinese. Native instructors from China taught various forms of empty-hand combat. *Further reading: Karate Illustrated Magazine,* Jan.-Mar. 1977.

401

DAI NIPPON BUTOKUKAI Founded in 1895, the Great Japan Martial Virtues Association. The **Butokuden** (Martial Virtues Hall), established in 1899 and located adjacent to the Heian Shrine in Kyoto, became the headquarters and central training area of the association, and was operated by leading martial artists of the period. Naito Takaharu, a master swordsman of the hokushin-itto ryu, was elected head instructor and lecturer of the section devoted to the study of **kendo**; Isogai Hajime headed the judo section. Leaders of the Butokukai stressed the importance of kendo and judo in the general education of all citizens.

Establishment of the Dai Nippon Butokukai Bujutsu Semmon Gakko (Great Japan Martial Virtues Association of Martial Arts Specialty School) in 1911 gave employment to martial arts experts and produced skilled exponents in both classical and modern combative forms. The Dai Nippon Butokukai was instrumental in getting judo and kendo accepted into the Japanese Public School system.

The institution originates with Emperor Kanmu, 50th emperor of Japan (A.D. 781-805), who held the first martial arts tournament on Boy's Day, May 5; the event is still held every spring, in May, in Kyoto. The Butokukai grew to a membership of several million, and established branches throughout the world. **Richard Kim** founded branches in America, Canada, France, and Germany.

EUROPEAN AMATEUR KARATE FEDERATION (EAKF) Governing body of European karate formed on March 15, 1979 as part of the world body, the International Amateur Karate Federation. Its original president was Desiderio Maggioni; **Masatoshi Nakayama** and **Hidetake Nishiyama** are the EAKF's advisors. Upon its founding it was composed of 16 nations. The 1st EAKF European karate Championships took place on May 22, 1975 in Milan, Italy, where representatives from 11 countries competed in the individual events, as well as eight national teams.

EUROPEAN JUDO UNION The EJU was founded in 1948 by 15 member countries and today represents most of the nations of Europe. It is a member of the International Judo Federation, and holds its own annual judo championships, the prestigious European Championships. This tournament has been ongoing since 1951, and some of the world's greatest judo champions first came to prominence here.

EUROPEAN KARATE UNION The EKU is the oldest karate organization in Europe, founded in 1962. It holds its own European Karate Championships annually, and has done so since 1966. Many top karate champions like Dominic Valera have been among its champions.

EUROPEAN KENDO FEDERATION The EKF was founded in 1969 and is the governing body of kendo in Europe. The organization sponsors a European Kendo Championship.

FEDERATION OF ALL-JAPAN KARATE-DO ORGANIZATIONS (FAJKO) Central organization of Japanese **karate-do** systems. Founded in 1964, when the Olympic Games were conducted in Tokyo, its purpose is to achieve a degree of standardization and coordination among Japanese karate-do styles. The majority of Japanese karate bodies, however, have no affiliation with it. Its principal original members were the AJCKF, the All-Japan Workers Karate-do Federation, the JKA, Goju-kai, Wado-kai, Rembu-kai, Rengo-kai, and Shito-kai. The first two have since rescinded membership. FAJKO's function is to set standards for techniques, and to advise on teaching methods and instructor qualifications. It also pays notice to the ethical standards of its individual members.

Since 1964 it has set about creating amateur noncontact rules that would allow inter-style competition. By the early 1970s, these had been widely accepted among Japanese stylists, and the first all-style world championships was held in Tokyo in 1970 under the auspices of the **WUKO,** for which the FAJKO is Japanese representative.

FRENCH FEDERATION OF JUDO AND ASSOCIATED SPORTS Known as the Federation Francaise de Judo et Discipline Assimilee (FFJDA). It is the regulating body in France for judo, aikido, savate and kendo.

FRENCH KARATE UNION The regulating body for karate and related arts in France. Jacquest Delcourt is its president.

GI TODAN Order of the Fighting Sons of Japan, a secret society located in San Francisco during the 1920s. Membership was composed of Japanese-Americans and recent immigrants from Japan. Many members of the soceity trained in jujutsu as a means of maintaining a link with their native land.

GOJU-KAI KARATE-DO U.S.A. U.S. organ of the International Karate-Do Goju-Kai supervised by **Gogen Yamaguchi.** It was founded in 1964 by **Gosei Yamaguchi,** who is now its chief instructor. The organization, headquartered in San Francisco, maintains branches throughout the U.S.

GREAT BRITAIN, KARATE UNION OF (KUGB) Founded in 1966 by **Hirokazu Kanazawa,** the KUGB promulgates Shotokan karate and is affiliated with the **Japan Karate Association.** When Kanazawa returned to Japan in 1971, **Keinosuke Enoeda** was named chief instructor, assisted in the 1970s by representatives M. Kawasoe and Hideo Tomita. By 1977, KUGB membership numbered 12,000, organized into five regions: northern, central, southern, Welsh, and Scottish. The organization conducts free seminars throughout the year, as well as numerous regional tournaments culminating in a major national event, the KUGB Championships, which was first conducted in 1967; the 16th KUGB Championships in 1982 attracted approximately 1,000 competitors. Winners of the tournament usually also participate in larger international and world tournaments.

HAWAII KARATE ASSOCIATION (HKA) Formed in June 1959 by Carlton Shimoeni of shorin-ryu karate; Paul Yamaguchi, a kempo student of **James Mitose;** and instructors Mitsugi Kobayashi, George Miyasaki, and Kenneth Murakami of goju-ryu. In 1961 these and other instructors united to form the Hawaii Karate Congress, with nine clubs under its leadership. On November 5, 1961, the Hawaii Karate Congress sponsored a karate exposition at the Honolulu Civic Auditorium featuring guest performers from Japan, including 10th dan Kanki Izumikawa, Shotokan's Hidetaka Nishiyama, and Hirokazu Kanazawa, former all-Japan sparring champion.

IKATAN PENTJAK SILAT INDONESIA Organization formed to unify Indonesian **pentjak-silat** systems under one technical administration. Formed in 1947, the organization is headquartered in Djakarta under the direction of Rachmad Soeronagoro; branches are in Sumatra, Borneo, and the Celebes. *Further reading: Weapons and Fighting Arts of the Indonesian Archipelago,* Donn F. Draeger, 1972.

INTERNATIONAL AMATEUR KARATE FEDERATION (IAKF) One of the two largest organizations governing amateur karate worldwide (the other is WUKO). It was formulated in 1968, but was actually established in September 1974. At this time the purposes and objectives of the Federation were outlined as follows:

Typical Japanese karate contest with a center referee and four corner judges. Most karate matches are conducted on wooden floors.

Master Miyata

"The IAKF intends, by popularizing and developing amateur karate in the proper direction and by promoting and strengthening friendly relations among its member organizations and their members in all countries, to achieve the advancement of world amateur sports spirit and thereby to contribute to the perfection of human character."

Today, the IAKF is made up of over 70 national karate federations. Through dedication and cooperation between these members, th elAKF has been able to establish karate standards, provide for the development and certification of judges, and present the World Karate Championship, etc.

In working toward its purpose and objectives, the IAKF initiates many activities. It has established regional organizations which include the European Amateur Karate Federation, the Pan American Karate Union, the Asia-Oceania Karate Federation, and the Arab-Africa Karate Federation. Certain other areas have established championship committees, such as the Mediterranean Karate Championship Committee, the Bolivariana Karate Confederecion and the Central America-Caribbean Karate Organization, in order to carry out IAKF business and activities in the area.

Presently, the IAKF presents the following championships on a regular basis:

1. World Karate Championship (odd-numbered years)
2. European Karate championship (annual)
3. Pan American Karate Championship (odd-numbered years)
4. Asia Oceania Karate Championship (even-numbered years)
5. Arab-Africa Karate Championship (annual)
6. Mediterranean Karate Championship (annual)

The main activities carried out for the fulfillment of the IAKF purpose are:

1. Hold the World Karate Championship Tournaments and related activities.
2. Hold or support regional tournaments, inter-country friendship tournaments and other related events.
3. Establish, conduct and supervise various rules and regulations for karate contests.
4. Establish, conduct and supervise various standards pertaining to the techniques of karate.
5. Establish, conduct and supervise various standards pertaining to the qualifications of instructors and judges.
6. Establish, conduct and supervise the standards pertaining to the amateur status.
7. Hold or support lecutres and seminars pertaining to karate.
8. Establish various educational and research institutions for the development of karate.
9. Publish and distribute official publications related to the activities of the organization and karate in general.
10. Exchange information and provide useful material for member organizations.
11. Carry on other necessary activities for the achievement of the aims of this organization.

INTERNATIONAL KENDO FEDERATION (IKF) Founded in Japan in 1971. Kendo is practiced by some 8 million devotees throughout the world; the IKF is the central regulatory association for all kendo practitioners.

INTERNATIONAL SHOTOKAN KARATE FEDERATION (ISKF) Founded in 1977; the representative organization for the **Japan Karate Association** in the U.S. Prior to 1977, ISKF members had belonged to the Japan Karate Association International of America. Administrative problems led to the formation of a new organization co-existent with the JKA International; thus the JKA is represented in the U.S. by two groups. The federation is divided into regions with regional directors as follows:

Southwest	Ray Dalke
Central	John Rappo
North Central	Richard Gould
Northwest	A. Richard Allen
Western	Shojiro Koyama
East Coast	Teruyuki Okazaki
Mountain States	Yutaka Yaguchi
South Atlantic	Shigeru Takashina
Southern	Takayuki Mikami
Great Lakes	Greer Golden

National headquarters of the ISKF are at 22 South 45th Street, Philadelphia, Pa. 19104.

JKA masters active in the federation are Teruyuki Okazaki, 8th dan; Takayuki Mikami, 7th dan; and Shigeru Takashina, 6th dan. The senior American members, all 5th dan, are Ray Dalke, Greer Golden, Maynard Miner, Robin Rielly, Leslie Safar, Leon Sill, and Frank Smith. See also Shotokan.

INTERNATIONAL TAEKWON-DO FEDERATION (ITF) In 1965, Gen. **Choi Hong Hi** was appointed by the Republic of Korea to lead a tae kwon do goodwill mission to West Germany, Italy, Turkey, the United Arab Republic, Malaysia, and Singapore. The trip led to the establishment of tae kwon do associations in these countries and creation of the ITF, on March 22, 1965. It initially had nine member nations. Gen. Hi currently supervises the ITF from Canada.

The ITF claims some two-million members throughout the world. Branches have been established in Vietnam, Malaysia, Singapore, West Germany, Turkey, Italy, United Arab Republic, England, Netherlands, the U.S., and several South American nations. The organization conducted its 1st World Taekwon-Do Championships in Montreal, Canada on Oct. 4-5, 1974. See also tae kwon do.

INTERNATIONAL BANDO ASSOCIATION The IBA was founded by U Ba Than Gyi in 1946, in Thailand. It is now the governing bando association for the art which is practiced in numerous countries outside of Thailand.

INTERNATIONAL JUDO FEDERATION Founded in 1952, the IJF is the senior world body for judo, comprising national federations from more than 70 countries. Some of the aims and purposes of the IJF are: to promote cordial and friendly relations among its members; to supervise judo activities around the world; to organize and conduct the World Judo Championships, as well as competitions in the Olympic Games; and to establish technical standards. See also Europe, history of judo in.

INTERNATIONAL KARATE-DO GOJU-KAI The IKG is the international governing body for Japanese style Goju-ryu karate. It is headed by **Gogen Yamaguchi,** and has its headquarters in Japan. The organization oversees schools all over the world and has a very large following.

INTERNATIONAL KARATE ASSOCIATION The IKA was founded by **Takayuki Kubota,** a high ranking karate master who now resides in Los Angeles. The Association oversees schools all over the world but is headquartered in Southern California.

INTERNATIONAL KENPO KARATE ASSOCIATION (IKKA) The governing body for **kenpo** karate. Created by **Ed Parker** in 1956 in California as the Kenpo Karate Association of America, it was changed to the IKKA in 1960 when association members began migrating to foreign countries. Association member John McSweeney introduced kenpo to Ireland in 1962; Arturo Petit to Chile in the mid-1960s; and Rainer Schulte to Germany in the mid-1960s. The organization has also spread to England, Spain, Holland, Guatemala, Venezuela, New Zealand and Australia. See also kenpo.

JAPAN KARATE ASSOCIATION Nippon Karate Kyokai in Japanese, established in 1949 with **Gichin Funakoshi,** the founder of **Shotokan** karate, as chief instructor. The JKA grew out of an earlier association, the **Shoto-kai,** organized by Funakoshi's son **Yoshitaka.** In 1958 the association was approved as a corporation by Japan's ministry of education. That same year the JKA conducted the first **All Japan Karate Championships,** now an annual event. The JKA now claims a membership of more than 100,000 active karate students and 300 affiliated karate clubs throughout the world. World membership reportedly numbers 5 million.

The association sends instructors to foreign countries to assist in establishing karate clubs and to help maintain a high standard in the art. Only 2nd-degree black belts and up who hold physical education degrees are accepted for instructors' training. Instructors study physical dynamics, sportsmanship, psychology, and gym management, among other subjects. Only after reaching 3rd dan can they instruct for the association. The JKA also sponsors a training program for inspectors and judges, and standardizes rules for Shotokan karate. *See also* Shotokan.

KARATE UNION OF GREAT BRITAIN (KUGB) Organization formed in 1966 to develop and propogate **Shotokan** karate. It is affiliated with the **JKA** and supervised by **Keinosuke Enoeda.** The organization holds seminars and tournaments, and its members compete in international events.

KEBUDAJAAN ILMU SILAT INDONESIA (KISI) Name both of an organization and a fighting form. This combative art, headquartered in Makassar in southwest Celebes, is headed by Lie Tjien Jan. The KISI is based chiefly on hand and arm techniques; kicking is minimal. It is a synthesis of **kuntao** and **pentjak-silat** methods.

KI SOCIETY Organization founded by **Koichi Tohei** in 1971 to propagate the teaching of **ki.** Tohei, who studied under **aikido** founder **Morihei Ueshiba,** organized the federation without official sanction of the aikido headquarters in Japan.

KODOKAN Nonprofit educational institution whose functions are to train judoka, provide seminars for instructors, to conduct research in judo techniques, award **dan** promotions, send instructors to dojo in Japan and abroad, and promote judo as a sport. The world's first judo school, it was opened in Tokyo in 1882 by Dr. **Jigoro Kano** at the age of 23. In its first year, the Kodokan had only nine students. There were nine other kodokans before the present one was constructed. Today, its students number in the hundreds of thousands, and the 500-mat facility is considered the mecca of all judoka. Kodokan means "hall for teaching the way."

Headquarters of the All Japan Judo Federation, it is the largest single establishment for the practice and promotion of judo. Located in the Suibodashi area of Tokyo, the present Kodokan is a seven-story building completed in 1958 at a cost of more than $750,000. It has more than 60 rooms, including seven dojo. Its staff of coaches and administrators numbers well over 100. The main training hall has a capacity of 500 mats; three smaller dojos with over 100 mats and three with 54 mats. There are showers, changing rooms, weight room, and 20 dormitory rooms on the 6th and 7th floors. A library, basement dining room, administrative offices, and lounges occupy the remaining areas.

The Kodokan offers training to foreigners, women, children, beginners, and advanced students. Contests, called tsukinami-shiai, are held every month except January, May, and October. The All Japan Judo Championships, for 5th-degree black belts and above, is also held at the Kodokan. Co-sponsored with the All Japan Judo Federation, it is usually conducted close to May to commemorate the death of Dr. Kano.

The first Kodokan was located at the Eishojo temple and contained 12 mats. Dr. Kano moved the dojo to a 360 square foot area in Kaminibacho. In 1886 the dojo again moved, this time to Fujimicho, Kudansakwe, where it grew to 40 mats (720 square feet). In 1889, the dojo was relocated to Hongo Masago (70 mats, 1,260 square feet), and in 1894, to Shimo Fujisaka Koishikawa (270 mats, 3,500 square feet). In 1933 the dojo moved to a building in Suidobashi, which had more than 500 mats, and remained there until 1958. *See also* judo.

KODOKAN JOSHI-BU Women's section of the famed **Kodokan,** it was formally opened in November 1926 by its founder, Prof. **Jigoro Kano.**

KOREA ARCHERY ASSOCIATION Organized in 1922 by 35 charter members at Hwang Jak Jung, Seoul, this organization regulates all archery tournaments and demonstrations. It is headquartered in the Korean Amateur Sports Association Building.

KOREA KUM DO ASSOCIATION Organized on June 3, 1948, in Seoul, it affiliated with the Korean Amateur Sports Association on Nov. 20, 1953. Highest ranking members are Ho Ik-ryong, Suh Jung-hak, and Lee Jong-ku. Headquartered in the Korean Amateur Sports Association Building in Seoul, it regulates all rank promotions, tournaments and other **kum do** functions.

KOREAN JUDO ASSOCIATION (KJA) In Sept 1945, 40 organizing committee members of the KJA met at Seoul's YMCA, and in October the KJA was officially formed by president Lee Mum-suk, and vice-president Han Jin-hee. The Korean judo team has participated in the World Judo Championships since 1959, in Tokyo.

Rank promotion, referee certification, and technical administration are the main functions of the KJA. Its headquarters are in the Korean Amateur Sports Association Building in Seoul.

KOREAN YUDO COLLEGE Established in 1952 in Seoul by Dr. Je-Hwang Lee, a prominent educator and philosopher, the Korean Yudo College is a four-year college offering a major in physical education and specializing in the training of martial arts instructors, particularly in judo, tae kwon do, and **cireum.** Graduates have become top competitors and leading instructors in Korea and throughout the world.

KOREA TAEKWONDO ASSOCIATION The popularity of tae kwon do declined during the Korean War (1950-53), but revived with the closing of the war. On Sept. 14, 1961, the KTA held its inaugural meeting to unify all tae kwon do schools. On June 25, 1962, the KTA became an affiliate of the Korea Amateur Sports Association, and on Oct. 24, tae kwon do became an official event at the 43rd annual National Games of the Republic of Korea.

On Nov. 19, 1971, construction began on the **Kukkiwon** in Seoul. Tae kwon do was officially included in the physical education curriculum of Korea's primary schools on Feb. 14, 1973. From May 25-28 the 1st World Tae Kwon Do Championships was staged at the Kukkiwon under the auspices of the KTA. On Aug. 31, 1973, tae kwon do was accepted into the physical education curriculum of middle schools. On Dec. 5 the National High School and Middle School Taekwondo Federation was established, followed soon after by the National Collegiate Taekwondo Federation, on Dec. 28.

Un Yong Kim, president of the KTA, was elected concurrently the first vice-president of the Korea Amateur Sports Association and vice-president and honorary secretary general of the Korean Olympic Committee on Feb. 25, 1974.

The KTA oversees activities of the **WTF,** and has devoted itself to the propagation and development of tae kwon do throughout the world. (Ken Min)

KUKKIWON Located in Seoul, Korea, the Kukkiwon is the headquarters of the **WTF.** The million-dollar structure was inaugurated on Nov. 30, 1972. Besides serving as an arena for tae kwon do training and competition, the Kukkiwon conducts black belt promotion tests and issues certificates. The Kukkiwon was the site of the 1st and 2nd World Tae Kwon Do Championships, the 1st Asian Tae Kwon Do Championships, and other national Korean contests, as well as the 1st and 2nd International Referee Seminar, Instructor Referee's Seminars, and various tae kwon do demonstrations. (Ken Min)

NEW ENGLAND KARATE REFEREE'S ASSOCIATION In 1969 **George Pesare** of Rhode Island, Robert Cheezic of Connecticut, and **George Mattson** of Massachusetts formed the New England Karate Referee's Association (NEKRA). The first organization of its kind in the U.S., NEKRA trained referees and promoted safety regulations and clean facilities for karate competitors.

The association established in New England the first regional circuit of elemination competitions, culminating in the New England Tournament of Champions. A number of NEKRA members formed the Karate Referee Association of New England (KRANE) in 1975.

NORTH AMERICAN TAE KWON DO UNION (NATU) Formed in May 1977, at Berkeley, Calif., charter members were Canada, Mexico, and the U.S. Its annual championship is held on a rotating basis. Its president is **Ken Min,** and vice-presidents are Dong J. Yang and **David Moon.** NATU has produced annually since 1977 the North American Tae Kwon Do Championships.

OKINAWA ASSOCIATION FOR THE SPIRIT OF THE MARTIAL ARTS With Shoko Makaina, head of the Okinawa Prefecture Library, and Bakumonto Sueyoshi, managing editor of the *Okinawa Times,* **Gichin Funakoshi** established this organization around 1921 to further the unification of karate-do.

OKINAWA KARATE-JUTSU KENKYU KAI (Okinawan Karate Research Club) Organization established in 1926 by **Chojun Miyagi** to improve and unify karate in Okinawa.

PAN-AMERICAN TAE KWON DO UNION (PATU) Organized at the 3rd World Tae Kwon Do Championships, in Chicago, its charter member countries include: Argentina, Bolivia, Brazil, Canada, Colombia, Costa Rica, Ecuador, El Salvador, Guatemala, the Honduras, Mexico, Nicaragua, Paraguay, Puerto Rico, Dominican Republic, Surinam, Trinidad y Tobago, Uruguay, U.S., and Venezuela. Don Morrow is president, **Ken Min** secretary-general, and Dong J. Yang and **David Moon** the technical committee.

PERSATUAN PENTJAK-SILAT SELURAH INDONESIA Organization founded to synthesize a national style of **pentjak-silat.** Originally under the direction of Maj.-Gen. Kasasih, it is now under the technical guidance of Lt. Col. Soedarjanto. The movement has succeeded in integrating many of the **tji** systems. PPSI members are skilled in three special weapons: **kujungi, arbir,** and **paku.** *Further reading: Weapons and Fighting Arts of the Indonesian Archipelago,* Donn F. Draeger, 1972.

PHYSICIANS MARTIAL ARTS ASSOCIATION (PMAA) Association to further martial arts medicine as a specialty, bringing together physicians who are practicing both medicine and some form of martial arts and to furnish qualified doctors to serve as tournament physicians.

LEE, BRUCE, THE WORLD OF Museum dedicated to the memory of the late kung-fu superstar, **Bruce Lee.** Originally housed in Glendale, Calif., it moved in 1980 to Hollywood—at 1 Hong Kong Alley. The museum, founded and directed by Norman Borine, officially opened its doors on March 23rd.

Borine, who worked with Columbia Studios to promote the U.S. release of Lee's final film, *Game of Death,* has been recognized in the martial arts field as "the world's leading authority on Bruce Lee." Borine also owns a portable showcase of Bruce Lee memorabilia which he takes on the road for public exhibitions. The portable exhibition has been shown in England, Canada, and parts of the U.S.

The main gallery, more than 2,000 square feet, houses photographs recalling Lee's theatrical and martial arts career. Two glass cases contain personal artifacts belonging to Lee, donated by both his wife and his mother. Other rooms and corridors feature posters, motion pictures advertisements, and memorabilia. On weekends Lee's movies and television appearances are screened. Occasionally, the main gallery is used as a site for seminars and lectures conducted by distinguished martial artists.

PROFESSIONAL KARATE ASSOCIATION Conceived in Aug. 1974 by **Don** and **Judy Quine** and **Mike Anderson** in Los Angeles, the PKA is the original sanctioning body for the sport of **full-contact**

karate. Since then, the organization has developed standardized rules, training requirements, and safety regulations that have been used in the U.S., Canad, Mexico, and parts of Europe.

The objective of the PKA has been to establish professional full-contact karate as a major sport complete with recognizable champions, standardized rules, and television coverage for its events. When Mike Anderson resigned as an executive officer in 1975, the Quines founded Sport Karate, Inc., a separate corporation that, among its various activities, functions as a promoter of full-contact events.

In Dec. 1979 **John Corcoran,** who had worked as a consultant for the PKA's individual promotions until 1977 when he then became a full-time consultant, resigned. Shortly afterward, Atlanta's **Joe Corley,** who began working with the Quines in 1977, became a full partner. Today, Corley and the Quines oversee the organization from offices in Beverly Hills and Atlanta.

Eight regulatory committees, composed of some of the sport's most respected leaders, have been established by the PKA. The committees are responsible for administrating the improving rules, ratings, sanctions, and official certification. The PKA Players Association claims some 2,000 members, more than 1,000 of them professional fighters. Player's annual dues is $75.

Safety has always been a hallmark of PKA bouts. No fight is sanctioned without insurance policies for all fighters, a doctor and medical emergency equipment at ringside, and an ambulance waiting outside the arena. Since 1974, there have been no fatalities or crippling injuries. Only twice has a fighter in a PKA-sanctioned bout sustained an injury requiring overnight hospitalization.

Trans World International (TWI), a major sports agency, represents the PKA. Programming executive Barry frank has played the most instrumental role in getting the PKA—and the sport of full-contact karate—on television.

Like all new sports, full-contact karate got off to a slow start under the newly-formed organization. It had only one sanctioned event in 1974, the World Professional Karate Championships conceived and promoted in Los Angeles by Mike Anderson. It was the event at which Anderson created the sport. The PKA had thre sanctions in 1975; 19 in 1976, with two of its bouts aired on network TV and one 90-minute syndicated special; ten sanctions in 1977, with three network airings; 19 in 1976, with three network broadcasts; and more than 20 sanctions in 1979.

In late 1979, the PKA signed a pact with the Entertainment and Sports Programming Network (ESPN), a new 24-hour all-sports cable channel, marking a significant turning point for the PKA and the sport. By 1980, PKA bouts were appearing weekly on ESPN. In fact, PKA-sanctioned events in 1980 reportedly reached an all-time high of 250, with each card averaging seven fights. Some 42 bouts aired on ESPN that year, and a *Mediastat Report* that summer determined that PKA karate was the highest-rated show on ESPN, a full point ahead of football, with boxing in third place. It lost that exalted position, however, to basketball and boxing in the following years.

In 1981, the number of sanctioned events dropped 20 percent, to 200, stemming from 70 U.S. cities. ESPN aired 48 bouts, the USA Cable Network three, and "NBC SportsWorld" three. PKA bouts were broadcast in South America for the first time that year. In 1982, the number dropped again, to 196 sanctions in some 100 cities, with 32 matches televised. ESPN, by this time, claimed some 17.5 million subscribers.

In return for licensing fighters, sanctioning fights, and promoting the sport, the PKA negotiates television contracts and controls all TV rights to all taped fights. Further, the association maintains exclusive contracts with all its world champions and all challengers to PKA world titles, whereby fighters agree not to defend their title for any rival organization in a live or televised bout. Essentially, this arrangement gives the PKA total control over its athletes and kills free agentry by PKA fighters. Any world champion violating this contract is stripped of his world title. Both of these contractual arrangements will clearly make the PKA principals very wealthy as the sport continues to grow in popularity; yet, the largest purse offered to a PKA fighter to date was the reported $25,000 earned by Bill Wallace for his final title fight. The contracts have been the most controversial practice engendered by the PKA.

The PKA rulebook runs to 26 pages. All pro matches consist of between 5 and 12 (for world title fights) rounds. Rules call for a

Ross Scott *(left)* jabs Demetrius Edwards during PKA World Heavyweight title fight in Ottawa, Ontario, Canada. Scott suffered his first title-defense loss because of a seventh rough knockout. Courtesy of Jay T. Will

Bill Wallace who held the PKA middleweight title for six years until his retirement was the best known full-contact fighter in the U.S. He and Benny Urquidez were the only two superstars in full contact karate.

minimum of eight kicks per round, none below the waist. Three judges and one referee are used in each bout. The PKA weight divisions are as follows: bantamweight (118-124.9 pounds); super lightweight (125-132.9); lightweight (133-140.9); super welterweight (141-147.9); welterweight (148-155.9); super middleweight (156-163.9); middleweight (164-171.9); light heavyweight (172-183.9); and heavyweight (184 and above). Monthly ratings of PKA champions and contenders were created in 1978 and were subsequently published each month in *Official Karate Magazine*. It was the esoteric nature of these ratings and their curious compilation that in 1980 led to the creation of the **STAR System** independent full-contact ratings, a rival rating method created by **Paul Maslak** and John Corcoran.

The PKA Point Circuit of semi-professional (**semi-contact**) tournaments was created by Corcoran in 1978. It was composed of 12 regional U.S. events culminating in the PKA Nationals, promoted by **Francisco Conde** in Baltimore. In 1979, the PKA Nationals were conducted in Los Angeles. Each annual grand champion was awarded the rotational Joe Lewis Perpetual Cup. Bobby Tucker was its first recipient in 1978, and it was passed to **Keith Vitali** in 1979. Idle in 1981, the circuit was resumed in 1982, with the PKA Nationals promoted by **Glenn Keeney** in Anderson, Ind. and cable-TV coverage by ESPN. (JOHN CORCORAN) *See also* full-contact karate; STAR System; U.S., history of karate in. *Further reading: Fighting Stars*, Apr. 1983; *Karate Illustrated*, Yearbook, 1980, 1982; *Sports Illustrated*, May 2, 1977, Jan. 24, 1983.

SEISHIN-KAI KARATE UNION Organization founded in 1964 by **Richard P. Baillargeon** to organize all karate instructors, regardless of style, and supervise the awarding of certificates. The association has members from all styles of Japanese and Okinawan karate and is affiliated with the Seishin-kai in Japan.

SHOTO-KAI Organized in 1949 by **Shigeru Egami**, Genchin Hironishi, and Hiroshi Noguchi, students of **Gichin Funakoshi**, this organization was the forerunner of the Nippon Karate Kyokai **(Japan Karate Association)**. Shoto was Gichin Funakoshi's calligraphic penname. *See also* Shotokan.

SHOTOKAN KARATE INTERNATIONAL An organization formed in 1977 under the leadership of top Shotokan instructor **Hirokasu Kanazawa**, a former member of the Japan Karate Association. The SKI advocates the practice of karate as a budo form with the sportitive part of karate being downplayed.

SHOTOKAN KARATE OF AMERICA The SKA is an American based karate organization headed by **Tsutomu Oshima**, who founded the organization in 1957 to promote karate in the true spirit of budo. The organization has member clubs all over the U.S. as well as in a number of foreign countries, such as Canada, England, France, Israel, Mexico and Switzerland.

SHUNYOKAN Probably the oldest judo club in the U.S. Founded Mar. 17, 1909, in Hawaii, it was first located at the home of Naomatsu Kaneshigo, the school's first head instructor. By 1920 and 1921 two branches were established, one in Waianae and the other in Ewa. In 1920 **Jigoro Kano** demonstrated judo at Shunyokan. The club, located in Honolulu, continues to teach judo.

TRIAS INTERNATIONAL SOCIETY Group of competitors, champions, and instructors drawn exclusively from the membership of the **USKA**. The association is a successor to the Trias International Award, first conceived in 1946 as a school patch awarded to the most dedicated students of **Robert Trias**. Only brown or black belt students that had won state or national championships in judo or karate were considered for this honor.

In 1948, in conjunction with the founding of the USKA, all previous awards were rescinded. From that time on it became a national award presented only to outstanding USKA members; it was renamed the Trias International Society, in honor of its founder. The first member of the new association was inducted in 1961. Until 1973 all society members were selected by Trias, based on outstanding achievement, competitive spirit, knowledge, ability, and unselfish contributions to the art of karate.

In 1973 Trias appointed **Parker Shelton** of Indiana the first president of the society. Since then deserving inductees have earned the award by the majority vote of society members. All USKA black belt national champions are eligible for acceptance, subject to 50 percent of the majority vote of the membership. Others must be recommended by a member and are subject to an 80 percent majority approval. At times as many as five individuals have been eligible or recommended for admission.

The majority of the members are past national champions including two world full-contact champions, **Bill Wallace** and Ross Scott. Members include: Parker Shelton; **Phil Koeppel**; James Kennedy; James McLain; Roberta Jane Kelly (Trias' daughter); Mel Wise; **Algene Caraulia; John Pachivas**; Artis Simmons; **Jim Harrison**; Thomas Pisut; Victor Moore; Randy Webb; Robert Bowles; Gerald Giles; Tom Benich; Dirk Mosig; Richard Rogers; Jim Hawkes; **Janet Walgren Harrison**; Jan Garrett; Larry Davenport; **Glenn Keeney**; Pete Rabino; **Robert Yarnall**; Randall Holman; Kathy Sullivan Morrica; Mike Awad, and Dale Benson.

Members wear a patch to denote membership.

T'SING-WU One of the largest kung-fu training institutes outside the **Shao-lin Temple.** Founded by the famous Huo-Yuan-Chia, the T'sing-wu housed a wide variety of kung-fu styles including, to name must a few, My-Jong-Law Horn, northern Shao-lin, **praying mantis**, and **eagle claw Fan-Tzu.** Headquartered in Shang-Hai, the T'sing-wu, known in Cantonese as the Ching-mo, helped to spread kung-fu styles throughout China. *See also* T'sing-Wu-Hwei Erh-Lang-Men.

UNITED STATES JUDO FEDERATION The USJF is one of the two leading judo organizations in the country (the other is the U.S. Judo Federation). It was known as the Armed Forces Judo Association till 1969 and was a member of the USJF till it broke away that year to form an independent organization with its own leaders and grading procedures. The USJF is a member of the AAU and has many high ranking American born Judo men among its members.

U.S. KARATE ASSOCIATION GRAND NATIONAL CHAMPIONSHIPS A tournament conducted annually since 1963 (when it was known as the "World Karate Championships") by the **USKA** and its president, Robert Trias.

U.S. WADO-KAI KARATE—DO FEDERATION The governing organization in the U.S. which teaches the classical Japanese **wado-ryu** style of karate-do. Founded in May 1964 by **Yoshiaki Ajari**, the Wado-kai has spread widely throughout northern California, but not throughout the U.S. *See also* U.S., history of karate in; wado-ryu.

U.S. TAE KWON DO FEDERATION (USTF) Formed in Chicago, Ill. on July 20, 1974, it is the American branch of the **International Taekwon-do Federation.** Composed of five committees and four subcommittees, its purpose is to set supervise, maintain and improve the standards of tae kwon do, providing technical advice and recommending awards and promotions. The original officers are: Congressman Bob Mathias (the two-time Olympic decathlon champion), president; **Tae Hi Nam**, senior vice-president; **Dong Ja Yang**, secretary; John Mecholsky, treasurer; and regional vice-presidents Gerald Walston (East), Joon San Chung (Midwest), and **Chuck Sereff** (West). Committee chairman included: Mecholsky (finance); Larry McGill (public relatins); Moon Gul Baek (standards); Nick Boodris (national rank registration); Cha Kyo Han (examination and promotion); dong Ja Yang (tournament rules); Gerald Walston (legislative); Yang (collegiate); Greg Youstra (interscholastic); Young Il Kong (junior development); and Sue Kong (women's).

USSR KARATE FEDERATION Governing body of karate in the Soviet Union, also known as the Soviet Karate Federation. It was founded at a constituent assembly held in Moscow in late 1978 and attended by representatives from karate schools from almost 50 Soviet cities. A karate commission, set up earlier at the USSR Sports Committee, carried out preparatory work by establishing contact with the various schools and clubs, which then operated independently, and laid the foundation for the new federation.

The first order of business for the new federation was the organization of a national seminar for karate instructors, conducted at Moscow's largest karate school, the Frunzenets, headed by Alexei Shturmin. It then produced a set of uniform competition rules, ratings system and titles, and drafted a standard program for karate schools, clubs, and groups. The Soviet Union joined the European Karate Union in 1979. After staging a series of elimination trials, the 1st National Karate Tournament was conducted in Dec. 1979 in Tallinn. Promoted by the Central School of Karate of Moscow, it drew more than 100 competitors from various union republics of the USSR, as well as from Moscow and Leningrad. Victor Smekalin of Moscow won the 75-kilo division; Moscow's Kamil Musin took the 60-kilo title; Estonia's Ivar Neemre, Belorussia's Oleg Kirienko, and Ukraine's Stanislav Bliznyuk captured the remaining titles. *See also* Europe, history of karate in.

UNITED KINGDOM KARATE-DO WADO-KAI (UKKW) Founded on Jan. 1, 1968 in London by **Tatsuo Suzuki**, its chief instructor, the UKKW is the governing body for this style in the U.K. and is recognized by British Karate Control Commission. The aims of the UKKW are the fostering and development of **wado-ryu** along traditional lines; the promotion of area and national championships; and the training of a karate team to represent Great Britain in international wado-ryu competition.

U.S. KARATE ASSOCIATION (UKSA) Organized by **Robert Trias** in 1948. The first karate organization established in America, it is today one of the largest in the nation. Membership fluctuated between 13 and 20 affiliates for the first several years, but within ten years, nearly every martial arts pioneer in the U.S. had joined.

Originally open to practitioners of all martial systems, the USKA, under Trias' direction, gradually limited membership after 1960 to exponents of his eclectic shorei-goju-ryu style.

WONG WEN SUN CHINESE BENEVOLENT ASSOCIATION This association, located in Los Angeles, was the earliest known group of kung-fu students in the mainland U.S. Membership exceeded 50 by 1931; chief instructor was **Ark-Yuey Wong.**

WORLD KARATE ASSOCIATION One of the major sanctioning bodies for professional karate. Conceived in Oct. 1976 by **Howard Hanson** and **Arnold Urquidez,** the World Karate Association (WKA) is a non-profit organization governing professional and amateur full-contact karate, with major events promoted throughout the world. The WKA is the first non-profit governing body for the sport, the first governing body to use an independently controlled rating list, the first to establish a world championship division for women, and the first to include countries from the Orient. The WKA has sanctioned events in Japan, Hong Kong, Korea, Australia, Mexico, South America, Europe, Canada, as well as throughout the U.S.

The WKA uses the independent **STAR** system for ratings, and requires its world champions to defend their titles against the highest ranked world-class fighter available. Because most Oriental fighters refuse to compete in the professional karate ring without the use of thigh kicks, WKA rules permit roundhouse kicks to the outer thigh region above the knee and below the hip joint. Anti-joint techniques as well as knee and elbow strikes are strictly forbidden. The WKA seeks to elevate professional karate to a major international sport with recognizable stars and network television coverage of its events. To this end the WKA cooperates with the press, and requires that only top-caliber competition be shown to national media and television audiences.

On Mar. 12, 1977, at the Olympic Auditorium in Los Angeles, the first WKA sanctioned event featured **Benny Urquidez,** the WKA Super Lightweight World Champion, against Narong Noi, the kick-boxing champion of Thailand. On the undercard Earnest Hart, Jr., soon to become a **PKA** world champion, was knocked out by Nate Saknarong, the international kick-boxing champion of Thailand; and Lilly Rodriguez TKOed Carlotta Lee. A riot broke out in the audience during the fierce Urquidez-Noi bout, however, and the California State Athletic Commission declared the outcome to be a no-contest.

Later that same year, with the help of Ron Holmes, Hisashi Shima, and Antonio Inoki (who once faced Muhammad Ali in a mix-match), the WKA made several promotional inroads into Japan. On Aug. 2, 1977 Benny Urquidez defended his title with a 6th-round knockout over the number 1 Japanese kick-boxing contender, Katsuyuki Suzuki, before a sold-out crowd at the Budokan in Tokyo. The bout was broadcast live on prime-time Japanese national television, and set a record for the largest monetary gate in sport karate history ($300,000).

Then, on Nov. 14, 1977, the former judo and kick-boxing champion of Japan, Kunimatsu Okao, embarrassed by the defeat of his countryman at the hands and feet of an American, came out of retirement to challenge Urquidez for the WKA world title. Even with ringside seats at $200.00 apiece, the bout again sold out the Budokan, setting a new gate record in excess of $500,000. Again, the bout was broadcast live on prime time Japanese national television. Okao was KOed in the 4th round, two rounds earlier than Suzuki.

Benny Urquidez immediately became a Japanese folk hero, complete with *Benny "The Jet"* comic books distributed throughout Japan. He was recognized there, and in the homeland of karate, Okinawa, as the first world champion in professional karate. Other champions soon followed. Kunimasa Nagae defeated Tony Lopez in Tokyo for the WKA lightweight world championship.

Meanwhile, on May 2, 1979, Benny Urquidez returned to the U.S. to defend his title successfully against Rick Simerly at South Lake Tahoe. The event was telecast on *NBC Sportsworld.* Later that month, on May 26, **Steve Sheperd** defeated Chris Gallegos in West Palm Beach, Fla., for the WKA Middleweight World Championship. Then in Oct. 1979, Urquidez again defended his title in Tokyo against the kick-boxing champion of Japan, Yoshimitsu Tamashiro. The bout was carried live on prime time Japanese national television.

Soon afterwards, Hanson announced that women's professional karate activity warranted the creation of two women's world championship divisions. As with men's divisions, the women's divisions would be sanctioned and expanded to reflect the volume of activity. On Dec. 23, 1979, **Graciela Casillas** defeated Irene Garcia in Las Vegas for the WKA women's bantamweight world championship. Casillas, who simultaneously held the Women's World Boxing Association (WWBA) bantamweight title, was not only the first world champion in the history of the sport, but also the first professional athlete to hold a world title in both karate and boxing.

On Jan. 26, 1980, the WKA prepared for another network telecast, this time from the Tropicana Hotel in Las Vegas. **Howard Jackson** defeated Yoshimitsu Tamashiro for the WKA Welterweight World Championship. Benny Urquidez successfully defended his title against number 1 Japanese kick-boxing contender Shinobu Onuki. And WKA U.S. Champion Refugio Flores knocked out PKA world champion Vernon Mason. The Jackson and Urquidez bouts aired on NBC-TV opposite the Winter Olympics on ABC-TV. Despite the strong competition, the telecast reportedly received the highest audience rating of any professional karate event since 1974.

On July 15, 1980 WKA president Hanson replaced the WKA world rating list, which had been published monthly in *Official Karate Magazine* since mid-1979, with the independent STAR system full-contact karate ratings. At the time, the new rating system was the only rating that ranked professional fighters in accordance with their actual ring performances, independent of organizational affiliations.

On Oct. 13, 1980, Don Wilson knocked out U.S. Champion Andy White in Cocoa Beach, Fla., for the WKA Light Heavyweight World Championship. The Wilson championship set two precedents. First Don Wilson, being half Japanese, was the first world champion of Asian descent to win his title in the U.S. And second, Wilson was also the first kung-fu stylist to hold a world title in professional karate.

The year of 1981 saw the WKA bring Hong Kong into professional karate. On April 9, 1981, a WKA World Team, headed by champions Benny Urquidez, Don Wilson, Tony Morelli, and Graciela Casillas, traveled to Hong Kong to defend thier titles against its leading full-contact fighters. All of the WKA champions distinguished themselves with early-round knockouts over their challengers. Other team members were Dennis Crawford, Frank Holloway, Stewart Lauper, and Darlina Valdez.

At the time of this writing, the WKA had 52 television shows in syndication in Japan, Canada, Mexico, Brazil, Chile, Panama, Costa Rica, Venezuela, Australia, Taiwan, Korea, the Philippines, Europe, as well as throughout the U.S., very possibly producing the largest viewing audience for professional karate in the world. (PAUL MASLAK) *See also* U.S., history of karate in.

WORLD TAEKWON-DO FEDERATION (WTF) The first organizational assembly of the WTF was held at the **Kukkiwon** on May 26, 1973, with participation by 35 tae kwon do representatives from around the world. The WTF was officially established two days later, on May 28, and Un Yong Kim, president of hte Korea Taekwondo Association, was elevated to the WTF's presidency for a four-year term. Among the resolutions passed at the inaugural meeting were the holding of the World Tae Kwon Do Championships every two years, and investing Kim with authority to select and designate officials for the WTF.

On June 1, 1973, 29 executive members throughout the world were appointed by Kim, and two days later, the secretariat of the WTF was installed at the Kukkiwon. Goals set by the WTF include: introduction of a universal system of black belt promotions; establishing unified rules and regulations for tae kwon do competition; sponsoring referees and officials courses and instructors refresher courses. Major activities to date include:

May 15-18, 1974: The 1st Internaitonal Referee Seminar was held at the Kukkiwon; 46 referees form 11 countries participated.

October 18-20, 1974: The 1st Asian Tae Kwon Do Championships was held at the Kukkiwon, Seoul, with the participation of 10 countries. The event was promoted by the WTF and sponsored by the Korea Taekwondo Association.

Aug. 22-23, 1975: The 2nd International Tae Kwon Do Referee Seminar was held at the Kukkiwon; 218 applicants from 29 countries participated; 87 passed the qualification test for third-class international referee certificates.

Oct. 8, 1975: The WTF became an affiliate of the General Assembly of the International Sports Federation (GAISF) by unanimous vote at its annual meeting in Montreal, Canada, which president Kim attended as tae kwon do's official representative.

Apr. 9, 1976: Tae kwon do was adopted by the International Military Sports Council (CISM). The decision to introduce tae kwon do in the CISM event as the 23rd official sport was made by the CISM executive committee meeting held April 7-9.

May 19-20, 1976: The 3rd International Tae Kwon Do Referee Seminar was conducted in Barcelona, Spjain; 16 of the 57 participants passed the tests.

May 21, 1976: The European Taekwon-do Union was organized at the inaugural meeting held in Barcelona, Spain, with the participation of 12 European member federations from Spain, Belgium, Austria, Portugal, West Germany, Italy, France, the Netherlands, Turkey, Greece, Denmark, and England.

Aug. 5, 1976: The first issue of *World Taekwondo,* the official organ of the WTF, was published.

October 12-15, 1976: The 4th International Tae Kwon Do Referee Seminar was held in Melbourne, Australia, with participation by 21 referees.

Oct. 16-17, 1976: The 2nd Asian Tae Kwon Do Championships was hosted by the Australia Taekwondo Association in Melbourne. Particiapting were 10 national delegations including Australia, Indonesia, Singapore, Malaysia, the Philippines, New Zealand, Iran, Japan, Tahiti, and Korea.

Dec. 13, 1976: The 1st Middle East International Goodwill Championships were held in Cairo, Egypt; 40 contestants, representing Egypt, Jordan, Saudi Arabia, Senegal, West Germany, Morocco, Turkey, Ivory Coast, and Lebanon, took part in the tournament.

By 1976, the WTF reported a membership in 58 countries with a total of 1,005 affiliated instructors. The number of instructors in the five leading countries, excluding Korea, were 637 (U.S.), 62 (Canada), 46 (Germany), 38 (Spain), and 19 (China). (KEN [KYUNG HO] MIN)

WORLD UNION OF KARATE-DO ORGANIZATIONS Known as WUKO, this international body was founded in 1970 to unify amateur karate. Currently a large number of nations are members of WUKO; in the U.S. the Amateur Athletic Union (AAU) is karate's representative in WUKO. WUKO sponsors the World Karate Championships, which have been held in Japan, France, the U.S., and Spain.

ZEN NIHON JUKEN-DO REMMEI (All Japan Juken-do Federation) Organization established in Japan in 1956 to bring official recognition for the modern discipline of **juken-do** (bayonet way). Its first president was Gen. Hitoshi Imamura. Ichiro Hatta, its current president, directs the activities of nearly 300,000 juken-do proponents, who are chiefly members of the Japanese Self-Defense Force.

ZEN NIHON KYUDO REMMEI (All-Japan Kyudo Federation) Organization founded in Japan in 1948 to establish and regulate a form of **kyudo.** These concepts have become the national kyudo standard in Japan. The mdoern form of kyudo is characterized by a blend of spiritual and sport values, and is studied by more than four million Japanese citizens in training programs conducted in schools, industry, and private organizations throughout the country.

ZEN NIHON NAGINATA-DO REMMEI (All Japan Naginata-do Federation) Organization founded in Japan in 1953 with the express approval of the Ministry of Education to promote a national standard of **naginata** technique. Training conducted under the auspices of the federation is threefold: athletic, and competitive.

Members of the World Taekwon-do Federation organizing committee at the 1973 World Tae Kwon Do Championships in Seoul. Courtesy of D. W. Kang and *Traditional Taekwon-Do*

BIBILIOGRAPHY

ACUPUNCTURE

Chang, Stephen Thomas. THE COMPLETE BOOK OF ACUPUNCTURE. California: Celestial Arts, 1976. 244p.

Kim, Myung Chil. ACUPUNCTURE FOR SELF-DEFENSE. U.S.A.: Traditional Taekwon-Do, n.d. 96p.

Lawson-Wood, Denis. CHINESE SYSTEMS OF HEALING: AN INTRODUCTION TO ACUPUNCTURE. London: Health Science Press, 1951.

Manaka, Yoshio and Ian A. Urquhart. THE LAYMAN'S GUIDE TO ACUPUNCTURE. New York: John Weatherhill, 1972. 143p.

Mann, Feliz. ACUPUNCTURE: THE ANCIENT CHINESE ART OF HEALING AND HOW IT WORKS SCIENTIFICALLY. New York: Vintage Books, 1971. 234p.

Serizawa, Katsuske. TSUBO: VITAL POINTS FOR ORIENTAL THERAPY. Japan: Japan Publications, 1976. 256p.

AIKIDO

Baygents, Jeffrey I. AIKIDO: A SUPPLEMENT TO DOJO TRAINING. M. E. Publications, 1981, 150p.

Clapton, M. J. AIKIDO: AN INTRODUCTION TO TOMIKI-STYLE. Great Britain: Paul H. Crompton, 1975. 85p.

Makiyama, Thomas H. THE POWER OF AIKIDO. New York: Lancer Books, 1960. 190p.

———. THE TECHNIQUES OF AIKIDO. England: Herbert Jenkins, 1963. 96p.

St. Denice, Claude. THE POWER OF AIKIDO. New York: Lancer Books, 1965. 190p.

Saito, Morihiro. AIKIDO: ITS HEART AND APPEARANCE. Japan: Minato Research & Publishing Co., 1975. 128p.

———. TRADITIONAL AIKIDO, Vol. II: ADVANCED TECHNIQUES. Japan: Minato Research & Publishing Co., 1973. 179p.

———. TRADITIONAL AIKIDO, Vol. III: APPLIED TECHNIQUES. Japan: Minato Research & Publishing Co., 1973.139p.

———. TRADITIONAL AIKIDO, Vol. I: BASIC TECHNIQUES. Japan: Minato Research & Publishing Co., 1973. 134p.

———. TRADITIONAL AIKIDO, Vol. IV: VITAL TECHNIQUES. Japan: Minato Research & Publishing Co., 1973. 165p.

Shioda, Gozo (trans. Geoffrey Hamilton). DYNAMIC AIKIDO. New York: Kodansha, 1968. 160p.

Tegner, Bruce. AIKIDO AND JIU-JITSU HOLDS AND LOCKS. California: Thor Publishing, 1969. 125p.

———. AIKIDO SELF-DEFENSE: HOLDS AND LOCKS FOR MODERN USE. California: Thor Publishing, 1961. 125p.

———. BRUCE TEGNER'S COMPLETE BOOK OF AIKIDO AND HOLDS AND LOCKS. California: Thor Publishing, 1970. 253p.

Tohei, Koichi (ed. Morihei Ueshiba). AIKIDO: THE COORDINATION OF MIND AND BODY FOR SELF-DEFENSE. London: Souvenir Publishing, 1966. 174p.

——— (trans. Richard L. Gage). AIKIDO IN DAILY LIFE. Japan: Rikugei Publishing, 1966. 202p. Tokyo: Japan Publications, revised to KI IN DAILY LIFE, 1978.

———. THIS IS AIKIDO, WITH MIND AND BODY COORDINATED. Tokyo: Japan Publications, revised edition, 1975. 180p.

———. WHAT IS AIKIDO? Japan: Rikugei Publishing, 1962. 118p.

Tourda, Wayne F. BASIC AIKIDO. Custom Publishing, 1981. 77p.

Uyeshiba, Morihei. AIKIDO. New Jersey: Wehman, 1968.

Westbrook, Adele and Oscar Ratti. AIKIDO AND THE DYNAMIC SPHERE: AN ILLUSTRATED INTRODUCTION. Vermont: C. E. Tuttle, 1970. 375p.

Wilkinson, John A. W., J. Elkin, R. F. Webb, and R. C. Maddock. AIKIDO. J & A Publications, 1966. Unpaged.

Yamada, Senta and Alex MacIntosh. THE PRINCIPLES AND PRACTICE OF AIKIDO.

Yamada, Yoshimitsu. AIKIDO COMPLETE. New York: Lyle Stuart, 1969. 127p. Citadel Press, 1974. 128p.

BUDDHISM See ZEN

CINEMA
See also BRUCE LEE

Bock, Audie. JAPANESE FILM DIRECTORS. New York: Kodansha, 1978. 370p.

Campbell, Sid. FALCON CLAW: THE MOTION PICTURE. California: Diamond Publications, 1980. 115p.

Glaessner, Verina. KUNG-FU: CINEMA OF VENGEANCE. Great Britain: Bounty Books, 1974. 134p.

Mellen, Joan. VOICES FROM THE JAPANESE CINEMA. New York: Liveright, 1975, 295p.

———. THE WAVES AT GENJI'S DOOR. New York: Pantheon, 1976. 433p.

Mintz, Marilyn D. THE MARTIAL ARTS FILM. New York: A. S. Barnes, 1978. 243p.

Richards, Jeffrey. SWORDSMEN OF THE SCREEN. London: Rutledge & Kegan, 1977. 293p.

Richie, Donald. THE FILMS OF AKIRA KUROSAWA. Berkeley: University California Press, 2nd edition, 1970. 223p.

———. THE JAPANESE MOVIE. New York: Kodansha, 2nd edition, 1982. 212p.

Silver, Alain. THE SAMURAI FILM. New York: A. S. Barnes, 1977. 242p.

Svensson, Arne. SCREEN SERIES: JAPAN, AN ILLUSTRATED GUIDE. New York: A. S. Barnes, 1971. 189p.

Weverka, Robert. CIRCLE OF IRON. New York: Warner Books, 1979. 221p.

HAND-TO-HAND COMBAT/MILITARY & POLICE TACTICS & DEFENSE/UNARMED COMBAT

AMERICAN COMBAT JUDO. New York: Leisure Library, n.d. Unpaged.

Applegate, Rex. KILL OR GET KILLED: RIOT CONTROL TECHNIQUES, MANHANDLING AND CLOSE COMBAT, FOR POLICE AND THE MILITARY. Pennsylvania: Military Service Publishing, 1943. 175p. Colorado: Paladin Press, revised and enlarged, 1976. 421p.

Aziz, Harry. POLICE PROCEDURES AND DEFENSIVE TACTICS TRAINING MANUAL. Tokyo: Japan Publications, 1979. 240p.

Bartels, Scott R. and Royal J. West. POLICE KARATE U.S.A.: American Taekwon-Do Federation, 1975. 80p.

Ben-Asher, David. FIGHTING FIT: THE OFFICIAL ISREAL DEFENSE FORCE GUIDE TO PHYSICAL FITNESS AND SELF-DEFENSE. New York: Putnam, 1982. 320p.

Biddle, A. J. Drexel. DO OR DIE: A SUPPLEMENTARY MANUAL ON INDIVIDUAL COMBAT, SHOWING ADVANCED SCIENCE IN BAYONET, KNIFE, JIU-JITSU, SAVATE, AND BOXING FOR THOSE WHOSE DUTIES MAY LEAD THEM INTO A TIGHT SPOT. Washington, D.C.: The leatherneck Association, 1937, 1944. 108p. Colorado: Paladin Press, revised, 1975. 74p.

Billings, H. C. and H. B. Johnson. HAND TO HAND FIGHTING, THE USE OF BAYONET. Wisconsin: George Banta, 1918. 89p.

Cahn, Irvin. A DEFENSE MANUAL OF COMMANDO JIU-JITSU. Chicago: Wilcox & Follet, 1943. 162p.

Carlin, Robert J. COMBAT JUDO. Toledo: n.p., 1945. 64p.

Carpenter, George. STREET FIGHTING: AMERICA'S MARTIAL ART. Arizona: Desert Publicatons, 1979. 113p.

Chicago Police Department. POLICE GUIDE FOR OFFENSE AND DEFENSE. Chicago: Self-published, 1957. Unpaged.

Cogdill, J. C. VICTORY GUIDE. Detroit: Oranson Printing, 1942. 133p.

Cosneck, B. J. American Combat Judo. New York: Sentinel Book Publishers, 1944. 125p.

D'Eliscu, Francois. HAND TO HAND COMBAT. Washington, D.C.: U.S. Navy Dept., n.d. Unpaged.

———. HOW TO PREPARE FOR MILITARY FITNESS. New York: W. W. Norton, 1943. 216p.

Dempsey, Jack and F. G. Menke. HOW TO FIGHT TOUGH. New York: Hillman Periodicals, 1942. 127p.

Dept. of the Army. DEAL THE FIRST DEADLY BLOW. Arizona: Normount Technical Publications, 1963. 332p.

Diagram Group. ENJOYING COMBAT SPORTS. New York; Paddington Press, 1977. 159p.

Diaz-Cobo, Oscar. UNARMED AGAINST THE KNIFE. Colorado: Paladin Press, 1981. 88p.

Fairbairn, William E. ALL-IN FIGHTING. London: Faber and Faber, n.d. Unpaged.

———. GET TOUGH! HOW TO WIN IN HAND-TO-HAND FIGHTING AS TAUGHT TO THE BRITISH COMMANDOS AND THE U.S. ARMED FORCES. New York: D. Appleton-Century Co., 1942. Colorado: Paladin Press, 1974. 121p.

Feldenkrais, M. PRACTICAL UNARMED COMBAT. London: F. Warne & Co., 1942. 96p.

Fleischer, Nat S. COMMANDO STUFF. New York: Ring Publishing, 1942. 128p.

Futsiaka, Kato and Butch. POLICE JIU-JITSU AND VITAL HOLDS IN WRESTLING. New York: Padell Book Co., 1937, 1942. 93p.

Gillespie, Harold K. METHODS OF UNARMED OFFENSIVE AND DEFENSIVE TACTICS. Miami: n.p., 1943. 48p.

GREEN BERET COMBATIVES FOR SELF-DEFENSE. New York: Parallax Publishing, 1967. 63p.

Hanley, R. E. COMBAT CONDITIONING MANUAL: JIT-JITSU DEFENSE. Chicago: Gordy Publishing, 1943. 159p.

Harris, Malcolm. EFFECTIVE UNARMED COMBAT. New York: Arco Publishing, 1972.152p.

———. LETHAL UNARMED COMBAT: SECRETS OF SELF-DEFENSE. New York: Drake Publishers, 1972. 150p.

———. UNARMED CLOSE COMBAT: A MANUAL OF SELF-DEFENSE. London: Pelham, 1972. 151p.

Haupt, Lester E. and H. J. Adamson. COMMANDOS. Kansas City: Superior Printing, 1942. 99p.

Hibbard, Jack and Bryan A. Fried. WEAPONLESS DEFENSE: A LAW ENFORCEMENT GUIDE TO NON-VIOLENT CONTROL. Illinois: Charles Thomas, 1980. 184p.

Hipkiss, James. UNARMED COMBAT. London: F. W. Bridges, 1941. 78p.

Jorgensen, S. J. AMERICAN POLICE JIU-JITSU. Seattle: n.p., 1937. 109p.

———. COME ALONG HOLDS. Seattle: n.p., 1938. 24p.

———. OFFICIAL POLICE JIU-JITSU. Seattle: n.p., 1938. 33p.

Jowett, George F. THE MODERN COMMANDO SCIENCE OF GUERILLA SELF-DEFENSE. New York: n.p., 1943. 45p.

Kenny, H. E. ROUGH AND TUMBLE FIGHTING. Illinois: Stipes Publishing, 1942. 48p.

Koga, Robert K. and John G. Nelson. THE KOGA METHOD: POLICE WEAPONLESS CONTROL AND DEFENSE TECHNIQUES. California: Glencoe Press, 1968. 151p.

Leather, E. H. COMBAT WITHOUT WEAPONS. Aldershot: Gale & Polden, 1942, 3rd edition, 1950. 37p.

Linck, S. R. COMBAT JIU-JITSU FOR OFFENSE AND DEFENSE. Portland: Stevens-Ness Law Publishing, 1943. 126p.

McDonald, Hugh. SURVIVAL. New York: Ballantine Books, 1982. 192p.

McLaglen, S. L. POLICE JIU-JITSU. England: Police Review Publishing Co., 1922. 83p.

Mclaglan, Leopole. UNARMED ATTACK AND DEFENSE FOR COMMANDOS AND HOME GUARDS. London: Harrison & Sons, 1942. 64p.

Marriott, Arhtur E. HAND TO HAND FIGHTING: A SYSTEM OF PERSONAL DEFENSE FOR THE SOLDIER. New York: Macmillan Co., 1918. 80p.

Martin, Wayne, H. Nichols, and R. Berry. HAND TO HAND COMBAT. Hollywood: The Authors, 1944. Unpaged.

Mashiro, N. BLACK MEDICINE, THE DARK ART OF DEATH: THE VITAL POINTS OF THE HUMAN BODY IN CLOSE COMBAT. Colorado: Paladin Press, 1978. 92p.

———. BLACK MEDICINE III: LOW BLOWS. Colorado: Paladin Press, 1981. 140p.

———. BLACK MEDICINE II: WEAPONS AT HAND. Colorado: Paladin Press, 1980. 88p.

Moynahan, James M. POLICE JIU-JITSU. Illinois: C. C. Thomas, 1962. 120p.

O'Donnel, G. and M. Stevens. AN AMERICAN METHOD IN HAND TO HAND COMBAT. New York: The Authors, 1943. 82p.

Parsons, Kevin. TECHNIQUES OF VIGILANCE: A TEXTBOOK FOR POLICE SELF-DEFENSE. Vermont: C. E. Tuttle, 1980.

Paurice, Torindo. PISTOL & REVOLVER MANUAL & DEFENSE WITHOUT ARMS. Virginia: Virginia Fifth Naval District Headquarters, n.d. 36p.

Perrigard, G. E. ALL OUT HAND TO HAND FIGHTING. Montreal: The Author, 1943. 263p.

Ramsey, George E. MAN TO MAN COMBAT. Georgia: North Georgia College, 1944. Unpaged.

Roth, Jordon and Robert Downey. OFFICER SURVIVAL: ARREST AND CONTROL. California: Davis Publishing, 1976. 122p.

Schultz, Donald O. and Michael Slepecky. POLICE UNARMED DEFENSE TACTICS. Illinois: C. E. Thomas, 1973. 82p. Revised, 1981. 102p.

Shaw, T. M. SECRETS OF DEFENSE AND ATTACK PRACTICED BY GREATER NEW YORK POLICE. Chicago: The Author, 1922. 78p.

Steiner, Bradley J. MANUALS ON MAYHEM: AN ANNOTATED BIBLIOGRAPHY OF BOOKS ON COMBAT MARTIAL ARTS AND SELF-DEFENSE. U.S.A.: Loompanics, 1979.

———. THE TACTICAL SKILLS OF HAND-TO-HAND COMBAT (SELF-DEFENSE). U.S.A.: Cobra Publications, 1977. 43p.

Sylvain, Georges. DEFENSE AND CONTROL TACTICS. New Jersey: Prentice-Hall, 1971. 74p.

Tappan, Mel. SURVIVAL GUNS: A GUIDE TO THE SELECTION, MODIFICATION, AND USE OF FIREARMS AND RELATED DEVISES FOR DEFENSE, FOOD GATHERING, PREDATOR AND PEST CONTROL, UNDER CONDITIONS OF LONG TERM SURVIVAL. California: Janus Press, 1977. 458p.

Tegner, Bruce. DEFENSE TACTICS FOR LAW ENFORCEMENT, Vol. I: WEAPONLESS DEFENSE AND CONTROL. Calfornia: Thor Publishing, 1972. 128p. Revised and enlarged, 1978. 191p.

———. JUDO-KARATE FOR LAW OFFICERS: DEFENSE AND CONTROL, A SIMPLE METHOD. California: Thor Publishing, 1962. 125p.

———. HAND TO HAND COMBAT. Washington, D.C.: U.S. Printing Office, 1943. 228p.

U.S.A. War Office. UNARMED DEFENSE FOR THE AMERICAN SOLDIER. Washington, D.C.: U.S. Printing Office, 1942. 311p.

U.S. Library of Congress (Division of Bibliography). JUDO, JIU-JITSU AND HAND-TO-HAND FIGHTING. A list of references compiled by Helen D. Jones under the direction of Florence S. Hellman. Washington, D.C.: 1943. 18p.

U.S. Naval Institue. HAND TO HAND COMBAT. Annapolis: Self-published, 1943. 228p.

Vairamuttu, Robert A. SCIENTIFIC UNARMED COMBAT: THE ART OF DYNAMIC SELF-DEFENSE. London: W. Foulsham, 1954. 91p.

Wise, Arthur. THE ART AND HISTORY OF PERSONAL COMBAT. Connecticut; Arma Press, 1971. 256p.

Wood, Micky. UNARMED ACTION. London: Chatto & Windus, 1941. Practical Press, 1943. 63p.

HISTORY, CULTURE & TRADITION (General)

Allyn, John. THE 47 RONIN STORY. Vermont: C. E. Tuttle, 1970. 240p.

Bailey, Paul. CITY IN THE SUN. Westernlore Press, 1971. 222p.

Brinkley, Capt. F. JAPAN: ITS HISTORY, ARTS AND LITERATURE. New York: J. B. Millet Co., 1901.

Denning, Walter. JAPAN IN DAYS OF YORE (4 Vols.). London: East-West Publications, reprint of the 1887-88 edition, 1978. Unpaged.

Dillon, Richard H. THE HATCHET MEN: THE STORY OF THE TONG WARS IN SAN FRANCISCO'S CHINATOWN. New York: Ballantine Books, 1962. 270p.

Gardiner, E. Norman. ATHLETICS OF THE ANCIENT WORLD. England: Oxford University Press, 1930.

———. GREEK ATHLETIC SPORTS AND FESTIVALS. England: Oxford University Press, 1910.

Gardiner, K. J. H. THE EARLY HISTORY OF KOREA. Canberra: Australian University Press, 1969.

Glick, Carl and Hong Sheng-Hwa. SWORDS OD SILENCE: CHINESE SECRET SOCIETIES PAST AND PRESENT. New York, n.p., 1947.

Han, Woo-Keun (trans. Lee Kyung-shik). THE HISTORY OF KOREA. Honolulu: East/West Center Press, 1971.

Ilyon (trans. T. H. Ha and G. K. Mintz). SAMGUK YUSA (LE GENDS AND HISTORY OF THE THREE KINGDOMS OF KOREA). Korea: Yonsei University Press, 1972.

Ivan, Dan TOKYO UNDERCOVER. California: Ohara Publications, 1976. 112p.

Kerr, George H. OKINAWA: THE HISTORY OF AN ISLAND PEOPLE. Vermont: C. E. Tuttle, 1958. 542p.

Kidder, J. E. JAPAN BEFORE BUDDHISM. New York: Praeger, 1966.

THE KOREAN HANDBOOK. Seoul: Yungmoonsa Publishing, 1960.

Lee, Calvin. CHINATOWN, U.S.A. New York: n.p. 1965.

Rutt, R. (ed.) HISTORY OF THE KOREAN PEOPLE. Seoul: Taewon Publishers, 1972.

Sansom, Sir George. A HISTORY OF JAPAN (3 Vols.). California: Stanford University Press, 1958-63. London: Barrie & Jenkins, 1959-64.

Smith, Robert J. and Richard K. Beardsley (eds.). JAPANESE CULTURE: ITS DEVELOPMENT AND CHARACTERISTICS. New York: Wenner-Gren Foundation for Anthropological Research, 1962.

Soko, Yamaga (comp. by R. Tsunoda, et al). SOURCES OF JAPANESE TRADITION, Vol. I. New York: Columbia University Press, 1958.

Tsunoda, R. SOURCES OF JAPANESE TRADITION. New York: Columbia University Press, 1964.

Welty, Paul T. THE ASIANS: THEIR HERITAGE AND THEIR DESTINY. New York: J. B. Lippincott, 1966.

JEET KUNE DO See BRUCE LEE

JIU-JITSU see JUJUTSU

JUDO

Aida, Hikoichi (trans./ed. E. J. Harrison). JUDO. London: W. Foulsham, 1956. 282p.

Amateur Athletic Union of the U.S. OFFICIAL AAU JUDO RULES. Indiana: Self-published, 1974, 1978. Unpaged

Arima, Sumitomo. JUDO: JAPANESE PHYSICAL CULTURE. Tokyo: Mitsumura & Co., 1906, 1908. 137p.

Arpin, Louis. THE COMPLETE GUIDE TO JUDO. Quebec: Habitex Books, 1975. 264p.

Athletic Institute (consultants: Sadaki Nakabayashi, et al). HOW TO IMPROVE YOUR JUDO. Illinois: n.p., 1965. 96p.

Bachman, A1. INTRODUCTION TO JUDO. IN: ROCKY MARCIANO'S BOOK OF BOXING AND BODYBUILDING. U.S.A.: n.p., 1957. 14p.

Barnett, Peter M. BARNETT'S JUDO GROUNDPLAY TO WIN. Louisiana: U.S. Judo Association, 1974. 60p.

———. BARNETT'S JUDO TO WIN. Louisiana: U.S. Judo Association, 1973. 58p.

Bartlett, Eric G. BASIC JUDO. New York: Arco Publishing, 1974. 112p.

———. JUDO AND SELF-DEFENSE. New York: Arco Publishing, 1962. 199p.

Black, Ishi. THE KEY TO JUDO AND JIU-JITSU. Maryland: Ottenheimer Publishers, 1958. 95p.

Blanchard, Robert G. THE MECHANICS OF JUDO. Vermont: C. E. Tuttle, 1961. 134p.

Bowen, R. and H. M. Hodkinson. JUDO. London: William Collins Sons, 1963. 128p.

British Judo Association. KNOW THE GAME: JUDO. London: Educational Productions (published annually).

Bruce, Jeannette. JUDO: A GENTLE BEGINNING. New York: Harper & Row, 1975. 160p.

Budokwai, The. KATAME-NO-KATA: 36 DRAWINGS ILLUSTRATING GROUNDWORK. London: Self-published, taken from Japanese originals; Japanese and English text, n.d. Unpaged.

———. NAGE-NO-KATA: 48 DRAWINGS ILLUSTRATING 15 FORMAL THROWS. London: Self-published, taken from Japanese originals: Japanese and English text, n.d. Unpaged.

Butlet, Pat. JUDO COMPLETE. London: Faber and Faber, 1963, 1971. 240p.

———. POPULAR JUDO. Great Britain: Thorson's Publishers, 1958. 78p.

Campbell, Ben. CAHMPIONSHIP DRILL TRAINING, Vol. II. California: Zenbei, 1974. 128p.

Clark, Buddy and Craig Davis. ALONE, UNARMED, BUT SAFE! AN ILLUSTRATED GUIDE TO JUDO DEFENSE. New York: Exposition Press, 1981. 128p.

DEADLY JUDO, FIERCEST FIGHTING TECHNIQUE (3 Vols.). New York: Variety House, n.d. Unpaged.

Dominy, Eric N. THE ART OF JUDO. England: Stellar Press, 1949. 83p.

———. JUDO. London: English University Press, 1954. 192p.

———. JUDO: BASIC PRINCIPLES. New York: Sterling Publishing Co., 1958. 156p.

———. JUDO: CONTEST TECHNIQUES AND TACTICS. New York: Sterling Publishing Co., 1966. 181p.

———. JUDO FROM BEGINNER TO BLACK BELT. London: W. Foulsham, 1958. 157p.

———. JUDO SELF-TAUGHT. New York: Barnes & Noble, 1963. 200p.

———. JUDO: TECHNIQUES AND TACTICS (CONTEST JUDO). New York: Dover Publications, 1968, 1969. 181p.

———. JUDO THROWS AND COUNTERS. London: W. Foulsham, 1956. 111p.

———. TEACH YOURSELF JUDO. London: English University Press, 1954. 192p. New York: Emerson Books, 1962. 200p.

Draeger, Donn F. and Ken Tremayne. THE JOKE'S ON JUDO. Vermont: C. E. Tuttle, 1966. 72p.

————and Tadao Otaki. JUDO FORMAL TECHNIQUES: A COMPLETE GUIDE TO KODOKAN RANDORI NO KATA. Vermont: C. E. Tuttle, 1982.

————and Isao Inokuma. WEIGHT TRAINING FOR CHAMPIONSHIP JUDO. California: Kodansha, 1966. 280p.

Edwards, George A. and Alan R. Menzies. JUDO HANDBOOK. New York: Bell Publishing, 1964. 104p.

Ewen, Harry and Pat Butler. MODERN JUDO AND SELF-DEFENSE. New York: Emerson Books, 1957. 84p. London: Faber and Faber, revised edition, 1968. 84p.

Ewen, Harry. YOUR BOOK OF JUDO. London: Faber and Faber, 1959. 36p.

Farrar, Arthur H. AMERICAN JUDO. New York: Padell Book Co., 1943. 88p.

Feldenkrais, M. HIGHER JUDO: GROUNDWORK. London: F.Warne & Co., 1952. 224p.

————. JUDO: THE ART OF DEFENSE AND ATTACK. London: F.Warne & Co., 1944. 176p.

Fergg, William and Paul Zippel. JUDO FIRST FOR SELF-DEFENSE. New York: n.p., 1942. 96p.

Fromm, Alan and Nicolas Soames. JUDO: THE GENTLE WAY. Routledge & Kegen, 1982. 144p.

Fukuda, Keiko. BORN FOR THE MAT: A KODOKAN KATA TEXTBOOK FOR WOMEN. California: n.p., 1973. 139p.

Gardner, Ruth B. JUDO FOR THE GENTLE WOMAN. Vermont: C. E. Tuttle, 1971. 147p.

Geesink, Anton. GO-KYO: PRINCIPLES OF JUDO. New York: Arco Publishing, 1967. 96p.

————. JUDO PRINCIPLES: NE-WAZA. New York: Arco Publishing, 1967. 95p.

————. MY CHAMPIONSHIP JUDO. New York: Arco Publishing, 1966. 135p.

Gibson, Walter Brown. JUDO: ATTACK AND DEFENSE. New York: Vista House, 1961. 136p.

———— (aka Ishi Black). THE KEY TO JUDO AND JIUJITSU. New York: Key Publishing, 1958. 95p.

Girshov, Mark. ESSENTIAL JUDO. Leisure Press, 1982. 224p.

Glass, George. COMPETITIVE JUDO: THROWING TECHNIQUES AND WEIGHT CONTROL. London: Faber and Faber, 1977. 93p.

Gleeson, Geoffrey Robert. ALL ABOUT JUDO. England: EP Publishing, 1975. 143p. New York: Sterling Publishing Co., 1979.

————. ANATOMY OF JUDO: ANALYSIS OF JUDO SKILLS IN DYNAMIC SITUATIONS. London: Kaye and Ward, 1969. 176p. New York: A. S. Barnes, 1969. 176p.

————. BETTER JUDO. London: Kaye and Ward, 1972, 1981. 96p.

————. JUDO AS A SPORT. London: Kaye and Ward, 1971. 94p.

————. JUDO FOR THE WEST. New York: A. S. Barnes, 1967. 207p.

Goodbody, John. JUDO: HOW TO BECOME A CHAMPION. London: Mitchell Beazley, 1974. 127p. London: W. Luscombe, 1975.

Harrington, Anthony P. DEFEND YOURSELF WITH JUDO. London: S. Paul, 1957. 128p. New York: Emerson Books, 1960.

————. JUDO GUIDE TO BLACK BELT. London: S. Paul, 1970. 228p.

————. THE SCIENCE OF JUDO. New York: Emerson Books, 1963. 160p.

Harrison, E. J. JUDO. London: The Anglo-Japanese Society, 1930. Unpaged.

————. JUDO. London: W. & G. Foyle, 1950. New York: Dover Publications, 1950. 104p.

————. JUDO AT-A-GLANCE. Maryland: I & M Ottenheimer, 1954. 91p.

————. JUDO FOR BEGINNERS. London: W. Foulsham, 1954. 63p.

————. JUDO FOR WOMEN. London: W. Foulsham, 1957. 92p.

————. JUDO ON THE GROUND: THE ODA—9TH DAN—METHOD. London: W. Foulsham. 1954. 199p.

————. KODOKAN JUDO: HIKOICHI AIDA. London: W. Foulsham, 1956. 282p.

————. THE MANUAL OF JUDO. London: W. Foulsham, 1952. 172p.

————. MY METHOD OF JUDO: M. KAWAISHI. London: W. Foulsham, 1955. 246p.

————. THEORY AND PRACTICE OF JUDO. London: n.p., 1928. Unpaged.

Harvey, Maurice G. THE JUDO INSTRUCTOR. London: Nicholas Kaye, 1957. 120p. New York: Emerson Books, 1957. 121p. London: Kaye & Ward, 1973. 128p.

Hoare, S. R. and J. M. Goodger. FAMOUS JUDO THROWS II: OSO-TOGARI. London: Leonard Hill Books, 1968. 110p.

HOW TO IMPROVE YOUR JUDO. Illinois: The Athletic Institute, n.d., 93p.

ILLUSTRATED KODOKAN JUDO. New York: Kodansha, 1955. 293p.

Inokuma, Isao and Nobuyuki Sato. BEST JUDO. New York: Kodansha, 1979. 255p.

International Judo Federation. JUDO KODOKAN REVIEW (Vol. XII, No. 5). Washington, D.C.: Judo Kodokan Review, 1962.

Ishikawa, Takahiko and Donn F. Draeger. JUDO TRAINING METHODS: A SOURCEBOOK. Vermont: C. E. Tuttle, 1961. 324p.

Ito, Kazou. THIS IS JUDO. Japan: Tokyo News Service, 1964. 259p.

Jacks, Brian. JUDO. London: Pelham, 1976. 64p.

James, Stuart. THE COMPLETE BEGINNER'S GUIDE TO JUDO. New York: Doubleday, 1978. 115p.

JUDO AND THE TECHNIQUES OF SELF-DEFENSE. Belgium: Edward Gerard & Co., 1970. 157p.

JUDO INTERNATIONAL. Paris: Editions A.M.I., 1950. 400p. Text in English and French.

JUDO, JIU-JITSU, SELF-DEFENSE. U.S.A.: Universal Bodybuilding, 1973. 38p.

JUDO, 30 LESSONS IN MODERN JIU-JITSU. Chicago: Popular Mechanics Press, n.d. Unpaged.

Kawaishi, Mikonosuke (trans./ed. E. J. Harrison). THE COMPLETE SEVEN KATAS OF JUDO. London: W. Foulsham, 1957. 203p. New York: The Overlook Press, 1982. 208p.

———— (trans./ed. E. J. Harrison). MY METHOD OF JUDO. London: W. Foulsham, 1955. 246p.

———— (trans. Jean Gailhat). STANDING JUDO: THE COMBINATIONS AND COUNTERATTACKS. London: W. Foulsham, 1963. 136p.

Kano, Prof. Jigoro. JUDO (JIU-JITSU). Tokyo: Tourist Library, 1937. 70p.

Kawamura, Teizo (trans./ed. G. Hamilton). JUDO COMBINATION TECHNIQUES. London: W. Foulsham, 1960. 61p.

Kelly, Vince. FELL'S GUIDE TO JUDO FOR PROTECTION AND SELF-DEFENSE. New York: F. Fell, 1965. 122p.

Kerr, George. JUDO: BASIC TRAINING MANUAL FOR BEGINNERS. London: W. Foulsham, 1964. 64p.

Kim, Daeshik. JUDO. Iowa: W.C. Brown, 1969. 64p. Second edition, 1977. 86p.

Klinger-Klingerstorff, Hubert. JUDO AND JUDO-DO. London: Herbert Jenkins, 1953. 144p.

————. JUDO SELF-TAUGHT IN PICTURES. London: Herbert Jenkins, 1952, 1953. 160p.

Kobayashi, Kiyoshi. ILLUSTRATED JUDO, KYU & DAN. Tokyo: Obun-Intereurope, 1975. 144p.

Kobayashi, Kiyoshi and Harold E. Sharp. THE SPORT OF JUDO AS PRACTICED IN JAPAN. Tokyo: Pacific Stars and Stripes, 1955. Vermont: C. E. Tuttle, 1956. 104p.

Kodokan, The. ILLUSTRATED KODOKAN JUDO. Tokyo: Kodansha, 1955. 286p.

———. KODOKAN JUDO: A GUIDE TO PROFICIENCY. Japan: Kodansha, 1963. 150p.

———. WHAT IS JUDO? Tokyo: Self-published, 1947. 78p.

Koizumi, Gunji. EIGHT JUDO EXERCISES. London: The Budokwai, 1950. 40p.

———. JUDO: THE BASIC TECHNICAL PRINCIPLES AND EXERCISES. LONDON: W. Foulsham, 1958. 64p.

———. MY STUDY OF JUDO: THE PRINCIPLES AND THE TECHNICAL FUNDAMENTALS. New York: Cornerstone Library, 1960. 200p.

———. ON STARTING A DOJO. London: The Budokwai, 1950. 4p.

———. TWELVE JUDO THROWS AND TSUKURI. London: The Budokwai, 1948. 40p.

Kudo, Kazazu. DYNAMIC JUDO: GRAPPLING TECHNIQUES. Tokyo: Japan Publications, 1967. 224p.

———. DYNAMIC JUDO: THROWING TECHNIQUES. Tokyo: Japan Publications, 1966. 224p.

———. JUDO IN ACTION: GRAPPLING TECHNIQUES. New York: Japan Publications, 1967. 127p.

———. JUDO IN ACTION: THROWING TECHNIQUES. New York: Japan Publications, 1967. 128p.

Kurihara, Tamio and Howard Wilson. CHAMPIONSHIP JUDO: ORIGIN AND DEVELOPMENT, TECHNIQUES, TRAINING, SELF-DEFENSE. London: Arthur Barker, 1966. 120p.

Kuwashima, T. Shozo and Ashbel R. Welch. JUDO. FORTY-ONE LESSONS IN THE MODERN SCIENCE OF JIU-JITSU. New York: Printice-Hall, 1938. 146p.

Kuwashima, T. Shozo. JUDO, JIU-JITSU AND THE ART OF SELF-DEFENSE. Chicago: The Authors, 1922. 14p.

Lawson-Wood, Denis and Joyce Lawson-Wood. JUDO, REVIVIAL POINTS, ATHLETES' POINTS AND POSTURE. London: Health Science Press, 1960. 43p.

LeBell, Gene and L. C. Coughran. THE HANDBOOK OF JUDO: AN ILLUSTRATED STEP-BY-STEP GUIDE TO WINNING SPORT JUDO. New York: Cornerstone Library, 1962. 186p.

LeBell, Gene. JUDO AND SELF-DEFENSE FOR THE YOUNG ADULT. Vermont: C. E. Tuttle, 1971. 128p.

Leggett, Trevor P. and K. Watanabe. CHAMPIONSHIP JUDO. England: W. Foulsham, 1964.

Leggett, Trevor P. THE DEMONSTRATION OF THROWS (NAGE-NO-KATA). London: W. Foulsham, 1963. 70p.

Lowell, Frederick P. THE WAY TO BETTER JUDO. New York: Exposition Press, 1952. 248p.

Matsushita, Saburo and Warwick Stepto. CONTEST JUDO: TEN DECISIVE THROWS. London: W. Foulsham, 1961. 100p.

Maynard, Ken and Allan R. Menzies. ATTACKING JUDO: INTEGRATED MOVEMENT PATTERNS. London: Pelham, 1968. 135p.

———. JUDO FOR SCHOOLS. London: Pelham, 1970. 158p.

Mifune, Kyuzo (trans. K. Sugai). THE CANON OF JUDO: PRINCIPLE AND TECHNIQUE. Japan: Seibundo-Shinkosha Publishing, 1956. 245p.

Nakabayashi, Sadaki, Yoshihiro Uchida, and George Uchida. FUNDAMENTALS OF JUDO. New York: Ronald Press, 1964. 273p.

———. JUDO. New York: Sterling Publishing Co., 1965. 128p. Revised edition, 1968. 160p.

Nakanishi, Chikashi. THE KEY TO JUDO. London: Pelham, 1963. 99p.

Neff, Fred. MANUAL OF THROWS FOR SPORT JUDO AND SELF-DEFENSE. Minnesota: Lerner Publications, 1976. 59p.

Nishioka, Hayward and James R. West. THE JUDO TEXTBOOK, IN PRACTICAL APPLICATION. California: Ohara Publications, 1979. 192p.

Norwood, Jr., W. D. THE JUDOKA. NEW YORK: Knopf, 1973. 221p.

Ohashi, Takumi. A GUIDE TO JUDO GRAPPLING TECHNIQUES. Japan: Nihon Kogyo Shimbun, 1962. 125p.

———. A GUIDE TO JUDO THROWING TECHNIQUE, WITH ADDITIONAL PHYSIOLOGICAL EXPLANATIONS. Japan: Nihon Kogyo Shimbun, 1964. 108p.

Okano, Isao. VITAL JUDO: GRAPPLING TECHNIQUES. Tokyo: Japan Publications, 1982. 192p.

Pearson, F. W. THE BASIS OF JUDO. England: G. Bell & Sons, 1966. 116p.

———. JUDO COACHING MANUAL. England: W. Foulsham, 1966. 112p.

Pohl, Donald (ed.). OFFICIAL A.A.U.-U.S.J.F. JUDO HANDBOOK. U.S.A.: Amateur Athletic Union and U.S. Judo Federation, 1968. 352p.

Porter, Philip S. JUDO FROM THE BEGINNING, Vol. I: NATIONAL COACHING STANDARDS. California: Zenbei, 1974. 128p.

Pujol, Jean. SOUTH AFRICAN JUDO SYLLABUS. South Africa: Tafelberg-uitgewers, 1975. 135p.

Reay, Tony and Geoffrey Hobbs. THE ILLUSTRATED GUIDE TO JUDO. England: Van Nos Reinhold, 1979.

Rex. JUDO FIGHTING. New Jersey: n.p., n.d. Unpaged.

Robinson, Jack. COMPLETE COURSE OF JUDO IN THE BLACK BELT SYSTEM OF JUDO-KWAI. Johannesburg: The Author, 1932. 32p.

Ross, A. J. TEXTBOOK OF JUDO (JIU-JITSU). Brisbane: The Author, 1950. Unpaged.

Ross, R. F. and J. M. Goodger. FAMOUS JUDO THROWS: I, HARAIGOSHI England: Leonard Hill, 1969. 111p.

——— (ed. P. H. Hargreaves). HARAIGOSHI. London: L. Hill, 1969. 111p.

St. Denice, Claude. COMBAT JUDO MADE EASY. New York: Lancer Books, 1963. 174p.

Sathaye, Margot. JUDO FOR WOMEN. London: W. & G. Foyle, 1964. 92p.

Sato, Tetsuya and Isao Okano. VITAL JUDO. Tokyo: Japan Publications, 1973, 1982. 192p.

Shaffer, George. JUDO AND SELF-DEFENSE. U.S.A.: A-B-S, n.d. 36p.

Sharp, Paul W. NEW IMPROVED AMERICANIZED JUDO (2 Vols.). California: Improved Judo, 1949. 124p.

Smith, Don. JUDO FOR SPORT AND SELF-DEFENSE. New Jersey: Troll Associates, 1974. 32p.

Smith, Ken. JUDO DICTIONARY. London: Avis, 1968. 240p.

Smith, Robert W. A BIBLIOGRAPHY OF JUDO AND OTHER SELF-DEFENSE SYSTEMS INCLUDING COGNATE WORKS AND ARTICLES. Vermont: C. E.Tuttle, 1958. Unpaged.

———. A COMPELTE GUIDE TO JUDO: ITS STORY AND PRACTICE. Vermont: C. E. Tuttle, 1958. 249p.

Smith, Tat. JUDO MASTERY IN SELF-DEFENSE. Montreal: A. Weider, 1947. 25p.

Starbrook, Dave with Neil Wilson. JUDO, STARBROOK STYLE. London: MacDonald and Jane's, 1978. 128p.

Steers, W. E. A PERFECT MANHOOD OR JUDO OF THE KODOKAN. London: The Budokwai, 1918. Unpaged.

Stuart, James. THE COMPELTE BEGINNER'S GUIDE TO JUDO. New York: Doubleday, 1978. 115p.

Stewart, Paul SPORTS ILLUSTRATED JUDO. New York: J. B. Lippincott, 1976. 96p.

Sweeney, A. J. and B. C. Goodger. FAMOUS JUDO THROWS: 3 SEOINAGE. New York: Leonard Hill, 1969. 96p.

Takagaki, Shinzo and Harold E. Sharp. THE TECHNIQUES OF JUDO. Vermont: C. E. Tuttle, 1956. 143p.

Tegner, Bruce. BRUCE TEGNER'S COMPLETE BOOK OF JUDO (formerly COMPLETE BOOK OF JUDO). California: Thor Publishing, completely revised, 1975. 223p.

———. COMPLETE BOOK OF JUDO. California: Thor Publishing, 1967. 256p.

——— (ed. Alice McGrath). JUDO: BEGINNER TO BLACK BELT. California: Thor Publishing, 1982. 207p.

———. JUDO FOR FUN: SPORT TECHNIQUES. California: Thor Publishing, 1970. 125p.

———. JUDO FOR FUN: SPORT TECHNIQUES MADE EASY. California: Thor Publishing, 1961. 121p.

———. JUDO: SPORT TECHNIQUES FOR PHYSICAL FITNESS AND TOURNAMENT. California: Thor Publishing, 1976. 127p.

Thibault, Claude (trans./ed. Iain Morris). JAPANESE JUDO CHAMPIONS: THEIR METHODS AND TECHNIQUES. London: W. Foulsham, 1966. 96p.

Tomiki, Kenji (trans. Ko Masuda). JUDO. APPENDIX: AIKIDO. Tokyo: Japan Travel Bureau, 1956. 176p.

United States Judo Federation (eds. Toyosaburo Fujiwara, George S. Uchida, and George L. Wilson). JUDO FOR HIGH SCHOOL (A HANDBOOK FOR INSTRUCTORS AND STUDENTS). U.S.A.: Self-published, 1970. 133p.

——— (ed. John W. Hunter). OFFICIAL UNITED STATES JUDO FEDERATION JUDO HANDBOOK. Michigan: Self-published, 1974. 228p.

Watanabe, Jiichi and Lindy Avakian. THE SECRETS OF JUDO: A TEXT FOR INSTRUCTORS AND STUDENTS. Vermont: C. E. Tuttle, 1960. 186p.

Weider, Ben. JUDO AND JU-JITSU. Montreal: Your Physique Publishing, 1950. 41p.

White, David. JUDO: THE PRACTICAL WAY. London: Barrie and Jenkins, 1977. 91p.

Yerkow, Charles. CONTEST JUDO. Pennsylvania: The Stackpole Co., 1961. 193p.

———. JUDO KATAS: FUNDAMENTALS OF THROWING AND MAT TECHNIQUES. New York: Prentice-Hall, 1955. 163p. London: Herbert Jenkins, 1956. 143.

———. MODERN JUDO: THE COMPLETE JU-JUTSU LIBRARY. Pennsylvania: Military Service Publishing, 1942. 295p.

———. MODERN JUDO, Vol. II: ADVANCED TECHNIQUE. Pennsylvania: Military Service Publishing, 1954. 253p.

———. MODERN JUDO, Vol. III: FORTY GOKYO TECHNIQUES. Pennsylvania: Military Service Publishing, 1955. 164p.

———. OFFICIAL JUDO: THE AUTHENTIC GUIDE TO SPORT JUDO AND SELF-DEFENSE. New York: A. A. Wyn, 1953. 98p. New York: Hill & Wang, 1957. 98p.

———. SPORT JUDO. Pennsylvania: Stackpole & Heck, 1950. 162p.

Yokohama, Sakujiro and Eisuke Oshima. JUDO. Tokyo: Nishodo, 1915. 175p.

JUJUTSU (JIU-JITSU)

Allen, Edward L. AMERICAN JIU-JITSU. New York: Hall Publishing, 1943. 76p.

American School of Jiu-Jitsu. ORIGINAL AND EXCLUSIVE GRAPHIC COURSE ON JIU-JITSU. Los Angeles: Self-published, 1934. 74p.

Ashikaga, Kara. JIU-JITSU, THE JAPANESE METHOD OF ATTACK AND SELF-DEFENSE. Liverpool: n.p., n.d. 4. Vols. 218p.

Bankier, William. JIU-JITSU, WHAT IT REALLY IS. London: n.p., 1905. 176p.

Benson, C. E. EVERYDAY JIU-JUTSU. London: G. Routledge & Sons, 1920. 48p.

COMPLETE COURSE IN SUPER JIU JITSU FOR HOME STUDY. Chicago: Nelson-Hall Co., 76 lessons in 6 volumes, 1942. 180p.

Crewe, L. JIU-JUTSO—JUDO—ADVANCED JAPANESE WRESTLING. U.S.A.: Police Review Publishing, 1933. 19p.

Dennis, R. D. THE NEW JIU-JITSU. Texas: n.p., 1944. 75p.

DePasquale, Jr., Michael. JU-JITSU. New York: Messner, 1977. 141p.

———. MONARCH ILLUSTRATED GUIDE TO JUJITSU. New York: Monarch Press, 1977. 141p.

Drayton, E. JU-JITSU, THE JAPANESE PHYSICAL TRAINING AND SELF-DEFENSE. London: Huddersfield, 1905. Unpaged. London: Health & Strength, 1907.

Feldman, Frank. THE JAPANESE ART OF WRESTLING OR THE AMERICAN ART OF SELF-DEFENSE JIU-JITSU. New York: np., nd. 25p.

Garrud, W. H. THE COMPLETE JIUJITSUAN. New York: E. P. Dutton, 1914. London: Methuen & Co., eigth edition, 1953. 125p.

Grose, Douglas. JIU-JITSU TRAINING MANUAL. U.S.A.: American Jiu-Jitsu Association, 1977. 52p.

Hall, Nelson. A COMPLETE COURSE IN SUPER JUJITSU. U.S.A.: The Author, 1958. Unpaged.

Hancock, H. Irving and Katsukuma Higashi. THE COMPLETE KANO JIU-JITSU. New York: G. P. Putnam's Sons, 1905, 1926. 526p. New York: Dover Publications, revised edition, 1961. 500p.

Hancock, H. Irving. JIU-JITSU COMBAT TRICKS: JAPANESE FEATS OF ATTACK AND DEFENSE IN PERSONAL ENCOUNTER. New York: G. P. Putnam's Sons, 1904. 151p.

Harrison, Ernest John (E. J.). THE ART OF JU-JITSU. Philadelphia: David McKay Co., 1932. 91p.

Hunter, H. H. SUPER JU-JITSU. Montreal: n.p., 1926. Unpaged. Liverpool: n.p., 2 Vols., n.d. 132p. London: Marshall Simpkin, revised edition, 1928. Unpaged.

Hutton, Alfred. EXAMPLES OF JIU-JITSU FOR SCHOOLBOYS. London: n.p., n.d. 16p.

Jay, Prof. Wally. DYNAMIC JUJITSU. Canada: Masters Publications, 1981. 129p.

JIU-JITSU, JAPANESE FEATS OF ATTACK AND DEFENSE. Detroit: Johnson-Smith, 1935. 64p.

Judoka. JU-JITSU: SECRETS OF SELF-DEFENSE MADE EASY. London: Buchanan Books, 2nd edition, 1954. Unpaged.

King, I. C. HOW TO USE JIU-JITSU. Chicago: Beckley Ralston Co., 1944. 48p.

Kodokwan Jiu-Jitsu Association. KODOKWAN JIU-JITSU (3 Vols.). Cape Town: Self published, n.d. Unpaged.

Koyama, K. and A. Minami. JIU-JITSU. New York: American Sports Publishing, 1905, 1922. 78p.

Lanius, Len. AMERICAN JIU-JITSU, THE NEW ART OF SELF-DEFENSE. Ohio: The Author, 1922. 42p.

Leiderman, E. E. THE SCIENCE OF WRESTLING AND THE ART OF JIU-JITSU. New York: The Author, 1923, 3rd edition, 1925. 223p.

Longhurst, Percy. JIU-JITSU AND OTHER METHODS OF SELF-DEFENSE. London: Link House, 1939. 110p.

———. JU-JITSO AND JUDO. London: F. Warne, 1928. 64p. Colorado: Paladin Press, 1980. 64p.

Lowell, Frederick P. AMERICA FIT—WITH JIU-JITSU-JUDO. New York: Business Course, 1944. 248p.

———. JIU-JITSU. New York: The Ronald Press Co., 1942. 83p. New York: A. S. Barnes, 11th printing, 1947. 83p.

McLaglan, Leopold. JIU-JITSU, A MANUAL OF THE SCIENCE. London: Harrison & Sons, 1918.

McLaglen, S. L. CAPT. LEO McLAGLEN'S JIU-JITSU LESSONS. Sydney: n.p., 1939. Unapged.

Marshall Stillman Association. JIU-JITSU DEFENSES AGAINST VIOLENT ATTACKS. New York: Self-published, 1920. 46p.

Martell, Jules. JIU-JITSU SIMPLIFIED. New York: The Author, 1944. 32p.

Mombasa Jiu-Jitsu Association. CORRESPONDENCE COURSE IN JIU-JITSU. N.p., n.d. Unpaged.

Nakae, Kiyose and Charles Yeager. JIU-JITSU COMPLETE. New York: Lyle Stuart, 1958. 165p. Citadel Press, 1974. 178p.

Nakae, Kiyose. MODERN SCHOOL OF JIU-JITSU. New York: Charles Yeager, 1942 85p.

Neff, Fred. BASIC JUJITSU HANDBOOK. Minnesota: Lerner Publications, 1976. 59p.

O'Brien, John J. A COMPLETE COURSE OF JIU-JITSU. Chicago: Self-Preservation League, 1904. Boston: Physicians' Publishing, 1905. 118p.

Ogata, W. E. KIMON KUDO REVEALS THE SECRETS OF JIU-JITSU. Los Angeles: The Author, 1935. 32p.

Ohashi, M. SCIENTIFIC JIU-JITSU. New York: Richard K. Fox, 1904, 1912. 69p.

Panzen, B. JIU-JITSU MADE EASY. Montreal: Your Physique Publishing, 1944. 29p.

Poindexter, Luther H. SIMPLIFIED JIU-JITSU. Oklahoma, E. V. Watt, 1919. 5p.

Robinson, Jack. COMPLETE SUPER JIU-JITSU SELF-DEFENSE CORRESPONDENCE COURSE. Johannesburg: The Author, 1932. Unpaged.

Saito, K. JIU-JITSU TRICKS. New York: Richard K. Fox, 1905. 119p.

Sato, J. THE SECRET TEACHINGS OF SELF-DEFENSE: JUJUTSU OF THE YAMATO SCHOOL. California: Tasuke Hagio, 1952. 170p.

Skinner, Harry H. JIU-JITSU, THE JAPANESE METHOD OF ATTACK AND DEFENSE. New York: Japanese Publishing Co., 1904. 118p.

Smith, A. C. THE SECRETS OF JIU-JITSU (7 Vols.). Georgia: The Author, 1920. 240p.

Smith, G. Malcom. DYNAMIC JIU-JITSU. Montreal: The Author, 1942. 16p.

Stein, Max. JIU-JITSU, A SUPERIOR LEVERAGE FORCE: THE JAPANESE ART OF WRESTLING AND SELF-DEFENSE. Illinois: The Author, 1940. 130p.

Sutherland, W. Bruce. JU-JITSU SELF-DEFENSE. London: Thomas Nelson & Sons, 1916. 126p.

Tani, Yukio and Taro Miyake. THE GAME OF JU-JITSU. London: Hazell, Watson & Vinly, 1906. 86p.

Tegner, Bruce. BRUCE TEGNER'S COMPLETE BOOK OF JIU-JITSU. New York: Bantam Books, 1977. 191p.

Thornberry, Richard W. A GENERAL COURSE IN JIU-JITSU. California: The American School of Jiu-Jitsu, 1933. 59p.

Turner, T. JIU-JITSU AND OTHER METHODS OF SELF-DEFENSE SIMPLIFIED. Sydney: n.p., n.d. 72p.

Uyenishi, Sada Kazu. THE TEXT BOOK OF JU-JITSU AS PRACTICED IN JAPAN. London: Link House, 1905. 106p.

Watts, E. D. THE FINE ART OF JIU-JITSU. London: William Heinemann, 1906. 146p.

Yabe, Yae K. A COURSE OF INSTRUCTION IN JIU-JITSU. London: Clark, Dudley & Co., 5 volumes, 1904. 652p.

–––. JIU-JITSU. New York: n.p., 1904. 32p.

Yamanaka, K (ed.). JIU-JITSU. New Jersey: Kondo & Co. Ohio: Rikko Art Co., 1918. 212p.

KARATE

Adams, Brian C. THE MEDICAL IMPLICATIONS OF KARATE BLOWS. New York: A. S. Barnes, 1969. 128p.

Amateur Athletic Union of the United States. OFFICIAL AAU KARATE RULES. Indiana: Self-published, 1977–78. Unpaged.

Anderson, Dan. AMERICAN FREESTYLE KARATE. California: Unique Publications, 1981. 200p.

Anderson, John L. THE BASIC FORMS OF SHOTOKAN KARATE: THE HEIAN KATAS AND TEKKI SHODAN. London: Paul H. Crompton, 1974. 83p.

–––. BASSAI-DAI KATA (TO STORM THE FORTRESS). London: Paul H. Crompton, 1974. 34p.

Armstrong, Steve (Ed. John Corcoran). SEISAN KATA OF ISSHIN-RYU KARATE. California: Ohara Publications, 1973. 206p.

Arneil, Steve and Bryan Dowler. BETTER KARATE: THE KEY TO BETTER TECHNIQUE. London: Kaye & Ward, 1976. 96p.

–––. KARATE: A GUIDE TO UNARMED COMBAT. Toronto: Coles, 1975.

–––. MODERN KARATE. London: Kaye & Ward, 1974. Illinois: H. Regnery Co.,1975. 182p.

Bartlett, E. G. BASIC KARATE. London: Faber & Faber, 1980. 96p.

Bassett, Randall. ZEN KARATE. New York: Warner Books, 1975. 238p.

Bitanga, Donald S. KARATE: QUESTIONS AND ANSWERS. Maryland: Mars Publishing, 1970. 78p.

Boehm, David. THE COMPLETE BOOK OF (KARATE &) SELF-DEFENSE. New York: Doubleday, 1968. 542p. New York: Sterling Publishing Co., revised edition, 1974. 542p.

Burns, Donald J. AN INTRODUCTION TO KARATE FOR STUDENT AND TEACHER. Iowa: Kendall Hunt Publishing, 1977. 173p.

Carter, Dan. TALLAHASSEE SEVIN-ZUKU-KARATE-DOJO. n.p., n.d. Unpaged.

Chapnick, David. DEFEND YOURSELF! A COMPLETE KARATE MANUAL. New York: New American Library, 1980. 144p.

Cho, Sihak Henry. SELF-DEFENSE KARATE. New York: Stravon Educational Press, 1969. 64p.

Church, Jr. Albert C. KARATE AS THE BUSHIDO WAY. N.p., 1968. 90p.

Conley, Chuck. KING-FU-DO KARATE. U.S.A.: n.p., 1972. 197p.

Crompton, Paul H. KARATE TRAINING METHODS. Great Britain: Pelham Books, 1971. 124p.

Demura, Fumio. SHITO-RYU KARATE. California: Ohara Publications, 1971. 95p.

Dominy, Eric. TEACH YOURSELF KARATE. London: English Universities Press, 1967. New York: Emerson Books, 1967. 192p.

Egami, Shigeru. THE HEART OF KARATE-DO. New York: Kodansha, 1981. 127p.

–––. THE WAY OF KARATE: BEYOND TECHNIQUE. New York: Kodansha, 1976. 127p.

Enoeda, K. and J. Chisholm. KARATE: DEFENSE AND ATTACK. London: Paul H. Crompton, 1972. 91p.

Enoeda, K. and C. J. Mack. SHOTOKAN KARATE: FREE FIGHTING TECHNIQUES. London: Paul H. Crompton, 1974. 88p.

Funakoshi, Gichin (trans. Tsutomu Ohshima). KARATE-DO KYOHAN: THE MASTER TEXT. New York: Kodansha, 1973. 256p.

Funakoshi, Gichin. KARATE-DO; MY WAY OF LIFE. New York: Kodansha, 1975, 1981. 127p.

Gambordella, Ted. THE ONE HUNDRED DEADLIEST KARATE MOVES. Colorado: Paladin Press, 1981. 88p.

Garcia, Darnell. KARATE: EXPLOSIVE INSTINCTS AND MIND POWER. California: Koinonia Productions, 1978. 76p.

Goldstein, Gary and Alex Sternberg. FROM KATA TO COMPETITION: THE COMPLETE KARATE HANDBOOK. New York: Arco Publishing, 1982. 208p.

Golomb, Robert. KARATE FOR BEGINNERS. New York: Brown Book Co., 1974. 50p.

Haines, Bruce A. KARATE'S HISTORY AND TRADITIONS. Vermont: C. E. Tuttle, 1968. 192p.

–––. KARATE AND ITS DEVELOPMENT IN HAWAII TO 1959. Unpublished thesis, University of Hawaii, 1962.

Hamada, Hiroshi, SPIRIT OF KARATE-DO. Iowa: Kendall/Hunt Publishing, 1976–1976–77; 1982–96p.

Hara, Naraki and Russell Kozuki. KEMPO SELF-DEFENSE. New York: Sterling Publishing Co., 1968. 96p.

Harrington, A. P. DEFEND YOURSELF WITH KARATE. London: Stanley Paul, 1970. 190p.

Harrison, Ernest John (E. J.). THE MANUAL OF KARATE. New Jersey: Wehman Brothers, 1959. 139p. New York: Sterling Publishing Co., 1966. London: W. Foulsham, revised, 1974. 139p.

Hassell, Randall G. THE KARATE EXPERIENCE: A WAY OF LIFE. Vermont: C. E. Tuttle, 1980. 107p.

Hibbard, Jack. KARATE BREAKING TECHNIQUES: WITH PRACTICAL APPLICATIONS TO SELF-DEFENSE. Vermont: C. E. Tuttle, 1981.

Hisataka, Masayuki. SCIENTIFIC KARATE-DO: SPIRITUAL DEVELOPMENT OF INDIVIDUALITY IN MIND AND BODY. Tokyo: Japan Publications, 1976. 296p.

Ingber, Lester. KARATE KINEMATICS AND DYNAMICS. California: Unique Publications, 1981. 186p.

Jennings, Joseph. WINNING KARATE. Illinois: Contemporary Books, 1982. 224p.

Kanazawa, Hirokazu. BASIC KARATE KATAS. London: Paul H. Crompton, 1968. 84p.

——— and Nick Adamou. KANAZAWA'S KARATE. England: Sakura-Dragon Corp., 1981. 225p.

———. KANKU-DAI (SHOTOKAN KARATE KATAS, No. 1). London: Paul H. Crompton, 1969. 33p.

KARATE, BOOK 1 AND BOOK 2. U.S.A.: Universal Bodybuilding, 1973. 38p (both editions).

Kim, Daeshik and Tom W. Leland. KARATE. Iowa: W. C. Brown, 1978. 93p.

———. KARATE AND PERSONAL DEFENSE. Iowa: W. C. Brown, 1971–64p; 1978–96p.

Kim, Richard (ed. John Scura). THE WEAPONLESS WARRIORS: AN INFORMAL HISTORY OF OKINAWAN KARATE. California: Ohara Publications, 1974. 112p.

Kozuki, Russell. COMPETING IN KARATE. New York: Sterling Publishing Co., 1974. 112p.

———. THE KARATE ROAD TO POWER. New York: Sterling Publishing Co., 1969. 192p.

———. KARATE POWER: THE BASIC KATAS (Condensed from THE KARATE ROAD TO POWER). New York: Sterling Publishing Co., 1975. 144p.

Kresge, Ted. THE ENCYCLOPEDIA OF KARATE AND RELATED ARTS. Florida: Pelican Print, 1972. 1,055p.

Kubota, Shihan Tak. THE ART OF KARATE. New York: Peebles Press, 1977. 221p.

———. GOSOKU RYU KARATE: KUMITE 1. California: Unique Publications, 1980. 160p.

Lomack, Craig. HOW TO PROTECT YOURSELF WITH KARATE. New York: Simon & Schuster, 1966. 118p.

Long, Harold and Allen Wheeler. THE DYNAMICS OF ISSHINRYU KARATE. Tennessee: National Paperback Book Co., 1978. 153p.

——— (ed. Steve Condry). THE DYNAMICS OF ISSHINRYU KARATE: BLACK AND BROWN BELT, BOOK 3. Tennessee: National Paperback Book. Co., 1980. 146p.

———. THE DYNAMICS OF ISSHINRYU KARATE:: BLUE AND GREEN BELT, BOOK 2. Tennessee: National Paperback Book Co., 1979.

Lowe, Bobby, MAS OYAMA'S KARATE AS PRACTICED IN JAPAN. New York: Arco Publishing Co., 1964. 216p.

Maccarrone, Terry and Joyce Santa Maria. SHORIN-RYU KARATE U.S.A. MANUAL OF INSTRUCTION. New York: Hegashi, 1979. 36p.

Mac, C. J. KARATE TEST TECHNIQUES. England: Merrimack Book Service, 1971. 91p.

Marchini, Ronald L. THE ULTIMATE MARTIAL ART: RENBUKAI. California: ROMARC, 1981. 128p.

Mattson, George E. UECHIRYU KARATE-DO (CLASSICAL CHINESE OKINAWAN SELF-DEFENSE.). Massachusettes: Peabody Publishing Co., 1974. 492p.

———. THE WAY OF KARATE. Vermont: C. E. Tuttle, 1963. 199p.

Morris, Iain (ed.). BASIC KARATE. London: W. Foulsham, 1969. 96p.

Morris, PMV THE ILLUSTRATED GUIDE TO KARATE. London: Barrie and Jenkins, 1979. 176p.

Motobu, Choki. OKINAWAN KEMPO: KARATE-JUTSU ON KUMITE. Kansas: Ryukyu Imports, an unaltered reproduction of the 1927 original, 1977. 74p.

Nagamine, Shoshin. THE ESSENCE OF OKINAWAN KARATE-DO (SHORIN-RYU). Vermont: C. E. Tuttle, 1976. 278p.

Nakayama, Masatoshi, BEST KARATE, COMPREHENSIVE, Vol. 1. New York: Kodansha, 1977. 144p.

———. BEST KARATE, FUNDAMENTALS, Vol. 2. New York: Kodansha, 1978. 144p.

———. BEST KARATE, KATA: BASSAI AND KANKU, Vol. 6. New York: Kodansha, 1980.

———. BEST KARATE, KATA: GANKAKU, JION, Vol. 8. New York: Kodansha, 1981. 144p.

———. BEST KARATE, KATA: HEIAN AND TEKKI, Vol. 5. New York: Kodansha, 1979.

———. BEST KARATE, KATA: JUTTA, HANGETSU, EMPI, Vol. 7. New York: Kodansha, 1981. 144p.

———. BEST KARATE: KUMITE 1, Vol. 3. New York: Kodansha, 1978. 143p.

———. BEST KARATE: KUMITE 2, Vol. 4. New York: Kodansha, 1979.

———. (trans. Harman Kauz). DYNAMIC KARATE. California: Kodansha, 1966. 308p.

———. KARATE KATA: HEIAN 1, TEKKI 1. New York: Kodansha, 1970. 143p.

———. KARATE KATA: HEIAN 2, HEIAN 3. New York: Kodansha, 1970. 140p.

———. KARATE KATA: HEIAN 4. New York: Kodansha, 1968. 104p.

———. KARATE KATA: HEIAN 5. New York: Kodansha, 115p.

———. KARATE KATA: TEKKI 2, TEKKI 3. New York: Kodansha, 1970. 128p.

———. and Donn F. Draeger. PRACTICAL KARATE, BOOK 1, FUNDAMENTALS. Vermont: C. E. Tuttle, 1963. 112p.

———, ———. PRACTICAL KARATE, BOOK 2, AGAINST THE UNARMED ASSAILANT. Vermont: C. E. Tuttle, 1963. 120p.

———, ———. PRACTICAL KARATE, BOOK 3, AGAINST UNARMED ASSAILANTS. Vermont: C. E. Tuttle, 1964. 120p.

———, ———. PRACTICAL KARATE, BOOK 4, AGAINST ARMED ASSAILANTS. Vermont: C. E. Tuttle, 1964. 122p.

———, ——— PRACTICAL KARATE, BOOK 5, FOR WOMEN. Vermont: C. E. Tuttle, 1965. 118p.

———, ———. PRACTICAL KARATE, BOOK 6, IN SPECIAL SITUATIONS. Vermont: C. E. Tuttle, 1966. 132p.

Neff, Fred. BASIC KARATE HANDBOOK. Minnesota: Lerner Publications, 1976. 55p.

———. FOOT-FIGTHTING MANUAL FOR SELF-DEFENSE AND SPORT KARATE. Minnesota: Lerner Publications, 1977. 63p.

———. HAND-FIGHTING FOR SELF-DEFENSE AND SPORT KARATE. Minnesota: Lerner Publications, 1977. 63p.

———. KARATE IS FOR ME. Minnesota: Lerner Publications, 1980.

Nicol, C. W. MOVING ZEN: KARATE AS A WAY TO GENTLENESS. New York: Morrow, 1975. London: Bodley Head, 1975. 151p.

Nishiyama, Hidetaka and Richard C. Brown. KARATE: THE ART OF EMPTY HAND FIGHTING. Vermont: C. E. Tuttle, 1959. 251p.

Norris, Chuck (ed. Dick Tirschel). CHUCK NORRIS KARATE SYSTEM. Georgia: Fitness Media, (retitled from CHUCK NORRIS' BASIC KARATE FUNDAMENTALS, 1973. Unpaged.

Norris, Chuck (ed. John Corcoran). WINNING TOURNAMENT KARATE. California: Ohara Publications, 1975. 127p.

Okazaki, Teruyuki and Milorad Stricevic. THE TEXTBOOK OF MODERN KARATE. New York: Kodansha, n.d. 350p.

Oyama, Masutatsu. ADVANCED KARATE. Tokyo: Japan Publications, 1970. 156p.

———. THE KYOKUSHIN WAY. Tokyo: Japan Publications, 1979. 112p.

——— (trans. Tomoko Murakami and Jeffrey Cousminer). MAS OYAMA'S ESSENTIAL KARATE. New York: Sterling Publishing Co., 1978. 256p.

———. MASTERING KARATE. New York: Grosset & Dunlap, 1969.

———. THIS IS KARATE. Tokyo: Japan Publications, 1965. 368p. Revised, 1978. 368p.

——— (trans. Richard L. Gage). VITAL KARATE. Tokyo: Japan Publications, 1967. 128p.

———, (———). WHAT IS KARATE? Japan: Tokyo News Co., 1957. 98p. Third edition, 1958. 144p. Tokyo: Japan Publications, new edition, 1963–140p; 1966–176p.

Parker, Edmund. SECRETS OF CHINESE KARATE. New Jersey: Prentice-Hall, 1963. 239p. New York: T. Y. Crowell, 1968. 239p.

———. ED PARKER'S INFINITE INSIGHTS INTO KENPO. VOLUME 1: MENTAL STIMULATION. Los Angeles: Delsby Publications, 1982. 122p.

Patterson, Cecil T. AN INTRODUCTION TO WADO-RYU KARATE. California: Ohara Publications, 1974. 95p.

Persons, Michael. KENPO. California: Unique Publications, 1982. 180p.

Pfluger, Albrecht. KARATE: BASIC MANUAL. New York: Sterling Publishing Co., 1982. 160p.

——— (trans. Dale S. Cunningham and Paul Kuttner). KARATE: BASIC PRINCIPLES. New York: Sterling Publishing Co., 1967. 144p. New York: Barnes & Noble, 1970. 144p.

———. KARATE KIAI!! PERFECTING YOUR POWER. New York: Sterling Publishing Co., 1977. 160p.

Pitss, Gary. KARATE HUMAN DEVELOPMENT. U.S.A.: Morley House, n.d. 41p.

Plee, H. D. (trans./ed. Iain Morris). KARATE: BEGINNER TO BLACK BELT. London: W. Foulsham, 1967. 128p.

———. KARATE BY PICTURES: THE SCIENCE OF SELF-DEFENSE BY THE EMPTY HAND. London: W. Foulsham, 1962. 51p.

Reilly, Robin L. THE HISTORY OF AMERICAN KARATE. New Jersey: Semper Fi Co., 1970. 203p.

Rone, Moja. SUPER KARATE MADE EASY. New York: Lancer Books, 1960. 191p.

Roth, Jordon. BLACK BELT KARATE. Vermont: C. E. Tuttle, 1974. 379p.

Russell, W. Scott. KARATE: THE ENERGY CONNECTION. New York: Dealcourt Press, 1976. 216p.

Sampayo, Carlos (trans. Alice L. Hobson). KARATE: WITHIN YOUR GRASP. New York: Sterling Publishing Co., 1976. 128p.

Schroeder, Charles Roy and Bill Wallace. KARATE: BASIC CONCEPTS AND SKILLS, Massachusetts: Addison-Wesley Publishing Co., 1976. 162p.

Siegel, Hank. KARATE TECHNIQUES, ADVANCED SUPER JUDO; THE ORIENTAL ART OF FOOT AND HAND DEFENSE. N.p., 1960? 97p.

Smith, Don. KARATE FOR SPORT AND SELF-DEFENSE. New Jersey: Troll Associates, 1974. 32p.

Smith, John BASIC KARATE KATAS, Vol. 2, PINAN 1, 2, 3, 4, 5. London: Paul H. Crompton, 1973. 50p.

Stratford Karate-Kai. KARATE MADE EASY. England: Health & Leisure, 1974. 122p.

Sugano, Jun. BASIC KARATE FOR WOMEN: HEALTH AND SELF-DEFENSE. New York: Trans-Pacific Publishers, 1976. 119p.

———. KARATE AND SELF-DEFENSE FOR WOMEN. London: Ward Lock, 1976. 119p.

Suzuki, Tatsuo. KARATE-DO. London: Pelham Books, 1967. Second edition, 1975. 160p.

Tabata, Kazumi. POWER KARATE TECHNIQUES FOR COLLEGES. Bermuda: Bermuda Press, 1974. 110p.

Tegner, Bruce. BRUCE TEGNER'S COMPLETE BOOK OF KARATE. New York: Bantam Books, 1966. 224p. California: Thor Publishing, 1967–256p; 1970–254p.

——— (ed. Alice McGrath). KARATE: BEGINNER TO BLACK BELT. California: Thor Publishing, 1982 224p.

———. KARATE: THE OPEN HAND AND FOOT FIGHTING, Vol. 1, SELF-DEFENSE. California: Thor Publishing, 1959. 104p.

———. KARATE: THE OPEN HAND AND FOOT FIGHTING, Vol. 2, TRADITIONAL FORMS FOR SPORT. California: Thor Publishing, 1961. 119p.

———. KARATE: SELF-DEFENSE AND TRADITIONAL SPORT FORMS. California: Thor Publishing, 1973. 160p.

Toguchi, Seikichi (comp. Toshio Tamano). OKINAWAN GOJU-RYU: THE FUNDAMENTALS OF SHOREI-KAN KARATE. California: Ohara Publications, 1976. 191p.

Trias, Robert A. THE HAND IS MY SWORD: A KARATE HANDBOOK. Vermont: C. E. Tuttle, 1973. 182p.

———. THE PINNACLE OF KARATE: METHODS AND PHILOSOPHY OF OKINAWAN SHURI-RYU. Phoenix: The Author, 1975. 367p.

Tulleners, Tonny (ed. John Corcoran). BEGINNING KARATE. California: Ohara Publications, 1974. 191p.

Urban, Peter. THE KARATE DOJO: TRADITIONS AND TALES OF A MARTIAL ART. Vermont: C. E. Tuttle, 1967. 145p.

Urquidez, Benny with Emil Farkas and Stuart Sobel. TRAINING AND FIGHTING SKILLS. California: Unique Publications, 1981. 222p.

Valera, Dominique. KARATE COMPETITION. London: Paul H. Crompton, 1973. 44p.

Ventresca, Peter. SHOTO-KAN KARATE: THE ULTIMATE IN SELF-DEFENSE. Vermont: C. E. Tuttle, 1970. 158p.

Williams, Bryn. KNOW KARATE-DO. New York: Berkley Publishing Corp., 1977. 203p.

Will, Jay T. ADVANCED KENPO KARATE. California: Unique Publications, 1980. 115p.

——— (ed. Tom Sulak). KENPO KARATE FOR SELF-DEFENSE. California: Ohara Publications, 1977. 157p.

Wong, Tim Yuen and K. H. Lee CHINESE KARATE KUNG-FU. California: n.p., 1961. 192p.

Yamaguchi, Gogen (trans. Gosei Yamaguchi). KARATE: GOJU-RYU BY THE CAT. Tokyo: International Karate-Do Goju-kai, n.d. 287p.

Yamaguchi, Gosei. THE FUNDAMENTALS OF GOJU-RYU KARATE. California: Ohara Publications, 1972. 175p.

———. GOJU-RYU KARATE II. California: Ohara Publications, 1974. 255p.

Yamashita, Tadashi. SHORIN-RYU KARATE: JAPANESE ART OF SELF-DEFENSE. California: Ohara Publications, 1976. 128p.

KENDO/KENJUTSU

SEE ALSO SWORDS

All Japan Kendo Federation. FUNDAMENTAL KENDO. Tokyo: Japan Publications, 1973. 179p.

Kammer, Reinhard (trans. Betty J. Fitzgerald). ZEN AND CONFUCIUS IN THE ART OF SWORDSMANSHIP: THE TENGUGEI-JUTSU-RON OF CHOZAN SHISSAI. London: Routledge & K. Paul, 1978. 118p.

Lidstone, R. A. AN INTRODUCTION TO KENDO. London: Judo Limited, 1964. 140p.

Lovret, Frederick J. KENJUTSU SHODEN. California: Bookmaker Publications, 1977. 160p.

Sasamori, Junzo and Gordon Warner. THIS IS KENDO: THE ART OF JAPANESE FENCING. Vermont: C. E. Tuttle, 1964. 159p.

KI

Barclay, Glen. MIND OVER MATTER: BEYOND THE BOUNDS OF KARATE. London: Barker, 1973. 142p.

Barnes, Steve (ed. David Goodman). KI: HOW TO GENERATE THE DRAGON SPIRIT. California: Sensei's Dojo Supply, 1976. 51p.

Tohei, Koichi. BOOK OF KI: CO-ORDINATING MIND AND BODY IN DAILY LIFE. Tokyo: Japan Publications, 1976. 102p.

———. KI IN DAILY LIFE. Japan: Ki No Kenkyukai, 1978. 136p.

KUNG-FU
See also T'AI-CHI-CH'UAN

Berk, William R. CHINESE HEALING ARTS: INTERNAL KUNG-FU. California: Peace Press, 1979. 209p.

Chao, K. T. and J. E. Weakland. SECRET TECHNIQUES OF WING CHUN KUNG-FU. London: Paul H. Crompton, 1976. 111p.

Chema, Sifu P. A. SHAOLIN KUNG FU. New York: Chemson Corp., 1974. 32p

Cheng, Joseph. CHONG WOO KWAN WING CHUN. London: Paul H. Crompton, 1977. 171p.

Chin, David and Michael P. Staples. HOP GAR KUNG-FU. California: Unique Publications, 1976. 94p.

CHINESE KUNG FU. U.S.A.: Informative Publications, 1963. 59p.

Chow, David and Richard Spangler. KUNG FU: HISTORY, PHILOSOPHY, AND TECHNIQUE. New York: Doubleday, 1977. 228p. California: Unique Publications, 1980. 220p.

Chua, Jose P. BOK PAI KUNG FU: NORTHERN LONG HAND FORM. California: Koinonia Productions, 1975. 84p.

———. THE EAGLE CLAW OF CHOI LAY FUT. California: Koinonia Productions, n.d. Unpaged.

———. GO CHU KUEN KUNG FU: THE FIVE FIST STYLE OF CHINESE BOXING. California: Koinonia Productions, 1976. 119p.

———. THE LOCKING HAND OF PRAYING MANTIS. California: Koinonia Productions, n.d. Unpaged.

Clausnitzer, R. WING CHUN KUNG FU. London: Paul H. Crompton, 1969. 80p.

CLAWS: TIGER CLAW SYSTEM OF SELF-DEFENSE. Great Britain: Fu-Jow-Pai, 1975. Unpaged.

Crompton, Paul H. KUNG-FU THEORY AND PRACTICE. London: Pelham Books, 1975. 72p.

Dennis, Felix and Paul Simmons. THE BEGINNER'S GUIDE TO KUNG-FU. New York: Pinnacle Books, 1974. Unpaged.

Fong, Leo T. (ed. Pat Alston). CHOY LAY FUT KUNG-FU: CHINESE ART OF SELF-DEFENSE. California: Ohara Publications, 1972. 191p.

———. COMBAT KUNG-FU: STREETFIGHTING ART. California: Koinonia Productions, n.d. Unpaged.

———. IRON PALF OPEN-HAND FIGHTING. California: Koinonia Productions, n.d. Unpaged.

———. KUNG-FU FREE FIGHTING TECHNIQUE. California: Koinonia Productions, n.d. Unpaged.

———. MODIFIED WING CHUN: Vol. 1, BASIC TECHNIQUES. California: Koinonia Productions, n.d. Unpaged.

———. MODIFIED WING CHUN: Vol. 3, STICKING TECHNIQUES. California: Koinonia Productions, n.d. Unpaged.

———. MODIFIED WING CHUN, Vol. 2, TRAPPING HANDS. California: Koinonia Productions, n.d. Unpaged.

——— (ed. Pat Alston). SIL LUM KUNG-FU: THE CHINESE ART OF SELF-DEFENSE. California: Ohara Publications, 1971. 159p.

———. TIGER CLAW TRAINING AND TECHNIQUES. California: Koinonia Productions, 1976. 53p.

———. WEI KUEN DO: THE PSYCHO-DYNAMIC ART OF FREE FIGHTING. California: Koinonia Productions, 1976. 218.

Harrington, A. P. DEFEND YOURSELF WITH KUNG-FU: A PRACTICAL GUIDE. London: Paul, 1975. 164p. New York: Emerson Books, 1975. 159p.

Hsu, Dr. Hong-Yen and Dr. William G. Peacher. CHINESE HERB MEDICINE AND THERAPY. California: Oriental Healing Arts Institute, 1976.

Jakab, Lajos. A PRACTICAL INTRODUCTION TO KUNG-FU. London: Paul H. Crompton, 1974. 56p.

Jwing-Ming, Yang. SHAOLIN CHIN NA: THE SEIZING ART OF KUNG-FU. California: Unique Publications, 1980. 159p.

———. SHAOLIN LONG FIST. California: Unique Publications, 1981. 250p.

Kenn, Charles W. A BRIEF HISTORY OF GUNG-FU. U.S.A.: n.p., 1963. 5p.

Khim, P'Ng C. and Donn F. Draeger. SHAOLIN: AN INTRODUCTION TO LOHAN FIGHTING TECHNIQUES. Vermont: C. E. Tuttle, 1979.

Kiong, Tjoa Khek, Donn F. Draeger, and Quintin T. G. Chambers. SHAUNTUNG BLACK TIGER: A SHAOLIN FIGHTING ART OF NORTH CHINA. New York: Weatherhill, 1976. 149p.

Kong, Bucksam and James Hughes. SIU LUM GUNG-FU, SERIES 1. Hong Kong: O. L. Printing, n.d. Unpaged.

——— and Eugene H. Ho (ed. John Scura). HUNG GAR KUNG-FU: CHINESE ART OF SELF-DEFENSE. California: Ohara Publications, 1973. 224p.

Kozuki, Russell and Douglas Lee. KUNG-FU FOR YOUNG PEOPLE: THE VING TSUN SYSTEM. New York: Sterling Publishing Co., 1975, 1982. 128p.

KUNG-FU. Kung-Fu International, 1973. 70p.

Lee, Alan. KUNG-FU WU-SU. New York: Lancer Books, 1972. 141p.

Lee, James Yimm. MODERN KUNG-FU KARATE, BOOK 1, PART A. U.S.A.: n.p., 1963. 116p.

———. WING CHUN KUNG-FU: CHINESE ART OF SELF-DEFENSE. California: Ohara Publications, 1972. 223p.

Lee, Ying-arng. THE SECRET ARTS OF CHINESE LEG MANEUVERS IN PICTURES. Hong Kong: Sin Poh Amalgamated, 1972. 114p.

Lee, Ying-arng. PA-KUA CHANG FOR DEFENSE. Hong Kong: Unicorn Press, 1972. 85p

Lee, Yung C. THEORY AND SCIENCE OF KUNG-FU: (SERIES 1) TWENTY AND TWENTY METHODS OF STRAIGHT LINE MOTIONS. California: Li Yung Co., 1975. 219p.

Lee, Ying-arng. IRON PALM IN 100 DAYS. n.p., n.d. 69p.

Leong, Cheong Cheng and Donn F. Draeger. PHOENIX-EYE FIST: A SHAOLIN FIGHTING ART OF SOUTH CHINA. New York: Weatherhill, 1977. 170p.

Leung, Ting. FIVE PATTERN HUNG KUEN, Vol. 1. Hong Kong: The Author, 1982. 146p.

———. FIVE PATTERN HUNG KUEN, Vol. 2. Hong Kong: The Author, 1982.

———. WING TSUN KUEN. Hong Kong: The Author, 1979. 323p.

Lin, Willy. CHIN-NA: THE GRAPPLING ART OF SELF-DEFENSE. California: Ohara Publications, 1981.

———. T'IEN SHAN P'AI KUNG -FU. California: Ohara Publications, 1976. 160p.

Marks, Tom (ed.). CHINESE CHING KUNG FOR PHYSICAL AND MENTAL HEALTH. Taiwan: Martial Arts, Inc., 1975. 39p.

Mart, Harry. KUNG BIBLE. New York: Todd & Honeywell, 1979.

Medeiros, Earl C. THE HISTORY AND PHILOSOPHY OF KUNG-FU. Vermont: C. E. Tuttle, 1974. 118p.

Meng, Choo. SHAOLIN KUNG-FU: THE CHINESE ART OF SELF-DEFENSE. Malaysia: Leong Fu, 1972. 408p.

Minick, Michael. THE KUNG-FU EXERCISE BOOK: HEALTH SECRETS OF ANCIENT CHINA. New York: Simon & Schuster, 1974. 128p.

———. THE WISDOM OF KUNG-FU. New York: William Morrow & Co., 1974. 121p.

O'Malley, Martin J. THE LUN YU OF KUNG-FU. U.S.A.: The Author, 1975. 20p.

Robinson, Richard. KUNG FU: THE PEACEFUL WAY. New York: Pyramid Books, 1974. 125p.

Sawal, Kenichi. TAIKI-KEN: THE ESSENCE OF KUNG-FU. Tokyo: Japan Publications, 1976. 160p.

Scott, William D. CHINESE KUNG-FU (KENPO): AN INTRODUCTION. Vermont: C. E. Tuttle, 1976. 196p.

Siou, Lily. CH'I KUNG: THE ART OF MASTERING THE UNSEEN LIFE FORCE. Vermont: C. E. Tuttle, 1975. 173p.

Smith, Robwer W. CHINESE BOXING: MASTERS AND METHODS. New York: Kodansha, 1974. 141p.

———. HSING-I: CHINESE MIND-BODY BOXING. New York: Kodansha, 1974. 112p.

———. PA-KUA: CHINESE BOXING FOR FITNESS AND SELF-DEFENSE. New York: Kodansha, 1967. 160p.

———. SECRETS OF SHAOLIN TEMPLE BOXING. Vermont: C. E. Tuttle, 1964. 71p.

Staples, Michael P. TIBETAN KUNG-FU: THE WAY OF THE MONK. California: Unique Publications, 1976. 80p.

——— (ed. John Corcoran). WHITE CRANE GUNG-FU: CHINESE ART OF SELF-DEFENSE. California: Ohara Publications, 1973. 96p.

———. and Anthony Chan. WU SHU OF CHINA. California: Willow Publications, 1976. 117p.

Tackett, Tim (ed. Gilbert Johnson). HSING-I KUNG-FU. California: Ohara Publications, 1975. 175p.

———. HSING-I KUNG-FU, Vol. II. California: Ohara Publications, 1982.

Tang, Peter P. THE NEW MANUAL OF KUNG-FU. New York: Arco Publishing, 1976. 109p.

Tegner, Bruce. KUNG-FU AND TAI CHI: CHINESE KARATE AND CLASSICAL EXERCISES. California: Thor Publishing, 1968, 1973, 1981, 127p.

Un, H. B. PAK MEI KUNG-FU: WHITE EYEBROW. London: Paul H. Crompton, 1974. 81p.

———. PRAYING MANTIS KUNG-FU. London: Paul H. Crompton, 1973. 84p.

Wong, Douglas. THE DECEPTIVE HANDS OF WING CHUN. California: Unique Publications, 1977. 111p.

———. KUNG-FU: THE WAY OF LIFE. California: Curtis Wong Enterprises, 1976. 111p.

———. SHAOLIN FIGHTING: THEORIES AND CONCEPTS. California: Curtis Wong Enterprises, 1975. 112p.

Wong, James. GREAT SAGE MONKEY KUNG-FU. California: Koinonia Productions, 1982. 79p.

———. A SOURCE BOOK IN THE CHINESE MARTIAL ARTS: HISTORY, PHILOSOPHY, SYSTEMS, AND STYLE, Vol. 1. California: Koinonia Productions, 1978. 176p.

———. A SOURCE BOOK IN THE CHINESE MARTIAL ARTS: MEDICINE, MEDITATION, AND MILITARY HISTORY, Vol. 2. California: Koinonia Productions, 1979. 113p.

Yeow, Lee Yew. CHINESE PRAYING MANTIS BOXING. The Author, 1973. 54p.

Yip, Chun and Jing Yip. WING CHUN WOODEN DUMMY TECHNIQUES, Part I. U.S.A.: Wing Jak Printers, 1976. 59p.

———. WING CHUN WOODEN DUMMY TECHNIQUES, Part II. U.S.A.: Wing Kai Enterprises, 1977. 71p.

Yuen, Kam. BEGINNING KUNG-FU. California: Ohara Publications, 1975. 191p.

BRUCE LEE/JEET KUNE DO

Block, Alex Ben. THE LEGEND OF BRUCE LEE. New York: Dell Publishing Co., 1974. 171p.

DeMile, James W. BRUCE LEE'S CHI SAO TAO OF WING CHUN DO, Vol. 2. California: Tao of Wing Chun Do, 1978. 128p.

———. BRUCE LEE'S 1 AND 3 INCH POWER PUNCH. Hawaii: Wing Chun Do Publications, 1975. 34p. California: Tao of Wing Chun Do, 1978. 40p.

———. TAO OF WING CHUN DO, Vol. 1: MIND AND BODY IN HARMONY. California: Tao of Wing Chun Do, 1977. 223p.

Dennis, Felix and Don Atyeo. BRUCE LEE: KING OF KUNG-FU. California: Straight Arrow Books, 1974. 96p.

——— and Roger Hutchinson. THE WISDOM OF BRUCE LEE. New York: Pinnacle Books, 1976. 168p.

Friedman, Stephen Alan. FAREWELL TO THE DRAGON. Pennsylvania: The Cinema Attic, 1974. Unpaged.

Glover, Jesse. BRUCE LEE: BETWEEN WING CHUN AND JEET KUNE DO. Washington: The Author, 1976. 96p.

———. BRUCE LEE'S NON-CLASSICAL GUNG-FU. U.S.A.: The Author, 1978. 129p.

———. BRUCE LEE'S NON-CLASSICAL STICKING HANDS. U.S.A.: Glover Publications, 1982. 200p.

Inosanto, Dan. ABSORB WHAT IS USEFUL: A JEET KUNE DO GUIDEBOOK, Vol. 2. California: Know Now Publishing, 1982.

——— with Alan Sutton. JEET KUNE DO: THE ART AND PHILOSPOHY OF BRUCE LEE. California: Know Now Publishing, 1976. 176p.

Kung-Fu Monthly (eds.). THE SECRET ART OF BRUCE LEE. New Jersey: Castle Books, 1976. 64p.

Lee, Bruce and M. Uyehara. BRUCE LEE'S FIGHTING METHOD: ADVANCED TECHNIQUES, Vol. 4. California: Ohara Publications, 1977. 126p.

———, ———. BRUCE LEE'S FIGHTING METHOD: BASIC TRAINING, Vol. 2. California: Ohara Publications, 1977. 125p.

———, ———. BRUCE LEE'S FIGHTING METHOD: SELF-DEFENSE TECHNIQUES., Vol. 1. California: Ohara Publications, 1976. 125p.

———, ———. BRUCE LEE'S FIGHTING METHOD: SKILL IN TECHNIQUES, Vol. 3. California: Ohara Publications, 1977. 128p.

———. CHINESE GUNG-FU: THE PHILOSPOHICAL ART OF SELF-DEFENSE. California: Oriental Book Sales, 1963. 102p.

———. TAO OF JEET KUNE DO. California: Ohara Publications, 1975. 208p.

Lee, Linda. BRUCE LEE: THE MAN ONLY I KNEW. New York: Warner Books, 1975. 208p.

St. Denice, Claude and Jacques Anton. BRUCE LEE'S BASIC KUNG-FU TRAINING MANUAL. New York: Zebra Books, 1976. 184p.

Uyehara, Mitoshi. BRUCE LEE: FAREWELL, MY FRIEND. California: Ohara Publications, 1976.

MARTIAL ARTS

Adams, Andy, Arthur Tansley, and John Robertson. JAPAN SPORTS GUIDE. Tokyo: BAT Publications, 1978. 161p.

Alexander, Howard, Quintin Chambers, and Donn F. Draeger. PENTJAK-SILAT: THE INDONESIAN FIGHTING ART. New York: Kodansha, 1970. 142p.

Aoki, Hiroyuki (trans. Michael Thompson and Haruyoshi Ito). SHINTAIDO: A NEW ART OF MOVEMENT AND LIFE EXPRESSION. California: Shintaido of America, 1982. 120p.

Arvanitis, Jim. MU TAU: THE MODERN GREEK KARATE. New York: Todd & Honeywell, 1979. 193p.

Baldwin, Lisa (comp.). THE MACCARRONE-KRESGE MARTIAL ARTS BOOK COLLECTION AT THE PATCHOGUE-MEDFORD LIBRARY: AN ANNOTATED BIBLIOGRAPHY. New York: The Patchogue-Medford Library, 1982. 233p.

Baltazzi, Evan S. KICK-BOXING: A SAFE SPORT, A DEADLY DEFENSE. Vermont: C. E. Tuttle, 1976. 72p.

Birrer, Richard B. and Christina D. Birrer. MEDICAL INJURIES IN THE MARTIAL ARTS. Illinois: C. E. Thomas, 1981. 240p.

Burke, M. D., Deniis R. TREATING MARTIAL ARTS INJURIES. California: Ohara Publications, 1981.

Campbell, Sid, et al. TWO THOUSAND & ONE MARTIAL ARTS KUNG-FU, KARATE, TAE KWON DO, KENPO STUDENTS SHOULD KNOW. California: Diamond Publications, 1980. 150p.

Cho, Hee 11. THE COMPLETE MARTIAL ARTIST. California: The Author, 2 vols., 1981. 654p.

———. MAN OF CONTRASTS. California: The Author, 1977. 226p.

Corcoran, John and Emil Farkas. THE COMPLETE MARTIAL ARTS CATALOGUE. New York: Simon & Schuster, 1977. 224p.

———, ———. THE OVERLOOK MARTIAL ARTS DICTONARY. New York: The Overlook Press, 1983. 288p.

Dowd, Steven. KUNTAW: FILIPINO FIGHTING. California: Koinonia Productions, n.d. Unpaged.

Draeger, Donn F. and Robert W. Smith. ASIAN FIGHTING ARTS. New York: Kodansha, 1969. 207p. Paperback reissue (as COMPREHENSIVE ASIAN FIGHTING ARTS), 1981. 207p.

———. CLASSICAL BUDO (MARTIAL ARTS AND WAYS OF JAPAN, Vol. 2). New York: Weatherhill, 1973. 127p.

———. CLASSICAL BUJUTSU (MARTIAL ARTS AND WAYS OF JAPAN, Vol. 1). New York: Weatherhill, 1973. 111p.

———. MODERN BUJUTSU AND BUDO (MARTIAL ARTS AND WAYS OF JAPAN, Vol. 3). New York: Weatherhill, 1974. 190p.

———. WEAPONS AND FIGHTING ARTS OF THE INDONESIAN ARCHIPELAGO. Vermont: C. E. Tuttle, 1972. 254p.

Fitzbarnard, L. FIGHTING SPORTS. U.S.A.: Saiga Publications, 1981.

Fong, Leo. AGRESSIVE DEFENSIVE FIGHTING. California: Koinonia Productions, n.d. Unpaged.

———. HITTING WITHOUT GETTING HIT. California: Koinonia Productions, n.d. Unpaged.

———. OFFENSIVE FIGHTING. California: Koinonia Productions, n.d. Unpaged.

———. POWER KICKING. California: Koinonia Productions, n.d. Unpaged.

———. STRATEGIES FOR WINNING IN KARATE AND KUNG-FU. California: Koinonia Productions, 1977. 80p.

———. THE THEORY AND PRACTICE OF KNOCKOUT PUNCHING. California: Koinonia Productions, 1977. 80p.

———. WINNING BY DECEPTION. California: Koinonia Productions, n.d. Unpaged.

Frommer, Harvey. THE MARTIAL ARTS: JUDO AND KARATE. New York: Atheneum, 1978. 125p.

Gilbey, John F. (aka Smith, Robert W.). SECRET FIGHTING ARTS OF THE WORLD. Vermont: C. E. Tuttle, 1963. 150p.

Gluck, Jay. ZEN COMBAT. New York: Ballantine Books, 1962. 224p.

Goodbody, John (ed.). THE JAPANESE FIGHTING ARTS. London: Arlington Books, 1967. New York: A. S. Barnes, 1969. 242p.

Gwon, Pu Gill. BASIC TRAINING FOR KICKING. California: Ohara Publications, 1981.

———. THE DYNAMIC ART OF BREAKING. California: Ohara Publications, 1977. 144p.

———. SKILL IN COUNTERATTACKS. California: Ohara Publications, 1979.

Gyi, Maung. BURMESE BANDO BOXING. Maryland: American Bando Association, 1978. 83p.

Hancock, H. Irving. JAPANESE PHYSICAL TRAINING. New York: Putnam's Sons, 1903. 156p.

Harrison, Ernest John (E. J.). THE FIGHTING SPIRIT OF JAPAN: THE ESOTERIC STUDY OF THE MARTIAL ARTS AND WAY OF LIFE IN JAPAN. New York: T. Fisher Unwin, 1912. Revised edition, 1913. London: W. Foulsham, 1955. 250p.

Herrigel, Eugen (trans. R. F. C. Hull). ZIN IN THE ART OF ARCHERY. New York: Pantheon, 1953. London: Routledge, 1953. New York: Random House, 1971. 109p.

Huard, Pierre and Ming Wong (trans. Donald N. Smith). ORIENTAL METHODS OF MENTAL AND PHYSICAL FITNESS: THE COMPLETE BOOK OF MEDITATION, KINESTHERAPY, AND MARTIAL ARTS IN CHINA, INDIA, AND JAPAN. New York: Funk & Wagnalls, 1971. 279p.

Hyams, Joe. ZEN IN THE MARTIAL ARTS. California: J. P. Tarcher, 1979. 143p.

Inosanto, Dan. A GUIDE TO MARTIAL ARTS TRAINING WITH EQUIPMENT: A JEET KUNE DO GUIDEBOOK. Vol. 1. California: Know Now Publishing, 1981. 160p.

———, Gilbert Johnson, and George Foon. THE FILIPINO MARTIAL ARTS, AS TAUGHT BY DAN INOSANTO. California: Know Now Publishing, 1977. 176p.

Jalmaani, Abu. SILAT: THE MALAYA ART OF HAND AND FOOT FIGHTING. California: Koinonia Productions, 1978. 60p.

Jorgensen, S. J. THIRTY-SIX SECRET KNOCKOUT BLOWS WITHOUT THE USE OF THE FISTS. Seattle: n.p., 1930. 24p.

Kang, Shin Duk. THE PRACTICAL APPLICATIONS OF ONE-STEP SPARRING IN KARATE, KUNG-FU, TAE KOWN DO. California: Ohara Publications, 1978. 143p.

———. TECHNIQUES IN FREE FIGHTING. California: Ohara Publications, 1980.

Kauz, Herman. THE MARTIAL SPIRIT: AN INTRODUCTION TO THE ORIGIN, PHILOSOPHY, AND PSYCHOLOGY OF THE MARTIAL ARTS. New York: The Overlook Press, 1977. 141p.

Keane, Christopher (aka Logan, William) and Herman Petras. HANDBOOK OF THE MARTIAL ARTS AND SELF-DEFENSE. New York: Funk & Wagnalls, 1975. 282p.

Kjostolf, Kjell. BIBLIOGRAPHICAL NOTES ON SOME WORKS ABOUT JIU-JITSU AND JUDO INCLUDING REFERENCES TO VARIOUS SUBJECTS CONNECTED WITH JAPAN AND THE JAPANESE ART OF SELF-DEFENSE. Norway: The Author, 1950. 38p.

Kozuki, Russell. BLACKBELT TECHNIQUES IN THE MARTIAL ARTS. New York: Sterling Publishing Co., 1976. 160p.

Kurban, Roy. KICKING TECHNIQUES FOR COMPETITION AND SELF-DEFENSE. California: Ohara Publications, 1979. 111p.

Laiken, Deidre S. MIND/BODY/SPIRIT: THE MARTIAL ARTS AND ORIENTAL MEDICINE. New York: J. Messner, 1978. 189p.

La Tourrette, Jon M. MENTAL TRAINING OF A WARRIOR: AN ADVANCED MANUAL OF STRATEGY AND PRINCIPLES FOR THE NON-CLASSICAL MARTIAL ARTIST. Idaho: Warrior Pbulications, 1981. 184p.

LEARN SIMPLIFIED SAVATE, BOXING AND WRESTLING. U.S.A.: Universal Bodybuilding, 1973. Unpaged.

Lederman, Milton. ANCIENT FIGHTING ARTS FOR THE MEN OF OUR TIMES. Amity Hallmark, 1976.

Lee, Chong. ADVANCED EXPLOSIVE KICKS. California: Ohara Publications, 1978. 143p.

——— (ed. Gilbert Johnson). DYNAMIC KICKS: ESSENTIALS FOR FREE FIGHTING. California: Ohara Publications, 1975. 96p.

———. KICKS FOR COMPETITION. California: Ohara Publications, 1982.

———. SUPER DYNAMIC KICKS. California: Ohara Publications, 1980.

Lee, Kein H. FIGHTING ARTS OF THE ORIENT. California: n.p., 1958. Unpaged.

LeShan, Lawrence. HOW TO MEDITATE. New York: Bantam Books, 1975.

Lew, James. THE ART OF STRETCHING AND KICKING. California: Unique Publications, 1977. 104p.

Liu, Da. TAOIST HEALTH EXERCISE BOOK. New York: Links Books, 1974. 135p.

Marchini, Ron and Leo Fong (eds. John Corcoran and John Scura). POWER TRAINING IN KUNG-FU AND KARATE. California: Ohara Publications, 1974. 224p.

Maslak, Paul. STRATEGY IN UNARMED COMBAT. California: Unique Publications, 1980. 131p.

———. WHAT THE MASTERS KNOW. California: Unique Publications, 1980. 108p.

Moynahan, James M. A GUIDE TO JUDO, JUJITSU AND ASSOCIATED ARTS. Washington: n.p., 1961. 100p.

Musashi, Miyamoto (trans. Victor Harris). A BOOK OF FIVE RINGS: A GUIDE TO STRATEGY. New York: The Overlook Press, 1974. 96p.

Nardi, Thomas. THE MIND IN THE MARTIAL ARTS. California: Koinonia Productions, n.d. Unpaged.

Nishioka, Hayward. FOOT THROWS: KARATE, JUDO AND SELF-DEFENSE. California: Ohara Publications, 1972. 95p.

Payne, Peter (ed. Jill Purce). MARTIAL ARTS: THE SPIRITUAL DIMENSION. New York: Crossroad, 1981. 96p.

Random, Michel. THE MARTIAL ARTS. London: Octopus Books, 1978. 286p.

Reisberg, Ken. THE MARTIAL ARTS. New York: F. Watts, 1979. 86p.

Reps. Paul. TEN WAYS TO MEDITATE. New York: Weatherhill, 1969. 56p.

Reumann, Wallace W. FORBIDDEN ORIENTAL FIGHTING ARTS, DEADLY DEFENSE AND ATTACK. U.S.A.: Informative Publications, 1963. 66p.

Ribner, Susan and Richard Chin. THE MARTIAL ARTS. New York: Harper & Row, 1978. 181p.

Robbins, Desmond. THE THROW, THE BLOW, AND THE KNOW: THIS IS JAPAN, 1958. Tokyo: n.p., 1958.

Shapiro, Amy. RUNNING PRESS GLOSSARY OF MARTIAL ARTS LANGUAGE. Pennsylvania: Running Press, 1978. 112p.

Shim, Sang Kyu. THE MAKING OF A MARTIAL ARTIST. Michigan: The Author, 1980. 141p.

Simon, Olaf E. THE LAW' OF THE FIST: INTRODUCING THE MOO SYSTEM. New York: Vantage Press, 1969. 202p.

Smith, David. THE EAST/WEST EXERCISE BOOK. New York: McGraw-Hill, 1976. 208p.

Smith, Don. AIDIDO AND KUNG-FU: THE ANCIENT ARTS. New Jersey: Troll Associates, 1974. 32p.

———. FROM BEGINNER TO BLACK BELT. New Jersey: Troll Associates, 1974. 32p.

So, Doshin. SHORINJI KEMPO: PHILOSOPHY AND TECHNIQUES. Tokyo: Japan Publications, 1970. 256p.

———. WHAT IS SHORINJI KEMPO? Tokyo: Japan Publications, 1970.

Sollier, Andre and Zsolt Gyorbiro. JAPANESE ARCHERY: ZEN IN ACTION. New York: Weatherhill, 1969.

Stockmann, Hardy. KICK-BOXING, MUAY-THAI: THE ART OF SIAMESE UNARMED COMBAT. California: Ohara Publications, 1976. 96p.

Tanjaworm, Samyon. THAI BOXING: THE DEVASTATING FIGHTING ART OF THAILAND. California: Divine Wind, 1975. 84p.

Tegner, Bruce, BLACK BELT JUDO, KARATE, AND JUKADO: ADVANCED TECHNIQUES FOR EXPERTS. California: Thor Publishing, 1967–94p; 1973–125p; 1980.

———. JUDO AND KARATE BELT DEGREES: REQUIREMENTS, RULES, REGULATIONS. California: Thor Publishing, 1963–96p; 1967–94p.

———. JUDO AND KARATE EXERCISES: PHYSICAL CONDITIONING FOR THE UNARMED FIGHTING ARTS. California: Thor Publishing, 1963. 93p.

———. KARATE AND JUDO EXERCISES: PHYSICAL CONDITIONING FOR ORIENTAL SPORT FIGHTING ARTS. California: Thor Publishing, 1972, 1981. 127p.

———. SAVATE: FRENCH FOOT FIGHTING. California: Thor Publishing, 1965. 125p.

———, and Alice McGrath. SOLO FORMS OF KARATE, TAI CHI, AIKIDO AND KUNG-FU. California: Thor Publishing, 1981. 112p.

Tomiki, Kenji. JUDO AND AIKIDO. Japan: Japan Travel Bureau, 1970. 184p.

Tsirakis, Jack K. THE ART OF JEET-KUNG-TAO. New York: Exposition Press, 1977. 194p.

TWENTIETH CENTURY WARRIORS: PROMINENT MEN IN THE ORIENTAL FIGHTING ARTS.

From the pages of Black Belt Magazine and Karate Illustrated. California: Ohara Publications, 1971. 254p.

Van Clief, Ron. THE MANUAL OF THE MARTIAL ARTS: AN INTRODUCTION TO THE COMBINED TECHNIQUES OF KARATE, KUNG-FU, TAE KWON DO AND AIKI-JUTSU FOR EVERYONE. New York: Rawson, Wade, 1981. 188p.

von Durckheim, Karlfried. HARA: THE VITAL CENTER OF MAN. London: George Allen & Unwin, 1962.

Wall, Bob (ed. John Corcoran). WHO'S WHO IN THE MARTIAL ARTS AND DIRECTORY OF BLACK BELTS. California: R. A. Wall Investments, 1975. 254p.

Wallace, Bill. DYNAMIC STRETCHING AND KICKING. California: Unique Publications, 1981.

Williams, Al. HOW TO OUTTHINK YOUR OPPONENT. San Francisco: John Newbegin, 1918. 75p.

Williams, Bryn (ed.). MARTIAL ARTS OF THE ORIENT. New York: Hamlyn, 1975. 168p.

Winderbaum, Larry. THE MARTIAL ARTS ENCYCLOPEDIA. Washington, D. C.: INSCAPE Publishers, 1977. 215p.

Wong, Harry. DYNAMIC TENSION. California: Unique Publications, 1980. 134p.

Zarrilli, Phillip B. (ed.). MARTIAL ARTS IN ACTOR TRAINING. U.S.A.: Drama Books, 1982.

MARTIAL ARTS/SELF-DEFENSE FOR JUVENILES

Butler, Pat. JUDO FOR JUNIORS. London: Faber & Faber, 1966. 62p.

Cho, Sihak Henry. BETTER KARATE FOR BOYS. New York: Dodd, Mead & Co., 1970. 61p.

Goldstein, Frances. KARATE FOR KIDS. New York: Arco Publishing Co., 1977. 247p.

Harrington, Anthony. EVERY BOY'S JUDO. New York: Emerson Books, 1960. 140p. London: Stanley Paul, 1966. 175p.

———. EVERY GIRL'S JUDO. New York: Emerson Books, 1961. 131p.

Harrison, Ernest John (E. J.). JUDO FOR GIRLS. New York: Sterling Publishing Co., 1954. 110p.

———. JUNIOR JUDO. New York: Sterling Publishing Co., 1958, 1965. 144p.

Kozuki, Russell. JUNIOR KARATE. New York: Sterling Publishing Co., 1971. 128p.

———. KARATE FOR YOUNG PEOPLE. New York: Sterling Publishing Co., 1974, 1982. 128p.

Lewis, Tom G. KARATE FOR KIDS. National Paperback, 1980. 120p.

Lichello, Robert. JU-JITSU SELF-DEFENSE FOR TEENAGERS: THE CLIFF FREELAND SYSTEM. New York: J. Messner, 1961. 189p.

McLaglan, S. L. JIU-JITSU FOR GIRLS. London: C. A. Pearson, 1922. 46p.

Mancuso, Ted and Frank Hill. KUNG-FU FOR YOUNG PEOPLE. California: Ohara Publications, 1982. 96p.

Manners, David. TEACH YOUR CHILD SELF-DEFENSE. New York: Arco Publishing, 1976. 159p.

Otaki, Tadao and Donn F. Draeger. JUDO FOR YOUNG MEN, BASIC AND INTERMEDIATE: AN INTERSCHOLASTIC AND INTERCOLLEGIATE STANDARD. Tokyo: Kodansha, 1965. 336p.

Oyama, Masutatsu. BOYS' KARATE. Tokyo: Japan Publications, 1968. 88p.

Tegner, Bruce. SELF-DEFENSE YOU CAN TEACH YOUR BOY: A CONFIDENCE-BUILDING COURSE. California: Thor Publishing, 1970. 125p.

———, and Alice McGrath. SELF-DEFENSE FOR YOUR CHILD: PRACTICAL DEFENSES AND ASSAULT PREVENTION. California: Thor Publishing, 1976. 127p.

———. TEACH YOUR BOY SELF-DEFENSE AND SELF-CONFIDENCE. California: Thor Publishing, 1961. 117p.

MILITARY TACTICS & DEFENSE
See HAND-TO-HAND COMBAT

NINJA/NINJUTSU

Adams, Andrew. NINJA: THE INVISIBLE ASSASSINS. California: Ohara Publications, 1970. 190p.

Draeger, Donn F. THE ART OF INVISIBILITY: NINJUTSU. Japan: Simpson-Doyle & Co., 1971. 118p.

Hatsumi, Dr. Masaaki. NINJUTSU, HISTORY AND TRADITION. California: Unique Publications, 1981. 205p.

Hayes, Stephen. THE NINJA AND THEIR SECRET FIGHTING ART. Vermont: C. E. Tuttle, 1981. 160p.

Hayes, Stephen K. (ed. Bill Griffith). NINJA: SPIRIT OF THE SHADOW WARRIOR. California: Ohara Publications, 1980.

———. NINJA: Vol. 2, WARRIOR WAYS OF ENLIGHTENMENT. California: Ohara Publications, 1982. 140p.

Kim, Ashida. SECRETS OF THE NINJA. Colorado: Paladin Press, 1981. 160p.

THE SECRETS OF NINJUTSU. New York: C. P. Exports, 1975. 43p.

Weiss, Al and Tom Philbin. CLAN OF DEATH: NINJA. New York: Pocket Books, 1980.

PHILOSOPHY
See also ZEN

Blofeld, John (trans.). THE ZEN TEACHING OF HUANG PO ON THE TRANSMISSION OF MIND. New York: Grove Press—1958. 136p.

Bonsall, B. S. CONFUCIANISM AND TAOISM. London: Epworth Press, 1934.

Brown, Brian. WISDOM OF THE CHINESE: THEIR PHILOSOPHY IN SAYINGS AND PROVERBS. California: Ohara Publications, 1975. 96p.

Bueler, William H. CHINESE SAYINGS. Vermont: C. E. Tuttle, 1972. 143p.

Butler, Kenneth D. THE HEIKE MONOGATARI AND THE JAPANESE WARRIOR ETHIC. Massachusetts: Harvard Journal of Asian Studies, 1970.

Chai, Ch'u and Winberg Chai. I-CHING. New York: Bantam Books, 1964.

Chau, Wing-tsit (trans. and comp.). CHINESE PHILOSOPHY. New Jersey: Princeton University Press, 1973.

Chau, Wing-tsit (trans. and comp.). CHINESE PHILOSOPHY. New Jersey: Princeton University Press, 1973.

Confucius (trans. Ch'u Chai and Charles Winberg). THE SACRED BOOKS OF CONFUCIUS AND OTHER CONFUCIAN CLASSICS. New York: University Books, 1965. 384p.

Fujisawa, Chikao. ZEN AND SHINTO: A HISTORY OF JAPANESE PHILOSOPHY. New York: Philosophical Library, 1959. 92p.

Fung, Yu-Lan (trans. Derek Bodde). A HISTORY OF CHINESE PHILOSOPHY, Vol. II. New Jersey: Princeton University Press, 1953.

Hanayama, Shinsho. A HISTORY OF JAPANESE BUDDHISM. Tokyo: Bukkyo Dendo Kyokai, 1966. 131p.

Hua, Ellen Kei. KUNG-FU MEDITATIONS AND CHINESE PROVERBIAL WISDOM. California: Farout Press, 1973. Unpaged.

———. WISDOM FROM THE EAST: MEDITATIONS, REFLECTIONS, PROVERBS AND CHANTS. California: Farout Press, 1974. 126p.

Humphreys, Christmas. THE WISDOM OF BUDDHISM. New York: Harper Colophon Books, 1960.

THE I-CHING (THE SACRED BOOKS OF CHINA). New York: Dover Publications, 1963. 448p.

(Trans. Cary F. Baynes). THE I-CHING OR BOOK OF CHANGES. New Jersey: Princeton University Press, 1967. 740p.

Lao-tze (trans. R. B. Blakney). TAO-TE-CHING. New York: New American Library, 1955.

Lau, D. C. (trans.). TAO-TE-CHING. New York: Penguin Books. 1967.

Luk, Charles. CH'AN AND ZEN TEACHING, First Series. California: Shambala Publications, 1970. 255p.

Nitobe, Inazo. BUSHIDO: THE SOUL OF JAPAN. California: Ohara Publications, an unaltered reproduction of the original 1899 work, 1969. 146p.

———. BUSHIDO: THE WARRIOR'S CODE. California: Ohara Publications, 1975. 112p.

Parulski, George. A PATH TO ORIENTAL WISDOM: INTRODUCTORY STUDIES IN EASTERN PHILOSOPHY. California: Ohara Publications, 1976. 192p.

Scarborough, William. CHINESE PROVERBS. London: n.p., 1873.

Singer, Kurt. MIRROR, SWORD AND JEWEL: THE GEOMETRY OF JAPANESE LIFE. New York: Kodansha, 1981. 176p.

Smith Arthur H. PROVERBS AND COMMON SAYINGS OF THE CHINESE. 1902.

Suzuki, D. T. BRIEF HISTORY OF CHINESE PHILOSOPHY. London: Probsthain & Co., 1914.

Ta-Kao, Ch'u. TAO-TE-CHING. England: George Allen & Unwin, 1937. 96p.

Tanaka, Minoru. BUSHIDO: WAY OF THE SAMURAI. New Mexico: Sun Publishing, 1975. 85p.

Tzu, Lao (trans. Gia-Fu Feng and Jane English). TAO-TE-CHING. New York: Vintage Books, 1972.

Watts, Alan. TAO, THE WATERCOURSE WAY. New York: Pantheon Books, 1975.

Wieger, Leo. TAOISM: THE PHILOSOPHY OF CHINA. California: Ohara Publications, 1976. 192p.

Wilhelm, Richard (trans. Cary F. Baynes). THE I-CHING: BOOK OF CHANGES. New Jersey: Princeton University Press, 1950.

Wright, Arthur R. BUDDHISM IN CHINESE HISTORY. California: Stanford University Press, 1959.

Yutang, Lin. THE WISDOM OF CHINA AND INDIA. New York: Modern Library, 1942.

——— (ed). THE WISDOM OF CONFUCIUS. New York: Modern Library, 1938. 290p.

POLICE TACTICS & DEFENSE
See HAND-TO-HAND COMBAT

SAMURAI
See also PHILOSOPHY

Abelard, Max. THE MAGNIFICENT SAMURAI. London: Paul H. Crompton, 1974. 188p.

Brinkley, Capt. F. SAMURAI: THE INVINCIBLE WARRIORS. California: Ohara Publications, 1975. 96p.

Gibson, Michael. THE SAMURAI OF JAPAN. London: Wayland, 1973. 96p.

Jennings, William Dale. THE RONIN. Vermont: C. E. Tuttle, 1968. New York: Signet, 1975. 146p.

Mishima, Yukio (trans. Kathryn N. Sparling). THE WAY OF THE SAMURAI: YUKIO MISHIMA ON HAGAKURE IN MODERN LIFE. New York: Basic Books, 1977. 166p.

Norman, J. F. THE FIGHTING MAN OF JAPAN: TRAINING AND EXERCISES OF THE SAMURAI. London: n.p., 1905. 78p.

Ratti, Oscar and Adele Westbrook. SECRETS OF THE SAMURAI: A SURVEY OF THE MARTIAL ARTS OF FEUDAL JAPAN. Vermont: C. E. Tuttle, 1973. 483p.

Seward, Jack. HARA-KIRI: JAPANESE RITUAL SUICIDE. Vermont: C. E. Tuttle, 1968. 116p.

Turnbull, Stephen R. THE SAMURAI: A MILITARY HISTORY. New York: Macmillan Publishing Co., 1977. 304p.

Wilson, William Scott (trans.). IDEALS OF THE SAMURAI: WRITINGS OF JAPANESE WARRIORS. California: Ohara Publications, 1982.

Yamamura, Kozo. A STUDY OF SAMURAI INCOME AND ENTREPRENEURSHIP. Massachusetts: Harvard University Press, 1974. 243p.

Yoshikawa, Eiji. MUSASHI: AN EPIC NOVEL OF THE SAMURAI ERA. New York: Kodansha, 970p.

YOUNG SAMURAI: BODYBUILDERS OF JAPAN. New York: Grove Press, 1967. 75p.

SELF-DEFENSE (General)

Accas, Gene and John H. Eckstein. HOW TO PROTECT YOURSELF ON THE STREETS AND IN YOUR HOME. New York: Pocket Books, 1965. 62p.

Adams, Ronald J., et al. STREET SURVIVAL: TACTICS FOR ARMED ENCOUNTERS. U.S.A.: Calibre Press, 1980. 416p.

ALL AMERICAN SYSTEM OF SELF-DEFENSE. Chicago: Eastern Press, n.d. 15p.

Allred, Sam H. DYNAMIC SELF-DEFENSE. Louisiana: U.S. Judo Association. 1967. 96p. New York: A. S. Barnes, 1969. 127p.

Armour-Milne, J. ("Slip" Saxon). FITNESS IN DEFENSE. London: Link House, n.d.

Baltazzi, Evan S. AMERICAN SELF-PROTECTION (THE ART OF SELF-PROTECTION): ASP, SYSTEM OF MIND-BODY SELF-PROTECTION FOR SELF-DEFENSE, FOR FITNESS, FOR SPORT. Ohio: Evanel Associates, 1972. 64p.

Bartlett, Eric G. NEW WAYS OF SELF-DEFENSE. New York: Hart Publishing, 1967. 125p.

———. SELF-DEFENSE IN THE HOME. London: Thorsons, 1967. 125p.

Braun, Matt. THE SAVE-YOUR-LIFE DEFENSE HANDBOOK. Connecticut: Devin-Adair Co., 1977. 189p.

Brown, Jr., Wesley, SELF-DEFENSE. New York: A. S. Barnes, 1951. 91p.

Bullard, Jim (ed. Craig Cowles). LOOKING FORWARD TO BEING ATTACKED. Tennessee: The Author, 1977. 85p.

Butler, Pat. SELF-DEFENSE COMPLETE. London: Faber & Faber, 1962. 96p. New York: Emerson Books, 1962. 100p.

———. YOUR BOOK OF SELF-DEFENSE. London: Faber & Faber, 1968. 53p.

Cacciolli, Peter R. ENCYCLOPEDIA OF SELF-DEFENSE. Missouri: International University, 1979. 225p.

Cahn, Rolf. SELF-DEFENSE FOR GENTLE PEOPLE. New Mexico: John Muir Publications, 1974. 183p.

Callum, Myles. BODY BUILDING AND SELF-DEFENSE. New York: Harper & Row, 1962. 141p.

Campbell, Sid and Jim Logsdon. THIS BOOK COULD SAVE YOUR LIFE. California: The Authors, n.d. 16p.

Carciofini, A. P. AMERICAN AND JAPANESE METHODS OF SCIENTIFIC SELF-DEFENSE. Minneapolis: Tribune Printing, n.d. 24p.

Cavendish, Marshall. ILLUSTRATED GUIDE TO THE ART OF ORIENTAL SELF-DEFENSE. London: The Author, 1975. 88p.

Chin, David. PERSONAL SURVIVAL. California: Creative Associates, 1982. 28p.

Chitwood, Terry. HOW TO DEFEND YOURSELF WITHOUT EVEN TRYING. U.S.A.: Polestar, 1981. 96p.

Clark, Eric. EVERYBODY'S GUIDE TO SURVIVAL. London: Collins, 1969. 159p.

Collingridge, W. H. TRICKS OF SELF-DEFENSE. London: Athletic Publications, 1949. 48p.

Collins, Blackie and Chris McLoughlin. PERSONAL DEFENSE. Georgia: The Authors, 1977. 160p.

Conroy, Mary and Edward R. Ritvo. COMMON SENSE SELF-DEFENSE: A PRACTICAL MANUAL FOR STUDENTS AND TEACHERS. Missouri: Mosby, 1977. 146p.

Cooper, Jeff. PRINCIPLES OF PERSONAL DEFENSE. Colorado: Paladin Press, 1972. 30p.

Cummings, Samuel B. THE ART OF SELF-DEFENSE. Hollywood: n.p., 1942. 31p.

———. TEACHING AMERICAN ART OF SELF PROTECTION FROM HOLLYWOOD TO GUADALCANAL. Hollywood: n.p., 1943. 59p.

D'Amoric, G. THE FRENCH METHOD OF THE NOBLE ART OF SELF-DEFENSE. N.p.; 1898. Unpaged.

Dante, Count (aka Keehan, John). WORLD'S DEADLIEST FIGHTING SECRETS. Illinois: Black Dragon Fighting Society. 1968. 72p.

Demura, Fumio and Dan Ivan. STREET SURVIVAL: A PRACTICAL GUIDE TO SELF-DEFENSE. Tokyo: Japan Publications, 1979.

Dobson, Terry and Victor Miller. GIVING IN TO GET YOUR WAY: THE ATTACK-TICS SYSTEM FOR WINNING YOUR EVERYDAY BATTLES. New York: Delacourt Press, 1978. 257p.

———, with Judith Shepherd-Chow. SAFE AND ALIVE: HOW TO PROTECT YOURSELF, YOUR FAMILY, AND YOUR PROPERTY AGAINST VIOLENCE. Los Angeles: J. P. Tarcher, 1981. 153p.

Dominy, Eric. TEACH YOURSELF SELF-DEFENSE. London: English Universities Press, 1957. 191p. New York: Emerson Books, 1964. 191p.

Edmundson, Joseph. THE HANDBOOK OF SELF-DEFENSE AND JUDO. London: Barker, 1967. 189p.

———. SELF-DEFENSE AND JUDO. London: Pan, 1967. 188p.

Ellison, Bob and Jill Shipstad. THIS BOOK CAN SAVE YOUR LIFE. New York: New American Library, 1968. 128p.

Fairbairn, W. E. DEFENDU, SCIENTIFIC SELF-DEFENSE. Shanghai: North China Daily News, 1925. 171p.

———. SCIENTIFIC SELF-DEFENSE. Shanghai: Chinese American Publishing Co., 1931. 165p.

FIFTY SIMPLE TRICKS OF SELF-DEFENSE. Detroit: Johnson-Smith & Co., 1935. 64p.

Fosler, F. S. A MANUAL FOR SELF-DEFENSE. Indianapolis: n.p., 1942. 95p.

Fu, Leong. SELF-DEFENSE IN EVERY EMERGENCY. London: Herbert Jenkins, 1963. 94p.

Gambordella, Theodore L. SEVEN DAYS TO SELF-DEFENSE. Illinois: Contemporary Books, 1980.

Geer, Alpheus. BOXING AND SELF-DEFENSE TAUGHT BY THE MARSHALL STILLMAN PRINCIPLE. New York: Marshall Stillman Association, 1919. 46p.

Gough, Galen. SIMPLIFIED SELF-DEFENSE. Los Angeles: W. G. Scholts, 1943. 52p.

Griffith, Liddon R. MUGGING: YOU CAN PROTECT YOURSELF. New Jersey: Prentice-Hall, 1978. 212p.

Grover, Jack. DEFEND YOURSELF! New York: Ronald Press, 1958. 82p.

Harrison, Ernest John (E. J.). MY METHOD OF SELF-DEFENSE: M. KAWAISHI. London: W. Foulsham, 1957. 119p.

Harvey, Maurice G. COMPREHENSIVE SELF-DEFENSE. New York: Emerson Books, 1967. 175p.

———. SELF-DEFENSE BY JUDO. New York: Emerson Books, 1959. 149p.

Heinrich, Joseph. SELF-DEFENSE. New Jersey: n.p., 1934. 96p.

Hepler, Don. SELF-DEFENSE SIMPLIFIED IN PICTURES. Vermont: C. E. Tuttle, 1969. 128p.

Horn, R., D. D. Jenkins, and W. J. R. Price. ATTACK AND DEFENSE. London: Longman's Green, 1942. 49p.

Hunter, George. HOW TO DEFEND YOURSELF, YOUR FAMILY, AND YOUR HOME: A COMPLETE GUIDE TO SELF-PROTECTION. New York: David McKay Co., 1967. 307p.

Jacomb, William J. PRACTICAL SELF-DEFENSE. New York: Lea & Febiger, 1918. 99p.

Johnson, R. H. and J. A. Blair. LOGICAL SELF-DEFENSE. New York: McGraw-Hill, 1980.

Laughlin, J. JISHUKAN-HONBU: THE CENTRAL SCHOOL OF SELF-DEFENSE. England: Thumbflix International, 1970.

THE LAW OF SELF-DEFENSE. Georgia: The Institute for Self-Defense, 1975. 16p.

LeBelle, Gene and L. C. Coughran. YOUR PERSONAL HANDBOOK OF SELF-DEFENSE. New York: Cornerstone Library, 1964, 1976. 144p.

Lee, Ching-nan and Ruben Figueroa. THE TECHNIQUES OF SELF-DEFENSE. New York: A. S. Barnes, 1963. 128p.

Lee, Eric. FIGHT BACK: YOUR GUIDE TO SELF-DEFENSE. California: Unique Publications, 1982. 214p.

Lewis, Frank S. THE NEW SCIENCE, WEAPONLESS DEFENSE. California: The Author, 1906. 157p.

McGrath, Alice (Greenfield). SELF-DEFENSE FOR COWARDS: A GUIDE TO NONCOMBATIVE ACTION FOR THE RATIONAL, RESOURCEFUL MAN. California: Thor Publishing, 1973. 69p.

Madison, Arnold. DON'T BE A VICTIM: PROTECT YOURSELF AND YOUR BELONGINGS. New York: Messner, 1978. 64p.

Mager, N. H. and S. K. Mager. PROTECT YOURSELF: COMPLETE GUIDE TO SAFE-KEEPING YOUR LIFE AND HOME. New York: Dell Publishing, 1978.

Martone, John, HANDBOOK OF SELF-DEFENSE IN PICTURES AND TEXT. New York: Greenberg, 1955. New York: Arco Publishing, 1961. 111p.

Masters, Robert V. THE COMPLETE BOOK OF SELF-DEFENSE. New York: Doubleday, 1968. 542p. New York: Sterling Publishing Co., 1974. 542p.

Mendall, Brooks. PROTECT YOURSELF. New York: Duel, Sloan & Pierce, 1944. Unpaged.

———. YOUR HANDS . . . SECRET WEAPONS. New York: American Physical Fitness Institute, 1943. 33p.

Miller, Olga Katzin (aka Sagittarius). EVERYBODY'S SELF-DEFENSE. London: Vawser & Wiles. 1944. 63p.

Mitchell, Dewey. SELF-DEFENSE OR JIU-JITSU. Cleveland: The Author, 1942. 95p.

———. SKILLED DEFENSE. Cleveland: The Author, 1936. 175p.

Mitose, James M. WHAT IS SELF DEFENSE? California: California State University, 2nd edition (reprint of the 1953 original), 1980. 109p.

Natividad, John. INTERNATIONAL SELF-DEFENSE. California: Martial Arts Publications, eight courses, 1974. Unpaged.

Neff, Fred. BASIC SELF-DEFENSE MANUAL. Minnesota: Lerner Publications, 1976. 63p.

———. EVERYBODY'S BOOK OF SELF-DEFENSE: A COMPREHENSIVE MANUAL FOR BEGINNERS. Minnesota: Lerner Publications, 1978. 255p.

Ochiai, Hidy. THE ESSENCE OF SELF-DEFENSE. Illinois: Contemporary Books, 1979. 210p.

Price, E. E. SCIENCE OF SELF-DEFENSE. New York: n.p., n.d. Unpaged.

———. BRUCE TEGNER'S COMPLETE BOOK OF SELF-DEFENSE. New York: Stein & Day, 1963. 224p. Revised, 1975. 223p.

———. INSTANT SELF-DEFENSE. New York: Grosset & Dunlap, 1965. 63p.

———. SELF-DEFENSE, A BASIC COURSE. California: Thor Publishing, 1979. 111p.

———. SELF-DEFENSE FOR BOYS AND MEN: A PHYSICAL EDUCATION COURSE. California: Thor Publishing, 1969, 1973. 125p.

———. SELF-DEFENSE FOR BOYS AND MEN: A SECONDARY SCHOOL AND COLLEGE MANUAL. California: Thor Publishing, 1968. 93p. New York: Grosset & Dunlap, 1969. 125p.

———. SELF-DEFENSE: NERVE CENTERS AND PRESSURE POINTS FOR ATEMI-WAZA, JUKADO, AND KARATE. California: Thor Publishing, 1968. 93p. Revised and enlarged, 1978. 124p.

Thornberry, Risher W. TWENTY LESSONS IN DISARMING A HOLDUP MAN. California: American School of Jiu-Jitsu, n.d. 9p.

Walston, Gerald M. THE LEGAL IMPLICATIONS OF SELF-DEFENSE: A REFERENCE MANUAL FOR THE MARTIAL ARTS. New York: Vantage Press, 1979. 169p.

Wernz, Jack. DEFENSE AGAINST CRIMINAL ATTACK MADE EASY. New York: Carlton Press, 1960. 56p.

Wheeldon, G. H. SELF-DEFENSE. London: J. Kimpton, 1905. Unpaged.

Wilson, Jim. ILLUSTRATED GUIDE TO THE ART OF SELF-DEFENSE. England: Marshall Cavendish, 1975. 88p.

PROTECTING YOURSELF AND YOUR FAMILY. New York: Dell Publishing, 1965. 64p.

Robert, Hank. DEFEND YOURSELF! KETSUGO: COMPLETE SELF-DEFENSE. New York: Key Publishing, 1961. 66p.

Robertson, Michel and Michel Benoit. SELF-DEFENSE KARATE. Montreal: Beauchemin, 1974. 143p.

Rocca, Antonino. SELF-DEFENSE AND PHYSICAL FITNESS. New York: Pocket Books, 1965. 75p.

Sagittarius. EVERYBODY'S BOOK OF SELF-DEFENSE. London: Vawser & Wiles, 1943. 64p.

Samuels, Dale. SELF-DEFENSE THROUGH THE EYES OF THE LAW. N.p., 1976. 88p.

Sandow, Billy C. SELF-DEFENSE. New York: Sandow-Lewis, 1926. 63p.

———. SELF-DEFENSE FOR THE INDIVIDUAL. New York: The Author, 1919. 18p.

Seidler, Armond H. DEFEND YOURSELF: SCIENTIFIC PERSONAL DEFENSE. Massachusetts: Houghton-Mifflin, 1978. 240p.

Stegne, Lillian R. THE PREVENTION AND MANAGEMENT OF DISTURBED BEHAVIOR. Ontario: Ministry of Health, 1976. 50p.

Tamura, Vince and Gene Shelton (ed. John Corcoran). COMMON SENSE SELF-DEFENSE. California: Ohara Publications, 1974. 152p.

Tegner, Bruce. BRUCE TEGNER METHOD OF SELF-DEFENSE. California: Thor Publishing, 1960–143p; 1969–127p. London: Corgi, revised and enlarged, 1972. 190p.

———. BRUCE TEGNER'S COMPLETE BOOK OF JUKADO SELF-DEFENSE. New York: Grosset & Dunlap, 1968. 256p.

Wilson, T. E. MASS ATHLETICS AND PERSONAL DEFENSE. Chicago: Wilson Athletic Library, 1923. 51p.

Woo, Moon Y. KONGSU: THE ART OF DEFENSE AGAINST VIOLENCE. U.S.A.: n.p., 1964. 140p.

Wyness, G. B. "Jerry." PRACTICAL PERSONAL DEFENSE. New York: Barnes & Noble, 1975. 103p.

SELF-DEFENSE FOR WOMEN/RAPE PREVENTION

Barthol, Robert G. PROTECT YOURSELF: A SELF-DEFENSE GUIDE FOR WOMEN FROM PREVENTION TO COUNTERATTACK. New Jersey: Prentice-Hall, 1979. 222p.

Bateman, Py, FEAR INTO ANGER: A MANUAL OF SELF-DEFENSE FOR WOMEN. Illinois: Nelson-Hall, 1978. 123p.

Blackman, Honor with Joe and Doug Robinson. HONOR BLACK-MAN'S BOOK OF SELF-DEFENSE. London: Andre Deutsch, 1965. 127p. New York: Macmillan, 1966. 125p.

Bochank, Elizabeth, et al (eds.). WOMEN'S SELF-DEFENSE CASES: THEORY AND PRACTICE. Mithcie-Bobbs, 1981. 330p.

Burg, Kathleen Keefe. THE WOMANLY ART OF SELF-DEFENSE: A COMMON SENSE APPROACH. New York: A & W Publishers, 1979. 175p.

Butler, Pat and Karen Butler. JUDO AND SELF-DEFENSE FOR WOMEN AND GIRLS. London: Faber & Faber, 1968. 180p.

Cahill, Willy. KICK AND RUN: SELF DEFENSE FOR WOMEN. California: Ohara Publications, 1978. 96p.

Conroy, Mary and Edward Ritvo. EVERY WOMAN CAN: A COMMON SENSE GUIDE TO SAFETY. New York: Grosset & Dunlap, 1982. 224p.

———. THE RATIONAL WOMAN'S GUIDE TO SELF-DEFENSE. New York: Grosset & Dunlap. 1975. 128p.

Davis, Linda J. and Elaine M. Brody. RAPE AND OLDER WOMEN: A GUIDE TO PREVENTION AND PROTECTION. Maryland: U.S. Dept. of Health, Education, and Welfare, 1979. 171p.

DePasquale, Jr., Michael. WOMAN'S GUIDE TO SELF-DEFENSE. New York: Cornerstone, 1980.

Erickson, Marion and Allen R. Steen. SELF-DEFENSE MANUAL FOR WOMEN. Texas: The Authors, 1966. 48p.

Fairbairn, W. E. HAND OFF! SELF-DEFENSE FOR WOMEN. New York: D Appleton/Century, 1942. 41p.

Farkas, Emil and Margaret Leeds. FIGHT BACK: A WOMAN'S GUIDE TO SELF-DEFENSE. New York: Holt, Rinehart and Winston, 1978. 159p.

Filson, Sidney. HOW TO PROTECT YOURSELF AND SURVIVE: FROM ONE WOMAN TO ANOTHER. New York: F. Watts, 1979. 151p.

Groth, A. Nicholas with H. Jean Birnbaum. MEN WHO RAPE: THE PSYCHOLOGY OF THE OFFENDER. New York: Plenum Press, 1979. 227p.

Hamada, Hiroshi and Patrick K. Tow PERSONAL SELF-DEFENSE MANUAL FOR WOMEN: MIND AND BODY. Iowa: Kendall-Hunt, 1982. 80p.

Horan, Ruth. JUDO FOR WOMEN: A MANUAL OF SELF-DEFENSE. New York: Crown Publishers, 1965. 149p.

Hudson, Kathleen. EVERY WOMAN'S GUIDE TO SELF-DEFENSE. Glasgow: Collins, 1977. New York: St. Martin's Press, 1977. 93p.

Kaufman, Doris, et al. SAFE WITHIN YOURSELF: A WOMAN'S GUIDE TO RAPE PREVENTION AND SELF-DEFENSE. Visage Press, 1980.

Keefe-Burg, Kathleen THE WOMANLY ART OF SELF-DEFENSE. N.p., 1979. 192p.

Krone, Chester W. THE WOMANLY ART OF SELF-DEFENSE. New York: Award Books, 1967. 127p.

Luchsinger, Judith A. H. PRACTICAL SELF-DEFENSE FOR WOMEN: A MANUAL OF PREVENTION AND ESCAPE TECHNIQUES. Minnesota: Dillon Press, 1977. 91p.

Mc Dermott, M. Joan. RAPE VICTIMIZATION IN 26 AMERICAN CITIES. Washington, D. C.: U. S. Dept. of Justice, 1979. 63p.

Molmen, Marcia E. AVOIDING RAPE WITHOUT PUTTING YOURSELF IN PROTECTIVE CUSTODY. Athens Press, 1982. 160p.

Monkerud, Donald and Mary Heiny. SELF-DEFENSE FOR WOMEN. New York: W. C. Brown, 1980. 96p.

Neff, Fred. SELF-PROTECTION GUIDEBOOK FOR GIRLS AND WOMEN. Minnesota: Lerner Publications, 1977. 63p.

Offstein, Jerrold N. SELF-DEFENSE FOR WOMEN. U.S.A.: National Press Books, 1972. 76p.

Okazaki, H. S. THE SCIENCE OF SELF-DEFENSE FOR GIRLS AND WOMEN. Hawaii: The Author, 1929. 72p.

Parker, Edmund. THE WOMAN'S GUIDE TO SELF-DEFENSE. Nebraska: Iron Man Industries, 1968. 77p.

Peterson, Susan Goldner. SELF-DEFENSE FOR WOMEN: THE WEST POINT WAY. New York: Simon & Schuster, 1979. 255p.

Pickering, Michael G. V. A WOMAN'S SELF-DEFENSE MANUAL. California: World Publications, 1979. 138p.

Pirnat, J. PERSONAL DEFENSE SKILLS FOR WOMEN. Stipes, 1975.

Sanford, Linda Tschirhart and Ann Fetter. IN DEFENSE OF OURSELVES: A RAPE PREVENTION HANDBOOK FOR WOMEN. New York: Doubleday, 1979. 177p.

Smith, James A. RAPISTS BEWARE. New York: Collier Books, 1978. 192p.

Sobol, Donald J. (aka Jo Miyasheta). SECRETS OF SELF-DEFENSE FOR WOMEN. New York: Studio 444, 1954. 48p.

Steiner, Bradley J. BELOW THE BELT: UNARMED COMBAT FOR WOMEN. Colorado: Paladin Press, 1976. 168p.

Stock, F. Patricia Pechanec. PERSONAL SAFETY AND DEFENSE FOR WOMEN. Minnesota: Burgess Publishing, 1968–128p; 1975–157p.

———. WOMAN ALERT! PERSONAL AND PROPERTY DEFENSE TECHNIQUES WITH BODY EXERCISES. Minnesota: Buegess Publishing, 1968, 1975. 157p.

Tegner, Bruce and Alice McGrath. SELF-DEFENSE AND ASSAULT PREVENTION FOR GIRLS AND WOMEN. California: Thor Publishing, 1977. 125p.

———. SELF-DEFENSE FOR WOMEN, A SIMPLE METHOD. California: Thor Publishing, 1961. 71p.

———, and Alice McGrath. SELF-DEFENSE FOR GIRLS AND WOMEN: A PHYSICAL EDUCATION COURSE. California: Thor Publishing, 1969. 125p.

———, ———. SELF-DEFENSE FOR GIRLS AND WOMEN. New York: Bantam Books, 1970. 95p.

———, ———. TEACHERS GUIDE FOR SELF-DEFENSE FOR GIRLS: A SECONDARY SCHOOL AND COLLEGE MANUAL. California: Thor Publishing, 1967. 31p.

Underwood, W. J. SELF-DEFENSE FOR WOMEN: COMBATO. Toronto: Blue Ribbon Books, 1944. New York: Garden City Publishing, 1944. 93p.

SWORDS
See also WEAPONS

Compton, Walter A. et al. NIPPON-TO ART SWORDS OF JAPAN: THE WALTER A. COMPTON COLLECTION. New York: Japan Society, 1976. 134p.

Dobree, Alfred. JAPANESE SWORD BLADES. England: Arms & Armour Publications, 1967. 39p.

German, Michael C. A GUIDE TO ORIENTAL DAGGERS AND SWORDS. London: The Author, 1967. 59p.

Hamilton, John D. THE PEABODY MUSEUM COLLECTION OF JAPANESE SWORD GUARDS. Massachusetts: The Museum, 1975. 86p.

Hawley, Willis M. JAPANESE SWORDSMITHS: 13,500 NAMES USED BY ABOUT 12,000 SWORDSMITHS FROM 700 to 1900. California: The Author, 2 volumes, 1966. 729p.

Homma, Junji (ed. National Museum). JAPANESE SWORD. Tokyo: Kogei-sha, 1948. 72p.

Inami, Hakusui. NIPPON-TO, THE JAPANESE SWORD. Tokyo: Cosmo Publishing Co., 1948. 222p.

Otake, Risuke. THE DEITY AND THE SWORD, KATORI SHINTO RYU 1. Japan: Minato Research & Publishing, 1977. 165p.

Robinson, Basil W. THE ART OF THE JAPANESE SWORD. Vermont: C. E. Tuttle, 1961. 212p. London: Faber & Faber, 2nd edition, 1970. 110p.

———. A PRIMER OF JAPANESE SWORD-BLADES. England: n.p., 1955. 95p.

Sasano, Masayuki. EARLY JAPANESE SWORD GUARDS—SUKA-SHI TSUBA. London: Robert G. Sawers, 1974. 292p.

Trousdale, William. THE LONG SWORD AND SCABBARD SLIDE IN ASIA. Washington, D.C.: Smithsonian Institution Press, 1975. 332p.

Yumoto, John M. THE SAMURAI SWORD: A HANDBOOK. Vermont: C. E. Tuttle, 1958. 191p.

SUMO

Kenrick, Doug. THE BOOK OF SUMO: SPORT, SPECTACLE, AND RITUAL. New York: Weatherhill, 1969. 171p.

Kuhaulaua, Jess and John Wheeler. TAKAMIYAMA: THE WORLD OF SUMO. New York: Kodansha, 1973. 176p.

Sargeant, J. A. SUMO: THE SPORT AND THE TRADITION. Vermont: C. E. Tuttle, 1959. 96p.

TAE KWON DO/KOREAN ARTS AND STYLES

Benko, James S. TAEKWON-DO HYUNGS FOR BLUE AND RED BELT LEVELS. U.S.A.: Midwest Taekwon-Do, 1981. 118p.

———. TAEKWON-DO HYUNGS FOR WHITE, YELLOW AND GREEN BELT LEVELS. U.S.A.: Midwest Taekwon-Do, 1981. 118p.
———. TAEKWON-DO: SELF-DEFENSE AGAINST WEAPONS. U.S.A.: Midwest Taekwon-Do, 1980. 108p.

Caputo, Robert. TANG SOO TAO: THE LIVING BUDDHA IN MARTIAL VIRTUE. Australia: Coleman's Printing, 1981. 254p.

Cho, Sihak Henry. KOREAN KARATE: FREE FIGHTING TECHNIQUES. Vermont: C. E. Tuttle, 1968. 249p.

Chun, Richard. MOO DUK KWAN TAE KWON DO: KOREAN ART OF SELF-DEFENSE. California: Ohara Publications, 1975. 207p.

———. MOO DUK KWAN TAE KWON DO: KOREAN ART OF SELF-DEFENSE, Vol. II. California: Ohara Publications, 1982.

———. with Paul Hastings Wilson. TAE KWON DO: THE KOREAN MARTIAL ART AND NATIONAL SPORT. New York: Harper & Row, 1976. 522p.

Garcia, Darnell. TANG SOO DO. California: Unique Publications, 1982. 180p.

Han, Bong Soo (ed. John Corcoran). HAPKIDO: KOREAN ART OF SELF-DEFENCE. California: Ohara Publications, 1974. 193p.

Hi, Choi Hong. TAEKWON-DO: THE ART OF SELF-DEFENSE. Seoul: Daeha Publication Co., 1965. 304p.

———. TAEKWON-DO (THE KOREAN ART OF SELF-DEFENSE): A TEXTBOOK FOR BEGINNING AND ADVANCED STUDENTS. Seoul: International Taekwon-do Federation, 1972. 518p.

Huan, B. S. Singapore: Russ International, 1975. 421p.

Jee, Joon M. ELEMENTARY HAPKIDO, Vol. 2. California: International Hapkido Association, n.d. 113p.

———. INTRODUCTION TO HAPKIDO, Vol. 1. California: International Hapkido Association, 1974. 135p.

Kee, Hwang. TANG SOO DO (SOO BAHK DO). New Jersey: U.S. Tang Soo Do Moo Duk Kwan Federation, 1978. 425p.

Kim, Pyung Soo (ed. John Corcoran). PALGUE 1, 2, 3 OF TAE KWON DO HYUNG. California: Ohara Publications, 1973. 144p.

———. PALGUE 4, 5, 6 OF TAE KWON DO HYUNG. California: Ohara Publications, 1975. 159p.

Kim, Un Yong. TAEKWONDO. Seoul: Korean Overseas Information Service, 1976. 54p.

Korean Overseas Information Service. TAEKWONDO. Seoul: Self-published, 1975. 44p.

Lee, Jae M. and David H. Wayf. HAPKIDO: THE KOREAN ART OF SELF-DEFENSE. New York: Arco Publishing, 1976. 122p.

Lee, Joo Bang. THE ANCIENT MARTIAL ART OF HWARANG-DO. California: Ohara Publications, 1978. 192p.

———. HWARANG-DO, Vol. 2. California: Ohara Publications, 1979.

Murphy, Hank. TANG SOO DO. Colorado: Paladin Press, 1980. 112p.

Myung, Kwang Sik. KOREAN HAPKIDO: ANCIENT ART OF THE MASTERS. Korea: World Hapkido Association, 1976. 310p.

Read, Stanton E. TAEKWONDO: A WAY OF LIFE IN KOREA. Taiwan: L-C Publishing Co., n.d. 64p.

Rhee, Jhoon. CHON-JI OF TAE KWON DO HYUNG. California: Ohara Publications, 1970. 136p.

———. CHUNG-GUN AND TOI-GYE OF TAE KWON DO HYUNG. California: Ohara Publications, 1971. 167p.

———. HWA-RANG AND CHUNG-MU OF TAE KWON DO HYUNG. California: Ohara Publications, 1971. 150p.

———. TAN-GUN AND TO-SAN OF TAE KWON DO HYUNG. California: Ohara Publications, 1971. 192p.

———. WON-HYO AND YUL-KOK OF TAE KWON DO HYUNG. California: Ohara Publications, 1971. 159p.

Sell, Edward B. KOREAN KARATE TRAINING MANUAL, Vol. 1 (TAE KWON DO, CHUNG DO KWAN). U.S.A.: The Author, 1973. 94p.

Shim, Sang Kyu. PROMISE AND FULFILLMENT IN THE ART OF TAE KWON DO. Michigan: The Author, 1974. 80p.

Son, Duk Sung and Robert J. Clark. BLACK BELT KOREAN KARATE. New Jersey: Prentice-Hall, n.d. 256p.

———, ———. KOREAN KARATE: THE ART OF TAE KWON DO. New Jersey: Prentice-Hall, 1968. 312p.

Tirschel, Richard L. TANG SOO DO KARATE. California: Tirschel & Associates, 1973. 191p.

Too, Jimmy M. S. THE TECHNIQUES OF TAEKWON-DO: A MODERN INTERNATIONAL MARTIAL ART. Singapore: Bushido Publishers, 1975. Vermont: C. E. Tuttle, 1975. 276p.

World Taekwondo Federation. TAEKWONDO (POOMSE). Seoul:Self-published, 1975. 295p.

Yates, Keith D. THE COMPLETE BOOK OF TAEKWON-DO FORMS. Colorado: Paladin Press, 1982. 200p.

T'AI-CHI-CH'UAN

Chang, Major G-Hand. TAI CHI CHUAN (THAI SUPREME BOXING FOR BEGINNERS). Taipei: Taiwan English Press, 1976. 233p.

Cheng, Man-ch'ing and Robert W. Smith. T'AI-CHI: THE SUPREME ULTIMATE EXERCISE FOR HEALTH, SPORT AND SELF-DEFENSE. Vermont: C. E. Tuttle, 1966. 112p.

Chen, Yearning K. TAI-CHI CHUAN: ITS EFFECTS AND PRACTICAL APPLICATIONS. Hong Kong: Unicorn Press, 1967. 184p.

Chung, Yeung Sau. PRACTICAL USE OF TAI CHI CHUAN (ITS ULTIMATE APPLICATIONS AND VARIATIONS). Massachusetts: Tai Chi Co., 1976. 42p.

Delza, Sophia. BODY AND MIND IN HARMONY: TAI CHI CH'UAN—AN ANCIENT CHINESE WAY OF EXERCISE TO ACHEIVE HEALTH AND TRANQUILITY. New York: David McKay Co., 1961. 184p.

Feng, Gia-Fu and Jerome Kirk. TAI CHI: A WAY OF CENTERING AND I-CHING. New York: Macmillan, 1970. 157p.

Huang, Al Chung-Liang. EMBRACE TIGER, RETURN TO MOUNTAIN. Utah: Real People Press, 1973. 188p.

Huang, Wen-Shan. FUNDAMENTALS OF TAI CHI CH'UAN. Hong Kong: South Sky Book Co., 1973. 559p.

Hui-Ching, Lu. T'AI CHI CH'UAN: A MANUAL OF INSTRUCTION. New York: St. Martin's Press, 1973. 166p.

Kauz, Herman. TAI CHI HANDBOOK: EXERCISE, MEDITATION AND SELF-DEFENSE. New York: Doubleday, 1974. 192p.

Lee, Douglas. TAI CHI CHUAN: THE PHILOSOPHY OF YIN AND YANG AND ITS APPLICATION. California: Ohara Publications, 1976. 160p.

Lee, Ying-arng. LEE'S MODIFIED TAI CHI FOR HEALTH. Hong Kong: Unicorn Press, 1968. 200p.

———. TAI CHI CHUAN FOR HEALTH. n.p., n.d. 200p.

Liang, T. T. T'AI CHI CHUAN FOR HEALTH AND SELF-DEFENSE. Massachusetts; Redwing Book Co., 1974. 84p.

———. TAI CHI CH'UAN FOR HEALTH AND SELF-DEFENSE: PHILOSOPHY AND PRACTICE. New York: Vintage Books, 1977. 137p.

Liu, Da. T'AI CHI CH'UAN AND I-CHING: A CHOREOGRAPHY OF BODY AND MIND. New York: Harper & Row, 1972. 86p.

Lum, Andrew. ADVANCED TAI CHI CHUAN. Hawaii: Golden Unicorn, 1975. 160p.

———. COMBAT TAI CHI CHUAN. Hawaii: Golden Unicorn, 1974. 147p.

Maisel, Edward. TAI CHI FOR HEALTH. New Jersey: Prentice-Hall, 1963.

Ming-Shih, Yang. T'AI CHI CH'UAN. Tokyo: Japan Publications, n.d. 60p.

———. TAI-CHI CHUAN FOR HEALTH AND BEAUTY. Japan: Bunka Publishing Bureau, 1976. 164p.

Po, Li and Amanda. WAVE HANDS LIKE CLOUDS. New York: Harper's Magazine Press, 1975. 112p.

Ruben, W. S. TAI CHI. New York: Lancer Books, 1970. 192p.

Stone, Justin F. T'AI CHI CHIH: JOY THROUGH MOVEMENT. New Mexico: Sun Publishing, 1974. 128p.

WEAPONS
See also SWORDS

Baillargeon, Richard P. WEAPONS KATAS SIMPLIFIED. N.p., n.d. 33p.

BASIC FORMAL EXERCISE OF NUNCHAKU. (ANCIENT MARTIAL ARTS OF THE RYUKYU ISLANDS, Series 1). Tokyo: Tokaido Co., n.d. Unpaged.

BASIC FORMAL EXERCISE OF TONFA OF HAMAHIGA . (ANCIENT MARTIAL ARTS OF THE RYUKYU ISLANDS, Series 3). Japan: N.p., n.d. 39p.

Demura, Fumio and Dan Ivan (eds. Gilbert Johnson and Geraldine Adachi). ADVANCED NUNCHAKU. California: 1976. 159p.

———, (eds.———, ———). BO: KARATE WEAPON OF SELF-DEFENSE. California: Ohara Publications, 1976.

———. Nunchaku: KARATE WEAPON OF SELF-DEFENSE. California: Ohara Publications, 1971. 143p.

———, (ed. John Corcoran). SAI: KARATE WEAPON OF SELF-DEFENSE. California: Ohara Publications, 1974. 160p.

———, (ed. Gregory Lee). TONFA: KARATE WEAPON OF SELF-DEFENSE. California: Ohara Publications, 1982. 144p.

Echanis, Michael D. BASIC STICK FIGHTING FOR COMBAT. California: Ohara Publications, 1978. 192p.

———. KNIFE FIGHTING, KNIFE THROWING FOR COMBAT. California; Ohara Publications, 1978. 191p.

———. KNIFE SELF-DEFENSE FOR COMBAT. California: Ohara Publications, 1977. 103p.

Gambordella, Theodore. THE COMPLETE BOOK OF KARATE WEAPONS. Colorado: Paladin Press, 1981. 256p.

Gardner, G. B. KERIS AND OTHER MALAY WEAPONS. Singapore: n.p., 1936.

Griffith-Williams, G. C. SUGGESTED ORIGIN OF THE MALAY KERIS. Singapore: n.p., 1937.

Gruzanski, Charles V. SPIKE AND CHAIN: JAPANESE FIGHTING ARTS. Vermont: C. E. Tuttle, 1968. 103p.

Hatsumi, Masaaki and Quintin Chambers. STICK FIGHTING: TECHNIQUES OF SELF-DEFENSE. New York: Kodansha, 1971. 147p.

Hess, Joseph C. NIGHT STICK. California: Ohara Publications, 1982.

Hill. A. H. THE MALAY KERIS AND OTHER WEAPONS. Singapore: n.p., 1937.

Hiroshi, Sakaida. NUNCHAKU TECHNIQUE, Vols. 1 and 2. California: Divine Wind, 1974. Unpaged.

Jalmaani, Abu. ARNIS: THE FILIPINO ART OF STICK FIGHTING. California: Koinonia Productions, n.d. Unpaged.

———. ARNIS: THE FREE FIGHTING TECHNIQUES. California: Koinonia Productions, n.d. Unpaged

———, and Jun Garcia. ARNIS: FILIPINO ART OF STICK FIGHTING. California: Koinonia Productions, 1976. 111p.

Jee, Joon M. NUNCHAKU TECHNIQUES. California: International Hapkido Association, 1975. 113p.

Kaneshiro, Hansei S. THE FIRST BOOK ON NUNCHAKU FOR SELF-DEFENSE. Illinois: The Banker's Print, 1971. 82p.

Kubota, Takayuki and Paul F. McCaul. BATON TECHNIQUES AND TRAINING. Illinois: Charles Thomas, 1974. 305p.

———. KUBOTAN: NEW POLICE TECHNIQUE. New Hampshire: Monadnock Lifetime Products, 1978. 30p.

Linick, Andrew S. NUNCHAKU: KARATE'S DEADLIEST FIGHTING STICKS. New York: Okinawan Kobujitsu Kyokai Association, 1975, 1982. 113p.

McEvoy, Harry K. KNIFE THROWING: A PRACTICAL GUIDE. Vermont: C. E. Tuttle, 1973. 108p.

MacLaren, I. S. and G. D. Thompson. THE TECHNIQUE OF THE TONFA. London: Paul H. Crompton, 1979. 61p.

———, ———. NUNCHAKU TRAINING MANUAL. England: Paul H. Crompton, 1974. 72p.

Mark, Bow-Sim. BASIC BROADSWORD. Massachusetts: Chinese Wushu Research Institute, 1977. 92p.

Marks, Tom (ed.). CHINESE KUNG-FU: ADVANCED STAFF FIGHTING TECHNIQUES. Taiwan: Martial Arts, Inc., 1975. 121p.

———. CHINESE KUNG-FU: TAI CHI SABRE FOR SELF-DEFENSE. Taiwan: Martial Arts, Inc., 1975. 51p.

NUNCHAKU. New York: Shuriken, n.d. 16p.

Parker, Edmund. ED PARKER'S GUIDE TO THE NUNCHAKU. California: The Author, 1975. 150p.

Phillips, James. THE NUNCHAKU AND POLICE TRAINING. New Jersey: The Author, 1973. 68p.

———. NUNCHAKU II: A NUNCHAKU ENCYOCLOPEDIA. New Jersey: The Author, 1975. 272p.

Presas, Remy. MODERN ARNIS: PHILIPPINE MARTIAL ART OF STICK FIGHTING. Manila: Modern Arnis Publishing, 1974. 168p.

Sakagami, Ryusho. NUNCHAKU AND SAI: ANCIENT OKINAWAN MARTIAL ARTS. Tokyo: Japan Publications, 1974. 174p.

———. SAI OF TSUKENSHITAHAKU. (ANCIENT MARTIAL ARTS OF THE RYUKYU ISLANDS, Series 2). Japan: Ogawa Trading Co., n.d. 20p.

Sanchez, John. FLEXIBLE WEAPONS. Colorado: Paladin Press, 1981. 80p.

———. SLASH AND THRUST. Colorado: Paladin Press, 1980. 72p

Santos, Neofito. ARNIS: THE FIGURE EIGHT SYSTEM. California: Koinonia Productions, n.d. Unpaged.

———. ARNIS: THE UP AND DOWN SYSTEM. California: Koinonia Productions, n.d. Unpaged.

Tegner, Bruce. STICK FIGHTING FOR SELF-DEFENSE: YAWARA, AIKIDO, CANE, POLICE CLUB, QUARTER STAFF. California: Thor Publishing, 1965. 127p.

Un, H. B. TONG LONG (DOUBLE END STICK) KUNG-FU (PRAYING MANTIS STYLE). London: Paul H. Crompton, 1976. 37p.

Werner, E. T. C. CHINESE WEAPONS. California: Ohara Publications, 1972. 128p.

Wooley, G. C. THE MALAY KERIS: ITS ORIGIN AND DEVELOPMENT. Journal of the Malayan British Royal Asiatic Society, Vol. 20, 1947.

Yuen, Kam. TECHNIQUE AND FORM OF THE THREE SECTIONAL STAFF IN KUNG-FU. California: Ohara Publications, 1979. 191p.

YOGA

Bhikshu. KARMA YOGA. Chicago: Yogi Publishing Society, 1928. 138p.

Bragdon, Claude. YOGA FOR YOU. New York: Lancer Books, 1943. 173p.

Danielou, Alain. YOGA: THE METHOD OF REINTEGRATION. New York: University Books, 1955. 165p.

Day, Harvey. THE STUDY AND PRACTICE OF YOGA. New York: University Books, 1954. 160p.

———. YOGA ILLUSTRATED DICTIONARY. New York: Emerson Books, 1971. 186p.

Devi, Indra. RENEW YOUR LIFE THROUGH YOGA. New York: Prentice-Hall, 1963. 256p.

———. YOGA FOR AMERICANS. New Jersey : Prentice-Hall, 1959. 208p.

Dunne, Desmond. YOGA FOR EVERY MAN: HOW TO HAVE LONG LIFE AND HAPPINESS. London: Gerald Dukeworth & Co., 1952. 116p.

Evans-Wentz, W. Y. TOBETAN YOGA AND SECRET DOCTRINES. New York: Oxford University Press, 1968. 389p.

Francis, Maj. P. G. YOGA: THE AMAZING SCIENCE. London: Thorson's, 1958. 88p.

Gervis, Pearce. NAKED THEY PRAY: THE MEANING AND PRACTICE OF YOGA. New York: Duell, Sloan and Pearce, 1956. 217p.

Grewal, Rishi Sigh. COMPLETE YOGA. California: The Author, 1937. 174p.

Hewitt, James. A PRACTICAL GUIDE TO YOGA. New York: Funk & Wagnalls, 1960. 188p.

Hittleman, Richard L. GUIDE TO YOGA MEDITATION. New York: Bantam Books, 1969. 192p.

———. YOGA FOR PHYSICAL FITNESS. New York: Paperback Library, 1964. 255p.

Iyengar, B. K. S. LIGHT ON YOGA. New York: Schocken Books, 1965. 342p.

Kiss, Michaeline. YOGA FOR YOUNG PEOPLE. New York: Archway, 1973.

Kriyanandam Swami. YOGA POSTURES FOR SELF-AWARENESS. California: Ananda Publications, 1967. 88p.

Kuvalayananda, Swami. POPULAR YOGA ASANAS. Vermont: C. E. Tuttle, 1971. 210p.

Liebers, Arthur. RELAX WITH YOGA. New York: Sterling Publishing Co., 1960. 95p.

McCartney, James. YOGA: THE KEY TO LIFE. New York: E. P. Dutton, 1969.

Mulbagala, K. V. THE POPULAR PRACTICE OF YOGA. Pennsylvania: M. B. Lippincott, n.d. 238p.

Ramacharaka, Yogi. HATHA YOGA, OR THE YOGI PHILOSOPHY OF WELL-BEING. Illinois: Yogi Publications, 1930. 286p.

———. THE HINDU-YOGI SCIENCE OF BREATH. Illinois: Yogi Publications, 1905. 88p.

———. RAJA YOGA OR MENTAL DEVELOPMENT. Illinois: Yogi Publications, 1907. 298p.

Rawls, Eugene S. A HANDBOOK OF YOGA FOR MODERN LIVING. New York: Pyramid Publications, 1964. 158p.

Shultz, Dodi. SLIMMING WITH YOGA. New York: Dell Publishing, 1968. 64p.

Slater, Wallace. RAJA YOGA: A SIMPLIFIED AND PRACTICAL COURSE. Illinois: Theosophical Publishing, 1968. 106p.

———. A SIMPLIFIED COURSE OF HATHA YOGA. Illinois: Theosophical Publishing, 1966. 52p.

Stearn, Jess. YOGA, YOUTH, AND REINCARNATION. New York: Bantam Books, 1968. 344p.

Taylor, Renee. THE HUNZE-YOGA WAY TO HEALTH AND LONGER LIFE. New York: Constellation International, 1969. 215p.

Vishnudevananda, Swami. THE COMPLETE ILLUSTRATED BOOK OF YOGA. New York: Julian Press, 1960. 361p.

Vithaldas, Yogi. THE YOGA SYSTEM OF HEALTH AND RELIEF FROM TENSION. New York: Cornerstone Library, 1957. 128p.

Volin, Michael and Nancy Phelan. YOGA FOR BEAUTY. New York: Bell Publishing, 1967. 92p.

Wood, Ernest. GREAT SYSTEMS OF YOGA. New York: Philosophical Library, 1954. 168p.

———. PRACTICAL YOGA: ANCIENT AND MODERN. California: Wilshire Books, 1948. 252p.

———. YOGA WISDOM. New York: Philosophical Library, 1970. 101p.

Yeats-Brown, F. THE RIGHT STEPS TO YOGA. New York: Blue Ribbon Books, 1933. 23p.

Young, Frank Rudolph. YOGA FOR MEN ONLY. New York: Parker Publishing, 1969. 214p.

Zorn, William. BODY HARMONY: THE EASY YOGA EXERCISE WAY. New York: Hawthorn Books, 1971. 172p.

ZEN/BUDDHISM

Albertson, Edward. ZEN FOR THE MILLIONS. California: Sherbourne Press, 1970. 167p.

Blyth, R. H. ZEN AND ZEN CLASSICS, Vol. 5. Tokyo: Hokuseido Press, 1962. 225p.

Chang, C. C. THE PRACTICE OF ZEN. New York: Perennial Library, 1959.

———. THE PRACTICE OF ZEN. New York: Harper & Row, 1959. 256p.

Deshimaru, Taisen (ed. Paul De Angelis). THE ZEN WAY TO THE MARTIAL ARTS: A JAPANESE MASTER REVEALS THE SECRETS OF THE SAMURAI. New York: Dutton, 1983. 128p.

Hanh, Thich What. ZEN KEYS. New York: Anchor Books, 1974.

Hayakawa, Sessue. ZEN SHOWED ME THE WAY. . .TO PEACE, HAPPINESS, AND TRANQUILITY. New York: Bobbs-Merrill, 1960. 256p.

Herrigel, Eugen. ZEN. New York: McGraw-Hill, 1960. 124p.

Hirai, Tomio. ZEN AND THE MIND: SCIENTIFIC APPROACH TO ZEN PRACTICE. Tokyo: Japan Publications, 1978. 144p.

Holmes, Stewart W. and Chimyo Horioka. ZEN ART FOR MEDITATION. Vermont: C. E. Tuttle, 1973. 115p.

Humphreys, Christmas. ZEN: A WAY OF LIFE. New York: Emerson Books, 1968. 199p.

Iino, Norimoto. ZEAL FOR ZEN. New York: Philosophical Library, 1967. 94p.

Kapleau, Philip (ed.). THE THREE PILLARS OF ZEN. Massachusetts: Beacon Press, 1965. 363p.

Kubose, Gyomay. ZEN KOANS. Illinois: Henry Regnery Co., 1973. 274p.

Leggett, Trevor (trans. and comp.). A FIRST ZEN READER. Vermont: C. E. Tuttle, 1960. 236p.

Ling, T. O. A DICTIONARY OF BUDDHISM. New York: Charles Scribner's Sons, 1972. Linssen, Robert. ZEN: THE ART OF LIFE. New York: Pyramid Communications, 1969. 242p.

Lu, Ku'an Yu. ZEN AND ZEN TEACHINGS: Second Series. New York: Shambala, 1973.

McCandless, Ruth S. and Nyogen Senzaki. BUDDHISM AND ZEN. New York: Philosophical Library, 1953. 90p.

Miura, Isshu and Ruth Fuller Sasaki. THE ZEN KOAN. New York: Harcourt, Brace & World, 1965. 156p.

Ogata, Sohaku. ZEN FOR THE WEST. New York: Dial Press, 1959. 182p.

Reps, Paul (comp.). ZEN FLESH, ZEN BONES: A COLLECTION OF ZEN AND PRE-ZEN WRITINGS. Vermont: C. E. Tuttle, 1972. 211p.

Ross, Nancy Wilson. THE WORLD OF ZEN: AN EAST-WEST ANTHOLOGY. New York: Vintage Books, 1960. 362p.

Sato, Koji and Sesei Kuzunishi. THE ZEN LIFE. New York: Weatherhill, 1972. 190p.

Sekiguchi, Shindai. ZEN: A MANUAL FOR WESTERNERS. Tokyo: Japan Publications, 1970. 111p.

Senzaki, Nyogen and Paul Reps. ZEN: A PATHWAY TO ENLIGHTENMENT. California: Ohara Publications, 1977. 126p.

Soothill, William E. and Lewis Hodous. A DICTIONARY OF CHINESE BUDDHIST TERMS. London: Kegan Paul, 1937.

Suzuki, Saisetz Teitaro (D. T.). ESSENTIALS OF ZEN BUDDHISM. New York: E. P. Dutton, 1962.

———. THE FIELD OF ZEN. New York: Harper & Row, 1969. 105p.

———. MANUAL OF ZEN BUDDHISM. New York: Grove Press, 1960. 192p.

———. SHIN BUDDHISM. New York: Harper & Row, 1970. 93p.

———. WHAT IS ZEN? New York: Harper & Row, 1971. 116p.

———. ZEN BUDDHISM: SELECTED WRITINGS OF D. T. SUZUKI. New York: Doubleday, 1956. 249p.

———. ZEN AND JAPANESE CULTURE. New York: Pantheon Books, 1959.

Suzuki, Shunryu. ZEN MIND, BEGINNER'S MIND. New York: Weatherhill, 1970. 134p.

Uchiyama, Kosho. APPROACH TO ZEN: THE REALITY OF ZAZEN/ MODERN CIVILIZATION AND ZEN. Tokyo: Japan Publications, 1973. 122p.

Watts, Alan W. THE SPIRIT OF ZEN: A WAY OF LIFE, WORK, AND ART IN THE FAR EAST. New York: Grove Press, 1958. 128p.

———. THE WAY OF ZEN. New York: Vintage Books, 1957.

Wood, Ernest. THE ZEN DICTIONARY. New York: Philosophical Library, 1957. New York: Citadel Press, 1962. 165p.

Yu, Lu K'uan (ed.). CH'AN AND ZEN TEACHING, Second Series. California: Shambala Publications, 1960. 254p.

Zaehner, R. C. ZEN, DRUGS, AND MYSTICISM. New York: Pantheon Books, 1972. 223p.

ZEN BUDDHISM. Japan: Japan Times, 1970. 111p.

PUBLISHERS

The following publishers each have published at least ten books on martial arts and related subjects. Most have a catalog available upon request.

Arco Publishing Co

A. S. Barnes

Paul H. Crompton
638 Fulham Rd.
London S.W. 6, England

Faber & Faber

W. Foulsham

Japan Publications
2–1, Saragaku-cho 1-chome
Chiyoda-ku, Tokyo, Japan

Kodansha International
10 E. 53rd St.
New York, NY 10022

Koinonia Productions
P.O. Box 7174
Stockton, CA 95207

Ohara Publications
1813 Victory Place
Burbank, CA 91504

Paladin Press

Prentice-Hall

Sterling Publishing Co.

Thor Publishing

Charles E. Tuttle Co.
Rutland, VT

Unique Publications
7011 Sunset Blvd.
Hollywood, CA 90028

John Weatherhill

INDEX